AF213858

INSTITUTIONAL INVESTOR ACTIVISM

INSTITUTIONAL INVESTOR ACTIVISM: HEDGE FUNDS AND PRIVATE EQUITY, ECONOMICS AND REGULATION

Edited by
WILLIAM W. BRATTON
and
JOSEPH A. McCAHERY

OXFORD
UNIVERSITY PRESS

OXFORD
UNIVERSITY PRESS

Great Clarendon Street, Oxford, OX2 6DP,
United Kingdom

Oxford University Press is a department of the University of Oxford.
It furthers the University's objective of excellence in research, scholarship,
and education by publishing worldwide. Oxford is a registered trade mark of
Oxford University Press in the UK and in certain other countries

© Introduction and Compilation William W. Bratton and Joseph A. McCahery
2015 and chapters 15, 17, and 20 Oxford University Press

The moral rights of the author have been asserted

First Edition published in 2015

All rights reserved. No part of this publication may be reproduced, stored in
a retrieval system, or transmitted, in any form or by any means, without the
prior permission in writing of Oxford University Press, or as expressly permitted
by law, by licence or under terms agreed with the appropriate reprographics
rights organization. Enquiries concerning reproduction outside the scope of the
above should be sent to the Rights Department, Oxford University Press, at the
address above

You must not circulate this work in any other form
and you must impose this same condition on any acquirer

Published in the United States of America by Oxford University Press
198 Madison Avenue, New York, NY 10016, United States of America

British Library Cataloguing in Publication Data
Data available

Library of Congress Control Number: 2015937040

ISBN 978–0–19–872393–6

Links to third party websites are provided by Oxford in good faith and
for information only. Oxford disclaims any responsibility for the materials
contained in any third party website referenced in this work.

Preface

Since the 1960s, institutional investing has been an important element of financial markets. The increase in institutional ownership was accompanied by an enhanced role played by institutions in monitoring companies' corporate governance behaviour. In fact, hedge funds and private equity firms have achieved a degree of success in actively shaping the business plans of target firms, encouraging corporate restructurings, mergers, increased leverage, dividend recapitalizations, and the replacement of management and board members. Yet, with the passage of time, activist shareholders have encountered opposition from lawmakers, analysts, and some sectors of the business community.

The global turbulence in the credit markets, triggered by the turmoil in the subprime mortgage market in the United States in 2007, was significant for activist investors. As has been widely noted, not only did the crisis end the private equity bonanza, but it contributed to an even steeper decline in hedge fund activism. The experience of the last decade lends support to the view that there are immense swings in shareholder activism. Fortunately, governments have recently promulgated some reforms that affect activist investors. Indeed, the effect of the reforms in some countries, such as the US, has led to lowering the costs of activism and increasing the ability of institutional investors to vote. And there is evidence that the huge rebound in activism after 2012 has led to the improved performances of target companies and significant returns for investors in activist hedge funds.

Most of our focus in this book is on role of the hostile activist shareholder that has been taken up by a set of hedge fund and private equity firms. These activists typically target and research companies, take large positions in their stock, criticize their business plans and governance practices, and confront their managers, demanding action enhancing shareholder value. Our aim here is to explore the implication that hedge fund activists, vulture funds, and private equity, taken together, may have revolutionized shareholding and lending, and thereby solved layers of agency problems without any assistance in the form of regulatory reform. Many of the chapters in this collection offer sustained insights into these important questions about the role and lessons of activist shareholders for corporate governance and regulation.

This volume emerged out of a March 2007 Conference on Activist Investors, Hedge Funds and Corporate Governance, organized by the University of Amsterdam Center for Law and Economics, Vanderbilt University School of Law, and the European Corporate Governance Institute in Amsterdam. We are grateful to the Amsterdam Center for Corporate Finance for their support of our examination of the economic and governance effects of institutional investor engagement in Europe and the US. We were also fortunate to have received financial assistance from the Netherlands Ministry of Economic Affairs, Agriculture and Innovation and the Netherlands Ministry of Finance.

We would like to thank the many individuals who have provided us with helpful advice and encouragement. We would particularly like to thank John Armour, Lucian Bebchuk, Marco Becht, Arnoud Boot, Mike Burkart, Brian Cheffins, John Coffee, Jill Fisch, Merritt Fox, Leo Goldschmidt, Henry Hu, Rajkamal Iyer, April Klein, Paul Koster, Florencio López de Silanes, Ronald Masulis, Enrico Perotti, Ludo Phalippou, Theo Raaijmakers, Robert Rasmussen, Luc Renneboog, Edward Rock, Zacharias Sautner, Dirk Schoenmaker, Armin Schwienbacher, Randall Thomas, Robert Thompson, Erik Vermeulen, Michael Wachter, Jaap Winter, Guy Wyser-Pratte, and Emanuel Zur. We would also wish to acknowledge our gratitude to Irene Wamelink for her work in organizing the conference. During the course of editing the collection, we benefited from the administrative and financial support provided by the Department of Business Law at Tilburg University and the University of Pennsylvania Law School. We would like to thank our authors for their contributions to the volume.

We would also like to extend our thanks to those who have helped us in preparing the collection. We are grateful to James J. Risser for his expert assistance in preparing the manuscript for submission to the press. We thank Barend van Drooge, Olaf van Pennen, Natashka Ramada, and Stanislav Wald for their able research assistance. We owe special thanks to our editor at Oxford University Press, David Musson, for his long-standing support, and helpful comments and feedback in preparing the collection. Finally, we thank the Institute of Law and Economics at the University of Pennsylvania and the Center for Company Law, and Tilburg Law and Economics Center (TILEC) for the stimulating environments that they provide.

Acknowledgements

Stuart L. Gillan and Laura T. Starks, 'The Evolution of Shareholder Activism in the United States'. Reprinted from *Journal of Applied Corporate Finance* (© 2007, John Wiley and Sons) with permission of John Wiley and Sons.

Lucian E. Bebchuk, 'The Myth of the Shareholder Franchise'. Reprinted from *Virginia Law Review*, Volume 93, 2007 with permission of *Virginia Law Review*.

John Armour and Brian Cheffins, 'The Rise and Fall (?) of Shareholder Activism by Hedge Funds'. Reprinted from *Journal of Alternative Investments*, Volume 14, No. 3, 2012, with permission of the author.

Marcel Kahan and Edward Rock, 'Hedge Funds in Corporate Governance and Corporate Control'. Reprinted from *University of Pennsylvania Law Review*, Volume 155, 2007 with permission of *University of Pennsylvania Law Review*.

Marco Becht, Julian Franks, Colin Mayer, Stefano Rossi, 'Returns to Shareholder Activism: Evidence from a Clinical Study of the Hermes UK Focus Fund'. Reprinted from *Review of Financial Studies*, Volume 22, No. 8, 2009 with permission of Oxford University Press, Inc.

Alon Brav, Wei Jiang, Frank Partnoy, and Randall Thomas, 'Hedge Fund Activism, Corporate Governance, and Firm Performance'. Reprinted from *Journal of Finance* (© 2008 The American Finance Association), with permission of John Wiley and Sons.

April Klein and Emanuel Zur, 'Entrepreneurial Shareholder Activism: Hedge Funds and Other Private Investors'. Reprinted from *Journal of Finance* (© 2009 The American Finance Association) with permission of John Wiley and Sons.

William Bratton and Michael Wachter, 'The Case Against Shareholder Empowerment'. Reprinted from *University of Pennsylvania Law Review*, Volume 158, 2010 with permission of *University of Pennsylvania Law Review*.

Douglas G. Baird and Robert K. Rasmussen, 'Antibankruptcy'. Reprinted from *Yale Law Journal*, Volume 119, 2010 with permission of *Yale Law Journal*.

Henry T. C. Hu and Bernard Black, 'Debt, Equity and Hybrid Decoupling: Governance and Systemic Risk Implications'. Reprinted from *European Financial Management* with permission of John Wiley and Sons (© 2008 Henry T. C. Hu Journal compilation, Blackwell Publishing Ltd).

Wei Jiang, Kai Li, and Wei Wang, 'Hedge Funds and Chapter 11'. Reprinted from *Journal of Finance* with permission of John Wiley and Sons (© 2012 the American Finance Association).

Steven N. Kaplan and Per Strömberg, 'Leveraged Buyouts and Private Equity'. Reprinted from *Journal of Economic Perspectives*, American Economic Association, Volume 23, No. 1, with permission of American Economic Association

Lucian A. Bebchuk and Robert J. Jackson, Jr., 'The Law and Economics of Blockholder Disclosure'. Reprinted from *Harvard Business Law Review*, Volume 2, 2012 with permission of *Harvard Business Law Review*.

Peter Cziraki, Luc Renneboog, and Peter G. Szilagyi, 'Shareholder Activism through Proxy Proposals: The European Perspective'. Reprinted from *European Financial Management* with permission of John Wiley and Sons (© 2010 Blackwell Publishing Ltd).

Jill E. Fisch, 'The Destructive Ambiguity of Federal Proxy Access'. Reprinted from *Emory Law Journal*, Volume 61, 2012 with permission of the author and *Emory Law Journal*.

Ludovic Phalippou, 'Performance of Buyout Funds Revisited?' Reprinted from *Review of Finance*, Volume 18, 2014 with permission of Oxford University Press, Inc.

Dan Awrey, 'The Limits of EU Hedge Fund Regulation'. Reprinted from *Law and Financial Markets Review*, Volume 5, No. 2, with permission of Hart Publishing Ltd (an imprint of Bloomsbury Publishing plc).

Contents

List of Figures

List of Tables

Table of Cases

ACC Bondholders Group v. Adelphia Commc'ns Corp. (In re Adelphia Commc'ns Corp.), 361 B.R. 337 (S.D.N.Y. 2007).

AFSCME v. AIG, Inc., 462 F.3d 121 (2d Cir. 2006).

Air Prods. & Chems., Inc. v. Airgas, Inc., 16 A.3d 48 (Del. Ch. 2011).

Am. Equity Inv. Life Ins. Co. v. SEC, 572 F.3d 923 (D.C. Cir. 2009), amended by 613 F.3d 166 (D.C. Cir. 2010).

Am. Fed'n of State, County & Mun. Employees v. Am. Int'l Group, Inc., 462 F.3d 121 (2d Cir. 2006).

AutoStyle Plastics, Inc. v. MascoTech, Inc. (In re AutoStyle Plastics, Inc.), 269 F.3d 726 (6th Cir. 2001).

Bebchuk v. CA, Inc., 902 A.2d 737 (Del. Ch. 2006).

Benchmark Capital v. Vague, 2002 WL 1732423 (Del.Ch. July 15, 2002).

Bershad v. Curtiss-Wright Corp., 535 A.2d 840 (Del. 1987).

Blasius Indus. v. Atlas Corp., 564 A.2d 651 (Del. Ch. 1988).

Brodie v. Jordan, 857 N.E.2d 1076 (Mass. 2006).

Business Roundtable v. SEC, 905 F.2d 406 (D.C. Cir. 1990).

Business Roundtable v. SEC, 647 F.3d 1144 (D.C. Cir. 2011).

Business Roundtable, et al. v. SEC, No. 10-1305 (D.C. Cir., filed Sept. 29, 2010).

CA, Inc. v. AFSCME Employees Pension Plan, 953 A.2d 227 (Del. 2008).

Camden Asset Mgmt., L.P. v. Sunbeam Corp., No. 99-8275-CIV-MIDDLEBROOKS, 2001 U.S. Dist. LEXIS 11022 (S.D. Fla. July 3, 2001).

Century Glove, Inc. v. First American Bank of New York, 860 F.2d 94 (3d Cir. 1988).

Chamber of Commerce v. SEC, 412 F.3d 133 (D.C. Cir. 2005).

Contrarian Funds, LLC v. Westpoint Stevens, Inc. (In re Westpoint Stevens, Inc.), 333 B.R. 30 (S.D.N.Y. 2005).

CSX Corporation v. The Children's Investment Fund Management (UK) LLP, 562 F. Supp. 2d 511 (S.D.N.Y. 2008), aff'd in part, vacated in part, 654 F.3d 276 (2d Cir. 2011).

CTS Corp. v. Dynamics Corp. of Am., 481 U.S. 69 (1987).

Danis v. USN Commc'ns, Inc., 189 F.R.D. 391 (N.D. Ill. 1999).

Edgar v. MITE Corp., 457 U.S. 624 (1982).

Emerald Partners v. Berlin, 787 A.2d 85 (Del. 2001).

Erickell Partners v. Emerging Commc'ns, Inc., No. 16415-NC (Del. Ch. Jun. 27, 2000).

Fin. Planning Ass'n v. SEC, 482 F.3d 481 (D.C. Cir. 2007).

Hoyt v. Thompson's Ex'rs, 19 N.Y. 207 (1859).

In re ACR Management LLC, No. 04-27848 (W.D. Pa. filed June 14, 2004).

In re Adelphia Commc'ns Corp., 368 B.R. 140 (Bankr. S.D.N.Y. 2007).

In re Allegheny Int'l, Inc., 100 B.R. 241 (Bankr. W.D. Pa. 1988).

In re American Remanufacturers, No. 05-20022 (Bankr. D. Del. Nov. 7, 2005).
In re Bank One S'holders Class Actions, 96 F. Supp. 2d 780 (N.D. Ill. 2000).
In re Calpine, No. 05-60200 (Bankr. S.D.N.Y. Dec. 20, 2005).
In re Cendant Corp. Sec. Litig., 109 F. Supp. 2d 273 (D.N.J. 2000), *aff'd*, 264 F.3d 286 (3d Cir. 2001).
In re Chrysler LLC, 405 B.R. 84 (Bankr. S.D.N.Y. 2009).
In re Cox Commc'ns Inc. S'holders Litig., 879 A.2d 604 (Del. Ch. 2005).
In re Critical Path, Inc. Sec. Litig., 156 F. Supp. 2d 1102 (N.D. Cal. 2001).
In re Donnkenny Inc. Sec. Litig., 171 F.R.D. 156 (S.D.N.Y. 1997).
In re Dow Corning Corp., 244 B.R. 634 (Bankr. E.D. Mich. 1999).
In re Drexel Burnham Lambert Group, Inc., 138 B.R. 717 (Bankr. S.D.N.Y. 1992).
In re Dura Auto. Sys., No. 06-11202 (Bankr. D. Del. Oct. 30, 2006).
In re Emerging Commc'ns, Inc. S'holders Litig., No. 16415, 2004 Del. Ch. LEXIS 70 (Del. Ch. May 3, 2004).
In re Enron Corp. Sec. Litig., 206 F.R.D. 427 (S.D. Tex. 2002).
In re FiberMark, Inc., 349 B.R. 385 (Bankr. D. Vt. 2006).
In re Kmart Corp., 359 F.3d 866 (7th Cir. 2004).
In re Lyondell Chem. Co., 402 B.R. 57 (Bankr. S.D.N.Y. 2009) (No. 0910023).
In re Meridian Automotive Sys., Inc., No. 65-11168 (Bankr. D. Del. Apr. 23, 2005).
In re MONY Group, Inc. S'holder Litig., 853 A.2d 661 (Del. Ch. 2004).
In re Network Assocs., Inc., Sec. Litig., 76 F. Supp. 2d 1017 (N.D. Cal. 1999).
In re New World Pasta, No. 04-02817 (M.D. Pa. *filed* May 10, 2004).
In re Owens Corning, 419 F.3d 195 (3d Cir. 2005).
In re Pure Resources Shareholder Litigation, C.A. No. 19876, 2002 Del. Ch. LEXIS 116 (Del. Ch. Oct. 9, 2002).
In re Snyder, 51 B.R. 432 (Bankr. Utah 1985).
In re Tarragon Corp. Sec. Litig., No. 07 Civ. 07972 (PKC), 2007 U.S. Dist. LEXIS 91418 (S.D.N.Y. Dec. 6, 2007).
In re Tyson Foods, Inc. Sec. Litig., No. 01-425-SLR, 2003 U.S. Dist. LEXIS 17904 (D. Del. Oct. 6, 2003).
In re Walt Disney Co. Derivative Litig., 907 A.2d 693 (Del. Ch. 2005).
In re WorldCom, Inc., No. 02-13533, 2003 WL 23861928 (Bankr. S.D.N.Y. Oct. 31, 2003).
Invacare Corp. v. Healthdyne Technologies, Inc., 968 F. Supp. 1578 (N.D. Ga. 1997).
JANA Master Fund, Ltd. v. CNET Networks, Inc., 954 A.2d 335 (Del. Ch. 2008).
Mason Capital, Ltd. v. Kaman Corp., No. 3:05CV1470, 2005 WL 2850083 (D. Conn. Oct. 31, 2005).
MONY Group, Inc. v. Highfields Capital Mgmt., L.P., 368 F.3d 138 (2nd Cir. 2004).
Moran v. Household Int'l, Inc., 500 A.2d 1346 (Del. 1985).
Nixon v. Blackwell, 626 A.2d 1366 (Del. 1993) (en banc).
Paramount Commc'ns, Inc. v. Time Inc., 571 A.2d 1140 (Del. 1989).
People ex rel. Manice v. Powell, 94 N.E. 634 (N.Y. 1911).
Perlman v. Catapult Entm't, Inc. (In re Catapult Entm't, Inc.), 165 F.3d 747 (9th Cir. 1999).
Phillip Goldstein et al. v. SEC, 451 F.3d 873 (D.C. Cir. 2006).
Prescott Group Small Cap, L.P. v. The Coleman Co., No. 17802, 2004 Del. Ch. LEXIS 131 (Del. Ch. Sept. 8, 2004).
Regal Entertainment Group v. Amaranth, LLC, 894 A.2d 1104 (Del. Ch. 2006).

Rosenfeld v. Fairchild Engine & Airplane Corp., 128 N.E.2d 291 (N.Y. 1955).
Sanders v. Devine, 1997 WL 599539 (Del.Ch. Sept. 24, 1997).
Smith v. Van Gorkom, 488 A.2d 858 (Del. 1985).
Stone v. Ritter, 911A.2d 362 (Del. 2006).
Theatre Enters., Inc. v. Paramount Film Distrib. Corp., 346 U.S. 537 (1954).
UniSuper Ltd. v. News Corp., 898 A.2d 344 (Del. Ch. 2006).
Unitrin, Inc. v. Am. Gen. Corp., 651 A.2d 1361 (Del. 1995).
Unocal Corp. v. Mesa Petroleum Co., 493 A.2d 946 (Del. 1985).
Versata Enters., Inc. v. Selectica, Inc., 5 A.3d 586 (Del. 2010).
Waterbury v. Temescal Water Co., 105 P. 940 (Cal. Ct. App. 1909).
Williams v. Geier, 671 A.2d 1368 (Del. 1996).
Yucaipa Am. Alliance Fund II, L.P. v. Riggio, 1 A.3d 310 (Del. Ch. 2010).

List of Contributors

John Armour is the Hogan Lovells Professor of Law and Finance at the University of Oxford. He was previously a University Senior Lecturer in Law and Fellow of Trinity Hall at Cambridge University. He studied law at the University of Oxford before completing an LLM at Yale Law School and taking up his first post at the University of Nottingham. He has published widely in the fields of company law, corporate finance, and corporate insolvency. His main research interest lies in the integration of legal and economic analysis, with particular emphasis on the impact on the real economy of changes in the law governing company law, corporate insolvency, and financial regulation. He has been involved in policy-related projects commissioned by the Department of Trade and Industry, the Financial Services Authority, the Insolvency Service, and the Jersey Economic Development Department.

Dan Awrey is an Associate Professor of Law and Finance at the University of Oxford. He holds a BA and an LLB from Queen's University, an LLM from the University of Toronto, and a DPhil from Oxford. Before entering academia, he served as legal counsel to a global investment management firm and, prior to that, as an associate practising corporate finance and securities law with a major Canadian law firm. His teaching and research interests reside in the area of financial regulation and, more specifically, the financial markets, institutions, and instruments, which together comprise the shadow banking system.

Douglas G. Baird is the Harry A. Bigelow Distinguished Service Professor of Law at the University of Chicago Law School. He received a BA from Yale and a JD from Stanford Law School, where he was elected to the Order of the Coif and served as the Managing Editor of the *Stanford Law Review*. He later served as a law clerk to Judge Shirley M. Hufstedler and Judge Dorothy W. Nelson, both of the US Court of Appeals for the Ninth Circuit. He served as Dean of the University of Chicago Law School from 1994 to 1999. His research and teaching interests focus on corporate reorganizations and contracts. He is a member of the Board of Directors of the American Law and Economics Association and has been a member of the Board of Directors of the American Law Deans Association and a Director of the American College of Bankruptcy. He is also a Fellow of the American Academy of Arts and Sciences and a Fellow of the American College of Bankruptcy.

Lucian A. Bebchuk is the William J. Friedman and Alicia Townsend Friedman Professor of Law, Economics, and Finance and Director of the Program on Corporate Governance at Harvard Law School. Bebchuk is also a Fellow of the American Academy of Arts and Sciences, Research Associate of the National Bureau of Economic Research, Inaugural Fellow of the European Corporate Governance Network, and Director of the SSRN Corporate Governance Network. Trained in both law and economics, Professor Bebchuk holds an LLM and SJD from Harvard Law School and an MA and a PhD in Economics from the Harvard Economics Department. His research focuses on corporate governance, law and finance, and law and economics.

Marco Becht is Professor of Finance and Economics at Université Libre de Bruxelles, a Resident Fellow at the European Centre for Advanced Research in Economics and Statistics at ULB, and the Executive Director of the European Corporate Governance Institute. In 2003 and 2012, he was Visiting Professor and Fellow at the Saïd Business School, University of Oxford; in 2008 Max Schmidheiny Visiting Professor for Entrepreneurship and Risk at the University of St. Gallen; and in 2011 Visiting Professor at Stanford Law School and a Visiting Fellow at the Rock Center for Corporate Governance. His research currently focuses on law and finance, with particular emphasis on corporate governance. He is a member of the Belgian Corporate Governance Commission, the Group of Financial Market Law Experts of the German Ministry of Finance, and a Senior Adviser to Oxera, the Economic Consultancy.

Bernard S. Black is the Nicholas D. Chabraja Professor at Northwestern University School of Law and Kellogg School of Management. He is also Managing Director of the Social Science Research Network and Founding Chairman of the annual Conference on Empirical Legal Studies. He received a BA from Princeton University, an MA in physics from the University of California, Berkeley, and a JD from Stanford Law School. He was Professor of Law at Stanford Law School from 1998 to 2004 and at Columbia Law School from 1988 to 1998. His principal research areas are law and finance, international corporate governance, health care and medical malpractice, and corporate and securities law. His books include *To Sue is Human: A Profile of Medical Malpractice Litigation* (with David Hyman, William Sage, Charles Silver, and Kathryn Zeiler, 2010), *The Law and Finance of Corporate Acquisitions* (with Ronald Gilson, 1995), and *Guide to the Russian Law on Joint Stock Companies* (with Reinier Kraakman and Anna Tarassova, 1998).

William W. Bratton is Nicholas F. Gallicchio Professor of Law at the University of Pennsylvania Law School and Co-Director of its Institute for Law and Economics. He holds a BA and a JD from Columbia University. His work brings an interdisciplinary perspective to a wide range of subject matters that encompass corporate governance, corporate finance, accounting, corporate legal history, and comparative corporate law. His work has appeared in the California, Cornell, Michigan, Northwestern, Pennsylvania, Stanford, and Virginia law reviews, and the Duke and Georgetown law journals, along with the *American Journal of Comparative Law* and the *Common Market Law Review*. His book, *Corporate Finance: Cases and Materials* (7th edn., 2012), is the leading law school text on the subject. He is a member of the American Law Institute, a Research Associate of the European Corporate Governance Institute, and a former Anton Philips Professor at the Faculty of Law of Tilburg University.

Alon Brav is Professor of Finance at the Fuqua School of Business, Duke University. He obtained a PhD in Finance in 1998 from the University of Chicago Booth School of Business. He is a Faculty Research Fellow at the National Bureau of Economic Research in the Corporate Finance Program. His current research focuses on hedge fund activism. This research has been featured in the *Journal of Finance*, the *Journal of Financial Economics*, and the *Financial Analysts Journal*. He was awarded the Smith Breeden Distinguished Paper Prize at the *Journal of Finance* with Paul Gompers, the Barclays Global Investors Michael Brennan Award for the best paper at the *Review of Financial Studies* with J. B. Heaton, and the Jensen Prize for the best corporate finance paper published in the *Journal of Financial Economics* with John Graham, Cam Harvey, and Roni Michaely.

Brian Cheffins has been the S. J. Berwin Professor of Corporate Law at Cambridge University since 1998. He began his academic career at the University of British Columbia's Faculty of

Law, where he taught from 1986 to 1997. He has held visiting appointments at Duke, Harvard, Oxford, and Stanford, and was named a Guggenheim Fellow in 2002. His primary research interests are corporate governance and corporate law, with particular reference to economic and historical aspects. Professor Cheffins is the author of *Company Law: Theory, Structure and Operation* (1997), *The Trajectory of (Corporate Law) Scholarship* (2004), and *Corporate Ownership and Control: British Business Transformed* (2008).

John C. Coffee, Jr is the Adolf A. Berle Professor of Law at Columbia University Law School and Director of its Center on Corporate Governance. He is a Fellow at the American Academy of Arts and Sciences and has been repeatedly listed by the *National Law Journal* as among its '100 Most Influential Lawyers in America'. Professor Coffee has been a member of the Legal Advisory Board to the NYSE, the Legal Advisory Board of the NASD, the Market Regulation Committee of the NASD, and the Economic Advisory Board to NASDAQ. He served as a Reporter to the American Law Institute for its *Principles of Corporate Governance: Analysis and Recommendations*, was a member of the SEC's Advisory Committee on the Capital Formation and Regulatory Processes, and served as Chairperson of the Section on Business Associations of the Association of American Law Schools. Professor Coffee is the author or editor of several widely used casebooks on corporations and securities regulation, including Coffee and Sale, *Securities Regulation: Cases and Materials* (12th edn., 2012); Choper, Coffee, and Gilson, *Cases and Materials on Corporations* (8th edn., 2013); and Klein, Coffee, and Partnoy, *Business Organization and Finance* (11th edn., 2010). His books include Coffee, *Gatekeepers: The Professions and Corporate Governance* (2006); Coffee, Lowenstein, and Rose-Ackerman, *Knights, Raiders and Targets: The Impact of the Hostile Takeover* (1988); and Ferran, Moloney, Hill, and Coffee, *The Regulatory Aftermath of the Global Financial Crisis* (2012). According to a recent survey of law review citations, Professor Coffee is the most cited law professor in law reviews over the last ten years in the combined corporate, commercial, and business law field.

Douglas Cumming is Professor of Finance and Entrepreneurship and the Ontario Research Chair at the Schulich School of Business, York University. His research spans areas that include entrepreneurship, entrepreneurial finance, venture capital, private equity, IPOs, law and finance, market surveillance, and hedge funds. He has won numerous academic awards and has consulted for a number of private and governmental organizations in North America, Europe, and Australasia.

Peter Cziraki is an Assistant Professor at the University of Toronto, Department of Economics, and a Junior Extramural Fellow at the Tilburg University, CentER Graduate School. He holds an MSc in Economics and an MA in English Translation from the University of Pécs, as well as an MPhil and a PhD in Finance from Tilburg University. He has been a Visiting Scholar at the Stanford Graduate School of Business. His particular areas of interest cover corporate finance, corporate governance, law and finance, shareholder activism, and insider trading.

Na Dai is Associate Professor at the University at Albany's School of Business. She holds a BA and an MA in Accounting, both from the Renmin University of China, and a PhD in Finance from the University of Kansas. She was previously an Assistant Professor at the Anderson School of Management, University of New Mexico, and an Assistant Professor at the School of Business, University at Albany. Her particular areas of research interest cover corporate finance, private investment in public equity, venture capital and private equity, financing of entrepreneurship and innovation, and hedge fund governance.

Jill E. Fisch is the Perry Golkin Professor of Law and Co-Director of the Institute for Law and Economics at the University of Pennsylvania Law School. Her work, which consists of more than fifty scholarly articles, has appeared in the top law reviews, including the *Harvard Law Review*, the *Yale Law Journal*, and the *University of Pennsylvania Law Review*. Current projects include the regulation of mutual funds, an empirical analysis of securities arbitration, and a reconceptualization of the structure of private securities fraud litigation. She is a member of the American Law Institute and a former chair of the Committee on Corporation Law of the Association of the Bar of the City of New York.

Julian Franks is Professor of Finance at the London Business School. He obtained a BA at the University of Sheffield, an MBA at Columbia University, and a PhD at London University. He was, previously, Visiting Professor at the University of North Carolina at Chapel Hill, and the University of California at both Berkeley and Los Angeles. His publications include works on takeovers, European corporate restructuring, financial regulation, corporate bankruptcy, and ownership and control. He is a member of the joint DTI–Treasury working party reviewing the insolvency code and of the Company Law Review's working party examining corporate governance. He is Associate Editor of the *Journal of Empirical Finance*, the *European Journal of Financial Management*, the *Journal of Corporate Finance*, and the *Journal of Financial Services Research*. He is also a member of various advisory boards including Stern Stewart and PwC.

Stuart L. Gillan is an Associate Professor at the University of Georgia, Department of Finance. He was previously Visiting Assistant Professor at Arizona State University and Associate Professor at the Texas Tech University. His particular research interests encompass corporate governance, ownership structure, and executive compensation. During the period 2011–13 he was also Associate Editor of the *Review of Financial Studies journal* and Co-Editor of the *Journal of Corporate Finance*.

Henry T. C. Hu is the Allan Shivers Chair in the Law of Banking and Finance at the University of Texas Law School. He teaches corporate law, modern finance and governance, and securities regulation. He has also taught at Harvard Law School, where he was the Bruce W. Nichols Visiting Professor of Law. He has been Chair of the Association of American Law Schools' Business Associations Section and a member of the Legal Advisory Board of the NASD (now FINRA), the NASD and NASDAQ Market Regulation Committees, and the Board of Trustees of the Center for American and International Law. He is on the Editorial Board of the Oxford University Press's *Capital Markets Law Journal*. He has testified before Congress, including on behalf of the SEC with regard to landmark derivatives legislation. In 2010, the National Association of Corporate Directors named him as one of the 100 most influential people in corporate governance ('Directorship 100'), based on a survey of 15,000 directors and executives. He holds a BS (Molecular Biophysics and Biochemistry), an MA (Economics), and a JD, all from Yale.

Robert J. Jackson, Jr is Professor of Law and Co-Director of the Ira M. Millstein Center for Global Markets and Corporate Ownership at Columbia Law School, where his research emphasizes empirical study of executive compensation and corporate governance matters. Before joining the Columbia faculty, he served as an advisor to senior officials at the Department of the Treasury and in the Office of the Special Master for TARP Executive Compensation. Before that, he practised in the Executive Compensation Department of

Wachtell, Lipton, Rosen & Katz. His most recent projects include the first empirical study of incentives throughout the managerial hierarchy of a large investment bank and the first comprehensive study of CEO pay in firms owned by private equity.

Wei Jiang is Arthur F. Burns Professor of Free and Competitive Enterprise in the Finance and Economics Division, and Director of Chazen Institute of International Business at Columbia Business School. Jiang received her BA and an MA in International Economics from Fudan University (China), and a PhD in economics from the University of Chicago in 2001, after which she joined Columbia Business School. She also has taught in the Master, MBA and EMBA programmes at Chicago, Columbia, Wharton, and Berkeley. She was an investment banking associate at Prudential Securities (Shanghai) before pursuing her PhD degree. Her main research interest lies in the strategies of institutional investors and their role in corporate decisions and financial markets. Her research has been published in top academic journals as well as featured in major media, including the *Wall Street Journal, The Economist, Institutional Investors, Money, Fortune, Business Week*, the *New York Times*, and the *Financial Times*. She is currently the Finance Area Editor of *Management Science*, and Associate Editor at the *Journal of Finance* and *Review of Financial Studies*.

Sofia A. Johan is an Adjunct Professor of Law, Entrepreneurship and Finance at the Schulich School of Business, York University. She has an LLB from Liverpool, an LLM in International Economic Law from Warwick, and a PhD in Law from Tilburg. Her research is primarily focused on law and finance, market surveillance, hedge funds, venture capital, private equity, and IPOs. Her work has been presented at the American Law and Economics Association, the European Law and Economics Association, the European Financial Management Association, and other leading international conferences. Her recent publications have appeared in numerous journals including the *American Law and Economics Review*, the *Journal of Banking and Finance, European Financial Management*, the *European Economic Review*, and *Entrepreneurship Theory and Practice*. Prior to her PhD, she was the head legal counsel at the largest government-owned venture capital fund in Malaysia. She has also consulted for a variety of governmental and private organizations in Australasia and Europe.

Marcel Kahan is the George T. Lowy Professor of Law at the New York University School of Law. His main areas of teaching and research are shareholder voting, hedge funds, corporate governance, mergers and acquisitions, and bondholder rights. He has written more than forty articles for law reviews, finance journals, and professional publications. He has received the Merton Miller Prize for the best paper submitted to the *Journal of Business* and the De Brauw Blackstone Westbroek Law Prize for the best paper in the European Corporate Governance Institute (ECGI) Law Working Paper series. In addition, the *Corporate Practice Commentator* has selected seventeen of his articles as among the best corporate and securities papers. He has been a Visiting Professor at Harvard Law School, Columbia Law School, and Hebrew University. He is a member of the American Academy of Arts and Sciences, a Fellow at the European Corporate Governance Institute, and a Director of the Pollack Center for Law & Business at NYU School of Law.

Steven N. Kaplan is the Neubauer Family Distinguished Service Professor of Entrepreneurship and Finance at the University of Chicago Booth School of Business. He conducts research on issues in private equity, venture capital, entrepreneurial finance, corporate governance, mergers and acquisitions, and corporate finance. He has published papers in a number of academic and business journals. He is a Research Associate at the National Bureau of Economic Research and an Associate Editor of the *Journal of Financial Economics*. He serves on the board or advisory board of Accretive Health, Columbia Acorn Funds, Morningstar, Sandbox Industries, and the Illinois Venture Capital Association. He also serves on the board of the Kauffman Fellows Program, an educational programme for new venture capitalists. He received an AB, in Applied Mathematics and Economics from Harvard College and a PhD in Business Economics from Harvard University.

April Klein is Professor of Accounting at New York University Stern School of Business. She teaches courses in financial accounting, financial statement analysis, and mergers and acquisitions. She also teaches financial accounting at the New York University Law School. Her primary research areas include audit committees, corporate governance, earnings management, hedge fund activism, financial accounting, and securities law. She has been published in numerous journals including the *Journal of Accounting & Economics*, the *Accounting Review*, the *Journal of Law and Economics*, the *Journal of Finance*, and the *Journal of Financial Economics*. She received a BA from the University of Pennsylvania, and an MBA and PhD in Finance from the University of Chicago.

Kai Li is the W. M. Young Professor of Finance, Associate Professor, at the Sauder School of Business, University of British Columbia. She also has been a Visiting Associate Professor of Finance at the MIT Sloan School of Management. She holds a BSc in International Business from the School of Management, Jiaotong University, an MA in Economics from Concordia University, and a PhD in Economics from the University of Toronto. Her areas of research interest include corporate governance, mergers and acquisitions, executive compensation, capital structure, and self-selection models.

Colin Mayer is the Peter Moores Professor of Management Studies at the Saïd Business School and the former Peter Moores Dean of the School between 2006 and 2011. He is an expert on all aspects of corporate finance, governance and taxation, and the regulation of financial institutions. He has consulted for numerous large firms and for governments, regulators, and international agencies around the world. His areas of expertise include corporate finance, corporate governance, corporate taxation, and the regulation of financial institutions.

Joseph A. McCahery is Professor of International Economic Law at Tilburg University Law School, where he is also a Fellow at the European Banking Center and TILEC. He clerked for Judge Nathaniel R. Jones in the US Court of Appeals for the Sixth Circuit and earned his PhD at the University of Warwick. He has been a Visiting Professor at Columbia University Law School, Leiden University Law School, University of Pennsylvania Law School, and ULB-Solvay Business School. He has contributed to the literature on banking and securities law, corporate law, corporate governance, the political economy of federalism, and taxation, and has published in a wide range of top academic journals. He has also served as a legal expert for the Centre for European Policy Studies, Dutch Central Bank, European Bank for Reconstruction, Monitoring Committee of the Netherlands on Corporate Governance, Netherlands Ministry of Economic Affairs, Netherlands Ministry of Finance, OECD, and other governmental and private organizations.

Frank Partnoy is the George E. Barrett Professor of Law and Finance at the Law School of the University of San Diego. He is also a Co-Director of the Center for Corporate and Securities

Law. He has obtained a BA and BS at the University of Kansas, and a JD at Yale Law School. His area of expertise covers business and corporate law. Prior to joining the Law School University of San Diego he worked as a Derivatives Structurer at Morgan Stanley and then practised law at Covington & Burling. Partnoy testified as an expert regarding various aspects of financial markets and regulation before both Houses of Congress, and frequently advises regulators and major corporations. He writes for the *New York Times* and the *Financial Times*, and has appeared on numerous media programmes, such as *60 Minutes*, *NewsHour* with Jim Lehrer, and *The Daily Show* with Jon Stewart.

Ludovic Phalippou is an Associate Professor of Finance at Saïd Business School, University of Oxford, and specializes in private equity. His research papers have been published in leading academic journals such as the *Journal of Finance*, the *Review of Financial Studies*, and the *Journal of Economic Perspectives*. He focuses on the areas of private equity that are of interest to investors and potential investors in that asset class, such as risk management, liquidity, and measurement of returns.

Robert K. Rasmussen is Dean and Carl Mason Franklin Chair and Professor of Law and Political Science at the University of Southern California Gould School of Law. His scholarly expertise is focused on the interaction of market forces and corporate reorganization law, and his most recent work addresses fundamental changes in corporate reorganization practice. He has a BA from Loyola University of Chicago and a JD from the University of Chicago Law School, where he was Comment Editor of the *University of Chicago Law Review*. He clerked for the Honourable John C. Godbold, Chief Judge of the United States Court of Appeals for the Eleventh Circuit, and worked in the Civil Division Appellate Staff at the US Department of Justice, handling litigation in the US Courts of Appeals and the Supreme Court. He later joined the Vanderbilt law faculty and has been a Visiting Professor at the University of Chicago and University of Michigan law schools.

Luc Renneboog is Professor of Corporate Finance at the Finance Department of Tilburg University and Director of Graduate Studies at the CentER for Economic Research. He graduated from the University of Leuven with a BSc/MSc in Commercial Engineering and a BA in Philosophy. He has an MBA from the University of Chicago and a PhD in Financial Economics from the London Business School of the University of London. He is also a research member of CentER for Economic Research, TILEC, and ECGI (Brussels). He has published in the *Journal of Finance, Management Science, American Economic Review, Journal of Financial Intermediation, Journal of Law and Economics, Journal of Corporate Finance, Strategic Management Journal, Journal of Banking and Finance, Journal of Law, Economics & Organization, Oxford Economic Papers, Cambridge Journal of Economics, Oxford Review of Economic Policy, European Financial Management*, and others. His research interests are corporate finance, corporate governance, mergers and acquisitions, rights issues, law and economics, the economics of sports, socially responsible investing, and the economics of art.

Edward B. Rock is the Saul A. Fox Distinguished Professor of Business Law at the University of Pennsylvania Law School and Senior Advisor to the President and Provost of the University and Director of Open Course Initiatives. He writes widely on corporate law and corporate governance. In recent years, working with Marcel Kahan at NYU, he has written a series of award-winning articles on hedge funds, corporate voting, proxy access, corporate federalism, and mergers and acquisitions.

Stefano Rossi is Associate Professor of Finance in the Finance Area in the Krannert School of Management. He is a Research Affiliate of the Centre for Economic Policy Research (CEPR), a Research Associate of the ECGI, and an Associate Editor of *European Financial Management*. His research interests include corporate governance, bankruptcy and financial distress, debt financing, international finance, sovereign borrowing, financing of innovations, and market mispricings due to institutional frictions and strategic trading. His research has been published in top peer-reviewed journals such as the *Journal of Financial Economics* and the *Review of Financial Studies*, and has been featured in publications such as the *Financial Times* and *The Economist*.

Laura T. Starks is the Charles E. and Sarah M. Seay Regents Chair in Finance and Associate Dean for Research, and Director of the AIM Investment Center in the McCombs School of Business at the University of Texas at Austin. She received a BA and a PhD from the University of Texas at Austin, and an MBA from the University of Texas at San Antonio. Her research and teaching interests include valuation of financial assets, portfolio management, corporate governance, the influence of institutional investors in financial markets, managerial incentives, and environmental, social, and governance investing.

Per Strömberg is the SSE Centennial Professor of Finance and Private Equity at the Stockholm School of Economics. He is also is the Director of the Swedish House of Finance (SHOF), a new Swedish national centre for financial research, which is a cooperation between SIFR, the Stockholm School of Economics, and Vinnova. He is also Adjunct Associate Professor of Finance at the University of Chicago Booth School of Business. He received a PhD in Financial Economics from Carnegie Mellon University and an MBA (civilekonom) from the Stockholm School of Economics. His research has primarily focused on the two areas of bankruptcy and private equity finance. His work has been published in the *Journal of Finance, American Economic Review*, the *Review of Economic Studies*, the *Review of Financial Studies*, and the *Journal of Financial Intermediation*, and has been presented at numerous conferences and universities.

Peter G. Szilagyi has been the University Lecturer in Finance since 2007 and the Director of the MPhil in Finance Programme since 2012 at the University of Cambridge. He holds an MA in International Relations and Economics from the Budapest University of Economic Sciences, an MA in Applied Finance from the University of Western Sydney, and a PhD in Finance from Tilburg University. Before taking his appointment at Cambridge, he was a Research Fellow at the University of Oxford as a member of the European Corporate Governance Training Network. He has been an external fixed-income consultant to the World Bank and the Asian Development Bank and, before entering academia, worked for the BBC World Service. He is the Corporate Finance Subject Editor of the *International Review of Financial Analysis* and a member of the Cambridge Corporate Governance Network (CCGN).

Randall S. Thomas is the John S. Beasley II Professor of Law and Business and the Director of the Law & Business Program at Vanderbilt Law School, and Professor of Management, Owen Graduate School of Business. His recent work addresses issues such as hedge fund shareholder activism, executive compensation, corporate voting, corporate litigation, and mergers and acquisitions. He previously served on the law faculties of the University of Iowa, the University of Michigan, Duke University, Boston University, and the University of Washington. Prior to teaching law, Professor Thomas was in private practice for four years, and clerked for US District Judge Charles Joiner of the Eastern District of Michigan.

Erik P. M. Vermeulen is Professor of Business and Financial Law at Tilburg University and TILEC. He is also Senior Counsel Corporate/Vice President at the Corporate Legal Department of Philips International B.V., where he advises on corporate governance issues, including the global corporate structure of the Philips Group of companies. He has worked on national and international projects for organizations such as the European Commission, OECD, the Dutch Development Finance Institution, and local governments in the Netherlands, concerning financial and venture capital markets, corporate law, and corporate governance.

Michael L. Wachter is the William B. Johnson Professor of Law and Economics and Co-Director of the Institute for Law and Economics at the University of Pennsylvania Law School. He is a prominent cross-disciplinary scholar in the fields of law and economics, with his current research focusing on topics of corporate law, corporate finance, and labour law and economics. Since 1970, when he joined the University of Pennsylvania faculty, he has held full professorships in three of Penn's schools: Arts and Sciences, where he has been Professor of Economics since 1976; the Wharton School, where he was Professor of Management from1980 to 1992; and the Law School, where he became Professor of Law and Economics in 1984. In that year he also took on the directorship of the Institute for Law and Economics. His current research focuses on corporate governance and topics in the intersection of corporate law and finance.

Wei Wang is Assistant Professor and Distinguished Faculty Fellow of Finance at the Queen's School of Business. He is also Director of Queen's Master of Finance—Beijing (Renmin-Queens Master of Finance) Program. He obtained a PhD in Finance from Queen's University, an MA in Economics from the University of Liverpool, and a Bachelor of Civil Engineering and Urban Planning from Northwest University (China). He has worked in commodity derivative trading and financial engineering. His current research interests are in bankruptcy, distressed securities, active investors, capital structure, credit ratings, CEO compensation, and behavioural finance. His papers have been published in the *Journal of Finance* and the *Journal of Fixed Income*, and his research has been featured in various media including the *Wall Street Journal*.

Emanuel Zur is Assistant Professor of Accounting and Information Assurance at the Robert H. Smith School of Business of the University of Maryland. He was previously Assistant Professor of Accounting at Baruch College and Visiting Assistant Professor at MIT's Sloan School of Management. He holds an LLB in Law and a BA in Economics from Tel-Aviv University, as well as an MPhil in Management and a PhD in Business Administration from New York University's Stern School of Business. His research has been published in the *Journal of Finance* and the *Review of Financial Studies*, and he has presented research papers at leading universities in Asia, Europe, and North America.

CHAPTER 1

INTRODUCTION

WILLIAM W. BRATTON
AND
JOSEPH A. McCAHERY

Agency theory posits that separation of ownership and control opens up a governance deficit. The shareholder principals, it says, have a collective action problem that leaves them without an economic incentive to monitor their manager agents. The theory, in its original form, held out the hostile takeover as a cure. But, in practice, the hostile takeover has never filled the role described, its incidence constrained by regulatory and other costs. The world of mergers and acquisitions has evolved to favour friendly transactions, even as hostile offers continue to appear in small numbers. The classic problem of the Berle and Means corporation persists accordingly.

To be sure, agency theorists have inquired into alternative possibilities for making up the governance deficit. For example, two decades ago the exercise of transnational governance comparison led observers in the United States, inspired by German main banks and Japanese *keiretsu*, to look to holders of large blocks of stock to provide quality oversight on a going concern basis. The blockholder, thus hypothesized as the solution to the governance problem, holds out two manifest advantages. First, it can monitor from an interior position, surmounting the information asymmetry problem that disables outside shareholder-monitors. Second, the blockholder, posited as an underdiversified, long-term investor, can monitor with a cooperative disposition, avoiding the costs and disruptions attending hostile engagement. But there also are problems. Separation of ownership and control holds out for shareholders the advantages of liquidity and easy exit through the trading market, even as it creates a manager–shareholder incentive problem. Blockholder governance implies reduced liquidity even as it addresses the incentive problem. As a result, blockholding poses its own incentive problem. A rational blockholder would be unlikely to give up the benefits of liquidity in order to extract gains from improved governance only to have to share those gains with the rest of a free-riding population of small shareholders who enjoy liquidity's benefits. A different sort of governance dysfunction follows—a rational blockholder will seek compensation for its governance contribution through self-dealing transactions, insider trading, or some other unshared mode of return.

Agency theory continues to look for means to circumvent these trade-offs. The search turns again and again to the sleeping giant of corporate governance: the institutional investor. Institutions hold an increasing percentage of shares outstanding and interest themselves in governance problems. Rational apathy respecting matters presented for shareholder approval, long a shareholder trait under the separation of control, no longer prevails amongst them. At the same time, however, sustained, active monitoring and affirmative governance input have not been the rule. Most institutions are passive, well-diversified investors. The same factors that complicate the incentives of blockholders come to bear more preclusively with these institutions. Active monitoring presupposes investment in information gathering and governance participation. Diversified mutual and pension fund managers have no incentive to make such investments because they bear the costs unilaterally and share the gains with the rest of a free-riding shareholder population.

These constraints determine and limit the modes of institutional investor governance engagement. Large repositories of corporate information and expertise do exist, but in the hands of intermediary firms that came into existence for the very purpose of providing passive institutional investors with the means of acquitting themselves of governance responsibilities.

Activists do exist among traditional investment institutions, but not institutions acting on pure financial incentives. Public sector pension funds and labour unions take the lead roles, acting through agents incentivized by prospects of reputational advancement. These actors target companies and challenge their managers with shareholder proposals and 'just vote no' campaigns. They thereby register their voice and affect outcomes, but from a secondary position and on an occasional basis. The cumulated governance activity is impressive, but none of it assures or very often results in constructive engagement by shareholders in the formulation of business policy at individual firms. As to that, collective action problems and the problems of separation of ownership and control persist.

There have long been two significant exceptions to the rule of institutional shareholder disability. Activist shareholders do appear, from time to time, to take significant stakes in companies and bargain with their managers towards the end of effecting productive changes in business policy. These actors, whose initial appearance dates back 150 years, intervene from outside corporate and financial power structures and operate out of small, independent, underdiversified investment entities. The second exception, of more recent vintage, is the private equity firm, an intermediary that raises capital for the purpose of buying publicly traded companies in friendly, negotiated transactions, for the purpose of profiting from redirection of their business policies. These too operate from small, independent, underdiversified investment entities. Since the turn of this century, we have seen unprecedented levels of activity from both of these exceptional types.

1.1 Hedge Funds as Activist Shareholders

The role of the hostile activist shareholder has been taken up by a set of hedge funds. This group targets and researches companies, takes large positions in their stock, criticizes their business plans and governance practices, and confronts their managers, demanding action enhancing shareholder value. When one hedge fund announces a 5 or 10% position in company, others can follow, forming a 'wolf pack' that sometimes has the voting power to force management to address its demands. The demands, in turn, likely include one or more actions assuring a quick return on investment—sale of the company at a premium, unbundling of the company through the sale or spin-off of a large division, or a large cash payment to the shareholders in the form of a special dividend or share repurchase. The hedge fund activists pack their biggest punch at small companies, in which their investments translate into large voting blocks. But they also have confronted giants like DuPont, Kraft, McDonald's, Proctor & Gamble, and Time Warner. The list of big targets has lengthened notably in recent years. In 2013, Apple, Sony, UBS, PepsiCo, Dell, and Microsoft all came under attack.

The activist hedge funds' financial power has increased steadily. According to Hedge Fund Research, funds in the activist sector had $12 billion at their disposal in 2003. In 2013, this stock of 'dry powder' had risen to $73 billion, amounting to a tangible outpouring of investor confidence in the sector. The continued investor support partially answers a question regarding the permanence of hedge fund activists' place on the governance stage, a question that only recently loomed large when activist intervention almost disappeared in the wake of the financial crisis of 2008 (Bratton 2010). Hedge fund activism rose after 2002, subsided after 2008, and then rose again. The first rise accordingly cannot be dismissed as a flash in the pan and a pro-cyclical aspect can be noted.

Money talks on Wall Street and respectability has followed for the activists. Where interveners in this mould were once dismissed as rogues and widely shunned, these funds have become the clients of the most prominent investment banks and law firms. More importantly, their model of governance engagement has proved robust. While hostile in approach, they rarely seek to take over their targets, distinguishing them from the hostile raiders of the 1980s. Today's activists pursue more focused, discreet governance agendas. They are flexible about the means to the end, joining target boards of directors and softening their hostile postures as the occasion demands.

The activist hedge funds' record of success is historically impressive. Prior to their appearance, activist institutional investors did not have much of an impact. Some studies showed that activist intervention caused the stock price to go up. But, unless the intervener proceeded to buy the company or trigger a takeover by a third party, there was little evidence of resultant change inside the target firm. Meanwhile, studies focused on activism by public pension funds showed no stock price effect at all. Nor did the activists have a favourable record of success with full-dress proxy contests for control. The hedge fund activists have changed this, causing stock prices to rise, directing changes in business policy, and entering boardrooms. One detects a palpable sense of frustration on the defensive side. With hostile tender offers, management's lawyers erected reliable protective walls in the form of poison pills and staggered boards. With activist hedge funds, the best the lawyers can counsel is good shareholder relations and constant monitoring.

Unsurprisingly, there are allegations of perverse practices and effects. Short-termism is the main complaint, relentlessly mooted by management and its legal representatives. Questions also come up regarding tactics. It is said that hedge funds use derivatives to evade reporting requirements imposed on large blockholders and manipulate voting outcomes. Regulatory reform initiatives have followed in response, and some changes have occurred, none of them as yet fundamental.

1.2 Hedge Funds as Activist Debtholders

Activist hedge funds also have played a role in the transformation of US bankruptcy reorganization. Traditionally, Chapter 11 reorganizations have been dominated by the distressed company's managers under a system that accorded them agenda control. The managers had exclusive power to present a plan of reorganization and took advantage of this, delaying presentation of a plan even as the company's creditors received no interest on their claims during the proceedings. The creditors, wanting above all to return their investments to paying status, tended to accede to unfavourable terms. Power shifted in the creditors' direction after 2000. Significantly, the shift happened without any structural reform of the system. Creditor classes picked up contractual tools that were already on the table, successfully deploying them to push management into a corner. New borrowing, termed 'DIP (debtor-in-possession) loans', is critical in many Chapter 11 proceedings. Under the US Bankruptcy Code, new loans can receive priority status. A bankruptcy declaration, accordingly, can imply an instant return to creditworthy status for the distressed company. After 2000, DIP lenders, with the concurrence of the bankruptcy courts, started using their debt contracts to impose timetables and performance metrics on the bankrupt company and its managers. As result, Chapter 11 reorganizations now move more quickly and more often conclude with asset sales rather than confirmed reorganization plans. New managers armed with new business plans are more likely to take over as the proceeding runs its course. In effect, a different separation of ownership from control—this one between creditors and incumbent managers—has been remedied.

Banks and other primary lenders are prominent among the newly empowered creditors. But activist hedge funds also sit at the table, playing complicated arbitrage strategies. The hedge funds are established Chapter 11 players. They first showed up in the 1980s, along with new trading markets in bankruptcy claims. Conservative lenders dump their paper into the claims trading markets where specialist hedge funds, termed 'vultures', pick up the paper at distressed prices. The hedge funds then aggressively use their claims positions to influence the outcomes of Chapter 11 proceedings, even looking to take control of the reorganized company.

Questions arise regarding the desirability of hedge fund aggression in Chapter 11. At a minimum the hedge funds impart an uncooperative aspect to bankruptcy proceedings. More worrisome are accusations of obstructionist and manipulative tactics. Some think that the costs of hedge fund disruption are uncompensated by any value added. But the matter is far from clear, for others plausibly look to hedge fund activism as the mainspring of bankruptcy's new efficiencies.

1.3 Private Equity Funds

We turn now to a contrasting mode of activist government intervention, going private transactions conducted by private equity firms. We acknowledge that our application of the term 'activist' will strike many as inappropriate, for, with private equity, friendly and cooperative engagement with target management is the byword in contrast to the hedge fund interventions just described. We do not, however, delimit activism to hostile engagement. Private equity buyouts are governance interventions and anything but passive.

A buyout carries blockholding out to its logical conclusion. It completely removes the target firm from the equity trading market, entailing the utmost liquidity sacrifice on the blockholder's part. The limited partnership that conducts the buyout (the buyout fund) emerges with the majority equity stake, with the target's managers as the only minority shareholders. Significantly, the interposition of this separate entity as the holder of a majority block of the target firm's shares solves the blockholder incentive problem. The buyout fund is organized and promoted by a private equity firm, with the risk capital coming from the institutional investors who take its limited partnership shares. The private equity firm selects the going private target, effects the buyout, and undertakes the role of target firm monitor. The buyout fund's limited partnership agreement and other operative contracts allocate the risks and returns between the buyout firm and the outside institutional investors. Meanwhile, the buyout target emerges from the control transfer with a governance structure that approaches the agency ideal. Its incumbent managers get high-powered incentives as minority shareholders even as control moves to a highly incentivized shareholder-monitor. At the same time, an arm's-length contract governs relations between that control party and outside equity investors. Returns from monitoring are thus allocated up front.

Private equity firms made their first appearance thirty-five years ago. They played a prominent role in the 1980s mergers and acquisitions market, in particular as promoters of leveraged corporate restructurings. But the 1980s buyout boom was followed by a spectacular bust. Figure 1.1 shows the per capita percentage of private equity buyouts amongst public company acquisitions peak at 27% in 1988, only to slide in 1994 to less than 2% of a thin market. By all appearances, private equity had, by the mid-1990s, disappeared in tandem with the 1980s bust-up takeover.

It looked for a time as if the private equity business model had seen its best days. Holmström and Kaplan, looking back to the 1980s in 2001, described a period of shock therapy that redirected management priorities in a more productive direction. Managers had needed the therapy because they had proved slow to adapt to changed conditions (Holmström and Kaplan 2001). The newly enabled capital markets imposed responsive strategies instead. Management learned its lesson, in turn. In the 1990s, managers, incentivized by stock option compensation, voluntarily downsized their operations and unbundled conglomerates. As the shareholder value approach became dominant, the private equity buyout's moment seemed to have passed. Effective management and high leverage were no longer seen as inevitable concomitants. Now that the shock effectively had been administered, other, less drastic, incentive devices could do the job.

But, as Figure 1.1 shows, buyouts came back to claim a per capita share of 41% of public company acquisitions in 2006. Buyouts then held their share of acquisitions in the diminished merger market that followed the financial crisis, reaching a highest-ever share of 42.6% in 2012. They did so in a shareholder value era, absent either a concomitant reappearance of hostile takeovers or a manifest need for a control shock. Their reappearance implies that, even in an era focused on best governance practices and shareholder value maximization, the incentive problems bound up in the separation of ownership and control retain economic salience.

Indeed, the fundamentals of the buyout business model have changed little across the period, even as there have been changes at the buyout firms themselves. In their original

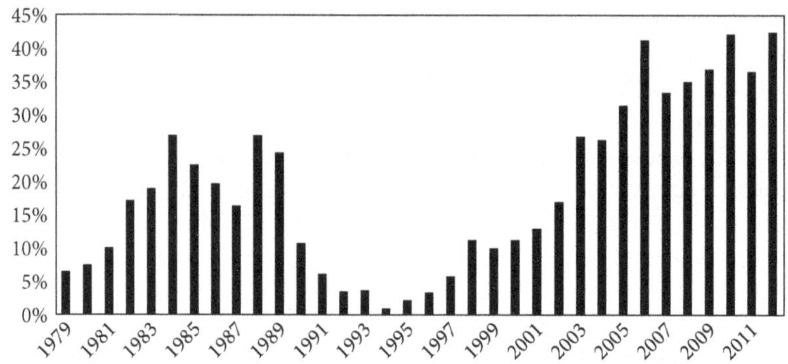

FIGURE 1.1 US going private transaction as a percentage of US public company acquisitions, 1979–2012
Source: Mergerstat.

iteration, private equity firms were small shops that lacked the in-house expertise and information needed for direct management of portfolio companies. Hence, a going private transaction was, by definition, a 'management buyout'—the incumbent managers stayed on. Today it depends on the deal. Buyout transactions are still almost invariably friendly, but the incumbent managers no longer necessarily remain with the target; private equity buyers frequently assemble teams to replace them. Meanwhile, as private equity firms have grown, their funds' investment portfolios have become more varied, including energy and real estate and a range of financial assets. But buyouts themselves have changed little, with their leveraged purchase prices and post-closing cost-cutting and asset sales.

1.4 Funds—Structural Comparison

We have then three categories of activist intervention—the first entails the holding of non-controlling share blocks with the holder wielding the shareholder franchise, the second entails the holding of debt claims in a Chapter 11 reorganization proceeding with the holder wielding votes within a class of bankruptcy claimants, the third entails the outright purchase of the control in the mergers and acquisitions market. All of the activists are funds, funds falling into two categories.

Hedge funds and private equity funds share a common, largely unregulated space, at least in the United States. If one puts periodic reporting to government authorities to one side, they remain outside the bounds of federal regulation of mutual funds, other investment companies, and their advisors. They market participations through the unregulated vehicle of the private placement. In other national economies, both types of funds are subject to more significant modes of regulatory control, including reporting requirements and sometimes capital structure rules.

Organizational structures are similar worldwide. Contracts control. Both hedge and private equity funds are limited partnerships organized by management firms, with risk capital coming from the institutional investors who purchase limited partnership shares. The management firm selects, makes, and monitors the investments. The limited partnership agreement of the hedge or private equity fund, along with other operative contracts, allocates the risks and returns between the management firm and the outside investors. Portfolios are likely to be leveraged in both cases, but more steeply on the private equity side. Compensation to the management firm also runs along parallel lines, with the management firm taking up to 2% per year of committed capital and a 20% 'carry' respecting annual profits, subject to negotiated percentage reductions in the asset fee, negotiated limitations of the asset fee percentage to capital actually invested, and negotiated hurdles and clawbacks respecting the carry. Finally, both types of funds implicitly promise to deliver above-market returns, a task that becomes harder and harder as more funds pursue the same strategies.

Until recently, hedge and private equity funds could be distinguished by the characteristics of their investments. Private equity takes companies private, investing long term in their equity from a control position. Hedge funds, in contrast, play securities markets worldwide. Private equity firms possess expertise in company analysis. The typical hedge fund, in contrast, employs 'numbers guys' expert in complex market arbitrage. Different hedge funds concentrate on different market plays. Some specialize in securities of distressed firms. Others make directional bets on the movement of currency exchange or interest rates. Still others pursue convertible arbitrage, going long in a convertible bond and shorting the underlying common stock. Many follow market momentum, moving in groups in and out of different asset classes. Some have taken up risky lending, funding leveraged buyouts and firms in bankruptcy reorganization, and trading in junk bonds and credit derivatives.

The activist hedge funds derive from a subset of the sector that invests in equities in the classic, value investor mode. These funds maintain concentrated portfolios and, in some cases, avoid the hedged or multi-strategy approaches followed by other funds, with their managers tending to be former investment bankers or research analysts rather than quantitative experts. They do the research and know their targets well, much like the private equity firms. Some of their managers even profess to be followers of Graham and Dodd, the mid-twentieth-century financial writers whose work remains a fundamental text of value investment. But their activist interventions break with the Graham and Dodd tradition. The leading value exponent, Warren Buffett, invests long term and stays patient, following the same cooperative strategy as the private equity investors. The hedge fund activists lack this patience. They look for value but want it realized in the near or intermediate term. Their strategy is to tell managers how to realize the value and to challenge publicly those who resist their advice. The vulture funds follow a similar playbook tailored to the context of bankruptcy reorganization. Instead of buying companies outright, they purchase significant, non-controlling stakes and then seek to magnify returns by influencing the bankruptcy decision-making process; if control follows purchased at a bargain price, all the better.

Private equity also actively reshapes business plans, but does so behind closed doors over periods of years, after buying the company with mostly borrowed money and taking it private. Differences in governing investment contracts parallel these different behaviour patterns. Contracts governing investment in hedge funds typically lock up investor capital for six months, although some impose terms of two years or longer. Contracts governing private equity investment tend to lock up investments for ten years. These more liberal arrangements facilitate not only large, illiquid, and long-term equity positions, but patience. In contrast, the hedge funds' shorter durations, when coupled with the large, illiquid positions, invite aggression and impatience. But it should be noted that nothing in present practice dictates the terms of the activists' future arrangements with their investors. If they obtain longer lock-ups, modified strategies may follow.

Despite all the differences, activist hedge funds and private equity firms may be characterized as pursuing a common goal—in the words used in the OECD Steering Group on Corporate Governance (2007), both seek:

> to increase the market value of their pooled capital through active engagement with individual public companies. This engagement may include demands for changes in management, the composition of the board, dividend policies, company strategy, company capital structure and acquisition/disposal plans which are normally regarded as governance issues.

Thus committed, activist hedge funds and private equity have a track record of management intervention reputedly so successful as to give rise to an unprecedented, even radical question: have they together in some meaningful sense solved the problem of separation of ownership and control? To the extent that they have, a conventional wisdom about management dominance of the machinery of corporate governance needs to be reconsidered. At the same time, hedge funds and private equity continue to confront an objection that descends from the bust-up takeover era of the 1980s. They are accused of short-termism—they are said to focus on shareholder value maximization myopically, causing productive enterprises to forego investment opportunities necessary for long-term viability.

This book collects descriptive expositions and empirical analyses essential for an understanding of both varieties of interventionist shareholder. The chapters herein detail these investors' strategic approaches, the financial returns they produce, and the regulatory frameworks within which they operate. The chapters also provide historical context, both of activist investment and institutional shareholder passivity. Finally, the collection facilitates comparison between the US and the EU, juxtaposing not only regulatory patterns but investment styles. A more particular description of the book's chapters follows.

1.5 Part I The Disempowered Shareholder

Part I sets the stage, describing the received context of separation of ownership and control and shareholder disempowerment.

In Chapter 2, Stuart L. Gillan and Laura T. Starks trace the evolution of shareholder activism in the US from the introduction of the SEC (Securities and Exchange Commission) shareholder proposal rule in 1942, through the takeover wars of the 1980s, and beyond, to the mutual and pension fund interventions of more recent years. Gillan and Starks go on to review the empirical literature on the effects of activism. News of shareholder proposals has consistently been shown, taken in aggregate, to lack a short-term impact on stock prices, although studies of proposals on particular issues (e.g., poison pills) have shown some effects. Studies of subsequent long-term operating results of target companies also, on the whole, fail to show positive effects. Voting patterns respecting non-binding shareholder proposals have evolved along a more successful path, with governance-oriented proposals doing well in the present context. The authors close with an overview of recent hedge fund activity.

Many attribute the historical ineffectiveness of shareholder activism to the inherited legal institution of the shareholder franchise, which in the US historically has done nothing to facilitate shareholder challenges, at least apart from the SEC provision for non-binding shareholder proposals. In Chapter 3, Lucian A. Bebchuk subjects the legal regime to critical inspection, asserting that it fails to legitimate the considerable power that the law delegates to the board of directors. Legitimacy, in Bebchuk's view, means adherence to the goal of shareholder value maximization, a goal not forwarded by the prevailing process barriers to shareholder challenges. Bebchuk presents the results of an empirical study of proxy challenges to incumbent directors in the period 1996–2005: twelve challenges per year overall, including three challenges per year at companies with market capitalizations exceeding $200 million, of which only less than one annually results in a victory. Unfavourable process and cost allocation rules are held to be responsible.

Bebchuk would revamp the prevailing legal structure, according the shareholders access to the ballot every other year with expense reimbursement for challengers garnering one-third of the votes cast, along with shareholder access to the bylaws to propose legislation related to election processes. In addition, he would accord the shareholders a periodic right to replace all of the directors, institute a default rule of majority rather than plurality voting, allow 'no' votes, and provide for confidential voting.

Chapter 4 changes the venue to Europe. Peter Cziraki, Luc Renneboog, and Peter G. Szilagyi report on shareholder intervention through the proxy process at European companies, analysing a sample of 290 proposals submitted in nine countries between 1998 and 2008. The regulatory background is quite different from that in the US: immediate adoption of the proxy access provisions in place in a number of European countries would go some distance in satisfying the law reform agenda presented by Bebchuk. In Europe, shareholders who meet specified thresholds have the right to call meetings at which directors can be removed and elected, governance legislation amended, and business plans altered. The door is opened widest in the UK, which accords power to summon a meeting to a 5% shareholder block or, alternatively, to 100 shareholders with at least £100 invested. The UK goes on to extend a corporate subsidy to solicitation. Other countries ask for more, but as the value of a given shareholder's block increases the percentage requirement can drop as low as 1% of shares outstanding; solicitation subsidies are unavailable.

A US observer surveying these European provisions readily might predict a steady flow of challenges to the boards of underperforming companies and activist victories. Cziraki, Renneboog, and Szilagyi confirm that European activists target underperforming firms, particularly those operating under deficient governance regimes. But activity is sporadic and management incumbents tend to win—challenges in the UK average 38.6% of the votes, while challenges on the Continent average only 21.1%. Most challenges arise in the UK (195 to 95) and concern board personnel changes and corporate strategy. Challengers on the Continent tend to focus on governance issues. The stock market reacts negatively to the outcomes. The authors conclude that, in Europe, shareholder interventions serve as 'an emergency brake rather than a steering wheel'.

The US–Europe comparison raises a series of questions. If the shareholder access door were opened in the US would there follow a materially larger volume of challenges along with different outcomes? Perhaps relations between institutional shareholders and managers in UK work differently from those in the US, rendering statutory access relatively less important than would be the case were it available in the US. Perhaps family holdings and stock pyramids on the Continent relegate shareholder intervention to a secondary governance role. Alternatively, perhaps lack of access in the US has become less of a problem in the wake of the rise of hedge fund activism. Part II contains several chapters reporting that the hedge fund activists have had a precedent-smashing run of success at telling US boards what do to. Ironically, the activist success record suggests a defence of the inherited legal model of the shareholder franchise: when a properly incented shareholder does come along, the system allows its voice to register. For some it follows that no law reform is necessary. But for other observers, Bebchuk assuredly among them, the appearance of hedge fund activists only further enhances the case for reform: that it took decades for a properly incented variety of investment institution to appear only proves the case. Meanwhile, activist intervention is not a universal fact of life at listed companies, and questions arise regarding the business model's sustainability.

1.6 Part II Hedge Fund Activism

Part II takes up hedge fund activism with a series of chapters that describe the funds in question, their strategies, and financial results.

1.7 Patterns and Policy Questions—Dark Sides and Light Sides

All of Part II's chapters, in one or another mode, address the question whether activist attacks hold out negative economic consequences. The lead questioner is the lawyer Martin Lipton, acting in his customary role as head of the management defence team. Says Lipton, 'We have gone from the imperial CEO to the imperial stockholder.' Critics like Lipton ask why, as between a team of managers who have been running a firm for years and an outside activist looking for above-market returns in the current period, the activist's judgement about the best way to run the business should command respect. The activists, they say, survey a target with a bias towards short-term gain, regardless of its future, the interests of its long-term investors, and the productivity of the wider economy. Hedge fund pressure on present and potential targets is thought negatively to constrain investment policy, skewing managers away from promising but difficult-to-value projects towards less promising but more easily valued projects. Where an activist extracts a payout financed by debt, the ongoing cash drain could leave the target vulnerable to distress in the economy's next downturn. Others warn of darker possibilities like lucrative side deals between unscrupulous funds and frightened managers or feigned interventions that create short-term trading opportunities.

Chapter 5 contains Marcel Kahan and Edward B. Rock's description of activist activity and their answer to the question just posed. They conclude that while hedge funds may not be the perfect embodiment of the long sought solution to the incentive problems of separated ownership and control, there is no basis for predicting an outbreak of short-term opportunism with long-term negative effects for individual firms and the wider economy.

Kahan and Rock begin with a description of hedge fund tactics, distinguishing both the tactics and the situations that trigger intervention from those characteristic of more conventional institutions. They go on to detail the incentive alignments that incline the respective institutions to activism. With conventional mutual funds, collective action problems, conflicts of interest, and investment duration all deter investment in interventionist strategies. The free-rider problem discourages investment managers from incurring the costs of challenges—gains must be shared with competitors who do not share costs. At the same time, many fund advisors sell services to managers, importing an independent business reason to stay cooperative. Finally, mutual fund investors can redeem at any time, inhibiting investment in large, illiquid positions. Public pension funds operate under a different set of constraints, largely political, that choke off financial incentives and constrain activist agendas. Hedge funds face none of these barriers. Their unregulated status frees them of diversification requirements imposed on mutual funds or restrictions on the setting of performance fees. The funds' managers have every reason to be aggressive in realizing value, given the carry of 20% of the profits. Small size and focused strategy minimize conflicts of interest. Finally, the governing investment contracts allow them to lock up capital for longer periods than do the mutual funds.

Kahan and Rock then detail a number of potential conflicts of interest and regulatory issues arising in the course of activist engagement—opportunities for voting manipulation, traversal of the federal securities laws' group disclosure rule, and greenmail. They go on to assay the short-termism charge, concluding that the allegations follow from speculative premises and predicting that operating companies will make appropriate adjustments that will deflect any threat to productivity. New regulation, in short, is not justified.

Chapter 6 follows, with a contrasting overview from John Armour and Brian Cheffins. They describe hedge fund activism as a 'market for corporate influence' and situate it historically, distinguishing today's hedge funds from the bust-up raiders of the 1980s, and detailing structural and secular changes that coalesced to produce a sudden burst of activist engagement in the mid-2000s. Amour and Cheffins look: (1) to the supply side, that is, the presence of profitable opportunities to exercise influence; and (2) to the demand side, that is, the presence of investors willing pursue the opportunities. Supply calls for underperforming or underpriced companies and a conducive legal environment. Demand calls for ready and cheap financing, and low costs, including regulatory costs. The authors show that much necessary stage-setting occurred long before the recent hedge fund surge, with information technology lowering search costs, bid-ask spreads dropping, access to private investment vehicles easing, and the SEC reforming the proxy rules to permit inter-investor communications. Their list of more particular supply side causes includes the post-tech bubble decline in stock prices and a concomitant climate of dissatisfaction within the institutional investor community, along with growing corporate cash accounts. On the demand side, cheap and ready credit both lowered the hedge funds' financing costs and facilitated defensive accommodations by targets.

Amour and Cheffins close with the distressed economic environment of 2008, asking some questions about the future. While depressed stock markets may keep up supply, the demand side suffered a temporary lapse. The disappearance of credit, along with a period of disappointing hedge fund returns plus consequent redemptions at many funds, impaired the sector, contributing to a drop off in activity beginning in mid-2009. But the activist sector, viewed broadly, coped 'tolerably well' with the market turmoil and was rousing itself again by 2010. Amour and Cheffins predict that the activists will retain a prominent place in US corporate governance for the foreseeable future.

1.8 Ownership Stakes, Operating Results, and Financial Returns

Chapter 7 presents an intensive case study of a single, activist fund from Marco Becht, Julian Franks, Colin Mayer, and Stefano Rossi. This work opened up a new era in the history of financial studies of institutional investors, reporting the first substantive evidence showing that activism can result in financial gain. The study focuses on the Hermes UK Focus Fund (HUKFF), a UK pension fund founded as an experiment in shareholder activism. HUKFF was to take positions in underperforming companies in which its parent, Hermes, already had invested through its index fund, taking stakes significantly large to make investment in intervention cost beneficial. Becht et al., taking advantage of access to the funds' records, study HUKFF's positions, tactics, and returns for the period 1998–2004.

The authors focus on the subset of HUKFF investments that involved active engagement with investee companies (30 of 41). The positions' sizes varied depending on the relational posture of the case. Sometimes confrontation resulted, and in those cases the average stake amounted to 6.9% of stock outstanding. Other target managers responded cooperatively; there the average stake amounted to only 3.2%. Whether in confrontational or cooperative mode, HUKFF conducted its engagements in private, concentrating on direct contact with company executives and board members and the company's other institutional holders, and for the most part avoiding proxy solicitations and public announcements.

In twenty-eight of the active cases HUKFF invested with a view to substantial restructuring through the sale of non-core assets and limits on further diversification. The targeted results were achieved most of the time—targeted asset sales occurred in six of ten cases; diversifying acquisitions were blocked in nine out of ten cases; and capital expenditures were contained in six out of seven cases. CEO or chairman replacement showed up on the list of objectives in half of the cases, a result achieved in around three-quarters of that subset. Stepped up payouts were an objective in seventeen cases, a goal achieved at eleven companies. Favourable effects on operating results are reported, with increases in median return on assets and market-to-book. Total assets, and numbers of employees, decline drastically.

Becht et al., show that HUKFF beat the market with raw annual returns of 4.9% (after adjustment for the Financial Times Stock Exchange (FTSE)) and a positive monthly alpha. Sorting out the portion of returns attributable to activist intervention presents a statistical challenge, however. The authors claim 90% causality, noting the novelty of their methodology. The study is not only ground-breaking but prescient. Many of the elements that Becht, Mayer, Franks, and Rossi detail at a single UK fund formed in 1998 later became common to a set of hedge fund investors operating on both sides of the Atlantic. There also would be variations in strategy. Where HUKFF proceeded gently and privately, their hedge fund successors proved rough and used publicity. The two chapters that follow provide intensive analyses of the hedge funds, their approaches, and their results.

In Chapter 8, Alon Brav, Wei Jiang, Frank Partnoy, and Randall S. Thomas gather data on activist hedge fund engagements with 882 target companies commenced between 2001 and 2006. The evidence adduced, they claim, justifies a distinctive profile for this new set of activists: they occupy an 'important middle ground' between internal blockholder monitoring and external monitoring by hostile offerors. The hedge funds, they assert, are more flexible, incentivized, and independent than internal blockholders, and, as opposed to corporate raiders, take smaller stakes, benefit from cooperation with management, and have support from other shareholders. Brav et al. make three more particular claims to this end: (1) hedge fund activism is about value creation through agency cost reduction; (2) the activists have succeeded in creating value; and (3) taking the record of success together with the persistence of the agency cost problem, this mode of activist engagement will take a permanent place in the governance picture. There is a subsidiary, negative assertion: hedge fund activism is not about stock picking.

Nor is hedge fund activism necessarily hostile. Brav et al., characterize only 30% of the engagements in their sample as 'openly hostile', entailing an actual or threatened proxy contest, a takeover threat, litigation, or confrontational public statements. The mode of engagement, note the authors, follows from a tactical decision. Hostility greets perceived management resistance, and entails greater cost.

Brav et al., profile the set of target companies as value opportunities, combining profitability and sound operating cash flows and return on assets with low market-to-book ratios. The targets tend to be small companies, as such well-suited to the amassing of significant shareholding stakes. At the same time, they have significant trading liquidity and higher institutional ownership than do their comparables, with the latter factor implying the presence of potential supporters in the shareholder population.

The authors go on to detail the market's reaction to public announcements of activist initiation. Positive abnormal returns in the [-20,+20] announcement window lie in the 7% to 8% range, with no reversal over the subsequent year. The returns are sorted according to the activists' stated objectives, with the highest returns (8.54%) accompanying a stated intent to effect sale of the company and the next highest (5.95%) accompanying a stated intent to change business strategy. In contrast, campaigns looking towards debt restructuring, recapitalization, dividend increases, and share repurchases, or alternatively, governance reform, yield positive but insignificant stock price reactions. The authors assert that the price effect reflects expectations of successful activist engagement, and reject the inference that the gains result a stock picking effect—the public revelation of the stock's selection by a respected value investor. To this end, the authors show that public revelation of a passive investment by the same funds has only a marginally lower positive abnormal return. At the same time, hedge fund withdrawal from an engagement triggers a price decline. The targets make significant governance concessions to the hedge funds in about two-thirds of the cases.

The chapter's statistical abstracts offer a concrete picture of the tactical parameters. The median initial stake taken in the target is 6.3%; a stake that grows to a median maximum of 9.1%. Hostile engagements command larger stakes. The median holding period for the engagements in the sample is one year, a result shortened by the necessity of imposing an arbitrary cut-off date on continuing engagements. The implication is that the activists in fact hold for more than one year, rebutting the short-termism allegation made by their detractors.

The authors go on to examine operating results at the targets. They focus on payout policy and leverage, consistent with the agency theory focus on the problem of management misuse of free cash flow. Payouts increase on a two-year time frame, beginning one year before the engagement. The increase is 0.3% to 0.5% relative to market capitalization and as against an across-the-board sample mean of 2.2%; leverage increases by 1.3% to 1.4% as against an across-the-board mean of 33.5%. Operating results improve two years after the engagement's commencement, with increases in earnings before interest, taxes, depreciation, and amortization (EBITDA)/assets and EBITDA/sales. The figures, while amounting to early returns, enhance the defensive case.

Although hedge funds make up the most prominent and newsworthy subset of activists in recent years, we see from the study of a special purpose pension fund by Becht et al., that not all of today's shareholder activists happen to be hedge funds. Individuals, private equity firms, and asset managers also enter the scene. Questions arise: which interventions involve hedge funds and which involve other institutional actors, and does anything distinguish one activist from another?

April Klein and Emanuel Zur address these questions in Chapter 9. They collect two samples for comparison, drawing on filings made between 1 January 2003 and 31 December 2005. The first is comprised of 151 activist campaigns conducted by hedge funds, and the second is comprised of 154 activist campaigns conducted during the same period by actors other than hedge funds. In the second group the entrepreneurs were individuals (including a set of the target firms' former CEOs), private equity and venture capital firms, and asset managers. Having broken the activists into two groups, Klein and Zur show both similarities and differences in their approaches and effects.

As with the sample of Brav et al., small firms with low market-to-book ratios predominate amongst the targets. Also in Chapter 8, there are positive abnormal stock returns during the period [−30,+30] surrounding public disclosure of the stock holding—here 10.2% for the hedge fund group and 5.1% for the second group. In contrast to the Brav group's results, however, the gains continue into the engagement's second year—11.4% for the hedge fund group and 17.8% for the non-hedge fund group. Levels of success are comparable—the hedge funds achieve their stated goals within one year in 60% of their engagements (gaining board membership in 31 out of 40 cases), and the other activists in 65% of their engagements (gaining board representation in 35 out of 45 cases). Interestingly, the market anticipates the engagements' eventual outcomes, with higher abnormal returns on filing respecting the targets where the intervention later proves successful.

Differences between the two activist groups open up when Klein and Zur break out target characteristics. Levels of research and development and capital expenditures and dividends are comparable across the two sets of targets. But the hedge funds tend to engage profitable, financially healthy firms, many of which are cash rich. They then demand share buy-backs or dividend increases and tend to get them—the targets on average double their dividends, increase their debt ratios, and decrease their cash and cash equivalents. The non-hedge fund activist group, in contrast, focuses on investment policy and operating strategies, the targets responding by reducing research and development and capital expenditures.

Klein and Zur associate levels of success with the level of aggression displayed in the activist's initial public filing, terming as aggressive demands for changes in the board, CEO firing, CEO salary cuts, termination of a merger, initiation of sale of the firm, dividend payments, and shareholder repurchases.

Finally, Klein and Zur collect operating data on the target companies one year after the engagement's commencement. They find no evidence of increased profitability at the hedge fund or other activist targets, measured as EBITDA/assets and cash flows from operations. Indeed, relative to comparable firms, the targets' EBITDA/assets and cash flows from operations, and cash balances, show statistically significant declines.

Overall, Klein and Zur offer a somewhat darker picture of hedge fund activism than do Brav et al. Even so, there is no direct conflict in the results—the positive operating returns reported by Brav et al., show up only on a two-year time frame, compared to Klein and Zur's one-year analysis.

The pattern described in these chapters has persisted. A study of the period 2008 to 2014 from Krishnan, Partnoy, and Thomas reports abnormal overall announcement period returns of 6% [−21, +21], with no sign of declining returns over time. The subset of hedge funds making the largest investments by dollar amount trigger an even more positive response of 10.91% (Krishnan, Partnoy, and Thomas 2015).

This collection of empirical results supports a number of generalizations. First, an activist posture in a hostile case presupposes a 6% to 10% stake in the target. Second, investment durations do not tend to be short, even as the need to liquidate investments precludes investment for an indefinite, patient term. Third, stock prices react favourably to activist intervention. Fourth, activist investors, thus situated and armed with the threat of an open proxy contest, extract significant concessions from managers. Fifth, and more tentatively, approaches to targets differ across the Atlantic. In the UK the relational environment favours quiet, private communication. In the US, in contrast, loud voices and publicity prevail. Sixth, economic results range from 'highly favourable' to the activists to 'mixed'.

An additional generalization can be supported if we make reference to some additional results from Alon Brav, Wei Jiang, and Hyunseob Kim: the case for the hedge funds improves as more data accumulate. Brav, Jiang, and Kim (2012) report on 1,927 fund-target pairs formed from 1994 to 2007 and follow the longer-term average returns of the targets. They show that not only do target stock prices bump up once the engagement is made public, but that the stock prices stay up, failing to revert to pre-engagement levels for up to three years. This is argued to refute the claim that the stock market overreacts to news of activist intervention and to imply that long-term shareholder value is created. Brav, Jiang, and Kim (2013) also have gathered data on the targets' return on assets. They find that target companies outperform their industries three years prior to activist engagement, that target performance declines to underperformance by the time of engagement, and that target performance returns to the positive side in the three years following intervention. Drawing on US census data, the authors make similar findings respecting the productivity of the target companies' plants, and of plants sold by target companies in the wake of activist intervention. They conclude that hedge fund activism is not a 'purely financial' phenomenon. That is, activist impact is not just a function of balance sheet leverage and cash in the till; positive productivity effects occur also.

Summing up, the empirical studies strongly suggest (even if they fall short of proving) that hedge fund activism will have a permanent place in the corporate landscape. We also note that there emerges little concrete support for the 'dark side' possibilities highlighted by Kahan and Rock. Even so, the 'dark side' questions continue to come up. The two chapters that follow pick up a prominent line of such questions, exploring the problem of strategic voting.

1.9 Strategic Holding versus Collective Interest: Empty Voting and Bankruptcy Reorganization

Hedge funds are highly strategic about their shareholding, sometimes seeking to effect specific outcomes in the short or intermediate term, and deploying (or avoiding deployment of) the shareholder franchise as a means to the end. It is not always apparent that the activist hedge fund's interest is well aligned with those of the shareholders as a group. Misalignment is particularly likely when a hedge fund takes advantage of technical opportunities to separate the power to vote the stock from the underlying economic interest in the stock. In Chapter 10, Henry T. C. Hu and Bernard S. Black take up salient incidences of this, the problem they term 'empty voting'.

Let us illustrate the problem with the story of activist shareholder Carl Icahn's intervention against Mylan Laboratories' announced acquisition of King Pharmaceuticals in 2004. The deal valued King at $16.66 per share, a generous 61.8% premium over its pre-announcement price. Too generous, thought traders in Mylan stock, leading to the stock promptly dropping from $18.51 to $15.51. But the stock had at least one buyer on the announcement day, Icahn, who purchased 1 million shares. He continued buying over the next six weeks, investing $307 million and finally revealing himself as the owner of 6.8% of the company in a public filing. He simultaneously denounced the deal as an overpriced acquisition of a weak company and announced his intention to mount a proxy fight against it at the shareholders' meeting to be convened for its approval. Mylan eventually mooted the matter by terminating the merger agreement, citing adverse facts discovered in the due diligence process. Meanwhile, Icahn's frontal attack on the merger put him at odds with other Wall Street players making the more conventional 'risk arbitrage' move of buying shares of the target (so as to benefit from any increase in the merger price) and simultaneously selling shares of the acquirer short (so as to benefit from any further decline in its price due to the merger). Richard C. Perry, a hedge fund manager and risk arbitrage player, did just that in Mylan's case, but with a twist. Wishing to protect the merger (and thus his investment) he purchased Mylan stock in an amount matching his short position, thereby gaining control of 10% of the votes at the upcoming meeting. Icahn called a foul on the ground that Perry's long/short position left him without an economic interest in Mylan. It followed, said Icahn, that Perry, despite his record ownership, should not have the privilege to vote the shares. Icahn sued, but the merger's cancellation mooted the matter.

Perry, with his long/short position, was positioned to vote 10% of Mylan's shares in favour of a merger when he had no economic stakes in Mylan and, as a long holder of King, had every interest in Mylan overpaying. The proliferation of equity derivatives makes it easier and cheaper to decouple the equity interest from the vote in this way. Alternatively, an actor can have an economic interest in a stock and lack the votes, but have the means to access the votes as needed. Hu and Black term this a 'hidden (morphable) voting interest'. We can illustrate with another Richard Perry incident. Perry used equity swaps to acquire a 16% economic interest in a New Zealand firm, Rubicon, Ltd, circumventing New Zealand's blockholder disclosure rule in so doing. As a swap counterparty, however, Perry had no votes. But when Perry needed voting rights at a Rubicon shareholders meeting, he unwound the swaps and caused the swap dealers to convey to him the Rubicon shares they had held to hedge their short swap positions.

Hu and Black note that the scale of this new vote buying is unknown due the lack of effective disclosure rules but compile a list of over ninety examples, most of them occurring in recent years and many involving hedge funds. They argue that disclosure rules need to be substantially revised so as to be adequate to the task of dealing with the problem described, picking up economic as well as voting interests in stock, treating short positions symmetrically with long positions, and exposing all cases of vote buying. They also would completely deny voting rights to shareholders with negative overall economic interest and would allow companies to amend their charters to address the voting rights of those whose economic interest in the company is compromised.

Hu and Black extend their discussion of voting distortions to the debtor–creditor context. Creditors also vote, particularly creditors of distressed borrowers called on to approve out-of-court restructurings or bankruptcy reorganization plans. Credit default swaps and other credit derivatives permit formal ownership of debt claims to be decoupled from economic exposure to the risk of default or credit deterioration. Yet formal ownership usually still conveys control rights under the debt contract. Incentives can become misaligned as a result. Where, for example, a given creditor buys protection under a credit default swap in a notional amount equal to or greater than the principal amount of debt held directly, it has an incentive to vote against a pre-bankruptcy composition that benefits the issuer and the creditors as a whole. The reason is that blocking the composition can force the borrower into bankruptcy so as to trigger full payment under the swap. Hu and Black contend that securitization of debt claims also decouples economic risk from contractual control rights and bankruptcy rights, and that widespread uncoupling can increase systemic risk across the overall economy.

In Chapter 11 Douglas G. Baird and Robert K. Rasmussen deepen and extend this picture of creditor incentive misalignment, discussing problems stemming from the strategic activities of the subset of hedge funds that specialize in distressed debt. Hedge funds have long been major, aggressive investors in the debt markets, specializing in arbitrage activity respecting distressed issues. Indeed, it is in the debt markets that hedge funds made their first appearance as activist holders of interests in corporations two decades ago. There were immediate benefits. As the hedge funds became major market players, debt claims became more liquid. Syndicated loans now trade freely in a secondary market. Bankruptcy claims trade freely as well. Liquidity also has enabled hedge funds to become leading, sometimes outcome-determinative, players in negotiations respecting work outs and bankruptcy reorganizations.

Baird and Rasmussen describe the stresses and strains that result for the scheme of bankruptcy reorganization in the US, a system designed on the assumption that stable creditor groups coalesce around identifiable and common interests. Things work differently in a liquid world populated by strategic hedge funds acting free of the reputational constraints imposed on primary lenders. Major creditors now can come and go quickly, disrupting the committee representation system. Control acquisition schemes often drive these transactions—the hedge fund buys bankruptcy claims (and hence votes) with a view to manoeuvring itself into control of the post-reorganization entity. When such a strategically minded hedge fund shows up, the bargaining process can be disrupted and distorted. For example, a hedge fund seeking control does not necessarily bargain for an outcome that maximizes returns to all creditors. Control comes cheaper with a low valuation of the bankrupt firm, leading to an alliance between the hedge fund and the firm's managers against the interests of the classes of creditors. Alternatively, a hedge fund might be motivated by an interest in a competing company.

Voting strategies matter in the new liquid world. A hedge fund without votes sufficient to dictate its favoured result may still have enough votes to block a reorganization plan. Indeed, hedge funds key their purchases of distressed claims with an eye to consequences respecting voting outcomes. They also form informal groups for the purpose of coordinating their votes, moving by stealth. Similar gaming occurs in votes on out-of-bankruptcy compositions, where the proliferation of credit derivatives complicates things further.

Baird and Rasmussen term all of this the 'anti-commons problem'. In their view, more good than harm results from the new instruments and markets. But bankruptcy judges will inevitably be presented with cases where strategic behaviour by hedge funds invites discretionary sanction. Baird and Rasmussen counsel caution at this point. In contrast to Hu and Black, they recommend mandated transparency over outright invalidation of votes.

Chapter 12 provides empirical backup for the cautious approach taken by Baird and Rasmussen. Indeed, it provides a basis for concluding that the problems associated with the strategic actions of hedge fund creditors have been somewhat overstated. Here Wei Jiang, Kai Li, and Wei Wang report on their examination of hedge fund participation in 474 Chapter 11 cases from the period 1996 to 2007. The hedge funds prove ubiquitous, with observable involvement in 90% of the proceedings. More importantly, they take strategic positions with positive productive implications.

Jiang, Li, and Wang depict Chapter 11 reorganization as a field of conflict between two opposing groups. On one side stands the historical power holders—incumbent managers and by implication the pre-bankruptcy shareholders. On the other side stand the newly empowered creditors—banks holding secured claims, whether as pre-bankruptcy secured lenders or post-bankruptcy DIP lenders. In contrast to the banks, the hedge funds buy unsecured claims. Unsecured claims stand in the priority ladder between those of the more empowered interests, and, significantly, can import a more productive incentive posture than either as regards deployment of the debtor's assets. To the extent that the property under the secured creditors' liens amply covers the dollar amount of their claims, their incentives are compromised—as, between a suboptimal liquidation that certainly covers the amount of their claims and a value-maximizing reorganization as a going concern, they rationally choose the former. The performance of incumbent management, meanwhile, needs to be appraised by an appropriately incentivized claimant. Enter a hedge fund seeking a 'fulcrum' position in unsecured debt—a claim that will lead to a controlling interest in the common stock of the post-reorganization going concern. Arguably, it has high-powered incentive to maximize the firm's value, higher than any other claimant with a seat at the table.

Jiang, Li, and Wang provide a great deal of indirect support for the above picture of Chapter 11. They show that hedge funds target bankrupt companies in which unsecured creditors are likely to emerge in a control position. Given a hedge fund holding a large unsecured claim, the incumbents are more likely to lose their exclusive right to propose a plan of reorganization, the post of CEO is more likely to turn over, a key employee retention plan is more likely to be adopted, the entity is more likely to emerge from Chapter 11, and the proceeding more likely to result in payoffs to junior creditors. There is also evidence of efficiency gains: higher total recovery by all debt claimants and a more positive stock market performance at the time of filing.

We close noting that the chapters in Part II leave the hedge funds with a mixed scorecard. Interestingly, the strongest confirmations come from the empirical studies of financial economists. The most pointed questions come from legal academics citing anecdotal evidence.

1.10 Part III Private Equity and Corporate Governance

Part III looks at the structure and development of the private equity sector, including transactional motivations, performance drivers, fund returns, and exit opportunities.

1.11 Structure and Motivation

Private equity funds are usually structured as limited partnerships, with the private equity firm as general partner and the limited partners comprised of pension funds, insurance companies, hedge funds, other investment institutions, and wealthy individuals. The limited partnership form allows both the internal and external participants to use contracts to reduce opportunism and agency costs. The private equity firm, as general partner, uses the limited partnership agreement to achieve extensive control over operations subject to few intrusive legal obligations. Other features, such as tax benefits, flexibility respecting structure and terms, and fixed life, also contribute to the limited partnership's continuing dominance as the business form of choice for collective investment vehicles.

The relationship between the limited partners and the general partners tends to follow from explicit contract terms. The capital comes from the limited partners—the private equity firm typically invests only between 1% to 3% of the private equity fund's total committed capital. Table 1.1 shows the most common contractual measures developed for dealing with the investment activities of general partners, and the relationship between general and limited partners.

Table 1.1 Limited partnership agreement: negotiating the terms

General partners	Limited partners
Carry calculations	Carry calculations
Management fees	Clawback provisions
Clawback provisions	General partner conflict issues, including limitations of opportunities
General partner capital commitment	Key-man provisions
Limitations of liability	Management fees
Indemnification by general and limited partners	General partner capital commitment
Investment strategy, limitations, and guidelines	Side letters
Fundraising period, investment period, and term	Investment strategy, limitations, and guidelines
Permitted activities of general partners	Permitted activities of general partners
Limited partner approval rights	Portfolio company fee offsets

Source: Adapted from Center for Private Equity and Entrepreneurship, Tuck School of Business at Dartmouth.

The compensation arrangement between the general partner/fund manager and the limited partner/investors is the critical provision in the contract. Compensation derives from two main sources. First, fund managers typically receive 20% of the profits generated by each of the funds. The second source is the management fee. Historically, a significant majority of funds assessed management fees as a constant percentage of committed capital. But management fees have decreased in recent years due to a number of economic factors. More particularly, some funds now receive a fixed fee of 2% of the fund's assets paid annually for the first five years with the fee thereafter decreasing by 25 basis points yearly for the next five years. Other contracts reduce the fixed fee based on a shift from a base in committed capital in years 1-5 to net invested capital in years 6-10. Given these changes, a substantial proportion of buyout firms' median off-the-top draw of committed capital has been reduced to 12% (Metrick and Yashida 2009). Some contracts also limit access to the carry, imposing hurdle rates that climb upwards to 15%-20%, which must be met before any profits are distributed. Finally, in order to protect the 80/20 deal, a clawback provision will be included in the agreement, that is, an over-distribution to a general partner will be clawed back to the fund and then distributed to the limited partners.

Agency cost reduction is held to be the primary motivation for buyouts. For the classic account, one looks to the agency story that accompanied the buyout's first rise during the 1980s. The story followed from Michael Jensen's (1988) description of suboptimal management performance and correction through capital market intervention. For Jensen, the 1980s outbreak of manager–shareholder conflict stemmed from the managers' habit of reinvesting more corporate cash flow than necessary to fund positive return investments, termed 'free cash flow'. Managers retained profits that should have been paid out to the shareholders and put them into unproductive plant and value-reducing acquisitions. Hostile takeovers and friendly leveraged buyouts were said to address the problem. Both paid shareholders a premium over market, in effect making up for past deprivations of cash flow. They then led to divestment of subpar acquisitions and redirection of investment policy in productive directions. Leverage also played a part in this disciplinary redirection of corporate focus. A higher level of corporate borrowing raised the rate of return on the equity even as it lowered the corporation's overall cost of capital due to tax savings. More debt also encouraged management discipline on a going-concern basis. Given the mandatory nature of the debt payments, they deterred ongoing waste of cash, returning the capital to the markets.

Jensen (1999) took the governance and capital structure of the buyout as an agency solution to separated ownership and control, suggesting that the 'LBO Association', with its combination of high leverage, control in the hands of market intermediaries, and high-powered incentives for managers, amounted to a robust one-size-fits-all mode of governance. But the buyouts' disappearance in the early 1990s put an end to the claim of early, levered disappearance for the Berle and Means corporation and the separation of ownership and control. At no time since has high leverage been seen as suited to a permanent place in corporate capital structures or as the *sine qua non* of shareholder value maximization.

The buyout retained its prestige in agency theory even as new going private deals disappeared. This stemmed partly from the attribution of the early 1990s shift away from leverage to regulatory constraints on institutional investors, a point that had some validity so far as risky lending by regulated institutions like savings banks and insurance companies was concerned. The continued vitality of the shareholder value norm and its dispersion into management suites also played a role. Empirical studies also offered support. These looked at the 1980s deals from various points of view and confirmed the story of governance improvement. The increased leverage and incentive realignment was shown positively to affect operating performance and productivity. There was evidence of increased sales and cash flows, decreased expenditures, improved margins, and reduced capital requirements.

In Chapter 13, Steven N. Kaplan and Per Strömberg offer an overview of the private equity sector as we know it today, describing its cycles over time and evaluating its performance. They begin with the structure of the buyout firms and then turn to the terms of the typical leveraged buyout transaction. They go on to present evidence respecting the evolution of private equity fundraising and transaction characteristics. In the first phase, during the 1980s, most targets were relatively large companies in mature industries like manufacturing and retail, with going private transactions accounting for almost half of transactional value. The junk bond bust brought not only substantial contraction in transaction value but a shift of target characteristics. 'Middle-market' buyouts of non-publicly traded firms came to account for the bulk of private equity transactions, with activity extending to industries such as information technology, telecommunications, financial services, and health care. The resurgence that began in the mid-1990s brought going private deals back into the mix to dominate at the recent peak. Activity also went global. Kaplan and Strömberg complete their picture with a survey of exit practices, showing a median holding period of six years, with 38% of exits achieved by sale to a strategic buyer, 24% by sale to another private equity fund ('secondary leveraged buyouts'), 14% by a public stock offering, and 6% in bankruptcy.

Kaplan and Strömberg also consider the effects of private equity, gathering evidence on its impact on capital structure, management incentives, and corporate governance. The evidence suggests that private equity activity creates economic value on average. But there is also evidence consistent with private equity investors taking advantage of market timing (and market mispricing) between debt and equity markets, particularly in the public-to-private transactions of the last fifteen years.

Finally, Kaplan and Strömberg review empirical evidence on performance and returns to private equity at the fund level. They show that private equity activity experiences recurring boom and bust cycles related both to past returns and the level of interest rates relative to earnings. They predict that while the recent market boom will eventually lead to some defaults and investor losses, the magnitude is likely to be less severe than after the 1980s boom because capital structures are less fragile and private equity firms are more sophisticated. They accordingly expect that a significant part of the growth in private equity activity and institutions is permanent.

Kaplan and Strömberg's prediction has turned out to be correct, at least as of 2015. Observers during the financial crisis looked at the capital structures of the bulge of buyouts that had closed through 2007 and noted a maturity wall. Bank borrowings were going to come due, and given the disappearance of liquidity and collapse of the market for going concern assets, private equity owners had no apparent means to pay them down. The maturity dates, however, came and went without a wave of bankruptcies. Where maturity occurred but takeout credit was unavailable, the portfolio companies and banks effected out of court compositions.

1.12 How Has Private Equity Performed?

We now turn to attempts to benchmark the performance of private equity funds.

There is an issue about measurement. Even though private equity funds disclose soft information to investors about current returns, it is often difficult to obtain accurate hard information due to long durations, the absence of public trading, and, until recently, the lack of a legal obligation to disclose to a central data repository. Most financial economists accordingly rely on databases collected from voluntary reports of private equity investors rather than reports of private equity firms.

There are two leading measures of fund manager performance, internal rate of return (IRR) and public market equivalent (PME). The latter is a ratio of the present value of all cash distributions (including undistributed assets taken on book value) over the present values of all drawdowns using the year by year realized return of S&P 500 as the discount rate. A PME less than 1 means that the fund investor would have been better off putting capital in the market index.

In a path-breaking study, Stephen Kaplan and Annette Schoar (2006) analysed the returns of 169 buyout funds that were close to fully liquidated during the period 1980 to 2001.[1] They benchmarked performance using the IRR of the funds calculated by Venture Economics and their own calculation of the funds' PMEs. Kaplan and Schoar broke the results down into two time periods to show that both PMEs and IRRs were better for funds raised in the early 1980s and poorer for funds raised in the early 1990s. They showed average PMEs for buyout funds of 0.93. Further, they find that the average returns net of fees (for buyout funds taken together with venture capital funds in the sample) of 0.96 (equal-weighted) and 1.05 (value-weighted). Kaplan and Schoar also found that the performance net of fees depended on a range of factors including fund size, fund sequence, past performance, and public market returns during the investment phase of the fund's life.

The Kaplan and Schoar study's overall message was negative: it seemed that private equity was not the bonanza that institutional portfolio managers assumed it to be and that the private equity industry's own reports of extraordinary IRRs were unreliable. But other studies showed different results (see Higson and Stücke 2012; Robinson and Sensoy 2013). In a recent study, Harris, Jenkinson, and Kaplan (2013) make reference to different and larger databases, reversing the results of Kaplan and Schoar and attributing the earlier results to shortcomings in the earlier database. The new data, from Burgiss, pick up cash flows from nearly 1,400 private equity funds as reported by 200 institutional investors. The study finds that, since 1984, most US buyout fund have beaten the market. The net-of-fees PME outperformance versus the S&P 500 averages 20% to 27% over the life of the fund and more than 3% per year. Furthermore, the study finds that within a given vintage year, a fund's PMEs are reliably predicted by its multiple of invested capital and IRR. The substitution of other benchmarks, such as the (small-cap) Russell 2000, leads to lower but still positive results,

[1] A caveat respecting these studies needs to be entered: here, as with many empirical studies of private equity, the data set sweeps in venture capital funds as well as buyout funds, breaking out the numbers separately.

Dispute over private equity returns persists, however. In Chapter 14, Ludovic Phalippou questions the recent results. The results follow, he notes, from analysis of proprietary data. But he replicates the results of Harris, Jenkinson, and Kaplan by reference to a publicly available data source, yielding mean (median) PMEs of 1.20 (1.13) using the S&P 500 as a benchmark. The critical response commences at this point: Phalippou stresses that the outcome depends on the choice of benchmark. He argues that private equity targets being largely small-cap companies, a small-cap benchmark should follow. He employs the DFA micro-cap, an unlevered small-cap mutual fund. As a result, the PMEs drop to 1.04 (0.99), with similar results following benchmarking directly to the Fama-French small cap index. The implication is that the market beating results found in other studies follow not from actual performance but from the Fama-French equity size premium.

Significantly, Phalippou makes no claim to employment of the 'correct' benchmark. His point instead is that correctness is hard to determine and that the only thing that is very clear is that results are highly sensitive to the choice. It follows that the bottom line question as to the competiveness of private equity returns remains open and debatable.

1.13 Part IV The Regulatory Framework

Part IV takes up regulation, where issues emerge in sharp relief as new initiatives change the landscape in the wake of the financial crisis of 2008. There are two tranches of materials. Part IV's first three chapters look at the treatment of hedge funds and private equity funds under legal regimes worldwide that promote investor protection and the safety and soundness of financial institutions. There follow two chapters on recent developments and controversies under US securities law that impact directly on the costs and benefits of shareholder activism. The final chapter offers a retrospective overview, suggesting that corporate governance world's law reform agendas need adjusting in the wake of the activist sector's appearance on the scene.

1.14 Structural Treatment of Hedge Funds and Private Equity: Investor Protection and Systemic Risk

We begin with global survey of regulation conducted during the years preceding 2008. In Chapter 15, Douglas Cumming, Na Dai, and Sofia A. Johan describe a series of studies of hedge fund regulation in twenty-four countries. The studies inquire into regulation's impact on the structure and performance of 2,137 investment entities. The presentation is eye-opening, for it negates the widespread notion that hedge funds were an 'unregulated' sector prior to the financial crisis. The notion does turn out to have been correct as regards the US. But, viewed comparatively, the US stands out as an unregulated environment, having (briefly) required registration in 2006, but otherwise prior to the financial crisis having imposed only insider trading constraints. Meanwhile, in other countries investor protection concerns brought hedge funds inside the regulated fold. Some countries subject hedge funds to minimum capital requirements. Some countries also bar hedge fund access to foreign-based service providers, an economically important restriction in a sector of small shops that rely on outsourcing. In addition, some countries impose marketing restrictions, in contrast to the US where hedge funds go to market as unregulated private placements. Under the restrictions, a hedge fund must be marketed in a package (a 'wrapper') with the offering materials for its sponsor's fund, opening up a conflict of interest between the sponsor and the hedge fund managers.

The authors find little support for the common notion that hedge funds thrive only in unregulated environments and can be expected to gravitate geographically to unregulated comfort zones. Hedge fund managers pursuing riskier strategies or strategies otherwise holding out more pronounced agency problems do not systematically select jurisdictions with less stringent regulations. If anything, the data indicate the contrary, with potentially problematic funds more likely to operate under stringent regulation. Investor-protective regulations like minimum capital requirements are associated with higher levels of hedge fund capital inflows and better-quality informational reports. At the same time, not all regulation encourages hedge fund activity: constraints on choice of service provider dampen investment, presumably because they potentially constrain the quality of human resources. From all of this it follows that regulation plays an important role in influencing the size and stability of the hedge fund market, and the inquiry is not a simple one of plus (regulation) and minus (deregulation) or minus (regulation) and plus (deregulation) but of avoiding both under- and overregulation.

Our pre-2008 comparative inquiry thus highlights notable differences in regulatory outcome between the US and the EU. Differences persist in the wake of substantial regulatory reforms enacted since 2008. The US, under the Dodd-Frank Act of 2010,[2] now imposes substantial informational reporting requirements on hedge funds and private equity funds towards the end of collecting information regarding systemic risk. But it remains unclear whether Dodd-Frank's accompanying regime of substantive systemic risk regulation will ever extend to the sector. Even if an extension eventually occurs, it seems highly unlikely that more than a few large funds would be impacted. The EU, in contrast, has instituted an exhaustive new regime, the Alternative Investment Funds Managers (AIFM) Directive, covering all significant hedge and private equity funds. The Directive not only mandates a full range of investor protection measures but extends also to regulation of risky investments and capital structures.

Dodd-Frank's new registration and reporting requirements cover all hedge funds and private equity funds whose assets under management exceed a modest threshold. The stated purpose is the facilitation of data collection that would permit the new Financial Stability Oversight Council (FSOC) to assess the funds' potential for generating systemic risk.[3] The new reporting requirements are intended to generate data to enable to the FSOC to make the relevant determinations, potentially bringing hedge funds and private equity funds into the regulated tent as systemically significant financial institutions (SIFIs). The determination

[2] Dodd-Frank Wall Street Reform and Consumer Protection Act, Pub. L. 111–203, H.R. 4173.

[3] Dodd-Frank Act, §§ 112–15.

process remains at an early stage, so for now the reporting requirements are the one clear thing that Dodd-Frank holds out for hedge funds and private equity.

Dodd-Frank's Title IV[4] requires investment advisers to private funds (including private equity funds and hedge funds) to register as such with the SEC.[5] A long list of new regulations follows.

- Registered investment advisers are required to adopt and implement written policies and compliance procedures and designate a chief compliance officer to administer its compliance policies and procedures.
- Extensive record-keeping requirements covering both advisers and funds are to be monitored by the SEC through both routine and 'for cause' inspections. The reporting requirements are designed to allow the SEC to collect proprietary information concerning leverage, counterparty credit risk exposure, trading and investment positions, valuation policies and practices, and side letters.
- The SEC will be permitted to require the disclosure of the identities of an adviser's clients and related client information for the purpose of systemic risk assessment. The information will be shared with the FSOC for the purpose of assessing systemic risk and with other federal regulators and self-regulatory organizations upon request, subject to certain conditions to protect confidentiality.
- There will be regulation of sales materials, relationships with solicitors, and custody of client assets. In addition, adviser must adopt each of (1) an ethics code; (2) a proxy voting policy; and (3) a business continuity plan.

It does not appear that any of these regulations threaten the business models of hedge funds or private equity funds. The required disclosure of propriety information is the most invasive of the new provisions. If the Act's confidentiality assurance turns out to be effective, then the private investment sector could emerge with an added cost burden but otherwise unimpaired. Early returns from empirical studies are mixed, however. Where one study finds a short-term positive impact on hedge fund performance from Dodd-Frank implementation (Kaal 2014), another takes a longer time period and associates Dodd-Frank implementation with lower alphas, lower information ratios, and higher risk, also detecting capital outflow. (Cumming, Dai, and Johan 2015).

That said, the FSOC is indeed inquiring into systemic risk creation in the non-bank financial sector towards the end of imposing new regulation on non-bank financials that make significant systemic risk contributions. Regulations under Dodd-Frank allow the FSOC to differentiate among companies that are potentially subject to heightened prudential standards on an individual basis or by category. The FSOC has authority to name any predominantly financial company that could 'pose a significant threat to U.S. financial stability', but the FSOC has narrowed by regulation the category of subject companies to those with more than $50 billion in assets and either $30 billion in credit default swaps, $3.5 billion in

[4] Dodd-Frank Act §§ 401–16.

[5] Under Dodd-Frank § 402(a), 'private fund' is defined as an investment vehicle relying on one of the so-called private fund exemptions under the Investment Company Act of 1940: Section 3(c)(1) (privately offered funds with fewer than 100 investors) or Section 3(c)(7) (privately offered funds for which all of the investors are qualified purchasers).

derivatives liability, $20 billion in total debt outstanding, 15-to-1 leverage ratio or a 10% ratio of short-term debt to assets. The FSOC has estimated that fifty companies might fall into this scheme of classification, and presently is in the process of identifying and examining them. At this stage, the FSOC's process has led to the identification and designation of three companies: two large insurers, Prudential and AIG, and General Electric's massive financial subsidiary, GE Capital. As of this writing, Prudential has appealed its designation.

A positive determination brings the SIFI appellation and subjection to bank regulatory capital and leverage requirements, a formal liquidity standard, a single counterparty exposure standard set at 25% of capital and surplus, process requirements respecting risk management, periodic stress testing, and remediation actions in the event of distress.

Treatment of large hedge fund advisors and private equity firms remains an open question. As asset management firms, their structures and risk profiles differ materially from those of companies like Prudential and GE Capital, which own their risky assets (and finance them with risky capital structures) rather than manage them on behalf of others. Asset management companies themselves own few assets and do not rely heavily on leverage to finance them. The FSOC has acknowledged this difference. But, in an October 2013 report, the FSOC also assets that the activities of asset management firms implicate vulnerabilities that could 'pose, amplify, or transmit threats to financial stability'. It has commenced a review of the status of two of the largest asset managers: BlackRock Inc. and Fidelity Investments.

Dodd-Frank, then, puts hedge funds and private equity funds into a new class of reporting companies but withholds substantive regulation pending a finding respecting each fund's contribution to systemic risk. If it emerges that a fund (or collection of funds) as a practical matter operates like a big bank, then the fund ultimately can be regulated as such.

The EU, with its AIFM Directive, is taking the converse approach. The Directive also puts hedge funds and private equity funds into a new class of reporting companies, but lays down prudential regulation in tandem. In other words, in the EU hedge funds and private equity funds are treated like banks whether or not they perform a bank-like function in the wider economy.

The AIFM Directive harmonizes requirements for intermediaries that manage and administer alternative investment funds (AIFs) in the EU. AIFs are defined negatively to include collective investment schemes not requiring authorization under the EU's Collective Investments in Transferable Securities Directive. The definition picks up hedge funds and private equity funds, among others, but does exempt venture capital funds pursuant to a *de minimis* exception. The Directive contemplates that each subject fund will register in a home member state; home state authorization will then serve the fund manager as a regulatory passport authorizing it to advise and market funds throughout the EU. Registration and compliance is also required of AIFMs from outside of the EU that seek to market funds within.

Once registered and authorized, the AIFM is subject to requirements respecting its conduct of business and governance, in particular its risk management, with requirements covering liquidity risk and including periodic stress testing. There is also a modest minimum capital requirement. Disclosure mandates are included, with an emphasis on liquidity management. Investors and regulators are not the only disclosure recipients: if an AIFM acquires a controlling interest in an EU company exceeding a stated size threshold, it must make prescribed disclosures to the company and its shareholders and employees.

The Directive's investor protection provisions do not stop with mandated disclosure. Third party protectors also are contemplated: the AIFM must appoint an independent appraiser for an annual valuation of assets under management and securities issued. A third party depository is also required. This must be a credit institution with a registered office within the EU. It acts as recipient for capital raised from investors and, on a going-concern basis, as the safekeeper of the AIFM's portfolio assets.

Dan Awrey takes a critical look at the AIFM Directive in Chapter 16. Awrey explains the Directive in political terms as a European challenge to the heretofore dominant Anglo-Saxon mode of market regulation. But, for Awrey, what might make sense politically to some observers does not make sense as public policy. The Directive ring-fences and defines a capacious class of financial institutions, applying a set of rules on a one-size-fits-all basis despite manifest differences within the class. The fit is particularly bad in the case of private equity. Meanwhile, the Directive's proponents have not made a persuasive case for its superiority to existing national-level regimes of investor protection. Nor, as a unilateral initiative, does the Directive amount to an effective measure of systemic risk regulation.

In Chapter 17, Joseph A. McCahery and Erik P. M. Vermeulen take a look at the AIFM Directive in connection with private equity fundraising in the EU, which is now recovering after a steep decline that began in 2008. The chapter asks two prospective questions. First, what can be done to increase investors' interest in private equity while at the same time increasing the responsibility of private equity managers? Second, does the AIFM make a positive contribution to increasing investor interest and management responsibility? The regulation's proponents argue that the AIFM label will not only help reduce uncertainty and information asymmetry in the industry, but also provide an international stamp of quality. If they are correct, institutional and other investors will be more inclined to invest again in private equity. McCahery and Vermeulen question this position, predicting that the AIFM label will amount to little more than a 'boilerplate' formality to be observed in future fundraising. Most private equity funds have already taken measures to deal with the new requirements, either by enhancing their back office capacity or outsourcing their compliance units to specialized consultants.

McCahery and Vermeulen point out that the more important changes regarding private equity fundraising are occurring in contracting rather than in regulation. They show that investors are demanding changes in private equity limited partnership agreements, getting more investor-favourable compensation terms and conditions. The old 'two and twenty' compensation arrangements are giving way to scaled down provisions and preferred returns. Private equity limited partners also are getting more control over the funds' investment decisions. Finally, private equity general partners now contribute more equity capital than did during the pre-crisis boom, better aligning the fund managers' interests with those of their investors. The appearance of these new limited partnership terms can largely be attributed to post-crisis problems in private equity fundraising and returns. Private equity managers have been forced to make concessions.

McCahery and Vermeulen conclude that these changes will better protect investors and have a more positive impact on the private equity industry than the need to comply with the cumbersome AIFMD rules.

1.15 Regulation and the Costs and Benefits of Shareholder Activism

In recent years, three topics have emerged as regulatory focal points for proponents and opponents of shareholder activism in the US-proxy access under section 14 of the Securities Exchange Act of 1934 (34 Act), reporting requirements under section 13(d) of the same statute, and poison pills incorporating novel constraints on stock purchases by activists conducting proxy contests. The first topic, proxy access, poses the question whether the SEC can make a positive contribution to corporate governance by substantially amending its proxy rules to facilitate activist challenges to incumbent boards of directors. In Chapter 18, Jill E. Fisch addresses this question, suggesting that the goal of governance enhancement would be better served by SEC withdrawal from the field in favour of contractual solutions determined pursuant to state corporate law. The latter two topics pose the converse question of whether existing regulatory structures should be altered in order to *discourage* activist intervention. In Chapter 19, Lucian A. Bebchuk and Robert J. Jackson Jr examine proposed changes to reporting requirements under section 13(d), making a case for the regulatory status quo towards the end of protecting the financial incentives of hedge fund activists. In contrast, in Chapter 20, John C. Coffee Jr defends new modes of drafting poison pills that raise the bar against activist intervention.

1.15.1 Proxy Access

Proxy access would permit qualifying shareholders to include their own nominees for the board of directors in management's proxy statement at corporate expense. In the US it amounts to a sort of Holy Grail of shareholder rights, and the SEC has proposed proxy access rules on repeated occasions. One such proposal was mooted by the SEC in 2009. But business interests undertook to challenge the proposal in court on the ground, among others, that proxy access was not included in the SEC's grant of regulatory authority in section 14 of the 34 Act. The agency delayed promulgation until it received a supplemental grant of rulemaking authority in the Dodd-Frank Act.[6] The SEC thereupon went ahead with a rule requiring proxy access for candidates taking up to 25% of the seats on a given board of directors. The rule threw up a strict qualification requirement—the shareholder or group of shareholders proposing a candidate must have held 3% of the company's shares outstanding for a three-year period.[7] As a practical matter, only coalitions of investment institutions would have been able to meet the test. Thus constructed, proxy access held out no cost advantages for activist hedge funds. But the point was moot in any event. A federal appeals court voided the rule on the procedural ground that the SEC had supported it with an inadequate cost-benefit analysis.[8] The SEC is free to try again in another rulemaking proceeding but has not done so.

[6] Dodd-Frank Act §971. [7] Rule 14a-11(b), 17 C.F.R. 240.14a11(b)(2010).

[8] *Business Roundtable and Chamber of Commerce of the United States of America v. SEC*, 613 F.3d 166 (D.C. Cir. 2011).

In Chapter 18, Jill Fisch questions the value of the entire enterprise. If, on the one hand, the SEC intended to facilitate shareholder nomination of directors, why make a rule that insulates companies from shareholder inputs? If, on the other hand, the SEC had no desire to shift the balance of power in publicly traded companies, why bother with rulemaking at all? For Fisch, the SEC's enterprise suffered from debilitating ambiguity because it lacked a normative vision respecting governance benefits to be obtained.

She suggests a radically different approach grounded in state law, in particular Delaware's recent amendment of its code to permit proxy access to be promulgated by means of a shareholder-initiated bylaw. In Fisch's view, the thoroughgoing set of rules through which the SEC regulates the proxy process holds out barriers to shareholder access, thereby inadvertently influencing the balance of power between managers and shareholders. She recommends that the agency step back from the regulation of corporate governance, contenting itself with creating a level playing field on which states, companies, and shareholders can experiment with governance structures. More particularly, all matters concerning director nominations, including shareholder access, should be left to state corporate codes and corporate charters and bylaws. The SEC proxy rules should limit themselves to requiring disclosure of all properly nominated director candidates (whatever the origin of the nomination) and the provision of a ballot containing all nominees. Meanwhile, groups of shareholders coalescing to support candidates should be left free of ancillary SEC controls.

1.15.2 Blockholder Reporting Under Section 13(d)

Section 13(d) requires parties acquiring more than 5% of a public company's stock to make a public filing disclosing their position and intentions respecting the issuer. Once the activist block becomes public information, the door opens for market free-riding, as stock watchers pile into the stock to take advantage of the positive price bump that tends to result from a disclosure of activist blockholding. Publicity accordingly constrains the activist's ability to make a profit from its investment in the target. But there are loopholes. Under a long-standing regulatory treatment, long positions held through equity swaps have been deemed outside of the section's scope. An activist accordingly can take an equity swap position during the pre-disclosure and filing stage of the engagement, acquiring what amounts in substance to an equity stake exceeding 5%, before the stock price bumps upward, ameliorating the free-rider problem.

A ruling from a US federal court in *CSX Corp. v. The Children's Investment Fund Management (UK) LLP.*,[9] for a time appeared to close the loophole, with negative implications for the activist sector. But the matter remains in doubt. An appeals court affirmed the ruling without opinion. Then, upon publishing its opinion three years later, the appeals court rejected the rationale of the lower court opinion even as it left the result in place.[10] Pressure accordingly mounts on the SEC to promulgate a rule that brings derivative instruments within the concept of 'beneficial ownership' under section 13(d). The SEC has

[9] 562 F. Supp. 2d 211 (S.D.N.Y. 2008).

[10] *CSX Corp. v. The Children's Investment Fund Management (UK) LLP*, 654 F.3d 276 (2nd Cir. 2011).

undoubted power to do this under the Dodd-Frank Act,[11] but has not yet undertaken to exercise it.

The *CSX* ruling inhibits activist activity in another respect. When a 'group' of shareholders forms, the members' stockholdings are aggregated for purposes of applying section 13(d)'s 5% test. Prior to *CSX*, cases under section 13(d) read the group concept narrowly, and practitioners in turn read the cases to condition group status on entry into a formal contract by the putative group members. Thus, activists, like the funds involved in the case The Children's Investment Fund Management (TCI) and 3G Capital Partners, communicate with one another and informally coordinate activities without aggregating their holdings for filing purposes. The *CSX* court read the group concept more broadly, sweeping in the activities of Children's and 3G. Legal uncertainty has resulted.

The uncertainty bears particularly on activist 'wolf pack' activity. In many hedge fund activist engagements, after one fund makes a public appearance and a 13(d) filing, another, or sometimes two others, quickly appear in tow. A 5% block thereby can double or triple in size. The rules under 13(d), as presently drafted, grant a 5% holder ten days to file from the date of acquisition of shares triggering the filing. To the extent that informal coordination is permitted, one hedge fund can signal to potential allies with all accumulating stock positions before the disclosure date, ten or so days hence. To the extent that informal coordination is not permitted, and any advance communication to another fund means a compliance problem, wolf pack formation is deterred. Risk-averse legal advisors now counsel activists to avoid having any contact with potential follower hedge funds.

The ten-day filing window, which dates from the statute's enactment in 1968, has also become controversial. The Dodd-Frank Act extends the SEC authority to shorten the filing window by rule.[12] Management advocates, most prominently the law firm of Wachtell, Lipton, Rosen & Katz, now are pressuring the SEC to exercise that authority. In a famous petition delivered to the SEC in 2011, the Wachtell firm laid out the case for a shorter window,[13] suggesting that two days would suffice. Transparency, fairness, and equality of information are the stated grounds. Technical developments since 1968 also figure in: back in those days, a two-day reporting timetable was not practically feasible, whereas now it imposes no special reporting burden. Moreover, countries such as the UK, Germany, Australia, and Hong Kong have shortened their windows, in some cases also lowering acquisition thresholds.

In Chapter 19, Lucian A. Bebchuk and Robert J. Jackson Jr make the rebuttal case. Bebchuk and Jackson caution that a window reduction could harm investors and undermine efficiency. This is not a simple case where it safely can be assumed that investors are better off because information becomes public on an earlier date. There is a trade-off between enhancing disclosure and encouraging activist intervention, and activist intervention holds out the benefits because it makes mangers more accountable and reduces agency costs. For the SEC, it follows that any change in the rule should be preceded by exhaustive empirical analysis. For Bebchuk and Jackson, the better the empirical preparation the weaker the case for amending the rule.

[11] Dodd-Frank Act § 766(e).

[12] Dodd-Frank Act § 929R.

[13] Letter of Wachtell, Lipton, Rosen & Katz to Secretary, Securities and Exchange Commission, 7 March 2011.

1.15.3 Poison Pills and Proxy Contests

The chapters in this book have so far focused mainly on the positive effects of hedge fund activism. Based on a comprehensive analysis of the empirical literature, John C. Coffee Jr seeks to offer, in Chapter 20, a balanced account of the impact of activism. He indicates that, on the one hand, hedge fund activism can generate positive short-term returns for shareholders. Indeed, earlier scholars have identified the strategies of activist investors that increase value of target firms and enhance the returns to investors. Based on more recent empirical research, Coffee shows, on the other hand, that there is little evidence of long-term positive returns following the announcement of a filing of a 13D or that positive returns tend to be concentrated in those firms that ultimately get acquired.

Moreover, the available evidence shows that as hedge fund activism has grown, there has been a significant growth in fundraising and an increased focus on the biggest companies as targets. Coffee argues that the emergence of new tactics of hedge funds, such as aggressive proxy fights and takeovers, have become important mechanisms for influencing target firms' management to accommodate the agenda of activist fund managers. In fact, there is growing use of the discriminatory poison pill to erect barriers to those who challenge incumbent management's control by proxy context as well as to those who launch hostile tender offers. More particularly, the pill's 'flip in' trigger goes off once a proxy contestant acquires a 20% stake in the target's shares, diluting the contestant's blockholding. The use of the 20% figure amounts to a long-standing drafting practice. Still, nothing in US corporate law says that the trigger cannot be set lower than 20%, even as legal barriers against impairment of the integrity of the shareholder franchise and against arrangements that unassailably entrench incumbent management strongly imply that at some point a threshold trigger becomes so low as to become illegal.

In a recent case, *ThirdPoint LLC v. Ruprecht*,[14] the Delaware Chancery Court addressed the legality question in connection with a poison pill triggered at 10% and deployed against the hedge fund Third Point in its proxy solicitation to elect a dissident short slate of directors to the board of Sotheby's. The Chancery Court sustained the low trigger, even though the pill effectively blocked the hedge fund from adding shares to its 10% ownership block and thereby constrained its ability to increase its vote total.

Drawing on the business context surrounding Third Point's campaign against the incumbent board of Sotheby's, Coffee shows that activist hedge fund interventions can harm corporate business plans and thus the interests of the target corporations' long-term shareholders. The possibility of harm significantly bolsters the corporate law case for a lower trigger. A key component of Coffee's analysis is his 'creeping control' account of activist tactics. Under this view, a hedge fund 'wolf pack' that accumulates more than 20% of a target's stock can thereby acquire the power to effect or block a control transfer, potentially trading off a best price payable to all shareholders as a group for private benefits. Thus Coffee concludes that, given the uncertainty about the impact of hedge fund activism, firms may have good evidence in support of seeking protection against creeping control acquisitions.

[14] 2014 WL 1922029.

1.15.4 Law Reform: The Burden of Persuasion

Fisch's suggestions regarding proxy access would once have been dismissed as misplaced contractarianism. Shareholders, according to a still widely held assumption, are structurally incapable of bootstrapping themselves into positions of empowerment by exercising their franchise; that lack of capability makes the separation of ownership and control corporate law's great unsolved problem, and justifies aggressive and preclusive regulation by the SEC. Yet in today's context it is not at all unreasonable to suggest that private ordering is the best means to the end of proxy access. What has changed?

William W. Bratton and Michael L. Wachter take up that question in this collection's final chapter, suggesting that enough has changed in respect of the balance of power between shareholders and managers to undermine the US case for shareholder empowerment through law reform. They, in effect, explore the implications of this collection's cumulated point: hedge fund activists, vulture funds, and private equity taken together have revolutionized shareholding and lending, solving layers of agency problems without any assistance in the form of regulatory reform.

In Bratton and Wachter's characterization, the case for law reform for the purpose of empowering shareholders comes down to the proposition that managers should manage to the market price of the stock. The case for shareholder empowerment through law reform begins with the principal-agent point: all other things equal, agency cost reduction enhances value, and enhanced principal control can conceivably lower agency costs. The shareholders, as principals, are well suited to provide value-enhancing inputs, for their investment in the residual interest lends them a pure financial incentive to maximize the company's value. The question is whether these pure shareholder incentives can be harnessed by the governance system despite the fact that dispersed, diversified shareholders labour under information asymmetries and lack business expertise. Here the market price of the stock comes in as the means to the end: if the stock price holds out an objective and accurate measure of the purely motivated shareholder maximand, then it provides the best source of instructions for governance and business policy. From this it follows that a manager-agent with correct incentives should manage to the market price. With the market price as the management yardstick, value-enhancing opportunities to merge, sell, or dissolve will no longer be frustrated by the managers' desire to hold on to control. Administrative coherence also would follow because the yardstick provides a means with which to evaluate management performance.

For Bratton and Wachter, shareholder empowerment proponents thus purport to offer a win-win, holding out benefits without asking about unintended costs. They counter on the cost side: what policy content, they ask, does the market price of the stock have to teach? Very little, in their view, once one puts aside a case like a hostile takeover, which poses a simple governance question in an information-enriched environment. As one moves away from an offer on the table for the whole to continuous business decision-making, the meaning of a market price signal becomes less and less clear and information asymmetries present more of a problem. Stock prices are less objective reports on particular value outcomes, than inputs for informed interpretation. Meanwhile, information asymmetries are real and unavoidable and market prices can be subject to speculative distortion.

More importantly, for present purposes, Bratton and Wachter ask whether agency costs remain wildly out of control. The shareholder empowerment advocates, they charge, pose as a static constant an agency cost picture that dates from the 1980s takeover era. In so doing, they have lost their way in history, failing to appreciate their own paradigmatic roots. Indeed, the shareholder proponents cost picture is the exact opposite of what Jensen and Meckling described in their fundamental exposition. Jensen and Meckling predicted, first, that actors will address agency costs as they arise over time, with managers bonding their fidelity to their investors and investors monitoring their investments, and, second, that when agency costs remain unaddressed, it is because their removal is too costly. In other words, markets and institutions work at agency cost reduction on a going-concern basis; at the same time, agency costs do not reduce to zero and a heroic attempt at agency cost reduction could be counterproductive.

Bratton and Wachter argue that post-1980s history acts out Jensen and Meckling's predictions. It has been a dynamic process of cost-reductive adjustment both inside corporations and outside in the market. Managers emerged from the 1980s sensitized to the benefits of shareholder value maximization. The board of directors simultaneously emerged as a more robust monitoring institution. Together, managers and boards used equity compensation plans to redirect management incentives in the shareholders' direction. Merger volume reached new records, with friendly rather than hostile deals as the means of moving assets to higher-valuing users. In addition, the corporate cash payout pattern underwent a notable shift to yield an unprecedented volume of share repurchases, a central shareholder agenda item.

Institutional investor activism comes to bear at this crucial point in the argument. Discipline, a factor supposedly lacking in the wake of antitakeover regulation, made a remarkable return to the governance front line when the private equity buyout re-emerged in the mid-1990s. With this business model, managers looking for enhanced upsides voluntarily put themselves under the control of market intermediaries who monitor costs intensively. And, on the market side of the line, activist hedge funds emerged to show that the shareholder collective action problem is not as preclusive as everybody assumed. The activists brought back hostility, but on a new platform independent of control transfer. They come forth as value investors, and pursue the very financial items that sit at the top of the shareholder proponents' agency cost agenda—increased leverage, payouts of excess cash, premium asset sales, and cost-cutting. In contrast to the accelerated share turnover that accompanied the shift to institutional holding, they, on average, invest for a period of two years. They have entered boardrooms in large numbers, all without any change in the legal model. The difference lies in the economics of their shareholding, and has to do with institutional incentive alignment.

In sum, where the shareholder proponents depict a governance system that chronically leaves big money on the table, Bratton and Wachter claim to depict dynamic adaptation towards the end of removing the money. Patterns of shareholding play a critical role in the process of adaptation. Much of the change can be attributed to the move away from individual to institutional holding and its role in ameliorating collective action problems. Critical changes in management policy follow when shares accumulate in three pockets—those of private equity funds, of hedge funds, and of corporate managers themselves. These critical shareholders have two things in common that distinguish them from the market price setters idealized by shareholder proponents. To wit, they are underdiversified (and thus highly incented to improve performance at individual firms) and well informed about the business (and thus positioned to offer productive planning and performance inputs). It follows that particular shareholders can be highly relevant so far as concerns value enhancement, even as their socio-economic status remains irrelevant.

1.16 Closing Questions

Our closing chapters bear close comparison with our opening chapters, bringing the collection full circle. The comparison triggers questions. Some focus on the persuasiveness of Bratton and Wachter's claim that activism, taken together with other shareholder favourable developments since the close of the takeover era, sufficiently ameliorates agency costs as to obviate the need for fundamental corporate law reform in the US. Does the evidence presented in this collection sustain the claim, or just open the door for a tentative suggestion? Other questions focus on the connection Bratton and Wachter make between shareholder empowerment, law reform, and the perverse effects of managing the market price. Given the open door to shareholder access in the UK, should not managing the market already have manifested itself there as a distinct problem? Alternatively, if shareholder activism has fundamentally changed the US governance context, should not managing to the market price already be an acute problem in the US, as an observer like Martin Lipton would claim? Either way, how important is law reform? If the balance of power between shareholders and managers in the UK lies differently than that in the US, is the difference due to company law or to institutional relationships of long standing? If US law were reformed in line with Bebchuk's agenda, would fundamental relational changes follow or would endogenous market adjustments lead us back to the present equilibrium? Finally, should lawmakers in the US, following Fisch, make sure pathways are open for management–shareholder contracting, but otherwise let shareholder empowerment take care of itself?

References

Bratton, W. W. (2010). Hedge Funds and Governance Targets: Long-Term Results, University of Pennsylvania Institute for Law & Economics Research Paper No. 10-17, available at <http://ssrn.com/abstract=1677517>.

Brav, A. P., Jiang, W., and Kim, H. (2012). Hedge Fund Activism: Updated Tables and Figures, Working Paper, available at <https://faculty.fuqua.duke.edu/~brav/HFactivism_March_2012.pdf>.

Brav, A. P., Jiang, W., and Kim, H. (2013). The Real Effects of Hedge Fund Activism: Productivity, Asset Allocation, and Industry Concentration, Working Paper (May), available at <http://ssrn.com/abstract=2022904>.

Cumming, D., Dai, N., and Johan, S. (2005). Dodd-Franking the Hedge Funds, Working Paper (May), available at <http://ssrn.com/abstract=2527679>.

Harris, R. S., Jenkinson, T., and Kaplan, S. N. (2014). Private Equity Performance: What Do We Know?, *Journal of Finance* 69, 1851–82.

Higson, C. and Stücke, R. (2012). The Performance of Private Equity, Working Paper (Mar.), available at <http://ssrn.com/abstract=2009067>.

Holström, B. R. and Kaplan, S. N. (2001). Corporate Governance and Merger Activity in the US: Making Sense of the 1980s and 1990s, *Journal of Economic Perspectives* 15, 121–44.

Jensen, M. (1988). Takeovers: Their Causes and Consequences, *Journal of Economic Perspectives* 2, 21–48.

Jensen, M. (1989). The Effects of Management Buyouts on Operations and Value, *Journal of Financial Economics* 24, 217–54.

Kaal, W. A. (2014). The Impact of Dodd-Frank Act Compliance Cost on the Hedge Fund Industry, Working Paper (Feb.), available at <http://ssrn.com/abstract=2389423>.

Kaplan, S. N. and Schoar, A. (2006). Private Equity Performance: Returns, Persistence and Capital Flow, *Journal of Finance* 60, 1791–1823.

Krishnan, C. N. V., Partnoy, F., and Thomas, R. S. (2015). Top Hedge Funds and Shareholder Activism, available at <http://ssrn.com/abstract=2589992>.

Metrick, A. and Yashida, A. (2009). The Economics of Private Equity Funds, *Review of Financial Studies* 23, 2303–41.

OECD (The OECD Steering Group on Corporate Governance) (2007). The Role of Private Pools of Capital in Corporate Governance: Summary and Main Findings: About the Role of Private Equity Firms and 'Activist' Hedge Funds, available at <http://www.oecd.org/corporate/ca/corporategovernanceprinciples/38672168.pdf>.

Robinson, D. T. and Sensoy, B. A. (2013). Cyclicality, Performance Measurement, and Cash Flow Liquidity in Private Equity. Charles A. Dice Center Working Paper No. 2010-021; Fisher College of Business Working Paper No. 2010-03-021, available at <http://ssrn.com/abstract=1731603>.

PART I

THE DISEMPOWERED SHAREHOLDER

CHAPTER 2

THE EVOLUTION OF SHAREHOLDER ACTIVISM IN THE UNITED STATES

STUART L. GILLAN AND LAURA T. STARKS

2.1 Introduction

Shareholder activism in the Untied States is by no means a new phenomenon. In the early 1900s, American financial institutions such as insurance companies, mutual funds, and banks were active participants in US corporate governance. In many cases, the representatives of such institutions—among them J. P. Morgan and his associates—served on corporate boards and played major roles in the strategic direction of the firm.

But over the next three or four decades, laws passed with the aim of limiting the power of financial intermediaries also prevented them from having an active role in corporate governance (Roe 1990). The Glass-Steagall Act prohibited US banks from owning equity directly. And the regulatory reforms that followed the stock market crash of 1929 limited the liquidity of, and otherwise raised the costs to, investors of active participation in corporate affairs. The consequence of such laws and regulations was a progressive widening of the gap between ownership and control in large US public companies—a process that continued until the emergence of corporate raiders and leveraged buyouts (LBOs) in the 1980s (Bhide 1990, 1993).

The current wave of US shareholder activism can be seen as dating from the Securities and Exchange Commission's (SEC) introduction in 1942 of a rule (the predecessor of today's Rule 14a-8) that first allowed shareholders to submit proposals for inclusion on corporate ballots. Since that time, the identities of shareholder activists have changed along with the focus of their efforts to bring about change. From 1942 to the end of the 1970s, shareholder activism was dominated by individual investors. The 1980s, by contrast, saw an increase in the involvement of institutional investors, which at first were mainly public pension funds. These pension funds submitted shareholder proposals, pressured management 'behind the scenes' for corporate reforms, and used the press to target the management and boards of poorly governed or performing companies. The 1980s also saw the rise of corporate raiders—perhaps the ultimate activists—who used the market for corporate control to try to impose discipline on boards and managements.

But with the decline of the takeover market during the 1990s, and regulatory changes that enhanced the ability of shareholders to communicate on voting issues, activist institutional investors again came to the fore. At the same time labour union pension funds began to assume a major role in investor activism. Indeed, as discussed later, a number of innovations in the use of shareholder proposals can be attributed to union-based funds.

While these different varieties of activism can still be seen today, the evolutionary process continues. In particular, during the past few years, hedge funds and private equity funds have assumed prominence in the activist arena. These funds have become increasingly important players in financial markets, particularly in their capacity as monitors of corporate performance and agents of change. In many respects, the hedge funds that take large, relatively long-term positions in underperforming companies (and, contrary to popular perception, there are a significant number of such funds) can be viewed as the modern-day equivalent of the active investors who disciplined US managers at the turn of the last century.

In the pages that follow, we review the evolution of shareholder activism since the establishment of the SEC in the 1930s, with emphasis on three main subjects: the kinds of companies that are targeted by activists; the motives of institutional investors for activism; and the effectiveness of activists in bringing about economically significant change at targeted companies. We finish with an analysis of the most recent changes that have occurred with the entry of hedge funds into shareholder activism.[1]

2.2 Varieties of Shareholder Activism

Shareholder activists are often viewed as investors who, dissatisfied with some aspect of a company's management or operations, try to bring about change within the company without a change in control. But one can also think of shareholder activism more broadly as encompassing a continuum of possible responses to corporate performance and activities. At one end, we could view shareholders who simply trade a company's shares as being 'active'. Through their initial purchases and subsequent decisions to hold or sell, shareholders are expressing their views of the corporation's performance. At the other end of the continuum is the market for corporate control, where investors initiate takeovers and LBOs aimed at accomplishing fundamental corporate changes. Between these extremes are intermediate points on the continuum that include, for example, blockholders who purchase minority stakes with the intent of influencing managerial decision-making.

Dissatisfied shareholders can simply vote with their feet—a practice known as the *Wall Street Walk*—by selling their shares. And theoretical and empirical studies provide evidence that the act of selling shares can have disciplinary effects on companies that lead to changes in governance (Admati and Pfleiderer 2009; Parrino, Sias, and Starks 2003). For example,

[1] For previous surveys of shareholder activism, see Black (1998); Gillan and Starks (1998); Karpoff (2001); and Romano (2001). Partnoy and Thomas (2007) contrast shareholder activism by hedge funds and institutional investors.

the probabilities of CEOs being fired and replaced by executives from outside the firm are higher after large sell-offs by institutional investors. Dissatisfied shareholders who choose instead to hold their shares (perhaps because they are 'indexed' and so unable to sell) have two choices: (1) do nothing (and thereby exhibit 'loyalty'); or (2) express their dissatisfaction using some means ranged on the continuum discussed above (Hirschman 1971). Our primary interest in this chapter is in the variety of ways that shareholders have 'voiced' their dissatisfaction with managements and boards over the past six decades and how both the identity of the shareholders and the focus of their dissatisfaction have changed.[2]

2.3 A Short History of Shareholder Activism

In 1942, after a series of new laws and regulations forced active investors out of corporate governance, the SEC adopted a rule that was the predecessor of and paved the way for the current Rule 14a-8, which states that management must allow shareholder proposals that constitute a 'proper subject for action by the security holders'. In 1943, shareholders began to submit proposals aimed at improving corporate governance and performance. And the next three decades saw a flood of shareholder resolutions aimed at improving performance and raising share values.

But that was not the only intent of such proposals. In 1970 a federal court decision allowed a shareholder proposal to forbid the sale of napalm by Dow Chemical, and other proposals on social responsibility issues began to appear (Manne and Wallich 1972). To get a sense of the proportion of shareholder proposals devoted to social issues at this time, consider that the member companies of the American Society of Corporate Secretaries (1979) reported that 611 of the 790 proposals they received during the 1978 proxy season dealt with governance issues and the other 179 with social issues. As for the disposition of these 790 proposals, 439 were voted on, 197 were excluded from the proxy statements, 125 were withdrawn, and the fate of the remaining twenty-nine is unknown.

Until the mid-1980s, the major proponents of shareholder proposals were individuals that came to be called 'gadfly' investors.[3] For example, in 1982, almost 30% of the 972 resolutions submitted to 358 companies came from three individuals: Lewis and John Gilbert, and Evelyn Davis (Ross 1983). From the the mid-1980s, however, shareholder activists began to work in numbers, and a number of groups have arisen—and some met their demise. For example, T. Boone Pickens established the United Shareholders Association in 1986 with the expressed intent of 'upgrading shareholder awareness'. After monitoring and targeting corporations and submitting corporate governance shareholder proposals for seven years, the

[2] Our focus in this review is on studies of corporate governance issues and attempts to link governance-based activism to shareholder value. This is notably different from the intent of, say, Tkac (2006), which provides an analysis of shareholder proposals with particular focus on social issues.

[3] Some of the gadflies had been submitting proposals since they were first allowed in 1942. In fact, according to Talner (1983), the activism of the Gilbert Brothers can be traced to a 1932 annual shareholders meeting of Consolidated Gas in which the chairman never recognized any of the shareholders who had raised their hand to ask questions. Lewis Gilbert was reportedly appalled by the lack of communication between management and shareholders.

group's board voted to disband in 1993 (Pickens 1998; Strickland, Wiles, and Zenner 1996). Another coalition of individual shareholders, the Investors' Rights Association of America, began submitting proposals in 1995 and did so for a short time.

Perhaps the newest group of prominent shareholder activists, known as The Investors for Director Accountability, was organized in March of 2006. Headed by luminaries that include John Bogle, T. Boone Pickens, and Robert Monks, the group has declared its goal to be the restoration of directors' accountability to shareholders (Kary 2006).

2.3.1 The Growing Role of Institutional Investors

With the suspension of hostile takeovers at the end of the 1980s, and the steady growth in their ownership of US companies, US institutional investors were forced to play a more active role in corporate governance. As can be seen in Figure 2.1, institutional investors held only about 10% of US equities in 1953, but their percentage ownership had jumped to over 60% by the end of 2005.

The beginnings of shareholder activism by institutional investors can be identified in the formation, in 1985, of the Council of Institutional Investors, which was led by Jesse Unruh, then treasurer of the state of California. As state treasurer, Unruh was responsible for the performance of two large institutional investment funds, the California Public Employees Retirement System (CalPERS) and the California State Teachers Retirement System (CalSTRS). Both of these funds were heavily invested in Texaco.

Unruh formed the Council in response to learning that the Bass Brothers, after acquiring a 9.8% block in Texaco, sold the shares back to Texaco at a $137 million premium over the current market price—a repurchase offer that was not extended to other shareholders like CalPERS and CalSTRS. The purpose of the Council of Institutional Investors was to act as a lobbying group for shareholder rights (Monks and Minow 2003).

Still in existence today, the Council has evolved to the point of becoming a focal point for many institutional shareholder activists. Although founded as an organization primarily for public pension funds, it now consists of more than 140 public, labour, and corporate pension funds that control in excess of $3 trillion in financial assets. Its stated objective is to

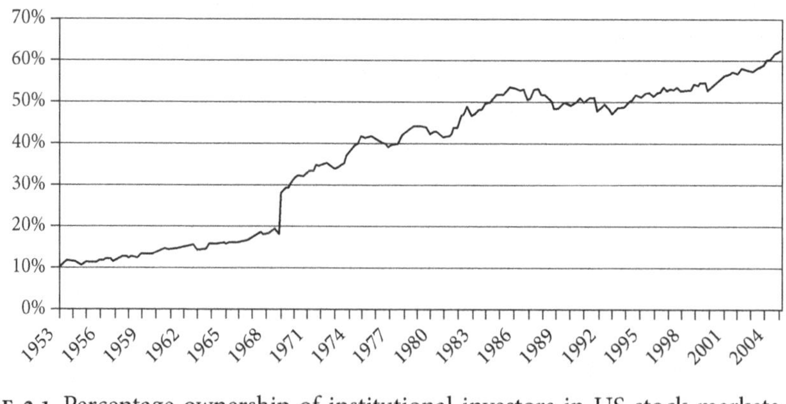

FIGURE 2.1 Percentage ownership of institutional investors in US stock markets

enable institutional investors to pool their resources and 'use their proxy votes, shareowner resolutions, pressure on regulators, discussions with companies, and, when necessary, litigation to protect plan assets'.[4]

Such institutional activism expanded greatly in 1986 and 1987, as large public pension funds began to submit shareholder proxy proposals, both individually and in collaboration with one another. In our own study (Gillan and Starks 2000) of proposals by institutional investors during the 1980s and 1990s, we found that the three most common objectives of such proposals were the repeal of antitakeover amendments, the adoption of cumulative voting, and greater board independence. But, as we also discovered, public pension funds changed their approach to activism in the early 1990s. One important change was to submit fewer proxy proposals while trying harder to initiate a dialogue with targeted companies' managements and boards. Another was to make greater use of the media in targeting companies, while alerting other investors to the firm's problems and the activist's proposals.

Until the recent emergence of hedge funds, the most activist institutional investors have been public pension funds and union funds. In the mid-1990s, union funds began to account for a larger proportion of shareholder proposals while the public pension funds' share started to fall. But their labour affiliation notwithstanding, the goals of the union funds have been similar to those of other institutional investors. As Schwab and Thomas (1998: 1019) commented in a *Michigan Law Review* article, 'In most cases it is hard to find a socialist or proletarian plot in what unions are doing with their shares. Rather labor activism is a model for any large institutional investor.' And since publication of this article, the union funds appear to have persisted in this behaviour. Besides submitting shareholder proposals, the unions have pursued innovative forms of activism, not only in terms of developing new proposals, but also by using the media to pressure management (the Teamsters publicly target individual directors rather than just a particular company), and making proposals from the floor at annual meetings (Prevost, Rao, and Williams 2009; Schwab and Thomas 1998).

Along with the rise of institutional investor activism in the mid-1980s, the Department of Labor, through its oversight of ERISA portfolios, began to pressure corporate pension funds to assume a more active role in monitoring the companies in their portfolios. They advocated the voting of proxies by the pension funds rather than delegating that responsibility to their external managers, arguing that voting was part of their fiduciary duty.[5]

Although private pension funds and mutual funds did not generally participate in public shareholder activism, money managers purportedly played a major role in the ouster of some high-profile CEOs. For example, according to Pensions and Investments, the removal of James D. Robinson as chairman of American Express was the result of pressure by private money managers, not public pension funds. And Fidelity reportedly had a behind-the-scenes role in Kay Whitmore's departure as the CEO of Eastman Kodak (Myerson 1993; Pensions and Investments 1993). Money managers have been involved

[4] Council of Institutional Investors website, 2006, available at <http://www.cii.org>.

[5] The 1994 release of the Department of Labor's Interpretative Bulletin 94-2 (IB 94-2) took an even stronger stance on the responsibility of corporate pension funds by stating that,

> active monitoring and communication with corporate management is consistent with a fiduciary's obligations under ERISA where the responsible fiduciary concludes that there is a reasonable chance that such activities... are likely to enhance the value of the plan's involvement, after taking into account the costs involved.

in other types of activism as well. For example, in 2002, Fidelity announced that it would vote against directors if executive compensation were not sufficiently linked to corporate performance. And in that same year, Fidelity took private activism further by appointing one of its own executives, Steve Akin, as chief executive of Colt Telecom, the troubled US telecommunications group.

While the efficacy of institutional activism continues to be the subject of debate, these activists achieved a considerable measure of influence. As one observer noted in 1996, '[f]ifteen years ago, the CEO and CFO did not know major holders and really didn't care. CEOs are now more accessible to money managers' (Ettorre 1996).

2.4 Motives for Shareholder Activism

Shareholder activism is, at bottom, a response to the potential gains from addressing the agency conflict at the core of large publicly traded companies with absentee owners. In such companies, shareholders effectively delegate decision-making responsibility to managers whose interests can diverge from those of their shareholders (Jensen and Meckling 1976). The board of directors has a significant role in controlling such agency problems that comes with its fiduciary obligation to shareholders, which includes the responsibility to hire, fire, compensate, and monitor top management. The demand for activism arises when boards fail to perform these tasks.

There are a number of remedies for inadequate boards, starting with the fact that common stocks are bought and sold in a marketplace.[6] Precisely because investors can sell their shares to the highest bidder, there is a market for corporate takeovers—or, in academic parlance, a 'market for corporate control'—that gives competing management teams, as well as unaffiliated active investors, the ability to gain control of companies, thereby circumventing ineffective managers and boards. But even in cases where there appear to be no bidders, the stock market performs an inherent monitoring function that exerts pressure on managers and boards to make decisions that serve the interests of shareholders. As Holmström and Tirole (1993) have argued, the stock market may be the most reliable monitor of managerial performance because stock prices incorporate a variety of kinds of information about future performance and value that cannot be found in financial statements alone.

We now have substantial theoretical and empirical evidence that documents the monitoring role played by institutional investors (Agrawal and Mandelker 1992; Almazan and Suarez 2003; Black 1992; Del Guercio and Hawkins 1998; Gillan and Starks 2000; Hartzell and Starks 2003; Kahn and Winton 1998; Kaplan and Minton 1994; Noe 2002; for shareholders in general, see Admati, Pfleider, and Zechner 1994; Black 1990; Bolton and von Thadden 1998; Chidambaran and John 1998; Coffee 1991; Huddart 1993; Maug 1998; Maug and Rydqvist 2008; Noe 2002; Shleifer and Vishny 1986). When interpreting such evidence, however, it's important to recognize that such investors differ in terms of their trading styles, incentives for managers, clienteles, legal and regulatory environments, and ability to gather

[6] Fama and Jensen (1983) suggest that the unrestricted nature of common stock residual claims allow special market and organizational mechanisms for controlling these problems.

and process information. These differences in turn imply differences among institutions' motives and capabilities for monitoring—and the evidence supports this contention. For example, empirical studies suggest that the presence of certain kinds of institutional shareholders in a company's ownership base influences (and is often influenced by) its executive compensation policy, its operating performance, and the market for corporate control that surrounds it. For example, companies with disproportionate holdings by independent investment advisers and mutual funds tend to place greater emphasis on pay for performance, produce consistently higher returns on capital, and avoid value-reducing mergers (Almazan, Hartzell, and Starks 2005; Borokhovich et al. 2006; Brickley, Lease, and Smith 1988; Bushee 1998; 2001; Chen, Harford, and Li 2007; Cornett et al. 2007; Gaspar, Massa, and Matos 2005; Pinkowitz 2003; Qiu 2006).

On the other hand, institutional investors, such as corporate pension funds or insurance companies, may be reluctant to undertake activism against other corporations, particularly those with which the sponsoring company does business. Because of business relations with the corporation, some institutional investors may feel compelled to vote with management even though such behaviour runs contrary to their fiduciary interests (Brickley, Lease, and Smith 1988; Pound 1988).

Consistent with the idea that institutional investors may face potential conflicts of interest in monitoring companies, a study by Romano (1993) investigated a widely held hypothesis that public pension funds are more effective monitors of management because they vote their own shares, whereas private pension funds typically delegate their voting to external money managers. However, she found no evidence to support this hypothesis. Furthermore, according to a survey of institutional investors from the Investor Responsibility Research Center (IRRC), there has been no significant difference in voting policy between public and private pension funds: both groups tended to support management over the survey period.

A 1993 survey of the forty largest US pension funds, forty largest investment managers, and twenty largest charitable foundations reported finding major differences among institutions—even institutions of the same type—in their attitudes and approaches to shareholder activism. For example, although we might expect to find indexed portfolios more engaged in activism, the survey indicated that while some index fund managers were highly active, most were completely passive. Based on follow-up interviews, the authors of the survey also reported that activist institutions preferred direct negotiation to proxy proposals, in large part because of the difficulty of persuading other institutions to agree on unified proxy strategies. Besides the need for arduous coalition-building among investors, another reason for avoiding proxy campaigns—at least prior to 1993—were regulatory constraints on communication among investors (Bradley et al. 2005; Useem et al. 1993).

Although some public pension funds have been praised for their advocacy of shareholder interests, a number of studies have shown that the incentives of the decision-makers at public pension funds may not be consistent with value-increasing shareholder activism (Murphy and Van Nuys 1994; Woidtke, Bierman, and Tuggle 2003). Woidtke's (2002) study comparing the relative value of companies held by public and private pension funds reported that corporate values were positively related to private pension fund ownership and negatively related to (activist) public pension ownership. In attempting to explain this finding, the author focused on political and social influences on public pension fund managers that divert their focus from maximizing value.

Some legal scholars have even suggested that the costs of shareholder activism are likely to exceed the benefits, and that the SEC should accordingly consider raising the hurdles for submitting shareholder proposals (Romano 2001). In a similar spirit, others have argued that activist institutions often pursue narrow agendas that, rather than aimed at increasing value, have the potential to undermine the effectiveness of corporate boards (Bainbridge 2005).

2.5 What Companies Get Targeted?

Until recently, the main criterion for the targeting of a corporation by shareholder activists has been poor performance. The targets have also often been characterized by large shareholdings by other institutional investors, low inside ownership, and what investors perceive to be a poor governance structure (Carleton, Nelson, and Weisbach 1998; Huson 1997; John and Klein 1995; Karpoff, Malatesta, and Walkling 1996; Smith 1996). Although some of the early targeting by public pension funds and TIAA-CREF focused primarily on companies with questionable governance structures, that practice largely disappeared in the early 1990s. For example, CalPERS, after experimenting with a variety of indicators of substandard governance, settled on poor performance as its primary criterion for targeting in 1990 (Thomas and Cotter 2006). While in some cases poor performance and poor governance still trigger activist campaigns, recent hedge fund activism has rekindled the focus on profitable companies (Brav et al., Chapter 8, this volume; Klein and Zur, Chapter 9, this volume).

2.5.1 The Evolution of Shareholder Proposals: Issues and Sponsors

The findings of our own (previously cited) study of corporate governance shareholder proposals submitted during the period 1987–94, when set against the findings of a later study by the proxy firm Georgeson (2005) for the period 2001–05, allows us to see the main issues of interest to shareholder activists and how they have changed over time.[7] As can be seen in both Table 2.1 and Figure 2.2, both periods saw extensive efforts by activist shareholders to remove poison pills, classified boards, and supermajority antitakeover amendments from corporate charters. Concerns about board independence and executive pay, while certainly in evidence in the earlier period (accounting for 13.7% and 11.4%, respectively, of all proposals), became much more prevalent in the later period (at 20.4% and 33.1%). And while the general focus of some of the proposals remained unchanged, there were also notable changes. For example, in the earlier period, the two

[7] Data for the early period come from Gillan and Starks (2000). Data for the latter period come from Georgeson Shareholders (2005).

Table 2.1 Number of corporate governance proposals submitted over two separate periods

Major issues	1987–94	2001–05
Repeal classified board	314	199
Eliminate poison pill	249	220
Cumulative voting	274	93
Supermajority	21	47
Audit-related	19	62
Board-related	279	353
Executive compensation	233	573
Other	653	183
Total	2,042	1,730

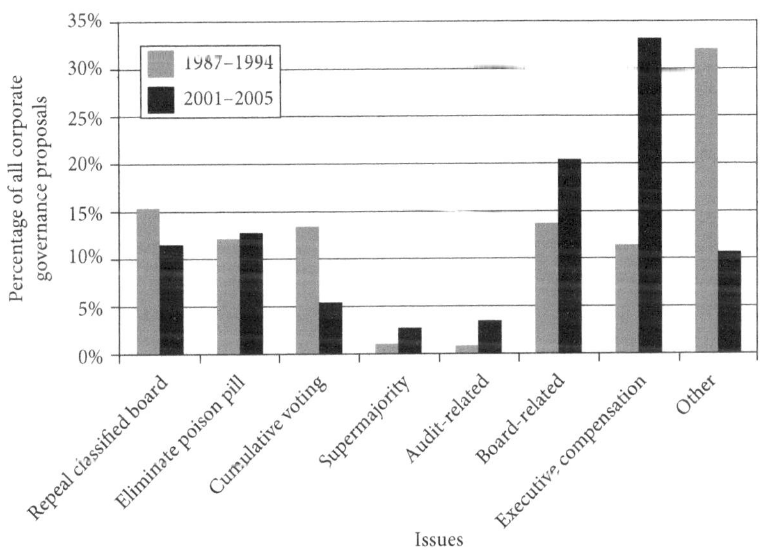

FIGURE 2.2 Corporate governance proposal issues across two periods

most common board-related proposals aimed at increasing director share ownership and limiting directors' terms. During the more recent period, the two most common board-related proposals were aimed at achieving director elections through majority vote and independent board chairmen.

Figure 2.3 shows that there were also large changes in the sponsors of the corporate governance proposals between the two periods. Union funds became a much larger force in shareholder activism, submitting over 40% of the proposals in 2004 and 2005, as compared with less than 10% during the 1987–94 period. In contrast, public pension funds accounted for a much smaller share of proposals (4%, as compared with an earlier 14.2%), as did unaffiliated individuals (44.5%, as compared with an earlier 70.4%).

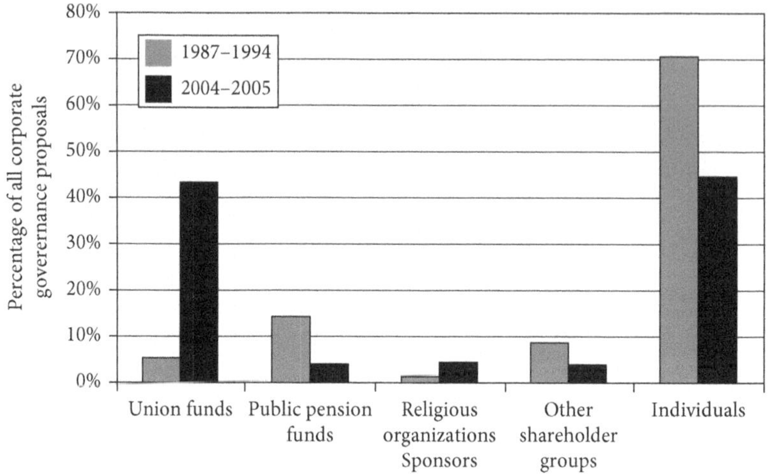

FIGURE 2.3 Sponsors of corporate governance proposals

2.5.2 Does Shareholder Activism Work?

Measuring the effectiveness of shareholder activism is a difficult task for several reasons. First, identifying cases of shareholder activism can be problematic. For example, when activists negotiate behind the scenes, there may be no external sign of the activity. Take the case of CalPERS and Texaco cited earlier. CalPERS submitted a shareholder proposal to the company calling for the creation of an advisory committee of major shareholders to work with management. After directly negotiating with Texaco and getting an agreement that management would nominate a pro-shareholder candidate to its board of directors, CalPERS withdrew its proposal (Parker 1989). Such activities are not detected by most studies of shareholder activism.

One exception is a study of direct negotiations with targeted companies by one notably activist shareholder, TIAA-CREF (Carleton, Nelson, and Weisbach 1998). The study found that, of the forty-five companies contacted by TIAA-CREF, 71% reached a negotiated settlement prior to the vote on the proposal. The remaining 29% of the firms resisted TIAA-CREF's pressures and the proposals went to a vote. These results suggest both the challenge for researchers posed by unreported events and the understatement of the extent of shareholder activism by studies that focus only on proposals that get put to a vote.

A second problem with such studies is the difficulty in establishing a causal link between shareholder activism and subsequent changes in governance, and between such governance changes and changes in corporate performance. In other words, are observed changes in governance the result of shareholder proposals, public pressure, behind-the-scenes negotiations with activists, or some other influence? And did the changes actually result in increases in the efficiency and value of the targeted firms?

For example, one major aim of shareholder activists has been to get more independent directors on the board. Although we can observe whether there are more independent directors, it is often difficult to attribute the increase to a particular shareholder action. And it is even harder to assess whether the change in the composition of the board led to higher profits and share values.

With these caveats in mind, we now present and discuss the empirical evidence on the effects of shareholder activism. Table 2.2 provides a summary of existing studies of shareholder activism, including the sample period, the type of activism, the identity of the shareholder activists, and the number of proposals and firms. As can be seen in the table, the sample periods all begin after 1985, the beginning of institutional investor activism.[8] Although many of the studies include all active institutions ('sponsors'), some focus on subsets of sponsors such as public pension funds, labour unions, coordinated groups, or individual pension funds. Finally, the studies vary widely in the number of firms and activist 'events' examined.

As might be expected with such a range of issues and sponsors, the studies produce some strikingly different assessments of the extent and effects of shareholder activism. In addition to analysis of the kinds of companies targeted by activists, researchers have devised and tested numerous measures of the influence of shareholder activism. Chief among them are short-term stock market reactions to announcement of shareholder initiatives, longer-term stock market and operating performance, outcomes of votes on shareholder proposals, and changes in corporate strategy and investment decisions in response to activism. In the following sections, we discuss the empirical evidence concerning each of these different ways of evaluating the effectiveness of shareholder activism.

2.5.3 Short-term Stock Market Reactions

One potential measure of the effects of shareholder activism is whether the announcement of such activism is accompanied by an increase in the company's value. That is, do other investors change their expectations about the value of the firm because they believe that activism will lead to real economic changes? To measure such an increase, researchers commonly examine changes in stock prices around the date of the announcement of the activism. But this kind of analysis has a number of limitations.

One problem is the difficulty in ascertaining exactly when investors first receive the information that a company has been targeted by a shareholder activist. For example, in examining shareholder proposals, the researcher needs to decide whether the critical date is the date of any initial letter to the firm, the proxy mailing, the shareholders' annual meeting, or a separate press release. Given the private nature of communications between corporate management and public pension funds, most studies consider the date of the proxy mailing to be the earliest release of news of a shareholder proposal. If this news caused investors to reassess the firm's valuation, we would expect to be able to detect the change around this date.

[8] The shortest analyses focus on proposals in a single year (e.g., Gordon and Pound 1993; Campbell, Gillan, and Niden 1999). The longest is our own study of the eight year period 1987–94 cited earlier (Gillan and Starks 2000). Most of the studies examine the submission of shareholder proposals related to corporate governance, but some studies also include shareholder proposals aimed at social reforms (Campbell, Gillan, and Niden 1999; John and Klein 1995). In addition, some studies emphasize other types of activism: firms on focus lists (Anson, White, and Ho 2004; Barber 2006; Caton, Goh, and Donaldson 2001; Crutchley, Hudson, and Jensen 1998; English, Smythe, and McNeil 2004; Nelson 2006; Opler and Sokobin 1998; Song and Szewczyk 2003), negotiated agreements (Carleton, Nelson, and Weisbach 1998; Strickland, Wiles, and Zenner 1996), and all activism aimed at a single firm (Gillan, Kensinger, and Martin 2000; Smith 1996).

Table 2.2 Empirical studies of shareholder activism

This table shows by study the sample period, the type of activism examined, the sponsors examined, the number of firms and activism events and the overall conclusions regarding outcomes.

Study	Sample period	Type of activism	Sponsor of activism	No. of firms and activism events	Conclusions regarding outcomes
Gordon and Pound (1993)	1990	Governance proposals	All sponsors	266 proposals	Voting outcomes depend on governance and performance of target firm and ownership by insiders, institutions, ESOPS, and blockholders.
Nesbitt (1994)	1987–92	All governance activism	CalPERS	42 firms	Targeted companies underperformed S&P 500 by 66% in five years before targeting and outperformed by 41% in five years after targeting.
Gillan (1995)	1986–91	Governance proposals	All sponsors	1,019 proposals at 305 firms	While there is a positive stock market reaction to shareholder proposals in some subsamples, on average there is no improvement in long-term stock market performance or operating performance. Public pension fund sponsorship of shareholder proposals is positively associated with the percentage of votes received.
John and Klein (1995)	1991–92	Social and governance proposals	All sponsors	344 proposals	The likelihood of a firm being the target of corporate governance proposals is significantly affected by firm size, presence of negative net income, percentage of outside directors with outside directorships in other S&P 500 firms, the percentage of institutional ownership and whether or not shareholders vote on the choice of auditor and last year's vote.

(continued)

Table 2.2 (Continued)

Study	Sample period	Type of activism	Sponsor of activism	No. of firms and activism events	Conclusions regarding outcomes
Karpoff, Malatesta, and Walking (1996)	1986–90	Governance proposals	All sponsors	522 proposals at 269 firms	There is no persuasive evidence that shareholder proposals increase firm values, improve operating performance, or influence firm policies.
Smith, D.G. (1996)	1990–95	Activism aimed at Kmart	All sponsors	1 firm	Concludes that problems were due to managerial incompetence and that shareholder activism is an ineffective mechanism for dealing with this type of problem.
Smith, M. (1996)	1987–93	All governance activism	CalPERS	51 firms	Shareholder wealth increased for firms that settled with CalPERS and decreased for firms that resisted. There were no statistically significant changes in operating performance.
Strickland, Wiles, and Zenner (1996)	1986–93	Proposals and negotiated settlements	United Shareholders Association	216 proposals at 85 firms	Votes on proposals were higher when target had poor performance and more institutional investors. Out of proposals sponsored by United States found fifty-three negotiated agreements, which had a small average positive announcement return. Authors concluded US's actions were successful.
Wahal (1996)	1987–93	All proposals	Public pension funds	356 proposals at 146 firms	Finds no significant target firm wealth effects from shareholder activism.
Carleton, Nelson, and Weisbach (1997)	1992–96	Negotiated agreements	TIAA-CREF	62 targetings of 45 firms	Negotiated agreements are generally successful in achieving goals, but whether there are short-term wealth effects depends on issue.

(*continued*)

Table 2.2 (Continued)

Study	Sample period	Type of activism	Sponsor of activism	No. of firms and activism events	Conclusions regarding outcomes
Johnson, Porter, and Shackell (1997)	1992–95	Executive compensation proposals	All sponsors	184 firms	Find no effect of proposals on executive compensation.
Johnson and Shackell (1997)	1992–95	Executive compensation proposals	All sponsors	169 proposals at 106 firms	Find no effect of proposals on executive compensation.
Bizjak and Marquette (1998)	1987–93	Poison pill rescission proposals	All sponsors	191 proposals at 116 firms	Pill recission proposals are submitted more frequently when firm performance has been poor, when the initial market reaction to the adoption of the pill is negative, and when insider and block ownership of stock is low. Firms that receive shareholder proposals regarding poison pills are more likely to restructure or rescind the pills.
Campbell, Gillan, and Niden (1998)	1997	All proposals	All sponsors	681 proposals at 394 firms	Governance-related proposals generally receive higher support than social-issue proposals. A high proportion of proposals sponsored by individual investors are omitted on technical grounds.
Crutchley, Hudson, and Jensen (1998)	1992–97	Target list firms	CalPERS	47 firms	Success of CalPERS activism depends on time period studied. Unless management is pressured into making substantial changes, investors will not benefit from activism.
Del Guercio and Hawkins (1998)	1987–93	Governance proposals	5 public pension funds	266 proposals at 125 firms	Shareholder proposals are not associated with accounting or stock market performance, but are associated with subsequent changes in corporate governance and corporate activities such as asset sales or restructurings.

(continued)

Table 2.2 (Continued)

Study	Sample period	Type of activism	Sponsor of activism	No. of firms and activism events	Conclusions regarding outcomes
Huson (1998)	1990–92	All governance activism	CalPERS	18 firms	Found significant changes in the real activities of targeted firms. In addition, market reaction to such transactions was significantly more positive, on average, than to comparable transactions before the targeting.
Martin, Gillan, and Kensinger (1998)	1989–92	Activism aimed at Sears Roebuck	All sponsors	1 firm	Suggestive of activism having a positive influence on Sears' value and that management was pressured to restructure faster than they would have done absent shareholder pressure.
Opler and Sokobin (1998)	1991–94	Targeted firms on focus lists	Council of Institutional Investors (CII)	117 firms	In year after being listed, firms averaged an 11.6% increase in share price suggesting that coordinated shareholder activism creates shareholder wealth.
Schwab and Thomas (1998)	1996–97	Governance proposals	Labour unions	126 proposals at 91 firms	Argues that unions need to align with shareholders and in so doing, they shift from an antagonistic player to a strategically cooperative player in corporate governance.
Thomas and Martin (1998)	1994	Governance proposals	All sponsors	309 proposals	Find that labour union proposals receive at least as much support as other shareholder group proposals.
Gillan and Starks (2000)	1987–94	Governance proposals	All sponsors	2,042 proposals at 452 firms	Shareholder reaction and voting outcome on proposals depend on issue and identity of sponsor. Proposals sponsored by institutions receive much higher votes and more positive reactions.

(*continued*)

Table 2.2 **(Continued)**

Study	Sample period	Type of activism	Sponsor of activism	No. of firms and activism events	Conclusions regarding outcomes
Prevost and Rao (2000)	1988–94	Governance proposals	Public pension funds	146 proposals	Find strong negative wealth effects on announcement of targeting.
Choi (2000)	1991–95	Governance proposals	Institutions	362 proposals at 278 firms	Examines proposals before and after SEC changes in proxy reform rules and finds no difference In voting outcomes after the changes.
Caton, Goh, and Donaldson (2001)	1991–95	Targeted firms on focus lists	Council of Institutional Investors (CII)	108 firms	Negative market reaction to list release, but increased earnings estimates by financial analysts for a subsample companies with solid growth opportunities.
Hann (2002)	1989–96	Targeted firms	5 public pension funds	150 targeted firms	Characteristics of target can explain whether activism results in successful changes. Can explain why so few studies find significant changes in target.
Song and Szewzcyk (2003)	1991–96	Targeted firms on focus lists	Council of Institutional Investors (CII)	156 firms	Find little evidence of the efficacy of shareholder activism by institutional investors.
English, Smythe, and McNeil (2004)	1992–97	Target list firms	CalPERS	63 targetings of 47 firms	Announcement effects depend on index used. For some, significantly positive announcement effects, but no long term abnormal performance after six months.
Wu (2004)	1988–95	Target list firms in Forbes 500	CalPERS	37 firms	Public targeting is associated with a decrease in the number of inside directors, an increase in the likelihood of CEO dismissal, and an increase in the sensitivity of CEO turnover to performance.

(*continued*)

Table 2.2 (Continued)

Study	Sample period	Type of activism	Sponsor of activism	No. of firms and activism events	Conclusions regarding outcomes
Thomas and Cotter (2005)	2002–04	Governance proposals	All sponsors	1454 proposals	Examines shareholder proposals post-Enron and finds many similarities in voting outcomes and market reactions as compared to previous studies. Also reports that recent targeting is not restricted solely to poor performers, and that private investments groups and individuals are most effective in garnering voting support.
Barber (2006)	1992–2005	Target list firms	CalPERS	115 firms	Short-term market reaction to target announcements suggests positive returns
Del Guercio, Wallis, and Woidtke (2006)	1996–2003	Just vote no campaigns	All sponsors	92 firms	Activism is associated with higher forced CEO and director turnovers and that forced CEO turnovers have positive valuation effects. Activism affects market for directors.
Nelson (2006)	1990–2003	Target list firms	CalPERS	91 firms	Studies on CalPERS activism have used biased parameters, too long a window and do not exclude contaminating events. Once these are corrected, there are positive results pre-1994, but none post-1994.
Akyol and Carroll (2006)	1990–2004	Poison pill rescission	All sponsors (including company initiated removals)	126 firms	Companies remove pills due to shareholder pressure, including pressure by way of pill rescission proposals. Company initiated pill removals are also associated with potential pressure from shareholders.

(continued)

Table 2.2 (Continued)

Study	Sample period	Type of activism	Sponsor of activism	No. of firms and activism events	Conclusions regarding outcomes
Prevost, Rao, and Williams (2006)	1998–2002	Governance proposals	Union funds	481 proposals at 232 firms	Results do not support the hypothesis that union fund proposals are indicative of conflicts of interest on the part of such funds seeking to extract gains for employees.
Zenner, Shivdasani, and Darius (2005)	2004–05	All types of activism	Hedge funds	31 firms	Found significant returns on announcement of activism, primarily driven by returns to targets where the activism was related to merger and acquisition activity.
Bradley et al. (2006)	1989–2003	Activism with regard to closed-end funds	All sponsors, most were hedge funds	Over 200 open-ending attempts	Activists target closed-end funds with high discounts but discounts shrink on activism.
Klein and Zur, Chapter 9, this volume	2003–05	All types of activism	Hedge funds	194 firms	Found significant returns for period surrounding 13D filing date; no improvement in accounting performance for year after filing but hedge fund goals were at least partially met about 60% of time.
Brav et al., Chapter 8, this volume	2004–05	All types of activism	Hedge funds	374 firms	Found significant returns for period surrounding 13D filing date; Hedge fund achieved their goals in a third of cases and partially achieved their goals in another third of cases.

On the other hand, some shareholder activists, including CalPERS and the Council of Institutional Investors, announce the list of companies they are targeting at the beginning of the proxy season. When this happens, some of the information has already reached other investors. In addition, many companies are repeat targets, in which case their inclusion may not convey news about the firm in that particular year.

Some studies have also examined stock returns around the date of the shareholders' annual meeting, with the idea that investors may change their expectations based on the voting outcome of the shareholder proposals. The problem with this approach, however, is that other important information is often made public during annual meetings. And the same objection can be made to the use of the proxy mailing date, given the other information disclosed in corporate proxy statements.

The second problem with analysis of short-term market reactions is that it is not clear what the investors' responses should be on learning that a company has been targeted by an active shareholder. Shareholder proposals are advisory in nature, which means that even if the proposals pass with 100% of the vote, management is not required to implement their directives. In addition, there is a question as to whether the announcement is good news (because it means there is increased monitoring) or bad (because it implies institutional investors could not come to a negotiated agreement with management).

In general, for the overall samples of shareholder proposals, the studies have found no significant abnormal returns around the assumed date of information release (see Carleton, Nelson, and Weisbach 1998; Del Guercio and Hawkins 1998; Gillan and Starks 2000; Karpoff, Malatesta, and Walkling 1996; Prevost and Rao 2000; Smith 1996; Song and Szewczyk 2003; Wahal 1996). This result tends to be true regardless of whether the study used the announcement date of the target list, the mailing dates of proxies, the annual meeting date, or the *Wall Street Journal* announcement date.

Nevertheless, some studies have reported significant responses to subsamples of the proposals or announcements. For example, some studies found a negative abnormal return for proposals to rescind poison pills, while others reported negative abnormal returns for board-related and antitakeover proposals (which could be driven by the poison pill rescission proposals in this category).[9] The study of proposals by TIAA-CREF discussed earlier found that for specific issues like board diversity and blank check preferred there were significant market responses—negative in cases involving board diversity and positive for blank check preferred—around the dates of targeting letters from TIAA-CREF (see Carleton, Nelson, and Weisbach 1998). A more recent study by Andrew Prevost and Ramesh Rao (2000) focused on two subsamples—companies targeted by CalPERS' proposals and firms receiving proposals from public pension funds—and reported significantly negative stock returns in the three days surrounding the mailing date of the proxy statement containing the proposal.[10] One interpretation is that the failure of management to negotiate with activist shareholders is viewed as bad news in the marketplace. Another is that the event date is noisy, and the abnormal return being captured reflects information other than that related to the shareholder proposal or targeting event.

Some studies have examined the reaction to other aspects of shareholder activism. For example, Strickland, Wiles, and Zenner (1996) found that the announcement of a negotiated settlement with a target firm is associated with significantly positive returns, on average. One interpretation of this finding is that such settlements bring about a reduction of

[9] Bizjak and Marquette (1998) and Gillan and Starks (2000) find negative abnormal returns for pill rescission proposals. Del Guercio and Hawkins (1998) focus on board-related issues and the repeal of antitakeover measures (including pills).

[10] Generalizing from some of these results should be viewed with caution, for the number of observations in the subsamples are small: twenty-two and sixteen in the Carleton, Nelson, and Weisbach paper (1998), and fifteen and twenty-three in the Prevost and Rao study (2000).

uncertainty about some potential liability while also conveying management's commitment to avoid the offending behaviour in the future.

Another recent study examines a particular activist practice in which institutional investors target the board rather than corporate governance practices by conducting 'Just Vote No' campaigns during director elections (Del Guercio, Wallis, and Woidtke 2008). The authors report that such campaigns are associated with higher forced CEO and director turnover and that the reputations of the targeted directors are affected by the campaigns.

2.5.4 Voting Outcomes on Shareholder Proposals

Another test of the efficacy of shareholder activism is to examine the voting outcomes of shareholder proposals. In so doing, several factors must be considered. First, shareholder proposals, as already noted, are only advisory; management is not required to adopt the proposal if it receives majority support. Moreover, shareholder activism conducted through the proxy process is subject to considerable managerial control in that managers have the ability to influence both the voting turnout and results. They can do so by excluding shareholder proposals from the proxy (subject to SEC oversight) and by hiring proxy solicitors to garner support for their position.[11]

Studies of voting outcomes on shareholder proposals for earlier periods (late 1980s to early 1990s) have reported that voting support for proposals has depended on a number of variables: the issue addressed by the proposal; the identity of the sponsor; insider ownership; institutional ownership; the number of times a proposal had been submitted; the governance structure and performance of the target firm; and whether the proposal was related to the removal of antitakeover mechanisms. Specifically, favourable votes have been higher in cases involving poison pill repeal proposals, proposals sponsored by public funds, companies with fewer insiders, smaller companies, and companies that had performed poorly in the stock market. Proposals sponsored by institutions, labour unions, or coordinated shareholder groups have also received substantially more support than proposals sponsored by individual investors (see Bizjak and Marquette 1998; Gillan and Starks 2000; Gordon and Pound 1993; Thomas and Martin 1998). Our own study (2000) also found a general increase in votes supporting governance proposals over the period we studied (1987–94).

In addition, research shows that governance proposals typically receive greater support than do social responsibility proposals. For example, a study of the 1997 proxy season reported that governance proposals received an average 24% of votes cast during that year, while social proposals received an average of just 6.6%. Furthermore, less than one-third of all social proposals were voted on in contrast to almost 50% of governance proposals (Campbell, Gillan, and Niden 1999).

According to the IRRC, 8,600 shareholder proposals were put on proxies during the period 1973–2004. Less than 10% of these won majority support, but, strikingly, more than half of the majority votes occurred in the 2000–04 period. Figure 2.4 shows differences in voting outcomes for types of shareholder proposals submitted in 2005 as compared to the

[11] When seeking support for management proposals, management can bundle hard-to-pass decisions with other proposals and classify proposals as routine in order to increase the number of votes in their favour Bethel and Gillan (2007).

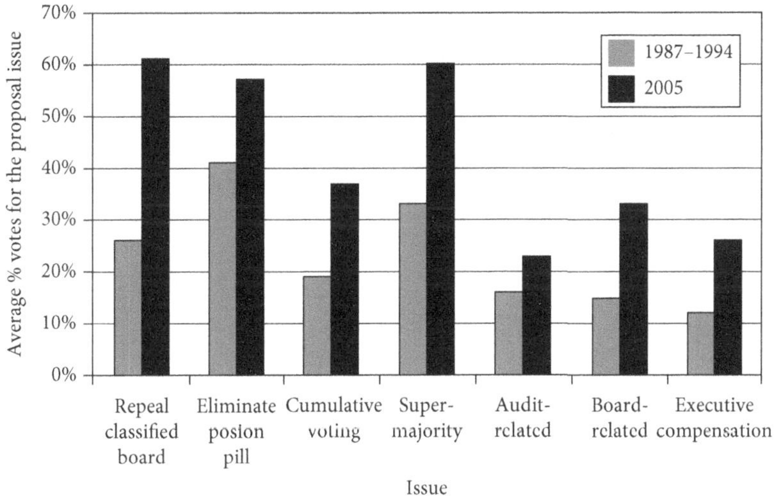

FIGURE 2.4 Voting outcomes for proposals

earlier 1987–94 period. As the figure shows, votes in support of proposals have increased significantly, as have the number of proposals aiming to repeal classified boards, eliminate poison pills, and remove supermajority amendments that have commanded over 50% of the shareholder vote. Votes in favour of shareholder proposals on executive compensation have more than doubled, from 12% to 26%. The general increase in voting support for many shareholder proposals likely reflects a number of factors: more concerted action by institutional investors, the existence of proxy voting advisory firms, and the public disclosure of mutual fund proxy votes.[12] One example of more concerted action are the 'Just Vote No' campaigns targeting boards of directors (Del Guercio, Wallis, and Woidtke 2008).

Several studies have also examined the potential conflicts of interest faced by investment managers when voting on management and shareholder proposals. An early study by Brickley, Lease, and Smith (1988) suggested that institutional investors that have business dealings with portfolio companies may be pressured to vote with management. However, the more recent evidence on this issue does not suggest that institutions, on average, are 'captured' by their business ties.[13]

Studying potential conflicts of interest on the part of mutual funds has resurfaced with new SEC regulations requiring that funds disclose the way they vote their shares in portfolio firms. Two recent studies examining the voting practices of large mutual fund families suggest that the funds studied are no more likely to vote with management at client than non-client firms. But if there is little direct evidence of conflicts of interest (Davis and Kim

[12] According to Alexander et al. (2006) proxy advisory services have significant effects on voting outcomes and their recommendation announcements are associated with significant abnormal returns.

[13] To consider one example, Van Nuys (1993), when examining the 1987 proxy fight at Honeywell, found that banks and insurance companies were more supportive of management-sponsored antitakeover proposals than public pension funds and independent investment managers. But, on closer inspection, Van Nuys found no evidence of business ties between Honeywell and its shareholders that would account for this pattern of voting.

2007; Rothberg and Lilien 2005), investment style does seem to influence voting decisions, with stock pickers tending to vote with management and passive indexers more likely to vote against management.

Such studies have also reported that funds with longer investment horizons tend to vote in favour of shareholder proposals that are likely to increase shareholders' wealth and rights, and in cases involving companies with weaker governance or entrenched management (Ashraf and Jayaraman 2007; Rothberg and Lilien 2005). Finally, other work suggests that, while shareholder support for management proposals has declined over time, there is no evidence to suggest that the requirement that funds disclose their votes has led to a change in mutual fund voting (Cremers and Romano 2007).

2.5.5 Voting on Management Proposals

Here the studies suggest that management proposals generally pass (they are generally put to shareholder vote only when management is confident of a victory) and uncontested directors receive most of the votes. The evidence also suggests that the degree of shareholder support varies with corporate performance, ownership structure, and a number of characteristics of the proposal. For example, several studies conclude that the percentage of votes cast in favour of stock option plan proposals decreases with the perceived cost to shareholders, typically measured as the potential dilution from the plan (see Bethel and Gillan 2007; Martin and Thomas 2005; Morgan and Poulsen 2001; Morgan, Poulsen, and Wolf 2006).[14] Finally, while there is relatively little variation in voting for directors, recent evidence suggests that voting support for directors has been related to firm performance, director performance, and a firm's shareholder rights. More specifically, directors receive fewer votes when they attend less than 75% of board meetings, and when Institutional Shareholder Services recommends that their clients vote against them (Cai, Garner, and Walkling 2009; Fischer et al. 2008).

2.5.6 Long-term Performance

The two previous measures of the effects of shareholder activism—stock market reactions to announcements of initiatives and voting outcomes on proposals—are both short-term in nature. But the effects of such activism are likely to show up only gradually over time. To investigate this possibility, studies have examined the long-term performance of the targeted companies, both their returns to shareholders and their operating performance.

The studies' definitions of what constitutes 'long-term' have varied from one year to five years. The problem noted earlier of uncertainty about the linkage between cause and effect is exacerbated by long-term performance measures. Even in cases of activism that lead to significant improvements in operating performance or stock appreciation over the next several years, it is difficult to ascertain whether it was activism per se that caused the changes.

[14] In the context of mergers, Burch, Morgan, and Wolf (2004) report that voting support varies substantially with firm and deal characteristics.

The general results of studies of the long-term stock performance of targeted companies have been mixed. An early study by Gillan (1995) focusing on companies targeted for the first time in 1990 or 1991 found no evidence of significant wealth effects. Similarly, two other studies reported no evidence of significant wealth changes for companies targeted over the 1987–93 period (Del Guercio and Hawkins 1998; Wahal 1996). But studies of interventions by a single institutional investor come to a different conclusion. For example, Stephen Nesbitt's (1994) study of CalPERS' governance initiatives showed significant gains for shareholders. And Michael Smith (1996) found that those of CalPERS' targets that cooperated with the fund's suggestions saw significant increases in shareholder wealth, while the shareholders of companies that resisted CalPERS' pressure experienced reductions in wealth.[15]

Virtually all studies of long-term operating performance have reported no statistically significant changes in the operating performance of targeted companies (Del Guercio and Hawkins 1998; Karpoff, Malatesta, and Walkling 1996; Smith 1996; Strickland, Wiles, and Zenner 1996; Wahal 1996). Another potential problem with studies of long-term performance is the choice of an appropriate control group when measuring 'abnormal' performance. Since the control firms are usually selected on the basis of being in the same industry and having similar performance, two related questions arise: First, did other activists not included in the study target the control firms? Second, if the control firms were not targeted, yet operate in the same industry and had the same performance, then why were the control firms not targeted as well (i.e., there must be important differences between them)?

With regard to the first question, there may be a time-period effect. That is, the activism may be attributed to one activist, or set of activists, when in fact the activism process had been initiated earlier by other investors. For example, a case study of Sears Roebuck (involving one of the present writers) showed that while Sears appeared on CalPERS' target list, the firm was also subject to a proxy fight for board representation by shareholder activist Bob Monks. Moreover, the activism at Sears, although leading to changes in the company's real activities and governance structure, took over three years to reach a 'satisfactory' conclusion.

With regard to the second question, researchers need to be careful when assessing why the control firms were somehow insulated from targeting. Given the previous studies of the characteristics of targeted firms, one has to consider a number of possibilities: were the control firms already in the process of change? Or were there other factors at work, such as lower institutional ownership or greater insider ownership? A related issue is whether any such differences in firm characteristics had an effect on the long-term performance, regardless of the targeting.

2.5.7 Changes in Other Aspects of the Target Firm

A number of studies have investigated how other aspects of the targeted companies have changed in response to shareholder activism. The primary focus of these studies has been on changes in governance structure, investment decisions, and management.

[15] Another study, Opler and Sokobin (1998), reported that stock market performance improved after a company appeared on the Council of Institutional Investors' focus list. But more recent papers call this result into question. However, more recent papers call this result into question. See, particularly Song and Szewczyk (2003).

On changes in governance structure, Michael Smith reported that 72% of the companies targeted by CalPERS between 1988 and 1993 either adopted CalPERS' proposed changes or made changes resulting in a settlement with the investor. Similarly, poison pills were more likely to be restructured, removed, or put to a shareholder vote after being the subject of a shareholder proposal. Moreover, shareholder pressure has been particularly effective in pill-removal post-Enron (Akyol and Carroll 2006; Bizjak and Marquette 1998). One study of pension fund activism showed that, during the three-year period after targeting, the targeted companies saw a greater frequency of governance events, including shareholder lawsuits, non-pension-fund-sponsored shareholder proposals, or public 'no' votes for directors (Del Guercio and Hawkins 1998). On the other hand, another study conducted around the same time found no evidence that the submission of a shareholder proposal on executive compensation was followed by significant changes in compensation levels or pay-for-performance sensitivities (Johnson and Shackell-Dowell 1997; Johnson, Porter, and Shackell-Dowell 1997).

In an extensive study of the effect of CalPERS' activism on the real activities of targeted companies, Mark Huson (1997) found significant changes in the real activities of these firms. In particular, the targeted firms had significantly more divestitures, fewer acquisitions, and more joint ventures. The study also reported that the market reaction to such transactions was significantly more positive, on average, than to comparable transactions before the targeting. Similarly, in their study of companies targeted by five major public pension funds, Del Guercio and Hawkins (1998) found a greater incidence of restructurings including asset divestitures and employee layoffs than for a comparable control group of companies.

In contrast, the results of studies focusing on management turnover have been mixed. Some studies reported finding no relation between CEO turnover and shareholder proposals, although there is evidence of higher turnover for other senior managers.[16] But other studies reported higher CEO turnover, as well as a decrease in board size, in companies targeted by CalPERS.[17]

One other way to test the effectiveness of investor activism is to examine the extent to which boards have implemented majority vote shareholder proposals, and how that has changed, if at all, over time. A recent study concluded that the frequency of implementations has more than doubled, from 16% in 1997 to over 40% in 2003–04. Moreover, the probability that a proposal was implemented has increased with the percentage of votes cast in favour of the proposal and the percentage of stock owned by activist shareholders. At the same time, however, shareholder proposals related to board issues and executive pay have been less likely to be implemented than other kinds of proposals (Ertimur, Ferri, and Stubben 2008).

[16] Smith, M. (1996); Karpoff, Malatesta, and Walkling (1996); and Del Guercio and Hawkins (1998) find that the target firms do not have a higher frequency of CEO turnover; however, Del Guercio and Hawkins (1998) do find a higher frequency of turnover for other executives.

[17] Huson (1997) and Wu (2004), report increased turnover, Wu, in particular, reports that board size declines.

2.5.8 New Kids on the Block: Hedge Funds and Shareholder Activism

During the past decade or so, hedge funds have not only entered the shareholder activism arena, but have become a dominant force. Recent examples include Relational Investors and Home Depot, Pershing Square and Wendy's International, Icahn Partners and Time Warner, and Breeden Partners and Applebee's International.

These hedge funds have a variety of goals in their activism. The most common ones are as follows: changing management strategy or board decisions; seeking a board seat for either input, control, or information purposes; effecting corporate governance changes; forcing a buyout or sale of a division; and increasing cash distributions to shareholders through dividends or share repurchases. While the hedge funds use some of the same strategies as those employed by the traditional institutional activists—including shareholder proposals, direct negotiations, and use of the media—they also use other means such as proxy contests, litigation, or outright takeover (Kahan and Rock, Chapter 5, this volume; Pearson and Altman 2006; Zenner, Shivdasani, and Darius 2006). Even their use of traditional institutional activist strategies is often different in its application. For example, one study concludes that the Hermitage Fund has been successful in lobbying the media to cover corporate governance violations of Russian public corporations, and thereby helping to bring about the Fund's desired changes in those companies (Dyck, Volchkova, and Zingales 2006).

One form of shareholder activism that is sometimes practiced by hedge funds is relationship investing. By definition, this is an ongoing relationship between the institutional investors and the firm.[18] And for a number of reasons, the shareholder consequences of such activism are difficult to measure. As noted earlier in Section 2.5.6 (when discussing the case of Sears), when activism occurs over a number of years and often involves different investors, it is difficult to attribute the outcome to any single activist or strategy.

Although proxy contests were a traditional form of shareholder voice that was used extensively in the 1980s, the rising expense of waging a proxy battle caused use of this tactic to fall off sharply. But with the rise of hedge funds, the proxy contest has staged a comeback. For example, there were ninety-one proxy contests over board elections in 2006, up from forty in 2005 and thirty in 2004; most of the increase has been attributed to the growth and proliferation of hedge funds engaged in such contests (Whitehouse 2007). Another likely contributor to the recent jump in proxy contests was the SEC's 1992 easing of rules limiting communication between shareholders (see, e.g., Collins and DeAngelo 1990; DeAngelo 1988; DeAngelo and DeAngelo 1989; Faleye 2004; Ikenberry and Lakonishok 1993; Mulherin and Poulsen 1998; Pound 1988).

A number of questions have arisen about the effectiveness of hedge fund activism: For example, have hedge funds really succeeded in adding value to the companies they have

[18] Any long-term relationship between large shareholders and companies can be termed relationship investing. For studies on block shareholders, see, e.g., Bethel, Liebiskind, and Opler (1998); Denis and Kruse (2000); and Denis and Serrano (1996). For studies on relationship investing specifically, see Bethel and Gillan (2007); Bhagat, Black, and Blair (2004); Gillan, Kensinger, and Martin (2000); Martin and Kensinger (1996); Rock (1994); and Wruck and Wu (2009).

targeted; or have most of the returns to hedge funds been short-terms profits at the expense of other, longer-term shareholders? Do hedge funds have the appropriate organizational structure to bring about change in the underlying target firms? And do hedge funds' incentives for activism differ from those of other kinds of institutional activists (Kahan and Rock, Chapter 5, this volume).

While there is no shortage of anecdotal reports of the failures (such as Icahn Partners's efforts with Blockbuster) and successes (Relational Investors's recent ouster of the CEO of Home Depot) of hedge fund activism, the general lack of information about hedge funds' activities and holdings has prevented researchers from assessing benefits and costs. Nevertheless, a handful of studies have attempted systematic investigations of the consequences of hedge fund activism using the information provided in the funds' filings of 13Ds. For example, in a recent study of 194 Schedule 13D filings by 102 hedge funds during the period 2003–05 period, the authors reported a 61-day announcement period return of 10.3% (Klein and Zur, Chapter 9, this volume). Another study (by different authors) of 374 Schedule 13D filings by 110 hedge funds during 2004–05 reported a 20-day announcement period return of 5–7% (Brav et al., Chapter 8, this volume).

These results indicate that there are short-term gains associated with hedge fund activism. But one problem with drawing firm conclusions from these results is our inability to ascertain when the hedge funds purchased and sold the shares, making it difficult to determine whether the hedge funds themselves earned abnormal returns on their investments. One study that may help resolve this issue examined the actual trades of a UK fund (the Hermes UK Focus Fund) and reported that the fund earned returns in excess of the benchmarks (Becht et al., Chapter 7, this volume). In the United States, a study of Relational Investors' activities provides evidence that the fund has succeed in targeting underperformers and beating benchmark returns (Bethel and Gillan 2007).

It is also difficult to distinguish announcement effects that derive from the knowledge that a hedge fund is engaging in shareholder activism from the longer-term effects that actually result from the activism. The study of the Hermes fund cited above accomplished this by linking the (longer-term) excess returns derived from the fund's activism directly to the success of specific initiatives, such as replacing directors, blocking diversifying acquisitions, and increasing payouts. And consistent with these findings, two studies of US hedge fund activism have reported that management often acquiesces to the hedge funds' demands (at least partially in over 60% of the cases examined) (Brav et al., Chapter 8, this volume; Klein and Zur, Chapter 9, this volume).

A study of the role of activism in 'opening-ending' closed-end funds provides further evidence of the success of shareholder activists, primarily hedge funds. Activists pressing for the open-ending of closed-end funds have used a variety of tactics, including negotiations, shareholder proposals, and proxy contests, with the latter accounting for a little over half of the attempts. No strategy has been completely reliable, as the authors report that the number of successful open-endings is much smaller than the number attempted. But even unsuccessful attempts at open-ending closed-end funds have tended to narrow the discounts at which the funds trade in relation to their NAVs (Bradley et al. 2005).

On the other hand, legal scholars have expressed concerned about potential problems related to some aspects of hedge fund activism. For example, Hu and Black have noted potential problems associated with the separation of economic ownership from voting rights—a separation that, according to Hu and Black, has been exploited by hedge funds in their relatively new practice of voting shares they no longer own (2007). (Such a practice, known as 'empty voting', could conceivably be used by short sellers to advocate measures that would reduce firm value.) Hedge funds can also achieve and maintain effective economic ownership without having to reveal it by foregoing voting rights (a condition that authors term 'hidden ownership'). And if, as some have argued, hedge funds have a shorter-term orientation than other investors, such ownership could cause problems (Kahan and Rock, Chapter 5, this volume).

2.6 Conclusion

Investor activism in the form of shareholder proposals has existed since the SEC's adoption in 1943 of Rule 14a-8. Between 1943 and the mid-1980s, the shareholder proposal process was almost exclusively the domain of individual shareholders and religious or political groups. But with the initiation of public pension fund activism in 1985, the involvement of large institutional shareholders increased dramatically.

The main motive for active participation by institutional investors in the monitoring of corporations has been the potential to enhance the value of their investments. But since the active investors incur all the costs associated with such activism (while the benefits accrue to all shareholders), only shareholders with large positions are likely to obtain a large enough return on their investment to justify the costs.

The evidence provided by empirical studies of the effects of shareholder activism is mixed. While some studies have found positive short-term market reactions to announcements of certain kinds of activism, there is little evidence of improvement in the long-term operating or stock-market performance of the targeted companies. Studies have reported significant changes in the business activities of companies targeted by shareholder initiatives, but it is difficult to establish a causal relationship between shareholder activism and these changes. The relatively recent entrance of hedge funds into shareholder activism has provided more evidence of gains from activism, but the long-term effects are still unknown and warrant more research.

References

Admati, A. R. and Pfleiderer, P. C. (2009). The 'Wall Street Walk' and Shareholder Activism: Exit as a Form of Voice, *Review of Financial Studies* 22(7), 2445–85.

Admati, A. R., Pfleiderer, P. C., and Zechner, J. (1994). Large Shareholder Activism, Risk-Sharing, and Financial Market Equilibrium, *Journal of Political Economy* 102, 1097–130.

Agrawal, A. and Mandelker, G. (1992). Shark Repellants and the Role of Institutional Investors in Corporate Governance, *Managerial and Decision Economics* 13, 15–22.

Akyol, A. C. and Carroll, C. A. (2006). Removing Poison Pills: A Case of Shareholder Activism, Working Paper, available at <http://ssrn.com/abstract=935950>.

Alexander, C., Chen, M., Seppi, D., and Spatt, C. (2006). The Role of Advisory Services in Proxy Voting, University of Maryland Working Paper, available at <http://ssrn.com/abstract=1434658>.

Almazan, A., Hartzell, J., and Starks, L. (2005). Active Institutional Shareholders and Cost of Monitoring: Evidence from Executive Compensation, *Financial Management* 34, 5–34.

Almazan, A. and Suarez, J. (2003). Managerial Compensation and the Market Reaction to Bank Loans, *Review of Financial Studies* 16, 237–61.

American Society of Corporate Secretaries (1953). *Analysis of Stockholder Proposed Resolutions Submitted under Rule X-14a-8 of the Securities and Exchange Commission.*

American Society of Corporate Secretaries (1979). *Report on Shareholder Proposals July 1, 1978 to June 30 1979.*

Anson, M., White, T., and Ho, H. (2004). Good Corporate Governance Works: More Evidence from CalPERS, *Journal of Asset Management* 5, 149–56.

Ashraf A. and Jayaraman, N. (2007). Determinants and Consequences of Proxy Voting by Mutual Funds on Shareholder Proposals, Working Paper, available at <http://ssrn.com/abstract=962126>.

Bainbridge, S. (2005). Shareholder Activism and Institutional Investors, UCLA School of Law, Law-Econ Research Paper No. 05-20, available at <http://ssrn.com/abstract=796227>.

Barber, B. (2006). Monitoring the Monitor: Evaluating CalPERS' Activism (Nov.), Working Paper, available at <http://ssrn.com/abstract=890321>.

Bethel, J. and Gillan, S. (2007). Relationship Investing, Corporate Change and Shareholder Value, Babson College and Texas Tech University Working Paper.

Bethel, J., Liebiskind, J., and Opler, T. (1998). Block Share Purchases and Corporate Performance, *Journal of Finance* 53, 605–34.

Bhagat, S., Black, B., and Blair, M. (2004). Relational Investing and Firm Performance, *Journal of Financial Research* 27, 1–30.

Bhide, A. (1990). Efficient Markets, Deficient Governance: US Securities Regulations Protect Investors and Enhance Market Liquidity: But Do They Alienate Managers and Shareholders?, *Harvard Business Review* 72(6), 129–39.

Bhide, A. (1993). The Hidden Costs of Stock Market Liquidity, *Journal of Financial Economics* 34, 31–51.

Bizjak, J. M. and Marquette, C. (1998). Shareholder Proposals to Rescind Poison Pills: All Bark and No Bite, *Journal of Financial and Quantitative Analysis* 33, 499–521.

Black, B. S. (1990). Shareholder Passivity Reexamined, *Michigan Law Review* 89, 520–608.

Black, B. S. (1992). Agents Watching Agents: The Promise of Institutional Investor Voice, *UCLA Law Review* 39, 811–93.

Black, B. S. (1998). Shareholder Activism and Corporate Governance in the US, in P. Newman (ed.), *The New Palgrave Dictionary of Economics and the Law* (London and Basingstoke, UK, Palgrave Macmillan), 459–65.

Bolton, P. and von Thadden, E. (1998). Blocks, Liquidity, and Corporate Control, *Journal of Finance* 53, 1–25.

Borokhovich, K., Brunarski, K., Harman, Y., and Parrino, R. (2006). Variation in the Monitoring Incentives of Outside Blockholders, *Journal of Law and Economics* 49, 651–80.

Bradley, M., Brav, A., Goldstein, I., and Jiang, W. (2005). Costly Communication, Shareholder Activism, and Limits to Arbitrage, AFA 2007 Chicago Meetings Paper, available at <http://ssrn.com/abstract=838165>.

Brickley, J. A., Lease, R. C., and Smith, C. W (1988). Ownership Structure and Voting on Antitakeover Amendments, *Journal of Financial Economics* 20, 267–92.

Burch, T. R., Morgan, A. G., and Wolf, J. G. (2004). Is Acquiring Firm Shareholder Approval in Stock-for-Stock Mergers Perfunctory?, *Financial Management* 33, 45–69.

Burkart, M., Gromb, D., and Panunzi, F. (1997). Large Shareholders, Monitoring and the Value of the Firm, *Quarterly Journal of Economics* 112, 693–798.

Bushee, B. J. (1998). The Influence of Institutional Investors on Myopic R&D Investment Behavior, *Accounting Review* 73, 305–33.

Bushee, B. J. (2001). Do Institutional Investors Prefer Near-Term Earnings over Long-Run Value?, *Contemporary Accounting Research* 18, 207–46.

Cai, J., Garner, J. L., and Walkling, R. A. (2009). Electing Directors, *Journal of Finance* 64, 2389–421.

Campbell, C., Gillan, S., and Niden, C. (1999). Current Perspectives on Shareholder Proposals: The 1997 Proxy Season, *Financial Management* 28, 89–98.

Carleton, W. T., Nelson, J. M., and Weisbach, M. S. (1998). The Influence of Institutions on Corporate Governance through Private Negotiations: Evidence from TIAA-CREF, *Journal of Finance* 53, 1335–62.

Caton, G., Goh, J., and Donaldson, J. (2001). The Effectiveness of Institutional Activism, *Financial Analysts Journal* 57, 21–6.

Chen, X., Harford, J., and Li, K. (2007). Monitoring: Which Institutions Matter?, *Journal of Financial Economics* 86, 279–305.

Chidambaran, N. and John, K. (1998). Relationship Investing: Large Shareholder Monitoring with Managerial Cooperation, NYU Working Paper No. FIN-98-044, available at <http://ssrn.com/abstract=1297123>.

Choi, S. (2000). Proxy Issue Contests: The Impact of the 1992 Proxy Reforms, *Journal of Law, Economics and Organizations* 16, 233–68.

Coffee, J. (1991). Liquidity versus Control: The Institutional Investor as Corporate Monitor, *Columbia Law Review* 91, 1277–368.

Collins, D. W. and DeAngelo, L. (1990). Accounting Information and Corporate Governance: Market and Analyst Reactions to Earnings of Firms Engaged in Proxy Contests, *Journal of Accounting and Economics* 13, 213–48.

Cornett, M., Marcus, A., Saunders, A., and Tehranian, H. (2007). The Impact of Institutional Ownership on Corporate Operating Performance, *Journal of Banking and Finance* 31, 1771–94.

Cremers, M. and Romano, R. (2007). Institutional Investors and Proxy Voting: The Impact of the 2003 Mutual Fund Voting Disclosure Regulation, Yale ICF Working Paper No. 07-10; Yale Law & Economics Research Paper No. 349; ECGI—Law Working Paper No. 83/2007, available at <http://ssrn.com/abstract=982493>.

Crutchley, C., Hudson, C., and Jensen, M. (1998). Shareholder Wealth Effects of CalPers Activism, *Financial Services Review* 7, 1–10.

Davis, G. F. and Kim, E. H. (2007). Business Ties and Proxy Voting by Mutual Funds, *Journal of Financial Economics* 85, 552–70.

DeAngelo, L. E. (1988). Managerial Compensation, Information Costs, and Corporate Governance: The Use of Accounting Performance Measures in Proxy Contests, *Journal of Accounting and Economics* 10, 3–36.

DeAngelo, L. E. and DeAngelo, H. (1989). Proxy Contests and the Governance of Publicly Held Corporations, *Journal of Financial Economics* 23, 29–59.

Del Guerio, D. and Hawkins, J. (1998). The Motivation and Impact of Pension Fund Activism, *Journal of Financial Economics* 52, 293–340.

Del Guercio, D., Seery, L. J., and Woidtke, T. (2008). Do Boards Pay Attention When Institutional Investor Activists 'Just Vote No'?, Working Paper, available at <http://ssrn.com/abstract=575242>.

Denis, D. and Kruse, T. (2000). Managerial Discipline and Corporate Restructuring Following Performance Declines, *Journal of Financial Economics* 55, 391–424.

Denis, D. and Serrano, J. (1996). Active Investors and Management Turnover Following Unsuccessful Control Contests, *Journal of Financial Economics* 40, 239–66.

Dyck, I. J. A., Volchkova, N., and Zingales, L. (2006).The Corporate Governance Role of the Media: Evidence from Russia, ECGI—Finance Working Paper No. 154/2007, available at <http://ssrn.com/abstract=891206>.

English, P. C., Smythe, T. I., and McNeil, C. R. (2004). The CalPERS Effect Revisited, *Journal of Corporate Finance* 10, 157–74.

Ertimur, Y., Ferri, F., and Stubben, S. (2008). Board of Directors' Responsiveness to Shareholders: Evidence from Shareholder Proposals, HBS Working Paper Series, available at <http://ssrn.com/abstract=1106375>.

Ettorre, B. (1996). When Patience is a Corporate Virtue, *Management Review* 85, 28–32.

Faleye, O. (2004). Cash and Corporate Control, *Journal of Finance* 59, 2041–60.

Fama, E. and Jensen, M. (1983). Separation of Ownership and Control, *Journal of Law and Economics* 26, 301–25.

Fischer, P. E., Gramlich, J. D., Miller, B. P., and White, H. (2008). Investor Perceptions of Board Performance and Board Response to Those Perceptions: Evidence from Uncontested Director Elections, Working Paper, available at <http://ssrn.com/abstract=928843>.

Gaspar, J. M., Massa, M., and Matos, P. (2005). Shareholder Investment Horizon and the Market for Corporate Control, *Journal of Financial Economics* 76, 135–65.

Georgeson Shareholder (2005). *Annual Corporate Governance Review—2005*, available at <http://georgesonshareholder.com/html/1703.asp?locid=1>.

Gillan, S. L. (1995). Shareholder Activism through the Proxy Mechanism: An Empirical Investigation, Dissertation, University of Texas at Austin.

Gillan, S. L., Kensinger, J. W., and Martin, J. D. (2000). Value Creation and Corporate Diversification: The Case of Sears Roebuck & Co., *Journal of Financial Economics* 55, 103–37.

Gillan, S. and Starks, L. (1998). A Survey of Shareholder Activism: Motivation and Empirical Evidence, *Contemporary Finance Digest* 2, 10–34.

Gillan, S. and Starks, L. (2000). Corporate Governance Proposals and Shareholder Activism: The Role of Institutional Investors, *Journal of Financial Economics* 57, 275–305.

Gordon, L. and Pound, J. (1993). Information, Ownership Structure, and Shareholder Voting: Evidence from Shareholder-sponsored Corporate Governance Proposals, *Journal of Finance* 47, 697–718.

Hann, R. (2002). On the Effectiveness of Pension Fund Activism, University of Southern California Working Paper.

Hartzell, J. C. and Starks, L. T. (2003). Institutional Investors and Executive Compensation, *Journal of Finance* 58, 2351–74.

Hirschman, A. (1971). *Exit, Voice and Loyalty: Responses to Decline in Firms, Organizations, and States* (Cambridge, MA, Harvard University Press).

Holmström, B. and Tirole, J. (1993). Market Liquidity and Performance Monitoring, *Journal of Political Economy* 101, 678–709.

Hu, H. T. C. and Black, B. (2007). Hedge Funds, Insiders, and Decoupling of Economic and Voting Ownership in Public Companies: Empty Voting and Hidden (Morphable) Ownership, *Journal of Corporate Finance* 13, 343–67.

Huddart, S. (1993). The Effect of a Large Shareholder on Corporate Value, *Management Science* 39, 1407–21.

Huson, M. (1997). Does Governance Matter? Evidence from CalPERS Interventions, University of Alberta Working Paper.

Ikenberry, D. and Lakonishok, J. (1993). Corporate Governance through the Proxy Contest: Evidence and Implications, *Journal of Business* 66, 405–36.

Jensen, M. and Meckling, W. (1976). Theory of the Firm: Managerial Behavior, Agency Costs, and Capital Structure, *Journal of Financial Economics* 3, 305–60.

John, K. and Klein, A. (1995). Shareholder Proposals and Corporate Governance, NYU Working Paper No. FIN-98-046, available at <http://ssrn.com/abstract=1297750>.

Johnson, M. F., Porter, S. L., and Shackell-Dowell, M. B. (1997). Stakeholder Pressure and the Structure of Executive Compensation, Working Paper, available at <http://ssrn.com/abstract=41780>.

Johnson, M. F. and Shackell-Dowell, M. B. (1997). Shareholder Proposals on Executive Compensation, Working Paper, available at <http://ssrn.com/abstract=121>.

Kahn, C. and Winton, A. (1998). Ownership Structure, Speculation, and Shareholder Intervention, *Journal of Finance* 53, 99–129.

Kaplan, S. and Minton, B. (1994). Appointments of Outsiders to Japanese Boards: Determinants and Implications for Managers, *Journal of Financial Economics* 36, 225–58.

Karpoff, J. M. (2001). The Impact of Shareholder Activism on Target Companies: A Survey of Empirical Findings, Working Paper, available at <http://ssrn.com/abstract=885365>.

Karpoff, J., Malatesta, P., and Walkling, R. (1996). Corporate Governance and Shareholder Initiatives: Empirical Evidence, *Journal of Financial Economics* 42, 365–95.

Kary, T. (2006). Upstart Investors for Director Accountability Target Pfizer, Marketwatch.com, available at <http://www.law.harvard.edu/programs/corp_gov/MediaMentions/4-13-06_MarketWatch.pdf>.

Manne, H. G. and Wallich, H. C. (1972). *The Modern Corporation and Social Responsibility* (Washington, DC, American Enterprise Institute for Public Policy Research).

Martin, J. and Kensinger, J. (1996). *Relationship Investing: What Active Institutional Investors Want from Management* (Newark, NJ, Financial Executives Research Foundation).

Martin, K. and Thomas, R. (2005). When is Enough, Enough? Market Reaction to Highly Dilutive Stock Option Plans and the Subsequent Impact on CEO Compensation, *Journal of Corporate Finance* 11, 61–83.

Maug, E. (1998). Large Shareholders as Monitors: Is There a Trade-off between Liquidity and Control?, *Journal of Finance* 53, 65–98.

Maug, E. G. and Rydqvist, K. (2008). Do Shareholders Vote Strategically? Voting Behavior, Proposal Screening, and Majority Rules, Mannheim Finance Working Paper No. 2006-15; ECGI—Finance Working Paper No. 31/2003; EFA 2004 Maastricht Meetings Paper No. 2516, available at <http://ssrn.com/abstract=471362>.

Monks, R. A. and Minow, N. (2003). *Corporate Governance* (Cambridge, MA, Blackwell Publishers).

Morgan, A. G. and Poulsen, A. B. (2001). Linking Pay to Performance: Compensation Proposals in the S&P 500, *Journal of Financial Economics* 62, 489–523.

Morgan, A. G., Poulsen, A. B., and Wolf, J. (2006). The Evolution of Shareholder Voting for Executive Compensation Schemes, *Journal of Corporate Finance* 12, 714–37.

Mulherin, J. H. and Poulsen, A. (1998). Proxy Contests and Corporate Change: Implications for Shareholder Wealth, *Journal of Financial Economics* 47, 279–313.

Murphy, K. and Van Nuys, K. (1994). State Pension Funds and Shareholder Inactivism, Harvard Business School Working Paper.

Myerson, A. (1993). Wall Street, the New Activism at Fidelity, *New York Times* (8 Aug.), § 3, at 15.

Nelson, J. (2006). The CalPERS Effect Revisited Again, *Journal of Corporate Finance* 12, 187–213.

Nesbitt, S. (1994). Long Term Rewards from Shareholder Activism: A Study of the CalPERS Effect, *Journal of Applied Corporate Finance* 6, 75–80.

Noe, T. (2002). Investor Activism and Financial Market Structure, *Review of Financial Studies* 15, 289–319.

Opler, T. C. and Sokobin, J. S. (1998). Does Coordinated Institutional Activism Work? An Analysis of the Activities of the Council of Institutional Investors, Dice Center For Research In Financial Economics, Working Papers Series 95-5, available at <http://ssrn.com/abstract=46880>.

Parker, M. (1989). It's Almost Spring, and That Means Proxy Fever, *New York Times* (5 Mar.), § 3, at 8.

Parrino, R., Sias, R., and Starks, L. (2003). Voting with their Feet: Institutional Ownership Changes Around CEO Turnovers, *Journal of Financial Economics* 68, 3–46.

Partnoy, F. and Thomas, R. S. (2007). Gap Filling, Hedge Funds, and Financial Innovation, in Y. Fuchita and R. E. Litan (eds.), *Brookings-Nomura Papers on Financial Services* (Washington, DC, Brookings Institution Press); Vanderbilt Law and Economics Research Paper No. 06-21; San Diego Legal Studies Paper No. 07-72, available at <http://ssrn.com/abstract=931254>.

Pearson, R. and Altman, K. (2006). Hedge Funds and Shareholder Activism: The Corporate Governance Advisor, *Corporate Governance* 14, 25–7.

Pickens, T. B. (1998). Speeches of T. Boone Pickens (unpublished).

Pinkowitz, L. F. (2003). Monitoring by Transient Investors? Institutions and Corporate Control, Working Paper, available at <http://ssrn.com/abstract=247004>.

Pound, J. (1988). Proxy Contests and the Efficiency of Shareholder Oversight, *Journal of Financial Economics* 20, 237–65.

Prevost, A. and Rao, R. (2000). Of What Value are Shareholder Proposals Sponsored by Public Pension Funds? *Journal of Business* 73, 177–204.

Prevost, A. K., Rao, R. P., and Williams, M. A. (2009). Labor Unions as Shareholder Activists: Champions or Detractors?, Working Paper, available at http://ssrn.com/abstract=1119328.

Qiu, L. X. (2006). Which Institutional Investors Monitor? Evidence from Acquisition Activity, Brown Economics Working Paper Series No. 2004-21; Yale ICF Working Paper No. 04-15, available at <http://ssrn.com/abstract=521803>.

Rock, E. (1994). Controlling the Dark Side of Relational Investing, *Cardozo Law Review* 15, 987–1031.

Roe, M. (1990). Political and Legal Restraints on Ownership and Control of Public Companies, *Journal of Financial Economics* 27, 7–41.

Romano, R. (1993). Public Pension Fund Activism in Corporate Governance Reconsidered, *Columbia Law Review* 93, 795–853.

Romano, R. (2001). Less is More: Making Shareholder Activism a Valued Mechanism of Corporate Governance, *Yale Journal on Regulation* 18, 174–252.

Ross, N. (1983). Gadflies Set to Buzz Shareholders' Meetings, *The Washington Post* (17 Apr.), at G1.

Rothberg, B. G. and Lilien, S. B. (2005). Mutual Fund Proxy Votes, Working Paper, available at <http://ssrn.com/abstract=669161>.

Schwab, S. and Thomas, R. (1998). Realigning Corporate Governance: Shareholder Activism by Labor Unions, *Michigan Law Review* 96, 1018–94.

Shleifer, A. and Vishny, R. (1986). Large Shareholders and Corporate Control, *Journal of Political Economy* 94, 461–88.

Smith, D. G. (1996). Corporate Governance and Managerial Incompetence: Lessons from Kmart, *North Carolina Law Review* 74, 1038–139.

Smith, M. (1996). Shareholder Activism by Institutional Investors: Evidence from CalPERS, *Journal of Finance* 51, 227–52.

Song, W. and Szewczyk, S. (2003). Does Coordinated Institutional Investor Activism Reverse the Fortunes of Underperforming Firms? *Journal of Financial and Quantitative Analysis* 38, 317–36.

Strickland, D., Wiles, K., and Zenner, M. (1996). A Requiem for the USA: Is Small Shareholder Monitoring Effective?, *Journal of Financial Economics* 40, 319–38.

Talner, L. (1983). *The Origins of Shareholder Activism, Investor Responsibility* (Washington, DC, Research Center Inc.).

Thomas, R. and Martin, K. (1998). Should Labor be Allowed to Make Shareholder Proposals?, *Washington Law Review* 73, 41–80.

Thomas, R. and Cotter, J. (2006). Shareholder Proposals Post-Enron: What's Changed, What's the Same?, Vanderbilt Law School Working Paper, available at <http://www.claremontmckenna.edu/fei/events/2006sec/papers/Thomas.pdf>.

Tkac, P. (2006). One Proxy at a Time: Pursuing Social Change through Shareholder Proposals, *Federal Reserve Bank of Atlanta Economic Review*, 1–20.

Useem, M., Bowman, E., Myatt, J., and Irvine, C. (1993). US Institutional Investors Look at Corporate Governance in the 1990s, *European Management Journal* 11, 175–89.

Wahal, S. (1996). Pension Fund Activism and Firm Performance, *Journal of Financial and Quantitative Analysis* 31, 1–23.

Whitehouse, K. (2007). Proxy Fights Hit High in 2006, and More Seen for 2007, Market Watch, available at <http://www.marketwatch.com/story/proxy-fights-hit-high-in-2006-and-more-seen-for-2007>.

Woidtke, T. (2002). Agents Watching Agents? Evidence from Pension Fund Ownership and Firm Value, *Journal of Financial Economics* 63, 99–131.

Woidtke, T., Bierman, L., and Tuggle, C. (2003). Reigning in Activist Funds, *Harvard Business Review* 8(3), 22–3.

Wruck, K. H. and Wu, Y. (2009). Relationships, Corporate Governance, and Performance: Evidence from Private Placements of Common Stock, *Journal of Corporate Finance* 15, 30–47.

Wu, Y. (2004). The Impact of Public Opinion on Board Structure Changes, Director Career Progression, and CEO Turnover: Evidence from CalPERS' Corporate Governance Program, *Journal of Corporate Finance* 10, 199–227.

Van Nuys, K. (1993). Corporate Governance through the Proxy Mechanism: Evidence from the 1989 Honeywell Proxy Solicitation, *Journal of Financial Economics* 34, 101–32.

Zenner, M., Shivdasani, A., and Darius, D. (2006). Growing Activism in Hedge Funds, in M. Zenner (ed.), *Hot Corporate Finance Topics 2006* (New York, Citigroup), available at <http://wenku.baidu.com/view/081f2bed102de2bd9605882e.html>.

CHAPTER 3

THE MYTH OF THE SHAREHOLDER FRANCHISE

LUCIAN A. BEBCHUK

3.1 Introduction

A well-known, often-quoted Delaware opinion states that '[t]he shareholder franchise is the ideological underpinning upon which the legitimacy of directorial power rests'.[1] Similarly viewing the shareholder franchise as a key mechanism for making boards accountable, another landmark Delaware opinion states: 'If the stockholders are displeased with the action of their elected representatives, the powers of corporate democracy are at their disposal to turn the board out.'[2] I shall argue in this chapter, however, that shareholders do not in fact have at their disposal those 'powers of corporate democracy'. As a result, the shareholder franchise does not provide the solid foundation for the legitimacy of directorial power that it is supposed to supply. I shall also offer proposals for reforming corporate elections and thereby making directors truly accountable to shareholders.

Before proceeding, I should stress that my analysis of election reform in public companies will focus on the sole objective of enhancing shareholder value. From this perspective, increased shareholder power to replace directors would be desirable if, and only if, such a change would improve corporate performance and value. Some critics have argued that proponents of reforming corporate elections inappropriately conflate political ideas with market institutions. It is therefore worth stressing that I do not view 'shareholder voice' and 'corporate democracy' as ends in themselves—or as necessary corollaries of the nature of shareholders' ownership rights.

My support for reforming corporate elections is not motivated by political ideas but rather by the goal of making a market institution—the modern publicly traded company—function better. If the absence of viable shareholder power to replace directors was expected to produce better corporate performance and higher shareholder value, I would fully support a corporate governance system lacking such power. I support a viable

[1] *Blasius Indus. v. Atlas Corp.*, 564 A.2d 651, 659 (Del. Ch. 1988).
[2] *Unocal Corp. v. Mesa Petroleum Co.*, 493 A.2d 946, 959 (Del. 1985).

shareholder power to replace directors only because I view it as a valuable instrument for enhancing shareholder value by making boards more accountable and more attentive to shareholder interests.

3.2 The Myth and Reality of Corporate Elections

3.2.1 The Critical Role of the Shareholder Franchise

Boards play a central role in the standard view and the legal structure of the modern publicly traded corporation with dispersed ownership. It is widely recognized that full-time executives managing such a company have an agency problem. Their private interests might provide them with an incentive to engage in empire-building, take excessive compensation, enjoy excessive perks, pursue pet projects, elevate cronies, refuse to accept beneficial acquisition offers, remain in power too long, and so forth. Such agency problems are supposed to be addressed by the board.

Under the rules of corporate law, the power to run the company is not vested in the CEO or the company's senior executives. Rather, this power is vested in the board of directors, under whose direction the business and affairs of the corporation are supposed to be managed. The members of the board have a fiduciary duty to the corporation and are expected to serve as the shareholders' guardians.

Although the board has the formal authority and power to make all corporate decisions, directors are not expected to manage the company themselves. Most of the directors of publicly traded companies perform their board roles part-time. Directors are generally expected to delegate ongoing management decisions to the company's officers and especially to the CEO. Nonetheless, the board is supposed to perform several crucial functions.

The board selects the CEO and other top executives. The board sets the executives' compensation arrangements and thereby shapes their incentives. After selecting and hiring executives, the board is supposed to monitor their strategy and performance, replacing them if necessary. Finally, major corporate decisions, such as how to respond to an acquisition offer, are made by the board, which has full power to accept or reject executives' recommendations.

Given the central role of the board, selecting directors with the appropriate abilities and characteristics is important. Furthermore, given that directors necessarily exercise significant discretion, it is important for them to have incentives to serve shareholder interests. Shareholder power to replace directors is supposed to play a key role in both areas. If incumbent directors are not well chosen, shareholders possessing such power will be able to replace them. Furthermore, the fear of replacement is supposed to make directors accountable and provides them with an incentive to serve shareholder interests.

The importance of shareholder power to replace directors in the corporate legal structure is reinforced by the legal system's choice to insulate directors' decisions from judicial review. According to established principles of corporate law, courts abstain from substantive review of the merits of director decisions and do not impose liability for decisions that could have been shown to be wrong had such a review been undertaken. In adopting this approach, courts have been influenced by their belief that shareholders have available to them an alternative, superior accountability mechanism—shareholder power to replace directors whose performance they find unsatisfactory. Thus, for example, in the recent decision in the Disney shareholder suit, Chancellor Chandler stated that 'redress for [directors'] failures... must come . . . through the action of shareholders . . . and not from this Court'.[3]

Shareholder power to replace the board has also been used as a basis for providing boards with the power to block tender offers. In the classic *Unocal* decision, which introduced the principle under which boards have since been permitted to use defensive tactics, the Delaware Supreme Court relied on shareholders' ability to vote out the board; the court reasoned that stockholders displeased with directors' decision to block an offer would be able to replace them with directors who would pursue a different course of action.[4] The insulation of directors from hostile takeovers under existing rules increases again the importance of shareholder power to replace directors via the ballot box.

Finally, the importance of the shareholder franchise is reinforced by the long-standing limits on shareholders' power to initiate major corporate decisions. Under existing corporate statutes, shareholders cannot adopt decisions to amend the corporate charter, merge, reincorporate, or dissolve the company; such decisions must be initiated by the board. These limitations have been justified on the ground that, under the republican paradigm of our corporate laws, shareholders dissatisfied with the board's decisions with respect to such issues have the power to replace incumbent directors with a new team that would make different decisions.

The importance of the shareholder franchise is not undermined by the fact that recent stock exchange requirements provide independent directors with a key role in board decision-making. Even though director independence is beneficial, it is hardly sufficient to ensure that directors are well chosen and incentivized. While independence requirements disqualify some undesirable director candidates, they still leave a vast number of individuals from whom a choice needs to be made.

Furthermore, while independence requirements rule out some undesirable motives that directors might otherwise have, they do not by themselves provide directors with affirmative incentives to serve shareholder interests. Thus, notwithstanding independence requirements, a viable shareholder power to replace directors is important in our board-based corporate governance system. Such power is necessary to provide directors with strong affirmative incentives to focus on shareholder interests.

3.2.2 The Incidence of Electoral Challenges

But do shareholders have real power to replace the board, as the accepted theory of the corporation and court decisions assume they do? Supporters of the existing state of affairs have asserted that this assumption is indeed valid.

3 *In re Walt Disney Co. Derivative Litig.*, 907 A.2d 693, 698 (Del. Ch. 2005).

4 *Unocal Corp. v. Mesa Petroleum Co.*, 493 A.2d 946, 959 (Del. 1985).

Table 3.1 Contested solicitations, 1996–2005

Year	Number of contested solicitations
2005	24
2004	27
2003	37
2002	38
2001	40
2000	30
1999	30
1998	20
1997	29
1996	28
Total	**303**

To assess the view that running an election contest is a viable alternative and that election contests occur regularly, I conducted an empirical examination of the frequency and outcome of such challenges. The starting point of this examination was the universe of all cases of contested solicitations of proxies identified by Georgeson Shareholder, a well-known proxy solicitation firm.

Table 3.1 reports the number of such solicitations in each of the ten years from 1996 through 2005. As the table indicates, there were about 300 contested solicitations during this decade, or about thirty per year.

However, the set of contested solicitations is larger than the set of electoral challenges by a rival slate of directors seeking to take over management of the firm as a stand-alone entity. To identify the nature of the contest, target company SEC filings were reviewed. In a few rare instances where the challenge was newsworthy, press accounts of the contest were also reviewed. To be conservative, a contest was classified as an electoral challenge by a rival slate seeking to run the target differently as a stand-alone entity whenever the documents reviewed did not enable a confident classification of a contest as something other than such a challenge. The analysis led to the classification of contested solicitations into several groups:

(i) Contested solicitations not involving the election of directors: In each of the years of the examined decade, there were a number of contested solicitations that did not involve a contest over the election of directors. Rather, shareholders opposed the board on matters such as whether a merger proposal should be approved or whether bylaws should be amended.

(ii) Director contests focusing on takeover/sale of the company: In a significant fraction of the contested solicitations, the contested proxy solicitations formally sought to replace directors but were essentially a mechanism to facilitate the takeover or sale of the company. When a company is protected by a poison pill, the only option for a bidder seeking to acquire the company is to replace the directors with a slate of directors that will redeem the pill. In such a case, the shareholder vote on the election of directors is essentially a referendum on the bidder's offer. If the bidder's team gains control of the board, the company will not be run differently; rather, it will be sold to the bidder. Of course, the number of contests in this category is relevant for assessing the disciplinary force of the market for corporate control. But the question we are examining here concerns the incidence of election contests over the management of a company as a stand-alone entity.

(iii) Director contests focusing on opening or restructuring a closed-end fund: The data also include some instances in which the contested solicitation primarily focused on the opening of a closed-end fund, restructuring a fund, or some other fund management issue.

(iv) Director contests in which a rival slate of directors sought to manage the company: This is the category on which I focus—contested solicitations seeking a change in the director team at the helm of the company are the primary concern of the policy debates over corporate elections. In these contests, the dissident team seeks to replace current director(s) to alter the management of the corporation as a going concern.

Table 3.2 displays the incidence of different types of contested solicitations. As the table indicates, electoral challenges by a rival team seeking to run the company differently were mounted in 118 companies during the 1996–2005 decade, an average of about twelve per year.

In the second half of the decade, the incidence of such challenges was somewhat higher. There were forty-seven such challenges in the first half of the decade, and seventy-one challenges, about 50% more, in the second half. Thus, although shareholder activism (as expressed, for example, in the incidence of shareholder precatory resolutions) was markedly higher in the second half of the decade, the incidence of electoral challenges remained small—an average of about fourteen per year.

Table 3.2 Classification of contested proxy solicitations, 1996–2005

Year	Number of contested solicitations	Director contests not involving the election of directors	Director contests focusing on takeover/sale of company	Director contests focusing on opening or restructuring a closed-end fund	Director contests focusing on an alternate team for governing company
2005	24	8	2	4	10
2004	27	8	3	1	15
2003	37	5	13	3	16
2002	38	5	13	6	14
2001	40	8	15	1	16
2000	30	7	13	4	7
1999	30	10	4	2	13
1998	20	4	5	1	13
1997	29	10	12	1	5
1996	28	9	8	0	9
Total	**303**	**74**	**88**	**23**	**118**

3.2.3 The Targets and Outcomes of Electoral Challenges

Which companies become targets of electoral challenges by rival teams of directors? Table 3.3 displays statistics about the company size (as measured by market capitalization) of such targets. As the table indicates, the great majority were small. Only twenty-four companies, or less than three per year on average, had a market capitalization exceeding $200 million at the time of the electoral challenge.

Any assessment of the viability of shareholder replacement of directors should take into account not only the incidence of electoral challenges but also the incidence of successful electoral challenges. Assuming hypothetically that the incidence of challenges was large, this incidence would still have limited influence on incumbents if they generally expected to defeat such challenges.

Table 3.4 displays statistics concerning the number of successful electoral challenges, ranked by market capitalization of the target. About two-thirds of the challengers lost. The absolute numbers make the picture especially stark: putting aside contests over a sale of the company or open-ending a closed-end fund, rivals seeking to oust incumbents succeeded in gaining control in only eight companies with a market capitalization above $200 million during the decade.

3.2.4 Impediments to Electoral Challenges

We have seen that the incidence of electoral challenges by a rival team seeking to run the company better is quite small—and successful challenges are quite rare. One possible interpretation is that shareholders are uniformly happy with incumbent directors. However,

Table 3.3 Size distribution of the targets of electoral challenges, 1996–2005

Market capitalization	Number	Percentage of total
$0–$50M	61	52%
$50M–$100M	20	17%
$100M–$200M	13	11%
> $200M	24	20%
Total	**118**	**100%**

Table 3.4 Successful challengers, 1996–2005

Market capitalization	Number	As percentage of electoral challenges in size group
$0–$50M	23	38%
$50M–$100M	8	40%
$100M–$200M	6	46%
> $200M	8	33%
Total	**45**	**38%**

given the large number of public companies, one would still expect substantial shareholder dissatisfaction in a significant number of the companies that belong, say, to the set of firms performing in the bottom 10% of their peers. Given the hundreds of firms that restated earnings in recent years, and the large number of companies whose boards elect not to follow majority-passed shareholder resolutions, one would expect to see more challenges by rival teams.

A more plausible interpretation of the evidence is that, even when shareholder dissatisfaction with board actions and decisions is substantial, challengers face considerable impediments to replacing boards. I discuss the existing impediments, which are partly a product of existing legal arrangements.

3.2.4.1 *Costs*

A rival team seeking to replace incumbents will bear significant costs—often to the amount of hundreds of thousands of dollars. To begin, even assuming that all shareholders recognize the rival team's superiority and are willing to vote for it, the rival team would have to incur significant 'procedural' costs. Because rival teams cannot place the names of their director candidates on the corporate ballot, they have to pay to mail proxy cards to individual shareholders and receive them back. Furthermore, rivals have to bear the legal costs involved in filing a proxy statement with the SEC and possibly also in dealing with incumbents' legal challenges to the proxy statement's completeness or accuracy. In the recent proxy contest at Six Flags, insurgent Red Zone LLC spent about $850,000 on legal fees and the cost of preparing, printing, and mailing proxy materials.

In addition to these procedural expenses, rivals must commonly incur additional costs. Even when shareholders are dissatisfied with incumbents, they must still be persuaded that the rival team offers a superior alternative. Doing so is far from straightforward and likely involves significant costs beyond the baseline procedural costs. The rival team needs to communicate with shareholders, develop and present its strategy and plans for the company, address questions or concerns that shareholders may have, and respond to the incumbents' criticism of its plans and candidates.

Furthermore, when persuasion is necessary, it will likely be important to communicate directly with shareholders. Many shareholders hold shares in street names and are thus not automatically known and accessible. To identify and reach such shareholders, challengers may well have to use the expensive services of proxy solicitors as well as incur significant travel expenses. In the proxy contest at Six Flags, Red Zone incurred $2,400,000 in investment banking fees, about $950,000 in travel expenses, and about $600,000 in fees and expenses for professional proxy solicitors.

The issue of costs is especially difficult because of the existence of a 'free-rider' problem. At first glance, it might be thought that, while the presence of the above costs will discourage some contests, it will not deter those that would produce benefits exceeding these costs. This is not the case, however, because potential rivals would not fully internalize the potential benefits from a contest. Although challengers must bear their full costs, they can capture only a fraction of the benefits that the contest confers on the shareholders collectively.

To illustrate, consider a potential challenger that holds a 3% block in a company with a market capitalization of $200 million. Suppose the challenger believes that, if it were to mount a contest, it would have to spend $0.5 million; that incumbents would counter by spending $2 million (1% of firm value); that the rival's probability of winning would be 50%; that in the event of such a victory the rival would be able to increase share value by 5%; and that even an unsuccessful challenge would still give incumbents a 'kick in the pants' that would increase share value by 2%. In this case, a challenge would increase shareholder value: while incumbents' spending would reduce firm value by 1%, improved performance would increase it by 5% or 2% (depending on whether the rival wins or loses), resulting in a net increase in stock value of either 4% or 1%—or 2.5% on average. The expected benefit from a contest would thus be $200 million x 2.5% = $5 million, which easily exceeds the challenger's $0.5 million cost.

However, even though mounting a challenge would be beneficial in these circumstances from the perspective of the shareholders collectively, it would not be worthwhile from the potential challenger's private perspective. The challenger would be able to capture only 3% of the expected benefit of the contest, that is, $5 million × 3% = $0.15 million. And even though the challenger would be able to reimburse its expenses if it wins, it would have to bear the cost of $0.5 million in the event (which has a 50% probability) that its challenge fails. Thus, the challenger's expected cost would exceed their expected benefit from mounting a contest.

The problem of costs is exacerbated by the asymmetric treatment of challengers and incumbents by existing legal arrangements. Although challengers get no reimbursement in the event that they lose, incumbents can charge their full expenses to the company regardless of the outcome. With such carte blanche, incumbents facing a meaningful chance of ouster will be prepared to spend substantial amounts. While potential challengers have insufficient incentive to invest in mounting a proxy contest, incumbents have excessive incentive to invest in opposing a challenge: they have an incentive to spend more than is optimal from the shareholders' collective perspective. The incumbents' easy access to the company's coffers further increases the amount that challengers must spend to counter incumbents' campaigning.

In examining the importance of challengers' costs as a barrier to proxy contests, it should be noted that, for some shareholders with significant stakes, the potential costs of mounting a challenge go beyond the out-of-pocket costs involved in running a contest. Mutual funds, including those belonging to the main mutual fund family groups, would be unlikely to mount challenges even if they had to bear only a small fraction of these out-of-pocket costs. As Robert Pozen observed, for mutual fund families such as Fidelity or Vanguard, mounting a proxy contest is not part of the modus operandi (1994: 140). Running a contest that demands management time and attention and might displease incumbents does not sit well with the business model of such funds. Such funds are at most 'reluctant activists', to use Pozen's term, which could conceivably vote for a challenger but could not be expected to initiate contests themselves.

Nonetheless, there is a pool of potential challengers whose business model is consistent with mounting a challenge. This pool is comprised of individuals, family firms, and 'activist' mutual funds or hedge funds that have or are willing to take on a significant stake in a target company. While these candidates are open to the idea of mounting a challenge, their behaviour is likely to be sensitive to the magnitude of costs they would have to bear in mounting a proxy contest. The low incidence of contests has likely been due, at least in part, to cost barriers.

3.2.4.2 *Uncertainty about the Rival*

Even when a rival team would be better at leading the firm, convincing shareholders that this is the case would likely require significant efforts with no guarantee of success. Shareholders would be making their choices under conditions of uncertainty: to vote for the rival team, they must be convinced not only that the incumbents' performance is subpar, but also that the rival team would likely perform better. Otherwise, shareholders might well choose to stay with the devil they know.

The important point to recognize is that shareholders cannot infer from a rival team's mounting a challenge that the rival directors would perform better. To begin, even a rival team that believes it would perform better may be acting out of hubris. Furthermore, and very important, a rival's decision to mount a challenge does not even imply that the rival itself believes it would perform better. After all, a challenge could be motivated instead by a desire to obtain the private benefits associated with control.

Thus, a challenger that knows it would in fact perform better may still have to do a significant amount of work—and may still fail—to convince shareholders to vote its way. The challenger must persuade shareholders that it is not merely attracted by private benefits, and must present them with a credible and convincing case that its slate of directors and its plans for the company would likely produce an improvement.

This task is made difficult by the fact that many shareholders pay little or limited attention to the question of how to vote. While one externality problem leads rivals to underinvest in launching contests and running them, another externality problem leads shareholders to underinvest in assessing which slate of directors would be better: a shareholder would have to bear the full costs of such an investment in decision-making, but would share the benefits from an improved decision with fellow shareholders.

One difficulty rivals have in this connection is that they generally are unable to give as complete a picture of their plans as the incumbents can. For shareholders assessing a slate of directors, one important consideration is the identity of the person who would serve under the directors as CEO. Shareholders know who the CEO chosen by the incumbents is, but rival teams may have difficulties specifying their CEO candidates in advance. Potential candidates for the CEO position may be executives in other companies. When incumbents wish to attract a new CEO, they can hold confidential discussions with such candidates. The willingness of the candidate to take the CEO position will be made public only when the board offers and the candidate accepts the position. In contrast, if a rival team of directors approaches such a candidate, the candidate may be reluctant to be named even if he or she is in fact willing to become CEO in the event of the rival's victory.

Finally, the reluctance of some money managers to vote against incumbents also makes it difficult for even highly qualified rival teams to attract sufficient support. Money managers interested in attracting business from companies may be concerned that voting for a challenger may make it more difficult for them to get business from incumbents in general or from the incumbents of the target company in particular. Indeed, there is some evidence suggesting that the voting decisions of money managers are distorted towards positions favoured by management.

All of the above factors make it difficult for a rival slate of directors to win, even a rival slate superior to the incumbents. As a result, these factors also discourage rivals from mounting challenges in the first place. Given that rivals must bear the costs of running the challenge themselves if they fail, anything that operates to reduce the likelihood of winning also affects challengers' willingness to initiate contests. Thus, the difficulties that even a superior rival slate faces in persuading shareholders to vote for it reinforce the current cost barriers to mounting challenges. Since even a rival superior to the incumbents cannot be certain of winning, it is worthwhile to consider (as I propose in section 3.3.1.2) providing reimbursement of costs to rivals who attract significant support but fall short of winning.

3.2.4.3 *Staggered Boards*

A majority of US public companies have a staggered board of directors (Bebchuk and Cohen 2005: 410). In such cases, directors are divided into classes, usually three, and only one class comes up for re-election each year. To gain control of a company whose directors are protected by a three-class staggered board, a rival needs to win two elections, held at least one year apart.

The need to win two elections discourages and impedes electoral challenges in two ways. First, it makes mounting a challenge more costly. Rivals need to run a slate of directors twice, which increases costs, and be prepared to sustain a campaign for more than a year. Furthermore, having to win two elections before gaining control makes it all the more difficult to specify during the campaign the identity of the CEO whom the rival directors will appoint if they gain control. That individual will have to sit on the sidelines, in a stand-by position as it were, for more than a year.

Second, assuming that a rival team did mount a challenge to incumbents protected by a staggered board, the very existence of the staggered board makes it less likely that the rival will be able to win. In the first round, shareholders will recognize that a victory by the rival would lead to a period of at least a year in which the incumbents would still be in control but the board would have internal divisions and friction. As a result, shareholders may be reluctant to vote for the rival in the first round even if they view the rival's candidates as superior to the incumbents.

3.3 Reforming Corporate Elections

Section 3.2's analysis of the impediments to mounting and winning an electoral challenge to incumbents provides a basis for identifying arrangements that could provide shareholders with a viable power to replace directors. I now turn to putting forward a detailed proposal for such a reform.

3.3.1 Periodic Facilitation of Electoral Challenges

3.3.1.1 *Frequency*

At the outset, I would like to stress that, while it is essential to have periodic elections in which shareholders have a genuine option to replace incumbents, the frequency of such elections is a matter on which there is room for reasonable disagreement. Under existing arrangements, elections are held each year, but they are held under arrangements that make it difficult for shareholders to replace directors. Having frequent elections is of little significance if they do not offer a genuine opportunity to replace the incumbents. Having 'real' elections less often would be superior to having annual elections under arrangements that make it difficult for challengers to run and win.

Furthermore, a priori, there is no reason to assume that the optimal frequency of scheduled elections for directors is once a year. On the one hand, the more often shareholders get a genuine opportunity to replace the board, the faster they will be able to do so if they conclude this is necessary. On the other hand, if elections are more meaningful, scheduling them frequently could 'shorten the horizon' of incumbents and lead to short-termism. Furthermore, scheduling elections less frequently than once a year might enable institutional investors, which generally have positions in many public companies, to devote more attention to making the right voting decision when an election does take place.

For these reasons, while I support giving shareholders a genuine opportunity to replace the board from time to time, I am open to the possibility of giving them such an opportunity less often than once a year. For concreteness, I will discuss a system under which the arrangements facilitating challenges are triggered every two or three years.

In-between the points in time at which these arrangements are triggered, it could be desirable to have a 'safety valve'. For example, elections could still occur at each year's annual meeting, but the arrangements facilitating challenges (access to the ballot, cost reimbursement, etc.) would be triggered only every two or three years. Alternatively, one could have no 'interim' elections scheduled, but enable shareholders in certain circumstances to call a special meeting to have a vote on replacing the directors.

Finally, I should note that the arrangements proposed in Section 3.3.1.2 for periodic facilitation of challenges should not apply to potential buyers running a slate to overcome or bypass board opposition to a hostile takeover. The proposed reform focuses on lowering the existing impediments facing challengers that seek to run a company differently as a stand-alone entity.

3.3.1.2 *Access to the Ballot*

Putting aside the question of when corporate elections should take place, I now turn to how they should be conducted when they do take place, and I start with the problem of contest costs. Under the historical arrangement, challengers incur the costs of sending their own proxy materials to shareholders and getting them back. These 'mechanical' costs can be reduced by allowing challengers who satisfy some threshold ownership and holding requirements to place their candidates on the corporate ballot. Given that the company is already mailing and receiving shareholders' proxy cards, the need for rivals to do the same separately imposes costs that can easily be avoided.

Of course, a system with shareholder access to the ballot should have some threshold criteria of minimum ownership for any shareholder or shareholder group wishing to place a candidate on the ballot. The ownership requirement would seek to prevent a situation in which the firm's ballot becomes stuffed with candidates nominated by fringe investors. Shareholder access to the ballot is intended to facilitate challenges that might succeed, not to offer a mode of expression for all shareholders.

In 2009, the SEC proposed an access rule under which only shareholders with 1% ownership would be able to make proposals.[5] In my view, the 1% threshold was probably too high, especially in the case of very large companies. The SEC's proposed rule also limited access to the ballot limits to shareholders who held shares for at least one year. Although the case for an ownership threshold is strong, it is less clear that such a minimum holding requirement is desirable. This limitation seems to be motivated by a desire to limit access to shareholders who might have an interest in improving the company's long-term value rather than making a short-term profit. However, if one seeks to limit access to shareholders with a long-term perspective, what matters is not how long a shareholder has already held shares in the company, but rather how long the shareholder plans to hold the shares going forward. Accordingly, it might be better to require shareholders who nominate a candidate to commit to maintaining their position for a certain period of time in case the candidate is elected.

The SEC withdrew its 1%–one-year proposal in the wake of a threatened court challenge to its rulemaking authority by business groups. Congress responded in section 971 of the Dodd-Frank Act by confirming the SEC's rulemaking power to require corporations to include in their proxy statements candidates nominated by shareholders. The SEC, thus authorized, produced a new rule that raises the thresholds, allowing access only to a 3% shareholder who has held for three years (or to a group of shareholders all of whom satisfy the three-year holding period requirement).[6]

The SEC's new rule largely eliminates the benefits that proxy-access reform could provide. The 3% ownership threshold makes the proxy provisions largely useless for the main set of investors whose involvement the proxy-access reform is intended to facilitate. To be sure, a proxy-access rule with a 3% threshold might still be used in some cases where activist shareholders or hedge funds hold large stakes. When players holding such blocks of stock wish to replace incumbent directors, however, they commonly have an incentive to bear the costs of running a separate proxy solicitation. While proxy access might save such players some costs, it cannot be expected, nor is it intended, to have a substantial effect on their willingness to get involved.

The primary purpose of a proxy-access reform is to facilitate increased involvement by long-term institutional investors that have 'skin in the game' but not large blocks of shares. Consider, for example, the asset manager TIAA-CREF, a long-term investor holding on the order of 0.5% of the shares of many large public companies. Because such an investor would be able to capture only a very small fraction of the benefits of improved governance, it cannot be expected to undertake a costly proxy solicitation even when it believes that replacing directors would significantly enhance firm value. But if this investor could place a director on the ballot, it might do so when it views governance as especially poor. And the ability of such institutional investors to do so might make boards more attentive to shareholder interests in the first place.

Under the SEC's earlier 1% threshold, involvement by such institutional investors might have remained viable. The 3% threshold makes the proxy-access provisions practically irrelevant for such long-term institutional investors. Even if the ten largest public pension funds

[5] SEC Rel. 33–9136, Facilitating Shareholder Director Nominations, Aug. 25, 2010.

[6] Rule 14a-11, 17 C.F.R. 240.14a-11. The rule has been stayed during the pendency of a litigation challenging its validity, *Business Roundtable, et al. v. SEC*, No. 10-1305 (D.C. Cir., filed Sept. 29, 2010).

hypothetically banded together—a concerted action that would involve overcoming significant coordination costs and collective action barriers—they might still fail to reach the 3% threshold. For example, data put together by CalPERS, the giant California state pension fund, indicates that the ten largest pension funds hold less than 2.5% of Bank of America, Microsoft, IBM, and Exxon Mobil. The three-year ownership requirement compounds the problem.

Fortunately, the 3%–three-year threshold is not hardwired under Dodd-Frank and can be relaxed in the future. Certainly, the Commission has a legitimate interest in preventing submission of proposals for direct access by shareholders with nominal holdings. But a threshold under 1% could still ensure that proposing shareholders have a non-trivial stake. In particular, a lower threshold should be used for large or very large companies.

3.3.1.3 *Reimbursement of Expenses*

Although shareholder access to the ballot would much reduce challengers' 'mechanical' costs, these are commonly not the main expenses involved in mounting a successful challenge. Therefore, as long as challengers have to bear their own costs fully, contest costs would remain a substantial impediment and deterrent to some beneficial challenges.

Under existing arrangements, challenges are impeded by incumbents' financing advantage: incumbents can fully charge their expenses to the company, but challengers have to pay their own way. This asymmetry should be reduced. Under the system I support, challengers would get reimbursement of their reasonable expenses under certain conditions.

Under what circumstances should challengers receive reimbursement of costs? In answering this question, it is important to recognize two points. First, not all rivals running a campaign should be reimbursed. Such a universal reimbursement arrangement would facilitate 'frivolous' challenges that are expected to get little support. Therefore, it would be desirable to provide no reimbursement to challengers that perform poorly at the ballot box.

Second, requiring a rival team to obtain the majority support needed to elect one or more candidates to the board as a condition for reimbursement would be too demanding. Even rivals superior to the incumbents cannot be certain of winning. Such rivals will have to take into account the possibility that they will fail to gain a majority. Thus, making reimbursement conditional on obtaining majority support will go too far and discourage some beneficial challenges.

Putting these two points together leads to the conclusion that it would be desirable to encourage challenges when potential rivals believe they have a substantial likelihood (even though no certainty) of winning. Thus, the condition for reimbursement should be obtaining sufficiently wide support. For example, consider an arrangement that would provide reimbursement in the event a rival garnered support from one-third of the shareholders voting on the election of directors. Such a requirement would not encourage challenges that are expected to have little practical significance. At the same time, because rivals who have a meaningful chance of winning might also have a significant likelihood of getting, say, only 40% of the votes, such an arrangement will facilitate challenges by such rivals.

It is worth noting why the proposed reimbursement arrangement is superior to a proportional reimbursement arrangement under which rivals obtaining X% of the votes would have X% of their costs reimbursed. A proportional reimbursement arrangement has two disadvantages relative to the one proposed. First, in cases in which the challenger obtains little support—say, 10% of the votes—a proportional reimbursement arrangement would provide excessive reimbursement. In such cases, the challenger should receive nothing (as with the proposed arrangement), because in all likelihood it had no meaningful likelihood of winning in the first place.

Second, in cases in which a challenger falls just short of winning a majority, proportional reimbursement would provide insufficient reimbursement. Under proportional reimbursement, the challenger in such cases would still have to bear a substantial fraction of the challenge costs. As a result, the 'public good' problem of underinvestment by challengers with a substantial likelihood of winning would not be eliminated.

The above discussion indicates that the optimal reimbursement schedule should: (1) provide no reimbursement to the challenger at sufficiently low levels of shareholder support; and (2) provide full reimbursement at levels below majority support that are sufficiently high. A proportional reimbursement arrangement does not have either one of these features. While the reimbursement arrangement that I propose does fall within the class of such schedules, there are other schedules that fall within this class, and I do not wish to claim that the proposed reimbursement arrangement is the best within this class; I am putting it forward merely as a simple rule that has certain attractive features the optimal rule must have, and I leave the examination of whether and how this rule could be refined and improved to future work.

The recent addition of Section 113 to the Delaware General Corporation Law removes any doubts regarding the validity of corporate by laws providing for reimbursement.[7] But it does little else. It leaves in place no reimbursement as the default arrangement and lets the provision of reimbursement evolve through the adoption of reimbursement arrangements on a company-by-company basis. Those who commend this approach stress the virtues of 'private ordering' that tailors arrangements to companies' particular circumstances. However, it is a mistake to conflate a preference for private ordering and 'one size does not fit all' with a preference for a no-reimbursement default. A preference for private ordering merely implies a preference for allowing opting out from whichever default is set, and does not imply that the ideal default is no reimbursement. No matter what the default rule, it is possible to have private ordering: if the default rule provides for reimbursement, there can be private ordering by allowing corporations to opt out of the regime; if the default rule is no reimbursement, there can be private ordering by allowing shareholders to opt in to reimbursement. Therefore, although arguments against a reimbursement regime cite a preference for private ordering, such a preference cannot provide a basis for opposition to the provision of a reimbursement default. A preference for private ordering is fully consistent with a reimbursement regime as long as opting out is permitted by the regime. The opposing position is thus grounded not in a preference for private ordering but in a preference for a no-reimbursement default over a reimbursement default.

3.3.1.4 *Replacement of All Directors*

Shareholders should be able to vote to replace all of the incumbent directors with new candidates at least every two or three years. There should be a point in time at which shareholders have an opportunity to vote for a full slate of new directors. As was explained in Section

[7] Del. Code Ann. tit. 8, § 113 (Supp. 2010).

3.2.4.3, requiring rivals to win two elections in a row to gain control is a substantial impediment to challengers.

Note that this proposal would not eliminate certain advantages cited by supporters of staggered boards (Koppes, Ganske, and Haag 1999: 1051–4). Such supporters believe that electing independent directors for a term longer than one year protects them from insiders and thus bolsters their independence. Such supporters also argue that a staggered board ensures that the roster of directors changes only gradually, thus ensuring stability.

The elections system that I support is consistent with largely maintaining these advantages. A company could still have a bylaw (or a company policy) requiring that the composition of the company's slate—that is, the slate put forward by the incumbent directors—be structured in the same way as it would be under a staggered board. Under such an arrangement, independent incumbent directors would know that their place on the company's slate would be reassessed only once every three years, and they would thus be fully protected from earlier replacement by the incumbent team. They could be removed earlier if shareholders revolt, but this possibility would certainly not undermine their independence from insiders.

Furthermore, with such a company bylaw (or policy), stability in the composition of the company's board of directors would be ensured absent a shareholder revolt. Replacement of more than one-third of the board would occur only in the rare event of shareholder revolt, when dissatisfaction with the incumbent team as a whole should take precedence. Thus, the proposed system would be consistent with maintaining whatever advantages might flow from commitment by the incumbent board to maintain stability in the composition of its slate. However, it would not insulate incumbents from ever losing control of the board in one election.

The proposed system would also be consistent with an arrangement under which all directors are elected for two- or three-year terms, provided that they all then come up together for re-election. Providing directors with a longer time horizon would be acceptable as long as shareholders at some point get a genuine opportunity to replace the full board. Such an arrangement would provide independent directors with the security of remaining on the board for the two or three years that supporters of staggered boards deem desirable, but would do so without insulating the incumbent directors from being replaced by a rival team.

3.3.2 Arrangements Applying to All Elections

I have thus far discussed the ways in which election arrangements should periodically facilitate electoral challenges. I now turn to discussing some additional changes in existing default arrangements which should apply to all elections. First, directors should not serve when more votes are cast against them than for them. Second, shareholders should vote by secret ballot.

3.3.2.1 *'Withhold' and 'Against' Votes*

For shareholders to be able to replace incumbent directors with outside candidates, some such outside candidates need to be on the ballot. However, even with the just arrangements proposed, most elections will likely be uncontested, with no candidates on the ballot other than those put forward by the company. In such situations, it will still be desirable for shareholders to be able to vote down a candidate put forward by the company.

Under existing default arrangements, shareholders do not have any meaningful power to veto candidates put forward by the board in an uncontested election. To begin with, under the existing default arrangements established by state law, whether a candidate is elected is determined according to a plurality standard: the candidate with the most votes is elected, which means that a candidate placed on the ballot by the board will be elected in an uncontested election as long as the candidate obtains one 'for' vote. Furthermore, if no one is elected to fill a board seat, the incumbent remains in place. Both arrangements make it possible for a director to serve on the board even following an election in which that director failed to obtain support from most voting shareholders.

This state of affairs has attracted a great deal of shareholder criticism. This shareholder opposition has led to changes that facilitate the adoption of bylaws that establish 'majority voting'—that is, prevent or constrain the election of candidates who failed to gain the support of a majority of the shareholders—both in the Delaware Code and in the Model Business Corporation Act. Given that majority voting has been extensively discussed, and that my interest is in majority voting as one element of a comprehensive reform of corporate elections, I will limit my discussion of the subject to four general points.

First, given the clear and widely accepted flaws of plurality voting, majority voting should be the default arrangement. Although Delaware and the Model Business Corporation Act have now moved to facilitate opting into majority voting arrangements, they have not made majority voting the default arrangement. Although there is room for reasonable disagreement about which of the variations of majority voting should be adopted as the default, there is little basis for continuing to maintain a default arrangement that enables directors to hold office even after an election in which they obtained, say, a single shareholder vote.

Second, shareholders should be able to cast 'against' votes, and director candidates should be viewed as voted down only if a majority of the votes are cast against them. Shareholders now generally have the choice only between a 'for' and a 'withhold' vote, and majority voting proposals therefore seek to prevent or constrain the election of directors who receive more 'withhold' than 'for' votes. The problem with this approach, however, is that shareholders withholding support from a candidate might be seeking to register a signal of dissatisfaction rather than prevent the candidate's election.

Given that 'withhold' votes might currently reflect two very different preferences, it is desirable to enable shareholders to clearly express each of these preferences. If both 'withhold' and 'against' votes are permitted, shareholders wishing to register dissatisfaction but willing to allow the candidate to serve will cast a 'withhold' vote, whereas shareholders who prefer to block the director's election will cast an 'against' vote. Under the proposed arrangement, directors will be prevented from serving only when a majority of the voting shareholders clearly prefers that outcome over merely sending a warning signal to the board.

Third, although majority voting has attracted a great deal of attention, it is not a substitute for the arrangements discussed in Section 3.3.1 for facilitating electoral challenges. Boards often act as a team and shareholders cannot isolate the separate contribution of each director to the team's collective decisions and performance. As a result, when shareholders are dissatisfied with the board, their dissatisfaction is often not limited to one or a few directors but rather extends to the team as a whole. In such a situation, improving matters might require adding to the board one or more new directors who are not part of the existing team.

Majority voting, however, does not facilitate such changes; if majority voting prevents the election of a director targeted by shareholders, the seat either will not or will be filled by the incumbent team, which will continue to call all the shots either way. Thus, even if most companies end up opting into majority voting, shareholders should not become complacent about corporate elections. Without the adoption of the other arrangements discussed in this section, shareholders will not obtain the viable power to replace incumbents with a new team that is necessary for corporate elections to perform their critical role.

Finally, while majority voting is hardly a substitute for the adoption of arrangements that facilitate electoral challenges, it is a useful complement to them. Even with such arrangements, challengers will not have sufficient incentive to mount a contest in all cases in which shareholder dissatisfaction might be substantial. Majority voting provides shareholders with an inexpensive and decentralized way to discipline directors without any shareholder having to bear the cost of mounting a challenge.

Furthermore, even though majority voting cannot adequately address situations in which shareholders are dissatisfied with the board and its decisions in general, it can be effective with respect to problems limited to a small subset of the directors or to a specific board decision. For example, the ability to use majority voting to block the election of the chair of the compensation committee might make that committee and its chair more attentive to shareholder interests—and thereby discourage the adoption of pay packages likely to outrage shareholders.

3.3.2.2 *Confidential Voting*

All voting on directors, in both contested and uncontested elections, should be by secret ballot. At present, although precatory resolutions calling for confidential voting have long attracted substantial support (Romano 2003: 466), voting is not confidential in the lion's share of public companies (Bebchuk 2004). This lack of confidentiality distorts voting decisions by some institutional investors in favour of incumbents.

Many institutional investors, including mutual funds, banks, insurance companies, and other money managers, have an interest in being on good terms—or at least not on adversarial terms—with management in public companies. Such good terms might facilitate getting business from such companies, including managing the retirement accounts of their employees or providing various other financial services. Given that a particular money manager's vote is unlikely to be pivotal, and that whatever benefits may arise from an efficient outcome of a vote will largely be captured by others, a money manager's other business interests may have a substantial influence on its vote in such a contest. In particular, the money manager might elect to support the incumbent even if the challengers appear to be somewhat better for shareholder value.

There is empirical evidence that institutions' voting decisions may be influenced by their other business interests. One study divided institutions into those that are 'pressure-sensitive' (because of their interest in public firms' business, such as insurance companies and banks), 'pressure-resistant' (because of the absence of such dealings, such as public pensions funds, endowments, and foundations), and 'pressure-indeterminate'. The study found that the percentage of votes cast against antitakeover provisions was positively correlated with the ownership stake of pressure-resistant and pressure-indeterminate institutions, but not with the ownership stake of pressure-sensitive institutions (Brickley, Lease, and Smith 1988: 276–80).

While the Brickley, Lease, and Smith (1988) study contrasted the voting behaviour of different categories of institutions, a more recent study investigated differences among institutions belonging to the same category (Davis and Kim 2007). In particular, this latter study examined whether mutual funds that vary in the weight they place on obtaining pension business differ in how they vote. It found a positive correlation between the volume of pension business that a mutual fund family does and its propensity to vote with incumbents.

Finally, a recent study (Cai, Garner, and Walkling 2009) provides direct evidence that confidentiality matters and that lack of confidentiality could discourage some shareholders from voting against incumbents. Examining director elections during 2003 and 2004, the study finds that lack of confidential voting had a negative and statistically significant effect on the percentage of shares casting 'withhold' votes in director elections. In particular, lack of confidentiality reduced the number of withhold votes on average by about 1.5–2.0% of outstanding shares.

Recognizing the problem of potential conflicts of interest, the SEC adopted, in 2003, a rule requiring mutual funds to disclose their votes.[8] However, because investors in mutual funds base their choices on investment performance and not on how funds vote, the adopted requirement cannot be expected to eliminate the pro-incumbent bias of mutual funds that have a significant interest in obtaining business from public companies. The best approach, therefore, is not to make the funds' voting decisions in proxy contests transparent to both incumbents and outside investors, but to keep them secret from both. Similarly, confidentiality is the best way of dealing with potential conflicts of interest on the part of institutions other than mutual funds.

Whatever the magnitude of the potential benefits of confidentiality, there is simply no reason not to make voting in corporate elections confidential. The default arrangement for public companies should therefore provide for such confidentiality. As is currently done in companies using confidential voting, an outside tabulator should count the votes and announce the vote's outcome without disclosing to either incumbents or challengers how any given individual shareholder voted.

3.3.3 Opting Out of Default Arrangements

The system I have put forward is proposed as a default arrangement. One size does not fit all, and companies should be able to opt into different arrangements. I therefore now turn to discussing the process through which such opting out should take place.

Whatever set of default arrangements public officials choose to adopt with respect to corporate elections, shareholders should play a decisive role in any opting out of these default arrangements. The election system is in place to provide a check on the board and to ensure its accountability to shareholders. Therefore, it would be desirable to prevent directors from having control over changes in the arrangements governing how difficult it would be to replace them. In particular, it would be desirable for public officials: (1) to facilitate

[8] Disclosure of Proxy Voting Policies and Proxy Voting Records by Registered Management Investment Companies, Securities Act Release No. 8188, Exchange Act Release No. 47,304, 68 Fed. Reg. 6564 (Feb. 7, 2003) (to be codified at 17 C.F.R. pts. 239, 249, 270, 274), reprinted in [2002–3 Transfer Binder] Fed. Sec. L. Rep. (CCH) P86,826 (Feb. 12, 2003).

shareholder initiation and adoption of election bylaws; and (2) to constrain directors from adopting election bylaws that make it more difficult for them to be replaced by shareholders.

3.3.3.1 *Facilitating Stockholder-Initiated Bylaws*

As long as public officials accept that increasing shareholder power to replace directors might be desirable, and that there is a role for private ordering in this area, facilitating shareholder adoption of such arrangements is desirable. Directors cannot be counted on to adopt bylaw provisions making their replacement easier even if such provisions would increase share value. Therefore, to ensure that directors do not have a veto power over such moves, shareholders should have the practical ability to initiate and adopt such arrangements.

To facilitate shareholder adoption of election arrangements, shareholders should be permitted to place on the corporate ballot any proposed bylaw concerning elections that would be valid under state law if adopted. Under SEC Rule 14a-8, as historically drafted, companies were permitted to exclude from the ballot any proposals relating 'to an election for membership on the company's board of directors'.[9] And the SEC Division of Corporation Finance interpreted this provision as allowing exclusion of proposals to adopt a bylaw provision providing shareholders with access to the corporate ballot on grounds that such proposals relate to an election.

The rule and the SEC's narrow interpretation became controversial. In the *AFSCME* case of 2006, the United States Court of Appeals for the Second Circuit prohibited American International Group from excluding a proposal relating to election arrangements from the corporate ballot.[10] The court reached its decision on the narrow basis that the SEC has not provided an explanation for switching from an earlier policy of opposing such exclusion to one that supports it. Together with colleagues, I filed an *amicus curiae* brief in the *AFSCME* case, opposing exclusion of shareholder bylaw proposals concerning corporate elections.[11] Allowing shareholders to place election bylaws on the corporate ballot is, in my view, necessary to advance the policy goals of Rule 14a-8 and called for by a reasonable interpretation of the rule. The provision allowing exclusion of a proposal that 'relates to an election for membership on the company's board of directors' should be understood as permitting the exclusion of proposals that relate to the election of a particular individual to membership on the board of directors. It should not be understood as permitting the exclusion of 'rules-of-the-game' provisions that relate to the procedural and substantive rules governing the elections process.

The elections exclusion should have been interpreted only to allow companies to omit proposals necessitating disclosures in the proxy statement by the proposing shareholders. For example, when a proponent seeks to elect a particular individual to the board, an informed shareholder vote requires a proxy statement that would supply particularized information about the characteristics and plans of the proposed individual. In such a case, the 500 words allotted by Rule 14a-8 to shareholder proposals do not enable shareholders

[9] 17 C.F.R. § 240.14a-8 (2006).

[10] *Am. Fed'n of State, County & Mun. Employees v. Am. Int'l Group, Inc.*, 462 F.3d 121 (2d Cir. 2006).

[11] *Brief of Amicus Curiae Harvard Law School Professors Lucian Bebchuk et al. in Support of Appellants, AFSCME*, 462 F.3d 121 (No. 05-2825-cv), available at <http://www.law.harvard.edu/faculty/bebchuk/Policy/AmicusCuria_Brief.pdf>. The following discussion draws on this *amicus curiae* brief.

to cast an informed vote without a proxy statement. This is not the case, however, when the proposal concerns not the board membership of a particular individual or individuals but rather a governance arrangement—whether one regulating the election process or pertaining to some other aspect of corporate governance.

The SEC modified Rule 14a-8 in the wake of the *AFSCME* decision to allow a company to exclude from its proxy statement a shareholder proposal that relates to a nomination or an election for membership on the company's board of directors or a procedure for such nomination or election.[12] The modified provision properly permitted the exclusion of a proposal that would result in an immediate election contest, but also permitted exclusion of proposals that would set up a process for future shareholder proxy access. The latter provision required a conforming amendment when SEC returned to the rule in connection with its adoption of a 3%-three-year proxy-access provision.[13] As further amended, the rule makes it clear that only proposals that deal with particular elections and candidates may be excluded.

3.3.3.2 *Constraining Board-Adopted Bylaws*

While it is desirable to facilitate private ordering through shareholder-adopted bylaws, it is also desirable to constrain board-adopted election bylaws. In particular, it is necessary to constrain board-adopted election bylaws that opt out of the provided default arrangement to make it more difficult to replace incumbent directors. Given that the corporate elections system is intended to make directors accountable, allowing directors to make it more difficult to replace them is counterproductive.

One way to deal with this problem is for the legal rules that establish default arrangements concerning corporate elections to allow opting out only through a bylaw adopted by shareholders. This approach is not unfamiliar to drafters of corporate codes: under the Delaware Code, a bylaw establishing a staggered board must be adopted by a vote of the shareholders.[14] This provision is presumably intended to prevent boards from adopting unilaterally a bylaw establishing a staggered board and thereby making director replacement more difficult. The same logic should be extended to aspects of the election system other than board classification.

If board-adopted bylaws that make replacement more difficult are not categorically ruled out, boards should, at a minimum, be prevented from repealing or amending election bylaws adopted by shareholders. A recent amendment to the Delaware Code prohibits boards from repealing shareholder-adopted bylaws that prescribe majority voting.[15] It is difficult to see any reason for prohibiting directors from undoing election bylaws adopted by shareholders concerning majority voting and, at the same time, allowing directors to undo shareholder-adopted election bylaws concerning other aspects of the directors' re-election process.

Furthermore, if the law elects not to categorically rule out board adoption of some bylaw amendments that make it more difficult to replace directors (whether or not such

[12] Press Release, SEC, Commission Calendars Proposed Amendment to Rule 14a-8 Governing Director Nominations by Shareholders (Sept. 7, 2006), available at <http://www.sec.gov/news/press/2006/2006-150.htm>.

[13] SEC Rel. 33-9136, Facilitating Shareholder Director Nominations, Aug. 25, 2010.

[14] Del. Code Ann. tit. 8, § 141(d) (2001).

[15] Del. Code Ann. tit. 8, § 216 (2001).

amendments undo provisions adopted earlier by shareholders), then directors' decisions to adopt such amendments should be subject to demanding judicial scrutiny. In *Blasius Industries, Inc. v. Atlas Corp.*, Chancellor Allen invalidated a board decision that he viewed as disenfranchising shareholders and lacking a compelling justification. In my view, a compelling justification test should be applied to any board decision to adopt a bylaw that makes it more difficult to replace directors even if the bylaw does not make such replacement practically impossible.

It should be stressed that the approach advocated in this section would not prevent boards from initiating changes in election arrangements when such changes are desirable. It would only constrain boards from making changes that make it more difficult to remove directors without shareholder approval. When such changes happen to be value increasing, directors can be expected to obtain shareholder approval for them.

3.4 Objections to Reform

Thus far I have argued that the shareholder franchise is largely a myth, and I have proposed a set of arrangements that would make shareholder power to replace the board real. But some opponents of reform believe that, even if the shareholder franchise is now largely a myth and shareholders lack real power to remove directors, this state of affairs is in fact optimal and should be maintained. On this view, giving shareholders effective power to replace boards—the power that they are assumed to have under the accepted theory of the corporation—would operate to the detriment of shareholders and the economy. This section therefore examines a wide range of possible objections and concerns. I conclude that they do not provide a basis for opposing election reform.

3.4.1 Is There Empirical Evidence in Support of Reform?

Opponents of election reform might argue that corporate arrangements, even those serving as defaults, should not be significantly changed without empirical evidence indicating that such changes would increase shareholder value. In the case under consideration, there is a significant body of empirical evidence that is relevant to assessing the proposed reform, and this body of evidence is consistent with the view that making boards more accountable by invigorating corporate elections would tend to increase shareholder value.

To begin, empirical studies consistently found that proxy fights are associated with accompanying increase in shareholder wealth (Borstadt and Zwirlein 1992; DeAngelo and DeAngelo 1989; Dodd and Warner 1983; Ikenberry and Lakonishok 1993; Mulherin and Poulsen 1998). These studies focus only on the *ex post* effects of proxy contests (their effects on shareholder wealth once a proxy contest takes place) and do not attempt to assess the *ex ante* effects of proxy contests (the effects of the prospect of a proxy contest on boards in general). But even though these studies focus only on a subset of the effects of proxy contests, their results are clearly consistent with a favourable view of such contests.

Furthermore, there is substantial evidence that the general direction in which the proposed reform would go—reducing incumbents' insulation from removal—has an overall beneficial *ex ante* effect on the management of public companies. To begin, there is evidence that insulation of boards from replacement via a hostile takeover leads to increase in managerial slack. A study by Marianne Bertrand and Sendhil Mullainathan (1999: 545), and a study by Gerald Garvey and Gordon Hanka (1999: 520) found that the passage of antitakeover statutes is accompanied by increases in managerial slack. Another study (Gompers, Ishii, and Metrick 2003) found that companies whose managers enjoy more protection from takeovers (as measured by a governance index taking into account both corporate arrangements and state antitakeover provisions) are associated with poorer operating performance—including lower profit margins, return on equity, and sales growth. This study also found that companies with stronger antitakeover protection are more likely to engage in empire-building (Gompers, Ishii, and Metrick 2003: 136–7). Yet another study found that acquisitions made by companies with stronger antitakeover protection are more likely to be value-decreasing. (Masulis, Wang, and Xie 2007).

There is also evidence that insulation from removal results in greater consumption of private benefits by executives. Kenneth Borokhovich, Kelly Brunarski, and Robert Parrino (1997) found that executives with stronger antitakeover defences enjoy higher compensation levels. Marianne Bertrand and Sendhil Mullainathan (1998) obtained similar findings for executives who are more protected due to antitakeover statutes. And a study by Olubunmi Faleye (2007) found that antitakeover protection is associated with lower compensation incentives in the CEO's compensation as well as with lower sensitivity of CEO turnover to firm performance.

Finally, there is evidence of a correlation between antitakeover protections and lower firm value. Alma Cohen and I found that staggered boards, with the substantial protection from removal they provide, are correlated with an economically significant reduction in firm value (Bebchuk and Cohen 2005: 430). In a subsequent study, Alma Cohen, Allen Ferrell, and I found that firm value is negatively correlated not only with staggered boards, but also with several other provisions associated with greater takeover protection, as well as with an entrenchment index based on these provisions (Bebchuk, Cohen, and Ferrell 2009).

To be sure, empirical evidence about the effects of insulation from removal via a takeover does not directly identify the effects of reducing insulation from removal via a proxy fight. But the evidence indicates clearly that current levels of board insulation are costly to shareholders and the economy. It thus provides support for reforms, such as the one under consideration, which would reduce the insulation of boards from removal.

3.4.2 Market Forces Provide Sufficient Accountability

There are some who believe that viable shareholder power to remove directors is unnecessary because market forces provide a sufficient source of accountability (Bainbridge 2006: 1741). As explained in this subsection, however, even though market forces impose some constraints on boards, they do not obviate the need for the power to replace directors.

1. *The market for corporate control.* Many economists and economically inclined legal scholars have looked to the market for corporate control to provide boards with incentives to perform well. However, under existing legal rules, boards have the power to resist and block hostile takeover bids. As a result, a hostile takeover is

possible only if the bidder is willing to offer a high premium and be sufficiently patient and determined, a situation that leaves a lot of room for slacking off in board performance. Thus, under the existing arrangements governing hostile bids, the threat of such bids cannot prevent even significant deviations from maximizing shareholder value.

2. *The market for new capital.* It might be suggested that the need to go back to the capital market to raise additional capital is an important source of discipline. However, many public companies do not raise additional capital for long periods after they go public, but rather finance investment through retained earnings. Furthermore, failure to focus on shareholder interests would not generally prevent raising additional capital. It would mean only that the company would have to sell shares at a slightly lower price. The costs of raising capital at somewhat worse terms would be borne mainly by shareholders, with the members of the board bearing only a fraction.
3. *The product market.* It might be argued that companies whose boards do not maximize shareholder interests would suffer a substantial disadvantage in competitive product markets, or even fail in such markets and be forced to exit, which in turn would discourage boards from deviating from shareholder interests in the first place. However, deviation from shareholder interests does not necessarily result in increased product prices or a reduced market share. It might simply result in lower profits and cash flows for shareholders without worsening the company's product market performance. Furthermore, even if a given deviation from shareholder interests were to produce an increased likelihood of business failure, that might not be enough to discourage such a deviation if the directors' private benefits from such a deviation exceed the costs resulting from this increased risk of failure.
4. *The market for shares and the Wall Street rule.* Defenders of the current state of corporate affairs argue that shareholders dissatisfied with incumbent directors can '"vote with their feet" by selling the company's stock', and that '[t]he purest form of corporate suffrage takes place in the capital markets' (Business Roundtable 2003: 24–45). The ability of shareholders to sell their shares on the market, however, is hardly a substitute for a viable route for replacing directors.

   Consider shareholders who believe that their board is and has been underperforming and that, as a result of this poor performance, the company's stock price is only $40 per share rather than the $60 per share it would be with adequate board performance. If the board performance cannot be improved, being able to sell shares on the market would not address the shareholders' problem: selling would still provide them with only $40 per share. Thus, for shareholders concerned that poor board performance is reducing the value of their investment, the freedom to sell their shares is hardly an adequate remedy.

5. *Pressure from institutional investors.* Finally, one could look to institutional investors and large outside blockholders to monitor board performance and put pressure on those who perform inadequately. There is evidence that the presence of such shareholders has a beneficial influence on how firms are governed (Bertrand and Mullainathan 2001: 920–1). The influence that institutions and large outside shareholders have, however, critically depends on the power that the background rules of corporate law give them. In particular, this influence is likely to depend on the extent

to which institutional investors are able to vote out directors if the latter decline to follow the institutions' recommendations and requests. The less meaningful shareholders' voting power is, the less clout institutions and other holders of large blocks of stock have with boards.

One way of thinking about the arguments considered in this section is that, if they were correct, it would not matter if investors' shares had no votes attached to them at all (or, in the case of the market for corporate control, carried with them voting rights only when held by a buyer that has obtained a majority block). Readers who believe that it is important for shares in companies with dispersed ownership to have voting rights should not be prepared to accept these arguments.

3.4.3 The Proposed Reform Would Not Have Practical Significance

The proposed reform, it might be argued, would have little practical significance. On this view, institutional investors tend to be passive and therefore cannot be expected to make much use of arrangements making it easier to challenge incumbent directors.

Indeed, most money managers cannot be expected to initiate or to sponsor a dissident slate even after the adoption of the proposed reforms. Most mutual funds are 'reluctant activists' and active involvement in corporate governance is not part of their business model (Pozen 2003). It is reasonable to expect, however, that challenges would come from individuals, family firms, and activist mutual funds and hedge funds that have or will acquire significant blocks in companies with boards that fail to maximize shareholder value. When such shareholders launch a contest whose success would likely raise share value, money managers that are unwilling to be active themselves could well vote for this slate. The past voting patterns of private money managers indicate that they commonly do not vote against management on social issues, but they do occasionally vote against management when its position appears to be value-decreasing.

Finally, suppose that election reform would have only a limited effect on the viability of an electoral challenge and thus on the accountability of incumbents. Such a conclusion could justify lowering one's expectations of what the proposed reform would accomplish, as well as considering more expansive reforms, but it could not provide a basis for opposing the proposed changes. To provide a basis for such opposition, opponents must argue that making it easier to replace directors would have significant negative consequences. I therefore now turn to such arguments.

3.4.4 Adverse Effects on Shareholders

3.4.4.1 *Waste and Disruption*

This objection runs in the opposite direction of the preceding one. Rather than claim that election reform would have little practical significance, this objection suggests that it would lead to large-scale disruption of corporate management. Making it easier to run a competing slate, opponents of reform worry, would make contested elections the norm. The Business Roundtable (2003) opposed even the SEC's modest proposal for a limited access to the ballot by shareholders on the grounds that it 'has the potential to turn every director election into a divisive proxy contest'. Such contests, it is argued, would not only require companies to incur substantial out-of-pocket costs, thereby wasting corporate resources, but also (and more importantly) divert management's effort and attention.

However, the proposed reform should not be expected to lead to full-scale contests becoming the norm. To begin with, in companies that are adequately governed and lack widespread shareholder dissatisfaction, incumbents would largely remain secure in their board seats and challenges would continue to be unlikely. The past voting patterns of institutional investors indicate that their voting en masse against incumbents is the exception, occurring only when motivated by some strong reasons for doing so. Without broad shareholder dissatisfaction resulting from a poor record, an electoral challenge would be futile. While the proposed reform would provide cost reimbursement to challengers, it would do so only when they attract a sufficiently substantial number of votes, and thus it would provide no encouragement to futile challenges.

Furthermore, even in the case of firms that would otherwise be inadequately governed, the proposed reform would often improve matters not directly, through proxy contests, but indirectly, by changing the incentives of incumbents. The mere existence of viable shareholder power to remove directors could well have a beneficial effect on the performance of such boards without an actual exercise of this power. The benefits of reform would be system wide—coming from increased accountability—and would not be limited to cases in which actual contests, with their accompanying costs, take place.

Granted, some boards might fail to improve performance even in the face of viable shareholder power to remove them. In such cases, the proposed reform is likely to increase the incidence of contests somewhat from its current low level. However, the small number of companies in which contests would occur in any given year would not be randomly drawn from the set of all companies. Rather, they would be concentrated among companies with high shareholder dissatisfaction and subpar performance. Although these contests would involve some costs, these costs would be a price worth paying for a process that could improve corporate governance in these companies as well as produce system-wide benefits.

It should be stressed that, by appropriate adjustment of the parameters of the system, it should be possible to permit the incidence of contests to grow somewhat without their becoming too common. In particular, the incidence of contests will likely increase as: (1) the (ownership and holding) thresholds that must be passed to gain access to the ballot are lowered; and (2) the (support) threshold that must be passed to gain reimbursement decreases. Conversely, the more demanding these thresholds, the lower the expected incidence of contests. Setting these thresholds at zero would likely result in a very high incidence of contests, whereas setting them at a very high level would result in no change compared with the existing state of affairs. By moving the thresholds along the continuum in-between, the incidence of contests can be reduced or raised.

Thus, if election reform initially produces an increase in the incidence of contests that is deemed to be too high, the thresholds set in the default arrangement could be tightened. More importantly, because the proposed system would be a default, firms themselves would be able to tighten the default thresholds if their shareholders find the likelihood of a contest too high and therefore are willing to approve such tightening. Thus, as long as the existing incidence of electoral challenges is viewed as too low, the desirability of reform is not undermined by concerns that it will result in too many electoral challenges.

3.4.4.2 *Shareholders with Special Interests*

Increases in shareholder power are also opposed on grounds that they would be used by a shareholder or a shareholder group that has a 'special interest' not shared by other shareholders to advance this interest at the expense of long-term share value (Anabtawi 2006: 564–5; Lipton and Rosenblum 2003: 82–3). In this view, a shareholder might, for example, seek to protect labour interests, advance a 'social' agenda, or extract 'greenmail' benefits. The proposed reform, it might be argued, would enable shareholders with special interests to get one or more representatives on the board or to extract concessions from the board by threatening to mount challenges.

While the proposed reform would make it easier for directors not nominated by the board to be elected if they are supported by a majority of shareholders, directors still could not be elected without majority support. A slate proposed by a special-interest shareholder to advance its particular agenda would have no meaningful chance of obtaining the majority of votes necessary to be elected. Given the tendency of most money managers to focus on shareholder value and to support incumbents absent some strong reason to the contrary, a special-interest candidate would not be able to attract their votes.

The patterns of shareholder voting on shareholder precatory resolutions support this prediction. The only resolutions that systematically obtain majority support are those calling for changes that are viewed as value-enhancing by a wide range of financial institutions—such as destaggering the board or rescinding poison pills. In contrast, proposals that focus on social or special-interest issues uniformly fall far short of a majority. For example, in 2003, while precatory resolutions to expense options obtained an average of 46% support, precatory resolutions to abolish stock options obtained an average of only 6%, and precatory resolutions seeking to highlight the ratio of highest to lowest compensation paid by the company obtained an average of only 12% of shareholder votes (Georgeson Shareholder 2003: 7–8).

Another concern is that, by threatening to run a competing slate, special-interest shareholders would be able to obtain 'leverage' and pressure the board into actions that serve the special interest but not shareholder value; labour unions, for example, could, in this way, extract concessions for workers (Castellani and Goodman 2007). However, given that a labour union's candidates will generally be unable to win electoral contests, the electoral reform under consideration would not provide unions with any significant 'extortion' power. Indeed, because the threat to incumbents' continued service would come only from losing the support of a majority of the shareholders, the proposed reform would make boards more reluctant, not more willing, to take actions that serve the special interests of one shareholder or shareholder group at the expense of shareholder value.

3.4.4.3 *Bad Choices*

Reform may also be opposed on the grounds that shareholders seeking to enhance share value would still misuse any increase in their power to remove directors by making uninformed and poor choices. Shareholders, it might be argued, simply do not have the full information available to the board's nominating committee. Consequently, they could make bad choices, electing directors who would not be as well qualified as candidates selected by the board.

The question, however, is not whether board nominating committees or shareholders have better information about candidates. Granting that the former commonly have superior information does not resolve the issue at hand. First, however informed the members of board nomination committees are, they do not always have adequate incentives to replace fellow directors or themselves when desirable. Accountability is important precisely because, given the divergence between directors' and shareholders' interests, directors may choose not to act in a certain way even if they recognize that it would likely increase share value.

Furthermore, although institutional shareholders may not have the same information as the board, there is no reason to assume that they are unaware of the informational advantages possessed by the board and its nominating committee. Indeed, institutional shareholders usually display a substantial tendency to defer to boards. They would likely continue to display substantial deference to the board's choices after the adoption of the proposed reform. Thus, the question is whether shareholders, in the infrequent cases in which they prefer to do so, should have the real power not to elect the board's candidates.

In some cases, the past record of the incumbent directors might lead shareholders to conclude that they would be better off replacing some or all of the incumbents. Of course, shareholders may not always get it right. But given that their money is on the line, shareholders naturally have incentives to make the decision that best serves their interests. There is no reason to expect that choices they make in favour of a shareholder-nominated candidate are generally likely to be wrong. When circumstances convince shareholders to overcome their tendency to defer to the board, there is little basis for a paternalistic view of their choices as misguided.

3.4.4.4 *Short-Termism*

The strongest objection to election reform comes from concerns about short-termism. The fear of being replaced, it might be argued, could lead boards seeking to please shareholders to take actions that improve short-term results but are not optimal from a long-term perspective (Stein 1989: 655–6).

If this consideration is given sufficient weight, it should be taken into account in designing reform. This consideration weighs in favour of reducing the frequency of occasions in which shareholders have a viable power to replace directors. This consideration, therefore, might lead one to support having such occasions, say, only once every two or three years.

Thus, the short-termism concern might justify providing boards with periods of significant length during which they do not face a meaningful chance of ouster. But the short-termism concern cannot provide a basis for a system under which shareholders, however long they wait, never have real power to replace directors. While short-term insulation might induce directors to focus on long-term performance, indefinite insulation would enable boards to deviate from focusing on shareholder interests in both the short run and the long run.

3.4.4.5 *Deterring Directors from Serving*

The proposed reform, it might be argued, would deter some potentially good directors from serving on boards of publicly traded companies (Lipton and Rosenblum 2003: 82–3). In this view, some good candidates would not be willing to serve if they faced any meaningful prospect of a contested election or even removal when they stand for re-election.

Clearly, any position on the margin is more attractive (and, other things equal, easier to fill) if the holder of the position has complete security from removal. But most individuals occupying business positions are not granted security by their firms, even though doing so might well attract more job seekers and reduce the required level of compensation. In most cases, firms find that the benefits of retaining the power to replace employees—the ability to make desirable replacements and the provision of incentives to perform well—exceed the costs.

Because directors' use of their power and discretion can have major effects on corporate value, improving their selection and incentives is especially valuable. Thus, if reform would improve director selection and incentives, that consideration should be given much weight. Is there really no way to run our corporate system without granting the people at the top of the pyramid protection from any meaningful risk of removal?

Note that, even with reform, directors would face a rather small likelihood of removal relative to those holding other positions in the business world. Thus, it is far from clear that the proposed reform would have any meaningful adverse effect on the attractiveness of the well-paid and highly prestigious positions of directors. Even if reform did make these positions somewhat less attractive, shareholders could well be better off countering this effect with increased pay rather than with reduced accountability. Providing complete job security as a means of attracting directors is counterproductive.

3.4.4.6 *The UK Example*

In assessing the claims that a system in which shareholders have more power to replace or remove directors would have adverse effects, it is worth recognizing that the United Kingdom has long had such a system. Under mandatory UK rules, shareholders always have the power to replace all the directors, they may call a special meeting in order to do so, and they may place a candidate on the corporate ballot (Davies 1997: 188–93).

The UK experience disproves some of the doomsday scenarios suggested by those opposing reform of corporate elections in the United States. While the UK experience does not prove that such a reform would be positive on balance, it does undermine any warnings that reform would substantially undermine boards' and companies' ability to function.

There is no evidence that the UK system leads to contested elections being the norm, discourages good directors from serving, empowers special interests, or leads boards to pursue value-reducing strategies. Rather than lead to frequent contests, shareholders' greater power in the United Kingdom enables them to exert greater influence on boards and make boards more attentive to their interests and wishes. Indeed, a recent study of shareholder activism in the United Kingdom documents how large UK shareholders are able to use their power to influence companies to make changes that turn out to have significant value-increasing effects (see Becht et al., Chapter 7, this volume).

3.4.4.7 *Do Hedge Funds Make Election Reform Unnecessary?*

Recently, there has been a significant increase in 'activism' by hedge funds. A growing number of hedge funds have shown a willingness to acquire blocks in companies and press for changes in the company's strategy or governance. The funds have used an array of tactics, including mounting or threatening to mount a proxy contest. Recent work on hedge fund activism suggests that, relative to mutual funds, managers of hedge funds have stronger financial incentives to engage in such activism and do not face the same regulatory and conflict-of-interest problems (see Kahan and Rock, Chapter 5, this volume). Some writers question whether hedge funds' increased activism efforts would generate sufficient returns to be sustainable (Bratton 2007). Assuming that hedge funds' increased activism is here to stay, however, the question naturally arises whether it would make the proposed reform of corporate elections unnecessary. As explained in this subsection it would not.

Even with a well-functioning system of corporate elections, challenges would require a pool of players that are willing to hold a block of shares and make the effort involved in mounting a contest. Indeed, for any given set of rules, the larger this pool, the more contests will take place, other things being equal. A large number of activist hedge funds thus might well operate to increase the number of contests, but if it did not provide incumbents with large structural advantages it would not be a substitute for a well-functioning election system.

To begin, while hedge funds holding blocks might sometimes be willing to mount a contest even under the existing rules, the free-rider problem produced by these rules can be expected to lead them to underinvest in mounting such contests. A recent study reports that the median stake of a hedge fund engaged in 'aggressive' activist strategy is 6.6% of the target's outstanding shares (see Brav et al., Chapter 8, this volume). Under the existing rules governing corporate elections, a fund with a 6.6% stake would have to bear its full costs in mounting a contest while capturing only 6.6% of the aggregate benefits to the target's shareholders from the contest. In such circumstances, the prospect of appreciation in the value of the fund's stake would not be sufficient to induce it to mount a contest whenever such a contest would be beneficial for the target's shareholders.

This free-rider problem is especially likely to discourage contests in large-capitalization companies. The evidence indicates that hedge funds tend not to choose as targets for their activism firms in the top quintile in terms of market capitalization (see Brav et al., Chapter 8, this volume)—the companies whose effective governance is, practically, the most important for the economy's performance. In such companies, activist hedge funds might have difficulty committing sufficient capital to obtain a substantial stake that would enable them to capture a substantial fraction of the aggregate benefits to shareholders from a contest.

Activist hedge funds do not eliminate the need for the proposed rule providing reimbursement of challengers' costs, nor for my other proposals for reforming corporate elections. Even with the presence of active and highly incentivized players that might serve as potential challengers, a well-functioning election system requires that shareholders be able to replace all directors at some point in time and that shareholders be able to cast their votes by secret ballot; that, in the large majority of cases in which incumbents run uncontested, 'withhold' and 'against' votes are not ignored; and that incumbents do not control the choice of the corporate bylaws governing their own election.

The recent work on hedge fund activism documents that hedge funds' activist efforts are accompanied by increases in the market value of the target companies (see Brav et al., Chapter 8, this volume). Electoral reforms that increase shareholder power would likely increase the number of cases in which such benefits are produced directly as well as, perhaps most importantly, the number of cases in which the prospect of an electoral challenge would improve incumbents' performance in the first place. Overall, the expansion of the pool of potential challengers produced by activist hedge funds is a complement, not a substitute, for election reform. With an increased pool of players prepared to use a reformed system of corporate elections, such a reform is likely to begin producing significant benefits quickly.

3.4.4.8 *Invigorate the Market for Corporate Control Instead*

There are some who accept that boards are now insufficiently accountable but believe that a better mechanism for restoring accountability is the market for corporate control (Kroszner and Wallison 2004). On this view, instead of reforming corporate elections, we should dismantle the antitakeover defences that have been erected over the past two decades. A vigorous market for corporate control, it is argued, would be sufficient to discipline boards and ensure that they do not deviate from shareholder interests.

Although I support reforms that would eliminate antitakeover defences, I view such reforms as a complement to rather than as a substitute for reforming corporate elections. There are some types of board failure that could be more effectively disciplined by the prospect of a proxy fight than by a hostile takeover bid. Consider a board decision whether, say, to grant a CEO pushed out for bad performance an unwarranted golden goodbye in the form of extra payments not required by contract. Such a decision might produce some investor outrage that could hurt the board in a proxy contest, and the board might thus be deterred from making it under a system that facilitates contested elections. However, the decision might not reduce firm value enough to make a hostile takeover bid profitable. Even in a system that facilitates hostile bids, the takeover mechanism would be costly and thus triggered only in cases in which the bidder could make substantial profit from taking over the company.

Although the British City Code facilitates hostile takeovers by preventing incumbents from blocking hostile offers, UK law facilitates the removal of directors by shareholders via the ballot box much more than does US law. These two elements of UK law reinforce each other and both operate to make boards more accountable and more attentive to shareholder interests. The United States should follow a similar approach.

3.4.4.9 *Adverse Effects on Stakeholders*

Finally, increasing shareholder power may be opposed on the grounds that, even if it made directors more attentive to shareholder interests, it could well make them less attentive to stakeholder interests (Blair and Stout 1999). The board, it is argued, should take into account and balance all of the possibly competing interests of shareholders and other constituencies, such as creditors, employees, customers, and so forth. Indeed, it has been argued that it is in shareholders' *ex ante* interest to tie their own hands and let boards make decisions that will take into account the interests of stakeholders in order to induce the stakeholders to invest in their relationship with the firm (Blair and Stout 1999: 253–4).

Even if one fully accepts that it would be desirable to provide stakeholders with additional protections, whether as an end in itself or to serve shareholders' *ex ante* interests in inducing specific investments by stakeholders, it is far from clear that insulating boards from removal provides stakeholders with such protections. For one thing, there is little reason to expect that boards commonly use their discretion to serve stakeholder interests. Under existing rules, directors may sometimes take stakeholders' interests into account, but are generally not required to do so. Those who support insulating boards in order to serve stakeholders do not call for requiring boards to take stakeholder interests into account, but rather express hope that boards will do so.

The interests of directors are likely to be even less aligned with the interests of stakeholders than they are with the interests of shareholders. Whereas directors often hold shares and options, they do not usually have any instruments tying their wealth to that of bondholders, employees, suppliers, or other stakeholders. Thus, we can expect directors to be even less reliable agents for stakeholders than they currently are for shareholders. To be sure, directors may sometimes have self-serving reasons to favour a decision that serves stakeholders but not shareholders (such as rejecting an acquisition offer that would benefit shareholders but result in layoffs). But there is no systematic overlap between the interests of directors and stakeholders that could provide any basis for confidence that increased board discretion would commonly operate to benefit stakeholders.

Standard board practices do not generally reflect a conception of boards as an agent for both stakeholders and shareholders. The compensation schemes designed for officers and directors generally tie such compensation to shareholder wealth but not to stakeholder wealth. While equity-based plans and bonus plans based on financial performance are common, I know of no company that explicitly links the compensation of executives or directors to measures of stakeholders' interests, such as the average compensation paid to employees.

There is little reason to expect that reduced board accountability to shareholders will translate into increased attention to other stakeholders. Insulating boards from removal does not make them more accountable to stakeholders at the expense of accountability to shareholders. Rather, such insulation makes boards accountable to no one. Directors might use such lack of accountability to serve their own interests rather than to balance the interests of shareholders and stakeholders or give more weight to stakeholder interests. By protecting boards from removal even in the event of consistent poor performance, insulation from removal could well be costly to both shareholders and stakeholders.

3.5 Conclusion

The shareholder franchise is largely a myth. Shareholders commonly do not have a viable power to replace the directors of public companies. Electoral challenges are rare, and the risk of replacement via a proxy contest is extremely low. To restore accountability and place our corporate governance system on solid foundations, the shareholder franchise should be transformed from a myth into a reality. The reforms put forward in this chapter would provide shareholders with a viable power to replace directors. They would thereby improve the accountability and performance of corporate boards. Such reforms, which would benefit investors and the economy, are long overdue.

References

Anabtawi, I. (2006). Some Skepticism about Increasing Shareholder Power, *UCLA Law Review* 53, 561–99.

Bainbridge, S. M. (2006). Director Primacy and Shareholder Disempowerment, *Harvard Law Review* 119, 1735–58.

Bebchuk, L. A. (2004). Designing a Shareholder Access Rule, *Corporate Advisor* 12, 28–32.

Bebhcuk, L. A. and Cohen, A. (2005). The Costs of Entrenched Boards, *Journal of Financial Economics* 78, 409–33.

Bebchuk, L. A., Cohen, A., and Ferrell, A. (2009). What Matters in Corporate Governance?, *Review of Financial Studies* 22, 783–827.

Bertrand, M. and Mullainathan, S. (1998). Executive Compensation and Incentives: The Impact of Takeover Legislation, NBER Working Paper No. W6830, available at <http://ssrn.com/abstract=141883>.

Bertrand, M. and Mullainathan, S. (1999). Is There Discretion in Wage Setting? A Test Using Takeover Legislation, *RAND Journal of Economics* 30, 535–54.

Bertrand, M. and Mullainathan, S. (2001). Are CEOs Rewarded for Luck? The Ones Without Principals Are, *Quarterly Journal of Economics* 116, 901–32.

Blair, M. M. and Stout, L. A. (1999). A Team Production Theory of Corporate Law, *Virginia Law Review* 85, 247–328.

Borokhovich, K. A., Brunarski, K. R., and Parrino, R. (1997). CEO Contracting and Antitakeover Amendments, *Journal of Finance* 52, 1495–517.

Borstadt, L. F. and Zwirlein, T. J. (1992). The Efficient Monitoring Role of Proxy Contests: An Empirical Analysis of Post-Contest Control Changes and Firm Performance, *Journal of Financial Management* 21, 22–34.

Bratton, W. W. (2007). Hedge Funds and Governance Targets, *Georgetown Law Journal* 95, 1375–433.

Brickley, J. A., Lease, R. C., and Smith, C. W. (1988). Ownership Structure and Voting on Antitakeover Amendments, *Journal of Financial Economics* 20, 267–91.

Business Roundtable (2003). Detailed Comments of Business Roundtable on the 'Proposed Election Contest Rules' of the US Securities and Exchange Commission, Attachment to Letter from Henry A. McKinnell, Chairman, Business Roundtable, to Jonathan G. Katz, Secretary, SEC (22 Dec.).

Cai, J., Garner, J. L., and Walkling, R. A. (2009) Electing Directors, *Journal of Finance* 64, 2389–421.

Castellani, J. J. and Goodman, A. L. (2007). The Case against the SEC Director Election Proposal, in L. A. Bebchuk (ed.), *Shareholder Access to the Corporate Ballot* (Cambridge, MA, Harvard University Press).

Davies, P. L. (1997). *Gower's Principles of Modern Company Law* (6th edn.) (London, Sweet & Maxwell).

Davis, G. F. and Kim, E. H. (2007). Business Ties and Proxy Voting by Mutual Funds, *Journal of Financial Economics* 85, 552–70.

DeAngelo, A. and DeAngelo, L. (1989). Proxy Contests and the Governance of Publicly Held Corporations, *Journal of Financial Economics* 23, 29–59.

Dodd, P. and Warner, J. B. (1983). On Corporate Governance, A Study of Proxy Contents, *Journal of Financial Economics* 11, 401–38.

Faleye, O. (2007). Classified Boards, Firm Value, and Managerial Entrenchment, *Journal of Financial Economics* 83, 501–29.

Garvey, G. T. and Hanka, G. (1999). Capital Structure and Corporate Control: The Effect of Antitakeover Statutes on Firm Leverage, *Journal of Finance* 54, 519–46.

Georgeson Shareholder (2003). *Annual Corporate Governance Review: Shareholder Proposals and Proxy Contest*, available at <http://www.computershare-na.com/sharedweb/georgeson/acgr/acgr2003.pdf>.

Gompers, P., Ishii, J., and Metrick, A. (2003). Corporate Governance and Equity Prices, *Quarterly Journal of Economics* 118, 107–56.

Ikenberry, D. and Lakonishok, J. (1993). Corporate Governance through the Proxy Contest: Evidence and Implications, *Journal of Business* 66, 405–35.

Koppes, R. H., Ganske, L. G., and Haag, C. T. (1999). Corporate Governance Out of Focus: The Debate over Classified Boards, *Business Lawyer* 54, 1023–55.

Kroszner, R. and Wallison, P. (2004). Remarks at the SEC Roundtable on Proposed Security Holder Director Nominations Rules, available at <http://www.sec.gov/spotlight/dir-nominations/transcript03102004.txt>.

Lipton, M. and Rosenblum, S. A. (2003). Election Contests in the Company's Proxy: An Idea Whose Time Has Not Come, *Business Lawyer* 59, 67–94.

Masulis, R. W., Wang, C., and Xie, F. (2007). Corporate Governance and Acquirer Returns, *Journal of Finance* 62, 1851–89.

Mulherin, J. H. and Poulsen, A. B. (1998). Proxy Contests and Corporate Change: Implications for Shareholder Wealth, *Journal of Financial Economics* 47, 279–313.

Pozen, R. C. (1994). Institutional Investors: The Reluctant Activists, *Harvard Business Review* (Jan./Feb.), 140–9.

Pozen, R. C. (2003). Institutional Perspective on Shareholder Nominations of Corporate Directors, *Business Lawyer* 59, 95–108.

Romano, R. (2003). Does Confidential Proxy Voting Matter?, *Journal of Legal Studies* 32, 465–509.

Stein, J. C. (1989). Efficient Capital Markets, Inefficient Firms: A Model of Myopic Corporate Behavior, *Quarterly Journal of Economics* 104, 655–69.

CHAPTER 4

SHAREHOLDER ACTIVISM THROUGH PROXY PROPOSALS: THE EUROPEAN PERSPECTIVE

PETER CZIRAKI, LUC RENNEBOOG, AND PETER G. SZILAGYI

4.1 Introduction

Shareholders are the ultimate owners of public companies and should therefore have the final say in decisions such as corporate restructuring, changes in top management, payout policy, or governance structures. The proxy process is one of the means for shareholders to impose their (value-generating) suggestions. Some studies regard shareholder-initiated proxy proposals as a useful tool of corporate governance and the proposal sponsors as valuable monitoring agents (Bebchuk 2005; Harris and Raviv 2008; Renneboog and Szilagyi 2009). Others argue that the same proposals have no real control benefits due to their non-binding nature (Gillan and Starks 2000; Prevost and Rao 2000), and that the proponents either disrupt the board's authority unnecessarily or outright pursue their own self-serving agendas (Anabtawi 2006; Bainbridge 2006).

While shareholder proposals are rarely mentioned in the European context, the business press regularly cites prominent cases of dissenting shareholders targeting European firms. Activists ousted the chairman of African Platinum as the firm underperformed its industry peers (Bream 2006), and pushed Dutch banking giant ABN Amro into selling itself (Larsen 2007). In another well-known example, Acquisitor Holdings targeted the UK dotcom firm Baltimore Technologies. In March 2004, Acquisitor Holdings requisitioned an extraordinary general meeting to replace Baltimore's board of directors. Baltimore claimed that Acquisitor, which then owned 10% of its equity, was opportunistically trying to drive down its share price in a bid to increase its ownership stake (Stewart 2004). However, Acquisitor pointed out that Baltimore had accumulated trading losses of over £1 billion through its poor acquisition strategy, and even launched a website criticizing the CEO (Shah 2004a). Leading up to the meeting on 6 May, the battle continued in the press. Baltimore revealed plans to transform into a green energy firm and labelled Acquisitor a vulture fund but subsequently apologized (Harrison 2004). In response, Acquisitor called the green energy concept 'outrageous' and increased its stake to over 16% (Boxell 2004a). At the meeting, Baltimore directors survived a knife-edge vote as shareholders, many of whom had lost personal fortunes, were unhappy with the plans of both Baltimore and Acquisitor (Boxell 2004b). In his statement to the press, Baltimore's chairman struck a cordial tone when he called for cooperation with Acquisitor and invited negotiations to be conducted privately (Smyth 2004). As the firm's annual general meeting in July approached, management abandoned the clean energy plan, placing the blame on Acquisitor for a failed takeover (Wendlandt 2004), and proposed to pay shareholders a special dividend (Klinger 2004). Acquisitor, which by then had increased its ownership stake to over 25%, successfully blocked the dividend payout (Shah 2004b). The power struggle ended at the meeting, where Acquisitor replaced management with its own nominees (Nuttall 2004).

These and other notable cases of shareholder proposals show that European shareholders view the proxy process as a viable tool for expressing dissent and disciplining management. However, it is clear that US lessons on the corporate governance role of shareholder proposals may not be readily applicable in the European context. First, proposals in the US are non-binding even if they pass the shareholder vote, whereas they are legally binding in the UK and in most of Continental Europe. Second, the laws and regulations governing shareholder access to the proxy vary considerably across countries, thereby affecting the incentives of and costs borne by the proponent shareholders. And third, the market-oriented Anglo-American model of corporate governance is very different from the stakeholder-oriented regimes of Continental Europe. La Porta et al. (1998) show, and Martynova and Renneboog (2008) confirm, that minority shareholders enjoy much better protection under US and UK common law, with Continental European firms often violating the one share-one vote rule by issuing multiple classes of stock, setting up pyramids, or engaging in cross-shareholdings.[1] In Continental Europe, corporate ownership is also more concentrated (Barca and Becht 2001; Faccio and Lang 2002), and while banks are predominantly passive investors in the US, they actively engage in proxy voting in countries such as Germany (Franks and Mayer 2001). Finally, major creditors and employees are often given board representation in Continental Europe, which implies conflicts of interest between the board and outside shareholders (Roe 2004).

This chapter is the first to investigate the corporate governance role of shareholder proposals across Europe, using a sample of 290 proposals submitted in nine countries between 1998 and 2008. While Buchanan, Netter, and Yang (2010) provide an elaborate comparison of proposal submissions in the US versus the UK, our analysis also includes Continental Europe, which is both very different from a corporate governance perspective and quite diverse in itself.

We simultaneously investigate the selection of target firms and proposal success in terms of the voting outcomes and the stock price effects, and make several contributions to the literature. First, compared to the US, proposal submissions remain relatively infrequent in Continental Europe in particular. In the UK, proposals typically relate to a proxy

[1] See also Goergen and Renneboog (2004) and Martynova and Renneboog (2011).

contest seeking personal changes on the board to force a change in corporate strategy. In Continental Europe, the proposal objectives are more focused on specific governance issues, corresponding to the conventional use of shareholder proposals in the US.

Second, we show that the target firms tend to underperform as well as have low leverage, which Jensen (1986) regards as a remedy for free cash flow problems. This coincides with the results of Renneboog and Szilagyi (2009) for the US, and provides some indication that the activists sponsoring proposal submissions are valuable monitors. There is also evidence that the proposal sponsors observe the identity of the voting shareholders, to the extent that proposal probability increases in the target firm's ownership concentration as well as the equity stake of institutional investors.

Third, we find that shareholder proposals enjoy relatively modest voting success in both the UK and Continental Europe. The voting outcomes are most fundamentally driven by the issue addressed, and are strongest for proposals that seek personal changes on the board and therefore indicate major governance concerns. However, they are also affected by the characteristics of the target firm, most notably the extent to which the CEO is incentivized through stock-based pay to protect shareholder interests.

Finally, we find that, irrespective of the proposal objectives, the shareholder vote on proposal submissions induces significantly negative stock price effects. This suggests that, rather than attribute them control benefits, the market interprets proposals and their failure to pass the shareholder vote as a negative signal of governance concerns. Indeed, consistent with agency considerations, the market responds better to proposals submitted against large firms with low leverage. However, the stock price effects are more negative for poorly performing firms with low market-to-book ratios and ill-incentivized CEOs, which indicates that unsuccessful shareholder attempts to exert discipline only exacerbate governance concerns.

The remainder of this chapter proceeds as follows. Section 4.2 provides an overview of the theoretical and empirical literature on shareholder activism through the proxy process. Section 4.3 discusses the corporate governance structures of the US, the UK, and Continental Europe, and describes the country-specific laws and regulations governing shareholder initiated proxy proposals. Section 4.4 provides a description of our sample and investigates proposal success in terms of the voting outcomes and stock price effects. In Section 4.5 we use sample selection models to perform a multivariate analysis of both target selection and proposal success. Finally, Section 4.6 allows for some concluding remarks.

4.2 The Literature on Shareholder Activism through the Proxy Process

The separation of ownership and control in publicly listed firms gives rise to agency problems (Jensen and Meckling 1976), which shareholders of the firm can seek to resolve in several ways. Gillan and Starks (Chapter 2, this volume) place shareholder activism on a continuum of responses that dissatisfied investors can give to corporate governance concerns. At one extreme of the continuum, shareholders can simply vote with their feet by selling their shares (Admati and Pfleiderer 2006; Parrino, Sias, and Starks 2003). At the other extreme is the market for corporate control, where investors initiate takeovers and buyouts to bring about fundamental changes (Jensen and Ruback 1983). The role of shareholder activism arises when shareholders continue to hold their shares and seek changes within the firm without a change in control. These investors may then press for corporate reforms by negotiating with management behind the scenes, or—especially when management is unresponsive—by submitting proposals for shareholder vote. Armour (2008) views this process as a private and informal enforcement mechanism, with private and formal mechanisms comprising lawsuits and litigation, and public mechanisms initiated by public bodies.

Bebchuk (2005) and Harris and Raviv (2008) advocate shareholder participation in corporate governance, and argue that proxy proposals are a useful and relevant means of mitigating managerial agency problems. However, Prevost and Rao (2000) point out that, even if they pass the shareholder vote, proxy proposals are likely to be ineffective in disciplining management because they are non-binding in the US under the SEC's Rule 14a-8. The authors add that proposal submissions often convey a negative signal of failed negotiations with management, because institutional activists often try to negotiate behind the scenes and only sponsor proposals as a last resort. The main argument offered against shareholder proposals is that the sponsoring shareholders are likely to pursue their own self-serving agendas (Anabtawi 2006; Prevost, Rao, and Williams 2008; Woidtke 2002) or be simply too uninformed to make effective governance decisions (Lipton 2002; Stout 2007). Bainbridge (2006) goes as far as claiming that proposal submissions should be restricted by the SEC, because they do more damage than good by disrupting the decision-making authority of the board of directors. Notwithstanding, the theoretical results of Harris and Raviv (2008) show that shareholders should have control over corporate decisions, even though they are at an informational disadvantage, and even if their goals differ from maximizing the value of the company.

4.2.1 The Role of Shareholder Proposals in the US

The empirical US literature finds considerable evidence that shareholder proposals should be regarded as a useful governance tool and the proposal sponsors as valuable monitoring agents. Recent studies confirm that proposal submissions exert pressure on the target firms despite their non-binding nature, because as many as 40% of the proposals that win a majority vote end up being implemented (Bizjak and Marquette 1998; Ertimur, Ferri, and Stubben 2010; Martin and Thomas 1999; Thomas and Cotter 2007). Ertimur, Ferri, and Stubben (2010) show that targets ignoring passed proposals are penalized by drawing negative press and downgrades by governance rating firms, and that their directors are less likely to be re-elected and more likely to lose other directorships.[2]

Other studies find that the proposal sponsors tend to have the 'correct' objective of disciplining management, and, as such, claims of their agenda-seeking are exaggerated. Early studies report that proposal submissions tend to be directed at large, poorly performing firms (Karpoff, Malatesta, and Walkling 1996; Martin and Thomas 1999). Renneboog and

[2] Del Guercio et al. (2008) find that dissatisfied activists often target director elections with 'just vote no' campaigns.

Szilagyi (2009) add that the targets tend to be under-levered as well as have generally poor governance structures. Smith (1996) shows that the proposal sponsors also consider the identity of voting shareholders before deciding whether or not to submit proxy proposals, because the targets tend to have high institutional and low insider ownership.

The literature confirms that the target firm's governance quality is also observed by the voting shareholders. Gillan and Starks (Chapter 2, this volume) find that the voting results are mostly driven by the proposal objectives and the sponsoring shareholders. However, Ertimur, Ferri, and Stubben (2010) and Renneboog and Szilagyi (2009) show that, irrespective of the issue addressed, proposals draw more voting support if the target has heavily entrenched managers and ineffective boards. Cremers and Romano (2011) report that the identity of the voting shareholders is also relevant. On one hand, voting support increases in institutional and decreases in insider ownership. On the other, insurance firms and banks' trust departments are less likely to vote in favour of shareholder proposals than are other institutional investors. Brickley, Lease, and Smith (1988) and Pound (1988) regard these investors as pressure-sensitive due to their existing or potential business relationships with the firms they invest in, which increases the risk of conflicted voting.

The US literature examines the stock price effects of shareholder proposals around the dates the proxy statements are mailed (Bhagat 1983; Bhagat and Brickley 1984). Early event studies find no evidence that the market recognizes shareholder proposals as a relevant control mechanism (Bizjak and Marquette 1998; Del Guercio and Hawkins 1999; Karpoff, Malatesta, and Walkling 1996; Prevost and Rao 2000; Thomas and Cotter 2007). However, Renneboog and Szilagyi (2009) find that proposal announcements are actually met with significantly positive stock price reactions, which are sensitive to the proposal objectives but are most fundamentally driven by the target firm's past performance and quality of governance structures.

4.2.2 The Role of Shareholder Proposals in Europe

Shareholder activism through the proxy process is seldom discussed in the European corporate governance literature. Becht et al. (Chapter 7, this volume) examine the activist strategies of a single institutional investor, the Hermes UK Focus Fund. The study shows that, similar to US funds, Hermes rarely submits proxy proposals for shareholder vote, instead negotiating successfully with management behind the scenes. The authors attribute this to management concerns of the fund requisitioning an extraordinary general meeting, with the looming prospect of a proxy fight. While Klein and Zur (Chapter 9, this volume) make a similar point for the US, this threat is even larger in the UK where passed proposals are legally binding, and shareholders can remove directors by an ordinary resolution.

Results of a recent survey by McCahery, Starks, and Sautner (2009) show that the types of corrective actions considered by most US and Dutch institutional investors are selling shares (80%), voting against the company at the annual meeting (66%), and initiating a discussion with the executive board (55%). Their findings, similarly to Becht et al. (Chapter 7, this volume) suggest that institutions use a wide range of measures to impact the firm's decisions, some of which take place behind the scenes, unnoticed by the market.

Buchanan, Netter, and Yang (2010) are the first to perform a comparison of US and UK proposal submissions. The authors find that the target firms tend to be poorly performing in both countries, but report systematic differences in the proposal objectives, the sponsor identities, and the voting outcomes. An important insight of the paper is that UK proposals draw more voting support, especially when they target personal changes on the board, and that they are often implemented even if they are later withdrawn. However, subsequent performance improvements are only detected in US firms, as measured by profitability, dividend payout, leverage, and stock price effects.

Girard (2009) is the only study to discuss the governance role of shareholder proposals in Continental Europe, by investigating activist strategies in France. The author examines the success rate of behind-the-scenes negotiations, targeting firms through the media, proposal submissions, and civil law suits. The results show that launching lawsuits is the preferred method of activists engaging firms over governance concerns, and that this particularly aggressive strategy is also more likely to succeed than other forms of activism, including the submission of proxy proposals.

Previous studies report no evidence at all of the corporate governance role of shareholder proposals in Continental Europe. An interesting study by De Jong, Mertens, and Roosenboom (2006) examines the proposals presented to shareholders at the general meetings of Dutch firms. The authors find that, during their sample period, all proposals put to shareholder vote were in fact sponsored by the board of directors. Furthermore, the number of votes cast against these submissions was negligible, with only 9 out of 1,583 proposals either rejected or withdrawn.

Overall, the literature is clearly incomplete on the extent to which the proxy process is accessible to European shareholders as a disciplinary device, and if so, whether proposal submissions are useful and effective in mitigating corporate governance concerns. The available evidence implies considerable variation across Europe in this regard, as is discussed in the following sections of this chapter.

4.3 The Regulatory Environment in European Countries

The corporate governance role of shareholder proposals should heavily depend: (i) on the extent to which laws and regulations support shareholder access to the proxy process; and (ii) the rules and practicalities of proxy solicitation. We now assess the differences in this regard across European countries.

4.3.1 Shareholder Access to the Proxy Process

A key difference in the legal treatment of shareholder proposals between the US and Europe is that while passed proposals are only advisory in nature in the US, they are legally binding in the UK and most of Continental Europe, except the Netherlands. The corporate governance laws and best practices of European countries generally recognize that, in order to protect their interests, minority shareholders must be provided with access to general meetings as well as the right to submit proxy proposals for shareholder vote. Nonetheless, the provisions governing shareholder access to the proxy typically remain stringent compared to the US. US shareholders are not allowed to call extraordinary meetings unless the corporate charter or bylaws allow otherwise. However, shareholders owning 1% of the voting shares or $1,000 in market value may submit proxy proposals for shareholder vote.

Table 4.1 provides an overview of the legal requirements for submitting proxy proposals and convening extraordinary meetings in nine European countries. The table shows that the required voting capital varies considerably across countries. In the UK, shareholders owning no less than 5% of the firm's issued share capital may submit proposals to be voted upon at a general meeting. Alternatively, a group of at least 100 shareholders, each with no less than £100 invested, may also put forward a proposal. To call an extraordinary meeting, the support of at least 10% of the voting capital is required.

France is somewhat more lenient than the UK in that shareholders owning 5% of the voting capital may both submit proposals and call extraordinary meetings. This ownership requirement is gradually reduced with the increase of capital, to 4% between €750,000 and €4.5 million; 3% between €4.5 million and €7.5 million; 2% between €7.5 million and €15 million; and 1% over €15 million. A noteworthy provision of the French Commercial Code is that even though a meeting can only deliberate on items on its agenda, 'it may nevertheless remove one or more directors or supervisory board members from office and replace them, in any circumstances'.[3] Shareholders entitled to change the agenda of a meeting may also demand that a representative appointed by the court convene the meeting.[4]

The German Stock Corporation Act (*Aktiengesetz*) provides that new agenda items and extraordinary meetings can be set by shareholders owning a minimum 5% of the voting capital. However, any shareholder may add a proposal to the existing items of a meeting's agenda, thus the proposal sponsors often include even university professors.[5] The similar Austrian *Aktiengesetz* also provides that general meetings can be called by shareholders owning at least 5% of the voting capital, but proposals can be submitted by those owning 1% or €70,000 of capital.[6]

The Norwegian Code of Practice for Corporate Governance requires firms to inform all shareholders in the notice of the general meeting about their right 'to propose resolutions in respect of matters to be dealt with by the general meeting'. Shareholders owning at least 5% of the issued share capital have the right to convene an extraordinary meeting.

In the Netherlands, 10% or more of the voting capital is needed to requisition an extraordinary meeting. Proposals may be submitted by shareholders with a stake of at least 1% or €50 million of the firm's shares and certificates.[7] However, only management or the

[3] Commercial Code/Book II title II chapter V section III Article L225-105 and L225-120.

[4] Commercial Code/Book II title II chapter V section III Article L225-103; 2001 May.

[5] Ekkehard Wenger and Leonhard Knoll, both from the *Julius-Maximilians Universität Würzburg*. Knoll sponsored fifty-four of the sample proposals, either alone or jointly with Wenger.

[6] The Austrian *Aktiengesetz* also provides that when a meeting is convened by a shareholder, whether the costs are to be borne by the firm or the shareholder will be decided at the meeting.

[7] Dutch certificates are tradable depository receipts, issued at the initiative of the supervisory board, that carry cash flow rights but no voting rights. They are designed to replace ordinary shares, which are then deposited with the issuer, the administration office. The administration office takes over all voting rights on the retired shares, thus typically taking a voting majority in the firm. It is always friendly to the management board, and is run by members of the supervisory and/or management boards as well as outside individuals.

Table 4.1 Statutory requirements on requisitioning an extraordinary general meeting and putting forward a proposal (placing an item on the agenda) at a general meeting

This table presents the regulatory requirements for extraordinary general meetings and shareholder proposals for the countries in our sample. *LLSV origin* is the legal origin of the country according to La Porta et al. (1998). *Extraordinary general meeting* lists the percentage ownership needed to requisition an extraordinary general meeting. *Proposal* is the percentage ownership required to place a proposal on the agenda of a general meeting. *Call general meeting* shows the deadline for the firm to announce a general meeting. *Submit proposal* contains the deadline for shareholders to put forward a proposal for a general meeting.

Country	LLSV origin	EGM	Remark	Proposal	Remark	Call GM	Submit proposal
Austria	German	5%		5%		at least 14 days before the GM	at least 7 days before GM
France	French	0.5–5%	this fraction can demand the appointment of a court representative to convene an EGM	0.5–5%	decreasing in company size	A 'notice of the GM' at least 30 days before the GM. A 'notice of call' at least 15 days before the GM, with same information as the 'notice of the GM' and any modifications to the agenda and/or the proposals.	at least 25 days before the GM
Germany	German	5%		5% or share ownership of €500,000 in nominal value any shareholder if related to already existing agenda items		20 full days before	1 week after publication of notice
Netherlands	French	10%		1% or share ownership of €50 million in market value		at least 15 days before	in writing, at least 60 days before GM

Norway	Scandinavian	5%		any shareholder		at least 14 days before, but the articles may set a longer/shorter period	
Portugal	French	5%		5%		at least 30 days, or 21 if notification is by registered mail	within 5 days of the convocation of the GM
Russia	Other	10%		2%	specific to sample firm		within 30 days after the end of the fiscal year
Switzerland	German	10%		share ownership of ₣1 million in market value	firm-specific information also available for our sample	two notices, the first at least 20 days before	at least 60 days before GM
UK	English	10%		5% or a group of at least 100 shareholders with shares on which at least £100 has been paid up, on average	automatically if it was the shareholder who convened the GM	21 days for an AGM or 14 days if an extraordinary resolution is voted upon	6 weeks before the GM or, if later, the time at which notice of the meeting is given

supervisory board may propose resolutions on certain topics, including amendments to the articles of association, share issues and subscription rights, asset sales, and the dissolution of the firm itself. Furthermore, provisions of the articles of association that limit the general meeting's power to amend the articles may only be altered by a unanimous decision of a general meeting where 100% of the share capital is represented.

In Switzerland, shareholders must own ₣1 million of the issued share capital to place a resolution on the meeting agenda, unless the articles of association specify otherwise. In line with the recommendations of the Swiss Corporate Governance Code, large firms such as UBS and Novartis have lowered this threshold, with the minimum ownership requirement often less than 0.1%. To convene an extraordinary meeting, a petition submitted by shareholders owning no less than 10% of the share capital is required.

Finally, while governance standards in Russia are gradually improving, the resolution of disputes between management and minority shareholders is complicated by institutional loopholes and weaknesses in the protection of shareholder rights. Nonetheless, shareholders with 2% or more of the voting stock can propose items for the agenda of a general meeting, while 10% of the voting stock is required to convene an extraordinary meeting.

4.3.2 Proxy Solicitation and Corporate Ownership

An important consideration likely to affect proposal submissions is that the sponsoring activist must seek the support of other shareholders. The European Commission (2006) points out that the rules and formalities for proxy solicitation vary considerably within Europe. In the UK, the solicitation request would be included in the proxy documents and distributed to all shareholders at no major cost to the activist. In other countries, the solicitation of proxies at the firm's expense is prohibited, so the production and distribution costs of the solicitation request are borne by the activist (European Commission 2006).

Manifest (2008) finds that for large firms, shareholder participation at annual meetings is fairly consistent across European countries, at 55.5% of the voting capital in France, 54.8% in Germany, and 61.8% in the UK. However, the European Commission (2006) adds that the attendance rate of the free float tends to be low in Continental Europe, at 10.1% in Germany and 17.5% in France compared with 53.2% in the UK. There are many reasons why shareholders would be prevented or discouraged from voting in Continental Europe in particular. First, meeting attendance is often hindered by the late availability or incompleteness of meeting-related information, resolutions in summary form, and overly short notice periods. Second, national regulations in some countries make proxy voting unduly cumbersome and prohibitively costly, with stringent restrictions on who and how may be appointed as a proxy. And third, many jurisdictions maintain the practice of share blocking, whereby shareholders must deposit their shares for a few days before general meetings to be able to vote. Share blocking exists to ensure that those who show up to vote are actually shareholders on the day of the vote. However, it is very costly for shareholders, as it prevents them from negotiating shares up to weeks in advance of general meetings.[8]

[8] See European Commission (2006), DSW (2008), and Manifest (2008) for detailed discussions.

In terms of proxy solicitation, it is an important fact that while large US firms tend to have widely dispersed ownership structures, ownership is slightly more concentrated in the UK and considerably more concentrated in Continental Europe. Goergen and Renneboog (2001) find that in the average UK firm, eight or more shareholders must join forces to attain a majority vote, which renders it fairly difficult to forge voting coalitions. Nonetheless, Becht and Mayer (2001) find that, at 10%, the typical voting block in the UK is twice the size of that in the US.

The largest voting blocks in Continental Europe tend to be even larger, ranging from 20% on average in France to 44% in the Netherlands and 57% in Germany.[9] These are often accumulated through pyramidal ownership structures, with approximately 40% of the largest firms held through pyramids in Austria, France, and Germany. Continental European firms also often deviate from the one share-one vote rule by issuing multiple classes of stock, granting multiple voting rights, and introducing voting right ceilings. In France, for example, it is possible to establish a double voting right for registered shares that have been held for two years. DSW (2008) finds that such structures are allowed across Continental Europe, except a few countries such as Austria, Germany and Norway, while they are virtually absent in the US and the UK.

Becht (2001) finds that the blockholders of US firms tend to be managers or directors, followed by institutional investors. Institutional investors are likely to support shareholder-initiated proposal submissions, although they are often passive or simply tend to vote with their feet. Insider blockholdings should clearly reduce the probability that a proposal is submitted or later passes the shareholder vote. On one hand, managers and directors are unlikely to cast their votes in favour of a shareholder proposal. On the other, insider ownership should help realign insider and shareholder interests, thereby mitigating the expropriation concerns of minority shareholders.

In the UK, institutional investors are the most important corporate owners, and they tend to be as passive as their US counterparts. Goergen and Renneboog (2001) point out that this often lends considerable power to the board of directors. On one hand, the proxy votes not exercised by shareholders are controlled by the board. On the other, directors themselves are the second largest blockholders in UK firms.

Faccio and Lang (2002) find that while 63% of UK firms can be regarded as being widely held, 50–60% of Continental European firms are effectively owned by families. In addition, many large firms are controlled by banks and holding companies. While banks tend not to hold significant equity in US and UK firms, they control 15% of the largest firms in Germany and Portugal, and 5% in France and Switzerland (La Porta et al. 1999). Goergen and Renneboog (2001) point out that, in Germany, the effective voting power of banks extends well beyond their ownership stakes, because they tend to engage in proxy voting such that they exercise the voting rights on the shares deposited with them. Nibler (1998) reports that, in Germany, listed firms Deutsche Bank, Dresdner Bank, and Commerzbank have an overall equity stake of 6.8% on average, but control another 14.4% of the votes through proxies.

[9] The average market capitalization of the top ten non-financial firms is considerably lower in Europe compared to the US. Within Europe, the top firms are twice as large in the UK than in Continental Europe (La Porta et al. 1998).

4.4 Sample Description and Univariate Analysis of Proposal Objectives, Voting Outcomes, and Stock Price Effects

We investigate the corporate governance role of shareholder proposals in Europe using submissions reported by the Manifest database. The database contains a total of 720 proposals. However, the voting outcomes are only reported for 290 proposals in Manifest, articles compiled by the Factiva database, and corporate filings.[10] Of these, 195 were submitted in the UK at a total of sixty-two general meetings of forty firms between 1998 and 2008. The remaining ninety-five proposals were submitted between 2005 and 2008 at twenty-eight general meetings of twenty-three firms in Austria, France, Germany, the Netherlands, Norway, Portugal, Russia, and Switzerland.

We collect accounting and stock price data for the target firms from Compustat and Datastream. Ownership information is gathered from Manifest and Bureau van Dijk. We use the Manifest Governance database and Thomson ONE Banker to obtain information on governance structures, including board composition and CEO ownership and remuneration.

Preliminary analysis of the 720 submissions reported by Manifest shows that shareholder proposals are submitted less frequently in the UK and Continental Europe than in the US. Table 4.2 compares the frequency of proposal submissions using the US data reported by

Table 4.2 Shareholder proposals by geographic location and stock market size

This table shows the absolute and the relative number of shareholder proposals submitted in the UK, Continental Europe, and the US. Information on the number of listed companies, traded stock value, and market capitalization is obtained from the World Bank's World Development Indices. Data on US proposals are from Renneboog and Szilagyi (2009).

				Proposals per year		
Region	Year	Number of Proposals	Proposals per year	per listed company	per USD trillion of traded stock value	per USD trillion of market capitalization
UK	1998–2008	362	32.9	0.0140	8.39	11.4
Continental Europe	2005–08	358	89.5	0.0117	5.80	7.19
US	1996–2005	2,792	279.2	0.0407	14.56	20.31

[10] The dissemination of the voting results is not compulsory in many European countries including Belgium, France, Ireland, the Netherlands, Poland, and the UK. Manifest (2008) reports that it has been best practice historically in the UK, with the disclosure rate at 96% among the FTSE 250 firms. In Continental Europe, it has only recently become common practice even for the largest firms, with the disclosure rate increasing between 2005 and 2007 from 51% to 100% for the CAC 100 firms in France, and from 68% to 88% for the AEX 25 firms in the Netherlands.

Renneboog and Szilagyi (2009) for the period between 1996 and 2005. We find that, normalized by the size of the stock markets as reported by the World Bank, the number of proposals is 3–4 times as high in the US per publicly listed firm, and approximately twice as high per traded stock value and market capitalization. This implies that, on the whole, shareholder proposals play a lesser role in European corporate governance.

4.4.1 Proposal Objectives

Table 4.3 provides an overview of the 290 proposals for which the voting outcomes are available by the issue addressed, the year of submission, and whether the target firm was from the UK or Continental Europe. We classify the proposal objectives into nine mutually exclusive categories: (i) election or removal of directors; (ii) corporate governance issues; (iii) pro-management loosening of corporate governance; (iv) asset restructuring; (v) capital structure; (vi) payout policy; (vii) corporate social responsibility; (vii) routine issues related to the general meeting; and (ix) other miscellaneous issues.

Table 4.3 shows that 139 out of the 290 sample proposals related to a proxy contest seeking the election or removal of board members in order to trigger corporate changes. The number of proposals targeting directors was particularly high in the UK in the latter half of the sample period, with 24 submissions up to 2003, and 105 thereafter. Buchanan, Netter, and Yang (2010) point out that this is unsurprising, because UK shareholders can replace the board with their own nominees by a simple majority vote.

While two-thirds of the UK proposals targeted the board directly, sixty-five of the ninety-five proposals submitted in Continental Europe were directed at corporate governance issues. Several of these related to board quality and shareholder rights. However, twenty-seven of the proposals sought to exert discipline retrospectively by calling for a special audit on past matters. In the UK, governance issues were targeted by a total of twenty-one proposals.

It is notable that five of the Continental European submissions favoured management or the board rather than shareholders, and therefore sought to reinforce rather than discipline corporate insiders. These included three proposals (including a resubmission) to limit the number of mandates for directors representing shareholders, one to waive claims against directors, and a counterproposal on calling a special audit.

Of the remaining proposals, twenty-one related to corporate social responsibility issues such as employee rights, contacts with customers, and environmental matters. These were submitted almost exclusively in the UK, with only three submissions made in Continental Europe. There were a total of eleven proposals seeking asset restructuring, fifteen calling for payout policy changes, seven proposals submitted in the UK targeted capital structure issues, and five were directed at routine issues associated with the time and location of general meetings.

4.4.2 Voting Outcomes

Table 4.4 provides an overview of the voting outcomes and the number of proposals that actually passed the shareholder vote, by the issue addressed, the year of submission, and whether the target firm was from the UK or Continental Europe.

Table 4.3 Shareholder proposals by issue addressed, geographic location, and year of submission

This table shows the number of shareholder proposals in the UK and in Continental Europe by the year of submission and the issue addressed.

	UK												Continental Europe					
	1998	1999	2000	2001	2002	2003	2004	2005	2006	2007	2008	Total by issue		2005	2006	2007	2008	Total by issue
Elect/remove	–	11	–	1	10	2	37	16	19	27	6	129	Elect/remove	–	–	5	5	10
Elect director	–	4	–	1	4	1	10	6	14	15	3	58	*Elect director*	–	–	3	2	5
Remove director	–	7	–	–	6	1	27	10	5	12	3	71	*Remove director*	–	–	2	3	5
Corporate governance	2	2	3	2	3	1	2	1	–	2	3	21	Corporate governance	1	5	31	34	65
Reduce director power	–	–	–	–	–	–	–	–	–	1	2	3	*Reduce director power*	–	–	1	–	1
Director independence	–	–	1	–	–	–	–	–	–	–	–	1	*Board size*	–	–	2	–	2
Director ownership	–	–	–	–	–	–	1	–	–	–	–	1	*Board liability*	–	–	3	–	3
Board liability	–	–	–	–	–	–	1	–	–	–	–	1	*Age limit for directors*	–	–	2	–	2
Board representation	–	–	–	1	–	–	–	–	–	–	–	1	*Elect committee/special representative*	–	2	–	6	8
Enfranchise non-voting Shares	–	1	1	–	1	–	–	–	–	–	–	3	*Shareholder right to comment*	–	–	2	–	2

Reincorporation in US	–	–	–	–	–	1	–	–	–	–	–	1	*Special audit*	–	1	12	14	27
Convene EGM	1	–	–	1	–	–	–	–	–	–	–	2	*Verbatim minutes*	–	–	2	2	4
Remove auditor	–	–	–	–	–	–	–	–	–	1	–	1	*Voting issues*	1	–	3	1	5
Other	1	1	1	–	2	–	–	1	–	–	1	7	*Other*	–	2	4	5	11
Corporate governance–Loosening	–	–	–	–	–	–	–	–	–	–	–	–	Corporate governance–loosening	–	–	2	3	5
													Waive board liability	–	–	–	1	1
													Limit shareholder representation	–	–	2	1	3
													Counterproposal–special audit	–	–	–	1	1
Asset restructuring	–	–	1	3	1	–	–	–	1	–	1	7	Asset restructuring	–	–	3	1	4
Capital structure	4	–	–	–	–	–	–	–	–	3	–	7	Capital structure	–	–	–	–	–
Payout policy	–	2	1	4	4	–	–	–	–	–	–	11	Payout policy	–	1	2	1	4
Corporate social responsibility	–	1	2	2	1	1	4	2	2	2	1	18	Corporate social responsibility	–	–	3	–	3
Routine	–	–	–	1	1	–	–	–	–	–	–	2	Routine	–	–	3	–	3
Other	–	–	–	–	–	–	–	–	–	–	–	–	Other	–	–	1	–	1
Total by year	6	16	7	13	20	4	43	19	22	34	11	195	Total by year	1	6	50	38	95

Table 4.4 Percentage of votes *for* shareholder proposals and the number of passed proposals

This table shows the mean percentage of votes cast in favour of shareholder proposals grouped by the issue addressed, year of submission, and geographic region. The first number in parentheses indicates the number of passed proposals. The second number in parentheses stands for the total number of proposals submitted.

	UK												Continental Europe				
	1998	1999	2000	2001	2002	2003	2004	2005	2006	2007	2008	Total by issue	2005	2006	2007	2008	Total by issue
Elect/remove	–	29.3	–	18.9	23.3	19.5	54.2	38.6	42.1	25.2	30.6	38	–	–	44.8	48.2	46.5
	–	(0/11)	–	(0/1)	(0/10)	(0/2)	(30/37)	(4/16)	(8/19)	(3/27)	(0/6)	(45/129)	–	–	(2/5)	(1/5)	(3/10)
Elect director	–	29.1	–	18.9	21.2	35.3	60.9	34.3	38.8	28.8	29.1	36.8	–	–	72.7	69.6	71.5
	–	(0/4)	–	(0/1)	(0/4)	(0/1)	(10/10)	(1/6)	(4/14)	(3/15)	(0/3)	(18/58)			(2/3)	(1/2)	(0/5)
Remove director	–	29.4	–	–	24.7	3.7	51.6	41.2	51.4	20.8	32	39.5	–	–	3	33.9	21.5
	–	(0/7)	–	–	(0/6)	(0/1)	(20/26)	(3/10)	(4/5)	(0/12)	(0/3)	(27/70)			(0/2)	(0/3)	(0/5)
Corporate governance	14.5	17	22.1	9.1	14.6	10.8	3	1.9	–	3.1	66	19.7	7.3	39.4	8.9	18.8	15.5
	(0/2)	(0/2)	(0/3)	(0/2)	(0/3)	(0/1)	(0/2)	(0/1)	–	(0/2)	(3/3)	(3/21)	(0/1)	(2/5)	(2/31)	(3/28)	(7/65)
Corporate	–	–	–	–	–	–	–	–	–	–	–	–	–	–	2.7	33.5	21.2
governance–Loosening	–	–	–	–	–	–	–	–	–	–	–	–	–	–	(0/2)	(1/3)	(1/5)

Asset restructuring	– –	– –	15 (0/1)	10.2 (0/3)	7.7 (0/1)	– –	– –	– –	95.2 (1/1)	– –	66 (1/1)	30.6 (2/7)	– –	– –	60.1 (2/3)	5.3 (0/1)	46.4 (2/4)
Capital structure	4 (0/4)	– –	– –	– –	– –	– –	– –	– –	– –	4.6 (0/3)	– –	4.3 (0/7)	–	–	–	–	–
Payout policy	– –	17.9 (0/2)	23.2 (0/1)	17.3 (0/4)	12.8 (0/4)	– –	– –	– –	– –	– –	– –	16.3 (0/11)	– –	0.3 (0/1)	19 (0/2)	99.5 (1/1)	34.4 (1/4)
Corporate social responsibility	– –	19.1 (0/1)	15.2 (0/2)	3.2 (0/2)	10.3 (0/1)	5.9 (0/1)	8.4 (0/4)	4.2 (0/2)	6 (0/2)	5.8 (0/2)	8.9 (0/1)	8.1 (0/18)	– –	– –	2 (0/3)	– –	2 (0/3)
Routine	– –	– –	– –	3.5 (0/1)	14.1 (0/1)	– –	– –	– –	– –	– –	– –	8.8 (0/2)	– –	– –	1.8 (0/3)	– –	1.8 (0/3)
Other	– –	– –	– –	– –	– –	– –	– –	– –	– –	– –	– –	– –	– –	– –	93.3 (1/1)	– –	93.3 (1/1)
Total by year	7.5 (0/6)	25.7 (0/16)	19.3 (0/7)	11.3 (0/13)	18 (0/20)	13.9 (0/4)	47.5 (30/43)	33.1 (4/19)	41.3 (9/22)	21 (3/34)	41.5 (4/11)	30.3 (50/195)	7.3 (0/1)	32.9 (2/6)	16.5 (7/50)	25.6 (6/38)	21.1 (15/95)

Table 4.4 shows that the proposals submitted in the UK achieved 30.3% of the votes cast on average. The voting outcomes improved substantially after 2003, coinciding with the results reported for the US by Renneboog and Szilagyi (2009). Continental European proposals drew less voting support, with an average 21.1% of the votes.

In the UK, the proposals seeking the election or removal of directors were by far the most successful, with 38.6% of the votes on average. In the period after 2003 many of these actually received a majority vote, with as many as thirty out of thirty-seven proposals passing in 2004. Although less widely used, similar proposals submitted against Continental European firms also fared well, with an average 46.5% of the votes in 2007 and 2008. This indicates that the voting shareholders view proposals related to a proxy contest as a strong signal of governance concerns.

The proposals seeking asset restructuring won a similarly high 36.3% of the votes on average. These submissions were also more successful in the latter half of the sample period, with the majority passing the shareholder vote after 2006 in both the UK and Continental Europe.

The voting outcomes on the remaining proposal objectives were significantly weaker. The governance-related proposals won only 15.5% and 19.7% of the votes in the UK and Continental Europe, respectively. The five Continental European submissions that favoured management or the board rather than shareholders drew an average 21.2% voting support. The proposals targeting payout policy attracted 16.3% of the votes in the UK, and had little success in all but one case in Continental Europe. Consistent with the findings of Gillan and Starks (Chapter 2, this volume) for the US, the proposals related to corporate social responsibility received even less support, at an average 7.3% of the votes cast. Finally, the proposals targeted at routine and capital structure issues achieved 4.6% and 4.3% of the votes, respectively.

While management should contest shareholder proposals to the extent that they are used as disciplinary tool by the outside shareholders, this was not always the case with the sample proposals. Table 4.5 partitions the voting outcomes by the voting recommendations issued by management on the individual submissions. The results show two major differences between the UK and Continental Europe. First, while management recommended a no vote on 186 out of 195 UK submissions, they opposed only 68 of the 95 proposals submitted in Continental Europe. Second, we find evidence that the management-supported proposals mostly passed the shareholder vote in Continental Europe but were unsuccessful in the UK. These results again suggest that, in Continental Europe, proposals often reinforce the incumbent leadership rather than serve shareholder interests, whereas in the UK any such attempts are likely to fail.

4.4.3 Stock Price Effects

To examine the stock price effects of the sample proposals, we analyse the cumulative abnormal returns (CARs) around the general meeting dates. The prior US literature examines stock price changes around the dates the proposals are first announced in the proxy statements (Bhagat 1983; Bhagat and Brickley 1984). However, our cross-country study does not permit this type of analysis. On one hand, the content, timing, and dissemination methods of the materials related to a general meeting show huge variations

Table 4.5 Percentage of votes for shareholder proposals by issue addressed, geographic location, and management recommendation

This table shows the mean percentage of votes cast in favour of shareholder proposals partitioned according to proposal issue and management recommendation. Data span 1998–2008 for the UK and 2005–08 for Continental Europe.

	UK								Continental Europe							
	Against		Case-by-case		For		Total by issue		Against		Case-by-case		For		Total by issue	
Management recommendation	Mean	(N)	Mean	(N)	Mean	(N)	Mean	(N)	Mean	(N)	Mean	(N)	Mean	(N)	Mean	(N)
Elect/remove	38.4	(125)	32.0	(3)	2.9	(1)	38.0	(129)	26.0	(4)	3.7	(1)	71.5	(5)	46.5	(10)
Elect director	36.8	(58)	–		–		36.8	(58)	–		–		71.5	(5)	71.5	(5)
Remove director	39.8	(67)	32.0	(3)	2.9	(1)	39.0	(71)	26.0	(4)	3.7	(1)	–		21.5	(5)
Corporate governance	21.5	(19)	–		3.0	(2)	19.7	(21)	6.7	(49)	8.7	(4)	53.7	(12)	15.5	(65)
Corporate governance–Loosening	–		–		–		–		3.3	(3)	–		48.1	(2)	21.2	(5)
Asset restructuring	19.8	(6)	–		95.2	(1)	30.6	(7)	46.4	(4)	–		–		46.4	(4)
Capital structure	4.3	(7)	–		–		4.3	(7)	–		–		–		–	
Payout policy	16.3	(11)	–		–		16.3	(11)	19.0	(2)	–		49.9	(2)	34.4	(4)
Corporate social responsibility	8.5	(16)	–		5.4	(2)	8.1	(18)	2.0	(3)	–		–		2.0	(3)
Routine	8.8	(2)	–		–		8.8	(2)	1.8	(3)	–		–		1.8	(3)
Other	–		–		–		–		93.3	(1)	–		–		93.3	(1)
Total by recommendation	30.6	(186)	32.0	(3)	19.2	(6)	30.3	(195)	9.9	(68)	22.0	(6)	57.0	(21)	21.1	(95)

across countries, with no minimum standards even within the European Union. On the other, several countries allow proposals to be placed on the meeting's agenda with a very short notice period. For example, Germany allows proposals up to a week after the publication of the meeting's notice, while France has no provision at all governing the deadline for submitting proposals, such that shareholders may do so until the meeting is called to order.[11]

By analysing the CARs around the general meeting dates, we effectively measure the stock price reaction to the shareholder vote on the sample proposals, with some probability that the market is informed of the submission itself on the day of the meeting. The market response to the proposal outcome is difficult to ascertain, which is likely to lead to a downward bias in the size and significance of the results. On one hand, even if the market is aware of the proposal, it should have reasonable expectations on whether it actually passes, thus the voting results only reveal new information if they differ from this projection. On the other, shareholders receive a great deal of new information during the meeting as well as vote on multiple agenda items, such as director elections, dividend payout, the annual accounts, as well as any other proposals submitted by shareholders and management.

We calculate the CARs using the market model methodology. The model parameters are estimated over the 200-day period ending 21 days before the GM dates, using representative national indices to calculate market returns.[12] The significance of the CARs is tested using the standardized cross-sectional *Z*-test of Boehmer, Masumeci, and Poulsen (1991) and Cowan's (1992) non-parametric generalized sign test. For robustness, we compute bootstrapped versions of the parametric test with 3,000 repetitions.

Table 4.6 reports the CARs for the full sample across a number of event windows. The results indicate a strong negative market reaction to the general meetings at which the sample proposals were voted upon. In the three-day [−1,+1] window around the meeting dates, the average and median CAR were −1.20% and −0.71%, respectively, with all tests significant at least at the 5% level. We find similar results for all other event windows. These findings imply that the market associates proposals with a negative signal rather than attribute them control benefits as a disciplinary device. As Prevost and Rao (2000) argue, the market may view proposals as being disruptive from a corporate governance perspective. However, it is likely that the stock price effects are driven by the negative signal of both governance concerns as well as the failure to address them, because most proposal submissions tend to fail the shareholder vote.

Table 4.7 classifies the CARs by the issues addressed by the proposal submissions. For the general meetings where multiple proposals were presented, the CARs are assigned to each of the corresponding proposal objectives. While the results are mostly insignificant due to sample size issues, the average CARs were negative for each objective across almost all event windows. Nonetheless, there is some evidence that the market responds least favourably to proposals that seek governance improvements or personal changes on the board, with the

[11] We try to analyse stock price changes around the date information on the sample proposals first became available on Manifest, but the results are inconsistent.

[12] The market indices used are FTSE All Share, DAX30, PSI20, CAC40, AEX, SwissMarket Index [SMI], ATX, RTS, and Oslo BMI.

Table 4.6 Cumulative abnormal returns around general meeting dates

This table shows per cent cumulative abnormal returns around general meeting dates. Market model parameters are estimated over the 200-day period ending 21 days before the date of the general meeting, using the appropriate national stock exchange index. The significance of means is tested using a cross-sectional *t*-test, Boehmer, Masumeci, and Poulsen (1991) standardized cross-sectional *Z*-test, as well as bootstrapped versions of both. Bootstrap simulations are performed with 3,000 repetitions. The significance of medians is tested using Cowan's (1992) generalized sign test. *, **, and *** denote significance at the 10, 5, and 1% level, respectively. Data span 1998–2008 for the UK and 2005–08 for Continental Europe.

Event window	*N*	Mean	Median	Positive:negative	*Z*-test	Bootstrapped *Z*-test	Sign test (p^* = 47%)
[−1,+1]	90	−1.227	−0.713	34:56	−2.81***	−2.81***	−1.79**
[−1,0]	90	−0.906	−0.418	36:54	−1.87*	−1.87**	−1.36*
[0,+1]	90	−0.761	−0.103	41:49	−2.14**	−2.14**	−0.31
[−2,+2]	90	−1.142	−0.628	34:56	−2.65***	−2.65***	−1.79**
[−1,+5]	90	−1.323	−1.256	34:56	−2.65***	−2.65***	−1.79**
[−1,+7]	90	−1.584	−1.326	38:52	−2.64***	−2.64***	−0.95
[−5,+5]	90	−1.603	−1.016	36:54	−2.53**	−2.53***	−1.36*
[−10,+10]	90	−2.002	−0.794	38:52	−2.60**	−2.60***	−0.95

Table 4.7 Cumulative abnormal returns by issue addressed

This table shows per cent cumulative abnormal returns around general meeting dates. Market model parameters are estimated over the 200-day period ending 21 days before the date of the general meeting, using the appropriate national stock exchange index. The significance of means is tested using Boehmer, Masumeci, and Poulsen (1991) standardized cross-sectional *Z*-test. *, **, and *** denote significance at the 10, 5, and 1% level. Data span 1998–2008 for the UK and 2005–08 for Continental Europe.

	N	[−1,+1]	[−1,0]	[0,+1]	[−2,+2]	[−1,+5]	[−1,+7]	[−5,+5]	[−10,+10]
Elect/remove	42	−1.28	−1.25	−0.68	−0.92	−2.20*	−2.78**	−2.60	−3.51
Corporate governance	33	−1.09	−0.59	−0.61	−1.81**	−0.80*	−0.96**	−0.71*	−1.23**
Corporate governance–loosening	5	−2.52	−0.12	−2.29	−4.53*	−2.87	−4.14	−2.62	−2.90
Asset restructuring	8	−1.73	−1.39	−1.40	−3.14	4.16	3.97	3.83	5.93
Capital structure	2	−0.43	−0.75	−0.12	−1.97	−3.54	−0.81	−3.05	−2.16
Payout policy	12	−0.57	−1.03	−1.34	−0.28	−1.99	0.82	1.04	−0.23
Corporate social responsibility	18	−0.32	−0.06	−0.07	−0.57	−0.95	−0.34	−1.13	0.30
Routine	4	−2.12	−1.08	−1.21	−2.89	−5.75	−5.98	−5.80	−3.28
Other	1	−0.11	−0.37	−0.72	−1.09	−1.08	−0.16	−0.11	−1.07

negative CARs significant in five and two of the eight event windows, respectively. This corresponds to the strong governance implications of these proposal objectives, and thus supports the assertion that the market assesses proposals, irrespective of their voting success, on the severity of the governance problems they signal.

4.5 Multivariate Analysis of Target Selection, Voting Outcomes, and Stock Price Effects

To gain further insight into the governance role of shareholder proposals in Europe, we use sample selection models to determine: (i) how activists decide which firm to target with a proxy proposal; and (ii) conditional on the firm being targeted, what drives proposal success in terms of the voting results and the stock price effects. The use of the sample selection models is motivated by the fact that target selection and proposal success are likely to be endogenous. On one hand, the activist is likely to consider the potential outcome before deciding whether or not to submit the proposal, given the non-trivial costs involved. On the other, the market and the voting shareholders may respond to the act of the submission beyond the objective of the proposal itself, to the extent that this reveals a negative signal of governance concerns, or in fact a positive signal of close monitoring by the activist.

To identify the firm characteristics that drive target selection and proposal success, we use a comprehensive set of accounting, stock market, ownership, and governance data collected from the AMADEUS, Bankscope, Compustat, Datastream, Manifest, and Thomson ONE Banker databases, as well as corporate filings. The analysis of target selection is performed through a matching process, such that for each target we select a peer within its industry that is comparable in size. While this process does not cover the entire universe of publicly listed European firms, it decreases the likelihood of a systematic bias due to missing or inaccurate data.

4.5.1 Descriptive Statistics on Target and Non-Target Firms

Table 4.8 compares the descriptive statistics on the target firms and their non-target peers. The variable descriptions are provided in Appendix A. The differences in means and medians are tested using paired *t*-tests and Wilcoxon rank-sum tests, respectively.

Panel A of Table 4.8 shows how the targets and non-targets compared in terms of their financial characteristics, market performance, and institutional ownership. Fama and French's (2001) agency proxies show little evidence that governance concerns in the targets were exacerbated, with no discernible difference in the debt-to-equity and market-to-book ratios of the targets and the non-targets. The performance data show some evidence that the targets underperformed relative to the non-targets in the year up to two months before the general meeting dates. Their stocks delivered an average raw return of 5.5%, and

Table 4.8 Descriptive statistics of target and non-target firms

This table reports financial, performance, and ownership information as well as governance characteristics for European firms in our sample. Targets are defined as firms at which one or more shareholder proposal was submitted and voted on at the general meeting. Non-targets are size- and industry-matched peers of targets. Banks and insurance companies are classified as pressure-sensitive, whereas other institutional investors are categorized as pressure-insensitive. Shareholder concentration is measured by the Bureau van Dijk Independence Indicator, with the scale transformed from A, B, C, and D to 1, 2 3, and 4.

	Targets				Non-targets					
	N	Mean	Median	St. dev.	N	Mean	Median	St. dev.	Difference in means	Differences in medians
Panel A: Financial, performance, and ownership characteristics										
Assets (£ millions)	90	53,581	1,390	142,689	89	94,881	3593	265,195	−41,301*	−2,202
Sales (£ millions)	90	16,204	392	47,590	89	12,820	2,075	22,041	3,384	−1,683*
Debt-to-equity ratio	90	2.41	0.64	5.18	89	2.48	0.78	4.28	−0.07	-0.13
Market-to-book ratio	90	2.44	1.65	2.28	89	2.14	1.62	1.80	0.30	0.03
Prior one-year raw stock return (%)	90	5.46	4.80	38.34	89	12.24	10.95	55.14	−6.78	−6.15
Prior one-year abnormal stock return (%)	90	−0.77	−1.84	34.27	89	7.55	0.98	50.05	−8.32	−2.82
Prior one-year stock turnover	90	2.62	1.37	8.43	89	0.98	0.73	0.94	1.64*	0.64***
Institutional ownership (%)	90	32.98	25.24	24.72	89	21.6	19.9	17.68	11.37**	5.34***
Institutional ownership–pressure-sensitive (%)	90	6.34	0.00	15.12	89	3.35	0.00	5.22	2.99*	0.00
Institutional ownership–pressure-insensitive (%)	90	26.70	19.00	23.10	89	18.25	10.76	17.97	8.45**	8.24**
Shareholder concentration	90	1.88	1.00	1.27	89	1.55	1.00	0.93	0.33*	0.00
Panel B: Governance characteristics										
Board size	90	12.83	12.00	6.98	89	11.43	10.00	5.92	1.40***	2.00**
Executive directors (%)	90	36.39	37.50	18.45	89	38.00	36.08	0.17	36.01	37.14
Average age of non-executive directors	90	59.35	58.88	4.69	89	59.91	59.98	5.40	−0.56	−1.10
Separate chair and CEO (binary)	90	0.88	1.00	0.33	89	0.83	1.00	0.38	0.04	0.00
CEO ownership (%)	90	0.74	0.01	3.28	89	2.50	0.04	8.05	−1.76*	−0.04***
Stock-based to total CEO compensation (%)	90	30.83	27.46	30.31	89	27.61	24.45	28.63	3.22	3.01

underperformed their respective market indices by 0.8%. The raw return on the non-target stocks was 12.2%, and these actually outperformed their respective indices by 7.6%. Turnover was considerably higher in the target stocks, at 2.6 versus 1.0, which is likely to be symptomatic of shareholders voting with their feet.

Finally, Panel A confirms that there were significant differences in the ownership structures of the targets and the non-targets. First, institutional ownership was higher in the targets at 33.0% and 21.6%, respectively. Using the classification provided by Pound (1988) and Brickley, Lease, and Smith (1988), we also observe that both pressure-sensitive and pressure-insensitive institutions own a larger percentage of target firms' stock. Taken together, these results suggest that activist shareholders count on voting support from institutions and that this plays a role in their selection of target firms. Second, there is evidence that ownership in the targets was more concentrated. We measure shareholder concentration using the independence indicator of Bureau van Dijk, and find that the mean concentration in the targets was significantly higher, at 1.9 versus 1.6.[13, 14] This result on ownership concentration is further evidence that activist shareholders study the ownership structure of potential targets, because more concentrated ownership means that activists have to convince fewer shareholders to ensure voting support.

Panel B of Table 4.8 compares the governance quality of the targets and the non-targets in terms of board effectiveness and the exposure of CEO wealth to firm performance. We measure board effectiveness by: (i) size; (ii) the proportion of executive directors; (iii) the average age of non-executive directors; and (iv) the independence of the board chairman. The data show mixed evidence on how the two groups compared in terms of board quality. The targets had 12.8 directors on average, significantly more than the 11.4 directors non-targets had and the optimal board size of 6 to 8 directors (Jensen 1993; Yermack 1996). However, there is no evidence that the targets had fewer independent directors, with executives constituting 36.4% of the board in the targets and 38.0% in the non-targets. We also find no discernible difference between the age and thus experience of the non-executive directors, at 59.3 and 59.9 years, respectively. The posts of CEO and board chairman were separated in 12% of the targets and 17% of the non-targets, but the difference is again insignificant.

The exposure of CEO wealth to firm performance, which Jensen and Murphy (1990) view as a remedy to agency concerns, is measured by: (i) the CEO's equity ownership; and (ii) the proportion of stock-based compensation in the CEO's total pay. Panel B of Table 4.8 shows that the target CEOs held smaller equity stakes in their firm, at 0.7% versus 2.5%. However, there is no evidence that CEO compensation was less high-powered in the targets, with options and restricted shares comprising an average 30.8% and 27.6% of total pay, respectively.

[13] The independence indicator reported by Bureau van Dijk takes values of A, B, C, and D. We transform these values into a scale from 1 to 4, with D = 4 representing the highest level of ownership concentration.

[14] This variable is used as an exclusion restriction, and it is therefore omitted from the outcome equations in our regression analysis.

4.5.2 Methodology

We perform the multivariate analysis of target selection and proposal success using Heckman's (1979) sample selection model, often referred to as a type-2 Tobit model. The model is specified as follows:

$$y_{1it}^{*} = X_{1it}^{'}\beta_1 + \varepsilon_{1it},$$

$$y_{1it} = \begin{cases} 1 & if\ y_{1it}^{*} > 0 \\ 0 & if\ y_{1it}^{*} \leq 0 \end{cases}$$

$$y_{1it}^{*} = X_{2it}^{'}\beta_2 + \varepsilon_{2it},$$

$$y_{1it} = \begin{cases} y_{2it}^{*} & if\ y_{1it}^{*} > 0 \\ 0 & if\ y_{1it}^{*} \leq 0 \end{cases}$$

where $\{\varepsilon_{1i\,t}, \varepsilon_{2i\,t}\}$ are drawn from a normal distribution with mean 0, variances σ_1^2 and σ_2^2, and correlation ρ_{12} (Amemiya 1984). The variable y^{*}_{1it} is a dummy variable showing whether firm i is targeted in year t, while the variable y^{*}_{2it} is the outcome of interest, that is: (i) the voting outcome observed at the proposal level; or (ii) the CAR observed at the firm level around the GM date. We observe the sign of y^{*}_{1it}, that is, whether a particular firm was a proposal target or not, and we observe y^{*}_{2it} (the voting outcome or the CAR) only when $y^{*}_{1it} > 0$. The X variables correspond to the explanatory variables. $X_{1i\,t}$ is observed for all i, and includes firm-level variables (leverage, market-to-book, prior stock price performance, and institutional ownership). $X_{2i\,t}$ additionally includes proposal-related variables (such as the issue addressed and the number of times the proposal has been submitted) but does not contain ownership concentration to ensure identification. β_1 and β_2 are vectors of the model coefficients.

In a standard setting, the error terms are assumed to be i.i.d. drawings. We relax this assumption across t and allow for the clustering of observations corresponding to a given firm i, that is, we assume the error terms to be i.i.d. across firms but not necessarily for different observations within the same firm. This procedure enhances the robustness of our findings and allows us to take the structure of our sample explicitly into account.

Throughout the chapter we call Equation (1) the selection equation and Equation (2) the outcome equation. As has been discussed, estimating the outcome equation independently would not be a valid alternative, because the OLS (ordinary least squares) estimator of β_2 is biased when the selection of the outcome sample is endogenous, that is, $\rho_{12} \neq 0$. The sample selection model addresses the endogeneity of selection, and thus renders reliable parameter estimates for the outcome equation.

4.5.3 Target Selection

The sample selection models analysing the voting outcomes and the stock price effects are depicted in Tables 4.9 and 4.10, respectively. The selection equations, shown in Panel A, are configured identically in the two tables. However, the voting outcomes are observed at the proposal rather than the firm level, thus the selection equations of Table 4.9 overweight the

Table 4.9 Sample selection models explaining proposal probability and voting outcomes

Panel A shows selection equations where the dependent variable is a dummy equal to one if a shareholder proposal was submitted and zero otherwise. In the outcome equations of Panel B, the dependent variable is the percentage of votes cast in favour of the proposal. The firm-level independent variables included in both Panels A and B are described in Appendix A. The proposal-level independent variables in Panel B are dummies equal to one if the variable description holds and zero otherwise. Log of assets is the natural logarithm of the book value of assets. Wald $\chi2$ tests the joint significance of the selection and outcome equations. $\rho = 0$ tests the independence of the selection and outcome equations using a Wald $\chi2$ test. *T*-statistics use standard errors with White (1980) correction for heteroscedasticity and adjusted for clustering of observations on each firm. *, **, and *** denote significance at the 10, 5, and 1% level, respectively.

	Model 1		Model 2		Model 3		Model 4		Model 5	
	Coefficient	*t*-stat	Coefficient	*t*-stat	Coefficient	*t*-stat	Coefficient	*t*-stat	Coefficient	*t*-stat
Panel A: Selection equations										
Intercept	0.857	1.63	1.950	1.55	2.516*	1.95	2.619	1.54	2.640**	2.15
Debt-to-equity	−0.003	−0.14	−0.051	−1.64	−0.077**	-2.48	−0.077**	-2.13	−0.079***	-2.74
Market-to-book	−0.107**	-2.43	−0.097**	-2.20	−0.103**	-2.01	−0.131*	-1.72	−0.129***	-2.56
Prior one-year abnormal stock return	0.029	0.13	−0.216	−1.10	−0.506***	-3.03	−0.500*	-1.89	−0.482***	-2.78
Prior one-year stock turnover	0.317**	2.48	0.685***	6.77	0.653***	6.38	0.684***	4.33	0.669***	7.06
Institutional ownership—pressure-sensitive	2.258	1.56	3.579**	2.25	3.365*	1.88	3.166	1.43	3.568**	2.17
Institutional ownership—pressure-insensitive	0.822*	1.71	1.814***	3.83	1.714***	3.27	1.793**	2.33	1.811***	3.44
Shareholder concentration			0.174*	1.95	0.174*	1.64	0.166	1.34	0.166*	1.68
Board size			0.005	0.06	−0.030	−0.38	0.040	0.30	0.027	0.32
Board size squared			0.004*	1.68	0.006**	2.27	0.004	0.94	0.004	1.64
Executive directors			1.260**	2.13	1.305*	1.93	1.024	1.25	1.017	1.39
Average age of non-executive directors			−0.029*	−1.92	−0.031*	−1.94	−0.34	−1.14	−0.033**	−1.99
Separate chair and CEO			0.506**	2.22	0.435*	1.75	0.377	1.07	0.380*	1.65
CEO ownership			−1.123	−0.56	−1.480	−0.69	−1.152	−0.42	−1.112	−0.52
Stock-based to total CEO compensation			−0.099	−0.25	0.042	0.10	0.311	0.67	0.315	0.96

Panel B: Outcome equations										
Intercept	0.176*	1.82	0.170	1.52	0.142	0.78	0.324	1.31	0.092	0.28
Times submitted	0.006	0.23	0.003	0.09	−0.016	−0.89			−0.021	−1.28
Number of proposals at meeting	−0.005	−0.66	−0.008	−1.05	−0.007	−1.46			−0.007	−1.04
Elect director	0.278***	4.23	0.305***	4.14	0.290***	4.72			0.218***	2.63
Remove director	0.271***	3.73	0.297***	3.64	0.280***	4.53			0.206***	2.57
Corporate governance	0.094	1.52	0.110	1.60	0.051	0.98			0.081	1.37
Corporate governance–loosening	0.165	0.95	0.170	0.95	0.118	0.67			0.183	1.02
Asset restructuring	0.234**	2.08	0.255**	2.10	0.098	1.08			0.105	1.16
Capital structure	−0.087*	−1.75	−0.050	−0.97	−0.043	−0.90			0.008	0.12
Payout policy	0.086	1.09	0.102	1.31	0.060	0.88			0.055	0.70
Corporate social responsibility	−0.029	−0.60	−0.007	−0.12	−0.016	−0.37			0.007	0.11
Other	0.769***	11.25	0.784***	10.80	0.713***	3.82				
Log of assets					−0.002	−0.19	0.010	0.95	0.011	1.03
Debt-to-equity					0.018***	2.79	0.018***	4.20	0.018***	4.02
Market-to-book					0.003	0.29	0.036***	3.08	0.025*	1.90
Prior one-year abnormal stock return					0.239***	3.57	0.250***	5.54	0.250***	4.78
Prior one-year stock turnover					−0.002	−0.92	−0.002	−1.59	−0.002	−1.63
Institutional ownership–pressure-sensitive					−0.006	−0.03	0.318**	2.12	0.094	0.43
Institutional ownership–pressure-insensitive					0.161	1.59	0.069	0.63	0.028	0.34

(continued)

Table 4.9 (Continued)

Board size				−0.029	−1.36	−0.032	−1.15
Board size squared				0.000	0.64	0.001	0.75
Executive directors				−0.045	−0.33	0.077	0.52
Average age of non-executive directors				0.000	0.03	0.002	0.51
Separate chair and CEO				0.061	1.45	0.051	0.96
CEO ownership				0.664	1.54	0.092	0.17
Stock-based to total CEO compensation				−0.306***	-4.27	−0.223***	-2.66
Number of observations	380	380	380	380		380	
Number of uncensored observations	290	290	290	290		290	
Number of proposals	290	290	290	290		290	
Wald $\chi2$	5,170.69***	2,248.52***	4,540.54***	189.28***		7,065.09***	
Log-likelihood	−153.014	−105.014	−66.403	−57.136		−38.137	
P	−0.597***	−0.641**	−0.457	−0.521**		−0.495**	

Table 4.10 Sample selection models explaining proposal probability and cumulative abnormal returns

Panel A shows selection equations where the dependent variable is a dummy equal to one if a shareholder proposal was submitted and zero otherwise. In the outcome equations of Panel B, the dependent variable is the cumulative abnormal return in the days [−1,+1] surrounding the date of the general meeting where the proposal was presented. Market model parameters are estimated over the 200-day period ending 20 days before the date of the general meeting, using country-specific stock market indices. The firm-level independent variables included in both Panels A and B are described in Appendix A. The proposal-level independent variables in Panel B are dummies equal to one if the variable description holds and zero otherwise. Log of assets is the natural logarithm of the book value of assets. Wald $\chi2$ tests the joint significance of the selection and outcome equations. $\rho = 0$ tests the independence of the selection and outcome equations using a Wald $\chi2$ test. *T*-statistics use standard errors with White (1980) correction for heteroscedasticity and adjusted for clustering of observations on each firm. *, **, and *** denote significance at the 10, 5, and 1% level, respectively.

	Model 1		Model 2		Model 3		Model 4		Model 5	
	Coefficient	*t*-stat	Coefficient	*t*-stat	Coefficient	*t*-stat	Coefficient	*t*-stat	Coefficient	*t*-stat
Panel A: Selection equations										
Intercept	−0.569	−0.96	0.219	0.16	−0.232	−0.20	−0.146	−0.08	−0.162	−0.13
Debt-to-equity	−0.042*	−1.86	−0.045	−0.37	−0.038	−0.83	−0.066	−1.08	−0.069**	−2.02
Market-to-book	0.008	0.17	−0.054	−0.57	−0.024	−0.40	−0.039	−0.64	−0.036	−0.89
Prior one-year abnormal stock return	−0.229	−1.20	−0.481**	−2.40	−0.385**	−2.22	−0.302	−0.50	−0.379**	−2.02
Prior one-year stock turnover	0.346***	3.20	0.438	1.21	0.316**	2.32	0.4572	1.21	0.494***	4.10
Institutional ownership–pressure-sensitive	2.116	1.45	2.911	1.70	2.697**	2.48	3.588	1.16	3.331**	2.18
Institutional ownership–pressure-insensitive	1.290***	2.75	2.113**	2.25	1.387***	3.04	2.3745***	2.64	2.298***	5.63
Shareholder concentration			0.301***	2.79	0.178	1.11	0.347	0.98	0.310**	2.41
Board size			0.077	1.01	omitted to attain convergence		0.056	0.38	0.063	0.76
Board size squared			0.001	0.54	omitted to attain convergence		0.002	0.49	0.002	0.75
Executive directors			0.664	0.47	0.239	0.27	0.994	0.98	0.989	1.21
Average age of non-executive directors			−0.016	−0.66	−0.007	−0.42	−0.021	−0.72	−0.019	−1.18
Separate chair and CEO			0.277	0.73	0.138	0.56	0.282	0.64	0.256	0.93
CEO ownership			−1.548	−0.76	−2.010	−0.69	−0.659	−0.25	−0.787	−0.36
Stock-based to total CEO compensation			0.413	1.24	0.253	0.49	0.686	0.55	0.565	1.51

(continued)

Table 4.10 (Continued)

	Model 1		Model 2		Model 3		Model 4		Model 5	
	Coefficient	*t*-stat	Coefficient	*t*-stat	Coefficient	*t*-stat	Coefficient	*t*-stat	Coefficient	*t*-stat
Panel B: Outcome equations										
Intercept	−0.000	−0.12	−0.030	−0.90	−0.087*	−1.73	−0.049	−0.62	−0.019	−0.27
Number of proposals at meeting	−0.005*	−1.78	−0.005*	−1.73	−0.005**	−2.29			−0.004*	−1.85
Elect director	0.003	0.18	0.007	0.27	0.003	0.12			−0.006	−0.41
Remove director	0.026*	1.77	0.027	1.39	0.038**	2.14			0.02	1.21
Corporate governance	0.019	1.51	0.012	0.43	0.02	1.39			0.018	1.21
Corporate governance—loosening	0.023	1.25	0.019	1.00	0.023	1.22			0.042***	2.73
Asset restructuring	0.001	0.03	0.006	0.27	0.025	1.41			0.012	0.74
Capital structure	0.015	0.72	0.030*	1.84	0.02	0.98			0.015	0.64
Payout policy	0.017	0.94	0.012	0.30	0.017	1.12			0.017	1.03
Corporate social responsibility	0.024*	1.72	0.019	0.59	0.015	0.96			0.000	0.01
Other	0.003	0.16	0.033	0.66	−0.000	−0.02			−0.025	−1.07
Log of assets					0.004**	2.40	0.003	1.08	0.005**	2.49
Debt-to-equity					−0.003**	−2.33	−0.002	−0.96	−0.003***	−2.65
Market-to-book					0.004*	1.83	0.004	0.82	0.004**	2.15
Prior one-year abnormal stock return					0.02	1.29	0.027	0.67	0.029**	2.11
Prior one-year stock turnover					−0.001	−0.25	0.001	0.38	0.000	0.59
Institutional ownership—pressure-sensitive					−0.002	−0.03	0.039	0.65	0.036	1.14

Institutional ownership—pressure-insensitive					0.009	0.25	0.056	0.88	0.033	1.37
Board size							−0.000	−0.06	−0.005*	−1.80
Board size squared							0.000	−0.06	0.000	1.34
Executive directors							0.038	0.66	0.029	1.34
Average age of non-executive directors							−0.001	−0.53	−0.001	−1.17
Separate chair and CEO							−0.002	−0.18	0.008	0.64
CEO ownership							0.221	0.61	0.173	0.98
Stock-based to total CEO compensation							0.037*	1.75	0.039**	2.07
Number of observations	180		180		180		180		180	
Number of uncensored observations	90		90		90		90		90	
Number of firms	124		124		124		124		124	
Wald χ 2	10.23		14.88		44.67***		50.17***		77.00***	
Log likelihood	57.163		74.152		71.373		85.334		93.311	
ρ	−0.615		0.539		−0.265		0.568		0.207	

targets with multiple proposals in a given year.[15] As the CARs are observed at the firm level, the corresponding selection equations are unbiased. Therefore, the remainder of this section discusses the selection equations shown in Panel A of Table 4.10. The selection equations control for the firm characteristics discussed in Section 4.5.1 and described in Appendix A. Fama and French's (2001) agency argument dictates that the probability of a proposal submission is related negatively to the debt-to-equity and market-to-book ratios. However, market-to-book also serves as a proxy for informational asymmetries, thus the sign on this variable can be positive to the extent that proposal submissions have signalling effects. Proposal probability should be related negatively to prior stock performance and positively to prior stock turnover. We control separately for ownership by pressure-sensitive and pressure-insensitive institutional investors. Proposal probability should increase in both, but less so in the former due to the threat of conflicted voting by pressure-sensitive institutions. Finally, we expect proposal probability to be positively related to shareholder concentration. On one hand, voting coalitions should be easier to build when firm ownership is concentrated. On the other, activists may actually be wary of expropriation by powerful large shareholders, and use proposal submissions to protect minority shareholder interests.

The selection equations include seven variables capturing governance quality. Board effectiveness is proxied by: (i) size; (ii) the square of size; (iii) the proportion of executive directors; (iv) the age of non-executive directors; and (v) a dummy equal to one if the chairman is independent and zero otherwise. We expect the sign on size to be negative and on squared size to be positive, to the extent that boards should be neither too small nor too large. The sign should be positive on the proportion of executive directors, and negative on director age and chairman independence. As before, the variables pertaining to CEO wealth and compensation are: (i) ownership; and (ii) stock-based to total pay. We conjecture that the signs are negative on both variables, due to the incentive effects of the CEO's exposure to firm performance.

Panel A of Table 4.10 shows that these selection equations are quite effective in explaining why firms get targeted by shareholder proposals. Apart from the role the equation plays in the selection model, it also delivers several results in its own right and confirms that target firms systematically differ from their non-target peers. First, we confirm that proposal probability decreases in the prior market performance and increases in the prior stock turnover. Second, we find that highly levered firms are less likely to be targeted, consistent with the role of leverage in mitigating free cash flow problems. And third, there is evidence that activists consider the ownership structure of the firm before deciding whether or not to submit proxy proposals. In Model 5, proposal probability increases by 3.3% and 2.3% for every 1% stock held by pressure-sensitive and pressure-insensitive institutions, respectively. While this shows little indication of conflicted voting by pressure-sensitive investors, the statistical relation is considerably more significant for pressure-insensitive institutions. We find no statistical evidence that proposal probability is affected by the additional proxies for governance quality; the variables capturing board effectiveness and the exposure of CEO wealth to firm performance are insignificant in the models.

[15] Firm-level specifications would yield unbiased results for the selection equations but lead to considerable loss of information on the individual proposals. For robustness, we performed the analysis at the firm level by excluding firms targeted by multiple proposals in a given year, as well as by using the average voting outcomes. The results of the outcome equations were similar to those presented in Section 4.4.3, but the information loss was significant.

4.5.4 Voting Outcomes

The outcome equations analysing voting success are depicted in Panel B of Table 4.9 and summarized in Appendix B. The models incorporate a similar set of firm-level variables included in the selection equations. While the voting outcomes are conditional on the target selection process, we conjecture that the variables affect proposal probability and voting success in the same way. We additionally control for firm size in the outcome equations using the log of assets, and exclude shareholder concentration to avoid endogeneity problems. We expect that voting success is related negatively to firm size, because while Fama and French (2001) find agency concerns to be more severe in large firms with dispersed ownership, voting coalitions should be much more difficult to build.

In addition to the firm-level variables, the outcome equations include eleven variables capturing the characteristics of the proposals themselves. *Times submitted* is the number of times a proposal has been submitted in consecutive years. We conjecture that consecutive resubmissions of unimplemented proposals improve the voting outcomes, consistent with the earlier findings of Gillan and Starks (2000) and Renneboog and Szilagyi (2009) for the US. *Number of proposals at meeting* captures the number of proposals presented at the same general meeting. While it is not immediate how this should affect voting success, we expect that the more proposals submitted, the greater the support from the voting shareholders due to the stronger signal conveyed over governance concerns. Finally, we use nine dummy variables to control for the proposal objectives. All proposals are uniquely allocated to an issue type, such that the intercept represents proposals addressing routine issues. Corresponding to our univariate results, we expect that proposals seeking personal changes on the board attract the most voting support.

The model statistics in Table 4.9 confirm that target selection and voting success are endogenous, with ρ sensitive to the model specification but significant in all but one case. Results not reported here show that independent analysis of the voting outcomes produces somewhat different parameter estimates and has lower explanatory power overall. These findings confirm that the voting success of shareholder proposals needs to be analysed in a sample selection framework.

The results in Panel B of Table 4.9 confirm that the voting outcomes are largely driven by the proposal objectives. In Model 5, the intercept shows that routine proposals receive 9.2% of the votes cast. In comparison, proposals seeking to elect or remove directors win 21.8% and 20.6% more voting support, respectively, which is consistent with the strong signalling implications of outright proxy contests. We find no evidence that routine proposals are outperformed by other submissions, including those calling for asset restructuring, with the exception of the single miscellaneous proposal seeking to assert damage claims. The results also show no indication that consecutive resubmissions of the same proposal or multiple submissions at the same general meeting affect the voting outcomes.[16]

Despite the careful target selection process we documented earlier, the firm-level variables add significant explanatory power to the outcome equations. Beyond its impact on the selection decision, institutional ownership has no discernible effect on the voting outcomes.

[16] The results on company- and proposal-specific covariates are largely robust to the inclusion of country fixed effects.

Surprisingly, however, we find that voting success conditional on target selection increases rather than decreases in the target's prior market performance and debt-to-equity and market-to-book ratios. This implies that the voting shareholders view submissions against less likely targets as a negative signal of governance problems. Of the governance-related variables, only the CEO's pay-performance sensitivity affects the voting outcomes. The relation between the two is negative, which shows that the CEO's exposure to firm performance mitigates shareholder concerns over the agency and signalling implications of proposal submissions.

4.5.5 Stock Price Effects

The outcome equations analysing the stock price effects in the days [−1,+1] around the general meeting dates are shown in Panel B of Table 4.10 and summarized in Appendix B. We control for the same firm characteristics included in the outcome equations pertaining to the voting results, and conjecture that the variables affect the CARs in a similar way. The only exception is firm size, which should be related positively rather than negatively to the CARs. This conjecture assumes that while submissions against large firms are likely to win less voting support, their control benefits are greater due to agency considerations.

As the CARs are observed at the firm rather than the proposal level, the dummies controlling for the proposal objectives are now equal to one if a corresponding proposal was presented at the general meeting and zero otherwise. We conjecture that, in line with their signalling effects, proposals seeking personal changes on the board generate more negative stock price changes. We similarly expect that the CARs are related negatively to the *number of proposals at meeting* variable, to the extent that multiple submissions signal greater governance concerns.

The model statistics in Table 4.10 show that the outcome equations have considerable explanatory power, even though we measure the response to the general meetings rather than the individual proposals. Similar to Renneboog and Szilagyi (2009), we find no evidence that the CARs are endogenous to target selection, but, as with the voting outcomes, independent regressions are less powerful and produce slightly different parameter estimates.

The outcome equations in Panel B of Table 4.10 show only limited evidence that the negative market reaction to general meetings is driven by the objectives of the proposals presented. The intercept representing routine proposals is insignificantly negative across all model specifications. In Model 5, the dummy capturing proposals to loosen governance quality is significantly positive. This implies that, *ceteris paribus*, the market responds well to submissions that attempt and fail to relax governance standards, and thereby indicate considerable shareholder dissent *vis-à-vis* management. The remaining dummies, including those pertaining to proposals that seek governance improvements or personal changes on the board, are statistically insignificant. However, we confirm that the CARs are related negatively to the number of proposals presented, in line with the signalling effects of multiple submissions.

The model statistics show that the stock price effects are most fundamentally driven by Fama and French's (2001) agency proxies and the target's prior market performance. The CARs are less negative for large firms with low leverage, indicating that the market attributes at least some control benefits to the public vote on shareholder proposals in the presence of agency concerns. However, they increase rather than decrease in both the market-to-book ratio and the prior stock price performance. This is inconsistent with the role of shareholder proposals as a disciplinary device, because it shows that the proposal outcomes only intensify the market's concerns over firms that have previously underperformed.[17]

The results in Panel B of Table 4.10 provide some support for the relevance of the target's governance structures in explaining the stock price effects. There is evidence that the CARs show the expected non-linear relation with the number of directors, with board size significantly positive and the square of board size insignificantly negative in the final Model 5. It is notable, however, that the relation between the CARs and the CEO's pay-performance sensitivity is positive rather than negative. This again is inconsistent with the control function of shareholder proposals, in that it indicates that governance concerns over firms with ill-incentivized CEOs are only exacerbated.

4.6 Conclusion

While the control function of shareholder proposals as a disciplinary mechanism has been subject to much debate in the US academic literature, their role in European corporate governance is rarely discussed. There is evidence for the US that shareholder access to the proxy has non-trivial control benefits, and shareholder proposals should be regarded as a useful disciplinary tool and the proposal sponsors as valuable monitoring agents. In Europe, the empirical investigation of this issue has been complicated by data availability, and by the fact that European countries are very diverse in terms of their legal provisions governing shareholder access to the proxy, corporate ownership structures, as well as the monitoring incentives and costs borne by proposal sponsors.

This chapter has contributed to the shareholder activism literature by examining shareholder proposals across nine European countries for the first time. The results have shown that, relative to the US, proposal submissions remain less frequent in Continental Europe in particular. The different use of shareholder proposals on the two continents can be attributed to differences in the costs of activism as well as disparities in legislation concerning shareholder proposals, which are non-binding in the US but binding in most of Europe. The importance of regulation is shown by the fact that while UK activists conveniently use proposals in relation to a proxy contest to replace the board, the proposal objectives remain largely limited to specific governance issues in Continental Europe.

Despite these country-level differences, proposal success in terms of the voting results and the stock price effects remain limited across Europe irrespective of the issues addressed. In fact, proposals are met with significantly negative market reactions when they are put to vote at general meetings. This implies that rather than attribute proposals meaningful control benefits, the market often interprets the shareholder vote as a negative signal of

[17] Similarly to the model explaining voting support, the results on company- and proposal-specific covariates are largely robust to the inclusion of country fixed effects. Moreover, none of the coefficients on country fixed effects are significantly different from zero.

governance concerns. Indeed, although voting success and the stock price effects are both affected by agency considerations, the market responds particularly negatively to proposals submitted against firms that have already underperformed.

Overall, we have shown that proposal submissions are preceded by a careful selection process, whereby activists target firms that both underperform and are subject to governance concerns. We conclude that shareholder proposals are only rarely used (relative to the US). Still, we provide compelling evidence that—when they are used—proposals submitted at European firms serve an emergency brake rather than a steering wheel: they signal dissent to the market but fall short of providing a reassuring solution.

APPENDIX A.

Variable Descriptions

Variable name	Description and source
Panel A: Financial, performance, and ownership characteristics	
Assets ($ millions)	The book value of total assets. Source: Compustat.
Sales ($ millions)	The value of total net sales. Source: Compustat.
Debt-to-equity ratio	Total debt divided by the book value of equity. Source: Compustat.
Market-to-book ratio	Market capitalization of equity divided by the book value of equity. Source: Compustat.
Prior one-year raw stock return	The dividend-adjusted stock price return in the year up to two months before the GM date. Source: Datastream.
Prior one-year abnormal stock return	The dividend-adjusted stock price return minus the return on the appropriate national stock exchange index, in the year up to two months before the GM date. Source: Datastream.
Prior one-year stock turnover	The total number of shares sold during the year up to two months before the GM date, divided by the total number of shares outstanding. Source: Datastream and Compustat.
Institutional ownership	The number of shares held by institutions, divided by the total number of shares outstanding. Source: Manifest, Bureau van Dijk, and annual reports.
Institutional ownership—pressure-sensitive	The number of shares held by banks and insurance companies, divided by the total number of shares outstanding. Source: Manifest, Bureau van Dijk, and annual reports.
Institutional ownership—pressure-insensitive	The number of shares held by pension and labour union funds, investment funds and their managers, independent investment advisors, and university endowments, divided by the total number of shares outstanding. Source: Manifest, Bureau van Dijk, and annual reports.

(continued)

Variable name	Description and source
Shareholder concentration	An independence index indicating ownership concentration. (1) no shareholder with ownership over 25% (direct or total); (2) no shareholder with ownership over 50% (direct or total), but one or more shareholders with ownership over 25%; (3) shareholder is ultimate owner with ownership over 50% (direct or total); (4) shareholder is ultimate owner with direct ownership over 50%. Source: Bureau van Dijk.
Panel B: Corporate governance characteristics	
Board size	The number of directors on the board of directors. Source: Manifest, Thomson ONE Banker, and annual reports.
Executive directors	The number of directors employed by the firm, divided by total board size. Source: Manifest, Thomson ONE Banker, and annual reports.
Average age of non-executive directors	The average age of directors not employed by the firm. Source: Manifest, Thomson ONE Banker, and annual reports.
Separate chair and CEO	A dummy variable equal to one if the chairman of the board and the CEO are different persons, and zero otherwise. Source: Manifest and annual reports.
CEO ownership	The number of shares held by the CEO divided by total shares outstanding. Source: Manifest and annual reports.
Stock-based to total CEO compensation	The value of stock options and restricted stock grants, divided by total CEO compensation for the individual year. Source: Manifest and annual reports.

APPENDIX B.

Economic Effects

This table summarizes the economic effects of proposal and firm characteristics on the voting outcomes as shown in Model 5 of Table 7.9, and on the probability of proposal submissions and the cumulative abnormal returns as shown in Model 5 of Table 7.10. The variables are described in Appendix A. *, **, and *** denote significance at the 10, 5, and 1% level, respectively.

	Proposal probability		Voting outcomes		Cumulative abnormal returns	
	Exp. sign	Economic effect	Exp. sign	Economic effect	Exp. sign	Economic effect
Panel A: Proposal characteristics						
Times submitted			+	nss		
Number of proposals at meeting			+	nss	–	0.004*
Elect director				0.218***		nss

(continued)

(Continued)

	Proposal probability		Voting outcomes		Cumulative abnormal returns	
	Exp. sign	Economic effect	Exp. sign	Economic effect	Exp. sign	Economic effect
Remove director				0.206***		nss
Corporate governance				nss		nss
Corporate governance–loosening				nss		0.042***
Asset restructuring				nss		nss
Capital structure				nss		nss
Payout policy				nss		nss
Corporate social responsibility				nss		nss
Other				0.674***		nss
Panel B: Financial, performance, and ownership characteristics						
Log of assets			–	nss	+	0.005**
Debt-to-equity	–	−0.069**	–	0.018***	–	−0.003***
Market-to-book		nss		0.025*	–	0.004**
Prior one-year abnormal stock return	–	−0.379**	–	0.250***	–	0.029**
Prior one-year stock turnover	+	0.494***	+	nss	+	nss
Institutional ownership–pressure-sensitive		3.331**		nss		nss
Institutional ownership–pressure-insensitive	+	2.298***	+	nss	+	nss
Shareholder concentration	+	0.310**				
Panel C: Governance characteristics						
Board size		nss	–	nss	–	−0.005*
Board size squared		nss	+	nss	+	nss
Executive directors		nss	+	nss	+	nss
Average age of non-executive Directors		nss	–	nss	–	nss
Separate chair and CEO		nss	–	nss	–	nss
CEO ownership		nss	–	nss	–	nss
Stock-based to total CEO compensation		nss	–	−0.223***	–	0.039**

References

Admati, A. R. and Pfleiderer, P. C. (2006). The 'Wall Street Walk' and Shareholder Activism: Exit as a Form of Voice, *Review of Financial Studies* 22, 2645–85.

Amemiya, T. (1984). Tobit Models: A Survey, *Journal of Econometrics* 24, 3–61.

Anabtawi, I. (2006). Some Skepticism about Increasing Shareholder Power, *UCLA Law Review* 53, 561–600.

Armour, J. (2008). Enforcement Strategies in UK Corporate Governance: A Roadmap and Empirical Assessment, ECGI—Law Working Paper No. 106/2008, available at <http://ssrn.com/abstract=1133542>.

Bainbridge, S. M. (2006). Director Primacy and Shareholder Disempowerment, *Harvard Law Review* 119, 1735–58.

Barca, F. and Becht, M. (eds.) (2001). *The Control of Corporate Europe* (Oxford, Oxford University Press).

Bebchuk, L. A. (2005). The Case for Increasing Shareholder Power, *Harvard Law Review* 118, 835–914.

Becht, M. (2001). Beneficial Ownership in the United States, in F. Barca and M. Becht (eds.), *The Control of Corporate Europe* (Oxford, Oxford University Press) 285–99.

Becht, M. and Mayer, C. (2001). Introduction, in F. Barca and M. Becht (eds.), *The Control of Corporate Europe* (Oxford, Oxford University Press) 1–45.

Bhagat, S. (1983). The Effect of Pre-Emptive Right Amendments on Shareholder Wealth, *Journal of Financial Economics* 12, 289–310.

Bhagat, S. and Brickley, J. A. (1984). Cumulative Voting: The Value of Minority Shareholder Voting Rights, *Journal of Law and Economics* 27, 339–65.

Bizjak, J. M. and Marquette, C. J. (1998). Are Shareholder Proposals All Bark and No Bite? Evidence from Shareholder Resolutions to Rescind Poison Pills, *Journal of Financial and Quantitative Analysis* 33, 499–521.

Boehmer, E., Masumeci, J., and Poulsen, A. B. (1991). Event-Study Methodology under Conditions of Event-Induced Variance, *Journal of Financial Economics* 30, 253–72.

Boxell, J. (2004a). Baltimore Slams Biggest Investor as 'Vulture Fund', *Financial Times* (London), (23 Apr.), at 2.

Boxell, J. (2004b). Dissident Acquisitor Fails to Oust Baltimore Board, *Financial Times* (London), (8 May), at 1.

Bream, R. (2006). African Platinum Chairman Ousted Following EGM Motion, *Financial Times* (London), (26 July), at 1.

Brickley, J. A., Lease, R. C., and Smith, C. J. (1988). Ownership Structure and Voting on Anti-Takeover Amendments, *Journal of Financial Economics* 20, 267–91.

Buchanan, B., Netter, J. M., and Yang, T. (2010). Are Shareholder Proposals an Important Corporate Governance Device? Evidence from US and UK Shareholder Proposals, Seattle University Working Paper, available at <http://ssrn.com/abstract=1572016>.

Cowan, A. R. (1992). Nonparametric Event Study Tests, *Review of Quantitative Finance and Accounting* 2, 343–58.

Cremers, K. J. M. and Romano, R. (2011). Institutional Investors and Proxy Voting: The Impact of the 2003 Mutual Fund Voting Disclosure Regulation, *American Law and Economics Review* 13(1), 220–68.

De Jong, A., Mertens, G. M. H., and Roosenboom, P. G. J. (2006). Shareholders' Voting at General Meetings: Evidence from the Netherlands, *Journal of Management and Governance* 10, 353–80.

Del Guercio, D. and Hawkins, J. (1999). The Motivation and Impact of Pension Fund Activism, *Journal of Financial Economics* 52, 293–340.

DSW (Deutsche Schutzvereinigung für Wertpapierbesitz) (2008). *Shareholders' Meetings in Europe* (Düsseldorf, Deutsche Schutzvereinigung für Wertpapierbesitz).

Ertimur, Y., Ferri, F., and Stubben, S. R. (2010). Board of Directors' Responsiveness to Shareholders: Evidence from Shareholder Proposals, *Journal of Corporate Finance* 16, 53–72.

European Commission (2006). *Annex to the Proposal for a Directive of the European Parliament and of the Council on the Exercise of Voting Rights by Shareholders of Companies Having their Registered Office in a Member State and Whose Shares are Admitted to Trading on a*

Regulated Market and Amending Directive 2004/109/EC—Impact Assessment, available at <http://ec.europa.eu/internal_market/company/docs/shareholders/comm_native_sec_2006_0181_en.pdf>.

Faccio, M. and Lang, L. H. P. (2002). The Ultimate Ownership of Western European Corporations, *Journal of Financial Economics* 65, 365–95.

Fama, E. F. and French, K. R. (2001). Disappearing Dividends: Changing Firm Characteristics or Lower Propensity to Pay?, *Journal of Financial Economics* 60, 3–43.

Franks, J. and Mayer, C. (2001). Ownership and Control of German Corporations, *Review of Financial Studies* 14, 943–77.

Gillan, S. L. and Starks, L. T. (2000). Corporate Governance Proposals and Shareholder Activism: The Role of Institutional Investors, *Journal of Financial Economics* 57, 275–305.

Girard, C. (2009). Comparative Study of Successful French and Anglo-Saxon Shareholder Activism, Audiencia—Nantes School of Management Working Paper, available at <http://ead.univ-angers.fr/~granem08/IMG/pdf/CGirard-3.pdf>.

Goergen, M. and Renneboog, L. (2001). Strong Managers and Passive Institutional Investors in the UK, in F. Barca and M. Becht (eds.), *The Control of Corporate Europe* (Oxford, Oxford University Press) 259–84.

Goergen, M. and Renneboog, L. (2004). Shareholder Wealth Effects of European Domestic and Cross-Border Takeover Bids, *European Financial Management* 10, 9–45.

Harris, M. and Raviv, A. (2008). Control of Corporate Decisions: Shareholders vs. Management, CRSP Working Paper No. 620, available at <http://ssrn.com/abstract=965559>.

Harrison, M. (2004). Baltimore Apologises for Shares Claim, *The Independent* (London), (27 Apr.).

Heckman, J. J. (1979). Sample Selection Bias as a Specification Error, *Econometrica* 47, 153–61.

Jensen, M. (1986). Agency Costs of Free Cash Flow, Corporate Finance, and Takeovers, *American Economic Review* 76(2), 323–9.

Jensen, M. C. (1993). The Modern Industrial Revolution, Exit, and the Failure of Internal Control Systems, *Journal of Finance* 48, 831–80.

Jensen, M. and Meckling, W. H. (1976). Theory of the Firm: Managerial Behavior, Agency Costs and Ownership Structure, *Journal of Financial Economics* 3, 305–60.

Jensen, M. C. and Murphy, K. J. (1990). Performance Pay and Top-Management Incentives, *Journal of Political Economy* 98, 225–64.

Jensen, M. and Ruback, R. (1983). The Market for Corporate Control: The Scientific Evidence, *Journal of Financial Economics* 11, 5–50.

Karpoff, J. M., Malatesta, P. H., and Walkling, R. A. (1996). Corporate Governance and Shareholder Initiatives: Empirical Evidence, *Journal of Financial Economics* 42, 365–95.

Klinger, P. (2004). Baltimore to Limit Return of Cash Pile, *The Times* (London), (8 June).

La Porta, R., Lopez-de-Silanes, F., and Shleifer, A. (1999). Corporate Ownership around the World, *Journal of Finance* 54, 471–517.

La Porta, R., Lopez-de-Silanes, F., Shleifer, A., and Vishny, R. (1998). Law and Finance, *Journal of Political Economy* 106, 1113–55.

Larsen, P. T. (2007). The Dutch Bank and the Great Hold-Up, *Financial Times* (London), (28 Nov.).

Lipton, M. (2002). Pills, Polls, and Professors Redux, *University of Chicago Law Review* 69, 1037–65.

Manifest (2008). *Proxy Voting 2007—A Pan-European Perspective* (Manifest Information Services).

Martin, K. J. and Thomas, R. S. (1999). The Effect of Shareholder Proposals on Executive Compensation, *University of Cincinnati Law Review* 67, 1021–81.

Martynova, M. and Renneboog, L. (2008). Spillover of Corporate Governance Standards in Cross-Border Mergers and Acquisitions, *Journal of Corporate Finance* 14, 200–23.

Martynova, M. and Renneboog, L. (2011). The Performance of the European Market for Corporate Control: Evidence from the 5th Takeover Wave, *European Financial Management* 17(2), 208–60.

McCahery, J. A., Starks, L. T., and Sautner, Z. (2009). Behind the Scenes: The Corporate Governance Preferences of Institutional Investors, AFA 2011 Denver Meetings Paper; Tilburg Law School Research Paper No. 010/2010, available at <http://ssrn.com/abstract=1571046>.

Nibler, M. (1998). Bank Control and Corporate Performance in Germany: The Evidence, Doctoral Dissertation, University of Cambridge.

Nuttall, C. (2004). Activist Investment Group Wins Battle for Control of Baltimore, *Financial Times* (London), (7 July).

Parrino, R., Sias, R. W., and Starks, L. T. (2003). Voting with their Feet: Institutional Ownership Changes around Forced CEO Turnover, *Journal of Financial Economics* 68, 3–46.

Pound, J. (1998). Proxy Contests and the Efficiency of Shareholder Oversight, *Journal of Financial Economics* 20, 237–65.

Prevost, A. K. and Rao, R. P. (2000). Of What Value are Shareholder Proposals Sponsored by Public Pension Funds?, *Journal of Business* 73, 177–204.

Prevost, A. K., Rao, R. P., and Williams, M. A. (2008). Labor Unions as Shareholder Activists: Champions or Detractors?, Working Paper, available at <http://ssrn.com/abstract=1119328>.

Renneboog, L. and Szilagyi, P. (2009). Shareholder Activism through the Proxy Process, CentER Discussion Paper Series No. 2009-65; ECGI—Finance Working Paper No. 275/2010, available at <http://ssrn.com/abstract=1460578>.

Roe, M. (2004). Explaining Western Securities Markets, in A. Grandori (ed.), *Corporate Governance and Firm Organization: Microfoundations and Structural Forms* (Oxford, Oxford University Press) 279–96.

Shah, S. (2004a). Investor Threatens to Oust Baltimore Board, *The Independent* (London), (22 Mar.).

Shah, S. (2004b). Acquisitor to Oppose Plans at Baltimore AGM, *The Independent* (London), (26 June).

Smith, M. P. (1996). Activism by Institutional Investors: Evidence from CalPERS, *Journal of Finance* 51, 227–52.

Smyth, J. (2004). Key Baltimore Figures Survive Knife-Edge Vote, *The Irish Times* (City Edition), (8 May).

Stewart, H. (2004). Move to Oust Baltimore Board, *The Guardian* (London), (22 Mar.).

Stout, L. A. (2007). The Mythical Benefits of Shareholder Control, *Virginia Law Review* 93, 789–809.

Thomas, R. S. and Cotter, J. F. (2007). Shareholder Proposals in the New Millennium: Shareholder Support, Board Response, and Market Reaction, *Journal of Corporate Finance* 13, 368–91.

Wendlandt, A. (2004). Baltimore Abandons Plans for Clean Energy, *Financial Times* (London), (4 June).

White, H. (1980). A Heteroskedasticity-Consistent Covariance Matrix Estimator and a Direct Test for Heteroskedasticity, *Econometrica* 48, 817–38.

Woidtke, T. (2002). Agents Watching Agents? Evidence from Pension Fund Ownership and Firm Value, *Journal of Financial Economics* 63, 99–131.

Yermack, D. (1996). Higher Market Valuation of Companies with a Small Board of Directors, *Journal of Financial Economics* 40, 185–211.

PART II

HEDGE FUND ACTIVISM

A.

Patterns and Policy Questions—Dark Sides and Light Sides

CHAPTER 5

HEDGE FUNDS IN CORPORATE GOVERNANCE AND CORPORATE CONTROL

MARCEL KAHAN AND EDWARD B. ROCK

5.1 Introduction

Hedge funds have become critical players in both corporate governance and corporate control.[1] Recently, hedge funds have pressured McDonald's to spin off major assets in an IPO;[2] asked Time Warner to change its business strategy;[3] threatened or commenced proxy contests at H. J. Heinz,[4] Massey Energy,[5] KT&G,[6] InfoUSA,[7] Sitel,[8] and GenCorp;[9] made a

[1] For purposes of this chapter, and in general, hedge funds are funds exempt from regulation under the Investment Company Act of 1940, which invest primarily in publicly traded securities or financial derivatives. See SEC (2003: 3).

[2] Eisinger (2005a) notes pressure by Pershing Square, a hedge fund, on McDonald's to sell company-owned restaurants; Gray (2005) reports Pershing Square's response to McDonald's rejection of its proposal.

[3] Angwin (2005) details Carl Icahn's alliance with three other investors to 'agitate for changes' at Time Warner; Sorkin and Siklos (2005: C1) describe a plan by Icahn to 'form a faction with enough leverage to spin off Time Warner Cable, and possibly other divisions'.

[4] Adamy and Reilly (2006a) report that Trian Partners had nominated five directors to run for the board of H. J. Heinz Co.

[5] *Associated Press* (2006a) notes Third Point LLC's plan to nominate two candidates for Massey's board to 'present stockholders' perspectives on management direction', executive compensation, and other issues.

[6] Cha (2006) reports and analyses the proxy contest between a group of investors led by Carl Icahn and KT&G management; Santini (2006) describes the Icahn group as having 'won more support than expected' during the proxy contest.

[7] *Reuters* (2006) discusses the proxy contest between InfoUSA's founder and Dolphin, a Connecticut-based hedge fund.

[8] *PR Newswire* (2005a) notes Jana Partners' nomination of three director candidates for SITEL's board.

[9] Swett (2006) reports Pirate Capital's victory in a proxy battle to elect its slate of directors to GenCorp's board.

bid to acquire Houston Exploration;[10] pushed for a merger between Euronext and Deutsche Börse (DB);[11] pushed for 'changes in management and strategy' at Nabi Biopharmaceuticals;[12] opposed acquisitions by Novartis of the remaining 58% stake in Chiron,[13] by Sears Holdings of the 46% minority interest in Sears Canada,[14] by Micron of Lexar Media,[15] and by a group of private equity firms of VNU;[16] threatened litigation against Delphi;[17] and pushed for litigation against Calpine that led to the ousting of its top two executives.[18]

Even though most hedge funds are not activist,[19] the ones that are have captured attention. Martin Lipton, the renowned advisor to corporate boards and veteran of the takeover wars of the 1980s, lists 'attacks by activist hedge funds' as the number one key issue for directors.[20] The *Wall Street Journal*, the newspaper of record for executives, bankers, and investment professionals, calls hedge funds the 'new leader' on the 'list of bogeymen haunting the corporate boardroom' (Murray 2005a: A2).[21] *The Economist* (2006a) has run a special report on shareholder democracy focusing on activism by hedge funds, and several European governments are considering regulations designed to curb hedge fund activism.[22]

What should we make of this spate of shareholder activism by hedge funds? Are hedge funds the 'Holy Grail' of corporate governance—the long sought-after shareholder champion with the incentives and expertise to protect shareholder interests in publicly held firms? Or do they represent darker forces, in search of quick profit opportunities at the expense of other shareholders and the long-term health of the economy?

In this chapter, we analyse and evaluate the implications of the rise of hedge funds for corporate governance and corporate control. In Section 5.2, we examine and categorize a variety of presumptively 'happy stories'—that is, examples of different kinds of activism where hedge

[10] Cauchi (2006) reports the bid by Jana for Houston Exploration.

[11] Clark and Ahuja (2006) discuss Euronext's acquiescence to TCI's request for a vote; Hedge Fund Street (2005) notes the proposed merger and provides the historical context.

[12] Steyer (2006) discusses the use of the same strategy employed with Ligand Pharmaceuticals towards Nabi Biopharmaceuticals.

[13] Hamilton (2006a) discusses the challenges ValueAct's activism presented to the then proposed merger between Novartis and Chiron; *Business Wire* (2006) notes ValueAct's continued opposition to the merger.

[14] Norris (2006) details Sears Holdings' attempt to take Sears Canada private and Pershing Square's opposition to the transaction.

[15] Chappell (2006) reports the concerns of a consortium of hedge funds, including Icahn Associates Corporation, and Elliott Associates, L.P., that the merger paid an insufficient price for Lexar.

[16] Singer (2006a) describes Knight Vinke Asset Management's opposition to the transaction.

[17] McCracken (2006) discusses an attempt by David Tepper, the head of Appaloosa Management, to form an equity committee in the Delphi bankruptcy case.

[18] Smith and Sender (2005) detail the battle between Calpine's management and dozens of hedge funds over bankruptcy strategy.

[19] See Section 5.2.3.

[20] Client Memorandum from Martin Lipton (2006a, b), the latter presents a checklist for clients to avoid disruptions caused activist hedge funds; Lipton (2005) notes an 'environment of attacks by hedge funds' and advises companies on how to deal with it.

[21] See also Eisinger (2006: C1) stating that '[t]he shareholder activists with the most clout these days are hedge-fund managers . . .'.

[22] Taylor (2006) reports that the German finance minister wanted to discuss the transparency of hedge funds, a concern shared by managers worried about activist funds; Taylor and MacDonald (2006) describe regulations being considered by Germany and the Netherlands.

funds have no apparent conflict of interest. We argue that this hedge fund activism differs, quantitatively and qualitatively, from the more moderate forms of activism that traditional institutional investors engage in.

In Section 5.3, we analyse why hedge funds are so much more active than other institutional investors. We show that hedge funds have better incentives, are subject to fewer regulatory impediments, and face fewer conflicts of interest than traditional institutions, such as mutual funds and pension funds, which have never lived up to the hopes of their partisans. But the activism of hedge funds may also be due to the fact that many follow a different business strategy than traditional institutions. This strategy involves taking high stakes in portfolio companies in order to become activist, rather than diversifying and becoming involved (if at all) only *ex post* when companies are underperforming, thus blurring the lines between betting on and determining the outcome of contests.

In Section 5.4, we turn to potential problems generated by hedge fund activism. We first examine the 'dark side' of activism—instances where the interests of activist hedge funds conflict with those of their fellow shareholders—to see whether regulatory intervention is warranted. We then discuss other problems that arise from the stress that hedge funds put on the governance system.

In Section 5.5, we turn to the most severe attack levelled against hedge funds: that hedge fund activism increases the pressure for short-term results over more valuable long-term benefits. We accept that short-termism by hedge funds can aggravate short-termism in the executive suite. But we nevertheless conclude that, at this point, no regulatory intervention is warranted because: it is unclear to what extent hedge fund activism is driven by excessive short-termism; hedge funds usually need the support of other, less short-term oriented constituents to affect corporate policy; and, to the extent short-termism generates a problem, adaptive devices adopted by corporations are a better way to address it than regulation.[23] Section 5.6 concludes.

5.2 What's Going On Out There? Some Illustrative, Happy Stories

Hedge funds are emerging as the most dynamic and most prominent shareholder activists. On the bright side, this generates the possibility that hedge funds will, in the course of making profits for their own investors, help overcome the classic agency problem of publicly held corporations by dislodging underperforming managers, challenging ineffective strategies, and making sure that merger and control transactions make sense for shareholders. In so doing, if one looks at the bright side, hedge funds would enhance the value of the companies in which they invest for the benefit of both their own investors and their fellow shareholders. In Section 5.2.1, we examine and categorize the different ways in which hedge funds, without any apparent conflicts of interest, have confronted managers. This section illustrates the potential bright side of hedge fund activism.

[23] We do not address the question of whether additional regulation is needed to protect hedge fund investors from either investment risk or unscrupulous managers. While important and timely, this question is beyond the scope of this chapter.

But the bright side story of hedge funds—of large and sophisticated investors standing up to management for the benefit of shareholders at large—has an element of *déjà vu*. Twenty years ago, similar stories were told about another set of large and sophisticated investors: mutual funds, pension funds, and insurance companies—or 'institutional investors', as they became known (see, generally, Admati, Pfleiderer, and Zechner 1994; Black 1992, 1990; Gilson and Kraakman 1991; Rock 1991; Roe 1991a). While, on the whole, the rise of these traditional institutional investors has probably been beneficial, they have hardly proven to be a silver bullet.

Are there reasons to think that the newly prominent hedge funds will be more effective? In Section 5.2.2, we start answering this question by comparing the activism of hedge funds to the activism of traditional institutions. We show that hedge fund activism differs in degree and type from activism by traditional institutions.

In Section 5.2.3, we place hedge fund activism in the context of hedge fund investment strategies more generally. Because only a small portion of hedge fund assets are devoted to shareholder activism, activism does not dominate what hedge funds do. Hedge funds, however, dominate certain modes of activism and—if that activism is profitable and more hedge funds' assets become devoted to it—the extent of hedge fund activism could quickly increase.

5.2.1 Hedge Funds as Activists

5.2.1.1 *Corporate Governance Activism*

Hedge funds have increasingly tried to influence the business strategy and management of corporations. This activism takes a variety of forms, from public pressure on a portfolio company to change its business strategy, to the running of a proxy contest to gain seats on the board of directors, to litigation against present or former managers.

One of the better-known (and more entertaining) activist hedge funds is Third Point, which has about $4 billion under management (*PR Newswire* 2005b). Its list of recent targets includes Ligand, Salton, Western Gas Resources, Massey Energy, Potlatch, Intercept, Warnaco, Penn Virginia, and Star Gas Partners (Innisfree M&A Inc. 2006: slide 15). Star Gas, to pick one of the targets, is a heating oil distributor in which Third Point acquired a 6% stake (*PR Newswire* 2005c). In addition to severely criticizing then CEO Irik Sevin's management of the company, Third Point attacked him personally: '[i]t is time for you to step down from your role as CEO and director so that you can do what you do best: retreat to your waterfront mansion in the Hamptons where you can play tennis and hobnob with your fellow socialites' (*PR Newswire* 2005c). The governance practices of Star Gas were apparently not ideal. Third Point openly wondered:

> [H]ow is it possible that you selected your elderly 78-year-old mom to serve on the Company's Board of Directors and as a full-time employee providing employee and unitholder services? We further wonder under what theory of corporate governance does one's mom sit on a Company board. Should you be found derelict in the performance of your executive duties, as we believe is the case, we do not believe your mom is the right person to fire you from your job (*PR Newswire* 2005c).
> The tactic worked. Bowing to the pressure generated by Third Point, Sevin resigned one month later (Orol 2005).[24]

[24] Whether this was too little too late is an interesting but separate question. After a brief uptick, Star Gas's stock price continued to decline.

The exploits of Barington Capital Group provide another good example. In June 2003, a syndicate of investors led by Barington nominated three directors to the board of Nautica Enterprises, the sportswear company. At the time, Barington held about 3.1% of Nautica stock (Kapner 2003a). Shortly thereafter, the company indicated that it was discussing a possible sale (Kapner 2003b). Barington subsequently convinced Institutional Shareholder Services, a proxy voting advisory service, to recommend that its clients vote for two director candidates nominated by Barington (*PR Newswire* 2003a). By July 2003, Barington's tactics had worked: Nautica agreed to be acquired by VF Corporation for $587 million (Sundaramoorthy 2003), and Barington dropped its proxy fight (*PR Newswire* 2003b). The following July, Barington turned to Steve Madden, the shoe retailer, and urged it to explore 'strategic discussions with potential acquirers' (Padgett 2004). Barington, which had accumulated a 7.7% stake, sent outside directors a strongly worded letter demanding that Steve Madden hire a more seasoned CEO, reduce change in control compensation, reduce conflicts of interest on the board, and use its excess cash to buy back shares and pay dividends (*PR Newswire* 2004a). By February 2005, the Steve Madden board agreed to spend $25 million in 2005 for share repurchases and dividends and to meet with representatives of Barington on a regular basis in order to avoid a proxy fight (*PR Newswire* 2005d).

Carl Icahn, familiar to some from the takeover battles of the 1980s, has returned to the headlines by starting a hedge fund, buying blocks in companies, and pressuring them to change (Pulliam and Peers 2005). For example, he teamed up with Jana Partners to take a position in Kerr-McGee and push for change (thedeal.com 2005). The outcome was a restructuring in which Kerr-McGee sold off its chemicals unit and its North Sea oilfields (Koza 2005). Icahn has more recently put pressure on Blockbuster, where he gained a board seat (Sender 2005); Time Warner, where the company agreed to add some independent directors to its board and to increase the size of its share repurchase programme (Karnitschnig 2006); KT&G, where the group he led gained board representation (Santini 2006); and Motorola, where he is seeking board representation (Yuan and Rhoads 2007).

Other examples, many involving household names, abound. Targets of corporate governance activism include McDonald's, where Pershing Square has sought a spin-off of its real estate assets (Eisinger 2005a);Wendy's, where Trian Partners has provoked an asset spin-off and gained board seats (Politi 2006); Heinz, where Trian has nominated five directors to the twelve-member board (Adamy2006a); Pep Boys—Manny, Moe & Jack, where Barington has sought to induce the company 'to sell itself or replace its CEO' (McGee 2006); and Delphi Corp., where Appaloosa Management has sought board seats and the creation of (and representation on) an official equity committee to represent shareholder interests in the company's Chapter 11 proceeding (McCracken 2006).[25]

[25] See also Richardson (2006), reporting that Xerion Capital helped form a shareholder committee, which succeeded in increasing the sale price of Riverstone Networks' assets in Chapter 11 from $170 to $210 million. For other instances of hedge fund governance activism, see Hallinan and Berman (2005), noting that, under pressure from hedge fund Private Capital Management and the company's largest shareholder, Knight Ridder put itself up for sale; Murray (2005b), observing that hedge funds ratcheted up pressure on the Morgan Stanley board to remove its CEO; Sender (2005), discussing hedge fund activism at OfficeMax, Woolworths, and Wendy's; *PR Newswire* (2004b), discussing efforts by Steel Partners to influence the board of BKF capital group; *PR Newswire* (2005e), revealing Steel Partners' plans to nominate director candidates for BFK's board.

In the course of their general corporate governance activities, hedge funds often get involved in various legal disputes with the targets of their activism. While these disputes are usually an adjunct to broader activism—as when Jana Partners sued SourceCorp to invalidate changes in the company's bylaws in light of an impending proxy contest (*Dallas Business Journal* 2005), or when Mason Capital tried to block the recapitalization of Kaman, arguing that it violated the Connecticut antitakeover statute[26]—litigation is sometimes an essential part of the activist strategy. Take, for example, Cardinal Value Equity Partners, which owned about 1.5 million shares in Hollinger International. When allegations of self-dealing and other improper transactions by Conrad Black, Hollinger's CEO, and other members of Hollinger's management surfaced, Cardinal brought a lawsuit in Delaware to obtain records and corporate documents (Vaughan-Adams 2003). Six months later, in December 2003, Cardinal brought a derivative lawsuit for breach of fiduciary duty against Hollinger's board of directors (Kirk 2004). Cardinal subsequently agreed to stay the action until an internal investigation of the alleged misconduct was finished (Rushe and O'Donnell 2004). By May 2005, Cardinal had negotiated a $50 million settlement with the directors not directly implicated in the self-dealing, with Hollinger International Inc. (2005) continuing to pursue the self-dealing claims against Black and some of his associates in a separate litigation. Cardinal, moreover, has continued to pressure Hollinger's board and recently criticized its failure to remove some of the settling directors from its ranks (Siklos 2005).[27]

Tellingly, hedge funds have even sought appointment as lead plaintiffs in securities fraud class actions under the Private Securities Litigation Reform Act.[28] What makes these efforts noteworthy is that, even though hedge funds are often among the investors with the largest losses, their appointment as lead plaintiffs is fraught with problems. Because hedge funds often engage in short selling, they face issues of reliance that may render them 'inadequate' class representatives. A short strategy is based on the assumption that the current market price is inaccurate. This provides evidence that a short-selling hedge fund did not rely on the integrity of the market price, as required under the fraud on the market theory on which most securities fraud class actions are based. Indeed, as a result of this conflict, courts have often, though not uniformly,[29] rejected the appointment of hedge funds as lead plaintiffs.[30]

[26] *Mason Capital, Ltd. v. Kaman Corp.*, No. 3:05CV1470, 2005 WL 2850083, at *1 (D. Conn. Oct. 31, 2005); see also *PR Newswire* (2005f), reporting the ruling in favour of Kaman; *PR Newswire* (2005g), announcing an agreement between the two firms to end the suit.

[27] For examples of other instances where Cardinal engaged in litigation, see *In re Pure Resources Shareholder Litigation*, C.A. No. 19876, 2002 Del. Ch. LEXIS 116 (Del. Ch. Oct. 9, 2002); *Associated Press* (2006b).

[28] Private Securities Litigation Reform Act of 1995, Pub. L. No. 104-67, 109 Stat. 737 (codified as amended in scattered sections of 15 U.S.C.).

[29] See, e.g., *In re Tyson Foods, Inc. Sec. Litig.*, No. 01-425-SLR, 2003 U.S. Dist. LEXIS 17904, at *10–20 (D. Del. Oct. 6, 2003) certifying the class in a securities fraud suit and rejecting challenges to a hedge fund as a representative—challenges based on the alleged unsuitability of hedge funds to serve in that role; *Danis v. USN Commc'ns, Inc.*, 189 F.R.D. 391, 396 (N.D. Ill. 1999) rejecting a challenge to a hedge fund's typicality based on short sales, because the fund also sustained losses on long positions.

[30] See, e.g., *Camden Asset Mgmt., L.P. v. Sunbeam Corp.*, No. 99-8275-CIV-MIDDLEBROOKS, 2001 U.S. Dist. LEXIS 11022, at *54–6 (S.D. Fla. July 3, 2001), denying class certification in a class action brought by a fund that hedged its investment in convertible debentures, because individual issues of reliance were held to predominate; *In re Critical Path, Inc. Sec. Litig.*, 156 F. Supp. 2d 1102, 1109–10 (N.D. Cal. 2001), holding that a hedge fund, which had shorted stock, was an inadequate class representative in a fraud on the market class action because short strategy is premised on inaccuracy of current

5.2.1.2 *Corporate Control Activism*

Hedge funds have been particularly active in transactions involving potential changes in corporate control. This activism broadly falls into three categories. First, as shareholders of the potential acquirer, hedge funds have tried to prevent the consummation of the transaction. Second, as shareholders of the potential target, hedge funds have tried to block the deal or improve the terms for target shareholders. Third, hedge funds have themselves—sometimes on their own, sometimes as part of a group—tried to acquire companies.

5.2.1.2.1 Blocking Acquirers

Perhaps the best-known example of a hedge fund blocking an acquirer involves the proposed acquisition by DB of the London Stock Exchange (LSE). Having tried and failed to acquire LSE in 2000, DB announced a new bid in December 2004 (Jenkins and Cohen 2004). This quickly spurred Euronext, a competing exchange, to announce its interest in LSE (Cohen 2004).

DB's problems started in mid-January, when TCI,[31] a London-based hedge fund that had assembled more than a 5% stake in DB, announced its opposition. TCI argued that using DB's cash hoard to buy back shares 'would be far superior in value creation' (Wray 2005). Although the bid did not require shareholder approval, TCI held a large enough stake to call an extraordinary general meeting to dismiss DB's supervisory board.[32] Around the same time, Atticus Capital, a US-based fund, which then controlled around 2% of DB's shares, joined TCI in opposing the bid (Cohen 2005). By February, DB shareholders holding about 35% of its stock (including several mutual funds), prompted by TCI and Atticus, were planning to confront DB (Armitstead 2005a: Bus.1).[33] TCI started looking for a candidate to replace Rolf Breuer as DB's chairman, and came up with Lord Jacob Rothschild (Armitstead 2005b), who, as it happens, was the father of the president of Atticus (Ringshaw 2005).

In early March, DB's CEO, Werner Seifert, came to London to meet with the largest dissident shareholders, only to have the offer of a meeting refused (Cohen and Jenkins 2005). With more than 40%, and as much as 60%, of the shares opposing the bid (depending on reports), DB abandoned its bid in early March and promised to develop a plan to distribute the cash (Cohen and Jenkins 2005).[34] As the participants celebrated the victory, the division of labour between hedge

market price; *In re Bank One S'holders Class Actions*, 96 F. Supp. 2d 780, 784 (N.D. Ill. 2000), rejecting a hedge fund as a lead plaintiff that had 'engaged in extensive day-trading, first shorting Bank One stock (presumably because it was regarded as overvalued at market price) and then buying to cover the short position'. In an interesting development, Chancellor Leo Strine forced a hedge fund to serve as a defendant class representative in *Regal Entertainment Group v. Amaranth*, LLC, 894 A.2d 1104 (Del. Ch. 2006). The effect of this—and presumably why the hedge fund resisted—is that any settlement must be approved by the court and, moreover, that the class representative cannot settle separately.

[31] So named because 50% of TCI's annual management fee is paid to The Children's Investment Fund Foundation, which funds development projects focused on children in developing nations (Waller 2005).

[32] To call a meeting, TCI would have to register its shares with BaFin and hold them for three months (Reece 2005).

[33] See also Kollewe (2005), indicating that Fidelity held more than a 4.5% stake.

[34] See also *Agence France Presse* (2005), describing DB's actions as 'effectively throwing in the towel in the face of fierce and long resistance to the deal on the part of private equity firms'; Danny Fortson (2005) noting DB's plan to 'redistribute funds to investors'.

funds and traditional institutional investors became clear. As the representative of one institutional investor said, 'The hedge funds have done a marvelous job. No matter how we feel about companies, traditional managers simply cannot move as fast to achieve our aims. We were right behind [the hedge funds], but we couldn't have done it without them' (Armitstead 2005a (insertion in original)). In May 2005, Seifert resigned after DB's chairman was ordered by the supervisory board 'to change the composition of the Supervisory and Executive Boards in order to reflect the new ownership structure of the Company' (DB AG 2005).

Other instances where hedge funds have sought to block an acquisition in their role as the shareholders of the potential acquirer include Carl Icahn's efforts to prevent Mylan Laboratories from acquiring King Pharmaceuticals;[35] Knight Vinke, which followed Templeton in opposing VNU's proposed acquisition of IMS Health (Berman and Singer 2005); Duquesne Capital Management, which opposed the proposed acquisition of Public Service Enterprise Group by Exelon (*Chicago Tribune* 2006); OrbiMed Advisors, which succeeded in blocking the acquisition of EOS by Pharmacopia (*San Francisco Business Times* 2002); and Pirate Capital, Omega Advisors, and Jana Partners, which collectively opposed Mirant's offer to acquire NRG (Trincal 2006).

5.2.1.2.2 *Blocking Targets*

As shareholders of target companies, hedge funds have actively opposed several proposed acquisitions and have often succeeded in improving the terms of the transaction. A recent example involved Novartis's attempt to acquire the 58% of Chiron that it did not already own. Novartis initially offered $40 per share to the Chiron shareholders. An independent committee of Chiron negotiated this price up to $45 per share, a 23% premium over Chiron's pre-offer share price (Novartis International AG 2005). One month after the agreement was announced, ValueAct Capital, a hedge fund and the third largest shareholder of Chiron, sent a 'stinging' letter to Chiron's CEO announcing its opposition (Hamilton 2006a). This started a shareholder revolt, with mutual fund Legg Mason, the second largest shareholder of Chiron, joining ValueAct's opposition, and Institutional Shareholder Services recommending a vote against the deal (Hamilton 2006a). To get the transaction through, Novartis had to raise its offer to $48 a share (Hamilton 2006b), increasing the premium from 23% to 32%.

The fate of the Chiron–Novartis deal is not unusual. Other examples of hedge funds opposing acquisitions include Masonite International, where Eminence Capital and Greystone Management Investment succeeded in raising the price from C$40.20 to C$42.25;[36] ShopKo, where Elliott Management derailed a proposed acquisition for $24 a share (*Business Journal of Milwaukee* 2005); MONY, where Highfields led the opposition to the company's acquisition by AXA;[37] Molson, where Highfields forced Coors to improve the sale terms (Innisfree M&A Inc. 2006: slide 6); VNU, where Knight Vinke Asset Management opposed the company's acquisition by a consortium of private equity firms (Singer 2006a); Lexar Media, where Carl Icahn and Elliott Associates opposed a merger with Micron (Chappell 2006); Sears Canada, where Pershing Square tried to hold out against a bid by Sears—itself a company

[35] See Section 5.4.1.3.

[36] See *PR Newswire* (2005h), expressing discontent with the initial C$40.20 per share offer; Masonite International Corp. (2005), announcing approval of the sale to KKR by 91.8% of non-senior management shareholders after the higher price was offered.

[37] See Section 5.4.1.2.

run by hedge fund manager Eddie Lampert—to freeze out the minority shareholders (Norris 2006); Titan International, Inc. (2006), where Jana Partners thwarted the company's proposed acquisition by a private equity firm; and MCI, which faced the threat of a proxy contest by Deephaven Capital to derail an acquisition by Verizon (Berman and Latour 2005).[38]

When hedge funds are dissatisfied with the terms of an acquisition and unable to obtain better terms, they also resort to litigation. In particular, hedge funds have filed statutory appraisal actions, in which shareholders receive a court-determined fair value instead of the merger consideration. Take the acquisition of Emerging Communications (ECM) by its majority shareholder, Innovative Communications, for $10.25 per share.[39] Greenlight Capital, a hedge fund, held about 500,000 shares in the company. After the acquisition was announced, it increased its stake and sought appraisal for 750,300 shares.[40] As is commonplace in minority freeze-out mergers, a plaintiff's law firm also filed a fiduciary duty action.[41] The latter form of action is often settled for a relatively modest recovery (if any).[42] But, in this case, when a settlement was proposed that provided for no additional payments to shareholders and $115,000 in legal fees,[43] Greenlight, which had also acquired litigation rights for over 2 million ECM shares, objected.[44] Both the appraisal and the fiduciary duty action proceeded to trial, and the court determined that the fair value of an ECM share was $38.05. Greenlight was awarded that amount plus compounded interest in its appraisal shares, as well as damages of $27.80 per share—the difference between the fair value and the merger consideration—in the fiduciary duty action.[45]

Other instances of hedge funds exercising appraisal rights include Gabelli Asset Management's 2004 appraisal action against Carter Wallace (GAMCO Investors, Inc. 2004), Prescott Group's appraisal against Coleman,[46] and the pending appraisal action brought by Icahn and others in Transkaryotic Therapies, where hedge funds had tried, but failed, to block the acquisition and decided to pursue appraisal instead of accepting the merger consideration.[47]

[38] For additional accounts of hedge funds interfering with acquisition bids, see, for example, Singer (2005).

[39] *In re Emerging Commc'ns, Inc. S'holders Litig.*, No. 16415, 2004 Del. Ch. LEXIS 70, at *2 (Del. Ch. May 3, 2004).

[40] Greenlight held shares in ECM before the merger was announced, but increased its stake by 264,700 shares between the announcement and the merger vote. In its Schedule 13D, filed ten days later, Greenlight disclosed its intention to seek appraisal rights. Greenlight Capital, L.L.C., General Statement of Beneficial Ownership (Schedule 13D) (28 Sept.1998), available at <http://www.secinfo.com/dsN7p.74d.htm#1stPage>.

[41] *In re Emerging Commc'ns*, 2004 Del. Ch. LEXIS 70, at *3.

[42] See *In re Cox Commc'ns Inc. S'holders Litig.*, 879 A.2d 604, 622 (Del. Ch. 2005) (noting that the plaintiffs' lawyers in a shareholder litigation were 'pragmatic' in 'temper[ing] their fee requests' to seek a 'relatively small percentage of the "benefits" '); Weiss and White (2004: 1833) find that settlements in squeeze-out cases provided for small recoveries.

[43] Stipulation and Agreement of Compromise and Settlement at 10, *Erickell Partners v. Emerging Commc'ns, Inc.*, No. 16415-NC (Del. Ch. Jun. 27, 2000).

[44] *In re Emerging Commc'ns*, 2004 Del. Ch. LEXIS 70, at *3–4.

[45] *In re Emerging Commc'ns*, 2004 Del. Ch. LEXIS 70. at *155. ECM has appealed the judgment to the Delaware Supreme Court, where the case is pending. See also Fields (2006).

[46] *Prescott Group Small Cap, L.P. v. The Coleman Co.*, No. 17802, 2004 Del. Ch. LEXIS 131 (Del. Ch. Sept. 8, 2004).

[47] See Latham & Watkins (2005: slide 11), noting that 'more than one third of Transkaryotic shares, including Icahn and other hedge funds, have exercised their appraisal rights' after the acquisition by Shire Pharmaceuticals.

5.2.1.2.3 *Making Bids*

Unlike traditional institutional investors, hedge funds not only urge portfolio companies to be acquired by third parties, but also make attempts to acquire these companies themselves. These bids can be part of a strategy to improve the governance or capital structure of these companies or to put the target in play. In other instances, however, hedge funds have emerged as controlling shareholders of large industrial corporations.

As an example of an acquisition offer that induced corporate governance changes, consider GenCorp. GenCorp owned more than 12,000 acres of undeveloped land in Sacramento, an asset that attracted the interest of various investors (Marcial 2005). In November 2004, Steel Partners, a hedge fund, announced that it was interested in acquiring GenCorp for $17 per share (*PR Newswire* 2004c). When the board rejected Steel Partners' advance, the fund threatened a proxy contest (Orol 2004). By February 2005, GenCorp and Steel Partners had agreed that Steel Partners would cast its votes in favour of GenCorp's nominees, a representative of Steel Partners could attend board meetings, the board would appoint a new independent director with expertise in corporate governance (identified in consultation with Steel Partners), and the board would then consider corporate governance changes proposed by Steel Partners (Kasler 2005).

ShopKo, a retail and pharmacy store chain, provides another illustration of this approach. ShopKo had agreed to be acquired by Goldner Hawn, a private equity firm, for $24 per share. But Elliott Associates, a hedge fund with a major stake in ShopKo, opposed the proposed deal. Together with Sun Capital, a private equity firm, and some other investors, Elliott made a counter bid of $26.50. After an auction, the Elliott Group succeeded in acquiring ShopKo for $29 a share (*Business Journal of Milwaukee* 2005).

Finally, take Kmart. Kmart filed for bankruptcy in February 2002. When it emerged from Chapter 11 in May 2003,[48] its largest shareholder was the hedge fund ESL, run by Edward Lampert. ESL owned about 50% of the company, having acquired $2 billion in financial claims (for somewhere around $200 million) that were converted into stock in the reorganization (Byron 2003; *Crain's Detroit Business* 2003). At the time Kmart emerged from bankruptcy, its stock opened at $15 per share and drifted downward (Rosenberg 2004). But by July 2004, Kmart's stock was at $76 per share and Lampert, who had taken over the management of Kmart, was the toast of the town (Yerak 2004). By unlocking the value of Kmart's real estate through selling off stores, Kmart accumulated a '$2.2 billion cash hoard' (Berner 2004: 81). By November 2004, Lampert answered the market's question of what he was going to do with all that money: Kmart and Sears agreed to merge (Hays 2004). The news of the deal pushed Kmart stock up to $109 per share, and Sears shares rose as well (Hays 2004).[49]

Additional examples of hedge funds making bids include Appaloosa Management, which made a bid for Beverly Enterprises (Moreira 2005);[50] Highfields, which made a bid to acquire

[48] Emerging from Chapter 11 in fifteen months is very quick for a major bankruptcy, and can be explained by the incentives put in place for management. See Baird and Rasmussen (2003: 698), attributing Kmart's atypical emergence from Chapter 11 to Lampert's control over the appointments to the board of directors and his stake in the reorganized business.

[49] Prior to its investment in Kmart, ESL had owned a large block of Sears stock—a block which had increased to 15% by the time the merger was announced. See *The Economist* (2004).

[50] In response to the bid, the board of Beverly decided to auction the company, which was ultimately acquired by another bidder. See *Wall Street Journal* (2005a); Loftus (2005b).

Circuit City;[51] ValueAct, which repeatedly attempted to acquire Acxiom (Levey 2005); and Jana Partners, which made a bid for Houston Exploration (Cauchi 2006).

5.2.2 Activism by Traditional Institutions Compared

Over the last twenty years, traditional institutional investors—specifically public pension funds and mutual funds—have also engaged in shareholder activism. The mode of this activism, however, differs in important respects from activism by hedge funds.

Activism by traditional institutions generally falls into two categories. Starting in the mid-1980s, and continuing to a limited extent until today, traditional institutions have made shareholder proposals under Rule 14a-8. These proposals are usually precatory resolutions that relate to various aspects of the corporate governance rules, such as poison pills, confidential voting, and board structure. Most of these proposals were introduced by public pension funds—including CalPERS, various New York pension funds, and the State of Wisconsin Investment Board—and by TIAA-CREF (see, generally, Del Guercio and Hawkins 1999; Gillan and Starks 2000; Karpoff, Malatesta, and Walkling 1996; Smith 1996). Since the mid-1990s, however, institutions have increasingly engaged in private negotiations to get boards to make governance changes voluntarily, and have only resorted to formal proposals in some of the instances where boards failed to do so.[52]

Seeking governance changes through (actual or threatened) shareholder proposals has largely been the domain of public pension funds.[53] Other than TIAA-CREF, mutual funds have not themselves been active in this strategy, whether initially or after failed private negotiations. Mutual funds have, however, voted in favour of proposals introduced by others. In addition, mutual funds have adopted policies to vote against certain changes in governance rules that entrench the current board if such changes are proposed by the board of directors, and these funds have sometimes withheld votes (i.e., abstained) in director elections.[54]

These activities differ from activism by hedge funds in a variety of ways. They are directed to changes in the corporate governance rules, rather than to specific aspects of a company's business or management (such as share buy-backs, spin-offs, mergers, or the composition of the board of directors). In addition, the effect of the policy changes sought is usually minor, either because

[51] Barbaro (2005) reports the bid by Highfields for Circuit City and notes the increasing interest among hedge funds in pursuing takeovers.

[52] See Carleton, Nelson, and Weisbach (1998: 1336), emphasizing 'the importance of private negotiations between institutions and corporations'; Gillan and Starks (2000: 279), stating that 'institutional investors began having more direct negotiation with company management and less reliance on proxy proposals'; Gillan and Starks (2003: 10), noting that institutional shareholders had shifted away from their previous tactic of shareholder proposals towards 'negotiating directly with corporate management'.

[53] More recently, union-affiliated pension funds have increasingly sponsored shareholder proposals (Schwab and Thomas 1998: 1019–20).

[54] See Romano (1993: 834 tbl.5), categorizing institutional investors' proxy voting policies. Public pension funds—but not mutual funds—have also increasingly applied to become lead plaintiffs in securities fraud class action lawsuits. See also Choi and Thompson (2006: 1507). Securities fraud class actions, however, are at the periphery of corporate governance and control activities.

the subject matter is not very important,[55] because the shareholder resolution is precatory (and a favourable vote is thus not binding), or because a board, even if it agrees to adopt the proposed policy, is free to change it later. To the extent that the 'activism' takes the form of merely voting in favour of proposals by others (or against proposals made by the company's board), it represents a rather passive form. Finally, a group of portfolio companies tends to be targeted at the same time,[56] and often with respect to the same governance changes.

Viewed charitably, this mode of activism is designed to achieve small changes in multiple companies at little expense, but it is unlikely to result in big changes in specific companies. The prominent role of proxy advisory firms like Institutional Shareholders Services (ISS) is consistent with this focus on small, low-cost, systemic changes.

The second category of activities by traditional institutions consists of 'behind-the-scenes' discussions with company management and board members.[57] From what has become known about these activities after the fact, it appears that they seek the same modest changes in governance rules as do shareholder proposals. For example, Carleton, Nelson, and Weisbach, who obtained access to the private correspondence between TIAA–CREF and portfolio firms, report that the changes sought involved confidential voting, board diversity, and limitations on targeted stock placements (1998: 1346 tbl.2).[58] Known instances of institutions seeking more far-reaching changes are rare and often involve unusual fact patterns.[59]

As to activities that have remained non-public, we, of course, do not know their scale and scope. But we consider it unlikely that such activities resemble the activism of hedge funds. It is implausible that institutions could often succeed in achieving major changes through behind-the-scenes discussions without their efforts becoming public.[60] After all, if management is not receptive to the proposed changes, the institution must either give up or go public. And if management knows that institutions are reluctant to go public, it has little incentive to accede to the request for change. Moreover, the leverage that institutions can exercise behind the scenes is limited. If an institution wanted to coordinate its pressure with those of other institutions, it could become engaged in a solicitation or in the formation of a 'group' within the meaning of the Securities Exchange Act, which often would require a public filing.[61] The

[55] See, e.g., Romano (2003: 506), concluding that confidential voting proposals are immaterial.

[56] See, e.g., CalPERS (2006), illustrating CalPERS's practice of compiling an annual 'Focus List' to channel its activism.

[57] See, e.g., Carleton, Nelson, and Weisbach (1998), analysing the influence of TIAA–CREF over corporate governance through private negotiations; Gillan and Starks (2003: 11–12), discussing 'behind-the-scenes' activism and providing examples of its use by TIAA–CREF and CalPERS.

[58] See also Myerson (1993), discussing letters that Fidelity sent to 100 companies opposing certain executive pay plans; Murray (2006: A2), noting that public pension funds induced governance changes at AIG, including separating the posts of chairman and CEO, increasing the number of independent board members, and '[r]equiring independent board members to meet in "executive session"'.

[59] For example, Fidelity had one of its employees appointed as CEO of Colt Telecom (Gillan and Starks 2003: 10). But Colt was unusual in that it was founded by Fidelity, was close to bankruptcy, and Fidelity held 54% of its stock (*Boston Business Journal* 2002).

[60] Cf. Fisch (1994: 1030), observing that institutions considering 'more activist efforts to influence corporate policy... do not appear convinced that the game is worth the candle'; Lazaroff (2005: 7), quoting an investor as saying, 'rarely do you hear a mutual fund manager make a sound', as an indication of passivity among institutional investors.

[61] See Securities Exchange Act of 1934 §§ 13(d)(3), 14(a), 15 U.S.C. §§ 78m(d)(3), 78n(a) (2000) (imposing disclosure obligations on 'groups' of shareholders). By contrast, the tendency of hedge funds to conduct their activism in public reduces the need for public disclosure of any coordination. See Section 5.4.2.1.

scarcity of such filings and the absence of any reports to the contrary suggest that traditional institutions do not coordinate their behind-the-scenes pressure. We are sceptical whether uncoordinated pressure by a single institution will often result in meaningful change.

This being said, traditional institutions have recently, in the wake of hedge fund activism, become somewhat more active in matters involving corporate control. Thus, as discussed in this section, Franklin Mutual Advisers, an investment adviser for mutual funds and other accounts, has joined forces with a hedge fund and other investors in making a bid for Beverly Enterprises.[62] Additionally, mutual funds have supported the efforts of hedge funds to block the acquisition of the LSE by Deutsche Bank, of Chiron by Novartis, of MONY by AXA, and of IMS Health by VNU.[63] And we suspect that there are additional examples where traditional institutions have expressed support for hedge funds in private communications with management. Hedge funds, it thus appears, have not just been activist themselves; they have also been a catalyst for activism by traditional institutions conducted jointly with, or in the wake of, hedge funds.[64]

5.2.3 Hedge Fund Activism in Perspective

In assessing the many instances where hedge funds have adopted an activist posture in corporate governance and control transactions, one has to keep in mind that only a minority of hedge funds pursue shareholder activism. Some hedge funds do not own many equity securities because they pursue macroeconomic strategies or because they invest primarily in debt securities.[65] And even most hedge funds that focus on equity securities are not activist, because they pursue quantitative strategies, because they value their relationship with management, or for other reasons.[66] Indeed, according to a recent estimate by J. P. Morgan (2006: 89), only 5% of hedge fund assets, or about $50 billion, are available for shareholder activism.

Our point in discussing hedge fund activism is thus not that shareholder activism is predominant among hedge funds. It is not. Our point is rather that hedge funds—to the virtual

[62] See note 50 and accompanying text.

[63] See notes 31–3 and accompanying text. This kind of activism is relatively novel for mutual funds. See Carrns (2005: C3), quoting a bank analyst as describing the public opposition to acquisition by a mutual fund as 'a little bit unusual'.

[64] See Brownstein and Norwitz (2006), stating that:

> [e]ven traditional long-term institutional investors are on occasion becoming more outspoken than they have been in the past. The fusion of aggressive hedge fund activism and the power of large institutional holders is a potent formula that can energize an activist campaign.

The willingness of traditional institutions to become involved in activism with hedge funds may be enhanced by the adoption of Regulation FD, which made it harder for management to retaliate against institutional investors by engaging in selective disclosure of information. See 17 C.F.R. § 243.100 (2006) (preventing selective disclosure by requiring the immediate public disclosure of any material non-public information intentionally disclosed by the issuer); see also Black (1990: 602), hypothesizing that mutual funds may be passive because of a fear of such retaliation.

[65] For a table detailing the assets under management by various hedge fund strategies, see The Barclay Group (2007).

[66] See, e.g., Dobbs and Koller (2006: 9–10), quoting Lee Ainslie, the managing partner of Maverick Capital, who explains that his fund puts a 'premium on the value of our relationships with management teams'.

exclusion of traditional institutional investors—dominate certain modes of shareholder activism. The fact that only a minority of hedge funds engages in such activism makes this point, if anything, even more noteworthy.

But the fact that, at present, only a minority of hedge funds is engaged in shareholder activism is important for another reason as well. It indicates that there is a large untapped fund of money that could quickly become available for activism. If activist strategies are profitable—more so than the other investment strategies hedge funds pursue—it would not take much for the capital devoted to activism to double or even quadruple overnight.[67] Thus, whatever the extent of hedge fund activism today, it may become much larger—or much smaller—tomorrow.

5.3 Hedge Funds as Institutional Investors

The activities of hedge funds described in Section 5.2 give substance to the hope that hedge funds may act 'like real owners' and provide a check on management discretion. But similar hopes were generated in the 1980s, when commentators noted that a significant shift in the shareholder profile of public corporations—from small individual shareholders to large institutional holders—had taken place.[68] The rise of institutional investors, starting in the early 1990s, generated a series of articles analysing the potential implications of institutional shareholdings on corporate governance (Black 1992; Rock 1991).

In this section, we analyse hedge funds against the backdrop of the analysis of traditional institutional investors. Our comparison focuses on open-ended mutual funds, both because mutual funds are the most important institutional investors, holding about 24% of all corporate equities,[69] and because they are economically closest to hedge funds. But we also discuss, more briefly, public pension funds, the third-largest category of traditional institutions, which hold 10.5% of corporate equities.[70]

[67] Unlike mutual funds, which must abide by the investment policies described in their registration statement or obtain shareholder approval for a change, see Investment Company Act of 1940 § 8(b)(2), 15 U.S.C. § 80a-8(b)(2) (2000), hedge funds can quickly change their policies to respond to new profit opportunities.

[68] According to the Federal Reserve Board, the percentage ownership of corporate equities by households declined from 70% in 1975 to 56% in 1984, while ownership by pension funds, insurance companies, and mutual funds increased from 25% to 37% (Federal Reserve System 2006a: 82 tbl.L.213). This trend has continued, with the ownership by households declining to 28% in the Third Quarter of 2006 and ownership by insurance companies, pensions, and mutual funds increasing to nearly 55% (Federal Reserve System 2006b: 90 tbl.L.213).

[69] According to the Federal Reserve, mutual funds in the Third Quarter of 2006 held $4,597 of $19,306 billion (24%) of corporate equities (Federal Reserve System 2006b: 90 tbl.L.213).

[70] Private pension funds, the second largest holder, owned another 12.8% of corporate equities (Federal Reserve System 2006b: 90 tbl.L.213). We do not further discuss corporate pension funds for several reasons: they hold fewer assets than mutual funds, the literature on institutional investors has expressed scepticism about whether corporate funds will be activist, and corporate funds, unlike public funds, have not been activist.

5.3.1 Mutual Funds and Monitoring

5.3.1.1 *The Pluses: Size and Expertise*

Compared to individual investors, mutual funds enjoy a major advantage as corporate monitors: they are large. The average size of an equity mutual fund was $218 million in 1990 and $964 million in 2004 (Investment Company Institute 2005: 61 tbl.3, 63 tbl.5). The largest mutual funds manage assets in the tens of billions of dollars.[71] In comparison, the average capitalization of stocks is $25 billion in the S&P 500 index (2006a), and $2.8 billion in the S&P MidCap index (2006b).

Due to their size, mutual funds enjoy significant economies of scale that arise in two ways. For one, they will tend to own a greater number of shares of an individual company than individual investors do. To the extent that governance activities entail company-specific costs, these costs can be spread over a larger investment. Moreover, mutual funds will tend to own shares in a larger number of companies than individual investors do. To the extent that governance activities entail costs that are common for several companies, these costs can be spread over a larger number of investments.

5.3.1.2 *The Minuses: Regulation, Incentive Problems, and Conflicts*

Mutual funds also suffer from a number of disadvantages that impede their ability to act as effective monitors. These disadvantages fall into three categories: regulatory constraints, inadequate incentives, and conflicts of interest.[72]

5.3.1.2.1 Regulatory Constraints

Mutual funds are subject to a number of regulatory constraints that can affect their ability and incentives to monitor portfolio companies. For one, mutual funds are subject to special disclosure requirements not applicable to other types of investors. Specifically, mutual funds must file semi-annual lists showing the amounts and values of the securities they own.[73] This makes it harder for mutual funds to accumulate positions in portfolio companies without such companies, and the market at large, becoming aware of their activities.

In addition, in order to qualify for significant tax benefits, mutual funds must comply with the diversification requirements in Subchapter M of the Internal Revenue Code. Accordingly, 50% of the assets of a mutual fund are subject to the limitations that the fund may own no more than 10% of the outstanding securities of a portfolio company, and that the stock of any portfolio company may not constitute more than 5% of the value of the assets of the fund (Roe

[71] For example, Vanguard's S&P 500 index fund has assets of $121.2 billion (Vanguard 2007).

[72] See, generally, Black (1992: 873–6), examining the factors influencing institutional investors' effectiveness as monitors; Rock (1991), analysing the interaction between collective action and agency costs in influencing institutional shareholder activism.

[73] Investment Company Act of 1940, § 29(e), 15 U.S.C. §80a-29(e) (2000). In addition, under a recently passed regulation, mutual funds must disclose how they voted any shares of their portfolio companies. 17 C.F.R. § 270.30b1–4 (2006); see also Disclosure of Proxy Voting Policies and Proxy Voting Records by Registered Management Investment Companies, 68 Fed. Reg. 6564 (Feb. 7, 2003), describing the purpose of the regulation.

1991a: 20). Moreover, in order to advertise themselves as 'diversified'—the preferred mode for most funds (Roe 1991b: 1474)—funds must further satisfy the diversification requirements of the Investment Company Act. Under the Act, 75% of the assets of a mutual fund are subject to the above limitation that the fund may own no more than 10% of the outstanding securities of a portfolio company and that the stock of any portfolio company may not constitute more than 5% of the value of the assets of the fund.[74] These diversification requirements, in principle, limit the ability of funds to take large positions in a single company, though the constraints they pose may not be binding for larger mutual funds.

Open-end mutual funds, by definition and by statute, must also stand ready to redeem their shares at the request of any shareholder at short notice.[75] The redemption price of these shares is based on the fund's net asset value. These requirements make it difficult for mutual funds to have illiquid investments, such as restricted securities, as illiquid investments cannot be readily transformed into cash when fund shareholders want to redeem their shares and cannot be easily valued. In light of this limitation, the staff of the SEC issued a guideline limiting the aggregate holdings of a mutual fund in illiquid investments to no more than 15% of the fund's net assets (Laise 2006).

Finally, regulations make it difficult for mutual funds to base the fee paid to the fund management company on the performance of the fund. Performance fees must be symmetrical, such that if fees are higher than normal after a good year, they must also be lower than normal after a bad year.[76] But even symmetrical pay-for-performance fees are rendered impracticable by the requirement that performance fees be based on a period of at least one year. Thus, if a fund has a stellar performance in one month, fund managers will likely earn an increased performance fee for the following eleven months. This, of course, creates incentives for investors to sell their shares at the end of the first month, when they have fully benefited from the stellar performance in that month but only paid one-twelfth of the associated performance fee, and discourages investors from buying shares in a fund after a strong month, as they have to pay eleven-twelfths of the performance fee without getting the benefit of the stellar performance.

5.3.1.2.2 *Incentives to Monitor*

Activism of the variety described in Section 5.2 is not cheap. Fund managers first have to identify a company that would benefit from activism and develop a strategy for the company that would raise its share price. Then, fund managers have to pressure the company's management to adopt that strategy. All of this consumes significant resources, both in-house and from hiring outside advisors.

For mutual funds, the incentives to expend resources on such activism are limited to begin with.[77] The lack of incentives is particularly pronounced for managers of indexed

[74] Roe (1991a: 19–20) summarizes the restrictions placed on mutual funds by 15 U.S.C. § 80a-5(b) (2000).

[75] Investment Company Act of 1940 § 5(a)(1), 15 U.S.C. § 80a-5(a)(1) (2000).

[76] Investment Advisers Act of 1940, § 205(b)–(c), 15 U.S.C. § 80b-5(b) to (c) (2000). Hedge fund advisors are typically exempt from registration and from § 205 under the so-called 'private adviser' provision of 15 U.S.C. § 80b-3(b)(3) (2000).

[77] Rock (1991: 472–6) discusses the collective action problem inherent in mutual fund shareholder activism.

funds. The job of index fund managers is to replicate the performance of the index. An index fund thus competes with other funds replicating the same index principally on the basis of fund expenses. As activism is costly and raises the fund's expenses (or lowers the managing company's profits), index fund managers will be reluctant to engage in activism.

There is often a similar shortage of incentives for diversified mutual funds. As previously discussed, regulatory barriers make it difficult for mutual funds to charge performance-based fees. As a result, 97% of all funds, accounting for 92% of all mutual fund assets, charge fees based on a flat percentage of the fund's assets under management.[78] Asset-based fees, however, provide only small direct incentives to engage in costly activism. The median stock fund in 2004 charged investors total expenses of 1.45% of assets, of which roughly half were management fees.[79] Thus, for example, when a manager of a $1 billion mutual fund earns additional profits of $100 million (a 10% return), total annual fees increase by $1.45 million and management fees increase by about $750,000. Of course, a portion of these increased fees covers increased expenses associated with running a larger fund, and fees do not increase at all to the extent that investors withdraw some of the profits. To get a sense of how much a fund management company benefits from the increased profits, assume that $1 million of the $1.45 million in total increased fees constitutes profits for the fund managers and that investors keep any profits in the fund for three years before withdrawing them. Applying a 5% discount rate, the $100 million in fund profits would then generate $2.85 million in additional profits for the fund management company—amounting to a very modest implicit performance fee of 2.85%. Even this rough estimate probably overstates the implicit performance fees because most larger funds utilize 'breakpoints', where the marginal percentage fee declines as fund assets increase.[80]

Even for the few funds that charge explicit performance fees, incentives are not much stronger. In order to avoid the problem of strategic timing of withdrawals and contributions described, the mutual fund performance fees that do exist are relatively flat. Fidelity's Magellan Fund, for example, charges a performance adjustment of 0.02% of assets for each percentage point of outperformance or underperformance relative to the S&P 500 index, up to a maximum of plus or minus 0.2%.[81] This is the equivalent of an annual performance fee of 2% of the fund's profits (as long as the profits are within the range where the performance adjustment is made).[82]

Mutual funds, of course, also can benefit from good performance indirectly. Studies have shown that funds that outperform their peers generally attract inflows of new assets. A recent

[78] See Eisinger (2005b: C1), stating that '[o]nly 3% of mutual funds charge performance fees. Such funds . . . make up less than 8% of the . . . assets in mutual funds.'

[79] See Oversight Hearing on Mutual Funds: Hidden Fees, Misgovernance and Other Practices that Harm Investors: Hearing before the Subcomm. on Financial Management, the Budget, and International Security of the S. Comm. on Governmental Affairs, 108th Cong. 189, 193 (2004) (prepared statement of Jeffrey C. Keil, Vice President, Lipper Inc.) [hereinafter *Lipper Testimony*] (providing data on management fees and total expenses in 1992 and 2002–03); Waggoner (2005), observing a reduction in average fund fees from 1.50% to 1.45% in 2004.

[80] *Lipper Testimony*, at 190 (see note 79).

[81] Fidelity Magellan Fund, Management Contract Between Fidelity Magellan Fund and Fidelity Management & Research Company (Exhibit 5(a) to Form N-1A), at P 3(c) (22 May 1998).

[82] Fidelity Investments, Prospectus, Fidelity Magellan Fund 21 (30 May 2006).

study by Stephen Choi and one of the authors of this chapter, for example, finds that a 1% abnormal positive performance by a fund (relative to other funds with the same investment objective) is associated with increased inflows of roughly 1% over the following year, while a 1% abnormal negative performance is associated with outflows of about 0.6% over a year (Choi and Kahan 2007).[83] Increased inflows, of course, generate management and other asset-based fees. The implicit performance fee generated indirectly by the effect of positive performance on inflows is, thus, roughly of the same magnitude as the implicit performance fee generated directly by asset-based fees.

In one important respect, however, the incentive effect of performance on net assets via inflows differs from the incentive effect of performance on net assets via profits. While the latter is a function of the fund's absolute performance, the former turns on a fund's performance relative to other funds with similar investment objectives.[84] Activism, however, will increase a fund's relative returns only to the extent that the fund has a higher stake in the portfolio company (relative to the fund size) than competing funds do and the costs of activism to the fund are less than the profits from that differential. For any given portfolio company, this means that funds with a below-average stake in the company (relative to fund size) have no incentives—or indeed negative incentives—to take action to increase that company's value, and funds with an above-average stake have only attenuated incentives to expend resources on activism. [85]

For example, Table 5.1 lists the ten largest stock holdings—as of 31 March 2005—of the Fidelity Magellan Fund and the comparable holdings in these companies—as of 31 December 2004—of the Vanguard 500 Index Fund.[86]

The last column of the table indicates the degree to which the Magellan Fund's incentives to monitor are diluted by the fact that any increase in the value of these shares would not also raise the S&P 500 index. As the table shows, the degree of dilution is significant even for the largest holdings of the fund. For smaller holdings, the degree of dilution is likely to be even higher.[87]

[83] See Choi and Kahan (2007), providing an overview of the literature analysing the effect of past performance on fund flows; see also Ippolito (1992: 55, 67), explaining investor responses to fund performance.

[84] See Fisch (1994: 1020), stating that '[t]heir [mutual funds'] performance is evaluated not in absolute terms, but based on whether they are able to generate a higher rate of return than the competition or than the market'; Ubben and Haarmeyer (2006: 60), arguing that 'performance of traditional money managers is measured on a relative, not an absolute, basis'.

[85] See Rock (1991: 472–3), discussing the collective action problem that forms in this context. And even funds with an above-average stake relative to fund size have incentives to expend material resources only if the stake is significant in absolute terms.

[86] See Fidelity Magellan Fund, Certified Shareholder Report (Form N-CSR) (27 May 2005); Vanguard Index Funds, Certified Shareholder Report (Form N-CSR) (25 Feb. 2005).

[87] For example, for the ten companies in the Magellan Fund's 'Consumer Staples' industry group, which account for 7.9% of the fund assets, the weighted average dilution is 78%. As further discussed in Section 5.3.3.5, the degree of dilution in incentives is endogenous as it is a function of a fund's investment portfolio, which itself will be a function of the fund's desire to engage in activism. For purposes of this section, however, we use a fund's portfolio as a starting point to determine the incentive to engage in activism given the portfolio choice.

Table 5.1 Top 10 Magellan holdings relative to S&P 500 index

Company	Magellan investment (in %)	Vanguard 500 index (in %)	Difference	Dilution of Magellan's incentives
GE	4.1	3.4	0.7	83 %
Microsoft	3	2.6	0.4	87%
Exxon Mobil	3	2.9	0.1	97%
Citigroup	2.7	2.2	0.5	81%
AIG	2.7	1.5	1.2	56%
Home Depot	2.2	0.8	1.4	36%
Bank of America	2.2	1.7	0.5	77%
Viacom	2.1	0.5	1.6	24%
Pfizer	2	1.8	0.2	90%
Tyco Int'l	1.9	0.6	1.3	32%
All 10 stocks	25.90%	18%	7.9	69% (weighted)

5.3.1.2.3 *Conflicts of Interest*

Mutual funds also suffer from conflicts of interest between fund managers and fund beneficiaries that inhibit their activities as monitors of portfolio companies.[88] Many mutual fund management companies are affiliated with—and are, in effect, subsidiaries of and controlled by—another financial institution, such as an investment bank or an insurance company. For example, of the twenty largest mutual fund complexes in 2003, nine had such affiliations.[89] Managers of such funds may be reluctant to antagonize present or future clients of their parent company with their governance activities. Indeed, the effect of such affiliations on governance activism may be both more subtle and more pervasive. Consider, for example, a mutual fund affiliated with an investment bank. The mutual fund managers will, *ex ante*, often not know which portfolio companies have hired, or are about to hire, the investment bank as an underwriter or financial advisor. And, *ex post*, the investment banker, for public relations and legal reasons,[90] would not want to interfere directly with the governance activism of the mutual fund when an investment banking client becomes the target of such activism. Thus,

[88] See Black (1990: 595–608), examining the conflicts of interest that affect institutional shareholders; Rock (1991: 469–72), noting the divergent interests that give rise to this conflict; Bogle (2005) notes the conflicts that can be created by large corporate clients at financial institutions that manage both pension plans and mutual funds. Conflicts are regarded as particularly pronounced in defined benefit plans, where fund assets are usually managed by designated corporate pension fund managers. The managers of a corporate pension fund are appointed by the executives of the corporation that sponsors the pension plan. These executives are believed to pressure pension fund managers to cast pro-management votes. Accordingly, corporate pension funds have not become active in corporate governance and are not regarded as likely to do so (Black 1990: 596–8).

[89] The list of funds was derived from a study sent by Fidelity to the SEC, including a study by Geoffrey H. Bobroff and Thomas H. Mack assessing the potential impact of independent board chairs on mutual fund performance (Roiter 2004).

[90] The potential pitfalls facing a mutual fund are illustrated by the publicity that resulted when Deutsche Asset Management, an affiliate of Deutsche Bank, switched its votes from 'against' to 'for' the

the easiest and safest way to avoid any problems is for affiliated mutual funds not to engage in governance activism at all.[91] This way, mutual fund managers do not have to distinguish between portfolio companies that are investment banking clients and those that are not, and investment bankers do not have to worry about mutual fund managers interfering in their business.

Of course, many mutual fund companies, including the two largest—Fidelity and Vanguard—are not affiliated with other financial institutions. But even unaffiliated mutual fund managers, especially the larger ones, face potential conflicts. For many mutual fund complexes, the management of corporate pension plans is an important source of revenues.[92] Governance activism could lead to a loss of such business, not just with respect to the activist fund, but for the complex as a whole.[93] John Bogle, the founder and former head of Vanguard, even suggested that merely voting against management could 'jeopardize the retention of clients of 401(k) and pension accounts'.[94] And Don Phillips, a managing director of Morningstar, attributes the reluctance of funds to support shareholder proposals to rein in executive pay to their 'desire to solicit business from corporations' (Levitz 2006). As in the case of affiliated funds, the effect of such conflicts on governance activism may be to deter strong activism on a broader scale. It is certainly easy to imagine a mutual fund complex concluding that having a reputation as a governance troublemaker is not conducive to being picked as a manager for corporate pension plans, and that the profits to be made from managing these pension plans would exceed those from governance activism.

To assess the significance of these conflicts of interest, one must compare them to the affirmative incentives a fund would have, absent any conflicts, to engage in activism. As discussed in Section 5.2, activism is costly, and fund management companies only profit modestly from any fund profits generated by activism. Thus, in our view, even modest conflicts of interest can easily dissuade a fund management company from pursuing an activist strategy and induce it to rely instead on less conflict-prone strategies—such as quantitative research or fundamental value analysis—to generate excess returns.

5.3.1.2.4 Concluding Remarks

The actual activities of mutual funds are consistent with our analysis. Mutual funds have shied away from the more costly and more confrontational modes of activism. They have not instigated proxy contexts nor led the charge in pushing for changes in business strategy and management. Most mutual funds have not even made shareholder proposals, and, until recently, mutual funds have rarely been active in opposing or triggering corporate control

merger of Hewlett-Packard (HP) and Compaq, after it learned that Deutsche Bank provided investment banking advice to HP (see SEC 2003b).

[91] Cf. Davis and Kim (2007), who find that voting by mutual funds appears to be independent of whether the fund has client ties with the portfolio company, but notes that funds with multiple clients are generally more likely to vote in favour of management.

[92] See, e.g., Morgenson (2006), noting Pfizer's influence as a client to several of its institutional shareholders.

[93] See, e.g., Black (1990: 602), observing that Armstrong World Industries transferred its employee savings plan business from Vanguard to Fidelity after Fidelity stopped opposing a then proposed Pennsylvania antitakeover law that Armstrong supported.

[94] See Baue (2005), quoting a letter from Bogle to the SEC, but also noting that a Fidelity spokesperson disclaimed any link between voting and clients.

transactions. If they engage in behind-the-scenes communications—and we doubt that they do so extensively—these communications are largely just that: efforts to coax management to change its ways, without much follow-up if management is not amenable. Despite this passive tendency, by capitalizing on their economies of scale, mutual funds have developed general policies that have led them to support some governance proposals brought by other shareholders, withhold votes from some board nominees, and oppose some governance proposals made by the board.

5.3.2 Public Pension Funds and Monitoring

Like mutual funds, public pension funds enjoy significant economies of scale. The average member of the Council of Institutional Investors, an organization of large public pension funds as well as union and corporate pension funds, has assets exceeding $23 billion.[95] The concerns about the ability of public pension funds to act as effective corporate monitors differ from those related to mutual funds. Public pension funds must make quarterly disclosures of their public equity securities holdings.[96] But, unlike mutual funds, public pension funds are not subject to specific diversification requirements or regulatory constraints on performance fees,[97] face predictable liquidity requirements, and have no business ties with portfolio companies that would be jeopardized by activism.

The problem for public pension funds, rather, is that they are political entities and, thus, subject to political constraints and conflicts of interest. The make-up of their boards of trustees is governed by state law and differs from fund to fund. Generally, these boards consist of some combination of gubernatorial appointees, elected politicians who serve *ex officio*, and officials elected by fund beneficiaries (Romano 1993: 823–5 and tbl.2). For example, the trustees of CalPERS, the nation's largest public fund, include six members elected by beneficiaries, three political appointees, and four members who serve *ex officio* (CalPERS 2005a). The New York State Common Retirement Fund (2007), the second largest public fund, has the State Comptroller, a state-wide elected official, as its sole trustee. As should be evident, public pension fund trustees lack significant financial incentives to maximize fund performance.

To be sure, public pension funds can hire professional managers compensated by performance-based fees.[98] The funds, however, are subject to political constraints in setting the size of these fees. As officials who are, as some commentators have noted, 'accountable for their decisions to politicians or the press' (Murphy and Van Nuys 1994), state pension officials avoid calling negative publicity to their activities. The adverse publicity generated by the pay packages of the managers of Harvard University's endowment provides some indication of the nature of these constraints. Though Jack Meyer, Harvard's top investment manager, 'produced stellar investment results', alumni complained that the pay of Meyer and of some

[95] See Council of Institutional Investors (2009), noting that it has '130 public, labor, and corporate pension funds with assets exceeding $3 trillion'.

[96] For a discussion of disclosure requirements for institutional investors, see Section 5.3.3.2.

[97] Public pension funds are subject to a prudent person standard for diversification (Romano 1993: 800). But, given a fund's size, this would often not be an effective constraint on its ability to take large positions in portfolio companies.

[98] CalPERS pays performance-based fees to some of its external managers (CalPERS 2005b).

of his top managers was inappropriately high (Stein 2005). Meyer and some of his employees ultimately left Harvard to start a hedge fund (Grant and Buckman 2006). By private sector standards, however—and certainly by hedge fund standards[99]—Meyer's pay package ($7 million in 2004) and those of his top two managers ($35 million each in 2003 and $25 million each in 2004) (Stein 2005) were laughably small, considering that Harvard's endowment of $22 billion would have been more than $12 billion smaller had Meyer earned median returns (Stein 2004).[100] Consistent with the tendency illustrated by the Harvard endowment example, empirical evidence has shown that the compensation of public pension fund administrators is less frequently based on performance—and is less performance sensitive when it is—than that of private-plan administrators.[101]

Given the potential pitfalls of high pay packages, a politically safer course for pension fund boards that are willing to pay steep performance-based fees would be to entrust funds to an outside entity rather than to hire in-house managers. This, of course, is exactly what public pension funds do when they manage the indexed portion of their portfolio in-house and invest some of their other assets in private equity funds, venture capital funds, and hedge funds.[102] Political constraints can also inhibit public pension funds from pursuing some of the more aggressive activist strategies employed by hedge funds. It is one thing for public pension funds to sponsor shareholder resolutions demanding greater board accountability, to act as lead plaintiffs in securities lawsuits, or even to demand governance changes in underperforming companies. It is quite another matter for them to tell a CEO how to run her business—by opposing major strategic acquisitions, demanding asset spin-offs, or recommending a different business strategy—and then threaten a proxy contest if management fails to cooperate. Public pension funds simply lack the legitimacy to push beyond relatively uncontroversial 'motherhood and apple pie' issues. Unlike CEOs or hedge fund managers, these funds do not have to go out to the market to compete for investment capital; their managers have little financial stake in their success; they are not subject to market penalties for failure; they are run by politicians, bureaucrats, and union representatives; and, as political entities, they are subject to political pressure not to overstep their bounds.

Compounding these political constraints are political conflicts of interest. Pension fund trustees who are gubernatorial appointees or elected politicians may be tempted to pursue political ends, rather than work to maximize investment returns. In her 1993 article on pension fund activism, Roberta Romano details several instances of pension fund trustees pursuing political goals rather than profits. In 1992, for example, the Illinois state treasurer and trustee of the state pension fund threatened not to make future investments in a leveraged buyout fund unless the fund's operator preserved jobs in an Illinois plant it was selling to its employees (Romano 1993: 797 n.6, 807). The same year, 'Elizabeth Holzman, New York City comptroller and a trustee for the city's pension funds, publicized her active approach to corporate governance' in her campaign for the Democratic nomination for New York's senate

[99] For a discussion of hedge fund manager compensation, see Section 5.3.3.3.

[100] See, generally, Grant and Buckman (2006), discussing Meyer's departure from Harvard and the problem of low endowment compensation compared to the private sector.

[101] Woidtke (2002: 104) provides a statistical comparison of compensation structure for private and public pension fund administration.

[102] See, e.g., CalPERS (2001), noting that the CalPERS board agreed to establish a $1 billion hedge fund programme in October 2000.

seat (Romano 1993: 822). As related by Romano, both the New York and the California state pension funds have come under political pressure to tone down (and indeed did tone down) their governance activities (Romano 1993: 815–20).[103] More recently, Alan Hevesi, the very active New York State Comptroller and sole trustee of the $115 billion New York State Common Retirement Fund (New York State Office of the State Comptroller 2007),[104] has been criticized both for pursuing political goals,[105] and for having the fund hire law firms that made large contributions to his campaign.[106]

Trustees elected by fund beneficiaries are usually union representatives, who also have objectives that may conflict with their fiduciary duty to maximize investment returns.[107] For example, CalPERS, the largest and, traditionally, most active public pension fund, has come under increased criticism for the presence of union representatives on its board and the pro-union stance it has taken in various labour disputes.[108] When public pension funds do not pursue political or labour goals, the relatively low pay and incentives of public pension fund executives raise the spectre that their governance activities are designed more for self-promotion than to enhance returns.[109]

The political constraints and conflicts of public pension funds not only make the funds less likely to engage in certain kinds of activism, but can also make public funds less effective when they do become active. To the extent that others perceive public pension fund activism to be politically motivated or as serving the promotional interests of fund executives, they are less likely to support public funds when they do become active. Without such support, however, activism is less likely to affect changes in the portfolio companies. This, again, suggests that public funds will be most effective when their activism is perceived to be least affected by political or personal motives—such as uncontroversial 'apple pie' issues—and, thus, will be inclined to limit their activism to such issues.

[103] For another example of such pressure, see Barnard (1991: 1141 n.39), discussing the political fallout when Wisconsin's pension fund submitted a proposal critical of management to General Motors as it was considering expanding a plant in Wisconsin.

[104] See Dale (2004), noting that Hevesi is considered an 'activist comptroller' and detailing the investor suits he has filed.

[105] See *Wall Street Journal* (2005b) editorial, arguing that Hevesi was using his clout as pension fund trustee to aid John Kerry.

[106] See, e.g., *Wall Street Journal* (2005a); Donovan (2005); *New York Sun* (2005) editorial; see also Woidtke (2002: 127–8), concluding that public pension fund activism is motivated more by political and social goals than by firm performance.

[107] See *Wall Street Journal* (2005b), stating that 'the AFL-CIO and its friends are now using pension funds to advance their political agenda'; see also Schroeder (2005: A15), noting that labour representatives have sought trustee positions in order to 'bolster union power to influence corporate management'.

[108] See *Wall Street Journal* (2004) editorial discussing the political and union ties of CalPERS board members and accusing the board of basing investment decisions on political goals of Labour and the Democratic Party; Carlton and Weil (2004: C3), noting that CalPERS has been criticized for 'meddling in political and labor-union issues with little connection to improving shareholder returns'; Weil and Lublin (2004: A1), explaining CalPERS's controversial actions in interceding on behalf of the striking employees of a portfolio company.

[109] See Romano (1993: 822 and n.102), suggesting that veteran activist Dale Hanson, former head of CalPERS, may have been so motivated; Black (1990: 599), stating that '[Public fund managers] may become active shareholders partly to generate good publicity for themselves.'

The actual activities of public pension funds correspond to these incentives and constraints. Consistent with their lack of business relations with target companies and the political interests of some trustees, public pension fund activism is somewhat more open and confrontational than activism by mutual funds: public funds make more shareholder proposals, publish lists of target companies, and apply to become lead plaintiffs in securities class actions. But the choice of targets—companies that have been underperforming or have been accused of major fraud—and the substance of the activism—such as calling for greater board accountability and opposing excessive CEO compensation—insulate the fund from political backlash. Additionally, because they lack the requisite incentives and credibility to do so, public funds have steered clear of demanding specific changes in strategy or management, have not engaged in proxy contests, and, so far, have not even joined forces with hedge funds in opposing or triggering corporate control transactions.

5.3.3 Hedge Funds and Monitoring

5.3.3.1 *Size*

Since hedge funds are largely unregulated, significantly less data is available about them than about other institutional investors. However, the available evidence suggests that hedge funds enjoy significant economies of scale. According to one estimate, there are approximately 8,000 hedge funds with aggregate assets under management of over $1 trillion (*The Economist* 2006b). These figures indicate that the average hedge fund has assets of about $100 million, while the largest hedge funds have assets of over $10 billion (*PR Newswire* 2005i). Although smaller than the comparable figures for mutual funds and pension funds, these figures probably understate the effective assets of hedge funds. Unlike mutual funds and pension funds, hedge funds regularly use leverage and invest in derivatives, enabling them to take positions that are much larger than those of mutual funds with similar net assets. According to an industry report, 15% of hedge funds use a leverage ratio in excess of two—meaning that the total dollars invested are more than twice the total equity—and another 35–55% use leverage at a lower ratio (Osterberg and Thomson 1999: 2).

5.3.3.2 *Regulatory Constraints*

Hedge funds are not subject to any specific regulatory constraints. They must, however, comply with rules applicable to investors generally. These constraints include the disclosure requirements under section 13(d) of the Securities Exchange Act,[110] which requires disclosures by persons who own more than 5% of the equity securities of a public company, and the short-swing profit rules under section 16(b),[111] which are applicable to officers, directors, and 10% shareholders of a company.[112]

In addition, all institutional investment managers—including hedge fund managers—are subject to the disclosure requirement of section 13(f) of the Securities Exchange Act.[113] Under that provision, certain investment managers (including mutual fund, pension fund, and hedge

[110] Securities Exchange Act of 1934 § 13(d), 15 U.S.C. § 78m(d) (2000). [111] Section 16(b).
[112] Section 16(a). [113] Section 13(f).

fund managers) must make disclosures about their holdings on a quarterly basis. However, the disclosure requirements under section 13(f) differ from those applicable to mutual funds in two important respects. First, and most significantly, only holdings of registered equity securities—so-called '13(f) securities'—need to be disclosed. These 13(f) securities include traded shares and options listed on an exchange. Importantly, however, holdings of other options and derivatives need not be disclosed in one's 13(f) filings. As a result, hedge funds can use derivatives to accumulate large economic positions in portfolio companies without disclosure, unless they become subject to the disclosure requirements under section 13(d). In addition, no disclosures at all must be made if one's holdings of 13(f) securities are less than $100 million. Thus, small and even medium-sized hedge funds can avoid making any disclosures as long as a sufficiently large percentage of their holdings are in debt securities or in non-listed equity derivatives.

Hedge funds also have a greater ability to invest in illiquid assets than do mutual funds. While mutual funds are required to redeem shares on short notice, and SEC guidelines limit the percentage of assets that mutual funds can hold in illiquid investments, hedge funds are not subject to any similar regulatory requirements. Contractually, hedge fund investors have more limited withdrawal rights than mutual fund investors. Traditionally, hedge fund investors could make withdrawals only after an initial lock-up period of six months. More recently, some hedge funds have extended the initial lock-up period to two years or longer.[114] Once the initial lock-up period has expired, further restrictions apply. In particular, hedge funds usually require advance notice for withdrawals and sometimes permit withdrawals only at specific points in time, while also imposing limits on the amounts an investor can withdraw at any point.[115] In addition, hedge funds may refuse a withdrawal request if the withdrawal would be harmful to other investors in the fund, or may 'pay' a requested withdrawal 'in-kind', rather than in cash.[116] These provisions combine to make hedge funds much less sensitive than mutual funds to sudden liquidity shocks.[117]

5.3.3.3 *Incentives to Monitor*

As discussed in subsection 5.3.1.2, traditional institutional investors suffer from impaired incentives to monitor portfolio companies. The incentives for hedge funds to monitor portfolio companies differ in several important respects from those of traditional institutions. First, hedge fund managers are highly incentivized to maximize the returns to fund investors. The standard hedge fund charges a base fee equal to 1–2% of the assets under management

[114] See, e.g., Anderson (2005), reporting that investors in a new hedge fund only can redeem initial funds after two years, and thereafter only annually; Zuckerman and McDonald (2005), noting that several hedge funds have adopted a two-year lock-up period, in part to avoid SEC registration requirements. The increased lock-up may contribute to hedge fund activism (McTague 2006).

[115] See, e.g., Sender (2006), noting that Citadel charged a penalty on an investor that wanted to withdraw more than 3% of its money.

[116] Telephone Interview with Nathan Fischel, Managing Member, DAFNA Capital Management LLC, in L.A., Cal. (2 Jan. 2006).

[117] Hedge funds also have a greater ability to take on debt than mutual funds. Under the Investment Company Act, mutual funds are required to have a three-to-one asset-to-debt ratio. Investment Company Act of 1940 § 18(f), 15 U.S.C. § 80a-18(f) (2000). As most mutual funds have no debt to speak of, this regulatory constraint is unlikely to be binding. Hedge funds are not similarly limited and, by all accounts, are often far more leveraged.

and a significant incentive fee, typically 20% of the profits earned.[118] This fee structure gives hedge fund managers a very significant stake in the financial success of the fund's investments. These stakes are even higher when, as is frequently the case, a hedge fund manager has invested a significant portion of her personal wealth in the hedge fund (Haarmeyer 2006).

Second, many hedge funds strive to achieve high absolute returns, rather than returns relative to a benchmark (Financial Services Authority 2005). In particular, the industry standard 20% incentive fee is usually based on a fund's absolute performance. And while a few funds use a hurdle rate before the incentive fee is payable, this hurdle rate is generally a rate based on the yield of debt securities, not based on the performance of a market index or an index of hedge funds with similar investment objectives.

Thus, unlike mutual funds, hedge funds benefit directly and substantially from achieving high absolute returns. For successful managers, the resulting profits can be extraordinarily high. The average take-home pay for the top twenty-five hedge fund managers in 2003 was $207 million, and the lowest paid manager in that group still earned a respectable $65 million (Taub 2004). These figures increased in 2004, when the average manager earned $251 million and the lowest paid manager received $100 million (Taub 2005).

Of course, hedge fund managers, like mutual fund managers, also care about retaining existing investors and attracting new ones through their performance. But even to the extent that hedge fund performance is, for this purpose, assessed relative to a benchmark or to other hedge funds with comparable strategies, their incentives are diluted to a lesser extent than those of mutual funds. This is because hedge fund portfolios resemble the relevant index much less than those of mutual funds. Reliable data on hedge fund holdings are not available since hedge funds need only disclose their holdings in equity securities and listed options, and not any other derivatives. We are thus unable to calculate the percentage of dilution in hedge fund incentives in the manner we calculated Magellan's dilution in incentives.[119] But the hedge fund managers we talked to confirmed that hedge fund investments are definitely much more eclectic and less correlated with a market index, or with investments of another hedge fund with a similar investment style, than those of mutual funds.[120] As one manager put it: eclecticism 'is what we are selling'.[121] As a result, hedge funds need not worry much about competitor funds free-riding on their governance activism and getting higher returns with lower costs.

Even if the activism of one hedge fund boosts the returns of activist hedge funds generally, the result may not be all that bad. Investors use returns of funds with a certain investment style to determine the amount of money they invest in this sector of funds. If activism by one hedge fund boosts the returns of activist hedge funds generally, more money will flow into this sector, thereby benefiting all activist funds.[122]

[118] See Interview with Anonymous Hedge Fund Manager (30 Jan. 2006). This fee is usually structured to incorporate a high-water mark, but not a clawback. That is, if a fund produces losses, these losses have to be made up before any incentive fee is payable (this is the high-water mark requirement), but if a fund makes profits and earns an incentive fee, the fee does not have to be returned if the fund suffers subsequent losses (hence, no clawback).

[119] See Table 5.1.

[120] Interview with Anonymous Hedge Fund Manager, see note 118.

[121] Interview with Anonymous Hedge Fund Manager, see note 118. Hedge funds specializing in merger arbitrage may be an exception in this regard, since their investments are highly correlated with those of other hedge funds specializing in merger arbitrage.

[122] Moreover, investors in hedge funds tend to be highly sophisticated. As a result, they may tend to use more complex evaluation criteria and channel their investment to the funds that took the lead in activism, and not those that were free riders.

5.3.3.4 *Conflicts of Interest*

Hedge funds suffer from fewer conflicts of interest between fund managers and fund investors than traditional institutional investors. First, most hedge funds are independent investment vehicles and are not affiliated with any other institution. Of the twenty largest hedge funds in 2004, only one was affiliated with another financial institution, such as a bank or insurance company.[123] By contrast, as reported in subsection 5.3.3.3, of the twenty largest mutual fund complexes in 2003, nine were so affiliated.[124] Furthermore, anecdotal evidence suggests that even hedge funds that are affiliated with other financial institutions do not shy away from taking actions that are antagonistic to investment banking clients of their affiliates. Recently, for example, the Highbridge Fund, majority-owned by J. P. Morgan, accumulated a stake of over 25% in convertible bonds of Saks Inc. and then sent a 'notice of default' when Saks breached a covenant by failing to file financial statements with the SEC—even though Saks has an investment banking relationship with J. P. Morgan.[125] Indeed, some concern recently has been expressed that investment banks sacrifice the interests of other clients in order to cultivate and retain lucrative hedge fund business.[126]

In addition, unlike mutual funds, hedge funds do not manage companies' defined-contribution plans. Accordingly, they do not have to be concerned that activism will result in a loss of fund management business. In sum, hedge funds are, to a much greater extent than mutual funds, free from the most significant potential sources of conflicts of interest.[127]

To be sure, hedge funds may still face some conflicts of interest to the extent that they want to attract contributions by defined-benefit corporate pension funds that are run by management-appointed trustees. Mutual funds, of course, would also face similar conflicts. But we believe that, at least for hedge funds, these conflicts tend to be minor. First, hedge funds may not be all that interested in capital from private pension funds. If private pension funds, together with public pension funds, account for more than 25% of the capital of a hedge fund, the hedge fund becomes subject to regulations under ERISA[128]—a fate unattractive to a sector that is otherwise largely unregulated. More importantly, however, we do not think that corporate pension funds have been, or will become, a substantial source of direct funds for hedge funds. Historically, corporate pension funds have not

[123] Interview with Anonymous Hedge Fund Manager, see note 118.

[124] See note 89 and accompanying text.

[125] Esterl and Sender (2005) suggest that Highbridge had bet on Saks stock declining by taking a short position.

[126] See, e.g., Hedge Funds and Capital Markets: Hearing before the Subcomm. on Securities and Investment of the S. Comm. on Banking, Housing, and Urban Affairs, 109th Cong. (16 May 2006), Statement of Susan Ferris Wyderko, Director, Office of Investor Education and Assistance, SEC, available at 2006 WLNR 8468099, discussing potential dangers of such 'side-by-side' management; see also Forman (2005), announcing an FSA (Financial Services Authority) review of the relationships between hedge funds and large investment banks in the UK.

[127] Cf. Der Hovanesian and Byrnes (2006), noting that hedge funds, unlike mutual funds, are not trying to sell money management services to companies.

[128] 29 C.F.R. § 2510.3-101(f) (2006); see also Shearman & Sterling LLP (2004), providing a brief overview of the applicability of the 25% limit to hedge funds. Under the recently passed Pension Protection Act of 2006, investments in hedge funds by foreign and governmental plans no longer count towards the 25% limit. § 611(f), Pub. L. No. 109–280, 120 Stat. 780.

been significant contributors to hedge funds. Rather, hedge funds have obtained most of their capital from wealthy individuals and institutions such as foundations or university endowments.[129] More recently, corporate (as well as public) pension funds have started to make investments in hedge funds.[130] While we lack precise data, we do not believe that corporate pension funds are a major source of capital for hedge funds at this time. And, given the declining importance of corporate defined-benefit plans,[131] we are sceptical that they ever will become one. Finally, even to the extent that corporate pension funds invest in hedge funds, they tend to do so through funds of funds rather than directly.[132] Hedge fund managers do not know the identity of the investor in a fund of funds, and investors in a fund of funds do not always know to which hedge funds their money flows. The presence of funds of funds thus serves to further insulate hedge funds from pressure by corporate pension funds.

Whatever residual conflicts of interest may remain must be compared to the affirmative incentives to enhance investor returns. As explained, hedge fund management firms and individual managers derive substantially greater benefits from increased fund returns than do mutual fund management firms and managers. As a result, any conflict of interest is more likely to be resolved in favour of hedge fund investors. On the whole, therefore, we do not believe that conflicts of interests are likely to interfere with activism by hedge funds, and, even if such interference does occur, it occurs much less than in the case of public pension funds and mutual funds.

5.3.3.5 *Activism and Stakes*

In the end, the incentives for a fund to engage in activism depend on its stake in a portfolio company.[133] In this regard, it is noteworthy that activist hedge funds usually accumulate stakes in portfolio companies in order to engage in activism. There are numerous examples of hedge funds taking stakes whose values depend on firm actions, and then taking action to determine the outcome—everything from trying to influence strategy and running proxy contests, to instigating litigation and threatening to vote against mergers.

In this regard, hedge funds differ markedly from mutual funds and public pension funds. Mutual fund and public pension fund activism, if it occurs, tends to be incidental and *ex post*: when fund management notes that portfolio companies are underperforming, or that

[129] See, e.g., Singer (2006b), indicating that 25.7% of Yale's endowment is invested in hedge funds.

[130] The Hennessee Group LLC (2005) recently estimated that public and private pension funds combined account for 9% of the sources of capital to hedge funds.

[131] In 1995, private pension funds held corporate equities of nearly $1.3 trillion, amounting to 15% of the total market value of corporate equities. By 2005, private pension funds held corporate equities of approximately $2.4 trillion, amounting to 9% of the total market value of corporate equities (Federal Reserve System 2006a).

[132] Kenney et al. (2003) stated that: '[m]uch of the new pension money enters the market through funds of hedge funds'.

[133] In addition, hedge funds may structure their portfolios so that they profit from activism in various ways. As discussed in Section 5.3.1.2, for example, it is likely that Highfields stood to profit from a defeat of the MONY/AXA merger both through its holdings of MONY shares and through its holdings of ORANs. On the plus side, this can allow hedge funds to increase their returns from successful activism, thereby overcoming rational apathy or free-riding.

their governance regime is deficient, they will sometimes become active.[134] In contrast, hedge fund activism is strategic and *ex ante*: hedge fund managers first determine whether a company would benefit from activism, then take a position and become active. Hedge fund activism represents a blurring of the line between risk arbitrage and battles over corporate strategy and control.

This suggests that the differences in activism between hedge funds and other institutions may be, at least in part, endogenous. Because (activist) hedge funds pursue activism as a profit-making strategy, they take economic positions in portfolio companies that enable them to engage in, and make profits from, activism. In contrast, traditional institutions do not pursue activism as a profit-making strategy; thus they do not take positions for this purpose and, accordingly, engage in less activism.[135] Put differently, the difference in activism is, in part, due to the fact that hedge funds and traditional institutions pursue different profit strategies.

Viewed from this perspective, the relevant question becomes why (some) hedge funds pursue activism as a strategy, while (most) traditional institutions do not. The answer to this question may lie, in part, in the fact that traditional institutions face regulatory barriers, political constraints, and conflicts of interest that make activism less profitable for them than it is for hedge funds.

But the difference in strategies may also be due to the fact that mutual funds view and market themselves as vehicles for diversification, which enables their investors to gain broad exposure to markets at low costs. To be a successful activist, it is probably helpful for a fund to engage in activism as a principal strategy—activism presumably entails learning, with funds that have done more of it becoming better at it, and funds with an activist reputation more easily attracting support from other investors and inducing management changes. An activist strategy, however, does not mesh well with a diversification objective, because strategic activism is relatively expensive and requires a fund to take comparatively large positions in relatively few companies. Hedge funds, in contrast, do not see themselves as vehicles for diversification; they engage in targeted hedges, rather than diversification, to eliminate unwanted risk.[136] More narrowly tailored strategies—such as activism—are thus more appropriate for hedge funds than for mutual funds.[137]

[134] See, e.g., Smith (1996: 231–2), describing the criteria for target selection used by CalPERS.

[135] See Ubben and Haarmeyer (2006: 60), noting that traditional money managers own small positions in many companies and have poor performance incentives, whereas activist investors invest in a small number of companies and have powerful incentives.

[136] Perhaps more importantly, hedge funds have less of a need to diversify because investors in hedge funds, unlike many investors in mutual funds, are already substantially diversified through their other holdings. Put differently, hedge fund investors have a greater tolerance for risk generated by their hedge fund investment than mutual fund investors have with respect to their mutual fund investment.

[137] Even non-activist hedge funds tend to pursue narrowly tailored investment strategies such as merger arbitrage and convertible bond arbitrage. Of course, some 'multi-strategy' hedge funds pursue broader (or a combination of narrower) strategies, and some mutual funds—such as sector funds—offer lesser diversification benefits. Indeed, some mutual funds, such as Mutual Beacon Fund, are even relatively activist. Franklin Templeton Investments (2006: 9) describes the investment strategies used by the Mutual Series of funds, including 'activist' investments in distressed securities. On the whole, however, the mutual fund sector is dominated by funds with broadly diversified portfolios, while the hedge fund sector is characterized by funds with narrowly tailored strategies.

5.4 Problems Generated by Hedge Fund Activism: Conflicts and Stress Fractures

Although hedge funds hold great promise as active shareholders, their intense involvement in corporate governance and control also raises some concerns. Hedge funds are set up to make money for their investors without regard to whether the strategies they follow benefit shareholders generally. For example, a hedge fund that owns shares in Company A may try to use that position to increase the value of another position, say in Company B, rather than to maximize the share price of Company A. Indeed, because hedge funds frequently engage in hedges and other sophisticated trading and arbitrage strategies, such conflicts of interest are likely to arise more frequently for hedge funds than for other institutional investors. We examine these 'hedging-related conflicts' in Section 5.4.1.

In addition to these direct conflicts, we also address a secondary problem related to hedge fund activism. Hedge funds combine high-powered incentives with great sophistication and access to vast pools of capital. Together, these can put great stress on the existing governance system. We examine some of these potential 'stress fractures' in Section 5.4.2.

We conclude this section by commenting in Section 5.4.3 on the absence, so far, of a third set of problems: managers buying off activist hedge funds through the payment of greenmail or similar devices. We leave the most common, and potentially most serious, criticism levelled against hedge funds—that they, due to their short-term trading horizons, aggravate an already serious problem of 'short-termism' in the executive suite—to be analysed in Section 5.5.

In assessing the need for a regulatory response to these problems, there are several considerations. First, to what extent does the existing regulatory structure adequately address the concerns? Here, we consider whether the problems are of a familiar type, and whether the increased pressure on the system imposed by hedge funds overwhelms existing tools. When a problem is a standard corporate law problem, we presume that the existing regulatory structure is adequate, unless some specific aspect of hedge fund involvement changes the analysis. If, on the other hand, the problem is of a new type, new tools may be required.

If one concludes that the current structure is inadequate, one then needs to consider which of the various tools available is most appropriate. In this regard, there are three general categories of potential responses. One can rely on market forces (e.g., competition among hedge funds or reputation), employ self-help (e.g., charter amendments or contracts), or resort to regulation.

While the specific response depends on the precise nature of the problem, it is critical to bear in mind that hedge fund activism is not static. Hedge funds are among the most nimble market actors, with a track record of coming up with new strategies, some of which are designed to exploit imperfections in the very responses developed to the old strategies. Moreover, hedge funds are not only clever, but quick. Therefore, in choosing a mode of response, speed and flexibility are very important. This suggests that market forces and self-help are better designed to deal with these problems than regulation. The reason is twofold. First, private actors generally can react more quickly than regulators. Second, private actors have a greater ability to learn from each other to devise a proper response.

As we will see, many of the problems discussed in this section are familiar and classic corporate law problems. Despite the increased pressure applied by hedge funds, our general view is that the traditional solutions (perhaps with increased enforcement), supplemented by market responses, and, possibly, some additional disclosure requirements, should suffice. We are not indifferent to the possibility of illegal or improper behaviour; rather, our view is that the current regulatory structure can handle this, with minor exceptions.

5.4.1 The Dark Side: Hedging-Related Conflicts

5.4.1.1 *Buying (Control) versus Selling (Shares)*

As the earlier anecdotes show, hedge funds are sometimes potential buyers, as opposed to sellers. When a hedge fund is a potential buyer of a company in which it has a stake, its interests clearly diverge from those of its fellow shareholders. The hedge fund wants to buy at the lowest possible price, while the other shareholders want to sell at the highest possible price. A hedge fund's activities may not be so much directed at making sure that the target is sold at the highest price, but rather at increasing the likelihood that the hedge fund succeeds in its acquisition attempt.

This is a very old problem in corporate law that is analysed under the rubric of the duty of loyalty. While hedge funds' interests diverge from general shareholder interests when they are seeking to buy control, this conflict is obvious, with management and other shareholders aware of it and on guard against it. Moreover, hedge funds will generally have no control over the target company they are trying to buy. We therefore believe that no special response is necessary.

5.4.1.2 *Conflicts in Merger Votes*

A more subtle conflict can arise in control transactions when a hedge fund owns other securities, the value of which depends on whether the transaction is consummated. Such conflicts featured prominently in the proposed acquisition of MONY (a publicly traded life insurance company) by AXA (a large French financial conglomerate), where hedge funds both favouring and opposing the deal had conflicts of interest.[138] Highfields—a hedge fund holding nearly 5% of MONY—led the opposition by MONY shareholders, running a full-page ad in the *Wall Street Journal*, 'urging MONY shareholders to reject the sale' (Hansard 2004),[139] convincing Institutional Shareholder Services, a proxy advisory firm, to recommend a 'no'

[138] See *In re MONY Group, Inc. S'holder Litig.*, 853 A.2d 661, 668 (Del. Ch. 2004) ('[P]ersons who hold long positions in ORANs stand to gain a large profit on that investment if the MONY/AXA merger is consummated. Conversely, arbitrageurs who sell ORANs short stand to gain if that same merger is not completed.').

[139] Highfields even mailed a letter to shareholders urging them to vote 'no' on the merger. Highfields had originally intended to enclose a duplicate of the corporate proxy card so that shareholders, should they choose, could easily cast a 'no' vote, but MONY succeeded in obtaining an injunction preventing this additional step, despite Highfields' argument that it was an exempt solicitation under Rule 14a-2(b)(1). *MONY Group, Inc. v. Highfields Capital Mgmt.*, L.P., 368 F.3d 138, 141–5 (2nd Cir. 2004).

vote on the deal,[140] and establishing a website to aid MONY shareholders in exercising their appraisal rights (*PR Newswire* 2004d).

But Highfields' interests were not pure. In order to finance its cash acquisition of MONY, AXA had issued convertible debt securities—known as 'ORANs'—to its shareholders. These debt securities were to convert into AXA shares on completion of the acquisition, but could be redeemed at face value plus interest if the acquisition was not completed by 21 December 2004. Given the relative values involved, the ORANs would be significantly more valuable if the MONY/AXA deal went through. Highfields held a large short position in ORANs, a position that would become more valuable if the merger did not close.[141] Other hedge funds favouring the merger, in turn, were long on ORANs and apparently purchased MONY stock at a premium in order to vote for the merger (Innisfree M&A Inc. 2006: slide 11).[142] Eventually, after a postponement of the shareholder meeting (which allowed shareholders who bought stock after the previous record date to vote) and much litigation, the MONY merger squeaked through, with 53.8% of the outstanding shares voting in favour (Norris 2004).[143]

In a world in which more than half of all equities are held by institutional shareholders, such conflicts are pervasive. But, while pervasive, they are not necessarily bad. Index funds, for example, will own shares on both sides of many mergers between public companies. In such cases, their financial interest is to maximize the value of their portfolios. Thus, they should approve a merger if it is value-enhancing, without regard to the magnitude of the premiums paid to shareholders, even if shareholders of individual firms, qua shareholders, might prefer higher premiums. In contrast to index funds, which simply find themselves on both sides, hedge funds potentially exacerbate the pervasive conflicts because they choose to invest in both sides of a deal and acquire stakes in order to influence the outcome.

Corporate law has long lived with, and tolerated, conflicts of interest in voting by shareholders. Hedge funds may be more likely to have such conflicts than traditional institutional investors, and may even choose to create such conflicts, but the conflicts in the context of hedge funds pale compared to the conflicts of controlling shareholders in freeze-outs, whose votes will usually be outcome-determinative. And controlling shareholders are entitled to vote their shares in their (conflicted) self-interest, unencumbered by any fiduciary duties to minority shareholders.[144]

Therefore, we see little need to impose stricter duties on hedge funds, or on voting conflicts more generally,[145] for several reasons: absent empty voting, the effect of conflicted votes is

[140] Hansard (2004) states that 'ISS said the sale price "is outside the boundary of reasonableness when compared to precedent transactions coupled with open-market opportunities to sell above the offer price"'.

[141] *In re MONY Group*, 853 A.2d at 668.

[142] See also *In re MONY Group*, 853 A.2d at 669 (describing the trading activity surrounding the merger). In a presentation to the MONY board, CSFB, the board's independent financial advisor, 'noted that as of the Board meeting, anyone long ORANs would receive an approximate 46% profit if the merger was consummated, compared to a 2.4% profit if it was not'. *In re MONY Group*, 853 A.2d at 671 n.29).

[143] The article also notes that '[e]ssential to approval may have been a block of 8.7 percent of the shares owned by Deutsche Bank', which was not disclosed until shortly before the vote (Norris 2004: CA).

[144] See *Bershad v. Curtiss-Wright Corp.*, 535 A.2d 840, 845 (Del. 1987) ('Clearly, a stockholder is under no duty to sell its holdings in a corporation, even if it is a majority shareholder, merely because the sale would profit the minority.').

[145] We suspect that a more common occurrence is that hedge funds have economic interests that are disproportionate to their voting interest due to options or other derivatives that have a value that correlates with the stock price, but carry no voting rights.

self-limiting;[146] conflicted funds are often on both sides of the contested issue and their votes thus cancel each other out;[147] the market is often aware of, and can respond to, these conflicts; all diversified shareholders—including all institutional investors—will often find themselves with similar conflicts; and the board of directors, which does have fiduciary duties, can take measures to counteract any dangers.

5.4.1.3 *Empty Voting*

A particularly extreme form of a hedging-related conflict arose in the proposed Mylan–King merger. In July 2004, Mylan Laboratories entered into a merger agreement with King Pharmaceuticals, whereby, subject to shareholder approval, Mylan would acquire King in exchange for Mylan shares. Perry, a hedge fund, was a large shareholder in King, with approximately 7 million shares, and supported the merger. While the deal was seen as favourable to King, the market reaction to the merger for Mylan was negative, and some large shareholders of Mylan, including Carl Icahn, threatened to vote against it. As a result, approval of the merger by Mylan shareholders was in doubt (Steyer 2004).

Perry then acquired 9.9% of Mylan's shares. At the same time, Perry apparently entered into 'equity swaps' with Bear Stearns and Goldman Sachs that fully hedged its economic exposure to Mylan's share price. As a result, Perry acquired shares—and votes—in Mylan, which, because it had no economic stake in Mylan, it could use purely on the basis of its interest as a King shareholder—thus in favour of the merger (Hu and Black 2006).[148] Indeed, this, presumably, was Perry's purpose.

The divergence between the interests of Perry and those of other Mylan shareholders is evident. If the merger was good for King but bad for Mylan, as many Mylan shareholders apparently felt, Perry would still vote its sizeable position in Mylan in favour of the merger and could help push it through. As it happened, King had to restate its earnings, which caused Mylan management to terminate the merger agreement. The success and legal validity of Perry's strategy thus were not tested.[149]

'Empty voting', as this is called, is an example of an old problem—conflicts of interests created by exploiting the separation of legal and beneficial ownership—aggravated by modern financial innovation. Perry took advantage of modern financial instruments to acquire votes.

[146] As long as the economic interest of a hedge fund corresponds at least to its voting rights, the hedge fund will suffer proportionally with other shareholders from any value decline.

[147] See Section 5.4.1.3 (discussing conflicts in the Mylan–King merger vote).

[148] The issues relating to empty voting are extensively discussed in Hu and Black (Chapter 10, this volume) See also Martin and Partnoy (2005: 779–80).

[149] Other, more traditional conflicts of interest in voting were also present. Icahn had a stake of about 10% in Mylan, both in terms of economic exposure and in terms of voting rights. But Icahn also had shorted 5.3 million shares of King stock. See Forbes (2005), explaining Icahn's position in the failed merger. Icahn could thus have an economic incentive to oppose the merger, even if the merger were in the interest of Mylan, as long as the market thought that the merger would be significantly more beneficial to King. In that event, Icahn would gain more from a defeat of the merger through his short position in King than he would lose on account of his long position in Mylan. Suppose Icahn shorted the King shares at $30 per share, that the shares would go up to $40 per share if the merger were completed, but down to $20 per share if the merger failed. Icahn would then profit from defeating the merger if his profits from shorting were greater than the increase in the value of his Mylan stake from completing the merger.

While Perry's actions functionally appear to be a form of 'vote buying', legally they do not seem to fall within the existing jurisprudential framework. Indeed, as Hu and Black explain, the existing regulatory structure does not prohibit it (2006). If empty voting turns out to be a significant problem—and it is not clear that it will—new measures will be required, either through regulation or by common law decision-making.

That said, how exactly the law should be changed, if it should at all, is a highly complex question. The complexity has several sources: multiple mechanisms can generate empty votes; current legal rules do not treat these mechanisms equivalently; other problems related to the compilation of broker votes interact with the concerns raised by empty voting; and, at present, neither the market, nor companies, nor regulators have the information necessary to determine the presence and extent of empty voting schemes.

The development of a proper response is further complicated by the fact that companies and investors have an interest in determining the outcome of a vote speedily. Thus, any more intrusive legal regime that involves protracted litigation generates special problems in the context of voting rules. Moreover, it is unclear to what extent market responses (such as the increasing costliness of hedging strategies around critical votes) temper empty voting. For now, we agree with Henry Hu and Bernie Black that not enough is known about the extent of empty voting to prescribe anything more than an increase in disclosure of schemes generating empty votes (Hu and Black 2006).[150]

5.4.2 Stress Fractures

With billions of dollars available, and super-high-powered incentive compensation structures, hedge funds put stress on the existing governance structures. In doing so, they highlight and exacerbate existing structural weaknesses, albeit not necessarily in a manner that generates a conflict of interest with other shareholders. In this section, we address two such potential weaknesses: undisclosed concerted action and over-voting.

5.4.2.1 *Undisclosed Concerted Action*

In many of the battles between managers and hedge funds described earlier in this chapter, the shareholder base of companies can change almost overnight, with hedge funds sometimes ending up with more than 50% of the shares. Managers and their counsel have speculated that hedge funds act in concert, both in the acquisition of their shares and in the subsequent pressuring of management, without filing the required disclosure statements[151] under Section 13(d) of the Securities Exchange Act.[152] Indeed, say some, there is a pervasive problem of SEC under-enforcement of Section 13(d).

We do not know whether this is true or not. If there is, in fact, a problem of under-reporting, it presents an interesting parallel to the events of the 1980s. When hostile tender offers first

[150] Hu and Black (Chapter 10, this volume) advocate disclosure as a means to curb empty voting because the information disclosed would expose a need for empty voting reform.

[151] See Lipton (2005), noting the tendency of activist hedge funds 'to execute purchases so as to avoid detection'.

[152] 15 U.S.C. § 78m(d) (2000).

assumed prominence, management complained that hostile bidders and their allies operated behind the scenes to the disadvantage of shareholders and companies. Now one hears complaints that it is hedge funds (some run by the same raiders about whom managers complained in the 1980s) that are operating behind the scenes.

An important difference exists, however, between non-disclosure by raiders in the 1980s and any non-disclosure by activist hedge funds today. The acquisition of a 5% stake by a raider was highly material, market-moving information. By delaying a 13(d) filing, raiders and their allies could acquire additional shares at a substantially lower price. By contrast, hedge fund activism has much less of an immediate market impact. Moreover, hedge fund corporate governance activities are usually conducted publicly, with hedge funds issuing press releases long before they reach the 5% filing threshold under Section 13(d).[153] Finally, hedge funds (unlike most raiders) must disclose their equity holdings quarterly under Section 13(f).[154] Thus, while hedge funds, like all other investors, ought to comply with 13(d), one wonders what all the fuss about a failure to disclose is about.

To be sure, a 13(d) filing can yield information that would otherwise not become public. Specifically, a 13(d) filing could reveal the presence of a conflict of interest, such as an empty voting scheme. Section 13(d) requires the disclosure of any contracts and other arrangements in which hedge funds dispose of their economic interests.[155] Indeed, it was this 13(d) requirement that forced Perry to reveal its hedging positions in the Mylan–King battle. Where such conflicts exist, they would have to be disclosed in a 13(d) filing. A failure to make the filing constitutes a serious problem, but it does not appear that such conflicts are common.

In addition, most poison pills incorporate the 13(d) concept of a group into the pill trigger. Thus, it may sometimes be the case that an undisclosed formation of a 'group' would trigger the pill—to the serious harm of the participating hedge funds and, one assumes, to the delight of management and their lawyers.[156] In that case, however, management is in a good position to respond: it can argue that the hedge funds have formed a group, declare the pill triggered, dilute down the members of the alleged group, and wait to be sued. Given the incentives for management to pursue such cases, this does not seem to be an area to which the SEC need devote its limited enforcement resources.

Thus, the key issue is not the SEC's failure to bring enforcement actions, but the vagueness of the concept of 'group' underlying Section 13(d) and the poison pill. Rule 13d-5 provides that '[w]hen two or more persons agree to act together for the purpose of acquiring, holding, voting or disposing of equity securities of an issuer, the group formed thereby shall be deemed to have acquired beneficial ownership'.[157] Thus, concerted conduct—but not parallel action—will trigger section 13(d)'s reporting obligations. The fact that a variety of hedge funds crowd into the shares of a company at the same time does not per se establish the formation of a group, any more than the mere fact that competing manufacturers raise their prices at the same time establishes a price-fixing agreement in violation of Section 1 of

[153] See, e.g., Yuan and Rhoads (2007), detailing, in a front page article, Carl Icahn's purchase of a 1.39% stake in Motorola.

[154] Securities Exchange Act of 1934 § 13(f), 15 U.S.C. § 78m(f) (2000).

[155] Section 13(d)(1)(E), 15 U.S.C. § 78m(d)(1)(E) (2000). But § 13(d) does not have a per se requirement to disclose conflicts of interest.

[156] See Plitch (2005), discussing the limited ability of boards to deploy a pill against hedge funds.

[157] SEC Rule 13d-5(b)(1), 17 C.F.R. § 240.13d-5(b)(1) (2006).

the Sherman Act.[158] Proving that parallel conduct is concerted action is difficult, both in the anti-trust and in the 13(d) context.

In this regard, hedge fund activism may raise a somewhat novel problem. Until recently, the issue of unaffiliated parties acting in parallel to influence a public company—and the accompanying evidentiary ambiguity concerning whether a group has been formed—has not arisen that often. Rather than bring more enforcement actions, the SEC may want to provide regulatory clarification on the question of group formation.

5.4.2.2 *Overvoting*

The current voting technology is seriously flawed. Some argue that it is so flawed that in any reasonably close corporate vote—the number of which are increasing with more hedge fund involvement—it would be impossible to prove which side has prevailed.

Since 1973, to avoid the overwhelming record-keeping problems of paper shares, companies have used a book entry system with share certificates held by the Depository Trust Company (DTC). Individual brokerage houses each have accounts with DTC in which, under the standard arrangements between customers and their brokerage firms, holdings of customers are commingled in a single, fungible mass. DTC's records simply indicate that Merrill Lynch, for example, has 20,000 shares of Firm X, without indicating how many shares specific customers of Merrill hold. As Merrill Lynch's customers buy and sell, Merrill's net holdings will change and DTC's records will reflect this, but it is Merrill's responsibility to keep track of its customers' holdings.

When it comes time for the shareholders of Firm X to vote, the company will typically retain a firm, usually ADP, to handle the distribution of proxy materials, the solicitation of proxies, and the tabulation of the votes.[159] ADP receives a list of holdings, sorted by brokerage house, from DTC, and a list of customers' accounts from the participant broker. It then sends out proxy materials, including proxy cards indicating the number of shares in a customer's account, to all who appear on the brokers' lists. Customers fill out their cards, return them to ADP, and the results are then passed on to the firm.

This system breaks down when there is significant short selling, as is often the case when hedge funds are involved. Consider what happens when someone 'shorts' a stock.[160] In a short sale, a brokerage house typically arranges for a short seller to acquire shares from a broker (sometimes itself) or bank that holds shares (in a fungible mass) for its custodial clients, subject to an obligation to return a share at some later date. The short seller then sells the shares to some third party, who will take full title and be entirely oblivious of the source of the shares.

Because a short sale involves an actual transfer of shares, it creates substantial difficulties in determining who has a right to vote shares, principally because tracing is not possible, and record keeping and communication are incomplete.[161] Suppose that Merrill has

[158] *Theatre Enters., Inc. v. Paramount Film Distrib. Corp.*, 346 U.S. 537, 541 (1954) ('[T]his Court has never held that proof of parallel business behavior . . . itself constitutes a Sherman Act offense.').

[159] ADP Investor Communications Services claims a 95% market share (ADP Investor Communication Services 2007).

[160] For an excellent account of the consequences of short selling, see Parsons et al. (2001).

[161] Here we follow the excellent discussion of the complications attendant to short sales in Parsons et al. (2001).

20,000 shares of X in its DTC account, while Goldman has 30,000 shares in its account. A hedge fund 'borrows' 5,000 shares from Merrill and, to go short, sells them to a customer of Goldman. Once that sale is completed, DTC records will show that Merrill has 15,000 shares of X while Goldman has 35,000 shares.

The problem is now clear: DTC's omnibus proxy will transfer the right to vote 15,000 shares to Merrill, and will inform ADP of this. But Merrill will give ADP a list of all its customers' holdings in Firm X for a total of 20,000 shares. ADP will then send out proxy materials according to the brokers' customer lists, with the result that it will send out proxy cards for more shares than are, in fact, entitled to vote. In this example, although Merrill and Goldman collectively hold only 50,000 shares, their customers will receive proxy cards representing 55,000 shares. Because the shorted shares are often not attributed to specific customer accounts, it is unclear which customers are entitled to vote. If fewer than 15,000 Merrill shares are voted, this problem is shoved under the table by pretending that the Merrill customers who returned proxies were all entitled to vote and some of those who did not return proxies were not entitled to vote anyway. But if proxies for more shares are returned than are entitled to vote—because the level of short selling was high and the abstention rate was low—it is unclear what should be done.

There are several possible effects of this system for collecting votes. First, it may mean that some people who are shareholders are unable to vote their shares. Second, it may mean that others who may not, in fact, own any shares (because they have been lent out) will nonetheless be able to vote. Finally, it may result in a situation in which there is no answer to the question of who is entitled to vote.

The MONY/AXA deal, discussed in Section 5.4.1.2, is an example of a contested transaction that illustrates these problems. The controversial buyout was approved by a margin of 1.7 million votes out of a total of 50.1 million shares at a time when somewhere around 6.2 million shares had been shorted.[162]

Though the over-voting problem has been noted for a long time,[163] it is becoming more acute now, because hedge fund activism makes close votes more likely and hedge funds engage in short selling at the time of votes. We discuss this problem in greater detail, and examine possible solutions, in a separate article (Kahan and Rock 2008).

5.4.3 The Absence (So Far) of a Third Conflict: Paying Hedge Funds Off

It is worth noting that we have not found any evidence for the existence of a third potential conflict between hedge funds and other investors: hedge funds and managers making a side deal, such as greenmail, in which the firm pays the hedge fund to go away. We are not aware of a single instance of hedge funds receiving greenmail, one of the 1980s' classic examples of

[162] Drummond (2006) uses the MONY/AXA deal as an example of a short sale's effects on corporate democracy.

[163] A 1991 House Report recommended that the SEC promulgate a rule to handle this situation, and, specifically, a rule that would prohibit brokers and dealers from soliciting proxy voting instructions from or giving proxies at the direction of beneficial owners for more shares than the net amount owned

'dark side' behaviour. The absence of greenmail is interesting in its own right. One possible explanation is that greenmail got such a bad name during the 1980s that hedge funds are too embarrassed to touch it, or, perhaps more plausibly, that boards are too embarrassed to offer it. Alternatively, the absence of greenmail or similar devices may reflect the fact that there are so many hedge funds around that greenmail or similar devices will not provide firms with any protection and may well elicit even greater interest. Finally, it could be that accepting greenmail may not serve the long-term interests of activist hedge funds because it would undermine their credibility and their ability to obtain the support of other investors (which they may need to succeed in their activism) the next time around.

5.5 Pervasive Short-Termism?

Although many of the 'dark side' problems identified in Section 5.3 have generated comment and controversy, the sharpest and most comprehensive criticism of hedge fund activism is that it exacerbates an already serious problem of 'short-termism' in the executive suite. In this section, we take that criticism seriously.

5.5.1 A Real Problem?

Hedge funds come close to being the archetypal short-term investor.[164] For some funds, holding shares for a full day represents a 'long-term' investment. Short-termism may thus pervade much that hedge funds do, including their corporate governance and control activism. Leading opponents of hedge fund activism, such as Martin Lipton, argue that hedge fund short-termism could cause managers not to make crucial long-term investments.[165] And the German finance ministry set up a panel to assess the impact of, and consider regulation of, 'short-term profit-oriented foreign investors' (Taylor and MacDonald 2006: C5).

beneficially by each beneficial owner, as shown on the books and records of the broker or dealer, after subtracting the short security positions of each beneficial owner. H.R. Rep. No. 102-414, pt. 1, at 33 (1991). More recently, the New York Stock Exchange (2004) states that '[s]everal recent special examinations of member organizations' proxy departments have discovered significant areas of concern involving an apparent systemic over-voting of proxies and a general lack of effective supervision'.

[164] See De Ramos (2006), noting that hedge funds make up 40% to 50% of average daily trading volume in major financial markets.

[165] See *The Economist* (2006a), stating that: 'Martin Lipton, a veteran Wall Street lawyer, [complained] that "we have gone from the imperial CEO to the imperial stockholder"'; Lipton (2006b) outlines a 'checklist' for rebuffing hedge fund attacks. Even if they are short-term oriented, hedge funds' short-term strategies may perform valuable functions. For example, when hedge funds play their traditional role of arbitraging market inefficiencies, their pursuit of short-term profit will be one of the mechanisms that helps to bring the market price into alignment with the value of the firm. Thus, for example, when prices are too high because of excessive optimism, hedge funds can be expected to short the stock, thereby putting some necessary downward pressure on the price. Moreover, even if the interests of short-term and long-term investors may occasionally conflict, their interests will often coincide. To that extent, hedge funds, by furthering their own short-term interests, will also benefit long-term shareholders.

One's views about whether hedge fund activism, on the whole, is desirable or undesirable are likely to turn on one's stand on the short-termism problem.[166]

Looking at the specific activities of hedge funds, there is often an inherent ambiguity as to whether they sacrifice valuable long-term projects in favour of short-term gains. Consider DB's failed attempt to acquire the LSE, discussed earlier in this chapter.[167] DB's CEO wanted to acquire the LSE and convinced the board that doing so was a good idea. Hedge funds that had acquired large stakes in DB disagreed. They maintained that the plan to acquire the LSE represented wasteful managerial empire-building and that DB's cash reserves should instead be distributed to shareholders. Now, if the investment in acquiring the LSE was a valuable long-term project, then the involvement of the hedge funds would have had the effect of pushing the company towards the lower value outcome: an outcome worse for long-term shareholders than acquiring the LSE. If the hedge funds were right that the investment was simply a bad investment driven by delusions of grandeur, their opposition benefited both short- and long-term shareholders.[168]

For the short-term trading horizon of hedge funds to generate a short-term investment outlook for hedge fund managers, the stock market must suffer from myopia: that is, it must undervalue long-term investments relative to short-term investments. If the market does not itself suffer from such a bias, then the interests of investors with short-term trading horizons will not conflict with those of investors with long-term trading horizons. In the case of the DB's attempt to acquire LSE, for example, a conflict between hedge funds with short-term trading horizons and other investors with long-term horizons would exist only if the market myopically failed to incorporate the long-term benefits of acquiring LSE into the stock price of DB.

Whether and under what circumstances the market suffers from myopia has been the subject of substantial analysis and debate. Many managers, directors, private equity funds, investment bankers, and others involved in the management and sale of companies are convinced that the market is myopic. Others believe that the allegations of myopia are a foil

166 There is, so far, limited empirical evidence regarding the effect of activism on company value. See Klein and Zur (Chapter 9, this volume) finding that a company's stock price increases when an activist hedge fund files a Schedule 13D, but that accounting performance declines in the year following filing; Brav et al. (Chapter 8, this volume) finding abnormal stock price increases upon announcement of activism and no support for the assertion that activism destroys value or is short-term focused. Since hedge fund activism is a relatively recent phenomenon, these studies, by necessity, cannot measure the long-term effect of such activism.

167 See Section 5.2.1.2.1.

168 This analysis nicely illustrates the different ways in which hedge fund involvement, when it crosses a critical threshold, can affect shareholders. Were hedge funds only to hold a small percentage of either DB or the LSE, and were the market to overvalue the transaction's worth to the companies, they could bet against the DB bid for the LSE by shorting DB stock. If they could be short for a long enough time, they would make money if it turned out that they were right that this was empire-building and would lose money if it turned out that this was value-enhancing. While, in the DB case, the hedge funds were likely right, there are other cases in which they bet against a complex strategy and lost. The clearest case seems to be the investment strategies surrounding the transaction between Lampert, Kmart, and Sears. When Lampert acquired control of Kmart, the stock was heavily shorted (Byron 2003). But within a year, the stock had gone from $15 per share to $109 per share. See note 49. Had those with the short view held a controlling position, they may have blocked the strategy, to shareholders' detriment.

for managerial failure to deliver results.[169] Academics have developed theoretical models showing that market myopia can result in a number of circumstances.[170] Much of the current research in finance starts from the assumption that capital markets are not perfectly efficient.[171] But the empirical evidence on the extent and magnitude of myopia is sketchy at best.[172]

Arguably, the phenomenal growth of private equity funds—whose basic business model includes taking companies private so that they can be reconfigured away from the short-term pressures on public companies—indicates that there may well be a serious problem of myopia. KKR, Blackstone, Carlyle, Apollo, and TPG all have raised new funds in excess of $10 billion.[173] Then again, the business model of private equity funds also includes providing managers with high-powered incentives and monitoring them closely.[174] Whether private equity and activist hedge funds pursue complementary strategies for maximizing firm value

[169] For example, Rosenstein (2006); see also Ubben and Haarmeyer (2006: 60), arguing that it is important to distinguish between activists that are 'short-term saber rattlers' and those that are 'long-term value creators', and criticizing defenders of entrenched management for trying to tar all activists with the same brush.

[170] See generally Kihlstrom and Wachter (2005); Shleifer and Vishny (1990); Stein (1989, 1988). Although the common view is that market myopia leads to underinvestment in long-term opportunities, some have argued that it can lead to overinvestment as well. See, e.g., Bebchuk and Stole (1993).

[171] For a short survey of the prevailing theories on market efficiency, see Wachter (2003: 801–4).

[172] Some of the studies focus on the effect on managerial myopia of institutional investors, which has been argued to have a shorter-term trading horizon than other investors. See, e.g., Bange and De Bondt (1998: 156), finding that managers are less likely to manipulate R&D budgets to reduce discrepancies between analysts' forecasts and reported income when institutional investors own a higher stake; Bushee (1998: 306–7), arguing that institutions generally reduce myopic pressure, but that institutions with high turnover that engage in momentum trading encourage myopia; Majumdar and Nagarajan (1997: 50), concluding that institutional investors have a positive and significant effect on R&D spending; Wahal and McConnell (2000: 311) conclude that presence of institutional investors, regardless of investment style, leads to more investment in long-term projects; Majumdar and Nagarajan (1994) find that institutions prefer to invest in firms with long-term orientation. Other studies focus on the effect of threatened hostile takeovers—which Lipton and others have suggested generates undesirable short-termism—on R&D expenses and similar measures of long-term investments. While one study suggests that, consistent with the short-termism hypothesis, R&D expenses might increase after the enactment of antitakeover legislation, two other studies found that R&D declines after the adoption of antitakeover provisions. See Johnson and Rao (1997: 674 tbl.2), finding that R&D expenses decline after the adoption of an antitakeover provision; Muelbroek et al. (1990: 1108, 1114–15). But see Pugh and Jahera (1990: 221, 226 tbl.1), finding a marginal increase in returns following enactment of an antitakeover statute, which the authors link to long-term investment, such as R&D. Other studies look at other aspects of myopia. See, e.g., Abarbanell and Bernard (2000: 221–2), concluding that 'stock prices do not generally exhibit myopic behavior'; Agrawal and Jaffe (2000: 7, 37), rejecting EPS myopia as an explanation for negative long-run stock returns after mergers; Ballardini et al. (2005), finding that the market values $1 invested in R&D as much or more than $1 invested in tangible assets; Cheng, Subramanyam, and Zhang (2005), finding that firms dedicated to giving quarterly earnings guidance engage in more myopic R&D investments; Lundstrum and Holden (2005), finding that the introduction of long-term options (Long-Term Equity AnticiPation Security; LEAPS) is associated with an increase in long-term investments.

[173] Smith (2006) notes that TPG has raised more than $14 billion for its latest fund, while Blackstone raised at least $13.5 billion, and Apollo Management and KKR have each raised over $10 billion. More than $250 billion is estimated to have been raised by private equity funds in 2005.

[174] *Wall Street Journal* (2007) suggests that improved incentives and reduced pressure to achieve quarterly earnings allow private equity firms to enhance value.

(with both targeting managerial agency costs in a different fashion), whether they are competitors in the same markets (as private equity funds open hedge funds and hedge funds take companies private), or whether hedge funds aggravate market imperfections and thus drive firms into the arms of private equity remains unclear.

Short-termism thus presents the potentially most important, most controversial, most ambiguous, and most complex problem associated with hedge fund activism. The other dark side problems represent relatively isolated and narrow concerns that do not relate to hedge fund activism as a whole. Short-termism, by contrast, arguably pervades hedge fund activism, and the accusation that hedge funds induce managerial short-termism has become the main ammunition for hedge fund critics. At the same time, among the problems associated with hedge fund activism, the very existence of a short-termism problem is the least proven, its manifestations—if it does exist—are the most manifold, and potential solutions are the least evident.

5.5.2 Potential Responses?

Let us assume that hedge fund managers tend to prefer that companies engage in projects with short-term payoffs, even if there are projects with longer-term payoffs that are more valuable. Should the law intervene, and if so, how?

The answer to these questions depends on a number of factors. First, even if hedge funds have short-term biases, to what extent is hedge fund activism driven by excessive short-termism? Activist hedge funds are agents of change with specific goals that depend on the particular company. When the company is diversified, hedge funds often push for divestitures. When it is underperforming, they often push for the sale of the company or a change in management. When the company has excess cash on hand, they push for stock repurchases or dividends. When the company has assets on its balance sheet that can be monetized (e.g., real estate), they push to monetize those assets. When companies are pursuing capital-intensive investment plans, hedge funds sometimes oppose the plans and push for the cash to be returned to shareholders. In the control area, hedge funds sometimes make bids, sometimes advocate or oppose deals from either side of the transaction, and often try to get better terms for the target. Is it always the case that, when a hedge fund gets involved, it is pushing for business strategies with a short-term payoff over strategies with a more valuable long-term payoff? Or is the short-term payoff preferred by hedge funds sometimes the more valuable one? And how often is hedge fund activism motivated by altogether different concerns, such as bad management, an ill-advised strategy, or an insufficient price in an acquisition?[175] Is the controversy really about different investment horizons, or does it instead reflect a substantive dispute over the appropriate course of action for the firm?

Second, how long is the horizon of managers?[176] A plausible argument can be made that it is managers—not just markets—that suffer from myopia these days. Many CEOs are close to retirement age and, even among younger CEOs, turnover is high. Executives' stock options

175 See, e.g., Adamy (2006b), reporting that a hedge fund asked Heinz to, among other things, sell its line of Italian baby food and use new forms of marketing to increase ketchup consumption.

176 See, e.g, Singer (2006c), reporting a trend among private equity funds to enter the faster-paced business of hedge funds.

continually vest and are exercised or hedged, if only to diversify their portfolio. Bonuses are often based on short-term performance goals. Is it sometimes management's failure to invest in valuable long-term projects that creates the opening for hedge fund activism?

Third, when and to what extent do hedge funds succeed in affecting corporate policy? Though hedge funds have become highly active in the corporate governance area, they generally have not become powerful enough to exercise control over the targets of their activism.[177] Rather, they purchase a sizeable, but far from controlling stake—rarely more than 5% to 10%—and then seek to influence corporate strategies.[178] Even when hedge funds commence a proxy contest, they usually seek only minority representation on the board. Activist hedge funds often have a chair at the metaphorical table where corporate strategy is set, giving them an opportunity to present their views. In order to see their views prevail, however, hedge funds usually need the support of others[179]—which cannot be taken for granted.[180] These 'others' include, in particular, corporate management, independent directors, traditional institutional investors with large stakes, and other large shareholders. To the extent that the largest shareholders are effectively indexers, a strategy that results in a short-term increase in share price (which benefits hedge funds), but a long-term loss (that hurts long-term shareholders), will not be attractive. More generally, over time the degree of support that hedge funds receive will likely depend on whether long-term shareholders benefit.

Fourth, if the determination of corporate policy, once hedge funds are involved, depends on multiple constituents, how do these constituents interact? At present, it seems that hedge funds often act as a counterweight to the substantial power of management, with the consequence that the effective power partly shifts to other groups, such as independent directors and traditional institutional investors. Independent directors and large shareholders, of course, may sometimes make mistakes, but management is not infallible either. We are inclined to be optimistic about the resulting interaction, which often results in a compromise rather than an outright victory for either hedge funds or management.[181] But another possibility—though one that we have so far not witnessed—is that hedge funds will enter an unholy alliance, either by being bought off by management through the payment of greenmail or its functional equivalent, or by teaming up with other large shareholders to advance their respective parochial interests to the detriment of shareholders at large.

Given these questions, a sufficient case for legal intervention has not been made. Our conclusion partly results from the uncertainties: about whether short-termism is a real

[177] See Brownstein and Norwitz (2006: 1), stating that '[i]n larger transactions [the success of hedge funds in blocking a deal] will often require that the activists' position be supported by more traditional institutional investors and ISS'.

[178] See Section 5.2.1 (describing the tactics of corporate governance activism); see also Plitch (2005: 4), noting that hedge funds 'typically acquire a stake of less than 10%'. Even when several hedge funds become active in a specific portfolio company, they generally do not control it. See, e.g., Armitstead (2005a), describing the ownership of the institutions that eventually blocked the purchase of the LSE by DB.

[179] See Rosenstein (2006: 17), characterizing hedge fund activism as 'campaigns between [hedge funds and managers] for the supprt of the company's true owners, its shareholders'.

[180] See Wachtell, Lipton, Rosen, & Katz (2006), noting success by some firms in persuading large institutional shareholders to support their boards.

[181] Hovanesian and Byrnes (2006: 2) note that there is 'scope for the warring parties to find a mutually beneficial resolution'.

problem, about the nature of the problem, about how much it affects hedge fund activism, and about how hedge fund activism relates to potential managerial short-termism. This conclusion also partly results from our observations that, at present, hedge funds influence, but do not control, corporate policy, that they depend on the support of other shareholders, and that they have shied away from greenmail and other similar unsavoury tactics.

But our conclusion also rests, to a large extent, on our view, which we have developed elsewhere, that companies (and the market more generally) will adopt what we have called 'adaptive devices' to deal with the potential negative effects of hedge fund short-termism (Kahan and Rock 2002: 872). To see the shape of some of these devices, one need look no further than the 'Hedge Fund Attack Response Checklist' mailed by Martin Lipton (2006b) to the clients of his firm. In this widely circulated memo, Lipton recommends that companies prepare in advance for hedge fund activism by: periodically updating the board of directors, reviewing dividend policy, improving financial public relations, maintaining consistency in the company's strategic message, proactively addressing reasons for any shortfall in peer company benchmarks, maintaining regular and close contact with major institutional investors, and reviewing basic strategy with the board.[182] These are terrific ideas, not just to deal with activist hedge funds, but in general. If companies follow Lipton's advice, hedge funds will already have made significant positive contributions to the management of US companies. Moreover, if hedge funds can succeed, despite companies taking these measures, we think that chances are reasonably high that they have identified a real problem.

One adaptive device missing from Lipton's list, but one that merits particular attention, is private equity. Vast sums are now available to take companies private, sums largely provided by the same (allegedly myopic) institutional investors who hold the shares of public companies and invest in hedge funds. As we have noted in section 5.5.1, private equity can be an escape mechanism for companies that suffer from excessive short-term pressures in the public market.[183] If it is indeed hedge funds that contribute substantially to such short-term pressures, it is no small irony that hedge funds and traditional private equity funds are now converging.[184] In an increasing number of high-profile deals, hedge funds have taken on 'the type of long-term control investing previously the domain of private equity funds' (Campbell and Spiegel 2005). If hedge funds are part of the problem because their activism exacerbates short-termism, they may also be part of the solution as they develop private equity expertise. This, by itself, shows how multifaceted hedge funds are as an investment vehicle, and should caution against adopting hasty regulation.

[182] See also Brownstein and Norwitz (2006), recommending that companies 'be proactive in explaining the reasons for, and the benefits of, a transaction', ensure that the board's position is accurately understood, and engage in early and open communication with significant stockholders; Mayer Brown Rowe & Maw (2006) recommend that companies review their dividend policies, proactively address reasons for any shortfall in performance, and maintain close contact with major investors.

[183] See Mayer Brown Rowe & Maw (2006: 1), noting that private equity funds are looking to take private targets of shareholder activism.

[184] See Singer (2006c), noting that an increasing number of private equity firms are opening hedge funds; cf. *Securities Regulation and Law Report* (2006) references a report by CFA Centre that accuses corporate managers of a 'short-term obsession'.

5.6 Conclusion

We are observing an evolutionary process in real time. Hedge funds—highly incentivized, mostly unconflicted, and largely unencumbered by regulatory constraints—have become the prime corporate governance and control activists. They pursue activism as a profit-making strategy and make investments in order to become activist, rather than as an afterthought to a failed portfolio investment. Thus, they blur the line between risk arbitrage and governance and control battles. The emergence of hedge funds and the role they play prove that there is money to be made from being an active shareholder.

One of the most intriguing developments we are starting to observe is the division of labour between hedge funds and more traditional institutional investors. Because hedge funds are typically relatively undiversified, they show little interest in agitating for systemic changes, such as an anti-poison pill or staggered board campaigns. On the other hand, hedge funds engage in firm-specific agitation to a degree unheard of among traditional institutional investors, with traditional institutions sometimes tagging along. As a representative of one traditional institution said, in connection with the battle to stop DB's attempt to acquire the LSE, 'The hedge funds have done a marvellous job. No matter how we feel about companies, traditional managers simply cannot move as fast to achieve our aims. We were right behind [the hedge funds], but we couldn't have done it without them' (Armitstead 2005c).

But there is also a potential downside to activism. The interests of hedge funds sometimes diverge from those of their fellow shareholders, and activism creates stress fractures for the regulatory system. The most serious accusation levelled against activist funds, however, is that activism is designed to achieve a short-term payoff at the expense of long-term profitability. It is here that the challenge lies for boards, traditional institutional investors, and the market as a whole. If the proposals made by hedge funds are sometimes valuable and sometimes misguided, how good are we at figuring out which is which? While we do not pretend to know the answer to this question, we believe that market forces and adaptive devices adopted by companies individually in response to activism are better designed to help separate good ideas from bad ones than is additional regulation.

Hedge funds are here to stay. They are prominent in control transactions and elsewhere. Their influence is being felt, but their future is uncertain. As hedge funds grow, will they retain their separate identity (and get stronger) or will (some of them) morph into high-fee mutual funds? Will activist investment opportunities for hedge funds dry up as more money chases these opportunities, or will more hedge funds become activist in response to the profits to be earned? If smart hedge fund investors keep hedge fund managers honest, will an expansion of the investor base reduce the monitoring of hedge fund managers and make them worse agents for their investors?

Finally, one can predict a backlash, although the exact form it takes will depend on the nature of the scandal that leads to the regulatory intervention. We are already beginning to see a regulatory reaction at the SEC, with a (failed) attempt to adopt rules requiring the regulation of hedge fund advisers,[185] and preparation for such regulation in Europe. When

[185] See, generally, *The Economist* (2006b: 68), reporting the federal appeals court decision striking down 'an attempt by the Securities and Exchange Commission (SEC) to monitor the industry'.

the inevitable crisis occurs, there will be pressure to regulate further. At this point, the most important admonition—obvious in a period of calm but less so after an explosion—is to regulate cautiously and carefully.

REFERENCES

Abarbanell, J. and Bernard, V. (2000). Is the US Stock Market Myopic?, *Journal of Accounting Research* 38, 221–42.

Adamy, J. (2006a). Heinz Investors to Seek Board Seats, *Wall Street Journal* (25 Apr.), at A17.

Adamy, J. (2006b). Investor Peltz Urges Heinz to Shed More Lines, Pare Payments, *Wall Street Journal* (24 May), at C4.

Adamy, J. and Reilly, D. (2006). Heinz Says Investor's Company Plans to Nominate 5 Directors, *Wall Street Journal* (4 Mar.), at B2.

ADP Investor Communication Services (2007). *ADP Investor Communication Services Story*.

Agence France Presse (2005). Deutsche Boerse Bows to the Might of Investment Funds, *Agence France Presse* (7 Mar.), available at Factiva, Doc. No. AFPR000020050307e13700096q, available at <http://www.afp.com>.

Agrawal, A. and Jaffe, J. F. (2003). The Post-Merger Performance Puzzle, in C. Cooper and A. Gregory (eds.), *Advances in Mergers and Acquisitions* (Bingley, UK, Emerald Group Publishing Limited), 7–41.

Anderson, J. (2005). Ex-Chairman of S.E.C. Set to Start Hedge Fund, *New York Times* (13 Sept.), at C1.

Angwin, J. (2005). Icahn Confirms Time Warner Challenge, *Wall Street Journal* (16 Aug.), at A3.

Armitstead, L. (2005a). Shareholders Revolt in Bid to Topple Seifert, *Sunday Times* (London), (20 Feb.), at Bus. 1.

Armitstead, L. (2005b). Rothschild to Lead Battle for Börse Rebels, *Sunday Times* (London), (27 Feb.), at Bus. 1.

Armitstead, L. (2005c). Saved by the Growing Power of Hedge Funds, *Sunday Times* (London), (13 Mar.), at Bus. 14.

Associated Press (2006a). Investment Company Wants Representation on Massey Board, *Associated Press* (17 Mar.), available at Factiva, Doc. No. APRS000020060317e23h002ea.

Associated Press (2006b). Cardinal Value Sues InfoUSA CEO, HighBeam Res., Associated Press (24 Feb.), available at <http://www.highbeam.com/doc/1P1-118948139.html>.

Baird, D. G. and Rasmussen, R. K. (2003). Reply, Chapter 11 at Twilight, *Stanford Law Review* 56, 673–700.

Ballardini, F., Malipiero, A., Oriani, R., Sobrero, M., and Zammit, A. (2005). Do Stock Markets Value Innovation? A Meta-Analysis, Working Paper, available at <http://ssrn.com/abstract=717562>.

Bange, M. M. and De Bondt, W. F. M. (1998). R&D Budgets and Corporate Earnings Targets, *Journal of Corporate Finance* 4, 153–84.

Barbaro, M. (2005). Circuit City Rejects Hedge Fund's Cash Bid, *Washington Post* (8 Mar.), at E5.

Barnard, J. W. (1991). Institutional Investors and the New Corporate Governance, *North Carolina Law Review* 69, 1135–87.

Baue, W. (2005). Biting the Hand That Feeds: Mutual Fund Ties to Corporate Clients Can Affect Proxy Voting, *SocialFunds.com* (10 Mar.), available at <http://www.socialfunds.com/news/article.cgi/article1659.html>.

Bebchuk, L. A. and Stole, L. A. (1993). Do Short-Term Objectives Lead to Under- or Over-Investment in Long-Term Projects?, *Journal of Finance* 48, 719–30.

Berman, D. K. and Latour, A. (2005). Major MCI Holder Starts Proxy Fight to Thwart Verizon, *Wall Street Journal* (15 June), at B3.

Berman, D. K. and Singer, J. (2005). VNU's Largest Shareholders Deride Plan to Buy IMS Health, *Wall Street Journal* (1-2 Oct.), at B3.

Berner, R. (2004). Turning Kmart into a Cash Cow, *Business Week* (12 July), at 81.

Black, B. S. (1990). Shareholder Passivity Reexamined, *Michigan Law Review* 89, 520–608.

Black, B. S. (1992). Agents Watching Agents: The Promise of Institutional Investor Voice, *UCLA Law Review* 39, 811–93.

Bogle, J. C. (2005). Op-Ed., Individual Stockholder, R.I.P., *Wall Street Journal* (3 Oct.), at A16.

Boston Business Journal (2002). Colt Names Fidelity's Akin to Replace CEO Manning, *Boston Business Journal* (online edition), (24 July).

Brownstein, A. R. and Norwitz, T. S. (2006). Client Memorandum, Wachtell, Lipton, Rosen & Katz, Shareholder Activism in the M&A Context (15 May) (on file with authors).

Bushee, B. J. (1998). The Influence of Institutional Investors on Myopic R&D Investment Behavior, *Accounting Review* 73, 305–33.

Business Journal of Milwaukee (2005). ShopKo agrees to $29 a Share Offer from Sun Capital, *Business Journal of Milwaukee* (online edition), (19 Oct.), available at <http://www.bizjournals.com/milwaukee/stories/2005/10/17/daily17.html>.

Business Wire (2006). Value Act Capital Refuses to Meet with Chiron Directors Except to Discuss Ways to Increase Shareholder Value Beyond $45, *Business Wire* (15 Mar.), available at Factiva, Doc. No. BWR0000020060315e23f0041v.

Byron, C. (2003). Short-Sell Scramble; Investors are Betting that Kmart Won't Bounce Back, *New York Post* (19 May), at 37.

CalPERS (2001). Press Release, CalPERS Taps Blackstone Alternative Asset Management as Advisor to $1 Billion Hedge Fund Program (15 May).

CalPERS (2005a). Structure and Responsibilities (12 May), available at <http://www.calpers.ca.gov>.

CalPERS (2005b). External Manager Fees Report, in Annual Investment Report, Year Ended (30 June).

CalPERS (2006). Press Release, CalPERS Focus List Targets Six Underperforming Companies (19 Apr.).

Campbell, W. W. and Spiegel, J. A. (2005). Hybrid Vehicles, *TheDeal.com* (17 June), available at <http://www.thedeal.com/servlet/ContentServer?pagename=TheDeal/TDDArticle/TDStandardArticle&bn=NULL&c=TDDArticle&cid=1118184148575>.

Carleton, W. T., Nelson, J. M., and Weisbach, M. S (1998). The Influence of Institutions on Corporate Governance through Private Negotiations: Evidence from TIAA-CREF, *Journal of Finance* 53, 1335–62.

Carlton, J. and Weil, J. (2004). Ouster Isn't Expected to Alter CalPERS Policy, *Wall Street Journal* (2 Dec.), at C3.

Carrns, A. (2005). Putnam Cites Price in Plan to Vote against WaMu's Providian Deal, *Wall Street Journal* (2 Aug.), at C3.

Cauchi, M. (2006). Jana Partners Sets Energy Bid in Unusual Move for Hedge Fund, *Wall Street Journal* (13 June), at A18.

Cha, S-J. (2006). Icahn Group Demands Access to KT&G Books, *Wall Street Journal* (15 Mar.), at C4.

Chappell, J. (2006). Hedge Fund Investors Question Lexar–Micron Deal, Electronic News (7 Apr.), available at <http://www.edn.com/electronics-news/4319016/Hedge-Fund-Investors-Question-Lexar-Micron-Deal>.

Cheng, M., Subramanyam, K. R., and Zhang, Y. (2005). Earnings Guidance and Managerial Myopia (Nov.), available at <http://ssrn.com/abstract=851545>.

Chicago Tribune (2006). Exelon Merger Criticized, *Chicago Tribune* (13 May), at § 2, 1.

Choi, S. J. and Thompson, R. B. (2006). Securities Litigation and Its Lawyers: Changes during the First Era after the PSLRA, *Columbia Law Review* 106, 1489–533.

Choi, S. and Kahan, M. (2007). The Market Penalty for Mutual Fund Scandals, *Boston University Law Review* 87, 1021–57.

Clark, N. and Ahuja, V. (2006). Hedge Fund Forces Euronext Merger Vote, *Financial News Online US* (5 Apr.).

Cohen, N. (2004). LSE War Looms as Euronext Confirms Intent, *Financial Times* (London), (21 Dec.), at 22.

Cohen, N. (2005). Deutsche Börse 'Empire Building', *Financial Times* (London), (17 Jan.), at 19.

Cohen, N. and Jenkins, P. (2005). Deutsche Börse Withdraws LSE Offer, *Financial Times* (London), (7 Mar.), at 1.

Council of Institutional Investors (2009). About the Council, available at <http://www.cii.org/about_us>.

Crain's Detroit Business (2003). Week in Review: Kmart out of Bankruptcy, *Crain's Detroit Business* (12 May), at 34.

Dale, A. (2004). New York Fund Sues Merck, Citing Vioxx, Stock Drop, *Wall Street Journal* (1 Dec.), at B8.

Dallas Business Journal (2005). Jana Partners Sues SourceCorp, *Dallas Business Journal* (online edition), (6 July), available at <http://www.bizjournals.com/dallas/stories/2005/07/04/daily20.html>.

Davis, G. F. and Kim, E. H. (2007). Business Ties and Proxy Voting by Mutual Funds, *Journal of Financial Economics* 85, 552–70.

De Ramos, R. R. (2006). Concerns over Hedge Funds Rise as Market Volatility Rises Globally, *Wall Street Journal* (15 June), at C5.

Del Guercio, D. and Hawkins, J. (1999). The Motivation and Impact of Pension Fund Activism, *Journal of Financial Economics* 52, 293–340.

Der Hovanesian, M. and Byrnes, N. (2006). Attack of the Hungry Hedge Funds, *BusinessWeek* (online), (20 Feb.), available at <http://www.businessweek.com/stories/2006-02-19/attack-of-the-hungry-hedge-funds>.

DB AG (2005). Press Release, Changes to the Boards of Deutsche Börse AG (9 May).

Dobbs, R. and Koller, T. (2006). Inside a Hedge Fund: An Interview with the Managing Partner of Maverick Capital, *McKinsey on Finance* (Spring), available at <http://www.trendfollowing.com/whitepaper/ainslie.pdf>.

Donovan, K. (2005). Legal Reform Turns a Steward Into an Activist, *New York Times* (16 Apr.), at C1.

Drummond, B. (2006). Corporate Voting Charade, *Bloomberg Markets* (Apr.), at 96.

The Economist (2004). Merger at the Mall, *The Economist* (17 Nov.),

The Economist (2006a). Battling for Corporate America, *The Economist* (11 Mar.), at 69.

The Economist (2006b). Hedge Funds and the SEC: Still Free, *The Economist* (1 July), at 68.

Eisinger, J. (2005a). Hedge-Fund Man at McDonald's, *Wall Street Journal* (28 Sept.), at C1.

Eisinger, J. (2005b). Pay-for-Performance Bedevils Mutual Funds, *Wall Street Journal* (13 Apr.), at C1.

Eisinger, J. (2006). Memo to Activists: Mind CEO Pay, *Wall Street Journal* (11 Jan.), at C1.

Esterl, M. and Sender, H. (2005). Highbridge Fund Sent Default Note to Retailer Saks, *Wall Street Journal* (20 June), at C5.

Federal Reserve System (2006a). Flow of Funds Accounts of the United States, 1995–2005, available at <http://www.federalreserve.gov/RELEASES/z1/Current/annuals/a1995-2005.pdf>.

Federal Reserve System (2006b). Flow of Funds Accounts of the United States, Third Quarter 2006, available at <http://www.federalreserve.gov/releases/z1/20061207/z1.pdf>.

Fields, T. (2006). ICC-LLC, Emcom File for Chapter 11, *Virgin Islands Daily News* (online edition), (2 Aug.), available at <http://www.highbeam.com/doc/1P2-27435778.html>.

Financial Services Authority (2005). Hedge Funds: A Discussion of Risk and Regulatory Engagement (Financial Services Authority Discussion Paper 05/4), available at <http://www.fsa.gov.uk/pubs/discussion/dp05_04.pdf>.

Fisch, J. E. (1994). Relationship Investing: Will It Happen? Will It Work?, *Ohio State Law Journal* 55, 1009.

Forbes (2005). Icahn Wins as Mylan, King Deal Dies; Stewart Leaves 'Big House' for House Arrest, *Forbes.com* (4 Mar.), available at <http://www.forbes.com/2005/03/04/cx_gl_0304faceweek_print.html>.

Forman, M. (2005). FSA Bloodhounds Pursue Hedge Funds, *Security Industry News* (16 May), at 11.

Fortson, D. (2005). Deutsche Bvrse [sic] Drops LSE Hunt, TheDeal.com (7 Mar.), available at <http://www.thedeal.com/servlet/ContentServer?pagename=TheDeal/DArticle/TDStandardArticle&bn=NULL&c=TDDArticle&cid=1107993123143>.

Franklin Templeton Investments (2006). *A Guide to Investment Style.*

GAMCO Investors, Inc. (2004). Press Release, Gabelli Clients Realize a More than 40% Premium in Settlement of Carter-Wallace Appraisal Litigation (1 Nov.), available at <http://www.gabelli.com/Gab_pdf/PRs/GBL_1Nov2004.pdf>.

Gillan, S. L. and Starks, L. T. (2000). Corporate Governance Proposals and Shareholder Activism: The Role of Institutional Investors, *Journal of Financial Economics* 57, 275.

Gillan, S. L. and Starks, L. T. (2003). Corporate Governance, Corporate Ownership, and the Role of Institutional Investors: A Global Perspective, *Journal of Applied Finance* (Fall/Winter) 4.

Gilson, R. J. and Kraakman, R. (1991). Reinventing the Outside Director: An Agenda for Institutional Investors, *Stanford Law Review* 43, 863.

Grant, P. and Buckman, R. (2006). Fatter Pay Lures University Endowment Chiefs, *Wall Street Journal* (27 June), at C1.

Gray, S. (2005). Big Shareholder of McDonald's Urges Asset IPO, *Wall Street Journal* (9 Nov.), at A6.

Haarmeyer, D. (2006). E-mail from David Haarmeyer to Marcel Kahan, George T. Lowy Professor of Law, New York University School of Law (4 Apr.) (on file with authors).

Hallinan, J. T. and Berman, D. K. (2005). Knight Ridder Goes up for Sale, but a Bidding War is Unlikely, *Wall Street Journal* (15 Nov.), at A3.

Hamilton, D. P. (2006a). Shareholder Insurrection Infects Novartis's $5.1 Billion Chiron Bid, *Wall Street Journal* (3 Apr.), at C3.

Hamilton, D. P. (2006b). Novartis Raises Chiron Bid, Virtually Sealing Deal, *Wall Street Journal* (4 Apr.), at A2.

Hansard, S. (2004). MONY Delays Vote as Dissidents' Effort Gains Steam, *InvestmentNews* (23 Feb.), available at <http://www.investmentnews.com/article/20040223/SUB/402230718/mony-delays-vote-as-dissidents-efffort-gains-steam>.

Hays, C. L. (2004). Kmart Takeover of Sears Is Set; $11 Billion Deal, *New York Times* (18 Nov.), at A1.

Hedge Fund Street (2005). Hedge Funds Push for Merger of Deutsche Boerse & Euronext (23 Nov.).

Hennessee Group LLC (2005). Hedge Fund Industry Growth (Jan.), available at <http://www.magnum.com/hedgefunds/articles/2005/050101.pdf>.

Hollinger International (2005). Press Release, Hollinger International Inc. Announces Settlement by Certain of Its Current and Former Independent Directors of Claims Asserted in Derivative Action Filed by Cardinal Value Equity Partners, L.P. (3 May) (on file with authors).

Hu, H. R. C. and Black, B. (2006).The New Vote Buying: Empty Voting and Hidden (Morphable) Ownership, *Southern California Law Review* 79, 811–908.

Innisfree M&A Inc. (2006). *Presentation to Skadden, Arps, Slate, Meagher & Flom LLP.*

Investment Company Institute (2005). *Investment Company Fact Book* (45th edn.), available at <http://www.ici.org/pdf/2005_factbook.pdf>.

Ippolito, R. A. (1992). Consumer Reaction to Measures of Poor Quality: Evidence from the Mutual Fund Industry, *Journal of Law and Economics* 35, 45–70.

J. P. Morgan (2006). *Global Mergers and Acquisitions Review* (on file with authors)

Jenkins, P. and Cohen, N. (2004). Deutsche Börse Courts LSE for European Exchange Union, *Financial Times* (London), (14 Dec.), at 23.

Johnson, M. S. and Rao, R. P. (1997). The Impact of Antitakeover Amendments on Corporate Financial Performance, *Financial Review* 32, 659.

Kahan, M. and Rock, E. B. (2002). How I Learned To Stop Worrying and Love the Pill: Adaptive Responses to Takeover Law, *University of Chicago Law Review* 69, 871.

Kahan, M. and Rock, E. (2008). The Hanging Chads of Corporate Voting, *Georgetown Law Journal* 96, 1227–81.

Kapner, S. (2003a). Board Move Lifts Nautica 21 Percent, *New York Post* (12 June), at 41.

Kapner, S. (2003b). Nautica Rises 11% on News of Suitor, *New York Post* (21 June), at 20.

Karnitschnig, M. (2006). Time Warner, Icahn Reach Accord, *Wall Street Journal* (18–19 Feb.), at A3.

Karpoff, J. M., Malatesta, P. H., and Walkling, R. A. (1996). Corporate Governance and Shareholder Initiatives: Empirical Evidence, *Journal of Financial Economics* 42, 365–95.

Kasler, D. (2005). GenCorp Reaches Truce with Firm that Made Hostile Bid, *Sacramento Bee* (17 Feb.), at D1.

Kenney, J. B., Knox, L., Taub, S., Blake, R., Bickford, M., Kramer, L., and Watson, P. (2003). The Hedge Fund 100, *Institutional Investor's (Alpha Supplement)* 37(6), 40.

Kihlstrom, R. E. and Wachter, M. L. (2005). Why Defer to Managers? A Strong-Form Efficiency Model, University of Pennsylvania Institute for Law & Economic Research Paper 05-19, available at <http://ssrn.com/abstract=803564>.

Kirk, J. (2004). Hollinger Board Never Said No, Suit Alleges, *Chicago Tribune* (3 Jan.), at 1.

Kollewe, J. (2005). Fidelity Joins Börse Shareholder Revolt, *Independent* (London), (25 Feb.), at 37.

Koza, P. (2005). Kerr Pursues Revamp, *TheDeal.com* (8 Aug.).

Laise, E. (2006). Mutual Funds Delve into Private Equity, *Wall Street Journal* (2 Aug.), at D1.

Latham & Watkins (2005). *Hedge Fund Activist M&A Investing, Presentation to the 2006 Proxy Season Symposium.* (on file with authors).

Lazaroff, L. (2005). Hedge Fund Activist Turns Up Heat, *Chicago Tribune* (27 Nov.), at § 5, 7.

Levey, R. H. (2005). ValueAct Redoubles Acxiom Takeover Effort, Direct (online edition), (4 Oct.), available at <http://chiefmarketer.com/news/valueact-redoubles-acxiom-takeover-effort>.

Levitz, J. (2006). Do Mutual Funds Back CEO Pay?, *Wall Street Journal* (28 Mar.), at C1.

Lipton, M. (2005). Client Memorandum from Martin Lipton *et al.*, Wachtell, Lipton, Rosen & Katz, Be Prepared for Attacks by Hedge Funds (21 Dec.) (on file with authors).

Lipton, M. (2006a). Client Memorandum from Martin Lipton, Wachtell, Lipton, Rosen & Katz, Key Issues for Directors (6 Dec.) (on file with authors).

Lipton, M. (2006b). Client Memorandum from Martin Lipton, Wachtell, Lipton, Rosen & Katz, Attacks by Activist Hedge Funds (7 Mar.) (on file with authors).

Loftus, P. (2005a). Beverly Enterprises Agrees to Bid by Fillmore Despite Better Offer, *Wall Street Journal* (22 Nov.), at C4.

Loftus, P. (2005b). Beverly Enterprises to be Acquired by Investor Group for $1.63 Billion, *Wall Street Journal* (18 Aug.), at A5.

Lundstrum, L. L. and Holden, C. W. (2005). Costly Trading, Managerial Myopia, and Long-Term Investment (16 Sept.), available at <http://ssrn.com/abstract=809507>.

McCracken, J. (2006). Delphi Ripped for Bankruptcy Case, *Wall Street Journal* (17 Mar.), at A10.

McGee, S. (2006). US Shareholder Friendly Rankings, *Institutional Investor* (14 Apr.), available at <http://www.institutionalinvestor.com/Popups/PrintArticle.aspx?ArticleID=1025799>.

McTague, R. (2006). Two-Year Lock-Up for Hedge Funds Seen as Promoting Activist Strategies, *BNA Securities Law Daily* (29 Mar.).

McWilliams, G. (2005). Circuit City Rejects Takeover Bid, Won't Consider Any Other Offers, *Wall Street Journal* (8 Mar.), at A8.

Majumdar, S. K. and Nagarajan, A. (1994). The Long-Term Orientation of Institutional Investors: An Empirical Investigation (Oct.), available at <http://ssrn.com/abstract=6052>.

Majumdar, S. K. and Nagarajan, A. (1997). The Impact of Changing Stock Ownership Patterns in the United States: Theoretical Implications and Some Evidence, *Revue D'Économie Industrielle* 82, 39.

Marcial, G. G. (2005). GenCorp's Earthly Assets, *Business Week* (24 Jan.), at 100.

Martin, S. and Partnoy, F. (2005). Encumbered Shares, *University of Illinois Law Review* 775–814.

Masonite International Corporation (2005). Press Release, Masonite Shareholders Approve Proposed Acquisition by KKR (31 Mar.).

Mayer Brown Rowe & Maw (2006). Hedge Fund and Institutional Shareholder Activism, SEC Update (21 Apr.), available at <http://www.mayerbrown.com/publications/>.

Meulbroek, L. K., Mitchell, M. L., Mulherin, J. H., Netter, J. M., and Poulsen, A. B. (1990). Shark Repellents and Managerial Myopia: An Empirical Test, *Journal of Political Economy* 98, 1108–17.

Moreira, P. (2005). Four Funds Bid for Beverly, *TheDeal.com* (27 Jan.).

Morgenson, G. (2006). Investors vs. Pfizer: Guess Who Has the Guns?, *New York Times* (23 Apr.), § 3, at 1.

Murphy, K. J. and Van Nuys, K. (1994). Governance, Behavior, and Performance of State and Corporate Pension, Harvard University Working Paper.

Murray, A. (2005a). Hedge Funds Are New Sheriffs of Boardroom, *Wall Street Journal* (14 Dec.), at A2.

Murray, A. (2005b). Backlash against CEOs Could Go Too Far, *Wall Street Journal* (15 June), at A2.

Murray, A. (2006). At AIG, a First Glance at 'Good Governance', *Wall Street Journal* (17 May), at A2.

Myerson, A. R. (1993). The New Activism at Fidelity, *New York Times* (8 Aug.), at § 3, 15.

New York State and Local Retirement System (2007). About Us, available at <http://www.osc.state.ny.us/retire/about_us/>.

New York State Office of the State Comptroller (2007). Pension Investment and Cash Management, available at <http://www.osc.state.ny.us/pension/index.htm>.

New York Stock Exchange (2004). Information Memorandum from the New York Stock Exchange (5 Nov.) (on file with authors).

New York Sun (2005). Editorial, Hevesi by the Letter, *New York Sun* (12 Apr.), at 10.

Norris, F. (2004). Holders of MONY Approve $1.5 Billion Sale to AXA, *New York Times* (19 May), at C4.

Norris, G. (2006). Sears Holdings Says It Will Own 100% of Sears Canada Despite Hedge Fund, *CBC.ca* (7 Apr.).

Novartis International AG (2005). Press Release, Novartis Int'l AG, Novartis Announces Agreement to Acquire Remaining Stake in Chiron (31 Oct.).

Orol, R. (2004). GenCorp Rejects $700M Offer, *TheDeal.com* (15 Nov.).

Orol, R. (2005). Fortress GenCorp, *TheDeal.com* (24 Mar.).

Osterberg, W. P. and Thomson, J. B. (1999). Federal Reserve Bank of Cleveland, The Truth about Hedge Funds, available at <http://www.clevelandfed.org/Research/commentary/1999/0501.pdf>.

Padgett, T. (2004). A Proxy Fight Is Brewing for Steven Madden, *Newsday* (NY), (30 Dec.), at A45.

Parsons, J. E., Apfel, R. C., Schwert, G. W., and Stewart, G. S. (2001). Short Sales, Damages and Class Certification in 10b-5 Actions, Simon School of Business Working Paper No. FR 01-19, available at <http://ssrn.com/abstract=285768>.

Plitch, P. (2005). Lawyers See No Poison Pill to Feed Hedge Fund 'Wolf Packs', *Corporate Governance* (Dow Jones), (21 Dec.), at 4.

Politi, J. (2006). Wendy's Agrees Deal with Trian, *Financial Times* (London), (3 Mar.), at 15.

PR Newswire (2003a). Institutional Shareholder Services Recommends Election of Barington Companies Group Nominees, *PR Newswire* (2 July), available at Factiva, Doc. No. PRN0000020030702dz72000k6.

PR Newswire (2003b). Barington Companies Group Reacts Favorably to Proposed Acquisition of Nautica Enterprises by VF Corporation—Withdraws Proxy Solicitation, *PR Newswire* (7 July), available at Factiva, Doc. No. PRN0000020030707dz77001 1s.

PR Newswire (2004a). Barington Capital Group Sends Letter to Outside Directors of Steven Madden Ltd. Calls for the Board to Replace CEO Jamieson Karson and to Make Other Changes to Enhance Shareholder Value, *PR Newswire* (13 Dec.), available at Factiva, Doc. No. PRN0000020041213e0cd00d4a.

PR Newswire (2004b). Steel Partners Asks Board of BKF Capital Group to Redeem Poison Pill, Use Excess Cash to Up Dividend and Buy Back Stock, Add Representatives of Institutional Stockholders to Board Steel Partners Says Board Needs to Improve Operating Profits and Reduce Expenses, *PR Newswire* (16 Dec.), available at Factiva, Doc. No. PRN0000020041216e0cg00ahw.

PR Newswire (2004c). Steel Partners Offers to Acquire the Outstanding Shares of GenCorp Inc. in Letter to Board, *PR Newswire* (11 Nov.), available at Factiva, Doc. No. PRN0000020041111e0bb003ff.

PR Newswire (2004d). Highfields Capital Establishes Web Site for MONY Shareholders Exercising Appraisal Rights, *PR Newswire* (31 Mar.), available at Factiva, Doc. No. PRN0000020040331e03v00bkp.

PR Newswire (2005a). JANA Partners LLC Announces SITEL Board Nominees and Intention to Replace Additional Board Members, *PR Newswire* (23 Nov.), available at Factiva, Doc. No. PRN0000020051123e1bn0050s.

PR Newswire (2005b). James Kelly Joins Third Point as President and Chief Operating Officer, *PR Newswire* (7 Sept.), available at Factiva, Doc. No. PRN0000020050907e197003s1.

PR Newswire (2005c). Third Point Demands that Star Gas CEO, Irik Sevin, Resigns and Returns Keys to Company Car, *PR Newswire* (14 Feb.), available at Factiva, Doc. No. PRN0000020050214e12e00dqm.

PR Newswire (2005d). Steven Madden, Ltd. and the Barington Capital Group Reach Agreement—Company Will Allocate $25 Million to Share Repurchase and/or Dividends in 2005, *PR Newswire* (2 Feb.), available at Factiva, Doc. No. PRN0000020050202e12200bvv.

PR Newswire (2005e). Steel Partners Serves Notice to BKF Capital Group, Inc. that it Intends to Nominate Three Individuals for Election to BKF's Board at BKF's 2005 Annual Meeting of Stockholders, *PR Newswire* (14 Feb.), available at Factiva, Doc. No. PRN0000020050214e12e00e79.

PR Newswire (2005f). Judge Rules in Favor of Kaman's Proposed Recapitalization; Enjoins Closing until December 1, *PR Newswire* (31 Oct.), available at Factiva, Doc. No. PRN0000020051031e1av004v9.

PR Newswire (2005g). Kaman and Mason Agree to End Litigation Concerning Recapitalization, *PR Newswire* (3 Nov.), available at Factiva, Doc. No. PRN0000020051103e1b3004pv.

PR Newswire (2005h). Eminence Capital Presents Letter to Masonite Board of Directors, *PR Newswire* (27 Jan.), available at Factiva, Doc. No. PRN0000020050127e11r002jq.

PR Newswire (2005i). Institutional Investor Magazine's Alpha Names Farallon Capital Mgmt the World's Largest Hedge Fund Firm in their Annual Hedge Fund 100, *PR Newswire* (27 May), available at Factiva, Doc. No. PRN0000020050527e15r002ml.

Pugh, W. N. and Jahera, J. S. (1990). Antitakeover Legislation and Shareholder Wealth, *Journal of Financial Research* 13, 221–31.

Pulliam, S. and Peers, M. (2005). Once a Lone Wolf, Carl Icahn Goes Hedge-Fund Route, *Wall Street Journal* (12 Aug.), at A1.

Reece, D. (2005). Börse Could Bid Pounds 1.7 bn for LSE, Says Deutsche, *Independent* (London), (27 Jan.), at 48.

Reuters (2006). InfoUSA Tells Shareholders to Ignore Hedge Fund, Reuters (4 May), available at Factiva, Doc. No. LBA0000020060504e254001vp.

Richardson, K. (2006). New Way to Play Distressed Firms: Acquire the Stock, *Wall Street Journal* (1 May), at C1.

Ringshaw, G. (2005). Rothschilds Unite in Attack on Seifert, *Sunday Telegraph* (London), (27 Feb.), at City 1.

Rock, E. B. (1991). The Logic and (Uncertain) Significance of Institutional Shareholder Activism, *Georgetown Law Journal* 79, 445–506.

Roe, M. J. (1991a). A Political Theory of American Corporate Finance, *Columbia Law Review* 91, 10–67.

Roe, M. J. (1991b). Political Elements in the Creation of a Mutual Fund Industry, *University of Pennsylvania Law Review* 139, 1469–1511.

Roiter, E. D. (2004). Letter from Eric D. Roiter, Senior Vice President and General Counsel, Fidelity Management and Research Company, to Jonathan G. Katz, Secretary, US Securities and Exchange Commission (18 Mar.), available at <http://www.sec.gov/rules/proposed/s70304/fidelity031804.htm>.

Romano, R. (1993). Public Pension Fund Activism in Corporate Governance Reconsidered, *Columbia Law Review* 93, 795–853.

Romano, R. (2003). Does Confidential Voting Matter?, *Journal of Legal Studies* 32, 465.

Rosenberg, Y. (2004). The Man behind the Deal, *CNNMoney* (17 Nov.).
Rosenstein, B. (2006). Activism is Good for All Shareholders, *Financial Times* (10 Mar.), at 17.
Rushe, D. and O'Donnell, J. (2004). Lord Black 'Looted $300m', *Sunday Times* (London), (4 Jan.), § 3, at 1.
San Francisco Business Times (2002). Pharmacopia and EOS Call off Merger, *San Francisco Business Times* (online edition), (18 Jan.), available at <http://www.bizjournals.com/sanfrancisco/stories/2002/01/14/daily52.html>.
Santini, L. (2006). Icahn Group Lands KT&G Board Seat, *Wall Street Journal* (17 Mar.), at C4.
Shleifer, A. and Vishny, R. W. (1990). Equilibrium Short Horizons of Investors and Firms, *American Economic Review* 80, 148–53.
Schroeder, M. (2005). Council of Institutional Investors is Set to Focus on Morgan Stanley, *Wall Street Journal* (13 Apr.), at A15.
Schwab, S. J. and Thomas, R. S. (1998). Realigning Corporate Governance: Shareholder Activism by Labor Unions, *Michigan Law Review* 96, 1018–94.
SEC (Securities and Exchange Commission) (2003a), Implications of the Growth of Hedge Funds: Staff Report to the United States Securities and Exchange Commission, available at <http://www.sec.gov/news/studies/hedgefunds0903.pdf> .
SEC (Securities and Exchange Commission) (2003b), SEC Brings Settled Enforcement Action Against Deutsche Bank Investment Advisory Unit in Connection with its Voting of Client Proxies for Merger Transaction; Imposes $750,000 Penalty (19 Aug.).
Securities Regulation & Law Report (2006). Groups' Report Recommends Moving Away from Short-Term Corporate Thinking, *Securities Regulation & Law Report* 38, 1315.
Sender, H. (2005). Hedge Funds: The New Corporate Activist, *Wall Street Journal* (13 May), at C1.
Sender, H. (2006). Citadel Pulls Up its Withdrawal Bridge, as Hedge Funds Aim to Block the Exits, *Wall Street Journal* (13 Jan.), at C1.
Shearman & Sterling LLP (2004). Client Publication, Hedge Fund Compliance with ERISA 25% Limit (Sept.), available at <http://www.shearman.com/files/Publication/0527637a-386d-4edd-b83b-b4babc648872/Presentation/PublicationAttachment/a8795ffd-7839-4515-8787-d058684f9ae2/eceb_092004.pdf>.
Shleifer, A. and Vishny, R. W. (1990). Equilibrium Short Horizons of Investors and Firms, *American Economic Review* 80, 148–53.
Siklos, R. (2005). Rebuked, Even Sued, a Board Remains in Place, *New York Times* (26 Sept.), at C1.
Singer, J. (2005). With Rising Clout, Hedge Funds Start to Sway Mergers, *Wall Street Journal* (25 Jan.), at A1.
Singer, J. (2006a). Knight Presses VNU Overhaul Plan, *Wall Street Journal* (7 Apr.), at C4.
Singer, J. (2006b). Ivy Leave: Yale Parts Ways with Hedge Fund, *Wall Street Journal* (29 Mar.), at C1.
Singer, J. (2006c). Carlyle Will Join Financiers' Moves into Hedge Funds, *Wall Street Journal* (1 Aug.), at C1.
Smith, M. P. (1996). Shareholder Activism by Institutional Investors: Evidence from CalPERS, *Journal of Finance* 51, 227–52.
Smith, P. (2006). Texas Pacific Raises Record $14bn for New Fund, *FT.com* (2 Apr.).
Smith, R. and Sender, H. (2005). Executives' Ouster Shows Growing Hedge-Fund Clout, *Wall Street Journal* (1 Dec.), at A1.
Sorkin, A. R. and Siklos, R. (2005). Icahn Tries to Form a Team to Take On Time Warner, *New York Times* (10 Aug.), at C1.
Standard & Poors (2006a). S&P 500 (31 Dec.).

Standard & Poors (2006b). S&P MidCap 400 (31 Dec.).

Stein, C. (2004). Harvard's $12 Billion Man, *Boston Globe* (17 Oct.), at D1.

Stein, C. (2005). Harvard's High-Paid Star Investor Leaving, *Boston Globe* (12 Jan.), at A1.

Stein, J. C. (1988). Takeover Threats and Managerial Myopia, *Journal of Political Economy* 96, 61–80.

Stein, J. C. (1989). Efficient Capital Markets, Inefficient Firms: A Model of Myopic Corporate Behavior, *Quarterly Journal of Economics* 104, 655–69.

Steyer, R. (2004). New Player Joins Mylan–King Fray, TheStreet.com (Nov. 29), available at <http://www.thestreet.com/stocks/robertsteyer/10196467.html>.

Steyer, R. (2006). Hedge Funds Take Aim at Nabi, *TheStreet.com* (26 Apr.), available at <http://www.thestreet.com/story/10281755/1/hedge-funds-take-aim-at-nabi.html>.

Sundaramoorthy, G. (2003). Nautica Accepts $587m VF Bid, *Financial Times* (London), (8 July), at 26.

Swett, C. (2006). Shareholder Revolt Rocks GenCorp, *Sacramento Bee* (1 Apr.), at A1.

Taub, S. (2004). The Bucks Stop Here, *Institutional Investor* (Aug.), at 47.

Taub, S. (2005). Alpha's Top 25, *Institutional Investor's Alpha* (May–June), at 15.

Taylor, E. (2006). German Official Wants to Put Hedge Funds on G-8's Agenda, *Wall Street Journal* (1 Sept.), at C4.

Taylor, E. and MacDonald, A. (2006). Hedge Funds Face Europe's Clippers, *Wall Street Journal* (23 May), at C1.

The Barclay Group (2007). Hedge Fund Industry—Assets under Management, available at <http://www.barclaygrp.com>.

TheDeal.com (2005). News in Brief: Americas: Moody's Warns Kerr-McGee, *TheDeal.com* (4 Mar.), available at <http://www.thedeal.com>.

Titan International, Inc. (2006). Press Release, Titan International, Inc. Announces Termination of Proposed Buyout (12 Apr.).

Trincal, E. (2006). Mirant Up on Activist Agitation, *TheStreet.com* (21 June), available at <http://www.thestreet.com/author/1100616/Emma20Trincal/all.html>.

Ubben, J. and Haarmeyer, D. (2006). With Activism Comes Accountability, *Institutional Investor's Alpha* (July/Aug.).

Vanguard (2007). Vanguard 500 Index Fund Investor Shares.

Vaughan-Adams, L. (2003). Hollinger Investor Seeks Access to Internal Records, *Independent* (London), (9 July), at 19.

Wachtell, Lipton, Rosen & Katz (2006). Client Memorandum, *Financial Institutions Developments* (22 Feb.).

Wachter, M. L. (2003). Takeover Defense When Financial Markets Are (Only) Relatively Efficient, *University of Pennsylvania Law Review* 151, 787–824.

Waggoner, J. (2005). Many More Stock Funds Lower Management Fees after Scandal in 2003, *USA Today* (5 Dec.), at 5B.

Wahal, S. and McConnell, J. J. (2000). Do Institutional Investors Exacerbate Managerial Myopia?, *Journal of Corporate Finance* 6, 307–29.

Wall Street Journal (2004). Editorial, Calpers and Cronyism, *Wall Street Journal* (18 Oct.), at A18.

Wall Street Journal (2005a). Beverly Enterprises Receives Higher Bid, *Wall Street Journal* (22 Aug.), at C5.

Wall Street Journal (2005b). Editorial, Pension Fund Blackmail, *Wall Street Journal* (31 Mar.), at A10.

Wall Street Journal (2005c). Editorial, Comptrolling Legal Authority, *Wall Street Journal* (1 Apr.), at A10.

Wall Street Journal (2007). Private Equity's Successes Stir Up a Backlash That May Be Misdirected, *Wall Street Journal* (31 Jan.), at A9.

Waller, M. (2005). Fund Says Opposition to Börse's LSE Bid Is Mounting, *Times* (London), (18 Jan.), at Bus. 43.

Weil, J. and Lublin, J. (2004). Gadfly Activism at Calpers Leads to Possible Ouster of President, *Wall Street Journal* (1 Dec.), at A1.

Weiss, E. J. and White, L. J. (2004). File Early, Then Free Ride: How Delaware Law (Mis)Shapes Shareholder Class Actions, *Vanderbilt Law Review* 57, 1797–882.

Woidtke, T. (2002). Agents Watching Agents?: Evidence from Pension Fund Ownership and Firm Value, *Journal of Financial Economics* 63, 99–131.

Wray, R. (2005). Börse Rebel Threatens To Derail LSE Bid, *Guardian* (London), (17 Jan.), at 21.

Yerak, B. (2004). Exec Lifts Kmart's Stock into Blue Yonder, *Chicago Tribune* (11 July), at C1.

Yuan, L. and Rhoads, C. (2007). Icahn Bid Adds to Woes Dogging Motorola's CEO, *Wall Street Journal* (31 Jan.), at A1.

Zuckerman, G. and McDonald, I. (2005). Hedge Funds Avoid SEC Registration Rule, *Wall Street Journal* (10 Nov.), at C1.

CHAPTER 6

THE RISE AND FALL (?) OF SHAREHOLDER ACTIVISM BY HEDGE FUNDS

JOHN ARMOUR AND BRIAN CHEFFINS

6.1 Introduction

THE forthright brand of shareholder activism associated with hedge funds became a major corporate governance phenomenon in the United States in the 2000s. Financial economists and law professors responded promptly to the challenge posed, as the surge in shareholder activism by hedge funds prompted a series of papers on the phenomenon. While academics responded expeditiously to the rise of hedge fund-driven shareholder activism and have provided valuable evidence on key aspects of the phenomenon (e.g., Bratton 2007: 1390–401; Brav et al., Chapter 8, this volume; Klein and Zur, Chapter 9, this volume), the relevant literature glosses over various important contextual questions. For instance, what distinguishes the particular form of activism hedge funds have engaged in from that undertaken by 'mainstream' institutional investors, such as pension funds or mutual funds? What motivates investors to step forward in the manner hedge funds have done? In other words, given that activism is costly, in terms of time, effort, and diversification forsaken, how is it that, at least for some investors, the perceived benefits outweigh the costs? Why did activism by hedge funds achieve prominence in the 2000s? And is hedge fund activism likely to remain an important part of the US corporate governance landscape going forward? This chapter introduces the heuristic of a 'market for corporate influence' to analyse these important background questions and to argue ultimately that while market turmoil arising from the recent financial crisis hampered the 'offensive' brand of shareholder activism that became prominent in the 2000s, this form of intervention will, in all likelihood, play an important part in US corporate governance going forward.[1]

[1] This chapter is an updated synthesis for a non-legal audience of 'The Rise and Fall (?) of Shareholder Activism by Hedge Funds', European Corporate Governance Institute—Law Working Paper No. 136/2009, a revised version of which will be published in the *Journal of Corporation Law* as 'The Past, Present and Future of Shareholder Activism by Hedge Funds'. In the *Journal of Corporation Law* article, interested readers can find more details and the extensive citations customary in legal scholarship. In this version, we provide only essential citations.

6.2 What is Shareholder Activism, Hedge Fund-Style?

Shareholder activism has been described as 'the exercise and enforcement of rights by minority shareholders with the objective of enhancing shareholder value over the long term' (Low 2004: 185–6). This formulation is a legitimate departure point but is too general in nature to distinguish hedge fund interventions from shareholder engagements carried out by 'traditional' institutional investors such as mutual funds and public pension funds. Kahan and Rock (Chapter 5, this volume) have drawn attention to the key differences in approach:

> Mutual fund and public pension fund activism, if it occurs, tends to be incidental and *ex post*: when fund management notes that portfolio companies are underperforming, or that their governance regime is deficient, they will sometimes be active. In contrast, hedge fund activism is strategic and *ex ante*: hedge fund managers first determine whether a company would benefit from activism, then take a position and become active.

Or, as Macey has put it (2008: 247), while '(m)utual funds and other savvy investors' generally will decline to invest in poorly performing companies, 'rather than seeing bad performance as something to avoid, hedge funds . . . see investment opportunities'.

Employing the adjectives 'defensive' and 'offensive' provides a convenient way to distinguish the sort of activism in which traditional institutional shareholders engage from the sort for which hedge funds have achieved notoriety. Defensive shareholder activism is *ex post* in orientation, as it occurs when an investor already holding a stake in a company becomes dissatisfied with corporate performance or corporate governance and reacts by lobbying for changes, whether 'behind the scenes' or with a public challenge to management (e.g., proposing the election of directors the dissidents support). To the extent pension funds and mutual funds engage in shareholder activism, it will be of this sort, as they work 'defensively' to protect pre-existing investments.

While, with 'defensive' activism, the insurgent shareholder will have held a stake in the company before stepping forward, this 'initial endowment' is not a feature of 'offensive' shareholder activism. What happens here is that an investor lacking a meaningful holding in a company builds up one 'offensively' on the presumption that changes will be made to correct failures to maximize shareholder returns. The investor, crucially, will intend *ex ante* to agitate for change if management does not take the initiative. As the quotes from Kahan and Rock and from Macey indicate, this is precisely the sort of activism for which hedge funds have gained notoriety.

6.3 Market for Influence verses Market for Control

It is also helpful at this stage to distinguish between attempts to use a sizeable minority stake in a public company as a platform to press for change and bids to obtain full voting control. The latter is a key element of the market for corporate control famously identified by Manne

(1965). The former—offensive shareholder activism—can be thought of as underpinning what can be termed a market for corporate *influence*.

Theoretically, a shareholder engaging in offensive shareholder activism can change gears and opt to launch a fully-fledged takeover bid. Likewise, a corporate 'raider' who puts target companies on the back foot by acquiring a sizeable stake, criticizing management, and intimating a bid for voting control may ensue may never follow through with an offer that has a realistic chance of success. Hence, seeking influence and seeking control may, in principle, constitute points on a continuum rather than being fully distinct corporate governance phenomena. However, analytically it is helpful to draw a distinction between investors who intend to agitate for change without acquiring a block of shares sufficiently large to secure legal or *de facto* voting control from those determined to execute what Gilson and Schwartz label a 'transfer by sale' (2001: 790), which involves buying up a majority of the shares from existing investors (e.g., by way of a successful tender offer).

Activist hedge funds generally have no interest in obtaining full-scale voting control of the companies they target (Brav et al., Chapter 8, this volume). Instead, they prefer not to tie up capital in the form of majority or sole ownership of companies and anticipate profiting as minority shareholders when shareholder returns improve, due, if necessary, to changes the management makes in response to investor pressure. Hedge fund activists typically begin their engagements by buying up a block of shares in a targeted company and then sounding out management with a telephone call or letter pressing the incumbent board to make changes designed to increase shareholder value. If a quiet approach fails to yield the desired results, an activist hedge fund can step up the pressure. A particularly forceful strategy is to threaten what Gilson and Schwartz term a 'transfer by vote' (2001: 790), this being the securing of managerial control by winning a proxy contest intended to determine who serves on the board.

6.4 Elements of the Market for Corporate Influence

For insurgents to step forward and engage in offensive shareholder activism, they must anticipate that the benefits they will derive will outweigh their costs. However, while activist shareholders must typically bear all the costs associated with intervention, due to the fact they will have only a minority stake in the companies they target they will receive only a fraction of the improvements in shareholder return their efforts generate. This is a potentially powerful deterrent to offensive shareholder activism. Put more formally, if we denote the expected costs of exercising influence to improve shareholder returns at a target company as c_i, the expected benefits for the firm's shareholders from exercise of influence as b_i, and the proportion of the target firm's shares held by the potential activist as α (where $0 < \alpha < 1$), then the exercise of influence will be privately rational for the potential activist only if the following inequality is satisfied:

$$c_i < \alpha b_i \tag{1}$$

The costs associated with exercising influence (c_i) include the search costs associated with finding potential target companies, transaction costs related to buying and selling shares (e.g., brokers' commissions and the bid-ask spread), and communication costs (e.g., expenses incurred contacting other shareholders and charges involved with making required filings with securities regulators). Moreover, because potential activists will frequently not be rich enough themselves to buy up a significant stake in a public company—at least one traded on a major stock market—offensive shareholder activism involves financing costs. Individuals inclined to engage in activism who lack the financial wherewithal to buy a significant stake in a public company can potentially proceed by raising capital from investors willing to back an investment fund with a suitable mandate. Activist hedge funds in effect rely on this approach.

The benefits of activism to a target company's shareholders as a whole (b_i) will comprise any increase in shareholder return that an activist's intervention generates. The percentage of shares owned will set an upper bound for the proportion of these benefits the activist shareholder will derive (i.e., $\alpha\ b_i$). However, due to the fact investors typically anticipate a shareholder activist's efforts once the activist's stake becomes public knowledge, and drive the share price upward, any gains generated after an activist's stake is divulged must, in effect, be shared with the market. Correspondingly, the proportion of the total benefits generated by improved shareholder returns which an activist will capture will typically be measured by reference to when the market first becomes aware of the activist's involvement (e.g., when a Schedule 13D filing is made under section 13(d) of the Securities Exchange Act of 1934 to disclose a holding of 5% or more of the shares of the publicly traded target). Put more formally, if we take λ (where $0 < \lambda < 1$) to be the maximum block of shares which can be purchased by 'stealth', inequality (1) can be modified to state the conditions for activism as follows:

$$c_i < (\text{argmin}\ \{\alpha, \lambda\})b_i \qquad (2)$$

A range of variables operating at the firm level can affect the costs and benefits associated with offensive shareholder activism in a particular case. However, for our purposes—seeking to explain changes over time and predict future trends—systemic factors are of greater interest. The market for corporate influence heuristic is instructive on this count, as matters can be characterized in terms of a 'supply side' (opportunities for the profitable exercise of influence) and 'demand side' (factors influencing the willingness of investors to pursue such opportunities).

On the supply side, instances where shareholder engagement can be anticipated to improve shareholder returns (i.e., $b_i > 0$) constitute a necessary pre-condition for offensive shareholder activism.[2] Companies falling into this category are likely to share two characteristics. First, the companies will be 'underperforming', at least from the perspective of the potential activist, in the sense that the activist anticipates that changes in financial policy or strategic direction will increase shareholder returns (i.e., $b_i > 0$). Second, change must feasible. Given that a shareholder activist is unlikely to be able to make credible proposals for change if a 'core investor' controls a sufficiently large block of votes to veto unwelcome shareholder resolutions, target companies will typically have diffuse share ownership. Moreover,

[2] An exception is where private benefits of control are available, but this should not be a common scenario with hedge funds.

corporate law will typically have to provide the activist with sufficient shareholder rights to capture management's attention. Legal rules that dictate the leverage a shareholder activist will have include those governing the scope shareholders have to determine the composition of the board, to exercise a veto over board initiatives and to counteract the advantages management has in securing shareholder support through the solicitation of proxies.

Even taking it for granted that there are companies where $b_i > 0$, offensive shareholder activism will not occur if the costs associated with intervention (c_i) exceed the benefits available to the potential activist, factoring in the activist's partial ownership stake (α). Correspondingly, to ascertain the extent to which conditions are propitious for offensive shareholder activism it is necessary to consider not only the opportunities for the profitable exercise of influence but also the factors that may affect investors' ability and willingness to exploit such opportunities. These factors shape the demand function in the market for corporate influence.

To illustrate, as compared with a few decades ago, a dramatic decline in search costs has helped to facilitate shareholder activism. Due to massive improvements in information technology, it is now much easier for a potential activist to find suitable targets than it would have been at the beginning or even the middle of the twentieth century (Armour and Cheffins 2011: 260–1). Likewise, technological advances have revolutionized share dealing and thereby driven down transaction costs associated with accumulating and unwinding substantial stakes in publicly traded companies. Moreover, communication costs have decreased dramatically (Armour and Cheffins 2011: 263–4). Before the advent of the Internet, shareholder activists had to mail letters to shareholders or pay for ads in publications such as the *Wall Street Journal* to make their points. Now activists can use e-mail, websites, and social media (e.g., Facebook and Twitter) to communicate instantly and cheaply with potential allies and supporters.

With financing costs, while those who anticipate generating superior risk-adjusted returns by engaging in shareholder activism can potentially accumulate the financial resources required to proceed if they manage an investment fund that has sufficient capital, laws governing collective investment vehicles can be an obstacle. Lawmakers, to protect otherwise potentially vulnerable retail investors, might impose requirements on collective investment vehicles that circumscribe the investment strategies and compensation practices of approved funds. Regulations of this sort can deter shareholder activism by discouraging approved collective investment vehicles from adopting investment strategies required to make 'offensive' interventions viable, such as eschewing diversification to take large stakes in a small number of companies. The Investment Company Act of 1940 does this, for instance, with mutual funds.

6.5 The Rise of Shareholder Activism by Hedge Funds

In the US offensive shareholder activism was a feature of the free-wheeling 1980s 'Deal Decade', but prominent practitioners of this corporate governance tactic typically operated through the medium of a publicly traded firm (e.g., Victor Posner with NVF Co. and

T. Boone Pickens with Mesa Petroleum Co.) rather than via a collective investment vehicle such as a hedge fund. Edward Lampert's ESL Investments, which generated headlines in the 2000s with investments in retailers Kmart and Sears, began operating in 1988, and Steel Partners II, another prominent hedge fund activist during the 2000s, was founded by Warren Lichtenstein in 1993. Nevertheless, both funds operated on a modest scale during the 1990s, and hedge fund managers showed little inclination to engage in shareholder activism despite hedge funds growing in prominence as an investment option. Headlines from the *New York Times* reflect these trends, proclaiming in 1995 'Hedge Funds Still Steaming Ahead' and asking in 1996 'Where, Oh Where, Have All the Corporate Raiders Gone?'. Over the next decade, and particularly in the 2000s, hedge funds moved to centre stage in the US as shareholder activists.

Business Week featured hedge funds Highfields Capital Management and Chapman Capital LLC in a 2002 article on 'value investors' minded to challenge existing management for the sake of value creation, saying 'Their style of investing is taking off like a Fourth of July bottle rocket (2002: 124).' By 2005, the *Wall Street Journal* was proclaiming 'Hedge Funds are New Sheriffs of the Boardroom' and *Business Week* was referring to the 'exploding number of activist hedge funds' and the 'onslaught from hedge funds (2005: 118).' A year-by-year breakdown of a dataset of 784 hedge fund activism campaigns Greenwood and Schor (2009: 365), compiled from Schedule 13D filings, reveals that activism events became progressively more common between 1994 and 2006 (Figure 6.1).

The surge in offensive shareholder activism by hedge funds can be accounted for by reference to various elements of the supply and demand side of the market for corporate influence. On the supply side a sizeable and sustained fall in share prices following the end of the dot. com stock market boom meant there was a sizeable cohort of companies trading at prices well below recent peaks. Correspondingly, there should have been numerous companies where $b_i > 0$. Revelations of high-profile scandals at companies such as Enron, Tyco, and WorldCom cast doubts on the quality of management in US public companies and therefore reinforced

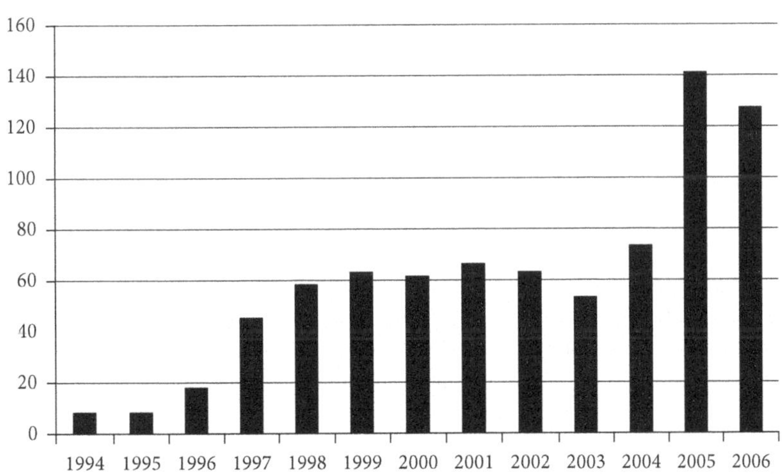

FIGURE 6.1 Hedge fund activism events, 1994–2006, identified by Schedule 13D filings

Source: Greenwood and Schor (2009).

the idea that shareholder value could be promoted more effectively. As the *New Yorker* observed, 'During the bull market, investors got lazy, leaving shareholder-rights advocacy to the gadflies and the geeks... The disasters at Enron and Tyco changed all that, and it has become fashionable again to question the judgment of the C.E.O...' (2003: 44).

Even though share prices rose smartly following the end of the bear market of the early 2000s, activist hedge funds still found numerous companies to pursue that were ostensibly underperforming. Most prominently, activist managers maintained public companies could readily unlock shareholder value by abandoning conservative financial policies. During the mid-2000s, corporate earnings grew smartly due to an expanding economy while executives, still shell-shocked by recessionary conditions, refrained from spending heavily on capital investment or increasing wages. Activist hedge funds argued that companies should return the rapidly accumulating cash on hand to shareholders by increasing dividend payouts, carrying out share buy-backs, or even putting the company up for sale.

Changes in ownership structure that affected the feasibility of change in publicly traded companies were an additional element of the supply side that helped to promote shareholder activism by hedge funds in the 2000s. The proportion of shares of US public companies held by domestic institutional investors (primarily pension funds and mutual funds) rose from 14% in 1965 to 45% in 1985 and again to 65% in 2002. This was accompanied by a change in mentality among institutional investors congenial to offensive shareholder activism. Whereas in the 1980s the *Wall Street Journal* suggested 'institutions are the worst constituency a dissident could have' (1986: 23), by the early 2000s key money managers had become quite receptive to activist overtures. *Institutional Investor* said of the change of heart 'A gruelling, two-year bear market is probably the biggest factor: What companies could get away with when most stocks were rising is no longer acceptable when they are plunging' (2003: 42).

Crucially, key institutional investors did not revert to old habits when share prices swung upwards in the mid-2000s. The *New York Times* spelled out the implications, saying 'the greatest shift in the influence that activist shareholders have gained is the role once-conservative institutional investors—big money managers like the mutual fund giant Fidelity—have begun to take' (2006: C1). This did not mean leading money managers were taking the initiative with underperforming companies; they still preferred to retain the option of cutting their losses by selling out and to avoid the adverse publicity that confronting public company executives could generate. Still, to a greater extent than had been the case previously, key institutional investors were prepared to offer backing to activists prepared to do the dirty work, thus lending valuable credibility to campaigns to challenge managers of target companies.

Switching to the demand side, regulatory changes the federal Securities and Exchange Commission (SEC) introduced in 1992 reduced communication costs considerably for hedge funds targeting US public companies. The SEC's 1992 reforms were intended to facilitate dialogue among shareholders by cutting back on instances where there had to be compliance with requirements imposed on parties seeking change through the proxy process, most notably an obligation to file relevant documentation for review by the SEC. For instance, a safe harbour was created for all oral communications and for discussions among fewer than ten investors, an exemption activists could rely upon to lobby privately in favour of their initiatives. Advertisements, speeches, and statements in the media were also exempted.

According to one study of hedge fund activism, the SEC's 1992 reforms were 'revolutionary', because '[r]estrained only by the general proxy antifraud rule, a hedge fund activist [was] now free to disseminate to the world near telephone books full of essentially unverifiable presentation slides' (Briggs 2007: 687). Correspondingly, when hedge funds were otherwise prepared to move to the forefront, as shareholder activists they could operate in a congenial legal environment as they targeted underperforming companies. Massive expansion of the hedge fund sector would soon help to put hedge funds in precisely this position.

As of 1990, there were approximately 300 hedge funds operating in the US with around $40 billion under management, compared with mutual fund portfolios totalling $1.6 trillion. By 2006 there were approximately 10,000 hedge funds managing assets of nearly $1.8 trillion (ISFL Research 2010). This sizeable pool of capital was ample to fund offensive shareholder activism on a reasonably wide scale, even if only a small subset of hedge funds actually engaged in activism (Brav et al., Chapter 8, this volume).

Correspondingly, while financing costs constitute a potential deterrent to offensive shareholder activism, the explosive growth of the hedge fund industry left hedge funds well placed to invigorate the market for corporate influence.

One factor that contributed to the dramatic expansion of the hedge fund sector was the deregulation of requirements concerning investor eligibility to invest in hedge funds. Hedge funds have historically operated largely outside US federal securities regulation by taking advantage of exemptions granted for 'private investment companies', with a key exemption being that investment funds that do not issue securities to more than 100 investors do not have to comply with the strictures of the Investment Company Act of 1940. Hedge fund sponsors found the 100 investor exemption difficult to work with, so in 1996, Congress, reasoning that highly sophisticated investors did not need the protection of the 1940 Act, exempted from the Act funds issuing securities only to 'qualified purchasers', defined to include individuals owning more than $5 million worth of investments or managing assets of greater than $25 million.

A key result of the 1996 change was that it helped to facilitate institutional investor participation in the hedge fund sector. As of 1993 institutional money made up only 5% of hedge fund assets. This figure ballooned to roughly 25% in 2001, with the 1996 rule changes meaning dozens of institutional investors could invest in a single hedge fund without giving rise to concerns the Investment Company Act of 1940 would come into operation.

Market trends worked in tandem with deregulation to foster institutional investment in the hedge fund sector. The slump in stock prices occurring at the beginning of the 2000s created pressure for those managing assets on behalf of pension funds, endowments, and charitable foundations to look beyond the stock market for satisfactory investment returns. The search led them to hedge funds, which were regularly outperforming mutual funds. A further attraction was that hedge funds could theoretically reduce overall portfolio risk by creating a level of diversification well above that which investors could get by relying on traditional asset classes. Accordingly, pension fund and endowment investment in hedge funds increased from $15 billion in 2000 to $100 billion in 2004, and the proportion of assets allocated to hedge funds by US pension funds, endowments, and foundations rose steadily from 1.6% in 2004 to 2.6% in 2007.

Market trends fortified activism by hedge funds in other ways in the mid-2000s. During this period debt was plentiful and borrowing was very 'cheap' by historical standards due to liberal lending by banks, and a booming market for credit derivatives hedge funds dominated. Correspondingly, hedge fund managers contemplating engaging in offensive shareholder activism were well positioned to boost available financial firepower by borrowing.

The credit 'bubble' that built up in the US in the mid-2000s also provided hedge funds with an ideal environment in which to lobby for change. Hedge fund activists commonly agitated for a target company to make a big cash payout, dispose of underperforming divisions, or put itself up for sale. With borrowing being cheap, it was relatively painless for target companies to respond by taking on more debt to distribute cash to shareholders and to find buyers for subsidiary operations. Even putting an entire company up for sale could be fairly straightforward, particularly with private equity firms using leverage to carry out buyouts during this era at an unprecedented rate.

6.6 Offensive Shareholder Activism and the 2008 Financial Crisis

While hedge fund-driven offensive shareholder activism had become an important feature of US corporate governance by the mid-2000s, the onset of the 2008 financial crisis cast doubt on the future of this form of shareholder intervention. On the supply side, a large drop in share prices occurring between the autumn of 2008 and the summer of 2009 meant there should have been numerous companies where there was a potentially sizeable discrepancy between the stock price and the intrinsic value of the underlying business. On the other hand, activist investors had fewer tools with which to work. While the cheap debt of the mid-2000s provided activists with market conditions well suited for lobbying target companies to distribute cash to shareholders or put the business up for sale, in the credit crunch associated with the financial crisis persuading boards to leverage their companies' balance sheets with debt or to thrust their companies into the arms of prospective bidders became considerably more difficult. Activism campaigns therefore had to focus on improving target company strategy and operations rather than financially oriented initiatives, a potentially unappealing prospect for many hedge fund activists.

Matters were not much more encouraging on the demand side. While the seemingly inexorable growth the hedge fund sector experienced up to the mid-2000s had ensured the deep pockets constraint impinged less on shareholder activism than had been the case in previous decades, the financial crisis threw a spanner into the works. Assets under management by hedge funds globally fell from $1.93 trillion in June 2008 to $1.3 trillion by mid-2009. Moreover, after the credit 'bubble' burst, hedge fund managers with an appetite to engage in shareholder activism that relied on borrowing as an element of their investment strategy found themselves unable to use debt to side-step financial constraints as readily as they could when hedge fund activism rose to full prominence in the mid-2000s. This helps to explain why, in 2009, companies targeted by hedge funds were considerably smaller than those targeted in 2008 (Bratton 2007).

For those in the hedge fund industry who specialized in shareholder activism their problems were compounded by the fact activist funds were among those worst affected during the market turmoil. The activist sector suffered disproportionately because activist funds tend to hedge less than other hedge funds, meaning they were fully exposed to falling stock prices, and because the small- and mid-cap companies in which they typically invest suffered outsized share price declines as compared with large-cap companies. Major activist hedge funds correspondingly experienced, even by the dismal standards of the hedge fund industry, heavy losses and sizeable redemption demands.

The reversal of fortunes was sufficient to disillusion various leading players in the activism field. Tim Barakett, founder of Atticus Capital and one of the fathers of hedge fund-oriented shareholder activism, closed the two big Atticus funds under his management in 2009 after assets invested plunged from $20 billion at the beginning of 2008 to $5 billion. TCI left the activism arena not long after its founder Christopher Hohn—widely regarded as one of the top activist investors in the world—complained in 2008 that activism was 'hard' and 'unpredictable and expensive'. Philip Falcone, chief of Harbinger Capital Partners, an activist hedge fund that controlled $26 billion in assets as of mid-2008 and only $8 billion as 2010 drew to a close, indicated in 2010 he intended to rely on a publicly traded shell company rather than a hedge fund to hold stakes in companies over the long term so as to protect himself from the whims of flighty investors.

6.7 Hedge Funds and Offensive Shareholder Activism—Future Trends

Prediction is a risky game. Those prescient enough to predict the 2008 financial crisis was in the cards were treated as Cassandras beforehand. Regardless, it seems a safe bet that offensive shareholder activism will remain an element of US corporate governance going forward. On the 'supply side' of the market for corporate influence, there should always be underperforming companies with a sufficiently dispersed ownership structure to mean $b_i > 0$. On the demand side, given how search costs, transaction costs, and communication costs have dropped dramatically over time, there no doubt will be instances going forward where $c_i < \alpha b_i$.

While the offensive form of shareholder activism in which hedge funds engage will not go away, it remains an open question whether the free-wheeling interventions that characterized the mid-2000s will become the norm again. One might anticipate that legal reforms introduced in response to the financial crisis would bolster offensive shareholder activism. As we have seen, legal rules that provide shareholders with leverage *vis-à-vis* a company's management team can potentially encourage adoption of influence-based activism strategies. However, while the 2010 Dodd-Frank Wall Street Reform and Consumer Protection Act (Pub. L. 111-203) bolstered shareholder rights in various ways, this legislation is unlikely to be a catalyst for hedge fund activism.

With respect to shareholder rights, the most important change the Dodd-Frank Act made was to authorize the SEC to revamp proxy access regulation; the SEC followed up by implementing rules giving shareholders meeting specified ownership thresholds the right to rely on a company's proxy materials to propose candidates for election to the board. Hedge funds engaging in offensive shareholder activism will quite often own a sufficiently large percentage of shares (3% or more) to qualify. On the other hand, given that a typical hedge fund activist only owns shares in a target company for about a year (Brav et al., Chapter 8, this volume), only the most patient hedge funds will be a stockholder in a company for a sufficiently long period—the SEC rules prescribe three years—to take advantage of proxy access. Given that the Dodd-Frank Act has likely exhausted the appetite in the US for further corporate governance-oriented statutory reform for the time being, legal changes are unlikely to foster offensive shareholder activism over the short to medium term.

Even if the corporate governance reforms in the Dodd-Frank Act have strengthened the hand of activist hedge funds to some degree, a different aspect of the legislation could discourage hedge fund activism. Due to the fact that the benefits a hedge fund will derive from engaging in shareholder activism will be defined primarily by the maximum block of shares which can be purchased by 'stealth', regulatory requirements for disclosure of block purchases do much to define the incentives to engage in hedge fund activism. While section 13(d) of the Securities Exchange Act of 1934 mandates the filing of an ownership report when an investor acquires 5% or more of a publicly traded company's shares, a hedge fund activist can build up a larger stake before disclosing by taking advantage of a ten-day reporting window section 13(d) provides for, and likely can rely on derivatives known as total equity return swaps to acquire an economic interest exceeding the 5% level without having to divulge its position under federal securities law. The Dodd-Frank Act specifically authorizes the SEC to close both loopholes and, as a result of a project to modernize disclosure procedures the SEC is currently undertaking, it could follow this up soon. Given that acquisition of a sizeable block of shares by 'stealth' is a key aspect of the business model of hedge fund activists, a major tightening of reporting requirements could reduce returns to activist hedge funds and thereby discourage future engagement with publicly traded companies.

While legal change could impinge upon future offensive shareholder activism, hedge fund interventions will likely remain a hallmark of US corporate governance in the aftermath of the 2008 financial crisis. Though the market turmoil was traumatic for the hedge fund industry, the sector rebounded quite smartly. Among institutional investors more than half were planning to increase target allocations to hedge funds as of the end of 2010, as compared with just 15% at the end of 2009 (SEI Knowledge Partnership and Greenwich Associates 2011). By the middle of 2011, industry-wide assets under management had reached a record \$2.04 trillion, with investment inflows exceeding \$62 billion during the first half of the year, the strongest half-year total since 2007 (Hedge Fund Research 2011).

As for activist hedge funds specifically, the technical innovations that drove down search, transaction, and communication costs remain as salient as they did before the financial crisis. A partial thawing of credit markets and an uptick in merger and acquisition activity that accompanied the end of the financial crisis has prompted speculation that the corporate governance environment is ripe for hedge funds to return fully to the shareholder activism fray (*The Economist* 2010). In addition, the accumulation of cash and short-term investments by publicly traded companies (\$1.1 trillion in the case of non-financial S&P 500 companies as of mid-2011) provides a tempting target for activist funds prepared to argue the funds should be returned to shareholders rather than earning paltry returns in the corporate treasury. Finally, the available evidence indicates that the financial crisis did not sideswipe hedge fund activism to the extent initially supposed.

The number of hedge fund interventions did drop between mid-2009 and early 2010 but, generally, hedge fund shareholder activism continued to occur with considerable regularity during and immediately following the financial crisis (Figure 6.2). Likewise, throughout the financial crisis hedge funds played a prominent role in shareholder activism incidents that escalated to a fully-fledged proxy battle. In 2007 hedge funds, despite their growing prominence as shareholder activists, initiated only a minority of proxy contests. By 2008, hedge funds were responsible for a majority of such incidents, a pattern that continued to prevail in 2009 and 2010 (Table 6.1).

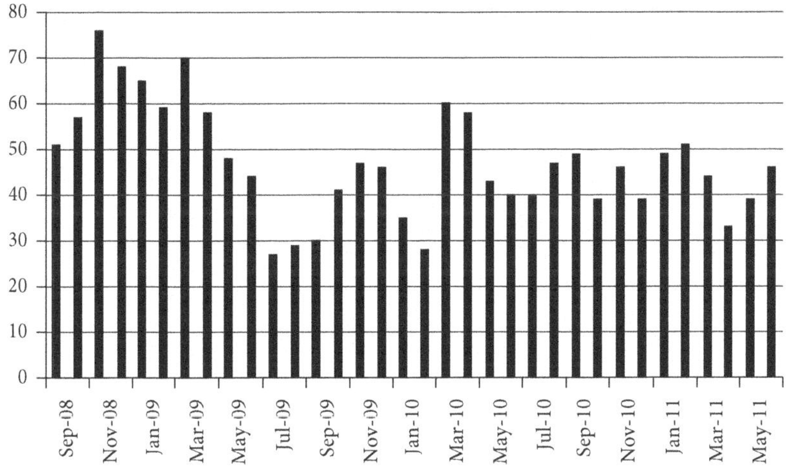

FIGURE 6.2 Companies targeted by activist shareholders, September 2008–June 2011

Source: Compiled from Hedge Funds Solutions' Catalyst Investment Research, Weekly Activist Investing Research.

Table 6.1 Proxy contests initiated by hedge funds, 2007–10

Year	Total number of proxy contests	Proxy contests initiated by hedge funds	Number of hedge funds involved
2007	46	20	16
2008	56	31	18
2009	57	31	27
2010	35	23	13

Source: Compiled from Georgeson (2007, 2008, 2009, 2010).

The dismal performance of activist hedge funds in the wake of the financial crisis generated doubts among investors that the benefits associated with shareholder activism outweighed the costs and demonstrated that even if returns were satisfactory over time they could be disturbingly volatile in the short to medium term (*Financial Times* 2010). Nevertheless, investor returns held up sufficiently well to mean investor confidence in shareholder activism should not have been fundamentally undermined. Activist hedge funds outperformed the stock market in both 2008 and 2009 (Figure 6.3), with the healthy returns generated in 2009 being partially attributable to the fact companies with low market capitalizations did especially well amid broadly stronger markets (*Wall Street Journal* 2009: 19). Ultimately, then, hedge fund activism coped tolerably well in the midst of the greatest stock market turmoil since the Great Depression, which implies a promising future under more conventional conditions. Indeed, the *New York Times* maintained in August 2011 that '[a]ctivist investors [were] escalating their fight for change' (2011: B1), a claim borne out by press reports of hedge fund activism campaigns affecting Fortune 500 constituents Kraft Foods Inc. and McGraw-Hill Companies.

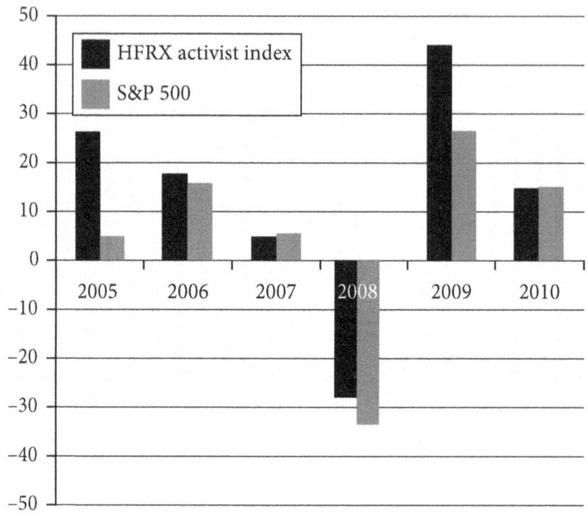

FIGURE 6.3 Annual performance of activist hedge funds/S&P 500, 2005–10
Sources: Hedge Fund Research; Standard and Poor's.

6.8 Conclusion

The hedge fund-driven shareholder activism which gained prominence in the 2000s generated a prompt academic response. This chapter has put the relevant literature into context by spelling out what is distinctive about the particular form of activism hedge funds have engaged in, by identifying the variables that affect the operation of the market for corporate influence hedge funds have come to dominate, and by explaining what prompted the hedge fund-oriented surge in offensive shareholder activism in the 2000s. The chapter has also analysed how matters are likely to develop going forward. As we have seen, the 2008 financial crisis was a blow to offensive shareholder activism in the US. However, hedge funds did not retreat fully from the activism arena even when the financial crisis was its height, and various features on the demand and supply sides of the market for corporate influence that contributed to the emergence of hedge funds as key players in corporate governance will continue to operate going forward. Correspondingly, hedge fund activism should remain a prominent feature of US corporate governance for the foreseeable future.

References

Armour, J. H. and Cheffins, B. R. (2011). Origins of 'Offensive' Shareholder Activism in the United States, in J. G. S. Koppell (ed.), *Origins of Shareholder Advocacy* (New York, Palgrave Macmillan) 253–76.

Bratton, W. W. (2007). Hedge Funds and Governance Targets, *Georgetown Law Journal* 95, 1375–433.

Briggs, T. W. (2007). Corporate Governance and the New Hedge Fund Activism, *Journal of Corporate Law* 32, 681–723.

Business Week (2002). The Ultimate Value Investors, *Business Week* (10 June), at 124.

Business Week (2005). Take Your Best Shot, Punk, *Business Week* (7 Nov.), at 118.

Financial Times (2010). Suspect Strategies, *Financial Times* (23 June), at 9.

Georgeson Shareholders (2007). *Corporate Governance: Annual Meeting Season Wrap Up*, available at <http://www.georgeson.com/us/Pages/default.aspx>.

Georgeson Shareholders (2008). *Corporate Governance: Annual Meeting Season Wrap Up*, available at <http://www.georgeson.com/us/Pages/default.aspx>.

Georgeson Shareholders (2009). *Corporate Governance: Annual Meeting Season Wrap Up*, available at <http://www.georgeson.com/us/Pages/default.aspx>.

Georgeson Shareholders (2010). *Corporate Governance: Annual Meeting Season Wrap Up*, available at <http://www.georgeson.com/us/Pages/default.aspx>.

Gilson, R. J. and Schwartz, A. (2001). Sales and Elections as Methods for Transferring Control, *Theoretical Inquiries in Law* 2, 783–814.

Greenwood, R. and Schor, M. (2009). Investor Activism and Takeovers, *Journal of Financial Economics* 92, 362–75.

Hedge Fund Research (2011). Hedge Funds Extends Record Asset Level with 2Q Inflows, Press Release (19 July), available at <https://www.hedgefundresearch.com/pdf/pr_20110719.pdf>.

IFSL Research (2010). *Hedge Funds 2010* (Apr.) (New York, ISFL).

Institutional Investor (2002). The Little Shareholder that Could, *Institutional Investor* (Apr.), at 33.

Low, C. K. (2004). A Road Map for Corporate Governance in East Asia, *Northwestern Journal of International Business Law* 25, 165–204.

Macey, J. (2008). *Corporate Governance: Promises Kept, Promises Broken* (Princeton, NJ, Princeton University Press).

Manne, H. G. (1965). Mergers and the Market for Corporate Control, *Journal of Political Economy* 73, 110–20.

New York Times (1995). Hedge Funds Still Steaming Ahead, *New York Times* (25 Jan.), at D1.

New York Times (1996). Where, Oh Where, Have All the Corporate Raiders Gone?, *New York Times* (30 June), at F10.

New York Times (2006). To Battle, Armed With Shares, *New York Times* (4 Jan.), at C1.

New York Times (2011). Investors Seek Change at Publisher, *New York Times* (2 Aug.), at B1.

New Yorker (2003). To the Barricades, *New Yorker* (9 June), at 44.

SEI Knowledge Partnership and Greenwich Associates (2011). *Institutional Hedge Fund Investing Comes of Age: A New Perspective on the Road Ahead* (Dubai, SEI).

Wall Street Journal (1986). Firms Face Gripes From New Gadflies, *Wall Street Journal* (19 May), at 23.

Wall Street Journal (2005). Hedge Funds are New Sheriffs of the Boardroom, *Wall Street Journal* (14 Dec.), at A2.

Wall Street Journal (Europe) (2009). Activist Hedge Funds Passively Rebound, *Wall Street Journal* (Europe), (29 Sept.), at 19.

B.

Ownership Stakes, Operating Results, and Financial Returns

CHAPTER 7

RETURNS TO SHAREHOLDER ACTIVISM: EVIDENCE FROM A CLINICAL STUDY OF THE HERMES UK FOCUS FUND

MARCO BECHT, JULIAN FRANKS, COLIN MAYER, AND STEFANO ROSSI

7.1 Introduction

SHAREHOLDER activism by institutional investors is controversial.[1] To some, activism holds the promise of resolving monitoring and incentive problems in widely held companies, thereby improving corporate performance (Black 1992). To others, shareholder activists lack the skills and the experience to second-guess the target firm's management (Lipton and Rosenblum 1991), with fund managers replacing corporate managers in the pursuit of private benefits and their own agenda (Romano 1993). As a result, activism is often described as disruptive, opportunistic, misguided, and, at best, as ineffective. For example, Black (1998: 465) declares:

> [a] small number of American institutional investors, mostly public pension plans, spend a trivial amount of money on overt activism efforts.... Institutions achieve the effects on firm performance that one might expect from this level of effort—namely, not much.

[1] Shareholder activism refers to a range of actions taken by shareholders to influence corporate management and boards. Actions range from threatening the sale of shares ('exit'), letter writing, and meetings with management and board, to asking questions at shareholder meetings, and the use of corporate voting rights. Under a common definition, an activist shareholder is a shareholder 'who tries to change the *status quo* through "voice", without a change in control of the firm' (Gillan and Starks 1998: 11).

Current empirical evidence, summarized in surveys by Black (1998), Gillan and Starks (1998), and Karpoff (2001), finds that US institutional investors on the whole engage in little activism and, even when they do, there is little or no link between activism and performance. The much-celebrated 'CalPERS effect' associated with the fund's own activism programme (Anson, White, and Ho 2004; Nesbitt 1994; Smith 1996) is reported to be very small or non-existent (English, Smythe, and McNeil 2004). The same holds for activism by other public pension funds (Del Guercio and Hawkins 1999), the Council of Institutional Investors (Opler and Sokobin 1995), and the United Shareholders Association (Strickland, Wiles, and Zenner 1996). Karpoff (2001: 1) concludes:

> [m]ost evidence indicates that shareholder activism [in the United States] can prompt small changes in target firms' governance structures, but has negligible impact on share values and earnings.

These repeated failures to link activism to performance are often blamed on three elements: inadequate monitoring due to free-riding, legal and institutional obstacles to activism, and incentive problems amongst institutional investors in the United States. With respect to the first, fund managers often hold relatively small stakes in listed companies, particularly in the case of diversified index funds. Pension fund trustees and fund managers will not spend sufficient resources on shareholder activism, because there is no market mechanism for internalizing the benefits of activism; the benefits accrue to all shareholders, including those who did not bear the cost of activism.

Second, the major US institutional investors are said to face conflicts of interest (Black 1998; Romano 2001). For example, the fund managers of mutual funds hold stakes in companies where they also have a pension fund mandate, which might be at risk if they were to engage. Also, company pension funds are not run independently of corporate management, while union pension funds are sometimes instruments of the struggle between the organized labour and management. Public pension funds are under the influence of politicians, who are elected by constituencies whose interests are not identical to those of the pension fund beneficiaries.

Third, the US legal and regulatory system limits the anti-director rights of shareholders. Black (1990: 531) notes that 'legal obstacles are especially great for shareholder efforts to nominate and elect directors, even for a minority of board seats'. As a result, activism in the United States is often confined to public 'naming and shaming' via focus lists and filing non-binding shareholder proposals in proxy statements. Highly regulated private intervention is mild and usually takes the form of letter writing (Carleton, Nelson, and Weisbach 1998). In contrast, Black and Coffee (1994) argue that the United Kingdom is an ideal institutional setting for shareholder activism, because it provides more legal tools than the United States to institutional investors (see also Bebchuk 2005). We describe the institutional differences between the United Kingdom and the United States with respect to shareholder activism in more detail in Section 7.2.1.

This chapter studies an experiment initiated by the trustees of one UK pension fund, the Hermes UK Focus Fund (HUKFF), to overcome free-riding problems in an institutional environment that is particularly friendly to activist shareholders. The investment correspondent of the *Financial Times* has characterized the HUKFF as a 'mix of traditional investor, private equity firm and hedge fund' (Tucker 2005).[2]

[2] The recent US literature has stressed the difference between traditional shareholder activism and hedge fund activism. Kahan and Rock (Chapter 5, this volume) argue that hedge funds are very promising activists because they face fewer regulatory barriers, political constraints, and conflicts of interest than

The HUKFF increases the stakes in companies that Hermes is already invested in through its index tracker fund; thereby the HUKFF partially internalizes the benefits of its activism. This chapter studies targeted, high-intensity shareholder activism over the period 1998–2004 by the HUKFF and takes advantage of unprecedented access to the entire records of the fund's activity from its inception. As a result, we were able to construct a private and comprehensive dataset of the fund's letters, memos, minutes, presentations, transcripts and recordings of telephone conversations, and client reports. To our knowledge, this is the first such database.[3] The HUKFF has been very successful in generating returns for its investors, measured by both annual raw returns net of fees of 8.2%, and abnormal returns net of fees of 4.9% a year against the FTSE All-Share Index over the period 1998–2004. We estimate that around 90% of such fund returns is due to activist outcomes.

To estimate the contribution of activism to performance, we develop a novel methodology for understanding and documenting the characteristics of shareholder activism, and linking them to the target companies' performance, and ultimately to the fund's returns. We begin by reporting the stated objectives of Hermes interventions under the headings of board changes (both executive and non-executive directors (NEDs)), financial goals of selling unfocused businesses and unprofitable assets, restricting capital expenditure, increasing payouts, and changing capital structure. We then classify the interventions under the headings of engagement with the management, engagement with other shareholders, public meetings, and other public interventions. We then address concerns about a potential selection bias in our sample, namely that Hermes invests in underperforming companies that intended to restructure even in the absence of shareholder engagement. Based upon target companies' responses to activism by Hermes, we classify these interventions as collaborative, confrontational, or a mixture of the two. Restructuring might have occurred in collaborative engagement events absent Hermes engagements. In contrast, it is unlikely that the management would have initiated restructuring it opposed in mixed and confrontational engagements. Using different categories of engagement objectives and the degree of hostility, we relate outcomes to measured abnormal returns to shareholders through an event study. Thus, we attribute an outcome to Hermes' engagement if and only if two conditions are met. First, the outcome must be listed as an objective prior to investing, and second, such an objective has to be specifically mentioned as such in private communications with the target management.

We record very different results from those previously reported. We find that shareholder activism is predominantly executed through private interventions as opposed to shareholder proposals at a company's annual meeting, or filings of proxy statements. The HUKFF

traditional investors. Partnoy and Thomas (2007) argue that hedge fund activists have more radical objectives than traditional activists (e.g., board changes and restructuring). The HUKFF has more in common with this 'new' US hedge fund activism than with traditional institutional investor activism.

[3] Carleton, Nelson, and Weisbach (1998) examine the correspondence between TIAA-CREF and their target firms to study the negotiation process in connection with the filing of proxy statements. In addition to the correspondence with target firms, our approach allows us to identify all the internal organization processes of a shareholder activist fund, from initial research into potential targets to investment objectives and outcomes, allowing us to estimate precisely the connections between an activist's actions and policies and stock returns.

invested in forty-one companies, and engaged with thirty of them. These engagements involved numerous meetings and telephone calls with chairmen, CEOs, and CFOs. In more than half of the cases, the HUKFF also engaged with other executives, such as divisional managers, heads of investor relations, and with non-executive board members. The HUKFF also privately contacted other institutional shareholders, with a view to communicating its engagement objectives and soliciting support for its activities. Strikingly, engagement rarely took a public form. From the cases we have seen, we believe that this in part reflects the potent threat of the Fund to requisition an extraordinary shareholders' meeting (EGM), alone or with others.[4]

What were the engagement objectives that gave rise to these events? We find that HUKFF's engagement objectives seek to bring about substantial changes in the governance structure of target companies. In twenty-eight out of thirty engagement cases, the HUKFF aims at a substantial restructuring of the operations of diversified firms in order to provide more focus (e.g., by selling non-core divisions and assets, and by limiting diversifying investments and acquisitions). In more than half of the cases, the HUKFF explicitly aims at replacing the CEO or the chairman, with a view to appointing new executives who are more willing to implement the required business restructuring of the target firm. Finally, also in more than half of the cases, the HUKFF seeks an increased cash payout to shareholders, who are often related to proposed divestment policies.

One of the most important objectives of this chapter is to determine if these engagement objectives are ultimately value-increasing. We find that when the fund's engagement objectives are achieved, there are economically large and statistically significant positive abnormal returns around the announcement date of the change. When events with confounding information, such as earnings announcements or profit warnings are excluded, the mean abnormal returns are 5.30% in the seven-day event window around the announcement date (median 3.69%). Importantly, the largest returns stem from mixed and confrontational engagements as opposed to collaborative.

The largest mean excess return, 6.6%, is associated with restructuring activities, including sales of assets and divisions. Changes of CEOs and chairmen give rise to large and positive excess returns of 6.0%, often in connection with prospective restructurings.[5] Further analysis of the company's restructuring shows that the size of assets and the number of employees are substantially lower post-Hermes intervention, and the return on assets is higher two years after the exit of the HUKFF. However, the latter results are only based on two-thirds of the sample because some interventions are so recent that insufficient time has elapsed for post-intervention performance to be observable.

[4] From conversations with the fund's managing partners and our reading of letters and meeting notes, 'soft' factors that are hard to measure might also play a role. These include a general desire of directors to 'do the right thing for the company' or deadlocks (e.g., a CEO who needs to overcome opposition to a restructuring plan from the chairman, or vice versa).

[5] For example, when company AAA announced the appointment of a new chairman, the *Financial Times* wrote: 'Mr X's appointment was welcomed in the City providing the first sharp upward movement in the group's shares in months. Yesterday AAA shares closed up almost 19 per cent at 57p. Current and former colleagues said he would not run away from making the difficult decisions required at AAA' ('New Chief Fuels Recovery Hopes', *Financial Times*, 2003). Note: names omitted. This example illustrates that the market associates the change of the chairman with the prospect of significant restructuring activities, and that this translates into large and positive announcement returns.

The question arises whether the changes in the target companies would have occurred in the absence of shareholder activism by the HUKFF. Three recent UK papers provide a measure of excess returns from restructuring and from board turnover. Dedman and Lin (2002) study CEO departures over the period 1990–95, Menon et al. (2004) study voluntary sell-offs over the period 2000–02, and Dimopoulos (2006) examines the excess returns around the announcement of board changes of underperforming companies, including CEO and chairman. The first two studies find zero or slightly negative announcement returns, while the third finds negative and significant returns, after adjusting for confounding events. Although these samples might not represent ideal control groups, they suggest that the returns to activism in our sample would not have accrued from a passive buy-and-hold investment strategy. We therefore find very different results from previous studies in three respects: (1) there is a large amount of active engagement, especially in private; (2) these engagements have a substantial effect on corporate activities; and (3) the returns to activism are economically large and statistically significant. There are a number of important qualifications to our results. First, they are for one fund only, and we cannot generalize to other shareholder activist funds in the United Kingdom or in other countries. Second, we provide evidence that the fund's trading activity gives rise to a risk profile that is significantly changing over time, both in the systematic and in the idiosyncratic components. This may raise the issue of appropriate benchmarks for calculating abnormal returns. Third, in our event study of outcomes, the abnormal returns might have been larger if the market had not anticipated the events prior to our window. These arguments imply that our methodology may actually *underestimate* the true impact of activism on stock returns. Finally, we are not in a position to compare the welfare costs of shareholder activism *vis-à-vis* other governance mechanisms. It could very well be the case that, for example, takeovers or electing large shareholder representatives to the board are less costly from the perspective of the various corporate constituencies. Equally, we do not provide evidence on the impact of shareholder activism on other corporate constituencies such as creditors or employees.

In contemporaneous work, Brav et al. (Chapter 8, this volume), Klein and Zur (Chapter 9, this volume), and Boyson and Mooradian (2007) study US hedge fund activism using publicly available information. They find large positive abnormal stock returns to target firms when hedge funds first disclose holdings larger than 5% in their 13D filings.[6] There are three main differences between these papers and the present chapter. First, unlike them we have full access to the private information on the fund's activism. Second, we have full information on stakes below the UK disclosure threshold of 3%. One striking implication of such differences is that reliance on public information alone in our sample would have excluded at least twelve out of thirty engagement cases.[7] Third, we have full access to the fund's trades and asset values, and as a result we can compute the fund's returns to activist outcomes, not simply the total fund return reported to the fund's investors.

[6] We also study the stock market reaction to the first disclosure of Hermes' stakes, but we find small, negative, and insignificant abnormal returns. One likely explanation is that disclosure is often done by the BT pension fund for the total holdings of all its funds, so that it is not easy to figure out that the HUKFF has invested.

[7] There are only three block disclosures that were explicitly linked to HUKFF engagements in the press.

In Section 7.2 we describe the data, and in Section 7.3 we present the results. Section 7.4 concludes the chapter.

7.2 Description of the Legal Environment, the Fund, and the Dataset

7.2.1 The UK and US Legal Environments for Shareholder Activism

Bebchuk (2005) compares the principal legal differences in four sets of shareholder rights: (1) rights relating to changes in basic governance arrangements; (2) director removal rights; (3) direct shareholder involvement in hostile bids; and (4) the speed of shareholder action.

A fundamental difference between the UK and US laws is the ability of UK shareholders to initiate a change in the basic contract by shareholder vote. Under the UK company law, it is mandatory that shareholders can change the articles and memorandum. Under the US state law, it is mandatory that the shareholder cannot initiate a change to the company charter (Bebchuk 2005). As a consequence, it is not possible for US shareholders to change the original charter without board approval; in the United Kingdom, shareholders can always change the basic contract without the agreement of the board.

A second difference is the power of UK shareholders to remove directors, which is related to the way shareholder meetings are called and voting is conducted (Table 7.1). At annual general meetings, the statutory rule in the United Kingdom is cumulative majority voting, meaning that each and every director must receive a majority of the 'yes' votes cast to be elected (excluding abstentions). A director coming up for (re)election might be removed from the board without an alternative director being proposed or appointed. In the United States, where state law rather than federal law applies, the default rule in Delaware is plurality voting, meaning that, in board elections, the candidate receiving the highest number of votes wins. Thus, a candidate does not need the majority of votes cast to be elected, as in the United Kingdom, nor is it possible to cast votes against candidates; institutional investors can only register their disapproval by abstaining or voting for another candidate.[8] The US legislation on voting is therefore more favourable to incumbent management (Bebchuk, Chapter 3, this volume).

In addition, in the United Kingdom, shareholders can call EGMs with 10% or more of the voting share capital, and put forward propositions to remove any and all directors at any time during their term. If more than 50% of the votes cast are in favour of such a resolution,

[8] In addition to plurality voting, the New York Stock Exchange (NYSE) listing rules contain a provision that results in shares held by brokers, but no voting instructions being cast for the management on proposals classified as routine. There is evidence that these 'broker votes' matter for voting outcomes and that management actively seeks to influence the classification (Bethel and Gillan 2002). The NYSE has published a special report on broker votes (2006), but postponed a final decision to a later date (Global Proxy Watch 2006).

Table 7.1 Comparison of the US and UK legal and institutional shareholder activism environment

Shareholder powers	United States	United Kingdom
Ordinary general meetings	Under Delaware Corporate Law, Subchapter VII, (2) (b) annual meetings deal with the election of directors and are called as set out in the bylaws	Ordinary general meetings must be called each year for the election of directors (Section 366 (1), Companies Act 1985)
Extraordinary general meetings (EGM)	Special meetings can be called under Delaware Corporation Law, Subchapter VII, (2) (d), but shareholders cannot call these meetings, unless the certificate of incorporation or the bylaws state otherwise. Thus, company's bylaws can deprive the shareholder of the right to call special meetings	Under the Companies Act 1985, Section 368, a shareholder, or group of shareholders, commanding at least 10% of the company's paid-up voting capital can requisition an EGM; the company's articles cannot deprive the shareholders of this right
Shareholder proposals	Shareholders can ask the company to add proposals to the company proxy under SEC Rule 14a-8, but this excludes all issues relating to elections; in general, proposals receiving a majority of votes under this rule are not binding on the board; the cost is borne by the company	At ordinary meetings, under the Company's Act 1985, Section 376, a shareholder, or group of shareholders, commanding 5% of the total voting rights of all members or 100 or more shareholders (each of whom have paid more than £100 of paid-up capital) can compel the company to put a resolution to the annual general meeting and to circulate a statement of not more than 1,000 words prior to the meeting
	Shareholder proposals—also on board appointments—can be made under SEC Regulation 14A via a full proxy solicitation; the cost of the solicitation is borne by the shareholder	At EGMs resolutions of shareholders requisitioning the meeting must be voted upon
Appointment/removal of directors		
Through board election	The voting rules set out in state law apply; in practice, these are determined by the bylaws; under Delaware Law, by default plurality voting applies; this means that the votes in favour are counted for each candidate; the candidates who receive most votes (not necessarily a majority of the votes attending) win; in a hostile vote, if there are, say, six candidates for three board positions, the candidates with the three highest vote counts win	Under the Companies Act 1985, election of directors must be by separate resolution for each director; (cumulative) majority voting applies

(continued)

Table 7.1 (Continued)

Shareholder powers	United States	United Kingdom
By other means	Under Delaware Corporation Law, Subchapter VII, (2) (b) shareholders can appoint directors (remove the board) by written consent, but this decision must be unanimous (a director holding one share could refuse to sign) and the bylaws can state otherwise	A director can always be removed by ordinary resolution (see above) regardless of how he or she was appointed and irrespective of provisions in the articles (Section 303, Companies Act 1985)
Tenure	Under Delaware Law, it is possible to stagger the terms of directors, ensuring that only one-third come up for election each year	A director's term of office is usually determined by the articles, but shareholders can always move to remove a director (see above)
Restrictions on voting power concentration	Under Delaware Law, it is possible to issue shareholder rights plans ('poison pills') that limit the ability of shareholders to concentrate voting power beyond certain thresholds, typically 10–15%; there is no mandatory bid requirement	Poison pills are largely absent from the United Kingdom; there is a mandatory bid requirement at 30%

then the director(s) is required to resign. Staggered boards do not constrain shareholders' ability to dismiss a director.[9] In Delaware, unless there are specific provisions in corporate charters, shareholders cannot call extraordinary meetings and therefore removing directors becomes much more difficult, particularly where there are staggered boards.[10] These legal differences are also discussed by practitioners. For example, Bob Monks (2005), the US shareholder activist who was instrumental in setting up the HUKFF, said:

> I fully acknowledge that the US is in a far worse state than the UK.... The UK market benefits ... from a clause in the Companies Act, stating that 10 percent of shareholders can requisition a meeting to dislodge any or all of the directors of a company at any time.

[9] The combination of UK company law with the City Takeover Code makes it much easier for activists to launch a hostile takeover bid than the combination of US state law and federal securities regulation. Under the UK City Code, target boards may not initiate an action that might frustrate a bid, and the whole purpose is to ensure that the bid is put to a shareholder vote as quickly as possible. Under US state law, an active board runs the takeover process, subject to judicial review. In the United States, boards can adopt poison pills without shareholder approval; in the United Kingdom, they cannot. In the United States, the combination of poison pills with staggered boards is a powerful deterrent to unsolicited takeover bids (Bebchuk, Coates, and Subramanian 2002). As discussed in Section 7.2.1, staggering of terms in the United Kingdom would not constrain hostile takeovers.

[10] Kraakman et al. (2004: 37) conclude that in the United Kingdom, unlike the United States, company law 'gives the shareholder majority a strong non-waivable right to remove directors without cause' midterm between AGMs.

Because of this, when, in the United Kingdom, activists write letters to the management of underperforming companies, the recipients are aware of the tools at the investors' disposal for changing the management. Moreover, institutions are well organized in the United Kingdom and frequently act collectively through, for example, the Association of British Insurers and the National Association of Pension Funds.[11] The largest institutional investors also have specialized employees and/or departments who maintain a direct relationship ('core engagement') with the boards of the companies in their portfolios.[12]

7.2.2 The Hermes UK Focus Fund

We study the HUKFF that is part of the Hermes Group, an investment management group owned by the British Telecommunication Staff Superannuation Scheme.[13] Hermes manages the assets of the BT Scheme and the Post Office Staff Superannuation Scheme, two of the four largest pension funds in the United Kingdom. In addition, since 1997 Hermes has been offering management services to third-party clients. As of 2005, Hermes has £61 billion under management.[14]

The Hermes asset split is heavily geared to equities, with 64% of total assets held in UK and other equities at the end of 2005. A large fraction of the UK equity is invested in index tracking funds, 28.5% of total assets versus 5.3% that was actively managed. It follows that the Hermes index fund alone represents approximately 1% of the total UK market capitalization.[15]

The HUKFF was created as a response to the problem of free-riding in institutional activism as perceived by the BT pension fund trustees. The trustees felt that the cost of higher intensity activism could not be sufficiently internalized through core engagement, and it was therefore necessary to overweight the fund's position in underperforming stocks that were to be engaged more intensively.[16]

[11] The Institutional Shareholders' Committee (2005), the association of the four UK institutional shareholder associations, has issued a statement of principle on institutional activism.

[12] The 'core engagement' programmes typically seek to ensure compliance with the UK's Combined Code and the funds' own corporate governance and other principles (e.g., its executive remuneration policies). Core engagement also acts as an early warning system that can trigger higher intensity engagement, often in collaboration with other institutions. There is little available evidence on core engagement. Faccio and Lasfer (2000: 71) examine occupational pension funds. They conclude that:

> the value added of these [pension] funds is negligible and their holdings do not lead companies to comply with the Code of Best Practice or outperform their industry counterparts. Overall, our results suggest that occupational pension funds are not effective monitors.

[13] Since the establishment of the HUKFF in 1998 as the first experiment of shareholder activism in the United Kingdom, one of the authors tried to convince the Hermes' staff to grant us access to their internal records. When they finally did grant us such access in 2004, they were certainly aware of their fund's performance, but they had not devised, or even attempted, a methodology to link their fund's performance to shareholder activism—as opposed to other determinants, such as stock picking.

[14] <http://www.hermes.co.uk/about/investment_style.htm> consulted on 14 March 2006.

[15] According to the LSE December Fact Sheet, the total market capitalization was £1,781.4 on 30 December 2005.

[16] Statement of A. Ross-Goobey at a *Journal of Applied Corporate Finance* roundtable, LBS, 9 February 2006.

The first HUKFF was established on 30 September 1998, as a joint venture with Lens Focus Management LLP (LENS) of the United States.[17] In addition to the BT Pension Scheme and LENS, there are several other investors, including several UK local authority (public) pension funds, another company pension fund, a Canadian public pension fund, and a Japanese life insurance company.[18] The composition of the HUKFF's investor base improves its independence from the sponsoring company of its main investor. In addition, there was a shareholder agreement between Hermes and LENS that ensured the independence of decision-making relating to investments and engagements in the Fund *vis-à-vis* the Hermes Group management. The agreement included the appointment of directors independent from the Hermes Group and the executives of the HUKFF.[19]

The HUKFF gives high-power incentives to its managing directors and other fund staff. These funds are established as partnerships, where the senior managers are special partners in the fund, receiving a share in the total payout. They also have a shadow equity stake in the fund management company. In addition, managing directors and other key fund staff are on bonus schemes. Hence, the remuneration of the fund staff is tied directly and substantially to the cumulative outperformance of the HUKFF. The incentive scheme could reward executives with seven-figure bonuses in years when performance is good.[20]

7.2.3 The HUKFF Activism Approach

The HUKFF applies a triple investment criterion, asking whether the company is underperforming, if the fund believes it can engage the company successfully, and whether the fund expects to obtain at least 20% more value over current share price. Only if the answer is a triple 'yes' does the fund invest with a view to bringing about governance changes.[21]

Once the fund is invested, it begins the engagement process by presenting the changes it seeks to the target management and/or board. Depending on the reaction of the target, three stylized engagement scenarios evolve. If the target reacts positively by accommodating the

[17] The LENS fund was founded in 1991 by veteran shareholder activists Robert A. G. Monks and Nell Minow.

[18] In practice, the HUKFF today consists of three separate funds that have been set up as limited partnerships. For legal reasons, the maximum number of partners (investors) each fund could accommodate was twenty. This legal requirement has recently changed. The partnerships are managed jointly and each partnership holds an equal amount of shares in each target company, so for practical purposes they act as, and we refer to them as, a single fund.

[19] When LENS sold its 25% stake in the management company to the Hermes Group, the shareholder agreement was replaced by a Memorandum of Understanding between the board of the new Hermes Focus Asset Management Limited, the manager of the HUKFF, and the Hermes Group, designed to ensure the continued independent decision-making of the fund. Bob Monks and the other independent directors continued to serve on the HUKFF board.

[20] 'The complex pay packages comprised a relatively low base salary . . ., benefits, an annual bonus triggered by better performance, payments from a long-term incentive plan and a share of profits under a "carried interest" plan' (Tucker 2005).

[21] Bethel and Gillan (2007) conduct a clinical study of the Relational Investor Fund, a fund that engages US companies, and has a partnership agreement with the HUKFF, as well as a similar investment strategy. Dyck, Volchkova, and Zingales (2008) conduct a clinical study of the Hermitage Fund that engages Russian companies through the press and the pressure of public opinion.

fund's requests, then the fund monitors the implementation of the changes and awaits the changes to be released to the market, so that the market can revaluate the target's shares, and the fund can realize a gain and exit.[22] If the target reacts negatively, the engagement may become confrontational and a range of actions are taken to press changes on the company. We report the frequency and nature of these actions below. Finally, if the company adopts a neutral attitude, discussions continue and the nature of the engagement turns either positive or negative.

7.2.4 Data Collection

The HUKFF provided full access to amounts invested, net asset values and fees, and all internal and external documents including letters, memos, minutes, and reports.[23] Fund staff coded additional information from agendas, personal notes, and memory. External data collected include stock prices from Datastream and the London Stock Price Database, news flow from Factiva regarding all board changes, takeovers, divestitures, and payout policies at target firms.

The HUKFF has invested in a total of forty-one companies between 1 October 1998 and 31 December 2004. The portfolio is dynamic. There are 4 to 8 new investments per year with a median duration of 517 trading days (Figure 7.1).

We collected data on significant holdings for each of the forty-one HUKFF investments. From (confidential) internal documents we know the date the fund first invested. This information is not observed by the market. From a Regulatory Information Service, we obtained notifications of significant holdings after the date of first purchase.[24] Under UK listing rules, investors having a material interest in 3% or more in the shares of a listed company should disclose such an interest to the market.[25] In addition to immediate notification through a Regulatory Information Service,[26] the UK listing rules stipulate that companies must use these notifications to disclose the distribution of significant holdings in the annual report. We collected such data to analyse the distribution of blocks.

In Table 7.2 we show statistics on the ownership stakes of the Hermes Group that includes the index trackers and the HUKFF. The mean stake is almost 4% (maximum of 13.5%) based on private information obtained from the Fund for all investments.[27]

[22] Note that the Hermes index tracker fund stays invested.

[23] Data access was provided on an arm's-length basis and subject to a confidentiality agreement. The agreement gave the HUKFF the right to read and comment on drafts of this chapter prior to publication and obliged the authors to give careful consideration to any comments received. If the fund had had 'reservations about the style or content of the paper' we would have recorded the fact in the chapter. No fees or expenses relating to this project were paid for by the Hermes Group or the HUKFF.

[24] We use the Hemscott Premium news database that collates information from all RNSs.

[25] Major holdings in a listed company incorporated in the United Kingdom must be notified under §§ 198 to 208 of the Companies Act 1985. To be more precise, § 199 states that a material interest in 3% or more of the nominal share value of any one class of shares that is acquired or ceased must be notified. It also states that a 10% or larger holding must be notified even when no material interest exists leading to notifications by large custodians, for example.

[26] The leading service is the RNS of the LSE.

[27] In the United Kingdom, under the Companies Act 1985 § 199, investors must disclose stakes greater than 3% to the market. Not all investor stakes reached 3%.

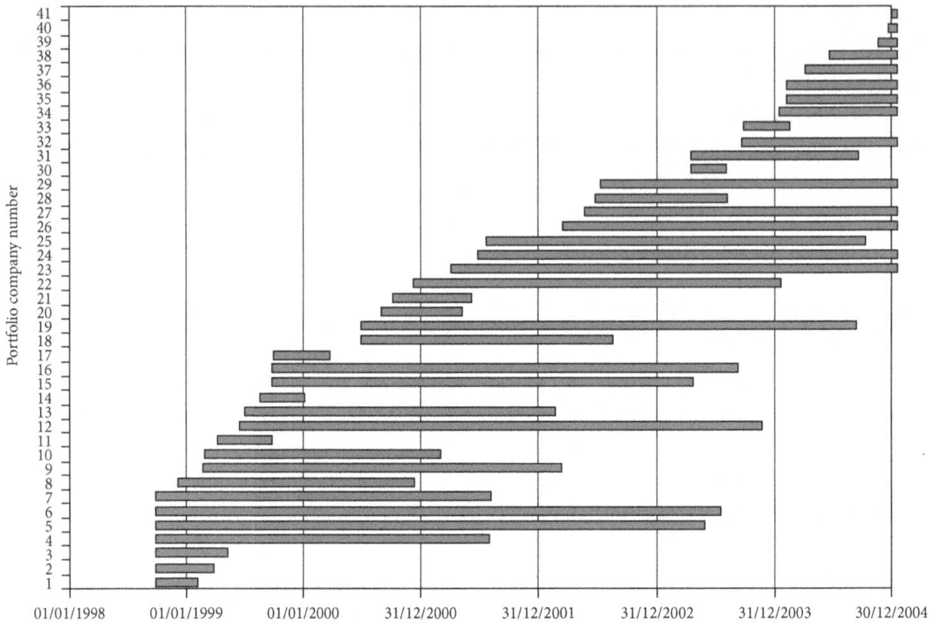

FIGURE 7.1 Timing and duration of the forty-one HUKFF portfolio investments made between the inception of the fund and 31 December 2004

Out of the forty-one investments, thirty companies were actively engaged, three companies were invested in shortly before 31 December 2004, and engagement had therefore not yet started. The remaining eight companies were sold relatively shortly after investment before the engagement had started, and after a sudden upward movement in stock prices prompted by exogenous events (e.g., unsolicited takeover bids).

Engagements can be further classified into collaborative, mixed, and confrontational. In collaborative engagements, the target agreed with the changes sought by the fund and implemented them in cooperation with Hermes. In confrontational engagements, there was disagreement about the Fund's objective from the outset and it was often necessary to remove the CEO and/or the chairman to implement the Fund's objectives. In the mixed engagements, the demands of the HUKFF were implemented reluctantly or grudgingly. In the Appendix, we illustrate the difference in attitudes with excerpts from letters, meeting memos, and press clippings.[28]

As one would have expected, ownership by the Hermes Group varies with the engagement attitude and is at its highest, at 6.9% on average, in confrontational engagements, compared with 3.2% in collaborative engagements (medians of 7.5% versus 2.4%).

[28] The attitude classification is subjective. We asked former and current fund staff to rank the attitude towards the Fund by the CEO and the chairman separately on a scale from 1 to 10, where 1 was fully collaborative and 10 very confrontational. There was little disagreement about the classification of the most confrontational engagements. The distinction between collaborative and mixed is more subjective (see the Appendix).

Table 7.2 Ownership in Hermes' targets

		Investments		Engaged by attitude		
		All	Engaged	Collaborative	Mixed	Confrontational
Panel A: Ownership by Hermes Group						
	Mean (%)	4.0	4.8	3.2	3.9	6.9
	Median (%)	2.5	3.9	2.4	3.3	7.5
	Min. (%)	1.0	1.0	1.1	1.0	1.0
	Max. (%)	13.5	13.5	8.4	9.4	13.5
	No. of companies	41	30	7	12	11
Panel B: Large stakes in Hermes' targets						
Top three stakes in Hermes' targets (%)	Mean	19.9	18.9	13.3	15.5	25.6
	Median	19.7	19.6	12.6	16.8	27.3
	Min.	3.1	3.1	3.1	4.0	3.1
	Max.	45.2	45.2	24.8	23.1	45.2
	Hermes' top three?	13	12	1	5	6
Sum of the stakes >3% in Hermes' targets (%)	Mean	26.1	26.1	18.3	22.6	34.3
	Median	24.3	22.6	17.5	16.9	36.6
	Min.	3.1	3.1	3.1	4.0	3.1
	Max.	60.9	60.9	34.4	60.9	52.6
Top stake >3%?	Count	35	28	7	10	11
Hermes' stake >3%?	Count	18	17	3	6	8
No. of stakes >3% in Hermes' Targets	Mean	4.4	4.6	4.3	4.4	5.1
	Median	4.0	4.0	4.0	3.0	5.0
	Min.	1.0	1.0	1.0	1.0	1.0
	Max.	12.0	12.0	6.0	12.0	1.0
Companies	Count	41	30	7	12	11
Investors	No. of stakes >3% in Hermes' targets					
Panel C: Most frequent holders of stakes >3% in Hermes' targets						
Legal & General Group	15					
Prudential	9					
Barclays	7					
Fidelity	7					
AXA	6					
Schroeder	6					
Sanford C. Bernstein	5					
Standard Life	5					
M&G	4					
Capital Group	3					
Silchester	3					
UBS	3					
Franklin	2					
Halifax	2					
Phillips & Drew	2					
Popeshead	2					

Panel B of Table 7.2 reports the various statistics on the largest outside stakes. The concentration of ownership is an important issue for Hermes and other activist funds since they must work with other large shareholders to bring pressure on the target management for change, if needed. The median size of the three largest outside shareholders with holdings of at least 3% is 19.7%, and Hermes is one of the three largest in thirteen out of the forty-one cases. The median size of the top three stakes is much larger in confrontational investments (27.3%) than in collaborative (12.6%) or in mixed engagements (16.8%). Similar results hold if one considers the sum of all stakes greater than 3%.

Panel C of Table 7.2 shows that the major UK institutional investors are frequent holders of outside stakes in Hermes' targets (e.g., the Legal and General Group has a stake greater than 3% in fifteen out of forty-one Hermes' targets). The Prudential holds a similar stake in nine cases, and Barclays and Fidelity in seven cases. These statistics on outside stakes show that it would be relatively easy to gather 10% of the votes to call an EGM in the face of a recalcitrant management.

Table 7.3 provides statistics on the duration of the investment and how it varies with the engagement attitude. Collaborative investments, where the changes are implemented in collaboration with the target management, are shorter, a median of 469 trading days. Confrontational engagements take longer to resolve, with a median duration of 1,284 trading days.

Table 7.4 reports performance prior to investments by the HUKFF. Panel A reports that the large majority of Hermes' targets were performing poorly, with more than 40% in the bottom quintile of performance in the six months prior to investment by Hermes. Panel B reports that Hermes' targets were underperforming the FTSE All-Share Index by more than 2% in the year before the investment. These results differ from the recent US hedge fund evidence, where Klein and Zur (Chapter 9, this volume) report that hedge fund targets outperformed market indices by more than 7% on average.

Table 7.3 Duration of investments

	Investments		Engaged by attitude		
	All	Engaged	Collaborative	Mixed	Confrontational
Number of days					
Mean	691.4	873.7	526.6	811.8	1,162.1
Median	517	958	469	930	1,284
Min.	1	104	104	180	197
Max.	1,744	1,744	1,043	1,433	1,744
No. of companies	41	30	7	12	11

This table reports descriptive statistics of the duration of the HUKFF investments for all forty-one companies invested between 1 October 1998 and 31 December 2004, computed as the number of calendar days from date of first purchase to the earliest between date of last sale and 31 December 2004. Statistics are reported for all thirty engagements, and separately for different engagement attitudes. Engagement attitudes are based on the target companies' response and can be collaborative, mixed, or confrontational.

Table 7.4 Performance prior to investment by HUKFF

Performance deciles	Six months prior	One year prior
Panel A: Relative performance prior to investment by HUKFF		
1	1	0
2	0	0
3	1	1
4	1	3
5	6	5
6	6	6
7	4	8
8	4	5
9	10	7
10	6	4
No. of companies	39	39

	Investments		Engaged by attitude		
	All	Engaged	Collaborative	Mixed	Confrontational
Panel B: Excess returns (percentage) over FTSE All-Share prior to investment by the HUKFF					
Six months prior	−2.54	−2.36	−0.94	−2.78	−2.55
Twelve months prior	−2.22	−2.02	−1.60	−1.92	−2.32
No. of companies	39	28	5	12	11

This table reports performance prior to investment by the HUKFF. Panel A reports the distribution of the target companies' relative performance to FTSE All-Share Index prior to investment by the HUKFF. Columns 2 and 3 of panel A report the number of target companies by performance decile based on a six-month and twelve-month periods prior to investment by the HUKFF. Performance decile 10 contains the companies in the lowest 10% performance interval. Panel B reports mean six-month and twelve-month excess returns prior to investment by the HUKFF.

7.3 Results

In this section, we report three sets of results. First, we examine the types of engagement activities initiated by the HUKFF and the extent to which they take a private or public form. Second, we report the fund's engagement objectives and evaluate the extent to which they are translated into outcomes. Third, using these outcomes we construct an event study to measure the effect of shareholder activism on stock prices.

7.3.1 Types and Frequency of Engagement Activities

Table 7.5 reports the type of engagement activities entered into by the HUKFF for the thirty companies in the portfolio in which they were engaged. Panel A examines contacts with the management of target companies and shows that, in all thirty cases, the HUKFF had numerous meetings with CEOs, chairmen, and CFOs. It also met with other executives, including the head of investor relations, the senior independent director, and the chairman of the executive remuneration committee. The HUKFF met target companies' executives repeatedly over the course of the engagements, on average 9.73 times (median 7) per company with a maximum of 48. In 60% of cases, the HUKFF had contacts with NEDs, whether by letter, telephone, or in person. In more than half of the cases, the HUKFF also sent representatives to visit the headquarters and operation sites of target companies.

Panel B of Table 7.5 examines contacts with other shareholders and other parties and reports that, in more than 80% of cases, the HUKFF contacted other institutional shareholders so as to communicate its engagement objectives and to solicit support for its activities, although this resulted in joint actions in only three cases, a meeting or letter to the target board. The HUKFF contacted company brokers in more than 70% of cases and headhunters in 26.6% of cases, with a view to helping target firms select suitable alternative candidates for senior executive positions. In no case did the HUKFF contact banks or bondholders to solicit support for its activities.

Panel C of Table 7.5 examines HUKFF activities in connection with shareholder meetings. For annual general meetings, we found that in only one case did the HUKFF pose a question or add an item to the agenda, and in only two cases did the HUKFF solicit votes against the management. For EGMs, shareholders had plans to requisition a meeting in three cases, but only one EGM was actually called: one EGM was planned by the HUKFF itself, one was planned by another shareholder, and one by the chairman of the target company. In at least one case, the plans had gone as far as preparing the necessary EGM papers.

Panel D of Table 7.5 examines US- and UK-style litigations and we observe only one US-style class action. The action was neither initiated nor joined by the HUKFF.[29] Panel E examines higher intensity actions such as threats to block rights issues, press campaigns, and takeover attempts. The HUKFF threatened twice to block a rights issue and was successful in both cases. Of the seven press campaigns that occurred in our sample, only two were initiated by the HUKFF. Finally, none of the four observed takeover attempts were induced or facilitated by the HUKFF.

In summary, Table 7.5 shows that engagement by the HUKFF tends to take a private rather than public form—a lot of letters, meetings, site visits, soliciting of support from other investors, and some press campaigns, but few interventions at public meetings. In contrast with our findings, Brav et al. (Chapter 8, this volume) report that engagements by US hedge funds take a much more public approach; in one-half of the cases they do not involve any private communication with the target management.[30]

[29] Actually, the HUKFF supported management, taking the view that the class action was not in the best interest of the HUKFF investment.

[30] Instead, US hedge funds often seek board representation and even public confrontation, through shareholder proposals, proxy contests, lawsuits, and takeover attempts.

Table 7.5 **Activism tactics**

	Meetings	Letters	Total
Panel A: Contact with the management			
CEO	30 (100.0%)	30 (100.0%)	
Chairman	30 (100.0%)	30 (100.0%)	
CFO	29 (100.0%)		
COO	8 (26.7%)		
Division manager	17 (56.7%)		
Head of strategy	11 (36.7%)		
SID	19 (63.3%)		
Head of IR	22 (73.3%)		
Chairman executive Remuneration Committee	15 (50.0%)		
Non-executive directors			18 (60.0%)
Site visits			19 (63.3%)

	Other shareholders				Banks and bondholders	Headhunters	Company brokers
	Calls/meetings	Solicit support	Joint letter	Joint meetings	Solicit support	Any contact	Any contact
Panel B: Contact and cooperation with other shareholders and relevant parties							
No. of cases observed	26	25	2	3	0	8	22
Percentage of sample (%)	86.7	83.3	6.7	10	0	26.7	73.3

(*continued*)

Table 7.5 (Continued)

	Annual general meeting				Extraordinary general meeting			
	Pose questions	Add item	Solicit hostile votes	Planned	Requisitioned	Planned by Hermes	Planned by other shareholders	Planned by a company chairman
Panel C: Shareholders general meetings								
No. of cases observed	1	1	2	3	0	1	1	1
Percentage of sample (%)	3.3	3.3	6.7	16.7	0.0	3.3	3.3	3.3

	UK litigation		US class action			
	Observed	Hermes induced	Observed	US lawyer induced	Shareholder induced	Hermes induced
Panel D: Litigation						
No. of cases observed	0	0	1	1	1	0
Percentage of sample (%)	0.0	0.0	3.3	3.3	3.3	0.0

	Threaten blockage rights issue	Hostile takeover attempt		Press campaign		
		Observed	Hermes induced	Observed	Shareholder induced	Hermes induced
Panel E: High-intensity actions						
No. of cases observed	2	4	0	7	4	2
Percentage of sample (%)	6.7	13.3	0.0	23.3	15.3	6.7

This table reports various engagement actions by Hermes Focus Fund. Panel A reports the number (%) of cases whereby Hermes had meetings with and wrote letters to various people within the organization. Panel B reports the number (%) of cases of contact and cooperation with relevant third parties. Panel C reports the number (%) of cases of intervention at shareholders GMs. Panel D reports the number (%) of cases of litigation in court. Panel E reports the number (%) of cases of high-intensity actions such as threats to block rights issues, hostile takeover attempts, and press campaigns.

Table 7.6 Governance objectives and outcomes

	Objective	Outcome conditional	Outcome % conditional
Restructuring			
Restructure diversified firms to more focus	28.0	15.5	55.36
Restructure non-diversified firms through asset sales	10.0	6.0	60.00
Stop acquisition	10.0	8.5	85.00
Discipline capital expenditures	7.0	6.0	85.71
Reduce discount on NAV	6.0	6.0	100.00
Board changes			
Change CEO	14.5	12.0	82.76
Change chairman	18.5	14.0	75.68
Change non-executive directors	17.0	10.0	58.82
Strengthen 'independent' element on board	15.0	7.0	46.67
Change remuneration policy	4.0	1.0	25.00
Financial policies			
Rights issue	2.0	2.0	100.00
Increase cash payout to shareholders	17.0	11.5	0.64
Other policies			
Improve operational management	8.0	4.0	50.00
Stop unequal treatment of shareholders	2.0	1.5	75.00
Improve investor relations	9.0	4.0	44.44

This table reports the governance objectives and outcomes in firms in the Hermes portfolio. Column 1 lists the possible governance issues. Column 2 reports the cases in which Hermes set out the governance issue as an objective in their investment committee papers: it adds 1 for firms in which the objective was set as primary, 0.5 for firms in which the objective was set as not primary, and 0 otherwise. Column 3 reports the number of cases in which the governance objective was achieved: it adds 1 for firms in which the governance issue was both set as an objective in the investment committee papers, and we could establish, based on a Factiva search, that the outcome was fully achieved, 0.5 for firms in which the outcome was partially achieved, and 0 otherwise. Column 4 reports the % conditional outcomes.

7.3.2 Engagement Objectives and Outcomes

Table 7.6 examines the objectives and outcomes of the HUKFF's engagement policy. In a large majority of cases, the HUKFF seeks to restructure the business; for example, selling non-core divisions by diversified firms is an objective sought in 28 cases, with an achieved outcome in 15.5 cases.[31] Selling non-core assets is an objective in ten cases and is achieved in six of these. The HUKFF also tries to stop diversifying acquisitions (ten) and limit capital expenditures (seven), and in more than 90% and 80% of the cases, respectively, target management agrees with the fund's demands. In six cases, the HUKFF seeks to reduce the discount on net asset values of investment trusts and property, and always achieves such a result.

[31] If the objective is mentioned in the Hermes investment committee report prior to investment, we code a dummy variable equal to 1 if the outcome is confirmed as fully achieved on Factiva, 0.5 when the outcome was partially achieved, and 0 otherwise.

HUKFF seeks also to bring about substantial board changes, including replacing the CEO and the chairman, an objective sought in 14.5 and 18.5 cases,[32] respectively, and achieved in more than 80% and 75% of the cases, respectively. These figures for CEO and chairman turnover compare with those reported by Dimopoulos (2006), who finds that in a sample of poorly performing companies in the United Kingdom, CEO turnover occurs in 11% of the cases, and chairman turnover occurs in 10% of the cases (see also Qiu 2006). This comparison suggests that the high level of top management turnover observed in our sample would not have occurred without activism by the HUKFF. In more than half of the cases, the HUKFF also seeks to replace or add NEDs, and strengthen the independent element of the board, often in conjunction with other top executive appointments. Appointments of non-executives and independent directors were part of Hermes' objectives and are observed in more than 60% of the cases.

The HUKFF also seeks to change financial policies such as promoting new equity issues by rights in two cases, and increasing cash payout to shareholders in seventeen cases. We observe three rights issues, the third being unwelcome to the HUKFF. In contrast, the objective of the increasing cash payout is achieved in eleven cases, often combined with restructuring activities.

In addition to restructuring, changing boards, and financial policies, HUKFF's other objectives included the improvement of operational management and investor relations in eight and nine cases, respectively, and stopping unequal treatment of shareholders in two cases. Outcomes consistent with these objectives were observed in a majority of cases.

In sum, the HUKFF seeks to restructure a large number of firms, focusing their activities, limiting acquisitions and capital expenditure, changing boards—CEOs, chairmen, non-executive and independent directors—and altering financial policy, in particular raising cash payouts.[33]

7.3.3 Returns to Disclosure of Activist Stakes

We analyse the market reaction to disclosure to the Regulatory News Service (RNS) of stakes at least as large as 3%, consistent with company law disclosure rules. In a review of the sample of engagements, we found either that there was no notification (because the stake was below the 3% threshold), the disclosure was made by the BriTEL trustees for the Hermes Group without the HUKFF being mentioned specifically, or the notification made by the BriTEL trustees (or another HUKFF investor) revealed that the Fund had acquired an interest. We also examine cases where the press mentioned the Fund as a shareholder, which on occasion happened even before official notification to the RNS.

To be more precise, in the thirty engagements we identified from the fund's internal records, thirteen were disclosed to the public on the RNS and fifteen were mentioned in the press, but only six were disclosed through both channels. In most cases, a substantial period of time had elapsed before the disclosure of the acquisition by the fund, on average 503 days for the RNS and 435 days for the press, conditional on disclosure. When the information was disclosed

[32] We add one-half when the objective is not board change per se, but it facilitates other objectives such as restructuring.

[33] BJPT report similar objectives sought by US hedge funds with one exception, namely that, unlike Hermes, US hedge funds frequently seek the sale of the target company itself.

through both channels, the press disclosure came, on average, 165 days after the RNS disclosure. Hence, in most cases the disclosure was routine and did not attract press interest.

This is confirmed by looking at the content of the press articles. Twelve of the fifteen press disclosures were not 'announcements', but retrospective pieces commenting on the outcomes of the HUKFF engagements.[34] There was only one instance where a purchase crossed the 3% threshold immediately and was disclosed in the press the day after with the headline 'Activist fund buys into Caledonia' (MacKintosh and Targett 2001).

We find negative, but small and statistically insignificant market reactions to the first disclosure of stakes of the HUKFF, be it by the regulatory authority RNS or by the press (Table 7.7). For the subsample where there is first disclosure by the press, cumulative average abnormal returns (CAARs) are positive, although small and statistically insignificant. For the subsample of first disclosure by the RNS, CAARs are negative and in general statistically insignificant, except for the window [−5, +5] days where we find statistically significant and negative returns of −3.7%.[35] These findings compare with Brav et al. (Chapter 8, this volume),

Table 7.7 Effect of disclosure of Hermes' stake on stock prices

Window	Mean (%)	*t*-stat	Median (%)	*z*-stat	Positive percentage (%)	*N*
First public disclosure—either the RNS or the press						
[−1, +1]	−0.33	−0.65	−0.46	−1.37	33.33	21
[−2, +2]	−0.01	−0.02	−0.22	−0.16	42.86	21
[−3, +3]	−0.04	−0.04	0.39	0.02	52.38	21
[−5, +5]	−1.85	−1.51	−1.90	−1.51	33.33	21
First disclosure by the RNS						
[−1, +1]	−0.41	−0.62	−0.64	−1.40	25.00	16
[−2, +2]	−0.66	−0.76	−0.64	−0.88	43.75	16
[−3, +3]	−1.23	−1.24	−0.63	−1.03	43.75	16
[−5, +5]	−3.69	−3.68	−3.53	−2.74	18.75	16
First disclosure by the press						
[−1, +1]	0.42	0.37	0.17	0.52	61.54	13
[−2, +2]	0.52	0.62	−0.40	0.25	38.46	13
[−3, +3]	1.23	1.04	−0.89	0.52	46.15	13
[−5, +5]	1.92	0.82	1.85	0.73	53.85	13

This table reports mean and median CARs (%) in various windows around the first disclosure dates of Hermes' ownership stakes.

[34] For example, on 20 August 2001 the *Financial News* published an article that contained the sentence 'The Focus funds have been active in taking stakes in companies such as Tomkins and Trinity Mirror, where management changes have subsequently taken place', thereby revealing the name of two companies that were engaged. A rare headline announcement in *The Observer* read 'Pub group Greenalls next on Hermes investor "hit list"' (Doward, Islam, and Hirst 1999).

[35] The Fund's management suggests a momentum argument that it tended to buy when prices were falling.

who report positive CAARs of between 5% and 7%, and with Klein and Zur (Chapter 9, this volume) who report CAARs of about 10% around the announcement of a 5% stake.

The most likely explanation of our findings is that it is very difficult for the market to determine whether the HUKFF holds shares in the target, because it is BriTel that discloses its holdings at the fund-family level. As a result, only in a handful of cases is it clear that the HUKFF is a separate shareholder, as distinct from other funds managed by the Hermes Group. In the rest of the cases, the media and the market are left to wonder whether that is the case.[36] This is corroborated by the absence of 'headline news' that coincided with the disclosure of a block. In the one case where this did happen—Caledonia—the [−2, +2] announcement abnormal return was 7.4%, in line with the hedge fund evidence from the United States.

7.3.4 Event Study on Outcomes

To examine whether the HUKFF engagement programme is value-increasing, we examine whether the fund's engagement objectives give rise to abnormal stock returns. To measure this, we examine a subset of engagement objectives that, by their nature, lead to announcement events, such as restructuring, board changes, and increases in the payout policy. Over the engagement period, we identify ninety-eight such events, an average of slightly more than three events for each of the thirty engaged firms.[37] For each event, we construct an event window and measure the abnormal returns over the event window, after adjusting for the FTSE All-Share Index. The event window varies from three to eleven days around the announcement date of the engagement outcome. Table 7.8 reports the results of such an event study. Depending on the window, mean cumulative abnormal returns (CARs) range from 3% to 4% (medians from 1.9% to 3.4%) for the three-day window [−1, +1] to the eleven-day window [−5, +5]; all are statistically different from 0 using a variety of tests. Focusing on the seven-day window [−2, +2], we find a mean CAR of 3.9% (median 3).

Frequently, these events coincide with other announcements such as a profit warning or an earnings announcement. As a result, the announcement returns include both the effect of the engagement, as well as other changes to the performance of the company. When events with confounding information, such as earnings announcements or profit warnings, are excluded, the mean abnormal returns increase and average 5.30% in the seven-day window [−3, +3] around the announcement date (median 3.69%). The largest excess returns, 6.6%, are associated with restructuring activities, including sales of assets and divisions. Changes of CEO and chairmen also give rise to large and positive excess returns of 6.0%. These are often accompanied by prospective restructurings. CARs for changes of NEDs are negative and insignificant.[38]

[36] As an illustration, in one case the *Financial Times* referred to rumours that Hermes had bought stakes in eight companies (Guerrera and Targett 2002). In reality, the HUKFF was only a shareholder in four of those eight cases.

[37] Regarding board changes, there are often two event dates for the same position, for example, when the previous CEO announces his intention to step down, and, subsequently, when the board announces the name of the newly appointed CEO. The same is true for some restructuring events, when, for example, a company announces an equity spin-off, and when the subsequent initial public offering (IPO) takes place. There are two carve-outs in our sample.

[38] In about a dozen cases, announcements of CEO or chairman changes are associated with the appointment of NEDs. These events are classified as CEO or chairman, and not as NED, changes.

Table 7.8 Effect of governance outcomes on stock prices, by type of outcome

Window	Mean (%)	*t*-stat	Median (%)	*z*-stat	Positive percentage (%)	*N*
Panel A: All investments						
[−1, +1]	2.97	4.21	1.86	3.95	68.37	98
[−2, +2]	3.92	5.07	3.02	4.61	68.37	98
[−5, +5]	3.94	4.03	3.38	3.95	66.33	98
Panel B: All investments, excluding events with confounding information						
[−1, +1]	3.72	4.49	2.15	4.38	74.63	67
[−2, +2]	4.60	4.96	3.20	4.42	68.66	67
[−5, +5]	5.74	4.67	4.17	4.41	71.64	67
Panel C: Restructuring						
[−1, +1]	3.57	3.13	2.27	2.90	68.89	45
[−2, +2]	5.22	4.41	4.79	3.75	71.11	45
[−5, +5]	4.97	3.05	3.32	3.00	68.89	45
Panel D: Restructuring, excluding events with confounding information						
[−1, +1]	4.58	3.85	2.59	3.51	77.14	35
[−2, +2]	5.86	4.67	5.16	3.83	74.29	35
[−5, +5]	6.66	3.69	4.98	3.33	74.29	35
Panel E: CEO and chairman turnover						
[−1, +1]	2.83	2.12	1.16	1.88	67.86	28
[−2, +2]	4.00	2.44	3.46	2.64	71.43	28
[−5, +5]	3.95	2.07	3.57	2.16	71.43	28
Panel F: CEO and chairman turnover, excluding events with confounding information						
[−1, +1]	3.71	2.13	1.65	2.27	73.68	19
[−2, +2]	5.21	2.69	3.85	2.78	73.68	19
[−5, +5]	5.92	2.37	3.61	2.50	78.95	19
Panel G: Payout						
[−1, +1]	3.30	2.24	3.18	2.22	81.25	16
[−2, +2]	2.97	2.62	3.08	2.17	75	16
[−5, +5]	2.81	1.64	2.77	1.40	62.5	16
Panel H: Non-executive directors' turnover						
[−1, +1]	−0.23	−0.15	−0.23	−0.06	44.44	9
[−2, +2]	−1.09	−0.56	−3.01	−0.77	33.33	9
[−5, +5]	0.82	0.44	−0.02	0.53	44.44	9
Panel I: Chairman turnover						
[−1, +1]	4.92	1.56	1.46	1.68	80	10
[−2, +2]	6.59	1.93	3.91	2.09	80	10
[−5, +5]	6.01	1.33	3.52	1.38	80	10

(continued)

Table 7.8 (Continued)

Panel J: CEO turnover						
[−1, +1]	1.67	1.49	0.54	1.18	55.55	18
[−2, +2]	2.56	1.51	3.16	1.72	66.66	18
[−5, +5]	2.81	1.7	3.75	1.68	66.66	18
Panel K: CEO turnover, excluding events with confounding information						
[−1, +1]	2.37	1.88	1.65	1.42	55.55	9
[−2, +2]	3.68	2.23	3.85	1.96	66.66	9
[−5, +5]	5.82	2.92	6.61	2.07	77.77	9

In sum, there are substantial share price reactions to engagement outcomes. There are particularly large gains associated with restructuring, and CEO and chairman turnover.

Table 7.9 partitions the share price reactions to engagement outcomes by engagement attitudes. Of the ninety-eight engagement outcome events, ninety-six occur in the thirty companies that are the targets of actual engagement by the HUKFF, and sixty-six events occur in the absence of confounding information (i.e., an average of 2.2 events per company). Focusing on the seven-day window [−3, +3] for events without confounding information, we find a mean CAR of 5.22% (median 3.5%). These figures may then be combined into an estimate of 11.5% 'agency costs' for the HUKFF target companies (i.e., abnormal returns of 5.22% per event times an average of 2.2 events per company). Such estimated 'agency costs' are largest in mixed engagements (12.7%, which is abnormal returns of 6.8% times 3.3 events per company), intermediate in collaborative engagements (11.5%, which is 4.04% times 2.9), and smallest in confrontational engagements (9.9%, which is 3.21% times 3.1).

7.3.5 Operating Performance

In this section, we provide a limited analysis of the operating performance of the target companies in the Hermes portfolio before and after the Hermes engagement. If focus fund activism is successful, we will expect to observe poor pre-engagement operating performance and improved performance after a completed intervention. Table 7.10 reports operating performance before and after the HUKFF engagements and two measures of restructuring intensity. Given the limited sample size, none of the reported differences in operating performance are statistically significant, but the changes in the numbers are economically large.

Panel A of Table 7.10 reports that the median return on assets recovers substantially from the levels seen one year before and one year after the engagement; however, it is only slightly higher than two years before the engagement. The means follow a similar pattern. They decline from 8% two years prior to the engagement to 6.8% one year prior to the engagement and rise back to 8.3% two years after the completed engagements.

Panel B of Table 7.10 reports restructuring intensity. The value of total assets is similar in medians both one and two years after the completed engagements. The means show a significant decline in total assets. The decline in the number of employees is more

Table 7.9 **Effect of governance outcomes on stock prices, by engagement attitude**

Window	Mean (%)	*t*-stat	Median (%)	*z*-stat	Positive percentage (%)	No. of events	No. of observations
Panel A: All engagements							
[−1, +1]	2.96	4.12	1.86	3.84	66.67	96	30
[−2, +2]	3.91	4.95	3.02	4.47	67.70	96	30
[−5, +5]	3.89	3.90	3.38	3.83	65.63	96	30
Panel B: All engagements, excluding events with confounding information							
[−1, +1]	3.68	4.38	2.12	4.27	72.73	66	30
[−2, +2]	4.58	4.86	3.11	4.31	68.18	66	30
[−5, +5]	5.65	4.53	3.89	4.32	71.21	66	30
Panel C: Collaborative							
[−1, +1]	3.26	2.08	1.98	1.83	65.00	20	7
[−2, +2]	4.11	2.95	4.31	2.54	70.00	20	7
[−5, +5]	1.92	1.19	3.12	1.60	70.00	20	7
Panel D: Collaborative, excluding events with confounding information							
[−1, +1]	4.30	2.05	2.40	1.89	80.00	10	7
[−2, +2]	3.58	1.72	4.70	1.68	60.00	10	7
[−5, +5]	2.51	0.90	3.21	1.27	70.00	10	7
Panel E: Mixed							
[−1, +1]	2.45	2.37	1.68	2.28	65.00	40	12
[−2, +2]	3.82	3.05	2.41	2.78	67.50	40	12
[−5, +5]	4.79	2.92	3.39	2.68	65.00	40	12
Panel F: Mixed, excluding events with confounding information							
[−1, +1]	3.68	3.12	2.21	3.33	73.33	30	12
[−2, +2]	5.37	3.83	3.60	3.50	76.67	30	12
[−5, +5]	7.23	3.87	5.19	3.67	76.67	30	12
Panel G: Confrontational							
[−1, +1]	2.76	2.30	1.84	2.18	67.65	34	11
[−2, +2]	3.10	2.36	2.79	2.18	64.71	34	11
[−5, +5]	3.30	1.92	3.50	1.99	61.76	34	11
Panel H: Confrontational, excluding events with confounding information							
[−1, +1]	2.60	1.99	1.29	1.77	66.67	24	11
[−2, +2]	2.92	2.06	1.53	1.66	58.33	24	11
[-5, +5]	4.15	2.01	3.50	2.06	62.50	24	11

This table reports mean and median CARs (%) in various windows around the announcement dates of Hermes' engagement outcomes, partitioned by engagement attitude. Engagement attitude can be collaborative, mixed, or confrontational.

Table 7.10 Restructuring and operating performance

		Pre-HUKFF years		Post-HUKFF years	
		Year −2	Year −1	Year +1	Year +2
Panel A: Return on assets					
Return on assets (%)	Mean	10.17	7.07	5.02	10.72
	Median	8.01	6.84	4.52	8.31
No. of observations		20	20	20	20
Panel B: Restructuring					
Total assets (million pounds)	Mean	5,388	5,735	3,463	3,725
	Median	1,439	1,589	1,495	1,570
No. of observations		20	20	20	20
Employees	Mean	25,817	26,689	16,438	16,336
	Median	13,459	12,340	7,506	7,451
No. of observations		19	19	19	19
Panel C: Market-to-book					
Market-to-book	Mean	3.02	0.37	2.63	2.75
	Median	2.08	1.60	1.64	2.52
No. of observations		20	20	20	20

This table reports measures of restructuring and operating performance of targets of the HUKFF engagement for selected years pre- and post-engagement. Panel A reports mean and median return on assets and total assets, panel B reports number of employees, and panel C reports market-to-book ratios. The data were taken from DataStream.

pronounced, with the median number of employees being approximately 40% lower in the two years after completed engagements than in the two years leading up to the engagement. This finding is consistent with the Fund's main restructuring objective—more focus (see Table 7.6).

Panel C of Table 7.10 reports statistics on the market-to-book ratio of Hermes' targets, both prior and subsequent to its engagements. The median market-to-book ratio shows a substantial rise in all previous years, consistent with the restoration of market valuations to the levels prior the decline in performance.

7.3.6 Case Studies

Three case studies are described in this section. The first case illustrates how an EGM can bring about board changes, and why the threat of an EGM can give 'real authority' (Aghion and Tirole 1997) over the target board and management. We find that the threat of an EGM may be as effective as its actual execution, as a way of forcing management to accept the proposed change, very much in the same way as the threat of a cramdown in Chapter 11 bankruptcies may force dissenting classes of creditors to vote for a proposed restructuring plan. The other two cases illustrate engagements by the HUKFF: the second case a collaborative one, and the third case a confrontational one.

Case 1: *Brazilian Smaller Companies Investment Trust*

The Brazilian Smaller Companies Investment Trust, better known as Brazit, was a closed-end fund managed by a subsidiary of Foreign and Colonial Management Limited. It had about $40 million under management. Hermes started a campaign for change in late 1996, which came to a head in 1997. The HUKFF was not yet established and this activism campaign was initiated by the index tracker fund. The case is important because it showed to Hermes that the requisitioning of EGMs was a powerful threat when management refused to engage. It also established the authority of the individuals who made up the original HUKFF team in 1998.

Hermes had three objections to the way Brazit was managed. It had significantly underperformed the main relevant indexes, the board of the investment trust was dominated by members of the management company or individuals closely associated with it, and the service contract was unusually long at three years, although it was subsequently reduced to two.

Hermes and another large shareholder in Brazit engaged with the board of the management company to bring about the change. When prolonged negotiations failed, the two shareholders requisitioned an EGM, with a proposal to dismiss the entire board of the target. A total of 70% of the shareholders voted, and 97% of them voted to dismiss the board. The new board eventually agreed to liquidate the investment trust. The ramifications of this engagement were felt throughout the investment trust industry. The parent company, along with many other investment management companies, changed their rules barring their employees serving on boards of investment trusts and allowed service contracts of only one year.

Case 2: Smith and Nephew

Smith and Nephew is an early collaborative engagement of the HUKFF. The Fund supported a new CEO's conglomerate transformation strategy while insisting on board transformation and cash payouts.

In 1998, Smith and Nephew was a health-care conglomerate with five divisions: wound management, casting, orthopaedic, endoscopy, and consumer products. The HUKFF invested in October 1998. Prior to making the investment, the Fund had identified a number of changes it felt could reduce the conglomerate discount.

In December 1998, the HUKFF met with the new CEO to discuss his strategic plans and vision for the road ahead. The Fund found that the restructuring plans of the new CEO and its own broadly coincided. However, the Fund still had concerns about the pending chairman's succession and excess free cash flow. These views were expressed in a letter to the CEO dated 31 December 1998.

The future course of the engagement followed the general line set out in this initial letter. In 1999, Smith and Nephew divested its bracing and support systems, as well as its cotton and wool business. In November, the chairman retired and was succeeded by an outsider. The ten-day abnormal returns around the announcement dates for these events were positive, but not very large, 4.7%, 1.1%, and 3.1%, respectively. At the beginning of 2000, the announcement of the Iruxol product from BASF resulted in a negative abnormal return of −13.8%. On 29 June, the company announced the sale of the female hygiene and toiletries division to an MBO, the sale of Elastoplast to Beiersdorf, and plans to return £415 million to shareholders. This announcement resulted in a 21% abnormal return over a −5 to +5 day window.

On 4 July 2000, the Fund wrote another letter to the CEO, congratulating him on completing the first stage of the transformation into a more focused company. In a final letter dated 17 August 2001, the HUKFF informed the CEO that it had divested from the company. The Fund also confirmed that Hermes would retain an overweight position in the stock in its mainstream portfolios. According to the HUKFF's own calculations, the internal rate of return of the Smith and Nephew investment (across all Hermes funds) was 46.77%, compared to an IRR of 2.99% had the same cash flows been invested in the FTSE All-Share Index.

Case 3: *Six Continents*

In 2001, Six Continents PLC was a leisure conglomerate with assets in the hotel, brewing, and pubs business. Until June 2001, it was known under the name Bass PLC. The HUKFF first acquired a stake in the company in late 1999. This holding was never disclosed to the RNS because it never crossed the 3% threshold, and was first mentioned in the press on 20 August 2001.[39]

The HUKFF invested because it was concerned about the lack of synergies between the conglomerate's divisions, its capital structure, and its acquisition track record. In previous years, Six Continents has successfully acquired the Holiday Inn and Intercontinental Hotel chains, but, in the view of the HUKFF, paid too much. These factors combined had led to a significant underperformance of the FTSE All-Share Index in the year prior to the investment by the HUKFF.

The Fund had four main engagement objectives for Six Continents: (1) simplify the conglomerate structure; (2) ask for cash to be paid out to shareholders through a share buy-back programme; (3) split the role of chairman and CEO; and (4) prevent further value-destroying acquisitions.

The role of chairman and CEO were split, although the press continued to assert that the chairman continued to dominate the company.

Six Continents divested its Bass brewing operations to Interbrew, and 1,000 smaller managed and tenanted pubs to Nomura of Japan. This generated £1.5 billion of cash holdings that, at this point, were not paid out to shareholders. Instead, the company looked for further acquisition opportunities in the hotel sector.

In January 2002, the Fund wrote a strongly worded letter to the company. The letter was leaked and direct quotes started to appear in the press:

> [w]e are concerned that Six Continents may contemplate a significant acquisition that will be value-destroying... both Intercontinental and Holiday Inn have destroyed huge amounts of

[39] The press report in the *Financial News* (2001) is illustrative of the Hermes investment disclosure and engagement style:

> [the companies] were not prepared to discuss Hermes' shareholdings. Hermes itself was also unwilling to comment on the extent of its involvement with the three FTSE 100 companies. The pension fund firm, [...], prefers to keep its brand of what it calls "shareholder engagement" quiet.

Financial News learned about the Hermes holding in Bass and two other companies from a well-known ownership database used by journalists and analysts.

shareholder value . . . this must not be allowed to happen again. (White 2002: <http://www.telegraph.co.uk/finance/2750117/Hermes-calls-for-1bn-Six-Continents-payout.html>).

In the same letter, the fund demanded for £1 billion of cash to be returned to shareholders.

On 14 April 2002, the press reported that Six Continents was preparing the requested £1 billion share buy-back. On 1 October 2002, further press reports announced the demerger of the hotels and the pubs division. On 3 March 2003, the entrepreneur Hugh Osmond launched a hostile bid.

7.3.7 Performance of the HUKFF and the Gains to Activism

In this section, we examine the performance of the fund and the contribution of activism to its performance.

Table 7.11 reports statistics for the fund over the six years and three months, until December 2004. From Hermes' detailed records, we reconstruct the complete cash flows of the fund, including inflows, dividends, and outflows. We then use such cash flows, together with the fund's market valuations at the end of each month, to compute the fund's monthly time-weighted returns for an investor who held shares at the beginning of the month.[40] Raw returns, net of fees, average 8.2% per year, and 4.9% after adjustment for the FTSE All-Share Index. These returns do not adjust for other factors such as size, book-to-market, and momentum. Table 7.12 addresses this issue by reporting performance attribution regressions. The Fund's monthly alpha is positive in all four regressions, and is significant or marginally significant in three of them, including the capital asset pricing model (CAPM), momentum, and the four-factor model. The fund's alpha is always economically large and is largest when controlling for momentum. The momentum factor is negative (and strongly significant in regression 3), indicating that the fund's performance is associated largely with reversal of the performance of previously underperforming companies.

Table 7.12 still does not adjust for potential issues arising from the dynamic trading strategy used by the fund. The risk profile of the HUKFF portfolio changes over time. The portfolio's beta changes from less than 0.6 to 1.2. However, much of this variation occurred over the first year of the fund, when the fund was invested in only eight companies or less. For the remaining period, the beta of the fund varies from slightly less than 1 to 1.2. The pattern of idiosyncratic risk is similar to that of systematic risk and ranges between 20% and 30%. The resulting monthly Sharpe Ratio of the fund is around 0.125, reflecting the risk of shareholder activism.[41]

Next, we link the event returns to the fund's overall performance, by defining and computing an activism contribution ratio (ACR) as follows:

$$ACR = \frac{\sum_{i=1}^{N} \sum_{j=1}^{J} \left[\left(MV\ of\ block \right)_{i,j,t-5} \times CAR_{j,[t-5,t+5]} \right]}{Total\ sterling\ excess\ return\ of\ fund} \qquad (1)$$

[40] Results are similar using IRRs.

[41] We also check whether the Fund's performance may be attributed to a trading strategy exploiting patterns in the higher moments of the returns' distribution. To verify this possibility, we include additional factors that have been used in the hedge funds literature (e.g., Agarwal, Daniel, and Naik 2007) to control

Table 7.11 Performance of the Hermes UK Focus Fund, 1 October 1998 to 12 December 2004

	Hermes UK Focus Fund raw returns	FTSE All	Hermes UK Focus Fund excess returns
Panel A: Raw returns and CAPM alpha over the sample period			
IRR monthly	0.660	0.270	0.390
IRR annual	8.209	3.285	4.925
Total return	63.741	22.385	41.356

Year	Management fees (%)	Performance fees (%)
Panel B: Fee structure of Hermes UK Focus Fund		
1998	100.0	0.0
1999	100.0	0.0
2000	100.0	0.0
2001	25.6	74.4
2002	31.0	69.0
2003	100.0	0.0
2004	45.6	54.4
Average	71.7	28.2

This table reports the performance of the Hermes Focus Fund asset management. Panel A reports the fund's buy-and-hold return, net of management, and performance fees. Panel B reports the fund's fee structure.

For each outcome j in the event study, we compute the sterling return of the fund for the event multiplying the market value (MV) of the block held at day −5 before the announcement by the CAR for the [−5, +5] window.[42] We then sum up these sterling returns across all the J outcomes and the N firms in the Hermes portfolio (a total of ninety-eight events) and compute them as a proportion of the total sterling excess return on the Fund between inception and 31 December 2004.[43] We find that 92% of the HUKFF's sterling excess return is accounted for by the sterling excess returns from the event study. Splitting up the total sterling return in the event study by engagement attitude, we find that 14.4% comes from engagements that we have previously described, in Section 7.1, as collaborative, whereas 30.5% occurs in engagements that are described as confrontational. The largest contribution to the overall fund return comes from the mixed engagements that contributed 55.1% of

for the time-varying risk profile, including the volatility, kurtosis, and skewness factors. In unreported regressions available upon request, we find that the additional factors are not statistically significant, and the fund's alpha is only minimally affected.

[42] We can do this because the fund gave us complete access to its portfolio holdings at any moment in time, so we exactly know how many shares were held over each event window.

[43] The sterling excess return for the Fund as a whole is the sum of annual returns in excess of the market index that Hermes computes for remuneration purposes; the numbers are audited.

Table 7.12 **Performance attribution regressions**

	CAPM (1)	FF (2)	Mom (3)	FF + Mom (4)
α	0.77	0.41	1.42	0.86
	(0.10)	(0.31)	(0.02)	(–0.1)
RMRF	1.16	1.13	1.04	1.10
	(0.000)	(0.000)	(0.000)	(0.000)
SMB		0.39		0.41
		(0.000)		(0.000)
HML		0.34		0.34
		(0.000)		(0.000)
Momentum			.0.34	.0.13
			(0.02)	(0.29)
No. of observations	75	75	57	57

The dependent variable is the monthly time-weighted rate of return net of both management and performance fees of the Focus Fund Hermes portfolio in excess of the risk-free rate, as proxied by the UK gilts rate. Factor regressions of value-weighted monthly returns are then estimated and the results reported below. The table reports the raw monthly return, the intercept α, and the coefficients (factor loadings) on the explanatory variables RMRF, SMB, HML, and Momentum. These variables are the returns to zero-investment portfolios designed to capture market, size, book-to-market, and momentum effects, respectively. RMRF, SMB, and HML are computed by Alan Gregory for the United Kingdom using the methodology of Fama and French (1993) and Carhart (1997); Momentum is computed by Chui, Titman, and Wei (2005) for the United Kingdom using the methodology of Jegadeesh and Titman (1993). The sample period is from October 1998 to December 2004 (seventy-five monthly observations) for the dependent variable. *p*-values are reported in parenthesis.

the sterling return in the event outcomes. Thus, hostility is related to higher gains than collaboration, but the highest returns come from mixed engagements. This result compares to the gains to hostile versus friendly takeovers, measured by target bid premiums, which are far larger in hostile transactions (Franks and Mayer 1996). It also stands in a sharp contrast to the evidence on bidder returns in takeovers, with bidders earning very small or negative returns in friendly and hostile takeovers; the returns of the HUKFF from the engagement outcomes are positive throughout.

7.3.8 Returns to Free-Riding on the HUKFF

Table 7.13 attempts to determine if other investors could have earned the same return as Hermes by buying into the engaged companies at the time of the first public announcement of a block purchase by the Hermes Group. If shareholders had bought shares in target firms on the date of the public disclosure of the stake purchases of the HUKFF, they would have earned a 12.58% raw return per year if they had rebalanced in the same way as Hermes, or a 14.25% if they had not rebalanced, but simply kept the shares until December

Table 7.13 Returns to various replicating portfolios

Replicating portfolio	Rebalancing	Annual raw return (%)
Hermes' net of fees	Yes	8.21
Hermes' gross of fees	Yes	10.07
Private info. (first day)	No	9.65
Private info. (first week)	No	10.65
Private info. (first month)	No	10.17
Public info.	Yes	12.58
Public info.	No	14.25

This table reports annual raw returns to trading strategies designed to replicate Hermes' trading strategy, based on private or public information, with or without rebalancing. Returns to Hermes' actual portfolio, net, and gross of fees are reported as a benchmark.

2004.[44] This compares with a raw return on the Fund of 8.2% annually. The crude comparison suggests that public shareholders would have done better than Hermes by buying at the public announcements of the disclosed stakes.

Next, we examine the returns that shareholders would have earned if they had invested on the private information of Hermes' first day (first week and first month, respectively) investments in target companies, and then fail to rebalance afterward. That is, we assume that (minority) shareholders heard the 'rumour' that Hermes had invested, but then did not have the subsequent information of Hermes' rebalancing activity. We find that such shareholders would have earned an annual return of about 10%, which is slightly better than the Fund's annual return of 8.2%. These results confirm that Hermes' returns are unlikely to be associated with trading on private information.[45]

Taken together, the findings confirm that when its stakes are disclosed, the HUKFF generates positive externalities. They also suggest that the Fund does not invest because it has insider information. It takes positions before starting the engagement process and—as shown in Table 7.7—takes small losses when its initial stakes are disclosed. *Ex post* the fund more than recovers these initial losses from positive abnormal returns on publicly observable outcomes.

7.3.9 Comparison with US Hedge Fund Activism Evidence

Two US studies (Brav et al., Chapter 8, this volume; Klein and Zur, Chapter 9, this volume) analyse how stock prices react to the announcement that a hedge fund has acquired a significant holding of 5% or more in a listed target company (Schedule 13D filing). They also investigate what kind of company is targeted, the stated objective of the engagement, and its outcome.

44 These portfolios are reported in Table 7.13 under the heading 'Public info portfolio'.

45 The evidence is also consistent with the Fund management's view that it tends to build up its initial stake when the share price has negative momentum.

Brav et al. (Chapter 8, this volume) identify 110 activist hedge funds in 2004 and 2005 that disclose 374 block holdings in 339 targets. They find that these announcements generate positive shareholder returns for the target, totalling 6% (median 4.8%) over a twenty-one-day window straddling the announcement.

Klein and Zur (Chapter 9, this volume) examine similar filings between 1 January 2003 and 31 December 2005. They identify 102 different hedge funds that engage 155 target firms disclosing 194 block holdings. They find abnormal returns of 7.3% for a window beginning thirty days prior to the announcement and five days after the announcement.

Whereas Brav et al. (Chapter 8, this volume) are positive about the activities of hedge funds, Klein and Zur (Chapter 9, this volume) are more sceptical, observing that hedge funds target companies that outperformed the market prior to the engagement.[46] Moreover, accounting measures of performance decrease one year after the engagement. Both studies document significant levels of CEO/chairman removal following the block disclosure. They also find that hedge fund activists often seek and obtain board positions. Klein and Zur (Chapter 9, this volume) find the activists achieve their goals more often when they bring or threaten a proxy fight.

A related set of studies present evidence that hedge funds use stock lending to enhance their voting power over their ownership stake; they also engage in swap and other derivative transactions to alter the relationship between their economic interest and voting power in the target companies (Christoffersen et al. 2007; Hu and Black 2006).

7.4 Conclusions

In contrast to much of the previous literature, this chapter has reported substantial effects and benefits associated with shareholder activism in the form of private engagements by an activist fund. This fund, the HUKFF, intervenes in the face of poor corporate performance where it believes that there is a significant probability of intervention being successful and resulting in substantial share price gains. It engages in meetings with board members, often seeking the support of other institutional investors, sometimes mobilizing press campaigns, but rarely relying on resolutions at shareholder meetings. It seeks corporate restructurings, changes to the boards of firms, and restrictions on corporate policies (e.g., takeovers and investments), sometimes requiring changes in financial policy, particularly dividend distributions. A high proportion of the interventions are successful and result in substantial shareholder gains, particularly in response to restructurings and board changes. These successful outcomes account for a large proportion of the significant outperformance of the fund relative to a variety of benchmarks over the sample period.

In sum, this study provides the first substantive evidence of gains to shareholder activism and suggests that well-focused engagements can result in substantial public returns to

[46] Klein and Zur (Chapter 9, this volume) observed that hedge fund activists appear to extract cash from the firm through increasing the debt capacity of the target firm and paying themselves higher dividends. The latter result, coupled with the positive stock price reaction surrounding the 13D filing date, suggests that stockholders perceive benefits to reducing agency costs associated with excess cash and short-term investments.

outside shareholders, as well as to those actually involved in the engagements.[47] This suggests an interesting line of research: that the legal environment might have a significant impact on activism by institutional shareholders.

APPENDIX

Classification of Engagement Attitude

The attitude of engagements was classified into confrontational, mixed, and collaborative. The classification is based on the subjective judgement of current and former fund staff and was corroborated by the authors using letters, memos of meetings and telephone conversations, and press reports.

For each of the thirty companies that were engaged, we asked the staff to classify the attitude towards the fund at the beginning of the engagement, recording the attitude separately for the chairman and the CEO (when the roles were split). The attitude was ranked using a score from 1 to 10, ranging from totally collaborative (1) to very confrontational (10). A score of 1 was never assigned, but a score of 2 was in several cases. A score of 10 was only assigned once.

Confrontational

Engagements were classified as confrontational when the target CEO initially rejected the proposals for change that were put to the company by the Focus Fund and this attitude did not change, or did not change voluntarily, throughout the engagement period. Engagements where the fund sought to replace the CEO and/or the chairman against their will were also classified as confrontational.

The confrontational attitude finds clear expression in the exchange of letters between the Focus Fund and the company and, often even more clearly, in meeting notes. The following examples provide illustrations of confrontational cases. Two were 'very confrontational' and were publicly hostile.

Case 1. The Focus Fund tried (and failed) to oust the chairman of the target company A and replace him with an independent outside chairman. The chairman and the target company resisted these changes. Press reports described the engagement as a 'battle' or 'storm'; another wrote 'Company A launched a blistering attack on two of its largest institutional investors yesterday, who had proposed the [company] be broken up in a radical restructuring.'

Case 2. The Focus Fund and other institutions worked with a blockholder to oust family members, who were considered to be responsible for the underperformance of the target company. One newspaper observed, 'the battle for control of company B, [. . .], is now pitting some

[47] Additional suggestive evidence stems from the observation that, after the results in the present chapter were presented, a number of UK institutional investors have started new activist funds.

of the City's richest and most prominent names against each other and threatening to spill some very blue blood on the carpet'.

The following are less obvious examples of confrontational cases:

Case 3. A letter from the fund to a NED of a target company:

> The purpose of this letter is to formally express our dissatisfaction with the performance of Company A PLC and advise that the current board can no longer rely on Hermes support as a representative of shareholders. Hermes believes that non-executive directors must be held accountable for long term destruction of shareholder value. We therefore support significant and early changes to the executive and non-executive components of the board and wish to see the process of restructuring completed before the end of the year.

Case 4. A letter to the executive chairman of the board of a company where the Fund sought a change in CEO:

> To recap, it seems sensible to leave any major strategic moves until the new CEO is appointed and to allow him, or her, to own the way forward. As you said, it is many years since there was any new thinking in the business. Having said that I think it is fair to say that I suspect shareholders will need a lot of convincing that only the operations need to change, not the shape of the business.

Mixed

In the mixed engagements, the demands of the Focus Fund were implemented reluctantly or grudgingly.

The following is a typical example of a mixed attitude engagement.

Case 5. Passage taken from the last paragraph of a letter written to the finance director:

> Thank you once again for a fascinating day. We were very impressed by XX, and by the progress and effort which has characterized the last few years. However, as this letter has outlined, there are some areas where we have concerns, and these may be reflected amongst investors generally.
>
> The mixed category is less extreme and therefore more subjective than either confrontational or collaborative.

Collaborative

In the vast majority of the collaborative engagements there is no doubt about the attitude of the engagement.

A letter from the Focus Fund, sent to the group CEO of a collaborative engagement towards the end of the engagement:

> I remember when we first met, you talked about your early days at Company XY, when the future of British industry looked bleak and you were negotiating your way around daft restrictive practices. I'm sure that if you had told people then, that you would end up creating a British based [...] company, employing over 30,000 people, which was a global leader in its field, they would never have believed it. It is a fantastic achievement.

References

Agarwal, V., Daniel, N. D., and Naik, N. Y. (2009). Role of Managerial Incentives and Discretion in Hedge Fund Performance, *Journal of Finance* 64(5), 2221–56.

Aghion, P. and Tirole, J. (1997). Formal and Real Authority in Organizations, *Journal of Political Economy* 105, 1–29.

Anson, M., White, T., and Ho, H. (2004). Good Governance Works: More Evidence from CalPERS, *Journal of Asset Management* 5, 149–56.

Bebchuk, L. A. (2005). The Case for Increasing Shareholder Power, *Harvard Law Review* 118, 833–917.

Bebchuk, L. A., Coates IV, J., and Subramanian, G. (2002). The Powerful Antitakeover Force of Staggered Boards: Further Findings and a Reply to Symposium Participants, *Stanford Law Review* 55, 885–917.

Bethel, J. E. and Gillan, S. L. (2002). The Impact of the Institutional and Regulatory Environment on Shareholder Voting, *Financial Management* 31, 29–54.

Bethel, J. E. and Gillan, S. L. (2007). Relationship Investing, Corporate Change and Shareholder Value, Babson College and Texas Tech University Working Paper.

Black, B. S. (1990). Shareholder Passivity Re-Examined, *Michigan Law Review* 89, 520–608.

Black, B. S. (1992). Agents Watching Agents: The Promise of Institutional Investor Voice, *UCLA Law Review* 39, 811–93.

Black, B. S. (1998). Shareholder Activism and Corporate Governance in the US, in P. Newman (ed.), *The New Palgrave Dictionary of Economics and the Law* (London and Basingstoke, Palgrave Macmillan) 459–65.

Black, B. S. and Coffee Jr, J. C. (1994). Hail Britannia? Institutional Investor Behavior Under Limited Regulation, *Michigan Law Review* 92, 1997–2087.

Boyson, N. M. and Mooradian, R. M. (2007). Hedge Funds as Shareholder Activists from 1994–2005, Working Paper, available at <http://ssrn.com/abstract=992739>.

Carhart, M. (1997). On Persistence in Mutual Fund Performance, *Journal of Finance* 52, 57–82.

Carleton, W. T., Nelson, J. M., and Weisbach, M. S. (1998). The Influence of Institutions on Corporate Governance through Private Negotiations: Evidence from TIAA-CREF, *Journal of Finance* 53, 1335–62.

Christoffersen, S. E. K., Geczy, C. C., Musto, D. K., and Reed, A. V. (2007). Vote Trading and Information Aggregation, *Journal of Finance* 62, 2897–929.

Chui, A. C. W., Titman, S., and Wei, K. C. J. (2005). Momentum, Legal Systems and Ownership Structure, University of Texas Working Paper, available at <http://ssrn.com/abstract=265848>.

Dedman, E. and Lin, S. W. J. (2002). Shareholder Wealth Effects of CEO Departures: Evidence from the UK, *Journal of Corporate Finance* 8, 81–104.

Del Guercio, D. and Hawkins, J. (1999). The Motivation and Impact of Pension Fund Activism, *Journal of Financial Economics* 52, 293–340.

Dimopoulos, T. (2006). Does Firing Top Management Improve Firm Performance? Evidence from the UK, London Business School Working Paper.

Doward, J., Islam, F., and Hirst, C. (1999). Pub Group Greenalls next on Hermes Investor 'Hit List', *Observer* (31 Jan.), at 1.

Dyck, A., Volchkova, N., and Zingales, L. (2008). The Corporate Governance Role of the Media: Evidence from Russia, *Journal of Finance* 63, 1093–135.

English, P. C., Smythe, T. I., and McNeil, C. R. (2004). The 'CalPERS Effect' Revisited, *Journal of Corporate Finance* 10, 157–74.

Faccio, M. and Lasfer, M. A. (2000). Do Occupational Pension Funds Monitor Companies in Which They Hold Large Stakes?, *Journal of Corporate Finance* 6, 71–110.

Fama, E. F. and French, V. (1993). Common Risk Factors in the Returns of Stocks and Bonds, *Journal of Financial Economics* 33, 3–56.

Financial News (2001). Hermes Sets Its Sights on UK's Largest Firms, *Financial News* (20 Aug.).

Franks, J. R. and Mayer, C. P. (1996). Hostile Takeovers and the Correction of Managerial Failure, *Journal of Financial Economics* 40, 163–84.

Gillan, S. L. and Starks, L. T. (1998). A Survey of Shareholder Activism: Motivation and Empirical Evidence, *Contemporary Finance Digest* 2, 10–34.

Global Proxy Watch (2006). *Global Proxy Watch X*, 33.

Guerrera, F. and Targett, S. (2002). Brussels Set to Shake Up Corporate Governance: The European Commission is Looking to Pave the Way for a Shareholder Democracy, *Financial Times* (London), (25 Feb.), at 1.

Hu, H. and Black, B. (2006). Empty Voting and Hidden (Morphable) Ownership: Taxonomy, Implications, and Reforms, *Business Lawyer* 61(3), 1011–70.

Institutional Shareholders' Committee (2005). *The Responsibilities of Institutional Shareholders and Agents—Statement of Principle* (London, Institutional Shareholders' Committee).

Jegadeesh, N. and Titman, S. (1993). Returns to Buying Winners and Selling Losers: Implications for Stock Market Efficiency, *Journal of Finance* 48, 65–91.

Karpoff, J. M. (2001). The Impact of Shareholder Activism on Target Companies: A Survey of Empirical Findings, University of Washington Working Paper.

Kraakman, R., Davies, P., Hansmann, H., Hertig, G., Hopt, K., Kanda, H., and Rock, E. B. (eds.) (2004). *The Anatomy of Corporate Law: A Comparative and Functional Approach* (Oxford, Oxford University Press).

Lipton, M. and Rosenblum, S. A. (1991). A New System of Corporate Governance: The Quinquennial Election of Directors, *University of Chicago Law Review* 58, 187–253.

MacKintosh, J. and Targett, S. (2001). Activist Fund Buys into Caledonia, *Financial Times* (London), (26 July), at 20.

Menon, A., Balachandran, B., Faff, R., and Love, R. (2004). Announcements of Voluntary Corporate Selloffs: A Comparative Country Analysis of their Impact on Shareholder Wealth, EFMA 2004 Basel Meetings Paper, available at <http://ssrn.com/abstract=499463>.

Monks, R. A. G. (2005). *Stock in Tirade: The Financial Communications Quarterly from the Exchange* (8th edn.) (London, London Stock Exchange).

Nesbitt, S. L. (1994). Long-Term Rewards from Shareholder Activism: A Study of the 'CalPERS' Effect, *Journal of Applied Corporate Finance* 6, 75–80.

NYSE (New York Stock Exchange) (2006). *Report and Recommendations of the Proxy Working Group to the New York Stock Exchange* (5 June) (New York, NYSE).

Opler, T. C. and Sokobin, J. S. (1995). Does Coordinated Institutional Activism Work? An Analysis of the Activities of the Council of Institutional Investors, Dice Center for Research in Financial Economics, Working Papers Series 95-5, available at <http://ssrn.com/abstract=46880>.

Partnoy, F. and Thomas, R. S. (2007). Gap Filling, Hedge Funds, and Financial Innovation, in Y. Fuchita and R. E. Litan (eds.), *Brookings-Nomura Papers on Financial Services* (Washington, DC, Brookings Institution Press) 101–40.

Qiu, L. (2006). Which Institutional Investors Monitor? Evidence from Acquisition Activity, Brown Economics Working Paper Series No. 2004-21; Yale ICF Working Paper No. 04-15, available at <http://ssrn.com/abstract=521803>.

Romano, R. (1993). Public Pension Fund Activism in Corporate Governance Reconsidered, *Columbia Law Review* 93, 795–853.

Romano, R. (2001). Less is More: Making Shareholder Activism a Valued Mechanism of Corporate Governance, *Yale Journal on Regulation* 18, 174–251.

Smith, M. P. (1996). Shareholder Activism by Institutional Investors: Evidence from CalPERS, *Journal of Finance* 51, 227–52.

Strickland, D., Wiles, K. W., and Zenner, M. (1996). A Requiem for the USA: Is Small Shareholder Monitoring Effective?, *Journal of Financial Economics* 40, 319–98.

Tucker, S. (2005). Putting Focus Funds under the Spotlight, *Financial Times* (28 Mar.), available at <http://www.ft.com/intl/cms/s/0/a1b8e3ae-9f25-11d9-82f0-00000e2511c8.html#axzz3Ls06M2T4>.

White, D. (2002). Hermes Calls for £1bn Six Continents Payout, *Daily Telegraph* (21 Jan.).

CHAPTER 8

HEDGE FUND ACTIVISM, CORPORATE GOVERNANCE, AND FIRM PERFORMANCE

ALON BRAV, WEI JIANG, FRANK PARTNOY, AND RANDALL S. THOMAS

8.1 Introduction

Although hedge fund activism is widely discussed and fundamentally important, it remains poorly understood. Much of the commentary on hedge fund activism is based on supposition or anecdotal evidence. Critics and regulators question whether hedge fund activism benefits shareholders, while numerous commentators claim that hedge fund activists destroy value by distracting managers from long-term projects. However, there is a dearth of large-sample evidence about hedge fund activism, and existing samples are plagued by various biases. As a result, even the most basic questions about hedge fund activism remain unanswered: which firms do activists target and how do those targets respond? How does the market react to the announcement of activism? Do activists succeed in implementing their objectives? Are activists short-term in focus? How does activism impact firm performance? In this chapter, we answer these questions by constructing the most extensive and thoroughly documented set of observations of hedge fund activism to date, extending from the beginning of 2001 through to the end of 2006.

We find that hedge funds increasingly engage in a new form of shareholder activism and monitoring that differs fundamentally from previous activist efforts by other institutional investors. Earlier studies showed that when institutional investors, particularly mutual funds and pension funds, followed an activist agenda, they did not achieve significant benefits for shareholders (Black 1998; Gillan and Starks, Chapter 2, this volume; Karpoff 2001; Romano 2001). Our results suggest that the opposite is true of hedge funds. Unlike mutual funds and pension funds, hedge funds are able to influence corporate boards and managements due to key differences arising from their different organizational form and incentives that they face. Hedge funds employ highly incentivized managers who manage large unregulated pools of capital. Lack of regulation implies that they are able to hold highly concentrated positions in small numbers of companies, and make use of leverage and derivatives. Hedge fund managers also suffer few conflicts of interest because they are not beholden to the management of the firms whose shares they hold. In sum, hedge funds are better positioned to act as informed monitors than other institutional investors.

Hedge fund activists tend to target companies that are typically 'value' firms, with low market value relative to book value, although they are profitable with sound operating cash flows and return on assets. Payout at these companies before intervention is lower than that of a matched sample. Target companies also have more takeover defences and pay their CEOs more than comparable companies. Relatively few targeted companies are large-cap firms, which is not surprising given the relatively high cost of amassing a meaningful stake in such a target. Targets exhibit significantly higher institutional ownership and trading liquidity. These characteristics make it easier for activists to acquire a significant stake quickly.

Our first piece of evidence regarding the impact of hedge fund activism is based on the market reaction to intervention announcements. We find that the market reacts favourably to activism, consistent with the view that it creates value. The filing of a Schedule 13D revealing an activist fund's investment in a target firm results in large positive average abnormal returns, in the range of 7 to 8%, during the [-20, +20] announcement window. The increase in both price and abnormal trading volume of target shares begins one to ten days prior to filing. We find that the positive returns at announcement are not reversed over time, as there is no evidence of a negative abnormal drift during the one-year period subsequent to the announcement. We also document that the positive abnormal returns are only marginally lower for hedge funds that disclosed substantial ownership positions (through quarterly Form 13F filings) before they file a Schedule 13D, which is consistent with the view that the abnormal returns are due to new information about activism, not merely that about stock picking. Moreover, target prices decline upon the exit of a hedge fund only after it has been unsuccessful, which indicates that the information reflected in the positive announcement returns conveys the market's expectation for the success of activism.

We next examine the cross-section of these abnormal returns. Activism that targets the sale of the company or changes in business strategy, such as refocusing and spinning-off non-core assets, is associated with the largest positive abnormal partial effects of 8.54% and 5.95%, respectively (the latter figure is lower than the overall sample average because most events target multiple issues). This evidence suggests that hedge funds are able to create value when they see large allocative inefficiencies. In contrast, we find that the market response to capital-structure-related activism—including debt restructuring, recapitalization, dividends, and share repurchases—is positive, yet insignificant. We find a similar lack of statistically meaningful reaction for governance-related activism—including attempts to rescind takeover defences, to oust CEOs, to enhance board independence, and to curtail CEO compensation. Hedge funds with a track record of successful activism generate higher returns, as do hedge funds that initiate activism with hostile tactics.

The positive market reaction is also consistent with *ex post* evidence of overall improved performance at target firms. On average, from the year before announcement to the year after, total payout increases by 0.3–0.5 percentage points (as a percentage of the market value of equity, relative to an all-sample mean of 2.2 percentage points), and book value leverage increases by 1.3–1.4 percentage points (relative to an all-sample mean of 33.5 percentage points). Both changes are consistent with a reduction of agency problems associated with free cash flow and subject managers to increased market discipline. We also find improvement in return on assets and operating profit margins, but this takes longer to happen. The post-event year sees little change compared to the year prior to intervention. However, EBITDA/Assets (EBITDA/Sales) at target firms increase by 0.9–1.5 (4.7–5.8) percentage points by two years after intervention. Analyst expectations also suggest improved prospects at target firms after hedge fund intervention. During the months before Schedule 13D filings, analysts downgrade (future) targets more than they upgrade them, whereas after intervention is announced analysts maintain neutral ratings. Given that successful activism often leads to attrition through the sale of the target company, *ex post* performance analysis based on surviving firms may underestimate the positive effect of activism.

Hedge fund activists are not short-term in focus, as some critics have claimed. The median holding period for completed deals is about one year, calculated as running from the date a hedge fund files a Schedule 13D to the date when the fund no longer holds a significant stake in the target company. The calculation substantially understates the actual median holding period, because it necessarily excludes a significant number of events for which no exit information is available by March 2007. Analysis of portfolio turnover rates of the funds in our sample suggests holding periods of closer to twenty months.

Because shareholders are by no means the only party affected by hedge fund activism we ask whether other stakeholders are impacted. In particular, we consider the possibility that the positive stock market reaction to activism might reflect wealth redistribution from creditors and executives. We find that hedge fund activism does not shift value from creditors to shareholders. Indeed, the 174 targets with no long-term debt have slightly higher announcement returns than the rest of the sample. On the other hand, we do see evidence that hedge fund activism shifts value away from senior managers. In particular, hedge fund activism is not kind to CEOs of target firms. During the year after the announcement of activism, average CEO pay declines by about 1 million dollars, and the CEO turnover rate increases by almost 10 percentage points, controlling for the normal turnover rates in the same industry, and for firms of similar size and stock valuation.

An important feature of our sample is that we include both hostile and non-hostile interactions between funds and targets. Although some commentators have characterized hedge fund activism as fundamentally hostile to managers, we actually find that hedge fund activists are openly hostile in less than 30% of cases (hostility includes a threatened or actual proxy contest, takeover, lawsuit, or public campaign that is openly confrontational). More commonly, hedge fund activists cooperate with managers, at least at the initial stages, and achieve all or most of their stated goals in about two-thirds of all cases. Managerial opposition to hedge fund activism may stem from its negative impact on CEO pay and turnover even if it ultimately creates value for shareholders.

Our findings have important implications for the policy debate about hedge fund activism. Although some prominent legal commentators, including leading corporate lawyers and European regulators, have called for restrictions on hedge fund activism because of its supposedly short-term orientation, our result suggest that activist hedge funds are not short-term holders. Activists also appear to generate substantial value for target firm shareholders. Indeed, our evidence of the market's positive response to hedge fund activism, and the subsequent success of activists, challenges the premises of proposals requiring increased hedge fund regulation.

For policymakers, our chapter shows important distinctions between the role of hedge funds and other private institutional investors, such as private equity firms. Despite their frequently aggressive behaviour, activist hedge funds do not typically seek control in target companies. The median maximum ownership stake for the entire sample is about 9.1%. Even at the 95th percentile in the full sample, the stake is 31.5%—far short of the level for majority control. Activists rely on cooperation from management or, in its absence, support from fellow shareholders to implement their value-improving agendas. This explains why hedge fund activists tend to target companies with higher institutional holdings and analyst coverage, both of which suggest a more sophisticated shareholder base. It is also common for multiple hedge funds to coordinate by cofiling Schedule 13Ds (about 22% of the sample) or acting in tandem without being a formal block. Although some regulators have criticized such informal block behaviour as anti-competitive, coordination among hedge funds can benefit shareholders overall by facilitating activism at relatively low individual ownership stakes.

The new evidence presented in this chapter suggests that activist hedge funds occupy an important middle ground between internal monitoring by large shareholders and external monitoring by corporate raiders. Activist hedge funds are more flexible, incentivized, and independent than internal monitors, and they can generate multiple gains from targeting several companies on similar issues. Conversely, activist hedge funds have advantages over external corporate raiders, because they take smaller stakes, benefit from cooperation with management, and have support from other shareholders. This hybrid internal/external role puts activist hedge funds in a potentially unique position to reduce the agency costs associated with the separation of ownership and control.

The rest of the chapter proceeds as follows. Section 8.2 provides the institutional background and literature review about shareholder activism. Section 8.3 describes the sample. Section 8.4 discusses the characteristics of target companies. Section 8.5 looks at stock market reaction to hedge fund activism. Section 8.6 analyses firm performance before and after activism. We present some conclusions in Section 8.7.

8.2 Institutional Background and Literature Review

The activist blockholders of the 1980s are probably the closest ancestors to hedge fund activists. Bethel, Liebeskind, and Opler (1998) compiled a sample of such blockholders including activists; financial organizations (including banks, pension funds, money managers, and insurance companies); and strategic investors, such as conglomerates. They found that activist blockholders targeted poorly performing companies, that their activism led to increased asset divestitures and share repurchases, and that their investments were associated with improvements in profitability and shareholder value. Financial and strategic blockholders also targeted underperforming companies, but their targets showed smaller changes in their operations and profitability, and the market reaction to these investors' block purchases was insignificant as well.

In response to these more successful forms of shareholder activism during the 1980s, firms implemented a variety of takeover defences, many of which were upheld by courts. These defences increasingly deterred control transactions by takeover activists. As hostile transactions seeking control declined, so did the role of control-driven shareholder activists (although such control-driven activism has recently resurfaced, particularly in going private transactions). Meanwhile, mutual funds and pension funds continued to press activist agendas, including corporate governance reform and a range of social and political issues, again with minimal impact.

For the past twenty years, institutional investors, religious organizations, labour unions, individuals, and other groups have engaged in shareholder activism, but with mixed results. Public pension funds and other activist investors have engaged in shareholder activism using Rule 14a-8, which permits shareholder proposals on a variety of topics (Karpoff, Malatesta, and Walkling 1996). Larger public pension funds and mutual funds have tried a variety of other techniques to influence corporate management (Smith 1996; Wahal 1996; Carleton, Nelson, and Weisbach 1998; Del Guercio and Hawkins 1999; Del Guercio and Hawkins 1999; Gillan and Starks 2000). As several literature surveys have shown, the results of this type of activism by these institutions have been disappointing: they cause only small changes to firms' corporate governance structures and do not measurably affect stock prices or earnings (Black 1998; Karpoff 2001; Romano 2001; Barber 2006; Del Guercio, Wallis, and Woidtke 2008; Gillan and Starks, Chapter 2, this volume). More recently Becht et al. (Chapter 7, this volume) gather data on non-public and public activism by Hermes UK, a leading UK pension fund. They do not find positive market reaction to public notification of Hermes's stake, although there is a significant 3% market reaction to governance outcomes of Hermes's activism.

Institutional investor monitoring generally has been plagued by regulatory and structural barriers, including: collective action issues that lead to free-riding on the efforts of others (Black 1990; Kahan and Rock, Chapter 5, this volume); conflicts of interest, such as those mutual funds face when considering activism with regard to future clients (Black 1990); regulatory constraints, including diversification requirements and insider trading regulations (Black 1990); political constraints where managers are constrained by local and state politics from engaging in activism (Romano 1993); and weak personal financial incentives for fund managers to engage in interventions (Rock 1992). Due to these limitations, the 'Wall Street Rule' often becomes the default form of institutional shareholder activism (Admati and Pfleiderer 2009).

For example, mutual funds are constrained by tax laws from taking overly concentrated positions in any one company or groups of companies. The Securities and Exchange Commission (SEC) also limits the types of fees that companies regulated by the Investment Company Act of 1940 may charge. Similarly, regulated funds are subject to restrictions on shorting, borrowing, and investing in illiquid securities. There are exemptions from SEC rules, but they generally require either that the fund remain private (by not offering investments to the public and maintaining no more than 100 investors) or that the fund have only 'qualified' high net worth investors (the current definition requires that a person must own at least $5 million of investments to be 'qualified'). As a result, any investment fund that is broadly sold to the public or that has investors without substantial net worth is prohibited, among other things, from holding concentrated positions and charging substantial performance fees.

Hedge funds are different. Although there is no generally agreed-upon definition of a hedge fund—a SEC roundtable discussion on hedge funds considered fourteen different possible definitions (SEC Roundtable on Hedge Funds 2003)[1]—hedge funds are

[1] See <http://www.connectlive.com/events/sechedgefunds/>.

usually identified by four characteristics: (1) they are pooled, privately organized investment vehicles; (2) they are administered by professional investment managers with performance-based compensation and significant investments in the fund; (3) they are not widely available to the public; and (4) they operate outside of securities regulation and registration requirements (Partnoy and Thomas 2007). More specifically, hedge funds avoid the Investment Company Act of 1940 by having a relatively small number of sophisticated investors.

The typical hedge fund is a partnership entity managed by a general partner; the investors are limited partners who are passive and have little or no say in the hedge fund's business. Hedge fund managers have sharp incentives to generate positive returns because their pay depends primarily on performance. A typical hedge fund charges its investors a fixed annual fee of 2% of its assets plus a 20% performance fee based on the fund's annual return. Although managers of other institutions can be awarded bonus compensation in part based on performance, their incentives tend to be more muted because they capture a much smaller percentage of any returns, and because the Investment Company Act of 1940 limits performance fees.

Hedge fund managers can take much larger relative positions than other institutions because they are not required by law to maintain diversified portfolios. Unlike mutual funds, hedge funds may hold large percentage stakes in individual companies and may require that investors agree to 'lock-up' their funds for period of two years or longer. In contrast, mutual funds are required by law to hold diversified portfolios, and to sell securities within one day to satisfy investor redemptions. Moreover, because hedge funds do not fall under the Investment Company Act regulation, they are permitted to trade on margin and engage in derivatives trading, strategies that are not available to other institutions, such as mutual and pension funds. As a result, hedge funds have greater flexibility in trading than other institutions.

Unlike many institutional investors, such as pension funds, hedge funds are generally not subject to heightened fiduciary standards, such as those embodied in ERISA. The majority of hedge fund investors tend to be wealthy individuals and large institutions, and hedge funds typically raise capital through private offerings that are not subject to extensive disclosure requirements or other regulations. Although hedge fund managers are bound by the anti-fraud provisions of United States securities laws, they are not otherwise subject to more extensive regulation, such as 'prudent man' investing standards.

Finally, hedge fund managers typically suffer fewer conflicts of interest than managers at other institutions. For example, unlike mutual funds that are affiliated with large financial institutions, hedge funds do not sell products to the firms whose shares they hold. Unlike pension funds, hedge funds are not subject to extensive state or local influence, or political control.

Therefore, hedge fund managers have powerful and independent incentives to generate positive returns. Although many private equity or venture capital funds also have these characteristics, those funds are distinguished from hedge funds because of their focus on particular private capital markets. Private equity investors typically target private firms or going private transactions, and acquire larger percentage ownership stakes than hedge fund activists. Venture capital investors typically target private firms exclusively, with a view to selling the company, merging, or going public, and therefore they invest at much earlier stages than both private equity and activist hedge funds. Nevertheless, the lines among these investors are not always crisp, and there is some substantive overlap, particularly between some private equity firms and activist hedge funds. Moreover, hedge funds (and private equity firms) frequently pursue multiple strategies, and some of the hedge funds in our sample are not exclusively activist in nature.

There have been a few attempts at studying hedge fund activism based on limited samples. Bradley et al. (2007) collect a comprehensive sample of hedge fund activism aimed at opening up discounted closed-end funds, and analyse its impact on closed-end fund governance and discount dynamics. A few recent papers have studied hedge fund activism in the US. Generally, these papers do not provide a complete explanation of the role of hedge fund activism due to the size and selection of the sample. For example, Bratton (2007) and Kahan and Rock (Chapter 5, this volume) assemble useful anecdotal evidence of hedge fund activism, but cover only a small percentage of the events in our sample and do not examine returns, performance, or cross-sectional variation in any detail.

Two recent papers study US hedge fund activism. Klein and Zur (Chapter 9, this volume) use a sample of 194 Schedule 13D filings by hedge fund activists from 2003 to 2005, although they omit activism below the 5% threshold and most of the non-confrontational hedge fund activism, where hedge fund managers worked collaboratively with portfolio firm management. Clifford (2008) collects a sample of 1,902 firm-fund observations over the period 1998–2005, but only examines stock price reaction and changes in operating performance without analysing the pattern of targeting, company response, and outcome of the interventions. Both papers find that hedge fund activism generates significantly higher abnormal stock returns than a control sample of passive blockholders, indicating the value of intervention.

8.3 Data and Overview

8.3.1 The Activism Sample

There is no central database of activist hedge funds. We therefore construct an independent sample based mostly on Schedule 13D filings, the mandatory federal securities law filings under section 13(d) of the 1934 Exchange Act that investors must file with the SEC within ten days of acquiring more than 5% of any class of securities of a publicly traded company if they have an interest in influencing the management of the company. Congress intended that the filing of a Schedule 13D would notify the market that the filer might seek to force changes or seek control at target companies.[2] In particular, Item 4 of Schedule 13D requires the filer

[2] In contrast, passive institutional investors that acquire more than 5%, but less than 10%, of the company's stock and do not intend to seek to influence control at the target company, but are merely investing in the ordinary course of business, file a Schedule 13G within forty-five days of the end of the calendar year in which they crossed this ownership threshold. Those passive investors accumulating more than 10% of the stock must file within ten days after the end of the first month in which they exceed 10%. Alternatively, any person that would be otherwise obligated to file a Schedule 13D may file a Schedule 13G if they do not intend to attempt to change control of the issuer and do not hold more than 20% of the issuer's stock. If they elect this option, then they must file within ten days of crossing the 5% threshold. Typically, the filing of a Schedule 13G does not foreshadow an activist event. However, if an institutional investor changes its initial passive purpose and decides to become active, it would need to file a Schedule 13D to announce this shift to the market.

to declare its reasons for acquiring the shares, particularly if the intention is to engage in merger and acquisition activity, seek a sale of any material amount of the issuer's assets, pursue a change in its capitalization or dividend policy, or propose other types of corporate changes.

Our data collection is based on a three-step procedure. As a first step, we purchased a list of all Schedule 13D filers during the period 2001–06 from LiveEDGAR, a for-profit organization that offers access to SEC filings in a user-friendly format. There are a total of 11,602 such filers. Based on the names and the descriptions of the filer type listed in Item 2 ('Identity and Background') of Schedule 13D, we were able to manually filter out the following filer types: banks, brokerage companies, regular corporations, foreign institutions, individuals, insurance companies, pension funds, trusts, and other miscellaneous categories. The remaining filers are hedge funds, private equity/venture capital funds, and some non-fund investment advisors, categories that are often difficult to distinguish. We searched the Internet for the websites of these filers and news articles describing them. In most cases, we were able to classify these remaining entities into hedge funds and non-hedge funds using web-based information. For the remaining cases, we called the filers using the phone numbers listed on their Schedule 13D filings and asked for their self-classification. From this set we further excluded filers that made only one Schedule 13D filing during the whole 2001–06 sample period and whose disclosures in Item 4 of the Schedule 13D filing indicated no explicit purpose (see more details about this in Section 8.3.3.1). This preliminary step led to a list including 311 hedge funds.

In our second step, we gathered all Schedule 13D filings and their amendments made by the 311 hedge funds on the SEC's EDGAR filing system. Filers are required to disclose the number of shares and percentage share ownership, plus all purchases and sales within the previous sixty days. Exchange traded derivatives must be disclosed, but equity swaps and other over-the-counter (OTC) derivatives generally do not have to be fully disclosed (Hu and Black 2006). After the initial Schedule 13D filing, the fund is required to 'promptly' file an amendment to its Schedule 13D (Schedule 13D/A) if there is any 'material' change in its position. Thus, the Schedule 13D filings provide information about the filing date, ownership and its changes, cost of purchase, and the stated purpose of the filing (from Item 4 'Purpose of Transaction'). Based on the information from Item 4, we further excluded events where: (1) the primary purpose of the filer is to be involved in the bankruptcy reorganization or the financing of a distressed firm; (2) the primary purpose of the filer is to engage in a merger and acquisition-related risk arbitrage where the filer takes long position in the target stock (and possibly short positions in the acquirer's stock) before a pending acquisition deal in order to exploit any price convergence when the takeover goes through; (3) the target is a closed-end fund or other non-regular corporation. We excluded (1) and (2) since the motive and consequence of risk arbitrage and distress financing are quite different from those of shareholder activism. We apply filter (3) since the primary interest of this study is hedge fund activism in regular corporations (see Bradley et al. 2007 for an exclusive study on shareholder activism in closed-end funds). After imposing these additional screens the number of hedge funds was reduced to 236, with a total number of 1,032 events. Although mutual funds are not technically hedge funds because they are required to register under the Investment Company Act of 1940, we made one exception, Franklin Mutual Advisers, because it behaves like the other activist funds in our sample.

In the third and final step, we conducted extensive news searches in Factiva using the hedge fund and target company names as keywords. From the news articles, we gathered information that was not available on the 13Ds, such as the hedge fund's motive, the target's response, and the development and resolution of the events. When necessary, we retrieved additional SEC filings, such as Schedule 14A, to obtain additional information.[3]

Given the amount of capital required to acquire a 5% stake in a large-cap company, the Schedule 13D-based search could bias the sample towards smaller targets. At very large firms, some hedge funds have engaged in activism with less than 5% stake in the target company. A notable example is Carl Icahn's investment in Time Warner, where Icahn was a 2.6% shareholder of Time Warner when he launched activism against the firm in 2005. To incorporate activism events without 13D filings, we collected information about such events through news searches (as in the 'third step' described in this section) for our sample hedge funds, plus a general search using various combinations of 'hedge fund' and 'activism' as keywords.

We further checked the completeness of the news search using the Thomson Financial Form 13F database. Specifically, for those funds in our sample for which we could find their Form 13F filings, we retrieved all companies whose shares were held by our sample hedge funds during the 2001–05 period, and conducted individual targeted news searches if: (i) the company's market value was more than $1 billion; and (ii) the ownership by the hedge fund was greater than 2%.[4] This process generated twenty-seven events that were not accompanied by 13D filings because they involve ownership levels in the target that were below the 5% threshold. Not surprisingly, target companies involved in these events tend to be larger and more mature (lower growth and higher cash flows). Though our sample might not be exhaustive of all potential hedge fund activist events without Schedule 13D filings during our sample period, we believe it includes all the important events, because any events we missed must also have failed to catch the attention of the media and are therefore unlikely to be economically meaningful.

With the addition of these events our final sample consists of 236 activist hedge funds and 1,059 hedge fund-target pairs for the period 2001–06, involving 882 unique target companies (97% of them have matched permanent numbers in the Center for Research in Security Prices (CRSP), 82% of which have complete data for return analyses). The target companies span 183 (respectively, 62) 3-digit (respectively, 2-digit) standard industrial classification (SIC) code industries. The number of funds and events increases almost monotonically during this time period, from 39 (97) funds (events) in 2001 to 126 (252) funds (events) in 2006. By compiling our own database, we avoid some problems associated with survivorship bias, reporting selection bias, and backfill, which are prevalent among other hedge fund databases.[5]

[3] At various stages during this process, we have also shown our list of hedge funds to participants in the hedge fund industry and obtained comments and suggestions for additions or deletions.

[4] This restriction was necessary to make the search tractable. Given that the data selection issue of activism ownership below 5% is likely to be more serious among the top quintile-sized firms, we restricted the search to firms that have market capitalization above $1 billion (about the median market capitalization of NYSE firms covered by CRSP at the beginning of our sample).

[5] Indeed, we find that publicly available databases, such as TASS, CISDM, contain only about a quarter of the activist hedge funds in our sample.

8.3.2 Two Examples of Activist Events

To give the reader a flavour of the boundaries of the activism that we focus on in this chapter, we provide a description of two such cases. The first event illustrates a non-confrontational approach that management subsequently embraced and executed. The second event illustrates an initially hostile approach that management ultimately accommodated. Our sample includes these two categories as well as activist events that remained hostile throughout.

8.3.2.1 *MLF Investments and Alloy, Inc.*

On 19 November 2003, MLF Investments LLC filed a Schedule 13D indicating that it owned 5.8% of Alloy, Inc., a direct marketing and retail company. MLF Investments had purchased those shares at an average cost of approximately $5.17 per share. In the Schedule 13D, MLF Investments and its affiliates (the 'Reporting Persons') stated that:

> The Reporting Persons support management's restructuring efforts to the extent they are focused on maximizing shareholder value. In that regard, the Reporting Persons believe that a spin-off of the Company's 'merchandise business' into a separate publicly traded entity should enable the businesses to focus on their core competencies and perform better. In our experience this increased focus should lead to an increase in the valuation of each of the two businesses. The Reporting Persons plan to talk to management and the Board of Directors of the Company regarding its plan to maximize shareholder value and assist them if wanted or needed.

During the [-20,+20] event window surrounding the announcement of Schedule 13D filing date, Alloy's share price increased in value by approximately 11%.

As stated in the Schedule 13D, representatives of MLF Investments initiated discussions with management and the board. After one year, Alloy appointed Matthew Feshbach, the founder and managing partner of MLF Investments, to its board. After several additional months of discussions, on 31 May 2005 Alloy announced plans to spin off its 'merchandise business', and its shares closed on a split adjusted basis at $8.39. MLF Investments had continuously increased its stake in Alloy from time to time since its initial Schedule 13D filing. By 7 September 2005, MLF Investments owned 16.1% of the company. The fund executed a smooth exit from its investment in March 2007.

8.3.2.2 *Pirate Capital and James River Coal*

On 17 November 2005, Pirate Capital filed a Schedule 13D file with the SEC indicating a 7.9% stake in James River Coal Co. Pirate purchased its stake at an average price of about $33.45. On 10 February 2006, Pirate Capital sent a letter to the target stating that:

> We have become increasingly concerned that James River's valuation is being discounted relative to its peers—a discrepancy we attribute to management's failure to articulate to the investment community a cohesive operational and financial strategy, together with its demonstrated inability to meet earnings consensus . . . We attribute these missteps to CEO Peter Socha's lack of operating experience within the coal industry and to the Company's lack of a CFO . . . We are now convinced that the Company's senior management team is simply not up to the task of achieving such goals. As a result, we demand that (i) the Board immediately retain an investment banking firm to pursue strategic alternatives, including the potential sale of the Company and (ii) immediately redeem the shareholder rights plan effective no later than March 15, 2006.

On 10 March 2006, management announced that they had hired Morgan Stanley to 'look at alternatives and potential bidders'. James River Coal's stock price rose more than 10% to $39.77 on that day. From late April to July, Pirate demanded that its representatives be placed on James River's board and that the company's board of directors repeal several antitakeover by-laws. On 22 August 2006, Pirate and James River Coal announced that they had entered into a settlement agreement whereby three representatives from Pirate were elected to James River Coal's board, and, in turn, Pirate dropped the proposals it had submitted to shareholders for the upcoming annual shareholder meeting. The stock price was essentially flat on that day.

8.3.3 Summary of Events

8.3.3.1 *Hedge Funds' Stated Objectives*

Table 8.1 Panel A summarizes the stated objectives that the activist funds provide when they announce activism in the target firms as well as the associated success (and partial success) rates. The motives behind hedge fund activism can be classified into five major categories, each containing multiple subcategories. The objectives, except the first, are not mutually exclusive, as one activist event can target multiple issues. An event is classified as successful if the hedge fund achieves its main stated goal, a partial success if the hedge fund and the company reach some settlement through negotiation that partially meets the fund's original goal.

The first objective includes events in which the hedge fund believes that the company is undervalued and/or that the fund can help the manager maximize shareholder value. No further activism to achieve specific goals (beyond communicating with the management) has been launched before the end of 2006. This category represents 48.3% of the full sample. All events in this objective involve only communication with the management, without more aggressive tactics.

In the second category, we include activism targeting firms' payout policy and capital structure. In the first subgroup of this category, the hedge fund proposes changes geared towards the reduction of excess cash, increase in firm leverage, or higher payouts to shareholders using either dividends or stock repurchase. The second subgroup involves suggested equity issuance, such as stopping or reducing seasoned equity offerings by the target companies or proposed debt restructuring.

In the third set of events, we include activism targeting business strategy. There are five subgroups that fall within this group. The first subgroup implicates general operational efficiency, cost-cutting, and tax efficiency-enhancing proposals. Second, hedge funds target companies they believe lack business focus or exhibit excess diversification, and propose spinning-off some divisions or refocusing the business strategy. Third, hedge funds attempt to play a role in a pending merger or acquisition, generally by asking for a better price where the firm is the target of the acquisition or by trying to stop the pending acquisition.[6] Finally, hedge funds may make proposals for the target company to better pursue its growth strategy.

[6] Note that this is different from risk arbitrage where a fund takes long position in the target company of a pending acquisition deal and perhaps a countervailing short position in the acquirer in order to exploit the price convergence if the deal goes through. Such cases are excluded from our sample.

Table 8.1 Summary of events by hedge funds' stated goals

The sample includes 1,059 events. Panel A reports the summary of the events sorted by hedge funds' stated objective. Columns 1 and 2 report the number of events, and the percentage among all events, of each category. Columns 3 and 4 list the rate of success (including partial success) and number of hostile events within each category. Columns 5 to 8 break down each category into hostile and non-hostile events and record the success and partial success rate within each subcategory. Percentages sum up to more than 100% since one event can have multiple objectives (the first category and the other four categories are mutually exclusive). An event is classified as successful if the hedge fund achieves its main stated goal; a partial success if the hedge fund and the company reach some settlement through negotiation that partially meets the fund's original goal. Panel B provides information on the tactics undertaken by hedge funds, including a breakdown into five categories and the per cent of events in each category relative to the full sample. Since activist events can fall within more than one category the percentages in categories 2 through 7 total more than 51.7% (the remaining 48.3% fall into the first category).

	(1)	(2)	(3)	(4)	(5)	(6)	(7)	(8)	(9)
	All events					Hostile events		Non-hostile events	
Objective categories:	Num. of events	% of sample	% success	% partial success	Num. of hostile events	% success	% partial success	% success	% partial success
Panel A: Summary of hedge funds' stated objectives									
1. General undervaluation/maximize shareholder value	511	48.3%	–	–	–	–	–	–	–
2. Capital structure									
• Excess cash, under-leverage, dividends/ repurchases	134	12.7%	32.0%	32.0%	65	23.1%	47.7%	41.3%	15.9%
• Equity issuance, restructure debt, recapitalization	65	6.1%	37.3%	35.6%	38	18.4%	50.0%	71.4%	9.5%
3. Business strategy									
• Operational efficiency	131	12.4%	35.6%	27.6%	63	35.2%	37.0%	36.4%	12.1%
• Lack of focus, business restructuring, and spinning off	96	9.1%	27.8%	38.9%	62	17.7%	51.6%	50.0%	10.7%
• M&A: as target (against the deal/for better terms)	79	7.5%	36.7%	19.0%	42	33.3%	21.4%	40.5%	16.2%
• M&A: as acquirer (against the deal/for better terms)	25	2.4%	20.0%	52.0%	22	18.2%	59.1%	33.3%	0.0%
• Pursue growth strategies	12	1.1%	44.4%		0	–	–	22.2%	22.2

4. Sale of target company									
• Sell company or main assets to a third party	148	14.0%	37.0%	26.7%	93	30.1%	34.4%	49.1%	13.2%
• Take control/buyout company and/or take it private	44	4.2%	43.2%	25.0%	34	38.2%	32.3%	60.0%	0.0%
5. Governance									
• Rescind takeover defences	60	5.7%	21.7%	43.3%	43	18.6%	53.5%	29.4%	17.6%
• Oust CEO, chairman	59	5.6%	39.7%	29.3%	59	39.7%	29.3%	–	–
• Board independence and fair representation	159	15.0%	34.4%	35.7%	114	31.6%	40.4%	41.9%	23.3%
• More information disclosure/potential fraud	58	5.5%	42.1%	26.3%	42	38.1%	33.3%	53.8%	6.7%
• Excess executive compensation/pay for performance	50	4.7%	20.4%	44.9%	38	18.4%	50.0%	27.3%	27.3%
Sum of categories (2) through (5):	**548**	**51.7%**	**40.6%**	**25.8%**	**286**	**29.5%**	**38.6%**	**53.7%**	**10.7%**

	Tactic categories	
Panel B: Summary of hedge funds' tactics		
1. The hedge fund intends to communicate with the board/management on a regular basis with the goal of enhancing shareholder value		48.3%
2. The hedge fund seeks board representation without a proxy contest or confrontation with the existing management/board		11.6%
3. The hedge fund makes formal shareholder proposals, or publicly criticizes the company and demands change		32.0%
4. The hedge fund threatens to wage a proxy fight in order to gain board representation, or to sue the company for breach of duty, etc.		7.6%
5. The hedge fund launches a proxy contest in order to replace the board		13.2%
6. The hedge fund sues the company		5.4%
7. The hedge fund intends to take control of the company, e.g., with a takeover bid		4.2%

The fourth category of activist events involves activism urging the sale of the target. In this category, hedge funds attempt to force a sale of the target company, either to a third party (in the majority of the cases), or they try to take over the company themselves. Partial success in this group means that the firm remains independent, but agrees to undergo major changes. Last, in the fifth set of events we include activism targeting firm governance. There are multiple subgroups, including efforts to: rescind takeover defences (most often to declassify the boards or to revoke poison pills); to oust the CEO or chairman; to challenge board independence and fair representation; to demand more information disclosure and question potential fraud; and to challenge the level or the pay-for-performance sensitivity of executive compensation.

The success rate of activism across the objectives varies widely. Aggregated across both hostile and non-hostile events, hedge funds achieve success in 40.6% of the cases, which we define as achieving their main stated goals. In 25.8% of the cases, we observe a partial success where hedge funds gain major concessions from their targets. In 21.4% of the cases the fund fails its mission, or withdraws from the target. The remainder 7.4% of the cases in our sample are either still ongoing towards the end of the sample collection (March 2007), or we cannot find any mention of their outcome in any news service or securities law filings.[7] Given that hedge funds achieve success, or partial success, in nearly two-thirds of the cases, despite the targets' strong tendency to resist, this success rate is impressive and comparable to that reported by Ikenberry and Lakonishok (1993) on outcomes of proxy contests for corporate control from 1968 to 1988. Interestingly, ISS, a third-party voting advisory service catering to institutional investors, recommended a vote in favour of hedge funds in twenty-three of the thirty-two media-reported cases.

Panel A provides additional detail about specific subcategories that illustrates the considerable heterogeneity in success rates. For example, hedge funds succeed in attaining their goal of removing a CEO in 39.7% of such events. We find that all such events are hostile and that in 29.3% of the time hedge funds achieve partial success, involving the CEO staying on but agreeing to adopt policies along the lines proposed by the fund. In comparison, hedge funds succeed in rescinding takeover defences only 21.7% of the time, albeit with partial success in another 43.3% of events. The last row of Table 8.1 Panel A summarizes events in categories (2) through (5) in which a goal is explicitly stated. Hostile events are associated with lower success rates but higher partial success rates, indicating that a negotiated compromise is a more likely outcome for events with open confrontation. Overall, the total success rates (including partial success) between the hostile and non-hostile samples are not significantly different (68.1 versus 64.4%).

Obviously, tactics represent endogenous decisions by the hedge funds, so that this evidence is best interpreted as an equilibrium outcome reflecting that hostile tactics are most likely adopted when the perceived resistance from the target management is higher. On the other hand, given that hostile tactics (such as proxy contests) are more costly to the hedge fund compared to less aggressive ones (such as a shareholder proposal), the lack of difference in success rate in equilibrium implies that hedge funds should only resort to aggressive approaches when the potential benefits from activism are also higher. Finally, the likelihood of success is slightly negatively correlated with target size, and positively correlated with

[7] In computing success and partial success rates we include the 7.4% of the ongoing events in the denominator. Hence, our estimates of success are conservative as we are effectively maintaining that 'ongoing' implies 'less likely to succeed'.

hedge funds' ownership stake. The full sample correlation coefficients are -0.03 and 0.10, respectively.

8.3.3.2 *Hedge Fund Tactics and Target Responses*

Panel B of Table 8.1 provides a breakdown of the hedge funds tactics in our sample, from the least to most aggressive. Such information is often available in Item 4 ('Purpose of Transaction') of the initial Schedule 13D, but this source is not complete and so we supplement it using news searches. The first tactic category includes events in which the hedge fund states that it intends to communicate with the board/management on a regular basis with the goal of enhancing shareholder value. Almost all filings in this group do not reveal (to the public) any specific agenda by the hedge fund. Such cases comprise 48.3% of the sample. The second category includes events in which the hedge fund seeks board representation without a proxy contest or confrontation with the existing management/board. The third tactic group includes cases in which the hedge fund makes formal shareholder proposals, or publicly criticizes the company and demands change. Next, category four includes events in which the hedge fund threatens to wage a proxy fight in order to gain board representation, or to sue the company for breach of duty, etc. The fifth category is assigned to events in which the hedge fund launches a proxy contest in order to replace the board. The remaining two tactic groups include events in which the hedge fund sues the company and the hedge fund intends to take control of the company, for example, with a takeover bid. Since activist events can fall within more than one of these tactic categories, the percentages in the second through seventh categories total more than 51.7% (the remaining 48.3% fall in the first group). For example, if a fund launches a proxy contest to replace the board, and files suit against them as well, we would place the event within both the fifth and sixth tactic categories.

The subcategory of 'hostile' activist events involves events in the fourth through seventh tactic categories, or those that fall in the third category but include a stated hostile intention (such as to oust the CEO). By this criterion, there are a total of 295 such hostile cases (27.9% of the total sample). We determine whether an event is hostile or not based on information that is made public while the activism is ongoing. In later analysis, we further distinguish events that began as hostile and those where hedge funds switched to hostile tactics in the course of the event. Such conditioning is necessary for matching stock returns to the information available at the time that activism became public information.

In addition to the tactics described, we note that hedge funds frequently work together. In approximately 22.1% of the events, multiple hedge funds that are not directly affiliated report as one group in their Schedule 13D filing. This does not include cases where multiple funds follow one another in investing in targeted companies, forming a so-called 'wolf pack', that acts together to force the target to address their demands, but which does not require filing a Schedule 13D together because their actions do not rise to the level of 'group' activity under securities laws. Nor does it include other hedge funds or investors that 'cascade' into the target firm's stock after the lead hedge fund's Schedule 13D filing to free ride on the lead hedge fund's intervention effort. Compared to single-fund-filing cases, multiple-fund-filing groups tend to take higher stakes in the target (13.7% versus 11.9%) and are more likely to employ hostile tactics (41.9% versus 23.9%). The latter difference is statistically significant at 5%.

The large heterogeneity in fund tactics raises the question as to how target companies respond to this rich set of tactics and the resulting equilibrium outcomes. Given that events in the first tactic category previously described ('communication' between the hedge funds and the target company management) do not provide public and explicit agendas, it is difficult to classify target company responses and outcomes. In the remaining 548 events hedge funds state some explicit agenda, such as demanding higher payouts or more scrutiny on executive compensation. We track the evolution of these events using information from both news searches and subsequent securities law filings (such as Schedule 13D/A and 14A).[8] Over the course of the hedge fund's intervention, target companies choose to accommodate the activists 29.7% of the time, to negotiate 29.1% of the time, to fight/resist 41.3% of the time. While there is no striking relation between hedge funds' stated objectives and target response, the 'fight' response is more likely as they face a hostile tactic (the correlation is 0.35).

8.3.3.3 *Hedge Funds' Investment in Target Companies*

How large are hedge fund investments in their target companies? We report the size of the activists' stakes in their target firms, both in dollar value (at cost), and as a percentage of outstanding shares of the target in Panel A of Table 8.2. Information in the columns denoted 'Initial' comes from the Schedule 13D filing. For the non-Schedule 13D events, the information is collected based on news media or Form 13F. The columns labelled 'Max. Ownership' provide the maximum stake that the funds accumulated in the targets, which is retrieved from the subsequent amendments to the 13D filings, or Schedule 13D/A. We record the highest holdings by the filing party in the target. The last four columns in Panel A present this information for the subsample of hostile events.

The median initial (maximum) percentage stake that a hedge fund takes in the target is 6.3 (9.1)%, and the median dollar stake, at cost, is 11.9 (15.8) million in 2006-constant dollars. We note that the hostile cases exhibit greater capital commitments in the target firm by the hedge fund at the higher percentiles of the sample. For example, at the 95th percentile, an initial stake in a hostile event requires nearly twice as much capital as an intervention in the full sample.

An important pattern emerging from Table 8.2 is that the activism that we analyse does not generally involve control blocks of stock. The inter-quartile of hedge funds' initial stakes is from 5.4 to 8.8%, and the 75th percentile of the maximum ownership falls below 15%. Even at the 95th percentile of the sample, hedge funds hold 31.5% in the target companies, considerably lower than the majority requirement. It therefore appears that the activist hedge funds are generally not interested in taking control of the company. Rather, they hope to facilitate value-enhancing changes in the target company as minority shareholders, and they often need coordination with and support from other shareholders, especially on issues that require shareholder voting. For example, there are 140 proxy contests in our sample, in most of which (including the James River Coal example in Section 8.3.2.2) hedge funds seek to elect a short slate of directors rather than seeking majority

[8] After the initial Schedule 13D filing, the fund is required to file promptly an amended Schedule 13D/A if there is material change in the position or other items (changes of more than 1% are deemed 'material'). Schedule 14A contains all of the information that is required to be filed in an issuer's proxy statement, which will be mailed to its shareholders prior to the company's annual shareholders' meeting.

Table 8.2 Hedge funds' capital commitment and investment horizon

Panel A provides the size of the hedge funds' stakes both in terms of dollar values (at cost), and as a percentage of the outstanding shares of the target companies. We report the 5th, 25th, 50th (median), 75th, and 95th percentiles of the sample. The 'Initial' columns report the stakes that hedge funds take at their initial 13D filings. The 'Max' columns report the maximum reported stakes that the funds accumulated in the targets as revealed from subsequent 13D/A filings. Panel B gives the breakdown of various forms of hedge fund exit. Reported in the last row are the percentages of events that had no information about exit by the end of March 2007. Finally, Panel C lists the length of holding period (in number of days) at different percentiles of the sample for the subsample that has exit information. In each panel, the statistics for the full sample and the subsample of hostile events are reported separately.

	All events				Hostile events			
	Invested capital ($ million)		% ownership		Invested capital ($ million)		% ownership	
Percentile	Initial	Max.	Initial	Max.	Initial	Max.	Initial	Max.
Panel A: Capital commitment (in 2006 constant dollars)								
5%	0.69	1.0	5%	5.0%	1.5	1.9	3.5%	3.6%
25%	3.5	4.6	5.4%	6.5%	4.5	6.8	5.6%	6.9%
50%	11.9	15.8	6.3%	9.1%	14.7	20.45	6.6%	9.5%
75%	40.3	54.6	8.8%	13.2%	44.2	68.8	8.8%	13.0%
95%	186.8	272.5	23.1%	31.5%	321	363.8	19.8%	29.5%

Categories	Hostile	Non-Hostile	All events
Panel B: Breakdown of exit			
Sold shares on the open market	26.1%	39.3%	35.5%
Target company sold	16.2%	6.9%	9.5%
Target company merged into another	9.9%	3.8%	5.5%
Liquidated	1.8%	0.7%	1.0%
Shares sold back to target company	1.8%	0.5%	0.9%
Still holding/no information	44.1%	48.4%	47.6%

Percentile	Hostile (initial)	Non-hostile (initial)	All events
Panel C: Length of holding period (#days) for completed spells			
5%	32	45	43
25%	126	171	169
50%	319	375	369
75%	610	672	647
95%	1,550	1,679	1,649

control of the board. Moreover, the funds seek to accomplish their objectives by coordinating with, and obtaining support from, other shareholders, especially on issues that require a shareholder vote. These features distinguish the activist hedge funds from the corporate raiders in the 1980s who sought to obtain full control to internalize all the benefits from their intervention.

The stockholdings reported are confined to disclosure in the Schedule 13D or news reporting. As Hu and Black (2006) note, certain types of derivative investments (e.g., OTC derivatives and short positions) might not need full public disclosure. In approximately 16.1% of the cases in our sample hedge funds report derivative positions in the target companies, most common types being option/warrants, convertible debt, and convertible preferred. They are mostly securities with embedded option features issued by the target companies, and not derivatives representing countervailing positions that offset the economic interests from the long positions (Martin and Partnoy 2005). We believe, however, that this information is likely to be incomplete given that disclosure of the latter is not mandatory. As a sensitivity check for potential countervailing positions that hedge funds might take, we match our sample firms to the monthly short interest data from the NYSE and NASDAQ for the period 2001–05. We find virtually no change in the short interest (as a proportion of outstanding shares) of the target companies in our sample around the Schedule 13D filing time—the median short interest ratio remains at about 1.0 to 1.2% during the thirteen-month period centred on the filing month.

Finally, activist hedge funds' investment horizons have been an issue of contention. Critics accuse activist funds of aiming for short-term gains at the expense of long-term shareholder value (Kahan and Rock, Chapter 5, this volume). We use multiple sources to determine the 'exit date' when the hedge fund significantly reduces its investment in the target company. First, we retrieve from the Thomson Financial database Form 13F data for the first quarter-end when the hedge fund's holding in the target company drops below 1% or $1 million. When such information is not available, we use the last 13D/A filing date indicating that the ownership drops below the 5% disclosure threshold.[9] Finally, we supplement with news searches for other forms of exits (such as a liquidation of the company). These combined sources allow us to form estimates of the hedge funds' investment duration after the filing of the initial Schedule 13D. However, our sample period is from 2001–06, so that many recent events still unresolved as of the close of data collection in March 2007. As a result, we are unable to find the exit information for about 47.6% of the cases in the full sample.

Table 8.2, Panel B, lists the breakdown of various forms of hedge fund exit, indicating that selling in the open market is the predominant form, accounting for two-thirds of all complete spells. If we focus on the subsample of the completed events where the fund is reported to have significantly reduced its ownership level, Table 8.2 Panel C shows that the median duration from the first Schedule 13D filing to divestment is 369 days. The 25th and 75th percentile figures for the full sample are 169 days and 647 days. Furthermore, events that are initiated with hostility see somewhat shorter investment horizons than the non-hostile ones (319 days versus 375 days at the median).[10]

[9] If the hedge fund's stake falls below 5% after the first Schedule 13D filing, the last Schedule 13D/A would reveal the date, remaining stake, and sometimes sale prices of the transactions that free the hedge fund from future reporting obligations associated with the 5% or more investment.

[10] Since we are trying to assess the correlation between investment horizon and initial conditions, 'Hostile (Initial)' is defined as hostile tactics employed by hedge funds at the initial launching of activism. For events that start as non-confrontational but later switch to hostility the duration is longer because of the hedge funds' tendency to persist in their goals.

Needless to say, focusing on the events in which hedge funds have exited grossly underestimates the unconditional duration of hedge funds' investment in the target companies. To try to get a better handle on this value, we offer two estimates for the all-sample investment horizon. First, we conduct a regression of completed duration on a set of variables, including dummies for the five stated objectives (as defined in Table 8.1), lagged market cap, book-to-market, and ROA of the target companies, and a dummy variable for whether the events were initiated with hostility. We then applied the estimated coefficients to the ongoing cases (and cases without exit information) to calculate predicted durations. Incorporating the imputed duration values for the ongoing cases, the full sample median duration becomes 556 days, and the 25th (75th) percentile value is 317 (981). For our second estimate, we use the Form 13F holdings data from the Thomson Financial to impute the turnover rate of an institutional investor's overall portfolio from quarterly changes. Our sample hedge funds' median annualized equity long position turnover rate is 55%, implying an average holding period of 22 months. Overall, the data indicate that the hedge funds' investment horizon is not as short as suggested by critics of hedge fund activism.

8.4 Characteristics of Target Companies

What type of companies do activist hedge funds target? The first three columns of Table 8.3 report summary statistics of target firms' characteristics in the year before they are targeted. We utilize these data to examine how the target companies compare to their peers' two different approaches. First, we compare the characteristics of the target firms with a set of industry/size/book-to-market matched firms. These comparisons are reported in the next three columns of Table 8.3. When we describe target firms by size (market capitalization), the size matching criterion is dropped and when we describe target firms by book-to-market and Q, the book-to-market matching is dropped. A comparison of targets with only industry-matched firms yields qualitatively similar results.

Second, in Table 8.4, we present probit regressions to identify the partial effects of all covariates. The matched firms for each target company are assigned from the same year, same SIC 3-digit industry, and same Fama and French 10 x 10 size and book-to-market sorted portfolios. If the narrow criteria yield no match, we relax the industry group to SIC 2-digit, and the size/book-to-market to 5 x 5 sorted portfolios. The average difference between a sample firm i and matched firms is calculated as follows:

$$Dif_i = X_i - \frac{1}{m}\sum_{j=1}^{m} X_j,$$

where X is a characteristic variable, and firms $j=1,\ldots,m$ are from the match group. We reported in column (4) of Table 8.3 is $\frac{1}{n}\sum_{i=1}^{n} Dif_i$, where $i = 1,\ldots,n$ is the index for our sample target firms. To assess the statistical significance of the differences, column 5 presents the t-statistics associated with the difference statistics, and column 6 provides the Wilcoxon signed rank statistic, which is asymptotically normal, for the difference in

Table 8.3 Characteristics of target companies

This table reports the characteristics of target companies and a comparison to a set of matched companies. The first three columns report the mean, median, and standard deviation of the characteristic for the target companies. Columns (4) through (6) report the average difference between the sample firms and the industry/size/book-to-market matched firms, the *t*-statistic for the average difference, and the Wilcoxon signed rank statistic, which is asymptotically normal, for the median difference. Size matching is dropped for *MV* comparison, and book-to-market matching is dropped for *BM* and *Q* analysis. The last five columns list the proportion of target firms that fall into each of the quintile groups formed by the CRSP/Compustat universe. All variables are retrieved from the year prior to the event year. *MV* is market capitalization in millions of dollars; *Q* is defined as (book value of debt + market value of equity)/(book value of debt + book value of equity); *BM* is the market-to-book ratio defined as (book value of equity/market value of equity); *GROWTH* is the growth rate of sales over the previous year; *ROA* is return on assets, defined as EBITDA/assets (lag); *CF* is cash flow, defined as (net income + depreciation and amortization)/assets (lag); *STKRET* is the buy-and-hold return, in excess of that of the market, during the twelve months before the announced activism; *LEV* is the book leverage ratio defined as debt/(debt + book value of equity); *CASH* is defined as (cash + cash equivalent)/assets; *DIVYLD* is dividend yield, defined as (common dividend + preferred dividends)/(market value of common stocks + book value of preferred); *PAYOUT* is the payout ratio, defined as the total dividend payments divided by net income before extraordinary items; *RND* is R&D scaled by lagged assets; *HHI* is the Herfindahl-Hirschman index of sales in different business segments as reported by Compustat; *GINDEX* is the Gompers, Ishii, and Metric (2003) governance index where high index values represent lower shareholder rights or higher management entrenchment; *INST* is the proportion of shares held by institutions; *ANALYST* is the number of analysts covering the company from I/B/E/S. The characteristic *AMIHUD* is the Amihud (2002) illiquidity measure, defined as the yearly average (using daily data) of 1,000 $\sqrt{Return/(Dollar\ Trading\ Volume)}$.

	(1)	(2)	(3)	(4)	(5)	(6)	(7)	(8)	(9)	(10)	(11)
	Summary statistics			Difference with matched firms			CRSP/COMPUSTAT quintile breakpoints				
Firm Characteristic	Mean	Median	Std dev	Avg. diff.	*t*-stat of diff.	Wilcoxon	% in Q1	% in Q2	% in Q3	% in Q4	% in Q5
MV	726.56	160.07	1,669.17	−63.54	−1.52	−2.05	0.214	0.253	0.239	0.18	0.114
BM	0.773	0.615	0.914	0.081	4.28	3.93	0.133	0.143	0.169	0.195	0.360
Q	1.544	1.238	1.007	−0.397	−9.17	−13.19	0.307	0.203	0.209	0.176	0.106
GROWTH	0.084	0.041	0.357	−0.057	−4.44	−7.72	0.299	0.234	0.194	0.117	0.156
ROA	0.054	0.085	0.201	0.020	3.12	4.18	0.212	0.178	0.217	0.185	0.208
CF	0.022	0.047	0.180	0.018	2.86	3.23	0.231	0.191	0.214	0.195	0.169

STKRET	0.195	−0.010	1.200	−0.073	−3.11	−5.15	0.295	0.16	0.169	0.141	0.234
LEV	0.348	0.327	0.297	0.028	2.91	1.70	0.196	0.197	0.197	0.207	0.203
CASH	0.177	0.088	0.214	−0.026	−3.61	−4.86	0.207	0.178	0.225	0.208	0.183
DIVYLD	0.007	0.000	0.016	−0.001	−2.13	−5.48		--0.754-		0.129	0.118
PAYOUT	0.296	0.000	0.995	−0.035	−1.81	−4.15		--0.720--		0.161	0.119
RND	0.079	0.029	0.114	−0.01	−2.21	−4.51	0.262	0.210	0.157	0.19	0.181
HHI	0.80	1.000	0.251	−0.034	−3.64	−1.93	0.212	0.214		--0.594--	
GINDEX	9.005	9.000	2.702	0.353	2.27	2.33	0.176	0.251	0.142	0.210	0.220
ANALYST	4.387	2.000	5.959	0.547	3.01	0.99	0.123	0.156	0.226	0.175	0.320
INST	0.447	0.447	0.274	0.083	9.57	8.82	0.086	0.158	0.409	0.184	0.162
AMIHUD	0.466	0.193	0.699	−0.075	−3.99	−7.65	0.091	0.139	0.434	0.183	0.153

Table 8.4 Probit analysis of targeting

This table reports the effects of covariates on the probability of being targeted by activist hedge funds. The dependent variable is a dummy variable equal to one if there is hedge fund activism targeting the company during the following year (that is, all covariates are lagged by one year). All independent variables are as defined in Table 8.3. In the first column we exclude the variable *GINDEX*, while in column 2 we include it, to reflect the significant loss of observations due to the *GINDEX* data availability. In each column, we report probit coefficients, their *t*-statistics, and the marginal probability change induced by a one standard deviation change in the values of the covariates from their respective sample averages. * and ** indicate statistical significance at the 10% and 5% levels.

Dependent variable:	(1)			(2)		
Dummy (of being targeted)	Coefficient	t-statistic	Marg. prob.	Coefficient	t-statistic	Marg. prob.
MV	−0.08**	−7.35	−0.80%	−0.14**	−7.04	−1.01%
Q	−0.07**	−4.77	−0.49%	−0.09**	−3.01	−0.56%
GROWTH	−0.14**	−3.10	−0.23%	−0.10	−1.16	−0.145
ROA	0.44**	4.30	0.39%	0.33	1.35	0.19%
LEV	−0.02	−0.42	−0.03%	0.06	0.64	0.07%
DIVYLD	−5.26**	−4.57	−0.38%	−4.89**	−2.69	−0.34%
RND	−0.15	−0.77	−0.07%	−0.55	−1.12	−0.18%
HHI	−0.22**	−3.61	−0.23%	−0.08	−0.84	−0.09%
ANALYST	0.12**	6.12	0.59%	0.05	1.51	0.24%
INST	0.07**	3.65	0.12%	0.32**	3.34	0.44%
GINDEX	-	-	-	0.02**	2.59	0.28%
CNST	−1.42**	−18.59	-	−1.26**	−7.04	-
Num. of obs and pseudo *R*-sqr	39,085	2.68%		14,758	4.39%	
Per cent targeted	1.788%			1.83%		

medians. Given that the distributions of many of the variables display fat tails and skewness, the Wilcoxon statistic, which is less influenced by extreme observations, serves as a robustness check.

Finally, the last five columns of Table 8.3 list the proportion of the target firms that fall into each of the quintile groups formed by the CRSP/Compustat firms. This sorting is unconditional and is meant to offer an overview of where the target firms populate in the universe of US public firms.

In discussing the statistics, we say that the difference between the target and its peers is significant if both the *t*-statistic and the Wilcoxon statistics indicate a two-tail significance of at least 10%, and at least one of the two statistics is significant at less than the 5% level. The summary statistics on market value (*MV*) indicate that the target firms are under-represented in the top size quintile, but are otherwise roughly evenly distributed among the other four quintiles. This is consistent with the idea that larger firms are less likely to be targeted because of the large amount of capital a hedge fund would need to invest in order to amass a meaningful stake. Acquiring a sizeable stake in a top size-quintile firm might introduce inordinate amount of idiosyncratic risk even for an activist hedge fund. In order to support this hypothesis, we collected fund size information from WRDS

CISDM hedge fund database, news articles, and hedge fund websites, and were able to assemble it for about 52% of our sample. The median size of the hedge funds in our sample is $793 million, and the 25th and 75th percentile values are $278 and $4,446 million. The top quintile CRSP target firms have an average (median) market value of $15.2 ($5.7) billion in 2005. Hence, a 5% stake in the average (median) top quintile target firm implies an investment of $760 ($285) million dollars, a considerable amount relative to the size of the typical sample funds.

The significant difference between target and matching firms' valuation variables, book-to-market (*BM*, defined as (book value of equity/market value of equity)), and *Q* (defined as (book value of debt + market value of equity)/(book value of debt + book value of equity)), indicates that the activist hedge funds are 'value investors'. Unconditionally, about one-third of the target firms appear in the top (bottom) quintile sorted by *BM* (*Q*). In fact, in about two-thirds of our cases, the hedge fund explicitly states that it believes the target is undervalued. To the extent that activist hedge funds profit from the improvement of the companies' operations and strategies, it is also important that hedge funds target companies whose stock prices have yet to reflect the potential for improvement.

In terms of operational performance, measured by sales growth (Growth) and return on assets (*ROA*, defined as the ratio of EBITDA to lagged assets), target firms tend to be low growth firms, but are significantly more profitable. Profitability is higher when measured both in terms of return on assets, which is 2.0 percentage point higher than the matched peers, and cash flows generated (*CF*, defined as net income + depreciation and amortization), scaled by lagged assets, which is 1.8 percentage points higher than the peers. The stock performance of the target firms also lags considerably behind the market. This evidence is important as it sets hedge fund activism apart from earlier institutional activism targeting poorly performing companies (Gillan and Starks, Chapter 2, this volume).

The next set of variables relate to targets' capital structure. Target firms have slightly higher leverage: the average book value debt-to-capital ratio (*LEV*) is about 2.8 percentage points higher than that of the matching firms. The cash-to-asset ratio (*CASH*) is lower than that of the peers. Target firms' dividend payout is significantly lower relative to peers, measured by both the dividend yield (*DIVYLD*, defined as (common dividend)/(market value of common stocks)) and payout ratio (*PAYOUT*, defined as the total dividend payments divided by net income before extraordinary items). Using total payout yield (defined as the ratio of the sum of dividend and share repurchase to the market value of common stocks) delivers qualitatively similar results.

On the investment side, target firms spend significantly less than their peers on research and development, scaled by lagged assets (*RND*). Target firms also have slightly lower Herfindahl-Hirschman indices (*HHI*, measured as the HHI index of sales in different business segments as reported by the Compustat). This indicates that they are more diversified.

Next, we turn to governance characteristics. Measured by the Gompers, Ishii, and Metrick (2003) governance index (*GINDEX*), target firms tend to have slightly more takeover defences. The *GINDEX* tracks twenty-four takeover defences that firms could adopt, as well as the laws of the state in which the targets are incorporated. Our target firms have, on average, 0.4 more defences than comparable firms. Furthermore, a greater percentage of targeted firms have a large number of such defences: In the GIM data that covers approximately 2,000 firms in 2004, 8.8% of the firms have 13 or more takeover defences; whereas in our sample of target firms, the same measure shows that 14.9% of target firms exhibit this level of defences.

Targets also have significantly higher institutional ownership and analyst coverage: an average of 44.7% institutional ownership (8.3% higher than comparable firms); and an average of 4.4 analysts covering each firm (0.5 more than peer firms). Both institutional ownership and analyst coverage are indications of sophistication of shareholder clientele. This is an important factor for activist hedge funds because they often rely on understanding and support from fellow shareholders to implement the changes, given their minority stakes in the target firms (see Table 8.2). Since the latter two variables could also proxy for trading liquidity we use a direct trading liquidity measure, the Amihud (2002) illiquidity measure. It is defined as the yearly average of 1,000 $\sqrt{|\text{Return}| \,/\, (\text{Dollar Trading Volume})}$ using daily data.[11] We find that target companies exhibit higher trading liquidity than otherwise comparable firms. Higher liquidity makes it easier for the activists to accumulate a stake within a short period of time. However, given that large-cap companies are under-represented, target firms are no more liquid relative to the universe of firms. In fact, target firms concentrate in the third quintile, sorted by liquidity.

While Table 8.3 compares target firms with their peers along single dimensions, Table 8.4 reports results from probit multivariate regressions to assess the marginal effect of each covariate. The unconditional probability for a firm being targeted is 1.8% during our sample period. Since the *GINDEX* (retrieved from the WRDS IRRC database) is only available for about one-third of firms on Compustat, the regressions with *GINDEX* are reported separately. Further, the subsample of firms that have GINDEX information is overrepresented by large firms and firms with higher institutional ownership, and the results should therefore be interpreted accordingly. In an untabulated sensitivity check, we replace *q* with *B/M*, *ROA* and *CF*, *LEV* with *CASH*, and *DIVYIELD* with *PAYOUT*, and find qualitatively similar results.

The results in Table 8.4 are consistent with those in Table 8.3. In particular, they confirm the two patterns emerging from the previous analysis in this section. First, activist hedge funds resemble value investors. A one-standard deviation decrease in *q* is associated with a 0.49 percentage point increase in the probability of being targeted, other things equal. Relative to the unconditional probability of 1.8%, the marginal probabilities are substantial. This suggests that activist hedge funds are seeking to identify undervalued companies where the potential for improvement is high. The hedge funds' stated goals, as reflected in their Schedule 13D filings, are consistent with this conclusion. Indeed, even the names of activist hedge funds suggest that the funds and their investors believe they are value investors. A large proportion of the hedge fund names in our sample include words or phrases that connote value investing, such as 'value', 'contrarian', and 'distressed'.

Second, the potential problems that hedge funds identify at targeted firms are more often issues that are generalizable to all firms, such as changes in governance and payout policies, rather than issues that are specific to one or a small number of target firms (such as slipping sales of a particular product). Targeted firms do not seem to suffer from serious operational

[11] The measure follows the algorithm described in Hasbrouck (2006), and is downloaded from Joel Hasbrouck's website: <http://pages.stern.nyu.edu/~jhasbrou/>. This illiquidity measure is denoted 'I2' in Hasbrouck (2006).

difficulties. They are actually profitable and enjoy handsome cash flows, as indicated by the significant coefficient on *ROA* in the full sample regressions (and in untabulated results, a significant coefficient on *CF*). The potential problems that these companies face are likely related to the agency problem of free cash flows, such as relatively low dividend yield and diversifying investments (as indicated by *HHI*) that might not be in the best interest of shareholders. Governance issues, including rescinding takeover defences, ousting CEOs, promoting board independence, and curtailing executive compensation, are also commonly cited as reasons for activism.

These targeting patterns seem sensible given that many of the hedge funds in our sample are, in general, not experts in the specific business of their target firms. Focusing on issues that are generalizable to other potential target firms helps lower the marginal cost of launching activism on a new company (Black 1990). Another reason to avoid targeting an idiosyncratic firm issue is offered by Kahn and Winton (1998). They predict that investors are more likely to intervene in well-understood firms or industries so that the market can rapidly appreciate the effects of an intervention. Hedge funds should avoid 'opaque' and complicated business, such as those involved with high R&D, in order to avoid delay in the resolution (in the market price) of the intervention's impact. Our data offer some support to this hypothesis. As indicated in Table 8.3, hedge funds tend to avoid high-tech firms (as proxied by *RND*, the ratio of R&D to assets) among the universe of public firms. We do not wish to over-interpret this relation because the effect is not significant in Table 8.4 when we control for the full set covariates. We note, however, that book-to-market ratio, growth, cash flows, and HHI of business segments are also indirect proxies for high technology intensity, and they are all statistically significant in predicting activist targeting. The combined evidence is therefore consistent with the predictions in Black (1990), and Kahn and Winton (1998).

8.5 Stock Returns and Hedge Fund Activism

The fundamental question for hedge fund activism is whether it achieves its stated goal of creating value for shareholders. In our first attempt to address this question, we examine stock market returns, both short-term announcement event-day returns and the long-run returns. This analysis addresses the questions of how the market perceives the effect of hedge fund activism on shareholder value and whether the long-run measures are consistent with the market's perception.

8.5.1 Event-Day Returns and Trading around the Filing of Schedule 13Ds

We adopt both short and long event windows around the filing of a Schedule 13D. Figure 8.1 plots the average buy-and-hold return, in excess of the buy-and-hold return on the value weighted NYSE/AMEX/NASDAQ index from CRSP, from twenty days prior to the Schedule 13D filing date to twenty days afterwards. There is a run-up of about 3.2% between ten days to one day prior to filing. The filing day and the following day see a

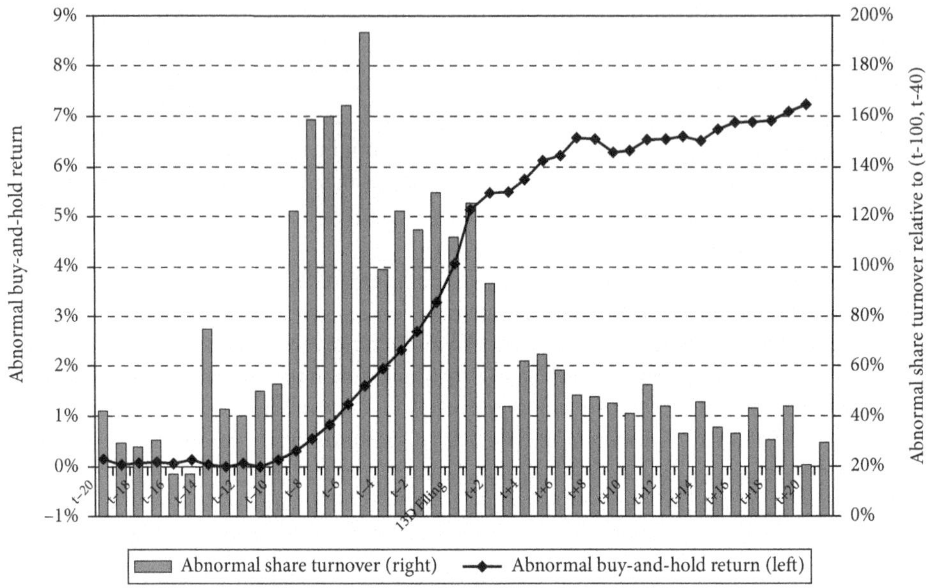

FIGURE 8.1 Buy-and-hold abnormal return around the filing of Schedule 13Ds

The solid line (left axis) plots the average buy-and-hold return around the Schedule 13D filing, in excess of the buy-and-hold return of the value-weight market, from twenty days prior the 13D file date to twenty days afterwards. The bars (right axis) plot the increase (in percentage points) in the share trading turnover during the same time window compared to the average turnover rate during the preceding [−100, −40] event window.

jump of about 2.0%. Afterward the abnormal return keeps trending up to a total 7.2% in twenty days. In the full sample, 62% of the events see positive abnormal return in the [-20, 20] window, the 25th, 50th, and 75th percentile values are -5.3%, 4.6%, and 17.3%, respectively.

Some hedge funds might file a Schedule 13D after publicly announcing their activist intent (at a lower ownership stake), while other hedge funds might launch aggressive activism only after they have filed a Schedule 13D. In such cases, the Schedule 13D file date might not be an accurate proxy for the event date when activism is first publicly known. As a sensitivity check, we focus on a subsample of 246 events in which the time of 13D filing coincides with the first public announcement of activism (that is, hedge funds describe a new and explicit agenda in the Schedule 13D beyond a general statement of maximizing shareholder value on the filing). The average buy-and-hold return of this sample (not plotted) displays a very similar pattern to that of Figure 8.1, although the magnitude is higher. The average (median) abnormal return during the [-20, 20] window is 8.4% (5.6%).

Figure 8.1 also includes the average abnormal turnover over the event window. We measure 'normal' turnover over the [-100, -40] window preceding the Schedule 13D filing date. The spike in abnormal trading volume, defined as the percentage increase in the share turnover rate, does not occur on the event day but rather during the ten-day period before the filing. This pattern is consistent with the fact that investors are required to file Schedule 13D no later than ten days after the transaction that causes them to go over the 5% level of stockholdings in the target firm, so that the filing fund may be engaging in additional buying prior to the public announcement of their activism. There are, however, two alternative explanations for the abnormal turnover in the days preceding the filing date. The first is 'wolf pack' investing, in which several hedge funds, which do not formally coordinate, buy into the target firm;[12] and the other is 'tipping', where the filing hedge fund reveals its intention to a small number of investors before the public filing for reciprocation of other favours. Given the informal and secretive nature of such communication, our data does not allow a formal testing of these two explanations.

We emphasize that market reactions are *not* an unbiased estimate of expected benefits from successful activism. If prices were to adjust fully to the *ex post* effect of success hedge fund activism, hedge funds, in the absence of reputation concerns and trading liquidity constraints, would have no incentive to continue with costly intervention. Rather, market prices adjust to a level reflecting the expected benefit of intervention adjusted for the equilibrium probability that the hedge fund continues with its activism and succeeds. Hence, the market reaction necessarily underestimates the value of *ex post* successful activism (e.g., Bond, Goldstein, and Prescott 2006). Moreover, the raw correlation between *ex post* success and announcement returns turns out to be low—it is 0.04. This low predictability of success, from the perspective of outside market participants, is consistent with the theoretical models of Maug (1998), and Cornelli and Li (2002), and the empirical evidence in Bradley et al. (2007). In such models, there cannot be an equilibrium with both outside market participants predicting the outcome (due to intervention) and the activist carrying out the action as expected.

8.5.2 Cross-Sectional Variation of Abnormal Returns

Equally important as the average abnormal return is its cross-sectional variation because it reflects the heterogeneity in market perceptions regarding the expected value generated by activism. Table 8.5 reports regressions exploring the cross-sectional variation in market response to shareholder activism. The dependent variable is the abnormal return in the [-20, 20] window around the filing of the Schedule 13D. We included as regressors dummy variables for the five broad stated objectives classified in Section 8.3.3.2, *MV* (the logarithm of market capitalization), *LTDebt* (the ratio of long-term debt to sum of debt and market value of equity), *Pre-13F* (a dummy variable equal to one if the hedge fund revealed a significant stake, defined as more than 1% or \$1 million, in the target company in its Form 13F

[12] There are open and controversial legal questions about what actions rise to the level of 'group' activity under the securities laws. Hedge funds argue that they are not required to file Schedule 13Ds if they are merely follow-on investors who take positions after they learn that another hedge fund has acquired 5% of a target. Relying on legal advice that this argument is correct, hedge funds frequently acquire significant stakes in targets within hours of learning that the initial fund has taken a position. Indeed, the fact that the hedge funds delay investing—even for a short time—is some evidence that they are not acting together with the initial fund. A counter-argument is that hedge fund networks are sufficiently close that they satisfy the legal definition of a group, even if the funds do not simultaneously acquire securities. Many defence-side attorneys have argued that the definition of a 'group' should include such funds. As of today, the legal issue is unresolved, but we note that hedge funds are commonly confident enough that they will not be classified as a group that they are willing to purchase significant stakes immediately after another fund files a Schedule 13D.

Table 8.5 Relation between abnormal return and type of activism

The dependent variable is the abnormal return during the [−20, +20]-day window around the Schedule 13D filing (or announced activism for events with lower than a 5% stake) date. There are five categories, not mutually exclusive, as defined in the Panel B of Table 8.1. All regressions control for the size of the target firm, *ln(MV)*, the log of market capitalization. Long-term debt, *LTDebt*, is the ratio of long-term debt to the sum of debt and market value of equity. *Pre-13F* is a dummy variable equal to one if the hedge fund had revealed significant ownership (more than 1% or $1 million) based on its previous 13F filing. *Avg Pre-Returns* is the average abnormal return from prior events belonging to the same hedge fund (first timers are coded as zero, the neutral value). All non-dummy variables are expressed as the deviation from the sample average values. Intercepts are suppressed in columns because of the full span of the dummy variables. The analysis in Column 1 is conducted on the full sample. Columns 2 and 3 offer the partition of subsamples of events that are hostile/non-hostile at initiation. All *t*-statistics adjust for heteroscedasticity. * and ** indicate statistical significance at the 10% and 5% levels.

	(1) Full sample		(2) Hostile (initial)		(3) Non-hostile (initial)	
Dependent variables: abnormal returns	Coefficient	*t*-statistic	Coefficient	*t*-statistic	Coefficient	*t*-statistic
ln(MV)	−1.27%**	−2.39	0.60%	0.50	−1.38%**	−2.09
LTDebt	−2.73%	−0.72	2.70%	0.37	−4.88%	−1.01
Pre-13F	−3.27%**	−2.1	−2.69%	−0.69	−4.43%**	−2.23
Avg Pre-Returns	0.08%	1.36	0.04%	0.28	0.09%	1.34
General	6.28%**	3.7	–	–	6.21%**	3.96
CapStructure	1.47%	0.78	1.23%	0.34	2.54%	1.17
BusStrategy	5.95%**	3.08	3.34%	1.17	8.11%**	3.49
Sale	8.54%**	4.1	10.70%**	3.43	8.33%**	3.15
Gov	1.73%	0.92	4.95%*	1.73	−0.02%	−0.01
Hostile	3.76%*	1.81	–	–	–	–
N ob & *R*-sqr	724	0.032	140	0.072	584	0.029

filings before the Schedule 13D filing), and *AvgPre-Returns* (the average [−20, 20] window abnormal return for all the previous events led by the same hedge fund). We provide the motivation for the construction and interpretation of these variables when we discuss the results in Sections 8.5.2 through 8.5.4.

In order to facilitate the interpretation of the coefficients on the dummy variables, all non-dummy covariates are expressed as the deviation from the mean, and the intercept of the regression is suppressed (because of the full span of the dummy variables). As a result, all the coefficients on the stated-objective dummy variables can be interpreted as the average partial effect on abnormal returns of one particular group of events, assuming that the target firms have average characteristics.

Column (1) shows how event-window abnormal returns vary with the stated goals of the hedge funds and other covariates in the full sample, while columns 2 and 3 provide estimates for the same relation separately for hostile and non-hostile subsamples, where hostility is measured at the initial filing of Schedule 13D (or the first announcement of activism for events without 13D filings) to reflect the information available to market participants in the announcement window. Turning first to column 1, we find that activism aimed at the sale of the target generates the highest abnormal return, with average abnormal return of 8.54% (t = 4.10). Business strategy-related activism also generates a significant abnormal return of 5.95% (t = 3.08). An announcement of a hedge fund's intention to intervene without revealing any specific goals generates a return of 6.28% (t = 3.70). On the other hand, though activism targeting capital structure and governance issues also generates somewhat positive average returns (1.47 and 1.73%), these estimates are not statistically distinguishable from zero. The latter estimates are consistent with the weak return effects documented by prior literature of traditional governance-oriented activism (with the exception of Bizjak and Marquette (1998), who document some value improvement from shareholder resolution to rescind poison pills). The weak returns associated with traditional institutional activism reflect those institutions' relatively small investments in targeted firms (unlike hedge funds), and the fact that institutions seek changes that do not seem to be important to firm value.

We further note that the hedge fund's stated objectives are not mutually exclusive (except the 'General' category). For example, if a hedge fund targets business strategy issues but also posts a governance agenda, the total return is expected to be 7.68 (= 5.95 + 1.73%).

Finally, to examine the effect of a hedge fund's track record on market reactions, we use the average announcement returns from the hedge fund's previous events as a proxy for the fund's historical success. A one-percentage point increase in return track record is associated with 0.08 percentage point increase in the current announcement return, but the statistical significance does not reach the conventional levels.

Columns 2 to 3 of Table 8.5 separate events by whether or not hedge funds initiate activism with hostile tactics (see definition in Section 8.3.3.2). Given that market reaction is based on information available at the time of the event, it is important to classify events based on their nature at initiation. Among all events that turn out to be hostile, about three-quarters begin with full-blown hostility, and the rest change into hostility after the targeted firms' management resists or ignores the hedge funds' friendly proposals. The two columns taken together indicate that the market seems to believe that hostile tactics are more effective in dealing with firm sales and governance issues, but not as effective for business strategy and capital structure issues. However, these differences are not statistically significant due to the large standard errors.

8.5.3 Returns to Hedge Funds Investment

The positive average abnormal returns at the announcement of activism indicate that activism is potentially a profitable investment strategy for the hedge funds. To provide a more comprehensive description of the returns accruing to hedge funds, we compute the deal holding period returns, that is, the buy-and-hold stock return between the month prior to the 13D filing date and the exit date, using a combination of information from 13F and 13D filings, as defined in Section 8.3.3.3, or 31 December 2006 if there is no information about the exit by that time. The summary statistics are reported in Panel A of Table 8.6.

Table 8.6 Long-term abnormal returns analysis

The table reports statistics on short- and long-term abnormal returns associated with hedge fund activism. Panel A reports the average raw and annualized deal holding period return for the hedge funds in the first two columns. Buy-and-hold returns are computed beginning in the month prior to the announced activism through the month in which the funds exits. Exit is defined as the first quarter-end when the 13F filing indicates that the holding falls below 1% or $1 million, or the last 13D/A filing date, indicating that the ownership drops below 5% if there is no 13F information. If no exit information is available, we assume that the holding lasts till December 2006, the end of our sample. The last two columns report the annualized holding period return in excess of the market and size-matched decile portfolio returns. Panels B and C report regression estimates and t-statistics from equal- and value-weighted calendar-time portfolio regressions. 'Window' indicates the buying time relative to the event (hedge fund activism targeting) and the holding period in months. 'Alpha' is the estimate of the regression intercept from the factor models. 'Beta(−1)' and 'Beta' are the factors loading on the lagged and concurrent market excess return (the Fama and French RMRF). 'SMB', 'HML', and 'MOM' are the estimates of factor loading on the Fama-French size and book-to-market factors, and the Carhart momentum factor. 'R2' is the R-squared from the regressions. * and ** indicate statistical significance at the 10% and 5% levels.

	Deal period raw return	Annualized raw return	Annualized market adjusted	Annualized size adjusted
Panel A: Hedge fund deal holding period return				
1%	−0.938	−0.933	−1.017	−1.233
5%	−0.609	−0.607	−0.708	−0.855
25%	−0.068	−0.062	−0.197	−0.250
50%	0.181	0.149	0.042	0.003
75%	0.602	0.411	0.283	0.249
95%	2.372	1.753	1.532	1.459
99%	4.674	4.659	4.393	4.39.0
Mean	0.420**	0.330**	0.206**	0.143**
Std. Dev.	0.979	1.025	1.004	1.013
P-Val (Mean = 0)	0.00%	0.00%	0.00%	0.01%

Window (months)	Alpha		Beta (−1)		Beta		SMB		HML		MOM		R^2
	Estimate	*t*-statistic	Estimate	*t*-statistic	Estimate	*t*-statistic	Estimate	*t*-statistic	Estimate	*t*-statistic	Estimate	*t*-statistic	
Panel B: Equal-weight four-factor model													
(−12,−10)	−1.023	−1.82	0.123	1.04	0.976**	6.81	0.663**	4.40	0.421**	2.41	−0.278**	−3.14	0.578
(−9,−7)	0.283	0.54	0.078	0.67	0.671**	4.94	0.913**	6.69	0.170	1.01	−0.493**	−5.88	0.657
(−6,−4)	−0.513	−1.02	0.252	2.27	0.805**	6.22	0.851**	6.15	0.322*	1.91	−0.243**	−2.84	0.648
(−3,−1)	−0.664	−1.30	−0.057	−0.50	0.57**	4.44	0.906**	5.20	0.333*	1.88	−0.164*	−1.79	0.516
Event	5.095**	6.72	0.371**	2.00	0.401*	1.90	0.644**	2.45	0.205	0.72	−0.274*	−1.77	0.302
(1,3)	1.093**	2.01	0.157	1.23	0.339**	2.26	0.611**	3.26	0.400*	1.74	−0.609**	−4.85	0.540
(4,6)	0.237	0.52	0.195*	1.71	0.727**	5.24	0.989**	5.99	0.428**	2.34	−0.092	−0.84	0.651
(7,9)	−0.093	−0.19	0.118	0.77	0.902**	5.45	0.655**	3.41	0.387	1.48	−0.163	−1.10	0.599
(10,12)	1.124	1.84	0.008	0.04	0.776**	3.65	0.602**	2.41	0.009	0.03	−0.019	−0.10	0.395

Window (months)	**Alpha**		**Beta (−1)**		**Beta**		**SMB**		**HML**		**MOM**		R^2
	Estimate	***t*-statistic**	**Estimate**	***t*-statistic**	**Estimate**	***t*-statistic**	**Estimate**	***t*-statistic**	**Estimate**	***t*-statistic**	**Estimate**	***t*-statistic**	
Panel C: Value-weight four-factor model													
(−12,−10)	−2.377**	−3.18	−0.060	−0.38	1.180**	6.17	0.413**	2.06	0.723**	3.10	−0.177	−1.50	0.383
(−9,−7)	−0.261	−0.42	0.161	1.17	1.025**	6.46	0.482**	3.03	0.145	0.74	−0.193**	−1.97	0.540
(−6,−4)	−2.122**	−3.34	0.054	0.39	1.032**	6.34	0.834**	4.79	1.054**	4.98	0.025	0.23	0.460
(−3,−1)	−1.663**	−2.33	0.159	0.99	0.731**	4.07	0.235	0.96	0.486*	1.96	−0.301**	−2.35	0.323
Event	1.616	1.18	0.820**	2.44	0.663*	1.74	0.678	1.43	0.112	0.22	−0.021	−0.07	0.173
(1,3)	0.141	0.28	0.211*	1.78	0.522**	3.75	0.450**	2.60	0.604**	2.84	−0.419**	−3.61	0.508
(4,6)	−0.683	−1.24	0.033	0.24	1.005**	6.04	0.959**	4.84	0.990**	4.52	−0.268**	−2.05	0.625
(7,9)	−0.005	−0.01	0.089	0.60	0.742**	4.57	0.587**	3.12	1.030**	4.03	−0.692**	−4.74	0.685
(10,12)	−0.041	−0.08	−0.132	−0.82	0.985**	5.50	0.778**	3.69	0.666**	2.181	−0.165	−1.05	0.610

The average (median) raw deal holding period return is 42.0 (18.1)%. On an annualized basis, the same figure becomes 33.0 (14.9)%. The average remains significantly (at less than the 1% level) positive after market and size adjustments. The sample annualized average return is 14.3% higher than the value-weighted portfolio returns of stocks in the same size decile. However, the median deal holding period return is no different from the size-adjusted benchmark. While it is apparent that the positive average returns are attributed to the right tail of the distribution, they are not driven by a few extreme outliers. The sample mean statistics remain qualitatively the same if we winsorize data at the 1% extremes. To summarize, while the typical deal does not earn abnormal returns, the upper 25% of the deals offer much more upside than the corresponding downside of the lower quartile.

8.5.4 Alternative Hypotheses

The large average abnormal stock return around the Schedule 13D filing date is consistent with the view that the market anticipates that hedge funds' activism will result in actual value improvement. However, it is possible that the reactions that we document are explained by alternative causes, which we now explore in detail.

8.5.4.1 *Market Over-Reaction and Temporary Price Impact*

One potential explanation for the high abnormal return is a temporary price impact caused by buying pressure from the filing hedge fund or other hedge funds. As shown by Figure 8.1, the run up in price around the announcement window is accompanied by abnormally high trading volume as well. If the price impact is purely temporary and reflects a trading friction rather than information about prospective value changes, we should observe negative abnormal returns shortly after the event. This turns out not to be the case. Figure 8.1 shows no reversal after twenty days (when the abnormal turnover declines to close to zero), and the pattern persists if we extend the window for another twenty days.

We conduct a more formal long-term return analysis using calendar-time portfolio regressions around the Schedule 13D filing date. For example, we form a [-3, -1] portfolio by buying all firms that will be targeted by a hedge fund in three months' time, and the firms are held for three months before selling. Similarly, we form a [1, 3] portfolio by buying all firms that were targeted by hedge funds one month earlier, and these firms are held for three months before selling. For each such portfolio we estimate a regression of the portfolio excess returns on the Fama-French RMRF, small minus big (SMB), and high minus low (HML) factors, and the daily momentum factor (MOM).[13] We then focus on the regression intercept, the alpha, as evidence for possible mean reversion in prices. Clearly, all portfolios in the pre-event windows do not represent a tradable strategy. They are presented for an *ex post* analysis of the stock return patterns of the companies in the pre-targeting period. The

[13] We obtain these factor returns and monthly risk-free rates from Ken French's website at Dartmouth College, available at <http://mba.tuck.dartmouth.edu/pages/faculty/ken.french/data_library.html>.

results are reported in Panel B and C of Table 8.6, using four factor models with equal and value-weighting of firms' returns.

The factor loadings in both Panels B and C indicate that targeted companies co-move with small value firms, evidence that is consistent with the results presented in Section 8.4 and Table 8.4. Targeted firms have a slightly subpar pre-event stock performance. However, the negative alphas are only significant in the value-weighting specification, implying that it takes larger stock return underperformance for large-cap firms to be targeted. The event (Schedule 13D filing or the first announcement of activism for non-13D events) month and the three months afterwards see quite robust positive abnormal returns. With equal weighting, the event month and [1, 3] window alpha is 5.10% (t = 6.72) and 1.09% (t = 2.01). The same numbers for value weights are much lower (1.62 and 0.14%) and are not significant; presumably the larger firms in the sample do not receive as favourable response from the market as the smaller targets. Abnormal returns are higher using the CAPM model (not tabulated), consistent with the size and value premium.

Most importantly, the alphas are positive and revert to close to zero during the nine months after the 13D filings in both models. This evidence clearly refutes the market overreaction hypothesis for up to a year post event.

8.5.4.2 *Stock Picking versus Value Improvement*

It is possible that hedge fund activists simply identify undervalued companies, but do not add to firms' fundamental value. According to this hypothesis, the positive market reaction is due to the announcement of new information that a hedge fund has identified an undervalued company, not to the announcement that a hedge fund has committed to intervene to add value to the company. Given the strong evidence in Tables 8.3 and 8.4 that hedge funds target 'value' firms (i.e., firms with high book-to-market, or low q), and the tendency of event-firm portfolios to load positively on the HML factor (Table 8.6), it is plausible that obtaining the value return is indeed part of the activist hedge funds' strategy.

However, we believe that the market response to activist hedge funds' targeting goes beyond the information effect of stock picking. We present several tests which all support this conclusion. First, we find that when hedge funds launch activism with hostile tactics, the abnormal return is on average 3.9% higher than non-hostile targeting (significant at the 5% level). Hostile deals, by definition, are resisted by the managers,and therefore the changes are unlikely to happen were it not for hedge funds' persistence. In Section 8.5.1, we argue that, upon announcement of activism, market prices adjust to a level reflecting the benefit of successful intervention adjusted for the equilibrium probability that the hedge fund continues with activism and succeeds. Accordingly, the hedge fund will only intervene when the probability-adjusted benefit is greater than the cost of intervention. Since in our sample hostility is not associated with a higher probability of success (including partial success) in equilibrium (the correlation is close to zero, 0.02), and it is reasonable that hostile deals involve higher costs of intervention, these two facts imply that the expected benefit when a hedge fund successfully carries out a hostile deal should be higher than a non-hostile one. As a result, the more favourable market response indicates that the perceived value improvement comes from imposed changes, rather than a mere discovery of undervaluation due to mispricing.

Second, we examine the abnormal announcement returns of the subsample where the hedge fund had revealed a significant ownership (more than 1% or $1 million) in the Form 13F filing before the Schedule 13D. To make sure that the block ownership information is known to the market, we require the portfolio date of the Form 13F filing to be at least sixty days before the Schedule 13D filing, taking into account the allowed forty-five-day delay between the quarter-end Form 13F filing. This subsample of 312 events is interesting because the new information in the subsequent 13D filing is not just about stock picking, but about intervention. In Table 8.5, the coefficient on the dummy variable, *Pre-13F*, indicating a revealed significant ownership by the same hedge fund in the most recent Form 13F, is indeed negative at -3.27 percentage points (t-statistic = -2.10). What is important is that this subsample of events still shows significant announcement window returns (3.96%, t–statistic = 3.01) even though there is little additional information regarding stock picking.[14] Needless to say, the significant ownership revealed through earlier Form 13F filings might also invite speculation about hedge fund intervention down the road, and therefore reduce the 'surprise' of the later Schedule 13D filing. If this is the case, then the coefficient on *Pre-13F* should be less negative in the subsample of hostile events where there is stronger new information about intervention. This is indeed the case. Columns (2) and (3) of Table 8.5 indicate that the coefficient on *Pre-13F* is much more negative in the subsample of non-hostile events. In fact, the coefficient in the hostile subsample is statistically insignificant.

Third, we find that abnormal returns upon hedge funds' exit show different patterns, contingent on whether the stated agenda has been adequately carried out. Figure 8.2 plots the average abnormal buy-and-hold return around the last Schedule 13D/A file date (indicating divestment by the hedge fund to below the 5% ownership level), which serves as a proxy for the time of exit. We plot two event-time series. The full sample series indicates positive returns leading up to the file date, and roughly flat afterwards. Trading volume tends to spike during the ten-day window leading to the filing. This pattern indicates that hedge funds tend to exit after positive stock returns, and their exit, overall, does not have positive or negative impacts on the stock price. On the other hand, if a hedge fund fails or withdraws from ongoing activism (because the prospect of success is poor) and exits, the market response tends to be quite negative. The average [-20, 20] window abnormal return is about -4%, about 8 percentage points lower than the full sample average (the difference is significant at the 5% level). These patterns are inconsistent with a simple stock picking story as it does not predict these varying abnormal return patterns.

Fourth, if activist hedge funds were merely picking stocks, they should sell immediately after the market price reflects their finding that a company's shares were undervalued. A 'pure' stock picker would capture this incremental value, and then employ its capital in other undervalued stock trades. A quick exit should not reveal negative information to the market either, if stock picking is considered to be the sole motive. However, we do not observe activist hedge funds selling immediately after the filing of a Schedule 13D. On the contrary, these funds continue to hold for relatively long periods of time (see Table 8.2, Panel C). Moreover, we find that, in 94% of the cases in which hedge funds had prescribed

[14] We obtain qualitatively similar results using a 4% ownership as the threshold for the construction of the pre-13F variable. To the extent that a 4% stake is not materially different from the 5% 13D threshold in terms of economic interest, the additional information of 13D filing should be about unexpected intervention rather than stock picking.

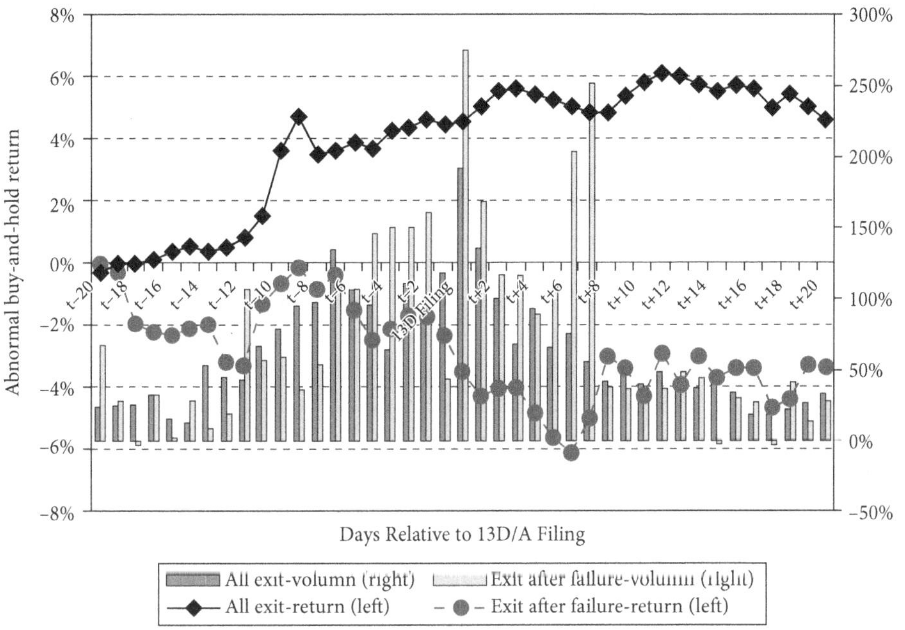

FIGURE 8.2 Buy-and-hold abnormal return and turnover around hedge fund exits

The lines (left axis) plot the average buy-and-hold return around the 13D/A file date, indicating a reduction of the hedge fund's position to below 5%, in excess of the buy-and-hold return on the value-weight market, from twenty days prior the 13D/A file date to twenty days afterwards. The two lines represent the full sample, and the subsample of hedge fund exits from unsuccessful activism. The bars (right axis) plot the share trading turnover (in percentage points) during the same time window compared to the average turnover rate during the preceding [−100, −40] event window.

an explicit agenda, they exit only after a resolution of the stated goals. It is consistent with the view that the positive abnormal return reflects the market expectation of hedge fund intervention, and it would be difficult for a hedge fund to exit at a high price without action. Given that the hedge fund needs to file an amendment to its Schedule 13D reflecting any material change in their position, including a reduction of the position to below 5%, 'promptly' after the change (some law firms recommend filing within one business day), it would have very little time to sell its block before making a public statement. Moreover, the typical stock has a turnover rate of about 0.4% a day and targeted firms tend to be mid- and small-cap stocks, making a quick exit very hard to execute. As a consequence, hedge funds can only cash out a large portion of their position at a price that no longer reflects the potential of value improvement if they exit before carrying out the stated agenda.

We conclude this section by noting that it is possible that activist hedge funds are merely stock pickers, but use long holding periods to sustain an (unwarranted) reputation for activism. Alternatively, it is possible that activist hedge funds are merely stock pickers, but believe (incorrectly) that they are activists and can add additional value after the filing of a Schedule 13D. We cannot rule out these possibilities, although we believe that a more plausible interpretation is that only a small portion of the positive abnormal return might be due to stock picking.

8.5.4.3 *Value Expropriation from Other Stakeholders*

Shareholders are by no means the only party affected by hedge fund activism. If other stakeholders are impacted, then some of the positive stock market reaction to activism might reflect wealth redistribution from other stakeholders. We consider two key stakeholders for our analysis: creditors and executives. We focus on these two groups mostly due to data availability and testability. We find no evidence that activist hedge funds redistribute wealth from creditors to shareholders, but we do find evidence of redistribution from managers to shareholders.

If shareholders of the target company gain at the expense of the creditors, then the gain should be higher in companies with higher levels leverage, especially long-term debt. Short-term debt will be renewed to reflect the new conditions within a year, and hence should not decline significantly in value. Long-term creditors, in the absence of renegotiation before the contracting term ends, therefore bear the cost of potential expropriation from shareholders. Given that we are interested in the effect of such expropriation on the market value of equity, the relevant leverage ratio should be market value (rather than book value) based. In Table 8.5, the corresponding covariate, *LTDebt*, is the ratio of long-term debt to the market value of capital (proxied by the sum of all debt and the market value of equity). The coefficient is far from significant statistically, and its economic magnitude is small as well. Every percentage point increase in the long-term leverage is associated with a 0.03 percentage point decrease in announcement return (t-statistic = −0.72).

In fact, the cleanest test of whether the gains to shareholders come at the expense of creditors is based on the subsample of 174 targets without any long-term debt. Obviously, shareholders cannot expropriate gains from long-term creditors if there are no such creditors. These firms actually see a somewhat *higher* announcement window returns (9.46%) than those that have some long-term debt (7.21%, the difference is not statistically significant). Overall, it is unlikely that the expropriation of bondholders is a meaningful source of shareholder gain in the wake of announced activism.[15]

To examine the effect of hedge fund activism on executives, we retrieve various variables from the Compustat Executive Compensation database. The results are reported in Table 8.7 Panel A. It shows the average differences of the listed variables between the targeted companies and their matched companies (from the same year, same SIC 2-digit industry, and same Fama and French 5 x 5 size and book-to-market sorted portfolios), and the associated t-statistics. In the first column of Panel A, the variable is total CEO compensation including option grants ('TDC1' by ExecuComp), which is an *ex ante* measure of total CEO compensation. In the event year, the target companies' CEO compensation is, on average, $914,000 higher ($t$ = 2.06) than CEO compensation at peer companies in the same industry and of similar size and stock valuation. We note that the compensation award levels are fixed in the year prior to the year in which they are paid. One year after hedge fund targeting, CEO pay is not distinguishable from peer levels. A related pattern is the increase in pay-for-performance sensitivity, measured as the percentage of CEO actual pay (including option exercise) that comes from equity-based incentives,

[15] Cremers, Nair, and Wei (2007) show that the relation between shareholder control and bondholder interest is ambiguous and depends on takeover vulnerability.

Table 8.7 Target firm performance before and after hedge fund activism

Panels A, B, and C report various statistics of target company performance in excess of a matched sample in years before and after being targeted by activist hedge funds. In the columns marked 'Year-by-Year Peer Match', a matching group for each target company is formed from other companies in the same industry/size/book-to-market group in each year. In the columns marked 't–2 Performance Match', a matching group consists of firms that have very close performance by the measure under consideration (the ratio being between 0.9 and 1.1) in year t–2, plus a best possible match along the industry and size dimensions. Difference is then taken between the target company and the average of the matching firms; and then averaged over all target companies ('Diff w/ Match'). Also reported are the associated *t*-statistics. 'CEO Contracted Pay' is the total CEO contracted pay including options valued at granting ('TDC1' from ExecuComp). 'CEO Pay-for-Performance' is the percentage of CEO take-home pay (including option exercise) that comes from equity-based incentive. '% CEO Turnover' is the rate of CEO turnover. 'Total Payout Yield' represents the sum of dividend and share repurchase scaled by the market value of equity. 'Leverage' is the ratio of debt to the sum of debt and book value of equity. * and ** indicate statistical significance at the 10% and 5% levels.

	CEO contracted pay ($1,000)		CEO pay-for-performance (%)		% CEO turnover	
	Diff w/ match	*t*-statistic	Diff w/ match	*t*-statistic	Diff w/ match	*t*-statistic
Panel A: Executive compensation and turnover (year-by-year peer match only)						
t–2	−445	−1.33	−7.10%**	−3.33	1.55%	0.62
t–1	18	0.05	0.29%	0.12	2.52%	1.03
Event	914**	2.06	5.70%**	2.56	5.82%*	1.88
t+1	−296	−0.73	6.14%**	2.02	12.42%**	2.85
(t+1)–(t–1)	−315	−0.6	5.85%*	1.94	9.90%**	2.34
(t+1)–(t)	−1,210**	−2.16	0.45%	0.14	6.60%	1.16

	EBITDA/assets				EBITDA/sales			
	Year-by-year peer match		(t–2) Performance match		Year-by-year peer match		(t–2) Performance match	
	Diff w/ match	t-statistic	Diff w/ match	t-statistic	Diff w/ match	t-statistic	Diff w/ match	t-statistic
Panel B: Operational performance								
t–2	1.99%**	3.56	0.01%	–	4.41%	1.26	−0.02%	–
t–1	1.16%**	2.17	0.12%	0.30	2.86%	0.81	−1.54%	−0.99
Event	0.01%	0.02	−0.49%	−0.95	2.79%	0.88	−3.03%*	−1.77
t+1	0.97%	1.48	0.29%	0.42	5.35%*	1.84	−2.31%	−1.08
t+2	2.67%**	2.79	1.04%	1.10	**	3.63	3.15%	1.05
(t+1)–(t–1)	−0.19%	−0.35	0.17%	0.44	2.49%	1.41	−0.77%	−0.23
(t+2)–(t–1)	1.51%*	1.94	0.92%	1.40	5.81%**	4.17	4.69%**	2.67

(*continued*)

Table 8.7 (Continued)

	Total payout yield				Leverage			
	Year-by-year peer match		(t-2) Performance match		Year-by-year peer match		(t-2) Performance Match	
	Diff w/ match	t-statistic	Diff w/ match	t-statistic	Diff w/ match	t-statistic	Diff w/ Match	t-statistic
Panel C: Payout and capital structure								
t-2	0.02%	0.14	0.01%	-	3.96%**	3.69	0.24%**	5.96
t-1	−0.007%	−0.60	−0.15%	−1.37	3.15%**	3.11	−0.91%	−1.48
Event	0.27%*	1.85	0.04%	0.28	3.28%**	3.05	0.18%	0.23
t+1	0.38%	1.88	0.13%	0.63	3.87%**	2.95	0.29%	0.28
t+2	0.16%	0.72	0.19%	0.8	4.45%**	2.69	0.49%	0.31
(t+1)-(t-1)	0.46%**	2.28	0.28%	1.36	0.72%	0.99	1.20%	1.59
(t+2)-(t-1)	0.23%	1.07	0.34%	1.58	1.30%**	2.70	1.40%	1.19

shown in the third column of Panel A: targeted firms experience significant increase in pay-for-performance during the event year and the year afterwards.

Accompanying the change in the level and composition of CEO pay is an increase in CEO turnover rate. We classify an event as CEO turnover if the name of the CEO of a company is different from that in the prior year. In the entire ExecuComp database, the CEO turnover rate for the 2001–06 period is 12.6%. Our sample companies have a slightly higher CEO turnover rate than their peer companies during the year before targeting, although the difference is not statistically significant. One year after targeting, however, the turnover rate at the sample companies is 12.4 percentage points higher than that of their matched peers ($t = 2.85$). This change in the turnover rate from the pre-event year is significant at the 5% level. We note that the estimates used here underestimate CEO turnover since they do not include CEO departures as a result of liquidation or sale of the company.

The combined effects of activism on CEO pay and turnover suggest that we examine whether the CEO pay cut is a result of replacing the old CEO with a lower-paid new one, or a cut in the pay of the incumbent. We find that, conditional on the subsample of surviving CEOs, their pay was $436,000 higher than that of their peers on average, and was cut to $709,000 below their peer level a year afterwards. Comparing those numbers with the full sample, it seems that CEO turnover is positively associated with preactivism compensation level, but (*ex post*) surviving CEOs received about the same level of pay cut on average.

Overall, hedge funds seem to have been successful in curtailing executive compensation, enhancing pay-for-performance, and ousting CEOs. The direct impact of these actions on shareholder gains can be considerable. Panel A of Table 8.7 shows that, relative to the matched sample, CEO pay is lower by about $1 million annually after activism. If all of the top executives combined are paid $5 million less for five years post-intervention due to activism, and this value goes to shareholders (assuming away tax issues, etc.), then the present value of such an income stream is on the order of magnitude of $20 million (using a 10% discount rate), which is a significant portion of the market capitalization of a typical targeted company (the average market capitalization of our sample firms is $706 million).

We also note that the change in CEO compensation and turnover is further evidence supporting the 'intervention' against the 'stock picking' hypothesis since it is highly improbable that such changes would occur absent intervention.

We have so far identified several potential explanations concerning the stock market reaction to hedge fund activism. The evidence in this section is consistent with the idea that the revision in equity prices around the filing of the Schedule 13Ds reflects the positive effect of activism on firm value. We now turn to a direct test and ask whether hedge fund activism affects target firms' *ex post* operating performance.

8.6 *Ex Post* Performance Analysis

Following the literature, we use ROA (return on assets, defined as EBITDA/lagged assets) and operating profit margins (defined as EBITDA/sales) as measures of operating profitability. These two measures are largely unaffected by non-operational factors such as leverage and taxes. Panel B of Table 8.7 reports target firms' average performance in excess of that of their matched sample from two years before the activism, to two years later. All variables discussed in this section were retrieved from Compustat, and updated to 2006.

We adopt two criteria to form a matched sample. With the first we match, year-by-year, along the industry/size/book-to-market dimensions as in Table 8.3. With the second matching procedure, we adopt the beginning-of-period performance matching as proposed by Barber and Lyon (1996). More specifically, a matched group for each target firm consists of firms from the same SIC two-digit industry (relaxed to one-digit if there is no match) and whose operating performance measure falls between 90 and 110% of that of the target in year (t−2). Target firms' performance in excess of the first type of benchmark indicates how these firms fare relative to their comparables at each point of time. The second type of benchmark serves to show how target firms go along a potentially different path of operational improvement from nontarget firms that had almost identical performance

Panel B shows that targeted companies, overall, have higher ROA and operating profit margin (OPM) than their industry/size/book-to-market matched peers. Their performance experiences a dip during the event year, and roughly recovers to the pre-event level one year after the event. The recovery continues into a significant improvement in year (t+2). ROA (OPM) is about 0.9 to 1.5 (4.7–5.8) percentage points higher than the pre-event levels, where the OPM change is significant at the 5% level. Both matching approaches yield a similar time-series pattern up to a level shift since the (t−2)–performance matching, by construction, starts with near-zero excess performance.

In comparison, the change in payout policies occurs sooner after the hedge fund intervention. Given that activist hedge funds often demand both dividends and share repurchases, a total payout measure is suitable for our analysis. We define the total payout yield as (dividend + share repurchase)/(lagged market value of equity). The ratio represents the return from all payouts that an equity investor obtains from his shares purchased at the market price. Panel C of Table 8.7 shows that payout increases during the year of intervention, and peaks in the year afterwards. Year (t−2) sees some reversion, but remains above benchmark levels. Compared to the level in the pre-event year, target firms' average total payout yield increases by 0.3–0.5 percentage points in the post-event year, and the change is significant at 5% using the year-by-year peer match.[16] Moreover, if we count activism that results in a target's liquidation, sale, or privatization, as a complete payout to existing shareholders, then the post-activism payout ratio is much higher than the conventional payout measures indicate.

Panel C traces out the change in leverage. There is some evidence of relevering after the event, but the magnitude is relatively small. In two years, the leverage ratio (by book values) on average increases by 1.3–1.4 percentage points compared to the level during the year before the event, out of an average leverage ratio of 34.8% for target companies (before the event). Furthermore, the correlation between dividend increase and leverage increase is weak (0.04). The moderate increase in leverage and its weak correlation with dividends are consistent with the analysis in Section 8.4.4.3, showing that expropriation of creditors is unlikely to be a significant source of shareholder gain.

Needless to say, *ex post* performance analysis can only be performed on firms that remain in the sample in post-event years and hence the challenge to address the potentially non-random attrition of target firms. If we define attrition as the state where a target firm, previously covered by Compustat, ceases to be so in the year after the event, then our sample attrition rate (for the 2001–05 subsample where attrition could be identified with Compustat data updated to 2006) is 18.2%. Moreover, the attrition rate is considerably higher among hostile events, especially events where hedge funds target for the sale of the firm (31.0%). If attrition, to a large extent, represents a successful outcome of hedge fund activism because it facilitates efficient reallocation of capital, the resulting absence of the firm from the *ex post* performance analysis can potentially induce a negative bias to inferences about firm performance.

The sample of surviving firms can help to test whether, indeed, activist hedge funds help create shareholder value through efficient reallocation of capital. We calculate the correlation between target firms' industry-adjusted assets change and their industry-adjusted ROA change in each of the two years after intervention (not tabulated). Specifically, for each target firm, we compute the percentage change in assets after activism: (Assets(t+1)–Assets(t–1))/Assets(t–1) and (Assets(t+2)–Assets(t–1))/Assets(t–1). We adjust these changes with the SIC three-digit industry level assets change during the same time period. We find that the correlation to industry-adjusted ROA change is 0.23 for the period from event year (t–1) to (t+1), and 0.25 over the period from event year (t–1) to (t+2). This evidence is important as it indicates that hedge fund activism is associated with a significant reallocation of capital to more efficient use. Similarly, the selective sale of target firms could be an even stronger form of capital reallocation. Moreover, hedge fund activism's direct effects on capital reallocation at target firms are supplemented by its indirect 'disciplinary' impact on other firms that are perceived as potential targets.

Finally, we look at analysts' forecasts as an additional sensitivity check. If activism improves firm performance, this effect should be reflected in forward-looking measures such as analyst forecasts. We retrieve analyst stock forecasts data from the I/B/E/S

[16] Hedge funds may also have contributed to dividend increases during the event year. We matched the 128 event-year dividend increase to the CRSP dividend declaration dates and found that in 15.5% of the cases, all dividends paid during the year are declared after the activism announcement date; in 56.9% of the events, part of the dividends are declared after activism and the post-event dividend sees increase over the same quarter last year.

and calculate, month by month, the proportion of all forecasts on the target firms that are upgrades (or downgrades) relative to the previous forecasts issues by the same analysts. During the twelve months before activism is announced, we find that there were more stock downgrades than upgrades among the (future) targets. In particular, downgrades outnumber upgrades by 54% to 22% during the three months leading to the event (where the remainder represents recommendations that maintain at the previous level). During the event month and the two subsequent months, we see significant decrease (increase) of downgrades (upgrades), and the overall analyst sentiment reverts to neutral thereafter (at 35% each). Therefore, analysts perceive improved prospects for the target firms subsequent to the hedge fund intervention. If one believes that stock analysts have at least as much information as hedge funds about the firms' prospects *without* hedge fund intervention, then the change in analyst sentiment represents analysts' updating their views about firms' prospects due to hedge fund intervention.

To summarize, we find that hedge fund activism is associated with an almost immediate increase in payout, heightened CEO discipline, and an improvement in analyst sentiment. On the other hand, the improvement in operating performance takes longer to manifest. In a recent paper, Cronqvist and Fahlenbrach (2009) show that there is large heterogeneity across different blockholders in their effect on corporate decisions along similar dimensions, but the average effect is small and insignificant (see also Bhagat, Black, and Blair 2004). Our study identifies one small group of blockholders—activist hedge funds—that are effective at influencing corporate policies.

8.7 Conclusion

This chapter is the first to examine hedge fund activism using a large-scale sample over the period 2001 to 2006. We document the heterogeneity in hedge fund objectives and tactics, and show how these factors relate to target firm responses. The positive market reaction to hedge fund intervention that we find is consistent with the improved post-intervention target performance, the effect of intervention on CEO pay/turnover, and changes in payout policy. Importantly, we show that the extent of hostility matters to market reaction and outcomes, and that the level of hostility among hedge fund activists is not as high as some have claimed.

Our findings are consistent with the view that informed shareholder monitoring can reduce agency costs at targeted firms. Hedge fund activists are a particularly nimble kind of shareholder, use a wide variety of tactics to pursue their objectives, and are largely successful even though they hold relatively small stakes. Sometimes hedge fund activists benefit from friendly interaction with management (and in this way resemble large blockholders), but other times they are openly confrontational with target boards when they perceive them as entrenched. Unlike traditional institutional investors, hedge fund managers have very strong personal financial incentives to increase the value of their portfolio firms, and do not face the regulatory or political barriers that limit the effectiveness of these other investors.

Although there is a large cross-sectional variation, hedge fund activism generates value on average, not because activists are good stock pickers, but because they credibly commit upfront to intervene at target firms on behalf of shareholders, and then follow through on their commitments. Thus, hedge fund activism can be viewed as a new middle ground between internal monitoring by large shareholders and external monitoring by corporate raiders. The benefit from their activism goes beyond the improved performance and stock prices at the actual target companies. The presence of these hedge funds and their potential for intervention exert a disciplinary pressure on the management of a large number of public firms to put shareholder value as a priority.

Finally, the abnormal positive returns to hedge fund activism appear to be consistent with the early arbitrage profits that hedge funds have previously captured using other strategies. During our six-year sample period, hedge fund activism becomes increasingly common, and, not surprisingly, the return to activism, measured as the average abnormal returns at the filing of Schedule 13D, has dropped monotonically from 15.9% in 2001 to 3.4% in 2006. If activism is viewed as another form of arbitrage, then it is likely that the abnormal returns associated with hedge fund activism will decline, or even disappear, as more funds chase after fewer attractive targets, and as the market incorporates the potential for investor intervention and improvement into security prices. Both effects suggest that decreasing returns to activists do not necessarily imply reduced benefits for shareholders from activism. Hedge fund activism might remain a staple of corporate governance, but at a lower equilibrium level of profitability.

References

Admati, A. R. and Pfleiderer, P. C. (2009). The 'Wall Street Walk' and Shareholder Activism: Exit as a Form of Voice, *Review of Financial Studies* 22(7), 2245–85.

Amihud, Y. (2002). Illiquidity and Stock Returns: Cross-Section and Time-Series Effects, *Journal of Financial Markets* 5, 31–56.

Barber, B. M. (2006). Monitoring the Monitor: Evaluating CalPERS' Activism, *Journal of Investing* 16, 66–88.

Barber, B. and Lyon, J. (1996). Detecting Abnormal Operating Performance: The Empirical Power and Specification of Test Statistics, *Journal of Financial Economics* 41, 359–99.

Bethel, J., Liebeskind, J., and Opler, T. (1998). Block Share Purchases and Corporate Performance, *Journal of Finance* 53, 605–34.

Bhagat, S., Black, B. S., and Blair, M. M. (2004). Relational Investing and Firm Performance, *Journal of Financial Research* 27, 1–30.

Bizjak, J. and Marquette, C. (1998). Are Shareholder Proposals All Bark and No Bite? Evidence from Shareholder Resolutions to Rescind Poison Pills, *Journal of Financial and Quantitative Analysis* 33, 499–521.

Black, B. S. (1990). Shareholder Passivity Reexamined, *Michigan Law Review* 89, 520–608.

Black, B. S. (1998). Shareholder Activism and Corporate Governance in the US in P. Newman (ed.), *The New Palgrave Dictionary of Economics and the Law* (London and Basingstoke, Palgrave Macmillan), 461–8.

Bond, P., Goldstein, I., and Prescott, E. S. (2006). Market-Based Regulation and the Informational Content of Prices, Working Paper, available at <http://ssrn.com/abstract=952031>.

Bradley, M., Brav, A., Goldstein, I., and Jiang, W. (2007). Shareholder Activism and Price Dynamics: Evidence from Closed-End Funds, Duke University, University of Pennsylvania, and Columbia University Working Paper.

Bratton, W. W. (2007). Hedge Funds and Governance Targets, *Georgetown Law Journal* 95, 1375–433.

Carleton, W. T., Nelson, J. M., and Weisbach, M. S. (1998). The Influence of Institutions on Corporate Governance through Private Negotiations: Evidence from TIAA-CREF, *Journal of Finance* 53, 1335–62.

Clifford, C. (2008). Value Creation or Destruction: Hedge Funds as Shareholder Activists, *Journal of Corporate Finance* 14, 323–36.

Cornelli, F. and Li, D. D. (2002). Risk Arbitrage in Takeovers, *Review of Financial Studies* 15, 837–68.

Cremers, M., Nair, V., and Wei, C. (2007). Governance Mechanisms and Bond Prices, *Review of Financial Studies* 20(5), 1359–88.

Cronqvist, H. and Fahlenbrach, R. (2009). Large Shareholders and Corporate Policies, *Review of Financial Studies* 22(10), 3941–76.

Del Guercio, D. and Hawkins, J. (1999). The Motivation and Impact of Pension Fund Activism, *Journal of Financial Economics* 52, 293–340.

Del Guercio, D., Seery, L. J., and Woidtke, T. (2008). Do Boards Pay Attention When Institutional Investor Activists 'Just Vote No'?, Working Paper, available at <http://ssrn.com/abstract=575242>.

Gillan, S. and Starks, L. (2000). Corporate Governance Proposals and Shareholder Activism: The Role of Institutional Investors, *Journal of Financial Economics* 57, 275–305.

Gompers, P., Ishii, J., and Metrick, A. (2003). Corporate Governance and Equity Prices, *Quarterly Journal of Economics* 118, 107–55.

Hasbrouck, J. (2006). Trading Costs and Returns for US Equities: The Evidence from Daily Data, NYU Stern School Department of Finance Working Paper, available at <http://ssrn.com/abstract=38836>.

Hu, H. and Black, B. (2006). Empty Voting and Hidden (Morphable) Ownership: Taxamony, Implications, and Reforms, *Business Lawyer* 61(3), 1011–70.

Ikenberry, D. and Lakonishok, J. (1993). Corporate Governance through the Proxy Contest: Evidence and Implications, *Journal of Business* 66, 405–35.

Kahn, C. and Winton, A. (1998). Ownership Structure, Speculation, and Shareholder Intervention, *Journal of Finance* 53, 99–129.

Karpoff, J. M. (2001). The Impact of Shareholder Activism on Target Companies: A Survey of Empirical Findings, University of Washington Working Paper, available at <http://ssrn.com/abstract=885365>.

Karpoff, J. M., Malatesta, P. H., and Walkling, R. A. (1996). Corporate Governance and Shareholder Initiatives: Empirical Evidence, *Journal of Financial Economics* 42, 365–95.

Martin, S. and Partnoy, F. (2005). Encumbered Shares, *Illinois Law Review* 3, 775–813.

Maug, E. (1998). Large Shareholders as Monitors: Is There a Trade-Off between Liquidity and Control?, *Journal of Finance* 53, 65–98.

Partnoy, F. and Thomas, R. S. (2007). Gap Filling, Hedge Funds, and Financial Innovation, in Y. Fuchita and R. E. Litan (eds.), *Brookings-Nomura Papers on Financial Services* (Washington, DC, Brookings Institution Press), 101–40.

Rock, E. (1992). The Logic and (Uncertain) Significance of Institutional Shareholder Activism, *Georgetown Law Journal* 79, 445–506.

Romano, R. (1993). Public Pension Fund Activism in Corporate Governance Reconsidered, *Columbia Law Review* 93, 795–853.

Romano, R. (2001). Less is More: Making Institutional Investor Activism a Valuable Mechanism of Corporate Governance, *Yale Journal of Regulation* 18, 174–251.
Smith, M. P. (1996). Shareholder Activism by Institutional Investors: Evidence from CalPERS, *Journal of Finance* 51, 227–52.
Wahal, S. (1996). Pension Fund Activism and Firm Performance, *Journal of Financial and Quantitative Analysis* 31, 1–23.

CHAPTER 9

ENTREPRENEURIAL SHAREHOLDER ACTIVISM: HEDGE FUNDS AND OTHER PRIVATE INVESTORS

APRIL KLEIN AND EMANUEL ZUR

9.1 Introduction

In this chapter, we examine recent aggressive campaigns by entrepreneurial shareholder activists. In the spirit of Pound (1992), we define an entrepreneurial activist as an investor who buys a large stake in a publicly held corporation with the intention to bring about change and thereby realize a profit on the investment.

We conduct our analyses on two samples of entrepreneurial activists. The common feature to both groups is that the investor is relatively free from the regulatory controls of the Securities Act of 1933, the Securities Exchange Act of 1934, and, most notably, the Investment Company Act of 1940. The first sample consists of 151 hedge fund activist campaigns conducted primarily between 2003 and 2005. Hedge fund activism has received widespread attention, both in the popular press and by legal and financial scholars.[1] Our chapter complements and extends this research by examining the determinants, methods, and consequences of hedge fund managers who undertake confrontational activist campaigns. The second sample contains 154 other entrepreneurial confrontational activist campaigns over the same time period. These activists consist primarily of individuals, private equity funds, venture capital firms, and asset management groups for wealthy investors. Although these investor activists have generated widespread interest, there is little large-sample evidence

[1] In Section 9.2, we include a literature review of past shareholder activism, as well as current studies on hedge fund activism. The research on hedge fund activism we discuss include those by Brav et al. (Chapter 8, this volume); Bratton (2007); and Kahan and Rock (Chapter 5, this volume).

on the determinants or outcomes of these campaigns. Thus, our chapter contributes to the recent shareholder activism literature by examining this group alone and also by comparing them to hedge fund activists.

We define the beginning of a confrontational activist campaign as the filing of an initial SEC Schedule 13D in which the activist clearly professes in the 'purpose' statement of the filing its goal to redirect managements' efforts. A Schedule 13D is triggered after an investor directly or indirectly acquires the beneficial ownership of 5% or higher of any equity security in a publicly traded firm with the stated intent of influencing the firm's policies. The redirections stated in the Schedule 13D purpose statement include (but are not limited to) seeking seats on the company's board, opposing an existing merger or liquidation of the firm, pursuing strategic alternatives, or replacing the CEO. We exclude 13D filings that are filed because the investor is 'unwilling to give up the option of affecting the firm' (Clifford 2007: 326). We also exclude 13D filings if the investor states an interest in working with or communicating with management on a regular basis. These restrictions limit our analyses to activist campaigns that can be characterized as aggressive or confrontational.

We find similarities and disparities between our samples of hedge fund and other entrepreneurial activists. The three main parallels are: a significantly positive market reaction around the 13D filing date, a further significant increase in share price over the subsequent year, and the activist's success in achieving its original objective.

Specifically, hedge fund targets earn 10.2% average abnormal stock returns during the period surrounding the initial Schedule 13D. Other activist targets experience a significantly positive average abnormal return of 5.1% around the SEC filing window. These findings suggest that, on average, the market believes activism creates shareholder value. Our findings are consistent with those of Holderness and Sheehan (1985), who document significant price increases for firms targeted by 'notorious' corporate raiders of the late 1970s and early 1980s, and also with those of Bethel, Liebeskind, and Opler (1998), who show similar results for firms targeted by individuals, rather than corporate or institutional large shareholders. The positive abnormal returns also are consistent with the work of Brav et al. (Chapter 8, this volume), who find positive market reactions for a sample of confrontational and non-confrontational hedge fund Schedule 13D filings. Furthermore, our target abnormal returns do not dissipate in the one-year period following the initial Schedule 13D. Instead, hedge fund targets earn an additional 11.4% abnormal return during the subsequent year, and other activist targets realize a 17.8% abnormal return over the year following the activists' interventions.

We also find that entrepreneurial activists experience great success in getting existing management to acquiesce to their demands as articulated in the initial Schedule 13D. Hedge funds enjoy a success rate of 60%, and other entrepreneurial activists accomplish their objectives 65% of the time. Moreover, *ex ante*, the market is able to differentiate between overall successful and non-successful campaigns. For both groups of activists, the abnormal return surrounding the initial Schedule 13D filing is significantly higher for firms in which the activist gains its objective within one year, when compared to those firms in which the activist is unsuccessful.

However, there are two striking differences between hedge fund and other entrepreneurial activism. The two main differences relate to the types of companies each group targets and the activists' post-13D filing strategies.

Hedge fund activists target more profitable and financially healthy firms than other entrepreneurial activists. Prior studies on activism almost always find that shareholder activists are more likely to target poorly performing firms (e.g., Gordon and Pound (1993); Bethel, Liebeskind, and Opler 1998; Faleye (2004); Becht et al., Chapter 7, this volume. Our results suggest that other entrepreneurial activists employ a similar screening mechanism to prior activists, but that hedge fund activists invest in a different subset of companies.

Given that the groups target firms with different characteristics, we expect and find that hedge funds and other entrepreneurial activists dissimilarly redirect target firms. Hedge funds appear to address the free cash flow problem, as articulated by Jensen (1986). Under this theory, firms can reduce agency conflicts between managers and shareholders by reducing excess cash on hand, and by obligating managers to make continuous payouts in the form of increased dividends and interest payments to creditors. Consistent with this view, hedge fund targets initially have higher levels of cash on hand than do other entrepreneurial activist targets. In addition, hedge fund activists frequently demand that the target firm buy back its own shares, cut the CEO's salary, or initiate dividends, whereas other activists do not make these demands. Consequently, over the fiscal year following the initial Schedule 13D, hedge fund targets, on average, double their dividends, significantly increase their debt-to-assets ratio, and significantly decrease their cash and short-term investments.

In contrast, other entrepreneurial activists appear to redirect the investment strategies of their targeted firms. In their initial Schedule 13Ds, they most frequently demand changes in the targets' operating strategies. Consistent with these requests, when comparing hedge fund and other entrepreneurial activist targets, we find significant differences in changes in R&D and capital expenditures in the year following the 13D filing, with the other entrepreneurial activist targets experiencing significant declines in both parameters.

Finally, we ask how the activist achieves these results. Overall, we find evidence that hedge fund and other entrepreneurial activists use the proxy solicitation process to gain board representation within one year of the initial 13D filing. We note that oftentimes the activist does not actually initiate a proxy fight, but instead threatens a proxy fight, which results in one or more board seats. These findings are inconsistent with earlier evidence on shareholder activism, which finds limited use of the proxy solicitation process as a weapon (e.g., Bebchuk 2005; Chapter 3, this volume).

The chapter proceeds as follows. Section 9.2 traces the recent history of shareholder activism and explains how the two samples fit the mould of a successful entrepreneurial activist. Section 9.3 describes the activist data, including the firms activists target. Section 9.4 examines the pre-13D filing market, financial, and discretionary spending characteristics of the target firms. In Section 9.5, we examine the market's response to initial 13D filings by hedge funds and other entrepreneurial activists. Sections 9.6 and 9.7 present the outcomes of the activists' campaigns, both in terms of the activists achieving their stated goals, and changes in firm characteristics for the one-year period between the pre- and post-13D filing dates. Section 9.8 summarizes and concludes the chapter.

9.2 Shareholder Activism

9.2.1 The Entrepreneurial Activist: Hedge Funds, Venture Capital Funds, Private Equity Funds, and Individual Investors

Hedge funds, asset management groups, private equity funds, and venture capital funds fall under a similar investment umbrella. Broadly, they can be characterized as classes of investments that are relatively free from the regulatory controls of the Securities Act of 1933, the Securities Exchange Act of 1934, and, most notably, the Investment Company Act of 1940.[2] They maintain their exemption from securities and mutual fund registration by limiting the number of investors and by allowing only experienced investors with significantly high net worth.[3] The funds are almost always organized as limited partnerships or occasionally as limited liability corporations (LLCs), and are managed by a small group of highly incentivized managers who are free from pay-for-performance restrictions imposed on mutual fund managers by the Investment Advisors Act of 1940. For example, whereas Kahan and Rock (Chapter 5, this volume) report that 97% of mutual funds charge investors a flat-rate fee based on the mutual fund's assets alone, a hedge fund manager's compensation typically includes both a percentage of invested funds and a percentage of the funds' profits, usually 5% to 40% over 0% or the risk-free rate. Private Equity Intelligence Ltd. (2007) reports similar percentages for private equity and venture capital funds.

The main difference among asset management groups, hedge funds, private equity funds, and venture capital funds lies in their investment strategies. Private equity funds tend to have large investments in a small number of private firms. Often, they invest in publicly traded companies and subsequently take them private. Venture capital funds invest in start-up or young companies, usually with new technologies or products. Hedge funds and asset management groups appear to be more eclectic investors and are more difficult to define by their investment strategies. Individual investors are also immune from most regulatory controls and generally are less diversified investors.

Pound (1992) discusses the active, entrepreneurial investor, whom he describes as an investor who buys stakes in publicly held corporations with the intention of bargaining with management to bring about productive change and thereby realize profits on his investments (Pound 1992: 7). Pound reviews the history of entrepreneurial investors from the mid-1800s on, and concludes that several primary characteristics distinguish successful activists from passive investors or unsuccessful activists.

Many of these characteristics are consistent with those described above in this section for our hedge fund and other entrepreneurial investor samples. First, as articulated by Pound, entrepreneurial investors are independent from corporate and financial power structures. This independence allows them to take positions without fear of economic or political reprisals.

Second, activists operate through small entities, for example, investment partnerships. This trait also minimizes their economic and political risks from their actions, thereby giving the general partners a great deal of control over their investment strategies.

[2] They are not exempt, however, from filing SEC Schedule 13D or 13G when crossing the 5% threshold of ownership or from filing an SEC Form 13F. The 13G filings are required for passive investors who acquire at least a 5% interest in a publicly traded equity security. See Clifford (2007) for an examination of Schedule 13G filings by hedge funds. A Form 13F must be filed within forty-five days after the end of March, June, September, and December by all institutional managers who exercise investment discretion over $100 million or more in total securities. Form 13F lists the securities, the number of shares owned, and the market value of each investment. It does not contain any indication of investment purpose.

[3] The investments are organized as '3(c)(1)' or '3(c)(7)' funds, referring to exemptions from mutual fund registration. Funds organized as 3(c)(1) funds are limited to ninety-nine 'accredited' investors. Section 3(c)(7) funds may have up to 499 'qualified' investors, but the net worth requirement is higher.

Third, the entrepreneurial activist is relatively undiversified and can risk a relatively large proportion of its wealth on individual ventures. Individual investors, hedge funds, asset management groups, private equity funds, and venture capital funds are wholly unrestricted in how they can invest in terms of diversification, illiquid assets, short-selling, and leverage. The funds need not have sufficient capital to cover redemptions and can restrict investors from exiting their funds. Furthermore, because the underlying investors are relatively wealthy, the activists have the financial resources to absorb large financial losses.

In addition to Pound's (1992) list, we note that our activists are not required to disclose their investment strategies, short-selling positions, or leverage ratios. One ramification of these disclosure exemptions is that activists have used the stock-lending (Christoffersen et al. 2007) or derivative markets (Hu and Black 2007) to acquire voting rights without owning a long position in the company's underlying stock. Thus, an activist can build up voting rights in a target company to buttress a threat of an impending proxy fight. Moreover, we argue that the pay-for-performance compensation structure described above in this section for fund managers is consistent with them pursuing confrontational activism if they believe this activism results in meaningful increases in the target's share price.

9.2.2 Prior Waves of Shareholder Activism

We trace shareholder activism over the past thirty years to allow comparisons between current and former waves of activism. Specifically, we discuss previous studies on the corporate raider, the large non-hedge fund blockholder, the institutional shareholder, and the hedge fund activist.[4]

Holderness and Sheehan (1985) and Walsh and Kosnik (1993) examine firms targeted by a handful of 'corporate raiders' during the 1977 to 1983 period.[5] In many respects, these raiders fit Pound's (1992) profile of the entrepreneurial activist. Most germane, their often-confrontational methods closely resemble those used by the managers and individual activists we examine in this chapter. Together, Holderness and Sheehan (1985) and Walsh and Kosnik (1993) find that although the stock market reacts positively to the public revelation of a raider's existence, there is little to no evidence that the raider influences the firm beyond, in several cases, subsequently buying out the raider at a profit to the raider. In particular, neither paper documents increased rates of board or top management turnover, nor an increased tendency for the targeted firm to be taken over or reorganized. In addition, Walsh and Kosnik (1993) report no association between prior firm performance and whether a firm is targeted by the raider.

Concurrent with and following the corporate raider is the large non-hedge fund blockholder (1978 to 1989).[6] These large shareholders include individuals, corporations, and

[4] See Gillan and Starks (Chapter 2, this volume) for an excellent and comprehensive review of shareholder activism.

[5] These raiders include Carl Icahn, Irwin Jacobs, Carl Lindner, David Murdock, and Victor Posner.

[6] With the exception of Bethel, Liebeskind, and Opler (1998), the studies we cite later in this section combine individual and corporate activists into their samples. Bethel, Liebeskind, and Opler (1998) divide their sample into activists (individuals who currently announce their intention to influence firm policies or in the past have done so), financial investors (banks, pension funds, mutual funds, and

financial institutions. Generally, a firm's stock price increases around the 13D filing date that identifies a new blockholder, indicating that the market interprets this event as value-increasing. The positive abnormal stock returns occur whether the block is bought on the open market (e.g., Mikkelson and Ruback 1985; Shome and Singh 1995) or through a negotiated transaction with the firm or a single shareholder of the firm (e.g., Barclay and Holderness 1989, 1991).

Shleifer and Vishny (1986) theoretically examine the positive monitoring effects of a large shareholder. They predict that the presence of a large shareholder increases: (1) the probability of a takeover (either by the blockholder or a third party); and (2) the target firm's future earnings over time. Shleifer and Vishny primarily envision the blockholder as achieving its goals through non-confrontational means. For example, they predict that it is not in the large shareholder's economic interests to pursue a proxy fight to achieve board representation or a successful takeover. In defence of the latter prediction, Shleifer and Vishny cite Dodd and Warner (1983), who report only seventy-one proxy contests over a seventeen-year period and a success rate of just 25%. Bebchuk (Chapter 3, this volume) using more recent data, comes to similar conclusions with regard to a shareholder's success in replacing sitting members of boards of directors.

The empirical literature on large blockholders both supports and refutes Shleifer and Vishny's (1986) conjectures. Barclay and Holderness (1991) find a positive correlation between the advent of an outside blockholder and the probability of a future takeover of the target over the 1978 to 1982 sample period. In contrast, Bethel, Liebeskind, and Opler (1998) report a reduction in merger activity, in the period after the activist investor stock purchase, for their sample of targets from 1980 through 1989. This drop in M&A activity might be a reflection of the overall decline in hostile or contested M&A activity that Holmström and Kaplan (2001) and Pound (1992) document for the post-1987 period.[7] In addition, Barclay and Holderness (1991) find that the reported positive abnormal returns surrounding the 13D filing are more likely only if the targeted firm is subsequently acquired either by the blockholder (usually a corporation) or a third party. As further evidence, they report that the original increase in stock price around the 13D dissipates within the first year after the filing if the firm is not subsequently acquired, whereas the abnormal return increases further if the firm is acquired within the first year. Thus, these blockholder studies envision the activist as a conduit to an eventual takeover.

Two studies measure changes in the target firms' future earnings. Bethel, Liebeskind, and Opler (1998) find a modest increase in the target's ROA the second and third year after a blockholder activist targets a firm (both changes around 1% each year), but report no changes in firm performance for corporate or institutional blockholders.[8] Shome and

individuals who do not adopt a public activist position), and strategic investors (non-financial investors, mainly companies). In addition, all of the studies, Bethel, Liebeskind, and Opler (1998) included, combine confrontational and non-confrontational activism.

[7] There are many reasons for this drop in M&A activity, including the rise of takeover defences and state takeover laws, along with the decline in the high-yield bond market following the demise of Drexel Burnham Lambert in 1987.

[8] Bethel, Liebeskind, and Opler (1998) attribute this result to the activist influencing the firm to be more focused, that is, less diversified following the initial stock purchase. However, it should be noted that their sample is for Fortune 500 firms in the 1980s, when investors viewed overly diversified companies as value-decreasing (e.g., Berger and Ofek 1995).

Singh (1995) report a 3.83% increase in operating income to total assets between years −3 and +2, but do not show which part of the increase occurs before and after the block purchase.

Beginning in the mid-1980s, financial institutions, most commonly pension funds and mutual funds, began a wave of non-confrontational shareholder activism. First, using Rule 14a-8, they tried to prod firms to make changes to their corporate governance and anti-takeover provisions by introducing shareholder proposals at annual corporate meetings. By and large, these proposals were unsuccessful and met with indifference by the market (e.g., Gordon and Pound 1993; John and Klein 1995; Wahal 1996; Del Guerico and Hawkins 1999; Gillan and Starks 2000). Second, large pension funds, for example, TIAA-CREF (Carleton, Nelson, and Weisbach 1998) and CalPERS (Smith 1996; Barber 2006), tried to engage firms through private negotiations or other relational investing techniques to influence corporate policies. These campaigns also had little impact on future firm performance or current stock price.

The main explanations offered by financial and legal scholars for these findings are that political costs and regulatory barriers exist that prevent mutual funds and pension funds from being entrepreneurial activists. Romano (2001), Woidtke (2002), Davis and Kim (2007), and Kahan and Rock (Chapter 5, this volume) analyse conflicts of interest that mutual funds and public pension funds face in voting against management. Black (1990, 1998) describes regulatory constraints that inhibit mutual funds from engaging in confrontational activism, including rules on maintaining liquidity, holding large blocks of any one company, and insider trading.

The most recent type of shareholder activism that has been examined is by the hedge fund activist. Bratton (2007), Briggs (2007), and Kahan and Rock (Chapter 5, this volume) present anecdotal data on hedge fund activism in the United States. These papers give interesting and often illuminating examples of the types of successful activist campaigns of hedge funds over the past few years. Becht et al. (Chapter 7, this volume) conduct a clinical study of one large UK pension fund, the Hermes UK Focus Fund, which is the pension fund of British Telecom. They find that this fund primarily targets poorly performing companies, but, contrary to most other blockholder studies, realizes a significantly negative abnormal return of −3.7% over a [−5, +5] window surrounding the notification by the Hermes Fund of their original stakehold in their UK companies.[9] They also document the fund's capacity to make significant changes to its target firms, most notably board changes and asset restructurings. One major difference between their study and ours is that Becht et al. (Chapter 7, this volume) describe almost all of the interactions between the Hermes fund and its target firms as non-confrontational, although they note that the fund uses the threat of calling a special or extraordinary shareholder meeting to vote on a shareholder proposal as a potent weapon towards achieving its goals.

Brav et al. (Chapter 8, this volume) analyse 888 events in the United States by 131 activist hedge funds from 2001 through 2005. Their larger sample size can be attributed to including both confrontational and non-confrontational activist events, to containing some events in which the hedge fund activist owns less than 5% of the target's shares, and their use of a longer time period. Despite these differences, many of our findings for hedge fund targets

[9] Under UK company law disclosure rules, all investments exceeding a 3% threshold must be disclosed.

are consistent with their chapter; for example, both report significantly positive price reactions around the initial 13D filing dates. However, there are several divergent results between the two studies, which might be due to the differences in sample selection.[10] Most notably, we report a decrease in operating performance and an increase in leverage for the target firm in the year following the Schedule 13D, whereas Brav et al. (Chapter 8, this volume) find an increase in operating performance and no such change in debt.[11]

9.3 Sample Selection and Data Description

9.3.1 Selection Criteria

We initially examine Schedule 13D and 13D/A filings between 1 January 2003 and 31 December 2005. Investors are required to file a Schedule 13D with the SEC within ten days after acquiring more than 5% of any publicly traded equity security class with the intent of influencing the firm's management.[12] A Schedule 13D/A is an amended filing by the same investor for the same firm and is filed subsequent to the original Schedule 13D. Because we are interested in examining first filings only, we trace these 13D/A schedules backwards in time to find the first event.

In either filing, the investor identifies name, background (including any criminal convictions within the last five years), number and type of shares purchased, the percentage of the class of equity owned, and the purpose of the transaction. For the hedge fund sample, we select only those transactions in which the investments: (1) are in a US publicly traded firm; (2) are purchased by a hedge fund or hedge fund manager; and (3) present an activist agenda in its purpose statement. For the other entrepreneurial activist sample, we use criteria (1) and (3), but select only those transactions that are purchased by individuals, venture capital firms, or private equity or asset management groups that invest for wealthy investors. Most importantly, we eliminate all activists that are required to file under the Investment Company Act of 1940 or the 1934 Securities Exchange Act, most notably mutual funds and corporations (both US and foreign). The one exception is GAMCO, formerly known as Gabelli Asset Management, a publicly traded fund.

[10] Boyson and Mooradian (2007), for example, find that the post-intervention changes in performance and cash holdings are related to whether the hedge fund practises more or less aggressive activism.

[11] Clifford (2007) examines Schedule 13D and Form 13G filings by hedge funds from 1998 to 2005. He includes all blocks purchased by 197 hedge funds. Similar to our chapter, Clifford (2007) finds a significant positive price reaction around the initial 13D filing date.

[12] Specifically, Rule 13d-1(a) states that:

> Any person who, after acquiring directly or indirectly the beneficial ownership of any equity security of a class which is specified in paragraph (i) of this section, is directly or indirectly the beneficial owner of more than five per cent of the class shall, within ten days after the acquisition, file with the Commission a statement containing the information required by Schedule 13D.

Rule 13d-2(b) further states that the investor could file a Schedule 13G if 'such person has acquired such securities in the ordinary course of his business and not with the purpose nor with the effect of changing or influencing the control of the issuer . . .'

Since there is no institutional or regulatory definition of a hedge fund, private equity fund, or venture capital fund, we rely on several sources to verify a blockholder's classification. These include the funds' websites, investor journals, Factiva, and newspaper and magazine articles, to determine if the filer is recognized as being a hedge fund or other type of fund. We use these sources to determine if the individual investors in our other entrepreneurial activist sample are investing for themselves (or him/herself if a solo investor) or are acting on behalf of a different entity's account. We also rely on the information in the 13D filing itself to help us determine the identity of the actual investor. When in doubt, we eliminate the filing—a rare event. We recognize that this search process may be imperfect, but we are confident that we correctly classify almost all (if not all) of our investors.

9.3.2 Descriptive Data

Table 9.1 describes the composition of the two samples of activist–target pairs. As Panel A shows, the hedge fund sample consists of 101 activists and 151 target events. The sample of other entrepreneurial activists consists of 134 investors and 154 target events. These activists fall into several categories: fifty-eight are individual investors; eight are *ex-officers* of the targeted firm; thirty-eight are investment advisors to wealthy investors; sixteen are private asset management firms; nine are private equity funds; and the remaining five are venture capital firms. We note that, although each sample contains roughly the same number of targets, hedge funds tend to be repeat activists when compared to the other activists in the sample. A total of 24 of the 101 hedge funds targeted two or more companies over our time period, with two, Steel Partners II and Carl Icahn's Hedge Fund, taking activist positions in eight or more firms. In contrast, only 12 of the 134 other entrepreneurial activists targeted more than 1 company, with only 1 investor, Gabelli Asset Management, engaging in a confrontational activist campaign against more than 3 firms.

As Panel B illustrates, most activists filed their original Schedule 13D from 2003 through 2005. However, we find a few examples of long-term activism. Carl Icahn's hedge fund filed its first Schedule 13D on National Energy Group in 1995, and Steel Partners II filed its first Schedule 13D on Ronson in 1998. Gabelli Asset Management originally invested in Liberty Corporation in 1998, and the Aokis began their activist campaign against Benihana (of which Rocky Aoki was the founder) in 1998.

In terms of trading venue, Panel C shows that hedge funds and other entrepreneurial activists invest in firms trading in a variety of markets, including the OTC bulletin board and the pink sheets. In addition, examination of whether these firms are in the S&P 500 index reveals (not tabulated) that only ten (seven) hedge fund targets (other entrepreneurial activist targets) were part of this index. Thus, entrepreneurial activists tend to target relatively smaller companies.

We also tabulate the target firms' industries. The hedge fund (other entrepreneurial activist) targets hail from thirty-six (forty-two) of the forty-eight Fama and French (1997) industry classifications. As Panel D shows, only two industries yield at least ten firms for the hedge fund sample: business services with twenty-nine firms and pharmaceutical products with ten firms. The top two industries in which other entrepreneurial activists invest are restaurants, hotels, and motels with nineteen firms, and banking with seventeen firms.

Table 9.1 Descriptive statistics

This table reports descriptive statistics for the final sample of hedge funds and other entrepreneurial activists along with their target firms. Panel A summarizes the number of activists and target firms in each of the samples. Panel B summarizes the number of firms targeted in each year by the hedge fund and other entrepreneurial activists. Panel C summarizes the number of target firms over the different exchanges or markets. Panel D summarizes the different industries of the target firms, where industry is defined according to Fama and French's (1997) forty-eight-industry classifications. Panel E summarizes the activists' initial stated reasons for targeting the firms, as collected from the Schedule 13D's 'Purpose of Transaction' section.

	Hedge fund activists	Other entrepreneurial activists
Panel A: Number of activists and target firms		
Total number of activists	101	134
Total number of target firms	151	154
Number of firms targeted by 2 activists	4	5
Number of firms targeted by 3 activists	3	2
Number of firms targeted by 4 activists	0	1
Number of activists that target:		
1 Firm	77	122
2 Firms	12	8
3 Firms	8	3
4 Firms	2	0
7 Firms	0	1
8 Firms	1	0
10 Firms	1	0
Panel B: Year of first 13D filing		
1995	1	0
1998	1	2
1999	3	0
2000	1	7
2001	3	4
2002	10	19
2003	28	31
2004	39	40
2005	65	51
Panel C: Exchange or market where target firm trades at time of initial investment		
New York Stock Exchange	45	56
American Stock Exchange	12	12
NASDAQ national market	79	63
OTC bulletin	6	11
Pink sheets	9	12

(*continued*)

Table 9.1 (Continued)

	Hedge fund activists	Other entrepreneurial activists
Panel D: Industry of target firm (eight or more firms for either group)		
Business services	29	11
Pharmaceutical products	10	5
Retail	9	3
Restaurants, hotels, motels	8	19
Banking	6	17
Communication	5	12
Panel E: Activists' stated reasons in Schedule 13D's 'purpose of transaction'		
Change board of directors' composition	41	35
Firm should pursue strategic alternatives	29	40
Oppose a merger	18	5
Sell the firm or merge with another company	16	5
Buy more stock with intention of buying the firm	12	24
Firm should buy back its own stock	4	0
Get list of shareholders	4	8
Become an active investor	4	10
Expresses concerns with corporate governance	3	8
Replace CEO	3	2
Cut CEO's salary	2	0
Firm should pay a cash dividend	2	0
Other reasons	13	17

Panel E presents the primary reasons stated in the original 13D filing for the investment under Item 4: 'Purpose of Transaction'. For the hedge fund sample, the most frequently stated purpose is to change the board's composition (forty-one filings), with the hedge fund manager usually asking to fill one or more seats. Pursuing alternative strategic goals is the second most frequently cited reason, accounting for twenty-nine filings. Opposing a merger (eighteen) or supporting a merger (sixteen) are common goals, as is the threat that the hedge fund would like to take over the firm in the future (twelve). In contrast, other activists are less concerned with merger and acquisition activity, but instead are more interested in steering the firm towards alternative strategic goals (forty), buying the target firm themselves (twenty-four), or becoming more active investors (ten). We note, however, that, similar to hedge funds, other activists frequently demand changes in the composition of board of directors (thirty-five). To determine if the differences in purpose statements are statistically significant, we use a χ^2 test of independence for the thirteen groups. The χ^2 value is 26.8 ($p < 0.01$); hence, we reject the null hypothesis that hedge fund activists and other entrepreneurial activists make a similar set of demands in their purpose statements.

9.3.3 Examples of Hedge Fund and Other Entrepreneurial Activism

In this section, we describe two confrontational campaigns to allow the reader to understand what is presented in the purpose statement and how these campaigns progress over time. The first example is a hedge fund that uses the 13D filing process to publicly wage its fight against the target firm. The second example is a venture capital fund that tried but failed to take over its target firm.

9.3.3.1 *Pirate Capital (a Hedge Fund) and Cornell Companies, Inc.*

On 23 June 2004, Pirate Capital (Pirate) filed a Schedule 13D indicating that it owned 5.2% of Cornell Companies, Inc. (Cornell). In the purpose statement, Pirate wrote:
'Pirate Capital LLC... may make proposals to the board of directors, seek to change the composition of and/or seek representation on the board of directors and/or solicit proxies or written consents from other shareholders of the Issuer.'

We consider this to be a confrontational activist filing and classify the purpose statement as indicating that the hedge fund wishes to gain board representation.

Between 9 July 2004 and 11 August 2005, Pirate filed twelve subsequent 13D/A filings. The overall purposes of these filings were to disclose additional holdings in the firm (which peaks at 14.8%) and, also, to make further demands of the company.

- 12 July 2004 (second filing): includes a letter to the CEO and Chairman Harry Phillips and to Cornell's Board of Directors, in which Pirate requests a complete list of shareholders and states that they 'are prepared to take every step necessary to maximize our investment including the removal of directors at the next annual meeting'.
- 5 August 2004 (third filing): includes another letter that proposes a special meeting of shareholders to vote on whether a sale of the company should be explored. In this letter, Pirate asks: 'How many failures will it take for you to actually start protecting the interests of shareholders?'
- 25 August 2004 (fourth filing) and 31 August 2004 (fifth filing): enclose letters to the board and to Mr Phillips, respectively, asking Cornell to immediately remove Mr Phillips as chairman of the board and CEO. By October 2004, Pirate Capital owned 11.8% of Cornell's shares and Mr Phillips had resigned as CEO of the firm. By October 2004, Pirate Capital owned 11.8% of Cornell's shares and Mr Phillips had resigned as CEO of the firm.
- 5 November 2004 (seventh filing): submits a plan to the board for Mr Phillips and another director to resign from the board and for Pirate to be given these two seats.
- 31 January 2005 (ninth filing): intends to run its own slate of board nominees at the next annual meeting.
- 24 February 2005 (tenth filing): intends to commence a proxy fight.
- 5 April 2005 (11th filing): files a preliminary proxy statement with the SEC with respect to the director slate. The 12th filing, dated 17 May 2005, discusses a letter of agreement between Pirate and Cornell, in which Cornell agrees to nominate seven Pirate Capital candidates (and two other candidates) to the board and to reimburse Pirate for up to

$750,000 in its proxy solicitation costs. In the last filing, dated 11 August 2005, it is revealed that the head of Pirate, Thomas Hudson, assumed the lead directorship of Cornell.

9.3.3.2 *Columbia Ventures Corporation (a Venture Capital Fund) and International Aluminum Corporation*

On 5 June 2000, Columbia Ventures Corporation (Columbia) filed a Schedule 13D in which it disclosed that it owned a 6.4% stake in International Aluminum Corporation. In its purpose statement, it proposes a transaction in which it would acquire all of the outstanding common stock of International Aluminum for $18.25. The filing also contains a letter to the target's board of directors in which it 'noted with disappointment the significant operating difficulties which have been reported recently' as well as the 'severe decline in the share price over the last several months'. The letter reiterates Columbia's desire to purchase the firm.

From Factiva, we find that, on 16 June 2000, the firm rejected the takeover offer. However, on 16 October 2000, it is reported that Kenneth D. Peterson, Jr, the CEO of Columbia, was elected to serve on the company's board of directors.

On 12 June 2002, Columbia filed a Schedule 13D in which they make another unsolicited offer to acquire 100% of International Aluminum's common stock. On 5 July 2004, a Schedule 13D/A reveals that Columbia had reduced its position in International Aluminum to under 5%.

International Aluminum remained a publicly traded company on the NYSE until 2 April 2007, when it was acquired by Genstar Capital LLC, a private equity firm, for $53.00 a share.

9.4 Properties of Targeted Firms Prior to 13D Filing Dates

What type of companies do entrepreneurial activists target? To address this research question, we examine the characteristics of hedge fund and other entrepreneurial activist targets. We make two comparisons. First, for each class of activist, we compare the properties of the target firms (for the year before they are targeted) to a matched sample of firms, where each target firm is matched with another firm by industry, size, and book-to-market ratio. Our matching algorithm is as follows. For each firm, we choose the ten closest firms in revenues (five above and five below) from all firms in the same Fama-French (1997) forty-eight-industry classification. From these ten possible matches, we choose the one firm with the closest book-to-market ratio. Second, we compare hedge fund targets to other entrepreneurial activist targets. This allows us to see if each group invests in firms with similar or different characteristics. In Section 9.4.1, we present univariate tests on mean and median values. In Section 9.4.2, we use logistic and probit models to identify the partial effects of all covariates.

9.4.1 Summary Statistics and Univariate Tests

Table 9.2 presents summary statistics. To give the reader a flavour of how the sample firms compare to their respective control samples, we show their means (medians) side by side. Columns 1 and 2 present the statistics for hedge fund targets and their control group, respectively. Columns 3 and 4 show the statistics for the other entrepreneurial activist targets and their control group, respectively. Columns 1 and 3 also present significance levels for tests for differences between sample and control firms' means and medians. Column 5 shows the *t*-statistic and the *Z*-statistic tests for differences between hedge fund target and other entrepreneurial activist target means and medians. For all tests, the *t*-statistics are for differences in means, assuming unequal variances between samples. The *Z*-statistics are from a Wilcoxon signed rank test, which does not require the assumption that the populations are normally distributed.

The first attribute we examine is firm performance. A firm's abnormal stock return is the difference between its buy-and-hold return from one year prior to the 13D filing date to thirty trading days before the date, and the buy-and-hold return for the same time period on the appropriate Fama-French size-matched portfolio of firms.[13] As Table 9.2 shows, hedge funds target good-performing firms, as evidenced by the prior one-year mean abnormal return for hedge fund targets of 12.3%. Furthermore, when we compare this return to the control sample's mean abnormal return of 8.1%, we find that the 4.2% difference is statistically significant at 0.01 level. In contrast, other entrepreneurial activist targets earn an average abnormal return of 2.8%, which is significantly less than their control group's mean abnormal return of 5.6% ($p < 0.05$). Testing for differences in the mean abnormal return between hedge fund and other activist targets yields a *t*-statistic of 1.74, suggesting that hedge fund activists target firms that perform better than those targeted by other entrepreneurial activists. Median values produce similar conclusions.

Table 9.2 also presents three measures of prior-period accounting profitability and financial health, namely, return on assets, defined as EBITDA/assets, cash flows from operations (CFO), defined as CFO/assets, and Altman's (1968) *Z*-score. These metrics are calculated over the one year ending on the fiscal year preceding the 13D filing date.[14] We present both raw and industry-adjusted metrics; the latter is defined as the difference between the firm's measure and the industry's median measure (Shah 1994).

[13] We winsorize extreme observations by setting the values in the bottom and top 1% to the values of the 1st and 99th percentiles to present more meaningful mean statistics. For each activist sample, there are two observations below the 1st percentile and two observations above the 99th percentile, respectively. As a sensitivity check to this process, we redo the analyses after dropping these extreme observations. The empirical results with the smaller samples are qualitatively the same, and therefore we do not include them. We employ the same winsorzing process for all variables throughout the analyses and include these results only.

[14] Compustat data are used for these and the other measures presented in Table 9.2. Nine hedge fund targets and twelve other entrepreneurial activist targets trade on the pink sheets and are excluded because they are exempt from filing financial statements with the SEC. Missing data further reduces our sample to 134 hedge fund and 139 other activist targets. For accounting flow data, that is, EBITDA, CFO, capital expenditures, and research and development (R&D) expenditures, we divide by mean assets, the latter defined as the average of beginning and ending total assets. For accounting balances, that is, cash, short-term investments, and debt, we divide by total assets at the fiscal year-end preceding the 13D filing date.

Table 9.2 Characteristics of target firms prior to the 13D filing date

This table summarizes characteristics of firms targeted by hedge funds (column 1) and other entrepreneurial activists (column 3), as well as each group's control sample (based on industry, size, and book-to-market; columns 2 and 4). For each variable the mean [median] is reported. All data are winsorized at the 1% and 99% levels. Columns 1 and 3 also contain significance levels for tests for differences between the means (medians) between sample and control firms. Column 5 shows the *t*-statistic (*Z*-statistic) testing for differences between hedge fund and other entrepreneurial activists' means (medians). The abnormal stock return is from one year prior to the 13D filing date to thirty trading days before day 0, where day 0 is the SEC 13D filing date. The accounting data are during (for flows) or (for balances) on the end of the year previous to the filing of the initial Schedule 13D. See Appendix A for variable definitions. *** significant at the 0.01 level; ** significant at the 0.05 level; * significant at the 0.10 level.

	Hedge fund activist target firms	Hedge fund control sample	Other entrepreneurial activist target firms	Other entrepreneurial activist control sample	*t*-statistic [*Z*-statistic] for difference between columns 1 and 3
	(1)	(2)	(3)	(4)	(5)
Profitability					
Abnormal stock return	12.3%***	8.10%	2.8%**	5.60%	1.74*
	[6.5%]***	[4.0%]	[0.5%]***	[6.8%]	[1.63]*
EBITDA/assets	0.062**	0.014	0.042	0.040	1.77*
	[0.071]	[0.055]	[0.044]	[0.049]	[1.97]***
Industry-adjusted	0.008**	−0.040	−0.004	−0.007	1.85***
	[0.008]**	[−0.008]	[−0.002]	[−0.005]	[1.88]**
CFO/assets	0.033	0.024	0.035	0.033	0.27
	[0.053]	[0.065]	[0.034]	[0.049]	[1.16]
Industry-adjusted	−0.007	−0.017	0.001	0.003	0.32
	[0.006]	[0.015]	[0.001]	[0.003]	[0.66]
Z-score	2.47	2.91	1.75**	2.65	2.51**
	[2.48]	[2.38]	[1.20]**	[2.61]	[3.72]***
Industry-adjusted	0.728	0.746	0.599*	0.848	1.97**
	[0.36]	[0.353]	[0.036]**	[0.046]	[1.56]
Discretionary spending					
Capital expenditures/ assets	0.032	0.023	0.029	0.0230	1.03
	[0.018]	[0.014]	[0.013]	[0.015]	[1.360]
Industry-adjusted	0.017	0.012	0.017	0.016	0.18
	[0.002]	[0.000]	[0.001]	[0.004]	[0.34]
R&D expenditures/assets	0.048	0.044	0.037	0.029	1.11
	[0.000]	[0.000]	[0.000]	[0.000]	[0.92]
Industry-adjusted	0.028	0.027	0.019	0.007	0.88
	[0.000]	[0.000]	[0.000]	[0.000]	[1.06]
Dividends/share	0.129	0.136	0.106	0.148	1.09
	[0.000]	[0.000]	[0.000]	[0.000]	[0.53]

(*continued*)

Table 9.2 (Continued)

	Hedge fund activist target firms	Hedge fund control sample	Other entrepreneurial activist target firms	Other entrepreneurial activist control sample	*t*-statistic [*Z*-statistic] for difference between columns 1 and 3
Industry-adjusted	0.099	0.103	0.055	0.105	1.11
	[0.000]	[0.000]	[0.000]	[0.000]	[0.38]
Cash balances and debt					
Cash/assets	0.137	0.118	0.094	0.100	2.73***
	[0.090]	[0.054]	[0.033]	[0.038]	[4.09]***
Industry-adjusted	0.109	0.095	.0.007	0.001	2.72***
	[0.096]	[0.060]	[0.006]	[0.010]	[4.17]***
(Cash + short-term investments)/assets	0.204	0.187	0.139	0.140	2.88
	[0.118]	[0.091]	[0.055]	[0.06]	[3.54]***
Industry-adjusted	0.052	0.049	−0.160	−0.162	2.96***
	[0.056]	[0.046]	[0.001]	[0.006]	[3.75]***
Total debt/assets	0.222	0.230	0.230	0.260	0.75
	[0.162]	[0.186]	[0.161]*	[0.226]	[0.19]
Industry-adjusted	−0.936	−.0.907	−0.618	−0.595	0.99
	[.0.462]	[.0.432]	[.0.252]	[.0.210]	[0.51]
Short-term debt/assets	0.049	0.051	0.042	0.065	0.71
	[0.007]	[0.015]	[0.011]	[0.019]	[−0.09]
Industry-adjusted	−0.717	−0.697	−0.487	−0.475	0.19
	[−0.210]	[−0.244]	[−0.116]	[−0.111]	[−0.25]
Long-term debt/assets	0.162	0.181	0.190	0.195	0.57
	[0.095]	[0.123]	[0.096]	[0.132]	[0.03]
Industry-adjusted	−0.186	−0.180	−0.124	−0.117	0.51
	[−0.168]	[−0.150]	[−0.057]	[−0.024]	[0.16]
Firm size and book-to-market ratio					
Assets ($ millions)	946.81	1,171.27	931.80	1,023.08	0.101
	[208.49]	[250.33]	[140.07]	[171.55]	[1.07]
Industry-adjusted	848.74	967.94	840.29	912.44	0.64
	[23.96]	[96.85]	[−23.91]	[−7.26]	[1.88]*
Revenues ($ millions)	796.03	902.73	439.33**	657.93	2.84***
	[148.31]	[130.25]	[68.42]**	[82.81]	[4.44]***
Industry-adjusted	591.45	680.08	571.69**	635.01	1.48
	[48.01]	[31.69]	[−7.99]*	[−2.84]	[1.83]*
Market value of equity ($ millions)	717.89	1, 071.03	461.02	484.23	1.73*
	[133.09]	[180.75]	[69.97]	[70.81]	[3.51]***
Industry-adjusted	635.15	935.41	312.89	341.75	1.45
	[47.10]	[85.93]	[4.93]	[6.89]	[2.69]***
Market-to-book ratio	1.460	1.699	1.294	1.303	1.04
	[1.241]	[1.303]	[1.095]	[1.080]	[0.91]
Industry-adjusted	0.108	0.337	0.030	0.040	0.59
	[0.080]	[0.091]	[−0.081]	[−0.069]	[0.34]
Number of firms	134	134	139	139	134/139

Consistent with the market return data, hedge funds target firms with positive earnings, (the mean EBITDA/assets of hedge fund targets is 0.062) and positive cash flows from operations (the average CFO/assets ratio of hedge fund targets is 0.033).[15] When compared to their sample of control firms, hedge fund targets have significantly higher earnings but similar cash flows from operations. Despite the fact that several hedge funds describe their investment strategies as investing in struggling or distressed companies (e.g., Contrarian Capital Management, Schultze Asset Management), the average Altman's Z-score, a predictor of bankruptcy, is 2.47, well above the predictive level of bankruptcy. Other entrepreneurial activist targets have similar EDITDA and CFO to their control sample, but significantly lower Altman Z-scores ($p < 0.05$). More significantly, perhaps, when we compare hedge fund targets to other activist targets, we find that hedge fund targets have significantly higher EBITDA/assets and Z-scores than other entrepreneurial activist targets. We note that raw and industry-adjusted performance measures yield similar results. Thus, whether we examine stock returns or accounting data, we conclude that hedge fund activists, on average, target better-performing firms than do other entrepreneurial activists.

These findings make an interesting comparison to those reported by Bethel, Liebeskind, and Opler (1998), who find that, between 1980 and 1989, activist investors were more likely to purchase large blocks of shares in firms with relatively low EBITDA/assets. In particular, our results support their findings when we focus on other entrepreneurial activists, but contrast with their findings when we examine hedge fund activists. Furthermore, our hedge fund target market returns are inconsistent with those reported by Becht et al. (Chapter 7, this volume) for the Hermes UK Focus Fund; they find that more than 40% of Hermes' targets are in the bottom quintile of performance in the six months prior to this fund's initial investment. They also differ from Barclay and Holderness (1991), who report negative market- and industry-adjusted returns for the three-year period (to day −40) for 106 negotiated block trades between 1978 and 1982.

Table 9.2 also presents data on discretionary spending items, for example, capital expenditures, research and development (R&D) expenditures, and dividends paid to common shareholders. We find no qualitative differences between either activist group or its control sample. Moreover, hedge fund targets and other entrepreneurial activist targets have similar discretionary spending ratios. Thus, these activists are neither more nor less apt to target firms with above- or below-average spending on investments or dividends paid to common shareholders.

We next examine prior-period cash holdings and debt-to-asset ratios. It has been argued in the financial press that hedge fund activists target firms to extract excess cash from them, either in terms of stock repurchases or increased stock dividends (Eisinger 2005; Wynn 2005). This claim is analogous to Jensen's (1986) discussion of agency costs between shareholders and management over 'free' cash flow. Under Jensen's theory, managers have incentives to grow their company beyond its optimal size and therefore may hoard cash to facilitate these purchases. Jensen (1986) also argues that excess cash-based agency costs are inversely related to the amount of firm debt because required interest payments reduce free

[15] As a sensitivity check, we also divide EBITDA by revenues, and by assets net of cash and short-term investments. Our results with these two specifications are qualitatively the same as those reported in Tables 9.2 and 9.8. For brevity, we do not report these numbers in the tables.

cash flow. Under Jensen's theory, targeted firms should have relatively high amounts of cash and relatively low amounts of debt on their balance sheet.

Cash is from the firm's balance sheet and, following generally accepted accounting rules (SFAS 95), is defined as cash plus interest-denominated investments with maturities of three months or less. We include a second measure, cash plus short-term investments, where the latter is defined as interest-denominated investments with maturities between three months and one year, or passive equity instruments.[16] Debt is measured as short-term (due within one year), long-term, and total debt. All variables are divided by total assets.

Table 9.2 supports the view that targets of hedge funds have substantially more cash than do other entrepreneurial activist targets on their balance sheets, be it cash or cash plus investments. Thus, there may be some basis to the argument that hedge funds target cash-rich companies, although we also note that none of the activist samples' cash ratios are significantly different from their control samples' ratios. There are no discernible differences in debt between the activist groups or between the activist groups and their control samples.

Table 9.2 also presents firm size and book-to-market data. Consistent with our earlier observation that few target firms are in the S&P 500 index, activists, on average, target relatively small companies. The median assets for firms targeted by hedge funds (other entrepreneurial activists) is \$208.49 (\$140.07) million; the mean assets is \$946.81 (\$931.80) million. These means compare to \$927 million for firms targeted by activist blockholders between 1980 and 1989 (a full twenty years earlier than our sample) studied by Bethel, Liebeskind, and Opler (1998). Similar observations can be made when using revenues or market value of equity as measures of firm size. Moreover, if we use revenues or market value as measures of firm size, we find that other entrepreneurial activists invest in smaller companies than hedge funds. For example, the median market value of equity for other entrepreneurial activist targets is \$69.97 million, compared to \$133.09 million for the hedge fund targets ($p < 0.01$ for difference). Finally, consistent with Brav et al. (Chapter 8, this volume), the hedge fund and other activist target samples have relatively low market-to-book ratios.

Taken together, our findings suggest that, when compared to each other, hedge funds and other entrepreneurial activists target firms with different characteristics. The targets of hedge funds have higher earnings, are financially healthier, and have more cash on their balance sheets when compared to targets of other entrepreneurial activists, who instead tend to target smaller firms in terms of revenues and market capitalization.

9.4.2 Logistic Models

We expand on the univariate analyses by using pooled logistic models. We fit the models separately for the pooled hedge fund activist–control samples, other entrepreneurial activist–control samples, and hedge fund activist–other entrepreneurial activist samples. The results, presented in Table 9.3, are consistent with the univariate tests presented above in Section 9.4.1. When compared to their respective control samples, hedge funds are more

[16] Between 2002 and 2005, the one-year Treasury constant maturity rate, as published by the Federal Reserve Bank of St. Louis, meandered between 1% and 3%. Thus, investments in short-term Treasury bills yield below-market returns, suggesting an additional agency cost of holding suboptimal assets. In addition, firms tend to place their excess cash in these short-term securities.

Table 9.3 Logistic models predicting targeting

This table reports the results of logistic regressions of the firms that are targeted by hedge funds and other entrepreneurial activists. Column 1 uses the firms in the control sample (based on industry, size, and book-to-market) in addition to the firms targeted by hedge funds. Column 2 uses firms targeted by other entrepreneurial activists in addition to firms in the control sample (based on industry, size, and book-to-market). The third set uses firms targeted by hedge funds in addition to firms targeted by other entrepreneurial activists. See Appendix A for variable definitions. All data are winsorized at the 1% and 99% levels. The table shows the coefficients and *p*-values. *** significant at the 0.01 level; ** significant at the 0.05 level; * significant at the 0.10 level.

	Hedge fund targets *vs* control sample	Other entrepreneurial activist targets *vs* control sample	Hedge fund target *vs* other activist targets
	(1)	(2)	(3)
Intercept	0.46	−0.684	0.564
	(0.38)	(0.26)	(0.28)
Abnormal stock return	0.179	−0.183	0.341
	(0.34)	(0.20)	(0.23)
EBITDA/assets	1.974	−0.778	1.300
	(0.02)**	(0.60)	(0.18)
Z-score	−0.065	0.008	−0.063
	(0.02)**	(0.61)	(0.05)**
Capital expenditures/assets	1.089	12.756	1.184
	(0.70)	(0.03)**	(0.59)
Dividends/share	0.005	−0.163	−0.483
	(0.95)	(0.79)	(0.19)
Total debt/assets	−0.703	1.236	−1.957
	(0.47)	(0.08)*	(0.01)***
Cash plus short-term investment/assets	1.417	2.012	0.736
	(0.06)*	(0.07)*	(0.40)
Log likelihood ratio	10.08	12.20	13.11
No. of observations	134/134	139/139	134/139

likely to target firms with higher earnings and cash plus investments, and to have lower Altman *Z*-scores, whereas other entrepreneurial activists are more likely to invest in firms with higher capital expenditures, total debt, and cash plus investments. Finally, when comparing hedge fund targets to other entrepreneurial activist targets, hedge funds activists are more likely to invest in firms with lower debt-to-asset ratios and Altman *Z*-scores.[17]

[17] To determine the sensitivity of our results to the choice of a logistic model, we replicate our analyses using probit models. Because the cumulative normal distribution and the logistic distribution are very close to each other, except at the tails, similar results should be observed (Maddala 1993). To examine the comparability of the two models, we examine the goodness-of-fit tests, the coefficients of the individual independent variables, and their significance levels. In all cases, the significance levels of the coefficients for the logistical and probit models are comparable to each other within a 0.02 range. The goodness-of-fit measures, the log likelihood ratios, are also comparable between specifications. Following Maddala

9.5 Market Response to Initial 13D Filings

Next, to determine how the market reacts to planned activism, we compute abnormal share price reactions around the initial 13D filing date. We define the filing date, as reported in www.sec.gov, as 'day 0'. Our event window begins on day −30 to allow for the ten-day 13D filing window, possible prior leakage of information, and pre-filing price pressure that may occur due to the activist accruing a large stake in a relatively short period of time. We extend the event window to day +5, and alternatively to day +30 to accommodate subsequent press coverage of the filing event.

To facilitate comparisons between our study and previous studies, we calculate and present three measures of abnormal stock returns. The target's size-adjusted return is the difference between its buy-and-hold return over a selected time period and the buy-and-hold return for the same time period on the Fama-French size-matched portfolio of firms. The market-adjusted return is the difference between the target's buy-and-hold return and the value-weighted NYSE/Amex/NASDAQ index from CRSP. The industry-adjusted return is the difference between the target's buy-and-hold return and the return for all firms (target excluded) in the target's Fama-French (1997) forty-eight-industry code.

9.5.1 All Schedule 13D Filings

Table 9.4 presents abnormal stock returns and both parametric and non-parametric test statistics to evaluate whether these returns are different from zero. Columns 1 and 2 present abnormal returns and significance levels for the [−30, +5] event window. Columns 4 and 5 show the abnormal returns and significance levels for the longer event window. Columns 3 and 6 contain test statistics for differences in means and medians between hedge fund and other activist targets for the shorter (column 3) and longer (column 6) windows.

We begin by discussing size-adjusted market returns. This measure is comparable to those presented by Bethel, Liebeskind, and Opler (1998). The portfolio of hedge fund targets earns statistically significant mean size-adjusted returns of 7.3% over the [−30, +5] window, and 10.2% over the [−30, +30] window. The medians are respectively 4.9% and 8.9%, also statistically different from zero. Thus, the market perceives substantial benefits upon learning that a firm is targeted by a hedge fund activist. Other entrepreneurial activist targets earn significantly positive mean (median) size-adjusted returns of 4.4% (3.6%) over the [−30, +5] window and 5.1% (6.7%) over the [−30, +30] window. These abnormal returns are consistent with those of Bethel, Liebeskind, and Opler (1998) for their sample of activist targets. When we compare abnormal returns between targets of hedge fund and other entrepreneurial activists, we find little to no statistical differences between the two groups. Thus, even though the size-adjusted returns for the hedge fund activists are larger than those for the other entrepreneurial activists, they are not statistically larger.

(1993), we transform the logistic estimates into approximations of the probit estimates by multiplying the logistic estimates by 1/1.6. This transformation produces estimates that, in all cases, are within 0.01 of the point estimates for the probit models.

Table 9.4 Abnormal stock returns surrounding the initial Schedule 13D filing dates

This table shows the distributions of size-adjusted stock returns, market-adjusted stock returns, and industry-adjusted stock returns surrounding the initial Schedule 13D filing dates for 134 firms targeted by hedge fund activists and 139 firms targeted by other entrepreneurial activists. The target's size-adjusted return is the difference between its buy-and-hold return for the time period and the return on the matched Fama-French size portfolio as calculated on Eventus. The market-adjusted return is the difference between the target's buy-and-hold return and the value-weighted NYSE/AMEX/NASDAQ index from CRSP. The industry-adjusted return is the difference between the target's buy-and-hold return and the return for all firms (target excluded) in the target's Fama-French (1997) forty-eight-industry code. The abnormal return is for the thirty trading days prior to the filing day of the Schedule 13D (day 0) through the five (30) trading days after the filing day of the Schedule 13D. All data are winsorized at the 1% and 99% levels. *** significant at the 0.01 level; **significant at the 0.05 level; * significant at the 0.10 level.

	Abnormal return [days −30, +5]			Abnormal return [days −30, +30]		
	Hedge fund targets	Other entrepreneurial activist targets	*t*-stat. [*Z*-stat.] for diff. between columns 1 and 2	Hedge fund targets	Other entrepreneurial activist targets	*t*-stat. [*Z*-stat.] for diff. between columns 4 and 5
	(1)	(2)	(3)	(4)	(5)	(6)
Size-adjusted returns						
Mean	7.3%***	4.4%***	1.34	10.2%***	5.1%***	1.97**
25%	−1.7	−4.2	[0.88]	0.1	−6.0	
50%	4.9***	3.6***		8.9***	6.7***	[1.49]
75%	13.9	15.9		20.3	17.8	
Market-adjusted returns						
Mean	5.7%***	2.2%*	1.53	7.2% . . .	1.9%.	2.03**
25%	.1.4	.6.1	[1.54]*	−2.7	−7.5	
50%	4.6***	3.0**		5.4***	2.6***	[1.92]**
75%	14.3	11.8		17.7	13.0	
Industry-adjusted returns						
Mean	7.0%***	4.4%***.		9.8%***	4.8%***	1.85*
25%	−1.8	−4.2	1.04	.0.1	.6.2	
50%	4.8***	3.5***		8.5***	6.5***	[1.79]**
75%	15.1	15.8	[0.57]	20.3	17.4	

Many current and previous activist and blockholder studies use market-adjusted returns to calibrate the market's perception of the effect of activism on shareholder wealth. Using this metric, we find that hedge fund targets earn a mean (median) market-adjusted return of 5.7% (4.6%) over the [−30, +5] window and 7.2% (5.4%) for the [−30, +30] period. The size and significance levels of these abnormal returns are consistent with those of Brav et al. (Chapter 8, this volume), who use a similar methodology for their sample of hedge fund activism, and with results of previous studies on corporate raiders (Holderness and Sheehan 1985) and block purchases (Barclay and Holderness 1989, 1991). They differ dramatically, however, from previous studies on institutional activism, which show little to no price reaction (see Karpoff 2001 for a summary of these studies). These differences can most likely be attributed to the fact that we are studying confrontational block purchase activism, whereas Karpoff summarizes papers that examine non-confrontational shareholder activism.

In contrast to the hedge fund targets, other entrepreneurial activist targets record smaller market-adjusted returns. The mean (median) abnormal return is 2.2% (3.0%) for the [−30, +5] time period and 1.9% (2.6%) for the [−30, +30] period. Although all are statistically significant at conventional levels, the t- and Z-statistics are lower than those reported for the size-adjusted returns. In addition, when we test for differences in market-adjusted returns between hedge fund activists and other entrepreneurial activists, we find statistically greater abnormal returns for hedge funds three out of four times.

We also present industry-adjusted returns to partially control for colinearities and possible contagion effects among firms in the same industry. Targets of hedge fund activists and other activists earn significantly positive abnormal returns around the 13D filing date. In addition, for the longer window, the abnormal returns for hedge fund activists' targets exceed those for the other entrepreneurial activists' targets.

In summary, Table 9.4 shows that the market reacts positively to activism in general and that the positive abnormal returns are robust across different methodologies. Table 9.4 also presents evidence that the market reacts more favourably to hedge fund activism than other entrepreneurial activism, particularly when comparing abnormal stock returns around the longer [−30, +30] window.

9.5.2 Abnormal Stock Returns by Purpose of Initial Schedule 13D Filing

Table 9.5 presents mean and median size-adjusted stock returns, for the −30 through +30 period surrounding the 13D filing date, by the stated purpose in the initial 13D filing. Since the number of occurrences of some of the cells are small, we concentrate only on the abnormal returns for which there are at least eleven occurrences. As the table shows, there are distinctly different market reactions by group (hedge fund versus other entrepreneurial activists) and by purpose statement. First, although the market reacts favourably to all hedge fund purpose statements (including those in cells with less than eleven observations), investors seem most intrigued when the hedge fund activist asks for at least one seat on the board (mean abnormal return = 12.60%) or hints at increasing its stake with the intention of buying the firm (mean abnormal return = 13.06%). In contrast, market reaction is relatively low when the hedge fund asks the firm to pursue alternative strategies (mean abnormal return = 4.30%). The latter two returns are consistent with those reported by Greenwood and Schor (2007) for a different sample of hedge fund targets.

Second, other entrepreneurial activist targets' mean abnormal returns are highest for the group of firms in which the activist intends to buy more stock in the firm (15.93%) or expects

Table 9.5 Abnormal stock returns by reason given in 'purpose statement' in initial 13D filing

This table presents mean [median] size-adjusted stock returns surrounding the initial Schedule 13D filing dates for 134 firms targeted by hedge fund activists and by 139 other entrepreneurial activists. The target's size-adjusted return is the difference between its buy-and-hold return for days [−30, +30] and the return on the matched Fama-French size portfolio as calculated on Eventus. All data are winsorized at the 1% and 99% levels. *** significant at the 0.01 level; ** significant at the 0.05 level; * significant at the 0.10 level.

Reason	Hedge fund targets	Other entrepreneurial activist targets
Change board of directors' composition	12.60%***	3.12%
	[9.50%]***	[4.18%]
	$N = 39$	$N = 33$
Firm should pursue strategic alternatives	4.30%	3.19%
	[2.21%]	[3.52%]
	$N = 27$	$N = 39$
Oppose a merger	8.37% . . .	9.81%**
	[6.32%]***	[9.81%]***
	$N = 16$	$N = 1$
Sell the firm or merge with another company	6.37%**	−2.19%
	[8.31%]**	[−2.19%]
	$N = 13$	$N = 1$
Buy more stock with intention of buying the firm	13.06%**	15.93%**
	[10.88%]***	[9.70%]***
	$N = 11$	$N = 23$
Firm should buy back its own stock	16.88%*	0.00%
	[18.12%]	[0.00%]
	$N = 4$	$N = 0$
Get list of shareholders	5.99%	5.39%
	[5.55%]	[9.43%]
	$N = 4$	$N = 8$
Become an active investor	2.30%	12.50%**
	[2.20%]	[11.10%]**
	$N = 4$	$N = 10$
Expresses concerns with corporate governance	11.88%	8.98%
	[7.48%]	[7.16%]*
	$N = 3$	$N = 6$
Replace the CEO	11.19%	−4.42%
	[20.43%]	[−4.42%]
	$N = 3$	$N = 2$
Cut CEO's salary	11.11%	0.00%
	[11.11%]	[0.00%]
	$N = 1$	$N = 0$
Firm should pay a cash dividend	9.83%	0.00%
	[9.83%]	[0.00%]
	$N = 2$	$N = 0$
Other reasons	19.40%*	−2.56%
	[20.28%]*	[−0.19%]
	$N = 7$	$N = 16$

to become more active (12.50%). The latter result is in contrast to hedge fund targets, which record a mean abnormal return of just 2.30%. Finally, when other activists ask for a seat on the board, the mean abnormal return is 3.12%, well below the 12.60% recorded by the hedge fund activist target firms.

9.6 Are Activists Successful in Achieving their Goals?

In this section, we document the success rates that activists have in achieving their initial goals, as articulated in the initial 13D filings. We also examine the association between success or non-success and activists' methods in trying to achieve these objectives. Finally, we compare market reactions around 13D filings by success and non-success, and also by certain outcomes to see if the market anticipates and values these outcomes.

9.6.1 Purpose of Investment and Success Rates

Table 9.6, Panel A, shows success rates for hedge fund and other entrepreneurial activists categorized by the purpose statements from the original 13D filings. We define success as achievement of the activist's goal within one year of the 13D filing. We gather this information by examining subsequent 13D/A filings and news articles disclosed on Factiva.

Hedge fund activists enjoy a 60% success rate. Most strikingly, they gain representation on the target's board thirty out of forty-one times, for an achievement rate of 73%. They are 100% successful in getting the firm to buy back its own stock, replace the current CEO, and initiate a cash dividend. Approximately 50% of the time, the target firm changes its operating strategies, drops its merger plans, or agrees to be taken over or merged.

Other entrepreneurial activists achieve their goals 65% of the time. Similar to hedge funds, other activists gain board representation twenty-five out of thirty-five times, for an achievement rate of 71%. They are 70% successful in getting the firm to pursue alternative strategies and 75% successful when wanting to change the company's corporate governance. We note that, unlike hedge funds, other activists do not demand that the company buy back its own stock or initiate a dividend. Instead, they appear to be most interested and successful in getting the firm to make organic changes to corporate governance (including board structure) and operations.

We interpret these high success percentages as evidence that both classes of activists are effective in making significant changes to their target firms. These findings are contrary to prior activism studies; in particular, they run counter to Bebchuk's (Chapter 3, this volume) evidence that US shareholders' ability to replace the board of directors is 'largely a myth'. However, our results are consistent with Becht et al. (Chapter 7, this volume) study on UK shareholder activism, in which they document the Hermes pension fund's capacity to make significant changes to its target firms, most notably board changes and asset restructurings.

Table 9.6 Outcomes of hedge fund and other entrepreneurial activism, and the proxy solicitation process

This table reports statistics for the outcomes of hedge fund and other entrepreneurial activism. Panel A summarizes the activists' purposes for the activism as stated in the original Schedule 13D filings' 'Purpose of Transaction', and the number and percentage of successes of these activist campaigns. We define a success as the activist having achieved its stated goal within one year of the initial 13D filing date. Panel B summarizes the relation between (proxy fight plus threaten proxy fight)/no proxy fight and the outcomes of the activist campaigns. Panel B also describes the relation between the proxy fight and the success in gaining a seat(s) on the target firm's board. *** significant at the 0.01 level.

Purpose	Hedge fund activists	Number of successes (%)	Other entrepreneurial activists	Number of successes (%)
Panel A: Stated purposes in Schedule 13D's 'purpose of transaction' and success rates of achieving their stated goals				
Change board of directors' composition	41	30 (73%)	35	25 (71%)
Firm should pursue strategic alternatives	29	14 (48%)	40	28 (70%)
Oppose a merger	18	10 (56%)	5	4 (88%)
Sell the firm or merge with another company	16	9 (56%)	5	2 (40%)
Buy more stock with intention of buying the firm	12	7 (58%)	24	13 (54%)
Firm should buy back its own stock	4	4 (100%)	0	0 (N/A)
Get list of shareholders	4	2 (50%)	8	5 (62%)
Become an active investor	4	4 (100%)	10	10 (100%)
Expresses concerns with corporate governance	3	1 (33%)	8	6 (75%)
Replace CEO	3	3 (100%)	2	0 (N/A)
Cut CEO's salary	2	1 (50%)	0	0 (N/A)
Firm should pay a cash dividend	2	2 (100%)	0	0 (N/A)
Other reasons	13	4 (31%)	17	8 (47%)
Total number	151 (100%)	91 (60%)	154 (100%)	101 (65%)

Table 9.6 (Continued)

	Hedge fund activists					Other entrepreneurial activists				
		Obtain Stated Goal?		Gain at least one seat on target's board?			Obtain stated goal?		Gain at least one seat on target's board?	
	Number	Yes	No	Yes	No	Number	Yes	No	Yes	No
Panel B: Associations between proxy fights and success rates of obtaining their stated goals or gaining at least one seat on the target's board										
Proxy fight	18 (12%)	13 (72%)	5 (28%)	13 (72%)	5 (28%)	13 (8%)	11 (84%)	2 (16%)	9 (69%)	4 (31%)
Threaten proxy fight	42 (28%)	26 (62%)	16 (38%)	24 (57%)	18 (43%)	35 (23%)	21 (60%)	14 (40%)	22 (63%)	13 (37%)
No proxy fight	91 (60%)	52 (57%)	39 (43%)	30 (33%)	61 (67%)	106 (69%)	69 (65%)	37 (35%)	34 (32%)	72 (68%)
Total	151 (100%)	91 (60%)	60 (40%)	67 (44%)	84 (56%)	154 (100%)	101(65%)	53 (35%)	65 (40%)	89 (60%)
χ^2 statistic for association between [proxy fight plus threaten proxy fight]/no proxy fight and the outcome		0.93		12.06***			0.03		14.31***	

9.6.2 Possible Reasons for Success Rates

We offer and examine several possible reasons behind the success rates of hedge fund and other activists. First, we consider whether the success rate is related to the relative level of aggressiveness of the initially stated objectives in the 13D. For example, management might be more willing to acquiesce to outside shareholders' demands if they believe the outcomes are less costly to the firm or to management itself. On the other hand, management might resist making concessions to aggressive demands for fear that future and more onerous demands might be in the offing.

We categorize eight of the thirteen purposes in Table 9.6, Panel A, as aggressive: change board, oppose a merger, sell the firm, buy more stock with intention of buying the firm, buy back its own stock, replace CEO, cut CEO's salary, and pay cash dividend.[18] This categorization is similar to that of Brav and colleagues (Chapter 8, this volume), with the exception that they consider board representation to be non-aggressive. Using our definition, we find that ninety-eight (65%) of the hedge fund activists' initially stated purposes are aggressive and fifty-three (35%) are not (not tabulated). Of the ninety-eight aggressive objectives, sixty-six (67%) ultimately are successful, whereas thirty-two (33%) are not. Of the fifty-three non-aggressive objectives, twenty-five (47%) are successful, whereas twenty-eight (53%) are not. Using a χ^2 test to determine if there is an association between the success rate and the purpose (aggressive or not) yields a χ^2 statistic of 5.85 ($p < 0.02$). Thus, we find a positive association between aggressive objectives and success rates for hedge fund activists' targets.

When we examine other entrepreneurial activists, a different picture emerges. For this group, seventy-one (46%) initial purpose statements are classified as aggressive, and eighty-three (54%) are non-aggressive (not tabulated). For the seventy-one aggressive objectives, the activist is successful forty-four (62%) times; for the eighty-three non-aggressive objectives, the activist succeeds forty-nine (59%) times. The χ^2 statistic for testing the association between aggression and success is 0.13, insignificant at conventional levels, suggesting no association between the two.

Next, we turn to the use of proxy fights by hedge fund managers and other activists, respectively, against the target firms. Bebchuk (Chapter 3, this volume); Briggs (2007); and Kahan and Rock (Chapter 5, this volume), suggest that a proxy fight is the shareholder's only effective weapon to bring about significant change in the target firm.

Table 9.6, Panel B, presents data on actual and threatened proxy fights for both samples of targets. Proxy solicitations are from the Georgeson Shareholder website, which presents a comprehensive list of 'contested solicitations' for each year in our data sample. Georgeson lists the target company, the dissident, the contested issue, and also whether the dissident or management won, or whether there was a settlement between the two parties. Threatened proxy fights are from Factiva and consist of all news reports that the activist was threatening to begin a proxy solicitation, but never got to the SEC level of an actual solicitation.

We find that 40% (12% + 28%) of the hedge fund campaigns involved an actual or threatened proxy solicitation. Of the eighteen realized proxy solicitations, Opportunity Partners

[18] Alternatively, we include 'get list of shareholders' as an aggressive purpose, and find similar results to those reported in this section.

engaged in three proxy fights, Steel Partners II and Santa Monica had two proxy fights apiece, and eleven other hedge funds were involved in one proxy fight each. In the remaining ninety-one cases (60% of the sample), there was no public information of an actual or threatened proxy fight, although we acknowledge there might be private correspondences between the activist and the firm did not come to our attention. Other entrepreneurial activists initiated thirteen proxy solicitations and publicly threatened thirty-five other proxy fights, for an overall rate of 31%. Of the thirteen proxy solicitations, five were conducted by individuals, two were by venture capital funds, and six were by asset management firms. No other entrepreneurial activist engaged in more than one proxy fight.

To gauge market reaction to these explicit and threatened proxy challenges, we calculate share price effects (size-adjusted returns) for the days [−5, +5], where day 0 is the first public disclosure from Factiva about the dissident's threat or initiation of a proxy challenge (not tabulated). For the hedge fund targets, the mean (median) abnormal return is 4.48% (4.15%), each significant at the 0.01 level. For the other entrepreneurial activist targets, the mean (median) abnormal return is 5.08% (2.57%), each significant at the 0.01 level. These findings support the view that investors treat activists' campaigns as value-increasing events.

We next examine if the overall success rates reported in Table 9.6, Panel A, are related to whether the activist used or threatened a proxy fight. As Panel B shows, the ninety-one successful hedge fund outcomes were accompanied by thirteen actual proxy fights, twenty-six threatened proxy solicitations, and fifty-two instances of no public action. For the sixty unsuccessful hedge fund campaigns, the activist filed a proxy solicitation five times, threatened a proxy fight sixteen times, but did not publicly use the proxy solicitation process thirty-nine times. When examining proxy fights and outcomes for the other entrepreneurial activism outcomes, we find that of the 101 successful campaigns, the investor initiated 11 proxy fights, threatened 21 proxy solicitations, and did not use the process 69 times. For the remaining fifty-three unsuccessful events, the other activists engaged in two actual proxy fights, threatened fourteen proxy fights, and had thirty-nine non-engagements.

To test for the association between the proxy solicitation process and the success rate of each group of activists, we perform a 2x2 χ^2 test, where we lump actual and threatened proxy fights together and compare them to non-engagements. For hedge fund activists, we report a χ^2 statistic of 0.93, insignificant at conventional levels. Similarly, the χ^2 statistic for other entrepreneurial activists is 0.03, also insignificant at conventional levels. Thus, we find no evidence of a relationship between proxy fights and the rate of success.

However, a perusal of the Georgeson database reveals that the vast majority of contested proxy solicitations are over board composition. We therefore determine if there is an association between proxy fights and whether a hedge fund or other activist gains at least one seat on the target firm's board of directors, independent of whether that change is in their original purpose statement.

As Table 9.6, Panel B, shows, 44% of the 151 hedge fund targets (67 events) resulted in the activist getting at least one seat on the target's board of directors. Of these firms, thirteen were engaged in a proxy fight with the activist, twenty-four were threatened with a proxy solicitation, and thirty were not public recipients of a real or threatened proxy fight. A 2x2 χ^2 test on the relation between proxy fights (real or threatened) and success in gaining board representation yields a χ^2 statistic of 12.06, indicating a significant association between the two. We find similar results for the other activists. Of the sixty-five board successes, nine activists engaged the firm in a proxy fight, twenty-two threatened a proxy fight, and thirty-four did not use the proxy solicitation as a threat. A χ^2 test on the relation between groups and success in gaining board representation yields a significant χ^2 statistic of 14.31.

In summary, an explicit or implicit proxy threat is positively related to whether an activist successfully gains a seat on the target's board. We interpret this finding as consistent with the activist's choice of tactics and probability of success being endogenous to the characteristics of the target firm. Similarly, we interpret the non-significant χ^2 values for the association between overall success and the proxy solicitation process as a reflection of the fact that most other demands made by activists are not voted on by shareholders, and thus the proxy ballot may not be the appropriate avenue to seek these changes.

9.6.3 Schedule 13D Abnormal Returns, Successful Campaigns, and Eventual Outcomes

In this section, we present size-adjusted stock returns around the initial 13D filings by: (1) the eventual success/failure of the campaign; (2) whether the activist received at least one seat on the board (irrespective of whether it initially asked for it) within one year; and (3) whether the firm was taken over or merged within one year.

Table 9.7 provides the results. When we compare abnormal returns between hedge funds that are successful in obtaining their goals within one year versus those that are not, we find sharp differences between the two groups of targets. As Table 9.7, Panel A, shows, the mean (median) abnormal return for successful campaigns over the [−30, +5] window is 10.7% (7.1%), which is significantly greater than the 2.6% (1.5%) mean (median) abnormal return for unsuccessful outcomes. The [−30, +30] window also produces significantly greater abnormal returns for the successful-outcome group than for the unsuccessful group.

We find similar differences in abnormal returns between successful and unsuccessful campaigns for firms targeted by other entrepreneurial activists. The mean (median) [−30, +5] initial Schedule 13D abnormal returns for successful outcomes is 6.4% (6.3%), which is significantly greater than the 1.1% (1.4%) abnormal return for the unsuccessful outcomes. The [−30, +30] window produces similar differentials; for successful outcomes, the mean (median) abnormal return is 7.1% (7.2%); for unsuccessful outcomes, it is 0.3% (2.4%). Thus, we conclude that investors, on average, are able to differentiate, albeit with error, between successful and unsuccessful campaigns.

Table 9.7, Panel B, presents abnormal stock returns by whether the activist obtains board representation within one year. These results differ from Panel A in that we observe significantly different abnormal returns between gaining or not gaining board seats for the hedge fund targets only. The mean (median) [−30, +5] 13D abnormal stock return for the hedge fund targets is 11.94% (9.33%), which is significantly larger than the 4.92% (2.01%) for those targets in which the hedge fund does not eventually get on the board. The longer window yields similar differentials. For the other entrepreneurial activist targets, the means and medians between subgroups are not significantly different from each other. We note that these results are similar to those reported in Table 9.5, in which the market reaction to a purpose statement of board representation is relatively high for the hedge fund targets, but relatively low for the other entrepreneurial activist targets.

Table 9.7 Abnormal stock returns surrounding the initial Schedule 13D filing dates by outcomes

This table presents mean [median] size-adjusted stock returns surrounding the initial Schedule 13D filing dates for three different outcomes. The target's size-adjusted return is the difference between its buy-and-hold return for the time period and the return on the matched Fama-French size portfolio as calculated on Eventus. Day 0 is the Schedule 13D filing date. Panel A shows abnormal stock returns by whether the activist achieved its goal within one year of the initial 13D filing, as stated in the purpose statement of the initial Schedule 13D filing. Panel B contains the abnormal stock returns by whether the activist obtains at least one seat on the target's board of directors within one year of the initial filing. Panel C presents the abnormal returns by whether the firm is ultimately merged or taken over within one year of the filing date. All data are winsorized at the 1% and 99% levels. The table presents test statistics for significance of the means [medians] as well as differences between groups. *** significant at the 0.01 level; ** significant at the 0.05 level; *significant at the 0.10 level.

	Activists obtain stated goals (1)	Activists do not obtain stated goals (2)	*t*-stat. [*Z*-stat.] for difference between (1) and (2)
Panel A: Activist does or does not obtain its goal within one year of initial schedule 13d filing			
Hedge fund targets			
[−30 to +5]	10.7%***	2.6%	2.29**
	[7.1%]***	[1.5%]**	[2.95]***
[−30 to +30]	13.2%***	5.6%**	2.03**
	[9.8%]***	[6.8%]***	[2.25]**
[+30 to +1 year]	12.3%***	10.0%**	0.99
	[5.4%]***	[4.2%]**	[0.81]
Other entrepreneurial activist targets			
[−30 to +5]	6.4%***	1.1%	1.98**
	[6.3%]***	[1.4]%	[1.79]**
[−30 to +30]	7.1%***	0.3%	1.99**
	[7.2%]***	[2.4%]	[1.98]**
[+30 to +1 year]	16.7%***	19.9%**	0.63
	[8.0%]***	[5.4]%**	[0.21]
	Activists receive board seat (1)	**Activists do not receive board seat (2)**	**t-stat. [Z-stat.] for difference between (1) and (2)**
Panel B: Activist does or does not receive at least one seat on target's board			
Hedge fund targets			
[−30 to +5]	11.94%***	4.92%***	1.91*
	[9.33%]***	[2.01%]***	[2.14]**
[−30 to +30]	14.62%***	7.30%***	1.89**
	[13.18%]***	[6.48%]***	[1.85]**
[+30 to +1 year]	10.18%**	13.41%***	−0.41
	[4.33%]**	[7.36%]***	[−0.28]

(*continued*)

Table 9.7 (Continued)

	Activists receive board seat (1)	Activists do not receive board seat (2)	t-stat. [Z-stat.] for difference between (1) and (2)
Other entrepreneurial activist targets			
[−30 to +5]	2.94%**	5.50%**	−0.89
	[2.78%]*	[4.23%]***	[.1.24]
[−30 to +30]	4.60%**	5.72%***	−0.38
	[3.29%]**	[8.14%]***	[−0.83]
[+30 to +1 year]	22.85%***	14.40%***	1.12
	[14.60%]***	[3.78%]**	[1.49]*
	Firm is merged or acquired (1)	**Firm is not merged or acquired (2)**	**t-stat. [Z-stat.] for difference between (1) and (2)**
Panel C: Firm is merged within one year of initial 13D filing			
Hedge fund targets			
[−30 to +5]	2.66%	8.63%***	−1.51
	[1.48%]	[5.17%]***	[.0.99]
[−30 to +30]	7.10%*	10.95%***	−1.01
	6.74%**	[8.94%]***	[−0.80]
[+30 to +1 year]	14.72%***	10.34%***	1.09
	[7.05%]***	[6.56%]**	[0.59]
Other entrepreneurial activist targets			
[−30 to +5]	17.39%***	3.25%***	2.59***
	[12.80%]***	[2.89%]**	[2.42]***
[−30 to +30]	12.24%	3.90%**	1.81*
	[14.06%]	[5.55%]***	[1.80]**
[+30 to +1 year]	21.50%***	14.30%***	2.42**
	[8.98%]***	[4.95%]**	[1.70]**

Finally, Barclay and Holderness (1991) find that the stock market reaction around the announcement date of the 13D filing date for a negotiated block trade is higher when the firm is acquired within one year. Barclay and Holderness (1991) examine 106 negotiated block trade announcements between 1978 and 1982. Their market-adjusted return for days −40 through 0 is 9.9% for the sixty-five firms that remain independent after one year of day 0 and 20.5% for the forty-one firms that are acquired within one year.

For our sample of 151 hedge fund targets, 22 firms are merged or acquired within one year and 129 remain independent. For the sample of 154 other activist targets, 19 targets are merged or acquired within a year, while 135 remain independent. Thus, the incidence of activist targets (hedge fund or other) being taken over within one year is less than that reported by Barclay and Holderness (1991). One possible reason for the different acquisition rates is that the majority of blockholders studied by Barclay and Holderness are other companies, whereas our blockholders are predominantly hedge funds, private investors, venture capitalists, or private equity managers. For example, as Table 9.6 Panel A shows, hedge funds and other entrepreneurial activists typically do not seek control of the target.

As Table 9.7 Panel C shows, there are distinct differences in abnormal returns by type of activist and whether the firm is acquired or merged within one year. For hedge fund activists, there are no significant differences in abnormal returns between firms that are merged or acquired within one year and firms that remain independent. In contrast, the abnormal returns are significantly greater for other entrepreneurial activists when the firm is acquired within one year when compared to firms that remain independent after one year. Over the [−30, +5] window, the mean (median) abnormal return for merged or acquired firms is 17.39% (12.80%), which is significantly greater than the 3.25% (2.89%) mean (median) abnormal return for those firms not merged or acquired. The [−30, +30] window also produces significantly greater abnormal returns for the merged group than for the group of targets that remain independent.

Taken together, these results suggest that the market places different weights on the 13D filing date on the probability that the target firm will be taken over in the future. These differences also reflect the disparity in incidences in which the activist professes an intent in having the target firm acquired, either by the activist or by a third party. Recall from Table 9.1 that other entrepreneurial activists declare an intention of buying more stock in the target firm twenty-four times versus twelve times for the hedge fund activist. Furthermore, as Table 9.1 shows, the incidence for both groups of activists to support or oppose a future merger is a wash.

9.7 Subsequent Abnormal Returns and Changes in Operating and Financial Structures after the Initial Filing Date

In this section we examine abnormal stock returns and changes in accounting performance, cash on hand, discretionary spending, leverage, and firm size for the one-year period after the initial 13D filing. Our primary purpose is to discern the short-term effects that activists have on the targeted firms.

Table 9.8 presents some of these results. Columns 1 and 2 contain the hedge fund targets and their control group, respectively. Columns 3 and 4 show the other entrepreneurial activist targets and their control group, respectively. Columns 1 and 3 also present significance levels for tests for differences between sample and control firms' means and medians. Column 5 shows the *t*-statistic and the *Z*-statistic for tests for differences between hedge fund target and other entrepreneurial activist target means and medians.

9.7.1 One-Year Abnormal Stock Returns following the Initial Schedule 13D Filing

We begin by computing size-adjusted stock returns for the target and control samples for the period from thirty trading days to one year after the filing date. The first row of Table 9.8 contains these returns. The mean one-year abnormal return for the sample of hedge fund

Table 9.8 One-year changes in target firm performance after activism

This table summarizes changes (Δ) in firm characteristics between the fiscal year following and prior to the filing of the Schedule 13D for firms targeted by hedge funds (column 1) and other entrepreneurial activists (column 3), as well as each group's control sample (based on industry, size, and book-to-market; columns 2 and 4). For each variable the mean [median] is reported. All data are winsorized at the 1% and 99% levels. The abnormal stock return is from thirty trading days after the 13D filing date to one year after day 0, where day 0 is the SEC 13D filing date. The accounting data are during (for flows) or (for balances) on the end of the year previous to the filing of the initial Schedule 13D. Columns 1 and 3 also contain significance levels for tests for differences between the means [medians] between sample and control firms. Column 5 shows the *t*-statistic (*Z*-statistic) testing for differences between hedge fund and other entrepreneurial activists' means [medians]. See Appendix A for variable definitions. *** significant at the 0.01 level; ** significant at the 0.05 level; * significant at the 0.10 level.

	Hedge Fund activist target firms (1)	Hedge fund control sample (2)	Other entrepreneurial activist target firms (3)	Other entrepreneurial activist control Sample (4)	*t*-statistic [*Z*-statistic] for diff. between columns 1 and 3 (5)
Profitability					
Abnormal stock return	11.35%***	3.17%	17.82%***	2.87%	1.97**
	[4.90%]***	[2.38%]	[7.09%]***	[2.11%]	[1.85]**
ΔEBITDA/assets	−0.024*	0.009	−0.008	−0.013	−1.36
	[−0.008]**	[0.002]	[−0.002]*	[−0.001]	[−0.19]
ΔIndustry-adjusted	−0.031**	0.003	−0.015	−0.020	−1.51
	[−0.015]**	[−0.003]	[−0.002]*	[−0.001]	[−0.23]
ΔCFO/assets	−0.001	0.005	−0.020	−0.004	0.87
	[−0.001]	[−0.000]	[−0.008]**	[0.000]	[1.00]
ΔIndustry-adjusted	−0.013	−0.003	−0.022	−0.005	0.69
	[−0.007]*	[−0.001]	[−0.011]**	[−0.000]	[−0.43]
Cash balances					
ΔCash/assets	−0.014	−0.003	−0.003*	0.018	−0.76
	[−0.000]	[0.000]	[.0.001]	[0.002]	[−0.80]
ΔIndustry-adjusted	−0.096**	−0.049	−0.005	0.016	0.93
	[−0.000]	[0.003]	[0.001]	[0.001]	[−0.90]
Δ(Short-term investments)/assets	0.004	0.003	−0.005**	0.009	−1.48
	[−0.003]*	[0.000]	[.−0.000]	[0.001]	[−0.56]
Δ Industry-adjusted	−0.103***	−0.013	.0.009**	−0.032	−1.48
	[−0.002]	[−0.001]	[−0.003]	[0.003]	[−0.24]
Δ(Cash + short-term investments)/assets	−0.011	−0.000	−0.007**	0.023	−0.51
	[−0.003]	[0.000]	[−0.001]	[0.002]	[−1.29]
ΔIndustry-adjusted	−0.199**	−0.045	−0.014***	−0.019	−0.48
	[−0.001]	[0.002]	[−0.003]	[0.001]	[−1.37]

(continued)

Table 9.8 (Continued)

	Hedge Fund activist target firms (1)	Hedge fund control sample (2)	Other entrepreneurial activist target firms (3)	Other entrepreneurial activist control Sample (4)	*t*-statistic [*Z*-statistic] for diff. between columns 1 and 3 (5)
Discretionary spending					
ΔCapital expenditures/assets	0.004	−0.002	−0.004	−0.001	1.71*
	[0.000]	[0.000]	[0.000]	[0.000]	[1.13]
ΔIndustry-adjusted	0.003	−0.003	−0.004	−0.001	1.78*
	[0.000]	[0.000]	[0.000]	[0.000]	[1.70]**
ΔR&D expenditures/ assets	0.003	0.001	−0.008***	0.005	2.35**
	[0.001]	[0.000]	[−0.001]	[0.000]	[0.77]
ΔIndustry-adjusted	0.003	0.002	−0.006***	0.007	2.29**
	[0.001]	[0.000]	[−0.000]	[0.001]	[1.27]
ΔDividends/share	0.112**	0.01	0.041	0.011	1.57
	[0.099]	[0.001]	[0.003]	[0.000]	[1.55]
ΔIndustry-adjusted	0.104**	−0.002	0.035	0.008	1.48
	[0.005]	[−0.010]	[0.001]	[−0.000]	[0.50]
Debt					
ΔTotal debt/assets	0.016*	−0.001	0.001	0.008	0.49
	[0.001]	[0.000]	[−0.000]	[−0.000]	[0.26]
ΔIndustry-adjusted	0.020*	0.001	0.009	0.017	0.34
	[0.004]*	[−0.000]	[0.007]	[0.012]	[0.19]
ΔLong-term debt/ assets	0.024***	−0.005	0.005	0.013	1.32
	[0.046]***	[0.000]	[0.000]	[−0.001]	[1.19]
ΔIndustry-adjusted	0.026***	−0.004	0.008	0.016	1.18
	[0.006]***	[−0.006]	[0.002]	[0.002]	[1.42]
ΔShort-term debt/ assets	−0.007**	0.004	−0.004	−0.008	−0.33
	[0.000]	[0.000]	[−0.001]	[0.000]	[−0.41]
ΔIndustry-adjusted	−0.006**	0.005	−0.001	−0.007	−0.74
	[0.000]	[0.000]	[0.000]	[0.001]	[−0.48]
Firm size					
ΔLn(assets)	0.007	0.048	0.014	0.003	0.15
	[0.026]	[0.041]	[0.016]	[0.032]	[0.11]
ΔIndustry-adjusted	−0.135	−0.090	−0.091	−0.096	−1.39
	[−0.106]*	[−0.088]	[−0.072]	[−0.076]	[−1.33]
Number of firms	132	132	129	129	132/129

targets is 11.35%, which is statistically different from zero at the 0.01 level, and is significantly greater than the abnormal return of 3.17% for the matched firm sample. Similarly, other entrepreneurial activist targets earn a significant abnormal return of 17.82% over the subsequent one-year period, which is significantly greater than the 2.87% for their control sample ($p < 0.05$). Median abnormal returns yield the same conclusions. Thus, the jump in share price around the 13D filing date continues throughout the first year after the activist engages the firm.

To examine possible sources of the subsequent one-year abnormal returns, we calculate the abnormal returns for subgroups of firms based on the outcome of the activist campaign. Table 9.7 contains these results. As the last column in the table illustrates, there are no significant differences in the one-year post-investment abnormal returns for hedge fund targets relative to whether the activist achieves its goal (Panel A), gains at least one seat on the target's board (Panel B), or is subsequently acquired during the year (Panel C). In light of the differentials we find for the abnormal returns surrounding the 13D filings for the first two categories, these one-year returns suggest that: (1) the market anticipated the success and/or the ability of the hedge fund activist to obtain board representation around the initial filing date; and (2) the positive overall subsequent rise in stock price is not related to these two outcomes. The positive, but insignificantly different, subsequent abnormal returns for the merged versus not merged targets is consistent with the view that the market return is not related to whether the company remains independent after one year. This result is contrary to that of Barclay and Holderness (1991), who find that the positive abnormal return around the 13D for firms targeted by blockholders dissipates if the target firms are not subsequently acquired or merged within one year.

For other activists, we see some evidence that outcomes are related to the one-year stock return. While there is no difference in abnormal returns between success and non-success (Table 9.7, Panel A), there is weak evidence that the abnormal return is greater when the activist receives board representation (Table 9.7, Panel B) and stronger evidence that the one-year abnormal return is higher for firms that are acquired within one year (Table 9.7, Panel C). Overall, the results support our previous findings that the market views hedge fund and other entrepreneurial activism as different types of activism.

9.7.2 One-Year Changes in Profitability, Discretionary Spending, Capital Structure, and Cash Reserves after the Initial Target Date

The one-year post-investment abnormal returns are consistent with the activist making short-term value-enhancing changes to the target firm. We explore several sources of these changes by calculating one-year changes in accounting profitability, cash balances, discretionary spending, leverage, and total assets. Specifically, we present mean and median changes in firm characteristics between the fiscal year after and prior to the filing of the initial Schedule 13D. Table 9.8 presents these changes for the activist firms and their control samples. Existing Compustat data extend to 31 December 2005, reducing our sample to 132 target and 129 control firms.[19]

We find no evidence that hedge fund targets become more profitable in terms of return on assets (EBITDA/assets) or cash flows from operations. On the contrary, there appears to be a deterioration of profitability. The mean and median EBITDA/assets ratios significantly decline, when measured in absolute (−0.024; −0.008) or industry-adjusted (−0.031; −0.015) terms. These decreases are statistically different from those reported for the control sample. We find weaker, but consistent, evidence that cash flows from operations drop in a similar manner. The median industry-adjusted change in CFO/assets is −0.007, significantly different at the 0.10 level than the −0.001 change for the control sample.

Other entrepreneurial activist targets experience similar changes in short-term profitability. The change in the targets' mean (median) EBITDA/assets is −.008 (−.002) in the year following the 13D filing; the mean (median) change in industry-adjusted ratio is −.015 (−.002). For both measures, the median values are significantly different from the respective control sample's median at the 0.10 level. CFO and CFO/assets decrease over the year, with median values (raw and industry-adjusted) that are significantly less than the control sample's values. Finally, when we test for differences between hedge fund activists and other entrepreneurial activists, we find little to no significant t- or Z-statistics, supporting the view that both groups of target firms display similar drops in one-year accounting profitability measures.

When examining changes in cash balances (broadly and narrowly defined), we find overall reductions in average cash balances for both groups of activist targets. For the hedge fund targets, the mean industry-adjusted changes in cash/assets, short-term investments/assets, and (cash plus short-term investments)/assets are each negative, indicating that cash on hand (relative to the industry norm) drops in the fiscal year following the initial 13D filing. Each measure is significantly less than its control sample mean. For the other entrepreneurial activist targets, both raw and industry-adjusted cash plus short-term investments drop significantly more than for the respective control sample, but the drop is due almost exclusively to a reduction in short-term investments and not to changes in cash balances.

Next, we examine changes in the target firms' discretionary spending, beginning with changes in the targets' investments in property, plant, and equipment (PP&E) and R&D. For the hedge fund targets, there is little to no one-year change in capital expenditures or R&D expenditures. In contrast, there is a drop in mean R&D expenditures for the other entrepreneurial activist targets, which is significantly less than the increase reported for their control sample. Furthermore, testing for differences in means and medians between the two activist samples (column 5) produces significant t-statistics for all four measures, suggesting that the reductions in capital and R&D expenditures for other entrepreneurial activist targets are greater than the changes in expenditures for the hedge fund targets.

These findings are consistent with the activists' stated reasons in their initial 13D filings as well as the rates of success obtained by these activists. As Table 9.1 shows, the most frequent demand made by other entrepreneurial activists is for the target to pursue strategic

[19] The reductions in sample size are due to time constraints as well as some of the firms leaving the Compustat database. We conduct the analyses with annual Compustat data because quarterly data are not currently available past 2004. When using quarterly data through 2004 for a smaller sample, we obtain qualitatively the same results as presented in Table 9.8.

alternatives; moreover, from Table 9.6, these activists are successful in achieving this goal within one year 70% of the time. In contrast, hedge fund activists have a 48% success rate in achieving this goal, suggesting they are less successful in changing the target's investment expenditures.

Next, we examine changes in dividends per share, another discretionary expenditure. For the hedge fund targets, mean dividends per share rise 11.2 cents per share (median = 9.9 cents per share)—almost doubling in size from the prior period (see Table 9.2). This change is significantly higher than the control sample mean dividend per share rise of one penny per share. We also find (not tabulated) that seven target firms initiate common stock dividends in the fiscal year following the 13D filing date, compared to four control firms. In contrast, average dividends per share for the other entrepreneurial activist targets rise by 4.1 cents per share (median = zero cents per share), which is not significantly different from these targets' control sample. We therefore conclude that the subsequent increase in dividends is most pronounced for the hedge fund targets.

The increase in dividends per share for the hedge fund targets is consistent with hedge funds addressing agency costs associated with Jensen's (1986) free cash flow theory. To investigate this further, we examine changes in leverage for the target firms. For the hedge fund targets, there are significant increases in leverage. The mean unadjusted total debt/assets ratio rises by 0.016 and the industry-adjusted ratio increases by 0.020. The average long-term debt/assets increase by 0.024 and the industry-adjusted long-term debt/assets increase by 0.026. When comparing the sample of hedge fund targets to its control group, each change is significantly different from each other, supporting the view that, following the initial 13D filing, hedge fund targets increase the amount of debt in their capital structures. In contrast, we find no discernible changes in the debt ratios for the other entrepreneurial activist targets. These findings, together, are consistent with the view that hedge fund activists more frequently address free cash flow issues whereas other entrepreneurial activists are more focused on the targets' investing patterns.

We also present changes in total firm assets. Industry-adjusted assets decline for both hedge fund and other entrepreneurial activists' targets, suggesting that target firms sell off unwanted assets within one year. These results are similar to those reported by Bethel, Liebeskind, and Opler (1998) for their sample of individual activist targets.

In summary, we conclude that activism does not result in an immediate increase in the firm's accounting profitability—on the contrary, earnings and/or cash flows decline in the year following the initial 13D investment. However, we do find evidence that hedge funds and other entrepreneurial activists pursue different post-intervention strategies. Hedge funds appear to address agency costs associated with excess cash balances by increasing dividends and the target's leverage. Other entrepreneurial activists appear to be more concerned with the investment strategies of the target firms and reduce investments in R&D and capital expenditures.

Finally, to see if these findings persist or are reversed in the second fiscal year, we calculate two-year changes as well as changes in the second year subsequent to the initial 13D filing. Since our data end on December 2005, we lose additional firms, resulting in sample sizes of sixty-nine for the hedge funds and seventy-three for the other activists. Because of the smaller sample sizes, we view these findings as preliminary and discuss them only briefly. Overall, there is no evidence that any of our one-year changes reverse in the second year. Nor do we observe large continuations of profitability, discretionary expenditures, and changes in debt, cash, and assets. We cautiously conclude that changes to the target occur mainly in the first year subsequent to the activism.

9.8 Summary and Conclusions

This chapter examines recent confrontational entrepreneurial shareholder activism. We define confrontational entrepreneurial activism as instances in which an investor files a 13D filing after taking an initial stake of 5% or more in the company and clearly states in the filing's 'purpose' section that it intends to proactively influence management's future decisions.

We examine two samples of entrepreneurial activists: hedge funds and other entrepreneurial investors, where the latter primarily consist of individuals, private equity funds, venture capital funds, and asset management firms. We find similarities and disparities between hedge fund and other entrepreneurial activism. The main parallels correspond to market returns and the activist's success in gaining its original objectives.

Hedge fund targets earn, on average, 10.2% abnormal stock returns during the period surrounding the initial Schedule 13D filing, and other activist targets experience abnormal returns of 5.1%. Furthermore, these returns do not dissipate in the one-year period following the initial 13D filings. Instead, hedge fund targets earn an additional 11.4% abnormal return during the subsequent year; other targets observe a 17.8% abnormal return.

Activists are extremely successful in getting existing management to acquiesce to their demands as articulated in the initial 13D filing, with hedge funds enjoying a success rate of 60% and non-hedge fund activists accomplishing their objectives 65% of the time. Both groups are particularly successful at gaining board representation on the target firm within one year of the initial finding. We present evidence that this success is based on activists' use of the proxy solicitation process (both actual and threatened), a finding contrary to Bebchuk (Chapter 3, this volume) and Dodd and Warner (1983).

However, there are distinct differences between hedge fund and other entrepreneurial activism. Hedge fund activists target more profitable and financially healthy firms than do other entrepreneurial activists. Hedge fund targets also have higher levels of cash on hand than evidenced by other activist targets. After the initial investment, hedge funds differentially redirect target firms relative to the redirection implemented by other entrepreneurial activists. Hedge funds address the free cash flow problem by frequently demanding the target firm to buy back its own shares, cut the CEO's salary, and initiate dividends. In the fiscal year after the initial 13D filing, hedge fund targets, on average, double their dividends, significantly increase their long-term debt, and significantly decrease their cash and short-term investments. In contrast, other activists most frequently demand changes in operating strategies. Consistent with these requests, there are significant differences in changes in R&D and capital expenditures in the year following the 13D filing between targets of hedge funds and other activists. Other entrepreneurial activist targets reduce expenditures in these investments, and the reductions are significantly less than the slight increases recorded by hedge fund targets.

Although many of our findings are consistent with studies on prior waves of shareholder activism, we conclude that hedge funds and other current, entrepreneurial activists take different approaches from each other, and that the current wave of confrontational entrepreneurial activism may represent a new breed of shareholder activist.

APPENDIX A

Variable Definitions for Tables 9.2 and 9.8

Abnormal Stock Return is the difference between the firm's buy-and-hold return for the time period and the buy-and-hold return for the same time period on the appropriate Fama-French size-matched portfolio, as computed by Eventus. There are five size-matched portfolios.

EBITDA/Assets is earnings before interest, taxes, depreciation, and amortization divided by mean total assets, the latter defined as the average of beginning and ending total assets.

CFO/Assets is net cash flow from operating activities divided by mean total assets.

Z-Score uses the Altman (1968) model to determine the likelihood of bankruptcy amongst companies.

Capital Expenditures/Assets is capital expenditures less the sale of PP&E divided by mean total assets.

R&D Expenditures/Assets is research and development expense divided by mean total assets.

Dividends/Share is dividends per share—*ex-date*.

Cash/Assets is total cash to total assets ratio.

(Cash plus Short-Term Investments)/Assets is the ratio of the sum of cash plus short-term investments to total assets.

Total Debt/Assets is the ratio of sum of long- and short-term debt to total assets.

Short-Term Debt/Assets variable is the ratio of debt in current liabilities to total assets.

Long-Term Debt/Assets is the ratio of total long-term debt to total assets.

Assets are total assets of the company.

Revenues are net sales of the company.

Market Value of Equity is the dollar value of common equity.

Market-to-Book Ratio is the ratio of the stock's market value to the difference in the value of total assets and total liabilities.

The *Industry-Adjusted* variable is the difference in the firm's value and the median value for all firms in the company's Fama and French (1997) forty-eight-industry classification.

References

Altman, E. (1968). Financial Ratios, Discriminant Analysis, and the Prediction of Corporate Bankruptcy, *Journal of Finance* 23, 589–609.

Barber, B. M. (2006). Evaluating CalPERS' Activism, Working Paper, available at <http://ssrn.com/abstract=890321>.

Barclay, M. J. and Holderness, C. G. (1989). Private Benefits from Control of Public Corporations, *Journal of Financial Economics* 25, 371–95.

Barclay, M. J. and Holderness, C. G. (1991). Negotiated Block Trades and Corporate Control, *Journal of Finance* 46, 861–78.

Bebchuk, L. A. (2005). The Case for Increasing Shareholder Power, *Harvard Law Review* 118, 835–914.

Berger, P. and Ofek, E. (1995). Diversification's Effect on Firm Value, *Journal of Financial Economics* 37, 39–65.

Bethel, J. E., Liebeskind, J. P., and Opler, T. (1998). Block Share Purchases and Corporate Performance, *Journal of Finance* 53, 605–34.

Black, B. S. (1990). Shareholder Passivity Reexamined, *Michigan Law Review* 89, 520–608.

Black, B. S. (1998). Shareholder Activism and Corporate Governance in the US, in P. Newman (ed.), *The New Palgrave Dictionary of Economics and the Law* (London and Basingstoke, Palgrave Macmillan), 461–8.

Boyson, N. M. and Mooradian, R. M. (2007). Hedge Funds as Shareholder Activists from 1994–2005, Working Paper, available at <http://ssrn.com/abstract=992739>.

Bratton, W. W. (2007). Hedge Funds and Governance Targets, *Georgetown Law Journal*, 95, 1375–433.

Briggs, T. W. (2007). Corporate Governance and the New Hedge Fund Activism: An Empirical Analysis, *Journal of Corporation Law* 32, 681–737.

Carleton, W. T., Nelson, J. M., and Weisbach, M. S. (1998). The Influence of Institutions on Corporate Governance through Private Negotiations: Evidence from TIAA–CREF, *Journal of Finance* 53, 1335–62.

Christoffersen, S. E. K., Geczy, C. C., Musto, D. K., and Reed, A. V. (2007). Vote Trading and Information Aggregation, *Journal of Finance* 62, 2897–929.

Clifford, C. (2007). Value Creation or Destruction? Hedge Funds as Shareholder Activists, Working Paper, available at <http://ssrn.com/abstract=971018>.

Davis, G. F. and Kim, E. H. (2007). Business Ties and Proxy Voting by Mutual Funds, *Journal of Financial Economics* 85, 552–70.

Del Guerico, D. and Hawkins, J. (1999). The Motivation and Impact of Pension Fund Activism, *Journal of Financial Economics* 52, 293–340.

Dodd, P. and Warner, J. B. (1983). On Corporate Governance: A Study of Proxy Contests, *Journal of Financial Economics* 11, 401–38.

Eisinger, J. (2005). Hedge Funds Set Sights on Company Cash Hoards, *Wall Street Journal* (12 Oct.).

Faleye, O. (2004). Cash and Corporate Control, *Journal of Finance* 59, 2041–60.

Fama, E. and French, K. (1997). Industry Costs of Equity, *Journal of Financial Economics* 43, 153–93.

Gillan, S. L. and Starks, L. T. (2000). Corporate Governance Proposals and Shareholder Activism: The Role of Institutional Investors, *Journal of Financial Economics* 57, 275–305.

Gordon, L. A. and Pound, J. (1993). Information, Ownership Structure, and Shareholder Voting: Evidence from Shareholder-Sponsored Corporate Governance Proposals, *Journal of Finance* 48, 697–718.

Greenwood, R. and Schor, M. (2009). Investor Activism and Takeovers, Harvard Business School Working Paper, available at <http://ssrn.com/abstract=1003792>.

Holderness, C. G. and Sheehan, D. P. (1985). Raiders or Saviors? The Evidence on Six Controversial Investors, *Journal of Financial Economics* 14, 555–79.

Holmström, B. and Kaplan, S. N. (2001). Corporate Governance and Merger Activity in the United States: Making Sense of the 1980s and 1990s, *Journal of Economic Perspectives* 15, 121–44.

Hu, H. and Black, B. (2007). Hedge Funds, Insiders, and Empty Voting: Decoupling of Economic and Voting Ownership in Public Companies, *Journal of Corporate Finance* 13, 343–67.

Jensen, M. C. (1986). Agency Costs of Free Cash Flow, Corporate Finance, and Takeovers, *American Economic Review* 76, 323–9.

John, K. and Klein, A. (1995). Shareholder Proposals and Corporate Governance, NYU Working Paper No. FIN-98-046, available at <http://ssrn.com/abstract=1297750>.

Karpoff, J. M. (2001). The Impact of Shareholder Activism on Target Companies: A Survey of Empirical Findings, University of Washington Working Paper, available at <http://ssrn.com/abstract=88536>.

Maddala, G. S. (1993). *Limited-Dependent and Qualitative Variables in Econometrics* (Cambridge, Cambridge University Press).

Mikkelson, W. H. and Ruback, R. S. (1985). An Empirical Analysis of the Interfirm Equity Investment Process, *Journal of Financial Economics* 14, 523–53.

Pound, J. (1992). Raiders, Targets, and Politics: The History and Future of American Corporate Control, *Journal of Applied Corporate Finance* 5, 6–18.

Private Equity Intelligence Ltd. (2007). *The 2007 Fund Terms Advisor: A Guide to Terms and Conditions of Private Equity Funds* (London, Preqin Ltd.).

Romano, R. (2001). Less is More: Making Shareholder Activism a Valued Mechanism of Corporate Governance, *Yale Journal on Regulation* 18, 174–251.

Shah, K. (1994). The Nature of Information Conveyed by Pure Capital Structure Changes, *Journal of Financial Economics* 36, 89–126.

Shleifer, A. and Vishny, R. W. (1986). Large Shareholders and Corporate Control, *Journal of Political Economy* 94, 461–88.

Shome, K. K. and Singh, S. (1995). Firm Value and External Blockholdings, *Financial Management* 24, 3–14.

Smith, M. P. (1996). Shareholder Activism by Institutional Investors: Evidence from CalPERS, *Journal of Finance* 51, 227–52.

Wahal, S. (1996). Pension Fund Activism and Firm Performance, *Journal of Financial and Quantitative Analysis* 31, 1–23.

Walsh, J. P. and Kosnik, R. D. (1993). Corporate Raiders and their Disciplinary Role in the Market for Corporate Control, *Academy of Management Journal* 36, 671–700.

Woidtke, T. (2002). Agents Watching Agents?: Evidence from Pension Fund Ownership and Firm Value, *Journal of Financial Economics* 63, 99–131.

Wynn, G. (2005). Hedge Funds Targets Cash-Rich Corporates, *Reuters* (23 June).

C.

Strategic Holding versus Collective Interest: Empty Voting and Bankruptcy Reorganization

CHAPTER 10

DEBT, EQUITY, AND HYBRID DECOUPLING: GOVERNANCE AND SYSTEMIC RISK IMPLICATIONS

HENRY T. C. HU AND BERNARD S. BLACK

10.1 Introduction

Ownership of shares customarily conveys economic, voting, and other rights, and disclosure and other obligations. Long-standing legal and economic theories of the public corporation assume that the elements of this package of rights and obligations are generally bundled together—and, in particular, that voting rights are linked to an economic interest in the corporation, and usually held in proportion to that economic interest.

Similarly, ownership of debt customarily conveys a package of economic rights (to receive payment of principal and interest); contractual control rights (to enforce, waive, or modify the terms of the debt contract); other legal rights (including rights to participate in bankruptcy proceedings and to sue company directors and officers under securities and other laws); and sometimes disclosure obligations. Both law and contracting practice assume that the elements of this package are generally bundled together. It is assumed, in particular, that creditors are normally interested in keeping a solvent firm out of bankruptcy and (inter-creditor conflicts aside) in maximizing the value of an insolvent firm.

These assumptions can no longer be relied on. Both debt and equity decoupling are widespread and often undisclosed. In prior work (Hu and Black 2006, 2007, 2008), we focused largely on equity decoupling.[1] Voting rights can be decoupled from economic interests quickly, at low cost, and on a large scale. Investors can have greater voting than economic

[1] Readers interested in specific disclosure and other policy proposals for equity decoupling should consult our *law* articles (Hu and Black 2006, 2008). These articles provide citations for the legal rules and decoupling examples we discuss here. Our predecessor *finance* article, Hu and Black (2007), provides useful background for a finance audience. We generally do not repeat here the many decoupling examples discussed in our prior work.

ownership, a pattern we termed 'empty voting'. Conversely, investors can have greater economic than voting ownership. This economic ownership is often not disclosed, resulting in 'hidden ownership'. In many cases economic ownership can be quickly transformed to include voting ownership as well, a pattern we termed 'morphable ownership'. The combination of hidden and morphable ownership (together, 'hidden (morphable) ownership') can permit stealth takeover bids. Some acquirers have amassed 30–45% stakes in target firms without prior disclosure. Conversely, target companies can defend against bids by using decoupling to place votes in friendly hands. Controlling families can formally retain shares and voting rights, while selling off much of their economic stake. Standard measures of corporate ownership and control (for example, Claessens, Djankov, and Lang 2000; Faccio and Lang 2002) ignore derivatives-based decoupling strategies, and thus overstate economic ownership and understate the disparity between controllers' voting and economic ownership.

On 11 June 2008, as this article was about to go to press, the first US court decision on the use of equity decoupling to avoid US 'large shareholder' disclosure requirements was rendered, in *CSX Corporation v. The Children's Investment Fund* (*CSX*). In Section 10.2.2 we briefly discuss this opinion, which will likely curtail the use of equity decoupling to create large hidden ownership positions in US companies.

The principal contribution of this chapter, however, involves debt and hybrid decoupling. There has been some prior writing on equity decoupling (in addition to our own work, see Brav and Mathews 2008; Kahan and Rock Chapter 5; Martin and Partnoy 2005; Nathan 2007; and Neeman and Orosel 2006). In contrast, there has been no systematic prior analysis of debt decoupling and its implications for debt governance and systemic financial risk. Credit default swaps and other credit derivatives now permit formal ownership of debt claims to be decoupled from economic exposure to the risk of default or credit deterioration. Yet formal ownership usually still conveys control rights under the debt contract and legal rights under bankruptcy and other laws. Securitization of debt claims also often decouples economic risk from contractual control rights and bankruptcy rights.

There are important parallels between equity and debt decoupling. Creditors can have greater contractual or legal rights than economic exposure, a pattern we can call 'empty crediting'. They can hold empty or economic-only positions with no disclosure, not even the limited disclosure required for formal holders of debt. If it becomes important to hold formal contractual rights, economic-only positions can sometimes be morphed to include these rights ('morphable crediting'). In both areas, investors can have control rights yet have negative economic ownership (sometimes loosely called a 'net short' position) and thus have incentives to cause the firm's value to fall.

Equity and debt decoupling can be combined, producing what one can call 'hybrid decoupling'. Investors can make bearish bets on a company's value by directly or indirectly shorting its shares, buying protection with credit default swaps, or both. They can use a long equity position to hedge a short debt position, or vice versa. Yet there is currently a disconnect between disclosure of equity and debt positions, with much more disclosure on the equity side.

Widespread debt decoupling can have important externalities, and can affect overall financial stability, both positively and negatively. The positives are well known—debt decoupling can contribute to economic efficiency and financial stability in a variety of ways, partly by allowing lenders to spread risk. We focus here on the negatives. Some of these are known, but some are not. Lenders' ability to shed risk weakens their incentives to assess and monitor debtors' repayment ability. Complex decouplings can pose model risks for both lenders and risk buyers, risks that become especially severe in times of market stress. New forms of intermediation raise new agency costs. Less obviously, decoupling also impedes what one might call 'debt governance'—the interactions between creditors and firms (or other debtors), such as negotiations to address loan terms and conditions. Financial restructurings are often made harder and sometimes infeasible, both in and out of formal bankruptcy. Spread across an economy, the 'freezing' of debtor–creditor relationships can increase systemic financial risk.

Widespread decoupling can also increase the economy's exposure to liquidity shocks. Lenders' business models evolve to rely on liquid risk-transfer markets. Borrowers can less easily renegotiate with lenders, and hence rely more heavily on an ability to refinance. And the resting place of credit risk can become hidden, which increases counterparty risk and can affect liquidity during financial downturns.

We focus on public companies. Section 10.2 discusses equity decoupling, Section 10.3 discusses debt decoupling. Section 10.4 discusses hybrid decoupling. Section 10.5 discusses the systemic risk implications of widespread debt decoupling. Section 10.6 concludes. References in this chapter to legal rules are generic, since these rules differ between countries, but are intended to capture the main lines of regulation in the United States, at the EU level in Europe, and (with less confidence in details) a few other jurisdictions.[2]

10.2 Equity Decoupling

We summarize here the principal forms of equity decoupling. With limited exceptions, the rules governing public firms presume that ownership of shares is a meaningful concept and conveys a standard package of shareholder rights ('full ownership'). Some of these rights are economic, including dividend, liquidation, and appraisal rights under corporate law. Some rights are not purely monetary, including voting rights, director fiduciary duties, rights to bring suits and inspect corporate records, access to corporate proxy machinery, and so on. Some of these rules are based on formal record ownership (even where the record owner passes voting rights to an economic owner); some are based on who holds voting rights. However, persons who have economic ownership but not voting rights are regulated lightly or, often, not at all.

Over the course of the last century, the assumption that most shareholders held full ownership mostly worked. Special rules for record owners handled the most important exception. This assumption works no longer. The derivatives revolution in finance, the growth of sophisticated, lightly regulated hedge funds, and the related growth in the share lending market now make it easy to decouple voting rights from economic ownership, and to

[2] In the United States, we assume corporations are incorporated in Delaware. In the EU, we assume they are governed by local laws which conform to relevant EU directives; including the recent Transparency Directive and Shareholder Rights Directive. For specific countries where decoupling has occurred, we are reasonably familiar with the UK and somewhat familiar with Australia, Canada, France, Germany, Italy, Korea, New Zealand, and Switzerland.

further decompose economic ownership—for instance, by separating appraisal or dividend rights from other economic rights.

10.2.1 The Elements of Equity Decoupling

Because of the many ways in which decoupling can occur, it is useful to summarize its functional elements and specify some terminology. By *formal voting rights*, we refer to the legal right to vote shares, including the power to instruct someone else how to vote. By *voting rights* or *voting ownership* of shares, we refer to either formal or informal rights to vote shares, including the informal power to instruct someone else how to vote or obtain formal voting rights. The company at which voting takes place is the *host company*.

By *economic ownership*, we will generally refer to the economic returns associated with shares. This ownership can be achieved directly by holding shares or, appraisal and some other rights aside, indirectly by holding a *coupled asset* that conveys returns that relate directly to those on the shares. Economic ownership can be either *positive* (the same direction as the return on shares), or *negative* (the opposite direction from the return on shares). Someone who owns voting shares has *full ownership*: he has all of the rights and obligations associated with shares, including voting rights and economic rights. Economic-only ownership may also be *hidden* (exempt or arguably exempt from the disclosure rules that apply to full ownership, and not voluntarily disclosed), *morphable* (accompanied by the informal ability to acquire voting rights), or both (hidden (morphable) ownership).[3] Hidden (morphable) ownership can be seen as one form of *soft parking* of shares: arranging for shares to be held in friendly hands to avoid regulatory or other burdens of direct ownership, yet retaining informal access to the desired shareholder rights.

Decoupling often depends on combining full ownership of shares with ownership of a coupled asset. Coupled assets include derivatives (such as options, futures, and equity swaps), contractual rights (such as rights under a share loan agreement), and other financial products. We will focus initially on decoupling of voting and economic rights, and return in Section 10.4 to other decoupling possibilities. The central idea is that the coupled asset affects economic ownership, but leaves voting rights unchanged. One could also decouple voting and economic rights by holding shares and having a side contract relating to the votes, but this is not common. We refer to anyone who has substantially greater voting than economic ownership as an *empty voter*.

Investors may also hold *related non-host assets*—assets, often securities of another company, whose value is related to the value of the host company's shares. For example, if the host company plans to acquire a target, the target's shares are a related non-host asset. The combined return from host shares, coupled assets, and related non-host assets produces an *overall economic interest* in actions that affect firm value, which can be positive, zero, or negative.

Empty voting, as we have defined it, includes some long-standing arrangements for concentrating voting power. These include dual-class capital structures, with one class

[3] Economic-only ownership, accompanied by morphable voting rights, is not truly 'economic-only'. We judged that this imprecision did not justify creating a specific term for this type of ownership.

holding greater voting power relative to economic rights, and pyramids and circular ownership structures, which concentrate effective voting control in the hands of the person, family, or group at the top of the pyramid or the 'centre' of the circular ownership structure. The efficiency and regulation of these techniques are beyond the scope of this chapter. More subtly, one might regard proxy voting advisors, such as Institutional Shareholder Services (ISS), as empty voters as well. These voting advisors have no direct economic interest in shares, yet wield substantial voting power through their advice to institutional investors. Analysis of voting advisors as empty voters is also beyond our scope.

10.2.2 Reasons for Equity Decoupling

Investors and firms can engage in equity decoupling for a wide variety of reasons, with differing efficiency properties.[4] We sketch here some of the principal reasons, and offer representative examples. See Hu and Black (2007, 2008) for a review of the theoretical justifications for linking voting and economic rights and additional details on the examples.

1. *Efficiency-enhancing, or potentially so.* Some forms of decoupling may be efficiency-enhancing. For example, transactions in equity derivatives can sometimes involve lower transaction costs than equivalent transactions in shares, can permit arbitrage between related markets (thus improving pricing efficiency in both), and can permit transfer of risk to lower-cost risk-bearers.

There are both pro- and anti-efficiency arguments specific to empty voting. On the pro side, Christoffersen et al. (2007) argue that more informed voters may acquire votes from less informed voters. Brav and Mathews (2008) model the efficiency properties of the ability of empty voters, who have private knowledge of their voting position, to trade on that knowledge between the record date for a shareholder meeting (henceforth, simply 'record date') and the voting date. In their model, this ability to trade can sometimes be efficiency-enhancing, and sometimes not.

2. *Efficiency effects likely neutral, or nearly so.* In some cases, equity decoupling is likely to have limited efficiency implications. The difference between voting rights, at a shareholder meeting, based on voting ownership on the record date, and economic ownership on the shareholder meeting date, offers an example with limited efficiency implications, assuming that the shareholders who vote have incentives similar to those of shareholders who acquire ownership between the two dates.

Tax-motivated strategies offer a family of examples in which efficiency effects are likely to be limited. These include dividend capture strategies (Christoffersen et al. 2005; Raghavan 2007), avoidance of transaction taxes on share trading (in the UK, for example, trading in the UK version of equity swaps, known as contracts for differences (CFDs) avoids a tax on share transactions), deferral of capital gain (Sheppard 2002), and avoidance by tax-exempt

[4] We use efficiency in a loose sense to refer to the overall social value of the firm, including investor claims, government claims (as tax collector), employee, customer, supplier, and community surplus, and other positive and negative externalities.

entities of unrelated business income tax (an issue in the US). To first order, wealth moves from the government to the arbitrageur, with limited impact on social wealth. However, to second order, evasion undermines the horizontal and vertical equity of the tax system and may prompt the government to raise tax rates, with likely efficiency costs. Whatever one thinks of, say, dividend or transaction taxes, it is difficult to develop an argument why ordinary investors should pay them, but clever hedge funds should not. Evasion also likely involves transaction costs.

3. *Avoiding ownership disclosure and other rules: efficiency uncertain.* In still other cases, decoupling is used to avoid regulatory requirements. A common goal has been to avoid rules requiring disclosure of share ownership. These rules are often based on formal voting rights, rather than economic ownership. A few jurisdictions (Australia, Hong Kong, Switzerland, and the UK during takeover bids) have modified their ownership disclosure rules to cover at least some economic-only positions, and further reforms are under consideration in various jurisdictions (Italy, the UK generally, and the US). In the US, the *CSX* decision will likely limit the use of equity swaps, and potentially other equity derivatives, to avoid large shareholder disclosure rules. Thus, there may be a trend towards greater disclosure of equity swaps and other cash-settled equity derivatives. Still, as of today, in most jurisdictions, in most circumstances, economic-only ownership is generally not disclosed. This ownership is often, as a practical matter, accompanied by morphable voting rights.[5]

On 11 June 2008, the first US judicial opinion addressing hidden (morphable) ownership was rendered, in the *CSX* case. A proxy fight target (CSX Corporation) claimed that two hedge funds (The Children's Investment Fund (TCI) and 3G Capital Partners), which held cash-settled equity swaps referencing CSX shares, violated the US large shareholder ownership disclosure rules that apply to activist investors (often referred to as the Section 13(d) rules, after the relevant statutory section) by not disclosing beneficial ownership of the shares referenced in the equity swaps. The trial judge found that the two hedge funds had violated the disclosure rules, principally under the pertinent SEC 'anti-evasion' rule. Loosely speaking, that anti-evasion rule deems, as a beneficial owner of shares, anyone who creates or uses any 'contract, arrangement, or device with the purpose or effect of divesting' such person of beneficial ownership 'as part of a plan or scheme to evade the [13(d)] reporting requirements'. The judge also found that, even apart from the anti-evasion rule, there were 'persuasive arguments' that these hedge funds held voting or investment power over the matched shares held by their dealers to hedge the equity swaps, though he did not rule on this question.[6]

The two hedge funds have said they will appeal. Subject to the outcome of the appeal, the *CSX* case will likely inhibit the use of equity swaps (and perhaps other equity derivatives)

[5] We discuss disclosure reforms and reform proposals in Hu and Black (2008) (current to year-end 2007). For the 2008 Australian reforms, see Takeovers Panel (Australia) (2008).

[6] *CSX Corporation v. The Children's Investment Fund Management (UK) LLP* (Southern District of New York, 11 June 2008). For the views of the staff of the SEC's Division of Corporation Finance on the scope of the Section 13(d) rules, provided to the judge at his request, see SEC (2008). The authors of this chapter were engaged, respectively, by counsel for the target and by counsel for the hedge funds to, among other things, offer views to the SEC on what advice the SEC should give to the court.

by activist shareholders to avoid Section 13(d) disclosure. A prospective user would fear being found by a court to have violated the SEC's 'anti-evasion' rule, or to have voting or investment power over matched shares, or both. Whatever the outcome of the appeal, the *CSX* case will likely put pressure on the SEC to adopt disclosure rules that explicitly address economic-only ownership.

Decoupling can also be used to avoid other rules. For many of these rules, coverage is based on formal voting rights, and does not include economic-only ownership. Depending on the jurisdiction, avoidable rules can include:

- *Rules against 'vote buying'.* Corporate law rules against vote buying are generally not triggered by empty voting strategies (for details, see Hu and Black 2006).
- *Mandatory bid rules.* Under these rules, a new controller must offer to buy all remaining shares at the price paid for the controlling shares. These are generally triggered by holding more than a threshold percentage of the target's shares, for which only enforceable voting rights count. Examples include *Victory-Unaxis* (Switzerland), *Banca Antonveneta Banco Populare* (Italy), *Fiat-Agnelli* (Italy), *SAI-Fondiaria* (Italy), and *John Fairfax Holdings-Brierley Investments* (Australia).[7]
- *Statutory, contractual, and other limits on voting power.* There can be a variety of limits on voting power, for particular firms or particular shareholders, arising from law or contract. Some countries restrict foreign ownership, the acquisition by anyone of a large percentage stakes, or both in particular industries (for example, banks, other financial firms, airlines, telecoms); some limit holdings by financial firms in non-financial firms, some impose special rules on investment companies or holding companies (whose principal assets are securities of other companies), and so on. In the US, some states limit the voting rights of shareholders who cross a specified ownership level; poison pill takeover defences limit stakes acquired without the target's consent. Many of these rules can be sidestepped through economic-only ownership. *Hyundai Elevator-Hyundai Merchant Marine* (Korea) offers an example involving holding company rules; *Endesa-Enel* (Spain) involves a strategic industry; *Kyivstar-Alfa Group* (Ukraine), and *MegaFon-Reiman* (Russia) involve contractual limits on voting power.[8]

[7] For discussion of *Banca Anton-veneta-Banco Populare* and *SIA-Fondiaria*, see Kirchmaier, Grant, and Kirchmaier (2009). The evasion can sometimes reach extreme proportions. For example, Victory currently holds a 68% economic stake in Unaxis (renamed Oerlikon), yet has kept its share ownership below the 30% level at which a bid for minority shares would be required.

[8] In *Hyundai Elevator-Hyundai Merchant Marine*, Elevator arranged for outside investors to hold Merchant Marine shares which, if held by Elevator, would have made Elevator a holding company, with adverse consequences under Korean law. Elevator retained voting rights and repurchase rights. In *Endesa-Enel*, Enel made a takeover bid for Endesa, and acquired 25% economic ownership. Its direct share position was limited to 10% ownership of shares by Spanish law, without approval of telecom regulators. In *Kyivstar-Alfa Group*, Russia's Alfa Group owned stakes in two competing Ukrainian mobile telephone companies; an arbitration award required it to cut its indirect ownership in one of them, Kyivstar, to below 5%. It complied by selling half of its stake to a Kazakh company, but retaining the right to repurchase the shares. In *MegaFon-Reiman*, Russian telecom minister Leonid Reiman held economic ownership of mobile phone company MegaFon through a Bermuda trust; he claimed that his lawyer, Mr Golmond, owned the MegaFon shares.

- *Income tax rules.* A family of strategies let shareholders hedge the risk on shares and obtain most of the shares' value in cash, while deferring income tax on gain. These strategies often involve some combination of short sales, over-the-counter derivatives, and sometimes other securities linked to the shares. Schizer (2001) and Sheppard (2002) discuss US strategies. *Estée Lauder* and *Ciber* offer examples.[9]
- *Recapture of 'short-swing' trading profits.* Under US rules, company directors, officers, and 10% shareholders must forfeit any profits made by buying and then selling shares within a six-month period. But only voting ownership counts towards the threshold. Thus, an investor can hold up to 9.99% in shares, have additional economic ownership through derivatives, and remain free to trade. Examples of this strategy include *Target–Pershing Square*.[10]
- *Limits on short sales, or 'margin borrowing' against the value of shares.* Some countries restrict short selling of shares, or limit leveraged purchases of shares. OTC equity derivatives can provide a way around these restrictions.
- *Antitrust rules.* US rules require the anti-trust regulators to consent in advance before one company can acquire a large stake in another. These 'Hart–Scott–Rodino' rules turn on ownership of voting securities; economic-only ownership is unlikely to count.

The efficiency properties of these avoidance strategies depend on the efficiency of the underlying rule. If the underlying rule is efficient, evasion is more likely to be inefficient, and vice versa. Yet the efficiency of particular rules is often unclear. For example, ownership disclosure rules can improve pricing efficiency because they give market participants better knowledge of the activities of large investors. Yet disclosure rules can also reduce incentives to search for undervalued shares, and hence reduce pricing efficiency. It is unclear, either theoretically or empirically, which disclosure rules are optimal. The efficiency of disclosure avoidance is thus also unclear.

4. *Separating ownership and control and takeover defences: efficiency doubtful.* Some uses of decoupling seem likely to be efficiency-decreasing, at least on average. First, controllers can use decoupling to reduce their economic ownership while preserving voting control. Often, they can do so without paying the market penalty which accompanies explicit sale of low-voting or non-voting shares. As we discuss in Hu and Black (2007), there are both theoretical and empirical reasons to think that this separation is likely to be inefficient on average.

Second, decoupling can form part of a takeover defence strategy. Often, this involves a firm arranging for the votes to be held in friendly hands, thus avoiding the legal ban in many countries on firms voting their own shares, held by the firm or a subsidiary. Given the

[9] In both *Estée Lauder* and *Ciber*, a major shareholder sought to cash out his holdings while deferring capital gains tax. *Estée Lauder* involved a prepaid forward short sale, to which the US tax rules responded by restricting simple sales. *Ciber* involved a prepaid variable forward sale, in which Ciber's CEO shed most of his economic risk, while retaining enough (5% downside risk, some upside potential) to satisfy US tax rules (as modified after *Estée Lauder*).

[10] In *Target–Pershing Square*, hedge fund Pershing acquired 12.6% economic ownership of Target, but kept its share ownership just under the 10% threshold for triggering short-swing profit recapture. Reuters, Hedge Fund Increases Its Stake in Target (25 December 2007).

general support from academic studies for an active corporate control market (for surveys, see Gilson and Black 1995; Becht, Bolton, and Roell 2004), these defences are likely to reduce efficiency, on average.

5. *Empty voting with conflicting or negative interests: efficiency doubtful.* A troubling empty voting possibility involves two firms whose fortunes are linked in some way, such as acquirer and target. In an extreme case, an empty voter can have negative net economic interest: the voter has incentives to vote to decrease company value, and often will have arranged to hold votes with that goal. There are several possibilities.

- *Target, its shareholders, or acquirer's managers influencing voting at an acquiring firm.* Any time an acquirer needs a vote of its own shareholders to complete an acquisition, the target and its shareholders may try to influence the acquirer's vote through empty voting. The target can potentially do so itself, either directly or through a friendly investment bank. Or the target's shareholders can do so (examples include *Perry–Mylan* and *Stark–M-Flex*).[11] The more the acquirer overpays, the more the target's shareholders will gain. Or the acquirer's managers can obtain empty votes, using one of the soft parking strategies discussed in Section 10.2.3.

  In a situation involving competing bidders, the target, its shareholders, or another bidder, may try to influence one of the bidders, either to encourage or discourage competition. In *Barclays–ABN-AMRO-Fortis*, for example, there was intense demand for borrowing Fortis shares just before a Fortis vote which determined whether it would bid. By whom, and for what purpose, is unclear.[12]
- *Acquirer, its shareholders, or target's managers influencing target.* It is similarly possible for the acquirer, its shareholders, or the target's managers to buy target votes, and cast them in favour of a takeover bid. Examples involving parent firms casting empty votes at subsidiaries in favour of freeze-outs include *Sears Canada* (Canada) and *Lindner Holding* (Germany).[13] *AXA–MONY* (US) involves investors in the acquirer's convertible bonds casting empty votes of the target's shares.[14]

[11] In *Perry–Mylan*, hedge fund Perry Corp. held a 9.9% voting stake in an acquirer (Mylan), but no economic ownership, in order to support Mylan's bid for a target (King) in which Perry held a large stake. Perry had an incentive to cause Mylan to overpay for King. *Stark–M-Flex* involves a similar scenario, where a large empty voter of M-Flex (the acquirer) would gain on the target side (MFS Technologies) if M-Flex acquired MFS.

[12] In *Barclays–ABN-AMRO-Fortis*, the target, ABN-AMRO, placed large orders to borrow shares of one of two competing bidders (Fortis), which needed shareholder approval to proceed with its bid. Whether ABN-AMRO did so for itself (which it denied) or for its clients is unclear.

[13] In *Sears Canada*, parent company Sears Holdings sought to buy the minority stake in subsidiary Sears Canada. The dealer-manager for its tender offer, Scotiabank, held a large voting stake in Sears Canada but no economic ownership (it held shares as matched shares to hedge an equity swap position with hedge fund Pershing Square). Scotiabank refused to unwind the swap and return the shares to Pershing, which opposed the bid, and planned instead to vote in favour of the offer. Scotiabank was blocked from voting by Canadian securities regulators. In *Lindner Holding*, a parent sought to use borrowed shares to reach the ownership threshold for completing a freeze-out under German law. The German courts did not allow the borrowed shares to count towards the threshold.

[14] In *AXA–MONY*, AXA issued bonds which were convertible into AXA shares at a discount, but only if AXA acquired MONY. Investors who were long (short) these bonds had incentives to vote MONY shares for (against) the takeover, for reasons unrelated to the merits of the deal.

- *Other possibilities.* More generally, hedge funds and other activist shareholders fairly often oppose buyouts and freeze-outs, seeking a higher price. Do some acquirers, when facing active opposition, directly or indirectly buy some target votes? Do deal opponents sometimes buy votes? Rumours abound, but no one knows for sure.

Finally, an empty voter may vote against a deal simply because it is net short. *Henderson Land* (Hong Kong) offers an extreme example in which a hedge fund was reported to have borrowed shares on the record date, voted them against a parent's buyout of outside shareholders, thereby killing the buyout, then sold the shares short, and profited from the price drop when the voting outcome became known.

10.2.3 Greater Voting than Economic Ownership: Empty Voting

1. *Techniques used by outside shareholders.* Hedge funds and other outside shareholders usually accomplish empty voting by relying on coupled assets (such as equity derivatives or stock loan agreements) or related non-host assets. We discuss the principal strategies in our prior work and do not repeat that discussion here.

One core strategy for empty voting is to hold shares but hedge the economic return on the shares. Various hedges are available, including a short equity swap position, buying put options (or selling call options), or a short position on a single stock future. Examples are numerous; see the Appendix.

An alternate empty voting strategy is known as record date capture. This strategy involves borrowing shares in the stock loan market just before the record date and returning the shares immediately afterwards. Under standard borrowing arrangements, the borrower has no economic exposure to the company. Taxes aside, the borrower holds votes without economic ownership, while the lender has economic ownership without votes. Examples include *British Land–Laxey Partners* and *Barclays–ABN-AMRO-Fortis*.[15]

2. *Market impact and scale.* These empty voting strategies do not directly require market trading of shares. Thus, they can often be carried out rapidly and on a large scale, with little impact on share price. Consider the share borrowing strategy. The empty voter borrows shares, and votes simply move from the share lender to the empty voter. No shares are bought or sold. This strategy will affect trading prices for shares only if the borrowing is on a scale which affects the access of short sellers or hedgers to borrowable shares. Consider next the strategy (buy shares, hedge with equity swaps). An empty voter can buy shares from a dealer and simultaneously take the short side of an equity swap with the same dealer. The dealer can hedge by borrowing the shares (with no share trading) at the same time it creates the swap. The empty voter and the dealer are both hedged, and votes have again moved from the share lender to the empty voter, without market purchase or sale of shares. The transaction between client and dealer is off-market.

[15] In *British Land–Laxey Partners*, hedge fund Laxey was an economic owner of 1% of British Land's shares, but borrowed an additional 8% to support a proposal to break up British Land. We discuss *Henderson Land* and *Barclays–ABN-AMRO-Fortis* in Section 10.2.2.

The borrowing directly affects the share lending market, but for most companies, at most times, this market includes a large pool of borrowable shares, available at a quite modest price, on the order of 15–20 basis points per year (Cohen, Diether, and Malloy 2007), or less than 0.1 basis points (0.001%) per day.

The principal non-regulatory constraint on the scale of empty voting will often be the number of shares that can be readily borrowed. Hard numbers are not available, but a conservative estimate from a knowledgeable source in late 2007 is that for most large US public companies, in normal (non-takeover) circumstances, 20% or more of the outstanding shares can be readily borrowed.[16] A 2007 survey indicates that $3.6 trillion of US equities (17% of the combined NYSE and NASDAQ market capitalization) were available for borrowing from just sixteen lending banks (Risk Management Association 2007). Additional shares are available from broker-dealers, institutional investors who run their own lending programmes, and other sources. In the United Kingdom, data from the Governance for Owners consultancy from 2006 suggests that as much as 50% of the shares of firms in the FTSE 100 index are generally borrowable (Butler 2006). The UK FSA estimates that, in 2007, equity swaps represented 35% of UK market capitalization (*Euromoney* 2008).

3. *Soft parking of votes by the corporation itself.* Empty voting is not limited to shareholders. Firms themselves can use decoupling techniques to provide insiders or other friendly third parties with votes on the firm's own shares, yet little or no economic exposure. In doing so, firms are effectively voting their own shares. This vote parking is often 'soft' and based on informal expectations about how the shares will be voted. A harder right to direct how shares are voted could be problematic under corporate law rules which bar a company from holding and voting its own shares, directly or through a subsidiary. Often the goal is to ward off changes in control. The basic strategy is for company insiders to arrange for voting ownership to be held by someone else, who has incentives to vote pro-management. Shares can be parked with a variety of people, in a variety of ways.

One strategy involves the corporation acquiring economic ownership of its shares through an equity swap or other equity derivative contract, say with a derivatives dealer. In substance, the corporation has repurchased its own shares; they are no longer economically owned by anyone. However, the shares remain outstanding and votable. But by whom?

Usually the dealer. The dealer will be short on the swap and will usually hedge its economic risk, often by holding 'matched shares', so that gain (loss) on the matched shares offsets loss (gain) on the equity swap. Assuming that the dealer holds matched shares and votes as company insiders want, the company (or the insiders, it does not matter which) can be seen as an empty voter. The scale of the transaction could well be large; the principal limit is the corporation's financial ability to repurchase its own shares. The dealer has incentives to hedge with matched shares (thus obtaining votes) and vote as its client would want, to stay on good terms with the client, and to preserve a reputation for treating clients well. The dealer will presumably understand that the company is acquiring swaps rather than shares for the purpose of leaving votes in friendly hands. Examples include *Portugal Telecom–Sonaecom*

[16] This estimate was provided to us by Irving Klubeck, President of the Securities Lending Division of the Securities Industry and Financial Market Association, the leading trade association for US broker-dealers, and a managing director of Pershing LLC.

and *Portugal Telecom–PT Multimedia*; we are also aware of one major derivatives dealer using PowerPoint outlines to market soft parking strategies to European corporations.[17]

Depending on context and amount, these strategies will often fall outside disclosure rules, and hence can be fully or partly hidden from investors. For example, the firm's use of equity swaps to effectively repurchase its own shares might well escape disclosure, where a direct purchase would be disclosable. The firm's informal control of now-empty votes will also be hidden. If a company lends treasury shares, the company's ownership of its own shares is disclosed, but not the loan and hence not the existence of voting rights.

Because these strategies are hidden, we don't know how common they are. But they offer one possible explanation for the finding by Listokin (2008) that US managers almost invariably win close votes. If managers anticipate a close vote, they may arrange for votes to be held by friendly hands, and then call in enough votes to win once they see how the voting is going.

Other variations on the soft parking theme are also possible. These include: (i) a forward transaction with a friendly shareholder, in which the company agrees to repurchase shares at a predetermined price, *after* a crucial vote; (ii) a nominal 'sale' of 'treasury shares'—shares which a company has repurchased—to a friendly dealer, with the company taking back an equity swap or otherwise protecting the dealer against loss; and (iii) a simple loan of treasury shares to a friendly holder. *UBS–Ebner* (Switzerland) and *MOL–OMV* (Hungary) offer examples of forward share purchase contracts and the loan of treasury shares, respectively.[18]

Netherlands firms have long used a variety of soft parking strategies, including: (i) issuing shares to a company-controlled foundation, which then sells depositary receipts to the public with limited voting rights;[19] and (ii) giving a call option to a company foundation, which the foundation can exercise to acquire high-voting shares if a threat to control arises (*Stork* is a recent example).[20]

4. *Employee stock ownership plans; restricted stock plans.* A company can also arrange for friendly, partly or mostly empty votes, through employee stock ownership plans (ESOPs) and like plans, and by granting restricted shares to its executives. Employees can be expected to support management against a hostile takeover, because they fear a threat to their jobs, correctly or not (Gordon and Pound 1990). Higher employee ownership indeed predicts lower probability of takeover (Rauh 2006).

[17] In *Portugal Telecom–Sonaecom*, Portugal Telecom attempted to park votes with Barclay's, as part of its defence against Sonaecom's takeover bid. *In Portugal Telecom–PT Multimedia*, Portugal Telecom used equity swaps with Barclay's to hold 10% of the shares in its subsidiary, PT Multimedia.

[18] In *UBS–Ebner*, UBS fought off a proxy fight by Martin Ebner in part by using forward contracts to park votes with two major shareholders (Loderer and Zgraggen 1999). In *MOL–OMV*, Hungarian firm MOL defended against a bid by OMV by repurchasing almost half its shares and then lending most of the repurchased shares to two Hungarian banks, which were expected to vote as MOL management wished.

[19] The holders of depository receipts can instruct the foundation on how to vote on ordinary matters, but not with regard to a takeover bid. The foundation can vote all shares in a takeover situation, and can otherwise vote shares for which it receives no instructions. See van der Horst and van Uchelen-Schipper (2007).

[20] In *Stork*, two hedge funds acquired 31% of Stork's shares. In response, the Stork Foundation exercised an option (granted back in 1990) to acquire preference shares with a high ratio of votes to economic rights; which represented almost half of Stork's total voting rights. The Dutch courts disallowed the issuance.

Employee ownership relates to empty voting in two principal ways. One way to structure an ESOP is to contribute a block of stock to an ESOP, with the shares to vest over an extended period. All shares carry voting rights, even though employees economically own only the vested shares. The trustees for the ESOP can either decides how to vote the unvested shares, or the ESOP documents can provide that unvested shares will be voted proportionately to the votes cast by employees on vested shares. In the former case, the trustees are empty voters, in the latter case, the employees are partially empty voters, because they have more voting power than economic ownership. Examples involving use of ESOPs as a takeover defence include *NCR-AT&T* (where NCR created an ESOP which conveyed 228 votes for each vested share); *Quanta Services-Aquila; LVMH-Gucci; Dunkin' Donuts-Kingsbridge Capital; Polaroid-Shamrock Holdings*; and *Macmillan-Maxwell Communications*.

A second possibility for empty voting arises from grants of restricted shares, often principally to managers and key employees, which vest over several years. Both vested and unvested shares usually carry voting rights; this will often make the holder a partially empty voter.

10.2.4 Economic-only Ownership

Empty voting positions involve greater voting than economic ownership. The opposite pattern of economic-only ownership—greater economic rights than formal voting rights—is also common. Economic-only ownership can often be used to achieve hidden ownership, morphable ownership, or both.

1. *Hidden and morphable ownership.* Some hedge funds and other investors have sought to avoid ownership disclosure rules that turn on voting rights or on full ownership of shares by taking the long side of an equity swap contract, with a derivatives dealer. The dealer will typically hedge its exposure, often by holding matched shares. Without more, the dealer is now an empty voter—it has voting rights but no economic interest. The investor has economic-only ownership, but no formal voting rights.

However, if the investor later wants to vote, it might well be able to return to the dealer, unwind the swap, and simultaneously purchase an equivalent number of shares either from the dealer or in the market, and thus obtain voting rights to accompany economic ownership. Practices vary, but the dealer may be willing to sell the matched shares directly to its client to accommodate its client's request. *Perry-Rubicon* offers an example.[21] Alternatively, an investor may ask its dealer to vote as it would have voted, and the dealer may oblige. Practices again vary, but *London Stock Exchange, Marks and Spencer*, and *Canary Wharf* offer UK examples.[22] Examples of hidden ownership are numerous; see the Appendix.

[21] In *Perry-Rubicon*, hedge fund Perry held a large, disclosed stake in Rubicon, sold it to derivatives dealers and acquired swaps instead to avoid disclosure, then terminated the swaps and reacquired the shares in order to vote at a shareholder meeting.

[22] In *Marks and Spencer* and *Canary Wharf*, hedge funds held equity swaps and favoured a takeover bid; their dealers held matched shares and supported the bid. In *London Stock Exchange*, several hedge funds, together holding 23% economic ownership, opposed NASDAQ's bid; their opposition was seen as crucial to LSE's defence; that they held swaps rather than shares was treated as a minor matter.

2. *Avoiding other rules.* Disclosure rules are only one of a number of rules which can often be avoided by holding economic-only ownership. We have discussed other possibilities in Section 10.2.2.

3. *Hidden takeover bids.* Decoupling, plus the often hidden nature of economic-only ownership, sometimes makes it possible for a takeover bidder to acquire a large, sometimes effectively controlling stake in a target, without public disclosure. The takeover battle may be essentially over before it has begun. Several recent European takeovers involve sudden emergence of a bidder with close to effective control of the target, including *Scor–Converium* (first disclosure at 33% ownership), *Vekselberg–Sulzer* (first disclosure at 32%), *Victory–Laxey-Saurer* (first Victory disclosure at 45%), and *Victory–Unaxis* (first disclosure at 30%). Several of these examples involved Swiss targets; Swiss regulators have since responded by requiring disclosure of most forms of economic-only ownership.

In the US, initial public disclosures have not yet been at Swiss levels. However, the Jana Partners and Castlerigg hedge funds recently made their first disclosure of a stake in CNET at 21% ownership, and TCI and 3G Capital Partners held a similar stake when they disclosed their positions in CSX. As discussed in Section 10.2.2.3, the *CSX* decision will affect US practices.

A variation on this theme involves a hedge fund, which does not want full ownership itself, buying a large stake, perhaps 20–30%, and announcing this. Potential acquirers will understand that the stake is for sale at the right price to a takeover bidder. One example is *Victory-Laxey-Saurer*, where Laxey Partners initially acquired 23% of Saurer. Victory Industrial acquired over 20% of Saurer separately, then bought Laxey's stake and announced that it held 45% of Saurer. Others include *Laxey-Implenia* (Laxey holds 23%), *Converium–Scor* (Martin Ebner accumulated 20% of Converium, then sold his position to Scor), and *Stork* (the Centaurus and Paulson hedge funds hold 31%).

10.2.5 Unbundling Other Aspects of Ownership

While the precise rights depend on each country's rules, full ownership of shares commonly conveys a package of rights, including the following:

- fiduciary duties owed by directors and officers to shareholders under corporate law, and the right to sue to enforce these fiduciary duties;
- disclosure obligations of companies, directors, officers, underwriters, and accountants under securities law, and the right to sue to enforce these obligations;
- the right to inspect the company's books and records;
- the right to nominate directors and to present resolutions at a shareholder meeting, and perhaps to include nominations and resolutions in the company's circular for its annual shareholder meeting; and
- several rights that can be seen as components of economic ownership:
    - appraisal rights;
    - rights to receive dividends;
    - pre-emptive rights; and
    - rights to be paid in liquidation (after everyone else).

For each of these rights, one must ask: how can this right be decoupled from others? What impact does decoupling of some rights, such as economic ownership from voting ownership, have on other rights? Which rights can be exercised by voting-only owners (independent of economic interest), and which by economic-only owners (independent of voting rights)? The answers are complex, and often unknown. We sketch here some elements of the complex landscape, focusing on US rules.

Fiduciary duties under corporate law and related rights to bring suit. Can holders of economic-only rights, such as holders of equity swaps, sue to enforce the fiduciary duties owed by officers and directors to the corporation and its shareholders, much as shareholders can? We don't know the answer. Our tentative view is that economic ownership should provide standing to bring a derivative suit, at least when the suit relates to the firm's economic value. The answer for direct suits is less clear, because allowing economic-only owners to sue could expand the ranks of potential plaintiffs, and thus damages.

How about empty voters, who hold shares but have hedged their economic ownership. 'Empty suing' is permitted, because courts normally don't ask whether apparent ownership is hedged. The *Deephaven* case offers an example.[23] But perhaps this should change—a better approach might be for plaintiffs to be required to routinely disclose net economic ownership, and for a positive stake in the firm to be necessary for the plaintiff to have standing.

Disclosure obligations and related rights to bring suit. Companies' disclosure obligations typically flow to all holders of the company's securities. Does this include persons who hold economic-only rights, say through equity swaps? The answer in the United States is—it depends. Holders of 'security-based swap agreements' are protected against company misrepresentations and omissions by general anti-fraud rules, but are not protected by the specific, pro-plaintiff liability rules available to purchasers in public offerings of securities. Thus, an economic-only owner, through equity swaps, can be a plaintiff, and potentially a lead plaintiff, in a securities class action based on general anti-fraud rules, but not in an action based on public offering rules. Conversely, can empty voters bring securities lawsuits? Similar to fiduciary duty suits, courts currently don't ask whether apparent ownership is hedged, but perhaps they should.

The right answers are not obvious. An investor who holds equity swaps is harmed by misdisclosure, just as if the investor held shares directly. Yet if the swaps were acquired from a dealer who hedged with matched shares, the dealer has suffered no economic loss, but can still sue. Similarly, if shares are borrowed both the borrower and lender are likely to be proper plaintiffs. In effect, the same loss can be sued for twice.

Inspection rights. Does an empty voter have rights to inspect the company's books ('empty inspecting')? Apparently yes, per *Deephaven.*

Director nominations and shareholder resolutions. Rights at shareholders meetings follow voting rights. Just as economic-only owners can't directly vote, they can't attend a shareholder meeting, nominate directors, or present shareholder resolutions, either at the meeting or through a process for including nominations or resolutions in the company circular

[23] In *Deephaven*, the plaintiff (Deephaven) wanted to participate in an offering which involved pre-emptive rights, without economic ownership. It borrowed shares, then 'sold' them from its account at one broker to its own account at a second broker. It used the long position at the second broker to exercise pre-emptive rights and to demand to inspect the company's books. The Delaware court allowed both manoeuvres.

for the annual shareholder meeting. Conversely, an empty voter can probably do all of these things, though it might have to disclose its hedging. Some US firms have begun to amend their bylaws to explicitly require this disclosure (Andrejcsak 2008).

Appraisal rights. 'Appraisal' rights are the rights of shareholders who are unhappy with elected major corporate actions, such as a merger or charter amendment, to vote against (or at least not for) the action, object to its completion, and have their shares bought at a court-determined fair value. In the United States, the *Transkaryotic* case apparently allows what we can call 'empty appraisal'.[24]

10.2.6 The Worldwide Scope of Equity Decoupling

How much decoupling activity is there? Without effective disclosure, we don't know. We can, however, collect examples—the visible tip of the potential iceberg. This list, included in the Appendix, currently includes over ninety examples of equity and hybrid decoupling from over twenty countries. Moreover, after a 2005 change in UK rules required disclosure of economic ownership through cash-settled derivatives during takeover bids, the number of ownership disclosures increased by about 20% during the first eighteen months after these rules came into force (Takeover Panel 2007). Our own preliminary search of these 'but-for' disclosures for May 2007 produced thirteen instances for that single month.

10.3 Debt Decoupling

Many elements of the framework for analysing equity decoupling can be extended to debt contracts. Still, in important ways, debt decoupling is more complex than equity decoupling. Companies often have only one class of common shares, each with identical rights. In contrast, multiple classes of debt are common, both with different seniority and with similar seniority but different rights. Holders of different classes often have differing incentives.

Debt decoupling markets are often larger, relative to the size of the underlying market, than their equity counterparts. For example, equity swap markets are a fraction of the size of the underlying equity markets, while credit default swap markets are a multiple of the underlying debt markets. Debt decoupling is also often more complex than equity decoupling. For example, there are large markets for collateralized debt obligations (CDOs) and other securitization vehicles, with no close equity-side parallels.

As we have seen, shareholders have disclosure and other obligations under a variety of laws. Creditors' obligations are more limited. Outside bankruptcy, there is almost no disclosure of who owns a company's debt, or derivatives on that debt. Within bankruptcy,

[24] In *Transkaryotic*, an investor bought shares in the market after the record date for a merger vote and then sought appraisal, on the grounds that someone else, from whom it might have bought the shares, had not voted for the merger. If courts do not ask about hedging, a future appraisal demand could be brought by someone who neither had voting ownership on the record date, nor economic ownership when the appraisal demand was brought.

direct claims against the company must be disclosed, but derivatives generally need not be. Thus, on the equity side, we offered many examples of the use of decoupling strategies at particular firms. On the debt side, we can offer far fewer firm-level examples. We rely instead—less satisfactorily—on possibilities, rumours, practitioner articles (which often don't name particular instances), and conversations with bankruptcy lawyers, bankruptcy judges, and other knowledgeable market participants. For representative practitioner discussions, see Berman (2007), Fisher and Buck (2006/7), and Flaschen and Mayr (2007).

The related literature which discusses the governance and systemic risk implications of debt decoupling is limited. Our work builds on initial discussions in Hu (2007), Hu and Westbrook (2007), and Hu and Black (2008). There are also brief discussions in Partnoy and Skeel (2007) and Baird and Rasmussen (Chapter 11, this volume).

We discuss firm-level decoupling in Sections 10.3.1–4; and decoupling through securitization in Sections 10.3.5–7. We turn to hybrid debt-equity decoupling in Section 10.4. Section 10.5 discusses the implications of debt decoupling for systemic financial risk.

10.3.1 Forms of Firm-level Debt Decoupling

Just as the conventional understanding of share ownership assumes a standard, bundled set of rights and obligations, so too a traditional conception of debt ownership includes a bundled set of rights under the debt contract, bankruptcy law, and other laws. Contractual rights commonly include rights to principal and interest payments, financial and other covenants, default rights, and voting rights on covenant or default waivers. Bankruptcy law gives creditors who are not paid in a timely fashion the right to force the company into bankruptcy, and the right to participate in bankruptcy proceedings, including voting on a plan of liquidation or reorganization, and perhaps the right to present such a plan to the court. Fraudulent conveyance law and some aspects of corporate law limit the ability of insiders to siphon money or other assets from a failing firm. For insolvent firms, directors' fiduciary duties to shareholders may switch and become instead duties to creditors.

The rights held by shareholders are more uniform across firms than the rights held by creditors. Many shareholder rights stem largely from corporate and other laws, customization in firm charters is often limited. Many creditor rights, in contrast, are contractual, and flow from the varying contracts negotiated by a particular firm with its creditors. Standardization and use of model forms coexist with tailoring of the terms of particular contracts.

Just as shareholders can hedge their economic exposure by holding equity derivatives and other coupled assets, creditors can often hedge through credit derivatives and other coupled assets. By analogy to empty voting, we will call a creditor who retains formal contractual control rights and legal rights, yet has partly or fully hedged its economic risk, an 'empty creditor'. Investors can hold economic-only debt claims, just as they can hold economic-only equity claims. Debt ownership, like equity ownership, can often be hidden; indeed non-disclosure is the norm. The extent to which economic-only debt is likely to be morphable, if the investor wants covenant rights or voting rights in bankruptcy, is unknown, but the possibility surely exists.

We discussed in Section 10.2.3 firms' ability to soft park their shares, in order to retain voting rights. This too has a parallel on the debt side. Most bond indentures let a company buy and then vote its own bonds. Companies, when in financial distress, regularly use this ability in coercive exchange offers. A typical strategy is to say to bondholders: 'Exchange Bond A for lesser valued Bond B, because if you don't and others do, we will vote to waive all covenants, leaving you worse off than if you had exchanged.' Even if a company can't directly vote its own bonds, soft or hard parking offer ways for a firm to influence a vote on a covenant waiver or other restructuring proposal.

One simple way for a creditor to hedge involves company-specific credit derivatives. One common derivative is a credit default swap. Today, most credit default swaps are settled through a cash payment by the credit protection seller to the protection buyer, and we will assume this here. In a simple credit default swap, if a 'credit event' (such as the bankruptcy of the company, a payment default, or an out-of-court restructuring) occurs during the term of the swap, the protection seller will compensate the protection buyer, based on the difference between the face value of the debt instrument and its estimated market value shortly after the credit event. The payment can be based on post-event bids for the debt instrument from market makers, or on an auction.[25] During the swap term, the protection buyer typically pays the seller a fixed periodic amount.

A creditor can thus hedge the default risk on debt by buying protection through a credit default swap, much as a shareholder can hedge equity risk by holding a short equity swap position. A creditor can also hedge through other credit derivatives, including transfers of the entire returns associated with a debt obligation ('total return swaps' or 'loan swaps'), options to buy credit default or total return swaps, and 'credit spread' options or swaps in which payoffs are linked to the spread between the yield on a particular bond and a reference yield.

Creditors can also hedge by being long one class of a company's debt, and short another. And they can hedge through strategies involving the company's common or preferred shares. We focus in this part on debt-only decoupling. We initially assume a single class of debt, and address multiple debt classes below. We address mixed debt–equity strategies in Section 10.4.

Dealers in debt and debt derivatives are likely to be an important class of empty creditors. Like their counterparts on the equity side, they will typically try to stay very close to fully hedged or 'net flat'—offsetting a long (short) debt position by, for example, buying (selling) credit protection.

Another general debt decoupling strategy arises from repackaging of debt. A 'loan participation' offers a simple example: a lead bank lends money to a corporation, but then transfers some, most, or all of its economic return to other lenders. Often, the lead bank agrees to exercise its rights under the loan agreement to declare or waive defaults, amend covenants, and so on, as instructed by the buyers of the loan participations, in proportion to dollar amount owned. But some loan participation contracts leave these control rights with the

[25] Most credit default swaps refer to standard terms developed by the International Swaps and Derivatives Association (ISDA) (2003). In a typical 'physically settled' swap, the protection seller pays off the buyer at par, and receives in return the underlying debt instrument. However, both parties often agree instead to cash settlement based on the value of the underlying debt instrument, determined through an auction held shortly after the credit event. There are both online auction sites and, for major bankruptcies, ISDA-organized auctions. Scholtes (2006) describes one such auction. In a standard 'cash-settled' swap, the protection seller pays the buyer for its estimated loss, based on bids from dealers.

lead bank.[26] If so, the lead bank will have greater formal control rights than economic exposure, and will be a partly or fully empty creditor. To be sure, in this case, the lead bank may still consult informally with the loan participation holders.

10.3.2 Implications for Debt Governance

In this section, we discuss some implications of corporate debt decoupling through 'direct derivatives', which relate to the value of a single company's debt. In Section 10.3.4, we consider hedging using different classes of a company's debt.

Decoupling can affect both how creditors exercise contractual control rights outside bankruptcy and how they exercise their legal rights within bankruptcy. We refer to creditors' overall relationship with the debtor, including the exercise or restructuring of contractual and legal rights, as 'debt governance'. We use credit default swaps as our main example. A creditor who has partly or fully hedged through a credit default swap nevertheless retains full contractual rights under the loan agreement or bond indenture, and full voting rights in bankruptcy. In contrast, the protection seller bears default risk, but normally has no control rights. Control rights are thus decoupled from economic rights.

Just as equity investors can have negative economic ownership (the value of their overall position rises if the firm's share price falls), so too creditors can have control and legal rights, yet negative exposure to a firm's credit risk (the value of their overall position rises if credit risk rises or a credit event occurs). We will again call this situation 'negative economic ownership'. An investor might, for example, hold $200 million of a company's bonds, but have bought credit protection on $500 million notional amount of bonds.

Creditors with negative economic ownership, like their equity counterparts, may have incentives to act to reduce the value of all debt claims, or the value of the specific debt class they formally hold. Such a creditor might prefer that the company fail, and hence oppose an out-of-court restructuring. Even a creditor with zero, rather than negative, economic ownership may want to push a company into bankruptcy, because the bankruptcy filing will trigger a contractual payoff on its credit default swap position.

Additional complexities may arise if an empty creditor has made a secured loan, and has additional rights relating to the collateral. Just as an empty unsecured creditor is less concerned with the firm's success, an empty secured creditor will be less concerned with the value of the collateral, and may make different decisions than other secured creditors.

No one knows how often creditors hold partly empty positions, fully empty positions (zero economic ownership), or negative economic ownership. But transfer of risk is clearly common. The credit default swap market has exploded over the last decade. One estimate is that the notional amount of credit default swaps on corporate debt exceeds the amount of underlying debt by a factor of ten, although this estimate may include both index and single-name swaps (Tett and Davies 2007). Major banks' use of credit derivatives and other forms of risk transfer has soared as well. Duffie (2007) reports that the net transfer of credit

[26] For a loan participation example involving decoupling of economic interest from control rights, see *AutoStyle Plastics, Inc. v. MascoTech, Inc. (In re AutoStyle Plastics, Inc.)*, 269 F.3d 726, 736–7 (6th Cir. 2001).

risk away from US banks in 2006, through credit default swaps and securitization, was about $3.2 trillion. The overall level of credit risk transfers grew at an 80% compound annual rate during 2001–06. By 2006, the risk transfer positions held by the major banks which relied on these transfers were more than double their loan assets. At the same time credit risk transfer is concentrated in a limited number of major banks: of the 5,700 banks which report to the Federal Reserve Board, only 40 engaged in credit derivative or securitization trading.

There are also several sources of qualitative evidence. We are informally advised that some credit default swap contracts now include customized terms which require the protection buyer, if it is also a creditor, to act in the interests of other creditors. This suggests concern that the protection buyer might not otherwise do so. But how this obligation can be enforced without disclosure is anyone's guess. We have also heard from bankruptcy judges that they sometimes see odd behaviour in their courtrooms, which empty crediting might explain. For example, one judge described a case in which a junior creditor complained that the firm's value was too *high*, even though a lower value would hurt the class of debt the creditor ostensibly held. Another is the recent discussion by the UK FSA of the greater potential complexity of workouts when creditors are often hedged, and of the potential for creditors to have no economic exposure or to be net short (FSA 2008: 52–3).

Partial hedging is rumoured to be common for 'distressed debt' investing—buying the debt of financially troubled or already bankrupt companies. Specialized 'distressed debt' or 'vulture' investors often accumulate large stakes in a debt class that are likely to be pivotal in a restructuring. For example, under US bankruptcy law, a one-third position in a pivotal debt class may let the holder block adoption of a reorganization plan favoured by other creditors, which ordinarily requires a two-thirds vote of creditors. The judge can approve a plan which does not receive this level of support, but the blocking position still conveys negotiating leverage. Unless hedged, these large positions convey large exposure to default risk. Distressed debt investors can often, however, hedge some of this risk, thus acquiring a large voting block without corresponding economic exposure. One sign of underlying activity is the recent skirmishing in several US bankruptcy proceedings over whether a member of ad hoc creditor committees must disclose coupled assets (Berman 2007; Flaschen and Mayr 2007).

In the Tower Automotive bankruptcy in 2005, some hedge funds were rumoured to have favoured a filing to benefit their short positions in Tower debt. One of them, Silver Point, told the *Wall Street Journal* that its 'policy' when net short was not to use a loan position to cause a company to file for bankruptcy (Sender 2005).

A final indirect sign of smoke is the interest in our work on debt decoupling among bankruptcy practitioners, bankruptcy judges, and derivatives dealers (for example, *Economist* 2008; Guerrera, White, and van Duyn 2008; Baird 2008). The analytic framework and 'empty crediting' terminology developed above offers them a language with which to describe activity that they see, or sometimes only suspect, on the ground.

Just as equity decoupling can undermine standard assumptions that underlie the equity side of corporate governance, so too for debt governance. Both loan contracts and bankruptcy laws are premised on the assumption that creditors are averse to downside risk, but otherwise have an economic interest in the company's success and will behave accordingly. Voting on loan contract waivers and amendments, and voting on restructuring plans in bankruptcy, is usually in proportion to the principal amount of debt held. This pattern rests on the same logic as a one share-one vote regime on the equity side—control rights should be held by those with an incentive to increase the value of the firm, or at least the value of a particular class of debt claims in proportion to that incentive. Empty crediting weakens these assumptions. Its hidden nature only makes the problem worse. Hidden empty crediting implicates other core aspects of the bankruptcy process, including which creditors should serve on creditor committees and the weight a court should give to the views of particular creditors.

10.3.3 Decoupling through Positions in Multiple Classes of Debt

We have thus far considered a single class of debt and a simple hedge with credit default swaps. But the world is more complex than this. Large public firms often have multiple classes of debt. These multiple classes offer additional possibilities for negative economic ownership. For example, a creditor's long position in class A may be offset, partly or fully, by his short interest in class B or C. Each of these positions can themselves be partly hedged, fully hedged, or over-hedged.

A creditor can be expected to vote its position in classes where it holds formal voting rights in support of its overall position. Moreover, if the vote of one class is expected to be pivotal in a reorganization, creditors holding other classes may scramble to acquire positions in the pivotal class (often hedged), to support their positions in other classes.

The divergent preferences of different classes on the value assigned to the firm already complicate restructuring negotiations, both in and out of bankruptcy. Holdings of stakes in different classes, potentially some long and some short, add further complexity. So does non-disclosure of hedges, which means that each creditor can't be sure of the incentives of other creditors.

The concept of economic ownership becomes more complex for firms with multiple classes of debt. Different classes of debt will have different 'deltas'—the fractional change in the value of a class of debt, for a $1 change in firm value. As a firm approaches bankruptcy, junior debt will often have a higher delta than senior debt. Yet if the firm's value continues to drop, to a level where the payoff to junior creditors is likely to be small, the junior debt delta will fall and the senior debt delta will increase. Thus, if an investor has interests in several classes of debt, the delta for its overall position will change with firm value. The investor's economic ownership could be positive over one value range, near zero over another, and negative over a third.

10.3.4 Firm-level Debt Decoupling: Legal and Contractual Implications

The potential for large-scale direct decoupling creates pressure for reform in both law and contracting practice. We sketch some of these implications here.

1. *Implications for bankruptcy proceedings.* Voting by empty creditors in bankruptcy can lead to less efficient decisions on liquidation versus continuation, or on post-reorganization capital structures. An initial response, similar to our proposal for enhanced disclosure of equity decoupling, would be disclosure in bankruptcy proceedings of significant disparities between nominal debt holdings and actual economic exposure. Put differently, above some *de minimis* threshold, creditors should disclose their hedges, and thus their 'hidden *non*-interest': their *lack* of economic exposure to the company.

This disclosure would ensure that the court, other creditors, and shareholders know where a creditor's economic interest lies. Even if an apparent creditor with negative net economic interest in a class of debt retained voting rights, its views would be discounted. Moreover, courts would likely be readier to override a creditor vote which was tainted by some creditors voting with little, no, or negative economic ownership. The details of such a disclosure regime, including exceptions for small positions or for general hedges tied to an asset class, are beyond the scope of this chapter.

Looking beyond disclosure, on the equity side, we propose in Hu and Black (2008) to deny voting rights to shareholders with negative overall economic interest, and to allow companies to amend their charters to address empty voting by shareholders with zero or positive economic interest. Creditor voting is more complex, and is often by class (for example, secured, senior, unsecured, junior unsecured). Voting rights may need to be limited to creditors with positive economic interest in a positive economic ownership in the debtor as a whole or in a particular debt class. The degree of voting rights may need to be based on net economic ownership instead of gross ownership of a debt class. The complexities of multiple classes of debt, and correspondingly complex economic interests, make it hard to design sensible voting rules. But it might be feasible to adopt crude rules that block voting with negative overall economic interest—either in the debtor or in a particular class. At least in the US, bankruptcy courts may have the power under current law to disregard or limit votes by empty creditors, if disclosure rules made it possible for them to identify these creditors.[27]

The difficulty in devising sensible voting rules may provide support for proposals to have the valuation of bankrupt firms rely more heavily on auctioning the firm's business and less on negotiations among investors (Adler 2005 surveys auction proposals). Yet auctions also become more problematic, especially if 'credit bids' are allowed. A hedged creditor who makes a credit bid is truly paying with funny money. Even for cash auctions, the opportunity to hedge makes it easier for a creditor to acquire a blocking or controlling stake in a pivotal debt class, which might discourage competing bidders, or let it negotiate auction terms favourable to itself (Harner 2008).

Where auctions are not available, outcomes may need to rely less on creditor voting and more on judicial discretion. Outside bankruptcy, we would leave it to debt contracts to specify when overall economic ownership should be disclosed, or should affect contractual control rights.

[27] To oversimplify complex law, approval of a reorganization plan under US law generally requires a two-thirds vote of each class of creditors, but courts can disallow votes that are 'not in good faith' (US Bankruptcy Code § 1126). There are no cases on whether empty voting by creditors can be disallowed as not in good faith. However, one case, *In re Allegheny International* (1990), disallowed voting by a 'lend-to-own' creditor who had acquired a blocking position in the debtor's secured debt, and sought to use that position to acquire post-bankruptcy control.

2. *Implications under other laws.* Creditors often have rights under a variety of other laws, in addition to bankruptcy laws, including corporate law, commercial law, securities law, and fraudulent conveyance law. For financially distressed firms, directors' duty to run the corporation principally in the interests of shareholders may become a duty to creditors. Directors may face requirements under 'wrongful trading' (the UK term) or similar laws to file for bankruptcy with reasonable promptness (Cheffins and Black 2006; Hu and Westbrook 2007).

Much as for equity decoupling, courts will need to address which rights can be exercised by empty creditors, who hold formal rights but no or even negative economic interest, and which can be exercised by economic-only creditors. Consider, for example, suits under securities law based on false or misleading disclosure. In the US, as we discussed in Section 10.2.3.2 for equity swaps, suits under general anti-fraud rules can be brought both by formal owners of debt and equity, and by holders of 'security-based swap agreements'.[28] The definition of this term is complex, but appears to include credit default swaps for bonds (Glass 2001).

3. *Implications for private ordering.* Beyond disclosure and formal legal proceedings, it seems likely that debt contracts and workout procedures will need to adjust to the new world of hedged interests. Financial covenants, especially in bank loan agreements, are often written fairly strictly, to provide an early warning of financial trouble and an opportunity for renegotiation. This pattern becomes less viable if there is a risk that, *ex post*, some holders of waiver rights will not care about the borrower's success, while others will hope it fails and may seek to use the 'technical default' provided by a covenant violation as leverage towards that end. If lenders are often hedged, they will have weaker incentives to monitor borrowers and participate actively in workouts (Partnoy and Skeel 2007). If workouts become less viable, optimal debt–equity ratios may decline.

A further problem with both debt trading and debt decoupling involves the transmission of confidential information about the company's business. For instance, Delphi has recently charged that some of its creditors shorted its bonds after obtaining private information from Delphi about its travails (McCracken 2008). Ivashina and Sun (2007) report quantitative evidence that lenders sometimes use credit-related information to trade in the company's shares. We are also informally advised that buyers of troubled debt (or sellers of credit protection for this debt) often receive detailed company information from loan sellers (protection buyers), both inside and outside bankruptcy. The disclosure may breach loan confidentiality provisions. Dissemination could facilitate insider trading in the company's debt or debt derivatives. Whether broader dissemination of company information aids or harms its survival prospects is not clear.

Notwithstanding the complexities in measuring economic ownership, we can imagine the emergence of covenants which limit contractual control rights for creditors who hold zero or negative economic interests. To make the covenants enforceable, one would need either a disclosure regime or, perhaps more likely, a requirement that creditors attest to their economic interest when exercising control rights. We can also imagine broader use of covenants which limit resale or hedging by the original lenders. Gande and Puri (2005) provide evidence that ownership restrictions can reduce borrowing costs for firms in emerging markets, most likely by facilitating renegotiation.

[28] US Securities Exchange Act of 1934, § 10.

Some protection sellers may also seek to obtain control rights from protection buyers. For example, monoline insurer XL Capital Assurance is currently seeking to cancel credit default swaps with Merrill Lynch, claiming that Merrill agreed to pass through control rights on the underlying debt, but reneged (Campbell 2008).

10.3.5 Securitization

Decoupling need not be limited to instruments that relate to a single borrower. Often, bonds or other debt obligations are securitized into CDOs; CDOs backed primarily by loans are referred to as collateralized loan obligations (CLOs) (Barnett 2002). In this section, we treat the term CDO as including CLOs. We refer to CDOs based primarily on 'real' debt obligations as 'cash' CDOs, and CDOs where the underlying assets are primarily credit default swaps, other CDO obligations, or other debt derivatives as 'synthetic' CDOs. These terms loosely match current practice. We focus here primarily on cash CDOs.

In a typical cash CDO, a financial institution collects a large number of bonds, and creates a special purpose entity (CDO issuer) that holds the bonds, normally as a single risk pool. The CDO issuer then issues securities which repackage the returns from the pool into different tranches. Typically, some tranches are structured as debt claims which have low default risk and receive an AAA rating. Other tranches are higher risk and thus lower-rated debt. The most junior tranche, in the form of equity in the CDO issuer, can be separately sold (Duffie and Garleanu 2001; Barnett 2002, 2007). The financial institution which creates the CDO pool may or may not retain interests in one or more tranches.

A CDO transaction will typically involve several service providers, of whom the most critical are the collateral manager and the indenture trustee. The division of tasks between the two can vary, but, typically, the collateral manager selects the assets which comprise the risk pool. Thereafter, some pools are actively managed, others are not. The trustee's role is similar to indenture trustees for non-securitized bonds, and often includes distributing the cash flow from the assets tranche holders, and interacting with tranche holders and the issuers of the pool securities. For simplicity, we initially assume that the pool contains a fixed set of assets and that the principal ongoing actor is the trustee. The trustee will exercise the formal creditor rights for the debt claims included in the portfolio. The rights of buyers of CDO tranches to instruct the trustee on how to act vary, both across CDOs and across tranches within a single CDO.

10.3.6 The Exercise of Creditor Rights

We consider here how creditor rights for pool securities will be exercised. We initially assume that the CDO vehicle holds bonds rather than loans. The CDO structure impedes active participation in a workout or other restructuring, whether the indenture trustee retains decision rights, or passes them to tranche holders.

Suppose, first, that the trustee retains decision rights. CDO trustees may have limited incentives to be actively involved in workouts. First, the trustee is a largely empty creditor. It has an interest in preserving the future stream of trustee fees, and may have a long-term reputational interest in behaving sensibly, but will typically have no other financial interest in the outcome. Second, many CDOs vehicles diversify widely, and own only a small piece of any one company's debt. Thus, the CDO trustee has a limited stake in a single company. Rational apathy, in which the trustee never acquires the information needed for an informed decision, and free rides on the efforts of larger creditors, could sometimes be a privately rational strategy, as apathy is rational for many small shareholders. Third, debt workouts require close knowledge of the debtor's business, and sometimes the willingness to lend additional amounts. CDO trustees often won't have the necessary knowledge, nor the ability to commit additional capital. Fourth, CDO trustees, like bond indenture trustees generally, are typically paid limited fees for a limited role, which may not cover the people cost of complex workout negotiations (out-of-pocket costs are typically recoverable from pool assets). To be sure, as workouts become more common, market practice is adjusting—some CDOs provide for higher servicing fees for troubled pools, and some trustees now specialize in CDO workouts.

Passing decision rights through to holders of CDO tranches raises a different set of issues. First, the economic interests of tranches can differ widely. The same action might benefit senior tranches yet wipe out juniors. Investors in CDO equity and in junior tranches are the most likely to be affected by a default on one or a small number of the bonds held by the CDO vehicle. Senior tranches will be affected only by widespread defaults. Yet senior tranches often hold decision rights. They have little incentive to participate in workouts, and often prefer to bail out early, before defaults impair their holdings. They can do so by encouraging the collateral manager to sell defaulted bonds, or by voting to wind up the CDO.[29]

Second, a typical CDO first packages a large number of bonds, and then sells tranches to a (usually moderate) number of investors. If the CDO trustee suffers from incentives for rational apathy, the CDO investors have these incentives squared. Third, CDO holders may be fully or partly hedged, or have other interests in the company's equity or debt. Fourth, the CDO holders may be spread throughout the world, some will hold their interests through nominees, some will trade into or out of positions. In some cases, interests in a cash CDO may form part of the assets of a 'downstream' synthetic CDO pool (called a CDO-squared), with its own trustee and investors. As a result, the CDO trustee may not even know who the ultimate economic holders are.

CDO-based decoupling thus has the potential to undermine debt governance. In particular, it can impede renegotiation of the contractual relationship between borrowers and lenders. This is likely to be the case whether the trustee retains decision rights or seeks instructions from tranche holders.

Thus far, we have assumed a CDO invested in bonds. The analysis of CLOs is generally similar. One difference is that loan agreements sometimes contain confidentiality provisions that can limit disclosure to the CLO investors of non-public information about the company. This can reduce the quality of decisions made by the CLO investors, or make it infeasible to pass decision rights to CLO investors.

[29] BIS data on derivatives is available at <http://www.bis.org/statistics/derstats.htm>.

10.3.7 Synthetic CDOs

Synthetic CDOs further separate economic owners from control rights, and raise additional possibilities for negative economic ownership. Suppose, for example, that a holder of a '*direct* asset' (a bond, loan, or CDO interest) in effect, sells that asset into a synthetic CDO. Depending on the nature of the direct asset, the synthetic CDO could hold the direct asset, hold a derivative whose value is tied to the value of the direct asset, or include the direct asset in a 'reference portfolio' for the synthetic CDO. The holder of the direct asset is then an empty holder, while the economic holders of interests in the synthetic CDO have no control rights.

Moreover, an investment bank (say) which holds a direct asset can use this asset as a reference asset for multiple synthetic CDOs. The investment bank will retain control rights, yet will be net short on the direct asset—it gains if the direct asset falls in value. Yet the bank is selling interests in the synthetic CDO to investors who will hold a portfolio which effectively includes the direct asset. The bank's net short position in some of the reference assets is often not disclosed. How often does repeat use of the same direct asset arise in practice? We don't know, but are informally advised that instances do occur. In one instance, an investment bank used the equity in a cash CDO as a reference asset for multiple CDO-squared structures—leaving itself with an incentive to mismanage the cash CDO.

10.4 Hybrid Decoupling: Mixed Equity and Debt Decoupling; Non-host Assets

10.4.1 Hedging Equity with Debt and Vice Versa

We have thus far discussed equity decoupling and debt decoupling separately. But they can readily be combined, a pattern one might call 'hybrid decoupling'. For example, creditors can hedge exposure to a company's default risk by buying put options on the company's shares, or taking a short equity swap position related to the common shares. They can buy credit protection on preferred shares, as well as debt. It is sufficiently common for credit protection sellers to hedge with equity so that equity market liquidity is a pricing factor for credit default swaps (Das and Hanouna 2007). Similarly, equity holders can hedge with credit default swaps.

A limited literature explores the pricing implications of hedging across debt and equity markets (Carr and Wu 2006; Das and Hanouna 2007) and discusses hybrid equity–debt derivatives, including equity default swaps (e.g., Medova and Smith 2004), and equity-collateralized debt obligations (EDOs). We know of no prior literature on the governance implications of hybrid decoupling.

The potential for hybrid decoupling expands the possibilities in both markets for empty voting or crediting, including negative economic ownership. For example, an investor could be long a senior class of debt but short shares. It would then want to recover on its debt position but see little or no value left over for equity holders. Or, an investor could be long both shares and debt, and seek to use its debt position primarily to ensure a valuation in bankruptcy sufficient to generate a gain on it share position. And so on.

Darker possibilities exist as well. An investor could manipulate share prices in order to profit on a credit default swap position. Manipulation is hard enough to detect in a single market. Cross-market manipulation is harder still, especially since there is no organized reporting for credit default swaps, similar to that for shares.

Debt investors could also acquire shares (often hedged) and vote to support their debt positions. The recent Bear Stearns collapse, addressed through a Federal Reserve-arranged acquisition by JP Morgan Chase (JPM), provides an example of this type of hybrid decoupling. Bear Stearns creditors wanted the acquisition go through at any price, because JPM had promised to support Bear's debt. They bought Bear shares in order to vote for the merger, helping to push the share price well above the $2 merger price (which JPM later increased to $10). Many creditors probably acquired hedged share positions. Meanwhile, other investors who were short Bear Stearns debt (directly or via credit default swap positions) may have bought shares to oppose the merger, hoping to cause Bear Stearns to file for bankruptcy. Shareholder votes are usually a way to assess whether a transaction is good for shareholders. However, at Bear Stearns, pre-crisis shareholders were only one of several groups jockeying for share ownership and associated voting rights. *AXA-MONY* provides another example.[30]

10.4.2 Related Non-host Assets

Decoupling need not be limited to a single company's debt and shares. Either within or across the equity–debt line there is the potential for an investor's economic interest to be affected by its positions in other companies—which we have called 'related non-host assets'. For example, a creditor could hold long or short positions in the shares or debt of the company's competitors. One can see these 'cross-company' positions as involving type of hybrid decoupling.

Cross-company positions can give rise to complex incentives with regard to each company's value. A 'long' investor in Company X might gain if competitor Y were to fail. Or Company X might want to push Company Y into a distress sale of assets, for which X would be a likely buyer. A hedged position in Company Y might provide a means towards those ends.

10.4.3 Towards Disclosure of Hybrid Positions

Once again, disclosure emerges as an important, if partial response. For equity disclosure, disclosable coupled assets will need to include the company's debt, and derivatives on this debt. Even the broadest of the current disclosure rules—for example, disclosure of economic ownership by insiders of public companies under US securities law—do not reach

[30] In some CDOs, the safety of payments on the AAA tranche is enhanced through credit insurance. The insurer will typically require the CDO to convey decision rights to it. The insurers' incentives will be similar to those of senior tranche holders.

this far. They will need to. And vice versa—if debt disclosure is expanded, as we propose, that disclosure will need to include equity positions in the same company.

The line between debt and equity is obscure in any event, once one adopts an option theory perspective in which a debt claim is equivalent, control and certain other rights aside, to a risk-free loan plus sale to the shareholders of a put option on the company's business, which enables the shareholders to 'sell' the company to the debtholders in exchange for the face amount of the debt. For equity disclosure, the line was sustainable as long as debt claims were infrequently traded and trading involved large transaction costs relative to the value of the embedded put option. Hedging debt with equity was feasible because of low transaction costs for equities and equity derivatives. Hedging equity with debt was less so.

But with the emergence of low-transaction-cost markets for credit derivatives and hybrid derivatives, hedging can now readily go both ways. Where hedging goes, so should disclosure, if one accepts the basic position that equity disclosure should include economic-only ownership, and debt disclosure, at least in bankruptcy, should include hedges.

Concerns about cross-market manipulation and insider trading in low-disclosure markets provide further reason for enhanced disclosure of transactions in debt, debt derivatives, and hybrid instruments. Acharya and Johnson (2007) provide evidence of insider trading in debt derivatives; Ivashina and Sun (2007) provide evidence of insider trading by lenders in shares. To address these risks, we are likely to need expanded disclosure of trades and large positions in debt and debt derivatives, similar to equity disclosure rules.

Writ large, cross-market hedging, hybrid derivatives, and the like are making the line between equity and debt ever blurrier. A regime of disclosure on the equity side, yet non-disclosure on the debt side, makes increasingly little sense.

10.5 Debt Decoupling and Systemic Risk

The combination of the large size of debt decoupling markets, relative to underlying debt claims, greater complexity of decoupling instruments, and limited disclosure in debt markets creates the potential for debt decoupling to involve externalities and perhaps create systemic financial risk. We sketch here some of the systemic risk implications of widespread debt decoupling. Full treatment is beyond the scope of this chapter. Prior discussion of the systemic risk from decoupling and other forms of financial innovation is limited. Hu (1993) discusses systemic risks from financial innovation generally. Rajan (2006) discusses agency risks from new forms of financial intermediation. Duffie (2007) discusses how credit risk transfer can affect financial stability.

We focus here on risks, especially those to which decoupling contributes, rather than benefits. We do not claim to outline all of the ways in which debt decoupling contributes or detracts from financial stability (for broader treatments, see, for example, Stulz 2004; Duffie 2007). Among other important positives, debt decoupling can lead to more efficient risk bearing and hence lower borrowing rates. At least in normal times, it can enhance liquidity. We make no claim that debt decoupling is 'bad', either in general or in particular situations.

10.5.1 Sources of Systemic Risk

As we discussed in Section 10.3, debt decoupling can complicate and impede renegotiation. For any one loan, these potential difficulties in renegotiating are simply a cost to be weighed against the efficiency gains from allowing securitization and other forms of decoupling. One can imagine separating equilibria, in which some loans permit repackaging, but tend to be covenant-light, others have tighter covenants but restrict repackaging to facilitate renegotiation, and still others are accompanied by standby refinancing facilities, to be resorted to if renegotiation fails.

Still, there are externalities lurking. First, spread across a large number of loans, the inflexibility of the relationships among creditors and debtors creates systemic risk. No one borrower can affect that risk. Moreover, any one borrower, by seeking to restrict decoupling, may signal that it expects to need to renegotiate, and thus is a poor borrower. For both of these reasons, privately optimal contracts might produce more decoupling than is socially optimal.

Some of the debt governance and other problems which can flow from widespread debt decoupling can be seen in the housing finance crisis that began in 2007. In the past, a homeowner facing financial difficulty could try to negotiate directly with his lender for waivers and loan modifications. This is harder today. Many home mortgage loans are resold by the initial lender, securitized, or both. If a loan has been securitized, the effective holder of the lender's contractual rights—the servicing agent for the loan that deals with the homeowner—may have limited authority to make accommodations. Even if the servicing agent has the authority, it has limited economic ownership—it holds, in effect, the future stream of servicing rights. (On the other hand, the tranche holders, rather than the servicer, will take the financial hit from loan modifications.)

As with corporate debt, pass-through of decision rights to investors may not help. The economic interests may be spread among a wide range of investors, potentially around the world. Even if these investors had congruent interests—and often they do not because they hold different tranches—the transaction costs to find them would be prohibitive. Sometimes it can be unclear who holds formal rights, notably the right to foreclose. The result, as we saw in 2007, can be gridlock—defaults which could have been avoided if loans could have been renegotiated, and a macro-level collapse in housing prices, which then drives up default risk for all lenders.

Decoupling can foster other potential sources of systemic risk. Some reflect the ways in which financial innovations in general can contribute to systemic risk (Hu 1993). These include: modelling errors (including underweighting low probability, large loss ('tail') risks, such as the loss of liquidity in times of market stress); buyer and seller failures to understand complex financial products; and new types of agency costs, both within financial institutions and between these institutions and their customers. Duffie (2007) offers the judgement that '[e]ven specialists in [CDOs] are currently ill equipped to measure the risks and fair valuation of tranches that are sensitive to default correlation', and discusses how this might contribute to liquidity shocks.

Debt decoupling raises both these general risks, and some additional systemic ones. Decoupling will tend to reduce the incentives for the initial lender or CDO packager to assess and monitor risks correctly. Investors Keys et al. (2008) report evidence of this effect in subprime lending; securitized loans performed worse than apparently similar, non-securitized loans are no longer eating their own cooking, as it were. To be sure, buyers of CDO tranches have incentives to assess risk, but they may have imperfect information or understanding. A CDO packager may, in practice, have a profitable product, if credit rating agencies bestow faultily high ratings. Packagers face reputational and legal risks, but in the 2007 crisis, these were clearly insufficient. Even packagers who placed internal bets against the value of mortgage-loan-based CDOs, notably Goldman Sachs, continued to package and sell these instruments.

The longer the ownership chain—which for corporate debt now often stretches from borrower to initial lender to CDO packager to CDO buyer (sometimes with a synthetic CDO repackager thrown in)—the greater the potential for agency costs and valuation errors to creep in. The initial lender and CDO packager can potentially profit by making bad loans, if the buyers misjudge risk. If the CDO buyer is a hedge fund or mutual fund, there is a further layer between the fund's managers and its investors. Money managers compete against each other for client funds based on relative past performance; some managers also earn a carry on returns. Money managers may, whether because of cognitive biases or inappropriate incentives, ignore or underestimate tail risks. These misjudgements can be systemic, as they were for mortgage loans, and thus have systemic consequences.

10.5.2 Liquidity Risks

Liquidity risks are a source of special concern. Liquidity often falls during a financial downturn, sometimes abruptly. Decoupling can exacerbate the risk of liquidity shocks in several ways. First, the resting place of risk can become uncertain. Market participants often want to deal only with reliably solvent counterparties. When a new source of risk emerges, if the holders of that risk cannot be readily identified, illiquidity can spread, and compound the losses from the initial risk event.

Second, the resting place itself may impede the resolution of financial crises. The principal holders of risk are no longer a relative handful of big banks with intricate past and expected future relationships, large individual stakes in troubled loans, and an incentive to resolve the crisis both for their own benefit and from fear of their regulators' raised eyebrows. Instead, risk is often dispersed, may be held by hedge funds and other investors who are less sensitive to publicity and regulatory risk, and is often hidden. An often-cited benefit of decoupling is risk spreading, and thus reduced concentration of default risk in a limited number of international banks and other financial institutions. Fair enough, but a less visible cost is the reduced ability of these financial institutions to address a widespread crisis.

Third, the business models of major financial institutions have come to depend on liquidity in debt decoupling markets. If that liquidity dries up, so does lenders' ability to make new loans, to good borrowers and bad alike.

Fourth, renegotiation and refinancing are potential substitutes: borrowers who, due to decoupling, have reduced ability to renegotiate will have their debt rely more heavily on ability to refinance. Yet that ability may dry up when they need it most. The housing finance crisis of 2007 again illustrates the fragile nature of the ability to refinance. Many homeowners took escalating rate mortgages, assuming they could refinance when the rate got too high. When the downturn hit, the borrowers who could least afford the escalating rates had the least ability to refinance.

To be sure, markets may evolve to provide standby sources of liquidity to borrowers, to address the risk that the borrower will face difficulty in refinancing at some time in the future. For example, banks already provide standby loan facilities for commercial paper issuers, available when a borrower is squeezed out of the commercial paper market. But it is unclear whether liquidity sources, available to particular borrowers expand market-wide liquidity. When a credit crunch hits, these liquidity backups may give some borrowers greater access to credit, at the expense of others.

Increased demands on market liquidity *may* induce a greater supply of crisis-time liquidity—but then again, they may not. Many of the same factors that lead lenders to underweight tail risks could lead liquidity users to undervalue protection against a low-probability liquidity shock. The potential (and, in 2007–08, actual) intervention of central banks as liquidity suppliers of last resort could further depress market demand for this protection, much as the likelihood of government disaster relief in flood zones suppresses the purchase of private flood insurance. Thus, liquidity shocks could become more frequent or more severe, other things being equal.

10.5.3 Towards a Disclosure-based Response

The systemic risks posed by debt decoupling suggest that current levels of disclosure need to be revisited generally, not just in the context of firm bankruptcies. Better overall disclosure by financial institutions and major institutional investors regarding who is holding which risks won't fully address the potential for systemic effects, but it will help. At a minimum, improved disclosure will let market participants decide which counterparties to trust.

A specific disclosure proposal is beyond the scope of this chapter. But the goal should be to provide investors, other institutions, and regulators with sufficient information about holdings of classes of instruments and aggregate risk levels so they can assess the risks which a particular institution faces. This aggregate disclosure should be on a close to real-time basis. We expect that real-time disclosure of specific positions will not be needed. But delayed disclosure of specific positions might be appropriate, partly as a check on the accuracy of aggregate disclosure. Delayed position-specific disclosure would be analogous to current US equity-side disclosure by major institutions.

The Bank for International Settlements (BIS) is a key source for data on worldwide derivatives activities.[31] It and the Basel Committee on Banking Supervision, which has long played a central role in addressing worldwide financial systemic risk, could be appropriate vehicles for the disclosures we contemplate.

10.6 Conclusion

The expectation that both shareholders and creditors hold standard bundles of rights and obligations as an integrated whole is central to legal, regulatory, and economic understandings of the public corporation. On the equity side, this presumed coupling ensures that shareholders

[31] In *AXA–MONY*, to finance a bid for MONY, AXA issued convertible bonds, which were convertible into AXA shares at a discount to AXA's price only if AXA acquired MONY. Some holders of AXA bonds acquired MONY shares to vote for the merger, while short sellers of AXA bonds acquired MONY shares to oppose the merger.

have an incentive to exercise voting rights to increase share value. The primary oversight mechanisms on which we rely to regulate public firms and their shareholders, and to constrain and incentivise managers to act in the interests of shareholder-owners presume this coupling.

On the debt side, this coupling ensures that creditors have an incentive to exercise their contractual and bankruptcy rights well, so that firms which are worth more alive than dead are reorganized, and other firms are sold or liquidated. The assumed coupling of creditors' rights and obligations pervades contracting practice, commercial law, and bankruptcy law.

Yet for both equity and debt, these couplings are increasingly optional. On the equity side, shareholders can decouple economic from voting rights, resulting in such patterns as empty voting, hidden ownership, morphable ownership, and empty appraisal. Corporations as well as shareholders can play the decoupling game. A corporation cannot directly vote its own shares, but it can often do so in practice by 'soft parking' shares in friendly hands.

On the debt side, the decoupling of contractual and bankruptcy rights from economic ownership poses important challenges, both for individual creditors and debtors and for the financial system as a whole. Some apparent creditors may now gain if a company fails. In workout negotiations, creditors cannot be confident they understand other creditors' motives; bankruptcy judges face similar issues.

Hybrid debt–equity decoupling raises additional challenges for regulation of both equity and debt. On the equity side, equity-only disclosure rules may no longer suffice; disclosure may have to include debt, debt derivatives, and debt–equity hybrids as well.

Widespread debt decoupling both enhances and detracts from financial stability, in poorly understood ways. Among the risks posed by decoupling are weakened debt governance, including reduced ability for debtors to renegotiate their way out of financial distress, and increased borrower and lender reliance on market liquidity, and hence increased exposure to liquidity shocks.

From a policy perspective, the first steps are surely to better understand when and how often decoupling occurs. Disclosure rules, however, have lagged behind market practice. Disclosure is weak on the equity side and nearly non-existent for debt. In this chapter, we have collected nearly 100 examples of equity decoupling; there are surely many more undisclosed instances. It is increasingly clear that equity decoupling is an important worldwide phenomenon.

On the debt side, decoupling is widespread, as indicated by the size of the debt derivative and securitization markets. Yet disclosure of debt derivative positions by individual financial institutions and other large market participants is limited, and disclosure of firm-level decoupling is almost non-existent. In Hu and Black (2006, 2008), we proposed expanded ownership disclosure rules and some substantive rules to address equity decoupling. Here, to address debt and hybrid decoupling we propose disclosure of coupled assets within bankruptcy, expansion of equity disclosure to include related debt instruments, and vice versa. For financial institutions, hedge funds, and other major investors, we propose disclosure of their aggregate holdings of debt and debt derivatives.

Large-scale equity and debt decoupling are still fairly new. Their extent and their benefits and costs remain imperfectly known. The hedging and risk-spreading benefits may well exceed the costs. But decoupling is occurring against the background of a corporate governance paradigm, contractual arrangements, equity and debt governance regimes, and legal rules which largely assume that shareholders and creditors hold bundled packages of rights and obligations. The granularity of analysis and regulation must change, to respond to new possibilities and risks.

No.	Date	Host company	Country	Vote buyer or hidden owner	Empty voting	Hidden ownership	Other goals	Coupled or related asset	Description
94	ongoing	many companies	US	company itself	X			ESOP	Empty voting of non-vested shares.
93	ongoing	many companies	US	company itself	X			restricted stock	Empty voting from being able to vote restricted shares.
92	ongoing	some companies	US and UK	insiders or company itself	X			various	Insiders expect close vote, arrange for friendly investors to engage in record date capture.
91	ongoing	many companies	various	Insiders	X			various	Insiders reduce economic stake by hedging, retain voting control.
90	ongoing	many companies	various	company executives	X			collars (put and call options)	Executives use collars to limit risk, become partly empty voters.
89	ongoing	many companies	various	Insiders	X		defer income tax	options, loans	Insiders use derivative strategies to 'monetize' shareholdings, shed most of their economic risk, but defer tax on gain.
88	ongoing	many companies	various	corporate shareholder	X		defer income tax	call options, debt exchangeable for shares	Company A holds shares in B, sells debt exchangeable for B's shares or long-duration call options on B's shares.

(*continued*)

(Continued)

No.	Date	Host company	Country	Vote buyer or hidden owner	Empty voting	Hidden ownership	Other goals	Coupled or related asset	Description
87	2008	Bear Stearns	US	Creditors	X		hybrid decoupling	Bear Stearns debt	Holders (short sellers) of Bear Stearns debt acquired shares to support (oppose) merger with JP Morgan Chase, which had promised to support this debt.
86	2008	CSX	US	TCI and 3G (hedge funds)		X		equity swaps	Hedge funds acquired 20% economic stake in CSX, but kept share ownership below 5% to defer 13D filing. See Section 2.2.3.
85	2008	CNET	US	Jana Partners and other hedge funds		X		equity swaps	Jana and Castlerigg announce holding 21% of CNET, launch proxy contest.
84	2007	Turkcell	Turkey	Alfa Group		X		repurchase agreement	Arbitration panel orders Alfa to reduce stake in Kyivstar to under 5%; Alfa sells part of Turkcell (which owns part of Kyivstar) to Kazakh company, retains repurchase rights.
83	2007	Endesa	Spain	Enel			avoid regulatory limit on share position	equity swaps	Enel uses swaps to acquire 25% of Endesa, direct holding of 9.99% is under 10% regulatory limit.
82	2007	Fortis	Netherlands	hedge funds (and rumours as to ABN-AMRO)				share loans	Record date capture, to influence Fortis's ability to raise funds to bid for ABN-AMRO.

81	2007	ABN-AMRO	Netherlands	Royal Bank of Scotland		X		equity swaps, call options	Takeover bidder quietly increases stake from 4% to 8%, then discloses new stake.
80	2007	OMX	Sweden	Borse Dubai		X		call options	Borse Dubai emerges with 28.4% of OMX, mostly through option agreements with hedge funds, competes with NASDAQ deal to buy OMX.
79	2007	MOL	Hungary	MOL	X			share loans	As defence to takeover bid, MOL buys 40% of own shares, lends them to Hungarian banks, which can vote them.
78	2007	Target	US	Pershing Square (hedge fund)	X (disclosed)		avoid short-swing profit recapture	call options, equity swaps	Pershing Square initially acquires 9.6% of Target, mostly through equity derivatives; later announces it holds 9.97% in shares and 12.6% total economic stake.
77	2007	TD Ameritrade	US	Jana Partners & SAC Capital (hedge funds)		X		unspecified	Hedge funds seek sale of company, advise it that they have 8.4% stake, no 13D filing.
76	2007	Implenia	Switzerland	Laxey Partners (hedge fund)		X		cash-settled call options	Laxey announces 23% stake in Implenia; no prior disclosure.

(*continued*)

(Continued)

No.	Date	Host company	Country	Vote buyer or hidden owner	Empty voting	Hidden ownership	Other goals	Coupled or related asset	Description
75	2007	Converium	Switzerland	Scor (France)		X		cash-settled call options	Scor acquires 33% stake in Converium as part of takeover bid, without prior disclosure.
74	2007	CVS Caremark	US	broker votes in director election	X			record ownership	Broker votes of client shares reelect director Roger Headrick despite 'vote no' campaign.
73	2007	Borders Group	US	Spencer Capital Management		X		options	Spencer obtains 6.8% stake in Borders, about one-third of which is in form of options.
72	2007	Freeport-McMoRan and others	US and Europe	Atticus Capital (hedge fund)		X		unspecified derivatives	Atticus Capital discloses that it owns 6.4% of Freeport but had 'long economic exposure' to 11.5% because of equity swaps and other derivatives.
71	2007	Sulzer	Switzerland	Victory Industrial & Viktor Vekselberg		X		cash-settled call options, other derivatives	ZKB and Deutsche Bank provide derivatives to let investor group acquire 32% hidden position in Sulzer.
70	2007	Tribune	US	Chandler family	X			Unspecified hedges	Chandlers own 20% of Tribune, support Zell merger proposal, expected to hedge economic interest but retain voting rights.

69	2007	LSE	UK	Heyman, K netics, and Paulson money managers	X (disclosed)			equity swaps	Money managers hold 23% of LSE through equity swaps, support LSE against NASDAQ bid.
68	2007	Ascom	Switzerland	Victory Industrial (Austria)		X		cash-settled call options	Victory announces holding of 20% of Ascom, through shares and options.
67	2007	PT Multimedia	Portugal	Portugal Telecom (parent)		X		equity swaps	Portugal Telecom holds 58% of PT Multimedia directly, another 10% through equity swaps with Barclays.
66	2007	Stork NV	Netherlands	company itself	X				Company responds to Centaurus and Paulson by placing high-voting preferred shares with foundation.
65	2007	Motorola	US	Carl Icahn			avoid anti-trust filing	call options	Icahn acquires Motorola stake, uses OTC call options to delay need for Hart-Scott-Rodino anti-trust filing.
64	2007	Stork NV	Netherlands	Centaurus and Paulson hedge funds		X		unspecified derivatives	Hedge funds holding 31% of Stork seek breakup, Stork claims they initially hid their ownership.
63	2007	U.S. Global Investors	US	Unspecified hedge funds	X				Company claims that share volatility 'may be amplified' by hedge funds engaging in empty voting who oppose charter amendments.

(*continued*)

(Continued)

No.	Date	Host company	Country	Vote buyer or hidden owner	Empty voting	Hidden ownership	Other goals	Coupled or related asset	Description
62	2007	Ceridian Corp.	US	Pershing Square (hedge fund)	X (disclosed)			OTC call options	Pershing makes initial disclosure because of share stake and later also acquires OTC call options.
61	2006	Multi-Fineline-Electronix	US and Singapore	Stark (hedge fund)	X			unspecified hedges	Freeze-out by parent company; Stark holds large position in parent plus hedged position in sub, supports freeze-out.
60	2006	EADS	Netherlands	Lagardère	X			convertible bonds	Lagardère issues bonds convertible into EADS shares, retains shares and hence votes until bonds are converted.
59	2006	Lindner Holding KGaA	Germany	Lindner Holding GmbH (controlling shareholder)	X		complete freeze-out	share borrowing	Parent uses borrowed shares to meet 95% threshold for freeze-out; effort blocked by Munich appeals court.
58	2006	Hyundai Merchant Marine	Korea	Hyundai Elevator	X		avoid holding company rules	repurchase agreement	Elevator seeks votes to block takeover bid by Hyundai Heavy Industries; will be regulated as holding company if holds shares directly; arranges for IXIS Bank to buy shares and vote as directed.

57	2006	Portugal Telecom	Portugal	company itself	X		unspecified hedges	Sonaecom bids for Portugal Telecom, which places Treasury shares with Barclays; Barclays will vote against bidder, is protected against loss.
56	2006	Arcelor	Luxembourg	unspecified hedge funds	X		unspecified hedges	Hedge funds, supporting Mittal's bid, rumoured to have acquired votes to oppose white squire deal with Severstal.
55	2006	Arcelor	Luxembourg	company itself	X		Dutch foundation	Arcelor places shares of major subsidiary with Dutch foundation as defence against Mittal takeover bid.
54	2006	Telnet PLC	UK	Polygon (hedge fund)	X		share borrowing and/or equity swaps	Polygon blocks acquisition of Telent, exercising voting power beyond its economic interest.
53	2006	Sears Canada	Canada	Pershing Square (hedge fund)	X (Scotiabank)	X (unsuccessfu , by Pershing Square)	equity swaps	Sears Holdings wants to freeze out minority in Sears Canada subsidiary, Pershing Square holds equity swaps in Sears Canada, Scotiabank is dealer manager for parent's offer, refuses to unwind swap, plans to vote for offer.

(*continued*)

(Continued)

No.	Date	Host company	Country	Vote buyer or hidden owner	Empty voting	Hidden ownership	Other goals	Coupled or related asset	Description
52	2006	Saurer	Switzerland	Victory Industrial (Austria)		X		cash-settled call options	Victory announces that it holds 45% stake—24% shares bought from Laxey Partners (see below) plus 21% through options—no prior disclosure, makes tender offer for rest of Saurer.
51	2006	Saurer	Switzerland	Laxey Partners (hedge fund)		X		unspecified	Laxey announces in July 2006 that it holds over 25% stake in Saurer, no prior disclosure.
50	2006	Euronext	France	company itself	X			unclear	French government recruits French banks to hold 'pool shares' of Euronext to defend against Deutsche Börse takeover bid.
49	2006	Henderson Investment	Hong Kong	hedge fund(s)	X	X (short position)		share borrowing + short sale	Parent Henderson Land proposed freeze-out of its subsidiary, Henderson Investment. Hedge fund borrows enough shares to let it kill the freeze-out, voted no, then sells short and profits when voting outcome is announced.

48	2006	Time Warner	US	Istithmar (private investment fund)		X	equity-linked notes	Istithmar acquires 2.4% economic ownership through equity-linked notes purchased from UBS, which agrees to 'consult' its client before voting or disposing of its matched shares.
47	2006	Phelps Dodge	US	Atticus Capital (hedge fund)		X	options	Atticus becomes largest shareholder in Phelps Dodge.
46	~ 2005	Confidential company	US	hedge fund(s)	X possible		??	Hedge fund holds 4.9% of shares, wants divestiture, rebuffed; two weeks later has 51% of votes, no apparent share accumulation (no market impact).
45	2005	Unaxis	Switzerland	Victory Industrial (Austria)		X	physical- and cash-settled call options	Victory uses shares and options to accumulate 30% stake without prior disclosure.
44	2005	OAO MegaFon	Russia	Leonid Reiman		X	Offshore trust	Reiman (Russian telecom minister) holds MegaFon shares through trust; his lawyer controls trust, claims to be beneficial owner.
43	2005	Wendy's Int'l	US	Pershing Square (hedge fund)	X (disclosed)		options	Pershing reports holding 9.3% stake, with more than 6% in form of options.
42	2005	Wendy's Int'l	US	Trian and allied hedge funds	X (disclosed)		matched call and put options	Trian mounts proxy campaign for spinoff of Wendy's subsidiary; its economic ownership is primarily through options.

(*continued*)

(Continued)

No.	Date	Host company	Country	Vote buyer or hidden owner	Empty voting	Hidden ownership	Other goals	Coupled or related asset	Description
41	2005	Banca Antonveneta	Italy	Banco Populare di Lodi		X	avoid mandatory bid rules	call options	Banco Populare holds 29.3% of Antonveneta directly, 46% total, Consob requires mandatory bid
40	2005	Fiat	Italy	Agnelli family		X	avoid mandatory bid rules	equity swaps	Agnelli family acquires equity swaps in Fiat, instead of shares, to preserve control without triggering mandatory bid rule, perhaps also to avoid disclosure and hence market impact.
39	2005	Austral Coal	Australia	Glencore		X		equity swaps	Glencore acquires 10% stake in Austral Coal through combination of disclosed share purchases and undisclosed swaps.
38	2005	Exar	US	GWA Investments (hedge fund)	X			short sales	GWA seeks minority board seats; its position in Exar is 96% hedged.
37	2003	Fuji TV	Japan	Nippon Broadcasting		X	deny voting rights to takeover bidder	stock lending	Nippon lends its shares in Fuji TV to others as a defence to takeover bid by Livedoor, Nippon's economic ownership is morphable but not hidden.
36	2005	Deutsche Börse	Germany	hedge funds	X			short sale of target shares	Opponents of Deutsche Börse bid for LSE go long Deutsche Börse, short LSE.

35	2005	Portman Mining	Australia	Seneca (hedge fund)		X		equity swaps	Cleveland Cliffs bids to acquire Portman. Seneca holds 9% economic interest in Portman through equity swaps.
34	2004–05	WMC Resources	Australia	BHP Billiton		X		equity swaps	Acquisition of 4.3% toehold through equity swaps.
33	2004–05	Mylan Laboratories	US	Perry Corp. (hedge fund)	X			equity swap	Perry and Citadel hold shares in King, which
32				Citadel (hedge fund)	X			unknown	Mylan proposes to acquire; they buy hedged positions in Mylan to vote for the merger.
31	2004	DFS	UK	Polygon (hedge fund)		X		equity swap	Polygon seeks to influence DFS despite owning only one share of stock (it had 3% economic ownership through equity swaps).
30	2004	Alvis	UK	hedge funds		X		equity swap	Hedge funds with equity swaps as to Alvis shares support BAe Systems' bid for Alvis.
29	2004	Hyundai Merchant Marine	Korea	Hyundai Elevator	X	X	avoid holding company rules	complex option and voting contract	Elevator wants to control more shares of Marine to block a takeover bid, arranges for Cape Fortune to hold them and vote as directed.
28	2004	Marks and Spencer	UK	Hedge funds (helping Philip Green to acquire Marks and Spencer)		X		equity swap	Dealers who hold matched shares to hedge equity swaps support Green's bid.

(continued)

(Continued)

No.	Date	Host company	Country	Vote buyer or hidden owner	Empty voting	Hidden ownership	Other goals	Coupled or related asset	Description
27	2004	Canary Wharf	UK	'Songbird' consortium (seeking to acquire Canary Wharf)		X		equity swap	Derivatives dealer UBS holds 7.7% of Canary as matched shares to support equity swaps held by Songbird members.
26	2004	MONY Group	US	Holders and short sellers of AXA convertible bonds	X		hybrid decoupling	acquirer's convertible bonds	Holders (short sellers) of AXA bonds support (oppose) merger with MONY, hoping to profit from AXA bond holdings.
25	2004	Disney Co.	US	broker votes in director election	X			record ownership	Broker votes of client shares reelect CEO Michael Eisner despite 'vote no' campaign.
24	2004	Unitedglobalcom	US	Deephaven (hedge fund)			empty exercise of appraisal rights	share borrowing	Deephaven borrowed shares in account at broker 1, sold them (short) to its own account at broker 2, and used second account to exercise pre-emptive rights
23	2004	News Corp.	Australia and US	Liberty Media	X	Hidden: yes Morphable: maybe		forward contract and equity swap	Liberty Media holds voting and non-voting News Corp. shares, uses derivatives to adjust its economic exposure.

22	2003	SK Corp.; SK Telecom	Korea	SK Networks			X	private contracts	SK Networks arranges for offshore money managers to hold SK Corp and SK Telecom shares, SK Networks retains economic risk and *de facto* voting rights.
21	2002	Middle East Tube Co.	Israel	controlling shareholders				informal put option	Controller lends money to friend to buy shares and vote them in favour of related party transaction, dispute over whether friend has informal put option.
20	2002	P&O Princess	UK	investor (favour Carnival bid for P&O Princess)	X	maybe		share borrowing	P&O shareholders who favour Carnival's bid reportedly borrow shares in order to vote for acceptance.
19	2002	Moss Brothers	UK	Legendary Investments			X	equity swap	Legendary uses equity swaps to obtain 20% economic interest, obtains formal assignment of voting rights of matching shares from the counterparty.
18	2002	Hewlett-Packard	US	holders of Compaq shares (target of HP merger bid)	X			target shares	Compaq shareholders are rumoured to have acquired hedged HP positions to support HP's merger with Compaq.
17	2002	Coles Myer	Australia	Solomon Lew (proxy contestant)	X	no		options	Lew buys additional shares, but hedges with options.

(continued)

(Continued)

No.	Date	Host company	Country	Vote buyer or hidden owner	Empty voting	Hidden ownership	Other goals	Coupled or related asset	Description
16	2002	Quanta Services	US	company itself	X			ESOP	Quanta adopts ESOP in response to takeover bid by Aquila.
15	2002	British Land	UK	Laxey Partners	X			share borrowing	Laxey holds 1% of British Land, borrows another 8% to support a breakup proposal.
14	2001	Telecom Italia	Italy	unknown share borrowers	X			share borrowing	Fidelity and Morgan Stanley hold 10% of Telecom Italia, oppose Pirelli bid, but can cast only 1% of the votes; their other shares were lent and can't be recalled in time.
13	2001	Fondiaria	Italy	SAI (acquirer)		X	avoid mandatory bid rule	call options	SAI parks Fondiaria shares with banks to avoid Italy's mandatory bid rule, retains call options on the shares.
12	2001	Rubicon	New Zealand	Perry Corp.		X		equity swaps	Perry holds equity swaps to conceal ownership in Rubicon, later unwinds swaps and votes at Rubicon meeting.
11	1999	Gucci	Netherlands	company itself	X			ESOP	LVMH buys 34% stake in Gucci, Gucci establishes ESOP to hold equal number of shares, neutralizing LVMH's interest.

10	1998	Ciber	US	CEO Bobby Stevenson	X		prepaid forward sale, options	CEO and founder forward sell $82M in company shares, sheds most risk, defers income tax
9	1997	Arad	Israel	Shlomo Eisenberg (controller)	X		put option	Controller places shares in friendly hands to obtain approval by non-conflicted shareholders of related party transaction, a put protects buyers against loss.
8	1997	John Fairfax Holdings	Australia	Brierley Investments		avoid mandatory bid rule	equity swaps	Brierley holds equity swaps instead of Fairfax shares to avoid Australia's mandatory bid rules.
7	1995	Estée Lauder	US	Lauder family	X	defer income tax	prepaid forward short sale	Estée and Ron Lauder borrow shares from other insiders, sell them short in IPO.
6	1994	Northern Electric	UK	Trafalgar House			equity swaps	Trafalgar enters into equity swaps before making bid for Northern Electric.
5	1994	UBS	Switzerland	company itself	X		share borrowing, forward contracts	In response to takeover bid by Martin Ebner, UBS seeks to amend charter, agrees to repurchase shares from two major shareholders *after* a shareholder meeting; the shares are voted in favour of the amendment.

(*continued*)

(Continued)

No.	Date	Host company	Country	Vote buyer or hidden owner	Empty voting	Hidden ownership	Other goals	Coupled or related asset	Description
4	1991	NCR	US	company itself	X			ESOP	NCR adopts ESOP as defence against bid by AT&T.
3	1989	Dunkin' Donuts	US	company itself	X			ESOP	Dunkin' Donuts adopts ESOP as defence against takeover bid Kingsbridge Capital and DD Acquisition
2	1988	Polaroid	US	company itself	X			ESOP	Polaroid adopts ESOP in response to takeover bid from Shamrock Holdings.
1	1988	Macmillan	UK	company itself	X			ESOP	MacMillan contributes additional shares to ESOP, replaces ESOP trustees with members of management.

References

Acharya, V. V. and Johnson, T. C. (2007). Insider Trading in Credit Derivatives, *Journal of Financial Economics* 84, 110–41.

Adler, B. (2005). *Foundations of Bankruptcy Law* (New York, Foundation Press).

Andrejczak, M. (2008). Update: Sara Lee, Coach Set Rules to Deter Devious Shareholders, *Dow Jones Business News* (3 Apr.).

Baird, J. (2008). CDS May Undermine Debt Governance—Law Professor, *Reuters* (18 Apr.).

Barnett, G. (2002). Collateralized Bond Obligations and Collateralized Loan Obligations, in *New Developments in Securitization 2002* PLI (ed.) (New York, Practicing Law Institute).

Barnett, G. (2007). CDO Equity Funds, in *New Developments in Securitization 2006*, PLI (ed.) (New York, Practicing Law Institute).

Becht, M., Bolton, P., and Roell, A. (2004). Corporate Governance and Control, in G. Constantinides, M. Harris, and R. Stulz (eds.), *Handbook of Economics and Finance* (Amsterdam: Elsevier), 343–61, also available at <http://ssrn.com/abstract=343461>.

Berman, M. (2007). Will the Sunlight of Disclosure Chill Hedge Funds?, *American Bankruptcy Institute Journal* (1 May).

Brav, A. and Mathews, R. D. (2008). Empty Voting and Efficiency, AFA 2009 San Francisco Meetings Paper, available at <http://ssrn.com/abstract=1108632>.

Butler, P. (2006). Address to the International Corporate Governance Network Conference: Creating Value—Building Trust (7 July) (Powerpoint slides).

Campbell, D. (2008). XL Capital Explains Decision to Sue Merrill, *Bond Buyer* (24 Mar.), at 1.

Carr, P. and Wu, L. (2006). Stock Options and Credit Default Swaps: A Joint Framework for Valuation and Estimation, Working Paper, available at <http://ssrn.com/abstract=748005>.

Cheffins, B. and Black, B. (2006). Outside Director Liability across Countries, *Texas Law Review* 84, 1385–480.

Christoffersen, S. K., Géczy, C. C., Musto, D. K., and Reed, A. V. (2005). Cross-Border Dividend Taxation and the Preferences of Taxable and Non-Taxable Investors: Evidence from Canada, *Journal of Financial Economics* 78, 121–44.

Christoffersen, S. K., Géczy, C. C., Musto, D. K., and Reed, A. V. (2007). Vote Trading and Information Aggregation, *Journal of Finance* 62, 2897–929.

Claessens, S., Djankov, S., and Lang, L. H. P. (2000). The Separation of Ownership and Control in East Asian Corporations, *Journal of Financial Economics* 58, 81–112.

Cohen, L., Diether, K. B., and Malloy, C. J. (2007). Supply and Demand Shifts in the Shorting Market, *Journal of Finance* 62, 2061–96.

Das, S. R. and Hanouna, P. (2007). Hedging Credit: Equity Liquidity Matters, Working Paper, available at <http://ssrn.com/abstract=1028735>.

Duffie, D. (2007). Innovations in Credit Risk Transfer: Implications for Financial Stability, BIS Working Paper No. 255; Rock Center for Corporate Governance Working Paper No. 6, available at <http://ssrn.com/abstract=1165484>.

Duffie, D. and Garleanu, N. (2001). Risk and Valuation of Collateralized Debt Obligations, *Financial Analysts' Journal* 57, 41–59.

Economist (2008). Bankruptcies in America: Waiting for Armageddon, *Economist* (29 Mar.), at 81.

Euromoney (2008). London turns its Attention to CFDs, *Euromoney* (Feb.), at 45.

Faccio, M. and Lang, L. H. P. (2002). The Ultimate Ownership of Western European Corporations, *Journal of Financial Economics* 65, 365–95.

FSA (Financial Services Authority) (UK) (2008). *Financial Risk Outlook 2008*, available at <http://www.fsa.gov.uk/pubs/plan/financial_risk_outlook_2008.pdf>.

Fisher, E. B. and Buck, A. L. (2006/7). Hedge Funds and the Changing Face of Corporate Bankruptcy Practice, *American Bankruptcy Institute Journal* (Dec.–Jan.), at 24.

Flaschen, E. D. and Mayr, K. A. (2007). Bankruptcy Rule 2019 and the Unwarranted Attack on Hedge Funds, *American Bankruptcy Institute Journal* (Sept.), at 46.

Gande, A. and Puri, M. (2005). Enhancing Security Value by Ownership Restrictions: Evidence from a Natural Experiment, *Financial Management* 34, 35–64.

Gilson, R. J. and Black, B. S. (1995). *The Law and Finance of Corporate Acquisitions* (2nd edn.) (Westbury, NY, Foundation Press).

Glass, A. W. (2001). CFMA Brings Legal Certainty, but Additional Liability for Credit Derivatives, *Euromoney* (Jan.) (Part 1), and (Apr.) (Part 2).

Gordon, L. A. and Pound, J. (1990). ESOPs and Corporate Control, *Journal of Financial Economics* 27, 525–55.

Guerrera, F., White, B., and van Duyn, A. (2008). Derivatives Boom Raises Risk of Bankruptcy, *Financial Times* (28 Jan.), at 13.

Harner, M. M. (2008). Trends in Distressed Debt Investing: An Empirical Study of Investors' Objectives, *American Bankruptcy Institute Law Review* 16(69), available at <http://ssrn.com/abstract=1147643>.

Hu, H. T. C. (1993). Misunderstood Derivatives: The Causes of Informational Failure and the Promise of Regulatory Incrementalism, *Yale Law Journal* 102, 1457–1513.

Hu, H. T. C. (2007). Shareholder and Creditor Decoupling: Separating 'Embedded Rights' and Contractual Rights from Economic Interests, Working Paper.

Hu, H. T. C. and Black, B. (2006). The New Vote Buying: Empty Voting and Hidden Ownership, *Southern California Law Review* 79, 811–908.

Hu, H. T. C. and Black, B. (2007). Hedge Funds, Insiders, and the Decoupling of Economic and Voting Ownership: Empty Voting and Hidden (Morphable) Ownership, *Journal of Corporate Finance* 13, 343–67.

Hu, H. T. C. and Black, B. (2008). Equity and Debt Decoupling and Empty Voting II: Importance and Extensions, *University of Pennsylvania Law Review* 156, 625–739.

Hu, H. T. C. and Westbrook, J. L. (2007). Abolition of the Corporate Duty to Creditors, *Columbia Law Review* 107, 1321–1403.

ISDA (International Swaps and Derivatives Association) (2003). *ISDA Credit Derivatives Definitions* (New York, International Swaps and Derivatives Association).

Ivashina, V. and Sun, Z. (2007). Institutional Stock Trading on Loan Market Information, AFA 2008 New Orleans Meetings Paper; EFA 2007 Ljubljana Meetings, available at <http://ssrn.com/abstract=972044>.

Kahan, M. and Rock, E. B. (2008). The Hanging Chads of Corporate Voting, *Georgetown Law Journal* 96, 1227–81.

Keys, B. J., Mukherjee, T. K., Seru, A., and Vig, V. (2008). Did Securitization Lead to Lax Screening? Evidence from Subprime Loans, EFA 2008 Athens Meetings Paper, available at <http://ssrn.com/abstract=1093137>.

Kirchmaier, T., Grant, J., and Kirschner, J. (2009). Financial Tunnelling and the Mandatory Bid Rule, FMG Discussion Paper No. 536, available at <http://ssrn.com/abstract=613945>.

Listokin, Y. (2008). Management Always Wins the Close Ones, *American Law and Economics Review* 10(2), 159–84.

Loderer, C. and Zgraggen, P. (1999). When Shareholders Choose Not to Maximize Value: The Union Bank of Switzerland's 1994 Proxy Fight, *Journal of Applied Corporate Finance* (Fall), 91–102.

McCracken, J. (2008). Delphi's Woes: Chapter 11 Insider Trading, *Wall Street Journal* (13 Mar.), at C1.

Martin, S. and Partnoy, F. (2005). Encumbered Shares, *University of Illinois Law Review* 775–813

Medova, E. A. and Smith, R. G. (2004). A Structural Approach to EDS Pricing, *Risk* 19, 84–8.

Nathan, C. M. (2007). 'Empty Voting' and Other Fault Lines Undermining Shareholder Democracy: The New Hunting Ground for Hedge Funds, *Corporate Governance Advisor* (Jan.–Feb.) 1–9.

Neeman, Z. and Orosel, G. O. (2006). On the Efficiency of Vote Buying when Voters Have Common Interests, *International Review of Law and Economics* 26, 536–56.

Partnoy, F. and Skeel, D. A., Jr (2007). The Promise and Perils of Credit Derivatives, *University of Cincinnati Law Review* 75, 1019–50.

Raghavan, A. (2007). Happy Returns: How Lehman Sold Plan to Sidestep Tax Man—Hedge Funds Use Swaps to Avoid Dividend Hit; IRS Seeks Information, *Wall Street Journal* (17 Sept.), at A1.

Rajan, R. G. (2005). Has Financial Development Made the World Riskier?, NBER Working Paper Series, Vol. w11728, available at <http://ssrn.com/abstract=842464>.

Rauh, J. D. (2006). Own Company Stock in Defined Contribution Pension Plans: A Takeover Defense?, *Journal of Financial Economics* 81, 379–410.

Risk Management Association (2007). *RMA Securities Lending Industry Composite, Averages for the Period: 2nd Quarter.*

Schizer, D. (2001). Frictions as a Constraint on Tax Planning, *Columbia Law Review* 101, 1312.

Scholtes, S. (2006). Dura Provides Test for New Settlement Rule, *Financial Times* (2 Nov.).

SEC (Securities and Exchange Commission) (2008). Division of Corporation Finance, Letter to Judge Lewis Kaplan, with regard to *CSX Corp. v. The Children's Investment Fund* (4 June).

Sender, H. (2005). Hedge-fund Lending to Distressed Firms Makes for Gray Rules and Rough Play, *Wall Street Journal* (18 July).

Sheppard, L. (2002). IRS Pursues Individual Constructive Sales Using Equity-Linked Securities, *Tax Notes* 96, 1797–801.

Stulz, R. (2004). Should We Fear Derivatives?, *Journal of Economic Perspectives* 18, 173–92.

Takeovers Panel (Australia) (2008). Guidance Note 20—Equity Derivatives.

Takeover Panel (UK) (2007). Code Committee: Derivatives and Options Regime: 2007 Review (June).

Tett, G. and Davies, P. J. (2007). Unbound: How a Market Storm Has Seen Derivatives Eclipse Corporate Bonds, *Financial Times* (8 Aug.), at 11.

Van der Horst, J. and van Uchelen-Schipper, M. (2007). The Netherlands, Working Paper.

CHAPTER 11

ANTIBANKRUPTCY

DOUGLAS G. BAIRD AND ROBERT K. RASMUSSEN

11.1 Introduction

Chapter 11 is now the last firewall protecting many of the country's largest corporations. It may hold. Over the last decade, and especially during the dot-com meltdown, Chapter 11 has been singularly successful. Long gone is the time when the managers of Eastern Airlines could allow it to wither away in bankruptcy with the creditors standing by helplessly (Lubove 1991: 99). A new breed of bankruptcy judges, lawyers, and turnaround specialists have come on the scene. They do not get caught up in emotion. They can cast a cold eye, harness markets, and make tough decisions. Billion-dollar corporations (United Airlines, Kmart, Budget Rent-A-Car) overcame financial distress in Chapter 11 and continued to operate.[1] Even in such fraud-ridden cases as Enron, assets were sensibly redeployed, general creditors received substantial recoveries, and wrongdoers and their fellow travellers were held to account.[2]

There is, however, considerable reason to doubt that reorganization law is up to the challenge it is about to face, at least in the largest cases.[3] The successes of recent years do not readily translate to the current economic environment. The players today are different from

[1] For a discussion of United's Chapter 11, see Armstrong (2006). For a discussion of Kmart's, see Harner (2008a: 725–7). Budget used Chapter 11 to effect a sale (see Brennan 2002).

[2] See *Investment Business Weekly* (2008): 'Today's distribution pushes the total amount returned to creditors past $20 billion, almost triple the amount originally anticipated. With this distribution, Enron creditors now are receiving 50.3 cents on the dollar and Enron North America Corp.... creditors are receiving 50 cents on the dollar, both excluding gains, interest and dividends.'

Financial institutions that participated in the off-balance sheet vehicles that masked Enron's financial condition were forced to make substantial settlements. See *Investment Business Weekly* (2008) (reporting a $1.866 billion settlement by Citigroup to resolve the claims of Enron's general creditors against it). For the fate of Enron's executives, see Hays (2007) (reporting that eight Enron former executives are serving prison terms of up to twenty-four years after reaching plea agreements).

[3] In this chapter, our focus is on the largest cases, those involving hundreds of millions or billions of dollars. The dynamic of small cases is utterly different and one cannot extrapolate from one to the other. See Baird, Bris, and Zhu (2007) (showing that capital structures of small and large cases are dramatically different).

those in past downturns.[4] For a long time, the capital structure of a firm in reorganization consisted of a senior bank with a security interest in all the firm's assets and a group of dispersed, but homogeneous, unsecured creditors that an active creditors' committee could represent.[5] The bank, the committee, and the debtor's managers bargained with each other against a backdrop of well-developed norms.

Today, we no longer have a single bank and dispersed general creditors. Dozens of constantly changing stakeholders occupy every tranche, each pursuing its own agenda.[6] Some seek long-term control of the business, while others are passive, short-term investors. Others may hold a basket of both long and short positions in multiple tranches and complicated hedges involving other businesses. Their concerns—such as whether a particular action will be a 'credit event' in a credit default swap—often have nothing to do with preserving the business or maximizing the value of its assets. Indeed, failure of the business can mean large returns to some creditors.[7] During the credit contraction of 2007–08, the sale of the company was sometimes done too quickly or sometimes not be done at all. In short, the new world of corporate reorganizations has more heterogeneous creditors whose rights against the business are deeply fragmented.

In the past, the bargains that parties reached among themselves followed a few familiar patterns. While there were many possible deals, the players naturally gravitated toward only a few.[8] In the new environment, with different players holding different stakes, the old patterns no longer apply and new ones have yet to take shape. There are no longer organized groups (like agented lenders or even creditors' committees), but instead investors have *one-off* relationships with the debtor entity (for example, counterparties with individual repos or swaps). The types of institution vary—from banks and broker-dealers to hedge funds and private equity firms. The current environment is one in which there are no natural leaders (or followers) among the creditors to perform the shuttle diplomacy required to

[4] Some of these changes have been under way for a time, but remained largely invisible during a period of enormous liquidity. In the early part of this decade, selling even the largest businesses on the market was usually an option. See Baird and Rasmussen (2003: 679) (reporting that, apart from the instances in which Chapter 11 was used to implement a deal arranged outside of bankruptcy, there were sixty-seven large reorganization cases in 2002 and fifty-two were sales of one kind or another).

[5] See Huebner and Tisdell (2008: 77, 78):

> Twenty-five years ago… [t]he major creditor participants in corporate reorganizations were usually large commercial banks and other institutional creditors (e.g., insurance companies), indenture trustees representing bondholders, and the debtors' vendors.

[6] See generally Harner (2008*b*: 93) ('Distressed debt investors with different investment strategies but the same investment target may lead to potential conflicts among creditors.'); Lubben (2007: 407) ('The operation of chapter 11 is premised on a perception of ownership that may no longer exist or is at the very least threatened by the expansion of credit derivatives.'); Miller (2007: 390):

> Distressed debt traders have different motivations and objectives than the old line relationship banks and trade creditors…. The explosion of distressed debt trading marked the end of the relationships that had been a major support structure of the reorganization paradigm of 1978.

[7] Denninger (2009) (speculating that GM bondholders were refusing to renegotiate because their bonds are backed by AIG credit default swaps that will pay in full if GM files for bankruptcy).

[8] To cast things in the language of game theory, there were many possible equilibrium agreements, but comparatively few were focal points. For the classic discussion of focal points, see Schelling (1960: 57–8).

build a consensus. Without familiar benchmarks, there is no shared understanding of what form a plan should take. Coalition formation is harder.[9] Worse yet, in some cases there may be no stable equilibrium at all. To use the language of cooperative game theory, the core may be empty.[10]

In this chapter, we review the changes in finance over the last decade and show how each is at odds with basic assumptions of Chapter 11. Our conclusion can be stated simply. The challenge the legal system faces is much like assembling a city block that has been broken up into many parcels. In this scenario, we face an anticommons problem, a world in which ownership interests are fragmented and conflicting.[11] This is quite at odds with the standard account of corporate reorganizations—that it solves a tragedy of the commons, the collective action problem that exists when general creditors share numerous dispersed, but otherwise similar, interests.[12] Bankruptcy has become antibankruptcy.

Section 11.2 examines how the prototypical general creditor has changed. It is no longer a small player holding a claim much like everyone else's. Moreover, this group changes constantly throughout the course of the case. Section 11.3 examines the changed nature of the secured creditor and, especially, the way in which it now enjoys much more control than it had even a decade ago. In Section 11.4, we focus on financial innovation and the way that derivatives and the ability to hedge alter the dynamics of Chapter 11. Section 11.5 draws on the lessons of cooperative game theory to show how in combination these changes are toxic. They undermine the coalition formation process that is central to Chapter 11.

11.2 The Changing Face of Unsecured Debt

11.2.1 The Bargaining Dynamic in Chapter 11

Bankruptcy law developed in a world of limited financial instruments. Secured debt (generally held by banks), unsecured debt (comprised of private debt, bonds, and trade credit), and publicly traded stock largely exhausted the types of investments that comprised the capital structure of large businesses.[13] The action lay at the level of the general creditors.

[9] In the recent Adelphia reorganization, for example, infighting among at least twelve unofficial groups of creditors resulted in seven proposed reorganization plans, and professional fees and expenses initially sought by these twelve groups alone totalled over $100 million (see Huebner and Tisdell 2008: 80).

[10] For a discussion of the 'empty core' and how it relates to corporate reorganizations, see Section 11.5.

[11] For a discussion of the anticommons problem, see Heller (1998). See also Heller (2008) (identifying anticommons problems in a variety of settings); Fennell (2009) (exploring the relationship among commons, anticommons, and semicommons).

[12] See Jackson (1986: 10–11) (noting that the role of bankruptcy to solve 'a common pool problem' is 'largely unquestioned').

[13] Tort claimants are comparatively rare. See Warren and Westbrook (2005: 1227–30) (excluding mass product liability cases, tort claims are present in as few as 1% of bankruptcy cases). Other types of claimants (most notably tax claimants) loom large in smaller cases, but this chapter focuses exclusively on the largest cases. While small Chapter 11s make up the vast majority in number, the total assets are overwhelmingly concentrated in a small handful of large cases. For a discussion of the empirical differences and the different dynamics between large and small cases, see Baird, Bris, and Zhu (2007).

The bankruptcy was for the benefit of the general creditors. Hence, the drafters of the Bankruptcy Code provided that administrative expenses be paid after the secured creditors, but before the general creditors.[14]

The creditors of the typical financially distressed business, whether bondholder or supplier, enjoyed at bottom the same legal right: the ability to sue and reduce their claim to judgment. If each were left to his/her own devices, they might tear the business apart. The Bankruptcy Code worked its magic by forcing the group to work together as one. The Code turned every variety of right against the debtor into a 'claim'.[15] A loan at 10% due in five years was treated the same as a loan at 5% due in ten years.[16] Someone who had a breach of contract action had a claim for the damages he/she would have received under nonbankruptcy law.

Because they held the same kind of legal right subject to the same treatment, all had the same incentive to maximize the value of the estate. Every claim entitled the stakeholder to exactly the same thing—a pro rata share of the bankruptcy estate.[17] A small committee of the largest creditors could thus look after everyone's interests.[18] The general creditors as a group bore the expenses of the committee.[19] Dispersed general creditors with small claims were spared the expense of vindicating their rights on their own. Because everyone had the same legal rights and received identical pro rata treatment, we could safely allow the decisions of the group as a whole to bind the dissenters.[20] There was no need to fear a tyranny of the majority. The plan had to treat those similarly situated in the same way.[21]

By the standard account, general creditors were dispersed (Jackson 1986: 11–19). Whereas the secured debt was primarily concentrated in the hands of a single institution, various parties held unsecured debt. The problem was one of collective action. As a group, the unsecured creditors would have been better off by taking concerted action, but no one creditor was willing to take the labouring oar. The costs of participation fell on those who participated, but the benefits were distributed to all creditors. While for creditors as a group the

[14] See 11 USC § 506 (2006) (determining secured status); § 507 (giving administrative expenses priority over most unsecured claims).

[15] See 11 USC § 101(5) (defining 'claim' for purposes of the Bankruptcy Code as generally any 'right to payment').

[16] See 11 USC § 502(b)(2) (disallowing claims for unmatured interest).

[17] See 11 USC § 726(b) (providing for pro rata distributions in Chapter 7 liquidations). Chapter 11 accomplishes this through requirements placed on the plan of reorganization. See *infra* note 20.

[18] See 11 USC § 1102.

[19] See 11 USC § 503(b)(3)(F) (including as administrative expenses of the estate the expenses incurred by members of the creditors' committee).

[20] Only substantially similar claims can be placed in the same class for purposes of voting on the plan, everyone in a class must be treated identically, and the plan cannot provide different treatment to classes at the same priority level. See 11 USC § 1122(a) (requiring that claims in the same class must be 'substantially similar'); 11 USC § 1123(a)(4) (requiring that the plan provide for the same treatment for each claim of a particular class 'unless the holder of a particular claim or interest agrees to a less favorable treatment'); 11 USC § 1129(b)(1) (mandating that, unless a class consents, it cannot be unfairly discriminated against). For a discussion of classification and related issues, see *In re Dow Corning Corp.*, 244 B.R. 634, 644 (Bankr. E.D. Mich. 1999), which states that:[c]laims may be classified together only if they are "substantially similar" to one another' and 'substantially similar claims may not be classified separately when it is done for an illegitimate reason'.

[21] There are a few exceptions, of course. Some claims (such as those of the tax collector, 11 USC § 507(a)(8), and those of workers for unpaid wages, 11 USC § 507(a)(4)(A)), are given priority. But these are the exceptions and they do not figure significantly in large cases (see Baird, Brisz, and Zhu 2007: 20–3).

best course of action was to participate in the reorganization discussions, for each individual creditor the rational thing to do was stay passive. The nonbankruptcy rights were insufficiently tailored to allow them to act in a way that was mutually beneficial. Just as the agency issuing fishing licenses or regulating drilling in an oil field attempts to maximize value, those charged with overseeing the reorganization took steps to preserve the value of the estate on behalf of general creditors, who were presumptively similarly situated and entitled to equal treatment.

In addition to the incentive towards passivity, unsecured creditors also lacked the information necessary to participate in the reorganization.[22] A central issue in most reorganization cases was valuation—the amount the company would be worth if liquidated and the amount if kept together. While creditors might have been able to piece together information on liquidation values from publicly available sources, putting a price on the company as a going concern was a more difficult endeavour. One had to know the future plans for the company and what the plausible projections were for the future revenue stream. These both required information that the company had but that outsiders did not. Indeed, the creditors had no legal entitlement to such information.[23]

The answer to these problems was to give a central role to a committee to represent the interests of the unsecured creditors (Skeel 1992: 523, 525–6). The committee would be staffed with creditors, presumptively those holding the seven largest claims against the debtor.[24] The existence of the committee provided a mechanism by which private information could be shared with the creditors. The committee would negotiate on behalf of the unsecured creditors as a group. Moreover, the committee would be able to collect the information that it needed in order to make an informed judgment. It could hire accountants to investigate the books of the company. It could hire investment bankers to assess what options the company had. It enjoyed the broad power to 'investigate the acts, conduct, assets, liabilities, and financial condition of the debtor, the operation of the debtor's business and the desirability of the continuance of such business, and any other matter relevant to the case'.[25] It could engage attorneys to help guide it through the bankruptcy proceeding.[26] Moreover, the debtor would pay for all of the committee professionals, such as investment bankers and accountants.[27] Because the Code assumed that the secured creditors would be paid in full and the general creditors would receive the residual, the effect of having the debtor pay was to spread the expenses among all of the general, unsecured creditors.

The creditors on the committee had both a fiduciary duty and an economic interest to represent the group of unsecured creditors as a whole. The case law established that those on the committee had to represent the interests of the unsecured creditors as a group.[28] By and

[22] Gappmayer (2006: 440):

> The balance between the creditors' need for disclosure and the debtor's need for confidentiality is struck in Chapter 11 proceedings by the appointment of a creditors' committee that is made up of specific creditors and is given access to all of the debtor's information, including nonpublic information.

[23] One of the authors discussed the central role valuation plays in Chapter 11 at length in Baird and Bernstein (2006).

[24] 11 USC § 1102(b)(1). [25] 11 USC § 1103(c)(2).

[26] 11 USC § 1103(a) (giving the committee, subject to court approval, the power to employ 'attorneys, accountants, or other agents').

[27] 11 USC § 330(a)(1).

[28] See, e.g., *In re Drexel Burnham Lambert Group, Inc.*, 138 B.R. 717, 722 (Bankr. SDNY 1992) (noting that the fiduciary duty 'extends to the class as a whole, not to its individual members').

large, this duty corresponded with the economic interest of the creditors. In theory, a creditor would maximize the value of its own claim by maximizing the value distributed to the unsecured creditors as a group.

The creditors' committee is a portal into the bankruptcy process. While any individual creditor has to pay its own costs should it seek to participate in the reorganization proceeding, the creditors' committee can hire counsel and advisors and have these fees reimbursed by the estate as an administrative expense.[29] Also, the creditors' committee can extract concessions from the debtor. The debtor would be hard-pressed to confirm a plan of reorganization over the active opposition of the creditors' committee. As such, the debtor has reason to listen to its concerns.

This approach—one that assumes common interests among dispersed creditors—fits awkwardly with what we find today. By the time of the bankruptcy, unsecured claims are in the hands of distressed debt professionals.[30] They often hold complicated positions, combining ordinary claims with derivative instruments. They pursue their own agendas. Rather than dispersed and homogeneous, they are close at hand, well informed, and radically different from one another. As a result, the idea of a committee as the principal vehicle for mediating the interests of the general creditors as a group may no longer work. Having a seat on the creditors' committee can provide an investor with a good deal of input into the way in which a bankruptcy case proceeds. At the same time, however, someone on the creditors' committee is supposed to attend to the interests of the general creditors as a whole. Reconciling the traditional committee structure with the new type of player requires forcing disclosures from the investor and limiting her range of action, especially with respect to the trading of claims.[31] Whether this can be done in a way that keeps the largest players at the bargaining table has proved hard to determine.[32] In an environment in which sitting at the bargaining table exposes participants to inside information, the most important players often want to stay in the shadows.[33] This is an inversion of the traditional process, one in which those with the most at stake wanted to be on the creditors' committee, rather than stay away from it.

The paradigm of the disparate but homogeneous general creditor is complicated for a further reason. Large corporations are typically not a single entity, but rather a corporate group. A single group of managers runs the business as a whole and cash from all operations flows into a single account, but many creditors have rights only against a particular subsidiary. In theory, each subsidiary files its own separate bankruptcy petition and should have its own

[29] 11 USC § 330(a)(1)(A) (providing for 'reasonable compensation for actual, necessary services rendered by the trustee, examiner, ombudsman, professional person, or attorney'); § 1103(a) (authorizing the committee to hire professionals).

[30] See *supra* note 6.

[31] For a discussion of disclosure obligations in bankruptcy and, in particular, the way they contrast with disclosure obligations outside of bankruptcy, see Drain and Schwartz (2002).

[32] For a discussion of how so-called 'Chinese Walls' may be used to mitigate this problem, see *infra* note 79.

[33] See Huebner and Tisdell (2008: 82):

> [M]embers of senior lender groups now frequently decline to receive company information so they can remain unrestricted and capable of purchasing and selling public subordinated debt. In some recent cases, only a handful of senior lenders have been willing to receive non-public information, making it impossible to include the vast majority of lenders in reorganization plan negotiations.

creditors' committee. Its assets should be segregated from those of the other entities. In practice, this is hard. Sorting out the relative rights of the different creditors requires both connecting creditors with specific entities and unscrambling the transactions among the different subsidiaries. Especially when there is widespread fraud, determining exactly how much each related entity owes the other is enormously expensive. In WorldCom, for example, there was approximately a trillion dollars in intercorporate transfers,[34] and, with a CFO facing years in prison,[35] hundreds were hired merely to create consolidated financial statements.[36]

For a long time, bankruptcy lawyers have navigated this problem by using the device of 'substantive consolidation', in which the different corporate groups are treated as one for purposes of the plan of reorganization. When enough of the affected groups are willing to consent to such a plan, bankruptcy judges tend to approve such plans, notwithstanding appellate opinions that make the practice suspect.[37] Hence, we have an odd world in which substantive consolidation takes place in more than half of the largest cases (Widen 2006: 53), even though black letter law unequivocally states that the practice is to be imposed only in the rarest of circumstances.[38]

Precisely because of the difficulty of valuing different claims against different corporate entities, it is often hard to assess exactly where one claim stands *vis-à-vis* another. When a business has hundreds or thousands of subsidiaries, there is no easy way to sort out the rights of the creditors, even though they are all nominally general creditors. Even if the general creditors of each of the entities can coordinate their actions (and for reasons that we shall discuss in the next section, they often can), it is hard for them to reach agreement with each other, as each is able to contest the value of their claims and there is not an easy way to resolve their dispute.

11.2.2 Claims Trading

The changing composition of creditors in Chapter 11 is primarily due to the rise in claims trading. The ability to trade in claims against a Chapter 11 debtor began to take hold in the 1980s.[39] At that time, however, some courts interpreted the Bankruptcy Rules to allow them to review claim trades and ensure that those selling them received full disclosure.[40] In 1991, however, the Rules Committee decided to deregulate claims trading, as existing judicial oversight was perceived to impair the liquidity of claims.[41] This newly deregulated market

[34] *In re WorldCom, Inc.*, No. 02-13533, 2003 WL 23861928, at *11 (Bankr. SDNY 31 Oct. 2003).

[35] See *Toronto Star* (2003); see also *In re WorldCom*, 2003 WL 23861928, at *13 (noting the 'loss of individuals with institutional knowledge').

[36] *In re WorldCom*, 2003 WL 23861928, at *13.

[37] See Baird (2005: 15) ('Substantive consolidation lacks the solid foundation one usually expects of doctrines so firmly embedded in day-to-day practice.').

[38] *In re Owens Corning*, 419 F.3d 195, 208–9 (3d Cir. 2005) (noting that there is nearly unanimous consensus among appellate courts that substantive consolidation is a remedy to be used 'sparingly').

[39] See Fortgang and Mayer (1990: 1–3) (describing claims trading in various bankruptcies dating back to 1986); Rasmussen and Skeel (1995: 101 n.71) (citing statistics on the growth of the claims trading market from the mid-1980s into the mid-1990s).

[40] See, e.g., *In re Allegheny Int'l, Inc.*, 100 B.R. 241, 243–4 (Bankr. W.D. Pa. 1988).

[41] Logan (1994: 501–2) (describing the decision of the Rules Committee to remove claims trading from judicial oversight to promote a liquid market in claims).

for claims provided opportunities that the highly regulated market for acquiring control through equity did not.[42] The increased presence and financial wherewithal of hedge funds heightened the importance of this aspect of reorganization practice.[43] This last decade saw the rise of hedge funds across the financial landscape.[44] It is not surprising that their influence extends to companies *in extremis*. Several funds exist whose sole purpose is to find value in the distressed end of the market. When a company is insolvent, investing in equity is not the safest route toward exercising influence. For those seeking outsized returns, debt is the instrument of choice. Claims trading, in essence, creates a market in all of the company's debt.

The basic rationale for claims trading is simple. It allows easy exit from a reorganization proceeding for those who are ill-equipped to navigate it. Chapter 11 cases can be drawn-out affairs.[45] When a debtor files for Chapter 11, the debtor is prohibited from paying prepetition debt.[46] Payments on such obligations await the end of the case, absent a showing that immediate payment makes creditors as a group better off.[47] But the holders of some claims, such as suppliers of goods and services, never expected to be long-term investors in the enterprise and do not want to wait until the end of the proceeding for payment. They are not set up to participate in the Chapter 11 proceeding. They have little knowledge of the ins and outs of bankruptcy practice. Perhaps even more importantly, their business model is not built around tying up capital in bankruptcy proceedings. Even if a trade creditor still wants an ongoing relationship with the debtor, it is eager to monetize its claim for prepetition goods and services. Similarly, small holders of long-term debts of a corporation may care primarily about regular payments to provide ongoing income. Claims trading allows the small, distant creditor an easy way out of the bankruptcy process. Undiversified small stakeholders can easily opt out of the bankruptcy process and receive fair value for their claims provided the market for claims is sufficiently liquid.[48]

[42] There is, for example, nothing comparable to the Williams Act. See Pub. L. No. 90-439, 82 Stat. 454 (1968) (codified as amended at 15 USC §§ 78m(d)–(e), 78n(d)–(f)) (requiring, among other things, disclosure of holding more than 5% of the equity of a publicly traded company).

[43] See Miller and Waisman (2004: 181) (noting that 'distressed debt trading has grown to proportions never contemplated at the time of the enactment of the Bankruptcy Reform Act'); Siegel (2003: 177):

> Perhaps nothing has changed the face of bankruptcy in the last decade as much as the newfound liquidity in claims.... Now, in almost every size case, there is an opportunity for creditors to exit the bankruptcy in exchange for a payment from a distressed debt trader...

See also Goldschmid (2005) (discussing the growing importance of the role that distressed debt investors play in Chapter 11).

[44] See Brav et al. (Chapter 8, this volume) (noting that hedge funds engage in new forms of active investment in corporations); Kahan and Rock (Chapter 5, this volume) (noting the recent emergence of hedge funds taking an active part in acquiring and managing corporations).

[45] For example, of the fifty-seven companies that were public at the time they filed for bankruptcy and confirmed reorganization plans in 2005, twenty-six were in bankruptcy for over a year, and one was in bankruptcy for almost seven years (see Mastroianni 2006: 46–7).

[46] 11 USC § 362(a) (2006). Over time, some exceptions have emerged, most notably for suppliers of goods within twenty days before the filing of the bankruptcy petition (§ 503(b)(9)).

[47] See, e.g., *In re Kmart Corp.*, 359 F.3d 866 (7th Cir. 2004) (disallowing immediate payment of 'critical vendors' in the absence of a showing that the payment benefited unsecured creditors as a group).

[48] As one of us has discussed elsewhere, whether the market for claims is in fact sufficiently liquid, however, is itself subject to doubt (see Baird 2009).

Claims trading flourishes because it is attractive to buyers as well as sellers.[49] Those with money to invest can make a profit. An investor with more knowledge about the likely outcome of the case and a longer time horizon can make a positive return. One way is by providing liquidity (Tung 1996: 1701). Investors can earn premiums from impatient creditors looking to turn their claims into cash. Creditors seeking liquidity are willing to forgo more in the future for a little less today.

Distressed debt players, however, rely on more than providing liquidity to justify their operations. The new investors may also profit from their ability to navigate the bankruptcy process (Tung 1996: 1702). They may be better able to assess how much the debtor will ultimately be able to pay on its claims. A hedge fund that examines a company in full is more likely to have a good sense of the entire value of the enterprise than is a trade creditor or small bondholder.[50] Moreover, the investor may be able to find overlooked value in the instruments that the debtor has issued. Either way, the new investor may be able to use its knowledge of the reorganization process to generate a higher return than could the party that owned the claim when the debtor filed for bankruptcy.[51]

In addition, in some instances the ability to buy claims allows strategic investors to gain control of the business. Here it might seem that claims trading plays the same role as a conventional takeover contest outside of bankruptcy, differing only in that the outsider buys debt rather than equity. Indeed, it is easy to identify bankruptcy cases where the fight for control was front and centre. The most notable example of buying claims to obtain control of a company in bankruptcy is the Kmart reorganization. ESL Investments, a well-heeled hedge fund, acquired control by buying up Kmart's debt (Harner 2008a: 725–7).[52] The reorganization plan gave ESL the right to appoint four directors. Edward Lampert, the head of ESL, appointed himself, two of his employees, and a major investor in ESL (Harner 2008a: 726).[53]

This market for corporate control, however, is different in a crucial respect from the one that exists outside of bankruptcy and comes with its own distinct risks. The Code's committee structure, by giving all large creditors a seat at the table, creates a situation where all parties battling for control of corporations in Chapter 11 are also given a large role in crafting the reorganization plan at the same time.

[49] For a discussion of the benefits of claims trading, see Tung (1996: 1701–3).

[50] See Baird and Bernstein (2006: 1949) (showing how large creditors acquire private information about the debtor).

[51] For example, just days after essentially buying Kmart out of Chapter 11 bankruptcy for nearly $1 billion, hedge fund ESL Investments sold some of Kmart's undervalued real estate assets for $900 million. ESL ultimately profited over $3 billion from selling off Kmart properties (see Bernstein 2008).

[52] Other recent examples of investors acquiring debt to exercise control include Loews Cineplex Entertainment Corp., Maidenform Brands, Inc., McLeodUSA Inc., National Equipment Services, Inc., New World Pasta Company, Rand McNally & Co., Regal Entertainment Group, and XO Communications, Inc. (see Harner (2008a: 707).

[53] See also *PR Newswire* (2003) (announcing the appointment of Lampert); Steven T. Mnuchin, <http://www.forbes.com/profile/steven-mnuchin/> (stating his position as Vice Chairman of ESL at the time); *Business Week* (2004) (describing Thomas Tisch as a member of the Tisch family, which was a large investor in ESL); William C. Crowley, <http://www.forbes.com/profile/william-crowley/> (describing his position as President and Chief Operating Officer of ESL).

The case of FiberMark illustrates some of the problems.[54] FiberMark was a specialty producer of paper products based in Vermont.[55] The company had been formed in 1989 by a management-led buyout of a division of Boise Cascade.[56] The capital structure of the company was relatively simple. It had a secured credit facility of $85 million.[57] Throughout the events surrounding FiberMark's financial distress, the company had more than sufficient assets to pay off the facility in full, and the secured lender, GE Capital, did not play a role in the fight that ultimately erupted.[58] Public bonds formed the bulk of the rest of FiberMark's financing. These bonds had a face amount of $346 million. The remaining unsecured debt was roughly $12 million.[59] In light of this capital structure, whoever controlled the bond debt would control the outcome of the case. It might seem that things should have gone smoothly, but they did not. The reorganization proceeding eventually became a brutal fight among three hedge funds that was only settled after the bankruptcy court intervened and appointed an examiner to investigate them.[60]

Two of the hedge funds, AIG Global Investment Corporation and Post Advisory Group, acquired FiberMark bonds before it filed for bankruptcy. At the time of the bankruptcy petition, AIG had about 19% of the outstanding notes, and Post held another 15% of the notes.[61] Neither was able to acquire any more notes during the case.[62] They thus had over a third of the outstanding notes at the time the case began (which meant that there would not be a consensual reorganization plan without their approval), and both were appointed to serve on the creditors' committee.[63] The indenture trustee for the notes and a trade creditor holding a $50,000 claim were also appointed to the committee.[64]

Because the other creditors were not actively involved, Post and especially AIG believed that they could control the committee, which would allow them to control FiberMark's reorganization.[65] Moreover, because their holdings were so large, their interests no longer corresponded with those of other claimholders. They were like a large controlling shareholder, while the other bondholders were more like minority shareholders. Outside bankruptcy, minority shareholders protect themselves through contract, and they may have some ability to enjoy the control premium.[66] By contrast, once in bankruptcy, a creditor holds only

[54] The fight in FiberMark is set out in detail in Report of Harvey R. Miller as Examiner, *In re FiberMark, Inc.*, 349 B.R. 385 (Bankr. D. Vt. 2006) (hereinafter *Miller Report*).

[55] *Miller Report*, 27. [56] *Miller Report*. [57] *Miller Report*.

[58] General Electric's secured claim was left unimpaired, and it stipulated to an adequate protection order early in the case. See Disclosure Statement With Respect to Amended Joint Plan of Reorganization Under Chapter 11, Title 11, United States Code of FiberMark, Inc., et al. as Debtors at 7–8, *In re FiberMark, Inc.*, No. 04-10463 (Bankr. D. Vt. 1 Nov. 2005).

[59] For a brief account of the history and prepetition debt structure of FiberMark, see *Miller Report, supra* note 54, at 27.

[60] See *In re FiberMark, Inc.*, 330 B.R. 480, 489–93 (Bankr. D. Vt. 2005).

[61] See *Miller Report, supra* note 54, at 2, 4. [62] *Miller Report*, 22. [63] *Miller Report*, 28.

[64] See *Miller Report*, 4. The trade creditor eventually sold its claim to Silver Point. As part of the sale, the trade creditor agreed to remain on the creditors' committee as an agent of Silver Point (*Miller Report*, 10, 21).

[65] *Miller Report*, 4.

[66] The extent to which minority shareholders must rely on contract varies by state. Compare *Nixon v. Blackwell*, 626 A.2d 1366, 1379–81 (Del. 1993) (*en banc*) (noting that minority investors must protect themselves through contract as the 'tools of good corporate practice are designed to give a purchasing minority stockholder the opportunity to bargain for protection before parting with consideration'), with *Brodie v. Jordan*, 857 N.E.2d 1076 (Mass. 2006) (noting that under Massachusetts law shareholders

a generic 'claim'. Any contractual protections that he/she obtained outside of bankruptcy disappear. The Bankruptcy Code homogenizes all claims, as it assumes that creditors at the same priority level share a common cause. Dissenting claimholders in a particular class have no ability to protect themselves through contract. As against the creditor holding a controlling position, they have the right only to insist that they be paid as much as they would receive in a liquidation.[67]

The representative of AIG dominated the creditors' committee. He took an active role in the case, worried about the amount of money being spent, and tried to direct the actions of the managers on the theory that the public debt holders were the residual claimants of the company.[68] At the beginning of the proceeding, he favoured a quick reorganization plan that basically wiped out the existing equity and converted the debt to equity.[69] Such a course of action would have left AIG as the largest shareholder and firmly in control of the business. He made it clear that he had no confidence in the CEO.[70]

AIG and Post were surprised to learn in the summer of 2004 that Silver Point, a fund noted for its expertise in investing in distressed companies, had begun acquiring large quantities of notes shortly before the case began and continued to do so while the case proceeded.[71] Silver Point was asked to join the creditors' committee, and, by the time it was appointed in October, it held 35% of the public notes.[72]

The drama of the case—one that lasted many months—consisted largely of the negotiations among the three hedge funds on a corporate governance agreement as to how the company was to be run after bankruptcy. Silver Point's arrival drastically altered the expectations of AIG and Post. Before they knew of Silver Point's investments in FiberMark, they believed that they would end up with de facto control of the reorganized company.[73] Silver Point's large stake and its intent to continue purchasing bonds made it clear that Silver Point would be the controlling shareholder of any reorganized company. Indeed, it appears that Silver Point eventually acquired more than 50% of the outstanding bonds, resulting in the three hedge funds holding well over 80% of the unsecured debt.[74] Once AIG and Post saw the changed landscape, they focused on minimizing the power that Silver Point would have as the controlling shareholder of the reorganized FiberMark.[75]

When Silver Point came into the picture, the prospects for a quick reorganization evaporated. Basically, the three hedge funds could never reach agreement among themselves as to what rights each would have in running the company post-reorganization. What had been a corporate reorganization transformed itself into an ugly takeover battle in which AIG and

of closely held corporations owe fiduciary duties to one another and the majority cannot frustrate the 'minority's reasonable expectations of benefit' from their ownership of shares). See generally Gilson and Gordon (2003) (exploring the limited ways in which legal doctrine constrains the actions of controlling shareholders).

[67] 11 USC § 1129(a)(7) (2006). [68] *Miller Report, supra* note 54, at 2–3.

[69] *Miller Report*, 98–9. [70] *Miller Report*, 69–70. [71] *Miller Report*, 4.

[72] *Miller Report*, 4–5. This ability to acquire such a significant stake in the company without attracting the attention of other major investors illustrates how opaque the claims trading market can be, even to those who participate in it on a regular basis.

[73] *Miller Report*, 302.

[74] *Miller Report*, 4 (stating that AIG and Post own 35% of debt); *Miller Report*, 8 (stating that Silver Point owns more than 50% of debt).

[75] *Miller Report*, 5–8.

Post, like entrenched board members, used their position on the creditors' committee to further their own interests rather than to advance the interests of the creditors[76] as a group.

In FiberMark, the parties reached agreement only after a blistering report issued by the court-appointed examiner.[77] To be sure, the parties involved took issue with many of the findings of the report,[78] but the highly public report did refocus the parties' negotiations. It resulted in an agreement under which Silver Point bought out the interests of the other hedge funds as well as the notes held by other investors (Brennan 2006). FiberMark illustrates the potential and perils of a world in which the liquidity of claims itself makes coalition building difficult. In addition, it underscores how one of the basic mechanisms of the Bankruptcy Code may no longer function effectively. Large creditors are active and pursue their own agendas (such as gaining control of the corporation), and they cannot be trusted to represent everyone's interests when serving on the committee. Moreover, because committee members receive confidential information which could prevent them from continued trading, some large players no longer even want to serve.[79] The days of a harmonious creditors' committee comfortably speaking on behalf of the interests of all creditors large and small have vanished.

11.3 The Transformation of Secured Debt

11.3.1 The Decline of the Traditional Bank

Twenty-five years ago the large bank was one of a handful of players on the scene (Huebner and Tisdell 2008: 78). The bank would make a large loan to the company and would have a security interest in most, if not all, of the company's assets. The financial interest of the bank, as a fully secured creditor, was relatively straightforward (Baird and Jackson 1984: 106–7). If it could realize the value of its collateral, it would be paid in full. As such, the lender had an incentive to turn its collateral into cash via some form of sale. Left to its own devices, the senior lender would sell the discrete asset in which it had a security interest, and this would lead to the closure of the business. The lender was biased toward liquidation (Adams 1993: 599; Westbrook 2004: 844–5). Because it did not share in the upside should the debtor's fortunes improve, it did not take such possibilities into account. Rather, if the lender could force a liquidation immediately, it could be paid in full. It saw no need to risk continuation that could only reduce its return. Even if the company was to be sold, the bank could not be

[76] See Lattman (2005) (calling FiberMark 'a controversial, "ugly" Chapter 11 proceeding' and summarizing much of the *Miller Report*), available at <http://www.forbes.com/forbes/2005/1031/060.html>.

[77] Lattman (2005). [78] See Lattman (2005: 62).

[79] Sometimes a hedge fund will be allowed to participate on the committee and be allowed to trade provided it erects a 'Chinese Wall' that blocks information acquired while sitting on the committee from being used. In practice, however, these walls have proved porous (see Sullivan 2008: 557) (noting that 'trading walls are not a panacea and there are certain harms they cannot prevent'). Such a screening wall was used in the FiberMark bankruptcy. Silver Point agreed to join the committee only on the condition that it be allowed to continue trading in debtors' notes, so the court entered an order establishing the wall. See *Miller Report, supra* note 54, at 5.

trusted if it was owed less than the company was worth. In this situation, the bank may not have sought top dollar. It would only look for a sale that would pay it in full. Given these incentives, the bank should not have had its hand on the levers of control.[80]

Changes in bank lending practice render this account obsolete. Central to the new dynamic is the rise of the syndicated loan.[81] Single banks no longer make loans to large businesses. Given the amount of these loans, any bank that funded the loan itself would be tying up a hefty portion of its capital with a single borrower. To take a simple example, assume that we have ten banks and ten borrowers. Each borrower wants to borrow $200 million, and there is a 10% chance that any given borrower will default during the term of the loan. In a world where loans were funded by a single bank, any bank loaning $200 million would have a 10% risk that a large portion of its capital would end up in default.

Syndication allows the banks to reduce this risk. By parcelling out each loan among a consortium of banks, each bank can lessen its default risk. In our example, if each bank signed up to fund 10% of each borrower, each would have mitigated its risk. To be sure, by participating in more loans it is more likely that some debtor in each bank's portfolio will default. Each bank expects to have to deal with a default on a $20 million commitment. It is much easier, however, for each bank to handle a $20 million default rather than a $200 million default. In exchange for taking on a greater risk that it will have to deal with some default, each bank has greatly reduced the risk that it will have a default that would threaten the viability of the bank.

For each loan, one of the banks takes the lead role.[82] It is charged with monitoring the debtor and overseeing the interests of the creditors as a group. Befitting the lead bank's status as the leader of the syndicate, the expectation developed that the lead bank would hold a portion of the loan that was larger than any other member.[83] By holding a share that was disproportionate to that of the other members of the syndicate, the lead bank would take a bigger economic hit should it fail to maximize the value of the loan (Simons 1993: 47–8). Making such a commitment made the loan easier to sell to other lenders.[84]

The lending agreement contained various covenants.[85] The documents provided the lender with access to information generally unavailable to other investors (Sufi 2007: 632–3). The lead bank could use this information to monitor the borrower. If the borrower tripped up a covenant, it would have to procure a waiver (Baird and Rasmussen 2006: 1211–12). The contract governing the syndicate did not grant the lead bank the unilateral right to grant a

[80] See Jackson (1986: 181–9) (asserting that secured creditors should receive the value of their rights, but the decision as to the fate of the corporation should be left to the general creditors).

[81] Syndicated loans grew from $137 billion in 1987 to more than $1 trillion dollars in 1997. See Dennis and Mullineaux (2000: 407). For a general discussion of syndicated lending, see Fight (2004) and Mugasha (2007).

[82] For a discussion of loan syndication and typical structures, see Simons (1993).

[83] See Sufi (2007: 633) ('[T]he lead arranger typically holds a larger share of the loan than any of the participants').

[84] See Sufi (2007: 663–5) (concluding that lead arrangers retain a larger portion of the loan when information asymmetry concerns are greatest, such as when the borrower is opaque). A number of factors, including the legal rights available to creditors in a particular jurisdiction, affect the composition of the lending syndicate. See Esty and Megginson (2003) (suggesting a relation between syndicate structure and legal risk).

[85] For a discussion of how loan covenants empower banks, see Baird and Rasmussen (2006: 1227–36).

waiver; rather, the waiver had to be approved by a requisite majority of the syndicate members (Sufi 2007: 633). For the most part, however, syndicate members would follow the recommendation of the lead bank as they had less knowledge about the borrower, but the same economic interests and instincts as the lead bank.[86]

Syndication is a long-standing practice that underwent enormous growth in the 1990s (Dennis and Mullineaux 2000: 407–10). Initially, it had little effect on bankruptcy practice. Many syndicate members were banks, and while at some level they were competitors, they were also repeat players. Any bank that reached an agreement with a borrower to fund a new loan would have to shop the loan to its brethren.[87] Other frequent participants in these syndicates were pension funds looking for a safe return on their assets who were more than content to follow the recommendation of the lead bank.[88]

The composition of lending syndicates, however, has changed recently. Membership is no longer limited to banks and pension funds. Hedge funds can participate in the syndication stage.[89] Moreover, there is a rapidly developing secondary market in syndicated loans.[90] The advantage of this market to those lenders participating in the syndicate is readily apparent. Unless restricted by the terms of the credit agreement, a member of the syndicate has an exit option. It can sell its portion of the loan to a willing buyer.[91] Trading of these loans has increased dramatically in recent times.[92] Thus, when a borrower trips up covenants in its loan or files for bankruptcy, it will not necessarily have to come to an understanding with the bank that has funded its senior debt. Today, hedge funds can purchase enough of a tranche in the secondary market so that they have the power to block any waiver of default, proposed amendment to the credit facility, or plan of reorganization that does not meet with their approval.[93]

Unlike the staid bank of an earlier era, a hedge fund that holds a position identical to the one held by a bank in an earlier time may view bad states of the world in a radically different

[86] See Sufi (2007: 633):'[T]he lead arranger typically also acts as the 'agent' bank that monitors the firm, governs the terms of the loan, administers the drawdown of funds, calculates interest payments, and enforces financial covenants.'

[87] See Simons (1993: 49): '[T]he lead banks' concern with maintaining their reputations in the marketplace may lead them not only to avoid abuses but to promote risky loans even less aggressively than safe loans.'

[88] See Mugasha (2004: 199) (noting that regular participants in the secondary loan market include banks and other financial institutions such as insurance companies, pension funds, and mutual funds).

[89] See Bobrow, Tech, and Redding (2006: 168) ('Hedge funds represented 29 percent of the primary market for institutional loans with spreads of LIBOR + 400 basis points or higher in 2005').

[90] See Coffey et al. (2006: 393, 415–16) (noting that from 2000 to 2005 hedge fund trading in the syndicated loan market has risen from 10% of JP Morgan's trading volume to nearly 30% of the total trading volume).

[91] See Güner (2006: 687, 689–90) (explaining why borrowers may dislike loan sales and suggesting that borrowers receive lower interest rates when they allow banks to sell participations in the loans); Lee and Mullineaux (2004: 118) (indicating consent on reselling the loan is required in fewer than half of the syndications). The options provided to banks by the secondary loan market are in many ways similar to the options that claims trading in bankruptcy provides to the holders of claims.

[92] See Mugasha (2004: 201) ('Secondary loan trading has increased tenfold in the last five years').

[93] See, e.g., Keehner (2009) (noting that private equity firms that held equity in Harrah's bought debt to gain control over the potential bankruptcy should Harrah's fail).

way.[94] It might seem that it would make no difference whether a hedge fund or a bank was the lender. Both ought to be interested in maximizing the value of their investments and hence it would seem that both would, in expectation, pursue the same path, especially when a business finds itself in economic distress, however, this may not be so. Banks and hedge funds, though owning the same instrument, often have drastically different business models. Banks are repeat players. A bank can have a relationship with a business that lasts for decades. The bank provides a large suite of services beyond simply making the loan. In addition, commercial norms and its reputation constrain its conduct in any particular relationship. While it might, for example, have the legal right to call a loan in default, commercial norms and its concern about its reputation with other borrowers may lead it to waive the covenant. A hedge fund, by contrast, has a limited life, provides no services, and acts under no reputational constraints.

In addition, those who work for banks and those who work for hedge funds bring different skill sets. Those who work for banks excel at monitoring the debtor and ensuring their collateral is safe.[95] Hedge funds hire entrepreneurs with industry expertise who have the skills needed to take a much more active role in the affairs of the company. When a loan covenant is violated, a bank might insist on additional collateral, while a hedge fund might insist on a new CEO. Finally, there are regulatory differences. A hedge fund can buy into a troubled debtor with a view to holding equity in the business for a number of years in the event it is reorganized. By contrast, a bank is limited in its ability to hold stock.[96]

Banks make their profit by lending money and having it paid back.[97] They do not seek to own and operate the business. Not so with hedge funds. A hedge fund may buy the loan with the view that in the event of default it would be left with the business, and given the amount at which it purchased the notes, it would not be a bad price at which to acquire it even if it were in financial distress. Banks want their money back; hedge funds loan to own.[98] The same dynamic that plays out with respect to publicly traded unsecured debt now plays out with respect to traditional bank debt as well.[99]

The increasing role of hedge funds in owning the secured debt of distressed companies calls into question the long-standing assumption that senior investors are biased towards

[94] See Circuit City Unplugged: Why Did Chapter 11 Fail To Save 34,000 Jobs?: Hearing Before the Subcomm. on Commercial and Administrative Law of the H. Comm. on the Judiciary, 111th Cong. 10–24 (2009) [hereinafter *Miller Testimony*] (statement of Harvey R. Miller, Senior Partner, Weil, Gotshal & Manges LLP) (observing, in the context of retailer bankruptcies, that financial institutions and members of lender syndicates have adopted a more distant and shorter-term relationship with debtors).

[95] For a discussion of the kind of monitoring in which banks engage, see James (1987) and Tung (2009).

[96] See 12 USC § 1843(a), (c)(2) (2006) (allowing banks to hold equity that has been converted from debt, but presumptively limiting the holding period to two years). For a discussion of the limits on banks to invest in, deal, and underwrite securities, see Carnell, Macey, and Miller (2009: 130–4).

[97] See Sarasvathy, Simon, and Lave (1998) (noting that bankers begin by identifying the return they seek and then focus on minimizing risks).

[98] Of course, one should not exaggerate these differences. Since the repeal of the Glass-Steagall Act, the differences between banks and hedge funds have diminished, but the process has been one in which banks have become more like hedge funds rather than the other way around. The effect is to magnify the changes that hedge funds have brought to the scene.

[99] Hedge funds look for the fulcrum security—the one that gives it control of the reorganization. They are equally content with owning secured and unsecured debt.

liquidation.[100] Far from having a liquidation bias, a hedge fund may affirmatively want to advance a reorganization plan in which it ends up with the equity of the business. Rather than push for a market sale, it prefers a judicial process it can control. Not only can it push for a low valuation, but the managers of the business (individuals whose options will be reset upon emergence from Chapter 11) will push for a low valuation as well.[101]

In short, the senior lender in the identical place within the capital structure is doing exactly the opposite of its traditional counterpart. Instead of fleeing from the Chapter 11 process, it embraces it. Rather than terminating its relationship with the business, the hedge fund wants to run it. Rather than fighting the managers, it takes control, both through conditions imposed on debtor-in-possession (DIP) financing and by installing new officers, most typically a chief restructuring officer (CRO).[102]

11.3.2 The Second Lien Loan

The first layer of secured debt often does not exhaust the borrowing capacity of the business. Borrowers in need of additional funds borrow from lenders who will take a junior position (in return for a higher interest rate). In years past, the debtor would access this additional value through mezzanine financing on an unsecured basis (Silbernagel and Vaitkunas 2006: 6–7). In the 1980s, this financing was provided by savings and loan associations and insurance companies (Silbernagel and Vaitkunas 2006: 6). These were relatively passive investors who had little ability to affect the operation of the company. To the extent that any investor was monitoring the debtor, it was the lead bank in the lending syndicate.

Today, however, we see a new trend in the capital markets. The debtor accesses the difference between the senior loan and full enterprise value through a second lien loan.[103] The lenders take a security interest in the same assets as does the first lender. Their right to payment, by and large, is not subordinated to the senior debt. Maturity schedules are set so that the borrower is required to make payments on both loans. The second lien lenders can seek to be repaid at the same time as the senior lender is being repaid. Moreover, unlike subordinated debt, they do not have to pay any monies that they collect to the senior debt. Rather, they are second only in terms of their claim on the collateral package. Only when collateral is sold for cash does the senior lender have first dibs.[104] The second lien market has exploded

[100] See, e.g., Baird and Jackson (1984: 106–8) (discussing the bias of secured creditors towards liquidation and the bias of junior parties for delay).

[101] In Section 11.4 of this chapter we take account of the rise of credit default swaps. These new investment vehicles can provide another reason for a party holding a part of a syndicated loan to favour a formal default rather than a workout.

[102] See *Miller Testimony, supra* note 94, at 14:

> The chapter 11 process, as contemplated in 1978, has been overwhelmed by marginalization of the debtor in possession, expansion of creditor (particularly secured creditor) control, the increasing imposition of creditor-designated chief restructuring officers (CROs), claims trading, more complex debt and organizational structures, and short-term profit motivation.

[103] See Hanrahan and Teh (2007: 109) (noting that second lien loan financings are now a widely used financing tool, often selected by borrowers in lieu of unsecured high-yield debt or traditional unsecured mezzanine financing).

[104] See Hanrahan and Teh (2007).

over the last several years.[105] As with syndicated first lien loans, there is a robust secondary market for second lien loans.[106] Hedge funds are primary purchasers of second lien debt (Harner 2008a: 715 n.45).[107]

The second loan benefits the first lender in that it puts more money into the business. This money can be used to generate additional revenues, some of which will be used to make payments to the senior lender. Yet the senior lender needs some assurances that the new lender—which, as with the senior loan, is usually a group of lenders—will not cause it undue hardship.[108] Granting a lien has consequences, both outside of bankruptcy and inside of bankruptcy. A second lien holder, by virtue of its lien, can grab its collateral.[109] After a bankruptcy petition has been filed, it can object to the use of its collateral and seek adequate protection of its interest.

The first and second lien holders sort out their respective rights in an intercreditor agreement.[110] This agreement specifies the relationship between the two lenders (Berman and Brighton 2009).[111] It addresses in detail their respective rights should the borrower file for bankruptcy. For example, the intercreditor agreement often grants the senior lender the right to sell the collateral without the consent of the second lien lender.[112] The intercreditor agreement also typically gives the senior lender the right to finance the debtor post-petition and provides that this financing will have priority over the loan of the second lien lender (Dobbs 2006: 211–25).

The effect of second liens has yet to be felt. The hedge funds that own the second lien debt after a bankruptcy proceeding is filed are not shy about testing the limits of the intercreditor agreement. Indeed, the enforceability of the intercreditor agreement, to the extent that the second lien holder agrees to waive statutory protections granted by the bankruptcy, is far from settled.[113] Litigation over the validity of the agreement, especially when the company is

[105] In 2003, second lien issuance in the North American market totalled just under $8 billion, but the amount was over $29 billion in 2006. See Chamblee (2008: 1) (citing statistics from the Loan Pricing Corporation). Although the market continued to grow, reaching $15.21 billion in the second quarter of 2007 alone, the credit crunch that hit the financial markets dropped the total back to $4.56 billion for the fourth quarter of 2007 (Chamblee 2008).

[106] See Hanrahan and Teh (2007: 110 n.3) (noting that collateralized debt obligation and collateralized loan obligation funds have started incorporating second lien loans into their portfolios since 2003).

[107] See also Futter and Wells (2007: 221) (noting that hedge funds 'have virtually created new financial markets, including the so-called second lien market').

[108] See Hanrahan and Teh (2007: 112) ('The concern [of first lien lenders] in times past has been that the existence of other secured creditors and their rights in collateral could result in complications for first lien lenders in the event of a workout or bankruptcy.').

[109] See UCC § 9-609 (2000).

[110] See Chamblee (2008) (discussing typical clauses in intercreditor agreements).

[111] See Dobbs (2006) (summarizing the significant issues faced in intercreditor agreements); see also Chamblee (2008) (discussing common provisions of the ABA Model Intercreditor Agreement); Singer (2008) (discussing common provisions of intercreditor agreements and issues that may arise should the debtor file for bankruptcy).

[112] See Berman and Brighton (2009: 64–5) (noting that it is common for second lien lenders to agree to this provision); Chamblee (2008: 18) (indicating that the ABA Model Intercreditor Agreement permits sales by the senior lender under § 363 of the Bankruptcy Code without consent of the second lien lender as long as the interest of the second lien lender attaches to the proceeds); see also Dobbs (2006: 218–19) (observing that the parties will negotiate over whether the intercreditor agreement will contain a clause prohibiting the second lien holder from objecting to a § 363 sale).

[113] First lien holders agreed to concessions to avoid litigation over intercreditor agreements in *In re Calpine*, No. 05-60200 (Bankr. SDNY 20 Dec. 2005), which was discussed in *Reuters* (2008), which

attempting to put its bankruptcy financing in place, could threaten to derail the reorganization effort at an early juncture.[114] The Code has proven sufficiently flexible (and the judges and the lawyers sufficiently creative) to overcome the problems that have arisen so far. For example, as a result of the increase in secured debt, many cases now enter bankruptcy administratively insolvent.[115]

After the secured creditors are paid, there are no funds to pay for the costs of the reorganization. But a practice has emerged in which the secured creditor agrees to 'carve out' a part of its lien to fund the costs of running the proceeding.[116] Now widely accepted, the debate is only over the extent of the carve-out. But doubt exists about other features of these new capital structures, especially the enforceability of provisions of the intercreditor agreement that tie the second lien holders' hands during the bankruptcy process.[117]

If parties find it in their interest to have a hierarchical capital structure with multiple tiers of secured debt, there seems to be no bankruptcy policy that justifies second-guessing them. To be sure, it does require a shifting of the way bankruptcy is paid for. If the second lien position is the fulcrum security—the security which is in the money, but not being paid in full—then the reorganization is being run for the second lien lenders' benefit and they should pay for it. The modern bankruptcy judge sees him/herself as charged with creating a forum in which the stakeholders, whoever they may be, come together and negotiate. As long as an agreement adequately deals with the substantive and procedural rights of all involved, it is not for her to question its details any more than it is for the New York Stock Exchange to review the price at which a given stock trades. She is indifferent to whether the agreement provides for an auction of the assets (as increasingly became the case over the past decade) or sets out a traditional plan of reorganization, spelling out in elaborate detail the capital structure of the reorganized firm (which has become increasingly rare, although

noted what second lien holders extract in exchange for giving up whatever rights they have under an intercreditor agreement. See *In re Dura Auto. Sys.*, No. 06-11202 (Bankr. D. Del. 30 Oct. 2006); Bracewell and Guiliani (2007):

> Disputes under intercreditor agreements can be postponed (and avoided) through consensual resolutions, as occurred in the *Dura Automotive* case where the parties agreed to provide the second lien lenders (represented by Bracewell) with adequate protection treatment in the form of current cash payment of interest during the bankruptcy case, which the intercreditor agreement, if enforceable, did not permit.

Conflicts between first and second lien holders loomed large as well in *In re Meridian Automotive Sys.*, Inc., No. 65-11168 (Bankr. D. Del. 23 Apr. 2005). See *Aftermarket News* (2006). Similar problems arose in *In re New World Pasta*, No. 04-02817 (M.D. Pa. filed 10 May 2004), and *In re ACR Management LLC*, No. 04-27848 (W.D. Pa. filed 14 June 2004). See Berman and Brighton (2006a).

[114] For example, in *In re American Remanufacturers*, No. 05-20022 (Bankr. D. Del. 7 Nov. 2005), the second lien holders objected to the debtor-in-possession financing package offered by the first lien holders. The bankruptcy court preliminarily agreed with the objections, the first lien holders eventually withdrew their financing offer, and the case converted to a Chapter 7 liquidation (see Berman and Brighton 2006b: 24–5, 57).

[115] Under the Code, secured creditors receive the value of their collateral first. After that, the administrative costs of bankruptcy are paid. See *supra* note 14 and accompanying text. A case is said to be 'administratively insolvent' when there are insufficient funds to pay off the administrative expenses.

[116] For an excellent discussion of the issues surrounding carve-outs, see Levin (2002).

[117] For example, a provision that takes away from the second lien holder its right to vote on the plan of reorganization is suspect. See Dobbs (2006: 221 n.64) (setting out the differing views of courts on whether junior creditors can give up voting rights in bankruptcy).

it could return in today's environment).[118] What matters is that the process is cost-effective and protects the rights of all the stakeholders.

11.3.3 The Rise of Control

Senior creditors over the last two decades have learned how to gain more control over their debtors outside of bankruptcy.[119] The security interest covers more assets and the lead lender controls all the cash that passes through the business. Moreover, secured creditors have learned, largely through terms contained in DIP financing, how to gain control over the debtor during the bankruptcy itself.[120] The increase in control rights, combined with the hetereogeneity in the most senior tranche, increases the risk that creditors pursuing their own individual agendas will not advance the interests of creditors as a group.

When the senior creditor is the DIP lender, many of the restraints on individual creditors, such as the automatic stay, loosen considerably. Typically, if there is a default under the DIP loan (which can include such things as a failure to meet income projections or maintain sufficient cash reserves), the DIP lender can pursue its rights notwithstanding the automatic stay.[121] This creates few problems when the DIP facility is in the hands of a single lead bank. Banks, however, are no longer the sole source of DIP financing as hedge funds have entered into this market (*Westlaw Business Currents* 2009). The formerly predictable situation becomes significantly more complicated when those providing the DIP financing are a group of competing hedge funds, each pursuing its own agenda.[122] In theory, an agreement

[118] Unsecured creditors and equity holders can take little solace in the rise of hedge fund activism in bankruptcy. While these funds may not have the liquidation bias normally associated with the senior bank, they are not charitable institutions. They seek to control the fulcrum security, and ensure that all of those who hold investments with a lower priority receive no interest in the reorganized company.

[119] See Kuney (2004: 24–5):

> [S]ecured creditors capitalizing upon agency problems to gain the help of insiders and insolvency professionals [have] effectively take[n] over—or "hijack[ed]"—the chapter 11 process and essentially create[d] a federal unified foreclosure process;

Lubben (2004–2005: 841–2) ('[I]t is not clear that this development promotes social welfare. Rather, lender control may only benefit lenders.'); Miller and Waisman (2003: 2) ('The exercise... of remedial rights given secured creditors upon the occurrence of default, in effect, puts those creditors in control of the debtor/borrower.'); Westbrook (2004: 799) ('[W]idespread adoption of a privatized system depending upon dominant security interests is as undesirable as it is unlikely').

[120] See *Miller Testimony, supra* note 94, at 11–12 (detailing commonly approved provisions in DIP financing orders, including:

> requiring the debtor in possession to hire a CRO... [c]ash-flow covenants that... can compel the sale of assets or downsizing[,]... [p]rovisions giving the lender control over disposition of the debtor's assets[,]... negative covenants that constrain management flexibility[, and]... [p]rovisions that subject the debtor's plan of reorganization to some form of lender control.

[121] See Cousins (2002: 793):

> Regardless of whether the DIP lender is also the prepetition lender, DIP orders often vacate the automatic stay upon the declaration of an event of default and after the expiration of a short period of time...

[122] We see exactly this problem in the Lyondell reorganization, where various hedge funds such as Silver Point and Appaloosa competed vigorously to gain shares of the DIP loan (see Kary 2009).

can be put in place that ensures that, at least with respect to the terms of the DIP loan, the disparate lenders act as one. But whether they can craft such agreements remains to be seen.

11.4 Financial Innovation

The changes described above drastically alter the bankruptcy landscape. They are changes, however, that standing alone, the bankruptcy system could well assimilate. Indeed, we see many parts of the company's capital structure crafted with a potential bankruptcy in mind. Intercreditor agreements, for example, focus explicitly on the relative rights two classes of creditors will have in bankruptcy.[123] All things being equal, one would expect that today's capital structures would aid the resolution of financial distress. Yet not all things are equal.

The Bankruptcy Code itself provides for secured claims, unsecured claims, interests, and pretty much nothing else.[124] Shareholders own shares; creditors have debt, with banks holding secured debt. When we think back to when the Code was drafted in the 1970s, these were the basic investments in a company. One could of course find some additional securities, but they were pretty much the exception. Put differently, the roots of the Bankruptcy Code predate Black–Scholes.[125]

In this world, it was relatively simple to ascertain the incentives of any investor. All wanted to maximize the return on their investment, but the nature of their investment dictated their optimal strategy. Secured creditors wanted safety; they were in the money and saw no need to take gambles. Equity holders, in contrast, wanted to swing for the fences. Only a dramatic turnaround would allow them to see a return on their investments. Unsecured creditors, by and large, tended to favour value-increasing changes. While no party had incentives aligned with the fortunes of the business as a whole, all were confident that they could identify the motives attending to each investor.

In this world, many companies could restructure their operations outside of a formal Chapter 11 proceeding. Chapter 11 provided the benchmark against which negotiations took place. Indeed, in recent years, even when Chapter 11 was used, it was part of a process where the company would file either to implement a restructuring already agreed upon or to sell off the company (Baird and Rasmussen 2002: 751–2). Fewer and fewer companies entered bankruptcy in a free-fall state. Bankruptcy was not a discontinuous event, but rather a tool in an arsenal of those deciding the fate of the business.

[123] See, e.g., Dobbs (2006: 202) (setting out the 'remedy block' first lienholders seek and limits second lienholders try to place on them).

[124] See 11 USC § 501(a) (allowing equity security holders to file an interest); § 506 (2006) (distinguishing between secured claims and unsecured claims); see also § 1129(b) (defining the cram down procedure for secured claims, unsecured claims, and interests). In recent years, the Bankruptcy Code has been amended so that many varieties of swap and derivative transactions entered into by the debtor are excepted from bankruptcy altogether. See, e.g., §§ 362(b)(27), 555, 556.

[125] See Black and Scholes (1973: 649–53) (deriving a valuation formula for options and applying it to corporate liabilities); Merton (1973: 141–2) (extending the Black-Scholes theory of option pricing). For an accessible discussion of how financial innovation alters our perception of capital structures, see Warren (1993: 465–70).

Events of the last few years, however, have altered the terrain. Addressing financial distress before the filing for bankruptcy has become much more difficult, as has making decisions once the company has filed for Chapter 11.

11.4.1 Derivatives

Ascertaining economic interests is crucial to assessing bankruptcy policy. Investments come with both cash flow rights and control rights.[126] Shareholders can vote for the board of directors (Easterbrook and Fischel 1991: 63–7). Credit agreements often give lenders the ability to affect the business in various ways. In the extreme case, the rights that a senior creditor has by virtue of its lending agreement give it the power to engineer a change in the corner office.[127] As a general matter, cash flow rights and control rights work in tandem. It is the investor's cash flow rights that give it the incentive to exercise its control rights in a certain manner.[128] We normally assume that an investor exercising a control right granted by a financial instrument is acting so as to maximize the value of that instrument.

Credit default swaps have rendered this assumption obsolete. A credit default swap is a two-party contract under which one party (the protection seller) acquires the credit risk of a loan from a counterparty (the protection buyer) in exchange for a fee (Lubben 2007: 405 n.2). If there is a default or some other 'credit event' (such as bankruptcy) on the loan, the protection buyer receives cash equal to the face value of the loan.[129] For example, a holder of a GM bond may enter into a credit default swap that provides that, if GM defaults on the bond, the holder can give the bond to its counterparty in exchange for the face amount of the bond. In essence, the parties have 'swapped' the risk of default. The extent of this market is quite large. There is no requirement that one actually own the underlying credit instrument in order to purchase a credit default swap. Indeed, the nominal value of credit default swaps is nearly $39 trillion, far greater than the amount of debt outstanding.[130]

Credit default swaps are in the first instance merely another way for a lender to reduce its risk exposure, just as lenders do with the syndication process. Just as a bank faces less risk when it only has a piece of a $200 million loan than when it funds the entire loan itself, a

[126] See Baird and Rasmussen (2006: 1217) ('The line between debt and equity is an entirely permeable one, in terms of both cash flow rights and control rights.').

[127] See Baird and Rasmussen (2006: 1209) ('When a business stumbles, creditors typically enjoy powers that public shareholders never have, such as the ability to replace the managers and install those more to their liking').

[128] See, e.g., Easterbrook and Fischel (1991: 68) ('As residual claimants, shareholders have the appropriate incentives... to make discretionary decisions').

[129] See Easterbrook and Fischel (1991: 411 (listing bankruptcy, failure to pay, and restructuring as typical credit events)). For more information on credit derivatives, see generally Partnoy and Skeel (2007), explaining the basics of credit derivatives and the ways in which they can be used.

[130] See Tett and Davies (2007) ('[T]he CDS market is now 10 times larger than the tangible cash bonds on which they [sic] are supposed to be based.'); International Swaps and Derivatives Association (2008):

> The notional amount outstanding of credit default swaps (CDS) was $38.6 trillion at year-end, down 29 percent from $54.6 trillion at mid-year 2008. CDS notional outstanding for the whole of 2008 was down 38 percent from $62.2 trillion at year-end 2007.

bank that buys a credit default swap reduces its exposure.[131] Indeed, the advocates for credit default swaps once argued that they promise to bring stability to the banking system.[132]

Banks by and large remain the originators of large loans.[133] Private institutions such as hedge funds simply do not (at least yet) have the back office operations necessary to service a large loan and often rely on prime brokers and investment banks to provide support services.[134] Credit default swaps allow the banks to offload some of the risk of default outside the banking system. Removing risk from the banking system should bolster the banks' position should the economy hit a downturn, or at least so the story went.[135]

Financing that leads to investment in the business occurs as part of a negotiating dynamic in which it was in the self-interest of everyone to take account of the interests of the company itself. By contrast, credit default swaps are created without the input of the borrowing company.[136] Some are even created by investors with no current interest in the company at all. They are often side bets in which parties care only about 'credit events', events that trigger settlement obligations under the swap. For example, the seller of a credit default swap will fight vigorously to prevent a bankruptcy filing from taking place (at least until the expiration of the swap) and the buyer will affirmatively encourage it, regardless of whether filing makes any sense for the company. This failure to attend to the interaction between these new investments and the bankruptcy process threatens to put unprecedented strain on the current system of addressing financial distress.

Buying a credit default swap differs from syndication in terms of control rights. When a lead bank sells part of the loan, it bundles with that loan any applicable control rights. Any waiver of an event of default needs to be agreed to by the syndicate. The agent may be able to cajole syndicate members to follow its recommendation, but it is still the case that those who own the loan have to make the decision. If a hedge fund sells its piece of the loan in the secondary market, it loses its ability to have an input on any decisions that the syndicate has to make. The economic exposure and the attendant control rights remain bundled, even if the package changes hands multiple times.

When a lender purchases a credit default swap, however, it retains the control rights that accompany the loan. The protection seller now bears the economic risks of the loan, but rights under the credit agreement remain lodged in the protection buyer. If a waiver of an event of default is needed, the holder of the loan is free to vote as it sees fit. But now its

[131] See Partnoy and Skeel (2007: 1023) (noting that credit default swaps give banks a method of shedding risk without the costs of negotiating the syndications and working with other banks and without sharing the benefits of the loan).

[132] See Partnoy and Skeel (2007:1024) (describing the view of Alan Greenspan and others that credit default swaps serve as a 'shock absorber' and provide systemic benefits).

[133] See Sufi (2007: 640) (showing that the largest lead syndicators are all banks).

[134] For a discussion of the industry that services hedge funds, see Bills (2006) (discussing JP Morgan's strategy for competing in the business of servicing hedge funds).

[135] Indeed, the proponents of credit default swaps have touted their ability to reduce the risk to the banking system. See *supra* note 132. But see Partnoy and Skeel (2007: 1040) (noting that credit default swaps also raise systemic concerns because a 'rush to unwind a vast array of interconnected contracts could create serious liquidity problems in the financial markets'). Credit default swaps have in fact been blamed for the current financial meltdown (see, e.g., Philips 2008).

[136] See Lubben (2007: 411) ('The debtor on the referenced obligation is not a party to the swap, and in most cases is unaware of the transaction').

economic interest has changed. In the extreme case, if the lender has purchased more in credit default swaps than it has at risk in terms of the loan itself, it may be the case that it will be to its financial advantage if the loan goes into default.[137] In the extreme, those who bought credit protection on loans they did not hold may subsequently buy loans in the secondary market for the sole purpose of preventing a workout and forcing a default.[138] While such a default and subsequent bankruptcy case may provide a lower return on its debt instrument than it would have received had the debtor procured a waiver, it may more than make up for this by collecting on its credit default swap contract. Blowing up the company may generate a higher return for these investors than saving it.

Such a shift in incentives is almost impossible for others in the process to observe. There is no public record of who has purchased a credit default swap. In the bankruptcy proceeding, all holders of claims and interests have to file their claims and interests with the bankruptcy court.[139] While it sometimes becomes unclear exactly who owns what, there is some information as to who holds the debtor's financial instruments. But since credit default swaps are private transactions to which the debtor is not a party, there is no way to know what the true financial incentives of anyone are.[140] A hedge fund that holds a large loan position that it has acquired in the secondary market may in fact be net short.

Credit default swaps shift the focus of negotiations outside of bankruptcy in a fundamental way. Ideally, the parties to the negotiation want to maximize the value of the business, and then fight over each party's relative share. Chapter 11 is often used as part of the process to implement what the parties have decided is a value-maximizing course of action. Credit default swaps alter this dynamic. The holders of the swaps, who may have a seat at the table by virtue of holding the underlying asset, may care more about whether any course of action is a 'credit event' than whether it increases the value of the company.[141]

Prior to credit default swaps, the filing of a bankruptcy petition was the midpoint in the process of resolving the company's financial distress. It was a step along a continuous path. Negotiations would start before bankruptcy, the outlines of a plan would be developed, a petition would be filed, and the plan would be implemented. Now, however, the stakes have changed. Credit default swaps make bankruptcy discontinuous. It is an event that fundamentally alters the payouts and identities of the investors. The day after a petition is filed, the old creditors may disappear and be replaced by those who now hold the debt in the company.

[137] See Hu and Black (2006) (describing how debt holders, like equity holders, may have negative economic ownership through derivative ownership that results in an incentive to act against the interest of other creditors).

[138] See Partnoy and Skeel (2007: 1034–5) (describing an analogous situation in the Tower Automotive bankruptcy where it was believed that hedge funds blocked a restructuring plan because a default would benefit their short positions in Tower stock).

[139] See 11 USC § 501 (2006); FED. R. BANKR. P. 3001–5.

[140] In light of the recent financial crisis, Treasury Secretary Timothy Geithner proposed regulating the trading of derivatives, which includes credit default swaps. See Letter from Timothy F. Geithner, Secretary of the Treasury, to Harry Reid, Senate Majority Leader (13 May 2009). This proposal, while addressing some problems with the extant market, would not require the public disclosure of the owners of credit default swaps.

[141] See Lubben (2007: 427) (indicating that creditors holding credit default swaps may try to 'jump the gun' by filing an involuntary petition to trigger default).

While the effects of the current economic downturn have just begun to play out in the bankruptcy process, we already can point to examples where credit default swaps have taken centre stage. Lyondell, a transnational corporation with assets in both the United States and the Netherlands, put its American operations into Chapter 11.[142] The operations in the Netherlands, however, remained outside of any insolvency proceeding (*Reuters India* 2009). This situation sparked a fight over whether the American bankruptcy court would enjoin the holders of bonds issued by the Dutch entity from seeking recovery on those bonds (*Reuters India* 2009). Were the bondholders to declare an event of default, the Dutch company would be forced into Dutch bankruptcy proceedings, where the outcome would most likely be a value-destroying liquidation. What explains this seemingly irrational behaviour on the part of the bondholders? The fact that they held a large amount of credit default swaps which would pay handsomely upon default by the Dutch company (*Economist* 2009).

Credit default swaps create a moral hazard problem only before the Chapter 11 begins and in its immediate aftermath. A Chapter 11 case is a 'credit event' that terminates the swap.[143] The accounts are settled up and soon the control of the claim against the debtor is again placed in the hands of the person who holds the economic interest in it. Credit default swaps may seriously complicate (and potentially even distort) workouts that take place before a 'credit event', but they are likely to matter in Chapter 11 only if crucial decisions are made at the start of the case and no one else is minding the store.

But credit default swaps still matter in bankruptcy.[144] Much of the action in a large case takes place on the first day.[145] Many issues—from the approval of the DIP financing to the composition of the creditors' committee—are resolved in the first month. In some cases, the entire case is effectively wrapped up within sixty days.[146] A case can arise in which the process of closing out positions takes place while the major controversies in the Chapter 11 proceedings are being resolved.[147] Credit derivatives may trade multiple times, but a credit derivative is only as good as the counterparty that issues it. If there are enough credit events across enough different firms, sorting out who ultimately takes the fall when some counterparties prove insolvent may need to be done at the same time that various Chapter 11s are already in motion.[148]

[142] See Complaint, *In re Lyondell Chem. Co.*, 402 B.R. 57 (Bankr. SDNY 2009) (No. 0910023).

[143] See *supra* note 129 and accompanying text.

[144] Of course, credit default swaps make it next to impossible for the creditors to agree to a prepackaged or prearranged bankruptcy. The bankruptcies of Chrysler and General Motors were able to be prearranged only because the federal government was able both to fund the cases and to cajole recalcitrant parties not to oppose the deals.

[145] See Grassgreen and Litvak (2006); Dickerson (2009: 909–10):

> First-day orders are entered in virtually all large reorganizations on an expedited basis in order to address time-sensitive matters such as obtaining DIP financing, using cash collateral, paying certain creditor claims, and retaining key executives (footnotes omitted).

[146] See Dickerson (2009: 911) (documenting the trend in recent years of large firms entering bankruptcy with a prenegotiated arrangement to sell the business).

[147] The most conspicuous example is the Lehman Brothers bankruptcy. While major assets were sold in the first week of the case, the credit derivatives involving Lehman were settled weeks later. Compare Bowers (2008) (reporting on the beginning of the unwinding of $200 billion in Lehman derivatives in mid-October), with White and Dash (2008) (reporting Barclays's purchase of the bulk of Lehman's assets only two days after Lehman filed for Chapter 11).

[148] This current problem of sorting out who owns what after a credit event could be ameliorated were Congress to require the central clearing of derivatives as proposed by Secretary Geithner. See *supra* note 140.

Moreover, credit default swaps are not the only new investment impacting the resolution of financial distress. The total return swap allows an investor (total return receiver) to enjoy the economic rights in a loan without the associated control rights. In a total return swap, the owner of a loan (total return payer) exchanges the income from the loan and any appreciation for a guaranteed income stream plus protection against capital depreciation (Morrison and Riegel 2005: 655 n.93).[149] While the owner thus offloads the economic risks associated with the loan, it retains the loan and all associated control rights. In these cases, the contracts are not necessarily settled in the event of default.

These are cases in which the owner of record is not the person with the economic interest and the holder of the economic interest is hidden from the rest of the world. The potential abuses of empty voting and hidden ownership are kept in check by the absence of any incentive on the part of the party that holds the control rights in the claim to exercise it in a way that runs contrary to the interests of its counterparty. Its return is fixed. Consider the dynamics when the party originating the loan is a bank. It is a repeat player that has transferred a portfolio of loans to the counterparty. It is not a strategic player who has another agenda. It faces a reputational penalty if it does something other than its counterparty's bidding. The risk here is not so much that the bank will vote contrary to its counterparty's interest, but rather that those with the economic interest are far away from the action.

Over time, this problem should prove self-correcting. Those buying the economic rights in a total return swap typically have the ability to sell the swap. The potential purchasers are likely to be the distressed debt professionals who will have both the expertise and the incentive to be active in the case. They too, of course, must rely on the willingness of the record owner to act as they wish, but in the typical case the record owner follows their wishes. To the extent that a tension exists, parties will try to recombine the control and formal ownership to overcome the agency problem that exists whenever ownership and control are separated.[150] Solving the problem, however, will likely take time, and winners and losers may appear while this is being sorted out.

Even if the big players could bargain among themselves and we no longer needed to worry about dispersed general creditors, there would still be a problem. You cannot negotiate with other stakeholders if you do not know who they are. The record owner, the person who files the claim, may not be the person who holds the economic stake. People who are stakeholders may not show up and when people do claim to be stakeholders, there is no way either to verify their claims or to know how large a stake they hold.[151]

[149] The major difference between a total return swap and a credit default swap is that the protection payer in a credit default swap purchases only the credit risk associated with the loan, whereas the total return receiver gets all the economic exposure of the loan.

[150] See Jensen and Meckling (1976) (showing that central problems of corporate finance are the agency problems that arise when ownership and control are separated).

[151] See Huebner and Tisdell (2008: 81–2):

> [N]ominal holders of claims are increasingly participating out or hedging their exposures (using outright participations or swaps). As a result, the apparent creditors of the troubled firm may not be the real parties in interest or even have the decision-making authority with respect to the claims they appear to own. This makes it increasingly difficult to communicate with the ultimate decision makers in the creditor body in order to negotiate a restructuring.

The need to ensure negotiations upon which Chapter 11 depends may require disclosure, at least as to who owns what.[152] To be sure, disclosure rules as a general matter discourage individuals from gathering private information and dampen the incentives of parties with private information to trade (Baird 2009). But there is another principle at work here as well. The easier it is to find the stakeholders, the more likely that a sensible plan of reorganization can emerge. The better defined the property rights, the more valuable they are. Land becomes more valuable when its owner and its boundaries are easy to identify from public records.[153] The law narrowly limits the types of ownership interests in land for exactly this reason (Merrill and Smith 2000). Quite apart from whether you want to buy or sell land, you can use your own land more effectively if it is easy for you to learn who your neighbours are. Knowing the identity of the holders of property rights is a key assumption of Coasean bargaining.

11.4.2 Wearing Multiple Hats

A change that is perhaps as large as any one of those discussed lies in the ability of individual investors to assemble together their own investment positions with the different instruments that are available. The proliferation of these various instruments allows particular investors to have conflicting positions in different tranches of the debtor and to have portfolios (perhaps with other firms in the same industry) that give them returns from different decisions that are dramatically different from those of other investors.

Hedge funds play an increasing role in this aspect of the bankruptcy process. Not only can a hedge fund buy into any part of a company's capital structure, but it can buy into multiple parts of the capital structure at the same time. Occupying multiple tranches is not inevitably a cause for concern. In theory, the hedge fund could acquire a position so that its economic interest was coextensive with the interest of the corporation. By holding slices throughout the capital structure, the hedge fund could focus on maximizing enterprise value rather than only maximizing the value of its investment. Yet such a benign outcome is by no means assured. Hedge funds can take actions which increase their returns but at the expense of other investors. For example, consider a company that files for bankruptcy. A hedge fund could, on the quiet, buy up a large portion of the unsecured debt. At the time, the equity is trading for trivial amounts. The hedge fund then buys up a large portion of the equity and makes this purchase public. Other investors, thinking that the hedge fund believes that there is value in the equity, reacts by bidding up the price of the unsecured debt. Surely, if the smart money thinks that equity is the place to be, the unsecured debt must be a relatively safe investment. But it may be that the purchase of the equity was simply a loss leader and the fund plans to recover the money spent on the equity through the increase in the prices of its bonds. Indeed, no one may ever know that the fund ever held the bonds. It can both buy and sell them in anonymity.

[152] See Hu and Black (2006) (discussing the need for disclosure of hidden debt hedges by creditors in bankruptcies).

[153] See Libecap and Lueck (2009) (reporting a study indicating that land in areas that use a centralized land demarcation system has a higher value than land in areas using the indiscriminate metes and bounds system).

Requiring all who hold claims against the debtor to reveal what they own does not completely solve the problem. A hedge fund can have a big investment in a competitor of the debtor, and the competitor may benefit from the debtor's demise. The hedge fund could use its rights under the Bankruptcy Code to slow down and perhaps ultimately undermine the reorganization. But a hedge fund's position need not be so crudely at odds with those of the other investors for its interests to be skewed. It might have entered into other kinds of derivative contracts, such as hedges on commodities that are crucial to the debtor's business, that make it look at a plan in a way that is different from a generic claim holder in the same class. The basic point is that the Code's assumption that all holders of the same type of claim have the same economic interest no longer holds. Just as credit defaults and total return swaps complicate bargaining outside of bankruptcy, the ability of a hedge fund to have multiple investments complicates bargaining inside of Chapter 11.

These complications are coming to the fore at the same time that liquidity, which often allowed for a sale of the company as a going concern,[154] is drying up. The ability by a group in interest to force a sale limits the opportunities for strategic investments in crafting a plan of reorganization. The sale settles the value of the assets, which are then divvied up roughly in accord with well-established priorities. To the extent that the current environment makes a sale of a large company difficult,[155] it increases the likelihood that the parties to the negotiation will not be able to assess each other's motivations. The inability to use the market sale as a benchmark for possible deals further complicates the task of forming a plan of reorganization.

11.5 Coalition Formation and the Problem of the Empty Core

The problems of identifying those with an interest in a large enterprise and their economic interests do not exhaust the challenges facing modern reorganization practice. Assume for the moment that a large enterprise that finds itself today in Chapter 11 can identify the relevant players and their economic interests; in other words, it has somehow navigated around the challenges we discussed above. Here, one would be tempted to think, the new world of corporate reorganization may be a more hospitable environment for deciding the future for the business. Those with investments in the enterprise seem to face few of the obstacles—high transaction costs and an abundance of private information—that hindered consensual agreement in earlier times. The key players are not hapless public investors and small trade creditors, but sophisticated parties who have invested in this business because of the special expertise they bring. They want to be at the bargaining table. After control rights are properly defined and sensible disclosure rules are in place, it might seem that the

[154] On the rise of sales of companies as a going concern, see Baird and Rasmussen (2003).

[155] Even in the days of abundant liquidity, it was still the case that the sale of very large companies was difficult to pull off. The market for two hundred million dollar companies is more robust than is the market for two billion dollar companies. For the largest companies, hedge funds need to pool their resources together. See Shearer (2006) (discussing how funds form 'clubs' to do larger deals).

bankruptcy judge needs to do relatively little other than provide rules that make trade reliable and transparent and a mechanism for resolving the disputes that arise. The chance of bargaining failure seems low. The players should reach agreement among themselves and the bankruptcy judge will have little more to do other than bless the agreement and adjudicate disputes among some of the players. But matters are not so simple.

Ironically, it is precisely here—a world in which everyone brings special expertise to the bargaining table and negotiates in an environment that is virtually frictionless—that a new difficulty arises. We should not assume that people will in fact strike deals somewhere along the Pareto frontier. When there is a zero-sum game, there are an infinite number of possible deals. The parties must form a coalition around one of many possible agreements. Bargaining works best when there are focal points that provide a basic understanding of the contours of an acceptable deal.[156] Someone is recognized as the person who takes the lead, and all of the parties have shared expectations about who gets what.

In the past, conventions emerged and coalitions formed along predictable lines. In the round of Chapter 11s in the early 2000s, for example, it was settled that out-of-the-money equity received nothing and played no role at the bargaining table. Plans that included equity, in the ordinary case, were no longer on the table (Baird and Rasmussen 2003: 692). Plans might include features that were in tension with appellate court decisions (such as the pervasive use of substantive consolidation[157]), but as long as everyone at the table followed existing norms, it caused few problems. Whether a feature of a plan was embedded in black letter law or even known to anyone else was not essential. As long as the repeat players who sat at the reorganization table knew it, that was enough.[158] The need to strike agreements in future cases held attempts at advantage taking in any particular case in check.

With the proliferation of new players and the introduction of new financial instruments, the old focal points may have disappeared. Reaching agreement is likely to become much harder, even though transaction costs are lower and information is complete. Consider the reorganization of Adelphia. Adelphia was the fifth largest operator of cable systems in the United States when it filed a Chapter 11 petition in 2002. As is common in large reorganizations, the debtor decided to sell its assets under § 363 as a going concern. In April 2005, it found a buyer willing to pay $17.6 billion, a substantial premium above its stand-alone value.[159]

[156] For a discussion of how focal points play an important role in the context of bargaining between two parties, see Young (1996: 116–21).

[157] See Baird (2005: 15) ('Substantive consolidation lacks the solid foundation one usually expects of doctrines so firmly embedded in day-to-day practice').

[158] Many practices in modern Chapter 11 are well known to insiders, but inaccessible to anyone else. For example, the fees of the indenture trustee are always paid, even though the Bankruptcy Code allows such fees only in the event of a 'substantial contribution' in a case. 11 USC § 503(b)(5) (2006). Experienced lawyers know not to expend any energy fighting them. The fees are routinely, indeed invariably, included in the plan, without inquiry into whether the indenture trustee's contribution was in fact 'substantial'. Junior associates sometimes find out about this feature of modern bankruptcy practice in a hazing ritual akin to the one in which the newest apprentice in a French restaurant is sent to retrieve soufflé weights lent to a rival. Aspiring bankruptcy lawyers are instructed to go to plan negotiations and to be unyielding on the question of allowing fees for the indenture trustee, only to be surprised when they are not taken seriously.

[159] See *In re Adelphia Commc'ns Corp.*, 368 B.R. 140, 146 (Bankr. SDNY 2007).

The purchase agreement required that the transaction close within fifteen months, and no creditor group raised serious objections either to the amount or the form of the sale.

By the traditional account, there would seem to be few impediments to wrapping up the case quickly. The only creditors were institutional investors owed fixed amounts of money. The only assets were either cash or stock in the buyer (Time Warner Cable). But things were not so simple. Adelphia was not a single corporation, but rather a group of 230 related entities.[160] Each creditor group could contest the valuation of its claim. Even though there were only a few large creditor groups, there was no easy way of putting a value on each one and there was no obvious focal point around which agreement might form. As a result, there was no way to 'assuage the concerns of one creditor faction without further alienating another.... This effectively froze progress on the confirmation of a reorganization plan, with the deadlock increasingly threatening the... sale.'[161]

The problem that we need to confront is that the core may be empty.[162] There is no deal that will stick. Consider the following stylized variation on the facts of Adelphia. There are four unsecured creditors, all of whom have claims of uncertain value. None brings any special value to the business, and each is focused only on maximizing the value of its debt. The plan of reorganization establishes the mechanism that will determine how each claim is valued.[163] There is no

[160] *In re Adelphia Commc'ns Corp.*, 368 B.R. 140, 146 (Bankr. SDNY 2007).

[161] *In re Adelphia Commc'ns Corp.*, 368 B.R. 140, 146 (Bankr. SDNY 2007), 159.

[162] An 'empty core' exists when three or more parties cannot reach a stable agreement with each other because some other agreement always exists that at least one party prefers. In other words, at least one person will always defect from any tentative agreement that might be made and, hence, none ever is reached. Low transaction costs create a frictionless environment in which agreements cannot stick. For an accessible introduction to the problem of the empty core, see Telser (1994). The problem of the empty core may require some qualification of the Coase theorem, as it is premised on the idea that parties can reach agreement with one another if transaction costs are low enough and information is perfect. See Aivazian and Callen (1981); Aivazian and Callen (2003) (expanding upon the argument that the Coase Theorem may break down when faced with an empty core). But see Coase (1981) (arguing that the empty core and the Coase Theorem can be reconciled through penalty clauses and time constraints). The empty core has been applied to antitrust and other areas of the law. See, e.g., Bittlingmayer (1982) (applying the empty core to the *Addyston Pipe* antitrust case); Dempsey (2008: 482–4) (summarizing the empty core as other scholars have applied it to the airline industry and deregulation); Hylton (1993: 502–5) (applying the empty core concept to labour law and unions); Smith (2002: 1969–70) (applying the empty core problem to structured settlements); Wiley (1987) (explaining the empty core's application to antitrust law but arguing that judges should ignore its implications). Some discussions of bankruptcy have mentioned the problem of the empty core in passing. See, e.g., Bussel (1996: 1605 n.219) (noting that coalitions formed in bankruptcy can experience problems similar to the empty core problem); Kornhauser (1998: 1575–9) (focusing on the empty core in the context of settlement and bankruptcy's pro rata sharing rule); Perino (1997: 122–3) (comparing collective action problems in class actions to those in bankruptcy and applying core theory to the problem); Stearns (1994: 1239 n.75) (warning that participants in bankruptcy cases may not be in the best position to determine how assets are divided due to the empty core problem). None of these analyses, however, has connected the problem to particular provisions of the Code, to the way in which bankruptcy judges can prevent an empty core, or to the way that changes in finance have greatly magnified the problem.

[163] Of course, in principle, it is possible for the court to keep the bankruptcy open and resolve each of the claims as best it can. In many cases, however, quite apart from the difficulty of determining the value of the claims, there is an efficiency loss from delay. In *Adelphia*, for example, even after the sale of the assets, the failure to get a plan of reorganization approved would require a premature IPO of stock received in the sale. *ACC Bondholders Group v. Adelphia Commc'ns Corp. (In re Adelphia Commc'ns Corp.)*, 361 B.R. 337, 353 (SDNY 2007).

efficiency loss in adopting one plan over another. Nevertheless, the plan does matter to the parties themselves, as each valuation mechanism tends to favour some at the expense of another. Section 1129 of the Bankruptcy Code allows any of the three to form a coalition in which they can cramdown a plan on the fourth.[164] Various rules in the Bankruptcy Code try to ensure that similar claims are treated alike,[165] but it is hard to bring this about in practice. For example, the plan of reorganization can provide that each receives 25% of the equity, but, as FiberMark suggests,[166] the three plan proponents can effectively divide governance rights among themselves in a way that leaves the fourth in the unhappy position of a powerless minority shareholder in a closely held corporation. In Adelphia, everything turned on how interdebtor disputes were resolved.

Let us assume that Firm is worth $14 and that any three of the creditors can form a coalition in which they divide $12 among themselves and leave $2 for the excluded creditor. The core here is empty. The creditor who is left out of the coalition can propose a deal that gives two members of the coalition more and still be better off than if he is left out of the deal entirely. We face a danger that the bankruptcy process degenerates into repeated and costly attempts at coalition building. To be sure, the Code's provisions provide some check. A plan that discriminated transparently in terms of allocating claims against the reorganized company would not pass muster, given the Bankruptcy Code's requirement that plans provide the same payout among claims in the same class without the adverse parties' consent.[167] Yet whenever valuation problems exist, even this requirement does not provide complete protection.

In an earlier era, one in which the dominant issue in corporate reorganizations was the collective action problem of bringing diverse stakeholders together, this sort of problem did not loom large. The costs of putting together any coalition were sufficiently high that once a coalition formed, it was unlikely that anyone else would be sufficiently organized to break it up. Transaction costs and the frictions they caused kept the problem at bay. Indeed, the very fact that most creditors were passive allowed a stable coalition to form. The dramatic decline in transaction costs and the ability of investors to interact with each other at such low costs, however, now makes the empty core a problem worth taking seriously.[168]

The problem worsens when the competing investors each bring value to the business. Consider the following hypothetical. Firm is in financial distress and has defaulted on its loans to both HedgeFund and Supplier. HedgeFund is owed $10 and has a security interest in all Firm's assets. Supplier is owed $10, but it is unsecured. Firm could be sold, but only $13 would be realized from the sale. (HedgeFund would receive $10 and Supplier will receive the balance of $3). The old equity holders would be wiped out. As Firm is being wound down,

[164] A class accepts a plan when a majority in number and two-thirds in amount of the claims in a class vote in favour of it, see 11 USC § 1126(c) (2006), and when a class accepts a plan, the judge can confirm it without going through the 'cramdown' procedure. See id. § 1129(a)(8).

[165] For a description of the provisions in Chapter 11 that bring this about, see *supra* text accompanying notes 14–21.

[166] See *supra* text accompanying notes 54–79.

[167] 11 USC § 1123(a)(4).

[168] For a description of how low transaction costs actually create empty core problems and how this relates to the Coase Theorem, see *supra* note 162. Barry Adler (2007) has suggested a reorganization mechanism in which junior creditors propose a plan that could include a take-it-or-leave-it offer for the senior creditor. Such a mechanism might avoid the empty core problem, as the ability to make take-it-or-leave-it offers dramatically narrows the range of possible equilibrium agreements.

Manager will be paid \$2. HedgeFund, Supplier, and Manager negotiate and attempt to settle on a plan of reorganization.

HedgeFund, Supplier, and Manager all bring value to the business. HedgeFund knows how to reshape and modify the business plan in a way that puts Firm back on track. Supplier provides a crucial component and has expertise in designing the next generation of the product. Manager knows the customer base and the best way to operate the business. If all three agree to work together, Firm is worth \$24. Any of the two, however, could also work together and bring added value to Firm. HedgeFund and Manager could work together and realize \$22, less the \$3 they must give Supplier if it is left out.[169] These two would then share the remaining \$19. Similarly, should Supplier and Manager agree to go it alone, the business would be worth \$20, \$10 of which they must give HedgeFund if it is left out.[170] This arrangement would allow Supplier and Manager to divide \$10 between them. Finally, HedgeFund and Supplier could reach a deal with each other, realize \$23, and exclude Manager. Manager would still capture \$2 while the deal is being arranged, but \$21 would still be left over to divide between the two other parties. All this is known to the parties, but not to the bankruptcy judge or to outsiders.[171]

Under these assumptions, the optimal outcome is for HedgeFund, Supplier, and Manager to reach a deal with each other and divide the \$24 that is realized among them. No other combination generates as high a total return. This deal, however, is not possible. No matter what share each is given in Firm, it will always be possible for one party to enter into a coalition with another that leaves them better off than they would be if they accepted the deal with the third.

Assume, for example, that a plan is put forward in which HedgeFund, Supplier, and Manager join forces and HedgeFund receives \$13, Supplier receives \$6, and Manager receives \$5. They are all receiving more than they would in the event of a liquidation of Firm, but it is not a plan that the parties will agree on. For example, Supplier, rather than accepting this deal, can propose to HedgeFund that they dump Manager and that HedgeFund take \$14, leaving \$7 for itself. HedgeFund and Supplier are both better off than they would be if they joined forces with Manager. Such a deal is not stable either. Manager would approach HedgeFund and suggest that it dump Supplier. Manager could offer HedgeFund a share of \$16 and still leave \$3 for itself. Supplier in turn could bribe either Manager or HedgeFund to abandon this coalition, and so forth. Under these assumptions, the core is empty. There is no agreement among the players that produces a stable equilibrium.[172]

This hypothetical is, of course, only that. When a relatively small group of sophisticated professionals cannot reach a deal over a long period of time, other factors are necessarily at work. The reorganization of Delphi, a former subsidiary of and still one of the principal suppliers of

[169] Note that although Supplier is due \$10, a plan can be confirmed so long as Supplier receives what it would have received in a liquidation. See 11 USC § 1129(a)(7)(A)(ii).

[170] As a secured claim holder, HedgeFund is entitled to its full claim up to the value of the underlying collateral, in this case all of Firm's assets. See 11 USC § 506.

[171] In this hypothetical, we have abstracted away many of the difficulties confronting modern reorganization practice. We have replaced shape-shifting creditors holding varying agendas with single actors, each of whom has a transparent economic interest.

[172] For a discussion and formal proof of the conditions necessary under these assumptions, see Aivazian and Callen (1981: 179–80).

General Motors, provides an illustration. The declining fortunes of General Motors and the automobile industry generally over the last several years made it hard to enforce any deal that took a significant amount of time to implement, as one party would have a strong incentive to back out. Nevertheless, as in Adelphia, we see sophisticated parties long unable to reach a deal with each other for reasons that seem unrelated to how the assets are used.[173] It is difficult for insiders—and may be impossible for outsiders—to ascertain in any given case whether the failure to reach a stable coalition stems from an empty core, radical disagreements about valuation, or strategic bargaining of various sorts. Nevertheless, paying attention to how coalitions come into being should inform our understanding of the Bankruptcy Code.

The possibility of an empty core creates a challenge for those designing bankruptcy policy. The solution to an empty core, however, raises challenges of its own. It is one thing to ensure that a plan will be formed; it is another to ensure that this plan will be the most efficient use of the debtor's assets. For example, consider a rule that gives the existing managers of the firm the exclusive right to propose a plan of reorganization at the outset of the case. This rule effectively removes one possible coalition from the table in our second hypothetical (namely, the coalition between HedgeFund and Supplier that eliminates Manager). Eliminating some coalitions may increase the chance that the core is not empty. This is the case with our example. There is an equilibrium plan in which Manager is given $10, HedgeFund $10, and Supplier $4. Neither HedgeFund nor Supplier can do a deal with Manager in which Manager receives more than $10 and either is left with more than it receives in the proposed plan.[174] HedgeFund and Supplier could, of course, do much better if they were able to propose a plan that excluded Manager, but the exclusivity rule prevents this from happening and thereby creates an equilibrium solution. Of course, while this sort of agenda control can prevent the core from being empty, this does not mean that the solution is optimal. Indeed, there is an extant literature that worries that managers can use agenda control to further their own interests at the cost of the enterprise as a whole.[175]

While some provisions of the Code may combat the empty core problem, others may exacerbate it. Most conspicuous are the rules governing solicitation of acceptances of plans. Section 1125 can be read to forbid agreements between creditors before the plan proponent writes a disclosure statement and has the judge approve it.[176] One-on-one discussions with another stakeholder rarely pose a problem, even if the communication is a draft plan. Negotiations per se are similarly unproblematic. Nor is § 1125 violated by obtaining informal assurances from a creditor to support a particular plan.[177] But in the new world of Chapter 11,

[173] See de la Merced (2009) (describing long and unsuccessful negotiations with shifting coalitions). Only when the government sought to engineer a sale of Delphi to a private equity firm at what the existing lenders thought was a bargain price did an agreement arise under which the existing lenders took control of the company.

[174] If HedgeFund and Manager worked together and left Supplier out, HedgeFund and Manager would have only $19 to split between themselves. If Supplier and Manager worked together, they would be left with only $10 to split.

[175] See, e.g., Skeel (2001: 214–15).

[176] The relevant statutory text is set out in 11 USC § 1125(b) (2006). For a discussion of relevant bankruptcy practice, see DeFranceschi (2003).

[177] For a narrow reading of § 1125(b), see *Century Glove, Inc. v. First American Bank of New York*, 860 F.2d 94, 100–03 (3d Cir. 1988), which interprets 'solicitation' narrowly so as not to inhibit negotiations. See also *In re Snyder*, 51 B.R. 432, 437 (Bankr. Utah 1985):

such informal assurances are sometimes not enough. The holder of a particular claim may be a bank today and a vulture investor tomorrow. Ensuring that you can rely next month on the support you garner this week by obtaining a writing that binds the party is useful. Such binding agreements, however, may not be enforceable. Indeed, if made, they expose their creators to the risk that their votes will not count.[178] Such doubt is itself an impediment to coalition building.

In practice, bankruptcy judges have allowed parties to form coalitions without going through the hoops of § 1125 (Baird 2006: 265–9). Nevertheless, it is not certain that this will always be the case. A court interpreting § 1125 might conclude that a disclosure statement must be approved before someone can be asked to make a binding commitment to vote in favour of a plan. Such an interpretation of § 1125 may run counter to some practices that have emerged in recent years and may be inconsistent with sensible bankruptcy policy, but some courts, especially appellate courts, have little sympathy for interpretations that are out of step with what seems to be the plain language of the statute.[179]

Other long-standing parts of the Code deserve re-examination as well. The Code has long had a two-prong rule for class-wide approval by a class of debt holders. For the class to vote in favour of the plan, half of the debt holders holding more than two-thirds of the amount of debt in the class need to support the plan. Both parts of this voting standard are subject to question in today's new environment. The best justification for the majority of the holders rule is that it allows for the pooling of information (Kordana and Posner 1999: 168–9). Such a rule makes sense in a world of many creditors, each of whom has differing information. This justification, however, runs aground in today's reorganization cases. The two-thirds in amount rule is equally suspect. The effect of this rule is to make it easier for any creditor to assemble a blocking position. Such a position will give that creditor a seat at the bargaining table. Multiplying the number of creditors who need to agree to a plan of reorganization may make it harder to find a stable coalition. Indeed, the current rules may lead to the situation that within each class there may be an empty core.

Other recent amendments compound the problem by increasing the fragmentation of claims. These include the expansion of priorities, such as requiring assurance of payment to utilities[180] and payment in full to vendors who ship within twenty days before the filing of the petition.[181] The proliferation of exclusions to the automatic stay has made matters worse as well. We can also take steps to improve the bankruptcy exchange. One can clarify exactly what rules govern claims trading and particularly what disclosure rules make sense. We can

> The terms 'solicit' and 'solicitation'... must be interpreted very narrowly to refer only to a specific request for an official vote either accepting or rejecting a plan of reorganization. The terms do not encompass discussions, exchanges of information, negotiations, or tentative arrangements...

[178] See 11 USC § 1126(e).

[179] See, e.g., *In re Kmart Corp.*, 359 F.3d 866, 871 (7th Cir. 2004) ('Answers to contemporary issues must be found within the Code (or legislative halls). Older doctrines may survive as glosses on ambiguous language enacted in 1978 or later, but not as freestanding entitlements to trump the text.'); *Perlman v. Catapult Entm't, Inc. (In re Catapult Entm't, Inc.)*, 165 F.3d 747, 754 (9th Cir. 1999) ('Policy arguments cannot displace the plain language of the statute; that the plain language... may be bad policy does not justify a judicial rewrite').

[180] See 11 USC § 366.

[181] See 11 USC § 503(b)(9) (classifying such payment as an administrative expense).

also figure out some way to identify stakeholders. Independent of optimal disclosure, you need to know who owns what in order to defragment capital structures.

But bolder steps may be needed to create focal points or otherwise ensure that the core is not empty. One way to prevent the bargaining breakdown is to give agenda control to a single party. A dictator can impose a solution on all of the parties. The bankruptcies of both GM and Chrysler were able to proceed at breakneck pace because one player—the United States government—was able to dictate the terms of the proceedings. Yet, giving power to one player raises concerns of its own. The bankruptcy judge in Delphi resisted the government's efforts to bring about a resolution of the case with its own plan, involving the participation of a private equity fund. As he put it, '[a]s far as I'm concerned, they're just guys in suits. Why can't other guys in suits pay more?' (Beales 2009).

The willingness of a bankruptcy judge to take unilateral action—such as insisting on an immediate sale of the assets—seems the most common way in which the problem of bargaining impasse is being solved. The costs of such a rule, of course, have been well explored.[182] In an illiquid market, if the sale takes place, the price may be less than its value in its best use and hence stakeholder recoveries decrease.[183] Moreover, sales often require buyers to assume some, but not all, of the debtor's existing obligations.[184]

Ordering the sale of the firm to the highest bidder is a way of putting a gun to the parties' heads. Judge Milton Pollock did essentially this in the bankruptcy of Drexel Burnham. He told the parties that if they could not reach agreement in short order, he would sell the firm's assets and retired to his chambers for a few minutes. Parties found the judge's threat credible and feared that a sale would make them all worse off (believing that the particular junk bonds were worth far more than the market would pay for them). Notwithstanding weeks of deadlock, they reached an agreement that was scribbled on a yellow legal pad just before time expired.[185]

The use of this 'nuclear' option may be a way to induce agreement, and the threat may only rarely need to be carried out. Moreover, little going-concern value may have been at risk in many cases. The social cost of carrying out the threat may be small. Again, the assets involved in Drexel were securities. Even if the market undervalued them, there is no social loss associated with selling them quickly. But we need to consider the cases in which there are a variety of different plans and only one of them preserves going-concern value. In such cases, relying on the parties to reach agreement has its greatest value. When the parties themselves know the highest and best use of the assets, but others do not, inducing such an agreement may be the best way to maximize the value of the assets.

[182] See LoPucki and Doherty (2007) (providing empirical evidence suggesting sales in bankruptcy yield lower values than when firms reorganize).

[183] See Shleifer and Vishny (1992) (showing that liquidation sales yield lower prices than actual value in best use as similarly situated firms are likely to be experiencing financial distress as well).

[184] See *In re Chrysler LLC*, 405 B.R. 84 (Bankr. SDNY 2009). The bidding procedures in *Chrysler* have been criticized because of the way in which the consideration offered by the only bidder consisted not only of cash, but also assumption of specified unsecured obligations of the business. For a critique, see Roe and Skeel (2009).

[185] See Miller (1992) (discussing how Judge Pollock threatened to dismantle the brokerage firm on his own if the parties did not reach a deal).

A judge who resists approaches that put value at risk is often left with the unpalatable alternative of approving plans that do not quite pass muster but do rough justice and are insulated from review by a court that would insist that square corners be cut. Adelphia may be an example of such a case. The district court stayed the confirmation of the plan as it had serious doubts about whether the letter of the law was being followed, but never heard the case, as the appellants were unwilling to post the required bond ($1.3 billion in cash; the first 10% due in twenty-four hours and the balance in seventy-two).[186]

Neither of these approaches, both of which are evident in recent bankruptcy cases,[187] can be reconciled neatly with traditional accounts of what bankruptcy judges are supposed to do. Indeed, the standard academic critique of bankruptcy judges is that they exercise too much discretion and are too quick to depart from the strict letter of the law. We are no longer in a world, however, in which judicial discretion is merely a way of neglecting the absolute priority rule. The push towards simple rules creates the risk of an empty core. Putting frictions and artificial barriers in place can accelerate rather than hinder consensual, value-maximizing bargains.

11.6 Conclusion

Judges are quite likely to follow the lead of professional investors when they present a united front. Modern judges are likely to enforce intercreditor agreements as written, but in a world in which the financial instruments are new, the agreements will likely be incomplete and some recourse to gap-filling is necessary. Even if things will sort themselves out eventually, life is not going to be easy during the interim.

The lifeblood of corporate reorganizations is and always has been negotiation. Creating the optimal environment for facilitating such negotiations is the principal business of those who shape the law. The most direct lesson of all this for the bankruptcy judge is likely one that the best intuited long ago: she should not interpret the Bankruptcy Code in a way that creates an empty core. A simple and transparent bargaining environment in some cases may not be enough. Precisely because it is simple and transparent, there is an increased danger that parties will find it hard for stable coalitions to emerge. It also suggests that much of recent bankruptcy reform—changes that have added complexity to the Code and sought to corral the bankruptcy judge's discretion—are headed in the wrong direction. The problem of ensuring coalition formation requires giving bankruptcy judges more discretion, not less.

If past is prologue, the uncertainties that financial innovation brings with it are likely to be resolved satisfactorily, even if not immediately. We do not believe that this anticommons problem—and the associated empty core problem that may come with it—will be an enduring feature of corporate finance, only that the emerging round of Chapter 11 will revolve around these problems precisely because they are new. Our experience with large

[186] See *ACC Bondholders Group v. Adelphia Commc'ns Corp. (In re Adelphia Commc'ns Corp.)*, 361 B.R. 337, 368 (SDNY 2007).

[187] For an example of a case in which the bankruptcy judge brought an end to a case through a sale in which the judge assessed competing non-cash bids, see *Contrarian Funds, LLC v. Westpoint Stevens, Inc. (In re Westpoint Stevens, Inc.)*, 333 B.R. 30, 55 (SDNY 2005).

corporations competing in a market economy is only about a century and a half old. Capitalism is still very much a work in progress, and the science of corporate finance is at an early stage.

References

Adams, E. S. (1993). Governance in Chapter 11 Reorganizations: Reducing Costs, Improving Results, *Boston University Law Review* 73, 581–635.

Adler, B. E. (2007). Game-Theoretic Bankruptcy Valuation, New York University Law & Economic Research Paper Series, Working Paper No. 07-03, available at <http://ssrn.com/abstract=954147>.

Aftermarket News (2006). Judge OKs Meridian Financing Changes, Aftermarket News, (22 Sept.), available at <http://www.aftermarketnews.com/Item/29395/judge_oks_meridian_financing_changes.aspx>.

Aivazian, V. A. and Callen, J. L. (1981). The Coase Theorem and the Empty Core, *Journal of Law & Economics* 24, 175–81.

Aivazian, V. A. and Callen, J. L. (2003). The Core, Transaction Costs, and the Coase Theorem, *Constitutional Political Economy* 14, 287–99.

Armstrong, D. (2006). United Plan Approved: Reorganization Will Let Airline Emerge from Bankruptcy, *San Francisco Chronicle* (21 Jan.), at C1.

Baird, D. G. (2005). Substantive Consolidation Today, *Boston College Law Review* 47, 5–22.

Baird, D. G. (2006). *The Elements of Bankruptcy* (4th edn.) (Westbury, CT, Foundation Press).

Baird, D. G. (2009). The Bankruptcy Exchange, *Brooklyn Journal of Corporate, Financial & Commercial Law* 4, 23–38.

Baird, D. G. and Bernstein, D. S. (2006). Absolute Priority, Valuation Uncertainty, and the Reorganization Bargain, *Yale Law Journal* 115, 1930–70.

Baird, D. G. and Jackson, T. H. (1984). Corporate Reorganizations and the Treatment of Diverse Ownership Interests: A Comment on Adequate Protection of Secured Creditors in Bankruptcy, *University of Chicago Law Review* 51, 97–130.

Baird, D. G. and Rasmussen, R. K. (2002). The End of Bankruptcy, *Stanford Law Review* 55, 751–89.

Baird, D. G. and Rasmussen, R. K. (2003). Reply: Chapter 11 at Twilight, *Stanford Law Review* 56, 673–99.

Baird, D. G. and Rasmussen, R. K. (2006). Private Debt and the Missing Lever of Corporate Governance, *University of Pennsylvania Law Review* 154, 1209–51.

Baird, D. G., Bris, A., and Zhu, N. (2007). The Dynamics of Large and Small Chapter 11 Cases: An Empirical Study, Yale International Center for Finance, Working Paper No. 05-29, available at <http://ssrn.com/abstract=866865>.

Beales, R. (2009). Delphic Dealings, *breakingviews.com*, (10 June), available at <http://www.breakingviews.com/obamas-latest-car-sector-bullying-hits-snag/1511389.article>.

Berman, M. N. and Brighton, J. J. (2006a). Second-Lien Financings Part IV: Good, Bad, and Ugly, June *American Bankruptcy Institute Journal* 25, 1, available at <http://www.highbeam.com/doc/1P3-1063742791.html>.

Berman, M. N. and Brighton, J. J. (2006b). Second-Lien Financings Part II: Good, Bad, and Ugly, March *American Bankruptcy Institute Journal* 25, 24.

Berman, M. N. and Brighton, J. J. (2009). *Handbook on Second Lien Loans and Intercreditor Agreements* (Alexandria, VA, American Bankruptcy Institute).

Bernstein, M. (2008). Hey, hat's This Guy Up To?, Ward's Dealer Business, (1 Dec.), at 33, available at <http://connection.ebscohost.com/c/articles/35686959/hey-whats-this-guy-up-to>.

Bills, S. (2006). JPM Buys Into Hedge Fund Middle Office, *American Banker* (14 Feb.), at 1.

Bittlingmayer, G. (1982). Decreasing Average Cost and Competition: A New Look at the *Addyston Pipe* Case, *Journal of Law & Economics* 25, 201–29.

Black, F. and Scholes, M. (1973). The Pricing of Options and Corporate Liabilities, *Journal of Political Economy* 81, 637–54.

Bobrow, B., Tech, M., and Redding, L. (2006). An Introduction to the Primary Market, in A. Taylor and A. Sansone (eds.), *The Handbook of Loan Syndications and Trading* (New York, McGraw-Hill) 186–207.

Bowers, S. (2008). Lehman Fallout: Derivatives Worth Hundreds of Billions Start To Unwind, *Guardian* (London), (11 Oct.), at 3.

Bracewell and Guiliani (2007), Legal Advisory: Intercreditor/Subordination Agreements in the Second Lien Generation, (20 July), available at <http://www.bracewellgiuliani.com/news-publications/updates/intercreditorsubordination-agreements-second-lien-generation>.

Brennan, T. (2002). Judge OKs Budget Sale to Cendant, *Daily Deal* (9 Nov.), available at 2002 WLNR 3561147.

Brennan, T. (2006). Turmoil Over, FiberMark Exits, *Daily Deal* (5 Jan.), available at 2006 WLNR 222106.

Business Week (2004). The Next Warren Buffett?, Business Week (22 Nov.), available at <http://www.businessweek.com/stories/2004-11-21/the-next-warren-buffett>.

Bussel, D. J. (1996). Coalition-Building through Bankruptcy Creditors' Committees, *UCLA Law Review* 43, 1547–633.

Carnell, R. S., Macey, J. R., and Miller, G. P. (2009). *The Law of Banking and Financial Institutions* (4th edn.) (Gaithersburg, MD, Aspen Publishers).

Chamblee, G. D. (2008). Reducing Battles between First and Second Lien Holders through Intercreditor Agreements: The Role of the New ABA Model Intercreditor Agreement Task Force, *North Carolina Banking Institute* 12, 1–20.

Coase, R. H. (1981). The Coase Theorem and the Empty Core: A Comment, *Journal of Law and Economics* 24, 183–7.

Coffey, M., Milam, R., Torrado, L., and Piorkowski, M. B. (2006). The Secondary Loan Market, in A. Taylor, and A. Sansone (eds.), *The Handbook of Loan Syndications and Trading* (New York, McGraw-Hill), 395–455.

Cousins, S. D. (2002). Postpetition Financing of Dot-Coms, *Delaware Journal of Corporate Law* 27, 759–802.

de la Merced, M. J. (2009). Delphi Is Said To Have a New Deal To Leave Bankruptcy, *New York Times* (17 July), at B2.

DeFranceschi, D. J. (2003). Delaware Bankruptcy Court Announces Bright-Line Rule for Use of Lock-up Agreements in Chapter 11 Cases, *American Bankruptcy Institute Journal* 22, 16–28.

Dempsey, P. S. (2008). The Financial Performance of the Airline Industry Post-Deregulation, *Houston Law Review* 45, 421–85.

Denninger, K. (2009). GM: Bankrupt, UNLESS...., *The Market Ticker* (1 Apr.), available at <http://market-ticker.org/akcs-www?singlepost=2138006>.

Dennis, S. A. and Mullineaux, D. J. (2000). Syndicated Loans, *Journal of Financial Intermediation* 9, 404–26.

Dickerson, A. M. (2009). Privatizing Ethics in Corporate Reorganizations, *Minnesota Law Review* 93, 875–932.

Dobbs, C. E. (2006). Negotiating Points in Second Lien Financing Transactions, *DePaul Business & Commercial Law Journal* 4, 189–234.

Drain, R. D. and Schwartz, E. J. (2002). Are Bankruptcy Claims Subject to the Federal Securities Laws?, *American Bankruptcy Institute Law Review* 10, 569–624.

Easterbrook, F. H. and Fischel, D. R. (1991). *The Economic Structure of Corporate Law* (Cambridge, MA, Harvard University Press).

Economist (2009). Burning Down the House: Why Credit-Default Swaps Make Restructuring Harder To Pull Off, *Economist* (7 Mar.), at 80.

Esty, B. C. and Megginson, W. L. (2003). Creditor Rights, Enforcement, and Debt Ownership Structure: Evidence from the Global Syndicated Loan Market, *Journal of Financial and Quantitative Analysis* 38, 37–59.

Fennell, L. A. (2009). Commons, Anticommons, Semicommons, University of Chicago Law & Economics, Olin Working Paper No. 457; University of Chicago, Public Law Working Paper No. 261, available at <http://ssrn.com/abstract=1348267>.

Fight, A. (2004). *Syndicated Lending* (Oxford, Butterworth-Heinemann).

Fortgang, C. J. and Mayer, T. M. (1990). Trading Claims and Taking Control of Corporations in Chapter 11, *Cardozo Law Review* 12, 1–115.

Futter, C. and Wells, A. E. (2007). What to Expect from Hedge Funds Today and in the Future: An Overview and Insolvency Perspective, *California Bankruptcy Journal* 29, 213.

Gappmayer, B. (2006). Protecting the Insolvent: How a Creditor's Committee Can Prevent Its Constituents from Misusing a Debtor's Nonpublic Information and Preserve Chapter 11 Reorganizations, *Utah Law Review* 2006, 439–63.

Gilson, R. J. and Gordon, J. N. (2003). Controlling Controlling Shareholders, *University of Pennsylvania Law Review* 152, 785–843.

Goldschmid, P. M. (2005). Note, More Phoenix than Vulture: The Case for Distressed Investor Presence in the Bankruptcy Reorganization Process, *Columbia Business Law Review* 2005, 91–274.

Grassgreen, D. and Litvak, M. (2006). *First Day Motions* (2d edn.) (Alexandria, VA, American Bankruptcy Institute).

Güner, A. B. (2006). Loan Sales and the Cost of Corporate Borrowing, *Review of Financial Studies* 19, 687–716.

Hanrahan, M. and Teh, D. (2007). Second Lien Loans, in A. Taylor and A. Sansone (eds.), *The Handbook of Loan Syndications and Trading* (New York, McGraw-Hill), 108–37.

Harner, M. M. (2008a). The Corporate Governance and Public Policy Implications of Activist Distressed Debt Investing, *Fordham Law Review* 77, 703–73.

Harner, M. M. (2008b). Trends in Distressed Debt Investing: An Empirical Study of Investors' Objectives, *American Bankruptcy Institute Law Review* 16, 69–110.

Hays, K. (2007). A Sordid Chapter on Enron Ending: Kenneth Rice Is the Final Figure To Be Punished After Pleading Guilty to Crimes in the Scandal, *Houston Chronicle* (18 June), at A1.

Heller, M. A. (1998). The Tragedy of the Anticommons: Property in the Transition from Marx to Markets, *Harvard Law Review* 111, 621–88.

Heller, M. A. (2008). *The Gridlock Economy: How Too Much Ownership Wrecks Markets, Stops Innovation, and Costs Lives* (New York: Basic Books).

Hu, H. and Black, B. (2006). Empty Voting and Hidden (Morphable) Ownership: Taxamony, Implications, and Reforms, *Business Lawyer* 61(3), 1011–70.

Hu, H. T. C. and Black, B. (2008). Equity and Debt Decoupling and Empty Voting II: Importance and Extensions, *University of Pennsylvania Law Review* 156, 625–739.

Huebner, M. S. and Tisdell, B. A. (2008). As the Wheel Turns: New Dynamics in the Coming Restructuring Cycle, in PricewaterhouseCoopers LLP (ed.) *Americas Restructuring and Insolvency Guide 2008/2009* (London, Globe Business Publishing), 77–83.

Hylton, K. N. (1993). Efficiency and Labor Law, *Northwestern University Law Review* 87, 471–522.

International Swaps and Derivatives Association (2008). Summaries of Market Survey Results, available at <http://www.isda.org/statistics/recent.html#2008end>.

Investment Business Weekly (2008). Recovery Rate Hits 50 Percent as Enron Creditors Receive More Than $6 Billion in Special Distributions, *Investment Business Weekly* (16 June), at 164.

Jackson, T. H. (1986). *The Logic and Limits of Bankruptcy Law* (Frederick, MD, Beard Books).

James, C. (1987). Some Evidence on the Uniqueness of Bank Loans, *Journal of Financial Economics* 19, 217–35.

Jensen, M. C. and Meckling, W. H. (1976). Theory of the Firm: Managerial Behavior, Agency Costs and Ownership Structure, *Journal of Financial Economics* 3, 305–60.

Kary, T. (2009). Lyondell Case Shows Bankruptcy Loans Are Available for a Price, *Bloomberg*, (4 Feb.), available at <http://www.bloomberg.com/apps/news?pid=newsarchive&sid=azqyUe8pwuUM>.

Keehner, J., Salas, C., and Kelly, J. (2009). Harrah's Owners Said To Hedge Against Bankruptcy (Update 1), *Bloomberg* (13 Mar.), available at <http://www.bloomberg.com/apps/news?pid=newsarchive&sid=aJzJ_THa9Pck>.

Kordana, K. A. and Posner, E. A. (1999). A Positive Theory of Chapter 11, *New York University Law Review* 74, 161–234.

Kornhauser, L. A. (1998). Fair Division of Settlements: A Comment on Silver and Baker, *Virginia Law Review* 84, 1561–604.

Kuney, G. W. (2004). Hijacking Chapter 11, *Emory Bankruptcy Developments Journal* 21, 19–36.

Lattman, P. (2005). Bankrupt, *Forbes* (31 Oct.), at 60, available at <http://www.forbes.com/forbes/2005/1031/060.html>.

Lee, S. W. and Mullineaux, D. J. (2004). Monitoring, Financial Distress, and the Structure of Commercial Lending Syndicates, *Financial Management* 33, 107–30.

Levin, R. B. (2002). Almost All You Ever Wanted To Know About Carve Out, *American Bankruptcy Institute Law Journal* 76, 445–60.

Libecap, G. D. and Lueck, D. (2009). The Demarcation of Land and the Role of Coordinating Institutions, ICER Working Paper No. 14/2009; CELS 2009 4th Annual Conference on Empirical Legal Studies Paper, available at <http://ssrn.com/abstract=1436986>.

Logan, W. A. P., III (1994). Claims Trading: The Need for Further Amending Federal Rule of Bankruptcy Procedure 3001(e)(2), *American Bankruptcy Institute Law Review* 2, 495–506.

LoPucki, L. M. and Doherty, J. W. (2007). Bankruptcy Fire Sales, *Michigan Law Review* 106, 1–60.

Lubben, S. J. (2004–05). The 'New and Improved' Chapter 11, *Kentucky Law Journal* 93, 839–66.

Lubben, S. J. (2007). Credit Derivatives and the Future of Chapter 11, *American Bankruptcy Law Journal* 81, 405–30.

Lubove, S. (1991). A Bankrupt's Best Friend, *Forbes* (1 Apr.), at 99.

Mastroianni, K. A. (ed.) (2006). *New Generation Research: The 2006 Bankruptcy Yearbook and Almanac* (Boston, George Putnam).

Merrill, T. W. and Smith, H. E. (2000). Optimal Standardization in the Law of Property: The *Numerus Clausus* Principle, *Yale Law Journal* 110, 1–70.

Merton, R. C. (1973). Theory of Rational Option Pricing, *Bell Journal of Economics and Management Science* 4, 141–83.

Miller, H. R. (2007). Chapter 11 in Transition—from Boom to Bust and into the Future, *American Bankruptcy Law Journal* 81, 375–404.

Miller, H. R. and Waisman, S. Y. (2003). The Creditor in Possession: Creditor Control of Chapter 11 Reorganization Cases, *Bankruptcy Strategist* 21, 1–5.

Miller, H. R. and Waisman, S. Y. (2004). Does Chapter 11 Reorganization Remain a Viable Option for Distressed Businesses for the Twenty-First Century?, *American Bankruptcy Law Journal* 78, 153–200.

Miller, N. (1992). Judge Rules with Rod, Impish Smile, *USA Today* (25 Mar.), at 5B.

Morrison, E. R. and Riegel, J. (2005). Financial Contracts and the New Bankruptcy Code: Insulating Markets from Bankrupt Debtors and Bankruptcy Judges, *American Bankruptcy Institute Law Review* 13, 641–64.

Mugasha, A. (2004). The Secondary Market for Syndicated Loans: Loan Trading, Credit Derivatives, and Collateralized Debt Obligations, *Banking & Finance Law Review* 19, 199.

Mugasha, A. (2007). *The Law of Multi-Bank Financing: Syndicated Loans and the Secondary Loan Market* (New York, Oxford University Press).

Partnoy, F. and Skeel, D. A., Jr (2007). The Promise and Perils of Credit Derivatives, *University of Cincinnati Law Review* 75, 1019–51.

Perino, M. A. (1997). Class Action Chaos? The Theory of the Core and an Analysis of Opt-out Rights in Mass Tort Class Actions, *Emory Law Journal* 46, 85–161.

Philips, M. (2008). The Monster that Ate Wall Street: How 'Credit Default Swaps'—an Insurance Against Bad Loans—Turned from a Smart Bet into a Killer, *Newsweek* (6 Oct.), at 46.

PR Newswire (2003). Edward S. Lampert Appointed Chairman of the Board, Kmart, *PR Newswire*, (6 May), available at <http://searsholdings.mediaroom.com/index.php?s=16310&item=25262>.

Rasmussen, R. K. and Skeel, D. A., Jr (1995). The Economic Analysis of Corporate Bankruptcy Law, *American Bankruptcy Institute Law Review* 3, 85–115.

Reuters (2008). Calpine Reaches Settlement with Second Lien Debtholders, *Reuters* (1 Feb.), available at <http://www.reuters.com/article/2008/02/01/idUS227576+01-Feb-2008+PRN20080201>.

Reuters India (2009). Lyondell Seeks to Stop Note Holders from Taking Action, *Reuters India* (10 Feb.), available at <http://in.reuters.com/article/2009/02/09/lyondellchemical-idINBNG38261720090209>.

Roe, M. J. and Skeel, D. A. (2009). Assessing the Chrysler Bankruptcy, Harvard Law and Economics Discussion Paper No. 645; University of Pennsylvania, Institute for Law & Economics Research Paper No. 09-22; University of Pennsylvania Law School, Public Law Research Paper No. 09-17; Harvard Public Law Working Paper No. 09-42, available at <http://ssrn.com/abstract=1426530>.

Sarasvathy, D. K., Simon, H., and Lave, L. (1998). Perceiving and Managing Business Risks: Differences between Entrepreneurs and Bankers, *Journal of Economic Behavior & Organization* 33, 207–25.

Schelling, T. C. (1960). *The Strategy of Conflict* (Cambridge, MA, Harvard University Press).

Shearer, B. (2006). Leading the M&A Pack: Private Equity's Party Is in Full Swing... but for How Much Longer?, *Mergers & Acquisitions: The Dealmaker's Journal* (Nov.), at 28.

Shleifer, A. and Vishny, R. W. (1992). Liquidation Values and Debt Capacity: A Market Equilibrium Approach, *Journal of Finance* 47, 1343–66.

Siegel, G. E. (2003). Introduction: ABI Guide to Trading Claims in Bankruptcy (Part 2), *American Bankruptcy Institute Law Review* 11, 177–8.

Silbernagel, C. and Vaitkunas, D. (2006). Mezzanine Finance, Working Paper, available at <http://pages.stern.nyu.edu/~igiddy/articles/Mezzanine_Finance_Explained.pdf>.

Simons, K. (1993). Why Do Banks Syndicate Loans?, *New England Economic Review* 1993, 45–56.

Singer, G. H. (2008). The Lender's Guide to Second Lien Financing, *Banking Law Journal* 125, 199–223.

Skeel, D. A., Jr (1992). The Nature and Effect of Corporate Voting in Chapter 11 Reorganization Cases, *Virginia Law Review* 78, 461–533.

Skeel, D. A., Jr (2001). *Debt's Dominion: A History of Bankruptcy Law in America* (Princeton, NJ, Princeton University Press).

Smith, H. R. (2002). Structured Settlements as Structures of Rights, *Virginia Law Review* 88, 1953–74.

Stearns, M. L. (1994). The Misguided Renaissance of Social Choice, *Yale Law Journal* 103, 1219–93.

Sufi, A. (2007). Information Asymmetry and Financing Arrangements: Evidence from Syndicated Loans, *Journal of Finance* 62, 629–68.

Sullivan, D. (2008). Comment, Big Boys and Chinese Walls, *University of Chicago Law Review* 75, 533–68.

Telser, L. G. (1994). The Usefulness of Core Theory in Economics, *Journal of Economic Perspectives* 8, 151–64.

Tett, G. and Davies, P. J. (2007). Unbound: How a Market Storm Has Seen Derivatives Eclipse Corporate Bonds, *Financial Times* (London), (8 Aug.), at 11.

Toronto Star (2003). Sullivan Plans To Plead Not Guilty to Fraud, *Toronto Star* (17 Sept.), at C12.

Tung, F. (1996). Confirmation and Claims Trading, *Northwestern University Law Review* 90, 1684–754.

Tung, F. (2009). Leverage in the Board Room: The Unsung Influence of Private Lenders in Corporate Governance, *UCLA Law Review* 57, 115–81.

Warren, A. C., Jr (1993). Commentary, Financial Contract Innovation and Income Tax Policy, *Harvard Law Review* 107, 460–92.

Warren, E. and Westbrook, J. L. (2005). Contracting Out of Bankruptcy: An Empirical Intervention, *Harvard Law Review* 118, 1197–254.

Westbrook, J. L. (2004). The Control of Wealth in Bankruptcy, *Texas Law Review* 82, 795–862.

Westlaw Business Currents (2009). Restructuring Terms: Hedge Fund Roll-Ups Steamroll Creditors, *Westlaw Business Currents* (1 July), available at <http://currents.westlawbusiness.com/Article.aspx?id=84b8c4cf-55d6-4b9c-88fd-dbf1de03ffc9&cid=&src=WBSignon.&sp=>.

White, B. and Dash, E. (2008). Barclays Reaches $1.75 Billion Deal for Lehman Unit, *New York Times* (17 Sept.), at C1.

Widen, W. H. (2006). Prevalence of Substantive Consolidation in Large Bankruptcies from 2000 to 2004: Preliminary Results, *American Bankruptcy Institute Law Review* 14, 47–68.

Wiley, J. S., Jr (1987). Antitrust and Core Theory, *University of Chicago Law Review* 54, 556–89.

Young, H. P. (1996). The Economics of Convention, *Journal of Economic Perspectives* 10, 105–22.

CHAPTER 12

HEDGE FUNDS AND CHAPTER 11

WEI JIANG, KAI LI, AND WEI WANG

12.1 Introduction

This chapter examines the roles of hedge funds in Chapter 11 and the effects of their presence on the nature and outcome of the bankruptcy process. Hedge funds' participation in the bankruptcy process takes a variety of forms, including investing in debt claims, buying equity stakes, serving on the unsecured creditors or equity committee, and pursuing a 'loan-to-own' strategy, whereby a hedge fund acquires the debt of a distressed borrower with the intention of converting the acquired position into a controlling equity stake upon the firm's emergence from Chapter 11.

Using a comprehensive sample of 474 Chapter 11 cases from 1996 to 2007 formed by merging a variety of data sources, we show that hedge fund presence has been prevalent in the Chapter 11 process—close to 90% of the sample cases have publicly observable involvement by hedge funds. This result is consistent with practitioners' observation that hedge funds have become the most active investors in the distressed debt market, generating approximately half of the annual trading volume in distressed debt, one-third of the trading volume in leveraged loans, and one-quarter of the trading volume in high-yield bonds during 2005 to 2006.[1] Yet despite anecdotal evidence on hedge fund vultures in the media and case studies by law scholars on various strategies favoured by hedge funds, to date no study has systematically examined hedge fund involvement in Chapter 11 over the past decade or so. Our chapter aims to fill this void.

In addition to updating earlier studies on bankruptcy, our chapter provides new insights on hedge funds as an emerging force in the Chapter 11 process. First and foremost, we find that, as large unsecured creditors, hedge funds balance the power between the debtor and secured creditors. This effect manifests in higher probabilities of the debtor's loss of exclusive rights to file a reorganization plan, CEO turnover, and adoptions of key employee retention plans (KERPs), and in higher probabilities of emergence and payoffs to junior claims. While the bankruptcy process was traditionally classified as either 'management driven'

[1] See Siegel (2006).

(Franks and Torous 1994; Berkovitch, Israel, and Zender 1998) or 'senior creditor driven' (Welch 1997; Baird and Rasmussen 2003), hedge funds have driven the transformation of the restructuring process into one that is best characterized as 'management neutral' (Skeel 2003; Harner 2008a), where managers facilitate and implement the distressed firm's restructuring plans but do not control the restructuring process.

Second, we find that hedge funds' choice of distressed targets and positions in the capital structure reflect both their firm-picking skills and their desire to have a larger impact on the reorganization process. Unsecured debt is the most popular entry point for hedge funds because of its 'fulcrum' nature and option-like payoffs, that is, unsecured debt is the most likely layer in the capital structure where the enterprise value fails to fully cover outstanding claims. Moreover, hedge funds prefer companies in which secured debt is more likely to be overcollateralized, leaving room for unsecured creditors to take a more active role. When investing in equity, hedge funds prefer firms with relatively strong operating performance and secured creditors with a weak liquidation bias.

We further find that hedge funds are effective in achieving their desired outcomes for the claims they invest in. Hedge fund presence increases the likelihood of a successful reorganization, which is usually associated with a higher recovery of junior claims (unsecured debt and equity) and an increased likelihood of their being converted into new equity. Moreover, hedge fund presence on the unsecured creditors or equity committee is associated with more favourable distributions to that class of claims, and hedge funds' pursuance of a loan-to-own strategy is associated with more favourable distributions to both types of junior claims.

Importantly, our evidence is more supportive of efficiency gains brought by hedge funds than of value extraction from other claims. The presence of hedge fund unsecured creditors is associated with both higher total debt (including secured and unsecured) recovery and a more positive stock market response at the time of a bankruptcy filing, suggesting a positive effect of hedge fund creditors on the firm's total value. Such value creation may come from overcoming secured creditors' liquidation bias (i.e., a higher probability of emergence), confronting underperforming CEOs (i.e., a higher CEO turnover rate), retaining key personnel (i.e., more frequent adoptions of KERP), and relaxing financial constraints (i.e., the loan-to-own strategy). Similarly, we show that hedge funds participating in bankruptcy do not have as short a horizon as their counterparts specializing in pure trading. These hedge funds benefit more from companies' emergence, where the long-term prospects of the firm are important.

This chapter adds to our understanding of the major forces underlying the patterns of, and changes in, the Chapter 11 process in the United States over the past decade, and contributes to the growing research on hedge fund activism in corporate decisions. By analysing the same hedge fund holding different types of stakes (e.g., debt, equity, or both) in a distressed firm over the course of Chapter 11 restructuring, our work may stimulate new theoretical research on bankruptcy that allows for complex and dynamic interactions among various stakeholders. Prior work most closely related to our study is Hotchkiss and Mooradian (1997), which examines the role of vulture investors (predecessors to hedge funds specializing in distress investing)[2] in distressed firms. We update the Hotchkiss and Mooradian

[2] See Rosenberg (2000) (especially Chapter 1) and Harner (2008a) for a discussion of the history of distress investing, and how distress investing hedge funds have evolved beyond their vulture predecessors over the past decade.

(1997) analysis of distress investing with new developments from the decade 2000 to 2010. We also expand the scope of analysis by investigating the different roles that hedge funds take on the debt side, the equity side, or both, and the effects of their involvement on a broad category of bankruptcy outcomes.

The outline of the chapter is as follows. Section 12.2 provides a brief review of the institutional background and outlines the main hypotheses that motivate our empirical tests. Section 12.3 describes the data collection process and presents an overview of hedge funds' participation in Chapter 11. Section 12.4 examines the determinants of hedge funds' participation on the debt and equity sides. Section 12.5 analyses the effects of hedge funds' involvement in Chapter 11 on the final outcomes. Finally, Section 12.6 concludes.

12.2 Institutional Background and Empirical Motivations

The bankruptcy of utility company Northwestern Corporation illustrates hedge fund involvement in the restructuring process. The company filed a voluntary petition under Chapter 11 on 14 September 2003. Hedge funds (AG Capital Funding Partners, Avenue Capital Management, Magten Offshore Partners, and Oaktree Capital Management) owned debt claims against the company and served on the unsecured creditors' committee. Northwestern's Restated Plan of Reorganization was confirmed by the court on 8 October 2004. Under the plan, existing shareholders received no distribution. Holders of senior unsecured notes and some general unsecured notes would receive 92% of newly issued common stock. On its first day of trading, the stock price of the reorganized Northwestern was \$24.95, implying a recovery rate of 90% for the senior unsecured creditors. The hedge funds emerged as major shareholders in the restructured company.

The above example highlights several features of hedge funds' distress investing strategies. First, unlike traditional creditors (such as banks and insurance companies) that strive to contain damages on their existing investment at the bankruptcy bargaining table, hedge funds seek out distressed claims for profitable investment. Secondly, hedge funds typically initiate their investment on the debt side, with the strategic goal of influencing the restructuring process; in many cases, they end up with a controlling stake in the company upon emergence. Finally, the presence of hedge funds specialized in distress investing could be behind some secular trends in the US Chapter 11 process, notably, the strengthening of creditors' rights (Bharath, Panchapegesan, and Werner 2007; Ayotte and Morrison 2009).

Exponential growth in the hedge fund sector, a more liquid debt market, and an increasingly activist stance among some hedge funds have all contributed to the increased presence of hedge funds among claimants of distressed companies over the last decade. The presence of hedge funds in turn promotes the development of an active secondary market for distressed claims, which changes the nature of in-bankruptcy governance and voting dynamics (Strömberg 2000; Thorburn 2000; Baird and Rasmussen 2003; Eckbo and Thorburn 2009).

Hedge funds are uniquely suited to pursuing activist strategies—that is, investing with the intention to intervene in distressed firms—for two reasons. First, compared to other institutional investors (such as banks, mutual funds, and pension funds), hedge funds have more incentives to pursue high returns and are less subject to conflicts of interest due to a lack of other business relationships with the portfolio firms.

Second, hedge funds are better able to hold highly concentrated, illiquid positions that strengthen their influence at the negotiation table. In contrast, mutual funds and pension funds are required by law to maintain diversified and prudent portfolios. Pension funds usually shun bankrupt firms because of the prudent man rule and the Employee Retirement Income Security Act of 1974 (ERISA), which discourage risk-taking at the individual security level. Mutual funds have limited capacity to invest in illiquid and especially non-traded securities due to their need to maintain an open-ended structure. Banks and mutual funds are also subject to regulatory restrictions that constrain their capacity for taking on legal liabilities.[3] and getting involved in the management of their portfolio firms. In comparison, the combination of lock-up provisions with their own investors, the ability to use derivatives, and minimal disclosure requirements affords hedge funds greater flexibility in investing in distressed firms and in influencing the restructuring process.

Being relatively new players in Chapter 11, hedge funds' strategies and impacts have not been systematically studied before. The key goal of our research is to inform the debate on whether hedge fund participation improves the efficiency of the bankruptcy process. Aghion, Hart, and Moore (1992: 532) succinctly summarize the two goals of an efficient bankruptcy procedure: '(1) it maximizes the *ex post* value of the firm (with an appropriate distribution of this value across claimants); (2) it preserves the (*ex ante*) bonding role of debt by penalizing management adequately in bankruptcy states'. Following their benchmark, our analyses focus on the following aspects of hedge fund incentives and their potential impact on the Chapter 11 process.

First, we examine whether hedge fund participation as creditor or shareholder impacts the outcome of bankruptcies that favour the payoff to the claims they hold. As sophisticated investors striving for high investment returns, hedge funds are expected to select firms and positions in the capital structure that offer the best prospects. Outcome variables considered include the likelihood of firm emergence from Chapter 11 (which is usually considered an outcome favourable to junior claims—unsecured creditors and shareholders—as opposed to being liquidated or acquired), debt recovery rate, and stock returns. Furthermore, we try to identify the causal effects of hedge funds' participation in bankruptcy. A comparison of the treatment effects and the total effects allows us to comment on hedge funds' ability to select firms based on unobserved characteristics.

Secondly, we test whether hedge funds help push the Chapter 11 process more in the direction of a senior creditor-driven process (with a pro-liquidation bias) or a management-driven process (with inadequate penalties for management), or if they manage to balance the power between the two parties and create a process somewhere in between these two extremes. Outcome variables considered for analysing hedge funds' impact on senior secured creditors' power include the likelihood of emergence, given the latter's bias for liquidation, and annual percentage rate (APR) deviation from secured to unsecured

[3] Holding a large position in a portfolio firm and/or being involved in the management of the firm brings legal uncertainties and obligations to an investor and often imposes restrictions on the latter's trading due to insider trading considerations. This is one major reason cited by Black (1990) for why most mutual funds (for whom liquidity is important) and institutional fiduciaries (to whom legal risks can pass through) remain passive shareholders.

creditors; those considered for analysing hedge funds' impact on managerial power include the probability of the debtor's loss of exclusive rights to file a reorganization plan, CEO turnover, and adoptions of KERP.

Finally and most importantly, we address the question of whether hedge funds bring efficiency gains to the Chapter 11 process by enhancing the total value of all claims, or merely engage in value extraction from other parties. While hedge funds' concentrated holdings reduce the free-riding problem in bankruptcy (Kahan and Rock 2009; von Thadden, Berglöf, and Roland 2010), they might also give rise to wasteful bargaining activities (Bris and Welch 2005) or a hold-out problem whereby hedge funds block the approval of a bankruptcy plan by accumulating large positions in a class of claims, which could prolong the process or add to the cost of restructuring (Rosenberg 2000). With anecdotal evidence supporting either view, the issue has been heatedly debated—mostly among legal scholars (Goldschmid 2005; Baird and Rasmussen 2008)—without the support of large-sample empirical evidence. To this end, we examine the impact of hedge funds as creditors on both debt recovery and stock returns, and also follow up on post-Chapter 11 firm financial and operating performance.

12.3 Sample and Data

12.3.1 Sample Formation

This study builds on one of the most comprehensive datasets used in the literature on US bankruptcies. Our sample spans all major Chapter 11 filings over the period 1996 to 2007, combining information from a variety of data sources—some of which requires intensive manual collection efforts. The status of cases is updated to the end of 2008. A comparison of our sample and those used in previous studies published in the recent decade[4] is provided in the Internet Appendix.[5]

12.3.1.1 *The Sample of US Chapter 11 Firms*

The Lynn M. LoPucki Bankruptcy Research Database is our starting point to form a sample of large US firms that filed for Chapter 11 during the period 1996 to 2007. For a firm to be included in our sample, we require that the firm have assets worth at least $100 million (measured in 1980 constant dollars using the consumer price index (CPI) deflator) at the time of a bankruptcy filing, and that it file form 10Ks with the Securities and Exchange Commission (SEC) within three years of its Chapter 11 filing. We obtain 500 such cases for the sample period, which we cross-check with New Generation Research's

[4] The list of studies includes Eisenberg and LoPucki (1999); Lopucki and Doherty (2002); Dahiya et al. (2003); Ayotte and Skeel (2004); LoPucki and Doherty (2004); Bris, Welch, and Zhu (2006); Adler, Capkun, and Weiss (2007).

[5] An Internet Appendix for this chapter is available online in the 'Supplements and Datasets' section at <http://www.afajof.org/supplements.asp>.

BankruptcyData.com to verify their Chapter 11 status and to obtain information on the final outcomes. Following this process, three cases drop out of our sample because one was in fact a Chapter 7 filing and two were duplicates of or affiliated with other cases. We drop another twenty-three cases from our sample because they were pending (twelve cases) or dismissed by court (eleven cases) as of 31 December 2008. Our final sample consists of 474 unique cases of Chapter 11 filings. The following industries have the highest representation in the sample: communications (sixty-nine cases), financial (thirty-seven cases), and business services (twenty-six cases).

The Bankruptcy Research Database provides basic information about the cases, including the date of filing,[6] major operational information (such as industry, sales, and assets), the type of filing (such as prepackaged, and pre-negotiated), and the outcomes and duration of the Chapter 11 process. Such information is cross-checked with BankruptcyData.com whenever possible. In case of an inconsistency, we resort to firms' 10K filings prior to their Chapter 11 filings to resolve the difference. Unless otherwise specified, all SEC filings are retrieved from the EDGAR website.

12.3.1.2 *Details about the Bankruptcy Process, Outcomes, and Key Stakeholders*

Before final outcomes such as emergence, acquisition, or liquidation, a Chapter 11 case may reach certain milestones or intermediate outcomes such as the extension of the exclusivity period, debtor-in-possession (DIP) financing, approval of KERP, and top management turnover. We obtain such information mainly from BankruptcyData.com, and supplement it with New Generation Research's Bankruptcy DataSource database, Public Access to Court Electronic Records (PACER), and news searches in Factiva and LexisNexis. BankruptcyData.com keeps bankruptcy reorganization and liquidation plans, and provides the following information for most of the cases: classes of claims, dollar amount of allowed claims, recovery, and whether a cash or security distribution is made to each class of claimant. For four cases in which the reorganization plans are not available, we purchased their plans directly from the US bankruptcy courts. Combining all the above sources with firms' 8K filings, we are able to code the key aspects of our 474 cases' Chapter 11 processes from the date of a Chapter 11 filing all the way up to the date of case resolution.

In addition, BankruptcyData.com provides names of the major stakeholders including the largest shareholders, the largest holders of unsecured debt claims, members of the unsecured creditors' committee, members of the equity committee, and providers of DIP financing during the restructuring process. We supplement and complete the above information using the Bankruptcy DataSource database, 8K and 10K filings, proxy statements, DealScan, the SDC Syndicated Loan Database, and news searches in LexisNexis and Factiva.

[6] We use the filing dates of the parent companies if there are also filings by subsidiaries. In practice, they usually get consolidated in the same court. We manually check the 'related filings' in LoPucki's database and find that fewer than 5% of the cases have affiliate filings elsewhere on the same day or before.

12.3.1.3 *Identifying Hedge Funds Among Key Stakeholders*

To track the various roles that hedge funds play at different stages of a bankruptcy and in different parts of the bankrupt firm's capital structure, we start with a master list of all key stakeholders, collected from the sources described in Section 12.3.1.2, then identify hedge funds from this list. It is worth noting that there is no official definition of 'hedge funds'. For the purpose of our research, we classify them as incentivized professional money managers whose pooled investment vehicles are not directly accessible to the general public. Due to these broad criteria, our list of 'hedge funds' includes managers of alternative investment vehicles that are sometimes not considered 'hedge funds' in the narrow traditional sense. For example, Cerberus Capital Management, a top player in our sample, markets itself as an investment firm that manages both hedge funds and private equity funds.

We identify hedge fund players at the management company level (which could manage multiple funds/portfolios) as this is the relevant unit of activist involvement in the target firms. All stakeholders in our master list (which consists of more than 5,000 entities) are manually checked for their business scopes. A stakeholder is classified as a hedge fund if it is reported by specialized publications (such as *Barron's, Alpha Magazine*, and *Institutional Investors*) as such, or if the company's own website lists hedge fund management or alternative investment management for pooled vehicles as part of its major business. Using this top-down approach, we identify 484 unique hedge fund companies in our sample.

Due to the nature of bankruptcy (which is usually triggered by a firm's failure to fulfil its obligations to its creditors), this list provides more detailed investor information on the debt side than on the equity side. To supplement information on the latter, we compile a list of institutions that make significant equity investments in the distressed firms—both before and during the Chapter 11 process—from two SEC filings: Schedule 13D and Form 13F. The Schedule 13D filing is a mandatory filing under Section 13(d) of the Securities Exchange Act that requires investors to disclose within ten days of acquisition of, or conversion into, more than 5% of any class of securities of a publicly traded company if they have an interest in influencing the management of the company (including the reorganization of the company). Form 13F filings (from the Thomson Reuters Ownership Database) require all institutions that have investment discretion over a minimum of $100 million in Section 13(f) securities (mostly publicly traded equity) to disclose their quarter-end holdings in these securities. The window to collect equity ownership information from both sources spans from one year before a Chapter 11 filing to one year after the confirmation of the plan. For ownership disclosed in the Form 13F, we impose a threshold of 2% of the shares outstanding for 'significant' equity ownership, as smaller stakes are unlikely to be effective in influencing the reorganization process.

12.3.1.4 *Firm-level Financial Information and Security Prices*

We merge our sample of Chapter 11 filers with the CRSP/Compustat (available through WRDS) and Capital IQ databases to retrieve additional firm-level financial information. While Compustat provides standard information from firms' income statements and balance sheets, Capital IQ provides more detailed information about capital structure, and in particular the ratio of secured debt to total assets. When such information is missing from

Capital IQ, we use data from BankruptcyData.com. We primarily rely on CRSP to retrieve stock price information for our sample firms, and turn to 'pink sheets', available through Bloomberg and Datastream, when there is no CRSP coverage.

Finally, we code two key outcome variables that characterize distribution to junior claims (unsecured debt and equity), possibly as a result of APR deviations (Eberhart, Moore, and Roenfeldt 1990; Betker 1995; Eberhart and Weiss 1998), using information from bankruptcy plans and supplemented by BankruptcyData.com and Datastream. The first variable, *APRCreditor*, measures the APR deviations for secured creditors (Capkun and Weiss 2008).[7] It is an indicator variable that is equal to one if unsecured creditors' recovery is greater than zero while secured creditors' recovery is less than 100%. The second variable, *DistEquity*, is an indicator variable that is equal to one if there is any distribution to existing equity holders.

Table 12.1 defines all the major variables used in this chapter and provides their data sources.

12.3.2 Sample Overview

Table 12.2, Panel A, reports Chapter 11 outcomes by year. Several patterns emerge from the table. First, bankruptcy filings are highly cyclical. The burst of the dot-com bubble in 2000 and subsequent recession is associated with a large number of Chapter 11 filings, while the boom prior to the 2008 financial crisis is associated with much fewer filings. Second, the adoption of KERP has been on the rise over the sample period, a trend also noted by Bharath, Panchapegesan, and Werner (2007). Third, APR deviations (as captured by APRCreditor) are not commonplace in our sample, occurring in about 15% of the cases, which is much smaller than in the 1980s and early 1990s, when APR deviations were the norm rather than the exception (see, e.g., Weiss 1990; Adler, Capkun, and Weiss 2007).[8] Finally, the average duration of bankruptcy has been substantially shortened, from twenty-one months at the beginning of our sample period to twelve months in the period 2004 to 2006.[9] In comparison, the average duration in Franks and Torous's (1994) sample over the period 1983 to 1988 is close to thirty months and the average in the Bharath, Panchapegesan, and Werner (2007) sample over the period 1979 to 2005 is eighteen months.

Panel B of Table 12.2 presents summary statistics of firm and Chapter 11 case characteristics. All firm-level variables are recorded at the fiscal year-end prior to the bankruptcy filing date. To mitigate the influence of outliers, we winsorize all potentially unbounded variables at the first and ninety-ninth percentiles. The median size of our sample firms, measured by total assets (*Assets*), is $706 million in 2008 constant dollars, putting the typical sample firm between the sixth and seventh size decile of the Compustat universe during the same period. Both the mean and median ratios of liabilities to total assets (*Leverage*) are close to one, much higher than the mean (median) leverage ratio of 68% (59%) for the Compustat universe—a direct sign of financial distress. Our sample firms also tend to have lower return

[7] We use market values of equity and warrants at emergence to calculate debt recovery.

[8] Our sample statistics are consistent with Bharath, Panchapegesan, and Werner (2007) and Capkun and Weiss (2008) using more recent data.

[9] The duration statistics for 2007 are not included to mitigate the truncation bias toward the end of our sample.

Table 12.1 Variable definitions

This table provides the definition of variables used in the study and data sources.

Variable	Definitions	Data Source
Assets	Book assets measured in 2008 dollars.	Bankruptcy Research Database, BankruptcyData.com, Compustat
AssetsChange	The change in book assets between the last fiscal year end and the time of filing Chapter 11, scaled by the former.	Bankruptcy Research Database, BankruptcyData.com, Compustat
Sales	Sales measured in 2008 dollars.	Bankruptcy Research Database, BankruptcyData.com, Compustat
Leverage	The ratio of total liabilities to book assets.	Compustat, EDGAR (10Ks), BankruptcyData.com
Cash	The ratio of cash and short-term investments to book assets.	Compustat, EDGAR (10Ks), BankruptcyData.com
Tangibility	The ratio of net PP&E to book assets.	Compustat, EDGAR (10Ks), BankruptcyData.com
ROA	The ratio of EBITDA to book assets.	Compustat, EDGAR (10Ks), BankruptcyData.com
SecuredDebt	The ratio of secured debt to book assets.	Capital IQ, BankrutpcyData.com, Compustat
Institution	Percentage of institutional ownership.	Thomson Reuters Ownership Database (13Fs)
NumClasses	Number of claim classes.	Bankruptcy Plans
CBLenders	An indicator variable that takes a value of one if at least one commercial bank is among the secured lenders.	BankruptcyData.com, DealScan, and SDC Syndicated Loan Database
Bankruptcy Case Characteristics		
Prepack	An indicator variable that takes a value of one if a bankruptcy is prepackaged or pre-negotiated. According to the definition by LoPucki, a case is prepackaged if the debtor drafted the plan, submitted to a vote of the impaired classes, and claimed to have obtained the acceptance necessary for consensual confirmation before filing. On the other hand, if the debtor negotiates the plan with less than all groups or obtains the acceptance of less than all groups necessary to confirm before the bankruptcy case is filed, then the case is regarded as pre-negotiated.	Bankruptcy Research Database, BankruptcyData.com, Bankruptcy Plans

(continued)

Table 12.1 (Continued)

Variable	Definitions	Data Source
Delaware	An indicator variable that takes a value of one if a bankruptcy case is filed in the state of Delaware.	Bankruptcy Research Database, BankruptcyData.com
LossExclusivity	An indicator variable that takes a value of one if the debtor loses its exclusive right to file a plan of reorganization after 180 days in bankruptcy.	Bankrutpcydata.com and Factiva
DIP	An indicator variable that takes a value of one if the bankrupt firm receives court approval of debtor-in-possession (DIP) financing.	BankruptcyData.com, Bankruptcy DataSource, Bankruptcy Plans, LexisNexis, Factiva
KERP	An indicator variable that takes a value of one if a KERP is approved by the court.	BankruptcyData.com, Bankruptcy DataSource, Bankruptcy Plans, LexisNexis, Factiva
Creditors' Committee	An indicator variable that takes a value of one if an unsecured creditors' committee is appointed by the court.	BankruptcyData.com, LexisNexis, Factiva
Equity Committee	An indicator variable that takes a value of one if an equity committee is appointed by the court.	BankruptcyData.com, LexisNexis, Factiva
CEOTurnover	An indicator variable that takes a value of one if the CEO of a bankrupt firm is replaced during the Chapter 11 restructuring.	BankruptcyData.com, LexisNexis, Factiva, EDGAR (Proxy Statements and 10Ks)
Emerge	An indicator variable that takes a value of one if the bankrupt firm emerges from bankruptcy.	Bankruptcy Research Database, BankruptcyData.com
Liquidated	An indicator variable that takes a value of one if the bankrupt firm is liquidated (liquidation in Chapter 11 or conversion to Chapter 7).	Bankruptcy Research Database, BankruptcyData.com
Duration	Number of months in bankruptcy, from the date of filing to the date of plan confirmation.	Bankruptcy Research Database, BankruptcyData.com
APRCreditor	An indicator variable that takes a value of one if there is an APR deviation for secured creditors, which occurs when unsecured debt holders receive a distribution before secured lenders are paid in full.	BankruptcyData.com, EDGAR (8K), Bankruptcy Courts
DistEquity	An indicator variable that takes a value of one if equity holders receive payoffs either through APR deviation or retaining pre-Chapter 11 shares.	BankruptcyData.com, EDGAR (8K), Bankruptcy Courts
DebtRecovery	Average recovery of all corporate debt (including both secure and unsecured debt) at plan confirmation.	BankruptcyData.com, EDGAR (8K), Bankruptcy Courts, CRSP, Bloomberg, Datastream

StkRet	Standardized abnormal monthly return, constructed by subtracting the contemporaneous holding period return of the CRSP equal-weighted index from the holding period return for Chapter 11 stocks from two days before filing to plan confirmation, normalized by the number of months in the Chapter 11 process.	CRSP, Bloomberg, Datastream
CAR[a,b]	CRSP equal-weighted index-adjusted CARs from *a* days before bankruptcy filing to *b* days after filing.	CRSP, Bloomberg, Datastream
Hedge Fund Presence		
HFCreditors Committee	An indicator variable that takes a value of one if at least one hedge fund is on the unsecured creditors' committee.	BankruptcyData.com, LexisNexis, Factiva
HFLargest Creditors	An indicator variable that takes a value of one if at least one hedge fund is one of the largest unsecured creditors as listed on the Chapter 11 petition forms.	BankruptcyData.com, LexisNexis, Factiva
HFEquity Committee	An indicator variable that takes a value of one if at least one hedge fund is on the equity committee.	BankruptcyData.com, LexisNexis, Factiva
HFJoint5%	An indicator variable that takes a value of one if the total equity ownership by all hedge funds is at least 5%.	Thomson Reuters Ownership Database (13Fs), EDGAR (13Ds, Proxy Statements, 10Ks)
HFLTO	An indicator variable that takes a value of one if at least one hedge fund appears to be a loan-to-own (LTO) player. A hedge fund is an LTO player if hedge funds are identified from a list of the largest unsecured creditors and unsecured creditors' committee and they are matched to 13D and 13F filings within one year after bankruptcy, or bankruptcy reorganization plans confirmed by the court show that the classes of claims held by hedge funds receive equity distribution.	BankruptcyData.com, Bankruptcy DataSource, Bankruptcy Plans, LexisNexis, Factiva, Thomson Reuters Ownership Database (13Fs), EDGAR (13Ds, Proxy Statements, 10Ks)
HFLTO DIP	An indicator variable that takes a value of one if at least one hedge fund appears to be a loan-to-own (LTO) player or at least one hedge fund is among the providers of DIP financing.	BankruptcyData.com, Bankruptcy DataSource, Bankruptcy Plans, LexisNexis, Factiva, Thomson Reuters Ownership Database (13Fs), EDGAR (13Ds, Proxy Statements, 10Ks)

Table 12.2 Summary of Chapter 11 cases

The sample includes 474 large US Chapter 11 filings from 1996 to 2007. This table presents summary statistics of key bankruptcy case and firm characteristics. Variable definitions are provided in Table 12.1. Panel A presents summary statistics of key case characteristics by year. Numbers presented are in percentages except for *Duration*. The variable *N* in Column (1) is the number of Chapter 11 filings in a given year (*N*). Panel B presents summary statistics of key firm characteristics.

	(1)	(2)	(3)	(4)	(5)	(6)	(7)	(8)	(9)	(10)	(11)	(12)	(13)
Filing Year	*N*	Loss Exclusivity	DIP	KERP	Creditors' Committee	Equity Committee	CEO Turnover	Emerge	Liquidated	Duration (months)	APR Creditor	Dist Equity	Debt Recovery
Panel A: Bankruptcy Case Characteristics by Year													
1996	15	13.3	73.3	26.7	73.3	6.7	60.0	40.0	46.7	20.5	13.3	33.3	56.8
1997	17	11.8	70.6	29.4	70.6	5.9	29.4	76.5	11.8	21.0	0.0	17.6	70.4
1998	31	16.1	64.5	29.0	90.3	16.1	30.0	71.0	22.6	17.0	9.7	19.4	49.4
1999	42	19.1	69.0	40.5	81.0	14.3	39.0	54.8	31.0	19.0	14.3	33.3	64.8
2000	77	19.5	62.3	28.6	88.3	6.5	23.4	55.8	32.5	20.6	20.8	14.3	48.6
2001	88	17.0	54.5	38.6	81.8	8.0	18.1	47.7	42.0	17.6	19.3	18.2	41.8
2002	80	21.3	57.5	40.0	83.8	8.8	18.3	58.8	25.0	14.1	21.3	20.0	46.8
2003	50	26.0	64.0	54.0	100.0	14.0	30.0	68.0	24.0	15.9	10.0	20.0	52.3
2004	28	35.7	82.1	57.1	82.1	17.9	21.4	85.7	14.3	11.6	3.6	28.6	58.0
2005	23	26.1	78.3	60.9	91.3	13.0	50.0	69.6	21.7	14.7	4.3	13.0	56.6
2006	13	7.7	84.6	46.2	84.6	38.5	23.1	84.6	15.4	11.4	15.4	38.5	65.1
2007	10	0.0	70.0	50.0	70.0	10.0	20.0	50.0	50.0	8.4	0.0	20.0	43.9
All	474	19.8	64.3	40.3	85.2	11.2	26.7	60.3	29.3	16.8	14.8	20.9	51.5

Firm/Case Characteristics	N	Mean	Standard Deviation	Min	25th	Median	75th	Max
Panel B: Summary Statistics of Key Firm and Case Characteristics								
Assets	474	2,718	8,975	220	424	706	1,686	124,363
Sales	474	1,901	6,914	0	323	615	1,324	122,787
Leverage	474	0.997	0.390	0.254	0.767	0.919	1.129	2.707
Cash	473	0.068	0.097	0.000	0.011	0.030	0.082	0.513
Tangibility	474	0.358	0.240	0.000	0.150	0.339	0.527	0.896
ROA	473	0.010	0.164	−1.073	−0.026	0.043	0.093	0.297
SecuredDebt	466	0.280	0.287	0.000	0.034	0.226	0.430	1.499
Institution	474	0.278	0.254	0.000	0.018	0.239	0.435	1.000
NumClasses	414	8.995	3.112	3	7	9	10	27
Prepack	474	0.293	0.456	0	0	0	1	1
Delaware	474	0.430	0.496	0	0	0	1	1

on assets and lower institutional ownership relative to the Compustat universe. The Internet Appendix reports the pairwise correlation coefficients among key firm/case characteristics and hedge fund participation variables.

12.4 Hedge Fund Presence in Chapter 11: Overview and Determinants

12.4.1 Overview of Hedge Fund Involvement

Table 12.3 presents an overview of hedge fund involvement during the Chapter 11 process, where statistics are grouped by year and by the timing of hedge fund presence. The table lists a set of indicator variables to capture the specific roles that hedge funds take on in Chapter 11 as creditors, equity holders, and loan-to-own players. While our formal analyses focus on hedge fund impact using the default measure in each category, sensitivity analyses using alternative measures are reported in the Internet Appendix.

Our default measure for hedge fund involvement as creditors is *HFCreditorsCommittee*, which refers to cases in which a hedge fund sits on the unsecured creditors' committee.[10] The alternative measure, *HFLargestCreditor*, refers to cases in which a hedge fund is one of the creditors holding the twenty (and in some cases information is available for fifty) largest unsecured claims according to the Chapter 11 petition forms.

Our default measure for hedge fund participation on the equity side is *HFEquityCommittee*, which refers to cases in which a hedge fund serves on the equity committee. The alternative measure is *HFJoint5%*, an indicator variable for hedge funds that jointly hold more than 5% of the outstanding shares based on their Schedule 13D and Form 13F filings, or information from BankrutpcyData.com, 10K filings, and proxy statements.

A hybrid role between creditors and shareholders that hedge funds take on in the Chapter 11 process arises when they adopt a 'loan-to-own' (LTO) strategy, whereby a hedge fund enters the restructuring process as a major creditor with the intention to emerge from the process as a significant shareholder. Our default measure for hedge funds playing the LTO strategy, *HFLTO*, takes a value of one if any of the following situations applies:[11] (i) a hedge fund identified from a list of the largest unsecured creditors or the unsecured creditors' committee members is matched to major shareholders from 13D and 13F filings within one year after bankruptcy, or (ii) bankruptcy reorganization plans confirmed by the court show

[10] In most Chapter 11 cases, the United States trustee appoints seven of the debtor's largest unsecured creditors to the unsecured creditors' committee as dictated by the US Bankruptcy Codes, § 1102. An appointment to the committee can enhance controlling creditors' involvement in the debtor's restructuring and further their investment agenda (Harner 2008a). The committee usually hires professionals (counsels and financial advisors) to serve as its representatives. Though it does not directly vote on a reorganization plan, the committee makes recommendations to creditors. On the other hand, it is rare to have secured creditors form a committee of their own given that their claims are already collateralized.

[11] The reorganization plan does not identify whether a particular creditor receives equity distribution. Instead, we infer this information from statements that indicate a certain class of creditors receives equity distribution.

Table 12.3 Hedge fund presence in Chapter 11 by year and timing

The sample includes 474 large US Chapter 11 filings from 1996 to 2007. This table presents an overview of hedge fund presence during the Chapter 11 process. Statistics are grouped by year and by the timing of hedge fund presence. *N* is the number of Chapter 11 filings in a given year. All numbers in Columns (1) to (12) are in percentages and track the presence of at least one hedge fund in the following roles: (1) among the twenty or fifty largest unsecured creditors as listed on the Chapter 11 petition forms (*Largest creditors*); (2) among the top shareholders at the time of filing (*Largest shareholders*); (3) filing Schedule 13D within one year before Chapter 11 filing (*13D filing*); (4) on the unsecured creditors' committee (*Unsecured creditors' committee*); (5) among the providers of debtor-in-possession financing (*DIP financing*); (6) filing Schedule 13D during the reorganization process (*13D filing*); (7) on the equity committee (*Equity committee*); (8) adopting a loan-to-own strategy (*Loan-to-own*); (9) adopting a loan-to-own strategy or providing debtor-in-possession financing (*Loan-to-own ˙DIP*); (10) being on the debt side including *largest creditors, unsecured creditors' committee*, and *DIP financing* (*Debt side*); (11) being on the equity side including *largest shareholders, 13D filing* both before and during bankruptcy, and *equity committee* (*Equity side*); and (12) the overall involvement by hedge funds (*Overall*).

		HF Presence Before Bankruptcy			HF Presence During Bankruptcy					Both Before and During Bankruptcy			
		(1)	(2)	(3)	(4)	(5)	(6)	(7)	(8)	(9)	(10)	(11)	(12)
Filing Year	*N*	Largest creditors	Largest shareholders	13D filing	Unsecured Creditors' committee	DIP financing	13D filing	Equity committee	Loan-to-own	Loan-to-own˙DIP	Debt side	Equity side	Overall
1996	15	16.7	27.3	0.0	30.8	0.0	6.7	6.7	28.6	28.6	46.2	36.4	72.7
1997	17	7.7	42.9	17.6	40.0	11.8	0.0	0.0	17.6	29.4 66.7	42.9	78.6	
1998	31	32.0	48.4	9.7	40.7	0.0	3.2	9.7	20.0	20.0	60.0	58.1	92.9
1999	42	39.5	50.0	4.8	50.0	4.8	0.0	2.4	35.6	39.0	64.9	52.5	83.8
2000	77	33.3	55.4	5.2	30.9	5.2	3.9	0.0	24.6	29.0	58.5	56.0	89.2
2001	88	11.3	44.7	5.7	29.4	3.4	2.3	3.5	18.5	23.1	51.2	48.2	88.3
2002	80	28.3	47.4	2.5	43.5	8.7	3.8	3.8	33.3	37.9	64.2	50.0	86.9
2003	50	20.9	50.0	8.0	47.6	14.0	2.0	10.2	34.0	44.7	66.7	59.2	89.1
2004	28	29.6	25.0	14.3	48.1	21.4	7.1	7.4	42.9	50.0	67.9	35.7	85.7
2005	23	21.7	59.1	13.0	40.9	21.7	17.4	13.0	30.4	47.8	59.1	73.9	91.3
2006	13	30.8	61.5	7.7	38.5	38.5	30.8	38.5	23.1	53.8	76.9	69.2	84.6
2007	10	0.0	80.0	20.0	20.0	20.0	0.0	10.0	0.0	20.0	30.0	80.0	90.0
All	474	25.1	48.5	7.0	39.5	9.1	4.4	5.8	27.7	34.5	60.7	53.4	87.4

w

that the classes of claims held by a hedge fund receive equity distribution. In recent years, DIP financing has become creditors' new power tool of corporate governance in Chapter 11 (Skeel 2003) because DIP lenders are able to take control of the bankrupt firm by bargaining for seats on the board of directors and receiving shares in the newly reorganized company. As a result, our alternative measure, *HFLTO DIP*, takes a value of one if conditions (i) or (ii) above, or (iii) a hedge fund is the provider of DIP financing, holds. DIP loans often turn into equity ownership because they have trigger clauses that replace the DIP debt with preferred or common equity to avoid default or that replace exit financing with debt-for-equity swaps.[12]

The most salient pattern emerging from Table 12.3 is that hedge fund participation in Chapter 11 bankruptcies is commonplace: 87% of the cases have publicly observable hedge fund involvement in some form. In 61% (53%) of the cases, hedge funds are present on the debt (equity) side. Moreover, the industry representation of our full sample is preserved in the subsamples of firms with various forms of hedge fund presence.

A few additional patterns are summarized as follows. First, despite the absence of an obvious time trend, hedge funds' participation on the debt side exhibits significant cyclicality: hedge fund presence on the unsecured creditors' committee or just among the largest unsecured creditors is relatively low in 1997, 2001, and 2007, years with tightened credit conditions. On the other hand, hedge fund provision of DIP financing rises steadily over our sample period, coinciding with the overall increasing trend of DIP financing since 1990 (Dahiya et al. 2003; Bharath, Panchapegesan, and Werner 2007). While the majority providers of DIP financing in the 1990s and early 2000s were banks and financial institutions that had prior lending relationships with the borrower, we show that hedge funds have become a new force in providing DIP financing since 2003.

Second, hedge funds' overall involvement on the equity side is smaller than their presence on the debt side. In about half of the cases hedge funds are among the largest shareholders at the bankruptcy filing. In about 6% of the cases hedge funds serve on the equity committee, but the percentage increases to double digits in recent years. This increase could be attributed to the fact that more equity committees have been formed in recent years.[13] Conditional on having an equity committee, hedge funds have representation in more than half of the cases, and in all cases during the 2005 to 2007 period. Therefore, it seems that hedge fund shareholders have strong incentives to represent other shareholders by forming and joining the equity committee.

Finally, based on our definitions of the loan-to-own strategy, hedge funds are creditors-turned-shareholders in 28% of the cases if DIP financing is not considered, and in 34% of the cases if it is. These numbers are remarkably close to the survey evidence in Harner

[12] A recent example is General Growth Properties Inc. in 2009. Farallon Capital Management LLC offered DIP financing that can be converted into 8% to 10% of the common stock on the effective date of the reorganization plan. For recent examples and related discussions, see Bravo and Hester (2009).

[13] Unlike the unsecured creditors' committee, the equity committee is not common (see Bharath, Panchapegesan, and Werner (2007) and our statistics in Table 12.2, Panel A). Parties (usually the seven largest equity holders as dictated by the US Bankruptcy Codes, § 1102) that have the intention to form the equity committee need to submit motions to the court. Once approved by the court, these parties will most likely become members.

(2008b).[14] Hedge funds' loan-to-own strategies are clearly cyclical. In the years of tightened credit conditions, the percentage of cases in which hedge funds engaged in the loan-to-own strategy ranges from 0% to 19%, which is considerably lower than the sample average.

In addition to the overall pattern of hedge fund participation at the event level, in the Appendix we list the five most active hedge funds by the particular roles they assume in Chapter 11. It is not surprising that Oaktree Capital Management, one of the world's largest distressed debt investors with $25 billion assets under management (Goldschmid 2005), is ranked at the top in the largest unsecured creditors and unsecured creditors' committee categories. Oaktree also appears on the lists of most active providers of DIP financing and largest shareholders. Cerberus Capital Management is the most active provider of DIP financing, but also holds large unsecured claims and often serves on the unsecured creditors' committee.

12.4.2 Determinants of Hedge Fund Participation

Hedge funds make calculated choices in their involvement in the distressed firm, especially with regard to the type of securities they purchase (e.g., debt versus equity). To analyse such choices, we start with predictive regressions that relate hedge fund investment strategies to firm and case characteristics. The dependent variables are the measures for hedge fund involvement as creditors, equity holders, and loan-to-own players, as defined in Section 12.4.1. The set of explanatory variables, described in Section 12.3, is chosen following prior literature on bankruptcy.[15] Table 12.4 reports the predictive regressions.

Our discussion of Table 12.4 focuses on the default measures for hedge fund participation. We find that overall hedge fund participation on the debt side is positively correlated with firm size. Not surprisingly, hedge funds appear as major creditors (measured by *HFCreditorsCommittee*) when the distressed firm has more cash and liquid assets on its balance sheet, which helps debt recovery. Interestingly, hedge funds prefer to invest in unsecured distressed debt when the ratio of secured debt to assets (*SecuredDebt*) is lower (significant at the 5% level). A low ratio of secured debt to total assets implies that the senior debt is more likely to be overcollateralized, which leaves room for a more active role for the unsecured creditors. Needless to say, the secured debt ratio and the leverage ratio are positively correlated (the correlation is 0.23). We confirm that the significance of the coefficient on *SecuredDebt* comes more from the amount of secured debt than from the amount of total debt because the coefficient remains significant regardless of whether we control for *Leverage*, while the latter becomes insignificant in the presence of *SecuredDebt*.

In contrast, hedge fund shareholders (as measured by *HFEquityCommittee*) prefer firms with lower leverage (significant at the 5% level) and are not averse to high levels of secured

[14] One of Harner's (2008b) survey questions is 'how often does your firm invest in a company's distressed debt to try to acquire the company or a controlling ownership position in the company, and how often is your firm successful in acquiring at least a controlling ownership position?' Some 32% of the respondents indicate that they engage and succeed in this practice.

[15] It is worth noting that adding year and industry (based on two-digit SIC codes) fixed effects does not qualitatively change our main findings in the chapter. Further, under most model specifications, these fixed effects are not individually statistically significant.

Table 12.4 Predicting hedge fund presence in Chapter 11

This table presents the probit regression results examining the determinants of hedge fund participation in Chapter 11. Columns (1) and (2) and Columns (3) and (4) examine the determinants of hedge fund participation on the debt side and the equity side, respectively. Columns (5) and (6) examine hedge funds adopting a loan-to-own strategy. Definitions of variables are provided in Table 12.1. Numbers in brackets are standard errors. ***, **, * correspond to statistical significance at the 1%, 5%, and 10% levels, respectively.

	Hedge Funds on Debt Side		Hedge Funds on Equity Side		Hedge Funds Loan-to-Own	
	(1)	(2)	(3)	(4)	(5)	(6)
Variable	HFCreditorsCommittee	HFLargestCreditors	HFEquityCommittee	HFJoint5%	HFLTO	HFLTO DIP
Ln(Assets)	0.163**	−0.083	0.104	−0.074	0.1A68***	0.105**
	[0.064]	[0.067]	[0.084]	[0.060]	[0.064]	[0.062]
Leverage	0.242	−0.257	−0.857**	−0.039	0.361*	0.429**
	[0.210]	[0.219]	[0.439]	[0.178]	[0.204]	[0.196]
Cash	1.538**	0.412	−1.851	1.518**	−0.909	−0.570
	[0.784]	[0.774]	[1.609]	[0.699]	[0.864]	[0.777]
Tangibility	0.286	0.087	−0.486	0.020	0.475	0.282
	[0.294]	[0.304]	[0.452]	[0.267]	[0.295]	[0.283]
ROA	0.828	0.063	0.539	0.759*	0.113	0.301
	[0.593]	[0.621]	[0.978]	[0.455]	[0.585]	[0.556]
SecuredDebt	−0.670**	−0.071	0.311	0.578**	−0.526**	−0.434*
	[0.288]	[0.290]	[0.428]	[0.235]	[0.272]	[0.260]
Institution	−0.197	0.115	1.474***	1.103***	−0.106	0.312
	[0.282]	[0.296]	[0.413]	[0.264]	[0.288]	[0.273]
NumClasses	0.012	0.036	0.013	−0.042*	0.082***	0.075***
	[0.024]	[0.025]	[0.036]	[0.023]	[0.025]	[0.025]
Prepack	−0.201	0.219	0.217	0.152	0.375**	0.281**
	[0.154]	[0.164]	[0.240]	[0.139]	[0.151]	[0.146]
Delaware	−0.169	0.129	−0.154	0.194	0.037	0.138
	[0.138]	[0.147]	[0.218]	[0.125]	[0.139]	[0.133]
Constant	−1.590***	−0.371	−2.020***	0.196	−2.957***	−2.424***
	[0.503]	[0.529]	[0.691]	[0.453]	[0.524]	[0.496]
N	369	361	459	447	416	416
Pseudo-R^2	0.050	0.016	0.148	0.058	0.087	0.077

debt. One possible explanation is that the secured creditor-driven fire sale bias is weakened (Ayotte and Morrison 2009) in firms where the senior debt is undercollateralized. In such cases shareholders enjoy more upside potential. Not surprisingly, hedge fund presence on the equity side is positively associated with institutional equity ownership (excluding the investing hedge funds) before bankruptcy (significant at the 1% level). Such stocks may possess characteristics that are appealing to institutional investors (which include hedge funds) in the first place, but, more importantly, hedge funds prefer to work with other institutional rather than individual investors when they intend to influence corporate policy and control, a phenomenon documented by Brav et al. (this volume, Chapter 8) and Bradley, Brav, and Goldstein (2010) among hedge funds that pursue activist agendas in underperforming companies and in discounted closed-end funds, respectively.

Certain firm and case attributes predict hedge funds' adopting loan-to-own strategies. In addition to firm size, we find that leverage, the number of claim classes, and prepackaged Chapter 11 cases are positively associated with adoption of the strategy (significant at the 10% level or better), while secured debt ratios are negatively associated with hedge funds' loan-to-own strategies (significant at the 5% level). The combination of high leverage and low secured debt indicates a high probability that unsecured debt will be converted into equity upon reorganization—a natural route for loan-to-own. The mean (median) number of claim classes (*NumClasses*) in our sample is nine.[16] A larger number of claim classes is usually associated with greater difficulty in reaching agreement among different groups of investors (Franks and Torous 1994; Betker 1995). However, the involvement of hedge funds in different parts of the capital structure through the loan-to-own strategy should help internalize such costs.

Prepackaged bankruptcies, constituting close to a third of the cases, are usually available to better-performing firms that are easier to reorganize. Tashjian, Lease, and McConnell (1996) find that unsecured creditors prefer prepackaged bankruptcies to traditional Chapter 11 reorganizations because the priority for secured creditors is less likely to be upheld in the former case. Their results are consistent with our evidence that hedge funds start their loan-to-own strategies by first investing in unsecured debt, which tends to enjoy higher recovery rates under prepackaged bankruptcies. Our main analyses include an indicator variable for prepackaged Chapter 11 as a control variable in all regressions to be consistent with the general practice in the literature. Sensitivity analyses excluding prepackaged cases are reported in Section 12.5.2.6.

Table 12.4, complemented by evidence from Tables 12.2 and 12.3, reveals hedge funds' strategic choice in seeking an entry point in the capital structure of the distressed firm that allows them to have a strong impact on reorganization. In general, hedge funds are more likely to approach distressed firms from the debt side than from the equity side, though a higher percentage of them become equity holders *ex post*. Within the debt category, the most popular entry point for hedge funds is unsecured debt (Baird and Rasmussen 2008; Harner 2008a). This preference is consistent with the argument put forth by recent legal studies,[17] that hedge funds have a strong preference for so-called 'fulcrum' securities in the

[16] The different classes of claims include, for example, tax claims, secured claims, priority nontax claims, bank loan claims, secured debt claims, unsecured debt claims, worker compensation claims, general unsecured claims, litigation claims, intercompany interests, convenience claims (smaller amount unsecured claims), subordinated claims, equity claims, and warrants and unexercised options.

[17] See, for example, Lichtenstein and Cheney (2008).

capital structure, which is the point in the capital structure where the enterprise value first fails to fully cover the claims. Secured debt is rarely fulcrum. Unsecured debt is thus appealing to hedge funds because of the potential upside gain due to their option-like features and, more importantly, the sensitivity of the securities' value to their actions.

Moreover, firms with high levels of secured debt are more likely to have undercollateralized secured debt, providing less room for unsecured creditors and hence less appeal for hedge funds to influence the process through the unsecured creditors' committee. In contrast, given senior creditors' weaker incentive to push for liquidation, the potential for reorganization and emergence gives shareholders more upside potential and thus attracts more hedge funds to the equity side.

12.5 Hedge Fund Presence and Bankruptcy Outcomes

12.5.1 Model Specification

This section examines the relation between hedge fund involvement and bankruptcy outcomes as measured by the following nine variables: (i) *Emerge*, which measures the emergence of the firm from bankruptcy (as opposed to being liquidated or acquired); (ii) *Duration*, which measures the number of months (measured in log) spent in bankruptcy until resolution (which includes emergence, liquidation, or acquisition); (iii) *LossExclusivity*, which measures the debtor's loss of its exclusive right to file a plan of reorganization after 180 days in bankruptcy; (iv) *APRCreditor*, defined in Section 12.2.1.4, which measures the occurrence of distributions to unsecured creditors before secured creditors are paid in full; (v) *DistEquity*, which measures distributions made to existing shareholders; (vi) *DebtRecovery*, which measures the average recovery of all corporate debt (including secured and unsecured debt) at plan confirmation; (vii) *CEOTurnover*, which measures CEO turnover during the reorganization process; (viii) *KERP*, which measures the existence of a KERP approved by the court; and (ix) *StkRet*, which measures the standardized abnormal return from Chapter 11 filing to plan confirmation. The variables (ii), (vi), and (ix) are continuous, while the rest are binary variables. The variables (iv) and (v) characterize distributions to junior claims as a result of APR deviation, and the variables (vii) and (viii) capture the incentives and stability of senior management during the Chapter 11 process. Each table presented below includes a subset of these nine outcome variables as relevant for the particular role that hedge funds assume.

Any relation between hedge fund presence and bankruptcy outcomes could result from two effects: (i) a pure selection effect, whereby informed hedge funds pick the targets that offer the best expected payoff,[18] and the value of the underlying assets is exogenous to hedge funds' action; and (ii) a pure treatment effect, whereby hedge funds change the outcome and

[18] See Li and Prabhala (2007) for an overview of self-selection in corporate finance.

hence the value of the underlying assets even if they were randomly assigned to distressed firms. This is the 'average treatment effect' of the full sample.

A priori a combination of these two effects is likely at work. Hedge funds are sophisticated investors that could potentially profit from their company-picking skills even if they remain passive stakeholders, and at the same time hedge funds are likely to choose cases in which they can more effectively influence the outcome in their favour. It is worth noting that our default measures for hedge fund participation (*HFCreditorsCommittee* and *HFEquityCommittee*) embed their activist roles. If hedge funds can achieve the desired outcome just by picking the right companies without exerting influence during the Chapter 11 process, they can remain passive large stakeholders without the costly voluntary effort of forming and serving on those committees.

As a large unsecured creditor, a hedge fund can accept or decline the invitation from the US Trustee's Office to join the unsecured creditors' committee; as a large shareholder, a hedge fund needs to submit motions to the court to form an equity committee. The duties of committee members range from reviewing the debtor's books to monitoring the debtor's business and legal activities and recommending a course of action to the holders of the claims they represent. However, their presence on such committees may infringe on their flexibility in trading claims due to their access to nonpublic material information. According to Ayotte and Morrison (2009), the unsecured creditors' committee often objects to key plan terms, such as the appointment of professionals, DIP loan terms, asset sales, and exclusivity extensions. It is, therefore, highly unlikely that hedge funds would put in such effort and incur the related costs if they did not intend to actively influence the Chapter 11 process.

Despite a lack of systematic public data sources that describe hedge funds' actual actions in court or in boardrooms, our search of news articles yields anecdotal evidence suggesting that they do actively engage in the process. In addition to the examples referred to in Section 12.2, two hedge funds (D.E. Shaw and Eton Park Master Fund) in the Allied Holdings case were on the unsecured creditors' committee that filed objections to exclusivity extensions. Also, in both the KCS Energy case (where DDJ Capital Management and Turnberry Capital Management were involved) and the Sunbeam case (where Oaktree Capital Management, HBK Investment, and KS Capital Partners were involved), hedge funds on the unsecured creditors' committees proposed alternative reorganization plans.[19]

To accommodate both the selection and the treatment effects, we use the following model:

$$\begin{aligned} &HFPart_i^* = X_i\beta + \varepsilon_i \\ &HFPart_i = 1 \text{ if } HFPart_i^* > 0; \text{ and } HFPart_i = 0 \text{ if otherwise,} \\ &\text{Outcome}_i = Z_i\gamma + \mu HFPart_i + \eta_i. \end{aligned} \tag{1}$$

In the above system, *HFPart* is an indicator variable for hedge funds' participation in various ways as analysed in Table 12.4, and Outcome is one of the outcome variables defined earlier in this section. Econometrically, a selection problem amounts to a nonzero correlation between the error disturbances of the two equations in (1), that is,

[19] For more detailed stories, see Beaudette (2006); *Federal Filings Newswires* (2000); and *Associated Press Newswires* (2002), respectively.

$corr(\varepsilon_i,\eta_i) \neq 0$. Consequently, the estimated ˆis upward (downward) biased if $corr(\varepsilon_i,\eta_i)$ is positive (negative).

For the purpose of identification, we need instrumental variables that effectively predict hedge funds' participation but do not affect outcome variables other than through hedge funds. That is, the vector of X in equation (1) must contain variables in addition to a full overlap with the vector of Z. We acknowledge that no firm-level variable is likely to satisfy the exclusion restriction because it is difficult to rule out a firm characteristic that attracts hedge fund participation as a simultaneous determinant of the outcome. Instead, we settle on the following two instrumental variables, both of which capture the capital supply conditions of hedge fund distress investing.

The first variable is *DistressHFRet*, which is the lagged return on an index of distress-investing hedge funds using data from CISDM (a hedge fund database available through WRDS). More specifically, we use the monthly average return over the three-month period (before the Chapter 11 filing) and find that our results are not sensitive to the particular estimation window chosen. This variable has explanatory power for hedge fund participation as creditors and shareholders. The second variable is *SP500Ret*, which is the lagged monthly return on Standard & Poor's (S&P) 500 index. To avoid collinearity, we use the residual from regressing the raw *SP500Ret* on *DistressHFRet*. Again, the three-month period (before the Chapter 11 filing) serves as our estimation window to form the lagged return variable. This variable has explanatory power for hedge fund participation as shareholders.

In general, a distressed firm is more likely to have hedge fund involvement if distress-investing hedge funds have been doing well, or if the overall stock market has been doing well, in the recent past before a particular firm's Chapter 11 filing. Because the two variables are recorded at a monthly frequency, they are able to generate cross-sectional variation despite being time-series variables. This is because the average (median) number of firms filing for bankruptcy in the same month during our sample period is only four (three) firms. Most importantly, these two variables are unlikely to directly impact the outcome of an individual bankruptcy case due to both the exogeneity of market-wide returns to an individual firm and the lack of autocorrelation in returns. Even if the market returns close to the confirmation date of a Chapter 11 case may affect its outcome, these returns are virtually uncorrelated with the earlier returns leading to the particular Chapter 11 filing that occurred, on average, seventeen months earlier.

When the outcome variable is binary (as in most cases), we adopt the estimation method for a 'binary outcome model with a binary endogenous explanatory variable' as prescribed in Wooldridge (2002: Ch. 15.7.3). When the outcome variables are continuous (e.g., *Duration* and *DebtRecovery*), we resort to the treatment regression method as prescribed in Maddala (1983: Ch. 5.7). Both models encompass a binary and endogenous key independent variable *HFPart* (measured by *HFCreditorCommittee*, *HFEquityCommittee*, and *HFLTO*), and both are estimated with the Maximum Likelihood Estimation (MLE) method. Results are presented in Tables V to VII. In addition to reporting the coefficients, we provide the sign of the estimated $\rho = corr(\varepsilon,\eta)$ (i.e., the correlation of the residuals from the selection equation and the outcome equation) as well as the χ^2 statistic and associated p-value from a likelihood ratio test for the null $H_0: \rho = 0$. The test is equivalent to testing the exogeneity of hedge fund participation with regard to bankruptcy outcomes because a nonzero ρ is the source of endogeneity (see equation (1)).

We present results both from the simple probit or OLS regression models (without instrumentation for *HFPart*) and from the instrumented regressions. While our emphasis is on the latter tables, especially when the exogeneity of hedge fund participation is rejected, we reference the un-instrumented results in discussing the nature of the selection effect due to hedge funds' strategic targeting. Comparison of the treatment effects and the total effects (without instrumentation) allows us to comment on the hedge funds' ability to select firms based on unobserved characteristics.

12.5.2 Relating Bankruptcy Outcomes to Hedge Fund Presence

12.5.2.1 *Hedge Fund Presence on the Unsecured Creditors' Committee*

Table 12.5, Panel A, shows that hedge fund presence on the unsecured creditors' committee is positively associated with all seven outcome variables, and the effects are significant (at the 5% level) for emergence, duration, APR deviations for the secured creditors, and the adoption of a KERP. Once the selection effect is taken into account, the coefficient on *HFCreditorsCommittee* in Panel B becomes significant in the outcome equations for the debtor's loss of exclusive rights to file a plan, debt recovery, and CEO turnover, but loses significance in other outcome equations.

The two panels of Table 12.5 indicate an interesting combination of investment selection abilities possessed by hedge fund creditors, as well as the activist roles they play. As skilled investors, hedge funds invest in the unsecured debt of distressed firms that are more likely to offer desirable outcomes for that class of claim holders, including emergence (as opposed to liquidation, which tends to favour secured creditors), more frequent APR deviations for secured creditors in favour of unsecured creditors, and retention of key employees (to ensure continuity of the going concern and to instill the incentive for recovery).[20] However, in these equations the likelihood ratio test cannot reject the null hypothesis of the exogeneity of hedge fund participation (i.e., H_0: $\rho = 0$) at conventional significance levels.

On the other hand, the debtor's loss of exclusive rights to file a reorganization plan after 180 days and higher CEO turnover rates appear to be caused by hedge fund actions. The magnitude as well as significance of *HFCreditorsCommittee* in these two outcome equations is much strengthened in the model where we control for the selection effect. Moreover, the likelihood ratio test rejects (at the 10% level or lower) the exogeneity of hedge funds' participation in favour of a negative selection (i.e., H_a: $\rho < 0$) for both outcomes. That is, hedge funds select firms in which, *a priori*, management has strong power over the creditors. As a result, hedge fund impact is strengthened after the selection effect is taken into account.

Such a contrast is intuitive given the confrontational nature of the two outcomes against management. The incumbent top management of the debtor would likely resist the loss of exclusivity or their jobs. It is, therefore, implausible that such outcomes would take place on their own were it not for the hedge funds' persistence. The strong relation between hedge fund presence and debt recovery suggests an overall efficiency gain, which could only be accomplished by hedge funds' ability to counter the power of the debtor.

[20] Gilson and Vetsuypens (1993) show that KERPs tie managers' pay to creditors' recoveries and the restructuring progress. See also Blumenstein (2002).

Table 12.5 Effects of hedge funds on unsecured creditors' committee

This table presents the effect of hedge fund presence on the unsecured creditors' committee (*HFCreditorsCommittee*) on Chapter 11 outcomes, including (1) emergence (*Emerge*), (2) the logarithm of the number of months in bankruptcy (*Duration*), (3) the debtor's loss of exclusive rights to file a plan of reorganization after 180 days in bankruptcy (*LossExclusivity*), (4) APR deviation for secured creditors (*APRCreditor*), (5) average recovery rate of all corporate debt at plan confirmation (*DebtRecovery*), (6) CEO turnover during Chapter 11 reorganization (*CEOTurnover*), and (7) adoptions of key employee retention plan (*KERP*). Variable definitions are provided in Table 12. Panel A presents results from a simple probit (when the outcome variable is binary, in Columns (1), (3), (4), (6), and (7)) or an OLS (when the outcome variable is continuous, in Columns (2) and (5)) regression model. Panel B presents results from a binary outcome model with a binary endogenous explanatory variable (when the outcome variable is binary) or a treatment regression model (when the outcome variable is continuous), as shown in equation (1). Instrumental variables in the selection equation are the lagged return on an index of distress-investing hedge funds (*DistressHFRet*) and the lagged monthly return on the S&P 500 index (*SP500Ret*), coefficients on which are reported. Also reported at the bottom of Panel B is the sign of ρ, the correlation coefficient of the residuals from the selection regression and the outcome regression, as well as the $\chi 2$ statistic and the associated p-value from a likelihood ratio (LR) test for the null $H0$: $\rho = 0$. Numbers in brackets are standard errors. ***, **, * correspond to statistical significance at the 1%, 5%, and 10% levels, respectively.

	(1)	(2)	(3)	(4)	(5)	(6)	(7)
	Emerge	Duration	LossExclusivity	APRCreditor	DebtRecovery	CEOTurnover	KERP
Panel A: Probit/OLS							
HFCreditorsCommittee	0.373*	0.173**	0.259	0.379**	0.011	0.158	0.324**
	[0.161]	[0.081]	[0.172]	[0.185]	[0.037]	[0.152]	[0.152]
Ln(Assets)	0.023	0.031	−0.474***	0.035	−0.020	0.140**	0.270***
	[0.072]	[0.036]	[0.100]	[0.081]	[0.017]	[0.066]	[0.071]
Leverage	0.893***	−0.133	0.006	−0.592*	−0.023	0.055	0.453**
	[0.289]	[0.118]	[0.231]	[0.302]	[0.052]	[0.237]	[0.225]
Cash	−1.712**	−0.920**	−0.455	−0.127	0.204	−1.905**	0.178
	[0.863]	[0.444]	[0.961]	[1.044]	[0.211]	[0.909]	[0.881]
Tangibility	0.162	−0.213	0.539	−1.331***	0.208***	−0.242	−0.416
	[0.337]	[0.167]	[0.350]	[0.411]	[0.074]	[0.319]	[0.321]
ROA	0.167	0.019	−0.138	−0.066	0.327**	−0.222	1.650**
	[0.663]	[0.335]	[0.654]	[0.897]	[0.149]	[0.621]	[0.703]
SecuredDebt	0.055	−0.264	−0.319	1.847***	−0.010	−0.325	0.171
	[0.360]	[0.161]	[0.340]	[0.375]	[0.070]	[0.324]	[0.309]

Institution	0.121	0.149	0.356	−0.088	0.092	0.449	0.700**
	[0.319]	[0.160]	[0.343]	[0.366]	[0.071]	[0.288]	[0.303]
NumClasses	0.149***	0.024*	−0.003	0.073**	0.006	−0.001	0.038
	[0.033]	[0.014]	[0.029]	[0.031]	[0.006]	[0.026]	[0.026]
Prepack	1.230***	−1.228***	−0.089	0.325*	0.195***	−0.357**	−1.212***
	[0.194]	[0.087]	[0.181]	[0.192]	[0.038]	[0.171]	[0.178]
Delaware	−0.297*	−0.088	−0.356**	0.237	−0.020	−0.010	0.100
	[0.155]	[0.079]	[0.166]	[0.181]	[0.035]	[0.149]	[0.150]
Constant	−2.229***	2.588***	2.192***	−1.918***	0.448***	−1.439***	−2.829***
	[0.594]	[0.283]	[0.688]	[0.648]	[0.130]	[0.522]	[0.556]
N	369	369	369	369	321	362	369
Pseudo-*R*2 or *R*2	0.242	0.449	0.112	0.154	0.131	0.062	0.218
Panel B: Binary Outcome with a Binary Endogenous Explanatory Variable Model/Treatment Regression							
HFCreditorsCommittee	0.779	0.355	1.884***	0.743	0.500***	1.306***	−0.085
	[1.056]	[0.490]	[0.109]	[1.148]	[0.141]	[0.379]	[1.036]
Ln(Assets)	−0.004	0.019	−0.363***	0.011	−0.059**	0.046	0.290***
	[0.100]	[0.046]	[0.071]	[0.110]	[0.023]	[0.074]	[0.079]
Leverage	0.837**	−0.150	−0.179	−0.616**	−0.067	−0.057	0.480**
	[0.346]	[0.125]	[0.182]	[0.303]	[0.066]	[0.222]	[0.227]
Cash	−1.918**	−1.030**	−1.334*	−0.325	−0.155	−2.247***	0.404
	[0.966]	[0.520]	[0.745]	[1.205]	[0.278]	[0.824]	[1.039]
Tangibility	0.118	−0.234	0.017	−1.352***	0.167*	−0.331	−0.365
	[0.357]	[0.174]	[0.268]	[0.407]	[0.092]	[0.295]	[0.352]
ROA	0.035	−0.040	−0.735	−0.169	0.158	−0.493	1.740**
	[0.748]	[0.354]	[0.544]	[0.945]	[0.189]	[0.584]	[0.713]

(continued)

Table 12.5 (Continued)

	Emerge	Duration	LossExclusivity	APRCreditor	DebtRecovery	CEOTurnover	KERP
SecuredDebt	0.153	−0.217	0.265	1.909***	0.088	−0.013	0.067
	[0.441]	[0.198]	[0.265]	[0.386]	[0.090]	[0.324]	[0.407]
Institution	0.148	0.162	0.374	−0.060	0.143	0.458*	0.654*
	[0.322]	[0.162]	[0.266]	[0.375]	[0.088]	[0.270]	[0.336]
NumClasses	0.144***	0.023*	−0.007	0.070**	0.005	−0.007	0.040
	[0.039]	[0.014]	[0.022]	[0.034]	[0.007]	[0.024]	[0.026]
Prepack	1.234***	−1.214***	0.091	0.347**	0.244***	−0.218	−1.220***
	[0.199]	[0.093]	[0.138]	[0.197]	[0.049]	[0.171]	[0.180]
Delaware	−0.264	−0.076	−0.110	0.257	0.019	0.070	0.071
	[0.184]	[0.084]	[0.128]	[0.186]	[0.045]	[0.140]	[0.167]
Constant	−2.138***	2.607***	1.305***	−1.851***	0.533***	−1.073**	−2.819***
	[0.689]	[0.285]	[0.506]	[0.709]	[0.162]	[0.540]	[0.571]
IV: DistressHFRet	2.499	2.486	2.180*	2.445	2.953**	2.512*	2.428
	[1.627]	[1.626]	[1.169]	[1.643]	[1.306]	[1.521]	[1.659]
IV: SP500Ret	1.561	1.665	0.851	1.594	0.493	1.952**	1.613
	[1.024]	[1.050]	[0.624]	[1.027]	[0.871]	[0.927]	[1.028]
Sign of ρ	−	−	−	−	−	−	+
LR Test of $\rho = 0$:							
$\chi 2(2)$	0.146	0.140	8.819***	0.090	1.940	3.158*	0.164
p-value	0.702	0.709	0.003	0.764	0.163	0.076	0.685

The mean (median) duration is seventeen (thirteen) months. The positive association between hedge fund presence on the unsecured creditors' committee and case duration has two potential explanations. First, unsecured creditors' committees are usually formed in more complex bankruptcies that take a longer time to resolve. For example, such committees are not usually formed in prepackaged cases. If we include in the regression both hedge fund presence on the unsecured creditors' committee and the existence of such a committee, we find that the latter variable overwhelms the former (results are reported in the Internet Appendix). That is, hedge funds do not lengthen the Chapter 11 process conditional on the formation of an unsecured creditors' committee. On the other hand, hedge fund presence on the unsecured creditors' committee remains significant in the regressions examining the likelihood of emergence, even when the existence of an unsecured creditors' committee is taken into account. The combination of the results from both emergence and duration indicate that, while unsecured creditors' committees are more likely to be formed in more complex cases, hedge fund presence on such committees favours the emergence outcome (which takes a longer time to materialize compared to straight liquidation).

Second, hedge funds' stake in unsecured debt is likely to be a fulcrum security that enjoys a lot of option value, especially when hedge funds participate in cases in which the unsecured debt is large relative to the secured (see Table 12.4). Given that the option value increases with duration, hedge funds may have an incentive to prolong the process.

12.5.2.2 *Hedge Fund Presence on the Equity Committee*

As discussed earlier, equity committees are less common than the committees for unsecured creditors. While 85% of our sample firms form unsecured creditors' committees during the restructuring process, the court appoints equity committees in only 11% of the cases. Bharath, Panchapegesan, and Werner (2007), while reporting an almost identical overall frequency, document a dwindling trend in the formation of equity committees after 1990. The declining role of shareholders in the Chapter 11 process is apparently matched by the rising importance of creditors in the process (Skeel 2003; Ayotte and Morrison 2009). However, we note that, during the most recent years (2005 to 2007), hedge funds are present on all equity committees when there is one.

The effects of hedge fund presence on the equity committee, reported in Table 12.6, share similarities to, as well as exhibit differences from, those related to their presence on the unsecured creditors' committee. Similar to their creditor counterparts, hedge fund equity holders are just as vigilant in pushing out failed CEOs. The effect is significant in both the simple probit model and the instrumented model, indicating that hedge funds constitute a strong force ousting CEOs of underperforming companies. Moreover, as in the case for hedge fund creditors, the exogeneity of hedge fund presence on the equity committee is rejected at the 1% level in favour of a negative selection ($\rho < 0$), that is, hedge fund shareholders target companies with more entrenched management. This evidence is consistent with the findings of Brav et al. (this volume, Chapter 8), who show that managerial entrenchment invites activism and that the CEO turnover rate among firms targeted by activist hedge funds doubles the normal level.

Equity holders in bankrupt firms seldom receive payoffs if the firm is liquidated. Hence, hedge fund equity holders should target firms that are more likely to survive and should exert their influence to favour emergence. Table 12.4 shows that hedge funds are more likely to have a presence on the equity committee in firms with lower leverage and higher

Table 12.6 Hedge funds on equity committee

This table presents the effect of hedge fund presence on the equity committee (*HFEquityCommittee*) on Chapter 11 outcomes, including (1) emergence (*Emerge*), (2) the logarithm of the number of months in bankruptcy (*Duration*), (3) equity holders receiving positive payoffs (*DistEquity*), (4) average recovery rate of all corporate debt at plan confirmation (*DebtRecovery*), (5) standardized equity abnormal monthly returns from two days before filing to plan confirmation (*StkRet*), (6) CEO turnover during Chapter 11 reorganization (*CEOTurnover*), and (7) adoptions of key employee retention plan (*KERP*). Variable definitions are provided in Table 12.1. Panel A presents results from a simple probit (when the outcome variable is binary, in Columns (1), (3), (6), and (7)) or an OLS (when the outcome variable is continuous, in Columns (2), (4), and (5)) regression model. Panel B presents results from a binary outcome model with a binary endogenous explanatory variable (when the outcome variable is binary) or a treatment regression model (when the outcome variable is continuous), as shown in equation (1). Instrumental variables in the selection equation are the lagged return on an index of distress-investing hedge funds (*DistressHFRet*) and the lagged monthly return on the S&P 500 index (*SP500Ret*), coefficients which are reported. Also reported at the bottom of Panel B is the sign of ρ, the correlation coefficient of the residuals from the selection regression and the outcome regression, as well as the χ^2 statistic and the associated p-value from a likelihood ratio (LR) test for the null H_0: $\rho = 0$. Numbers in brackets are standard errors. ***, **, * correspond to statistical significance at the 1%, 5%, and 10% levels, respectively.

	(1)	(2)	(3)	(4)	(5)	(6)	(7)
	Emerge	Duration	DistEquity	DebtRecovery	StkRet	CEOTurnover	KERP
Panel A: Probit/OLS							
HFEquityCommittee	0.390	0.160	1.246***	0.182***	0.157***	0.684**	−0.178
	[0.298]	[0.149]	[0.281]	[0.068]	[0.043]	[0.268]	[0.287]
Ln(Assets)	0.035	0.046	−0.075	−0.031**	−0.011	0.162***	0.312***
	[0.064]	[0.033]	[0.073]	[0.015]	[0.010]	[0.062]	[0.064]
Leverage	0.841***	−0.090	−0.025	−0.053	0.011	0.090	0.276
	[0.229]	[0.100]	[0.208]	[0.047]	[0.034]	[0.212]	[0.188]
Cash	−0.898	−0.931**	−0.376	0.145	0.041	−1.567*	0.215
	[0.774]	[0.398]	[0.906]	[0.193]	[0.127]	[0.825]	[0.768]
Tangibility	0.201	−0.116	0.883***	0.219***	0.019	−0.108	−0.260
	[0.293]	[0.148]	[0.312]	[0.067]	[0.046]	[0.292]	[0.280]
ROA	0.911*	0.001	−0.307	0.301**	0.043	0.109	1.010**
	[0.491]	[0.243]	[0.550]	[0.123]	[0.087]	[0.515]	[0.483]
SecuredDebt	0.038	−0.326**	−0.347	−0.037	−0.011	−0.659**	0.288
	[0.276]	[0.131]	[0.285]	[0.061]	[0.044]	[0.290]	[0.251]

Institution	0.124	0.152	0.112	0.009	0.033	0.213	0.714**
	[0.291]	[0.148]	[0.332]	[0.068]	[0.050]	[0.279]	[0.278]
NumClasses	0.126***	0.015	0.044*	0.012**	0.002	0.005	0.020
	[0.028]	[0.012]	[0.026]	[0.006]	[0.004]	[0.024]	[0.023]
Prepack	1.154***	−1.242***	1.205***	0.193***	0.027	−0.383**	−0.978***
	[0.171]	[0.078]	[0.157]	[0.035]	[0.026]	[0.159]	[0.155]
Delaware	−0.204	−0.117*	0.140	0.008	0.021	0.001	0.188
	[0.136]	[0.070]	[0.151]	[0.032]	[0.023]	[0.137]	[0.132]
Constant	−2.152***	2.616***	−1.526***	0.509***	−0.048	−1.591***	−2.870***
	[0.508]	[0.250]	[0.557]	[0.116]	[0.079]	[0.483]	[0.489]
N	459	459	459	388	334	442	459
Pseudo-R^2 or R^2	0.210	0.435	0.199	0.155	0.054	0.079	0.163
Panel B: Binary Outcome with a Binary Endogenous Explanatory Variable Model/Treatment Regression							
HFEquityCommittee	1.205*	−0.548*	−0.334	0.186	0.135**	2.332***	0.279
	[0.661]	[0.324]	[0.470]	[0.224]	[0.065]	[0.166]	[0.961]
Ln(Assets)	0.020	0.056*	−0.031	−0.031**	−0.011	0.127**	0.304***
	[0.065]	[0.034]	[0.071]	[0.015]	[0.010]	[0.058]	[0.068]
Leverage	0.878***	−0.123	−0.115	−0.052	0.009	0.140	0.296
	[0.229]	[0.102]	[0.207]	[0.048]	[0.034]	[0.207]	[0.191]
Cash	−0.762	−1.032**	−0.538	0.146	0.037	−1.309*	0.281
	[0.778]	[0.405]	[0.875]	[0.191]	[0.125]	[0.784]	[0.776]
Tangibility	0.246	−0.161	0.730**	0.220***	0.018	−0.043	−0.229
	[0.291]	[0.151]	[0.311]	[0.068]	[0.046]	[0.281]	[0.286]
ROA	0.898*	0.013	−0.207	0.301**	0.043	0.189	1.002**
	[0.491]	[0.246]	[0.541]	[0.121]	[0.086]	[0.506]	[0.483]
SecuredDebt	0.001	−0.302**	−0.268	−0.038	−0.009	−0.690**	0.269
	[0.276]	[0.133]	[0.278]	[0.061]	[0.043]	[0.273]	[0.254]

(*continued*)

Table 12.6 (Continued)

	Emerge	Duration	DistEquity	DebtRecovery	StkRet	CEOTurnover	KERP
Institution	−0.037	0.285*	0.459	0.008	0.038	−0.116	0.628*
	[0.316]	[0.160]	[0.334]	[0.082]	[0.050]	[0.266]	[0.331]
NumClasses	0.123***	0.016	0.043*	0.012**	0.002	0.001	0.019
	[0.028]	[0.013]	[0.024]	[0.005]	[0.004]	[0.023]	[0.023]
Prepack	1.106***	−1.227***	1.160***	0.193***	0.028	−0.375**	−0.980***
	[0.179]	[0.079]	[0.158]	[0.035]	[0.026]	[0.152]	[0.155]
Delaware	−0.179	−0.132*	0.093	0.008	0.020	0.046	0.196
	[0.137]	[0.071]	[0.146]	[0.032]	[0.023]	[0.132]	[0.132]
Constant	−2.075***	2.598***	−1.612***	0.509***	−0.049	−1.374***	−2.838***
	[0.513]	[0.253]	[0.528]	[0.115]	[0.078]	[0.460]	[0.500]
IV: DistressHFRet	10.134***	9.414***	10.542***	8.962**	9.383**	9.671***	10.035***
	[3.691]	[3.477]	[3.165]	[4.116]	[3.965]	[3.210]	[3.674]
IV: SP500Ret	4.066**	4.216**	3.348**	5.100**	4.366**	3.624***	4.058**
	[1.742]	[1.661]	[1.575]	[2.103]	[1.942]	[1.389]	[1.739]
Sign of ρ	−	+	+	−	+	−	−
			LR Test of $\rho = 0$:				
$\chi^2(2)$	1.220	2.210	4.129**	0.001	0.180	9.815***	0.204
p-value	0.269	0.138	0.042	0.985	0.674	0.001	0.652

profitability; such evidence suggests firm-picking by the hedge funds. Table 12.6 confirms that the coefficient on *HFEquityCommittee* is indeed positive in the outcome equation for *Emerge*. Importantly, the coefficient is significant (at the 10% level) in the instrumented model, which is also supportive of a causal relation.

The ultimate payoff to hedge fund equity holders can be summarized by the variable *DistEquity*, which indicates the occurrence of a distribution to existing shareholders and happens in 21% of the cases. Hedge fund presence on the equity committee is associated with a 43 percentage point increase in the probability of a positive distribution to existing equity holders, controlling for firm and case characteristics. The effect is rendered insignificant when the instrumented model is employed. Similarly, the log-likelihood ratio test rejects the exogeneity of hedge fund participation at the 5% level in favour of a positive selection. Together these results offer strong evidence in support of hedge funds' ability to pick stocks of distressed firms with better prospects for existing shareholders, but offer less evidence for hedge funds' activist role in making the distribution happen.

We next make two refinements to the analysis on emergence and distribution to equity holders. First, we collect information on the stated purpose in Item 4 of Schedule 13D filings by hedge funds in the bankrupt firms. It turns out that in twenty-one of the fifty Schedule 13D filings both before and during Chapter 11, hedge funds state that influencing the restructuring process is their goal, suggesting a strong activist bias in hedge funds' investment in distressed firms. When we include an indicator variable for the stated goal in the probit regression to explain emergence (results are reported in the Internet Appendix), the new variable is positively associated with the likelihood of emergence (significant at the 10% level). Moreover, the marginal effect associated with this new indicator variable is close to twenty percentage points, which is economically significant as compared to the sample average emergence frequency of 60%.

Second, we find that, in contrast to *HFEquityCommittee*, *HFJoint5%* does not bear a significant relation with *DistEquity* (results are reported in the Internet Appendix). Such a difference points to the importance of hedge fund actions (through their committee involvement) beyond their being mere investors. We also refine the finding of Bharath, Panchapegesan, and Werner (2007) that the formation of an equity committee is positively associated with APR deviations by clarifying that hedge fund presence on the committee has its own effect. Indeed, the coefficient on *HFEquityCommittee* retains its significance even if the existence of an equity committee is controlled for.

A subset of the sample in which we observe stock returns during the Chapter 11 process should directly indicate how hedge funds' presence as major equity holders is related to the returns to existing shareholders. For this purpose, the outcome variable is the abnormal holding period returns from the last trading day prior to the Chapter 11 filing to the date of plan confirmation (or case resolution). We have stock trading prices from before the filing to the plan confirmation date (the holding period) for 298 cases from both CRSP and the OTC/pink-sheet markets. We supplement the calculation of stock returns using information about distributions to common shareholders for another 43 cases. Therefore, we are able to calculate the standardized abnormal monthly return by subtracting the contemporaneous holding period return of the CRSP equal-weighted index—a benchmark commonly adopted in the bankruptcy literature (Dawkins, Bhattacharya, and Bamber 2007)—and then normalizing by the number of months in the Chapter 11 process for a total of 341 cases (StkRet).

Table 12.6 shows that the coefficients on *HFEquityCommittee* are statistically significant (at the 5% level or better) and economically large (between fourteen and sixteen percentage points), regardless of whether the selection effect is taken into account. These numbers are not necessarily proportional to the returns that hedge funds obtain from their own equity investment because they could buy into the equity at different times during the bankruptcy process. What we show here is that hedge fund participation is associated with more favourable returns to existing shareholders of the bankrupt firms.

12.5.2.3 *Hedge Fund Pursuance of Loan-to-own*

Table 12.7 examines the relation between hedge fund pursuance of a loan-to-own strategy and Chapter 11 outcomes. The results appear to be a natural blend of those in Tables 12.5 and 12.6, consistent with the hedge funds' dual roles—first as creditors and then as new shareholders. We do not examine emergence in this table because the coding of *HFLTO* favours emergence cases due to the requirement that hedge fund creditors become shareholders *ex post*.

Overall, hedge funds aiming at loan-to-own are pro-KERP (significant at the 10% level), and are associated with more distributions to both unsecured creditors (significant at the 1% level) and shareholders (significant at the 5% level). As in Table 12.5, the effects are significant (at the 1% level) on the debtor's loss of exclusivity, debt recovery, and CEO turnover in the instrumented model, and the test for the exogeneity of hedge fund participation rejects the null in favour of a significant negative selection. All these relations indicate that the loan-to-own players act like unsecured creditors in exerting their influence over management. At the same time, they value continuity by retaining companies' key employees given that they have a relatively long investment horizon in firms that emerge from Chapter 11.

12.5.2.4 *Relations Among Hedge Funds' Different Roles*

Tables 12.5 demonstrate that hedge funds appear to be effective in achieving their intended goals for the role they assume. Given that hedge funds could take different sides as unsecured creditors or shareholders, a natural question that arises is whether hedge funds' influence from one position works against the interests of another class of claim holders. Given the lack of shareholder power in bankruptcy relative to creditors, it is especially important to analyse the relation between hedge fund presence as creditors and the value implications for existing equity holders. To address this question, we relate changes in stock prices around the bankruptcy filing to hedge fund involvement on the debt side that is observable at the time. To the extent that equity prices are forward looking, they should incorporate information that is predictive of the effect of hedge funds on future outcomes.

In 277 of our sample cases information is available for both hedge fund presence and stock returns. We separate this event sample into two groups: seventy-five cases in which hedge funds are listed among the largest unsecured creditors on the petition forms on the day of bankruptcy filing, and 202 cases that have no publicly known hedge fund involvement on the debt side. Figure 12.1 plots the cumulative abnormal returns (CARs; using the CRSP equal-weighted return as the benchmark) of both groups for the [-10, +10] window, where day 0 is the date of the Chapter 11 filing. Though the stock market reacts negatively to bankruptcy filings in general, cases with hedge funds on the debt side fare much better. Immediately after the petition,

Table 12.7 Hedge funds loan-to-own

This table presents the effect of hedge funds adopting a loan-to-own strategy (*HFLTO*) on Chapter 11 outcomes, including (1) the logarithm of the number of months in bankruptcy (*Duration*), (2) debtor's loss of exclusive rights to file a plan of reorganization after 180 days in bankruptcy (*LossExclusivity*), (3) APR deviation for secured creditors (*APRCreditor*), (4) equity holders receiving positive payoffs (*DistEquity*), (5) average recovery rate of all corporate debt at plan confirmation (*DebtRecovery*), (6) CEO turnover during Chapter 11 reorganization (*CEOTurnover*), and (7) adoptions of key employee retention plan (*KERP*). Variable definitions are provided in Table 12.1. Panel A presents results from a simple probit (when the outcome variable is binary, in Columns (2), (3), (4), (6), and (7)) or an OLS (when the outcome variable is continuous, in Columns (1) and (5)) regression model. Panel B presents results from a binary outcome model with a binary endogenous explanatory variable (when the outcome variable is binary) or a treatment regression model (when the outcome variable is continuous), as shown in equation (1). Instrumental variables in the selection equation are the lagged return on an index of distress-investing hedge funds (*DistressHFRet*) and the lagged monthly return on the S&P 500 index (*SP500Ret*), coefficients which are reported. Also reported at the bottom of Panel B is the sign of ρ, the correlation coefficient of the residuals from the selection regression and the outcome regression, as well as the χ^2 statistic and the associated p-value from a likelihood ratio (LR) test for the null $H0: \rho = 0$. Numbers in brackets are standard errors. ***, **, * correspond to statistical significance at the 1%, 5%, and 10% levels, respectively.

	(1)	(2)	(3)	(4)	(5)	(6)	(7)
	Duration	LossExclusivity	APRCreditor	DistEquity	DebtRecovery	CEOTurnover	KERP
Panel A: Probit/OLS							
HFLTO	0.050	−0.084	0.668***	0.328**	0.059	−0.141	0.298*
	[0.085]	[0.182]	[0.182]	[0.166]	[0.037]	[0.165]	[0.159]
Ln(Assets)	0.048	−0.391***	0.069	−0.092	−0.035**	0.153**	0.271***
	[0.035]	[0.089]	[0.078]	[0.074]	[0.016]	[0.063]	[0.067]
Leverage	−0.118	−0.029	−0.390	−0.214	−0.042	0.144	0.324
	[0.111]	[0.217]	[0.271]	[0.226]	[0.050]	[0.222]	[0.206]
Cash	−0.934**	−0.111	0.082	−1.046	0.135	−2.114**	0.064
	[0.414]	[0.845]	[1.013]	[0.940]	[0.199]	[0.861]	[0.792]
Tangibility	−0.199	0.434	−1.506***	0.740**	0.204***	−0.248	−0.308
	[0.158]	[0.325]	[0.402]	[0.318]	[0.070]	[0.301]	[0.296]
ROA	−0.092	−0.311	−0.132	−0.839	0.326**	−0.127	0.902
	[0.295]	[0.550]	[0.772]	[0.613]	[0.140]	[0.593]	[0.553]
SecuredDebt	−0.333**	−0.476	1.730***	−0.308	0.017	−0.543*	0.390
	[0.147]	[0.310]	[0.329]	[0.304]	[0.064]	[0.304]	[0.277]

(continued)

Table 12.7 (Continued)

	Duration	LossExclusivity	APRCreditor	DistEquity	DebtRecovery	CEOTurnover	KERP
Institution	0.147	0.065	−0.203	0.694**	0.095	0.542**	0.757***
	[0.153]	[0.324]	[0.356]	[0.317]	[0.067]	[0.276]	[0.285]
NumClasses	0.021	−0.001	0.054*	0.029	0.005	0.004	0.023
	[0.014]	[0.028]	[0.030]	[0.026]	[0.006]	[0.026]	[0.026]
Prepack	−1.233***	−0.064	0.170	1.172***	0.190***	−0.331**	−1.197***
	[0.084]	[0.172]	[0.182]	[0.165]	[0.036]	[0.164]	[0.169]
Delaware	−0.113	−0.400***	0.286*	0.112	−0.027	−0.048	0.103
	[0.074]	[0.155]	[0.171]	[0.153]	[0.033]	[0.141]	[0.138]
Constant	2.594***	1.952***	−2.105***	−1.128**	0.573***	−1.510***	−2.626***
	[0.273]	[0.635]	[0.624]	[0.569]	[0.124]	[0.505]	[0.524]
N	416	416	416	416	359	407	416
Pseudo-R^2 or R^2	0.434	0.093	0.174	0.166	0.143	0.067	0.191
Panel B: Binary Outcome with a Binary Endogenous Explanatory Variable Model/Treatment Regression							
HFLTO	0.328	1.604***	−0.179	1.106	0.709***	1.086***	−0.176
	[0.569]	[0.285]	[0.771]	[0.737]	[0.0704]	[0.389]	[0.781]
Ln(Assets)	0.032	−0.381***	0.116	−0.129*	−0.074***	0.065	0.290***
	[0.046]	[0.079]	[0.084]	[0.077]	[0.022]	[0.068]	[0.070]
Leverage	−0.148	−0.172	−0.256	−0.286	−0.103	0.012	0.367*
	[0.127]	[0.192]	[0.299]	[0.224]	[0.068]	[0.209]	[0.213]
Cash	−0.872**	0.012	−0.169	−0.865	0.280	−1.670**	−0.054
	[0.432]	[0.776]	[1.012]	[0.929]	[0.270]	[0.830]	[0.810]
Tangibility	−0.240	0.110	−1.248**	0.581	0.107	−0.363	−0.234
	[0.179]	[0.298]	[0.512]	[0.355]	[0.095]	[0.283]	[0.322]
ROA	−0.100	−0.374	−0.114	−0.820	0.328*	−0.033	0.899
	[0.295]	[0.498]	[0.732]	[0.601]	[0.190]	[0.560]	[0.550]

ROA	−0.100	−0.374	−0.114	−0.820	0.328*	−0.033	0.899
	[0.295]	[0.498]	[0.732]	[0.601]	[0.190]	[0.560]	[0.550]
SecuredDebt	−0.285	−0.140	1.442***	−0.147	0.127	−0.300	0.299
	[0.177]	[0.283]	[0.495]	[0.337]	[0.087]	[0.297]	[0.318]
Institution	0.153	0.116	−0.209	0.665**	0.109	0.482*	0.729**
	[0.153]	[0.279]	[0.340]	[0.314]	[0.091]	[0.264]	[0.291]
NumClasses	0.014	−0.042*	0.074**	0.007	−0.012	−0.031	0.035
	[0.020]	[0.025]	[0.032]	[0.034]	[0.008]	[0.026]	[0.031]
Prepack	−1.266***	−0.201	0.262	1.015***	0.133***	−0.416***	−1.113***
	[0.107]	[0.149]	[0.190]	[0.259]	[0.050]	[0.152]	[0.248]
Delaware	−0.116	−0.328**	0.280*	0.103	−0.045	−0.044	0.106
	[0.074]	[0.139]	[0.166]	[0.148]	[0.045]	[0.132]	[0.137]
Constant	2.727***	2.191***	−2.440***	−0.706	0.878***	−0.714	−2.792***
	[0.382]	[0.541]	[0.629]	[0.695]	[0.170]	[0.574]	[0.548]
IV: DistressHFRet	4.466**	3.871**	5.013***	4.697***	4.803***	5.072***	4.568**
	[1.919]	[1.719]	[1.757]	[1.736]	[1.312]	[1.654]	[1.786]
IV: SP500Ret	0.590	−0.121	0.136	0.476	0.250	0.635	0.575
	[1.099]	[0.934]	[1.067]	[1.036]	[0.700]	[0.972]	[1.069]
Sign of ρ	−	−	+	−	−	−	+
LR Test of $\rho = 0$:							
$\chi^2(2)$	0.210	4.637**	1.089	0.615	18.210***	4.023**	0.385
p-value	0.646	0.031	0.297	0.433	0.000	0.045	0.535

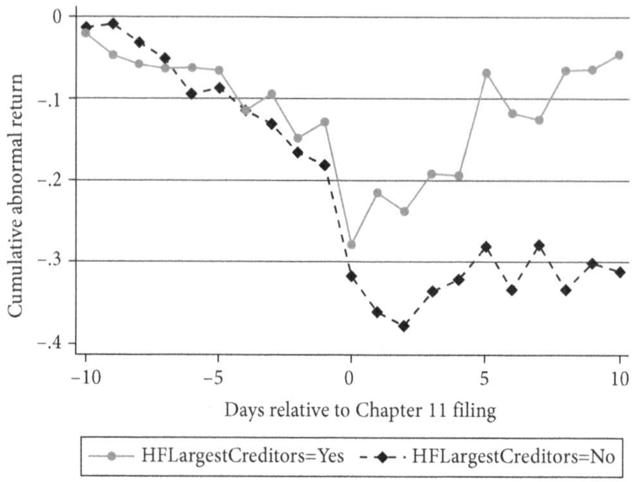

FIGURE 12.1 Event study around Chapter 11 filing

This figure shows the CARs (adjusted by the CRSP equal-weighted return) from the ten days before to the ten days after a Chapter 11 filing. The solid line represents CARs for seventy-five cases with at least one hedge fund listed as the largest unsecured creditor. The dashed line represents CARs for 202 cases without any hedge fund listed as the largest unsecured creditor.

the group with hedge funds among the largest unsecured creditors experiences price increases, while the group without hedge fund presence continues to experience price declines.

Table 12.8 presents the same result using univariate and multivariate regressions where the dependent variables are CARs over two event windows: [-10, +10] and [-5, +5]. The key independent variable of interest is hedge funds' presence as largest unsecured creditors (*HFLargestCreditor*), which is the only debt-side participation variable that is known at the time of a bankruptcy filing. The univariate results confirm the message of Figure 12.1 (a fifteen to twenty percentage point difference). Motivated by Bris, Welch, and Zhu (2006), we include the following control variables: the difference between Compustat-reported book assets at the last fiscal year end and the value at the time of bankruptcy filing, scaled by the former; the presence of banks among the secured creditors; the number of claim classes; an indicator variable for prepackaged Chapter 11; an indicator variable for filing in Delaware; and firm size (logbook assets). Except for the conventional size control, most covariates represent new information revealed upon the bankruptcy filing that could potentially impact the returns over the announcement window.

We find that the coefficient on *HFLargestCreditors* remains significant, and becomes even bigger in magnitude (twenty to thirty percentage points) in the presence of control variables, suggesting that the market perceives hedge funds to be the largest unsecured creditors favourable to the shareholders of Chapter 11 firms. As expected, the change in assets from the last annual filing to the SEC to Chapter 11 filing is positively related to announcement returns (significant at the 5% level using the [-5, +5] window). Prepackaged Chapter 11 is also greeted favourably by the stock market, though the effect (about seven to eight percentage points), while economically meaningful, is statistically insignificant. Finally, commercial banks being among the secured creditors and the Delaware venue choice do not have a meaningful return effect.

Results in Table 12.8 are closely related to our analysis on emergence. Emergence from Chapter 11 is generally good news to equity holders because the APR is most likely upheld in

Table 12.8 Market reactions to Chapter 11 filing

This table presents OLS regression results examining the determinants of CARs (adjusted by the CRSP equal-weighted return) measured over two event windows around Chapter 11 filing. Columns (1) and (3) present univariate regression results, and Columns (2) and (4) include control variables. Variable definitions are provided in Table 12.1. Numbers in brackets are standard errors.***, **, * correspond to statistical significance at the 1%, 5%, and 10% levels, respectively.

	(1)	(2)	(3)	(4)
	CAR[−5, +5]	CAR[−5, +5]	CAR[−10, +10]	CAR[−10, +10]
HFLargestCreditors	0.168**	0.220**	0.247**	0.323***
	[0.085]	[0.100]	[0.099]	[0.115]
AssetsChange	0.311**			0.245
	[0.142]			[0.164]
CBLenders	−0.084			−0.015
	[0.106]			[0.121]
Ln(Assets)	−0.048			−0.065
	[0.036]			[0.042]
NumClasses	0.010			0.010
	[0.014]			[0.016]
Prepack	0.066			0.076
	[0.099]			[0.113]
Delaware	−0.029			0.070
	[0.091]			[0.104]
Constant	−0.185***	0.165	−0.315***	0.042
	[0.044]	[0.273]	[0.051]	[0.315]
N	274	202	277	205
R^2	0.014	0.068	0.022	0.077

liquidation while the firm as a going concern leaves some upside potential for shareholders. Given the positive relation between hedge fund creditors and firm emergence, the favourable stock market reaction to hedge fund presence is expected.

12.5.2.5 *Effects of Other Firm and Case Characteristics*

In addition to the effects of hedge fund involvement on bankruptcy outcomes, Tables 12.5 also relate other firm and case characteristics to outcomes. Given that these relations are not central to our analysis and that most of our results are consistent with the prior literature (Bris, Welch, and Zhu 2006; Bharath, Panchapegesan, and Werner 2007; Lemmon, Ma, and Tashjian 2009), we only briefly summarize some interesting results below.

First, high leverage is associated with a higher likelihood of emergence, and high leverage and high return on assets are associated with more frequent adoptions of KERP. These relations indicate that firms that have strong fundamentals but suffer from financial distress are more likely to emerge from Chapter 11 and to retain their key employees in the future. Both relations are indicative of the overall efficiency of the Chapter 11 process, as shown in Lemmon, Ma, and Tashjian (2009). Second, higher levels of both cash holdings and secured debt are associated with shorter duration in bankruptcy. While cash provides liquidity, the latter effect might be due to the fact that secured creditors tend to be more concentrated, which leads to fewer conflicts among them and, in turn, faster resolution.

Third, cases with many classes of claims favour reorganization. This result might seem counter-intuitive, in that having more claim classes tends to make negotiations more difficult. Bolton and Scharfstein's (1996) model illustrates inefficient renegotiation following a default with multiple creditors. Welch (1997) provides a rationale for concentrated bank debt to be senior and dispersed public debt to be junior in reducing rent-seeking and avoiding deadweight loss in the bankruptcy process. On the other hand, our finding is consistent with the general goal of bankruptcy courts, which is to facilitate an outcome that creates the greatest economic gains rather than simply protecting the most senior parties (Harner 2008a). In cases with a large number of claim classes, liquidation will result in zero distributions to many classes in order to provide payments to the most senior classes. As a result, courts are more likely to lean toward reorganization.

12.5.2.6 *Sensitivity Analyses*

We conduct several sensitivity analyses to supplement our main results. First, we examine the relation between hedge fund presence and the likelihood of a company re-entering Chapter 11 after emergence (i.e., 'Chapter 22'), which happens in fifty-two of the 286 emergence cases in our sample. Tables 12.5 and 12.6 indicate that hedge funds favour emergence over liquidation (or acquisition). If their preference leads to underliquidation, in that firms with weak prospects are saved when liquidation would lock in a higher value, then we should observe a positive association between hedge fund presence and the incidence of Chapter 22. An ordered probit analysis, reported in Table 12.9, indicates that this is not the case.

In the ordered probit analysis, the outcome of emergence and no re-filing is coded as the high outcome (= 3), emergence with later re-filing is coded as the medium outcome (= 2), and liquidation (or acquisition) in the first round is coded as the low outcome (= 1). The coefficients on all three measures of hedge fund participation (*HFCreditorsCommittee*, *HFEquityCommittee*, and *HFLTO*) are positive, two of which are significant (at the 1% level). The results support a positive relation between hedge funds' involvement and eventual survival rather than a hedge fund bias toward underliquidating *ex post* unviable companies.

Second, we are able to replicate our main results on the subsample excluding prepacks. Results are presented in the Internet Appendix. Prepacks are potentially very different from regular Chapter 11 cases. In the Internet Appendix we relate hedge fund presence as the largest unsecured creditors[21] to the choice of pre-pack, and show that hedge funds do not exhibit any significant preference for prepack versus fighting in court. Therefore, using prepack as a control variable should not interfere with the effect of hedge funds. In the Internet Appendix we also examine the relation between hedge fund presence as the largest unsecured creditors and the likelihood of an involuntary filing (occurring less than 5% of the time). Again we find no significant hedge fund effect.

[21] We could not use our default measure of hedge funds' presence on the unsecured creditors' committee because the committee is usually formed during Chapter 11.

Finally, to ensure that our results are not driven by the 'credit boom' years of 2005 to early 2007 or affected by the Bankruptcy Abuse Prevention and Consumer Protection Act (BAPCPA) in effect since 2005,[22] in the Internet Appendix we replicate Tables 12.5 by restricting attention to the subsample spanning 1996 to 2004. Again, results are qualitatively similar.

12.5.3 Summary of Hedge Funds' Roles in Bankruptcy

To summarize Tables 12.5, we find that hedge funds favour emergence over the alternatives of liquidation or acquisition, even though they tend to participate in more complex cases that take longer to resolve. Our study indicates that hedge funds playing activist roles in distressed companies do not necessarily have as short an investment horizon as the typical hedge fund, which tends to have significantly quicker portfolio turnover than other institutional investors (Agarwal, Fos, and Jiang 2011). These hedge funds benefit more from companies' emergence where the long-term company prospects are important, and the increasingly popular loan-to-own strategy necessitates their transition to holding long-term stakes in the underlying firm.

Though hedge funds are often perceived as anti-management, our study reveals a more subtle picture whereby hedge funds could be better described as transforming the traditional 'management-driven' restructuring process to a 'management neutral' (rather than 'senior creditor control') process, a trend articulated by Skeel (2003); Harner (2008a); and Ayotte and Morrison (2009). Despite the high average CEO turnover rate of 27% in our sample, this number is lower than the 33% to 75% range reported in earlier studies (see Gilson 1989; Gilson and Vetsuypens 1993; Betker 1995; Hotchkiss 1995). Though hedge fund presence is associated with high CEO turnover, hedge funds are equally eager to retain key employees through KERP. KERP rose from about a quarter of the filings in 1996 to about half towards the end of our sample period in 2007. The correlation between the adoption of a KERP and CEO turnover among bankrupt firms in our sample is positive (0.15). While it seems counter-intuitive, the positive correlation indicates a common practice of replacing the former leader of a bankrupt company while striving to retain key employees at the same time. The WorldCom case provides such an example. While the company's CEO (Bernard Ebbers) and CFO (Scott Sullivan) were both forced out, a KERP was approved in order to retain 329 key employees.[23] Hedge funds (including Blue River Capital and Cerberus Capital), which were among the largest unsecured creditors and were also

[22] Two major changes have been brought by BAPCPA. First, BAPCPA curbs the usage of KERP. Second, debtors have exclusive rights to file a reorganization plan for only eighteen months after a Chapter 11 filing, instead of enjoying potentially unlimited extensions.

[23] For a more detailed story, see Blumenstein (2002). Movies Gallery Inc. is another example. Its 2008 10K filings stated that the company:

> expect[s] to make cash payments during the course of fiscal 2008 of approximately $13 million for employee retention and severance programs related to changes in our management team and consolidation of certain corporate functions.

On the other hand, the former chairman/CEO/founder, Joe Malugen, was replaced by C. J. Gabriel, Jr on 20 May 2008.

members of the unsecured creditors' committee, played an active role in selecting the new CEO of WorldCom and worked with the company management to develop long-term strategic plans.

Several of our findings are strongly suggestive of a favourable effect of hedge funds on firm value. The event study presented in Table 12.8 shows that hedge funds' influence as creditors does not come at the expense of shareholders. The fact that their presence greatly benefits the current shareholders is a strong indication that they successfully offset the power of secured creditors, which benefits all junior claim holders. Moreover, among a subset of sample firms in which secured debt is minimal (i.e., below 5% or 10% of assets), the

Table 12.9 Ordered probit analysis of Chapter 11 outcomes

This table presents the ordered probit regression results examining the determinants of Chapter 11 outcomes. The outcome of emergence and no re-filing is coded as the high outcome (= 3), emergence with later re-filing is coded as the medium outcome (= 2), and liquidation (or acquisition) in the first round is coded as the low outcome (= 1). Variable definitions are provided in Table 12.1. Numbers in brackets are standard errors. ***, **, * correspond to statistical significance at the 1%, 5%, and 10% levels, respectively.

	(1)	(2)	(3)
HFCreditorsCommittee	0.354**		
	[0.138]		
HFEquityCommittee		0.422	
		[0.270]	
HFLTO			0.931***
			[0.152]
Ln(Assets)	0.047	0.052	0.03
	[0.064]	[0.059]	[0.063]
Leverage	0.411**	0.511***	0.443**
	[0.205]	[0.179]	[0.198]
Cash	−1.422*	−0.703	−0.818
	[0.765]	[0.702]	[0.734]
Tangibility	0.123	0.163	−0.102
	[0.290]	[0.259]	[0.278]
ROA	−0.221	0.591	0.182
	[0.557]	[0.429]	[0.497]
SecuredDebt	−0.002	0.028	0.206
	[0.281]	[0.233]	[0.258]
Institution	0.163	0.167	0.289
	[0.275]	[0.258]	[0.269]
NumClasses	0.133***	0.117***	0.105***
	[0.028]	[0.024]	[0.028]
Prepack	0.805***	0.752***	0.644***
	[0.152]	[0.137]	[0.147]
Delaware	−0.258*	−0.209*	−0.290**
	[0.133]	[0.121]	[0.129]
N	369	459	416
Pseudo-R^2	0.122	0.114	0.157

positive relation between stock price reaction and hedge funds' presence as the largest unsecured creditors remains. Such evidence combined with the positive relation between hedge fund presence and debt recovery (as shown in Table 12.5) supports the hypothesis that hedge funds enhance the overall value of firms in Chapter 11. They apparently achieve this by alleviating financial constraints, reducing the frequency of inefficient liquidation, and mitigating conflicts among different classes of claims. Our result is consistent with Hotchkiss and Mooradian (1997), who show a positive stock price reaction to purchases of public debt by vulture investors, and supports the conclusion by Goldschmid (2005) that distressed debt investors 'are more like phoenix than vulture' as they add value to the restructuring process.

Examining the role of hedge funds in post-emergence firm performance, we find that hedge fund presence in Chapter 11 is positively associated with reduced leverage (measured as the change in leverage between the time of bankruptcy filing and one year after emergence), but do not find a significant relation with respect to *ex post* operating performance (such as industry-adjusted return on assets); results are reported in the Internet Appendix. Combined with results from Table 12.9 regarding the likelihood of re-filing, this suggests that hedge fund involvement is most conducive to reducing financial constraints faced by distressed firms. Such a pattern is consistent with practitioners' views about hedge funds picking firms with 'good fundamentals' but 'bad balance sheets', and echoes the results in Table 12.5, which shows that firms that emerge tend to be those suffering from financial distress but having strong operating performance.

12.6 Conclusion

Using a comprehensive sample of Chapter 11 firms from 1996 to 2007, this study documents the prevalence of hedge funds in the restructuring process, and demonstrates their activist role in shaping bankruptcy outcomes. We find that hedge fund presence is associated with a higher probability of the debtor's loss of exclusive rights to file a reorganization plan, a higher probability of emergence, more favourable distributions to the claims they invest in, greater CEO turnover, and more frequent adoptions of KERP. We further establish the causal effects of hedge funds, especially in their role as creditors, through instrumentation for hedge fund participation. Finally, we show that the favourable outcomes for claims in which hedge funds invest do not come at the expense of other claimholders—they are more likely to result from value creation by alleviating financial constraints and mitigating conflicts among different classes of claims.

APPENDIX

Top Hedge Fund Players in Chapter 11 by Categories

Rank	Largest Unsecured Creditors	Unsecured Creditors' Committee	DIP Financing	Largest Shareholders/13D Filing before Bankruptcy	Equity Committee/13D Filing during Ban	Overall Ranking
1	Oaktree Capital Management, LLC	Oaktree Capital Management, LLC	Cerberus Capital Management	Bain Capital Funds	Harbinger Capital Partners Master Fund	Oaktree Capital Management LLC
2	Appaloosa Management, LP	PPM America Special Investments Fund	Silver Point Capital Group, LP	Loomis Sayles & Co., LP	Xerion Capital Partners, LLC	Cerberus Capital Management
3	Apollo Advisors, LP	Cerberus Capital Management	Black Diamond Capital Management, LLC	Oaktree Capital Management, LLC	Lonestar Partners, LP	Loomis Sayles & Co., LP
4	Cerberus Capital Management	Appaloosa Management, LP	DDJ Capital Management, LLC	Rutabaga Capital Management, LLC	Appaloosa Management, LP	Appaloosa Management, LP
5	Loomis Sayles & Co., LP	Loomis Sayles & Co., LP	Oaktree Capital Management, LLC	Warburg, Pincus Ventures, LP	Prescott Group Capital Mgmt	PPM America Special Investments Fund

References

Adler, B. E., Capkun, V., and Weiss, L. A. (2007). Destruction of Value in the New Era of Chapter 11, New York University Working Paper, available at <http://ssrn.com/abstract=1291620>.

Agarwal, V., Fos, V., and Jiang, W. (2011). Inferring Reporting Bias in Hedge Fund Databases from Hedge Fund Equity Holdings, Georgia State University and Columbia University Working Paper, available at <http://ssrn.com/abstract=1536886>.

Aghion, P., Hart, O., and Moore, J. (1992). The Economics of Bankruptcy Reform, *Journal of Law, Economics, & Organization* 8, 523–46.

Associated Press Newswires (2002). Sunbeam Creditor Committee Wants to Propose Another Plan, *Associated Press Newswires* (18 Apr.).

Ayotte, K. M. and Morrison, E. R. (2009). Creditor Control and Conflict in Chapter 11, *Journal of Legal Studies* 1, 511–51.

Ayotte, K. M. and Skeel, D. A. (2004). Why Do Distressed Companies Choose Delaware? An Empirical Analysis of Venue Choice in Bankruptcy, University of Pennsylvania Institute for Law and Economics Research Paper No. 03-29, available at <http://ssrn.com/abstract=463001>

Baird, D. G. and Rasmussen, R. K. (2003). Chapter 11 at Twilight, *Stanford Law Review* 55, 101–29.

Baird, D. G. and Rasmussen, R. K. (2008). Financial Innovation and the New Chapter 11, Law and Economics Workshop Series, no. WS 2007-2008 (7), Law and Economics Programme, Faculty of Law, University of Toronto.

Beaudette, M. (2006). Allied Holdings Creditors Object to a 5-month Exclusivity Extension, *Dow Jones Newswires* (7 Apr.).

Berkovitch, E., Israel, R., and Zender, J. F. (1998). The Design of Bankruptcy Law: A Case for Management Bias in Bankruptcy Reorganizations, *Journal of Financial and Quantitative Analysis* 33, 441–64.

Betker, B. L. (1995). Management's Incentives, Equity's Bargaining Power, and Deviations from Absolute Priority in Chapter 11 Bankruptcies, *Journal of Business* 68, 161–83.

Bharath, S. T., Panchapegesan, V., and Werner, I. (2007). The Changing Nature of Chapter 11, Ohio State University, Charles A. Dice Center for Research in Financial Economics Working Paper Series, available at <http://www.cob.ohio-state.edu/fin/faculty/werner/papers/bankruptcy.pdf>.

Black, B. (1990). Shareholder Passivity Reexamined, *Michigan Law Review* 89, 520–608.

Blumenstein, R. (2002). Worldcom Judge Approves Plan to Keep Employees, *Wall Street Journal* (30 Oct.), at A7.

Bolton, P. and Scharfstein, D. S. (1996). Optimal Debt Structure and the Number of Creditors, *Journal of Political Economy* 104, 1–25.

Bradley, M., Brav, A., and Goldstein, I. (2010). Activist Arbitrage: A Study of Open-Ending Attempts of Closed-End Funds, *Journal of Financial Economics* 95, 1–19.

Bravo, R. and Hester, E. (2009). KKR Turns Vulture Investor as Distressed Debt Beckons *Bloomberg News* (3 Sept.), available at <http://www.bloomberg.com/apps/news?pid=newsarchive&sid=a5WF1xFH1Awk>.

Bris, A. and Welch, I. (2005). The Optimal Concentration of Creditors, *Journal of Finance* 60, 2193–212.

Bris, A., Welch, I., and Zhu, N. (2006). The Costs of Bankruptcy: Chapter 7 Liquidation versus Chapter 11 Reorganization, *Journal of Finance* 61, 1255–303.

Capkun, V. and Weiss, L. A. (2008). Bankruptcy Resolution and the Restoration of Priority of Claims, American Law & Economics Association Annual Meetings Working Paper, available at <http://law.bepress.com/cgi/viewcontent.cgi?article=2556&context=alea>.

Dahiya, S., John, K., Puri, M., and Ramirez, G. (2003). Debtor-in-Possession Financing and Bankruptcy Resolution: Empirical Evidence, *Journal of Financial Economics* 69, 259–80.

Dawkins, M. C., Bhattacharya, N., and Bamber, L. S. (2007). Systematic Share Price Fluctuations after Bankruptcy Filings and the Investors Who Drive Them, *Journal of Financial and Quantitative Analysis* 42, 399–420.

Eberhart, A. C., Moore, W. T., and Roenfeldt, R. L. (1990). Security Pricing and Deviations from the Absolute Priority Rule in Bankruptcy Proceedings, *Journal of Finance* 45, 1457–69.

Eberhart, A. C. and Weiss, L. A. (1998). The Importance of Deviations from the Absolute Priority Rule in Chapter 11 Bankruptcy Proceedings, *Financial Management* 27, 106–10.

Eckbo, B. E. and Thorburn, K. S. (2009). Bankruptcy as an Action Process: Lessons from Sweden, *Journal of Applied Corporate Finance* 21, 38–52.

Eisenberg, T. and LoPucki, L. M. (1999). Shopping for Judges: An Empirical Analysis of Venue Choice in Large Chapter 11 Reorganizations, *Cornell Law Review* 84, 967–1003.

Federal Filings Newswires (2000). KCS Energy/Plan -2: CSFB, Creditors Have Alternative Plan, *Federal Filings Newswires* (15 Aug.).

Franks, J. R. and Torous, W. N. (1994). A Comparison of Financial Recontracting in Distressed Exchange and Chapter 11 Reorganization, *Journal of Financial Economics* 35, 349–70.

Gilson, S. C. (1989). Management Turnover and Financial Distress, *Journal of Financial Economics* 25, 241–62.

Gilson, S. C. and Vetsuypens, M. R. (1993). CEO Compensation in Financially Distressed Firms: An Empirical Analysis, *Journal of Finance* 48, 425–58.

Goldschmid, P. M. (2005). More Phoenix than Vulture: The Case for Distressed Investor Presence in the Bankruptcy Reorganization, *Columbia Business Law Review* 191–274.

Harner, M. (2008a). The Corporate Governance and Public Policy Implications of Activist Distressed Debt Investing, *Fordham Law Review* 77, 101–71.

Harner, M. (2008b). Trends in Distressed Debt Investing: An Empirical Study of Investors' Objectives, *American Bankruptcy Institute Law Review* 16, 69–110.

Hotchkiss, E. S. (1995). Postbankruptcy Performance and Management Turnover, *Journal of Finance* 50, 3–21.

Hotchkiss, E. S. and Mooradian, R. M. (1997). Vulture Investors and the Market for Control of Distressed Firms, *Journal of Financial Economics* 43, 401–32.

Kahan, M. and Rock, E. (2009). Hedge Fund Activism in the Enforcement of Bondholder Rights, *Northwestern University Law Review* 103, 281–322.

Kalay, A., Singhal, R., and Tashjian, E. (2007). Is Chapter 11 Costly?, *Journal of Financial Economics* 84, 772–96.

Lemmon, M. L., Ma, Y.-Y., and Tashjian, E. (2009). Survival of the Fittest? Financial and Economic Distress and Restructuring Outcomes in Chapter 11, Third Singapore International Conference on Finance 2009, available at <http://ssrn.com/abstract=1325562>.

Li, K. and Prabhala, N. R. (2007). Self-selection Models in Corporate Finance, in B. E. Eckbo (ed.), *Handbook of Corporate Finance: Empirical Corporate Finance* (Amsterdam, Elsevier/North-Holland), 37–86.

Lichtenstein, M. S. and Cheney, M. W. (2008). Riding the Fulcrum Seesaw: How Hedge Funds Will Change the Dynamics of Future Bankruptcies, *New Jersey Law Journal* (1 Jan.).

LoPucki, L. M. and Doherty, J. W. (2002). Why are Delaware and New York Bankruptcy Reorganizations Failing?, *Vanderbilt Law Review* 55, 1935–85.

LoPucki, L. M. and Doherty, J. W. (2004). The Determinants of Professional Fees in Large Bankruptcy Reorganization Cases, *Journal of Empirical Legal Studies* 1, 111–41.

Maddala, G. S. (1983). *Limited-Dependent and Qualitative Variables in Economics* (New York, Cambridge University Press).

Rosenberg, H. (2000). *The Vulture Investors* (New York, John Wiley & Sons, Inc.).

Siegel, A. (2006). Hedge Funds Turn Up the Volume, *Investment News* (14 Sept.), available at <http://www.investmentnews.com/article/20060914/REG/609140707/hedge-funds-turn-up-the-volume>.

Skeel, D. A. (2003). Creditors' Ball: The 'New' New Corporate Governance in Chapter 11, *University of Pennsylvania Law Review* 152, 917–51.

Strömberg, P. (2000). Conflicts of Interests and Market Liquidity in Bankruptcy Auctions, *Journal of Finance* 55, 2641–92.

Tashjian, E., Lease, R. C., and McConnell, J. J. (1996). Prepacks: An Empirical Analysis of Prepackaged Bankruptcies, *Journal of Financial Economics* 40, 135–62.

Thorburn, K. S. (2000). Bankruptcy Auctions: Costs, Debt Recover, and Firm Survival, *Journal of Financial Economics* 58, 337–68.

von Thadden, E.-L., Berglöf, E., and Roland, G. (2010). The Design of Corporate Debt Structure and Bankruptcy, *Review of Financial Studies* 23, 2648–79.

Weiss, L. A. (1990). Bankruptcy Resolution: Direct Costs and Violation of Priority of Claims, *Journal of Financial Economics* 27, 285–314.

Welch, I. (1997). Why Is Bank Debt Senior? A Theory of Priority Based on Influence Costs, *Review of Financial Studies* 10, 1203–36.

Wooldridge, J. M. (2002). *Econometric Analysis of Cross Section and Panel Data* (Cambridge, MA, MIT Press).

PART III

PRIVATE EQUITY AND CORPORATE GOVERNANCE

A.

Structure and Motivation

CHAPTER 13

LEVERAGED BUYOUTS AND PRIVATE EQUITY

STEVEN N. KAPLAN AND PER STRÖMBERG

13.1 Introduction

In a leveraged buyout, a company is acquired by a specialized investment firm using a relatively small portion of equity and a relatively large portion of outside debt financing. The leveraged buyout investment firms today refer to themselves (and are generally referred to) as private equity firms. In a typical leveraged buyout transaction, the private equity firm buys majority control of an existing or mature firm. This arrangement is distinct from venture capital firms that typically invest in young or emerging companies, and typically do not obtain majority control. In this chapter, we focus specifically on private equity firms and the leveraged buyouts in which they invest, and we will use the terms private equity and leveraged buyout interchangeably.

Leveraged buyouts first emerged as an important phenomenon in the 1980s. As leveraged buyout activity increased in that decade, Jensen (1989) predicted that the leveraged buyout organizations would eventually become the dominant corporate organizational form. He argued that the private equity firm itself combined concentrated ownership stakes in its portfolio companies, high-powered incentives for the private equity firm professionals, and a lean, efficient organization with minimal overhead costs. The private equity firm then applied performance-based managerial compensation, highly leveraged capital structures (often relying on junk bond financing), and active governance to the companies in which it invested. According to Jensen, these structures were superior to those of the typical public corporation with dispersed shareholders, low leverage, and weak corporate governance. A few years later, this prediction seemed premature. The junk bond market crashed; a large number of high-profile leveraged buyouts resulted in default and bankruptcy; and leveraged buyouts of public companies (so-called public-to-private transactions) virtually disappeared by the early 1990s.

But the leveraged buyout market had not died—it was only in hiding. While leveraged buyouts of public companies were relatively scarce during the 1990s and early 2000s, private equity firms continued to purchase private companies and divisions. In the mid-2000s, public-to-private transactions reappeared when the United States (and the rest of the world) experienced a second leveraged buyout boom.

In 2006 and 2007, a record amount of capital was committed to private equity, both in nominal terms and as a fraction of the overall stock market. Private equity commitments and transactions rivalled, if not overtook, the activity of the first wave in the late 1980s that reached its peak with the buyout of RJR Nabisco in 1988. However, in 2008, with the turmoil in the debt markets, private equity appears to have declined again.

We start the chapter by describing how the private equity industry works. We describe private equity organizations such as Blackstone, Carlyle, and KKR, and the components of a typical leveraged buyout transaction, such as the buyout of RJR Nabisco or SunGard Data Systems. We present evidence on how private equity fundraising, activity, and transaction characteristics have varied over time.

The chapter then considers the effects of private equity. We describe the changes in capital structures, management incentives, and corporate governance that private equity investors introduce, then review the empirical evidence on the effects of these changes. This evidence suggests that private equity activity creates economic value on average. At the same time, there is also evidence consistent with private equity investors taking advantage of market timing (and market mispricing) between debt and equity markets, particularly in the public-to-private transactions of the last fifteen years.

We also review the empirical evidence on the economics and returns to private equity at the fund level. Private equity activity appears to experience recurring boom and bust cycles that are related to past returns and to the level of interest rates relative to earnings. Given that the unprecedented boom of 2005 to 2007 has just ended, it seems likely there will be a decline in private equity investment and fundraising in the next several years. While the recent market boom may eventually lead to some defaults and investor losses, the magnitude is likely to be less severe than after the 1980s boom because capital structures are less fragile and private equity firms are more sophisticated. Accordingly, we expect that a significant part of the growth in private equity activity and institutions is permanent.

13.2 Private Equity Firms, Funds, and Transactions

13.2.1 Private Equity Firms

The typical private equity firm is organized as a partnership or limited liability corporation. Blackstone, Carlyle, and KKR are three of the most prominent private equity firms. In the late 1980s, Jensen (1989) described these firms as lean, decentralized organizations with relatively few investment professionals and employees. In his survey of seven large leveraged buyout partnerships, Jensen found an average of thirteen investment professionals, who tended to come from an investment banking background. Today, the large private equity firms are substantially larger, although they are still small relative to the firms in which they invest. KKR's S-1 (a form filed with the Securities and Exchange Commission (SEC) in preparation for KKR's initial public offering) reported 139 investment professionals in 2007. At least four other large private equity firms appear to have more than 100 investment professionals. In addition, private equity firms now appear to employ professionals with a wider variety of skills and experience than was true twenty years ago.

13.2.2 Private Equity Funds

A private equity firm raises equity capital through a private equity fund. Most private equity funds are 'closed-end' vehicles in which investors commit to provide a certain amount of money to pay for investments in companies as well as management fees to the private equity firm.[1] Legally, private equity funds are organized as limited partnerships in which the general partners manage the fund and the limited partners provide most of the capital. The limited partners typically include institutional investors, such as corporate and public pension funds, endowments, and insurance companies, as well as wealthy individuals. The private equity firm serves as the fund's general partner. It is customary for the general partner to provide at least 1% of the total capital.

The fund typically has a fixed life, usually ten years, but can be extended for up to three additional years. The private equity firm normally has up to five years to invest the fund's capital committed into companies, and then has an additional five to eight years to return the capital to its investors. After committing their capital, the limited partners have little say in how the general partner deploys the investment funds, as long as the basic covenants of the fund agreement are followed. Common covenants include restrictions on how much fund capital can be invested in one company, on types of securities a fund can invest in, and on debt at the fund level (as opposed to debt at the portfolio company level, which is unrestricted). Sahlman (1990), Gompers and Lerner (1996), and Axelson, Strömberg, and Weisbach (2009) discuss the economic rationale for these fund structures.

The private equity firm or general partner is compensated in three ways. First, the general partner earns an annual management fee, usually a percentage of capital committed, and then, as investments are realized, a percentage of capital employed. Second, the general partner earns a share of the profits of the fund, referred to as 'carried interest', that almost always equals 20%. Finally, some general partners charge deal and monitoring fees to the companies in which they invest. Metrick and Yasuda (2010) describe the structure of fees in detail and provide empirical evidence on those fees.

For example, assume that a private equity firm, ABC Partners, raises a private equity fund, ABC I, with $2 billion of capital commitments from limited partners. At a 2% management fee, ABC Partners would receive $40 million per year for the five-year investment period. This would decline over the following five years as ABC exited or sold its investments. The management fees typically end after ten years, although the fund can be extended thereafter. ABC would invest the difference between the $2 billion and the cumulative management fees into companies.

[1] In a 'closed-end' fund, investors cannot withdraw their funds until the fund is terminated. This contrasts with mutual funds, for example, where investors can withdraw their funds whenever they like. See Stein (2005) for an economic analysis of closed- versus open-end funds.

If ABC's investments turned out to be successful and ABC was able to realize $6 billion from its investments—a profit of $4 billion—ABC would be entitled to a carried interest or profit share of $800 million (or 20% of the $4 billion profit). Added to management fees of $300 to $400 million, ABC partners would have received a total of up to $1.2 billion over the fund's life.

In addition, general partners sometimes charge deal and monitoring fees that are paid to the general partner by the portfolio companies, not by the limited partner. The extent to which these fees are shared with the limited partners is a somewhat contentious issue in fundraising negotiations. These fees are commonly split fifty/fifty between general and limited partners.

The *Private Equity Analyst* (2008) lists thirty-three global private equity firms (twenty-two US-based) with more than $10 billion of assets under management at the end of 2007. The same publication lists the top twenty-five investors in private equity. Those investors are dominated by public pension funds, with CalPERS (California Public Employees' Retirement System), CalSTERS (California State Teachers' Retirement System), PSERS (Pennsylvania Public School Employees' Retirement System), and the Washington State Investment Board occupying the top four slots.

13.2.3 Private Equity Transactions

In a typical private equity transaction, the private equity firm agrees to buy a company. If the company is public, the private equity firm typically pays a premium of 15% to 50% over the current stock price (Bargeron et al. 2008; Kaplan 1989b). The buyout is typically financed with 60% to 90% debt—hence the term, leveraged buyout. The debt almost always includes a loan portion that is senior and secured, and is arranged by a bank or an investment bank. In the 1980s and 1990s, banks were also the primary investors in these loans. More recently, however, institutional investors purchased a large fraction of the senior and secured loans. Those investors include hedge fund investors and 'collateralized loan obligation' managers, who combine a number of term loans into a pool and then carve the pool into different pieces (with different seniority) to sell to institutional investors. The debt in leveraged buyouts also often includes a junior, unsecured portion that is financed by either high-yield bonds or 'mezzanine debt' (i.e., debt that is subordinated to the senior debt). Demiroglu and James (2007) and Standard and Poor's (2008) provide more detailed descriptions.

The private equity firm invests funds from its investors as equity to cover the remaining 10% to 40% of the purchase price. The new management team of the purchased company (which may or may not be identical to the pre-buyout management team) typically also contributes to the new equity, although the amount is usually a small fraction of the equity dollars contributed.

Kaplan (2005) describes a large leveraged buyout—the 2005 buyout of SunGard Data Systems—in detail. Axelson et al. (2008) provide a detailed description of capital structures in these kinds of leveraged buyouts.

13.2.4 Commitments to Private Equity Funds

Private equity funds first emerged in the early 1980s. Nominal dollars committed each year to US private equity funds have increased exponentially since then, from $0.2 billion in 1980 to over $200 billion in 2007. Given the large increase in firm market values over this period,

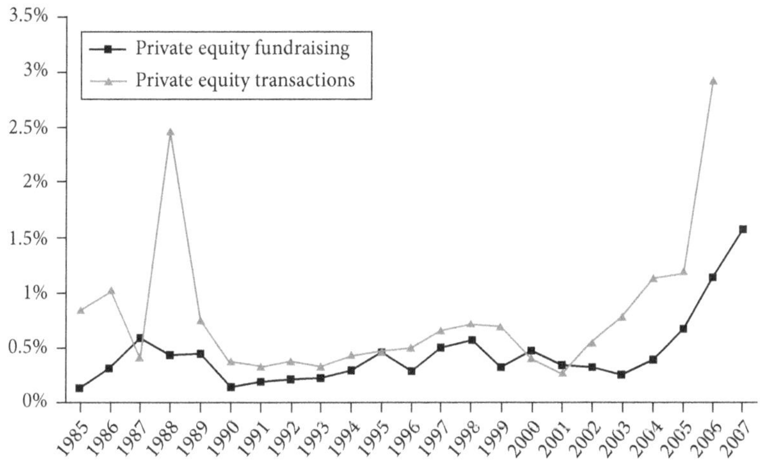

FIGURE 13.1 US private equity fundraising and transaction values as a percentage of total US stock market value, 1985–2007

Source: Private Equity Analyst, Capital IQ, Stromberg (2008), authors' calculations.

it is more appropriate to measure committed capital as a percentage of the total value of the US stock market. The deflated series, presented in Figure 13.1, suggests that private equity commitments are cyclical. They increased in the 1980s, peaked in 1988, declined in the early 1990s, increased through the late 1990s, peaked in 1998, declined again in the early 2000s, and then began climbing in 2003. By 2006 and 2007, private equity commitments appeared extremely high by historical standards, exceeding 1% of the US stock market's value. One caveat to this observation is that many of the large US private equity firms have only recently become global in scope. Foreign investments by US private equity firms were much smaller twenty years ago, so the comparisons are not exactly apples to apples.

Although we do not have comparable information on capital commitments to non-US funds, it is clear that they also have grown substantially. In 2007, the Private Equity Analyst lists three non-US private equity firms among the twelve largest in the world in assets under management.

13.2.5 Private Equity Transactions

Figure 13.2 shows the number and combined transaction value of worldwide leveraged buyout transactions backed by a private equity fund sponsor based on data from Capital IQ. In total, 17,171 private equity-sponsored buyout transactions occurred from 1 January 1970 to 30 June 2007. (This excludes transactions announced but not completed by 1 November 2007.) Transaction values equal the enterprise value (market value of equity plus book value of debt minus cash) of the acquired firms, converted into 2007 US dollars. When transaction values are not recorded (generally smaller, private-to-private deals), we impute values as a function of various deal and sponsor characteristics. Figure 13.1 also uses the Capital IQ data to report the combined transaction value of US leveraged buyouts backed by a private equity fund sponsor as a fraction of total US stock market value. Strömberg (2008) describes the sampling methodology and discusses potential biases. The most important qualification is that Capital IQ may underreport private equity transactions before the mid-1990s, particularly smaller transactions.

Overall buyout transaction activity mirrors the patterns in private equity fund-raising. Transaction and fundraising volumes exhibit a similar cyclicality. Transaction values peaked in 1988; dropped during the early 1990s, rose and peaked in the later 1990s, dropped in the early 2000s; and increased dramatically from 2004 to 2006. A huge fraction of historic buyout activity has taken place within the last few years. From 2005 through June 2007, Capital IQ recorded 5,188 buyout transactions at a combined estimated enterprise value of over $1.6 trillion (in 2007 dollars), with those two and a half years accounting for 30% of the transactions from 1984 to 2007 and 43% of the total real transaction value, respectively.

Although Figure 13.2 only includes deals announced through December 2006 (and closed by November 2007), the number of announced leveraged buyouts continued to increase until June 2007 when a record number of 322 deals were announced. After that, deal activity decreased substantially in the wake of the turmoil in credit markets. In January 2008, only 133 new buyouts were announced.

As the private equity market has grown, transaction characteristics also have evolved, as summarized in Table 13.1; Strömberg (2008) presents a more detailed analysis. The first, late 1980s buyout wave was primarily a US, Canadian, and to some extent a UK, phenomenon. From 1985 to 1989, these three countries accounted for 89% of worldwide leveraged buyout transactions and 93% of worldwide transaction value. The leveraged buyout business was dominated by relatively large transactions, in mature industries (such as manufacturing and retail); public-to-private deals accounted for almost half of the value of the transactions. These transactions in the first buyout wave helped form the perception of private equity that persisted for many years: leveraged buyouts equal going-private transactions of large firms in mature industries.

Following the fall of the junk bond market in the late 1980s, public-to-private activity declined significantly, dropping to less than 10% of transaction value, while the average

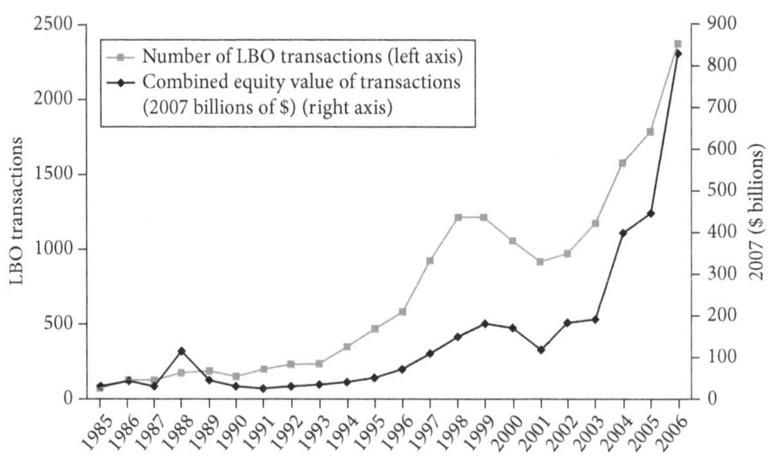

FIGURE 13.2 Global private equity transaction volume, 1985–2006

Source: Capital IQ, Strömberg (2008), authors' calculations.

Table 13.1 Global leveraged buyout transaction characteristics across time

	1985–89	1990–94	1995–99	2000–04	2005–30/6/2007	1970–30/6/2007
Combined enterprise value	$257,214	$148,614	$553,852	$1,055,070	$1,563,250	$3,616,787
Number of transactions	642	1,123	4,348	5,673	5,188	17,171
LBOs by type:						
(% of combined enterprise value)						
Public to private	49%	9%	15%	18%	34%	27%
Independent private	31%	54%	44%	19%	14%	23%
Divisional	17%	31%	27%	41%	25%	30%
Secondary	2%	6%	13%	20%	26%	20%
Distressed	0%	1%	1%	2%	1%	1%
LBOs by target location:						
(% of combined enterprise value)						
United States and Canada	87%	72%	60%	44%	47%	52%
United Kingdom	7%	13%	16%	17%	15%	15%
Western Europe (except UK)	3%	13%	20%	32%	30%	26%
Asia and Australia	3%	1%	2%	4%	6%	4%
Rest of World	0%	2%	2%	3%	3%	3%

Note: The table reports transaction characteristics for 17,171 worldwide leveraged buyout transactions that include every transaction with a financial sponsor in the Capital IQ database announced between 1/1/1970 and 30/6/2007. Enterprise value is the sum of equity and net debt used to pay for the transaction in millions of 2007 US dollars. For the transactions where enterprise value was not recorded, these have been imputed using the methodology in Strömberg (2008).

enterprise value of companies acquired dropped from $401 million to $132 million (both in 2007 dollars). Instead, 'middle-market' buyouts of non-publicly traded firms—either independent companies or divisions of larger corporations—grew significantly and accounted for the bulk of private equity activity. Buyout activity spread to new industries such as information technology/media/telecommunications, financial services, and health care, while manufacturing and retail firms became less dominant as buyout targets. Although aggregate transaction value fell, twice as many deals were undertaken in 1990–94 versus 1985–89.

As private equity activity experienced steady growth over the following period from 1995 to 2004 (except for a dip in 2000–01), the market continued to evolve. Public company buyouts increased, although buyouts of private companies still accounted for over 80% of transaction value and more than 90% of transactions. An increasing fraction of buyouts were so-called secondary buyouts—private equity funds exiting their old investments and selling portfolio companies to other private equity firms. By the early 2000–04 period, secondary buyouts comprised over 20% of total transaction value. The largest sources of deals in this period, however, were large corporations selling off divisions.

Buyouts also spread rapidly to Europe. From 2000 to 2004, the Western European private equity market (including the United Kingdom) had 48.9% of worldwide leveraged buyout transaction value, compared with 43.7% in the United States. The scope of the industry also continued to broaden, with companies in services and infrastructure becoming increasingly popular buyout targets.

The private equity boom from 2005 to mid-2007 magnified many of these trends. Public-to-private and secondary buyouts grew rapidly in numbers and size, together accounting for more than 60% of the $1.6 trillion leveraged buyout transaction value over this time period. Buyouts in non-manufacturing industries continued to grow in relative importance, and private equity activity spread to new parts of the world, particularly Asia (although levels were modest compared to Western Europe and North America). As large public-to-private transactions returned, average (deflated) deal sizes almost tripled between 2001 and 2006.

13.2.6 Manner and Timing of Exit

Because most private equity funds have a limited contractual lifetime, investment exits are an important aspect of the private equity process. Table 13.2 presents statistics on private equity investment exits using the Capital IQ buyout sample. The top panel shows the frequency of various exits. Given that so many leveraged buyouts occurred recently, it is not surprising that 54% of the 17,171 sample transactions (going back to 1970) had not yet been exited by November 2007. This raises two important issues. First, any conclusions about the long-run economic impact of leveraged buyouts may be premature. Second, empirical analyses of the performance of leveraged buyouts will likely suffer from selection bias to the extent that they only consider realized investments.

Conditional on having exited, the most common route is the sale of the company to a strategic (non-financial) buyer; this occurs in 38% of exits. The second most common exit is a sale to another private equity fund in a secondary leveraged buyout (24%); this route has increased considerably over time. Initial public offerings, where the company is listed on a public stock exchange (and the private equity firm can subsequently sell its shares in

Table 13.2 Exit characteristics of leveraged buyouts across time

Year of original LBO	1970–84	1985–89	1990–94	1995–99	2000–02	2003–05	2006–07	Whole period
Type of exit								
Bankruptcy	7%	6%	5%	8%	6%	3%	3%	6%
IPO	28%	25%	23%	11%	9%	11%	1%	14%
Sold to strategic buyer	31%	35%	38%	40%	37%	40%	35%	38%
Secondary buyout	5%	13%	17%	23%	31%	31%	17%	24%
Sold to LBO-backed firm	2%	3%	3%	5%	6%	7%	19%	5%
Sold to management	1%	1%	1%	2%	2%	1%	1%	1%
Other/unknown	26%	18%	12%	11%	10%	7%	24%	11%
No exit by Nov 2007	3%	5%	9%	27%	43%	74%	98%	54%
% of deals exited within								
24 months (2 years)	14%	12%	14%	13%	9%	13%		12%
60 months (5 years)	47%	40%	53%	41%	40%			42%
72 months (6 years)	53%	48%	63%	49%	49%			51%
84 months (7 years)	61%	58%	70%	56%	55%			58%
120 months (10 years)	70%	75%	82%	73%				76%

Note: The table reports exit information for 17,171 worldwide leveraged buyout transactions that include every transaction with a financial sponsor in the Capital IQ database announced between 1/1/1970 and 30/6/2007. The numbers are expressed as a percentage of transactions, on an equally weighted basis. Exit status is determined using various databases, including Capital IQ; SDC; Worldscope; Amadeus; Cao and Lerner (2007); as well as company and LBO firm websites. See Strömberg (2008) for a more detailed description of the methodology.

the public market), account for 14% of exits; this route has decreased significantly in relative importance over time.

Given the high debt levels in these transactions, one might expect a non-trivial fraction of leveraged buyouts to end in bankruptcy. For the total sample, 6% of deals have ended in bankruptcy or reorganization. Excluding post-2002 leveraged buyouts, which may not have had enough time to enter financial distress, the incidence increases to 7%. Assuming an average holding period of six years, this works out to an annual default rate of 1.2% per year. Perhaps surprisingly, this is lower than the average default rate of 1.6% that Moody's reports for all US corporate bond issuers from 1980 to 2002 (Hamilton et al. 2006). One caveat is that not all cases of distress may be recorded in publicly available data sources; some of these cases may be 'hidden' in the relatively large fraction of 'unknown' exits (11%). Perhaps consistent with this, Andrade and Kaplan (1998) find that 23% of the larger public-to-private transactions of the 1980s defaulted at some point.

The bottom panel of Table 13.2 shows average holding periods for individual leveraged buyout transactions. The analysis is done on a cohort basis, to avoid the bias resulting from older deals being more likely to have been exited. Over the whole sample, the median holding period is roughly six years, but this has varied over time. Median holding periods were less than five years for deals from the early 1990s, presumably affected by the 'hot' initial public offering markets of the late 1990s.

Recently, private equity funds have been accused of becoming more short-term oriented, preferring to 'flip' their investments rather than maintain their ownership of companies for a sustained time. In our analysis, we see no evidence that 'quick flips', defined as exits within twenty-four months of the private equity fund's investment, have become more common. Instead, holding periods of private equity funds have increased since the 1990s. Overall, only 12% of deals are exited within twenty-four months of the leveraged buyout acquisition date.

Finally, because of the high fraction of secondary buyouts in recent years, the individual holding periods understate the total time in which leveraged buyout firms are held by private equity funds. Accounting for secondary buyouts, Strömberg (2008) shows that the median leveraged buyout is still in private equity ownership nine years after the original buyout transaction. In comparison, Kaplan (1991), who also takes secondary buyouts into account, found the median leveraged-buyout target remained in private ownership for 6.82 years, which is consistent with privately owned holding periods having increased since the 1980s.

13.3 Is Private Equity a Superior Organizational Form?

Proponents of leveraged buyouts, like Jensen (1989), argue that private equity firms apply financial, governance, and operational engineering to their portfolio companies and in so doing improve firm operations and create economic value. In contrast, some argue that private equity firms take advantage of tax breaks and superior information, but do not create any operational value. Moreover, critics sometimes argue that private equity activity is influenced by market timing (and market mispricing) between debt and equity markets. In this section, we consider the proponents' views and the first set of criticisms about whether private equity creates operational value. In Section 13.3.1, we consider market timing issues in more detail.

13.3.1 Financial, Governance, and Operational Engineering

Private equity firms apply three sets of changes to the firms in which they invest, which we categorize as financial, governance, and operational engineering.

Jensen (1989) and Kaplan (1989a, b) describe the financial and governance engineering changes associated with private equity. First, private equity firms pay careful attention to management incentives in their portfolio companies. They typically give the management team a large equity upside through stock and options—a practice that was unusual among public firms in the early 1980s (Jensen and Murphy 1990). Kaplan (1989b) finds that management ownership percentages increase by a factor of four in going from public to private ownership. Private equity firms also require management to make a meaningful investment in the company, so that management has not only a significant upside, but a significant downside as well. Moreover, because the companies are private, management's equity is illiquid—that is, management cannot sell its equity or exercise its options until the value is proved by an exit transaction. This illiquidity reduces management's incentive to manipulate short-term performance.

It remains the case that management teams obtain significant equity stakes in portfolio companies. We collected information on forty-three leveraged buyouts in the United States from 1996 to 2004 with a median transaction value of over $300 million. Of these, twenty-three were public-to-private transactions. The median chief executive officer receives 5.4% of the equity upside (stock and options) while the management team as a whole gets 16%. Acharya and Kehoe (2008) find similar results in the United Kingdom for fifty-nine large buyouts (with a median transaction value of over $500 million) from 1997 to 2004. They report the median chief executive officer gets 3% of the equity; the median management team as a whole gets 15%. These magnitudes are similar to those in the 1980s public-to-private transactions studied by Kaplan (1989b). Even though stock-and option-based compensation have become more widely used in public firms since the 1980s, management's ownership percentages (and upside) remain greater in leveraged buyouts than in public companies.

The second key ingredient is leverage—the borrowing that is done in connection with the transaction. Leverage creates pressure on managers not to waste money, because they must make interest and principal payments. This pressure reduces the 'free cash flow' problems described in Jensen (1986), in which management teams in mature industries with weak corporate governance could dissipate cash flows rather than returning them to investors.[2] In the United States and many other countries, leverage also potentially increases firm value through the tax deductibility of interest. On the flip side, if leverage is too high,

[2] Axelson, Strömberg, and Weisbach (2009) also argue that leverage provides discipline to the acquiring leveraged buyout fund, which must persuade third-party investors—the debt providers—to co-invest in each deal.

the inflexibility of the required payments (as contrasted with the flexibility of payments to equity) increases the chance of costly financial distress.

Third, governance engineering refers to the way that private equity investors control the boards of their portfolio companies and are more actively involved in governance than public company boards. Private equity portfolio company boards are smaller than comparable public company boards and meet more frequently (Acharya and Kehoe 2008; Cornelli and Karakas 2008; Gertner and Kaplan 1996).[3] Acharya and Kehoe (2008) report that portfolio companies have twelve formal meetings per year and many more informal contacts. In addition, private equity investors do not hesitate to replace poorly performing management. Acharya and Kehoe (2008) report that one-third of chief executive officers of these firms are replaced in the first 100 days, while two-thirds are replaced at some point over a four-year period.

Financial and governance engineering were common by the late 1980s. Today, most large private equity firms have added another type that we call 'operational engineering', which refers to industry and operating expertise that they apply to add value to their investments. Indeed, most top private equity firms are now organized around industries. In addition to hiring dealmakers with financial engineering skills, private equity firms now often hire professionals with operating backgrounds and an industry focus. For example, Lou Gerstner, the former chief executive officer of RJR and IBM, is affiliated with Carlyle, while Jack Welch, the former chief executive officer of GE, is affiliated with Clayton Dubilier. Most top private equity firms also make use of internal or external consulting groups.

Private equity firms use their industry and operating knowledge to identify attractive investments, to develop value creation plans for those investments, and to implement the value creation plans. A plan might include elements of cost-cutting opportunities and productivity improvements, strategic changes or repositioning, acquisition opportunities, as well as management changes and upgrades (Acharya and Kehoe 2008; Gadiesh and MacArthur 2008).

13.3.2 Operating Performance

The empirical evidence on the operating performance of companies after they have been purchased through a leveraged buyout is largely positive. For US public-to-private deals in the 1980s, Kaplan (1989b) finds that the ratio of operating income to sales increased by 10% to 20% (absolutely and relative to industry). The ratio of cash flow (operating income less capital expenditures) to sales increased by roughly 40%. The ratio of capital expenditures to sales declined. These changes are coincident with large increases in firm value (again, absolutely and relative to industry). Smith (1990) finds similar results. Lichtenberg and Siegel (1990) find that leveraged buyouts experience significant increases in total factor productivity after the buyout.

Most post-1980s empirical work on private equity and leveraged buyouts has focused on buyouts in Europe, largely because of data availability. Consistent with the US results from the 1980s, most of this work finds that leveraged buyouts are associated with significant

[3] Empirical evidence on public firm boards (Yermack 1996) suggests that smaller boards are more efficient.

operating and productivity improvements. This work includes Harris, Siegel, and Wright (2005) for the United Kingdom; Boucly, Sraer, and Thesmar (2008) for France; and Bergström, Grubb, and Jonsson (2007) for Sweden. Cumming, Siegel, and Wright (2007) summarize much of this literature and conclude there 'is a general consensus across different methodologies, measures, and time periods regarding a key stylized fact: LBOs (leveraged buyouts) and especially MBOs (management buyouts) enhance performance and have a salient effect on work practices'.

There has been one exception to the largely uniform positive operating results—more recent public-to-private buyouts. Guo, Hotchkiss, and Song (2011) study US public-to-private transactions completed from 1990 to 2006. The ninety-four leveraged buyouts with available post-buyout data are concentrated in deals completed by 2000. The authors find modest increases in operating and cash flow margins that are much smaller than those found in the 1980s data for the United States and in the European data. At the same time, they find high investor returns (adjusted for industry or the overall stock market) at the portfolio company level. Acharya and Kehoe (2008) and Weir, Jones, and Wright (2007) find similarly modest operating improvements for public-to-private deals in the United Kingdom over roughly the same period. Nevertheless, Acharya and Kehoe (2008) also find high investor returns. These results suggest that post-1980s public-to-private transactions may differ from those of the 1980s and from leveraged buyouts overall.

While the empirical evidence is consistent overall with significant operating improvements for leveraged buyouts, it should be interpreted with some caution.

First, some studies, particularly those in the United States, are potentially subject to selection bias because performance data for private firms are not always available. For example, most US studies of financial performance study leveraged buyouts that use public debt or subsequently go public, and leveraged buyouts of public companies. These may not be representative of the population. Still, studies undertaken in countries where accounting data is available on private firms, which therefore do not suffer reporting biases—for example, Boucly, Sraer, and Thesmar (2008) for France and Bergström, Grubb, and Jonsson (2007) for Sweden—find significant operating improvements after leveraged buyouts.

Second, the decline in capital expenditures found in some studies raises the possibility that leveraged buyouts may increase current cash flows, but hurt future cash flows. One test of this concern is to look at the performance of leveraged buyout companies after they have gone through an initial public offering. In a recent paper, Cao and Lerner (2007) find positive industry-adjusted stock performance after such initial public offerings. In another test of whether future prospects are sacrificed to current cash flow, Lerner, Sorensen, and Strömberg (2008) study post-buyout changes in innovation as measured by patenting. Although relatively few private equity portfolio companies engage in patenting, those that patent do not experience any meaningful decline in post-buyout innovation or patenting. Furthermore, patents filed post-buyout appear more economically important (as measured by subsequent citations) than those filed pre-buyout, as firms focus their innovation activities in a few core areas.

Overall, we interpret the empirical evidence as largely consistent with the existence of operating and productivity improvements after leveraged buyouts. Most of these results are based on leveraged buyouts completed before the latest private equity wave. Accordingly, the performance of leveraged buyouts completed in the latest private equity wave is clearly a desirable topic for future research.

13.3.3 Employment

Critics of leveraged buyouts often argue that these transactions benefit private equity investors at the expense of employees who suffer job and wage cuts. While such reductions would be consistent (and arguably expected) with productivity and operating improvements, the political implications of economic gains achieved in this manner would be more negative (e.g., see comments from the Service Employees International Union 2007).

Kaplan (1989b) studies US public-to-private buyouts in the 1980s and finds that employment increases post-buyout, but by less than other firms in the industry. Lichtenberg and Siegel (1990) obtain a similar result. Davis et al. (2008) study a large sample of US leveraged buyouts from 1980 to 2005 at the establishment level. They find that employment at leveraged buyout firms increases by less than at other firms in the same industry after the buyout, but also find that leveraged buyout firms had smaller employment growth before the buyout transaction. The relative employment declines are concentrated in retail businesses. They find no difference in employment in the manufacturing sector. For a subset of their sample, Davis et al. (2008) are able to measure employment at new establishments as well as at existing ones. For this subsample, the leveraged buyout companies have higher job growth in new establishments than similar non-buyout firms.

Outside the United States, Amess and Wright (2007) study buyouts in the United Kingdom from 1999 to 2004 and find that firms that experience leveraged buyouts have employment growth similar to other firms, but increase wages more slowly. The one exception to the findings in the United States and United Kingdom are those for France by Boucly, Sraer, and Thesmar (2008), who find that leveraged buyout companies experience greater job and wage growth than other similar companies.

Overall, then, the evidence suggests that employment grows at firms that experience leveraged buyouts, but at a slower rate than at other similar firms. These findings are not consistent with concerns over job destruction, but neither are they consistent with the opposite position that firms owned by private industry experience especially strong employment growth (except, perhaps, in France). We view the empirical evidence on employment as largely consistent with a view that private equity portfolio companies create economic value by operating more efficiently.

13.3.4 Taxes

The additional debt in leveraged buyout transactions gives rise to interest tax deductions that are valuable, but difficult to value accurately. Kaplan (1989a) finds that, depending on the assumption, the reduced taxes from higher interest deductions can explain from 4% to 40% of a firm's value. The lower estimates assume that leveraged buyout debt is repaid in eight years and that personal taxes offset the benefit of corporate tax deductions. The higher estimates assume that leveraged buyout debt is permanent and that personal taxes provide no offset. Assuming that the truth lies between these various assumptions, a reasonable estimate of the value of lower taxes due to increased leverage for the 1980s might be 10% to 20% of firm value. These estimates would be lower for leveraged buyouts in the 1990s and 2000s, because both the corporate tax rate and the extent of leverage used in these deals have declined. Thus, while greater leverage creates some value for private equity investors by reducing taxes, it is difficult to say exactly how much.

13.3.5 Asymmetric Information

The generally favourable results on operating improvements and value creation are also potentially consistent with private equity investors having superior information on future portfolio company performance. Critics of private equity often claim that incumbent management is a source of this inside information. To some extent, supporters of private equity implicitly agree that incumbent management has information on how to make a firm perform better. After all, one of the justifications for private equity deals is that with better incentives and closer monitoring, managers will use their knowledge to deliver better results. A less attractive claim, however, is that incumbent managers favour a private equity buyout because they intend to keep their jobs and receive lucrative compensation under the new owners. As a result, incumbent managers may be unwilling to fight for the highest price for existing shareholders—thus giving private equity investors a better deal.

Several observations suggest that it is unlikely that operating improvements are simply a result of private equity firms taking advantage of private information. First, Kaplan (1989b) studies the forecasts the private equity firms released publicly at the time of the leveraged buyout. The asymmetric information story suggests that actual performance should exceed the forecasts. In fact, actual performance after the buyout lags the forecasts. Moreover, Ofek (1994) studies leveraged buyout attempts that failed because the offer was rejected by the board or by stockholders (even though management supported it) and finds no excess stock returns or operating improvements for these firms. It would be useful to replicate these studies with more recent transactions.

Second, private equity firms frequently bring in new management. As mentioned earlier, Acharya and Kehoe (2008) report that one-third of the chief executive officers in their sample are replaced in the first 100 days and two-thirds are replaced over a four-year period. Thus, incumbent management cannot be sure that it will be in a position to receive high-powered incentives from the new private equity owners.

Third, it seems likely that at times in the boom-and-bust cycle, private equity firms have overpaid in their leveraged buyouts and experienced losses. For example, the late 1980s was one such time, and it seems likely that the tail end of the private equity boom in 2006 and into early 2007 will generate lower returns than investors expected as well. If incumbent management provided inside information, it clearly wasn't enough to avoid periods of poor returns for private equity funds.

While these findings are inconsistent with operating improvements being the result of asymmetric information, there is some evidence that private equity funds are able to acquire firms more cheaply than other bidders. Guo, Hotchkiss, and Song (2011) and Acharya and Kehoe (2008) find that post-1980s public-to-private transactions experience only modest increases in firm operating performance, but still generate large financial returns to private equity funds. This finding suggests that private equity firms are able to buy low and sell high. Similarly, Bargeron et al. (2008) find that private equity firms pay lower premiums than public company buyers in cash acquisitions. These findings are consistent with private equity firms identifying companies or industries that turn out to be undervalued. Alternatively, this could indicate that private equity firms are particularly good negotiators, and/or that target boards and management do not get the best possible price in these acquisitions.

Overall, then, the evidence does not support an important role for superior firm-specific information on the part of private equity investors and incumbent management. The results are potentially consistent with private equity investors bargaining well, target boards bargaining badly, or private equity investors taking advantage of market timing (and market mispricing), which we discuss below.

13.4 Private Equity Fund Returns

The company-level empirical evidence suggests that leveraged buyouts by private equity firms create value (adjusted for industry and market). This evidence does not necessarily imply, however, that private equity funds earn superior returns for their limited partner investors. First, because private equity firms often purchase firms in competitive auctions or by paying a premium to public shareholders, sellers likely capture a meaningful amount of value. For example, in KKR's purchase of RJR Nabisco, KKR paid a premium to public shareholders of roughly \$10 billion. After the buyout, KKR's investors earned a low return, suggesting that KKR paid out most, if not all, of the value added to RJR's public shareholders. Second, the limited partner investors in private equity funds pay meaningful fees. Metrick and Yasuda (2010) estimate that fees equal \$19 in present value per \$100 of capital under management for the median private equity fund. As a result, the return to outside investors' net of fees will be lower than the return on the private equity fund's underlying investments.

Kaplan and Schoar (2005) study the returns to private equity and venture capital funds. They compare how much an investor (or limited partner) in a private equity fund earned net of fees to what the investor would have earned in an equivalent investment in the Standard and Poor's 500 index. They find that private equity fund investors earn slightly less than the Standard and Poor's 500 index net of fees, ending with an average ratio of 93% to 97%. On average, therefore, they do not find the outperformance often given as a justification for investing in private equity funds. At the same time, however, these results imply that the private equity investors outperform the Standard and Poor's 500 index gross of fees (i.e., when fees are added back). Those returns, therefore, are consistent with private equity investors adding value (over and above the premium paid to selling shareholders).

At least two caveats are in order. First, Kaplan and Schoar (2005) use data from Venture Economics which samples only roughly half of private equity funds, leaving an unknown and potentially important selection bias. Second, because of data availability issues, Kaplan and Schoar compare performance to the Standard and Poor's 500 index without making any adjustments for risk.

Kaplan and Schoar (2005) also find strong evidence of persistence in performance—that is, performance by a private equity firm in one fund predicts performance by the firm in subsequent funds. In fact, their results likely understate persistence because the worst-performing funds are less likely to raise a subsequent fund. In contrast, mutual funds show little persistence and hedge funds show uncertain persistence. This persistence result explains why limited partners often strive to invest in private equity funds that have been among the top performers in the past (Swensen 2000). Of course, only some limited partners can succeed in such a strategy.

Phalippou and Gottschalg (2009) use a slightly updated version of the Kaplan and Schoar (2005) dataset. They obtain qualitatively identical results to Kaplan and Schoar for the average returns and persistence of private equity/buyout funds relevant here.

13.5 Boom and Bust Cycles in Private Equity

13.5.1 Portfolio Company Level

The pattern of private equity commitments and transactions over recent decades suggests that credit market conditions may affect this activity. One hypothesis is that private equity investors take advantage of systematic mispricings in the debt and equity markets. That is, when the cost of debt is relatively low compared to the cost of equity, private equity can arbitrage or benefit from the difference. This argument relies on the existence of market frictions that enable debt and equity markets to become segmented. Baker and Wurgler (2000) and Baker, Greenwood, and Wurgler (2003) offer arguments that public companies take advantage of market mispricing.

To see how debt mispricing might matter, assume that a public company is unleveraged and being run optimally. If a private equity firm can borrow at a rate that is too low given the risk, the private equity firm will create value by borrowing. In the recent wave, interest rate spreads for private equity borrowing increased from roughly 250 basis points over the benchmark LIBOR (London Interbank Offered Rate) in 2006 to 500 basis points over LIBOR in 2008 (Standard and Poor's 2008). Under the assumptions that debt funds 70% of the purchase price and has a maturity of eight years, debt mispricing of 250 basis points would justify roughly 10% of the purchase price or, equivalently, would allow a private equity fund investor to pay an additional 10% (i.e., the present value of an eight-year loan for seventy discounted at the higher interest rate is sixty, not seventy).

The mispricing theory implies that relatively more deals will be undertaken when debt markets are unusually favourable. Kaplan and Stein (1993) present evidence consistent with a role for overly favourable terms from high-yield bond investors in the 1980s buyout wave. The credit market turmoil in late 2007 and early 2008 suggests that overly favourable terms from debt investors may have helped fuel the buyout wave from 2005 through mid-2007.
To study buyout market cyclicality, we make more detailed 'apples-to-apples' comparisons of buyout characteristics over time by combining the results in Kaplan and Stein (1993) for the 1980s buyout wave with those in Guo, Hotchkiss, and Song (2011) for the last ten years. Both papers study public-to-private transactions in the United States.

First, we look at valuations or prices relative to cash flow. To measure the price paid for these deals, we calculate enterprise value as the sum of the value of equity and net debt at the time of the buyout. Firm cash flow is calculated using the standard measure of firm-level performance, EBITDA, which stands for earnings before interest, taxes, depreciation, and amortization. Figure 13.3 reports the median ratio of enterprise value to cash flow for leveraged buyouts by year. The figure shows that prices paid for cash flow were generally higher at the end of the buyout waves than at the beginning. (The first private equity wave began in

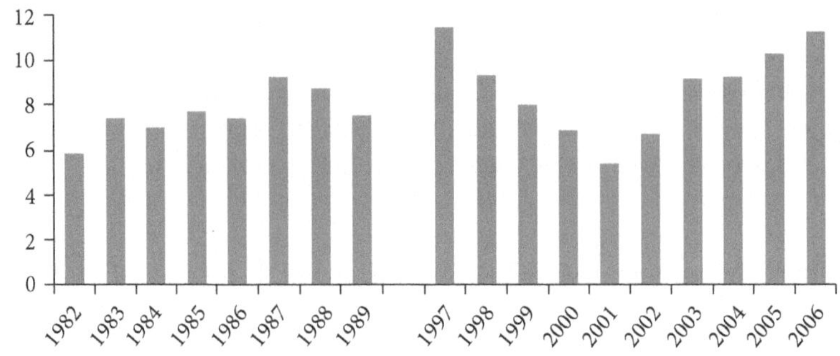

FIGURE 13.3 Enterprise value to EBITDA in large US public-to-private buyouts, 1982–2006 *('EBITDA', a measure of cash flow, stands for earnings before interest, taxes, depreciation, and amortization)*

Source: Kaplan and Stein (1993) and Guo, Hotchkiss, and Song (2007).

1982 or 1983 and ended in 1989; the second began in 2003 or 2004 and ended in 2007). The more recent period, in particular, exhibits a great deal of cyclicality, first dipping substantially from 2000 through 2002, and then rising afterwards.

Figure 13.3 also shows that valuation multiples in the recent wave exceeded those in the 1980s wave, although this conclusion is open to some interpretation. In general, ratios of all corporate values to cash flow were higher in the last decade than in the 1980s. When the ratios in Figure 13.3 are deflated by the median ratio for non-financial companies in the Standard and Poor's 500 index, the valuations of leveraged buyout deals relative to the Standard and Poor's 500 are slightly lower in the recent wave relative to the previous wave. Even after such a calculation, the cyclicality of the recent wave remains.

Next, we look at changes in leverage buyout firm capital structures. We compare the ratio of equity used to finance leveraged buyouts in each time period and find that the share of equity used to finance leveraged buyouts was relatively constant in the first wave, at 10% to 15%, and relatively constant in the second wave, but at roughly 30%. This striking increase in equity percentage from one era to the other is both a prediction of and consistent with the arguments in Kaplan and Stein (1993) that debt investors offered overly favourable terms, particularly too much leverage, in the buyout wave of the 1980s.

Valuations relative to a standardized measure of profits—EBITDA—were higher in the recent wave, but debt levels were lower. Interest rates also changed. Figure 13.4 combines these factors by measuring the ratio of EBITDA to forecast interest for the leveraged buyouts of the two eras. This interest coverage ratio is a measure of the fragility of a buyout transaction. When this ratio is lower, it implies that the buyout is more fragile, because the firm has less of a cushion from not being able to meet interest payments. Figure 13.4 has two interesting implications. First, interest coverage ratios are higher in the recent wave, suggesting the deals are less fragile. Second, the cyclical pattern of the second wave remains. Coverage ratios are higher from 2001 to 2004 than in the periods before and after.

Leveraged buyouts of the most recent wave also have been associated with more liberal repayment schedules and looser debt covenants. Consistent with this, we find patterns similar to (if not stronger than) those in Figure 13.4 when we factor in debt principal repayments.

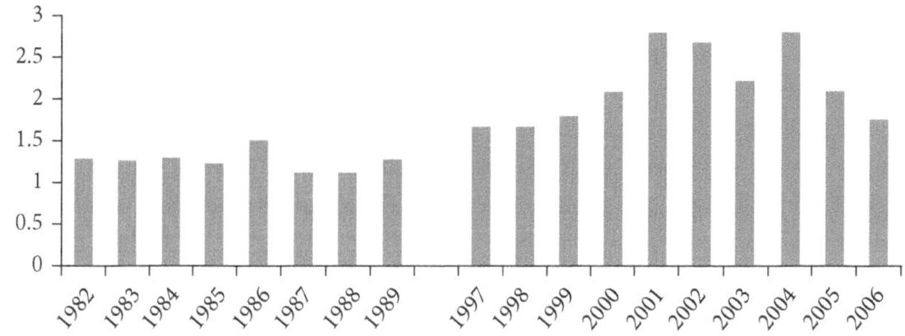

FIGURE 13.4 EBITDA to interest in large US public-to-private buyouts, 1982–2006 *('EBITDA', a measure of cash flow, stands for earnings before interest, taxes, depreciation, and amortization)*

Source: Kaplan and Stein (1993) and Guo, Hotchkiss, and Song (2007).

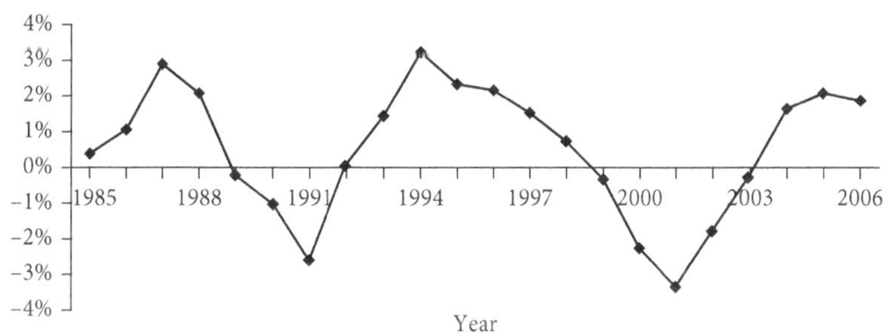

FIGURE 13.5 Standard & Poor's EBITDA/enterprise value less high-yield rates, 1985–2006 *('EBITDA', a measure of cash flow, stands for earnings before interest, taxes, depreciation, and amortization)*

Demoriglu and James (2007) and Standard and Poor's (2008) also confirm that loan covenants became less restrictive at the end of the recent wave.

Figure 13.5 considers cyclicality in private equity in one additional way. It compares the median ratio of EBITDA to enterprise value for the Standard & Poor's 500, to the average interest rate on high-yield bonds—the Merrill Lynch High Yield (cash pay bonds)—each year from 1985 to 2006. In particular Figure 13.5 looks at operating earnings yield net of interest rate. This measures the relation between the cash flow generated per dollar of market value by the median company in the Standard & Poor's 500 and the interest rate on a highly leveraged financing. One can interpret this measure as the excess (or deficit) from financing the purchase of an entire company with high-yield bonds.

The pattern is suggestive. A necessary (but not sufficient) condition for a private equity boom to occur is for earnings yields to exceed interest rates on high-yield bonds. This pattern held true in the late-1980s boom and in the boom of 2005 and 2006. When operating earnings yields are less than interest rates from high-yield bonds, private equity activity tends to be lower.

These patterns suggest that the debt used in a given leveraged buyout may be driven more by credit market conditions than by the relative benefits of leverage for the firm. Axelson et al.

(2008) find evidence consistent with this in a sample of large leveraged buyouts in the United States and Europe completed between 1985 and 2007. They find that leverage is cross-sectionally unrelated to leverage in similar size, same industry, public firms and is unrelated to firm-specific factors that explain leverage in public firms. Instead, leveraged buyout capital structures are most strongly related to prevailing debt market conditions at the time of the buyout. Leverage in leveraged buyouts decreases as interest rates rise. The amount of leverage available, in turn, seems to affect the amount that the private equity fund pays to acquire the firm. Similarly, Ljungqvist, Richardson, and Wolfenzon (2007) find that private equity funds accelerate their investment pace when interest rates are low. These results are consistent with the notion that debt financing availability affects booms and busts in the private equity market.

These patterns raise the question as to why the borrowing of public firms does not follow the same credit market cycles. One potential explanation is that public firms are unwilling to take advantage of debt mispricing by increasing leverage, either because managers dislike debt or because public market investors worry about high debt levels. A second explanation is that private equity funds have better access to credit markets because they are repeat borrowers, which enables them to build reputation with lenders. Recent papers by Ivashina and Kovner (2008) and Demiroglu and James (2007) suggest that more prominent private equity funds are able to obtain cheaper loans and looser debt covenants than other lenders. A third explanation is that the compensation structures of private equity funds provide incentives to take on more debt than is optimal for the individual firm (Axelson et al. 2009).

13.5.2 Private Equity Fund Level

In the time series of private equity fund commitments examined earlier, they appear to exhibit a boom and bust pattern. In this section, we consider this more closely by studying the relation between commitments and returns.

First, we consider the relation between private equity fundraising and subsequent private equity fund returns. Table 13.3 presents illustrative regressions in which the dependent variable is the capital-weighted return to all private equity funds raised in a particular year. We refer to this as the 'vintage year return'. We use the vintage year returns for US private equity funds from Venture Economics as of September 2007 for vintage years 1984 to 2004. The return measures are noisy because Venture Economics does not have returns for all private equity funds. In addition, the funds that comprise the more recent vintage years are still active and their returns may change over time. (This factor is probably unimportant because we obtain similar results when we eliminate all vintages after 1999). As independent variables, we use capital committed to private equity funds in the vintage year and the previous vintage year relative to the total value of the US stock market. Regressions 1 to 4 in Table 13.3 indicate a strong negative relation between fundraising and subsequent vintage year returns. Including a time trend does not affect the results. While this simple regression finding can only be considered illustrative of broader patterns, it suggests that inflows of capital into private equity funds in a given year can explain realized fund returns during the subsequent ten- to twelve-year period when these funds are active. It strongly suggests that an influx of capital into private equity is associated with lower subsequent returns.

Next we consider the extent to which past returns affect capital commitments. In these regressions, the dependent variable is the annual capital committed to US private equity

Table 13.3 Relation of private equity returns and fundraising in United States

	Dependent variable: Vintage year average internal rate of return to private equity (capital weighted) from 1984 to 2004			
	(1)	(2)	(3)	(4)
Panel A				
Constant	0.31	0.31	0.35	0.35
	(6.2)	(7.0)	(7.5)	(7.2)
Private equity commitments to stock market, t	−32.60**			−20.79*
	(−2.4)			(−1.6)
Private equity commitments to stock market, t−1		−36.87**		−28.66**
		(−3.0)		(−2.2)
Private equity commitments to stock market, t+t−1			−24.78***	
			(−3.5)	
Trend	−0.004	−0.003	−0.002	−0.002
	(−1.2)	(−1.0)	(−0.8)	(−0.8)
Adjusted R^2	0.28	0.36	0.44	0.41

	Dependent variable: Private equity commitments to stock market, t from 1984 to 2007 (as a fraction of the total value of the US stock market)	
	(1)	(2)
Panel B		
Constant	−0.091	−0.292
	(0.7)	(−1.8)
Annual private equity return t-1	0.007**	0.008***
	(2.1)	(2.6)
Annual private equity return t-2		0.007***
		(2.4)
Trend	0.031***	0.031***
	(4.1)	(4.6)
Adjusted R^2	0.40	0.50

Note: Private equity vintage year internal rate of return is the average internal rate of return to US private equity funds raised in a given year, according to Venture Economics. Mean vintage year internal rate of return is 16.5%. Private equity commitments are capital committed to US private equity funds from Private Equity Analyst as a fraction of the total value of the US stock market. Mean private equity commitments are 0.43%. Private equity annual return is the annual return to all US private equity funds according to Venture Economics. Mean annual return is 18.6%. Standard errors are in parentheses.

*, **, and *** indicate statistical significance at the 10%, 5%, and 1% levels, respectively.

funds as a fraction of the US stock market from 1987 to 2006. The independent variables are the two previous years' returns to private equity, again, as reported by Venture Economics. Note that the annual return to private equity is different from the vintage year return (which was the dependent variable in the previous regressions). The vintage year return measures the annual return to all funds raised in a particular year over the life of the fund—that is, the vintage year return is a geometric average of many years of returns. In contrast, the annual return to private equity is the return to all private equity funds of different vintages in a given calendar year.

Again, these regressions are meant only to be suggestive. In these two regressions in panel B, capital commitments are positively and significantly related to lagged private equity returns—in other words, investors seem to follow good returns. The positive trend is consistent with significant secular growth in private equity fund commitments over time above any cyclical factors.

To summarize the regressions, private equity fund returns tend to decline when more capital is committed to this asset class. Capital commitments to private equity tend to decline when realized returns decline. These patterns are consistent with a boom and bust cycle in private equity.

13.6 Some Speculations

The empirical evidence is strong that private equity activity creates economic value on average. We suspect that the increased investment by private equity firms in operational engineering will ensure that this result continues to hold in the future. Because private equity creates economic value, we believe that private equity activity has a substantial permanent component.

However, the evidence also is strong that private equity activity is subject to boom and bust cycles, which are driven by recent returns as well as by the level of interest rates relative to earnings and stock market values. This pattern seems particularly true for larger public-to-private transactions.

From the summer of 2007 into mid-2008, interest rates on buyout-related debt increased substantially—when buyout debt is even available at all. At the same time, corporate earnings have softened. In this setting, private equity activity is likely to be relatively low, particularly large public-to-private buyouts. Institutional investors are likely to continue to make commitments to private equity for a time, at least, because reported private returns have not declined, but are still robust. As of September 2007, Venture Economics reports private equity returns over the previous three years of 15.3% versus Standard and Poor's 500 stock market returns of 12.7%.

The likelihood that investors' commitments to private equity funds remain robust while debt markets remain unfavourable will create pressure for private firms to invest the capital committed. Given the fee structure of private equity funds, we do not expect that many private equity firms will return the money. However, these patterns suggest that the structure of private equity deals will evolve.

First, we suspect that private equity firms will make investments with less leverage, at least initially. While this change may reduce the magnitude of expected returns (and compensation), as long as the private equity firms add value, it will not change risk-adjusted returns.

Second, we suspect that private equity firms will be more likely to take minority equity positions in public or private companies rather than buying the entire company. Private equity firms have experience with minority equity investments, both in venture capital investments and in overseas investments, particularly in Asia. The relatively new operational engineering capabilities of private equity firms may put them in a better position to supply minority investments than in the past, because private equity firms can provide additional value without having full control. Moreover, top executives and boards of public companies may have an increased demand for minority equity investments. Shareholder and hedge fund activism and hostility have increased substantially in recent years (Brav et al., Chapter 8, this volume). In the face of that hostility, private equity firms are likely to be perceived as partners or 'white knights' by some chief executive officers and boards.

Finally, what will happen to funds and transactions completed in the recent private equity boom of 2005 to mid-2007? It seems plausible that the ultimate returns to private equity funds raised during these years will prove disappointing because firms are unlikely to be able to exit the deals from this period at valuations as high as the private equity firms paid to buy the firms. It is also plausible that some of the transactions undertaken during the boom were driven less by the potential of operating and governance improvements, and more by the availability of debt financing, which also implies that the returns on these deals will be disappointing.

If and when private equity returns decline, private equity commitments also will decline. Lower returns to recent private equity funds are likely to coincide with some failed transactions, including debt defaults and bankruptcies. The relative magnitude of defaults and failed deals, however, is likely to be lower than after the previous boom in the early 1990s, assuming a downturn of roughly similar magnitude. While private equity returns for this period may disappoint, the transactions of the recent wave had higher coverage ratios and looser debt covenants on their debt than those of the 1980s, which reduces the likelihood that those companies will subsequently default.

References

Acharya, V., Franks, J., and Servaes, H. (2007). Private Equity—Boom or Bust, *Journal of Applied Corporate Finance* 19(4), 44–53.

Acharya, V. and Kehoe, C. (2008). Corporate Governance and Value Creation Evidence from Private Equity, Working Paper, available at <http://www.ecgi.org/competitions/rof/files/Acharya_Kehoe_v5.pdf>.

Amess, K. and Wright, M. (2007). Barbarians at the Gate? Leveraged Buyouts, Private Equity and Jobs, Working Paper, available at <https://editorialexpress.com/cgi-bin/conference/download.cgi?db_name=IIOC2008&paper_id=191>.

Andrade, G. and Kaplan, S. N. (1998). How Costly is Financial (Not Economic) Distress? Evidence from Highly Leveraged Transactions that Became Distressed, *Journal of Finance* 53(5), 1443–93.

Asquith, P. and Wizman, T. (1990). Event Risk, Covenants, and Bondholder Returns in Leveraged Buyouts, *Journal of Financial Economics* 27(1), 195–213.

Axelson, U., Jenkinson, T., Strömberg, P., and Weisbach, M. (2008). Leverage and Pricing in Buyouts: An Empirical Analysis, Working Paper, available at <http://www.ecb.int/events/pdf/conferences/ecbcfs_conf9/Axelson.pdf?2e42473109fcbe654e230b3232520f0c>.

Axelson, U., Strömberg, P., and Weisbach, M. (2009). Why Are Buyouts Leveraged? The Financial Structure of Private Equity Funds, *Journal of Finance* 64(4), 1549–82.

Baker, G. (1992). Beatrice: A Study in the Creation and Destruction of Value, *Journal of Finance* 47(3), 1081–119.

Baker, M., Greenwood, R., and Wurgler, J. (2003). The Maturity of Debt Issues and Predictable Variation in Bond Returns, *Journal of Financial Economics* 70(2), 261–91.

Baker, M. and Wurgler, J. (2000). The Equity Share in New Issues and Aggregate Stock Returns, *Journal of Finance* 55(5), 2219–57.

Bargeron L., Schlingemann, F., Stulz, R., and Zutter, C. (2008). Why Do Private Acquirers Pay So Little Compared to Public Acquirers?, *Journal of Financial Economics* 89(3), 375–90.

Bergström C., Grubb, M., and Jonsson, S. (2007). The Operating Impact of Buyouts in Sweden: A Study of Value Creation, *Journal of Private Equity* 11(1), 22–39.

Bhagat, S., Shleifer, A., and Vishny, R. (1990). Hostile Takeovers in the 1980's: The Return to Corporate Specialization, in *Brookings Papers on Economic Activity: Microeconomics* (Washington DC, Brookings Institution Press), 1–72.

Boucly, Q., Sraer, D., and Thesmar, D. (2008). Do Leveraged Buyouts Appropriate Worker Rents? Evidence from French Data, HEC Paris (Groupe HEC)Working Paper.

Cao, J. X. and Lerner, J. (2007). The Performance of Reverse Leveraged Buyouts, Swedish Institute for Financial Research Conference on The Economics of the Private Equity Market, Working Paper, available at <http://ssrn.com/abstract=937801>.

Cornelli, F. and Karakas, O. (2008). Private Equity and Corporate Governance: Do LBOs Have More Effective Boards?, Working Paper, available at <http://www.ecgi.org/competitions/rof/files/Do%20LBOs%20have%20more%20effective%20boards,%20(Cornelli,%20Karakas).pdf>.

Cumming, D., Siegel, D., and Wright, M. (2007). Private Equity, Leveraged Buyouts and Governance, *Journal of Corporate Finance* 13(4), 439–60.

Davis, S., Haltiwanger, J., Jarmin, R., Lerner, J., and Miranda, J. (2008). Private Equity and Employment, US Census Bureau Center for Economic Studies Paper CES-WP-08-07, available at <http://ssrn.com/abstract=1107175>.

Demiroglu, C. and James, C. (2007). Lender Control and the Role of Private Equity Group Reputation in Buyout Financing, Working Paper, available at <http://www.bi.no/OsloFiles/ccgr/Demiroglu_James.pdf>.

Gadiesh, O. and MacArthur, H. (2008). *Lessons From Private Equity Any Company Can Use* (Boston, MA, Harvard Business School Press).

Gertner, R. and Kaplan, S. N. (1996). The Value Maximizing Board, Working Paper, available at <http://ssrn.com/abstract=1097>.

Gompers, P. and Lerner, J. (1996). The Use of Covenants: An Empirical Analysis of Venture Partnership Agreements, *Journal of Law and Economics* 39(2), 463–98.

Gompers, P. and Lerner, J. (1998). What Drives Venture Capital Fundraising?, in *Brookings Papers on Economic Activity: Microeconomics* (Washington DC, Brookings Institution Publishing), 149–92.

Gompers, P. and Lerner, J. (2000). Money Chasing Deals? The Impact of Fund Inflows on Private Equity Valuations, *Journal of Financial Economics* 55(2), 281–325.

Graham, J. (2003). Taxes and Corporate Finance: A Review, *Review of Financial Studies* 16(4), 1075–129.

Grossman, S. and Hart, O. (1980). Takeover Bids, the Free-rider Problem, and the Theory of the Corporation, *Bell Journal of Economics* 11(1), 42–64.

Guo, S., Hotchkiss, E., and Song, W. (2011). Do Buyouts (Still) Create Value?, *Journal of Finance* 66(2), 479–517.

Hamilton, D., Varma, P., Ou, S., and Cantor, R. (2006). Default and Recovery Rates of Corporate Bond Issuers, 1920–2005, Moody's Investors Service Global Credit Research (Special Comment).

Harris, R., Siegel, D., and Wright, M. (2005). Assessing the Impact of Management Buyouts on Economic Efficiency: Plant Level Evidence from the United Kingdom, *The Review of Economics and Statistics* 87(1), 148–53.

Holthausen, R. and Larcker, D. (1996). The Financial Performance of Reverse Leveraged Buyouts, *Journal of Financial Economics* 42(3), 293–332.

Ivashina, V. and Kovner, A. (2008). The Private Equity Advantage: Leveraged Buyout Firms and Relationship Banking, EFA 2008 Athens Meetings Paper, available at <http://ssrn.com/abstract=1017857>.

Jensen, M. (1986). Agency Costs of Free Cash Flow, Corporate Finance and Takeovers, *American Economic Review* 76(2), 323–9.

Jensen, M. (1989). Eclipse of the Public Corporation, *Harvard Business Review* 67(5), 61–74.

Jensen, M. and Murphy, K. J. (1990). Performance Pay and Top Management Incentives, *Journal of Political Economy* 98(2), 225–64.

Kaplan, S. N. (1989a). Management Buyouts: Evidence on Taxes as a Source of Value, *Journal of Finance* 44(3), 611–32.

Kaplan, S. N. (1989b). The Effects of Management Buyouts on Operating Performance and Value, *Journal of Financial Economics* 24(2), 217–54.

Kaplan, S. N. (1991). The Staying Power of Leveraged Buy-outs, *Journal of Financial Economics* 29(2), 287–313.

Kaplan, S. N. (2005). SunGard Data Systems, University of Chicago Graduate School of Business, Case Study, available at <http://faculty.chicagobooth.edu/steven.kaplan/teaching/sungard.pdf>.

Kaplan, S. N. and Schoar, A. (2005). Private Equity Returns: Persistence and Capital Flows, *Journal of Finance* 60(4), 1791–823.

Kaplan, S. N. and Stein, J. (1993). The Evolution of Buyout Pricing and Financial Structure in the 1980s, *Quarterly Journal of Economics* 108(2), 313–57.

Lerner, J., Schoar, A., and Wang, W. (2007). Smart Investors, Foolish Choices: The Limited Partner Performance Puzzle, *Journal of Finance* 62(2), 731–64.

Lerner, J., Sorensen, M., and Strömberg, P. (2008). Private Equity and Long Run Investment: The Case of Innovation, NBER Working Paper Series, Vol. w14623, available at <http://ssrn.com/abstract=1327245>.

Lichtenberg, F. R. and Siegel, D. (1990). The Effects of Leveraged Buyouts on Productivity and Related Aspects of Firm Behavior, *Journal of Financial Economics* 27(1), 165–94.

Ljungqvist, A., Richardson, M., and Wolfenzon, D. (2007). The Investment Behavior of Buyout Funds: Theory and Evidence, ECGI—Finance Working Paper No. 174/2007; AFA 2008 New Orleans Meetings Paper; 20th Australasian Finance & Banking Conference 2007 Paper, available at <http://ssrn.com/abstract=972640>.

Metrick, A. and Yasuda, A. (2010). Economics of Private Equity Funds, *Review of Financial Studies* 23, 2303–41.

Ofek, E. (1994). Efficiency Gains in Unsuccessful Management Buyouts, *Journal of Finance* 49(2), 637–54.

Phalippou, L. and Gottschalg, O. (2009). Performance of Private Equity Funds, *Review of Financial Studies* 22(4), 1747–76.

Private Equity Analyst. (2008). 2007 Review and 2008 Outlook (New York, Dow Jones).

Sahlman, W. (1990). The Structure and Governance of Venture Capital Organizations, *Journal of Financial Economics* 27(2), 473–521.

Service Employees International Union (2007). 'Behind the Buyout', available at <http://www.behindthebuyouts.org/>.

Smith, A. (1990). Capital Ownership Structure and Performance: The Case of Management Buyouts, *Journal of Financial Economics* 27(1), 143–64.

Standard and Poor's (2008). *Leveraged Lending Review* 1Q08, available at <http://www.lcd-comps.com/pg/research/us_reearch.html>.

Stein, J. (2005). Why Are Most Funds Open-End? Competition and the Limits of Arbitrage, *Quarterly Journal of Economics* 120(1), 247–72.

Strömberg, P. (2008). The New Demography of Private Equity, Working Paper, Stockholm Institute for Financial Research.

Swensen, D. (2000). *Pioneering Portfolio Management: An Unconventional Approach to Institutional Investment* (New York, Free Press).

Weir, C., Jones, P., and Wright, M. (2007). Public to Private Transactions, Private Equity and Performance in the UK: An Empirical Analysis of the Impact of Going Private, Working Paper, available at <http://ssrn.com/abstract=1138616>.

Yermack, D. (1996). Higher Market Valuation of Companies with a Small Board of Directors, *Journal of Financial Economics* 40(2), 185–211.

B.

How has Private Equity Performed?

CHAPTER 14

PERFORMANCE OF BUYOUT FUNDS REVISITED

LUDOVIC PHALIPPOU

14.1 INTRODUCTION

ALTHOUGH private equity investing on an institutional scale began in the 1970s, it took almost thirty years for the first large-scale academic study of investor returns to emerge. Using a similar dataset from Thomson Venture Economics, first Kaplan and Schoar (2005) and then Phalippou and Gottschalg (2009) found that the average buyout fund had underperformed stock market indices.[1]

This finding has now come into question. Robinson and Sensoy (2011 'RS'), Harris, Jenkinson, and Kaplan (2013 'HJK') and Higson and Stucke (2012 'HS') have access to proprietary, up-to-date and apparently high-quality data.[2] They find that the average buyout fund has significantly outperformed Standard & Poor's (S&P) 500 index (after fees) and argue that this overturns previous conclusions.[3]

This chapter first shows that publicly available data (albeit at a fee) is sufficient to closely replicate the findings of RS, HJK, and HS. Specifically, this chapter employs the Preqin dataset that contains the cash flows to and from 392 US buyout funds.[4] This data is primarily

[1] This chapter focuses on buyout funds, but it is noteworthy that the Preqin dataset also contains a large number of real estate and venture capital funds and thus a similar analysis could be executed on these asset classes. This chapter focuses on buyout funds as this is the largest of these asset classes. Also, and unless otherwise specified, 'return' means net of fees charged by the funds.

[2] The first draft of Robinson and Sensoy (2011) circulated in December 2010, the first draft of Harris, Jenkinson, and Kaplan (2013) circulated in September 2011, and the first draft of Higson and Stucke (2012) circulated in March 2012.

[3] A notable exception is the finding of Franzoni, Nowak, and Phalippou (2012) of a zero *alpha* gross-of-fees for a large sample of liquidated buyout investments when using the four factors model of Pastor and Stambaugh (2003) to correct for risk.

[4] The datasets of RS, HJK and Preqin mainly cover post-1993 vintage years, while the Thomson dataset used in early studies encompassed only pre-1993 vintage years. It is therefore not possible to tell whether the discrepancy in findings between early and recent studies results from the differences across datasets. HS claim to have a good coverage of early vintage years and find that Thomson returns are lower than theirs for these vintage years. It is possible that the Thomson dataset suffers from some biases which result

obtained from US pension funds using the Freedom of Information Act. I find an average and median Public Market Equivalent (PME) of 1.20 and 1.13 respectively when using the Vanguard S&P 500 index fund returns as a benchmark.[5] These numbers are virtually identical to those that RS, HJK, and HS report for their comprehensive but proprietary datasets. In addition, there is a high correlation between the time series of vintage year returns of the Preqin dataset and those of the proprietary datasets. The correlation is 76% and 90% between the Preqin and HJK returns and the Preqin and HS returns respectively.[6] Furthermore, the equally weighted average returns across vintage years are also virtually identical across datasets.[7] Taken together, these results indicate that publicly available fund cash-flow datasets are, a priori, sufficiently precise to be used for a range of applications in this field.[8]

The cross-funds average PME of 1.20 means that, on average, the present value of capital distributions surpasses the present value of capital investments by 20%. Spread over an effective holding period of 3.3 years (justified below), a PME of 1.20 translates into an outperformance of 5.7% per annum.[9] It is, however, difficult to determine the right benchmark, and this chapter aims to examine the sensitivity of results to the choice of the benchmark.

To begin with, I try to get a sense of the types of companies that private equity funds invest into. The most comprehensive publicly available data on private equity investment characteristics is Capital IQ (Strömberg 2007). Out of the 5,316 buyout transactions listed in the Capital IQ dataset, 95% have a reported enterprise value below $1.08 billion. As a comparison, the largest stock in the Fama-French small-cap index has a market capitalization of $1 billion. Hence, more than 95% of leverage buyout investments would fall within the Fama-French small-cap index and it would, therefore, be sensible to use this index as a benchmark.

An important issue when benchmarking against small stocks is the transaction cost incurred when investing in them. In addition, Asparouhova, Bessembinder, and Kalcheva (2013) show that small stock returns can be significantly mis-measured. For both of these reasons, I benchmark buyout funds to a small-cap mutual fund. I choose 'DFA micro-cap' (its ticker is DFSCX) as it is, to my knowledge, the only mutual with the objective to invest in small-caps without leverage, passively and at low cost.[10] This fund was created in 1981, has $3.6 billion under management (end of 2011) and has been studied in the academic

in too low a return (see Phalippou and Gottschalg 2009; Harris, Jenkinson, and Kaplan 2013; and Higson and Stucke 2012, for a discussion).

[5] The Vanguard S&P 500 index fund is the oldest index fund. As of December 2011, its Total Net Asset value was $26 billion. Returns are taken from the CRSP Mutual Fund database.

[6] Robinson and Sensoy (2012) do not provide a comparable time series of average PME per vintage year and their dataset is therefore omitted from this analysis.

[7] The equally weighted average return across vintage years is 1.30 in the Preqin dataset, 1.28 in the HJK dataset and 1.29 in the HS dataset.

[8] This result does not indicate that Preqin data is of equivalent quality compared with proprietary datasets. However, Preqin data appears to come close to those proprietary datasets as far as aggregate return statistics are concerned.

[9] This magnitude is similar to what the industry associations report (see Appendix).

[10] The fund prospectus indicates that the largest market capitalization considered is $1,130 million (as of December 2011) and, as shown above, this corresponds to an enterprise value that is higher than that of the 95th percentile of the largest leveraged buyout transactions.

literature (e.g., Keim 1999). Using this mutual fund as a benchmark, I find that the average and median PMEs fall to 1.04 and 0.99 respectively, neither of which is significantly different from 1 at the 5% level test. Similar results are obtained when benchmarking buyout funds directly to the Fama-French small-cap index. It thus appears that the average buyout fund return is similar to that of (similar-sized) listed equity. As a result, it could be argued that the premium found when using the S&P 500 as a benchmark is partly or fully due to the equity size premium (Fama and French 1993).

Exploring benchmark sensitivity further, it has been shown that small *growth* stocks exhibit very low returns and these low returns are difficult to rationalize (e.g. Fama and French 1993; Loughran and Ritter 2000). As a result, small growth stocks drive down the performance of the Fama-French small cap index. Furthermore, early observers argued that buyout firms are unlikely to invest in growth companies (Jensen 1986). Unlike size, the book-to-market ratio or other measures of 'value' are not available for a large sample of buyout fund portfolio companies. However, Capital IQ provides the book-to-market ratio for 537 US buyout investments (see Axelson et al. 2013, for use of that data). In this sample of 537 US buyout investments, the median book-to-market ratio is above 2, indicating that buyout investments are indeed more value investments than growth investments (the threshold for value stocks in the Fama-French portfolio is below 1).[11]

Using the Fama-French small-value index as a benchmark, the average PME of buyout funds becomes 0.96 and is statistically significantly below 1.00.[12] If DFA's value mutual fund is used as a benchmark (which is also old enough, passive and low cost), I find the average PME to be 1.00 and the median PME to be 0.96. Hence, the average buyout fund has exactly the same performance as the DFA value mutual fund.

Another interesting aspect to investigate is the sensitivity of the relative performance of private equity to the leverage assumption. For this purpose, I carry out the same empirical exercise as Robinson and Sensoy (2011) but employ different benchmarks. Consistent with Robinson and Sensoy (2011), I find that the relative performance of buyout funds is not very sensitive to beta. However, with a beta of 1.3 the average buyout fund underperforms any of the small stock benchmarks. Interestingly, when I employ a simple formula to adjust beta for leverage, I obtain a beta of 1.3 for buyout investments. If a 1.3 beta is used in conjunction with the small-value index, the average PME drops to 0.90. With the 3.3 years of effective holding period found in my sample, this corresponds to an underperformance of 3.1% per annum.

Up to now, I have assumed that the Net Asset Value (NAV) that is reported by a fund is equal to the market value of the non-liquidated investments of that fund. As it is difficult to know what the true market value of a buyout fund is and because these NAVs are self-reported, I examine the sensitivity of results to the value of the NAVs. I find that in order for the average buyout fund to match the return of the levered small-value index, its market value would have to be 125% of the stated NAV. In the secondary market, however, the observed average ratio of market value to reported NAV for buyout funds is only 75%,

[11] Consistent with Capital IQ data, Cao and Lerner (2009) show that the average reverse leverage buyout has a positive exposure to both the value factor (HML) and the size factor (SMB) of Fama-French; the betas are 0.17 and 0.55 respectively.

[12] I use the value-weighted index. Using the equally weighted indices of Fama-French further lowers the relative performance of buyout funds.

which corresponds to a 25% discount rather than a 25% premium (Kleymenova, Talmor, and Vasvari 2012).[13]

Although the investments made by the largest buyout funds would mostly fall into the Fama-French small-value category, they are likely to be larger and less value-tilted than those of small buyout funds. When splitting funds by their size, I observe that the average PME is similar across fund size quartiles when the S&P 500 is used as a benchmark. However, when using the small-value index as a benchmark, small buyout funds strongly underperform while large buyout funds show no abnormal performance (their average PME is close to one). When adding the leverage adjustment, it is again the smaller funds which suffer most. This is consistent with the idea that smaller funds have investments that are generally smaller than those of large funds. When average PMEs are weighted by fund size, the average performance comes close to that of the Fama-French small-value index and is below the levered Fama-French small-value index.

It may also be worth bearing in mind that buyout fund stakes are not readily tradable and that investors require an additional return premium for this lack of liquidity (e.g. Ang, Papanikolaou, and Westerfield 2012; Sorensen, Wang, and Yang 2012). Investors also grant credit lines to buyout funds, so-called fund commitments. Like any credit line, these pose a cost for the provider. Neither of these 'liquidity' costs is accounted for in the above analysis. Finally, investing in buyout funds requires additional expenses that are not included in the 'net-of-fees' cash flows available to researchers. These costs include internal staff salary and expenses, external consultants, and lawyers. Dyck and Pomorski (2012) show that these internal costs average 0.4% per annum for their sample of pension funds.

As a result, given the difficulty of determining the right benchmark and the sensitivity of results to the choice of benchmark, it remains unclear whether the implications drawn from previous research efforts remain valid. What is novel, however, is the notion that private equity may be viewed as a potentially efficient way for large institutional investors to access small and value equity premiums. For large allocations, listed equity may not have the required liquidity. This is especially true outside of the US, where the listed equity market for small and value companies can be very thin. Nonetheless, if private equity is mainly about capturing the small and value premiums, then it may be more efficient for large institutions to invest directly in private equity rather than going via funds. This seems to be one of the keys issues to be addressed by future research.

14.2 Empirical Analysis

14.2.1 Preqin Cash-Flow Data

I use the cash-flow dataset of Preqin downloaded in March 2012. Most data is as of June 2011 and the latest reports are from September 2011. Preqin collects the quarterly aggregated investments, distributions, and NAVs made by private equity funds as recorded by US pension funds. Preqin obtains the data under the Freedom of Information Act. There may be

[13] The discounts observed on the secondary market are just indicative. They cannot be taken at face value as they partly reflect liquidity.

more noise in these data than in the proprietary datasets used by RS, HJK, and HS, but pension funds would face serious legal issues if they were to deliberately misreport or only selectively report returns. In addition, data on a given fund can be cross-checked between the different pension funds who invest in it. The data is nonetheless backfilled to the extent that only pension funds that have been investing in private equity since Preqin started to collect these data (mid 2000s) provide their track record. Data for the 1980s and to a lesser extent for the 1990s is thus expected to have an upward bias and to be much less representative.

HJK and HS include only US-focused funds. RS employs both US and non-US funds, with the vast majority of their funds being US-based. Preqin data also mainly contains US funds. For this analysis, I selected funds classified as buyout, reported as 'closed' or 'liquidated', and based in the USA.[14]

As just mentioned, coverage in early years is poor, and data backfilling suggests that the performances of these funds are above average. From 1985 to 1991, the number of funds per vintage year oscillates between zero and six. Concerned about the backfilling bias, I somewhat arbitrarily selected vintage years from 1993 (first vintage year with more than ten funds) to 2010 by default. For completeness, the analysis will also show results when selecting other start and end points. There are 392 funds in this 'default sample'. In comparison, HJK consider 598 funds, RS analyse 542 funds, and HS employ a sample of 1,169 funds.

Despite the lower number of funds used in my analysis, I find similar average and median relative performance as those three recent studies. Table 14.1 shows the average and median

Table 14.1. Buyout fund performance and the size premium

Funds are from vintages 1993 to 2010. The last recorded cash flow (or NAV) is as of June 2011 for the majority of funds, and the most recent data is from September 2011. Selected funds are classified as 'buyout', 'closed' or 'liquidated', and 'US'. There are 392 funds in the sample. Cash-flow data on buyout funds are from Preqin. Data on CRSP indices are from CRSP, accessed via WRDS. Fama-French indices are the size tercile indices containing stocks classified as small, mid, and large respectively; they are downloaded from Ken French's website <http://mba.tuck.dartmouth.edu/pages/faculty/ken.french/data_library.html>, and are value-weighted. PME is the ratio of the present value of cash distributions (plus last reported NAV) to the present value of cash invested. Standard errors are equal to the standard deviation in sample divided by the square root of the number of observations. T-statistics are shown in italics and test whether the average PME is statistically different from one.

	CRSP US stock -market indices		Fama-French size indices		
Benchmark	Value-weighted	Equally weighted	Large	Mid	Small
Mean	1.19	1.03	1.19	1.02	1.03
Median	1.12	0.99	1.12	0.97	0.98
Std error	0.02	0.02	0.02	0.02	0.02
t-stat	*8.21*	*1.53*	*8.29*	*0.98*	*1.49*

14 I exclude an outlier called GCP California Fund, L.P. It is a partnership between Leonard Green and the California Public Employees' Retirement System (CalPERS) to invest in 'California-related industries and underserved markets'.

PME in my default sample with different benchmarks. PME is the ratio of the present value of cash distributed divided by the present value of cash invested. A PME above one thus indicates an outperformance of discount rate used to calculate the present values. The first column uses the value-weighted index of all US stocks compiled by the Center for Research in Security Prices (CRSP). The index captures the entire US listed equity market. As it is value weighted, its returns are similar to those of the S&P 500. The average PME is 1.19 and a median PME of 1.12. To compare, HJK calculate an average of 1.20 and a median of 1.11, whereas RS find an average of 1.19 and a median of 1.09. Finally, HS derive an average PME of 1.22 and a median PME of 1.13.

As shown below, the buyout funds in my sample exhibit an average duration of 3.3 years. A PME of 1.19 would then correspond to a 5.7% yearly outperformance of the S&P 500 index. This number is similar to that of Cambridge Associates, the data provider of the National Venture Capital Association. With data as of June 2011, they calculate returns over the past ten years to be 11.34% for buyout funds and 2.72% for the S&P 500; whilst for the past twenty years, returns reached 13.61% for buyout funds and 8.73% for the S&P 500 index.

14.2.2 The Size of Private Equity Investments

Previous research has employed the S&P 500 as the public market benchmark for buyout fund returns, probably because S&P 500 index returns are readily obtainable at a negligible cost for institutional investors. However, companies that belong to the S&P 500 index appear beyond the reach of most buyout funds. To illustrate this, let us consider the largest buyout ever: the takeover of 'TXU Corp.' on October 2007. At the end of year 2006 (pre-announcement year), TXU Corp. had a market capitalization of $25 billion and was the 120th largest US stock (source: CRSP). TXU Corp. and a handful of so-called 'mega-deals' are the exception. Indeed, 95% of the 5,316 buyout transactions listed in the Capital IQ dataset have an enterprise value of less than $1.08 billion.[15] The average enterprise value is $302 million.

In the literature, the performance of stocks of different size is typically captured by the Fama-French size indices. The largest stock in the Fama-French small cap index has a market capitalization of $1.1 billion. Such a market capitalization would typically correspond to an enterprise value of more than $1.2 billion. Hence, more than 95% of leveraged buyout investments would fall in the Fama-French small cap index.[16]

14.2.3 The Size Premium in Listed Equity

As shown in section 14.2.2, buyout funds invest mainly in companies that are similar in size to small-cap stocks. For the time period covered in earlier studies of buyout performance,

[15] Filter used is: 'Merger/Acquisition' classified as 'LBO' and 'closed or effective or successful' between 1993 and 2011 with enterprise value greater than zero, and US headquartered. Capital IQ often fails to report an enterprise value. As these transactions are probably the smaller ones, the 95th percentile of enterprise values is an upper estimate.

[16] The amount invested in a single deal is not observable in Preqin. One can only observe the aggregated quarterly investment made by a fund. 95% of these quarterly aggregated amounts invested are less than $156 million. Assuming these correspond to a single investment (to be conservative), and that there was twice as much debt as equity, the 95th percentile enterprise value would only be about $500 million.

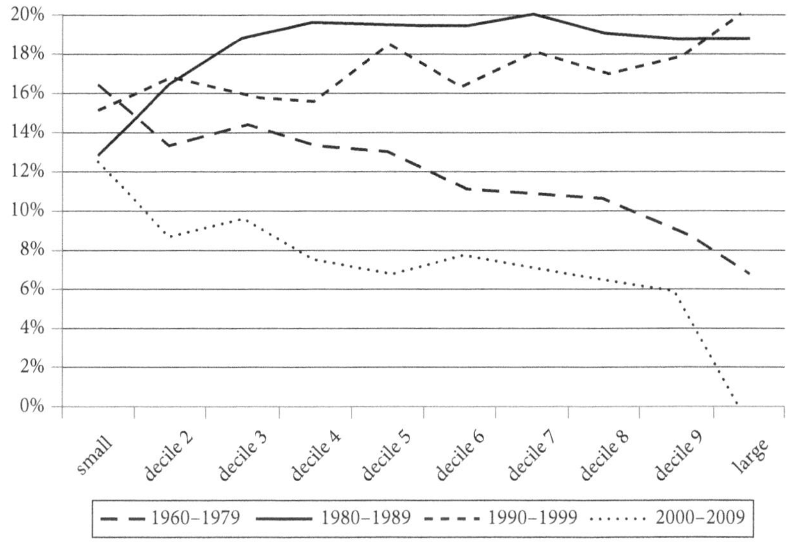

FIGURE 14.1 Annualized average value-weighted return of the Fama-French size portfolios

This figure plots the average monthly return (annualized) of the ten size-deciles portfolios of Fama-French. The data is broken down by time periods: 1960-79, 1980-89, 1990-99, 2000-09.

Source: Ken French website: <http://mba.tuck.dartmouth.edu/pages/faculty/ken.french/data_library.html>.

this fact did not matter since these were the only two decades without a size premium (1980-2000). As a result, the S&P 500 index had returns similar to those of small-cap, and the S&P 500 was used as a benchmark for simplicity.

Figure 14.1 shows the strong size premium of the 1960-1979 period that is documented in the literature (e.g. Fama and French 1993). The spread in average returns between the bottom size-decile and top size-decile is almost 10% per annum over that time period. Both in the 1980s and the 1990s, the size premium is small and is actually slightly negative. However, the size premium returns in the 2000s and is actually very strong. The difference in returns between the bottom size-decile and top size-decile is a staggering 12% per annum.

Another illustration is provided by Figure 14.2. It plots the 10-year forward-looking moving averages of the S&P 500 index, the CRSP equally weighted index, and the ten-year T-bond.[17] A ten-year horizon is chosen since it is the usual life span of a buyout fund. In a sense, Figure 14.2 shows alternative benchmark returns for private equity funds of any given starting date. For an illustration, consider a fund that began operations in 1980. Over the next ten years, the total return of the S&P 500 was just over 15% per annum—similar to the average US stock return. The S&P 500 would hence provide suitable benchmark return for this fund. However, for a fund starting in 2000, the picture is very different. The average

[17] The CRSP equally weighted index measures the return of the average US stock (CRSP-EW) and the CRSP value-weighted index measures the return of the average dollar invested in US stocks (CRSP-VW). CRSP-EW, CRSP-VW, and S&P 500 returns are obtained from Wharton Research Database Services (WRDS); select CRSP dataset, Index/S&P 500 indexes, monthly, returns include distributions). Treasury bond returns are also accessed via WRDS.

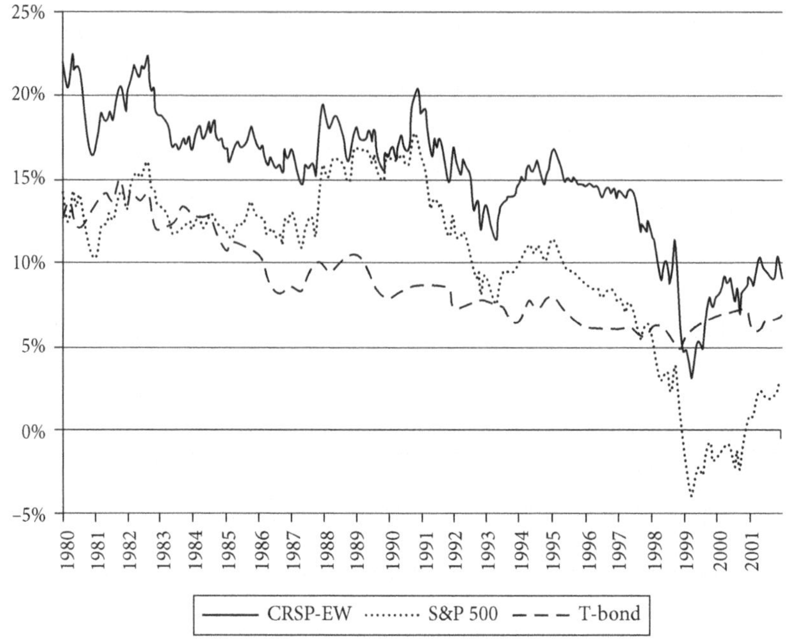

FIGURE 14.2 Annualized ten-year forward-looking moving average returns

Each point is calculated as the average monthly return over the next 120 months. The average monthly return is annualized. Data are from January 1980 to December 2011. The 10 year forward-looking moving average is thus from January 1980 to December 2001. The CRSP equally weighted index measures the return of the average US stock (CRSP-EW). CRSP-EW and S&P 500 returns are obtained from WRDS (Select CRSP dataset, Index/S&P 500 indexes, monthly, returns include distributions). The ten-year Treasury bond monthly returns are also obtained from WRDS (select CRSP dataset, Index/Treasury, annual frequency, return, ten-year bond).

return on the S&P between 2000 and 2010 is negative, but the return for the average US stock lies above 10%. Even Treasury bond returns significantly outperformed those of the S&P 500 over this period. Now suppose funds starting in 2000 have outperformed the S&P 500 by 3% per annum: this still implies that they have underperformed the average US stock by more than 7% per annum and have provided even lower returns than Treasury bonds.

14.2.4 Adjusting Buyout Fund Performance for the Size Premium

Even abstracting from risk-adjustment considerations, it is important to benchmark buyout investments against listed companies of similar size (and book-to-market) as the pricing of companies when buying and selling is based on comparable listed stocks. Suppose a buyout fund added no value but simply bought and sold a random small-cap company at market prices over the last decade. Doing this, it would have strongly outperformed the S&P 500 index but solely due to the existence of the equity size premium.

Table 14.1 shows the results when using the CRSP value weighted index *vis-à-vis* the CSRP equally weighted index. Next, it shows the results when the Fama-French size indices—large, mid-cap, and small-cap—are employed. The results for the CRSP value-weighted and the large cap index are virtually identical. Consistent with the conclusions of recent studies, the results exhibit a strong outperformance of buyout funds. In contrast, when using either the CRSP equally weighted index, the Fama-French small-cap index or Fama-French mid-cap index, the average PMEs are never statistically different from 1 at the 5% level. This shows that the average Net Present Value is not statistically different from zero after a simple adjustment for the size premium.

Put differently, these results show that the average buyout fund return is similar to that of listed equity of similar size. The premium found when using the S&P 500 as a benchmark could therefore be attributed to the size premium (Fama and French 1993).

It is worth noting that recent studies of buyout performance *partly* correct for the size premium, often presenting such results as part of their 'robustness tests'. Robinson and Sensoy (2011 'RS') report what they call the 'tailored PME'. To achieve this, they divide their buyout funds into three groups (terciles) based on size, and then benchmark these three groups against the three Fama-French size indices.[18] This implies that only one-third of their buyout funds are benchmarked against the size category that encompasses 95% of the transactions.[19] This partial adjustment reduces the average PME from 1.19 to 1.08 and the median PME from 1.09 to 0.96.

Harris, Jenkinson, and Kaplan (2013) show that average PME drops from 1.20 to 1.11 and the median PME from 1.11 to 1.02, if the Russell 2000 index is used instead of the S&P 500. The Russell 2000 index captures some of the mid-cap and small-cap stocks in the US and is frequently used in practice. Higson and Stucke (2012) employ the S&P 600 to capture mid-cap returns and find a similar drop in relative returns to Harris, Jenkinson, and Kaplan (2013), with their average PME dropping from 1.22 to 1.12.[20]

14.2.5 Adjusting Buyout Fund Performance for the Value Premium

The small stock benchmark contains many small-growth stocks. These stocks have been shown to have very low returns, which are generally difficult to rationalize (e.g. Fama and French 1993; Loughran and Ritter 2000). The inclusion of small-growth stocks in the benchmark thus significantly reduces the hurdle for buyout funds to outperform the index.

Thus, small-growth stocks should be included in the benchmark only if buyout funds do indeed invest in small growth companies. However, early observers argued that buyout funds target firms with large and stable cash flows rather than growth firms (Jensen, 1986). In contrast to size, the book-to-market ratio or other measures of 'value' are not widely available for buyout fund portfolio companies. However, Capital IQ provides an 'implied equity

[18] The largest size-tercile of buyout funds is matched to the large stock index, the smallest size-tercile of buyout funds is matched to the small stock index, and the in-between size-tercile of buyout funds is matched to the mid-cap index.

[19] As shown above, the bottom tercile would be the comparable size benchmark for 95% of buyout transactions.

[20] Appendix Table 14.1 compares the Russell 2000 index, the S&P 600 index, and the Fama-French size indices. The S&P 600 contains stocks with capitalizations of up to $1,000m which is similar to the small -cap index of Fama-French. The Russell 2000 contains stocks with capitalizations of up to $2,500m.

Table 14.2 Buyout fund performance and the value premium

Funds are from vintages 1993 to 2010. The last recorded cash flow (or NAV) is as of June 2011 for the majority of funds, and the most recent data is from September 2011. Selected funds are classified as 'buyout', 'closed' or 'liquidated', and 'US.' There are 392 funds in the sample. Cash-flow data on buyout funds are from Preqin. Data on mutual funds and on CRSP indices are from CRSP, accessed via WRDS. Fama-French indices are the six double-sorted portfolios containing stocks classified as small -growth, -neutral and -value; and large -growth, -neutral and -value, according to stocks' size and book-to-market ratios. Fama-French indices are downloaded from Ken French's website <http://mba.tuck.dartmouth.edu/pages/faculty/ken.french/data_library.html>. The value-weighted indices are used in Panel A and the equally-weighted indices are used in Panel B. PME is the ratio of the present value of cash distributions (plus last reported NAV) to the present value of cash invested. Standard errors are equal to the standard deviation in sample divided by the square root of the number of observations. t-statistics are shown in italics and test whether the average PME is statistically different from one.

	Fama-French indices (double sorted: size, book-to-market)					
	Small			Large		
Benchmark	Growth	Mid	Value	Growth	Mid	Value
Panel A: Value-weighted portfolio returns						
Mean	1.15	0.97	0.96	1.17	1.14	1.18
Median	1.05	0.94	0.92	1.09	1.07	1.14
Std-error	0.02	0.02	0.02	0.02	0.02	0.02
t-Stat	*6.46*	*−1.68*	*−2.17*	*7.33*	*6.25*	*8.29*
Panel B: Equally weighted portfolio returns						
Mean	1.13	0.94	0.90	1.07	1.02	1.01
Median	1.03	0.89	0.86	0.99	0.97	0.97
Std-error	0.02	0.02	0.02	0.02	0.02	0.02
t-Stat	*5.41*	*−3.18*	*−5.17*	*3.32*	*0.98*	*0.57*

value to book value' for 537 observations, based on data available when the transaction is announced. The average book-to-market ratio is 4.6 and the median book-to-market ratio is 2.1. To compare, the average book-to-market ratio in the Fama-French small value portfolio is about 1.2 (source: Ken French website at <http://mba.tuck.dartmouth.edu/pages/faculty/ken.french/data_library.html>). This confirms—although with limited data—that buyout investments are closest to small-value stocks in nature. As a result, a small-value benchmark seems most appropriate. Table 14.2 shows the average and median buyout fund PMEs when measured against any of the six (two by three) Fama-French size/book-to-market indices. Panel A shows the result for the value-weighted indices and Panel B shows the results for the equally weighted indices.

In Panel A, we see that the average buyout fund significantly outperforms all of the indices except for the small-mid and small-value ones. Moreover, the average buyout fund outperforms all large-cap indices as well as the small-growth index. However, as argued above, this does not correspond to the investment universe of buyout funds. The average buyout fund significantly underperforms the small-value index, with a PME of 0.96.

Panel B shows that using an equally weighted index significantly lowers relative returns. The average PME against the (equally weighted) small value index is only 0.90. In the remainder of this chapter, value-weighted indices are employed to produce conservative results. As a result, any further adjustments would lead to even lower performance if equally weighted indices were used.

14.2.6 Adjusting for Tradability

An important issue when benchmarking against small stocks or small value stocks is the transaction cost incurred when investing in them. Interestingly, starting in the early 1980s, Dimensional Fund Advisor has run a small-cap mutual fund whose objective is to offer a passive low-cost exposure to small-cap stocks in the US. At the end of 2011, the small cap fund had $3.6 billion under management. The fund is called 'DFA micro-cap' (its ticker is DFSCX), and its specific characteristics have been studied in the academic literature (e.g. Keim 1999). The fund prospectus indicates that the largest market capitalization considered was $1,130 million (as of December 2011) which, as shown above, corresponds to an enterprise value that is higher than that of the 95th largest leveraged buyout. In addition, in 1993 (the beginning of our sample), Dimensional Fund Advisor introduced a passive low-cost value mutual fund (the ticker is DFSVX).

Table 14.3 shows that when using the S&P 500 index of Vanguard, results are similar to those obtained with large cap indices or value-weighted indices. However, results are also similar when using DFA mutual funds versus small cap indices or value indices. Using DFA micro-cap mutual fund as a benchmark, I find that the average and median PME fall to 1.04 and 0.99, respectively. When using DFA value mutual fund as a benchmark, the average and median PME fall to 1.00 and 0.96, respectively. Hence the average buyout fund has returned exactly as much as the oldest and most prominent passive low-cost value mutual fund.

Table 14.3 Buyout fund performance and mutual funds

Funds are from vintages 1993 to 2010. The last recorded cash flow (or NAV) is as of June 2011 for the majority of funds, and the most recent data is from September 2011. Selected funds are classified as 'buyout', 'closed' or 'liquidated', and 'US'. There are 392 funds in the sample. Cash-flow data on buyout funds are from Preqin. Data are from CRSP, accessed via WRDS. PME is the ratio of the present value of cash distributions (plus last reported NAV) to the present value of cash invested. Standard errors are equal to the standard deviation in sample divided by the square root of the number of observations. t-statistics are shown in italics and test whether the average PME is statistically different from one.

Benchmark (ticker)	Vanguard S&P 500 (VFINX)	DFA micro-cap (DFSCX)	DFA value (DFSVX)
Mean	1.20	1.04	1.00
Median	1.14	0.99	0.96
Std-error	0.02	0.02	0.02
t-Stat	*8.85*	*1.83*	*0.23*

14.2.7 Adjusting Buyout Fund Performance for Leverage

The difference in leverage between buyout funds and listed equity is an additional dimension to control for. Hence, it seems more accurate to compare buyout fund returns with those of a hypothetical investor who has levered up a position in listed equity.

For example, assume an investor has $100, the DFA micro-cap return is 10%, and the investor can borrow at a rate of 5%—an amount that is one -to -one when giving the DFA micro-cap as collateral. This means the investor can have 50% leverage and can hence invest $200 in DFA micro-cap and obtain a return of 2*10%-5%=15%. In this simple example, if the average buyout fund has 50% leverage, then the benchmark should be 1.5 times the buyout fund returns.[21] This 1.5 can be interpreted as the beta in the CAPM formula (abstracting from the risk-free rate).

One way to estimate beta is to analyze the realized cash flows of buyout funds. Both Driessen, Lin, and Phalippou (2012) and Franzoni, Nowak, and Phalippou (2012) find a beta of 1.3 with respect to a broad value-weighted stock index. Neither research provides results with respect to a small cap index.

We can also compute a beta using the CAPM formula in conjunction with some classic assumptions. Ivashina and Kovner (2011) report an average yield of 3% (over LIBOR) for buyout debt. Assuming an equity risk premium of 8%, the CAPM formula thus implies a beta on debt of 3/8 = 0.375. Axelson et al. (2012) report an average leverage of buyout investments of 69%, which corresponds to a debt-to-equity ratio of 2.23. Their matched public companies have a debt-to-equity ratio of 0.5.[22] For this analysis, I assume a tax rate of 35%. Using the standard formula, we thus obtain:

$$\text{Beta unlevered of } 1/\left(1+\left(1-0.35\right)*0.5\right) = 0.75$$
$$\text{And a buyout beta of } (0.75*(1+\left(1-0.35\right)*2.23) - (0.375*\left(1-0.35\right)*2.23) = 1.3$$

Table 14.4 shows the average PMEs with beta set to 1.3. Results are shown for the main benchmarks, that is, the large-cap indices (S&P 500, CRSP value-weighted and Fama-French large-cap index) and the more relevant indices (DFA micro-cap, CRSP equally weighted, and Fama-French small-cap index and small-value index).

Having a beta of 1.3 reduces PMEs as expected. An important observation is that the effect is much stronger for the small-cap benchmarks. This is probably due to the fact that large-cap benchmarks exhibit returns close to zero and are thus less sensitive to changes in beta. For example, the PME with the large-cap index only decreases from 1.19 to 1.16. The PMEs with small-cap benchmarks decrease by about 5%. Hence with a beta of 1.3, the average buyout fund underperforms the DFA value fund (average PME is 0.96), the CRSP equally weighted index (average PME of 0.97) and both the small-cap index and the small-value index (average PME of 0.99 and 0.90 respectively). The average buyout fund thus underperforms a moderately leveraged small-value index by 3.1% per annum with an effective holding period of 3.3 years.[23]

[21] Buyout funds have more than 50% leverage, but the stocks in which DFA micro-cap invests in also have some leverage. This comparison also abstracts from the cost of levering up listed equity.

[22] They do not adjust for size when 'matching' companies, which would probably lower average leverage.

[23] $(1\text{-}3.1\%)^{3.3}$=0.90

Table 14.4 Buyout fund performance and leverage effect

Funds are from vintages 1993 to 2010. The last recorded cash flow (or NAV) is as of June 2011 for the majority of funds, and the most recent data is from September 2011. Selected funds are classified as 'buyout', 'closed' or 'liquidated', and 'US'. There are 392 funds in the sample. Cash-flow data on buyout funds are from Preqin. Data on mutual funds and on CRSP indices are from CRSP, accessed via WRDS. Fama-French indices are i) Size tercile indices containing stocks classified as small, mid, and large respectively; and ii) Six double-sorted portfolios containing stocks classified as small -growth, -neutral, and -value; and large -growth, -neutral, and -value, according to stocks' size and book-to-market ratios. Fama-French indices are downloaded from Ken French's website <http://mba.tuck.dartmouth.edu/pages/faculty/ken.french/data_library.html>, and are value-weighted. In Panel A, a 1.3 multiplier is applied to the benchmarks (i.e. beta is set to 1.3 instead of 1; ignoring risk-free rate). In Panel B, a 1.5 multiplier is applied to the benchmarks. PME is the ratio of the present value of cash distributions (plus last reported NAV) to the present value of cash invested. Standard errors are equal to the standard deviation in sample divided by the square root of the number of observations. t-statistics are shown in italics and test whether the average PME is statistically different from one.

	Mutual funds		CRSP				
	Vanguard	DFA	US stock-market indices		Fama-French indices		
Benchmark	S&P 500	Value	Value-Weighted	Equally weighted	Large	Small	Small & Value
Panel A: Beta is set to 1.3 (instead of 1)							
Mean	1.17	0.96	1.16	0.97	1.16	0.99	0.90
Median	1.11	0.90	1.10	0.93	1.10	0.94	0.86
Std-error	0.02	0.02	0.02	0.02	0.02	0.02	0.02
t-stat	*7.48*	*−1.95*	*6.93*	*−1.43*	*7.05*	*−0.62*	*−4.90*
Panel B: Beta is set to 1.5 (instead of 1)							
Mean	1.16	0.94	1.15	0.94	1.15	0.97	0.88
Median	1.10	0.87	1.09	0.90	1.08	0.92	0.84
Std-error	0.02	0.02	0.02	0.02	0.02	0.02	0.02
t-stat	*6.96*	*−2.64*	*6.33*	*−2.93*	*6.47*	*−1.37*	*−5.84*

The 3.3 years of effective holding period is calculated as with a fixed-income investment (see Phalippou and Gottschalg 2009). For each fund, the holding period is calculated as the difference between the weighted average time of cash distribution and the weighted average time of capital invested. The weights are the present value of each cash flow and the S&P 500 is used as a discount rate (which does not impact duration). The average holding period across the 392 buyout funds is thus 3.3 years. The duration is relatively short as many funds in the sample are quite young. The sample in Phalippou and Gottschalg (2009) contained only funds of ten years of age or more. That study finds an average (effective) holding period of six years.

Interestingly, as pointed out by Robinson and Sensoy (2011), a further increase in beta has little effect on relative returns. As shown in Table 14.4–Panel B, when beta increases to 1.5, the decrease in PME is small.

14.2.8 Adjusting Buyout Fund Performance for Self-reported NAVs

The analysis above assumes, just like the recent studies of buyout fund returns, that the NAV of a fund is equal to its market value. This implies that in order to compute performance, one can simply use the last reported NAV as the last cash flow.

Fund NAVs are set internally by buyout managers and it is well known that different buyout managers can estimate very different valuations for the same investment.[24] However, the secondary market for buyout fund positions is becoming increasingly liquid. The prices paid in this market for fund positions provide a better value estimate than the NAVs assigned by fund managers. Kleymenova, Talmor, and Vasvari (2012) present a comprehensive analysis of the pricing of fund positions on the secondary market. On average, they find that market prices reflect a discount of 25% to stated NAV.[25] Obviously, the discount only partially reflects the misvaluation of NAVs as it also reflects a compensation for liquidity provision. This leads to an interesting question: what market price, relative to NAV, would be required to raise the average buyout fund's return to break even against the levered small value index?

The answer is that the market price would need to be $1.25 per $1 of stated NAV (Table 14.5–Panel A). This is much higher than the $0.75 actual payment per $1 of NAV observed in Kleymenova, Talmor, and Vasvari (2012). Part of the gap reflects liquidity and differences between the funds that trade on the secondary market and the universe of funds. But it seems unlikely that such a large gap is fully reflected by these two factors alone.

HS calculate returns using a 12.5% discount to NAV. Table 14.5–Panel B shows the results when using this 12.5% discount, which represents only half of the observed discount on the secondary market. When using the S&P 500 as a benchmark, the average PME decreases from 1.20 to 1.13. When using the DFA value mutual fund as a benchmark, the average PME is significantly below one.

14.3 Additional Empirical Analysis

In this section, I first show the sensitivity of performance to benchmarks for different fund size categories and then for each vintage year. Next, I compare the time series of returns found in Preqin with that found in proprietary datasets. Then, I show the robustness of the results to the sample selection methodology. Finally, I discuss additional adjustments that would be necessary to evaluate buyout fund returns more precisely.

[24] Investors routinely report that when several funds invest in the same deal, they observe that each fund comes up with a different valuation and deviations may be substantial.

[25] 25% is the discount observed both on their full sample and for years 2010 and 2011.

Table 14.5 Buyout fund performance and self-reported NAVs

Funds are from vintages 1993 to 2010. The last recorded cash flow (or NAV) is as of June 2011 for the majority of funds, and the most recent data is from September 2011. Selected funds are classified as 'buyout', 'closed' or 'liquidated', and 'US'. There are 392 funds in the sample. Cash-flow data on buyout funds are from Preqin. Data on mutual funds and on CRSP indices are from CRSP, accessed via WRDS. Fama-French indices are i) Size tercile indices containing stocks classified as small, mid, and large respectively; and ii) Six double sorted portfolios containing stocks classified as small -growth, -neutral, and -value; and large -growth, -neutral and –value, according to stocks' size and book-to-market ratios. Fama-French indices are downloaded from Ken French's website <http://mba.tuck.dartmouth.edu/pages/faculty/ken.french/data_library.html>, and are value-weighted. Panel A shows results when the fund remaining market value is assumed to be 125% of the last reported NAV (instead of assuming they are equal) and Panel B shows results when the fund remaining market value is assumed to be 87.5% of the last reported NAV. PME is the ratio of the present value of cash distributions (plus last reported NAV) to the present value of cash invested. Standard errors are equal to the standard deviation in sample divided by the square root of the number of observations. T-statistics are shown in italics and test whether the average PME is statistically different from one.

	Mutual funds		CRSP				
	Vanguard	DFA	US stock-market indices		Fama-French Portfolios		
Benchmark	S&P 500	Value	Value-Weighted	Equally weighted	Large	Small	Small & Value
Panel A: Change last reported NAV to 125% of reported value							
Mean	1.30	1.07	1.28	1.08	1.28	1.10	1.01
Median	1.26	1.06	1.26	1.07	1.26	1.07	1.00
Std-error	0.02	0.02	0.02	0.02	0.02	0.02	0.02
t-Stat	*12.69*	*3.17*	*12.18*	*3.97*	*12.29*	*4.44*	*0.45*
Panel B: Change last reported NAV to 87.5% of reported value							
Mean	1.13	0.95	1.12	0.97	1.13	0.97	0.90
Median	1.06	0.89	1.05	0.92	1.05	0.92	0.86
Std-error	0.02	0.02	0.02	0.02	0.02	0.02	0.02
t-Stat	*5.76*	*−2.60*	*5.33*	*−1.31*	*5.43*	*−1.32*	*−5.12*

14.3.1 Performance and Fund Size

Although the investments made by large funds would mostly fall into the Fama-French small value category, they are likely to be larger and more growth-tilted than those of small funds. It is thus informative to break down results by fund-size categories.

Table 14.6 shows average PMEs with different benchmarks when splitting funds by their size. The average PME is similar across fund-size quartiles when the S&P 500 is used as a benchmark. However, when using the small-value index as a benchmark, small buyout funds strongly underperform while large buyout funds show no abnormal performance (average PME is close to one). When adding the leverage adjustment, it is again the smaller funds who suffer most. This is consistent with the idea that smaller funds have investments that are tilted more towards small and value companies than large funds.

Table 14.6 Performance and fund size

Cash-flow data on buyout funds are from Preqin. Funds are from vintages 1993 to 2010. The last recorded cash flow (or NAV) is as of June 2011 for the majority of funds, and the most recent data is from September 2011. Selected funds are classified as 'buyout', 'closed', or 'liquidated', 'US' and have a valid fund size that is reported. There are 386 funds in the sample. Data on mutual funds (DFA and Vanguard) are from CRSP, accessed via WRDS. The small-value size index of Fama-French is downloaded from Ken French's website <http://mba.tuck.dartmouth.edu/pages/faculty/ken.french/data_library.html>, and is value-weighted. The 'Small & value & leveraged' index is equal to 1.3 times the 'Small & value' index. The table shows the average PME within each fund-size quartile. The break points for the size quartiles are $343 million, $692 million and $1.5 billion respectively. Fund size is given by Preqin. PME is the ratio of the present value of cash distributions (plus last reported NAV) to the present value of cash invested.

Fund size Category	Benchmark is:	Vanguard S&P 500	DFA Micro-cap	Fama-French Small & Value	Small & Value & Levered
Small funds (less than $343 million)		1.22	0.99	0.93	0.86
2nd size quartile		1.17	0.95	0.90	0.84
3rd size quartile		1.19	1.04	0.99	0.95
Large funds (more than $1.5 billion)		1.24	1.05	1.02	0.97

Given this result, it is important to verify that the above findings remain similar if performance is value-weighted. The weighting issue is, however, difficult to tackle. Within vintage years, it is simple enough and the results for this are discussed in sub-section 14.3.2. However, size-weighting across funds is difficult because $1 invested in 1992 does not have the same value as $1 invested in 2007. In addition, funds vary both in their investing pace and in the fraction of their capital that is actually invested. The latter remark motivates the use of the present value of the actual amount invested as an alternative weighting variable.

Appendix Table 14.2 shows the results. When average PMEs are weighted by fund size, average performance is very close to that of the Fama-French small-value index and below the levered Fama-French small-value index.[26] Against the leveraged small-value index, the average PME reaches 0.95 (up from 0.90 when average PME is equally weighted). However, when funds are weighted by the present value of their investments, average PMEs are back to their equally weighted average. For example, against the leveraged small-value index the present-value-weighted average PME is 0.91.

To compute the present value, the small-value index is used. But this choice does affect results. As the discount rate increases, relative performance usually decreases towards the equally weighted performance. When the discount rate is closer to zero (e.g., when the S&P 500 is used), results converge to the size-weighted case and thus relative performance increases. Yet, even when funds are size-weighted, the average buyout fund slightly underperforms the small-value index and significantly underperforms the leveraged small-value index.

[26] Results with 'total capital invested' as weight are virtually identical to those with size as weight (which is defined as the total capital committed).

14.3.2 Performance Per Vintage Year

It is also interesting to investigate the average performance broken down per vintage year in order to appreciate the performance cycles of buyout funds. Table 14.7 shows the results. In Panel A, fund PMEs are equally weighted within each vintage year and the cycles are very clear. 1993–94 funds outperform the S&P 500, the DFA value fund and the small-value stock index (but not the leveraged small-value index). 1995–99 vintage years show poor performance when benchmarked to small-caps and to the small-value index. 2000–05 funds have very strong returns overall compared with any benchmark. Then 2006–10 funds display low returns against any benchmarks.

As pointed out by HJK, buyout funds outperform the S&P 500 in virtually all vintage years. However, when benchmarked against the value indices, only the 1993–94 and 2000–05 vintages outperform. Against the leveraged small-value index, only the vintage years 2001–05 outperform. Table 14.7–Panel B shows results when funds are value-weighted within a vintage year. The cycles are similar but overall returns are higher. The average PME across vintage years increases from 0.90 to 0.94 (against the leveraged small-value index).

14.3.3 Comparison of US Buyout Fund Cash-flows Datasets

While investigating the time series of average PMEs (across vintage years), it is interesting to compare them with those shown in Harris, Jenkinson, and Kaplan (2013 'HJK') and in Higson and Stucke (2012 'HS'). Both HJK and HS show results comparable to those in Table 14.7–Panel B.[27]

Table 14.8–Panel A displays the number of funds and the size-weighted average PMEs per vintage year for the Preqin, HJK, and HS datasets. In Section 14.2.1, it was already noted that the average and median PMEs across funds were virtually identical in these three datasets despite their differences in coverage. Table 14.8–Panel A exhibits the difference in coverage for these three datasets. The Preqin sample used in this analysis encompasses 356 funds, compared with 557 funds in the HJK sample (i.e. 56% more) and 992 funds in the HS sample (i.e. 179%) more. Despite this, the correlation between the number of observations in Preqin and in HJK sample is 89% and the correlation between the number of observations in Preqin and in HS sample is 95% (non-tabulated).

Importantly, the yearly average returns are similar across the three datasets and the average across years is almost equal: 1.30 in Preqin, 1.28 in HJK and 1.29 in HS. Table 14.8–Panel B reports the correlation matrix between the yearly average PMEs. The correlation is 90% between both the HJK and HS sample, and the Preqin and HS sample. It is 76% between the HJK sample and Preqin sample. These are obviously high coefficients of correlation, and it is also interesting to note that the highest correlation is achieved with the most comprehensive sample.

[27] Robinson and Sensoy (2011) only show vintage year performance for their subsample of liquidated funds, they include both US and non-US funds, and their dataset stops with vintage year 2005. Consequently, their results cannot be included in this analysis.

Table 14.7 Buyout fund performance per vintage year

Funds are from vintages 1993 to 2010. The last recorded cash flow (or NAV) is as of June 2011 for the majority of funds, and the most recent data is from September 2011. Selected funds are classified as 'buyout', 'closed' or 'liquidated', and 'US'. There are 392 funds in total, of which 386 funds have information about their size. Cash-flow data on buyout funds are from Preqin. Data on mutual funds are from CRSP, accessed via WRDS. The small-value size index of Fama-French is downloaded from Ken French's website <http://mba.tuck.dartmouth.edu/pages/faculty/ken.french/data_library.html>, and is value-weighted. The 'Small & value & leveraged' index is equal to 1.3 times the 'Small & value' index. The table shows the average PME of the funds raised in a given vintage year. In Panel A the average is equally weighted and in Panel B it is size-weighted. The average at the bottom of the table equally weight each vintage year.

Vintage year	Number of observations	Benchmark is:	Vanguard S&P 500	DFA value	Fama-French Small & value	Small & value & leveraged
Panel A: Equally weighted performance within vintage year						
1993	11		1.22	1.29	1.15	0.98
1994	13		1.18	1.16	1.06	0.93
1995	9		0.95	0.82	0.73	0.63
1996	15		1.03	0.80	0.72	0.65
1997	18		1.18	0.68	0.62	0.53
1998	30		1.34	0.68	0.62	0.52
1999	22		1.28	0.80	0.75	0.65
2000	33		1.58	1.15	1.10	0.98
2001	11		1.63	1.37	1.33	1.22
2002	13		1.30	1.16	1.11	1.05
2003	14		1.35	1.29	1.22	1.21
2004	23		1.52	1.48	1.40	1.41
2005	41		1.18	1.13	1.07	1.08
2006	38		1.02	0.96	0.93	0.92
2007	38		1.05	0.96	0.94	0.90
2008	31		0.97	0.90	0.89	0.84
2009	14		0.94	0.87	0.87	0.82
2010	18		0.87	0.89	0.88	0.88
Sum	392					
Average			1.20	1.02	0.97	0.90
Panel B: Size-weighted performance within vintage year						
1993	11		1.20	1.24	1.10	0.93
1994	13		1.27	1.25	1.14	1.00
1995	9		1.09	0.95	0.84	0.72
1996	15		1.09	0.84	0.75	0.67
1997	18		1.23	0.74	0.67	0.58
1998	30		1.21	0.60	0.55	0.46
1999	22		1.27	0.81	0.76	0.66
2000	33		1.54	1.13	1.08	0.96
2001	11		1.70	1.43	1.39	1.27
2002	13		1.48	1.34	1.28	1.21
2003	14		1.73	1.62	1.55	1.50
2004	23		1.58	1.53	1.45	1.46

(*continued*)

Table 14.7 (Continued)

Vintage year	Number of observations	Benchmark is:	Vanguard S&P 500	DFA value	Fama-French Small & value	Small & value & leveraged
2005	39		1.33	1.29	1.21	1.23
2006	37		1.05	0.97	0.93	0.93
2007	37		1.05	0.95	0.93	0.90
2008	31		0.97	0.89	0.89	0.83
2009	13		0.88	0.82	0.82	0.77
2010	17		0.89	0.90	0.90	0.90
Sum	386					
Average			1.25	1.07	1.01	0.94

Taken together, these results indicate that publicly available fund cash-flow datasets are, a priori, sufficiently precise to be used for a range of applications in this field.

14.3.4 Robustness to Sample Selection

Table 14.9 shows the results for various sample selections. As mentioned above, sample size increases over the years. Sample size exceeded ten funds per year for the first time in 1993, and then went beyond fifteen funds for the first time in 1996, and so on. The default sample somewhat arbitrarily started in 1993; but this choice does not impact results significantly. Table 14.9–Panel A shows results starting in the vintage year of 1996 instead of 1993. Relative performance with respect to the S&P 500 is not affected, and PMEs with respect to the small-cap indices are slightly reduced.

The ending vintage year may also be debated. The way fees work means that young funds mechanically have low returns.[28] However, young funds were hurt most by the financial crisis. Hence, simply removing vintage years such as 2007-10 would mechanically result in higher relative performance. In Table 14.9–Panel B, results are shown for funds raised up to 2001. These funds are all more than ten years old in 2011. Since ten years is the usual official time span of a fund, this makes for a natural cut-off and results are not affected by the boom vintage years 2004-06 and the bust vintage years 2007-10. In that sub-sample (vintage years 1993-2001), performance relative to the S&P 500 increases sharply, with the average PME moving from 1.20 to 1.31. The performance relative to small-caps, however, is sharply reduced. Average PME with respect to i) the small-cap index goes down to 1; ii) the small-value index falls to 0.87; and iii) the DFA micro-cap mutual fund decreases to 1.01.

As mentioned above, NAVs are difficult to value and different assumptions about their true valuation significantly impact on the results. One approach is to discard funds with high NAVs from the sample. However, the resulting sample may not be sufficiently

[28] Fees are charged up front based on total capital committed and the few investments made are usually held at cost in early years. This creates mechanically a low return in early years.

Table 14.8 Comparison of US buyout fund cash-flows datasets

This table compares the Preqin cash-flow dataset (i.e. the dataset used in this chapter) with the proprietary datasets of Harris, Jenkinson, and Kaplan (2012 'HJK') and Higson and Stucke (2012 'HS'). The sample of Robinson and Sensoy (2012) is excluded from the analysis because the authors do not show comparable statistics in their paper. Panel A shows the number of funds and the average size-weighted PMEs per vintage year. PME is the ratio of the present value of cash distributions (plus last reported NAV) to the present value of cash invested. The discount rate is the S&P 500 index. Panel B shows the correlation matrix for the three time-series of average PMEs shown in Panel A.

Vintage	Number of observations			Size-weighted average PME (wrt S&P 500)		
year	Preqin	HJK	HS	Preqin	HJK	HS
Panel A: Comparison per vintage year						
1993	11	11	23	1.20	1.24	1.14
1994	13	13	42	1.27	1.75	1.43
1995	9	17	36	1.09	1.20	1.26
1996	15	9	36	1.09	0.90	1.00
1997	18	30	56	1.23	1.30	1.37
1998	30	38	72	1.21	1.21	1.20
1999	22	28	58	1.27	1.27	1.28
2000	33	39	84	1.54	1.47	1.48
2001	11	26	47	1.70	1.38	1.55
2002	13	21	37	1.48	1.53	1.55
2003	14	13	34	1.73	1.58	1.59
2004	23	46	62	1.58	1.51	1.41
2005	39	57	92	1.33	1.23	1.28
2006	37	67	108	1.05	0.99	1.07
2007	37	74	107	1.05	1.02	1.00
2008	31	68	98	0.97	0.90	0.96
Sum	356	557	992			
Average				1.30	1.28	1.29
Vintage year average PMEs				Preqin (%)	HJK (%)	HS (5)
Panel B: Correlation matrix of vintage year average PMEs across datasets						
Preqin				100%	76%	90%
Harris-Jenkinson-Kaplan (HJK)				76%	100%	90%
Higson-Stucke (HS)				90%	90%	100%

representative. The results in Table 14.9–Panel C indicate that discarding the few funds with a reported NAV higher than the total amount invested decreases PMEs by about 0.02.

Table 14.9–Panel D shows that further discarding funds with a reported NAV higher than half of the total amount invested results in a much smaller sample of only 226 funds, versus 392 funds in the default sample. In the reduced sample, PMEs with respect to large-cap benchmarks are hardly affected, but those with respect to small-cap benchmarks decrease sharply. The average PME with respect to the small-value index, for example, reaches 0.86.

Table 14.9–Panel E shows that when European buyout funds are included, the number of funds increases from 392 to 509, but relative performance remains virtually identical.

Table 14.9 Buyout fund performance—robustness to sample selection

Funds are from vintages 1993 to 2010. The last recorded cash flow (or NAV) is as of June 2011 for the majority of funds, and the most recent data is from September 2011. Selected funds are classified as 'buyout', 'closed' or 'liquidated', and 'US'. There are 392 funds in the sample. Cash-flow data on buyout funds are from Preqin. Data on mutual funds and on CRSP indices are from CRSP, accessed via WRDS. Fama-French indices are i) Size tercile indices containing stocks classified as small, mid, and large respectively; and ii) Six double sorted portfolios containing stocks classified as small -growth, -neutral, and -value; and large -growth, -neutral, and -value, according to stocks' size and book-to-market ratios. Fama-French indices are downloaded from Ken French's website <http://mba.tuck.dartmouth.edu/pages/faculty/ken.french/data_library.html>, and are value-weighted. Panels A to F show results when a change is made to the original sample: change starting and ending vintage years, exclude some funds based on their relative last reported NAV, add European funds and use a wider definition of buyout funds (i.e. include funds classified as turnaround, special situation, balanced and growth). PME is the ratio of the present value of cash distributions (plus last reported NAV) to the present value of cash invested. Standard errors are equal to the standard deviation in sample divided by the square root of the number of observations. t-statistics are shown in italics and test whether the average PME is statistically different from one.

	Mutual funds		CRSP				
	Vanguard	DFA	US stock-market indices		Fama-French Portfolios		
Benchmark	S&P 500	Value	Value weighted	Equally weighted	Large	Small	Small & Value
Panel A: Change starting vintage year to 1996 (number of funds is 359)							
Mean	1.20	1.00	1.19	1.02	1.19	1.02	0.95
Median	1.14	0.96	1.13	0.99	1.13	0.98	0.92
Std-error	0.02	0.02	0.02	0.02	0.02	0.02	0.02
t-Stat	*8.50*	*−0.22*	*8.13*	*1.19*	*8.18*	*0.95*	*−2.32*
Panel B: Change ending vintage year to 2001 (number of funds is 162)							
Mean	1.31	0.94	1.29	1.05	1.31	1.00	0.87
Median	1.30	0.91	1.28	1.03	1.30	0.97	0.84
Std-error	0.04	0.03	0.04	0.03	0.04	0.04	0.03
t-Stat	*7.79*	*−1.83*	*7.41*	*1.59*	*7.66*	*0.02*	*−3.99*
Panel C: Exclude funds whose last reported NAV is more than capital invested (number of funds is 369)							
Mean	1.18	0.99	1.17	1.02	1.17	1.01	0.94
Median	1.12	0.95	1.10	0.97	1.11	0.97	0.91
Std-error	0.02	0.02	0.02	0.02	0.02	0.02	0.02
t-Stat	*7.77*	*−0.69*	*7.36*	*0.80*	*7.46*	*0.63*	*−3.04*
Panel D: Exclude funds whose last reported NAV is more than 50% of capital invested (number of funds is 226)							
Mean	1.17	0.91	1.16	0.98	1.17	0.95	0.86
Median	1.07	0.84	1.06	0.93	1.06	0.89	0.82
Std-error	0.03	0.03	0.03	0.03	0.03	0.03	0.03
t-Stat	*4.96*	*−3.11*	*4.64*	*−0.56*	*4.84*	*-1.56*	*−5.05*
Panel E: Include European funds (number of funds is 509)							
Mean	1.20	1.00	1.19	1.03	1.19	1.03	0.96
Median	1.13	0.96	1.12	0.99	1.12	0.99	0.92
Std-error	0.02	0.02	0.02	0.02	0.02	0.02	0.02
t-Stat	*9.46*	*0.16*	*9.04*	*1.84*	*9.11*	*1.62*	*−2.46*

(continued)

Table 14.9 (Continued)

	Mutual funds		CRSP				
	Vanguard	DFA	US stock-market indices		Fama-French Portfolios		
Benchmark	S&P 500	Value	Value weighted	Equally weighted	Large	Small	Small & Value
Panel F: Widening the definition of a buyout fund (number of funds is 447)							
Mean	1.20	1.00	1.18	1.03	1.19	1.03	0.95
Median	1.13	0.96	1.12	0.99	1.12	0.99	0.92
Std-error	0.02	0.02	0.02	0.02	0.02	0.02	0.02
t-Stat	*9.11*	*0.09*	*8.67*	*1.43*	*8.75*	*1.40*	*−2.52*

If funds from the rest of the world were included, however, relative performance would decrease (non-tabulated).

Finally, Table 14.9–Panel F shows results when a wider definition of buyout funds is employed. Some funds classified by Preqin as 'turnaround funds', 'balanced funds', 'growth funds', and 'special situations' could be considered as 'buyout funds'. When doing so, the number of funds in the sample increases to 447, and results are hardly affected. Taken together, these results show that the findings in section 14.3.3 are robust to sample choices.

14.3.5 Additional Adjustments

The above results show that the performance of the average buyout fund is significantly lower than that of a levered small-value benchmark. Yet, other important characteristics of buyout funds would require a premium and not a discount against listed equity.

The most important characteristic is what is broadly referred to as 'illiquidity' and which encompasses a number of related concepts. First, buyout fund stakes are not freely tradable and investors should command an additional return premium for this illiquidity, as recently shown by Ang, Papanikolaou, and Westefield (2012) and Sorensen, Wang, and Yang (2012). Second, an investor in a private equity fund usually has to provide what is known as a 'capital commitment'. This is the economic equivalent of a credit facility. It allows the fund's manager to draw down cash from the investor as and when convenient, over a period of (typically) five years. Again, one should expect investors to be compensated for granting a credit line.

It is also important to keep in mind that investing in buyout funds requires additional expenses that are not included in the 'net-of-fees' cash flows available to researchers. The largest private equity investors have teams of more than 100 people and may hire external advisors such as consultants and lawyers. For example, AlpInvest, one of the largest private equity investors, now owned by Carlyle, has an annual budget of €50 million (plus a carried interest) and invests about €5 billion a year. Dyck and Pomorski (2012) report that the average pension fund in their sample has an internal cost of 0.4% per annum for private equity investments. Some investors also use funds-of-funds and pay extra fees as a result.

Potential sample biases are also important to keep in mind. The extensive literature on mutual funds provides a good illustration of this. Moreover, sample biases are naturally magnified in high-volatility assets such as private equity or hedge funds. The datasets behind the three recent studies appear to be of higher quality than anything else that has been made available for research purposes. The data in Robinson and Sensoy (2011) come from one investor, but because the investor inherited the track record, they argue that the investor has no specific preferences for results being positive or negative. Harris, Jenkinson, and Kaplan (2013) examine the returns of funds that were selected by a large number of investors who agreed that their track record could be included in the study. Higson and Stucke (2012) use Cambridge Associates data, which they complement with data given directly to them by a large number of investors. In each case, it seems fair to say that the data providers stand to benefit from growth in the buyout industry; participating investors have survived for a number of years and have willingly shared their track record with academic researchers. A sample bias might arise as participating investors are more likely to have selected funds that are above average rather than below average.[29]

Nonetheless the size of the sample bias may turn out to be small because missing funds may be negligible on a value-weighted basis, especially in recent years when the buyout industry has shrunk dramatically. For the 1980s, however, it is more difficult to be optimistic about possible sample biases. However, as an empirical question, this remains open.

14.4 Conclusion

This study shows that a publicly available dataset for buyout fund cash flows is sufficient to replicate the findings derived from richer but proprietary datasets. Using this publicly available data, it is found that the average buyout fund outperforms the S&P 500 by about 5.7% per annum. This chapter investigates the sensitivity of that result to the choice of a benchmark.

When benchmarked to a leveraged small-value index, the average buyout fund underperforms by 3.1% per annum. However, the average buyout fund performance is similar to that of small cap stock indices, of a passive small-cap mutual fund (DFA small-cap), and of a passive value mutual fund (DFA value).

Given the nature of the data, there are a number of unknowns that matter for performance evaluation, such as the value of the NAVs. It also remains unclear how one should weight different vintage years. Choosing the right benchmark also poses a challenge. The -3.1% estimate is obtained with value-weighted benchmarks of Fama-French. However, other equally weighted benchmarks exhibit higher returns, and using those would thus result in even lower relative performance of buyout funds. In the absence of more detailed data, it is hence difficult to precisely benchmark funds. The use of the small-value index is probably a good approximation for most funds, but not all. As a result of these impediments, one cannot reach a definite conclusion regarding the performance of buyout funds. The results in this paper show that the choice of a benchmark plays an important role and that publicly available data are now sufficiently rich to explore various aspects of private equity fund performance.

[29] For example, the public pension funds which back a disproportionate number of underperforming local fund managers (see Hochberg and Rauh 2011) are unlikely to be part of these databases. As a result, these underperforming funds are unlikely to be included in the sample.

The findings of relatively low performance compared with certain stock market indices may provide a rationale for current trends in the industry. Investors have increasingly obtained co-investment opportunities, which allow them to increase the amount invested in selected deals whilst paying lower fees (Fang, Ivashina, and Lerner 2012). Investors are also increasingly bypassing funds and instead investing directly in private equity transactions. Ontario Teachers' Pension Plan pioneered this move and several investors are following suit (e.g. Abu Dhabi Investment Authority (ADIA), the largest asset manager in the world). Finally, there has been pressure to lower fees as witnessed by the document proposed by the Institutional Limited Partners Association (ILPA) entitled 'Private Equity Principles'. Recently raised funds seem to have adopted some of these principles and, as a result, lowered their fees. These developments broadly show that investors have more bargaining power over funds than in the past. Lower than expected performance of funds could well be the source of this bargaining power.[30]

APPENDIX

Press Release

Washington, DC, 21 June 2012—The presidential election thrust the private equity industry into the spotlight, but often lost in the discourse are the superior returns private equity delivers to public pensions, university endowments and charitable foundations. The Private Equity Growth Capital Council (PEGCC) released a new analysis today, highlighting returns provided by private equity investments compared to the S&P 500. The research shows private equity outperformed (net of fees) the S&P 500 for 1-, 5-, and 10-year time horizons by 7.1, 5.7, and 7.6 percentage points respectively. Private equity underperformed the S&P 500 during the 3-year time horizon due to the index's historic dip during the financial crisis, which inflated S&P returns during this period.

Appendix Table 14.1 Annualized average return of alternative small cap stock indices

Monthly returns are compounded to calculate annualized returns. Indices are the S&P 600 index, Russell 2000 index, and the size-based indices of Fama-French. Fama-French indices are the size tercile indices containing stocks classified as small, mid, and large respectively; they are downloaded from Ken French's website <http://mba.tuck.dartmouth.edu/pages/faculty/ken.french/data_library.html>, and are value-weighted.

	Small-cap Fama-French	Mid-cap Fama-French	S&P 600	Russell 2000
1990–1999	15.83%	17.21%	14.77%	14.11%
2000–2009	9.86%	7.26%	8.57%	4.37%

[30] This state of affairs might be expected in a world where capital is in abundant supply. The fact that many new investors allocated capital to private equity funds over the last two decades suggests that the provision of capital has been competitive. In this situation, the standard economic prediction is that fund managers should capture most of the value they are perceived to create. Consistent with this view, practitioners routinely state that only top quartile funds are worth investing in. In addition, a similar view has been expressed for hedge funds (e.g. Fung et al. 2008; Lack 2012), which have a similar investor base.

Appendix Table 14.2 Fund weighting choices

This table shows the average PME across buyout funds. The benchmarks and the sample are the same as in Table 14. 6-panel B. The average PME is computed with three different weighting schemes: i) equally weighted; ii) size-weighted; and iii) weighted by the present value of the capital invested, using the Small & Value Fama-French index to discount all the cash flows to January 1993.

Weighting choice	Benchmark is:	Vanguard S&P 500	DFA Micro-cap	Fama-French Small & value	Small & value & levered
Equally weighted		1.20	1.04	0.96	0.90
Size-weighted		1.19	1.06	0.99	0.95
Weighted by the present value of investments		1.24	1.06	0.97	0.91

References

Ang, A., Papanikolaou, D., and Westerfield, M. (2012). Portfolio Choice with Illiquid Assets, Columbia University Unpublished Working Paper, available at <http://ssrn.com/abstract=1697784>.

Asparouhova, E. N., Bessembinder, H., and Kalcheva, I. (2013). Noisy Prices and Inference Regarding Returns, *Journal of Finance* 68(2), 665–714.

Axelson, U., Jenkinson, T., Strömberg, P., and Weisbach, M. S. (2013). Borrow Cheap, Buy High? The Determinants of Leverage and Pricing in Buyouts. *Journal of Finance Journal of Finance* 68(6), 2223–67.

Cao, J. and Lerner, J. (2009). The Performance of Reverse Leveraged Buyouts, *Journal of Financial Economics* 91, 139–57.

Driessen, J., Lin, T. C., and Phalippou, L. (2012). A New Method to Estimate Risk and Return of Non-Traded Assets from Cash Flows: The Case of Private Equity Funds, *Journal of Financial and Quantitative Analysis* 47(3), 511–35.

Dyck, A. and Pomorski, L. (2012). Why Bigger Can Be Better: Alternative Assets and Pension Plan Management, University of Toronto Unpublished Working Paper, available at <http://www.nhh.no/Files/Filer/CPE/symposium/2012/dyck.pdf>.

Fama, E. and French, K. (1993). Common Risk Factors in the Returns on Stocks and Bonds, *Journal of Financial Economics* 33, 3–56.

Fang, L., Ivashina, V., and Lerner, J. (2012). The Disintermediation of Financial Markets: Direct Investing in Private Equity, INSEAD Unpublished Working Paper, available at <http://ssrn.com/abstract=2159229>.

Franzoni, F., Nowak E., and Phalippou, L. (2012) Private Equity Performance and Liquidity Risk, *Journal of Finance* 67(6), 2341–73.

Fung, W., Hsieh, D. A., Ramadorai, T., and Naik, N. Y. (2008) Hedge Funds: Performance, Risk, and Capital Formation, *Journal of Finance* 63, 1777–803.

Harris, R. S., Jenkinson, T., and Kaplan, S. (2013). Private Equity Performance: What Do We Know?, Fama-Miller Working Paper; Chicago Booth Research Paper No. 11-44; Darden Business School Working Paper No. 1932316, available at <http://ssrn.com/abstract=1932316>.

Higson, C. and Stucke, R. (2012). The Performance of Private Equity, London Business School Unpublished Working Paper, available at <http://www.collerinstitute.com/Research/Paper/181>.

Jensen, M. (1986). Agency Costs of Free Cash Flow, Corporate Finance and Takeovers, *American Economic Review* 76, 323–9.

Kaplan, S. and Schoar, A. (2005). Private Equity Performance: Returns, Persistence, and Capital Flows, *Journal of Finance* 60, 1791–823.

Keim, D. B. (1999). An Analysis of Mutual Fund Design: The Case of Investing in Small-cap Stocks, *Journal of Financial Economics* 51, 173–94.

Kleymenova, A., Talmor E., and Vasvari, F. (2012). Liquidity in the Secondaries Private Equity Market, London Business School Unpublished Working Paper, available at <http://www.rsm.nl/fileadmin/home/Department_of_Finance__VG5_/LQ5/Kleymenova.pdf>.

Lack, S. (2012). *The Hedge Fund Mirage: The Illusion of Big Money and Why It's Too Good To Be True* (Hoboken, NJ, John Wiley & Sons, Inc.).

Loughran T. and Ritter, J. (2000). Uniformly Least Powerful Tests of Market Efficiency, *Journal of Financial Economics* 55, 361–89.

Phalippou, L. and Gottschalg, O. (2009). The Performance of Private Equity Funds, *Review of Financial Studies* 22, 1747–76.

Robinson, D. T. and Sensoy, B. A. (2011). Cyclicability, Performance Measurement and Cash Flow Liquidity in Private Equity, Charles A. Dice Center Working Paper No. 2010-021.

Sorensen, M., Wang, N., and Yang, J. (2011). Valuing Private Equity, Columbia University Unpublished Working Paper , available at <http://wwwo.gsb.columbia.edu/faculty/nwang/papers/swy100.pdf>.

Strömberg, P. (2007). The New Demography of Private Equity, Swedish Institute of Financial Research Unpublished Working Paper.

PART IV

THE REGULATORY FRAMEWORK

A.

Structural Treatment of Hedge Funds and Private Equity: Investor Protection and Systemic Risk

CHAPTER 15

HEDGE FUND REGULATION AND GOVERNANCE

DOUGLAS CUMMING, NA DAI, AND SOFIA A. JOHAN

'... the results were suspiciously smooth. Mr. Madoff barely ever suffered a down month, even in choppy markets ...' The Economist, 18 Dec 2008, 'The Madoff Affair: The Con of the Century'.

15.1 Introduction

HEDGE funds have been the subject of media attention in the United States and around the world pursuant to the Bernard Madoff scandal and the more recent allegations against the Galleon Group. Given the pronounced growth of the hedge fund sector in recent years and the comparative dearth of regulations faced by hedge fund managers, this attention is probably appropriate. One concern shared by market participants and many regulators around the world is that the size of the hedge fund industry coupled with potential agency problems, activist investment practices and herding behaviour exacerbates financial instability. By 2005 hedge funds collectively accumulated over a trillion dollars in assets, while at the peak in the summer of 2008 industry estimates suggest the market grew above $2.5 trillion in assets (Ineichen and Silberstein 2008). This amount, while not trivial, is comparatively small compared with the size of worldwide mutual fund capital which is estimated at $24.32 trillion by the Investment Company Institute. There is, however, significant scope for the industry to move markets. For example, in the week of 6 August 2007, hedge funds following long/short equity strategies experienced massive losses. Empirical evidence on this event shows significant and growing systematic risk in the hedge fund industry (see Khandani and Lo 2007; Getmansky, Lo, and Makarov 2004).

Hedge funds are not prohibited from employing a variety of investment instruments in pursuing their investment strategies (i.e., the primary mandate of a hedge fund), many of which would not be permitted by other funds such as mutual funds and private equity funds. This is possible by compromising on the extent to which their products or funds are able to be offered to the public. In the US and the UK, for example, hedge funds can only be distributed by private placements. Hedge funds, for example, may utilize derivative instruments, may short sell and leverage rather highly to achieve their investment goals. Commonly observed hedge fund strategies include investment in distressed companies, commodity trading advisors/managed futures, short biased and small-micro capitalization (hereafter 'micro-cap') focused strategies, among numerous other strategies identified herein.

There are, as in any form of financial intermediation, inevitable agency problems associated with hedge fund management. While these specific agency problems will be described in more detail in Section 15.3 of this chapter, we would like to briefly outline the extent to which potential agency problems may arise. First, in a more direct manner, hedge funds might pursue investment strategies and/or prepare financial reports that benefit the hedge fund manager at the expense of their investors. For example, hedge funds are much more likely to report marginally positive monthly returns than returns that are marginally negative, and this type of returns manipulation significantly aids capital-raising efforts of hedge fund managers (see, e.g., Bollen and Pool 2008, 2009, 2006; Cumming and Dai 2009). Second, in a more oblique manner, hedge funds' investment strategies might be counter to the interests of the other shareholders of portfolio companies in which hedge funds invest (see Kahan and Rock, Chapter 5, this volume, for examples of this category of agency problem). For example, hedge funds that acquire significant voting rights in a company may seek to act in ways that primarily bring about financial benefit to the fund (and therefore its investors), at the expense of the company's other shareholders (see, e.g., Hu and Black 2006). Such active participation in portfolio companies by hedge funds have been labelled in both a flattering manner, as hedge fund activism, and in a more critical manner, as vulture fund activity.

Section 15.3 provides an overview of the potential agency problems associated with managing a hedge fund and associated rationales for hedge fund regulation. While hedge funds are hardly regulated in the US, other jurisdictions outside the US implement different and sometimes more onerous sets of regulatory requirements. Examples of international differences in hedge fund regulation include minimum capitalization requirements, restrictions on the location of key service providers, and different permissible distribution channels via private placements, banks, other regulated or non-regulated financial intermediaries, wrappers, investment managers, and fund distribution companies.

One argument consistently being put forward opposing more onerous regulation of hedge funds is the threat of regulatory arbitrage, or hedge funds moving from one jurisdiction to another less regulated one to avoid onerous regulatory oversight. Hedge funds are free to forum shop by registering in many different countries around the world subject to meeting the requirements of jurisdiction. A central issue considered in this chapter is therefore whether hedge funds that are pursuing riskier strategies are also practicing regulatory arbitrage to facilitate such strategies. If hedge funds pursuing risky investment strategies select jurisdictions with more onerous regulation, then it is possible to infer that hedge fund managers perceive regulation to be informative to the funds' potential investors as fund managers signal their interest in mitigating potential agency conflicts associated with fund management, thus being able to raise more capital. If hedge fund managers pursuing riskier strategies select jurisdictions that have less onerous regulatory oversight, then it may be possible to infer that the managers are practicing regulatory arbitrage, potentially at the expense of investors. If hedge fund strategies are invariant to international differences in regulation, then we may infer that regulatory differences provide little or no information to a fund's investors.

The latter part of this chapter provides an empirical analysis of hedge fund strategies, structure, fund flows, performance, and misreporting behaviour in the context of international differences in hedge fund regulation. The data offer little support for the view that hedge fund managers pursuing riskier strategies or strategies with potentially more pronounced agency problems systematically select jurisdictions with less stringent regulations. In fact, to the extent that there is evidence of forum shopping, it is for the most part suggestive that funds pursuing riskier strategies or strategies with greater potential agency problems select jurisdictions with more stringent regulations (for examples of consistent empirical evidence found in other unrelated contexts, see Romano 1985; Cumming and MacIntosh 2000). We may infer from the evidence that forum shopping by fund managers in relation to fund strategic focus is not consistent with regulatory arbitrage where funds select jurisdictions with limited regulation such that regulators have incentives to curtail regulation. Rather, the data suggest hedge funds select jurisdictions that are in funds' investors' interests in order to facilitate capital-raising by the hedge fund.

This chapter will also show that hedge funds registered in countries which have larger minimum capitalization requirements tend to have higher levels of inflows. This suggests minimum capitalization enhances investor confidence in terms of greater stability with larger funds. This finding holds even after controlling for minimum investment amounts per transaction. Hedge funds registered in countries which restrict the location of key service providers also have lower levels of inflows. This latter result is consistent with the view that locational restrictions are perceived by investors to mitigate human resource quality, and this perceived reduction in human resource quality is more pronounced than any associated perceived improvement in regulatory oversight. Data and empirical tests are also used to analyse hedge fund structure and performance, and finally the chapter will address the issue of hedge fund misreporting. In brief, it is possible to show empirically that hedge funds registered in countries which have larger minimum capitalization requirements tend to have higher levels of inflows, while funds registered in countries which restrict the location of key service providers have lower levels of inflows. Misreporting is also less common among funds in jurisdictions with minimum capital requirements and restrictions on the location of key service providers. Also, country-specific regulations related to distribution channels tend to impact fund flow-performance sensitivity and misreporting. These findings will be discussed in the following sections.

15.2 What Are Hedge Funds?

What are hedge funds? Financial regulators in the US and the United Kingdom have yet to promulgate a legal definition of hedge fund (see Garbaravicius and Diereck 2005). Other jurisdictions have differing views on what hedge funds are, and by taking into account the investment strategies used, they have specified such funds as Sophisticated Alternative Investment Vehicles, Highly Leveraged Institutions, and Leveraged Investment Funds (see Donaldson 2003). In view of the fact that highly competent regulatory bodies have themselves been unable to define the term hedge fund, we will not attempt to do so in this chapter. Therefore, for the purposes of this chapter, when reference is made to the term hedge fund, we believe the description as provided by Hodder and Jackwerth (2007) as *'a compensation scheme for a pool of money to be collectively managed and invested on behalf of the capital providers'* is apt.

It is said that no man is an island, and that holds true for hedge fund managers. Hedge fund investment strategies are facilitated by various external (and increasingly internal) service providers, as depicted in Figure 15.1. The hedge fund managers, rather obviously, have overall authority over the functions of the fund and determine the investment strategies. If they are successful, they may manage a few funds in tandem. They may have assisting them other investment and professional advisors such as lawyers, accountants, consultants, and tax and audit specialists. There are also the administrators that assist the fund managers in providing fund administrative and accounting services, including record keeping, independent valuation of investments, and meeting disclosure requirements. The registrar or transfer agent may assist the fund manager in processing subscriptions and redemptions and in maintaining the register of shareholders. Sometimes, depending on the structure of the fund and the human resources of the manager, these duties may be carried out internally by the fund manager. The actual financing arrangements and execution of investments more often than not are carried out by external prime brokers, which can be either securities firms or banks. Occasionally, the prime brokers themselves decide to set up their own fund, and they therefore also become hedge fund managers. There is, of course, another service provider, the custodian, that has custody over the fund assets. Again, this duty may sometimes be carried out internally by the prime broker.

A hedge fund manager is essentially just another financial intermediary, just as mutual fund managers or private equity managers are. There are, of course, significant differences among these three types of financial intermediaries, and we will very briefly set out the most

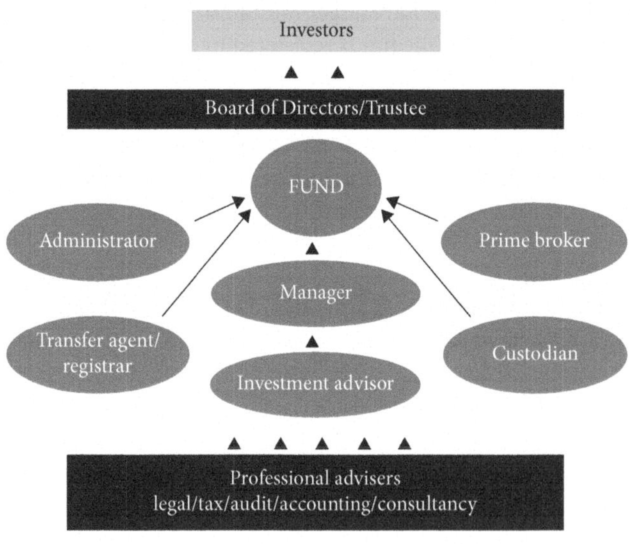

FIGURE 15.1 Typical parties appointed to operate a hedge fund

Note: Administrator: keep records and books and independently verify asset value of the fund. Registrar / Transfer Agent: process subscriptions and redemptions and maintain registrar of shareholders. Custodian: keep assets safe. Prime Broker: provide access to stock and loan financing, as well as a host of value-added services.

Source: PriceWaterhouseCoopers.

obvious differences, including but not limited to their investor base; transparency, liquidity, and pricing; strategies and leverage; regulatory oversight; and fees.

15.2.1 Investor Base

Generally speaking, mutual funds, hedge funds, and private equity funds could be categorized as public investment companies or pooled investment vehicles. What inevitably exempts hedge funds and private equity funds from the legal and regulatory requirements and ensuing oversight of public investment companies or pooled investment vehicles are the characteristics of their typical investors. Unlike mutual funds, hedge funds and private equity funds limit the number of investors as required by the relevant regulatory authorities. For example, in the US, hedge funds utilize the exemptions provided pursuant to Section 3(c)(1) of the Investment Company Act 1940 and the number of investors does not exceed ninety-nine in order to avoid regulatory oversight (see 15 U.S.C. § 80a-3(c)(1)). Hedge fund investors also comprise mainly institutional investors and high net worth or wealthy individuals. Taking the US example again, to take advantage of the exemption under the same act, hedge funds likely would not market their services to the retail public with assets below $5 million (see 15 U.S.C. § 80a-3(c)(7)).

15.2.2 Transparency, Liquidity, Valuation, and Pricing

Mutual funds, due to their investor base, have to meet stringent disclosure requirements, are obliged to implement established valuation principles, and have to price their portfolios on a daily basis. Hedge funds and private equity funds, in contrast, are extremely opaque with regards to the reporting of their operations and the valuation of their portfolio. Such is the case for private equity funds that, as a result of mandatory disclosure of private equity fund performance data, such as IRRs by public institutional investors investing in public equity funds, led to the decision by some funds to exclude public institutional investors. With regard to liquidity, hedge funds are more liquid than private equity funds, because private equity funds require investors to commit their capital for up to ten years, while hedge funds have at most lock-up periods of up to twenty-five months. Mutual funds are also the most liquid of the three funds.

15.2.3 Strategies and Leverage

Of the three types of funds, the hedge fund is the most autonomous in its ability to implement its rather innovative investment strategies. Mutual funds are usually constrained, to a certain extent, legally and by regulation in their asset choices and have to disclose to their investors the anticipated allocations in such asset classes. Private equity funds are equally constrained by contract, as they are required at the outset to specify the maximum amount of capital to be invested in any one company as well as the industry and stages of development of investee companies. Hedge funds, in contrast, are able to use a variety of investment strategies that, ironically, have far less to do with hedging, and these strategies include the use of facilities not normally accessible to mutual funds and private equity funds—short-selling and derivatives. While it is not possible to perfectly classify different hedge fund strategies, it is possible to carry out a rather rough grouping of strategies, and for the purposes of this chapter we will refer to the following strategies: convertible arbitrage, fixed income arbitrage, merger/risk arbitrage, capital structure arbitrage, statistical arbitrage, long/short equity, multi-strategy, CTA/Managed futures, emerging markets, technology sector, macro, event driven, distressed securities, Regulation D and high-yield low-grade fixed income securities, short bias, small-micro-cap, special situations, energy sector, and country specific.

Another rather significant difference is that both mutual funds and private equity funds are constrained in their ability to leverage. These constraints are usually legal and regulatory in form for mutual funds, and contractual for private equity funds. In contrast, hedge funds are 'leveraging' creatures in that they 'sell securities short and buy securities on leverage' (see House Committee on Banking and Financial Services 1999). They are not, however, leveraged in the more traditional sense of taking on more debt capital. They leverage themselves by the innovative use of derivatives instruments, the use of margin financing, and short selling.

15.2.4 Regulatory Oversight

Due to their accessibility to the retail public and their investment strategies, mutual funds are subject to rather strict legal and regulatory oversight. In the US, for example, the Securities and Exchange Commission (SEC) requires mutual fund managers to be registered. In addition, they are also subject to various regulations under the Investment Advisers Act of 1940, the Securities Act of 1933, the Investment Company Act of 1940, and the Securities Exchange Act of 1934. Hedge funds and private equity funds are not as strictly regulated, as they are enabled by their structure and investment strategies to meet the relevant requirements to be exempt from the laws and regulations that could limit their operational freedom. They essentially avoid regulation by following the letter of the law.

15.2.5 Fees and Proprietary Investment

Mutual funds are usually constrained in their ability to arbitrarily impose fees or sales charges, and more often than not they are required to disclose their fees to their potential investors. In contrast, hedge fund and private equity fund managers impose a management fee based on the size of fund managed (usually 2.5% for private equity funds and 1.5% for hedge funds), and a performance fee that is usually 20% of the profits. Private equity fund managers and hedge fund managers usually are required to put their money where their mouths are, or pay-to-play. This is not the case for mutual fund managers. Private equity fund managers, however, only really invest a minimal amount in the fund partnership to meet the requirements of general partnership, and for the most part they are restricted from co-investment in investee companies. Hedge fund managers, in contrast, are not restricted in the amount of proprietary capital that they may invest in the hedge funds they manage.

While there are significant differences among the three financial intermediaries, what is strikingly similar among them is that all three types of fund managers have a fiduciary duty to act in the best interest of the fund and fund investors. The duties of good faith and fair dealing, loyalty, and care have to be upheld by all hedge fund managers as well as their counterparts, and they are prohibited from engaging in fraudulent activities, as are other financial intermediaries. However, as with any form of financial intermediation, there will inevitably be conflicts of interest or agency problems. Such agency problems are exacerbated by the characteristics of hedge fund which we listed earlier. In the next section we will list the potential agency problems encountered in hedge fund management, how they are connected to the characteristics of hedge funds, and how regulatory measures have sought to mitigate such problems.

15.3 Agency Problems in Hedge Fund Management

The debate with regard to the regulation of hedge funds probably began in earnest with the Long Term Capital Management debacle in 1998, and will probably continue as capital increasingly floods into the industry. The systemic risks such funds pose to the stability of the financial industry as a whole is becoming more apparent. While demonized in the popular media, it would be incorrect to say that hedge funds are wholly unregulated, rogue entities. Across the globe, the activities of hedge funds are constrained to a certain extent by various laws and regulations which aim to protect investors and the stability of the financial market or economy within a given jurisdiction. However, even in the US and the UK, which are deemed to be the strictest regulatory regimes, such laws and regulations have been deemed to be insufficient in view of the potential systemic damage, and there has been a call by policymakers for a review of this 'regulation-lite' environment.

The agency problems that may arise within a hedge fund manager/client relationship comprise conflicts of interest between any of the parties involved in the management of the hedge fund. As we mentioned earlier in Section 15.2, depending on the structure, size, and jurisdictional base of the hedge fund, the duties carried out by the manager, its advisors, administrator, registrar or transfer agent, prime broker, and custodian may either be partly or wholly internally carried out or partly or wholly outsourced. There will, therefore, be a rather endless list of potential conflicts of interest that may arise between the parties depending on the nature and extent of their relationship. We will, for the purposes of this chapter, limit our discussion of conflicts to those most common and readily recognizable among the parties and regulatory bodies, and to how they relate to the characteristics unique to hedge funds. We will also provide a brief description of the nature of the conflict, be it operational in nature, related to the marketing process, or a legal conflict. These types of conflicts may also overlap. For example, the business conflict of the manager using his proprietary assets to allocate securities to his own account before implementing his investment strategy may be a business conflict as well as a legal conflict of insider trading and breach of fiduciary duty.

15.3.1 Potential Conflicts Arising from Investor Base

Hedge fund investors comprise institutional investors, endowments, and high net worth individuals. While the argument against the regulation of hedge funds may centre around the fact that its investors are sophisticated investors, it can also be argued that of the different types of investors, the least sophisticated of the above-mentioned purportedly sophisticated group may be the high net worth individual. The threshold to be deemed as a high net worth individual, or a sophisticated investor, may range from the holding of assets of $1 to $5 million and above. If we take the example of an average person with a home in an established US city, other recreational property, investments, and retirement savings, it is possible that the threshold of $1 million could easily be breached. The average age of a US-based investor with more than $5 million is 67, and with $1 million is 62. In 2009 in the US alone, the number of families with a net worth of more than $1 million (excluding primary residence) numbered 7.8 million, and there were more than 790,000 households with a net worth of more than $5 million (see Leondis 2010). Would these investors be as sophisticated an investor as an endowment fund? Unfortunately, we do not think this would be likely. Neither would a hedge fund manager. The hedge fund manager is aware that the level of due diligence carried out prior to investment by a high net worth investor will differ from that of an endowment. The high net worth individual may neither have the technical capabilities, nor want to incur the added expense of hiring experts, to carry out the due diligence. The institutional investor, however, has a fiduciary duty to its own clients and will therefore carry out a thorough search for appropriate fund managers and carry out a due diligence exercise. The hedge fund manager may therefore be incentivized to provide more information during the marketing exercise to different types of investors. The hedge fund manager also aims not only to attract new investors to a fund, but also to retain existing investors as potential investors in other hedge funds he will inevitably establish. The potential for conflicts to arise as a result of his preference to retain specific investors over others may result in preferential disclosure in different marketing efforts, preferential investment, and preferential redemption terms, among others. Such agency problems may give rise to a legal conflict with regard to allocation issues, breach of fiduciary duty, and disclosure issues (see Bollen and Pool 2006). A potential business conflict is the high net worth individual being given less favourable investment terms in the fund than other more sophisticated investors.

15.3.2 Potential Conflicts Arising from Fees and Proprietary Investment by Hedge Fund Managers

The fee structure for hedge fund managers may also bring about potential agency problems as the hedge fund manager may be incentivized to take unnecessary risks. The manager essentially has a 20% share of unlimited upside potential, but will not have shared any losses. Unlike the investor, the manager in essence has an option-like compensation structure, unless he invests his own proprietary capital. That said, as he has total control over the investment strategies, he may be able to protect his share of the fund from the additional risks that he is placing the rest of the fund. This total control over the investment of the fund also follows through to the fees to be paid to support service providers.

We mentioned earlier that some successful hedge fund managers manage a few funds, sometimes concurrently. There are also instances where prime broker banks that already manage a few mutual funds establish their own hedge funds. What is increasingly obvious is that other financial intermediaries, such as mutual fund managers and private equity fund managers, are joining the fray, so to speak, and establishing hedge funds alongside other types of funds. This is also the case for the support service providers, such as prime brokers, that may not have their own hedge funds to manage but provide services to both hedge funds and mutual funds. In these situations, where one institution wears two hats or where one party has to act in the interests of various side-by-side clients, there is the potential for agency problems to arise. This is especially the case where levels of fees acquired from different clients, or different types of clients, differ in that some funds or managers are willing to pay higher transaction fees for 'special' services. Some managers and prime brokers therefore may provide additional information regarding an investment, carry out preferential allocations, confer liquidity preferences, or provide other preferential treatments in favour of a specific hedge fund over others, either due to higher fees paid or the level of proprietary investment made in that specific fund. Specific hedge funds may also be favoured over other mutual funds, again due to the higher fees or the institution's dependency on the execution business of the hedge fund. It has been indicated that more prime brokers are becoming dependent on the income stream garnered form hedge funds, to the point of such income comprising an eighth of total revenue in one case (Bollen and Pool 2006). Such agency problems may give rise to a legal conflict with regard to allocation issues, breach of fiduciary duty, disclosure issues, and insider trading. A potential business conflict is the competition of allocations and investment opportunities between an institution (or manager), on a proprietary basis, and the hedge fund.

15.3.3 Potential Conflicts Arising from Lack of Regulatory Oversight

We mentioned earlier that in many jurisdictions, hedge funds are not as strictly regulated as, say, mutual funds as they are enabled by their structure and investment strategies to meet the relevant requirements to be exempt from the laws and regulations that could limit their operational freedom. This ability to operate freely may give rise to a gamut of potential agency problems. Lord Acton once said that 'Power tends to corrupt, and absolute power corrupts absolutely' (see Hirsch, Kett, and Trefil 2002).

Agency problems in hedge fund management often take a more basic form of simple fraud. In Bollen and Pool (2009), a recent study of hedge fund litigation cases, the authors found that the most common type of offence involved misappropriation whereby a fund manager diverts investor capital for personal expenses.

While it is true that regulatory oversight may not totally remove agency problems, proper regulation may mitigate the potential for them to arise as proper rules of behaviour by all parties involved and procedures to be adhered to are to be abided by at the threat of civil or criminal penalties. What is interesting to note is that just as hedge funds have utilized the letter of the law to be exempted from regulatory oversight, they are also using the law to protect themselves in the event they themselves or any of their support service providers become 'corrupted absolutely'.

In some private placement memoranda, the instrument with which they market their fund to sophisticated investors, they include a section specifically addressing a range of potential conflicts of interest or activities that could be construed as such, including but not limited to proprietary trading, managing side-by-side funds, and managing competing funds. With this disclosure, investors are then given notice and will have to agree that the disclosed potential activities will not be actionable, thereby protecting the fund and the manager from potential lawsuits or disciplinary measures.

The lack of regulatory oversight may provide the hedge fund manager and other support service providers with the necessary latitude to undertake behaviour that may be improper, if not illegal, but for the lack of regulation. On the other hand, this perception of the hedge fund industry wholly unregulated, rogue financial intermediaries may be detrimental to the participants, and therefore the lack of formal regulation may be made up for by self-regulating actions.

15.3.4 Potential Conflicts Arising from Lack of Transparency, Liquidity, Independent Valuation, and Pricing

Hedge funds are known for their opaqueness, illiquidity, highly subjective valuation methods, and inability (or rather unwillingness) to price themselves. If the investors in hedge funds find it difficult to obtain a full picture of the investment, they will find it almost impossible to determine the full extent of the related party transactions among the external support service providers and the fund itself. It is not difficult to see how agency problems may arise is this case. Also, note that even if most of the support services are provided internally, they will be provided by different departments or agents and therefore there is still the potential for conflicts of interest to arise. Take, for example, the simple valuation of investments carried out by the hedge fund. This is not usually carried out independently by an external agent, and this subjective valuation process gives rise to the potential for managers to over-value certain investments, under-value losses, and generally sugar-coat fund performance (see Bollen and Pool 2009).

Even where such valuation is carried out independently, the valuer is essentially carrying out the instructions of its client —the hedge fund manager—and valuations and disclosures are made on the basis of information which is in turn disclosed to him or justified by the hedge fund manager.

Conflict may also arise when all support services are provided internally, as different business units within an institution do not act in alignment and against the interest of the fund the institution is managing. For example, some banks have units which carry out M&A advising, underwriting activities, and advising distressed companies. These activities may have an effect on the companies in which a hedge fund unit of the bank is investing.

Conversely, where all business units do act in concert, conflict may also arise. For example, where a custodian acts in concert with the manager and against the interest of the fund, there is a potential for the manager to misuse the fund capital at the expense of fund investors. Such agency problems may give rise to a legal conflict with regard to disclosure issues, breach of fiduciary duty, insider trading or improper related party transactions, and allocation issues. A potential business conflict is the provision of such fee-generating services such as M&A advising, underwriting activities, and advising distressed companies by a unit of the bank at the expense of the investments made in such companies by the hedge fund unit of the same bank.

15.3.5 Potential Conflicts Arising from Strategies and Leverage

Hedge funds, in contrast to mutual funds or private equity funds, are able to use a variety of investment strategies that ironically have far less to do with hedging, and these strategies include the use of facilities not normally accessible to mutual funds and private equity funds, which are short-selling and derivatives. We will elaborate on the strategies utilized by hedge funds in Section 15.5. Contrary to popular belief, hedge funds no longer primarily hedge nor do they utilize uniform investment strategies or investment instruments. Roel Campos, a Commissioner of the US SEC, once remarked that, 'The complexity of the strategies employed by hedge funds as they aim for absolute returns adds to the barrier of understanding regarding the specific risk posed by the investments'. Fund managers may even pursue offsetting strategies that are disguised by marketing materials. For example, a fund manager might invest long in one index and short the same index within the same fund or with two different funds. Such a fund manager would collect management fees on both funds and performance fees on one of the two funds, at the expense of the investors. Further, hedge fund managers might 'style drift' and invest in a strategy that is different from their strategy that was stated to their investors (see Bollen and Pool 2009).

Different hedge fund strategies may pose conflicts of interest with the other shareholders or debt holders in the companies in which the fund invests (see Kahan and Rock, Chapter 5, this volume). For example, for micro-cap investments, while the hedge fund investors are very large, the investee companies themselves are very small and illiquid, and it is relatively easy to manipulate trading activity and returns among such investments. As another example, hedge funds can innovatively take advantage of derivatives instruments, margin financing, and short selling to make both debt and equity investments in financially distressed companies, and thereby profit by investing in ways that are counter to the interests of the company's other shareholders and/or debt holders. Further, hedge funds may engage in 'empty voting' when they acquire voting rights that are divergent from their ownership interests, and thereby vote in a way that is counter to the interests of the other shareholders and solely at a financial gain to the fund (see Hu and Black 2006). More generally, it is possible that hedge fund interests are much more short-term than that of the other shareholders, thereby leading to investment strategies and voting decisions by the hedge fund that are to the detriment of their investee companies and such companies' other shareholders (see Kahan and Rock, Chapter 5, this volume). Such practices, however, have not been prevalent or severe enough for legal analysts to conclude that a case for legal intervention has been made.

Hedge fund investment horizons also tend to be more short-term than banks. For instance, hedge funds may pursue strategies in which they trigger bankruptcy in a financially distressed company and then buy the debt of the company in the secondary loan market. Banks, for instance, face regulations that impose a 'Chinese Wall' to separate commercial and investment banking activities within the institution, and these restrictions were strengthened by the Sarbanes-Oxley Act of 2002 (Pub. L. No. 107-204, 116 Stat. 745). Hedge funds face a comparative dearth of oversight and are nevertheless able to lend and hold equity in the same company.

Below, in Section 15.5, we consider alternative fund strategies in more detail. Specifically, we address the question of whether differences in hedge fund strategies encourage managers to carry out regulatory arbitrage, or are associated with hedge fund forum shopping. That is, because hedge funds may register in different jurisdictions, it is possible that funds pursuing strategies with more pronounced agency costs select jurisdictions with comparatively less regulatory oversight. Before we turn to that question, we first explain international differences in hedge fund regulation in Section 15.4.

15.4 International Differences in Hedge Fund Regulation

Given the significant scope for potential agency problems and systemic risk, regulators in many countries around the world are calling for additional hedge fund regulation. For example, it is noteworthy that on 23 January 2008, fourteen of the largest hedge funds in the UK agreed to greater voluntary disclosure standards. The disclosure standards are designed to give rise to more information about investment strategies, risks, and asset valuation. It has been conjectured by media commentators that the hedge fund industry agreed to the voluntary standards in order to mitigate the possibility of more onerous regulatory standards being imposed in the future (see Mackintosh 2008). The possibility of more onerous regulation may still be rather far off on the horizon, as even in the US hedge funds still enjoy comparatively minimal regulation. In 2006, the US SEC Chairman, Christopher Cox, expressly indicated that hedge funds should not remain unregulated (see also Goldschmid 2004). Most hedge funds, however, remain largely unregulated irrespective of SEC initiatives (See Brown et al. 2008).

In view of the growing call towards increasing hedge fund regulation in certain countries, it is worthwhile to examine the international experience with hedge fund regulation. It was argued in *Phillip Goldstein et al. v. SEC* and elsewhere that hedge funds should not face greater regulation in the US since many fund managers would simply relocate abroad or 'forum shop to the bottom'.

International differences in hedge fund regulation are outlined in Table 15.1. For the purposes of this section, we will concentrate on differences in hedge fund regulation that fall within three primary categories: (1) minimum capital to operate as a hedge fund; (2) permissible marketing channels; and (3) restrictions on the location of key service providers. Specific details on these differences across countries are reviewed in detail in PWC (2006), and briefly summarized below.

Some jurisdictions require hedge funds to maintain minimum capitalization to remain in operation. One rationale is that greater minimum capitalization facilitates financial stability by mitigating the risk of fund failure. An additional rationale for minimum capitalization requirements is that lower quality and less reputable fund managers will have difficulty establishing funds in jurisdictions with higher minimum capitalization requirements. In view of the sophisticated investor base, it is perceived that the funds that are able to attract enough investors and pass their due diligence exercises to raise the minimum amount of capital required should be allowed to operate. Also, as the fees charged by the hedge fund managers are dependent on the capital raised, there needs to be sufficient capital to meet overhead costs of managing a fund and meeting relevant administrative, disclosure, and regulatory requirements.

Minimum capitalization also indirectly ensures that hedge funds limit their investors to high net worth individuals and institutional investors. They are restricted in the number of investors they may have, therefore each investor has to invest a rather substantial sum. The larger the amount an investor invests, the better his bargaining power with regards to seeking more transparency from the hedge fund, obtaining better liquidity terms, and ensuring that proper valuation and pricing methods are used. Minimum capitalization amounts indicated in Table 15.1 are, however, comparatively small relative to potential losses.

For some countries, minimum capitalization depends on fund operating costs and other things specific to the fund, and as such the values indicated in Table 15.1 are proxies. For details, see PWC (2006). Austria has the greatest minimum capitalization requirement at $6.75 million among the 23 countries enumerated in Table 15.1. Many jurisdictions such as Bermuda, Canada, New Zealand, and the US currently have no minimum capitalization requirements.

Different countries also have different permissible distribution channels. In the hedge fund industry, capital is most often sought through private placements. Jurisdictions limit the hedge funds' distribution channels to mainly private placements, as it precludes them from direct access to retail investors, and thereby limit potential conflicts of interests that might arise with unsophisticated retail based investors (see, e.g., Barclay, Holderness, and Sheehan 2007).

In view of their aim to limit their investor base to sophisticated institutional and high net worth individuals, this limitation on their distribution channels cannot, however, be said to be overly detrimental. In fact, this limitation may enable hedge funds to be less transparent with their initial disclosures, such as their fee structure and liquidity terms. Their private placement memoranda (and ensuing negotiations) may be tailored to meet the requirements of different types of investors, therefore the investors may not be playing on a level playing field. Private placements are permitted in most jurisdictions, except Austria, Luxembourg, and Switzerland.

In many countries outside the US, there are additional distribution channels through which funds may gain greater access to a wider range of investors. For example, twelve of the twenty-three countries in the sample permit distributions via wrappers. Wrapper products are typically insurance policies or structured products, purportedly used by investors for tax deferral (see Fink 2005). For example, as insurance policies, the insurance company will be treated as owning the assets being managed by the hedge fund in order to meet its obligations under the policy, and the investor will obtain the tax benefits from owning an insurance contract. Some jurisdictions, such as the Isle of Man and South Africa, permit wrappers distributions via insurance companies only (see PWC 2006).

Legal practitioners have noted potential conflicts of interest with respect to disclosures in the wrapper (see Gerstein 2006), and generally wrappers are used to overcome regulatory barriers in distributions to high net worth individuals (see Fink 2005). While it is possible that unsophisticated retail investors may take advantage of this potential access to hedge funds via wrapper products, these products are most probably characterized as higher

Table 15.1 Regulation of and channels for distribution of hedge funds by country

This table summarizes by country the regulation of hedge funds across twenty-nine countries including the minimum capital requirements, permissible marketing channels, and whether there exists restrictions on the location of key service providers (Figure 15.1). The minimum capital requirements to operate as a hedge fund manager vary in some countries depending on fund characteristics and, as such, are proxied, as summarized in this table.

Country	# Funds in Dataset 1994–2005	# Funds in Dataset 2003–05	Proxy for Minimum Capital Requirement to Operate as Hedge Fund Manager (2005 US $)	Main Marketing Channels: Banks	Fund Distribution Companies	Wrappers	Private Placements	Investment Managers	Other Regulated Financial Services Institutions	Non-Regulated Financial Intermediaries	Total Number of Marketing Channels	Restrictions on Location of Key Service Providers?	Legal Origin: English	French	German	Scandinavian	GDP per Capita (2005 US $)
Australia	1	1	0	1	1	1	1	1	1	0	6	0	1	0	0	0	$30,700
Austria	1	1	$6,750,000	1	1	1	0	0	0	0	3	0	0	0	1	0	$31,300
BWI, Anguilla	11	11	$500,000	1	0	0	1	1	0	0	3	1	1	0	0	0	$24,500
Bahamas	113	44	$25,000	0	0	0	1	1	0	0	2	1	1	0	0	0	$17,700
Bermuda	281	179		1	0	0	1	1	0	0	3	1	1	0	0	0	$36,000
Brazil	4	4	$362,000	1	1	0	1	1	1	0	5	1	0	1	0	0	$8,100
British Virgin Islands	497	260	$500,000	1	0	0	1	1	0	0	3	1	1	0	0	0	$24,500
Canada	20	15		1	1	1	1	1	1	0	6	0	1	0	0	0	$31,500
Cayman Islands	889	609	$500,000	1	0	0	1	0	0	0	2	1	1	0	0	0	$32,300
Channel Islands	78	76	$44,077	1	1	1	1	1	1	1	7	0	1	0	0	0	$35,264

France	14	14	$168,750	0	1	[illegible]	1	1	0	0	4	0	0	1	0	0	$28,700
Germany	2	2	$373,617	1	0	0	0	0	1	1	3	[illegible]	0	0	1	0	$30,635
Gibraltar	1	1	$155,674	1	0	0	0	1	1	0	3	1	0	0	1	0	$38,200
Guernsey	17	0	$45,517	1	1	1	1	1	1	1	7	0	1	0	0	0	$44,600
Hong Kong	1	0	$2,275,000	1	1	0	1	1	1	0	5	0	1	0	0	0	$34,200
Ireland	77	56	$67,500	1	0	0	1	0	1	0	3	1	1	0	0	0	$31,900
Isle of Man	21	18	$142,500	0	1	1	1	1	0	0	4	1	1	0	0	0	$35,000
Italy	5	5	$1,245,390	0	0	0	1	0	0	0	1	1	0	1	0	0	$28,108
Jersey	3	0	$45,517	1	1	1	1	1	1	1	7	0	0	1	0	0	$57,000
Luxembourg	78	57	$168,750	1	0	0	0	0	1	0	2	0	0	1	0	0	$58,900
Malta	2	2	$155,674	1	1	0	1	0	1	0	4	1	0	1	0	0	$14,686
Mauritius	2	2		0	0	0	1	0	0	0	1	1	1	0	0	0	$12,800
Netherlands	4	1	$303,750	0	0	1	0	1	1	0	3	1	0	1	0	0	$29,500
Netherlands Antilles	34	16		0	0	0	1	0	0	0	1	1	0	1	0	0	$11,400
New Zealand	1	0		1	1	1	1	1	1	0	6	0	1	0	0	0	$23,200
Sweden	2	2	$155,674	1	1	0	0	1	1	0	4	1	0	0	0	1	$28,400
Switzerland	13	11	$4,300,000	1	1	1	0	1	1	0	5	1	0	0	1	0	$33,800
US	1,602	827		0	0	0	1	0	0	0	1	0	1	0	0	0	$40,100
UK	6	1	$67,500	1	0	1	1	1	0	0	4	0	1	0	0	0	$29,600

risk products within the institutions that create them. As these institutions themselves are highly regulated and will have more stringent risk disclosure requirements, it is unlikely that the products would be marketed to, and included in, an unsophisticated retail investor's portfolio.

Distributions via banks are permitted in every country enumerated in Table 15.1 except the Bahamas, France, Isle of Man, Mauritius, Netherlands, Netherlands Antilles, and the US. Many (albeit not all) of these jurisdictions that permit distributions via banks also permit distributions via other regulated financial services institutions. Sixteen of the twenty-three jurisdictions permit distributions via investment managers and twelve of the jurisdictions permit distributions via fund distribution companies. These additional channels of distribution may be deemed by regulators to be appropriate in view of the strict regulatory oversight over these institutions themselves. Also, it is in the interests of the hedge funds themselves to avoid the inclusion of potentially unsophisticated investors to ensure the continuity of their ability to operate rather free of regulation. Therefore, the hedge fund managers will themselves ensure that investment managers market the product appropriately.

The final type of regulation we address in this section is the restriction on the use of key service providers based outside the jurisdiction. Of the jurisdictions, twelve impose restrictions on the location of key service providers. For example, the Isle of Man requires local residency for day-to-day operators for Professional Investor Funds and Experienced Investor Funds. For Germany, the investment manager and custodian bank are required to be based in, and regulated by, Germany. Additional details on the nature of the restrictions of location are provided by PWC (2006).

It is most probably the view of the regulatory authorities that the existing regulatory oversight of the key service providers providing support services to the hedge fund will suffice. Even if these services are carried out internally within an institution, the provision of such services by the specific department will be regulated by the relevant regulatory body or authority. Unlike the two types of restrictions mentioned earlier, which are related somewhat to the mitigation of exposure of the hedge fund to unsophisticated retail investors, this restriction is more in line with ensuring that the hedge fund utilizes only recognized (and thus potentially regulated) service providers. For example, the higher fees the hedge funds pay may not be that much of an incentive for service providers to act in concert with hedge fund managers contrary to the interest of hedge fund investors if there is a threat of disciplinary action or loss of reputation. The reputational concerns among service providers may instigate them to ensure that the hedge funds meet certain transparency, disclosure, liquidity, and valuation method benchmarks. Also, as hedge funds seek to build up their own reputations for professionalism to seek further capital, they will align themselves to the more reputable and professional service providers.

Suffice it to say that the international differences in hedge fund regulation broadly depicted in Table 15.1 do not capture all of the nuances of the differences across countries. They do, however, enable broad levels of comparison that can be used in our empirical analyses of forum shopping, which is carried out in the next subsection.

Based on the data used in the empirical analyses in this chapter, the prevalence of funds registered in each jurisdiction is summarized in Table 15.1. The data sources are described in Subsection 15.5.2 provided immediately below.

15.5 Hedge Fund Forum Shopping

This section considers the issue of whether hedge funds pursuing riskier strategies select jurisdictions that have less onerous regulation. In Cumming and Johan (2008), the authors looked at the average monthly return and standard deviation of returns to determine the riskiness of each strategy. In Subsection 15.5.1 we describe hedge fund strategies and relate different strategies to the extent to which risk and agency problems are more pronounced. In turn, we also conjecture hypotheses regarding fund strategies and forum shopping for different regulation. In Subsection 15.5.2 we describe the dataset used to test the hypotheses. Multivariate empirical tests are also provided in Subsection 15.5.2, as well as a discussion of the limitations and extensions with the tests. Thereafter we look at hedge fund structure and performance in Section 15.6.

15.5.1 Hedge Fund Strategies and Forum Shopping

Hedge fund strategies are classified into different investment strategies. Funds indicate to hedge fund data vendors, such as the Center for International Securities and Derivatives Markets (CISDM), HedgeFund.Net, and TASS, their primary strategies or investment focus. The range of strategies recorded differs slightly across different data vendors. The strategies indicated in the HedgeFund.Net and CISDM datasets are indicated in Cumming and Johan (2008). The range of strategies recorded in the HedgeFund.Net dataset is slightly broader than that found in CISDM.

Cumming and Johan (2008) also present the average monthly return and standard deviation of monthly returns over the period 2003 to 2005. These performance statistics provide a rough guide to risk and returns associated with different fund strategies (see also Malkiel and Saha 2005, for similar information over the period 1995 to 2003).

While it is not possible to perfectly classify different hedge fund strategies into different degrees of risk, it is possible to carry out a rather rough grouping of strategies into different risk profiles and potential agency problems with an analysis of average monthly returns and average standard deviation of returns. For example, strategies that involve risk-free arbitrage would of course be of minimal concern for either risk and/or agency problems. The arbitrage strategies indicated in Cumming and Johan (2008) include convertible arbitrage, fixed income arbitrage, merger/risk arbitrage, capital structure arbitrage, statistical arbitrage, and other arbitrage. Generally, the standard deviation of returns is lower for these arbitrage strategies relative to other non-arbitrage strategies. We may therefore infer that potential agency problems are less pronounced for these arbitrage strategies. For example, fixed-income arbitrage strategies have been described as analogous to steam rollers that pick up loose change on the street.

For reasons identified above, strategies for which agency problems may be more pronounced might include long/short equity, multi-strategy, CTA/Managed futures, emerging markets, technology sector, macro, event driven (in some classifications, event driven strategies encompass distressed securities, Regulation D, and high yield low grade fixed income securities), short bias, small-/micro-cap, special situations, energy sector and country specific. For example, long/short strategies have been associated with potential agency problems where the fund manager acts against the interests of its investor, and such strategies have been associated with massive volatility swings. Funds pursuing small-/micro-cap strategies and distressed investments also have significant scope for exacerbated agency problems.

While Cumming and Johan (2008) did not set out to precisely identify the severity and scope of agency problems within each fund or class of funds, they were nevertheless able to use the above-mentioned rough grouping to assess whether fund managers pursuing different strategies (be they less or more risky) tend to register their funds in different countries with different sets of regulations as identified in Table 15.1 and discussed in Section 15.4 above. As such, they pose three alternative hypotheses about forum shopping:

Hypothesis 1: Race to the Bottom: *Hedge fund managers pursuing riskier strategies and strategies for which potential agency problems are more pronounced select jurisdictions that have less onerous regulatory oversight.*

Hypothesis 2: Neutrality: *The relation between hedge fund strategies and hedge fund regulation is random.*

Hypothesis 3: Alignment of Interests: *Hedge funds pursuing risky investment strategies select jurisdictions with more onerous regulation.*

According to the authors, to the extent that we find evidence in support of Hypothesis 1, we may be concerned that international differences in hedge fund regulation facilitate a race to the bottom, where fund managers' interests are served at the expense of their investors. Alternatively, if the data are consistent with Hypothesis 2, such that hedge fund strategies are invariant to international differences in regulation, then we may infer that regulatory differences provide little or no information to a fund managers' intentions with regards to potential agency problems. Finally, if we find evidence in support of Hypothesis 3, then we may infer that hedge fund managers perceive regulation to be informative to the funds' investors, because fund managers signal their interest in mitigating potential agency conflicts associated with fund management by registering in a jurisdiction with greater regulatory oversight and thereby facilitating fundraising efforts.

15.5.2 Data and Empirical Findings

The data used in Cumming and Johan (2008) comprise 1,845 funds. Data were used from two sources: (1) CISDM; and (2) HedgeFund.Net (HFN) DataExport collected by Channel Capital Group Inc. Similar data have been used in prior work (see Cumming 2009, 2010).

The number of fund strategies in each country of fund registration is found in Cumming and Johan (2008). There the authors show some notable patterns, for example, a greater proportion of funds pursuing emerging market strategies are registered in offshore centres such as the Bahamas, Channel Islands, and Cayman Islands. While some patterns may appear, the authors nevertheless considered multivariate tests to ascertain patterns in fund registration relative to fund strategies. The results of the exercise are provided immediately below.

Table 15.2 provides eight different regression models to assess the extent of jurisdiction shopping for minimum capitalization (Model 1), restrictions on location (Model 2), and different distribution channels (Models 3 to 8). In the regressions they include as control variables fund size and age, as well as dummy variables for primary location of assets.

The data indicate very weak evidence of any jurisdiction shopping for fund strategies in relation to minimum capitalization, and Fixed Income Arbitrage funds are more likely to select jurisdictions with larger capital requirements. This is not surprising, as fixed income arbitrage strategies involve small gains on extremely large transactions. Market Timer funds tend to be registered in jurisdictions with lower minimum capitalization requirements. Some commentators have noted that market timing strategies may involve taking advantage of differences in market prices for funds that own assets in different parts of the world and differences in information after markets close at different points in time around the world, and possibly trading strategies that are associated with manipulating closing prices. While the evidence shows Market Timer funds tend to select jurisdictions with lower capital requirements, the authors do note that their data comprise five funds with a primary market strategy of market timing, and of these, four are registered in the US (where there are no minimum capitalization requirements for hedge funds) and one in Bermuda. Additionally, when they employed alternative estimation methods, they did not find evidence of a significant relation between market timing and minimum capitalization. It would thus be difficult to conclude from the evidence on a negative relation between market timing strategies and minimum capitalization that there is a 'race to the bottom' along the lines of Hypothesis 1 outlined above.

Table 15.2 show some evidence that fund strategies are related to choice of jurisdiction in terms of restrictions on the location of key service providers. In particular, the data indicate at the 5% level of statistical significance that Emerging Markets funds are 23.2% more likely to register in countries with restrictions on the location of key service providers. If we may infer that emerging market strategies potentially involve more pronounced agency problems than other strategies, then the fact that these funds select jurisdictions that restrict location is consistent with Hypothesis 3 described above in Subsection 15.5.1.

Consistent with the evidence on emerging markets and restrictions on location in support of Hypothesis 3, Table 15.2 also shows at the 10% level of statistical significance that funds pursuing CTA/Managed Futures strategies are 23.9% more likely to register in countries with restrictions on the location of key service providers. It is suggested that CTA/Managed Futures fund strategies involve potentially greater agency problems, and certainly this strategy is riskier than other strategies in terms of variance in returns (Cumming and Johan 2008). As such, we would again infer that the data are consistent with Hypothesis 3 insofar as funds pursuing riskier strategies register in countries with more onerous regulations.

Table 15.2 shows that Technology Sector funds pursuing technology sector strategies are 8.2% less likely to register in jurisdictions that restrict the location of key service providers, and this evidence is significant at the 10% level. There are potentially a variety of reasons why Technology Sector funds seek fewer location restrictions. One explanation is that Technology Sector funds exhibit greater agency problems since information asymmetries are more pronounced with high-tech investments, and as such there is greater scope for fund managers to pursue excessive risk-taking strategies.

Another explanation is that technology sector investments require greater geographical proximity to mitigate information asymmetries faced by the investee companies and the hedge fund manager and key service providers, and any restrictions on location may in turn

Table 15.2 Regression Analyses of Hedge Fund Form Shopping

Table 4 Panel A presents logit regression analyses of the determinants of forum shopping for different rules for minimum capitalization, restrictions on location, and distribution channels in the HFN and CISDM datasets. Fund strategy variables are dummy variables equal to one where the fund's primary strategy is indicated, as per the fund strategies as defined in Table 2. All regression models in Panel A use dummy variables equal to one for the location of fund assets and a dummy variable equal to one for the HFN Dataset. Model (1a) includes but does not report (for reasons of space) the coefficient estimates for dummy variables equal to one for statistical arbitrage, value, Regulation D, fixed income (non-arbitrage), finance sector, long only, energy sector, country specific, options strategies and other arbitrage (all of these strategy variable estimates were statistically insignificant in Model (1a)); Models (2a)–(8a) do not include any strategy variables not indicated; more parsimonious specifications were necessary in the logit models (2a)–(8a) due to collinearity and invariance with respect to the binary dependent variable. Fund size is excluded in Model (3a) to avoid colinearity problems. Marginal effects are reported and not the standard logit coefficients in order to highlight economic significance alongside statistical significance. *, **, *** Statistically significant at the 10%, 5%, and 1% level, respectively.

	(1a)	(2a)	(3a)	(4a)	(5a)	(6a)	(7a)	(8a)
	Minimum Capitalization Requirements	Restrictions on the Location of Key Service Providers	Marketing via Private Placements	Marketing via Wrappers	Marketing via Banks	Marketing via Other Regulated Financial Institution	Marketing via Investment Managers	Marketing via Fund Distribution Companies
Panel A. Combined CISDM and HFN Data								
Constant	380210.296***	0.296***	0.016	−0.057***	0.494***	−0.067***	0.466***	−0.069***
Hedge Fund Strategy								
Fixed Income Arbitrage	70454.269*	0.113	−0.038**	0.010	0.051	0.0003	0.071	0.011
Merger/Risk Arbitrage	47740.678	0.150		0.050	0.110	0.108	0.068	0.051
Convertible Arbitrage	−3312.301	0.078			0.063	0.036	−0.010	
Multi-Strategy	75605.281	0.041	−0.036***	0.024	−0.015	0.002	−0.022	0.016
Event Driven	−12643.066	0.241			0.054		0.018	
Short-term Trading	−11039.529							
Market Neutral Equity	−18918.861	0.008	−0.003	0.010	−0.015	0.024	−0.063	0.006
Small/Micro-Cap	−1872.101							
Short Bias	44861.133	0.039			0.040		−0.011	
Long/Short Equity	−2457.890	−0.102		0.029*	0.052	0.001	0.025	0.005

Technology Sector	−60895.931	−0.082*			−0.129**		−0.144***	
Emerging Markets	60490.056	0.232**		−0.001	0.082	0.008	0.188*	0.046
Macro	145446.365	0.160		0.009	0.117	0.039	0.071	0.032
Capital Structure Arbitrage	43149.933						0.001	
CTA/Managed Futures	70527.075	0.239*		−0.001	0.172	0.040		0.007
Market Timer	−139038.931***							
Distressed Securities	−23136.145	−0.040			−0.120**	−0.010	−0.105*	
Fund Characteristics								
Fund Size	0.00001*	1.06E-10***		−5.63E-12	2.74E-10***	1.10E-12	1.37E-10***	−5.71E-12
Fund Age	−488.661***	−0.0009***	0.00001	−0.0001	−0.002***	−0.0002**	−0.0014***	−0.00009
Model Diagnostics								
Number of Observations	1845	1845	1845	1845	1845	1845	1845	1845
Number of Observations with Dependent Variable =1	Not Applicable	612	1833	59	640	73	633	49
Loglikelihood Function	−25992.874	−749.307	−64.099	−233.041	−804.086	−286.646	−813.738	−215.631
Adjusted R^2 (Pseudo R^2 for Models 2–8)	0.110	0.361	0.117	0.108	0.325	0.067	0.314	0.046
F-Statistic (Chi-squared Statistic for Models 2–8)	25.38***	845.942***	16.572**	56.166***	773.709***	41.328***	745.427***	21.139

have a negative effect on the hedge fund value since better performing funds are more geographically proximate to their investee companies (see Coval and Moskowitz 1999, 2001). Overall, therefore, this is not conclusive evidence in support of Hypothesis 1 outlined above.

In terms of minimum capitalization and restrictions on location, the data in Cumming and Johan (2008) tend to suggest that fund strategies are largely invariant to fund regulation, hence providing support for Hypothesis 2. Where coefficients are statistically significant, they tend to be more consistent with Hypothesis 3 and do not support the race to the bottom view of Hypothesis 1.

Table 15.2 also analyses forum shopping for different marketing channels in relation to fund strategies. Funds pursuing fixed income arbitrage strategies are approximately 3.8% to 4.9% less likely to be registered in countries that offer distributions via private placements, and this evidence is statistically significant at the 5% level of significance. Distribution via private placements offers the potential of risk reduction to the investor since there is more room for negotiation, for example ratchet clauses may be used alongside various covenants to protect the investors, and if necessary, prices may be discounted in cases of riskier strategies. Since fixed income arbitrage is a comparatively risk- free strategy—analogous to steamrollers picking up nickels on the street—it is not surprising that fixed income arbitrage is less commonly associated with private place distribution jurisdictions. The authors also indicate that multi-strategy funds are 3.6% less likely to be registered in jurisdictions that offer private placements; however, that evidence is not robust in the subsample of CISDM data.

Funds pursuing long/short equity strategies are 2.9% more likely to be registered in jurisdictions that allow marketing via wrapper products. This might be suggestive of an exacerbated potential agency problem insofar as wrappers might facilitate the distribution of distorted information to investors with the combination of multiple products. However, the authors note that this evidence is only statistically significant at the 10% level, and not statistically significant with the subsample of CISDM data only.

Funds pursuing Technology Sector strategies and Distressed funds are less likely to be distributed via banks, and this evidence is statistically significant at the 5% level and at the 10% level. In terms of the economic significance, Technology Sectors are 12.9% and 19.2% less likely to be registered in bank distribution jurisdictions and Distressed funds are 12.0% and 19.7% less likely to be registered in jurisdictions involving bank distributions. As agency problems with Technology Sectors and Distressed securities are more pronounced, and bank distributions tend to facilitate greater access to retail customers (albeit of typically more inflated wealth), this evidence supports Hypothesis 3 in that funds are less likely to register in countries with strategies that are in conflict with their potential investors' interests. Cumming and Johan (2008) also find that Market Neutral Equity funds are 10.3% more likely to register in countries that permit distributions via other regulated financial institutions. Overall, this is suggestive of the absence of forum shopping for other regulated financial institution distributions (in support of Hypothesis 2), and in the alternative, to the extent there is forum shopping, it is not in conflict with the interests of potential investors (in support of Hypothesis 3 and not Hypothesis 1).

Funds pursuing emerging markets strategies are 18.8% to 19.0% more likely to register in jurisdictions that offer marketing via investment managers. Investment managers are of interest to hedge funds that seek assistance for facilitating easier access to potential investors that have an interest in the particular strategy employed by the fund. The investment manager provides services for regular assessment of strategy and execution, as well as services for risk management reduction and reporting of the hedge fund. This makes the fund more attractive to its investors (see Zimmermann 2002). In view of the idiosyncrasies of emerging market hedge fund strategies, it is not surprising that it is more attractive for Emerging Market funds to seek jurisdictions that offer investment manager distribution channels so that the investment manager can help particular fund strategies match with suitable investors. In net, therefore, we may view this evidence of a positive association between emerging markets funds and distributions via investment managers as supportive of Hypothesis 3.

The authors also, however, show that Technology Sector funds are 14.4% to 26.3% less likely to register in jurisdictions permitting distributions via investment managers. As well, Distressed funds are 10.5% to 22.6% less likely to register in jurisdictions that permit distributions via investment managers. Fund managers typically require a performance fee of 20% of fund profits and an eaxclusivity arrangement. It is possible that those terms are less suitable for hedge funds in the technology sectors and in distressed securities. It is also possible that the client base of investment managers is less interested in technology-focused funds and funds focused on distressed securities.

Finally, the authors note that there are no statistically significant relations between hedge fund strategies and registrations in jurisdictions that permit distributions via fund distribution companies. This is supportive of Hypothesis 2 outlined above.

Overall, there is not much evidence of forum shopping in relation to fund strategies. Where the authors do observe forum shopping, the evidence is less consistent with the race to the bottom view expressed in Hypothesis 1 and more consistent with the alignment of interests view in Hypothesis 3.

15.6 Hedge Fund Structure and Performance

We have thus far discussed how hedge funds raise the funds used to implement their various strategies. We also show that hedge fund managers perceive regulation to be informative to the funds' investors, because fund managers signal their interest in mitigating potential agency conflicts associated with fund management by registering in a jurisdiction with greater regulatory oversight to facilitate fundraising efforts. What we seek to do now is to discuss how hedge fund regulation has impacted fund structure and performance, which has always been the focal point in the debate on whether more regulatory insight should be introduced to the hedge fund industry.

While the growth of hedge funds worldwide has led regulators to re-evaluate the suitability and effectiveness of their existing regulatory oversight (PWC 2006, 2007), hedge fund registration in the US, however, only really commenced in 2006 (Partnoy and Thomas 2007; Brav et al., Chapter 8, this volume). This disparity in regulatory oversight is especially relevant with over a trillion US dollars of capital under management and at 5% alphas sought/promised by most hedge funds at fund raising, as this implies that there needs to be at least an aggregate $50 billion above systematic risk justified return (and more than $125 billion in excess returns in 2008). Given the implausibility of over $50 billion being readily available for hedge fund investors and managers who aim to 'beat the market', it seems highly likely that many hedge fund participants will be sorely disappointed in the future.

In other countries around the world, hedge funds face stricter regulations such as minimum capital requirements, marketing restrictions, and restrictions on retail investor participation, among other things. Many hedge fund managers are against stricter regulations, arguing that such regulation may hamper hedge fund performance. To provide insight on this debate, Cumming and Dai (2010a) examine the impact of various hedge fund regulations on fund governance and performance with a comprehensive dataset.

15.6.1 Theory and Hypotheses

In theory, there is an ambiguous correlation between hedge fund regulation on the one hand, and hedge fund structure and performance on the other. The first possibility is that lack of regulatory oversight may give rise to fund managers who disguise investment schemes and merely capture the fees. This view is consistent with theory and evidence in Bebchuk and Fried (2003), at least in other contexts, that the compensation structure is part of the agency problem rather than its solution. For instance, suppose there are two funds managed by the same group of fund managers. One has a strategy of shorting the Standard and Poor's (S&P) 500 index while the other has a strategy of going long on the S&P. The additional aspects of the hedge fund marketed to the hedge funds' investors hide the true nature of these hedge funds. In the end, half of the investors of these two hedge funds will lose, while the hedge fund managers reap the profits of the fixed management fees and carried interest performance fees of both hedge funds. The fund investors remain unaware of the scheme due to all of the 'mumbo jumbo' of the marketing and promotional material of the hedge funds. Further, without regulatory oversight and/or hedge fund registration requirements, regulatory authorities would also be unaware. Hedge fund registration and oversight would curb this type of behaviour, thereby improving hedge fund structure and average performance.

Alternatively, regulatory oversight may hamper fund performance where hedge fund managers and their investors lose freedom to contract and organize their resources in the way they deem to be most efficient, thereby exacerbating agency problems. The most common forms of regulation in different countries around the world include restrictions on minimum hedge fund size; restrictions on the location of key service providers such as the administrator, custodian, investment advisor, auditors, legal and tax advisors, accountants, and consultants; and limitations on the main market channels for hedge fund distribution. Such restrictions may constrain the fund to an inefficient scale, give rise to inefficient choices of human resources associated with fund management, create barriers to entry, and limit investor participation most suited to the particular hedge fund's strategy. If so, the authors expect worse hedge fund performance and less efficient hedge fund structures (that do not as efficiently align the interests of investors and managers) in terms of higher management fees and lower performance fees.

15.6.2 Data and Empirical Findings

As discussed above, the interaction between hedge fund regulation on the one hand, and hedge fund structure and performance on the other, is theoretically ambiguous and subject to whatever effect one believes dominates in the marketplace. Therefore, Cumming and Dai (2010a) sought to sort these issues out with an empirical analysis of pertinent data. In particular, the authors empirically examine the relationship between hedge fund performance (including Goetzmann et al. 2007) MPPMs, Fung and Hsieh (2004) multifactor alphas, average monthly returns and the standard deviation of returns, hedge fund structure (fixed management fees and carried interest performance fees), and various aspects of hedge fund regulation (minimum capitalization, restrictions on the location of key service providers, and restrictions on marketing channels) with an international dataset of 3,782 hedge funds from twenty-nine countries around the world (listed in Table 15.1). Cumming and Dai (2010a) demonstrate results for data spanning the years 1994–2005 and show robustness for the subsample over 2003–05.

At a broad level, the data indicate that regulatory requirements in the form of restrictions on the location of key service providers and marketing channels that permit wrappers (securities that combine different products) are associated with lower alphas, lower average returns, and higher fixed fees. Related evidence confirms that restrictions on location are also negatively related to MPPMs, while wrapper distributions are significantly negatively related to performance fees. There is further evidence that the standard deviation of returns is lower among jurisdictions with restrictions on the location of key service providers and higher minimum capitalization requirements.

In particular, in jurisdictions with restrictions regarding the location of key service providers, monthly returns are approximately 0.3% lower, MPPMs are approximately 0.2% lower (the MPPM is the average monthly welfare of a power utility investor in the portfolio over our sample periods), and 7-factor alphas are approximately 0.1–0.5% lower. These effects are statistically significant and robust to alternative specifications including alternative control variables, different sample periods (both 2003–05 and 1994–2005), exclusion of funds-of-funds, and instrumental variable framework correcting for the endogeneity of regulations.

There is fairly robust evidence that minimum capitalization restrictions lower the standard deviation of returns. The data indicate that an increase in required minimum capitalization for a hedge fund from $1 to $2 million tends to be associated with a reduction in standard deviation of monthly returns by 0.02%. Minimum capitalization restrictions, however, are statistically unrelated to other aspects of fund performance.

The evidence indicates that jurisdictions with marketing via wrappers have lower monthly average returns by approximately 0.2% and 7-factor alphas 0.2–0.5% lower. These effects are economically large, ranging from 2.4% to 6.2% per year. Furthermore, wrapper distributions lower standard deviations of monthly returns by 0.9%. These effects are robust for the 1994–2005 period, but not for the 2003–05 period.

Finally, there is evidence that jurisdictions permitting distributions via wrappers have lower performance fees by 0.43%. There is further evidence that jurisdictions with wrapper distributions and restrictions on the location of key service providers have higher fixed fees by 0.54% and 0.51%, respectively. Insofar as lower fixed fees and higher performance fees mitigate agency problems and better align the interests of fund managers and owners, this evidence is consistent with the related evidence demonstrating a negative association between performance and jurisdictions which permit distribution via wrappers and have restrictions on location.

15.7 Hedge Fund Capital Flows

We show above how regulations impact hedge fund performance and structure. In this section, we further consider how regulation influences hedge fund capital flows and the flow-performance relationship. In Cumming and Dai (2009), the authors believe this question is important because it is central to the efficient allocation of capital in the hedge fund industry. In Subsection 15.7.1 we describe the different distribution channels for hedge funds in different countries. In Subsection 15.7.2 we describe the dataset used and empirical tests in Cumming and Dai (2009).

15.7.1 Theory and Hypotheses

The flow-performance relation has been examined in the context of hedge funds in more recent studies given the availability of new industry data. Agarwal and Naik (2004), Goetzmann, Ingersoll, and Ross (2003), and Getmansky (2005) show there are decreasing returns to scale in the performance of hedge funds, and explain their findings by the limited availability of assets that provide superior hedge fund returns. Agarwal and Naik (2004) and Agarwal, Daniel, and Naik (2006, 2009) control for additional factors, such as managerial incentives and fees, size, and age of funds, and rank hedge funds based on non-risk adjusted return performance. They find that flows are positively associated with performance, which is different from the findings in Goetzmann, Ingersoll, and Ross (2003). Similarly, Fung et al. (2008) show that the alphas are associated with greater and steadier capital inflows of funds (see also Fung and Hsieh 1997, 2000, 2001, 2004, 2006). Convexity versus concavity of the flow-performance relationship has been debated in the hedge fund literature. Agarwal, Daniel, and Naik (2006) find a convex relationship in hedge fund flow-performance; Getmansky (2005) finds a concave flow-performance relationship; and Baquero, Horst, and Verbeek (2005) find a linear flow-performance relationship. The results depend on database used, time period analysed, and the frequency of the sample. Ding et al. (2007) reconcile these conflicting findings by showing that hedge funds exhibit a convex flow-performance relation in the absence of share restrictions (similar to mutual funds), but exhibit a concave relation in the presence of restrictions. Further, live funds exhibit a concave flow-performance relation due to diseconomies of scale, but defunct funds display a convex relation due to the various reasons that they had become defunct.

Cumming and Dai (2009) argue that both the level of hedge fund capital flows and the flow-performance relationship are subject to the regulatory factors in the jurisdictions where hedge funds are registered. For instance, they propose that restrictions on location of key service providers would reduce fund inflows if such restrictions limit the ability of a fund to freely contract with the service providers that are most likely to add value to the fund. Alternatively, if such restrictions improve regulatory oversight and enhance investor confidence, funds registered in jurisdictions that mandate restrictions on the location of key service providers would have higher fund inflows. Higher level of minimum capitalization requirement may help attract capital if it enhances investor confidence that hedge funds in the market are more stable or at least less likely to fail. The permissible distribution channels may influence the flow-performance relationship as different distribution channels influence marketing, products, and the types of buyers and sellers. For instance, wrappers involve tied selling and therefore capital flows do not depend merely on past performance of the fund but also the companion securities. Furthermore, there are other regulations that may affect investor confidence and the flow of funds to and from hedge funds, such as restrictions on the location of key service providers and minimum capitalization requirements. As well, tax considerations may influence the flow of funds. The central importance of these hedge fund regulations to the flow of funds of investors is made clear in industry analyses such as that provided by PWC (2006).

15.7.2 Data and Empirical Findings

Cumming and Dai (2009) use the CISDM dataset, which comprises hedge funds that are registered in sixteen countries around the world, for the time period 2003–05 for which there is a significant number of funds in the data.

Cumming and Dai (2009) find a very pronounced impact of hedge fund regulation on fund flows. They empirically show that hedge funds registered in countries with larger minimum capitalization requirements tend to have higher levels of inflows. This suggests minimum capitalization enhances investor confidence in terms of greater stability with larger funds. This finding holds even after controlling for minimum investment amounts per transaction. Cumming and Dai (2009) also empirically show that funds registered in countries which restrict the location of key service providers have lower levels of inflows. This latter result is consistent with the view that locational restrictions are perceived by investors to mitigate human resource quality, and this perceived reduction in human resource quality is more pronounced than any associated perceived improvement in regulatory oversight.

Further, Cumming and Dai (2009) find that the permissible distribution channels have a strong impact on the sensitivity of fund flows to past performance. Country-specific regulations which permit distribution channels in the form of wrappers mitigate the sensitivity of fund flows to past performance, while distribution channels via investment managers and fund distribution companies enhance flow-performance sensitivity. These findings are robust to different methods of measuring past performance, as well as different methods of accounting for non-linearities in the flow-performance relation. Also, the evidence is robust to controls for share restrictions, as well as fund fees, fund age, country -GNP and legal origin, among other control variables such as fund strategies and fund location of assets. As well, they explicitly show robustness to controls for selection effects using treatment regressions for the non-random decision of some funds to locate in an offshore jurisdiction.

In addition to these regulatory impacts on fund flows and flow-performance relationship, two findings in this chapter are consistent with tax effects on hedge fund flows. First, offshore funds tend to have higher capital flows, and there of course exist tax advantages associated with offshore funds. Second, we find pronounced seasonality effects in the data. Fund flows tend to be lower in later calendar months and higher in earlier calendar months, and as discussed further in Cumming and Dai (2009), this seasonality pattern is consistent with tax incentives for timing investment flows. This seasonality effect documented by Cumming and Dai (2009) is a new finding in the context of hedge fund flows (see Kamstra, Kramer, and Levi 2003).

15.8 Hedge Fund Misreporting

Hedge fund managers compete with each other to attract capital from institutional investors. Recent evidence has shown that fund managers report monthly returns that are much more likely to be marginally positive than zero or marginally negative, and this evidence is best explained by the incentive to attract investors (Bollen and Pool 2008, 2009). Cumming and Dai (2010b) address the issue of whether hedge fund regulation mitigates or exacerbates the tendency of fund managers to misreport returns.

They examine misreporting in reference to marginally positive versus marginally negative returns, and consider competing explanations for the observed patterns of returns. By examining cross-country evidence on misreported returns, the authors can infer, by holding other factors constant, the impact of international differences in hedge fund regulation on the propensity to misreport returns. Further, Cumming and Dai (2010b) examine and calculate explicitly whether it pays to misreport.

15.8.1 Theory and Hypotheses

Similar to Bollen and Pool (2008, 2009), Cumming and Dai (2010b) refer to 'marginally positive' monthly hedge fund returns as ones that are more likely to be 'misreported returns' (i.e., it is more likely that they would otherwise have been zero or marginally negative). They argue that if regulatory oversight in the form of minimum capitalization, restrictions on location, and restrictions on distribution channels facilitates additional value-added governance, then hedge funds in those jurisdictions are less likely to misreport monthly returns. For instance, it is possible that minimum size restrictions eliminate lower quality funds from the market. Further, it is possible that restrictions on the location of key service providers centralizes the regulatory oversight and better enables regulators to engage in surveillance of fund activities. Restrictions on distribution channels may afford superior investor protection and enable more effective regulatory oversight.

In the alternative, restrictions on minimum capital requirements for managers increase incentives to manage earnings to maintain capital above minimum thresholds (Degeorge, Patel, and Zeckhauser 1999). Restrictions on the location of key service providers limit human resource choices and lower the quality of governance provided, thereby making it easier for fund managers to manipulate reported earnings each month. Further, restrictions on hedge fund distribution channels may limit the governance provided by those involved in the distribution channels. It is likely, for instance, that there is less governance provided by wrapper distributions where funds are sold in conjunction with other products (Gerstein 2006). By contrast, investment managers and fund distribution companies might be more likely to provide active oversight and notice misreporting. If these effects are predominant, hedge funds in these jurisdictions may exhibit more misreporting behaviour.

15.8.2 Data and Empirical Findings

Using a sample of 8,641 hedge funds from 48 countries during the period from 1994 to 2003, Cumming and Dai (2010b) find strong evidence of a significant relation in the data between hedge fund regulation and misreporting, and the findings are robust to controls for selection effects, among other robustness checks. Returns in jurisdictions which permit distributions via wrappers are more likely to be misreported. Wrappers, by definition, are sold as tied products and appear to enable fund managers to avoid the same level of scrutiny as that provided via other distribution channels. This evidence is consistent with other work that shows wrappers have a 'flatter' flow-performance relation and lower overall levels of performance. They also find evidence that the sensitivity of wrappers to misreporting is stronger for funds without lock-up provisions, which is intuitive as funds without a lock-up risk losing capital allocations for poor performance each month, and hence have a stronger incentive each month to report marginally positive as opposed to marginally negative returns. Also, misreporting is less common among funds in jurisdictions with minimum capital requirements and restrictions on the location of key service providers. Minimum capitalization requirements prevent smaller lower-quality funds from entering, and these funds might otherwise have had a pronounced incentive to misreport, and most jurisdictions that have minimum capitalization requirements likewise have restrictions on location. Further, Cumming and Dai (2010b) empirically show that misreporting significantly affects capital allocations. Wealth transfer, which is an estimate of the distorted capital allocation due to misreporting, is particularly large in jurisdictions permitting distributions via wrappers.

15.9 Trends in Hedge Fund Regulation

A number of changes are likely to shape the future of the hedge fund industry as a result of the increased attention generated by the financial crisis, the increase in assets under management by hedge funds, and the increased potential of such funds to have a systematic effect on financial markets. For instance, in the US, the SEC has proposed to update the accredited investor definition under the 1933 Act to require such investors to hold at least $2.5 million in investable assets, an increase from the current reinvestment of $1 million. In 2010, Congress passed legislation requiring all managers of hedge funds with more than $150 million in assets under management to register under the Advisers Act. Congress is likely to establish a regulatory regime for monitoring systemic risk which would require hedge funds with assets under management in excess of $25 billion to meet stricter reporting requirements, including disclosure about the funds' degrees of leverage, ability to sell assets quickly at current prices, concentrated positions, and key counterparties for trading to the Federal Reserve and the SEC. These new requirements would subject managers of hedge funds to stricter SEC examinations and more extensive disclosures to investors, which would help to some extent to mitigate the various agency problems we discussed above. However, hedge funds managers would still be allowed to choose investment strategies, use leverage, and charge asymmetric performance fees.

15.10 Conclusion

The debate around hedge fund regulation in part involves the use of innovative investment strategies by hedge funds, coupled with the significant and growing systematic risk in the hedge fund industry (see Getmansky, Lo, and Makarov 2004; Khandani and Lo 2007). On the one hand, these innovative hedge fund strategies provide various benefits to the financial systems involved, including providing crucial liquidity to markets, limiting price distortions and anomalies via arbitrage trading, and taking on risk across instruments and markets as they are able to change portfolio composition rather quickly. On the other hand, as active risk takers across instruments and markets, hedge funds may also exacerbate the risk of systemic failure as their strategies involve multiple markets with as yet untested instrument links.

Opponents of more stringent regulation believe that such beneficial hedge fund activities are facilitated within a 'friendly' environment which allows for freedom and discretion. To curtail such freedom may just cause the players to leave for a much friendlier playing field, so to speak. To allow the players complete freedom, however, may just enable them to run amok. Regulation and oversight may be so heavy-handed that hedge funds and managers will move their operations to more accommodating, less regulated jurisdictions. Also, as more regulatory oversight will involve taking self-regulating functions away from hedge fund participants, this may encourage laxity with regard to investment decisions and risk management. The question now is not how to regulate the industry, but where to draw the line which divides under- and over-regulation.

In the first section of this chapter, we provided an overview of the potential agency problems associated with managing a hedge fund and associated rationales for hedge fund regulation. We also provided examples of international differences in hedge fund regulation including minimum capitalization requirements; restrictions on the location of key service providers; and different permissible distribution channels via private placements, banks, other regulated or non-regulated financial intermediaries, wrappers, investment managers, and fund distribution companies.

If it is assumed that all hedge fund managers want complete freedom to do what they do best, then it follows that any extra regulatory oversight will cause them to forum shop. And it also follows that they might forum shop in a 'race to the bottom'. What we sought to determine in the first part of this chapter is whether this is the case. We considered whether forum shopping exists across different hedge funds applying different strategies. The latter part of this chapter provides an empirical analysis of hedge fund strategies, structure, fund flows, performance, and misreporting behaviour in the context of international differences in hedge fund regulation. The data offer little support for the view that hedge fund managers pursuing riskier strategies or strategies with potentially more pronounced agency problems systematically select jurisdictions with less stringent regulations. Rather, the data suggest that hedge funds select jurisdictions that are in funds' investors' interests in order to facilitate capital-raising by the hedge fund. We then show that hedge fund regulation has an important role to play in influencing the size and stability of the hedge fund market.

In Cumming and Dai (2009), the authors show that the level of fund flows was negatively related to restrictions on location of key service providers and positively related to minimum capitalization requirements. This suggests minimum capitalization enhances investor confidence in terms of greater stability with larger funds. This finding holds even after controlling for minimum investment amounts per transaction. Hedge funds registered in countries which restrict the location of key service providers have lower levels of inflows. This latter result is consistent with the view that locational restrictions are perceived by investors to mitigate human resource quality, and this perceived reduction in human resource quality is more pronounced than any associated perceived improvement in regulatory oversight. Data and empirical tests are also used by Cumming and Dai (2008) to analyse hedge fund misreporting. The authors find strong evidence of a significant relation in the data between hedge fund regulation and misreporting.

References

Agarwal, V., Daniel, N., and Naik, N. Y. (2006). Flows, Performance, and Managerial Incentives in the Hedge Fund Industry, EFA 2003 Annual Conference Paper No. 501, available at <http://ssrn.com/abstract=424369>.

Agarwal, V. and Naik, N. Y. (2000). Multi-Period Performance Persistence Analysis of Hedge Funds, *Journal of Financial and Quantitative Analysis* 35(3), 327–42.

Agarwal, V. and Naik, N. Y. (2004). Risks and Portfolio Decisions Involving Hedge Funds, *Review of Financial Studies* 17(1), 63–98.

Baquero, G., Horst, J. T., and Verbeek, M. (2005). Survival, Look-ahead Bias, and Persistence in Hedge Fund Performance, *Journal of Financial & Quantitative Analysis* 40(3), 493–517.

Barclay, M., Holderness, C. G., and Sheehan, D. P. (2007). Private Placements and Managerial Entrenchment, *Journal of Corporate Finance* 13, 461–84.

Bebchuk, L. A. and Fried, J. M. (2003). Executive Compensation as an Agency Problem, *Journal of Economic Perspectives* 17, 71–92.

Bollen, N. P. B. and Pool, V. K. (2006). A Screen for Fraudulent Return Smoothing in the Hedge Fund Industry, Working Paper, available at <http://ssrn.com/abstract=686137>.

Bollen, N. P. B. and Pool, V. K. (2008). Conditional Return Smoothing in the Hedge Fund Industry, *Journal of Financial and Quantitative Analysis* 43, 267–98.

Bollen, N. P. B. and Pool, V. K. (2009). Do Hedge Fund Managers Misreport Returns? Evidence from the Pooled Distribution, *Journal of Finance*, 64, 2257–88.

Brown, S. J., Goetzmann, W. N., Liang, B., and Schwarz, C. (2008). Lessons from Hedge Fund Registration, *Journal of Finance* 63, 2785–815.

Campos, R. (2006). Speech by SEC Commissioner: Remarks before the SIA Hedge Funds & Alternative Investments Conference (14 June).

Coval, J. D. and Moskowitz, T. J. (1999). Home Bias at Home: Local Equity Preference in Domestic Portfolios, *Journal of Finance* 54, 2045–73.

Coval, J. D. and Moskowitz, T. J. (2001). The Geography of Investment: Informed Trading and Asset Prices, *Journal of Political Economy* 109, 811–41, available at <http://faculty.chicagobooth.edu/tobias.moskowitz/research/GeogInv.pdf>.

Cumming, D. and Dai, N. (2009). Capital Flows and Hedge Fund Regulation, *Journal of Empirical Legal Studies* 6, 848–73.

Cumming, D. and Dai, N. (2010a). A Law and Finance Analysis of Hedge Funds, *Financial Management* 39, 997–1026.

Cumming, D. and Dai, N. (2010b). Hedge Fund Regulation and Misreported Returns, *European Financial Management* 16, 829–57.

Cumming, D. and Johan, S. (2008). Hedge Fund Forum Shopping, *University of Pennsylvania Journal of Business and Employment Law* 10, 783–831.

Cumming, D. and MacIntosh, J. (2000). The Role of Interjurisdictional Competition in Shaping Canadian Corporate Law, *International Review of Law and Economics* 20, 141–86.

Ding, B., Getmansky, M., Liang, B., and Wermers, R. (2007). Market Volatility, Investor Flows, and the Structure of Hedge Fund Markets, University of Massachusetts Working Paper, available at <http://www.q-group.org/research/files/recently_funded/2005_market_volatility.pdf>.

Degeorge, F., Patel, J., and Zeckhauser, R. (1999). Earnings Management to Exceed Thresholds, *Journal of Business* 72, 1–33.

Donaldson, W. H. (2003). Testimony Concerning Investor Protection Implications of Hedge Funds by Chairman, US Securities and Exchange Commission, before the Senate Committee on Banking, Housing and Urban Affairs (10 April), available at <http://www.sec.gov/news/testimony/2006/ts072506cc.htm>.

Fink, S. (2005). The Distribution of Hedge Funds to Mass Affluent Investors, *Alternative Investment Management Association Journal* (Sept.), available at <http://www.aima.org/uploads/Fink68pdf>.

Fung, W. and Hsieh, D. A. (1997). Empirical Characteristics of Dynamic Trading Strategies: The Case of Hedge Funds, *Review of Financial Studies* 10(2), 275–302.

Fung, W. and Hsieh, D. A. (2000). Performance Characteristics of Hedge Funds and CTA Funds: Natural versus Spurious Biases, *Journal of Financial and Quantitative Analysis* 35(3), 291–307.

Fung, W. and Hsieh, D. A. (2001). The Risk in Hedge Fund Strategies: Theory and Evidence from Trend Followers, *Review of Financial Studies* 14(2), 313–41.

Fung, W. and Hsieh, D. A. (2004). Hedge Fund Benchmarks: A Risk Based Approach, *Financial Analyst Journal* 60, 65–80.

Fung, W. and Hsieh, D. A. (2006). Hedge Funds: An Industry in Its Adolescence, *Federal Reserve Bank of Atlanta Economic Review* (4th Quarter), No. 91, 1–33.

Garbaravicius, T. and Diereck, F. (2005). Hedge Funds and their Implications for Financial Stability, European Central Bank Occasional Paper Series No. 34, available at <http://ssrn.com/abstract=752094>.

Gerstein, K. S. (2006). *Hedge Fund Distribution: Regulatory Hot Buttons* (New York, Schulte Roth & Zabel, LLP).

Getmansky, M. (2005). The Life Cycle of Hedge Funds: Fund Flows, Size and Performance, University of Massachusetts Working Paper, available at <http://www.mtadata.org/eweb/docs/pdfs/Getmansky.pdf>.

Getmansky, M., Lo, A. W., and Makarov, I. (2004). An Econometric Model of Serial Correlation and Illiquidity in Hedge Fund Returns, *Journal of Financial Economics* 74(3), 529–609.

Goetzmann, W. N., Ingersoll, J. E., and Ross, S. A. (2003). High-water Marks and Hedge Fund Management Contracts, *Journal of Finance* 58(4), 1685–718.

Goetzmann, W. N., Ingersoll, J. E., Spiegel, M. I., and Welch, I. (2007). Portfolio Performance Manipulation and Manipulation-Proof Performance Measures, *Review of Financial Studies* 20(5), 1503–46.

Goldschmid, H. J. (2004). Speech by SEC Commissioner: Should Hedge Funds be Regulated (17 Nov.), available at <http://www.sec.gov/news/speech/spch111704hjg.htm>.

Hirsch, E. D., Kett, J. F., and Trefil, J. (eds.) (2002). *The New Dictionary of Cultural Literacy: What Every American Needs to Know* (3rd edn) (New York, Houghton Mifflin Company).

Hodder, J. E. and Jackwerth, J. C. (2007). Incentive Contracts and Hedge Fund Management, *Journal of Financial and Quantitative Analysis* 42, 811–26.

House Committee on Banking and Financial Services (1999). Hedge Funds, Leverage, and the Lessons of Long-Term Capital Management: Report of the President's Working Group on Capital Markets (Apr.), available at <http://www.treasury.gov/resource-center/fin-mkts/Documents/hedgfund.pdf>.

Hu, H. and Black, B. (2006). Empty Voting and Hidden (Morphable) Ownership: Taxonomy, Implications, and Reforms, *Business Lawyer* 61(3), 1011–70.

Ineichen, A. and Silberstein, K. (2008). *AIMA's Roadmap to Hedge Funds* (Alternative Investment Management Association).

International Financial Services (2006). *Hedge Funds: City Business Services* (Mar.)

Kamstra, M. J., Kramer, L. A., and Levi, M. D. (2003). Winter Blues: Seasonal Affective Disorder (SAD) and Stock Market Returns, *American Economic Review* 93, 324–43.

Khandani, A. E. and Lo, A. W. (2007). What Happened to the Quants in August 2007? *Journal of Investment Management* 5(4), 5–54.

Leondis, A. (2010). US Millionaires' Ranks Rose 16% in 2009, *Bloomberg Businessweek* (9 Mar.).

Mackintosh, J. (2008). Hedge Funds Agree to Greater Disclosure, *Financial Times* (22 Jan.).

Malkiel, B. G. and Saha, A. (2005). Hedge Funds: Risk and Return, *Financial Analysts Journal* 61, 80–8.

Partnoy, F. and Thomas, R. S. (2007). Gap Filling, Hedge Funds, and Financial Innovation in Y. Fuchita, and R. E. Litan (eds.), *Brookings–Nomura Papers on Financial Services* (Washington DC, Brookings Institution Press), 6–21.

PricewaterhouseCoopers (PwC) (2006). *The Regulation, Taxation and Distribution of Hedge Funds in Europe: Changes and Challenges* (London, PricewaterhouseCoopers).

PricewaterhouseCoopers (PwC) (2007). *Under the Spotlight: The Regulation, Taxation and Distribution of Hedge Funds Around the Globe* (London, PricewaterhouseCoopers).

Romano, R. (1985). Law as a Product: Some Pieces of the Incorporation Puzzle, *Journal of Law, Economics and Organization* 1, 225–83.

Zimmermann, V. (2002). Hedge Fund Marketing: Pros, Cons and Structuring Agreements with Third-party Marketers, *Alternative Investment Quarterly* (3rd Quarter).

CHAPTER 16

THE LIMITS OF EU HEDGE FUND REGULATION

DAN AWREY

16.1 Introduction

On the surface, the global financial crisis of 2007–09 (GFC) has served to galvanize support for the proposition that we need to fundamentally rethink the ways in which we regulate financial markets and institutions. This consensus is reflected in the Communiqué released by G20 finance ministers and central bank governors following their summit in Seoul, South Korea on 11–12 November 2010.[1] Prominent within this professed consensus is the conviction that we must strengthen public regulation and oversight of the so-called 'shadow banking system': non-bank financial institutions including structured investment vehicles, money market funds, and hedge funds.[2] Dig a little deeper, however, and it is possible to detect emerging fault lines between the Anglo-Saxon and Continental perspectives. Perhaps nowhere is this divergence of views more evident (or acute) than in connection with post-crisis regulatory reforms targeting hedge funds and other 'alternative' investment vehicles.

This brief chapter examines the mechanics of the recently adopted Alternative Investment Fund Managers (AIFM) Directive and offers some preliminary observations respecting its likely effectiveness.[3] On balance, the results of this examination are not encouraging. First, the EU has failed to mount a persuasive case for why the Directive represents an improvement over existing national regulatory regimes or prevailing market practices in several key

[1] G20 Seoul Summit Leaders Declaration, 11–12 November 2010 (G20 Communiqué), available at <http://www.g20.org/pub_communiques.aspx>.

[2] G20 Seoul Summit Leaders Declaration, 11–12 November 2010 (G20 Communiqué), available at <http://www.g20.org/pub_communiques.aspx>, 2. Other 'shadow banks' include finance companies, asset-backed commercial paper conduits, securities lenders and, in the US, government sponsored entities; see Pozsar et al. (2010).

[3] The AIFM Directive (alternatively, the Directive) was voted through by the European Parliament on 11 November 2010 and formally adopted by the Council of the European Union on 27 May 2011. The acronym AIFM is used to denote legal or natural persons whose regular business is to manage one or more AIFs; Directive, Art. 3(b).

areas. Second, by attempting to ring fence a disparate and essentially artificial class of financial institutions—as opposed to focusing on the various economic functions performed by these institutions, their operational models and the attendant risks—the Directive establishes what is in many respects a conceptually muddled regulatory regime. Untangling this morass is likely to preoccupy regulators and market participants well into the foreseeable future. Finally, and most importantly, the Directive's approach toward the amelioration of the potential systemic risks associated with alternative investment funds manifests an inherent and ultimately fatal structural flaw. It is this flaw which punctuates the necessity of translating the consensus embodied in the G20 Communiqué into a globally coordinated regulatory response.

16.2 Hedge Fund Regulation: A Reality Check

It can be difficult to cut through the rhetoric and demagoguery which surrounds the debate over the regulation of hedge funds, private equity funds and other alternative investment vehicles. Many observers view these institutions as mechanisms of market efficiency: providing greater diversification and liquidity, lowering market volatility and enhancing the process of price discovery.[4] Others, however, view them as conduits for fraud and market manipulation and as sources of potential systemic risks.[5] Some commentators herald them as would-be champions of more effective corporate governance.[6] Some, meanwhile, condemn them as inherently short-termist or,[7] somewhat more colourfully, 'hoodlums'[8] and 'locusts'.[9] There is a broad perception that hedge funds were unregulated prior to the GFC. Yet, within the EU at least, this was demonstrably not the case.[10] There is also a widely held

[4] See, for example, Grabaravicius and Dierick (2005); Timothy Geithner, 'Hedge Funds and Their Implications for the Financial System', Keynote Address at the National Conference on the Securities Industry (17 November 2004), and Staff Report of the US Securities and Exchange Commission (SEC), 'Implications of the Growth of Hedge Funds' (September 2003) (SEC Report).

[5] For a good summary of the potential systemic risks posed by hedge funds, see Boyson, Stahel, and Stulz (2010); Chan et al. (2007).

[6] See, for example, Brav et al. (Chapter 8, this volume); Kahan and Rock (Chapter 5, this volume); Briggs (2007).

[7] See, for example, the comments of veteran Wall Street lawyer Marty Lipton (2006).

[8] See *Financial Times* (2010a), quoting French MEP Jean-Paul Gauzès.

[9] See *Time* (2005), quoting Germany politician Franz Müntefering.

[10] In the UK, for example, which is home to the vast majority of EU-domiciled hedge fund managers, these institutions typically require authorization as investment managers and/or advisers under articles 37 and/or 53, respectively, of the Regulated Activities Order promulgated under the Financial Services and Markets Act (2000), c. 8 (FSMA). Once authorized, these managers/advisers are subject to, *inter alia*, the UK Financial Service Authority's (FSA) senior management arrangement, systems and controls and conduct of business rules for dealers and managers, and relevant EU regulation including the Markets in Financial Instruments Directive (2008/10/EC) (MiFID), Transparency Directive (2004/109/EC), and Market Abuse Directive (2004/72/EC). That said, the funds themselves and their administrators typically reside offshore. For a more detailed overview of the FSA's pre-GFC regulation of hedge funds, see FSA, 'Hedge Funds: A Discussion of Risk and Regulatory Engagement', Discussion Paper 05/4 (June 2005) (FSA Discussion Paper).

view that hedge funds are highly—if not excessively—leveraged. Again, empirical evidence perhaps suggests otherwise.[11]

So what do we know about hedge funds and other alternative investments? First, the universe of alternative investment funds encompasses a hugely diverse range of financial institutions engaged in a variety of different activities and posing very different prospective risks. Accordingly, there is likely to be no one-size-fits-all approach toward their regulation. Second, the risks posed by alternative investment funds are by no means unique to them. Proprietary trading desks, sovereign wealth funds, insurance companies and other institutional investors are frequently capable of playing similar roles within financial markets—and thus generating similar risks. Third, investors, counterparties and regulators require information respecting these funds and their managers in order to properly monitor these risks.[12] Insofar as private market mechanisms prove ineffective in this regard, there exists a potential role for public regulation in terms of subsidizing disclosure of this information and, more broadly, ensuring that these institutions implement appropriate policies and procedures respecting, inter alia, business conduct, governance and risk management. At the same time, however, more stringent regulation is not a panacea: Bear Stearns, Lehman Bros, and AIG were all heavily regulated. Finally, alternative investment funds were not a proximate cause of the GFC,[13] nor have the substantial number of fund failures which have followed in its wake triggered systemic instability. That said, it would be foolish to disregard the possibility that these institutions—and hedge funds in particular—might be the catalysts of future systemic crises.[14] It is within this complex and politically charged environment that the EU has introduced the AIFM Directive.

[11] Recent estimates of average hedge fund leverage have ranged from 1.3 to 3.9 times equity; see H.M. Treasury, Comment Letter in Response to the Commission Services Consultation Paper on Hedge Funds (12 March 2009) (Treasury Letter); Alternative Investment Fund Management Association, Comment Letter in Response to the Commission Services Consultation Paper on Hedge Funds (30 January 2009), and Shadab (2009) citing various studies. By way of comparison, a US congressional oversight panel recently estimated the average leverage ratio of institutions across the entire financial system at twelve times equity; Congressional Oversight Panel, 'Special Report on Regulatory Reform' (January 2009), 24. Unfortunately, the Panel chose to lump broker-dealers (historically the most leveraged financial institutions) and hedge funds into a single category for the purpose of its calculations. Utilizing the TASS database, Grabaravicius and Dierick (2005: 31) found that, as of 30 June 2005, 32% of hedge funds employed no leverage, while only 13% employed leverage of greater than one times equity. Notably, 23% of funds with assets of more than $1 billion employed leverage in excess of this threshold (Grabaravicius and Dierick 2005: 31). Ultimately, however, estimating hedge fund leverage is difficult owing to both (1) a relative dearth of publicly available data; and (2) the absence of methodological consistency in terms of how leverage is measured and reported.

[12] A. Lo, 'Hedge Funds, Systemic Risk, and the Financial Crisis of 2007–2008', Written Testimony prepared for the US House of Representatives Committee on Oversight and Government Reform (13 November 2008), 3, and SEC Report at x–xi and 78–80.

[13] See H. Sants, Chief Executive of the FSA, speech delivered at Hedge 2008 (22 October 2008).

[14] As outlined in Part IV, these systemic risks could theoretically be transmitted through several channels, some of which are more likely to materialize than others.

16.3 The AIFM Directive: The Basic Mechanics

The AIFM Directive introduces harmonized requirements for financial intermediaries engaged in the management and administration of alternative investment funds (AIFs) within the EU. The Directive defines an AIF as any collective investment scheme which does not require authorization under the Undertakings for Collective Investments in Transferable Securities (UCITS) Directive.[15, 16] This broad definition was designed to capture hedge funds, private equity funds, real estate funds and other institutional investment vehicles which had previously fallen outside the perimeter of EU financial regulation.[17, 18] Management and administration of AIFs are, subject to certain limited exceptions, reserved to EU-domiciled AIFMs authorized under the Directive.[19]

The Directive mandates that any AIFM seeking to manage or market an AIF within the EU obtain authorization from the competent authorities in its home Member State.[20] The Directive contains a *de minimus* exemption for managers which directly or indirectly manage AIF portfolios with total assets of less than €100 million.[21] This threshold is raised to €500 million for managers which (1) only manage AIFs which do not employ any leverage; and (2) do not grant investors redemption rights for at least five years from the date of a fund's inception.[22] As a precondition to authorization, an AIFM will be required to provide the competent authorities with detailed information respecting, inter alia, the identity of its owners, the characteristics of the AIFs it intends to manage, and any arrangements for the delegation of management functions and the valuation and safekeeping of portfolio

[15] 2009/65/EC. [16] Art. 3(a).

[17] Directive on Alternative Investment Fund Managers ('AIFMD'): Frequently Asked Questions, Memo/10/572 (11 November 2010) (FAQ). The breadth of this definition is curtailed somewhat by a number of exceptions. Specifically, the Directive does not apply to collective investment schemes regulated under the UCITS Directive, EU credit institutions, pension funds, life assurance or reinsurance companies or sovereign wealth funds; Art. 2, §§ 2(c)-(g). The Directive also does not apply to an AIFM established in the EU but which does not provide management services to an AIF domiciled or marketed in the EU; Art. 2, § 2(b).

[18] Which is not to say, however, that these institutions fell outside the perimeter of regulation in their home Member States.

[19] The Directive contemplates the delegation of administration (but not management) functions to offshore entities where (1) the third party is authorized to provide such services or is registered in the third country and subject to prudential supervision; (2) there is an appropriate cooperation agreement between the competent authority of the AIFM and the supervisory authority of the third party; and (3) the procedural requirements of the Directive relating to the delegation of functions are fulfilled; Art. 18 and 36.

[20] Art. 4, § 1. An AIFM may be authorized to provide management services in respect of all or only certain types of AIF; Art. 4, § 2.

[21] Art. 2, § 2(a). There is a potential ambiguity in the English language version of the Directive respecting whether the thresholds apply at the fund or manager levels. The Commission estimates that the €100 million threshold will capture 30% of all hedge fund managers (managing almost 90% of assets) of EU-domiciled hedge funds; Proposal for a Directive on Alternative Investment Funds, 2009/0064 (30 April 2009) (AIFM Proposal) at 6.

[22] Art. 2, § 2(a).

assets.[23] More broadly, an AIFM will be required to satisfy the competent authorities that it will be able to comply with the substantive requirements of the Directive.[24] Once authorized, an AIFM will be permitted to provide management services to AIFs domiciled in any Member State[25] and to market the securities of the AIFs it manages to 'professional investors'[26] across the EU.[27] In the short term, this passport will only be available to EU-domiciled AIFs and AIFMs. It is presently contemplated, however, that the passport will be extended to non-EU-domiciled managers and funds in 2013.[28]

An AIFM authorized under the Directive must ensure compliance with substantive requirements respecting, inter alia, (1) conduct of business, governance and risk management; (2) third party valuation and safekeeping; and (3) initial, periodic and event-driven disclosure to investors, the competent authorities and certain third party stakeholders. The Directive also empowers the European Commission and, in exceptional circumstances, the competent authorities within each Member State, to restrict the use of leverage by AIFs.[29]

16.3.1 Conduct of Business, Governance, and Risk Management Requirements

The Directive imposes uniform duties of care and loyalty on authorized AIFMs. Specifically, it mandates that an AIFM (1) act honestly, with due skill, care and diligence and fairly in conducting its activities; (2) act in the best interests of the AIFs it manages, the investors in those AIFs and the integrity of the market; and (3) ensure that all AIF investors are treated fairly.[30] An AIFM must also take all reasonable steps to identify conflicts of interest and,[31] thereafter, maintain and operate effective organizational and administrative arrangements with a view to preventing these conflicts from adversely affecting the interests of

[23] Art. 5. [24] Art. 6, § 1.

[25] Either directly or via the establishment of a branch, subject to (1) the scope of its original authorization; (2) the communication of its intention to do so to the competent authorities in its home Member State; and (3) meeting the relevant procedural requirements; Art. 34, §§ 1-3.

[26] As defined in Annex II of MiFID; Art. 2, § 1. The Directive permits Member States to allow the marketing of securities of AIFs to retail investors within their territory and, for that purpose, to impose requirements on AIFMs and/or AIFs more strict than those imposed under the Directive; Art. 32, § 1.

[27] Again, subject to communicating its intention to do so to the competent authorities in its home Member State (who must then pass the information on to the competent authorities in the applicable host Member States), and meeting the relevant procedural requirements; Art. 33, §§ 1-2.

[28] Provided that, inter alia: (1) the Commission has determined that the legislation regarding prudential regulation and ongoing supervision in the relevant third-party country is equivalent to the Directive and effectively enforced; (2) the third-party jurisdiction has granted EU-domiciled AIFMs reciprocal market access; and (3) the supervisor of the AIFM has signed a cooperation agreement with the competent authorities of the relevant Member State; Art. 39, §§ 1 and 3. The EU has characterized this phase-in period as necessary to ensure appropriate controls and cooperation agreements are put in place to enable regulators to effectively supervise non-EU-domiciled AIFMs; FAQ, *supra* note 17.

[29] Alternatively, the Commission.

[30] This includes a prohibition against any undisclosed preferential treatment of investors; Art. 9, §§ 1(a)-(c).

[31] This includes conflicts (1) between an AIFM (including its managers, employees, and those able to exercise direct or indirect control) and AIF investors; and (2) between different AIF investors; Art. 10, § 1.

an AIF or its investors.[32] Where an AIFM identifies a material conflict of interest within its operations—or where it determines that its conflict arrangements are not sufficient to ensure with reasonable confidence that the interests of AIF investors will not be adversely affected—it must disclose this fact to AIF investors.[33]

The Directive mandates that an AIFM implement risk management systems designed to measure and monitor all risks to which the AIFs it manages may be exposed by virtue of their investment strategies.[34] This requirement contemplates, inter alia, (1) the implementation of an appropriate, documented and regularly updated due diligence process for making investments; (2) ensuring that risks can be accurately identified, measured and monitored through appropriate stress testing procedures;(3) ensuring that the risk profile of each AIF corresponds to its size, structure, investment strategies and objectives;[35] and (4) where an AIF engages in short selling, the implementation of procedures to manage the related risks.[36] The Directive also requires an AIFM to implement systems designed to manage liquidity risk (i.e. ensure adequate liquidity matching) and to conduct regular stress tests of these systems under both normal and exceptional market conditions.[37] It further requires the separation of portfolio and risk management functions—along with their respective review processes—within the operational environment of an AIFM.[38] These risk management requirements are augmented by a requirement that an AIFM implement remuneration policies that are consistent with and promote sound risk management.[39]

Lastly, the Directive imposes modest initial and ongoing capital requirements. All AIFMs are required to maintain own funds of at least €125,000.[40] In addition, where the aggregate portfolio value of the AIFs it manages exceeds €250 million, an AIFM must set aside supplemental capital equal to 0.02% of the amount by which the portfolio value exceeds the €250 million threshold. Accordingly, for an AIF with a portfolio value of €1 billion, an AIFM would be required to put aside capital totalling €275,000 (or 0.0275% of aggregate portfolio

[32] Art. 10, § 1. This is in fact a purposive interpretation of what, it must be said, is a tortured piece of legislative drafting which contemplates the maintenance of '*effective*' arrangements 'with a view to taking all *reasonable steps designed* to prevent conflicts of interest' (emphasis added). It remains to be seen how authorities will interpret the interplay between the requirement of effectiveness, the subsequent reasonableness qualifier, and the notion that the arrangements need only be 'designed' to prevent conflicts of interest.

[33] Art. 10, §§ 1-2. This is, once again, a purposive interpretation of an ambiguously drafted provision. Specifically, the Directive contemplates disclosure where an AIFM's conflict arrangements are 'not sufficient to ensure, with reasonable confidence, *that the risks of damage* to investors' interests will be *prevented*' (emphasis added). However, if one acknowledges that preventing *the risk* of damage is not the same thing as preventing the damage itself, this language is potentially inconsistent with the 'adverse effects' standard articulated in the same Article.

[34] Art. 11, § 2. [35] Art. 11, §§ 3(a)-(c).

[36] Art. 11, § 4. The Directive further provides that Member States shall ensure that an AIFM has in place procedures which provide it with access to securities/financial instruments on the date it is required to deliver them pursuant to any short selling arrangement.

[37] Art. 12, § 1. As a corollary, an AIFM must ensure that the redemption policy of each AIF it manages is appropriate given the liquidity profile of its portfolio assets; Art. 12, § 2.

[38] Art. 11, § 1.

[39] On 11 February 2013, the European Securities and Markets Authority (ESMA) published its final report and guidelines on sound remuneration requirements under AIFM; see <http://www.esma.europa.eu/system/files/2013-201.pdf>. The guidelines on sound remuneration policies took effect on 22 July 2013.

[40] Art. 14.

value). These capital requirements are subject to any higher obligations imposed under Article 21 of the Capital Requirements Directive[41] governing the capital adequacy of investment firms and credit institutions.

Perhaps not surprisingly given the broad nature of many of these requirements—to say nothing of the wide diversity of investment strategies, business models, conflicts of interest and other risks typically encountered in connection with different types of AIF—the Directive contemplates that the Commission will adopt level two implementing measures further specifying the precise substance of these requirements as they are intended to apply to each species of AIF.[42] Accordingly, it is in many respects too early to evaluate the precise impact of these requirements in terms of the day-to-day conduct and practices of AIFMs.

16.3.2 Third-Party Valuation and Safekeeping Requirements

The Directive requires that an AIFM appoint an independent third party to value both the portfolio assets of the AIFs it manages and their issued securities.[43] This valuation exercise must be undertaken at least once a year and on each occasion on which securities of an AIF are issued or redeemed.[44] An AIFM must also appoint a depositary for the purposes of, inter alia, (1) receiving subscription proceeds from AIF investors and depositing them into a segregated account; and (2) safekeeping AIF portfolio assets.[45] The depositary must be a credit institution having its registered office in the EU.[46] The depositary is required to act independently and solely in the interests of AIF investors and will be liable to the AIFM and AIF investors for any losses suffered by them as a result of its failure to perform its obligations pursuant to the Directive.[47]

16.3.3 Disclosure Requirements

The Directive lays down a series of initial, periodic, and event-driven disclosure requirements designed to enhance the transparency of AIF activities to investors, the competent authorities, and certain other stakeholder constituencies. An AIFM will be required to provide potential investors with, inter alia, a description of the relevant AIF's

[41] 2006/49/EC. [42] Art. 9, § 2; Art. 10, § 3; Art. 11, § 5, and Art. 12, § 3.

[43] Art. 16, § 1. Third-party valuators domiciled in jurisdictions outside the EU must be subject to regulatory standards equivalent to those applicable within the EU; Art. 37, § 1(b).

[44] Art. 16, § 1.

[45] Art. 17, §§ 1(a)-(c). Where an AIF is domiciled in a third country, Member States will allow it to delegate the performance of its functions to a sub-depositary in the same third country provided that the legislation of that third country is equivalent to the Directive and effectively enforced; Art. 38, § 1. Such sub-depositaries must also, inter alia, be (1) subject to effective prudential regulation and supervision which is equivalent to the relevant EU law, and (2) domiciled in jurisdictions where cooperation between the home Member State and the relevant authorities of the third country is sufficiently ensured; Art. 38, §§ 1(a)-(c).

[46] Art. 17, § 3. An AIFM cannot, however, act as a depositary; Art. 17, § 2.

[47] Art. 17, §§ 2 and 5.

(1) investment strategy and objectives;[48] (2) valuation and redemption policies; (3) valuation, custody, administration, and risk management procedures; and (4) fees, charges, and expenses.[49] Thereafter, an AIFM will be required to make available to investors on an annual basis an audited report containing the AIF's balance sheet, income statement, activity report and auditor's report.[50] An AIFM must also submit these annual reports to the competent authorities in its home Member State.[51] The Directive contemplates additional periodic disclosure to both investors and the competent authorities respecting (1) the percentage of AIF portfolio assets which are subject to special arrangements arising from their illiquid nature; (2) any new arrangements for managing liquidity; and (3) the current risk profile of each AIF and the systems employed by the AIFM to manage these risks.[52] An AIFM will also be required to provide aggregated information to the competent authorities on a regular basis respecting the principal markets and instruments in which its AIFs trade, their principal exposures, and important concentrations of risk.[53] In addition, an AIFM must report to the competent authorities the main categories of assets in which its AIFs are invested and, where relevant, the use of short selling.[54] The Directive contemplates that the Commission will adopt implementing measures which ensure that the nature and frequency of these periodic disclosures—or at least those targeted at investors—will be tailored to each species of AIF.[55]

Finally, the Directive imposes event-driven and subsequent periodic disclosure obligations on an AIFM in connection with the acquisition of a controlling interest in a company domiciled in the EU which employs more than 250 persons and has an annual turnover exceeding €50 million and a balance sheet exceeding €43 million.[56] An AIFM will be deemed to have acquired a 'controlling interest' if either it or any of the AIFs it manages holds, either individually or in the aggregate, 30% or more of the voting rights of the target company.[57] Where an AIFM acquires a controlling interest, it must make available to the company, its shareholders, and employees (or their representatives) certain prescribed information.[58] In addition, an AIFM must include in its annual report information pertaining to each company in which it holds a controlling interest. More specifically, the report must include information respecting, inter alia: (1) its operational and financial affairs; (2) any financial risks associated with its capital structure; (3) employee turnover, termination, and recruitment; and (4) any significant divestment of assets.[59]

[48] Including descriptions of (1) the permitted assets and techniques and their attendant risks; (2) any investment restrictions; and (3) the circumstances in which the AIF may use leverage and the types and sources of permitted leverage; Art. 20, § 1.

[49] Art. 20, § 1. [50] Art. 19, §§ 1-3. [51] Art. 21, § 3(a). [52] Art. 20, § 2 and Art. 21, § 2.

[53] Art. 21, § 1. [54] Art. 21, §§ 2(d)-(e). [55] Art. 20, § 3.

[56] Arts. 26-29. This provision applies to both listed and non-listed companies, and includes the conclusion of an agreement which would allow an acquisition.

[57] Art. 26, §§ 1(a)-(b).

[58] The nature of the information required will depend on whether the company is listed or non-listed; see Arts. 27-28.

[59] Art. 29.

16.3.4 Leverage Requirements

Last, but by no means least, the Directive empowers the Commission to set leverage requirements for AIFs where it deems them necessary to ensure the stability and integrity of the financial system.[60] It further empowers national authorities to restrict the use of leverage in respect of individual AIFMs and AIFs in exceptional circumstances.[61] The Directive mandates that an AIFM evaluate on a quarterly basis whether any of the AIFs it manages employ high levels of leverage on a systematic basis.[62] An AIF will be deemed to have met this test where its combined leverage from all sources exceeds the value of its equity capital in two out of the past four quarters.[63] Where an AIF exceeds this threshold, its manager must make prescribed disclosures to both AIF investors[64] and the competent authorities in its home Member State.[65]

16.4 The AIFM Directive: Some Preliminary Observations

There exists a theoretically strong informational argument in support of bringing many alternative investment funds and their managers within the perimeter of financial regulation. This argument is the strongest for hedge funds which, by and large, raise the most acute potential investor protection and market integrity problems and pose the greatest potential systemic risks.[66] At the same time, there is obvious informational utility in casting a somewhat broader net in recognition of the fact that institutions—and their attendant risks—can be expected to evolve over time. Direct public oversight of these institutions through authorization and suitably tailored regulatory reporting

[60] The Directive defines leverage broadly so as to encompass any method by which an AIFM increases the exposure of an AIF to a particular investment, whether through borrowing of cash or securities, leverage embedded in derivative positions, or any other means; Art. 3(1). The Directive contemplates that the Commission will adopt implementing measures setting limits on the leverage an AIFM can employ taking into account, inter alia, the type of AIF, its investment strategy, and sources of leverage; Art. 25, § 3.

[61] Provided they are temporary in nature and comply with the Commission's leverage limits; Art. 25, § 4.

[62] Art. 22.

[63] Art. 22, § 4.

[64] An AIFM managing an AIF with high levels of leverage on a systematic basis must disclose to investors (1) the maximum level of leverage which the AIFM may employ as well as the right of re-use of collateral or any guarantee granted under the leveraging arrangement; and (2) on a quarterly basis, the total amount of leverage employed in the preceding quarter; Art. 23.

[65] An AIFM must regularly provide to competent authorities information respecting the level of leverage and a breakdown between leverage arising from borrowed cash or securities and that embedded in financial derivatives; Art. 24, § 1. This information must include the identity of the five largest sources of borrowed cash or securities for each AIF and the amounts of leverage received; Art. 24, § 2.

[66] Indeed, if not for the EU's fixation with the problem of adequately defining what constitutes a 'hedge fund', I suspect that many of the provisions of the Directive would have been more directly targeted at hedge funds and their managers. It is perhaps revealing in this respect that the consultation paper which preceded the Directive was exclusively focused on the regulation—and definition—of hedge funds; see Commission Services Consultation Paper on Hedge Funds (18 December 2008).

requirements would provide competent authorities with information necessary to engage in more effective monitoring and, ultimately, develop a better understanding of, amongst other matters, their evolving micro-and macro-prudential risk profiles (McGuire and Tsataronis 2008).[67] Enhanced disclosure to investors, meanwhile, would promote more informed contracting and, potentially, bring an end to questionable industry practices such as the provision of investor 'side letters'.[68]

What is ultimately unclear, however, is the extent to which the informational requirements embedded within the AIFM Directive will represent a marked improvement over existing national regulatory regimes or prevailing market practices. The issue here is not whether the Directive violates the principle of subsidiarity per se, but rather whether it is likely to have any real world impact. By way of illustration, the UK is home to the vast majority of EU-domiciled hedge fund managers. In total, the FSA oversees roughly 85% of managers[69] exercising discretion over approximately 80% of European hedge fund assets.[70] The FSA has long collected data from these managers in the context of its day-to-day supervisory activities and through thematic reviews, targeted surveys and non-supervisory dialogue.[71] Simultaneously—and perhaps not surprisingly given the influence of sophisticated institutional investors on the demand side—the marketplace has exhibited some sensitivity to investor protection concerns as evidenced by, among other things, the voluntary provision of comprehensive pre-sale disclosure. The Alternative Investment Fund Management Association (AIFMA), for example, has developed a due diligence questionnaire for prospective hedge fund investors which has purportedly become widely used within the industry.[72] Ultimately, the effectiveness of these (and other) existing mechanisms for subsidizing the production of potentially salient information undermines the practical case for pan-European regulatory intervention.

The EU has similarly failed to make a persuasive case for why the Directive will enhance conduct of business or risk management practices. Once again, the FSA and other national regulators already impose conduct of business and risk management requirements on authorized advisers and managers. Many of these institutions are also subject to the Capital Requirements Directive. EU regulatory intervention is rendered even less of an imperative by the fact that regulators in many of these jurisdictions—including the German Federal

[67] The alternative to direct public oversight—at least with respect to hedge funds—is 'indirect' (i.e. market) oversight via these institutions' prime brokerage relationships. However, insofar as it has become common practice within the hedge fund industry to allocate business among multiple prime brokers, these institutions frequently possess information in respect of only a fraction of a fund's overall portfolio; Grabaravicius and Dierick (2005); King and Maier (2009); and US Government Accountability Office, 'Hedge Funds: Regulators and Market Participants Are Taking Steps to Strengthen Market Discipline, but Continued Attention Is Needed', Report to Congressional Requesters (January 2008), 7. In this respect, public regulators can be understood as potentially more effective aggregators—if not necessarily analysers—of salient information.

[68] Employed primarily within the hedge fund industry, side letters are agreements between a manager and one or more investors which vary the terms of the agreement (typically set out in an offering document) by which other investors agree to invest.

[69] PricewaterhouseCoopers, 'Changing Rules: The Regulation, Taxation and Distribution of Hedge Funds Around the Globe' (June 2009), 8.

[70] Treasury Letter, *supra* note 11, 1.

[71] See FSA Discussion Paper, *supra* note 10.

[72] See Morgan Stanley, Comment Letter in Response to the Commission Services Consultation Paper on Hedge Funds (30 January 2009), 2.

Ministry of Finance,[73] a strong supporter of the AIFM Directive—have acknowledged the robustness of hedge fund risk management practices relative to those of other market participants.[74] Indeed, that the hedge fund industry has developed relatively robust practices in this area should not come as a surprise: the high-powered incentives generated by the combination of a carried interest,[75] managerial co-investment,[76] and the reputational market for investment management services make it in the economic interests of managers to design and implement effective safeguards against excessive risk-taking in the vast majority of circumstances.[77]

Proponents counter with the assertion that the AIFM Directive will ensure a harmonized approach toward disclosure, conduct of business and risk management requirements. There are three relatively straightforward rejoinders to this argument. First, it is far from certain that harmonization represents the optimal approach toward the regulation of financial markets or institutions. The primary source of uncertainty in this regard stems from the prospective, if empirically contestable, benefits of regulatory competition.[78] Second, the EU's own Impact Assessment[79]—the relevant portion of which, at three pages, might charitably be described as perfunctory[80]—reveals not a striking diversity of substantive approaches among Member States toward the regulation of alternative investments (and hedge funds in particular) but, rather, a broadly consistent one.[81] What is more, as exemplified by the AIFMA due diligence questionnaire, private mechanisms have already helped to promote a form of de facto harmonization—and all without the bother or expense of direct regulatory intervention at the EU level. Third, and most importantly, harmonization at the EU level is

[73] German Federal Ministry of Finance, Comment Letter in Response to the Commission Services Consultation Paper on Hedge Funds (30 January 2009), 7 stating: 'In Germany the supervisory authority demands high risk management standards for hedge funds, which has in our view proven to be successful'.

[74] Treasury Letter, *supra* note 11, 9.

[75] The carried interest is a performance fee contingent upon the manager exceeding some preset minimum annual rate of return (or 'hurdle rate'). In the prototypical case, the manager will be entitled to a fee of 20% of the amount by which a fund's return exceeds a hurdle rate of between 8% and 8.5%. Payment of the fee is typically subject to a high watermark designed to ensure that the fee is only paid where the fund's cumulative performance has recovered from any previous shortfalls.

[76] Agarwal, Daniel, and Naik (2009) have estimated that managerial co-investment accounts for 7.1% of hedge fund assets, with the median manager owning 2.4% of the equity in their funds.

[77] Agarwal, Daniel, and Naik (2009); Shadab (2009); King and Maier (2008). The one obvious circumstance in which these incentives might fail to disincentivize excessive risk-taking is where a fund is underperforming close to the end of its term (and where, as a result, its manager might be tempted to 'shoot for the moon').

[78] For a recent restatement of the case for regulatory competition in the field of securities law, see Romano (2010).

[79] Commission Staff Working Document accompanying the AIFM Proposal (30 April 2009) 2009/576 (Impact Assessment).

[80] Commission Staff Working Document accompanying the AIFM Proposal (30 April 2009) 2009/576 (Impact Assessment), 15–17.

[81] The Impact Assessment reveals, for example, that all canvassed jurisdictions (1) have an existing regulatory regime governing hedge funds; (2) place constraints on distributions of hedge fund securities to retail investors; (3) require the authorization of hedge fund managers; and (4) impose capital requirements on hedge fund managers; Commission Staff Working Document accompanying the AIFM Proposal (30 April 2009) 2009/576 (Impact Assessment), 15–17. Oddly, the Impact Assessment only canvassed seven jurisdictions: the UK, France, Denmark, Luxembourg, Ireland, Italy, and Spain.

ultimately illusionary within the broader context of globally integrated financial markets. As examined in greater detail below, nowhere is this more readily apparent than in connection with the regulation of potential systemic risks.

A second overarching problem with the Directive stems from the decision to shoehorn an economically, strategically, and operationally diverse population of financial institutions into a single, artificial class of regulated actors. This decision has opened the door to some potentially cumbersome (even nonsensical) rulemaking. The third-party valuation and safekeeping requirements provide a representative example. There exists a strong case in favour of imposing such requirements on institutions which (1) invest in relatively liquid assets (i.e. marketable securities); (2) invest in markets with limited price transparency (i.e. over-the-counter derivatives markets); and/or (3) provide investors with liquidity in circumstances not contingent on the prior realization of portfolio assets. We might expect the majority of hedge funds, for example, to fall squarely into all three categories. In such circumstances, third-party valuation requirements would eliminate the conflict of interest arising where a manager compensated on the basis of assets under management exercises discretion over the valuation of investments for which there is no current, publicly available market price.[82] Safekeeping requirements, meanwhile, would serve to mitigate custody risk: ring-fencing client assets in the event of insolvency and thwarting Madoff-type frauds in which the opacity of an institution's investment activities—combined with the ease, speed, and anonymity with which portfolio assets can be liquidated—render it relatively straightforward for managers to make off with client money.[83]

It is far more difficult, however, to understand the rationale for imposing these requirements on, for example, private equity funds. The long-term, illiquid, and typically very public nature of the investments made by these institutions virtually eliminates the potential for Madoff-type fraud. Put differently, the observability and verifiability of investment and divestment (and thus potential defection) to both investors and the marketplace provides an extremely powerful disincentive for would-be fraudsters. This practical constraint obviates much of the regulatory justification for placing the underlying assets—share certificates in private companies in this case—with a depositary.[84] It is similarly difficult to identify the justification for third-party valuation requirements. As a starting point, arm's length valuators will invariably find themselves at a comparative disadvantage *vis-à-vis* private equity firms in terms of the production and verification of salient information respecting the value of portfolio investments. This disadvantage is a function of both the general expertise possessed by private equity firms in evaluating the type of asset in question and, more importantly, their substantial asset-specific investments in due diligence and ongoing monitoring. More importantly, however, the mechanics of private equity funds eliminate the latent conflict of interest at the heart of the valuation problem. Specifically, distributions to investors are typically triggered by the disposition of portfolio

[82] And where, as a result, the manager will be able to inflate its compensation by manipulating asset values around redemption windows.

[83] Although, in reality, safekeeping requirements are perhaps best understood as merely shifting the source of these potential risks to custodians.

[84] Although there may be an argument for employing depositaries in a narrower capacity as subscription agents.

investments (including via IPO).[85, 86] Investor liquidity is thus contingent upon prior disposition, which provides a credible (indeed, some might say definitive) third-party valuation of the asset. This link between investor liquidity and disposition also makes it difficult to understand how the liquidity risk management and related disclosure requirements set out in the Directive would apply to private equity funds (or, indeed, most other alternative investments). It is equally difficult to understand precisely what regulatory objectives the imposition of these requirements on such funds would ultimately serve. The Directive is, unfortunately, awash in such ambiguities.

The EU has conceded that many of the core provisions of the Directive will need to be tailored to reflect different species of alternative investment fund. Indeed, it has gone so far as to acknowledge—without offering any specifics—that some of these provisions may 'make no sense' for certain types of funds.[87] It is the EU's view, however, that these more detailed, bespoke rules can and will be fleshed out in the process of formulating level 2 implementing measures, technical standards, and guidelines. The EU anticipates this process will take up to two years.[88] Here we find another curious policy choice. Citing the need to 'proceed quickly' in response to the GFC, the EU dramatically curtailed its normal consultation processes in connection with the formulation of the Directive.[89] Furthermore, at the time of this abridged consultation, the scope of the EU's proposal was expressly limited to hedge funds. Clearly, however, by electing to defer the articulation of many substantive requirements to the post-adoption rulemaking phase, the EU has now effectively negated any potential benefits to be derived from a swift regulatory response. Simultaneously, by expediting the consultation process (and then dramatically expanding the scope of the Directive), EU regulators have failed to effectively leverage the vast wealth of available technical expertise—expertise that would have undoubtedly helped to resolve many of the issues with which they must now grapple. In the short term, wrestling with these technical issues will consume precious time and other resources. In the long term, and more broadly, the Directive's myopic focus on the object of regulatory intervention—rather than the objectives of it—seems an unlikely strategy for generating effective regulation.

Nowhere is the nearsightedness of the AIFM Directive more clearly reflected than in its approach toward the amelioration of potential systemic risks.[90] There are at least four

85 That is to say, there are no periodic redemption windows enabling investors to withdraw money at their discretion. In general, this serves to distinguish hedge funds (which often allow for periodic redemptions) from other alternative investment vehicles.

86 It is also arguably the case that valuation is unnecessary in connection with the issuance of fund securities. This is certainly true at the time of initial closing (at which point the fund is in effect a blind pool and where, as a result, the aggregate value of the issued securities is equal to the subscription proceeds less any expenses accruing at the fund level). While the situation becomes somewhat more complicated where the fund raises capital through any subsequent closings, mechanisms typically exist in respect of such closings to ensure that all investors (both 'new' and 'old') are treated equally on a retrospective basis.

87 AIFM Proposal, *supra* note 21, 5.

88 See Letter from the Director General (2 December 2010), provisionally requesting advice on level 2 implementing measures, available at <http://ec.europa.eu/internal_market/investment/alternative_investments_en.htm#level2>.

89 See statement available at <http://ec.europa.eu/internal_market/consultations/2008/hedge_funds_en.htm>. The consultation period was cut to a mere eight weeks.

90 There is arguably no single, universally accepted definition of 'systemic risk'. Andrew Lo, however, provides a useful working definition: 'the risk of a broad-based meltdown in the financial system, often

channels through which alternative investment funds could, theoretically, undermine financial stability. The first and most straightforward channel would be through the failure of a fund (or group of funds) which was itself systemically important. Second, the failure of a fund (or funds) could destabilize a systemically important financial institution connected to the fund(s) by virtue of its ownership, prime brokerage and/or other counterparty relationships (Grabaravicius and Dierick 2005). Third, where a critical mass of funds coalesced to exploit the same opportunities within the same markets, simultaneous selling by these funds could—given the right circumstances—undermine market liquidity, exacerbate market volatility, and potentially precipitate wider financial instability (Lo 2008). Finally, the collapse of a fund (or funds) could trigger a forced liquidation of portfolio assets (King and Maier 2009). Depending on the size of the liquidated positions relative to the liquidity of the underlying market, a disorderly 'fire sale' could put significant downward pressure on prices—imposing substantial losses on (systemically important) counterparties and weakening the balance sheets of other (systemically important) financial institutions via mark-to-market accounting requirements (King and Maier 2009). However improbable, it is thus not inconceivable that the adverse effects of fund failure could reverberate throughout the global financial system.

The primary means by which the AIFM Directive attempts to address these risks is through the imposition of leverage constraints. Importantly, the EU is the only strategically significant jurisdiction to restrict the use of leverage by alternative investment funds. This includes the US—long home to the largest and most influential segment of the global alternative investment fund industry.[91] Broadly speaking, the rationale behind leverage constraints is that they reduce the probability of fund failure—in effect by making funds less sensitive to market fluctuations and, thus, less susceptible to margin and/or collateral calls which might trigger a forced liquidation of portfolio assets.[92] Implicit within this rationale is also the belief that—owing both to competitive forces within the prime brokerage industry and the status of financial stability as a public good—private counterparty credit risk management is unlikely to represent a comprehensive response to potential systemic risks.

This logic is not necessarily incorrect—but it is incomplete. As a preliminary matter, granting regulators the authority to change leverage constraints mid-course would appear to be a recipe for systemic instability insofar as the industry-wide (and inherently correlated) portfolio rebalancing thereby triggered might come to mimic the very fire sales which the EU is ostensibly attempting to prevent.[93] The key insight, however, is derived

realized as a series of correlated defaults among financial institutions, typically banks, that occurs over a short period of time and typically caused by a single major event'; Lo, *supra* note 12, 3-4.

[91] Title IV of the Dodd-Frank Wall Street Reform and Consumer Protection Act, Pub. Law. No. 111-203 (2010) (Dodd-Frank Act) does impose, inter alia, registration, recordkeeping and regulatory reporting requirements on many so-called 'private funds' and 'private advisers', categories broadly—if not completely—analogous to AIFs and AIFMs, respectively. The Dodd-Frank Act also contemplates that the US Federal Reserve can extend its regulatory powers to cover financial institutions which pose a potential threat to financial stability (which might include, for example, large, highly leveraged hedge funds).

[92] Thus simultaneously reducing financing risk (for the fund), counterparty credit risk (for the fund's counterparties) and systemic risk (for the rest of us). It is worthwhile noting, however, that all this assumes that what is being constrained is economic leverage (not, for example, accounting or balance sheet leverage).

[93] Setting aside the potential systemic repercussions, it is not difficult to see how a downward shift in leverage constraints could put funds investing in illiquid assets in a very difficult position *vis-à-vis* their portfolio assets and, ultimately, their investors.

from understanding that the transmission of systemic risks through each of the channels described above is in no way impeded by geopolitical boundaries. In a world of globally integrated financial markets and institutions, the failure of a US hedge fund will have the same systemic impact as the failure of an otherwise similarly situated EU-domiciled fund. As a result, the EU cannot insulate itself from the systemic repercussions arising from the failure of an alternative investment fund operating outside the reach of the AIFM Directive. The EU thus faces a bleak calculus: while it will bear all of the direct and indirect costs of attempting to address systemic risks, the benefits thereby generated will be negligible insofar as it will remain exposed to negative externalities stemming from the failure or refusal of other jurisdictions to adopt equivalent measures (Awrey 2011: 153). Simultaneously, any benefits will, at least in part, spill over to these other jurisdictions. Furthermore, relatively onerous leverage or other requirements serve to provide EU-domiciled managers with a marginal incentive to (re)locate their businesses offshore.[94] From the perspective of the EU (or any other jurisdiction for that matter), systemic risk regulation thus represents a bundle of potentially significant costs without the realistic prospect of any corresponding benefits. It is for this reason that a globally coordinated response to potential systemic risks is not only desirable, but an imperative.

16.5 Is the AIFM Directive a Harbinger of Things to Come?

The AIFM Directive was the product of a highly politicized process pitting the UK (and its substantial domestic financial services sector) against many of its Continental neighbours.[95] This process played out in the context of a broader power shift within the EU away from national financial regulators such as the FSA and toward three newly created pan-European institutions: the European Banking Authority, European Insurance and Occupational Pensions Authority, and European Securities and Markets Authority (ESMA). Brought into existence on 1 January 2011, it is ESMA which will ultimately be responsible for the administration of the Directive.

Understanding the Directive as the product of not only a policy process, but also a political one, serves to shed considerable light on many of its apparent shortcomings. For example, viewed from this perspective, the Directive can be understood not as a response to any perceived deficiency in existing national regulatory regimes or market practices but, alternatively, as an attempt to expand the scope of the EU's authority within the field of financial regulation. Similarly, the Directive's focus on the object of regulation, rather than its objectives, can be viewed as reflecting a desire on the part of some Member States—Germany and France key among them—to identify a suitable scapegoat for the excesses of Anglo-Saxon capitalism which they and many of their constituents perceive as having, amongst other

[94] Whether this marginal incentive will translate into a meaningful migration of business offshore is a complex issue requiring further empirical investigation and which, in any event, resides well beyond the scope of this chapter.

[95] See *Financial Times* (2010b, c, d, e, f, g); *Wall Street Journal* (2010).

things, precipitated the GFC.[96] That these Member States historically had been unable to compete with the UK in the financial services sector made the economic calculus almost as straightforward as the political one. Finally, the EU's relatively aggressive stance in terms of the imposition of leverage constraints and other requirements can be viewed as a laudable (if ill-fated) attempt to influence the direction of international reforms designed to mitigate systemic risks within the shadow banking sector. In each of these respects, it may ultimately not have been that EU policymakers had their heads in the sand so much as they were attempting to draw a line in it.

So is the AIFM Directive a harbinger of things to come? Potentially yes. The EU is already leading the charge to reform corporate governance and remuneration practices within financial institutions.[97] It also recently announced its intention to crack down on speculation within commodities markets, which it views as having contributed to excessive volatility in food prices.[98] Both of these initiatives have what might be characterized as a decidedly Continental flavour. Like the AIFM Directive, neither of these proposed reforms have been met with open arms outside the EU. If this emergent trend continues, the fragile consensus reflected in the G20 Communiqué will inevitability unravel. If it does, we will have failed to heed one of the most important lessons of the GFC.

16.6 Conclusion

It is in many respects still too early to pass definitive judgment on the AIFM Directive. The vast majority of its substantive requirements remain to be fleshed out through the articulation of level 2 implementing measures, technical standards and guidelines. The ESMA would be well advised to seek out and meaningfully engage with the alternative investment fund industry as part of this process. More broadly, it remains to be seen how the fledgling ESMA will grow into its new role as pan-European securities regulator. Will it soar on the wings of its substantial new powers? Or will it crash back down to earth under the weight of its broad remit and anaemic resources? Despite this lingering uncertainty, it is possible to make two important, if cautious, observations. First, the real world benefits flowing from the adoption of the Directive are—at best—unclear. Many of its requirements will likely mirror existing national regulatory regimes and/or prevailing market practices. Others, meanwhile, and in particular those aimed at ameliorating potential systemic risks, are simply not fit for purpose. Second, the adoption of the Directive was likely motivated as much by politics as by policy. In the end, neither observation generates much cause for optimism.

[96] Indeed, as the quotes from German and French politicians at the outset of this chapter suggest, Germany and France (along with countries like the Netherlands, Denmark, and Sweden) voiced concerns about the adverse impact of hedge funds and private equity funds on their domestic financial markets (and markets for corporate control) well in advance of the GFC; see Callum McCarthy, 'Hedge Funds: What Should be the Regulatory Response?', speech to the European Money and Finance Forum (6 December 2007).

[97] See note 39.

[98] See 'The Commission Calls for Action on Commodities and Raw Materials', IP/11/122 (2 February 2011). See also *Wall Street Journal* (2011).

References

Agarwal, V., Daniel, N., and Naik, N. (2009). Role of Managerial Incentives and Hedge Fund Performance, *Journal of Finance* 64(5), 2221–56.

Awrey, D. (2011). The FSA, Integrated Regulation and the Curious Case of OTC Derivatives, *University of Pennsylvania Journal of Business Law* 13(1), 39–43.

Boyson, N. M., Stahel, C. W., and Stulz, R. M. (2010). Hedge Fund Contagion and Liquidity Shocks, *Journal of Finance* 55(5), 1789–816.

Briggs, T. (2007). Corporate Governance and the New Hedge Fund Activism, *Journal of Corporation Law* 32, 681–723.

Chan, N., Getmansky, M., Haas, S., and Lo, A. (2007). Systemic Risk in Hedge Funds, in M. Carey and R. Stulz (eds.), *The Risks of Financial Institutions* (Chicago, University of Chicago Press), 235–330.

Financial Times (2010a). Hedge Fund Rules Defended by French MEP, *Financial Times* (16 May).

Financial Times (2010b). Germany Pushes UK on Hedge Fund Rules, *Financial Times* (17 Mar.).

Financial Times (2010c). UK Suffers Hedge Fund Blow, *Financial Times* (13 May).

Financial Times (2010d). Hedge Fund Rules Defended by French MEP, *Financial Times* (16 May).

Financial Times (2010e). Ministers Push for EU Hedge Fund Rules, *Financial Times* (17 May).

Financial Times (2010f). Haggling Over Legislation is Far From Over, *Financial Times* (18 May).

Financial Times (2010g). New Regulations for Hedge Funds, *Financial Times* (10 Oct.).

Grabaravicius, T. and Dierick, F. (2005). Hedge Funds and Their Implications for Financial Stability, European Central Bank Occasional Paper No. 34, available at <http://www.ecb.int/pub/pdf/scpops/ecbocp34.pdf>.

King, M. and Maier, P. (2009). Hedge Funds and Financial Stability: Regulating Prime Brokers will Mitigate Systemic Risk, *Journal of Financial Stability* 5, 283–97.

Lipton, M. (2006). Shareholder Democracy: Battling for Corporate America, *The Economist* (9 Mar.).

Lo, A. (2008). *Hedge Funds: An Analytical Perspective* (Princeton, Princeton University Press).

McGuire, P. and Tsataronis, K. (2008). Estimating Hedge Fund Leverage, Bank for International Settlements Working Paper No. 260 (Sept.).

Pozsar, Z., Adrian, T., Ashcraft, A., and Boesky, H. (2010). Shadow Banking, Federal Reserve Bank of New York Staff Reports No. 458 (July).

Romano, R. (2010). Against Financial Regulation Harmonization: A Comment, Yale Law & Economics Research Paper No. 414 (22 Nov.).

Shadab, H. (2009). The Law and Economics of Hedge Funds, *Berkeley Business Law Journal* 6(2), 240–97.

Time (2005). The Day of the Locusts, *Time* (15 May).

Wall Street Journal (2010). Osborne's Pyrrhic Victory, *Wall Street Journal* (15 July).

Wall Street Journal (2011). Regulating Commodity Speculation Back in EU Spotlight, *Wall Street Journal* (2 Feb.).

CHAPTER 17

RECASTING PRIVATE EQUITY FUNDS AFTER THE FINANCIAL CRISIS: THE END OF 'TWO AND TWENTY' AND THE EMERGENCE OF CO-INVESTMENTS AND SEPARATE ACCOUNTS

JOSEPH A. McCAHERY
AND
ERIK P. M. VERMEULEN

17.1 Introduction

Why has the alternative asset sector been subject to less regulatory scrutiny than the broader financial sector? Prior research provides insights into the contractual mechanisms that protect investors and compensation arrangements (also known as 'two and twenty') as the most effective means to align the interests of fund managers and private equity investors (Fleischer 2008; Litvak 2009; Metrick and Yasuda 2010). However, scholars are increasingly redirecting their attention towards basic questions regarding the optimal level of regulatory intervention in the alternative asset market. The global turbulence in credit markets, triggered by the turmoil in the subprime mortgage market in the United States in 2007–08, brought an end to the private equity bonanza as well as the laissez-faire era in the alternative asset sector. In response, governments introduced legislation subjecting fund managers to registration requirements and provisions targeted at improving fund monitoring and accountability.

According to analysts, the economic downturn has had a severe impact on all aspects of the private equity industry. Yet, if we compare the total amount of cash raised by private equity funds on a global scale in 2005 and 2012, the industry has not changed significantly. According to available data (Preqin 2013a), the aggregate annual fundraising amount in 2005 was $362 billion. In 2012 this amount was $373 billion. What has changed dramatically is that the economic downturn has affected the level of private equity fundraising and investment activity,[1] particularly in Europe. Market forces also continue to alter the dynamics of the private equity market. It is estimated that there were 601 funds in the market in 2005 (Preqin 2013a). By 2013, there were more than 2,000 funds engaged in fundraising activities, and it is evident that the economic downturn unleashed a wave of fierce competition among private equity funds. The increase in the average time to the final closing of a fund, which was approximately 11.3 months in 2006 and 17.8 months in 2012, is clear evidence of the competition in the private equity industry. The second important change is the increased scrutiny of private equity funds by regulators and policymakers, but also by investors (especially in the area of compensation arrangements) (Mulcahy, Weeks, and Bradley 2012).

From this discussion arises the question of what can be done to increase investors' interest in private equity while at the same time increase managerial responsibility. If we focus on Europe, reliance on a regulatory overhaul has been the core response to the effect of the financial crisis on the private equity industry. Having assumed that interventions should aim at increasing transparency towards investors and stakeholders, the regulators' approach has been to introduce a set of harmonized rules and regulations imposing stringent registration and reporting requirements for alternative investment fund advisers/managers. These regulations seek to reduce the systemic risk emerging from the operation of private equity funds and promote the stability and efficiency of the financial markets. The Alternative Investment Fund Managers Directive (AIFMD) offers a good example of these regulatory initiatives.

So, what can we expect from the post-financial crisis's legal and regulatory interventions? There is no easy answer. The response can be separated into two different categories. At the one extreme, many have argued that the AIFMD addresses the inconsistencies and gaps that currently exist in the fragmented European regulatory framework, thereby reducing risks and stimulating growth for EU fund managers. At another extreme, others expect that the AIFMD will increase costs and create regulatory uncertainty (Burrows 2013a). Some argue that the regulatory burden is overwhelming. For example, the one-off costs are estimated to range from $300,000 to over $1 million (Wang 2013). Indeed, the concern over high costs is likely to deter non-EU fund managers from offering portfolios to European investors and induce EU fund managers to shift offshore (Marriage 2013). The result might be that the AIFMD will significantly crowd out private equity investments that are (particularly in a declining stock market) necessary to create economic stability and jobs. In fact, there is some regulatory support for the latter view. The architects of the AIFMD have acknowledged that strict application of the stringent and costly rules and regulations would be detrimental to the formation of smaller private equity funds (that often operate as venture capital providers). As a consequence, the AIFMD includes certain exemptions applicable to venture capital funds.[2]

[1] See also State Street (2013). 82% of 391 alternative investment managers indicated that fundraising would be the most challenging activity over the next five years.

[2] See Articles 3(2), 16(1), 21(3) second subparagraph, and 26(2)(a) of the AIFMD.

Against this background, there is a general belief that the AIFMD will negatively impact the private equity industry in Europe. However, we take a different view. Those expecting a nightmare (or a miracle) from the AIFMD should not hold their breath. In the end, it is highly questionable whether the proposed regulatory initiatives will form the basis of a coherent and effective regulatory regime that sufficiently protects the interests of most sophisticated investors. For this reason, we predict that the AIFM label will just become a necessary 'boilerplate' formality to raise funds in the future. In fact, we already observe that most private equity funds take measures to deal with the regulatory requirements of the AIFMD by either enhancing their back office capacity or outsourcing their compliance units to specialized consultants (Duffel 2013).

The question that remains is: will the AIFMD make fundraising more efficient? The experience of fundraising during the financial crisis suggests that the fundraising levels per private equity fund will continue to lag behind the pre-financial crisis levels in Europe. Recent empirical evidence shows (Preqin 2013b) a number of trends in private equity finance and investments in the post-financial crisis era. One development is immediately noteworthy: the 'survival of the fittest' trend. To be sure, there are signs of a fundraising recovery in 2013 (Winfrey 2013). However, only high-quality funds with impeccable track records seem able to attract new investors. The results are clear. Another trend is the significant decline in the number of successful closings of private equity funds in the post-financial crisis era (and there are no indications that this trend will change any time soon).

In this chapter, we focus not only on the value of the AIFMD's new secondary reporting and transparency requirements, but also on the other factors that may influence investors to commit funds to private equity investment. This approach is supported by the evidence that compensation arrangements in private equity agreements between investors and fund managers may require updating and retooling in order to better deal with the high degree of information asymmetries. Although the literature has followed the pre-crisis trends, our evidence shows that investors are demanding the inclusion of more investor-favourable compensation terms and conditions in private equity fund agreements. Thus, the benefits ascribed to the new contractual terms provide investors with more favourable management fee and profit distribution arrangements, but also give them more control over a fund's investment decisions (Donato 2011), as well as more straightforward co-investment rights (Favas 2013).

In addition to examining the role of investor-favourable terms and the impact of such provisions on benefits for limited partners, this chapter also studies the extent to which general partners have more skin in the game as a natural market reaction to the pre-crisis transactions, where they had little skin in the game. The economic reasoning behind top-performing general partners making significant capital contributions to their own funds is that managers' interests can be better aligned with those of investors.

This chapter is divided into four sections. Section 17.2 briefly describes the regulatory measures introduced by the European AIFMD. We also address the exemptions to the AIFMD. Section 17.3 begins with a discussion of the traditional contractual framework that governs fund formation and operation, management fees and expenses, profit sharing and distributions, and corporate governance. It then discusses how the practice of private equity contracting is changing in the post-financial crisis era, making the dominant compensation arrangements obsolete (Private Equity International 2013a). Section 17.4 concludes.

17.2 The Regulatory Infrastructure of the Private Equity Industry in Europe

17.2.1 The Pros and Cons of Private Equity Regulation in Europe

In economics jargon, the private equity market is replete with information asymmetries. There is inevitably a high degree of information asymmetry between the fund managers, who play a relatively active role in the development (or restructuring) and growth of portfolio companies, and the passive investors, who are not able to closely monitor the prospects of each individual company. To be sure, national 'private placement' rules and regulations often offer some protection to investors. Here, private placement is understood as the marketing and sale of 'investment interests' in private equity funds to a limited number of professional investors, such as institutional investors and wealthy individuals. However, the downside of the application of these rules is that attracting investors significantly increases the compliance costs and fundraising complications. This is particularly true in Europe, where the regulatory systems of the member states are still fragmented and only partly harmonized.

In a controversial move, European regulators introduced a directive that (if implemented properly) will enable fund managers to obtain a European passport. A possible solution to the regulatory barriers of setting up a Europe-wide fund is to allow fund managers to ask for a European registration in the home member state, which would then automatically be mutually recognized in other member states. The application of a harmonized and uniform regulation that would govern the marketing and sale of 'investment interests' in private equity funds should make it easier for—and provide incentives to—investors to participate in foreign funds. The passport system would help defragment the private equity market, allegedly resulting in more cross-border oriented private equity funds. In the next section, we will turn to the AIFMD and explain the arguments in favour of and against this type of regulation in Europe.

17.2.2 The Alternative Investment Fund Managers Directive (AIFMD)

The AIFMD provides a marketing passport for managers of Alternative Investment Funds (AIFs) that fall outside the scope of the Undertakings for Collective Investment in Transferable Securities (UCITS) Directive, such as hedge funds, private equity funds and real estate funds. The rationale behind the AIFMD is to develop a uniform set of rules and regulations for AIFs that protect investors and other market participants. AIF managers that comply with the rules of the Directive and have obtained the 'passport' will be allowed to manage or market funds to professional investors throughout the European Union. Since AIF managers' decisions affect investors in different member states, the AIFMD aims to introduce a comprehensive and secure regulatory framework that ensures proper monitoring and prudential oversight of alternative investments that pose systemic risk. Strict rules on transparency and disclosure, valuation, risk and liquidity management, the use of leverage, remuneration, conflicts of interest, and the acquisition of companies are expected to enhance public accountability and the protection of investors (see also Table 17.1). In order to further reduce the problems arising from information asymmetries, the AIFMD requires the AIF's assets to be safe-kept by an independent depositary, which is subject to high liability standards.

We conjecture that the strict application of the stringent (and costly) AIFMD rules is likely to have a decreasing effect on the supply of private equity, thereby seriously hampering the working of the private equity cycle. Not surprisingly, therefore, the AIFMD contains certain

Table 17.1 The AIFMD in a nutshell

Categories of rules	AIFMD
Authorization and/or Registration Procedures	All AIFMs managing AIFs must apply for authorization with the authorities of their home MS (Art. 6 and 7 AIFMD). Disclosure of information concerning the AIFM, its members/shareholders, the managers of the AIFM, the program of activity and structure of the AIFM, remuneration policies and delegation/sub-delegation of functions (Art. 7(2) AIFMD), the AIFs, their investment strategies, leverage policies, risk profiles, countries of establishment, instruments of incorporation, appointment of depositaries and the additional information of Art. 23(1) AIFMD (Art. 7(3) AIFMD).
Initial Capital and Own Funds	For internally managed AIFs: at least €300,000 (Art. 9(1) AIFMD). For AIFs with an external manager: at least €125,000 (Art. 9(2) AIFMD). If the value of the portfolios managed by the AIFM exceeds €250 million: additional amount equal to 0.02% of the value of the difference between €250 million and the total value of the portfolios of AIFs managed by such AIFM (Art. 9(3) AIFMD).
Operating Conditions	(i) Fiduciary duties of AIFMs towards AIFs and their investors; (ii) restrictive remuneration policies; (iii) duty to identify, prevent and disclose conflicts of interest; (iv) duty to establish effective risk management systems; (v) strict rules on valuation and appointment of an internal/external valuer; (vi) strict rules on delegation/sub-delegation of functions; (vii) appointment of depositary for each AIF whose function's delegation is restricted (Arts. 12 to 21 AIFMD).
Transparency Requirements	(i) Audited annual report with audited financial statements for each managed AIF, to be disclosed to each of AIF's investors and to authorities of home MS of the AIFM (and of the AIF if applicable); (ii) pre-investment disclosure towards prospective investors of all material information items concerning the managed AIF; and, (iii) regular reporting duties to authorities of AIFM's home MS on the markets and instruments in which it deals and the principal exposures and most important concentrations of each managed AIF (Arts. 22 to 24 AIFMD).
Rules on Fund Managers Managing Specific Types of AIFs	Exemption of AIFMs managing AIFs that acquire control of non-listed companies that are SMEs (Art. 26(2)(a) AIFMD). AIFMs managing VC funds exempted.

exemptions that are applicable to smaller funds.[3] Article 3(2) states that, besides certain registration and notification duties, the AIFMD does not apply to (a) AIF managers which either directly or indirectly (through a company with which the AIF manager is linked by common management or control, or by a substantive direct or indirect holding) manage portfolios of AIFs whose assets under management, including any assets acquired through use of leverage, in total do not exceed a threshold of €100 million; or (b) AIF managers which either directly or indirectly (through a company with which the AIFM is linked by common management or control, or by a substantive direct or indirect holding) manage portfolios of AIFs whose assets under management in total do not exceed a threshold of €500 million, provided that the AIFs are unleveraged and do not provide for redemption rights exercisable during a period of five years following the date of initial investment in these AIFs.[4]

It should be noted that if investors are to benefit from the harmonizing effect of the proposed regulatory measures, we would expect an increase in investor confidence and interest in the private equity industry throughout the European Union. More specific details on the state of the trends in the private equity industry emerge from an examination of fundraising. Data provider Preqin observed that the aggregate amount of capital raised by funds closed was $78 billion in 2012, which is more than the $62.4 billion in 2011 and $58.9 billion in 2010 (Preqin 2012). It is striking, however, to observe that the number of private equity funds that had a final closing declined, from 414 in 2007 to 110 in 2012 (see Figure 17.1). Note that this trend continued into early 2013, but ended with a sharp upturn in fundraising during the second quarter of the year. While this increase reflects renewed confidence in markets, closer scrutiny of the deal volume (463 deals announced, with an aggregate deal value of $37 billion in Q2 2013), suggests that general partners will most likely find fundraising hard going in the future unless they can effectively locate new investments with significant aggregate deal value. Here it should be noted, however, that high-quality funds appear to receive continuous funding for their investment activities. This is confirmed by data derived from Dow Jones LP Source (which is based on multiple closings). The result is that the median fund size has significantly increased in Europe (see Table 17.2).

This brings us to the question whether it is reasonable to expect that financial governance reforms, such as the AIFMD, can stimulate private sector investments in the private equity industry. Does the Directive deal with the key investment issues? Attempts to answer this question have generated a great deal of discussion in the literature. On the one hand, optimists will argue that the AIFMD label will not only help reduce uncertainty and information asymmetry in the industry, but also provide an international stamp of quality. If they are correct, institutional and other investors will be more inclined to invest again in private equity (and not only high-quality funds). We claim, however, that the improved fundraising view is too optimistic. Our view is supported by a recent empirical study conducted by data

[3] In October 2013, the European Securities and Markets Authority (ESMA) published its final guidelines on the disclosure requirements for AIFMs.

[4] The AIFMD provisions deviate slightly from the registration measures introduced by the Dodd-Frank Act in the United States. The US counterpart of the AIFMD significantly extended the registration requirements under the Investment Advisers Act of 1940 to include advisers of private funds, such as hedge funds and private equity funds. The rationale behind the Dodd-Frank Act is, similarly to the AIFMD, to reduce financial market failures or systemic risk. Venture capital funds are exempted, because they do not threaten the stability and continuity of the financial system.

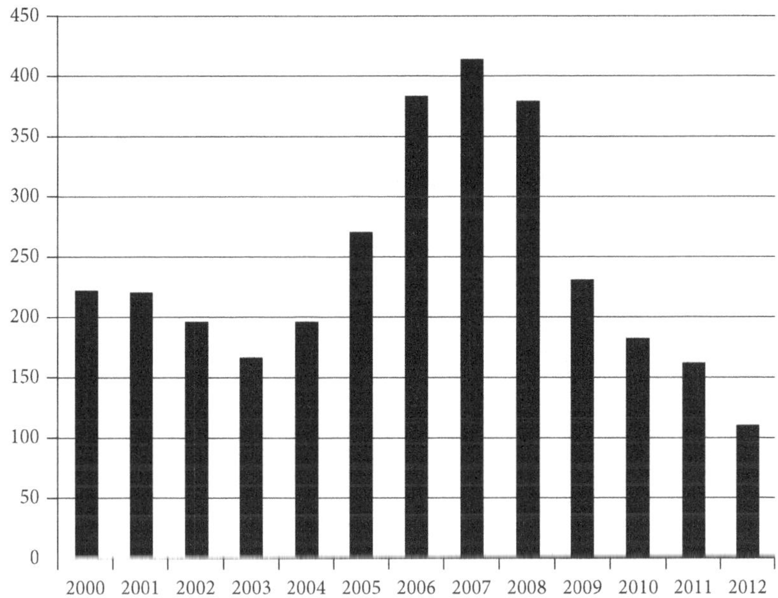

FIGURE 17.1 Closings of private equity funds in Europe
Source: Preqin.

Table 17.2 Private equity fundraising in Europe (based on multiple closings)

	Funds raised			Number of funds			Median fund size		
	2011	2012		2011	2012		2011	2012	
United States	$133.2b	$160.4b	+20%	453	426	−6%	$250m	$310m	+24%
Europe	$59.2b	$58.1b	−2%	182	157	−14%	$207m	$300m	+45%

Source: Dow Jones LPSource

provider Preqin (2013c). The study shows that only 19% of the 450 responding private equity investors (42% of the respondents were European investors and 40% were located in the United States) expected a positive impact from regulatory initiatives, such as the AIFMD. Not only did 41% state that an increasingly regulatory approach would not benefit the industry, but another 40% were still unsure.

In addition to showing that European investors are not overly optimistic about the benefits of regulation aimed at contributing governance improvements to the operation and efficiency of funds, the data indicates that, in order to deal more effectively with the post-financial crisis challenges of uncertainty, information asymmetry, and opportunism, investors in private equity funds are becoming tougher in negotiating the terms and conditions of the funds (Burrows 2013b; Preqin 2013a, b, c). Predictably, the more active approach of investors is likely to bring about a cultural change in the private equity industry. We already see a trend towards the demand of greater clarity in private equity fund terms. In our assessment, investors increasingly prefer to invest in private equity funds that are willing to better accommodate their specific concerns, particularly related to co-investment rights and compensation arrangements and disclosures. Potentially, the emergence and standardization of new disruptive contractual practices in the private equity industry will lead to their being adopted quickly to ensure better firm performance and productivity. The next section will provide an overall assessment of the changing fundraising landscape in more detail.

17.3 The Contractual Infrastructure of the Private Equity Industry

In Europe and elsewhere, the limited partnership form (or an equivalent flexible business form) is the dominant legal vehicle used in private equity structuring. The popularity of this form is due to its contractual nature that allows the internal and external participants to reduce opportunism and agency costs. Indeed, the limited partnership structure permits fund managers (general partners) to achieve extensive control over the operation of their funds subject to few intrusive legal obligations. Other features, such as tax benefits, the flexibility surrounding its structure and terms, and its fixed life, contribute to its continuing viability as the business form of choice for collective investment vehicles. The limited partnership has other important advantages as well. First, it is familiar to most investors and intermediaries, which contributes to its enduring popularity. Second, there is a risk that other business forms, operating internationally, could be treated as a non-transparent foreign entity and taxed as a corporate body.

In order to obtain fees and shield individual managers from the liabilities of the fund, two entities are usually created: a limited partnership and a management company, which is generally organized as a corporation. Moreover, the management company is either a separate entity from the general partner or affiliated with one of the general partners, or is a subsidiary of a bank or insurance company and, accordingly, will exercise effective control over the limited partnership. With a management company, the day-to-day management is separated from the fund, which may assist in resolving some tax issues while limiting doing business and other concerns.

We have seen that the flexibility of the limited partnership plays a critical role in aligning the interests of venture capitalists and investors. This brings us to the contractual provisions that are typically employed by private equity investors in Europe (as well as in the United States).

17.3.1 Private Equity Contracting and Compensation Arrangements

The relationship between the limited partners and general partners is, as we have seen, usually characterized as a principal–agent relationship. In order to make this work, legal practice tends to include boilerplate clauses in the limited partnership agreement that are designed to reduce agency costs by aligning the incentives of the general partners with the interests of the investors. The boilerplate arrangements in private equity limited partnerships can roughly be split into three separate categories: (1) fund formation and operation provisions, such as limits on the fundraising period, the lifespan of the fund, and the required managers' contribution; (2) management fees and carried interest; and (3) the governance structure to ensure that the fund is organized and managed in the most effective manner.

For example, a fund's duration is usually ten years with a five-year investment period, making it possible for investors to estimate with reasonable accuracy when the private equity firm can make fresh investments and, most importantly, when they ultimately will be able to recover their investments, including profits. In order to align the interests of the investors and the managers, the latter are also required to make a capital commitment. Typically the managers invest between 1% and 3% of the fund's total commitments. Another key contractual technique is the compensation arrangement between the fund managers and the investors. Compensation usually derives from two main sources (the so-called 'two and twenty' arrangement). First, fund managers are typically entitled to receive 20% of the profits generated by each of the funds, the carried interest. A second source of compensation for the fund managers is the annual management fee, usually 2% to 2.5% of a fund's committed capital.

Arguably, the tried-and-tested compensation arrangements in the limited partnership agreement lower transaction costs and offer the contractual transparency necessary to induce investors to make their money available for investments in start-up companies. However, limited partners are more and more convinced that they have been mistaken in believing that the boilerplate 'two and twenty' rule ensures a proper alignment of interests and incentives.

It should therefore come as no surprise that provisions in the limited partnership agreement increasingly include provisions that protect investors from managerial misbehaviour. What is interesting in this respect is that European funds demand more protective clauses than do investors that operate in the more mature US private equity market (see Figure 17.2). A plausible explanation for this is that the attention to the contractual and organizational structure of the fund arguably increases when the private equity market, which is prone to violent cyclical movements, lacks the implicit mechanisms against opportunistic behaviour and misappropriation that are found in mature markets, such as trust and reputation.

Figure 17.2 shows that European funds can generally be distinguished from their US counterparts in terms of the stricter rules regarding the distribution of profits to managers and the preferred return to investors. Yet, despite these differences, the increasingly global nature of the private equity industry as well as the financial crisis may well lead to substantial convergence of contractual arrangements in Europe and the US in a number of important ways, particularly in the area of management fees and profit distribution.

A key contractual technique, for example, is the scale down compensation arrangement between the fund manager and the investors. This technique is commonly used in the United States, but is also employed more and more by European private equity funds. What is a scale down arrangement? Historically, a significant majority of funds assess management fees as a constant percentage of committed capital. This is where the scale down arrangement comes into play. There has been a decrease in management fees in recent years due to a number of economic factors. In particular, some funds are more likely to have a fixed fee of 2% of the fund's assets, which is paid annually for five years and then decreases by

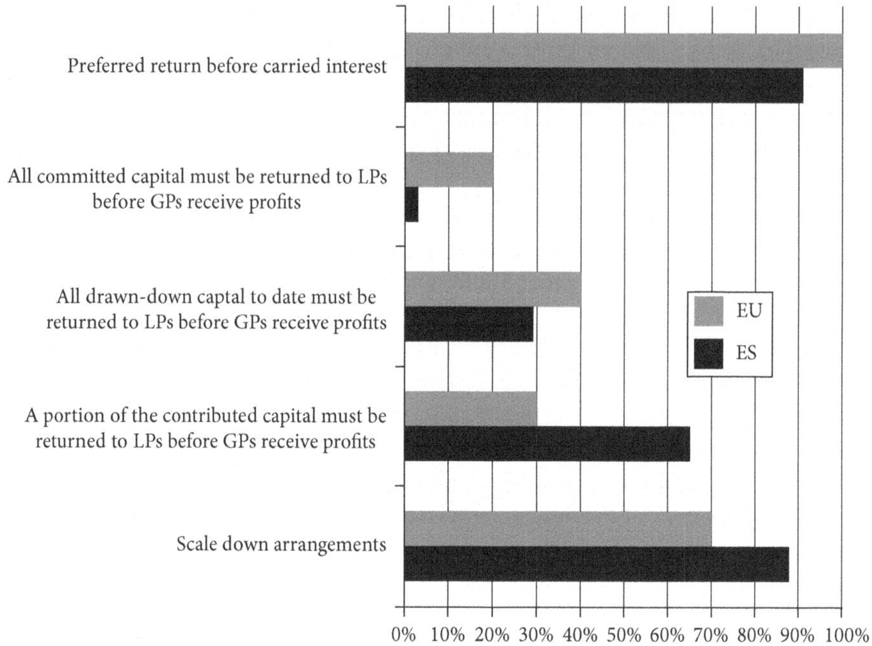

FIGURE 17.2 Differences between EU and US limited partnership agreements
Source: Dow Jones Private Equity Partnership Terms & Conditions, 2009 Edition.

twenty-five basis points for the next five-year period. Other fund managers will allow reductions of the fixed fee based on a change from committed capital in years one to five to net invested capital in years six to ten. Given these changes, a substantial proportion of buyout firms' median compensation has been reduced to 12% of the committed capital.

Another example of convergence in contract terms is the profit distribution provision for the preferred return (or hurdle rate) arrangement. According to this arrangement, profits can only be distributed to fund managers after a certain profit threshold—a minimum annual internal rate of return—has been satisfied. The preferred return rate ranges from 5% to 10% and can usually be found in European limited partnership agreements, but, as mentioned, are increasingly included in limited partnership agreements in the United States. The convergence is reflected in the introduction of such a provision by the Institutional Limited Partners Association (ILPA) (<http://www.ilpa.org>).

These profit distribution arrangements are an attempt to maximize fund managers' performance, which means that profits can only be distributed to the managers after a certain threshold has been reached. Clearly, these arrangements, which, as mentioned earlier, usually require private equity managers to first provide a preferred return to the investors before being able to distribute the 'carry', significantly reduce the chance that managers receive more than their fair share of the profits. In order to keep the managers focused and incentivized, most priority returns arrangements have a catch-up provision, which permits a reallocation of the profits to the general partner after the priority return has been distributed to the investors. In short, the catch-up provision entitles fund managers to receive most of the profits until the contractually agreed profit split between the investors and the managers has been reached. Certainly, if at a later stage it transpires that the general partners have received more than their fair share of the profits, investors will be entitled to call upon the clawback provisions under which the managers have to pay back the excess carry distributed earlier.

Overall, the contractual mechanisms for determining the general partners' compensation include both a profit sharing arrangement that balances investors' concerns regarding pay-for-performance, and a distribution scheme to investors to limit overall fund risk-taking. Moreover, there are a variety of factors that affect fund manager compensation. First, private equity funds' focus and characteristics can result in quite different outcomes for fund managers. For example, funds focusing on venture capital investment are more likely to require professional staff and expertise, which leads to lower yields and higher performance fees to align interests. Conversely, larger funds, such as buyout funds, are more likely to have lower fixed compensation because they require fewer staff than funds focusing on venture capital. Second, the type of institutional investor and their risk appetite may influence the fixed and variable fee structure of fund managers.

The question is whether we can expect to see more dramatic revisions to the fee and profit distribution provisions, rejecting the long-standing contractual practices. We will address the critical issues involved with this question in the next subsection of the chapter.

17.3.2 Post-Financial Crisis Trends in Private Equity Contracting

It follows from the previous subsection that private equity investors are increasingly successful in finding ways to improve management fee and profit distribution arrangements (Jannarone 2012). This is confirmed by empirical evidence, which found that 59% of the investors who were interviewed in June 2013 indicated that investor-favourable fee and profit arrangements were at the top of their priority lists (Preqin 2013c). One year earlier, this percentage was still 68%, which is an indication that private equity investors are increasingly successful in negotiating more favourable terms. Moreover, our work shows that an increasing number of investors still seek a higher degree of control and bargaining power over the terms of the limited partnership agreement or attempt to avoid the payment of management fees altogether (McCahery and Vermeulen 2013).

Consider Blackstone's Tactical Opportunities, which is a portfolio of separately managed accounts (Witkowsky 2012a). Separate accounts are different from the organization of traditional funds in that an investor's capital contribution will only be invested in accordance with its specific investment strategies and interests. From the perspective of the limited partners, the benefits are twofold. First, separate account arrangements are flexible in the sense that they are usually tailored to the investors' risk appetite and diversification needs. Second, and perhaps more importantly, it is obvious that the direct and close relationship between a single limited partner and a private equity firm enables investors to bargain for better terms and conditions, including 'disruptive' and investor-favourable management fees and carried interest provisions (Canada 2013; Kelleher 2013). Also, it is only to be expected that institutional investors will be more inclined to invest in separate accounts in the future. For instance, nineteen out of 100 surveyed institutional investors have set up a separate account arrangement in 2013, a significant increase compared with the 7% of investors who invested through a separate account arrangement in 2012 (Preqin 2013c).

Of course, it could be argued that these separate account arrangements should be viewed as a style or strategy that will gradually disappear in the aftermath of the financial crisis (Moix 2004). But since segregated accounts appear well designed to reduce investors' risks, it is unlikely that investors will change their preferences so long as the structure meets their needs. The evidence is consistent with this view: 64% of investors currently investing in separate accounts believe that these arrangements will be a permanent feature of the relationship between investors and fund managers (Preqin 2013c). Small and medium investors in particular, such as family offices and wealthy individuals, are more and more being lured to invest in funds that offer separate account arrangements (Myles 2013). Unsurprisingly, therefore, these arrangements have quickly gained in popularity. According to a recent survey among approximately 100 private equity fund managers from the United States, Europe and Asia, 7% of respondents have already set up separately managed accounts, with another 10% planning to do so in the next five years (State Street 2013).[5] This also explains why lawyers and advisers are attentive to separate accounts. In order to avoid conflicts of interest between the separately managed funds and the traditional (commingled) funds, they assist in setting out clear investment and disclosure policies for the separate accounts (Dai and Canada 2013).

These findings point to investors' search for greater control over both the investment decisions of general partners and the negotiations of fund terms, which has also led to an increase in direct investments in private equity opportunities. We would like to stress that the uncertainties and information asymmetries often deter institutional investors from investing directly in high growth companies. We observe, however, in an attempt to make investments in the best performing companies more lucrative (without the need to negotiate thorny compensation arrangements), an increase in private equity deals with institutional investors piggybacking on the due diligences and selection efforts of their fund managers by demanding the ability to pursue a co-investment strategy. Recent studies show that co-investments have gained in popularity. A study by Dineen (2012) indicated that co-investment rights provisions are already a must-have for institutional investors. Empirical evidence supports this view: (1) thirty-two out of 100 investors invest as co-investors with their fund manager; and (2) 97% of these investors expect to maintain (44%) or even increase (53%) their co-investment strategies (Preqin 2013c).

It is also likely that investors' increased demand for greater control over their portfolios will lead to greater use of alternative fund structures, such as pledge funds (Blake and Judd 2012). Pledge funds offer investors the opportunity to make investment decisions on a deal-by-deal basis. In order to get access to investment opportunities, investors must pay an annual fee and carry is calculated based on the amount invested. Although admitted investors can review potential portfolio companies, they are usually not obliged to participate in the deal. If the managers receive sufficient commitments from the 'member investors', they can prepare and negotiate the deal documents on behalf of the fund—in most cases a separate limited partnership is set up to make the investment. Again, the advantages are

[5] Separate account arrangements are already common in the area of hedge funds and real estate funds. The State Street (2013) study shows that 35% of hedge funds managers have set up separately managed accounts, while another 22% have indicated they intend to follow suit. For real estate funds, these percentages are 26% and 16% respectively.

Table 17.3 Skin in the game in the private equity industry

In the future, how much will management contribute to your own funds?

Contribution as % of committed capital	Respondents
<1%	21%
1–2%	28%
2–5%	35%
>5%	16%

Source: Private Equity International

clear. Besides the greater control over portfolio acquisitions, the pledge fund alternative also provides investors the possibility to avoid high management fees and carried interest. The downside is that the newly designed pledge funds structures usually come with higher transaction costs (Jesch 2010), and may suffer lower returns on investment due to lack of diversification and cherry-picking problems by general partners.

So far we have focused on the empirical research that shows that investors are taking an increasingly active approach in negotiations about the compensation terms of the limited partnership agreement. But there is more. Besides demanding 'improvements' to the limited partnership agreement, we observe that investors want to see more skin in the game from the managers/general partners. Recall that the industry norm is 1% to 3% of the committed capital. By requiring the general partners to make significant capital contributions to their own funds, the investors can reasonably expect that the managers' interests will be better aligned. It appears that 'higher-than-average' capital commitments (ranging from 5% to 10%) are gradually becoming the norm in the private equity industry (Witkowsky 2012b). This view is confirmed by a poll conducted among general partners during the Private Equity International Forum in January 2011 (see Table 17.3) (Mitchenall 2011).

17.4 Conclusion

This chapter analysed the regulatory alternatives for the private equity industry. We discussed important regulatory checks that limit managers' misbehaviour and misconduct. In this context, we examined some of the proposed changes recently introduced by the AIFMD in Europe.

Having explored the benefits and costs of a regulatory regime, we then turned to review the typical contractual measures in place that are designed to align investors' and fund managers' interests. This chapter argued that the fundraising landscape has evolved and changed significantly in the post-financial crisis era, leading to 'new' limited partnership compensation arrangements. The evolution of new limited partnership terms can largely be attributed to the major problems in private equity fundraising and returns.

This chapter identified two strategies that are currently being deployed by private equity fund managers in response to increased limited partner (LP) bargaining power. The first strategy relates to the negotiation of improvements to the 'two and twenty' compensation arrangements in the traditional limited partnership agreement. The adoption of scale down provisions and preferred returns provide substantial protections to potential investors. The second strategy involves the creation of 'innovative' private equity structures that constrain fund managers' discretion to make investment decisions. Greater customization through separate account arrangements and deal-by-deal investment opportunities will significantly increase investors' bargaining power and ability to negotiate more effective compensation arrangements. Together these results are consistent with the view that the 'end' of the traditional two and twenty rule will arguably have a more positive impact on the private equity industry than the need to comply with the cumbersome AIFMD rules.

References

Blake, J. and Judd, L. (2012). Fund Structures 2012, Bespoke Tailoring—Expert Commentary SJ Berwin, *Private Equity International* (Apr.).

Burrows, C. (2013a). Moulton: AIFMD 'Meaningless' and 'Unreadable', *Private Equity International* (19 Sept.).

Burrows, C. (2013b). GPs Shift Focus From Returns to Protection, *Private Equity International* (31 Oct.).

Canada, H. (2013). Fee Cuts Aside, PE Firms Have Much to Gain From Separate Accounts, *The Wall Street Journal* (Private Equity Beat), (17 Sept.).

Dai, S. and Canada, H. (2013). Lawyers, Advisers Weigh In on Separate Accounts, *Dow Jones LBO Wire* (18 Sept.).

Dineen, E. (2012). Changing Methods of Accessing Private Equity, *Preqin Private Equity Spotlight* (July).

Donato, N. (2011). LPs Demanding Greater Clarity in Fund Terms, *Private Equity International* (12 Aug.).

Duffel, T. (2013). AIFMD Sparks Hiring Spree, *Private Equity International* (24 July).

Favas, M. (2013). Study: Co-Investment to Increase Competition for Deals, *Private Equity International* (11 June).

Fleischer, V. (2008). Two and Twenty: Taxing Partnership Profits in Private Equity Funds, *New York University Law Review* 83(1), 1.

Jannarone, J. (2012). Fewer Blank Checks in Private Equity's Pocket, *Wall Street Journal* (Heard on the Street), (26 Mar.).

Jesch, T. A. (2010). Pledge Funds and Other Innovative Structures, *International Law Office* (20 Oct.).

Kelleher, E. (2013). Private Equity: Funds of Funds Falter in Battle for Survival, *Financial Times* (Investment Strategy), (7 July).

Litvak, K. (2009). Venture Capital Partnership Agreements: Understanding Compensation Agreements, *University of Chicago Law Review* 76, 161.

Marriage, M. (2013). Hedge Funds Shun New European Framework, *Financial Times* (13 Oct.).

McCahery, J. A. and Vermeulen, E. P. M. (2008). Private Equity and Hedge Funds Activism: Explaining the Differences in Regulatory Responses, *European Business Organization Law Review* 9, 535.

McCahery, J. A. and Vermeulen, E. P. M. (2013). Conservatism and Innovation in Venture Capital Contracting, ECGI—Law Working Paper No. 213.

Metrick, A. and Yasuda, A. (2010). The Economics of Private Equity Funds, *Review of Financial Studies* 23(6), 2303.

Mitchenall, T. (2011). Wanted: Skin in the Game, Fund Structures 2011, *Private Equity International* (Apr.).

Moix, P.-Y. (2004). Style Drift: Monitoring, Detection and Control, in L. Jaeger, (ed.), *The New Generation of Risk Management for Hedge Funds and Private Equity* (London, Euromoney Institutional Investor LLC), 387–98.

Mulcahy, D., Weeks, B. and Bradley, H. S. (2012). We Have Met the Enemy... And He Is Us: Lessons from Twenty Years of the Kaufmann Foundation's Investments in Venture Capital funds and the Triumph of Hope over Experience, Ewing Marion Kauffman Foundation (May), available at <http://ssrn.com/abstract=2053258>.

Myles, D. (2013). How Fundraising Models Will Bifurcate PE Market, *Private Equity International* (11 Sept.).

Preqin (2012), Preqin Special Report: European Private Equity, (Mar.), available at <https://www.preqin.com/docs/reports/Preqin_Special_Report_European_Private_Equity.pdf>.

Preqin (2013a). Private Equity Spotlight, (Oct.), available at <https://www.preqin.com/docs/newsletters/pe/Preqin_Private_Equity_Spotlight_October_2013.pdf>.

Preqin (2013b). 2013 Preqin Private Equity Fund Terms Advisor, (Sept.), available at <https://www.preqin.com/docs/newsletters/pe/Preqin_Private_Equity_Spotlight_September_2013.pdf>.

Preqin (2013c). Preqin Investor Outlook: Alternative Assets H2, available at <https://www.preqin.com/docs/reports/Preqin_Investor_Outlook_Alternative_Assets_H2_2013.pdf>.

Private Equity International (2013a). Flocking to Quality, Friday Letter, *Private Equity International* (19 Apr.).

Private Equity International (2013b). Blind Pool Blindness, Friday Letter, *Private Equity International* (8 Mar.).

State Street (2013). The Next Alternative: Thriving in a New Fund Environment, available at <http://www.Statestreet.com>.

Wang, W. (2013). AIFMD Compliance Remains Exclusive, *Global Custodian* (22 July).

Winfrey, G. (2013). Fundraising on Course for Post-Crisis Record in 2013, *Private Equity International* (2 Oct.).

Witkowsky, C. (2012a). Blackstone Sees Demand for Separate Accounts, *Private Equity International* (18 Apr.).

Witkowsky, C. (2012b). Fundraising GPs Put More 'Skin in the Game', *Private Equity International* (14 Nov.).

B.

Regulation and the Costs and Benefits of Shareholder Activism

CHAPTER 18

THE LAW AND ECONOMICS OF BLOCKHOLDER DISCLOSURE

LUCIAN A. BEBCHUK AND ROBERT J. JACKSON, JR

18.1 Introduction

A rulemaking petition recently submitted to the Securities and Exchange Commission (SEC) by the senior partners of a prominent law firm advocates tightening the rules that have long governed the disclosure of blocks of stock in public companies.[1] The Commission has subsequently announced a rulemaking project to develop proposals for tightening these rules, and members of the Commission's staff have signalled that the staff is prepared to recommend that the Commission adopt such proposals.[2] Chairman Mary Schapiro, acknowledging the 'controversy' surrounding these important rules, has indicated that the Commission is actively considering whether to adopt the changes proposed in the Petition.[3]

[1] Letter from Wachtell, Lipton, Rosen & Katz to Elizabeth M. Murphy, Secretary, US Securities and Exchange Commission (7 Mar. 2011), available at <http://www.sec.gov/rules/petitions/2011/petn4-624.pdf> (hereinafter Petition). Because the Petition provides a comprehensive statement of the arguments that might be raised in support of tightening these rules, we use the Petition as a basis for discussing those arguments—and the questions that the Commission should examine in evaluating them.

[2] See Beneficial Ownership Reporting Requirements and Security-Based Swaps, Exchange Act Release No. 34-64628, 76 Fed. Reg. 34,579, 34,581 (14 June 2011) (to be codified at 17 C.F.R. pt. 240) ('[O]ur staff is engaged in a separate project to develop proposals to modernize reporting under Exchange Act Section[] 13(d)'); Oral (2011):

> [T]he chief of the SEC's Office of Mergers & Acquisitions, Michele Anderson, said that she plans to recommend to the [C]ommission that they should shorten the number of days activist investors have before they must publicly disclose they have a 5% stake in the company.

[3] See Mary L. Schapiro, Chairman, US Securities and Exchange Commission, Remarks at the Transatlantic Corporate Governance Dialogue (15 Dec. 2011), available at <http://www.sec.gov/news/speech/2011/spch121511mls.htm>.

In this chapter, we provide a detailed framework for the Commission's examination of these rules. We argue that the Commission should not proceed with changes to these rules before undertaking a comprehensive examination of their economic implications for investors. In the meantime, the existing research and available empirical evidence provide no basis for concluding that the tightening of disclosure thresholds advocated by the petition would protect investors and promote efficiency, as the Commission's rules must;[4] indeed, the existing research and empirical evidence raise concerns that such tightening could harm investors and undermine efficiency.

Our analysis proceeds as follows. In Section 18.2, we explain why policy analysis weighing the advantages and disadvantages of tightening these rules is needed before the Commission proceeds with the proposed tightening. It might be argued that more prompt disclosure of information is unambiguously desirable under principles of market transparency and was the clear objective of the Williams Act, which first established these rules by adding Section 13(d) to the Securities Exchange Act in 1968. Thus, at first glance one might conclude that the Commission should tighten the rules without consideration of the costs and benefits of doing so. Unlike ordinary disclosure rules that require insiders to provide information to investors, however, the Williams Act imposed an exception to the general rule that outside investors in public-company stock are entitled to remain anonymous. The drafters of the Williams Act made a conscious choice not to impose a hard 5% limit on pre-disclosure accumulations of shares, instead striking a balance between the costs and benefits of disclosure of blockholders' activities to avoid excessive deterrence of the accumulation of these outside blocks. Thus, in deciding whether to tighten the rules in this area, the Commission should be guided by the general requirement that any costs associated with changes to its rules should be outweighed by benefits for investors.

We therefore proceed to provide a framework for the policy analysis that the Commission should conduct. In Section 18.3, we begin by considering the costs of tightening the rules on blockholders. We first explain the benefits of these blockholders for corporate governance. We review the significant empirical evidence indicating that the accumulation and holding of outside blocks makes incumbent directors and managers more accountable, thereby reducing agency costs and managerial slack. Thus, we argue, tightening disclosure requirements can be expected to reduce the returns to blockholders and thereby reduce the incidence and size of outside blocks as well as blockholders' investments in monitoring and engagement—which, in turn, could well result in increased agency costs and managerial slack.

In Section 18.4, we consider the asserted benefits of tightening the rules described in the Petition. We explain that there is no empirical evidence to support the Petition's contention that tightening these rules is needed to protect investors from the risk that outside blockholders will capture a control premium at shareholders' expense.[5]

Section 18.5 considers whether the proposed tightening is justified by changes in trading practices, legal rules in the United States, or legal rules in other jurisdictions that have occurred since the passage of Section 13(d). We first explain that there is no systematic

[4] See 15 USC § 78c(f).

[5] We emphasize that our analysis is based on existing research and empirical work. Future work on the issues we identify may well warrant reconsideration of the conclusions we reach below.

empirical evidence supporting the suggestion that investors can now acquire large blocks of stock more quickly than they could when Section 13(d) was first enacted. We then show that changes in the legal landscape since that time have tilted the balance of power between incumbents and blockholders against the latter—and therefore counsel against tightening the rules in a way that would further disadvantage blockholders. We also explain why comparative analysis of the regulation of blockholders in other jurisdictions does not justify tightening the rules governing blockholders in the United States. Overall, we argue, lawmakers should recognize that the rules governing the balance of power between management and outside blockholders are already tilted in favour of insiders—both in absolute terms and in comparison to other jurisdictions—rather than outside blockholders.

We conclude by recommending that the Commission pursue a comprehensive examination of the rules in this area along the lines we put forward. Such an examination should include an investigation of the empirical questions we identify. In the meantime, however, as we explain below, existing research and empirical evidence offer no basis for tightening the disclosure obligations of outside blockholders.

Before proceeding, we note that we focus on the timing of disclosure by blockholders and, in particular, the Petition's assertion that the Commission should shorten the ten-day period in which blockholders must disclose their presence after they have reached 5% ownership. Other questions, such as whether derivatives and similar securities should count toward the 5% threshold, are beyond the scope of this chapter.[6] We do, however, offer a framework for analysing these questions that should be considered in future work on any rules that affect the balance of power between incumbents and blockholders. As we explain below, any analysis of such rules should give adequate weight to the beneficial role played by blockholders described in this chapter.

18.2 The Need for Policy Analysis of Tightening the Rules on Blockholders

Before turning to an assessment of the advantages and disadvantages of tightening the rules governing blockholder disclosure, this section first explains why careful policy analysis of the proposed tightening is needed. It might be argued that the Commission need not conduct policy analysis of this kind before tightening its rules in this area. In particular, it might be argued that accelerating the disclosure of information is unambiguously beneficial for two reasons: first, more prompt disclosure is justified by basic principles of market transparency; and, second, more prompt disclosure is necessary to achieve the objectives of the Williams Act. We examine each of these claims in turn in Sections 18.2.1 and 18.2.2 below. We conclude that neither argument provides a sound basis for the Commission to proceed with the proposed tightening without first conducting a careful policy analysis of the costs and benefits of doing so.

[6] Petition, *supra* note 1, at 8 (arguing that the Commission's 13(d) rules should be amended to include ownership through these securities toward the threshold).

18.2.1 The Unique Disclosures Required by the Williams Act

At first glance, it may seem that requiring immediate disclosure of the accumulation of outside blocks of public-company stock will improve market transparency and, thus, is obviously desirable. On this view, principles of transparency compel such disclosure and make it unnecessary for the Commission to conduct a policy analysis before proceeding with the changes proposed by the Petition.

In considering this view, however, it is important to note that the disclosure rules we focus on here apply not to information that insiders must provide to investors, but rather to information that outsiders must disclose about their purchases of public-company stock. For such purchases, the general principle is that, outside the specific exception established by the Williams Act, buyers of shares are not required to disclose their purchases to the market—even when that information would be of interest to others.

Suppose, for example, that Warren Buffett chose to purchase 2% of the stock of a publicly traded company. Certainly this information would be the subject of a great deal of interest to other investors. But as a general rule the law does not require Buffett, or any other outside investor in similar circumstances, to disclose purchases of this kind. And for good reason: such a requirement might enable other investors to free-ride on Buffett's investments in information acquisition about undervalued companies, and thus could have an adverse effect on such investments. For this reason, the appeal of market transparency has not by itself been a sufficient justification for requiring outside investors to disclose their purchases of public-company stock.

To be sure, the Williams Act did establish an exception to the general principle that outside investors may remain anonymous. Rather than imposing a general requirement of transparency, however, the Williams Act delineated a limited exception requiring disclosure in certain prescribed circumstances. In the next section we consider whether tightening the rules is necessary to meet the objectives of the drafters of the Williams Act.

18.2.2 Is Tightening Necessary to Achieve the Williams Act's Objectives?

It might be argued that tightening the disclosure rules that apply to outside blockholders is necessary to achieve the purposes Congress sought to address in 1968 when it adopted the Williams Act's exception to the general rule that investors in public companies may remain anonymous. Indeed, the Petition contends that Congress hoped to 'compel the release of information to the investing public' about outside blocks of 5% or more, and that today 'this purpose is no longer being properly served', because 'the ten-day reporting lag leaves a substantial gap' when blockholders can continue to accumulate shares in secret.[7]

This argument proceeds on the mistaken assumption that the drafters of the Williams Act intended to place an absolute 5% limit on pre-disclosure accumulations of outside blockholders but failed to design the rules to achieve this objective. As explained below, however,

[7] Petition, *supra* note 1, at 2–3.

this account of the objectives of the Williams Act is incorrect. In fact, Congress expressly considered, and declined to adopt, that approach.

The history of the Williams Act makes clear that the ten-day period between the acquisition of a 5% stake and disclosure is not a 'gap' left open by incompetent drafters.[8] Instead, it reflects a careful balance that Congress struck, after extensive debate, between the need to provide information to investors and the importance of preserving the governance benefits associated with outside blockholders.

Senator Williams's initial proposal in this area, which he introduced in October 1965, would have made it unlawful for an outside blockholder to cross the 5% threshold without prior disclosure.[9] The senator abandoned that proposal, however, after its advance-notice provision was met with significant opposition from the Commission and others.[10]

Instead, following discussions with the Commission, members of the New York Stock Exchange, and private industry, Senator Williams introduced a new bill in January 1967 that would have required that an investor acquiring 10% of the equity of a public company disclose that stake within seven days.[11] When he introduced his new proposal, Senator Williams described his conscious effort to balance the effect of the new law on management and blockholders. He noted that he had 'taken extreme care' 'to balance the scales equally to protect the legitimate interests of the corporation, management, and shareholders'; 'every effort ha[d] been made to avoid tipping the balance of [the] regulatory burden in favor of management or in favor of' those subject to the new disclosure requirement.[12]

Even this new proposal, however, drew criticism from corporate law commentators of the time. During hearings on Senator Williams's second proposal, one observer expressed concern that the proposed disclosure would undermine the benefits of outside blockholders, arguing that blockholders make 'corporate management . . . recognize . . . that it will be subject to replacement if its performance' is substandard, and that these benefits were 'imperative' for effective corporate governance.[13]

Senator Williams later concluded that outside investors who acquire large blocks of public-company stock 'should not be discouraged, since they often serve a useful purpose by providing a check on entrenched but inefficient management'.[14] Thus, Senator Williams proposed a third bill. This proposal was the first to introduce a ten-day window between the acquisition of the investor's stake and disclosure, requiring any person acquiring beneficial ownership of 10% of a public company's stock to disclose that ownership within ten days.[15] When introducing the proposal, Senator Williams argued that the new bill 'carefully weighed both the advantages and disadvantages to the public' of the disclosure requirement and took 'extreme care to avoid tipping the scales either in favor of management or in favor of' large investors.[16] This

[8] For a detailed account of the legislative history of the Williams Act, see Wilmer Cutler Pickering Hale and Dorr LLP (2011).

[9] See A Bill Providing for Fuller Disclosure of Corporate Equity Ownership of Securities Under the Securities Exchange Act of 1934, S. 2731, 89th Cong. § 2 (22 Oct. 1965).

[10] See 112 Cong. Rec. 19004 (1966).

[11] See S. 510, § 1, 90th Cong. (introduced 18 Jan. 1967).

[12] 113 Cong. Rec. 854 (1967).

[13] Full Disclosure of Corporate Equity Ownership and in Corporate Takeover Bids: Hearing Before the Senate Sub. Comm. on Securities of the Senate Comm. on Banking and Currency, 90th Cong. 134 (1967) (statement of Stanley Kaplan, Professor, University of Chicago).

[14] 113 Cong. Rec. 24,664 (1967).

[15] S. 510, § 2, 90th Cong. (amended 31 Aug. 1967).

[16] 113 Cong. Rec. 24,664 (1967).

proposal later became law. Two years later, when Congress lowered the disclosure threshold from 10% to 5%, it chose to keep the ten-day disclosure window in place.[17]

This legislative history suggests that the ten-day window between the acquisition of a 5% stake and required disclosure is not a technical 'gap' left open by incompetent congressional drafters. Instead, the window reflects the balance that Senator Williams and his colleagues struck between the benefits that the holders of large blocks of stock convey upon public investors and the need for disclosure of these blocks.[18] The fact that blockholders have the ability to acquire additional stock during this ten-day period would not be surprising to the legislators who approved the Williams Act in 1968. Instead, this outcome is a product of Congress's careful consideration of the benefits that blockholders provide to public investors.

In a recent article, a partner in the law firm that submitted the Petition responded to a comment letter that we provided to the Commission regarding the Petition.[19] The article contends that our arguments 'do not address . . . the undeniable point that the current § 13(d) rules no longer effectively serve their stated purpose' (Katz and McIntosh 2012: 6). We think that this argument assumes, incorrectly, that the 'stated purpose' of these rules is to absolutely bar outside blockholders from pre-disclosure accumulations exceeding 5% of the company's stock. As we have explained, however, the legislative history of the Williams Act makes clear that Congress intentionally left open the ten-day window during which such accumulations may be made. What the article describes as a 'loophole', then, instead reflects the long-standing legislative compromise that Congress adopted when it enacted the Williams Act in 1968 (Katz and McIntosh 2012: 6).

To be sure, although Congress chose in 1968 to allow blockholders to acquire stock during the ten days before they are required to disclose, in 2010 Congress made clear in the Dodd-Frank Act that the SEC has the power to shorten the ten-day period if it so chooses.[20] The grant of this authority should not, however, be understood as a Congressional mandate that the Commission take whatever steps are necessary to ensure a firm 5% constraint on pre-disclosure accumulations. Had Congress wanted that outcome, it could have prohibited pre-disclosure accumulations exceeding 5%, instructing the Commission to adopt rules implementing this objective. Instead, by granting the Commission this authority, Congress has simply posed a question that deserves the Commission's attention: does it make sense to

[17] See Williams Act, Pub. L. No. 90-439, 82 Stat. 454 (1968); Act of December 22, 1970, Pub. L. No. 91-567, 84 Stat. 1497 (1970).

[18] Interpreting this legislative history, the Supreme Court has repeatedly concluded that the Williams Act is the product of Congress's balancing of these considerations. See, e.g., *Edgar v. MITE Corp.*, 457 U.S. 624, 633 (1982):

> There is no question that in imposing the [Section 13(d) disclosure] requirements, Congress intended to protect investors. But it is also crystal clear that a major aspect of the effort to protect the investor was to avoid favoring either management or the takeover bidder.

[19] Letter from Lucian A. Bebchuk, Professor, Harvard Law School & Robert J. Jackson, Jr, Associate Professor, Columbia Law School, to Elizabeth M. Murphy, Secretary, US Securities and Exchange Commission (11 Jul. 2011), available at <http://www.sec.gov/comments/4-624/4624-3.pdf>.

[20] See Dodd-Frank Wall Street Reform Consumer and Protection Act, Pub. L. No. 111-203, § 929R(a), 124 Stat. 1376 (2010).

strike the balance between outside blockholders and management differently than Congress did in 1968?

In making that decision, the Commission should not be guided by general intuitions about transparency or mistaken assumptions about the Williams Act's objectives—but instead by the principle that its rules must protect investors and promote efficiency. We therefore turn below to an analysis of the costs and benefits of the proposed tightening of the rules governing the disclosure of outside blockholders.

18.3 The Costs of Tightening the Rules on Blockholders

The literature in law, economics, and finance has long recognized that the presence of outside blockholders—and particularly blockholders willing to invest in monitoring and disciplining management—is beneficial for investors.[21] Shareholders who make these investments in monitoring must bear their full costs, but share the benefits with fellow shareholders, capturing only the shareholder's pro rata fraction of these benefits. For this reason, shareholders that hold only a small fraction of the firm's shares have little incentive to make such investments—even when those investments could produce a significant increase in value. By contrast, outside blockholders with a significant stake have stronger incentives to invest in monitoring and engagement. These investments can be expected to make incumbents more accountable and to reduce agency costs and managerial slack.

These investments, however, are costly, and it is well understood that the incidence and size of outside blocks depends on blockholders' ability to obtain returns that cover these costs. As we explain below, tightening the rules that apply to blockholders can be expected to reduce the incidence of outside blocks as well as blockholders' investments in monitoring and disciplining management.

18.3.1 Empirical Evidence on the Value of Blockholders

There is a substantial body of empirical evidence that is consistent with the view that outside blockholders improve corporate governance and benefit public investors. To begin, two recent studies examine situations in which outside blockholders announced their presence to the markets by making Section 13(d) filings. In one study, Alon Brav, Wei Jiang, Frank Partnoy, and Randall Thomas (Chapter 8, this volume) found that the filing of a Schedule 13D revealing an activist shareholder's position is associated with large, positive average abnormal returns. In another study, April Klein and Emanuel Zur (Chapter 9, this volume) concluded that the filing of a Schedule 13D in which an outside blockholder indicates that it aims to redirect management's efforts is also associated with large, positive average

[21] For an early article recognizing the importance of outside blockholders, see Shleifer and Vishny (1986); see also, e.g., Holderness and Sheehan (1985); Brav et al. (Chapter 8, this volume); Klein and Zur (Chapter 9, this volume).

abnormal returns. This evidence is consistent with the view that market participants expect the presence of blockholders to be beneficial for firm value.[22]

Furthermore, consistent with the findings of positive market reactions to the presence of an outside blockholder discussed above, there is substantial empirical evidence indicating that the presence of outside blockholders is associated with improved outcomes for shareholders on various dimensions. This body of work includes the following studies:

(i) A study by Marianne Bertrand and Sendhil Mullainathan (2001: 903) finds that CEO pay is less likely to reward 'luck' instead of performance when a blockholder is represented on the company's board;

(ii) A study by Lucian Bebchuk, Yaniv Grinstein, and Urs Peyer (2010: 2365) shows that the presence of representatives of blockholders on a board's compensation committee is associated with reduced incidence of stock option backdating;

(iii) A study by Anup Agrawal and Tareque Nasser (2012) shows that the presence on a company's compensation committee of an independent director associated with a significant shareholder is correlated with a stronger relationship between CEO pay and performance, a stronger relationship between CEO turnover and performance, and lower levels of CEO pay;

(iv) A study by James Brickley, Ronald Lease, and Clifford Smith (1988) shows that the presence of institutional blockholders is associated with increased shareholder opposition when management proposes entrenching anti-takeover amendments to the company's charter; and

(v) A study by Anil Shivdasani (1993) shows that the presence of outside blockholders is associated with an increased likelihood of transactions that discipline management.[23]

Finally, the presence of an outside blockholder benefits shareholders by making the possibility of a proxy fight more viable. The possibility of a proxy fight is generally understood to be a disciplinary mechanism that plays an important role in making directors accountable for corporate performance and constraining agency costs. There is significant evidence that the announcement of a proxy fight is associated with positive abnormal returns (Borstadt and Zwirlein 1992: 23),[24] and the disciplinary force of the prospect of a proxy fight could well produce additional benefits for shareholders in many cases in which a proxy fight does not actually take place. Without an outside blockholder, however, a proxy fight is unlikely even in a case of substantial underperformance because there may not be a shareholder with sufficient 'skin in the game' to bear the costs involved in a proxy challenge.

[22] This conclusion was also reached in an early empirical study by Clifford Holderness and Dennis Sheehan (1985: 557) (concluding that the filing of a Schedule 13D by six investors known to actively engage with management was associated with positive abnormal returns).

[23] The literature described here focuses on the effects associated with outside blockholders—that is, blocks held by shareholders not affiliated with management. By contrast, large blocks held by insiders may render insiders less rather than more accountable to shareholders.

[24] Cf. Ikenberry and Lakonishok (1993: 432–3) (finding that the targets of proxy contests exhibit negative abnormal returns, and worsening operating performance, immediately prior to the initiation of a proxy contest).

In contrast, the presence of an outside blockholder with a significant stake makes a proxy fight more viable. When a proxy fight might lead to an increase in shareholder value, the prospect of having its block appreciate in value might provide such an outside blockholder with sufficient incentive to bear the costs of mounting a proxy fight (Bebchuk and Hart 2002). Indeed, there is evidence that the shareholders mounting these challenges are likely to have a significant stake in the firm.[25] Thus, at companies without an outside blockholder (or the prospect of a blockholder emerging), incumbent directors and executives face a substantially reduced threat of a proxy fight in case of underperformance, and this insulation from the possibility of a proxy fight will be likely to have an adverse effect on shareholder interests, increasing agency costs and managerial slack.

18.3.2 The Effect of Tightening the Rules

Having discussed the benefits of outside blockholders for investors—taking their presence as given—we turn now to the factors that determine whether such blockholders are likely to emerge. It is well understood that the incidence and size of outside blocks, and the investments in value-enhancing activities made by outside blockholders, depends on the ability of outside blockholders to obtain returns that cover their costs. Outside blockholders make costly investments in monitoring and engagement and, in addition, may be forced to bear the costs of non-diversification associated with their large stake.

It has long been recognized in the literature that an important source of incentives to become an outside blockholder is the blockholder's ability to purchase shares at prices that do not yet fully reflect the expected value of the blockholder's future monitoring and engagement activities.[26] Once the presence of an outside blockholder is publicly disclosed, prices rise to a level reflecting these expected benefits. If an outside blockholder could not purchase an initial block at prices below this level, the returns to becoming an active outside blockholder would fall, and shareholders would lose the benefits of blockholders' presence. The ability to buy an initial block at prices below the post-disclosure level enables blockholders to capture a fraction—albeit a fairly limited fraction—of the expected benefits from their expected future activities. Other shareholders benefit from giving blockholders this ability, because other investors capture the lion's share of the benefits generated by the blockholder's monitoring and engagement activities—benefits that otherwise might not be produced.

Tightening the rules that govern the amount of time blockholders have to acquire shares before disclosing their stake can thus be expected to reduce the returns to outside shareholders considering acquiring a block and, in turn, to result in a reduction in the incidence and size of outside blocks.[27] In some cases, those considering becoming significant blockholders might be deterred from doing so altogether. In other cases, those becoming significant blockholders might elect to purchase a smaller block. Given the importance and

[25] See Pound (1988: 253 tbl.3).

[26] For early work recognizing this point, see Grossman and Hart (1980); Shleifer and Vishny (1986).

[27] We focus here only on the rules that govern the timing of disclosure that blockholders are required to provide after they have reached the 5% ownership disclosure threshold. We put to one side other questions, such as whether derivatives and similar securities should count toward the 5% threshold. See *supra* text accompanying note and note 6.

beneficial role of outside blocks, disincentives to the creation of such blocks can be expected to impose costs on investors, increasing agency costs and managerial slack, and rules creating such disincentives should be adopted only if they can be expected to produce benefits that exceed these costs.

The Petition suggests that, for sophisticated players with ample access to legal counsel—as most outside blockholders are—tighter disclosure rules will not impose any meaningful costs.[28] But the main cost of disclosure obligations in this context is not the transaction costs, such as legal fees, imposed by securities filings. Rather, the principal cost of tightened disclosure obligations for potential outside blockholders is that such tightening reduces the fraction of the benefits produced by their monitoring and engagement that the potential outside blockholders can expect to capture if they choose to acquire a block.[29] This cost to potential outside blockholders might, in turn, produce costs for investors by reducing the incidence and size of outside blocks.

Before tightening the rules governing the outside investors who hold large blocks of public company stock, regulators should carefully consider the valuable role that these outside blockholders play in corporate governance, the increased agency costs and managerial slack that would arise if outside blockholders are discouraged or suppressed, and the significant empirical evidence on the benefits produced by outside blockholders. These considerations should play a role in the Commission's examination of the rules governing outside blockholders.

18.4 The Asserted Benefits of Tightening the Rules on Blockholders

As we have noted, tightening the rules on blockholders may impose substantial costs on investors—including the increase in agency costs and managerial slack that might accompany a diminished role for blockholders in corporate governance. These costs, of course, must be weighed against any benefits that would arise from tightening these rules. The Petition argues that the key benefit of tightening these rules would be to protect public-company investors from losing the premium associated with corporate control.

To illustrate, consider a situation in which an outside blockholder identifies an under-performing company with 100 million shares and a market capitalization of $1 billion. Suppose that the blockholder purchases 5% of the company's shares for $10.00 each on 1 June, and an additional 2% for $10.10 each between 1 June and 9 June. Suppose, too, that the outside blockholder files a Schedule 13D on 10 June—and that, upon the filing of the Schedule 13D, the price per share rises by 5%, to $10.60. According to the Petition, the

[28] See Petition, *supra* note 1, at 5 (because blockholders are 'sophisticated, experienced investor[s]', tightened rules will not impose a substantial burden on them); see also Katz and McIntosh (2012: 3–4) (arguing that the 'sophistication of the investors' who trigger Section 13(d)'s disclosure requirements make tighter disclosure requirements 'feasible' for these investors).

[29] Cf. Brav et al. (Chapter 8, this volume) (finding that the filing of a Schedule 13D by hedge funds is associated with positive abnormal stock returns).

blockholder's ability to pay $10.10 per share, rather than $10.60 per share, for the additional 2% deprives the selling shareholders of a control premium of $1 million ($0.50 x 2 million shares), enabling the blockholders to capture control benefits of $1 million. Tightening Section 13(d)'s disclosure rules, the Petition claims, is necessary to protect investors from losing control premia in such situations.[30]

This claim, however, is unwarranted. In cases like these, the blockholder purchasing an additional 2% has not obtained control benefits, and shareholders have not lost a control premium. A buyer obtains a control block only when the block is large enough for the buyer to have the practical ability to determine corporate outcomes, which in turn permits the buyer to obtain substantial 'private benefits of control' not shared by other, non-controlling shareholders. Blocks that are large enough to convey control usually trade at a premium to the prevailing market price.[31] By contrast, the buyer of the outside block in cases like the example above does not obtain control and its private benefits.

A shareholder with a 7% block will be able to move the company in the direction the blockholder views as value-increasing only if the blockholder can convince other shareholders that doing so would be desirable (or if the incumbent directors and executives anticipate that the blockholder will be able to convince shareholders). If an outside blockholder is able to facilitate such a change, the blockholder would not be capturing a private benefit, but rather a gain that would be shared, on a pro rata basis, with fellow shareholders. Indeed, should the non-controlling outside blockholder decide to sell its 7% block, it would likely be unable to get a control premium over the market price for its block. While blocks that carry a control premium with them are generally sold as a block, outside blockholders that decide to exit after filing a Schedule 13D usually do not sell their block as a whole but rather, consistent with the view that they have not captured a control premium, sell shares in the market.[32]

The Petition relies heavily upon two recent anecdotes in which an outside blockholder influenced public companies—noting that in one case the company decided to pursue the strategy advocated by the blockholder, and in the other the company appointed a representative of the blockholder to its board—and suggests that these cases 'demonstrat[e] the influence and control' that blockholders enjoy.[33] But this sort of 'influence' should hardly be equated with the blockholder obtaining control and capturing a control premium at the expense of other shareholders. Indeed, there are many cases in which shareholders holding far less than a 5% stake were able to exert influence over a public company. Recently, for example, shareholders owning less than 1% of the stock of Massey Energy successfully urged that CEO Don Blankenship be removed (James 2010). CalPERS, which commonly holds far less than a 5% stake in most public companies, has had influence on companies it targeted

[30] See, e.g., Katz and McIntosh (2012: 3) (arguing that, under current rules, one blockholder was able to acquire shares of J.C. Penney 'at a substantially lower price from unwitting shareholders than would have been possible' under a tighter set of disclosure rules).

[31] For an empirical analysis of control premia, see Dyck and Zingales (2004).

[32] See, e.g., Brav et al. (Chapter 8, this volume) (describing the exit behaviour of blockholders such as activist hedge fund investors and concluding that 'hedge fund activism does not generally involve control blocks of stock').

[33] See Petition, *supra* note 1, at 6. Notably, in both cases the outside blockholder did not succeed in electing its nominees to a majority of the seats on the company's board of directors (see Brav et al., Chapter 8, this volume).

using its 'focus list'.[34] This type of influence, or the appointment of a single blockholder representative to the board, is by itself not evidence that the shareholder has obtained 'control'.

Of course, outside blockholders can derive benefits—even though these are not 'control' benefits—from the ability to buy additional shares at lower prices before their presence is made public. This ability allows the outside blockholder to capture an increased fraction of the benefits its activities are expected to produce, which in turn gives outside blockholders incentives to create value that will be shared with other investors. While tightening Section 13(d)'s disclosure requirements could give shareholders an increased fraction of the benefits from the blockholder activity that would still take place after the rules are tightened, these benefits would come at the cost of a reduction in the expected incidence and size of outside blocks—and, in turn, increased agency problems and managerial slack.

Thus, while it is far from clear that shareholders would obtain any net benefits from tightening these rules, what is clear is that such tightening would significantly benefit incumbent directors and executives—especially those at under-performing companies. Under-performing incumbents have much to gain from increased insulation from outside blockholders' monitoring and engagement, and therefore would benefit from changes in rules that would provide disincentives for the emergence of significant, active outside blockholders. For shareholders, however, such increased insulation would be detrimental, increasing agency costs and managerial slack. The Commission should carefully consider these potential costs before modifying the rules in this area.

18.5 Changes since the Passage of the Williams Act

The Petition also argues that changes since the passage of the Williams Act—and, in particular, changes in trading technology—justify tightening these rules. In this section we explain why changes in the decades since the passage of the Williams Act provide little support for the proposed tightening. Section 18.5.1 explains that there is currently no evidence that changes in trading practices provide a basis for tightening of disclosure rules. Indeed, we argue in Section 18.5.2, changes in the legal landscape since the passage of the Williams Act have imposed significant additional costs on blockholders over the past three decades—and therefore weigh against the Petition's proposed tightening of the rules on blockholders. Finally, in Section 18.5.3 we explain why developments in jurisdictions outside the United States do not provide support for tightening the rules, as the Petition suggests; to the contrary, US law places outside blockholders at a much greater disadvantage than they face in any of the jurisdictions that the Petition relies upon when arguing in favour of tightening the rules governing blockholder disclosure in the United States.

[34] See Reform Focus List Companies, CalPERS, available at <http://www.calpers-governance.org/focuslist/reform-companies>.

18.5.1 Changes in Trading Practices

The Petition stresses that much has changed since the passage of the Williams Act. In particular the Petition argues that, due to changes in trading practices and technologies, outside blockholders now tend to amass larger positions before filing a Schedule 13D than they did previously.[35] Indeed, the Petition contends, 'recent events have highlighted the potential extremes to which these acquisition tactics may be taken, and make clear the urgent need for ... reform'.[36] But we are aware of no empirical evidence to support the Petition's claim that outside blockholders have in recent years amassed larger pre-disclosure ownership stakes than they accumulated in earlier periods.

Data on pre-disclosure accumulations by blockholders are now, and long have been, publicly available from Schedule 13D filings. However, the Petition does not provide a systematic examination of these data—for example by comparing evidence from recent years to data from earlier periods—or refer to any empirical study doing so. Instead, the Petition refers to four anecdotes—two from 2010, involving J. C. Penney and Fortune Brands, and two from 2008, involving CSX and CNET.[37] In claiming that investors 'frequently do' engage in large accumulations during the period between the crossing of the 5% threshold and the time of disclosure, the Petition also relies on a newspaper article that refers to three of these four cases described but does not identify any other US cases.[38] And, as we have noted, a partner of the law firm that authored the Petition recently published an article supporting the Petition. Although that article was written nearly a year after the Petition was submitted, the article still mentions only one anecdote (drawn from the set of four anecdotes on which the Petition relied) and the same newspaper report, offering no systematic examination of the data that is publicly available from Schedule 13D filings (Katz and McIntosh 2012: 3).

Describing four cases occurring over the past four years, however, is not the type of systematic evidence that could provide a basis for concluding that Commission rulemaking is urgently needed to address changes in trading practices and technologies. Indeed, the existence of anecdotes like these is itself far from a new market development. A study by Clifford Holderness and Dennis Sheehan (1985: 563) examined Schedule 13D filings during the 1977–82 period and reported the existence of a small minority of cases with significant accumulation between the crossing of the 5% threshold and the filing of the Schedule 13D.

In addition, a recent study in this area suggests that the anecdotes described in the Petition are not representative of blockholders' accumulation practices today. In response to the Petition, Alon Brav, J. B. Heaton, and Wei Jiang submitted a letter to the Commission indicating that their study of certain blockholders' disclosures between 2001 and 2007 indicates that more than 50% of blockholders voluntarily disclose their stakes before the tenth day, when the disclosures are required. Indeed, the authors find that the relationship between the number of days that it takes the blockholder to report and the stake the blockholder reports

[35] See Petition, *supra* note 1, at 3 (stating that '[t]he advent of computerized trading ... allowing massive volumes of shares to trade in a matter of seconds' and 'the increasing use of derivatives has accelerated the ability of investors to accumulate economic ownership of shares ...').

[36] See Petition, *supra* note 1, at 2.

[37] See Petition, *supra* note 1, at 5–6, 8, 10; see also Katz and McIntosh (2012: 3).

[38] See Petition, *supra* note 1, at 3, n.9 (citing Sorkin 2010) (noting the cases of J. C. Penney, CSX, and CNET).

is negative. Based on their assessment of blockholder activity during this period, the authors conclude that the anecdotes described in the Petition are 'not typical'.[39]

In assessing the claim that accumulation practices by outside blockholders have markedly changed over time—creating an 'urgent' need to adjust the rules to changed market circumstances—the Commission should not rely on a few anecdotes. An adequate assessment of this claim requires a systematic empirical examination of publicly available Schedule 13D filings to determine what changes in pre-disclosure accumulations by outside blockholders, if any, have taken place since the passage of the Williams Act. Such a study could, for example, examine substantial samples of Schedule 13D filings in each five-year period since the passage of the Williams Act and compare the ownership stakes held by outside blockholders at the time they made these filings.

Of course, the results of such a study would not be dispositive with respect to whether changes in the rules governing outside blockholders would benefit investors and promote efficiency. In making that decision, the Commission should take into account the evidence we have previously described as well as the additional considerations described below. However, such an inquiry would help the Commission obtain an adequate factual understanding of whether pre-disclosure accumulations in recent years are significantly different from earlier patterns. To our knowledge, no existing empirical evidence provides sufficient support for that claim.

18.5.2 Changes in the Legal Landscape

While it is not clear at this stage what changes, if any, have occurred in the accumulation practices of outside blockholders since the passage of the Williams Act, the Commission should carefully consider significant legal changes that have clearly taken place during that period. Over the past three decades, legal rules have evolved in ways that impede outside blockholders and disadvantage them *vis-à-vis* incumbents. Given how the legal landscape has changed since the passage of the Williams Act, the Commission should be especially cautious before further tightening the rules that apply to blockholders.

To begin, those who might consider buying an outside block as a 'toehold' prior to acquiring a control block—the case that the drafters of the Williams Act devoted much attention to[40]—now face formidable impediments that did not exist when the Williams Act was passed. In particular, state law now allows boards to use poison pills to block hostile tender offers.[41] Because of the substantial legal impediments to hostile takeover bids, the incidence of such bids is low.[42] Today, active outside blockholders filing a Schedule 13D are commonly

[39] See Letter from Alon Brav et al. to Elizabeth M. Murphy, Secretary, US Securities and Exchange Commission (5 July 2011), at 2, available at <http://www.sec.gov/comments/4-624/4624-2.pdf>.

[40] See, e.g., H.R. Rep. No. 91-1711, at 2 (1968) (describing the focus of the drafters of the Williams Act on the use of cash tender offers in connection with takeover bids).

[41] In Delaware, boards' virtually absolute power to block hostile offers has been established by the courts. See *Air Prods. & Chems., Inc. v. Airgas, Inc.*, 16 A.3d 48 (Del. Ch. 2011). In other states, this power is enshrined in pill-endorsement statutes (Barzuza 2009).

[42] See, e.g., Baker and Subramanian (undated) (reporting that hostile tender offers represented approximately 3.6% of all merger and acquisition volume in the United States in 2002).

not expected to seek to acquire control, but rather to monitor and engage with management and fellow shareholders.[43]

More importantly, in addition to the limits on unsolicited offers for control, further legal changes since the passage of the Williams Act impede blockholders that seek merely to influence how their company is managed. To begin, companies have been adopting poison pills with low ownership thresholds—pills designed not to prevent an acquisition of control but to keep outside blockholders unfriendly to management from increasing their stake—and state law has been displaying tolerance toward such pills.[44] Among the 805 public companies in the Sharkrepellent dataset that currently have poison pills in place, 76% have pills triggered by an ownership threshold of 15% or less, while 15% have pills triggered by a threshold of 10% or less.[45] Furthermore, while most publicly traded companies do not currently have a pill in place, these companies always have an 'off-the-shelf' low-trigger pill available to them, and can instal one immediately if an outside blockholder disfavoured by the incumbents emerges—an important feature of the current landscape that a market participant considering becoming an outside blockholder must consider.

In addition, state law now allows companies to use poison pills selectively to disfavour some outside blockholders and to prohibit some shareholders—but not others—from holding stakes exceeding a specified threshold.[46] Companies have also been adopting poison pills with 'continuing director' provisions triggered when a majority of directors is replaced with new directors not approved by the incumbents, thereby discouraging outside blockholders from attempting to run a proxy fight for a majority of the seats on the board.[47]

To be sure, the Commission does not have the power to make direct changes to the state law rules that have, since the passage of the Williams Act, evolved to disfavour outside blockholders. But in considering whether to make changes in rules it does have the power to amend, the Commission should take these state law rules into account in deciding what changes, if any, would be desirable. Given the value of outside blockholders to investors, the Commission should be wary of adopting rules that would further discourage these blockholders and their activities without a clear showing that the benefits of any such rules would outweigh their costs.

[43] See, e.g., Brav et al. (Chapter 8, this volume) (blockholders such as 'activist hedge funds do not typically seek control in target companies').

[44] In *Versata Enters., Inc. v. Selectica, Inc.*, 5 A.3d 586, 599–607 (Del. 2010), the Delaware Supreme Court upheld the use of a poison pill with a 5% ownership trigger where the company had certain net operating loss assets that could lose value if that ownership level was breached. The Delaware courts have not yet established the lowest level at which pill triggers may be set in the absence of such an asset, but current practices indicate that practitioners expect (or hope) that companies will be permitted to use triggers at a 15% or 10% ownership level.

[45] See Factset Research Systems, Inc., Dataset, Sharkrepellent, available at <http://sharkrepellent.net>.

[46] See, e.g., *Yucaipa Am. Alliance Fund II, L.P. v. Riggio*, 1 A.3d 310, 312–313 (Del. Ch. 2010) (upholding the use of a poison pill triggered by the acquisition of 20% ownership by shareholders other than Leonard Riggio, the founder of Barnes & Noble, Inc.), *aff'd*, 15 A.3d 218 (Del. 2011).

[47] See generally Allen, Kraakman, and Subramanian (2009: 606 § 13.9.1) (describing the use of 'continuing director' pills); see also *Invacare Corp. v. Healthdyne Technologies, Inc.*, 968 F. SUPP. 1578 (N.D. Ga. 1997) (upholding the use of such pills under Georgia law).

18.5.3 Falling Behind the Rest of the World?

Finally, the Petition argues that the rules governing the timing of blockholder disclosure in other countries, including for example the United Kingdom, 'compel[] the Commission to enact related reforms'.[48] As we explain below, however, this claim is based on an unduly narrow comparison of the rules that apply to blockholders. In fact, when one considers the broad set of rules regulating the balance of power between incumbents and outside blockholders, it is clear that US law puts blockholders at a greater disadvantage than they face in other relevant jurisdictions.

The Petition and its supporters argue that support for their position is provided by rules in several foreign jurisdictions that require blockholders to disclose lower stakes, or to disclose stakes more quickly, than current US rules—the United Kingdom,[49] Australia,[50] Canada,[51] and Hong Kong.[52] Citing these jurisdictions, a partner in the firm that authored the Petition argues in recent work that, '[i]n the absence of updated requirements, the U.S. markets are more vulnerable than those in other jurisdictions to' 'exploitat[ion] of the 10-day window' (Katz and McIntosh 2012: 4).

This view fails to acknowledge, however, how the United States compares with these countries in terms of the overall treatment of outside blockholders. In no common law country other than the United States can an outside blockholder disclosing its presence fear being immediately subject to a poison pill precluding it from exceeding an ownership level that falls substantially below a control block. Indeed, in our view, to the extent there is a risk that American law puts our markets at a disadvantage, that risk is most acute with respect to state law rules that render the United States much more hostile to outside blockholders—which, as we have explained, play an important role in corporate governance.

To be sure, the Commission should consider developments in foreign jurisdictions, and their effects on US markets, when examining its rules on outside blockholders. But a narrow assessment of the law in these jurisdictions, limited only to the disclosure rules that apply to blockholders, offers an incomplete picture of the overall effect of legal rules on the role of blockholders in corporate governance. Instead, any comparative assessment of the United States' rules on blockholder disclosure should consider the broad set of rules governing outside blockholders—and recognize that the United States stands out among common law countries in the legal tools it gives incumbents seeking to impede outside blockholders who attempt to improve governance and increase firm value.

Indeed, lawmakers in the United States should be concerned that, overall, the rules governing the balance of power between management and outside blockholders have already moved some distance in favour of the former, particularly when compared with other jurisdictions.

48 See Petition, *supra* note 1, at 9.

49 See Katz and McIntosh (2012: 4) (citing Disclosure Rules and Transparency Rules, 2012, Fin. Servs. Auth. Handbook, ch. 5 (UK), available at <http://fsahandbook.info/FSA/html/handbook/DTR/5>.

50 See Katz and McIntosh (2012: 4) (citing Takeover Panels, Guidance Note 20: Equity Derivatives (Austl.)), available at <http://www.takeovers.gov.au/content/DisplayDoc.aspx?doc=guidance_notes/current/020.htm&pageID=&Year=>.

51 See Katz and McIntosh (2012: 4) (citing Province of Ontario Securities Act, R.S.O 1990, c. S.5, § 102.1 (Can.)).

52 See Katz and McIntosh (2012: 4) (citing Hong Kong Securities and Futures Ordinance, No. 571, (2003), pt. XV).

A partner in the firm that submitted the Petition has argued that the Commission's failure to tighten these rules further has worked 'to the detriment of the United States' ability to compete effectively in the global economy', and that tightening is needed to 'level the playing field'.[53] To the contrary, as we have explained, current law in the United States already tilts the playing field against blockholders further than the law in any other advanced economy. The United States is the only country in which incumbents can use shareholder rights plans to impose a ceiling on the size of the stakes that can be purchased by outside blockholders that incumbents do not favour. Combined with low-trigger rights plans, a further tightening of the rules requiring disclosure of outside blocks could give incumbents the power to keep outside blockholders at bay. This interaction between previously sanctioned defensive measures and disclosure rules is not present in any other advanced economy. Thus, lawmakers seeking to guard the United States' capital markets, and its ability to compete effectively, should be wary of any steps that would further tilt the legal playing field in favour of incumbents.

18.6 Conclusion

The SEC is currently considering tightening the rules that govern the timing of the disclosure of large blocks of stock in US public companies. Such tightening cannot be justified by an appeal to general intuitions about market transparency or by the claim that tightening is required to achieve the objectives of the Williams Act. Instead, before proceeding with the proposed tightening, the Commission should conduct a policy analysis of its expected costs and benefits. In this chapter, we have provided a framework for that analysis.

As we have explained, the Commission should consider the significant evidence that blockholders' presence and activities provide substantial benefits to public companies and their shareholders—and the adverse effect that tightening blockholders' disclosure obligations can be expected to have on these activities. Moreover, current evidence on changes in market practices since the passage of the Williams Act provides no basis for tightening these rules. Instead, changes in the legal landscape since that time make clear that blockholders face significant hurdles that are greater than those they face in other jurisdictions as well as those that were in place when Section 13(d) was first adopted in 1968.

We encourage the Commission to undertake a comprehensive examination of the rules governing blockholders. In our view, the Commission's examination should include a careful assessment of the empirical issues we have identified, including the following:

(i) An assessment, building on existing empirical work, of the magnitude of the benefits conferred on shareholders by the presence of outside blockholders and the factors that determine the size of these benefits in given cases;

(ii) An assessment of the effects of existing disclosure requirements, and of the expected effects of tightening or relaxing them, on both the incidence and size of the stakes held by outside blockholders and the investments in monitoring and engagement activities made by such blockholders;

[53] See Katz and McIntosh (2012: 4).

(iii) An assessment, based on an empirical study of Schedule 13D filings, of how pre-disclosure accumulations by outside blockholders have changed, if at all, since the passage of the Williams Act; and

(iv) An assessment of the extent to which the evolution of rules impeding the activities of outside blockholders, including rules allowing companies to use poison pills against outside blockholders not seeking to acquire control, adversely affect both the incidence and size of the stakes held by outside blockholders and the monitoring and engagement investments made by such blockholders.

In the meantime, the Commission should not pursue a piecemeal tightening of the rules governing the timing of blockholder disclosure. The received academic understanding and the available empirical evidence provide no basis for concluding that such changes would protect investors and promote efficiency. Indeed, there is a strong basis for concern that such changes would adversely affect investors and the performance of publicly traded companies.

References

Agrawal, A. and Nasser, T. (2012). Blockholders on Boards and CEO Compensation, Turnover and Firm Valuation, CELS 2009 4th Annual Conference on Empirical Legal Studies Paper, AFA 2012 Chicago Meeting Paper, available at <http://ssrn.com/abstract=1443431>.

Allen, W. T., Kraakman, R., and Subramanian, G. (eds.) (2009). *Commentaries and Cases on the Law of Business Organization* (3rd edn) (New York, Wolters Kluwer Law & Business/Aspen Publishers).

Baker, G. P. and Subramanian, G. (undated). The Global Market for Corporate Control (unpublished manuscript, on file with authors).

Barzuza, M. (2009). The State of State Antitakeover Law, *Virginia Law Review* 95, 1973.

Bebchuk, L. A., Grinstein, Y., and Peyer, U. (2010). Lucky CEOs and Lucky Directors, *Journal of Finance* 65, 2363–96.

Bebchuk, L. A. and Hart, O. (2002). Takeover Bids vs. Proxy Fights in Contests for Corporate Control, European Corporate Governance Institute—Finance Working Paper No. 04/2002; Harvard Law and Economics Discussion Paper No. 336, available at <http://ssrn.com/abstract=290584>.

Bertrand, M. and Mullainathan, S. (2001). Are CEOs Rewarded for Luck? The Ones Without Principals Are, *Quarterly Journal of Economics* 116, 901.

Borstadt, L. F. and Zwirlein, T. J. (1992). The Efficient Monitoring Role of Proxy Contests: An Empirical Analysis of Post-Contest Control Changes and Firm Performance, *Financial Management* 21, 22.

Brickley, J. A., Lease, R. C., and Smith, Jr, C. (1988). Ownership Structure and Voting on Antitakeover Amendments, *Journal of Financial Economics* 20, 267.

Dyck, A. and Zingales, L. (2004). Private Benefits of Control: An International Comparison, *Journal of Finance* 59, 537.

Grossman, S. J. and Hart, O. D. (1980). Disclosure Laws and Takeover Bids, *Journal of Finance* 35, 323.

Holderness, C. G. and Sheehan, D. P. (1985). Raiders or Saviors? The Evidence on Six Controversial Investors, *Journal of Financial Economics* 14, 555.

Ikenberry, D. and Lakonishok, J. (1992). Corporate Governance through the Proxy Contest: Evidence and Implications, *Journal of Business* 66, 405.

James, S. (2010). Massey Faces Shareholder Anger over Mine Disaster, *Reuters* (13 Apr.), available at <http://www.reuters.com/article/2010/04/13/us-massey-idUSTRE63C2Q920100413>.

Katz, D. and McIntosh, L. A. (2012). Corporate Governance Update: Section 13(d) Reporting Needs Updating, *New York Law Journal* (22 Mar.), available at <http://www.newyorklawjournal.com/PubArticleNY.jsp?id=1202546490293&Section_13d_Reporting_Requirements_Need_Updating&slreturn=20130228111652>.

Oral, R. D. (2011). SEC Eyes Faster Disclosure for Activist Funds, *CBS Marketwatch* (25 Feb.), available at <http://articles.marketwatch.com/2011-02-25/markets/30783592_1_activist-investors-damien-park-fund-managers>.

Pound, J. (1988). Proxy Contests and the Efficiency of Shareholder Oversight, *Journal of Financial Economics* 20, 237.

Shivdasani, A. (1993). Board Composition, Ownership Structure, and Hostile Takeovers, *Journal of Accounting and Economics* 16, 167.

Shleifer, A. and Vishny, R. W. (1986). Large Shareholders and Corporate Control, *Journal of Political Economy* 94, 461.

Sorkin, A. R. (2010). Big Investors Appear out of Thin Air, *Dealbook* (1 Nov.), available at <http://dealbook.nytimes.com/2010/11/01/sorkin-big-investors-appear-out-of-thin-air/>.

Wilmer Cutler Pickering Hale and Dorr LLP (2011). The Williams Act: A Truly 'Modern' Assessment (5 Aug.), unpublished manuscript, available at <http://www.sec.gov/comments/4-624/4624-5.pdf>.

CHAPTER 19

THE DESTRUCTIVE AMBIGUITY OF FEDERAL PROXY ACCESS

JILL E. FISCH

19.1 Introduction

UNDER US corporate law, the shareholders elect the board of directors.[1] In most cases, however, those shareholders do not nominate director candidates. Instead, the nominating committee of the board chooses a slate of candidates, and those candidates are submitted to the shareholders for approval.[2] Absent the infrequent phenomenon of an election contest,[3] shareholders do not participate in the nomination process.[4]

The Securities and Exchange Commission (SEC) has struggled for years to regulate the shareholders' role in nominating directors.[5] As early as 1942, the SEC proposed a rule that

[1] See, e.g., Del. Code Ann. tit. 8, § 211(b) (2001) ('[A]n annual meeting of stockholders shall be held for the election of directors . . .').

[2] See Order Approving NYSE and NASD Proposed Rule Changes and Amendments Relating to Corporate Governance, Exchange Act Release No. 48,745, 68 Fed. Reg. 64,154, 64,177 (4 Nov. 2003) (approving a New York Stock Exchange rule change requiring listed issuers to have an independent nominating committee).

[3] See Harris (2010: 120–1) (summarizing several reports on the frequency of contested elections and finding that, over the time period from 1996 to 2008, the number of contested elections at public companies averaged around thirty-six per year).

[4] Election contests, in which a challenger files a separate proxy card and conducts an independent solicitation, generally involve a substantial shareholder that is either seeking control of the company or seeking, through board representation, to effect a change in corporate strategy. See Cernich et al. (2009: 7–11) (describing how hedge funds use partial board representation to attempt to change corporate strategy). Few election contests are premised on differences in directors' personalities as opposed to the policies they propose to implement. Cf. *Rosenfeld v. Fairchild Engine & Airplane Corp.*, 128 N.E.2d 291, 293 (N.Y. 1955) (distinguishing between election contests premised on policy disagreements and those based on personal issues).

[5] State corporation law, rather than federal securities regulation, is the source of any shareholder power to nominate director candidates. Since the 1930s, however, the federal proxy rules have regulated

would have required issuers to include shareholder-nominated candidates in their proxy statements.[6] Ultimately, the SEC abandoned the proposal. In the ensuing almost seventy years, the SEC revisited the issue at least five times but failed to adopt a rule allowing proxy access.[7]

Adoption of a shareholder nomination rule faced several obstacles. First, from the outset, the rule faced strong opposition from business interests. Indeed, measured by the number of comment letters, proxy access is, by far, the SEC's most controversial rule-making initiative.[8] Second, as the SEC refined the federal proxy rules in response to on-going marketplace developments, the details of a proxy access rule became both increasingly important and impossible to perfect. Fundamentally, the SEC was unable to draft a proxy access rule that would satisfy everyone. Third, the DC Circuit declared in its 1990 decision in *Business Roundtable v. SEC* that the SEC lacked the authority to regulate corporate governance through the proxy rules.[9] A shareholder nomination rule was likely to raise a potential conflict with this holding and to trigger litigation seeking to invalidate the rule.[10]

When Congress authorized the SEC to adopt a federal proxy access rule as part of the Dodd-Frank financial regulatory reforms,[11] it removed the last of these hurdles, clearing

the procedures and disclosures associated with shareholder voting and the solicitation of proxies (see Fisch 1993: 1130–1).

Although the federal rules ostensibly do not modify shareholders' substantive voting rights, as a practical matter, federal regulation has substantially limited the exercise of those rights (Fisch 1993: 1134) ('[T]he SEC has affirmatively impeded the effectiveness of the shareholder voting process . . . .'); Strine (2008: 1087) ('[T]he use by stockholders of their state law rights had been stymied by the SEC itself . . .').

[6] Securities Act Release No. 2887, Exchange Act Release No. 3347, Holding Company Act Release No. 3988, Investment Company Act Release No. 417, 1942 WL 34864 (18 Dec. 1942).

[7] See Div. of Corp. Fin., Sec, 96th Cong., Staff Rep. on Corporate Accountability 29–32 (Comm. Print 1980) (describing task force and public hearings on proxy access in the late 1970s); Facilitating Shareholder Director Nominations, Securities Act Release No. 9046, Exchange Act Release No. 60,089, Investment Company Act Release No. 28,765, 74 Fed. Reg. 29,024 (proposed 18 June 2009) (to be codified at 17 C.F.R. pts. 200, 232, 240, 249, 274) (hereinafter Proposing Release) (proposing a proxy access rule); Shareholder Proposals, Exchange Act Release No. 56,160, Investment Company Act Release No. 27,913, 72 Fed. Reg. 43,466, 43,472 (proposed 3 Aug. 2007) (to be codified at 17 C.F.R. pt. 240) (proposing a rule that would allow 5% shareholders to propose proxy access by-law amendments); Security Holder Director Nominations, Exchange Act Release No. 48,626, Investment Company Act Release No. 26,206, 68 Fed. Reg. 60,784 (proposed 23 Oct. 2003) (to be codified at 17 C.F.R. pts. 240, 249, 274) (proposing a proxy access rule); Regulation of Communications Among Shareholders, Exchange Act Release No. 31,326, Investment Company Act Release No. 19,031, 57 Fed. Reg. 48,276, 48,288 (22 Oct. 1992) (to be codified at 17 C.F.R. pts. 240, 249) (considering a universal ballot as part of proposed amendments to the bona fide nominee rule).

[8] See Romanek (2010) (stating that the SEC had received almost 52,000 comment letters on proxy access as of February 2010). It should be noted that many of these were duplicate or form letters (Romanek 2010).

[9] See 905 F.2d 406 (D.C. Cir. 1990).

[10] See Letter from Henry A. McKinnell, Chairman, Bus. Roundtable, to Jonathan G. Katz, Sec'y, SEC 4–6 (22 Dec. 2003), available at <http://www.sec.gov/rules/proposed/s71903/s71903-381.pdf> (arguing that the 1990 *Business Roundtable* decision limited the SEC's power to regulate disclosures, not corporate governance).

[11] Dodd-Frank Wall Street Reform and Consumer Protection Act, Pub. L. No. 111-203, § 971, 124 Stat. 1376, 1915 (2010) (codified as amended at 15 U.S.C. § 78n(a)(2) (Supp. IV 2010)).

the way for the SEC both to adopt proxy access and more importantly, to consider explicitly the corporate governance implications of increasing shareholder access to the proxy. Yet Rule 14a-11,[12] the SEC's proxy access rule, adopted on 25 August 2010, when the ink on Dodd-Frank was barely dry,[13] was limited in scope and ambiguous in both its application and its justification. Indeed, once Congress authorized the SEC's adoption of proxy access, the SEC's most significant change to its prior proposals was to tighten the qualification requirements, sharply limiting the number of shareholders that would be able to use the rule.

Although the SEC described the proxy access rule as 'facilitat[ing] the rights of shareholders to nominate directors to a company's board',[14] it failed to do so. The restrictive limitations on which shareholders qualify to use the rule, coupled with new and existing burdens on shareholder collective action, suggested that the rule would be a non-starter, ineffective in enabling shareholders even to exercise their nominating power, much less to affect board composition or increase director accountability. In addition, the SEC battened down the hatches with respect to state law and private ordering efforts to facilitate shareholder nominating power. Although it purported to leave issuers the option of further extending shareholder nominating rights, the new rule burdened the use of issuer-specific alternatives to it—even though recent amendments to the Delaware statute explicitly authorized issuers to establish shareholder nominating procedures.[15]

When the DC Circuit invalidated Rule 14a-11,[16] it removed a largely ineffective tool for shareholder nomination of directors but not the pre-existing and continuing burdens on private ordering. Existing SEC rules continue to impose extensive regulatory requirements on the exercise of shareholder nomination rights and to frustrate shareholder efforts to enhance those rights through state law mechanisms.

Regardless of whether one supports shareholder nomination of directors, the Rule 14a-11 experience raises a puzzle. If the SEC intended to facilitate shareholder nomination of directors, why did it adopt a rule that largely insulates issuers from shareholder input into the selection of director candidates? If, instead, the SEC determined that increasing shareholder nominating power was a bad idea, why go through the pretence of adopting a proxy access rule at all? More broadly, the SEC's rulemaking releases offer no insight into the SEC's normative position as to whether proxy access will improve the corporate governance of public companies. Absent such justification, the exercise of rulemaking authority appeared disturbingly arbitrary. Yet the DC Circuit appeared untroubled by these deficiencies and,

[12] Rule 14a-11 was reserved from the 2010 Code of Federal Regulations pending litigation over its validity in the DC Circuit. After the rule was invalidated in *Business Roundtable v. SEC*, 647 F.3d 1144 (D.C. Cir. 2011), the 2011 Code of Federal Regulations omitted the rule entirely. The rule as it was adopted can be found at Facilitating Shareholder Director Nominations, Securities Act Release No. 9136, Exchange Act Release No. 62,764, Investment Company Act Release No. 29,384, 75 Fed. Reg. 56,668, 56,677–93 (16 Sept. 2010) (to be codified at 17 C.F.R. pts. 200, 232, 240, 249) (hereinafter Adopting Release). The remainder of this chapter will refer to the final rule as released in the Federal Register.

[13] President Obama signed the Dodd-Frank Act into law on 21 July 2010 (*Boston Globe* 2011).

[14] Press Release, SEC, SEC Adopts New Measures to Facilitate Director Nominations by Shareholders (25 Aug. 2010), available at <http://www.sec.gov/news/press/2010/2010-155.htm>.

[15] See Del. Code Ann. tit. 8, § 112 (Supp. 2011) (authorizing issuers to adopt proxy access by-laws).

[16] *Bus. Roundtable v. SEC*, 647 F.3d at 1146.

instead, took the unprecedented approach of second-guessing the conclusions of the SEC's economic analysis.

This chapter explores the destructive ambiguity of federal proxy access. It demonstrates the tension between the federal requirements for the exercise of shareholder nominating rights and the state law principles upon which the SEC purported to ground those rights. It unpacks the ambiguities in the SEC's conception of which shareholders should nominate director candidates. And it reveals the ambiguity resulting from the SEC's failure to confront, in adopting its rule, the appropriate allocation of power between shareholders and management, and the effects of proxy access on that balance. Ironically, these deficiencies highlight the advantages provided by state law regulation of corporate governance and strengthen the case for implementing shareholder nominating procedures through private ordering.

Because it is important to consider Rule 14a-11 in its historical context, Section 19.2 of this chapter briefly recounts the history of federal proxy access. In Section 19.3, the chapter describes the major features of Rule 14a-11, the SEC's accompanying changes to Rule 14a-8, and the subsequent history of the rules, including the DC Circuit's decision. Section 19.4 identifies the SEC's ambiguous rationale for adopting a federal proxy access rule. In Section 19.5, the chapter situates proxy access within the broader context of corporate governance and demonstrates how latent ambiguity in the appropriate allocation of power within the corporate structure and the inability of a mandatory federal rule to adjust as necessary to maintain a stable equilibrium render a federal standard inferior to state law and private ordering.[17] Section 19.6 proposes an alternative regulatory approach designed to facilitate such private ordering. Section 19.7 concludes.

The existing political climate makes it unlikely that the SEC will propose a revised proxy access rule, at least in the short term, and the revisions to the Delaware statute and Rule 14a-8 provide, at least nominally, the opportunity for shareholders to experiment with proxy access through private ordering. As described in this chapter, however, federal law continues to impede such experimentation. With the invalidation of Rule 14a-11, adoption of the reforms advocated in Section 19.6 of this chapter to remove such impediments becomes increasingly important.

19.2 The History of Federal Proxy Access

The tepid support offered by the SEC for proxy access and the limited scope of Rule 14a-11 are particularly surprising in light of the rule's long gestation period. The SEC has been considering proxy access for almost seventy years. Indeed, the SEC first considered a rule

[17] This chapter uses the term private ordering to describe issuer-specific corporate governance provisions, as distinguished from corporate law rules established by statute or regulation. Such governance provisions are contractual in nature and typically take the form of a charter or by-law provision, although they may alternatively be embodied in a traditional contract. See *UniSuper Ltd. v. News Corp.*, 898 A.2d 344, 345–6 (Del. Ch. 2006) (describing an agreement between a board and a corporation's shareholders regarding the board's power to adopt a poison pill); Smith, Wright, and Hintze (2011: 127 n.12) (discussing various uses of the term 'private ordering').

that would have required issuers to include shareholder-nominated director candidates on the proxy statement in 1942.[18] This consideration was part of the rulemaking process that resulted in the adoption of the shareholder proposal rule, now Rule 14a-8—rulemaking that resulted from the changes to the proxy solicitation process that reduced in-person attendance at shareholder meetings.[19] Although the SEC adopted a requirement that issuers include shareholder proposals in the proxy statement, the SEC abandoned the provision addressing shareholder nominations in the face of substantial opposition by corporate management (Fisch 1993: 1163).

Subsequently, the SEC revised the shareholder proposal rule to preclude proposals relating to director elections. As time went on, the SEC's interpretations of this exclusion became increasingly restrictive, leading the SEC to authorize the exclusion of proposals that nominated or advocated the election of a particular director, as well as proposals that addressed director qualifications or election procedures more generally (Fisch 2008: 63–4).

Investors repeatedly challenged the SEC's restrictive approach to shareholder voting and urged the SEC to reverse its position. In 1977, the SEC established a task force to undertake a comprehensive review of the federal proxy rules.[20] As part of the review process, the SEC held a series of public hearings in which it received testimony and submissions from a wide variety of constituents concerning the nomination process.[21] Critics of shareholder nominations, primarily corporate management, testified that the use of nominating committees would adequately address any perceived problems about the director nomination process.[22] At the conclusion of the process, the SEC did not propose a shareholder nomination rule.[23] Instead, as the SEC task force reported to the Senate, due to the emergence of nominating committees, a shareholder nomination rule was unnecessary.[24]

In response to continued investor complaints, the SEC undertook another 'comprehensive review' of the proxy rules in 1990.[25] Following two years of study, the SEC adopted a variety of controversial rule changes designed to reduce the 'chilling effect' and costs associated with shareholder participation in the proxy solicitation process.[26] Despite proposals for a universal ballot that would have facilitated investor choice among competing slates of candidates, the SEC did not adopt such a proposal, nor did it adopt a shareholder nomination rule.[27]

[18] See Fisch (2008: 63) (describing the 1942 rule proposal).

[19] Securities Act Release No. 2887, Exchange Act Release No. 3347, Holding Company Act Release No. 3988, Investment Company Act Release No. 417, 1942 WL 34864 (18 Dec. 1942).

[20] See Div. of Corp. Fin., Sec, Staff Report: Review of The Proxy Process Regarding the Nomination and Election of Directors 3 n.10 (2003), available at <http://www.sec.gov/news/studies/proxyreport.pdf> (describing the SEC's consideration of proxy access in 1977).

[21] See Div. of Corp. Fin., *supra* note 7, at 29–30.

[22] See Div. of Corp. Fin., *supra* note 7, at 122–7.

[23] In response to the task force report, the SEC developed three proposals, two of which would have substantially reduced the SEC's role in regulating shareholder access to the ballot (Fisch 1993: 1165 n.169). The SEC did not adopt these proposals (Fisch 1993: 1165 n.169).

[24] Div. of Corp. Fin., *supra* note 7, at 122–7.

[25] See Fisch (1993: 1165–6) (internal quotation marks omitted) (describing concerns leading up to the SEC's 1990 review of the proxy rules).

[26] See Regulation of Communications Among Shareholders, Exchange Act Release No. 31,326, Investment Company Act Release No. 19,031, 57 Fed. Reg. 48,276, 48,279 (22 Oct. 1992) (to be codified at 17 C.F.R. pts. 240, 249).

[27] See Regulation of Communications Among Shareholders, Exchange Act Release No. 31,326, Investment Company Act Release No. 19,031, 57 Fed. Reg. 48, 276, 48,287–9.

Finally, in the wake of the Sarbanes-Oxley Act of 2002[28] and the wave of corporate governance scandals that precipitated its adoption,[29] the SEC returned to the subject of proxy access. In May 2003, the SEC solicited public comment on its review of the proxy rules relating to the nomination and election of directors.[30] Several months later, the SEC proposed a proxy access rule.[31]

The proposed rule, in general terms, would have allowed shareholders that had held at least 5% of the company's stock for at least two years[32] to nominate from one to three director candidates, but only upon the occurrence of a triggering event.[33] Triggering events included one or more directors receiving a 35% withhold vote, submission of a direct access proposal by holders of at least 1% of the issuer's stock and approval of the proposal by a majority of votes cast, and, possibly, the issuer's failure to adopt a shareholder resolution or proposal that had received majority approval.[34]

As proposed, the extent to which Rule 14a-11 would have resulted in the inclusion of shareholder-nominated directors was unclear. With respect to the triggering conditions, the SEC found, in a study of director elections over the preceding two years, that roughly 1.1% of companies had total withhold votes in excess of 35% of the votes cast.[35] The SEC also observed that 84% of companies listed on an exchange or NASDAQ had at least one

[28] Pub. L. No. 107-204, 116 Stat. 745.

[29] Fisch (2010a: 924–5) (describing frauds at Enron and WorldCom as the most prominent examples of these scandals).

[30] Notice of Solicitation of Public Views Regarding Possible Changes to the Proxy Rules, Exchange Act No. 47,778, 68 Fed. Reg. 24,530 (7 May 2003).

[31] Security Holder Director Nominations, Exchange Act Release No. 48,626, Investment Company Act Release No. 26,206, 68 Fed. Reg. 60,784, 60,784–5 (proposed 23 Oct. 2003) (to be codified at 17 C.F.R. pts. 240, 249, 274). The rule was explicitly subject to state corporate law provisions concerning shareholder nomination rights (Security Holder Director Nominations, Exchange Act Release No. 48,626, Investment Company Act Release No. 26,206, 68 Fed. Reg. 60,808). In particular, the SEC noted that, to the extent that state law permitted a corporation to prohibit shareholder nominations through provisions in its charter or by-laws, the proposed proxy access procedure would not be available to shareholders of corporations choosing to do so (Security Holder Director Nominations, Exchange Act Release No. 48,626, Investment Company Act Release No. 26,206, 68 Fed. Reg. 60,808).

[32] Security Holder Director Nominations, Exchange Act Release No. 48,626, Investment Company Act Release No. 26,206, 68 Fed. Reg. 60,806. Where multiple shareholders were eligible to use the rule, the company would only be required to include the nominee(s) of the shareholder with the largest stake in the company (Security Holder Director Nominations, Exchange Act Release No. 48,626, Investment Company Act Release No. 26,206, 68 Fed. Reg. 60,798).

[33] Security Holder Director Nominations, Exchange Act Release No. 48,626, Investment Company Act Release No. 26,206, 68 Fed. Reg. 60,797. The proposed rule also included various disclosure and independence requirements, including a requirement that the nominee be independent of the nominating shareholder (Security Holder Director Nominations, Exchange Act Release No. 48,626, Investment Company Act Release No. 26,206, 68 Fed. Reg. 60,795–6). The independence requirement provided, inter alia, that a natural person could not nominate himself and that an entity could not nominate a current or former employee (Security Holder Director Nominations, Exchange Act Release No. 48,626, Investment Company Act Release No. 26,206, 68 Fed. Reg. 60,796).

[34] See Security Holder Director Nominations, Exchange Act Release No. 48,626, Investment Company Act Release No. 26,206, 68 Fed. Reg. 60,789–91 (describing triggering events).

[35] Security Holder Director Nominations, Exchange Act Release No. 48,626, Investment Company Act Release No. 26,206, 68 Fed. Reg. 60,790.

shareholder that would have been eligible to submit a proxy access resolution.[36] According to the SEC, in the event proxy access was triggered, 42% of filers had at least one shareholder that, individually, met the necessary ownership requirements to nominate a director candidate, and 18% had two or more such shareholders.[37] The SEC did not provide information about the characteristics of these shareholders that might provide a basis for assessing whether they would be likely to nominate a director. Based on this data, the SEC estimated that the proxy access rule would be triggered annually in seventy-three companies and that, in forty-five of these companies, at least one shareholder would make a nomination.[38]

Although the SEC's estimates may have been overly generous and, even under those estimates, shareholder nominations under the proposed rule were unlikely to occur frequently,[39] business interests mounted substantial opposition to the proposal. A total of 504 individuals and entities submitted comments on the proposal,[40] and an additional 185 comments were subsequently submitted in response to an additional solicitation of comments.[41] As the SEC explained in its summary, most of those supporting the proposal favoured a stronger rule—one providing greater proxy access rights.[42] Corporations, corporate executives, and corporate directors, however, 'were nearly unanimous in their opposition to the proposed rules'.[43] Faced with this business opposition, coupled with

[36] See Security Holder Director Nominations, Exchange Act Release No. 48,626, Investment Company Act Release No. 26,206, 68 Fed. Reg. 60, 790 (observing that 84% of these companies had at least one shareholder that owned at least 1% of the outstanding shares for at least one year).

[37] Security Holder Director Nominations, Exchange Act Release No. 48,626, Investment Company Act Release No. 26,206, 68 Fed. Reg. 60,794.

[38] Security Holder Director Nominations, Exchange Act Release No. 48,626, Investment Company Act Release No. 26,206, 68 Fed. Reg. 60,810. These estimates were made as part of the SEC's analysis under the Paperwork Reduction Act (Security Holder Director Nominations, Exchange Act Release No. 48,626, Investment Company Act Release No. 26,206, 68 Fed. Reg. 60,807). The SEC conceded that

> there is no reliable way to predict how many more security holder proposals would be submitted based on the proposed amendments, how often the events would be triggered or how many security holders would be able to meet the applicable requirements (e.g., minimum ownership threshold (Security Holder Director Nominations, Exchange Act Release No. 48,626, Investment Company Act Release No. 26,206, 68 Fed. Reg. 60,811)).

[39] In 2002, the SEC indicated that there were approximately 9,400 reporting issuers. See Acceleration of Periodic Report Filing Dates and Disclosure Concerning Web Site Access to Reports, Securities Act Release No. 8128, Exchange Act Release No. 46,464, 67 Fed. Reg. 58,480, 58,489 n.95 (16 Sept. 2002) (to be codified at 17 C.F.R. pts. 210, 229, 240, 249). By 2006, that number had increased to almost 12,000.

See Smaller Reporting Company Regulatory Relief and Simplification, Securities Act Release No. 8876, Exchange Act Release No. 56,994, Trust Indenture Act Release No. 2451, 73 Fed. Reg. 934, 935 (4 Jan. 2008) (to be codified at 17 C.F.R. pts. 210, 228, 229, 230, 239, 240, 249, 260, 269).

[40] Summary of Comments: In Response to the Commission's Proposed Rules Relating to Security Holder Director Nominations, U.S. SEC. & EXCH. COMM'N (5 Mar. 2004), available at <http://www.sec.gov/rules/extra/s71903summary.htm> (hereinafter Summary of Comments).

[41] Div. of Corp. Fin., Sec, File No. S7-19-03, Supplemental Summary of Comments Received on or after February 6, 2004: In Response to the Commission's Proposed Rules Relating to Security Holder Director Nominations 3–8 (2004).

[42] Div. of Corp. Fin., Sec, File No. S7-19-03, Supplemental Summary of Comments Received on or after February 6, 2004: In Response to the Commission's Proposed Rules Relating to Security Holder Director Nominations 9–10 ('[M]ore than half the Supporting Commenters desired a stronger rule.').

[43] Summary of Comments, *supra* note 40.

claims that any consideration of shareholder nomination should be deferred pending an assessment of the impact of Sarbanes-Oxley, Chairman Donaldson abandoned the proposal.[44]

The SEC's decision not to mandate proxy access in 2003 might have laid the issue to rest, but institutional investors were not satisfied. Having failed to persuade the SEC to adopt proxy access, they sought, through private ordering, to implement proxy access procedures at individual issuers.[45] In 2006, the Second Circuit upheld an effort by the American Federation of State, County and Municipal Employees (AFSCME), a union pension fund, to submit a proxy access by-law for a vote by AIG shareholders.[46] The decision, by holding that Rule 14a-8 permitted the submission of proxy access by-laws,[47] opened the door for investors to establish issuer-specific procedures for shareholder participation in the nominating process.[48]

The SEC promptly closed the door on these private ordering efforts. Expressing concern that the decision would lead to 'uncertainty and confusion' in the upcoming proxy season and that proxy access by-law amendments could result in contested director elections that did not comport with the disclosure requirements applicable to election contests, the SEC reopened the issue of proxy access.[49] The SEC proposed two alternatives. The first alternative would have authorized large shareholders that satisfied certain conditions to propose proxy access procedures through by-law amendments.[50] The second alternative proposed codifying the position that the SEC had advocated in *AFSCME v. AIG, Inc.*, authorizing issuers to exclude shareholder nomination by-law proposals.[51] On 6 December 2007, the SEC adopted the latter alternative, overturning the court's decision in *AFSCME*.[52]

44 Morgenson (2006) (explaining that corporate lobbying 'helped to defeat' the 2003 proxy access proposal).

45 See Fisch (2008: 66) (describing issuer efforts to obtain proxy access through by-law amendment proposals in the wake of the failed 2003 proposal).

46 *AFSCME v. AIG, Inc.*, 462 F.3d 121, 130–1 (2d Cir. 2006).

47 *AFSCME v. AIG, Inc.*, 462 F.3d 121, 130–1 (2d Cir. 2006).

48 The court noted that the SEC was free, however, to change the scope of the election exclusion (see *AFSCME v. AIG, Inc.*, 462 F.3d 121, 130 n.9 (2d Cir. 2006)):

> [I]f the SEC determines that the interpretation of the election exclusion embodied in its 1976 Statement would result in a decrease in necessary disclosures or any other undesirable outcome, it can certainly change its interpretation of the election exclusion, provided that it explains its reasons for doing so.

49 Shareholder Proposals Relating to the Election of Directors, Exchange Act Release No. 56,161, Investment Company Act Release No. 27,914, 72 Fed. Reg. 43,488, 43,491 (proposed 27 July 2007) (to be codified at 17 C.F.R. pt. 240).

50 Shareholder Proposals Relating to the Election of Directors, Exchange Act Release No. 56,161, Investment Company Act Release No. 27,914, 72 Fed. Reg. 43,470 (proposing a rule allowing shareholders that held at least 5% of the company's stock for at least a year and who had filed a 13G in addition to making a variety of further disclosures to propose a proxy access by-law amendment). The proposed rule did not seek to dictate any specific procedures or qualifications for proxy access.

51 Shareholder Proposals Relating to the Election of Directors, Exchange Act Release No. 56,161, Investment Company Act Release No. 27,914, 72 Fed. Reg. 43,493.

52 Shareholder Proposals Relating to the Election of Directors, Exchange Act Release No. 56,914, Investment Company Act Release No. 28,075, 72 Fed. Reg. 70,450 (11 Dec. 2007) (to be codified at 17 C.F.R. pt. 240).

The 2007 amendment, which precluded shareholders from establishing nominating procedures on an issuer-specific basis through private ordering, was the most restrictive approach to shareholder nomination that the SEC had ever taken. President Obama's election and his subsequent appointment of Mary Schapiro to serve as the new Chair of the SEC made proxy access appear more likely. In her confirmation hearings, Schapiro pledged to give large shareholders more say in the selection of corporate directors (Goldfarb 2009).

Subsequently, on 10 June 2009, the SEC introduced another proxy access proposal.[53] The proposal contained two components. First, the SEC proposed a revised version of Rule 14a-11 that would have authorized shareholders that owned from 1% to 5% of the issuer's stock (depending on the size of the issuer) for at least a year to nominate candidates for up to 25% of the board of directors.[54] Although the proposal required shareholder candidates to meet applicable standards of independence,[55] it eliminated the requirement of a triggering event[56] and the limitations on relationships between the candidate and the nominating shareholder that had been part of the 2003 proposed rule.[57] The rule also required new disclosures on proposed Schedule 14N—disclosures that the SEC described as 'substantially similar' to those proposed in 2003.[58]

Second, the SEC proposed amending Rule 14a-8 to permit shareholder proposals concerning nomination procedures or disclosures as long as the proposals did not conflict with proposed Rule 14a-11.[59] The amendment would have treated such proposals similarly to all other shareholder proposals—proposing shareholders would have been required to hold a minimum of $2,000 worth of stock for at least a year[60] and would not have been required to make any mandated disclosures or filings.[61] The SEC explained that this proposal, which essentially reversed its 2007 rule change, was feasible in light of the fact that any issuer-specific shareholder nomination process would now be subject to mandated disclosure under new Rule 14a-19, which included the requirement that a nominating shareholder file a Schedule 14N.[62]

The SEC received 537 comments in the initial sixty-day comment period (Ballard 2009). Some of these comments provided data and analysis suggesting that the SEC's review had been incomplete. As a result, in December 2009, the SEC reopened the comment period for

[53] Proposing Release, *supra* note 7.

[54] Proposing Release, *supra* note 7 at 29,032–44. The rule proposed to allow shareholders to nominate one director candidate or 25% of the board's directors, whichever was greater. Proposing Release, *supra* note 7 at 29,043. Where multiple qualifying shareholders sought to nominate director candidates, the company would only be required to include those candidates from the first nominating shareholder or group (Proposing Release, *supra* note 7 at 29,044).

[55] Proposing Release, *supra* note 7 at 29,040–2.

[56] Proposing Release, *supra* note 7 at 29,032 ('Today's proposal does not require a triggering event.').

[57] Proposing Release, *supra* note 7 at 29,041.

[58] Proposing Release, *supra* note 7 at. 29,045–6. The SEC described Schedule 14N as requiring 'disclosure similar to what would be obtained in an election contest' (Proposing Release, *supra* note 7 at 29,046).

[59] Proposing Release, *supra* note 7 at 29,056.

[60] Proposing Release, *supra* note 7 at 29,056 n.256.

[61] Proposing Release, *supra* note 7 at 29,056.

[62] See Proposing Release, *supra* note 7 at 29,056–8.

an additional thirty days, specifically inviting the public to comment on this additional material.[63] Approximately sixty comments were submitted during this additional period.[64]

As indicated above, commentators have repeatedly questioned the authority of the SEC to mandate proxy access.[65] With the adoption of the Dodd-Frank Wall Street Reform and Consumer Protection Act[66] on 15 July 2010 (Dennis 2010), Congress addressed these concerns. The new legislation explicitly authorized the SEC to adopt rules requiring proxy access, although Dodd-Frank did not require the SEC to adopt a proxy access rule.[67] President Obama signed the legislation on 21 July 2010 (Cooper 2010). Just a month later, on 25 August 2010, the SEC voted 3–2 to adopt a proxy access rule.[68]

19.3 The Federal Proxy Access Rule

The SEC's final rules contained the same two components as the 2009 proposal: new Rule 14a-11 (the proxy access rule) and an amendment to Rule 14a-8 permitting shareholder proposals relating to nomination procedures.[69] Both rules were similar to the 2009 proposals, but Rule 14a-11 reflected two significant changes. First, Rule 14a-11 limited proxy access to shareholders that have owned at least 3% of the issuer's stock, providing a uniform minimum ownership requirement for all companies rather than varying the threshold depending on company size.[70] For the largest companies, this change was a substantial increase from the 1% threshold originally proposed. Second, the final rule increased the required holding period before a shareholder could qualify to nominate a director candidate from one to three years.[71] Nominating

[63] Facilitating Shareholder Director Nominations, Securities Act Release No. 9086, Exchange Act Release No. 61,161, Investment Company Act Release No. 29,069, 74 Fed. Reg. 67,144, 67,145 (proposed 14 Dec. 2009) (to be codified at 17 C.F.R. pts. 200, 232, 240, 249, 274) (referencing four documents containing such data and analysis and included in the public comment file).

[64] Comments on Proposed Rule: Facilitating Shareholder Director Nominations, US SEC. & Exch Comm'n, available at <http://www.sec.gov/comments/s7-10-09/s71009.shtml> (last modified 1 Nov. 2010) (listing and providing links to submitted comments and including approximately sixty comments submitted after December 2009).

[65] See, e.g., Div. of Corp. Fin., *supra* note 20, at 6 (describing these objections).

[66] Pub. L. No. 111-203, 124 Stat. 1376 (2010) (codified as amended in scattered sections of 7, 12, and 15 U.S.C.).

[67] Compare Dodd-Frank Wall Street Reform and Consumer Protection Act § 971 (authorizing the SEC to adopt proxy access rules), with § 951 (adopting an explicit requirement of periodic shareholder votes on executive compensation).

[68] Adopting Release, *supra* note 12.

[69] Adopting Release, *supra* note 12. The description in this section summarizes the key features of the rule. The adopting release contained numerous technical details not discussed here including the basis upon which ownership was calculated, the procedures for contesting a shareholder nomination and the time periods applicable to such procedures, and the manner in which a disqualified nominating group or nominee was to be replaced. See generally Adopting Release, *supra* note 12, at 56,677–740 (detailing the specific provisions of the adopted changes to Rules 14a-11 and 14a-8).

[70] Adopting Release, *supra* note 12, at 56,674–5.

[71] Adopting Release, *supra* note 12, at 56,675. The rule addressed various technical details concerning these ownership requirements. Among these, ownership, for the purpose of using Rule 14a-11, was defined to include both voting and investment power (Adopting Release, *supra* note 12, at 56,675).

shareholders were required to continue to hold the stock through the annual meeting and to disclose their intentions with respect to continued ownership after the meeting.[72] As with the 2009 proposal, shareholders were limited to nominating a maximum of one director or candidates for 25% of the board, whichever was greater.[73]

The final rule included new disclosure requirements for nominating shareholders and their nominees. Under the rule, a nominating shareholder or group had to file a Schedule 14N between 120 and 150 days prior to the first anniversary of the mailing of the proxy statement for the issuer's prior annual meeting.[74] Rule 14a-18 (adopted at the same time) extended the requirement of filing a Schedule 14N to shareholder nominations made pursuant to state and foreign law as well.[75] Schedule 14N provides notice to the issuer and the SEC of the shareholder's intent to nominate one or more director candidates and requires, inter alia, information about the nominating shareholder's securities ownership; disclosures about the nominating shareholder and the nominees as well as any relationships between the nominating shareholder, the nominees, and the issuer; and disclosures about the nominees' qualifications, including a statement that the nominees meet the objective stock exchange independence criteria.[76]

Presumably recognizing that few shareholders would be able to satisfy the minimum ownership and holding period requirements individually, the adopting release contemplated—indeed, embraced—the formation of nominating groups.[77] The federal securities laws have traditionally treated collective shareholder action with suspicion. Indeed, the adopting release specifically warned that communications among shareholders for the purpose of forming a nominating group constitute proxy solicitations that are themselves subject to Regulation 14A.[78] Nonetheless, to facilitate the formation of nominating groups, the SEC adopted new Rule 14a-2(b)(7). Rule14a-2(b)(7) provided a limited exemption from certain of the proxy rules for oral and limited written communications in connection with the formation of a nominating group.[79]

The exemption applied only to shareholders seeking to form a nominating group pursuant to Rule 14a-11; it did not apply to communications that would have had the purpose or effect of changing control of the company, and it did not protect shareholders seeking to exercise nominating rights pursuant to state law or issuer-specific nominating procedures.[80] The rule limited the content of written solicitations to specified information, required that all written solicitations be filed with the SEC, and required disclosure of oral communications prior to the occurrence of the first such solicitation.[81]

Other aspects of the proxy rules impeded collective shareholder action (Fisch 1993: 1198). In response to concerns about these impediments, the SEC amended Rule 13d1(b)(1) to

[72] Adopting Release, *supra* note 12, at 56,675.

[73] Adopting Release, *supra* note 12, at 56,675.

[74] Adopting Release, *supra* note 12, at 56,675. This uniform notice period would have pre-empted an issuer's advance notice by-laws. For a discussion of advance notice by-laws, see *JANA Master Fund Ltd. v. CNET Networks, Inc.*, 954 A.2d 335, 343–4 (Del. Ch. 2008).

[75] Adopting Release, *supra* note 12, at 56,748–9.

[76] See Adopting Release, *supra* note 12, at 56,789–92.

[77] See Adopting Release, *supra* note 12, at 56,674 ('Shareholders will be able to aggregate their shares to meet the [ownership] threshold.').

[78] Adopting Release, *supra* note 12, at 56,725.

[79] Adopting Release, *supra* note 12, at 56,726.

[80] Adopting Release, *supra* note 12, at 56,726–7.

[81] Adopting Release, *supra* note 12, at 56,726.

provide that participation in a nominating group did not, by itself, require a shareholder to file a Schedule 13D, rather than a Schedule 13G.[82] This amendment was of particular significance for activist shareholders that might have been concerned, after *CSX Corp. v. Children's Investment Fund Management (UK) LLP*, about the implications of engaging in collective action.[83] Group formation could, however, trigger the obligation to file a Schedule 13G, and the rule did not provide an exemption.[84] In addition, the adopting release explicitly stated that nominating groups were not exempt from the provisions of section 16 of the Exchange Act, effectively precluding the formation of groups with aggregated holdings that exceed 10%.[85]

Finally, the adopting release made clear that Rule 14a-11 was not available to shareholders that sought to affect the control of the issuer.[86] Although the SEC attempted to justify this restriction by stating that the rule was not intended to serve as a substitute for the existing disclosures and other regulation of control contests—despite the expanded disclosure requirements of Schedule 14N—the resulting limitations were highly restrictive.[87] Each nominating shareholder or member of the nominating group was required to certify on Schedule 14N that it was not 'holding the company's securities with the purpose, or with the effect, of changing control of the company or to gain a number of seats on the board of directors that exceeds the maximum number of nominees that the company could be required to include under Rule 14a-11'.[88] In addition, no member of a nominating group was permitted to join with another shareholder or group in soliciting proxies, to conduct a separate proxy solicitation, or to be a participant in another person's solicitation.[89]

The amendment to Rule 14a-8 was similar to that in the 2009 proposal; it reversed the SEC's 2007 rule change and required issuers to include otherwise valid shareholder proposals to amend the issuer's governing documents relating to director nominating procedures or disclosures.[90] Proposals conflicting with Rule 14a-11 or applicable state law were not

82 Adopting Release, *supra* note 12, at 56,736 (describing the amendment to 17 C.F.R. § 240.13d1(b)(1)(i) (2011)).

83 See 562 F. Supp. 2d 511, 554 (S.D.N.Y. 2008), aff'd in part, vacated in part, 654 F.3d 276 (2d Cir. 2011) (finding that communications and common objectives of two hedge funds resulted in the formation of a group and triggered the disclosure requirements of section 13(d) of the Exchange Act). Qualification to file a Schedule 13G, rather than a Schedule 13D, also offers shareholders the opportunity substantially to delay disclosure of their intentions. See *infra* notes 206–8 and accompanying text (describing differences between Schedule 13G and 13D disclosure obligations).

84 Adopting Release, *supra* note 12, at 56,735 ('[I]t is possible that in aggregating shares to meet the ownership requirement, a nominating shareholder or group will trigger the reporting requirements of Regulation 13D–G. . . .').

85 Adopting Release, *supra* note 12, at 56,737:

> [A]n exclusion from Section 16 is not appropriate for groups formed solely for the purpose of nominating a director pursuant to Rule 14a-11, soliciting in connection with the election of that nominee, or having that nominee elected as director.

86 See Adopting Release, *supra* note 12, at 56,698.

87 Seemingly, however, the SEC did not view these limitations as sufficient. As it explained, the concern about control contests also warranted extending the required holding period from one to three years (Adopting Release, *supra* note 12: 56,697–8). '[A] longer holding period is another safeguard against shareholders that may attempt to inappropriately use Rule 14a-11 as a means to quickly gain control of a company.' (Adopting Release, *supra* note 12: 56,698).

88 Adopting Release, *supra* note 12, at 56,675.

89 Adopting Release, *supra* note 12, at 56,682.

90 Adopting Release, *supra* note 12, at 56,730–2.

permitted, nor were proposals focused on specific directors or director candidates.[91] As with the 2009 proposal, shareholders wishing to submit such proposals merely needed to satisfy the standard minimum ownership and holding requirements of Rule 14a-8.[92] As discussed further below, however, shareholders that use issuer-specific nominating procedures must comply with the complete filing and disclosure requirements of Regulation 14A in a similar manner to shareholders that mount a proxy contest.[93]

The new rules applied to all issuers that were subject to the federal proxy rules, including investment companies as well as controlled companies in which minority shareholders lack sufficient voting power to elect a shareholder nominee.[94] Many commentators objected to the one-size-fits-all approach and urged the SEC to allow private ordering.[95] Specifically, commentators argued that issuers should have been able to design proxy access procedures that were tailored to their individual circumstances.[96]

The SEC refused. The final rule explicitly precluded issuers from adopting more restrictive approaches to proxy access through charter or by-law provisions.[97] The SEC nonetheless purported to ground its approach in state law by stating that shareholders could not use the rule if state law (but not a specific issuer's charter) prohibited shareholder nominations.[98]

At the time it adopted the rules, the SEC intended them to be effective in time for the 2010–11 proxy season.[99] On 29 September 2010, however, the Business Roundtable and the

[91] Adopting Release, *supra* note 12, at 56,730. The rule, as amended, permitted the exclusion of any proposal that:

(i) [w]ould disqualify a nominee who is standing for election;

(ii) [w]ould remove a director from office before his or her term expired;

(iii) [q]uestions the competence, business judgment, or character of one or more nominees or directors;

(iv) [s]eeks to include a specific individual in the company's proxy materials for election to the board of directors; or

(v) [o]therwise could affect the outcome of the upcoming election of directors. Adopting Release, *supra* note 12, at 56,732.

[92] Adopting Release, *supra* note 12, at 56,730.

[93] Adopting Release, *supra* note 12, at 56,733.

[94] Adopting Release, *supra* note 12, at 56,682–3. The rule exempted companies that were subject to the proxy rules solely because they had a class of debt securities registered under section 12 of the Exchange Act (Adopting Release, *supra* note 12: 56,683).

[95] Adopting Release, *supra* note 12, at 56,670–4 (referencing and rejecting commentators' argument that proxy access rules should be determined through private ordering).

[96] Adopting Release, *supra* note 12, at 56,670–1. For an example of this argument, see Letter from Alexander M. Cutler, Chair, Corporate Leadership Initiative, Bus. Roundtable, to Elizabeth M. Murphy, Sec'y, SEC 2–3 (17 Aug. 2009), available at <http://www.sec.gov/comments/s7-10-09/s71009-267.pdf>:

> State law . . . provides shareholders and boards of directors with the opportunity to deal effectively with the myriad of different circumstances applicable to their companies in designing a proxy access and/or proxy reimbursement regime.

[97] Adopting Release, *supra* note 12, at 56,678–89.

[98] Adopting Release, *supra* note 12, at 56,674.

[99] See Adopting Release, *supra* note 12, at 56,668 (setting the effective date of the regulations at 15 November 2010). The SEC delayed the effective date of the new rules for 'smaller reporting companies' as defined in the Code of Federal Regulations. Adopting Release, *supra* note 12 (quoting 17 C.F.R. § 240.12b-2 (2011)) (internal quotation marks omitted).

US Chamber of Commerce brought suit challenging Rule 14a-11.[100] The suit alleged that the rule was arbitrary and capricious and that the SEC failed to comply with its statutory obligation to assess its effect on efficiency, competition, and capital formation.[101] The SEC voluntarily stayed the effectiveness of Rule 14a-11 and the other amendments, including the amendment to Rule 14a-8, pending the resolution of the litigation.[102]

On 22 July 2011, the DC Circuit vacated Rule 14a-11.[103] The DC Circuit noted that the SEC 'has a unique obligation to consider the effect of a new rule upon "efficiency, competition, and capital formation" '.[104] According to the court, the SEC acted arbitrarily and capriciously by failing 'adequately to assess the economic effects of' Rule 14a-11.[105] In particular, the court stated its belief that 'the Commission has not sufficiently supported its conclusion that increasing the potential for election of directors nominated by shareholders will result in improved board and company performance and shareholder value'.[106]

Following the announcement of the DC Circuit's decision, the SEC announced that it would not seek rehearing or appeal the decision to the US Supreme Court.[107] By the terms of the stay, it expired once the DC Circuit issued its mandate.[108] On 20 September 2011, the SEC published a brief notice indicating that the amendment to Rule 14a-8 and the additional amendments to the federal proxy rules, other than Rule 14a-11, would become effective on that day.[109]

19.4 Justifying Federal Proxy Access

19.4.1 The SEC's Explanation

Despite the years of attention that the SEC has devoted to proxy access, it offered a surprisingly limited defence of Rule 14a-11 in its proposing and adopting releases. The SEC did not defend the rule in terms of possible corporate governance objectives, such as increased shareholder voice, better board composition, or improved corporate performance.[110] Instead, the SEC's releases offered two narrow and ambiguous justifications. First, the SEC stated that the rule was necessary to ensure that shareholders enjoy the same rights that they

[100] Petition for Review, *Bus. Roundtable v. SEC*, 647 F.3d 1144 (D.C. Cir. 2011) (No. 10-1305).

[101] Petition for Review, *Bus. Roundtable v. SEC*, 647 F.3d 1144 (D.C. Cir. 2011) (No. 10-1305).

[102] See Bus. Roundtable, Securities Act Release No. 9149, Exchange Act Release No. 63,031, Investment Company Act Release No. 29,456, 2010 WL 3862548 (4 Oct. 2010).

[103] *Bus. Roundtable*, 647 F.3d at 1156.

[104] *Bus. Roundtable*, 647 F.3d at 1148 (quoting 15 U.S.C. §§ 78c(f), 80a-2(c) (2006)).

[105] *Bus. Roundtable*, 647 F.3d at 1148 (quoting 15 U.S.C. §§ 78c(f), 80a-2(c) (2006)).

[106] *Bus. Roundtable*, 647 F.3d at 1151.

[107] Press Release, SEC, Statement by SEC Chairman Mary L. Schapiro on Proxy Access Litigation (6 Sept. 2011), available at <http://www.sec.gov/news/press/2011/2011-179.htm>.

[108] Bus. Roundtable, Securities Act Release No. 9149, Exchange Act Release No. 63,031, Investment Company Act Release No. 29,456, 2010 WL 3862548, at *2 (4 Oct. 2010).

[109] Facilitating Shareholder Director Nominations, Securities Act Release No. 9259, Exchange Act Release No. 65,343, Investment Company Act Release No. 29,788, 76 Fed. Reg. 58,100, 58,100 (20 Sept. 2011).

[110] Ironically, these were nonetheless the criteria against which the DC Circuit evaluated the rule (*Bus. Roundtable*, 647 F.3d at 1150–1).

could exercise through personal attendance at an annual meeting.[111] Second, the SEC suggested that proxy access might increase director accountability to shareholders.[112]

As the SEC explained, the federal proxy rules were designed to replicate, as nearly as possible, an in-person shareholder meeting.[113] At an in-person meeting, shareholders have the power to nominate as well as elect director candidates.[114] The SEC acknowledged that, despite this objective, it has exercised its rulemaking authority to restrict, rather than enhance, shareholder voting power. One example of this restrictive approach is the SEC's refusal to adopt a universal ballot or form of proxy that would require issuers to disclose all validly nominated director candidates.[115] Another example is its approach to Rule 14a-8, which has limited shareholders' ability to establish nomination procedures through private ordering.[116] Recognizing that the federal proxy rules have imposed affirmative impediments on 'the exercise of shareholders' rights' to nominate and elect directors to company boards of directors, the SEC explained that Rule 14a-11 was designed to remove these impediments.[117]

Critically, the SEC did not defend either its historically restrictive approach to proxy access or its new regulations in terms of a normative perspective. In other words, the SEC did not purport to be identifying an appropriate level of shareholder nominating or voting power or to ground its regulations in identified deficiencies in existing corporate governance mechanisms. Instead, the SEC claimed simply to be implementing shareholder power under state law. As the SEC repeated throughout the adopting release, its objective was to 'facilitate the effective exercise of shareholders' traditional State law rights to nominate and elect directors to company boards of directors'.[118]

Second, the SEC drew a relationship between the impediments to the exercise of shareholder nominating rights and a lack of director accountability. As the SEC explained in the proposing release, the 2008 financial crisis led many commentators 'to raise serious concerns about the accountability and responsiveness of some companies and boards of

[111] Adopting Release, *supra* note 12, at 56,670.

[112] Adopting Release, *supra* note 12, at 56,670.

[113] Adopting Release, *supra* note 12, at 56,670.

[114] Although state statutes do not explicitly articulate shareholder nominating power, the claim is that such power is implicit in the statutory power to elect directors (see Check and Miller 2009: 300). In truth, existing director elections more closely resemble shareholder ratifications of the board's choice of directors.

Alternatively, shareholders might be viewed as 'confirming' the issuer's slate, in much the same way that the Senate confirms the President's appointment of judges and other public officials. Issuers appear, however, to assume that shareholders have the power to nominate director candidates. A recent empirical study found, for example, that in a sample of large US corporations, virtually all had by-law provisions that explicitly authorized shareholders to nominate director candidates (see Check and Miller 2009: 303–4).

[115] Rule 14a-4(d)(4), the bona fide nominee rule, explicitly precludes the use of a universal ballot by requiring nominees to consent to their inclusion on a proxy card (see, e.g., Fisch 1993: 1168–9) (describing the SEC's refusal to adopt a universal ballot and its continued efforts to preclude shareholders from having an opportunity to choose from among shareholder-nominated and issuer-nominated director candidates); Grossman and Denton (2009) (describing the inability of shareholders to split their votes when voting by proxy absent a universal ballot).

[116] See *supra* notes 45–52 and accompanying text (discussing the SEC's response to private ordering efforts by *AFSCME*).

[117] Proposing Release, *supra* note 7, at 29,025–6.

[118] Adopting Release, *supra* note 12, at 56,677.

directors to the interests of shareholders, and has resulted in a loss of investor confidence'.[119] The SEC suggested that the federal proxy rules 'may be impeding the ability of shareholders to hold boards accountable',[120] observing that the academic literature 'points to a link between board accountability and company performance'.[121] Although it did not specifically find either that boards were insufficiently responsive to shareholder needs or that Rule 14a-11 would increase board responsiveness, the SEC nonetheless concluded that its rule changes would 'significantly enhance the confidence of shareholders who link the recent financial crisis to a lack of responsiveness of some boards to shareholder interests'.[122]

The SEC's effort to defend Rule 14a-11 as facilitating the exercise of state law rights was disingenuous. By specifying qualifications and criteria for the exercise of nominating power, Rule 14a-11 attempted to create a federal nominating power—a power far narrower than that granted to shareholders by state law. State law gives all shareholders equal power to nominate directors without regard to the quantity of stock they own or the period for which they have held it. With limited exceptions, state law grants all shareholders governance rights proportionate to their economic interest without requiring a minimum ownership threshold or holding period.[123] State law does not condition the exercise of voting power on shareholder-specific characteristics, such as independence, lack of control, intent, and the like. Moreover, to the extent that shareholder nominating power is based on the power to elect directors, state law provides no basis for limiting such nominating power to a lesser number of nominees than those upon whom the shareholders vote, much less an arbitrary limit of 25% of the board.

At the same time, state law grants issuers substantial power to determine the scope of shareholder nominating rights, power that the SEC eliminates through the mandatory nature of the federal nominating power that it creates. Although the SEC asserted that shareholder nominating power is implicit in the shareholders' right to elect the board,[124] nothing in state corporation law requires corporations to give shareholders this power. The SEC's claim that this power is 'imposed by statute' and 'cannot be bargained away'[125] was simply incorrect. State law allows corporations to limit or eliminate shareholder nominating rights. Indeed, state corporate law does not even require that the board of directors be elected by the shareholders—shareholder election of directors is merely a default rule that may be modified in the corporate charter.[126] To the extent that Rule 14a-11 prohibited corporations

[119] Proposing Release, *supra* note 7, at 29,025.

[120] Proposing Release, *supra* note 7, at 29,025.

[121] Proposing Release, *supra* note 7, at 29,026.

[122] Adopting Release, *supra* note 12, at 56,670.

[123] Exceptions to this general principle include tenure voting rights, which increase voting power for long-term shareholders, see *Williams v. Geier*, 671 A.2d 1368, 1370, 1373 n.10 (Del. 1996) (discussing a tenure voting plan in which shares held for three years would enjoy ten times the voting power of shares held for a lesser period), and some state antitakeover statutes, which may have the effect of disenfranchising large shareholders, see *CTS Corp. v. Dynamics Corp. of Am.*, 481 U.S. 69, 73–5, 85 (1987) (upholding a state antitakeover statute that removed voting rights of acquired shares unless restored by a vote of minority shareholders).

[124] See Adopting Release, *supra* note 12, at 56,672–3.

[125] Adopting Release, *supra* note 12, at 56,672.

[126] See, e.g., Del. Code Ann. tit. 8, § 151(a) (2001) (authorizing corporations to issue one or more classes of stock that may have 'such voting powers, full or limited, or no voting powers' as set forth in the certificate of incorporation). Indeed, prior to the adoption of the federal securities laws, a number of corporations restricted or eliminated the voting rights of common shareholders (see Stevens

from adopting provisions that provide more limited nominating rights, it was flatly inconsistent with existing state law. Similarly, the continued burdens imposed by the proxy rules on nominations that do not conform to the requirements of Rule 14a-11 frustrate, rather than facilitate, the exercise of state law rights.

This frustration is most apparent in the context of Delaware corporation law.[127] Delaware, the state of incorporation for most publicly traded companies, recently amended its statute, explicitly authorizing corporations to establish by-laws requiring the inclusion of shareholder nominees in the issuer's proxy statement.[128] The Delaware amendments authorize shareholders to establish shareholder nomination procedures on an issuer-specific basis and to adopt (or reject) minimum ownership and holding period requirements appropriate to the issuer and its shareholder base.[129] Rule 14a-11, however, prohibited by-law provisions that were more restrictive than the federal rule and subjected more lenient provisions to the same federal regulatory requirements as mounting a proxy contest. In short, Rule 14a-11 eviscerated the enabling approach of the Delaware statute.

That state law does not offer a foundation for federal proxy access is illustrated most dramatically by the fact that Rule 14a-11 provided proxy access for shareholders of investment companies.[130] Most investment companies are not even organized as corporations under state law, but as business trusts.[131] State law does not require business trusts to have shareholder-elected directors (Newman 2008: 7, 9). Rather, the requirement of a shareholder-elected board stems from the Investment Company Act.[132] In responding to commentator suggestions that investment companies be excluded from Rule 14a-11, however, the SEC stated its belief 'that facilitating the exercise of traditional State law rights to nominate and elect directors is as much of a concern for investment company shareholders as it is for shareholders of non-investment companies'.[133] The adopting release contained no

1926: 357–60) (describing the use of non-voting common stock by major public corporations in the 1920s). It is worth noting that many state statutes require shareholder approval of specified transactions, such as mergers and charter amendments, and that those provisions may afford voting rights to otherwise non-voting stock (see Stevens 1926: 359) (observing that corporate law may have required a shareholder vote to ratify certain actions).

[127] Rule 14a-11 similarly frustrates the exercise of shareholder nomination rights under North Dakota law. North Dakota permits 5% shareholders to nominate director candidates without requiring a minimum holding period or limiting the number of director nominees (N.D. Cent. Code § 10-35-08 2007). In addition, the North Dakota statute explicitly limits the disclosures that an issuer may require from a nominating shareholder (N.D. Cent. Code § 10-35-08 2007).

[128] Del. Code Ann. tit. 8, § 112 (Supp. 2011). Delaware's legislation followed a debate over the validity of such by-laws under Delaware law. Although many commentators took the position that such by-laws would be valid, the SEC prevented courts from resolving this question for a number of years by allowing issuers to exclude shareholder by-law proposals (see Strine 2008: 1086–8) (describing the debate and the SEC's basis for exclusion).

[129] Del. Code Ann. tit. 8, § 112.

[130] See Adopting Release, *supra* note 12, at 56,683–5 (describing the application of Rule 14a-11 to investment companies).

[131] Newman (2008: 7, 9) (explaining that most mutual funds today are organized as Massachusetts business trusts, Delaware statutory trusts, or Maryland corporations).

[132] Investment Company Act of 1940, ch. 686, 54 Stat. 789 (codified as amended at 15 USC §§ 80a-1 to-64 (Supp. IV 2010)); Fisch (2010b: 1967).

[133] Adopting Release, *supra* note 12, at 56,684.

source of authority for the claim that the right to nominate and elect directors is a 'traditional State law right[]' for mutual fund shareholders.[134]

The SEC's conception of shareholder nominating groups similarly lacked a basis in state law. State law does not contemplate or require that shareholders exercise their nominating or voting power collectively by forming shareholder groups. Indeed, it is unclear how state law would respond to a shareholder group's exercise of corporate power—the selection of director candidates who will be included in the company's proxy statement—when that corporate power is not available to shareholders generally. Would members of the shareholder group, for example, owe fiduciary duties to other shareholders? More generally, to what extent did a rule like Rule 14a-11 infringe on existing board responsibilities such as determining the qualifications of the corporation's directors?[135]

Rule 14a-11 thus attempted to create a federal nominating power that was both narrower and broader than shareholders' traditional state law rights. Specifically, Rule 14a-11 reflected the SEC's ambiguous determination of which shareholders are eligible to exercise nominating power and under what conditions. Section 19.4.2 of this chapter examines that determination to gain a better understanding of the objectives of federal proxy access. Although Rule 14a-11 has been invalidated, the rule was the culmination of repeated SEC efforts to structure proxy access through arbitrary qualification requirements, and as such, the following analysis should operate as a constraint on future rulemaking proposals.

19.4.2 The Terms of Federal Proxy Access

The SEC's predictions about the effect of Rule 14a-11 were guarded. As indicated above, it defended the rule in terms of 'facilitating' shareholder nominating power, rather than expressing an intention to increase the number of shareholder nominees. Moreover, although the SEC predicted that the rule 'will result in a greater number of nominees appearing on a proxy card',[136] it offered no judgment that the existing level of shareholder nominations was insufficient and provided no benchmark by which to assess whether an increase would be appropriate.[137] Indeed, the SEC made all its substantive arguments in support of proxy access without attempting to quantify the extent to which shareholders would use it. It was only seventy-four pages into its adopting release (as published in the Federal Register), in the context of its statutorily required cost–benefit analysis under the Paperwork Reduction Act (PRA), that the SEC provided any quantitative analysis.[138]

Both the analysis and resulting statistics were underwhelming. The SEC estimated that, out of approximately 11,000 reporting companies other than investment companies,[139]

[134] See Adopting Release, *supra* note 12, at 56,684. Although the DC Circuit criticized the application of Rule 14a-11 to investment companies, its criticism was limited to concerns about the SEC's cost–benefit analysis. *Bus. Roundtable v. SEC*, 647 F.3d 1144, 1156–8 (D.C. Cir. 2011).

[135] The relationship of state law to federal proxy access is considered in more detail in Subsection 19.4.2.

[136] Adopting Release, *supra* note 12, at 56,673.

[137] See Macey (2007: 768–71) (questioning the availability of a baseline by which to determine whether the existing level of contested director elections is appropriate).

[138] Adopting Release, *supra* note 12, at 56,742.

[139] Adopting Release, *supra* note 12, at 56,751.

forty-five companies per year would receive a shareholder nomination under Rule 14a-11.[140] The basis for this estimate was 'the number of contested elections [fifty-seven] and board-related shareholder proposals [118] that have been submitted to companies'.[141] Although neither contested solicitations nor shareholder proposals bear any relationship to director nominations under Rule 14a-11, the SEC stated that these numbers indicate shareholders that 'have shown an interest in using currently available means under our rules to influence governance matters'.[142] Significantly, of course, shareholders did not need to meet any of the eligibility criteria of Rule 14a-11 to initiate an election contest or submit a shareholder proposal. The SEC also did not explain the methodology by which these numbers translated into an estimate of forty-five nominations.

Even if the statistics regarding election contests and shareholder proposals offered a measure of the number of shareholders interested in corporate governance, it is unlikely that any of those shareholders would have qualified to use federal proxy access. Hedge funds, which were unlikely to be eligible, for reasons discussed below, to use Rule 14a-11,[143] conducted virtually all of the contested solicitations in the Georgeson list upon which the SEC relied.[144] Shareholders submitted the '[b]oard related proposals'[145] pursuant to Rule 14a-8, which requires a shareholder to own just $2,000 worth of stock.[146] In neither case did the number of shareholders that chose to use these mechanisms provide the SEC with a basis for estimating the number of shareholders that would have been able and willing to use Rule 14a-11.[147]

To understand the SEC's expectations better, it is useful to consider more carefully the conditions upon which Rule 14a-11 allowed shareholders to nominate director candidates. The minimum required ownership level was perhaps the most controversial issue in the

140 Adopting Release, *supra* note 12, at 56,744. It further estimated that six investment companies would receive such a nomination (Adopting Release, *supra* note 12, at 56,744).

141 Adopting Release, *supra* note 12, at 56,743 n.408.

142 Adopting Release, *supra* note 12, at 56,743.

143 Any contest in which a dissident filed a proxy statement and distributed a separate proxy card was included in Georgeson's list (2009: 47). As a result, the list includes issue-based contests, such as proposals to remove a classified board, which involve a very different type of shareholder engagement than proposing a competing slate of directors. The list also includes at least twelve solicitations at investment companies (Georgeson 2009: 47), which raise very different issues than a contest at an operating company. Moreover, by definition, a contested election involves a shareholder that is willing to incur the costs of a separate solicitation.

144 Adopting Release, *supra* note 12, at 56,743 n.804 (citing Georgeson, *supra* note 143).

145 Adopting Release, *supra* note 12, at 56,743 n.804 (citing Georgeson, *supra* note 143).

146 17 C.F.R. § 240.14a-8(b) (2011).

147 The SEC considered and rejected, as alternative bases for its estimates, a variety of predictions made in connection with its earlier proposals, specifically the 2009 proposed rule. See Adopting Release, *supra* note 12, at 56,743. These earlier estimates were largely based on counting the number of shareholders that met the qualification criteria and then predicting what per cent of eligible shareholders might choose to submit a proposal. Specifically, the SEC estimated that 5% of those companies with at least one eligible shareholder would receive a 14a-11 nomination (Adopting Release, *supra* note 12, at 56,743). The SEC first recognized that it could not rely on these numbers because the 2009 rule had a much lower threshold for eligibility (Adopting Release, *supra* note 12, at 56,743). It then rejected the methodology behind this approach, reasoning that the presence of a qualifying shareholder did not provide evidence about that shareholder's interest in nominating directors (Adopting Release, *supra* note 12, at 56,743).

debate over the various formulations of the SEC's proposed proxy access rule. As the SEC observed in its proposing release, commentators argued in favour of minimum ownership levels ranging from the $2,000 ownership level required under Rule 14a-8 to a requirement that shareholders own 3%, 5%, 10%, or even 15% of the issuer.[148]

At the heart of the debate is the question of which shareholders should be able to nominate director candidates. The SEC accepted the position that shareholders should be required to have a substantial financial interest in the issuer to exercise nominating power.[149] A minimum ownership requirement could be defended as preventing nuisance nominations and unqualified candidates. Although state law does not impose this requirement, the SEC based federal proxy access on its own determination as to which shareholders would make the best use of this power.

Neither the comment letters in support of a minimum ownership requirement nor the SEC's various proposals contained any empirical justification for the claim that a minimum ownership requirement will result in higher-quality nominations. The releases did not show that investors with larger shareholdings are more sophisticated, better able to identify qualified directors, or more expert in corporate governance. Indeed, at least some academic commentary has criticized institutional investors for supporting governance reforms that are not correlated with improved corporate performance.[150] The releases did not demonstrate that investors with larger shareholdings spend more money to research and monitor their investments; many large investors have limited budgets and do not spend substantial resources on governance research. The releases did not show that the interests of investors with larger holdings are correlated with those of other shareholders.[151] Indeed, commentators have demonstrated that large institutions may have competing objectives with respect to their portfolio companies (Romano 2001).

Of course, a minimum ownership requirement drastically limits the number of shareholders that can use a proxy access rule. First, as a practical matter, any required ownership level beyond the most minimal precludes all retail investors from nominating director candidates. This preclusion is arguably at odds with the fact that, as a group, individual investors are most likely to benefit from the cost savings associated with proxy access since their interests are insufficiently large to make an independent solicitation cost-justified. Because retail investors, as a group, tend to be long-term investors, the exclusion is also at odds with the SEC's articulated objective of placing nominating power in the hands of long-term holders.[152]

The SEC did not explain why retail investors are presumptively disqualified from identifying appropriate director candidates. Concededly, corporate managers have long disparaged activism by individual shareholders. Yet activists such as John and Lewis Gilbert, early champions of the shareholder proposal rule, advocated a variety of corporate governance reforms that have been embraced by today's institutional investors, including proper auditing, the elimination of staggered boards, and limits on executive compensation.[153] Harvard

[148] Proposing Release, *supra* note 7, at 29,035.

[149] Proposing Release, *supra* note 7, at 29,035.

[150] See, e.g., Romano (2001) (reviewing empirical literature and concluding that institutional activism has little or no effect on the performance of targeted firms).

[151] See Fisch (2010b: 881) (observing that institutional intermediaries' objectives with respect to their portfolio companies may not be limited to maximizing firm value).

[152] See Proposing Release, *supra* note 7, at 29,035 (articulating this objective).

[153] See Fisch (2008: 50) (recounting the Gilbert brothers' shareholder initiatives).

law professor and retail investor Lucian Bebchuk has served as a type of modern corporate gadfly, challenging executive pay policies and crafting innovative by-law proposals to address the scope of a board's power to deploy a poison pill.[154] Denver activist Gerald Armstrong's frequent shareholder proposals have included requests to eliminate classified boards and to implement advisory shareholder votes on executive compensation (McKinney 2009)—both issues that have been the frequent focus of large institutional investors. Armstrong's proposals at Supervalu, where he has held 350 shares for approximately a dozen years, received the support of a majority of shareholders (McKinney 2009). Indeed, both Bebchuk and Armstrong are likely to be among the investors counted in the SEC's PRA analysis as those interested in using existing corporate governance mechanisms, although neither qualified to use Rule 14a-11. Retail investors may challenge management viewpoints, but the SEC's releases presented no evidence that, as a class, they are incapable of participating meaningfully in the election process.

Even if a minimum ownership requirement is appropriate, neither the SEC nor commentators offered any basis for selecting 3% as an appropriate minimum. If the threshold was designed to limit nominations to those with a substantial economic interest, one might have expected a threshold tied to the overall size of the interest rather than to the proportion of shares that it represented.[155] If 3% is a proxy for a large dollar value, one would have expected the release to contain statistics quantifying the typical dollar value of a 3% stake and explaining why investments of less than that amount are not economically significant. Such an analysis might note, for example, that a 3% stake in the toy company Mattel, currently number 392 on the Fortune 500 list (CNNMoney 2011), is worth more than $345 million[156] and explain why an investment of less than $345 million does not give its owner a sufficient incentive to make responsible director nominations.

In fact, existing evidence suggests that shareholders view investments of far less than 3% as economically significant and act accordingly. In 2001, the Regents of the University of California had purchased more than two million shares of Enron stock for the university's retirement funds.[157] The Board of Regents was selected by the court to serve as lead plaintiff in the Enron securities class action based on the size of the funds' losses in the company stock and a congressional determination, reflected in the Private Securities Litigation Reform Act of 1995[158] (PSLRA), that lead plaintiffs should be those whose economic interest

[154] See, e.g., Colvin (2007) (describing Bebchuk as 'America's most influential critic of CEO pay'). Bebchuk owned 140 shares of Computer Associates as of 2006. *Bebchuk v. CA, Inc.*, 902 A.2d 737, 738 (Del. Ch. 2006).

[155] Nor does the release consider relative significance—the size of a given investment relative to a particular investor's overall portfolio or total wealth. Consider, for example, the Florida State Board of Administration, the $100 billion state pension fund that was the subject of extensive public criticism for its loss of $334 million on its investment in Enron (see Frankel 2002) (describing the Florida State Board and the size of its loss); Hollis (2002) (noting mounting 'criticism . . . over the Florida pension fund's losses in Enron stocks and bonds'). Clearly the loss, which represented one-third of 1% of the fund's assets, was financially significant. Similar CalPERS' and CalSTRS' Enron stock represented less than 0.1% of each fund's total portfolio in June 2001 (Pender 2001).

[156] As of 30 March 2012, Mattel had a market cap of $11.51 billion. MAT Industry: Toys & Games, Yahoo! Fin., available at <http://finance.yahoo.com/q/in?s=MAT>.

[157] *In re Enron Corp. Sec. Litig.*, 206 F.R.D. 427, 454 (S.D. Tex. 2002).

[158] Pub. L. No. 104-67, 109 Stat. 737 (codified as amended in scattered sections of 15 U.S.C.).

in the litigation is substantial.[159] That the Regents had sufficient incentives to litigate vigorously was reflected by the fact that the Enron settlement included the rare requirement that outside directors contribute toward the settlement out of their personal assets.[160] The funds' interest, however, which at one time was worth nearly $200 million,[161] represented less than 0.3% of the company.[162] The Regents would not have come near to qualifying to nominate an Enron director under Rule 14a-11.

As the Enron example illustrates, the 3% ownership requirement would have had the effect of limiting proxy access to a very small subset of institutions. Public pension funds, union pension funds, foundations, and the like virtually never hold as much as 3% of a company—holdings of even 1% are comparatively rare because such concentrated holdings increase the risk of a portfolio. Hedge funds often buy stakes of more than 3% but, as discussed below, are unlikely to meet the three-year holding period requirement.[163] The only institutional investors that regularly hold 3% stakes for at least three years are mutual funds, and even then, only a small few funds are likely to achieve that ownership level for any given company.[164] At the same time, mutual funds have historically been among the least active investors in corporate governance. Mutual funds do not serve as lead plaintiffs or submit shareholder proposals.[165] Indeed, until they were forced to do so, mutual funds neither voted their shares[166] nor filed claims to recover their damages in securities fraud litigation.[167]

Indeed, the recognition that mutual funds and hedge funds were the most likely investors to meet the ownership threshold may provide some explanation for the second requirement to nominate directors under Rule 14a-11: a three-year holding period. The SEC stated that this requirement would limit nominating power to shareholders with a long-term perspective, based on the premise that a short-term perspective is detrimental to an issuer's long-term performance and that, as a result, the interests of shareholders with a short-term focus are in conflict with those of other shareholders.[168] The empirical support for this conclusion is limited. Although corporate America has cited the short-termism of institutional investors as a basis for restricting shareholder power,[169] there is little evidence that

[159] *In re Enron Corp.*, 206 F.R.D. at 442, 459. See generally Fisch (2001: 61–2) (describing the lead plaintiff provision of the PSLRA).

[160] See Black, Cheffins, and Klausner (2006) (describing the terms of the Enron settlement and demonstrating the infrequency with which directors are required to contribute personal assets).

[161] Enron stock peaked at approximately $83/share (*USA Today* 2002).

[162] At the time of its collapse, Enron had 754.3 million shares outstanding (*USA Today* 2002).

[163] See Bratton (2007: 1420 tbl.8) (finding a mean holding period of twenty-one months for hedge fund investments in a sample studied).

[164] See Davis (2008: 16–17) (documenting increased block ownership by mutual funds from 1999 to 2005).

[165] See Choi, Pritchard, and Fisch (2005: 880) ('Mutual funds have failed to participate in securities fraud litigation at all, despite their substantial holdings.'); Choi and Fisch (2008: 319); Gillan and Starks (Chapter 2: fig.2.3, this volume) (documenting sponsors of corporate governance shareholder proposals).

[166] See Nicholson (2004: 696–7) (describing the adoption of federal requirements for mutual funds to vote their stock).

[167] See Cox and Thomas (2002: 879) (reporting that mutual funds regularly failed to file claims in successful securities fraud class actions).

[168] Adopting Release, *supra* note 12, at 56,697.

[169] See, e.g., Lipton and Rosenblum (1991: 203) (describing '[t]he short-term bias imposed by institutional stockholders' and suggesting reforms to remedy the problem).

shareholders are able to convince managers to sacrifice long-term firm value in favour of short-term interests.[170] Indeed, short-term investors, because they trade actively, may be better informed (Yan and Zhang 2009: 920–2). A recent study by Yan and Zhang found that trading activity by short-term institutional investors forecasts future returns and that the resulting performance does not reverse over a longer time period—refuting the argument that short-term institutions pressure managers to maximize short-term earnings at the expense of long-term returns (Yang and Zang 2009: 920–2). The authors found no evidence that long-term institutional investors had superior long-term information or were superior monitors (Yang and Zang 2009: 922).

The three-year holding period, however, would likely have eliminated any remaining shareholders that could have used Rule 14a-11. Empirical studies of hedge fund activism show that, contrary to many claims, activist hedge funds are not particularly short-term in focus.[171] Nonetheless, their median holding period is about twenty months (Brav et al., Chapter 8, this volume), far less than required by Rule 14a-11. The average mutual fund turnover ratio has gradually increased to almost 100%, meaning that the fund turns over its entire portfolio in a year.[172] Of course, the ratio is an average—some securities are held for just a few months, some for much longer. Nonetheless, actively managed funds are likely to hold relatively few securities for more than three years. In addition, those securities held for longer are least apt to trigger board nominations because the longer holding period likely reflects the portfolio manager's satisfaction with the company's performance. A portfolio manager can more readily address a perceived problem by invoking the Wall Street Rule and selling the stock of a disfavoured issuer than by nominating candidates for the board.

Even indexed investors that do not actively trade were relatively unlikely to meet the holding requirement of Rule 14a-11. First, because they are indexed, such investors hold relatively small percentages of each portfolio company. Second, fluctuations in the underlying indices create a significant amount of fluctuation in the resulting portfolios. As CalPERS explained to the SEC, just two-thirds of the securities in its domestic index portfolio as of 30 June 2010 had been in the portfolio three years earlier.[173]

The SEC acknowledged the restrictive nature of these requirements. In its adopting release, the SEC admitted that two-thirds of publicly traded companies did not have even a single shareholder that met the holding and ownership requirements of Rule 14a-11.[174]

[170] See Dent (2010) (explaining that no one has demonstrated that shareholders are myopic and that myopic shareholder behaviour would conflict with basic principles of market efficiency).

[171] E.g., Brav et al. (Chapter 8, this volume). Bratton finds a similar median holding period of twenty-one months. Bratton (2007: 1420 tbl.8).

[172] See Reichart (2009) (explaining that a firm with a turnover ratio of 100% has an average holding period of one year for its portfolio securities).

[173] See Letter from Anne Stausboll, Chief Exec. Officer, CalPERS, et al., to Mary L. Schapiro, Chairman, SEC (17 Aug. 2010) (hereinafter Stausboll Letter), available at <http://www.calpers-governance.org/docs-sof/marketinitiatives/initiatives/proposed-proxy-disclosure-rules.pdf> (reporting that 1,570 of 2,322 securities were held three years earlier).

[174] See Adopting Release, *supra* note 12, at 56,692. The SEC 'estimate[d]' this data based on data collected and reported in its proposing release that related to a one-year holding requirement rather than the three-year requirement adopted in the final rule (Adopting Release, *supra* note 12, at 56,690 n.221). Given the significance, in assessing the rule's rationality, of determining the number of shareholders eligible to use it, it is unclear why the SEC viewed an estimation process as sufficient.

This statistic reflects the significance of the modifications made to the Rule shortly before its adoption.[175] The SEC had previously reported that more than 99% of large accelerated filers had at least one shareholder that could meet the ownership and holding period requirements of the proposed rule, more than 85% of accelerated filers had at least one such shareholder, and 'roughly 59% of [non-accelerated] filers . . . ha[d] at least one shareholder' that could meet the requirement.[176] Even under the provisions of the 2003 proposed rule, which would have required the occurrence of a triggering condition, a higher percentage of issuers—42%—had a shareholder that would have qualified for proxy access.[177]

The SEC's claim that Rule 14a-11 facilitated the exercise of shareholders' state law rights was seriously flawed if the majority of issuers lacked even a single qualifying shareholder.[178] Moreover, qualifying alone was not enough—for proxy access to have been meaningful, those shareholders that qualified must have been willing to use it.[179] Thus, the SEC's release should have included an analysis of the extent to which cost considerations, liability concerns, and institutional structure might have precluded eligible shareholders from seeking to nominate directors under Rule 14a-11,[180] an issue to which this chapter will return. The SEC's attempted solution to these eligibility concerns was the nominating group. Rule 14a-11 granted nominating power to a 'nominating shareholder or nominating shareholder group'.[181] Specifically, Rule 14a-11 provided that the 3% holding requirement could be met by a shareholder group that, 'in the aggregate, . . . hold[s] at least 3% of the total voting power'.[182] The SEC clearly expected that institutional investors would engage in collective action to form groups with holdings of sufficient size to meet the 3% threshold.

That the rule permitted aggregation did not mean that a qualifying group would have been easy to assemble. The SEC's own data indicated that, at 69% of issuers, a qualifying group would require the participation of six or more shareholders—six or more of the very largest institutional investors.[183] By way of concrete example, CalPERS explained to the SEC in its comments

[175] Adopting Release, *supra* note 12, at 56,690 n.221.

[176] Proposing Release, *supra* note 7, at 29,036; accord Adopting Release, *supra* note 12, at 56,693 (noting that other studies reporting investor ownership levels typically did not include the requirement of a continuous three year holding period).

[177] Security Holder Director Nominations, Exchange Act Release No. 48,626, Investment Company Act Release No. 26,206, 68 Fed. Reg. 60,784, 60,794 (proposed 23 Oct. 2003) (to be codified at 17 C.F.R. pts. 240, 249, 274).

[178] Somewhat anomalously, for purposes of its cost–benefit analysis, the SEC projected that eleven issuers would receive nominations made by a single shareholder. See Adopting Release, *supra* note 12, at 56,744 n.805. Given that two-thirds of public companies lacked even a single shareholder that was eligible to use Rule14a-11, it is unclear who would have submitted those nominations.

[179] In addition, the SEC did not exclude corporate insiders, such as founders, CEOs, and existing directors, from its statistics on qualifying shareholders, despite the fact that such insiders do not need Rule14a-11 to influence board composition. For example, the shareholders who own more than 3% of Yahoo! include founders David Filo and Jerry Yang. See Yahoo! Inc., Proxy Statement (Form DEF 14A), at 36 (29 Apr. 2010). Similarly, Warren Buffett and Bill Gates (through the Bill and Melinda Gates Foundation) own more than 3% of Berkshire Hathaway. Berkshire Hathaway Inc., Proxy Statement (Form DEF 14A), at 16–17 (11 Mar. 2011). Warren Buffett is the company's chairman and CEO, and Gates is a director (Berkshire Hathaway Inc., Proxy Statement (Form DEF 14A), at 7–8).

[180] The DC Circuit did not view this omission as a deficiency in the SEC's economic analysis. See *Bus. Roundtable v. SEC*, 647 F.3d 1144, 1148–56 (D.C. Cir. 2011).

[181] Adopting Release, *supra* note 12, at 56,781.

[182] Adopting Release, *supra* note 12, at 56,755 n.861.

[183] Adopting Release, *supra* note 12, at 56,692.

on the proposed rule that aggregating the holdings of the twenty largest pension funds on the share register of Goldman Sachs would result in a holding of only 2.88%.[184] Similar data previously released by CalPERS indicated that the ten largest public pension funds together hold less than a 2.5% stake at Bank of America, Microsoft, IBM, and Exxon Mobil (Bebchuk 2010). As will be described below, federal law imposes various burdens on group formation, but even in the absence of those burdens, overcoming the consent and coordination problems necessary to assemble a group of this size is not trivial.

To complicate matters, the SEC was ambiguous with respect to permissible group size and the appropriate methodology to be used in aggregating the holdings of group members. The SEC did not explain whether each individual group member had to satisfy the three-year holding requirement for the total number of shares that it contributed to the group's holdings or whether group members could tack their holding periods. Tacking, which is permitted in other regulatory contexts, such as the calculation of holding periods under Rule144,[185] would enable a shareholder that owns 3% for two years and then sells to another shareholder that holds for an additional year to meet the holding period by forming a group. Similar issues could arise with respect to members of a mutual fund family—would the group satisfy the requirements by holding a net position of at least 3% for three years, or would each fund's contribution to the total be limited to the number of shares that it held individually for the entire three-year period?

Aggregation highlights a more fundamental ambiguity in the SEC's stated objectives. Rule 14a-11 did not limit the number of shareholders whose holdings could be aggregated for the purpose of satisfying the rule. If group size is unlimited, dozens or even hundreds of shareholders might join together to meet the ownership threshold. Yet the SEC's stated rationale for the threshold was to limit nominating power to those shareholders that possess a substantial interest. A large group comprised of smaller holders would likely result in a delegation of power either to a shareholder that does not individually meet the 3% threshold or to a third-party agent or intermediary. Either delegation would be inconsistent with the concerns articulated in the adopting release.

The early experience with the selection of a lead plaintiff under the PSLRA highlights the potential challenges posed by allowing aggregation of shareholder interests.[186] Plaintiffs, often with the assistance of counsel, created lead plaintiff groups in an effort to assemble the largest collective interest in the litigation and thereby secure the lead plaintiff appointment (Fisch 2001: 54). In a few notable cases, courts were asked to approve the appointment of lead plaintiff groups consisting of hundreds or even thousands of shareholders that individually lacked substantial financial stakes.[187] The formation of these groups created agency costs both because the groups were themselves unwieldy mechanisms for making litigation decisions and because, in some cases, the group was effectively controlled by a third

[184] Stausboll Letter, *supra* note 189, at 2.

[185] See 17 C.F.R. § 230.144(d)(3) (2011) (combining the holding periods of acquirer and acquiree for certain transactions, including securities acquired through pledge, gift, or conversion).

[186] See generally Fisch (2001: 67) (describing formation of large lead plaintiff groups under the PSLRA).

[187] See, e.g., *In re Network Assocs., Inc., Sec. Litig.*, 76 F. Supp. 2d 1017, 1019 (N.D. Cal. 1999) (considering lead plaintiff applications from two competing groups, one consisting of more than 1,725 investors and the other consisting of over 100 institutions and thousands of individual investors).

party—in this case, lead counsel—whose financial interests differed from those of the group members.[188]

Ultimately, courts largely rejected extensive aggregation under the PSLRA as inconsistent with the statutory objectives.[189] Nonetheless, even smaller groups pose coordination and collective-action problems. For example, the lead plaintiff group in the Cendant case,[190] which consisted of three institutional investors, could not reach a consensus position with respect to challenging the fee awarded by the trial court through an auction procedure.[191]

Even if these ambiguities were resolved, formation of nominating groups would be hindered by existing federal regulatory burdens on collective shareholder action. The adopting release explicitly recognized these burdens,[192] but the rule changes did not offer adequate relief. In the absence of such relief, the potential for formation of nominating groups is substantially reduced. Regulation 14A, for example, requires shareholders that engage in proxy solicitations to file those communications, as well as a proxy statement, with the SEC.[193] The adopting release explicitly stated that shareholder communications in connection with the formation of a nominating group would be treated as proxy solicitations.[194]

The SEC offered two limited concessions to the need for shareholder collective action under Rule 14a-11. First, the SEC adopted a narrow exemption, in Rule 14a-2(b)(7), for solicitations in connection with the formation of a nominating group.[195] To qualify for the exemption, written communications were limited to four items: a statement of the shareholder's intent to form a nominating group; a description of the proposed nominees or the characteristics of intended nominees; the percentage of voting power held by the soliciting shareholder; and the means by which shareholders can contact the soliciting party.[196] Compliance with these limitations did not exempt the communications from a filing requirement—written communications had to be filed with the SEC as of the date they were first used,[197] precluding shareholders from testing the waters or exploring whether they wanted to proceed with a 14a-11 nomination before publicly disclosing their intentions.

[188] See Fisch (2001: 71–3) (explaining how large lead plaintiff groups transfer authority to counsel, creating agency costs).

[189] See, e.g., *In re Tarragon Corp. Sec. Litig.*, No. 07 Civ. 07972 (PKC), 2007 U.S. Dist. LEXIS 91418, at*4–5 (S.D.N.Y. 6 Dec. 2007) (citing *In re Donnkenny Inc. Sec. Litig.*, 171 F.R.D. 156, 157–8 (S.D.N.Y. 1997)). The courts premised their analyses on the explicit statutory purpose of the lead plaintiff: reducing litigation agency costs. See, e.g., *In re Donnkenny Inc.*, 171 F.R.D. at 157–8 (explaining that the appointment of a lead plaintiff group was inconsistent with the statutory goal of 'prevent[ing] lawyer-driven litigation'). In contrast to the PSLRA, the SEC's release adopting Rule 14a-11 contains no such specification of the rule's objectives, making it impractical for the SEC or a court to find that a particular example of aggregation frustrates those objectives.

[190] *In re Cendant Corp. Sec. Litig.*, 109 F. Supp. 2d 273 (D.N.J. 2000), aff'd, 264 F.3d 286 (3d Cir. 2001).

[191] See Fisch (2002: 717 n.363) (describing the disagreement among the Cendant group members).

[192] See Adopting Release, *supra* note 12, at 56,681 ('We remain concerned that the Federal proxy rules may not be facilitating the exercise of shareholders' ability under State law to nominate and elect directors. . . .').

[193] See Fisch (1993: 1140–1) (describing regulatory requirements for the solicitation of proxies).

[194] See Adopting Release, *supra* note 12, at 56,725.

[195] See Adopting Release, *supra* note 12, at 56,780–1. In addition to the new exemption under Rule 14a-2(b)(7), shareholders could continue to use the exemption under Rule 14a-2(b)(2) for solicitations made to no more than ten persons (Adopting Release, *supra* note 12, at 56,676).

[196] Adopting Release, *supra* note 12, at 56,781.

[197] Adopting Release, *supra* note 12, at 56,781.

The exemption did not limit the content of oral solicitations, but soliciting shareholders were required to file a Schedule 14N notice as of the time they commenced oral solicitations.[198]

Importantly, the exemption applied only to shareholder nominations conducted pursuant to Rule 14a-11. To the extent that shareholders attempted to nominate a director candidate through other mechanisms, such as state statutory rights or issuer-specific charter provisions, they would have been ineligible for the exemptive provisions of Rules 14a-2(b)(7) and (8). Now that Rule 14a-11 has been invalidated, shareholders' efforts to form a group for the purpose of meeting a required minimum of nominating shareholders or seconders under issuer-specific nominating procedures will be regulated as proxy solicitations.[199]

Second, once shareholders formed a nominating group pursuant to Rule14a-11 and filed a Schedule 14N, Rule 14a-2(b)(8) permitted them to solicit on behalf of their nominees, and against the issuer's nominees, without filing a formal proxy statement.[200] The rule only permitted such solicitations once the shareholders received notice from the issuer that their nominees would be included in the proxy statement.[201] In addition, the rule required specific disclosures and obligated soliciting shareholders to file all written solicitation materials with the SEC.[202]

Commentators raised the concern that these filing requirements imposed an unnecessary burden on shareholder efforts to organize a nominating group.[203] The SEC responded that the exemption was sufficient because it provided shareholders 'with the opportunity to engage in activities for which they would otherwise need to file a proxy statement or have another exemption available'.[204] The SEC did not explain how burdening efforts by shareholders to communicate about the prospect of nominating a director candidate was consistent with either the objectives of Rule 14a-11 or shareholders' state law nominating rights.

Other aspects of the federal securities laws increase the burden on shareholder collective action. Regulation 13D, for example, requires extensive disclosure from shareholder groups whose aggregate holdings exceed 5%.[205] Rule 13d-1(b) reduces the regulatory burden for most institutional investors by permitting them to file the less burdensome Schedule 13G.[206] Significantly, while a Schedule 13D must be filed within ten days after a shareholder passes the 5% threshold,[207] a 13G need not be filed until forty-five days after the end of the

[198] Adopting Release, *supra* note 12, at 56,727.

[199] See Adopting Release, *supra* note 12, at 56,729:

> Given the range of possible criteria that companies and/or shareholders could establish for nominations, we continue to believe it would not be appropriate to extend the exemption to those circumstances.

[200] See Adopting Release, *supra* note 12, at 56,781. The SEC previously adopted Rules 14a-2(b)(1) and (6) to exempt proxy solicitations by disinterested shareholders from certain of the proxy rules, including the obligation to file a proxy statement. See 17 C.F.R. § 240.14a-2(b)(1), (6) (2011). New Rule 14a-2(b)(8), which appears to be in effect despite the invalidation of Rule 14a-11, extends this protection to members of a nominating group, so long as they comply with the other requirements of Rule 14a-11. Adopting Release, *supra* note 12, at 56,781. It is unclear how this rule operates in the absence of a valid Rule 14a-11.

[201] Adopting Release, *supra* note 12, at 56,781.

[202] See Adopting Release, *supra* note 12, at 56,781.

[203] See Adopting Release, *supra* note 12, at 56,726–7 (describing objections raised by commentators).

[204] Adopting Release, *supra* note 12, at 56,727.

[205] See §§ 240.13d-1(a), 13d-101.

[206] See § 240.13d-1(b) (describing conditions under which an investor may file a Schedule 13G in lieu of a Schedule 13D); § 240.13d-102 (setting forth information that must be included in a Schedule 13G filing).

[207] § 240.13d-1(a).

calendar year in which the shareholder has passed the threshold.[208] A 13G filing is permitted, however, only for passive investors.[209] SEC Rule 13d-5(b)(1) explicitly extends the trigger for the disclosure requirements of section13(d) to group formation for the purpose of voting.[210]

As part of the adopting release, the SEC amended the beneficial ownership reporting rules to provide that participation in the 14a-11 nominating procedure would not, by itself, cause an investor to forfeit its eligibility to file a Schedule 13G.[211] The SEC refused, however, to relieve shareholders from the burden of filing a Schedule 13G if their aggregated holdings exceeded 5% and explicitly acknowledged that, as a result of aggregation, some new shareholders would be subject to the 13G filing requirement.[212] In addition, the adopting release warned that a Schedule 13G filing would only be available to those shareholders that limited their activity to that permitted under Rule 14a-11: '[A]ny activity other than those provided for under Rule 14a-11 [such as approaching the board and proposing strategic alternatives] would make the exception inapplicable'.[213]

The prospect of avoiding filing obligations or potential liability under section 13(d) might, in itself, have created an incentive for shareholders to use Rule 14a-11 to obtain proxy access, rather than to experiment with alternative procedures.[214] The invalidation of Rule 14a-11, however, appears to have rendered this amendment meaningless. As a result, shareholders that engage in collective action in connection with efforts to nominate director candidates or adopt proxy access procedures risk being treated as a group for purposes of section 13(d) and being subject to the resulting disclosure requirements.

Similarly, the SEC refused to create an exemption from the requirements of Exchange Act section 16 for shareholder groups with aggregated holdings that exceed 10%. The provisions of section 16, although triggered less frequently than those of Regulation 13D, are more onerous in that they are not limited to disclosure requirements. Members of a section 16 group are required to forfeit short-swing trading profits under appropriate circumstances to the corporation.[215] Again, the SEC explicitly declined to exempt 14a-11 groups from the scope of section 16, explaining merely that, '[b]ecause the ownership threshold . . . for Rule 14a-11 eligibility is significantly less than 10%, shareholders will be able to form groups with holdings sufficient to meet the Rule 14a-11 threshold without reaching the 10% threshold in Section 16'.[216]

Critical to the operation of Rule 14a-11 was new Schedule 14N.[217] Schedule 14N, which remains in effect despite the invalidation of Rule 14a-11and now applies to all shareholder

[208] § 240.13d-1(b)(2).

[209] See § 240.13d-1(b)(1)(i) (providing that an investor may not have acquired the securities 'with the purpose nor with the effect of changing or influencing the control of the issuer').

[210] § 240.13d-5(b)(1). See *CSX Corp. v. Children's Inv. Fund Mgmt. (UK) LLP*, 654 F.3d 276 (2d Cir. 2011) (describing how group formation triggers section 13(d) disclosure requirements).

[211] See Adopting Release, *supra* note 12, at 56,676, 56,680 (describing the amendment to § 240.13d-1(b)(1)(i)).

[212] Adopting Release, *supra* note 12, at 56,751.

[213] Adopting Release, *supra* note 12, at 56,736.

[214] This regulatory advantage would potentially be far more important than any cost savings that proxy access would provide to an activist investor. Cf. Kahan and Rock (2011: 1405) (arguing that activists such as hedge funds would not use proxy access because the trivial value of the cost savings of proxy access would be outweighed by its disadvantages).

[215] 15 U.S.C. § 78p(b) (Supp. IV 2010).

[216] Adopting Release, *supra* note 12, at 56,737.

[217] 17 C.F.R. § 240.14n-101 (2011).

efforts to nominate director candidates, requires extensive disclosure.[218] The SEC has characterized the required disclosure as 'similar to that currently required in a contested election'.[219] The requirements are not limited to information about the nominees but include information about the nominating shareholders, such as disclosure of any legal proceeding in which any member of the nominating group has been involved during the past ten years.[220] If members of the nominating group are corporations, the rule requires disclosure by officers, directors, and controlling persons.[221] Because the nominating shareholders are not themselves up for election, this disclosure requirement seems somewhat intrusive, but the SEC explained 'that the disclosures will enable shareholders to gauge the nominating shareholder's or group's interest in the company, longevity of ownership, and intent with regard to continued ownership in the company'.[222]

The disclosure requirements also present a liability risk for shareholders considering the formation of a nominating group. Schedule 14N requires the nominating group to make various representations regarding the net economic interest of its members, the independence of the nominee, and the group's intention to hold its stock through the date of the annual meeting.[223] In addition, a Rule 14a-11 nominating group was required to certify that it did not have the intention to change the control of the issuer or to seek more board seats than permitted by the rule.[224] The SEC explicitly noted in its adopting release that the nominee, nominating shareholder, and each member of any nominating group are potentially liable for any misrepresentations or omissions in the Schedule 14N and 'any other related communication'.[225] Nothing in the release limited liability to a group member's representations about itself. This created the possibility that the SEC or courts would impose on group members the responsibility of verifying the veracity of each other's shareholdings, relationships, and intentions.

In short, the impediments to group formation were substantial, a factor that had to be considered within the context of the large number of shareholders required to create a qualifying group under Rule 14a-11, especially at the larger public companies. The impediments are more substantial with the invalidation of Rule 14a-11 and its limited exemptions, and make it impractical for issuers to adopt nominating procedures that require the formation of nominating groups.

[218] The disclosure requirements in prior proposals were even more extensive. See, e.g., Annette L. Nazareth, Comm'r, SEC, Remarks Before the International Corporate Governance Network (29 Oct. 2007), available at <http://sec.gov/news/speech/2007/spch102907aln.htm> (stating that the proposed disclosure requirements were 'more extensive than those in a proxy contest' and 'more extensive than that required of someone seeking to take over the company').

[219] Facilitating Shareholder Director Nominations, U.S. Sec. & Exch. Comm'n, <http://www.sec.gov/info/smallbus/secg/14a-8-secg.htm> (last updated 19 Sept. 2011).

[220] § 240.14n-101(5)(d).

[221] § 240.14n-101(5)(c)–(d).

[222] Adopting Release, *supra* note 12, at 56,715.

[223] See § 240.14n-101 (setting forth disclosure requirements).

[224] § 240.14n-101(8)(a)(1).

[225] Adopting Release, *supra* note 12, at 56,676:

> Final Rule 14a-9(c) makes clear that the nominating shareholder or group will be liable for any statement in the Schedule 14N or any other related communication that is false or misleading with respect to any material fact, or that omits to state any material fact necessary to make the statements therein not false or misleading, regardless of whether that information is ultimately included in the company's proxy statement.

Disclosure, the practical and regulatory requirements associated with group formation, and the other elements of liability exposure make proxy access costly. Many institutional investors are already struggling with limited resources, making it difficult to allocate funding for proxy access. At public pension funds and unions, such allocations may generate political outrage. As Francis Byrd, a managing director at the Altman Group, a proxy solicitation firm, asks, 'Can you imagine CalPERS or CalSTRS trying to justify spending $500,000 on a proxy contest, while the state is struggling to keep libraries open?'[226] Similarly, many mutual funds, especially indexed funds, will have difficulty justifying the costs in the face of market pressure to reduce fees and provide competitive returns.[227]

19.4.3 The Exclusivity of Federal Proxy Access

The analysis in Subsection 19.4.2 suggests that few shareholders would have met the eligibility requirements of Rule 14a-11. Of those shareholders that qualified, many would not have been interested in shareholder activism. Those that both qualified and were interested would have faced major burdens in terms of compliance costs and liability exposure. One might infer from this analysis a lack of SEC enthusiasm for increasing shareholder nominations. Why did the SEC adopt a federal proxy access rule that did not provide proxy access?

As indicated above, the SEC faced substantial challenges in adopting a proxy access rule. These challenges may have led the SEC to draft its rule narrowly, leaving the market to respond to any perceived deficiencies by providing shareholders with more extensive proxy access rights than those available under Rule 14a-11. Indeed, in the adopting release, the SEC stated that any deficiencies in federal proxy access could be addressed through private ordering.[228] The SEC noted that shareholders can adopt issuer-specific nominating procedures that expand the rights provided under Rule 14a-11, such as reducing the requirements described in Subsection 19.4.2 above.[229] Indeed, the accompanying amendments to Rule 14a-8 explicitly permitted the use of shareholder proposals to adopt issuer-specific nominating procedures.[230]

Historically, federal regulation of proxy solicitation has disfavoured issuer-specific attempts at private ordering.[231] As recounted above, the SEC rules prohibit issuers from

[226] Preparing for the Dodd-Frank Act, ISS, available at <http://www.issgovernance.com/weekly/20100723DoddFrank>.

[227] See, e.g., Fisch (2010b: 1989) (describing Fidelity's and Charles Schwab's reductions of fund fees in an effort to compete with Vanguard funds).

[228] See Adopting Release, *supra* note 12, at 56,693:

> Of course, to the extent that shareholders believe the 3% threshold is too high our amendments to Rule 14a-8 will facilitate their ability to adopt a lower ownership percentage.

[229] See Adopting Release, *supra* note 12, at 56,755 (noting that issuers' governing documents may be modified to 'enhance[]' the benefits to shareholders by lowering the required ownership threshold or shortening the required holding period).

[230] See Adopting Release, *supra* note 12, at 56,759:

> With the adoption of the amendment to Rule 14a-8(i)(8), shareholders will be able to establish procedures that can further facilitate [their state law nominating power], if they wish.

[231] In its 2009 proposing release, the SEC observed that 'the director nomination and shareholder proposal processes are two areas in which our current proxy rules pose impediments to the exercise of

adopting a universal ballot combining shareholder and management nominees. Although shareholders have always had the option of nominating director candidates by conducting an independent proxy solicitation, such a solicitation requires the shareholder to file a proxy statement and all solicitation materials with the SEC.[232] The SEC directly opposed investor efforts to use the corporate by-laws to establish alternatives to a full-scale election contest.[233] Even with the amendments to Rule 14a-8, shareholders that successfully propose and adopt issuer-specific nominating procedures will have to comply with the proxy solicitation rules that apply to a full election contest. In addition, shareholders that engage in collective action are subject to the disclosure requirements of section 13(d)[234] and, to the extent their collective holdings exceed 10%, may also be subject to the short-swing trading limitations of section 16(b).[235]

The SEC's stated rationale for proxy access was to reduce existing impediments to shareholder exercise of state law nominating rights. With respect to shareholder nominations conducted through procedures other than now-invalid Rule 14a-11, however, the new rules did nothing to remove these impediments. Shareholders that nominate directors pursuant to state law, issuer-specific charter or by-law provisions, or foreign law are not relieved from the filing requirements associated with a full-scale proxy solicitation. The SEC's rule changes did not permit such shareholders, even if they did not seek control, to take advantage of the limited exemptions from the regulation of proxy solicitations under Rules 14a-2(b)(7) and 14a-2(b)(8). Indeed, shareholder efforts to experiment with nominating procedures by adopting firm-specific charter or by-law provisions offer a nominating shareholder little advantage under current law over conducting an independent solicitation. Absent a reduction in the regulatory burdens, shareholders have little reason to adopt such procedures.

19.4.4 Rationalizing Proxy Access

The foregoing discussion highlights the destructive ambiguity in Rule 14a-11. After so many years of debate, the SEC adopted a proxy access rule that held limited promise in terms of increasing shareholder access to the proxy. Even that limited promise was lost in the face of

shareholders' rights'. Proposing Release, *supra* note 7, at 29,026. Curiously, this statement is not included in the adopting release.

[232] Independent solicitations are also costly. The ministerial costs of printing and mailing a proxy statement may be limited, see Proposing Release, *supra* note 7, at 29,073 (estimating these costs at $18,000), although these costs depend on the size of the shareholder base. One proxy solicitation firm estimates that printing and mailing costs range from $4 to $6 per investor, resulting in a cost of $60,000 each time a shareholder conducts a mailing if the company has just 15,000 investors (Connelly 2010: 52). For General Electric, with five million shareholders, these costs are obviously much higher. Investing with GE: Investor Information, Investor Types, GE, available at <http:// www.ge.com/investors/investing/index.html>.

In addition to the ministerial costs, however, the costs of a contested election include, at a minimum, legal fees, advertising, the costs of a proxy solicitation firm, and the costs of seeking the support of proxy advisors (Connelly 2010: 51–2). By way of example, Carl Icahn stated that he spent over $1 million in his campaign to gain two board seats in 2009 at Biogen Idec (Connelly 2010: 51).

[233] See *AFSCME v. AIG, Inc.*, 462 F.3d 121, 127 (2d Cir. 2006) (describing the SEC's opposition to the inclusion of a shareholder-proposed by-law amendment).

[234] 15 U.S.C. § 78m(d) (2006).

[235] 15 U.S.C. § 78p(b).

the SEC's half-hearted defence of the rule. At the same time, the SEC's regulation of proxy solicitations continues to forestall further attempts to increase shareholder nominating power through state law and private ordering. What explains this regulatory approach? Several explanations for the ambiguity in Rule 14a-11 are possible.

First, Rule 14a-11 may simply have reflected caution. Faced with extensive controversy over the likely effects of proxy access, the SEC may have decided to draw the narrowest possible rule in an effort to test the waters. There are three problems with understanding Rule 14a-11 in these terms. First, as described in Subsection 19.4.2 above, the qualification requirements under Rule 14a-11 were so stringent as to preclude virtually all shareholders from using it, making it unlikely that the rule would have provided policymakers with a basis for evaluating the efficacy of expanding shareholder nominating rights. Second, the limited number of shareholders that would have qualified to use the rule were not representative of other shareholders generally or activist shareholders in particular. Third, those shareholders that would have qualified to use Rule 14a-11—those with the largest stakes—were precisely those shareholders that stood to gain the least from the rule because they had the financial resources and sophistication to nominate directors by running independent solicitations.

Finally, as was evident from the opposition to Rule 14a-11 and the immediate court challenge, the SEC will face a substantial battle if it seeks to broaden proxy access in the future. Rule 14a-11's brief life was likely the product of a rare opportunity—the confluence of the 2008 financial crisis and the impetus it supplied for regulatory reform coupled with a rise in the political power of Democratic officials who were more receptive to shareholder interests. The effectiveness of these forces in generating regulatory reform has already decreased. Given the history of proxy access, SEC officials were presumably aware that the political climate offered them a rare opportunity to adopt a proxy access rule. They could not reasonably have anticipated an opportunity to expand the rule later.

If Rule 14a-11 was not in fact an initial effort to ascertain the effects of increasing shareholder nominating rights, how should it be understood? Perhaps the SEC decided that this highly controversial battle was not the best use of its limited political capital. As indicated above, business interests expended tremendous resources opposing proxy access and predicting horrible effects that would flow from its adoption. The SEC was presented with empirical studies that, although seriously flawed, purported to demonstrate that proxy access would damage firm performance.[236] The adopting release failed to confront these comments or to identify their flaws, suggesting the possibility that, in the end, comments from business groups persuaded SEC officials that proxy access was an undesirable

[236] Commentators presented the SEC with two empirical studies purporting to show that the SEC's proposed proxy access rules reduce shareholder wealth (see Grundfest 2010: 2). The studies by Akyol and Larcker measured correlations between stock price movements and various significant news events concerning the likelihood that the SEC would adopt a proxy access rule (see Aykol, Lim, and Verwijmeren 2012; Larcker, Ormazabal, and Taylor 2010). A combination of problematic coding decisions and confounding events raises serious doubts about the studies' empirical claims. In addition, a subsequent study employing a similar methodology reached the opposite conclusion (see Becker, Bergstresser, and Subramanian 2011) (finding that the market placed a positive value on proxy access). Because the SEC does not discuss this research in its releases, it is impossible to determine the extent to which the research influenced the Commissioner's views.

governance change.[237] Indeed, one might have accused the SEC of sandbagging its economic analysis to provide the DC Circuit with an easy basis for invalidating the rule. After all, the DC Circuit had previously warned the SEC of its obligation to consider the economic consequences of its rules.[238]

Why then adopt a proxy access rule at all? The Obama administration and the SEC leadership had made a variety of public statements avowing their support for proxy access.[239] A failure to adopt any rule may have been viewed as a sign of weakness or as catering to the opponents of proxy access. Members of the press who had been following the battle over proxy access with interest touted the adoption of the rule as a shareholder victory despite the rule's limitations.[240] Some institutional investors publicly defended the rule, stating that its limitations would ensure that shareholders selected director candidates who enjoyed broad support.[241] Notably, the last-minute changes to the prerequisites for using Rule 14a-11, changes that dramatically limited the scope of the rule, received limited public attention.[242]

Alternatively, the SEC may justifiably have been concerned about the litigation challenge that any proxy access rule was likely to face. In recent years, the SEC's rulemaking, particularly rulemaking opposed by business groups, has been repeatedly challenged through litigation. A number of these challenges have been successful, resulting in the invalidation of SEC rules and, more significantly, the dismantling of controversial SEC reform efforts.

[237] It is worth noting that business interests conducted a substantial number of in-person meetings with SEC officials in connection with the proxy access rulemaking. See Comments on Proposed Rule: Facilitating Shareholder Director Nominations, *supra* note 68. Similar meetings were conducted with members of the institutional investor community (see Comments on Proposed Rule: Facilitating Shareholder Director Nominations, *supra* note 68). Although the existence of these meetings is disclosed in the SEC comment files, the substance of the meetings is not. See, e.g., Memorandum from Kayla J. Gillan, Deputy Chief of Staff, SEC, to File No. S7-10-09 (31 Mar. 2010), available at <http://www.sec.gov/comments/s7-1009/s71009-648.pdf> (reporting a meeting between SEC officials and the chair of the ABA's Corporate Laws Committee and stating that '[a]mong the topics discussed were the Commission's proposed rules regarding facilitating shareholder director nominations').

[238] See, e.g., *Chamber of Commerce v. SEC*, 412 F.3d 133, 143 (D.C. Cir. 2005) (invalidating SEC rules regulating mutual fund governance and noting the SEC's 'statutory obligation to determine as best it can the economic implications of the rule it has proposed').

[239] See, e.g., Lynch (2009) (describing SEC Chair Mary Schapiro as having 'championed the proxy-access proposal in response to the financial crisis'); Scannell (2009) (reporting that three of five SEC Commissioners publicly stated their support for proxy access). Although President Obama did not address proxy access directly, he publicly supported increased shareholder voice, including sponsoring Say on Pay legislation, while in the Senate (see Kirdahy 2008).

[240] E.g., Holz and Berman (2010) (stating that the rule gives investors 'greater sway' in the selection of directors).

[241] See, e.g., Letter from Donna F. Anderson, Vice President & Global Governance Analyst, T. Rowe Price Assocs., Inc., and Darrell N. Braman, Vice President & Managing Counsel, T. Rowe Price Assocs., Inc., to Elizabeth Murphy, Sec'y, SEC (17 Aug. 2009), available at <http://www.sec.gov/comments/s7-10-09/s71009-218.pdf>:

> [T]he rule should be structured to encourage collaboration among investors so as to increase the likelihood that contested elections of non-controlling slates of directors take place primarily at companies where there is broad consensus among shareholders that a change in the boardroom is warranted.

[242] The administration appeared to back away from proxy access at the eleventh hour, proposing a measure that would have required a 5% ownership threshold—even higher than that adopted by the SEC (see *Compliance Intelligence* 2010).

Notable examples include *Goldstein v. SEC*, in which the DC Circuit invalidated the SEC's effort to require registration of hedge funds,[243] and *Chamber of Commerce v. SEC*, in which the court overturned SEC rules imposing increased independence requirements on mutual fund boards.[244] The decisions have reduced the SEC's credibility and power in pursuing its regulatory agenda.

SEC Chair Mary Schapiro clearly anticipated a legal challenge to whatever proxy access rule the Commission adopted.[245] The SEC may have believed, however, albeit erroneously, that adopting a highly restrictive rule would reduce the incentive for business interests to challenge the rule or reduce the willingness of the DC Circuit to invalidate such a rule. It is plausible to believe that business interests might have been deterred from challenging a proxy access rule if its requirements were so stringent as to make its use virtually impossible. This may also explain the lack of protection afforded to private ordering; a regulatory approach that reduces the incentive for institutional investors to push for greater access through state law or private ordering favours business interests.

It is possible that the SEC saw proxy access, like the shareholder proposal rule, not as a tool for increasing the effectiveness of shareholder voting but as a communication device. The SEC has long defended the value of shareholder proposals in communicating share-holder views to management;[246] indeed, the shareholder proposal rule existed and was used for four decades despite the fact that shareholder proposals virtually never received majority approval.[247] The 'proposals-as-communication' perspective is reflected in the SEC's encouragement of non-binding or precatory proposals,[248] proposals that have no predicate in state law and that Vice Chancellor Strine has termed 'imaginary voting'.[249] Although precatory proposals have no legal effect even if they receive majority approval, they enable shareholders to communicate with each other.[250] Senator Dodd defended precatory proposals

[243] 451 F.3d 873, 874, 884 (D.C. Cir. 2006).

[244] 412 F.3d 133, 145 (D.C. Cir. 2005); accord *Am. Equity Inv. Life Ins. Co. v. SEC*, 572 F.3d 923, 936 (D.C. Cir. 2009) (invalidating SEC regulation of indexed annuities), amended by 613 F.3d 166 (D.C. Cir. 2010); *Fin. Planning Ass'n v. SEC*, 482 F.3d 481, 493 (D.C. Cir. 2007) (vacating an SEC effort to exempt broker-dealers from certain statutory requirements).

[245] See Graybow (2009) (paraphrasing Schapiro as saying that 'litigation may result from whatever rule change is endorsed').

[246] See, e.g., Amendments to Rules on Shareholder Proposals, Exchange Act Release No. 40,018, Investment Company Act Release No. 23,200, 63 Fed. Reg. 29,106, 29,108 (28 May 1998) (codified at 17 C.F.R. § 240.14a-8) (explaining, as basis for overturning its prior controversial Cracker Barrel no-action position, that:

> we have gained a better understanding of the depth of interest among shareholders in having an opportunity to express their views to company management on employment-related proposals that raise sufficiently significant social policy issues)).

[247] See Palmiter (1994: 883) ('As of 1981, only two contested shareholder proposals of the thousands submitted had ever won.').

[248] See Fisch (2008: 54–5) (describing the SEC's 'creat[ion]' of the precatory proposal in 1976).

[249] Roundtable Discussions Regarding the Federal Proxy Rules and State Corporation Law, U.S. Sec. & Exch. Comm'n (7 May 2007), available at <http://www.sec.gov/spotlight/proxyprocess/proxy-transcript050707.pdf>; *accord* Strine (2008: 1088) (describing precatory proposals as 'a pretend polity under Rule 14a-8 that had no reference to principles of state law' (footnote omitted)).

[250] See, e.g., Paul S. Atkins, Comm'r, SEC, Shareholder Rights, the 2008 Proxy Season, and the Impact of Shareholder Activism, Address Before the U.S. Chamber of Commerce (22 July 2008), available at

as providing shareholders with 'an essential democratic shareholder right to speak to each other'.[251] This view of shareholder voting as a communication device is also reflected in the advisory votes on executive compensation mandated by Dodd-Frank.[252]

Like the submission of a precatory proposal, filing a Schedule 14N enables shareholders to communicate their dissatisfaction with the issuer's board candidates even if the shareholders do not succeed in assembling a nominating group or electing a shareholder nominee to the board. Indeed, the practical obstacles to successful shareholder use of Rule 14a-11 were unimportant if the rule was not designed to enable shareholders to nominate and elect director candidates.

Further support for this communication reading of Rule 14a-11 can be found in the SEC's decision to extend its coverage to controlled companies. In controlled companies, minority shareholders—those other than the controlling shareholder—lack sufficient voting power to influence director elections. Despite the seeming futility of a rule allowing minority shareholders at such companies to nominate directors, the SEC refused to exempt controlled companies from the rule.[253] In so doing, the SEC conceded that the purpose of allowing proxy access at these companies was not to further the election of shareholder-nominated directors: '[T]hough applying Rule 14a-11 to controlled companies would be unlikely to result in the election of shareholder-nominated directors . . ., we appreciate that shareholders at controlled companies may have other reasons for nominating candidates for director'.[254]

A related theory is that Rule 14a-11 was designed to raise the level of director discomfort without presenting a real threat of contested elections. Public-company directors are highly sensitive to visible criticism. Withhold votes and negative Institutional Shareholder Services (ISS) recommendations, even in the context of an uncontested election in which the directors face no realistic threat of replacement, cause them concern.[255] As a result, proxy access may be understood to offer institutions a bargaining chip with which they could demand board responsiveness or at least board attention in exchange for foregoing the steps associated with forming a nominating group.

Finally, the SEC may simply have lost perspective. After years of considering proxy access—years in which opponents raised vigorous challenges to every proposed rule-making effort—the SEC was derailed by the effort to address each of these potential challenges.[256]

<http://www.sec.gov/news/speech/2008/spch072208psa.htm> (describing and criticizing precatory proposals).

[251] Press Release, U.S. Senate Comm. on Banking, Hous., & Urban Affairs, Dodd Stands Up for Shareholder Rights (1 Nov. 2007), available at <http://www.banking.senate.gov/public/index.cfm?FuseAction=Newsroom.PressReleases&ContentRecord_id=796095f1-ade9-4777-9b56-587b06cf6430&Region_id=&Issue_id=>.

[252] Dodd-Frank Wall Street Reform and Consumer Protection Act, Pub. L. No. 111-203, § 951, 124 Stat. 1376, 1899–900 (2010) (codified as amended at 15 U.S.C. § 78n-1 (Supp. IV 2010)) (requiring the SEC to adopt rules requiring advisory votes on Say on Pay).

[253] See Adopting Release, *supra* note 12, at 56,685–6.

[254] See Adopting Release, *supra* note 12, at 56,685–6.

[255] See Goodman, Olson, and Fontenot (2010: § 10.03) (describing issuer compliance with ISS policy guidelines to avoid withhold recommendations).

[256] In part, this response may be a by-product of the notice-and-comment rulemaking process. Over the years, as the SEC has attempted to structure its rulemaking to consider all possible arguments and objections to proxy access, its proposals have become increasingly complex. As James McRitchie (2009) puts it:

Each response led, in turn, to additional line-drawing. Commentators argued, for example, that activist shareholders would use proxy access to circumvent the rules governing control contests.[257] Rather than evaluating whether the disclosure requirements of Schedule 14N and the other restrictions of Rule 14a-11 provided adequate protection in the context of a control contest,[258] the SEC attempted to identify the appropriate percentage of director candidates that would not pose a control threat.[259] Limiting the number of nominees forced the SEC, in turn, to formulate procedures to choose among candidates proposed by multiple nominating groups.[260]

The same can be said for the required ownership threshold and holding period. Critics warned that proxy access would give union pension funds and other special interest groups a tool to use against existing management.[261] The SEC responded by adopting a 3% ownership requirement—effectively precluding unions and similar special interest groups from using the rule. Critics expressed concern about the short-term objectives of hedge funds, which frequently assemble holdings of greater than 3%.[262] The SEC again responded by imposing a three-year holding period designed to preclude hedge funds as well. As former Commissioner Paul Atkins explained it, the SEC was attempting 'to find the magic number where "good" shareholder groups (like state pension funds) are in, but "bad" groups (politically incorrect shareholders, like hedge funds) are out' (Atkins 2010).

The SEC's efforts to avoid all possible bad effects or 'unintended consequences' (Aguilar 2009) may have led it to choose instead a rule that would have had no consequences, intended or otherwise. Importantly, the SEC's focus was seemingly on avoiding bad consequences rather than identifying an affirmative value to increasing shareholder nominating power and determining the changes necessary to achieve that value. This evaluation, of course, would have brought the SEC into the core of the corporate governance debate, an area the SEC has struggled to avoid since the 1990 Business

> I'm afraid too many will be distracted by the hundreds of questions raised by the SEC, the labyrinth of language only an SEC attorney could love, and the need to arrive at a consensus document that all with a vested interest in the status quo can at least live with.

[257] See, e.g., Letter from Cravath, Swaine & Moore LLP et al. to Elizabeth Murphy, Sec'y, SEC 3–4 (17 Aug. 2009), available at <http://www.sec.gov/comments/s7-10-09/s71009-212.pdf> (identifying provisions of Rule 14a-11 that, in combination, might allow shareholders to obtain a change in control).

[258] Significantly, most contested solicitations for director elections include shareholder nominations for only a minority of board seats. See Gibson Dunn (2009) (explaining that running a 'short slate' has become 'the preferred approach for dissidents seeking board representation' (internal quotation marks omitted)). Among the reasons for this approach is that proxy advisors, such as ISS, are more likely to support activists who are not seeking to replace a majority of the board (Gibson Dunn 2009).

[259] Adopting Release, *supra* note 12, at 56,706–7 (explaining the rationale for the limitation of 25% in terms of preventing the use of Rule 14a-11 for control contests).

[260] Adopting Release, *supra* note 12, at 56,710–11.

[261] See, e.g., Hall (2010) (reporting that a coalition of seventeen groups expressed these concerns in opposition to Dodd-Frank's proposed proxy access provision).

[262] See, e.g., Letter from Darla C. Stuckey, Soc'y of Corporate Sec'ys & Governance Prof'ls, to Elizabeth M. Murphy, Sec'y, SEC 1 (19 Jan. 2010), available at <http://www.sec.gov/comments/s7-10-09/s71009610.pdf>:

> [M]any hedge funds seek to direct the operations of a company with a view to short-term profitability or otherwise to the detriment of the long-term interest of companies and their shareholders.

Roundtable decision.[263] Any debate over proxy access that fails to evaluate its effect on the allocation of power between shareholders and managers is, however, destructively ambiguous because the best argument in favour of proxy access—increasing board accountability—requires that proxy access increase shareholder power. Similarly, the most potent arguments against proxy access are based on claims that increasing shareholder power is ill-advised. In the following section, this chapter turns to the corporate governance debate and demonstrates how the role of proxy access within the context of corporate governance highlights the limitations of federal rulemaking.

19.5 Proxy Access and Corporate Governance

The SEC's failure to articulate a normative justification for proxy access was the primary source of the ambiguity in Rule 14a-11. The SEC did not offer empirical support for the proposition that US corporate governance is defective or explain how the proxy access provided by Rule 14a-11 would improve it.[264] Nor did the SEC provide a theory as to how shareholders might, through proxy access, increase board accountability. The SEC did not demonstrate that public company boards are insufficiently responsive to shareholder interests; indeed, some scholars have argued that the 2008 financial crisis was exacerbated by an excessive focus on shareholder interests.[265] Nor did the SEC explain how the nomination and election of directors representing a minority of the board is likely to impact board decision-making.[266]

These questions about the desirability of proxy access implicate fundamental issues of corporate governance—determining the optimal equilibrium between management and shareholder power, evaluating the extent to which the existing allocation of power has deviated from that optimal balance, and assessing whether the regulatory reform under consideration is likely to restore that balance. Critics and commentators strongly disagree about these points.[267] Reviewing and evaluating that debate is a difficult task that extends beyond

[263] See Loewenstein (1994: 783–4) (explaining the SEC's caution in regulating corporate governance because of ongoing questions over its statutory authority to do so).

[264] Commentators are divided on this point. Compare Cheffins (2009) (arguing that the financial failure did not demonstrate the existence of a governance problem), with Kirkpatrick (2009) (identifying failures in board oversight as a substantial factor contributing to the financial crisis).

[265] See, e.g., Bratton and Wachter (Chapter 21, this volume) (explaining that focus on shareholder value maximization led financial firms to take excessive risks).

[266] At least one study has considered the impact on stock returns of a dissident obtaining minority board representation. See Cernich et al. (2009: 25–37) (surveying 120 hybrid boards and evaluating their effect on governance structures and shareholder value).

[267] Compare Bebchuk (2005: 836) (arguing that the existing allocation of power is insufficient to enable shareholders to initiate value-increasing changes), with Anabtawi (2006: 579–83) (arguing that large shareholders will use any increase in shareholder power to obtain private gains at the expense of the firm and other shareholders), and Bainbridge (2006: 1758) (claiming that the existing system of limited shareholder voting rights provides 'substantial efficiency benefits').

the scope of this chapter. The challenges presented by this task create substantial impediments to SEC efforts to regulate shareholder nominating power through a federal proxy access rule. In this section, this chapter identifies the problems inherent in mandatory federal regulation of corporate governance.

19.5.1 Proxy Access and Corporate Governance

Shareholder nominating power—which, in turn, is an element of shareholder voting power—is a component of corporate governance: the mechanisms that allocate power between shareholders and management.[268] This allocation of power addresses operational decision-making and, in the public corporation, attempts to minimize the agency costs that result from the separation of ownership and control.[269] Critically, to function well, corporate governance must maintain a balance between managerial and shareholder power (Jensen and Meckling 1976: 308–10). Excess managerial power increases managerial agency costs (Jensen and Meckling 1976: 308–10). Excess shareholder power creates inefficiency and may, in some cases, create intra-shareholder agency costs.[270]

A variety of governance mechanisms contribute to the balance of power in the public corporation. Internal governance mechanisms include the allocation of decision-making authority established by the corporation's statute, charter, and by-laws as well as the ability of shareholders to impose accountability on director decisions through their power to elect and remove board members. Internal governance mechanisms also include the poison pill, which increases management power in the takeover context,[271] and the ability of shareholders to call a special meeting, which enhances shareholder power.[272] External governance mechanisms include gatekeepers such as credit rating agencies, regulators, and the disciplinary effect of the capital markets (Macey 2008: 50 tbl. 3.1).

Evaluating the effect of corporate governance mechanisms or changes to those mechanisms is difficult. First, a specific governance mechanism does not exist in isolation. Its effectiveness is based on its interaction with other aspects of a firm's governance structure. Bebchuk, Coates, and Subramanian, for example, found that the impact of a staggered board on management power to resist a takeover attempt was greatly enhanced when the staggered board was coupled with a poison pill.[273] Similarly, Coates has noted that the effects of staggered boards, which are typically viewed as a powerful management entrenchment device, are avoidable in companies at which shareholders have the right to expand the board

[268] See Macey (2008: 2) (explaining that corporate governance is a 'framework of institutions and processes' that, '[t]aken together, .. determine how power within a company is exercised'); Macey (2008: 50 tbl.3.1) (listing major corporate governance mechanisms for US public companies).

[269] See Jensen and Meckling (1976: 308–10) (describing agency costs that result from separation of ownership and control).

[270] See Walton (2011).

[271] See Ovide (2010) (paraphrasing Marty Lipton as explaining that he invented the poison pill 'to give boards of a target company a chance to "level the playing field" ').

[272] See Allen (2010) (explaining the controversy over proposals that give shareholders the right to call special meetings).

[273] Bebchuk, Coates, and Subramanian (2002: 904) ('Pills made staggered boards important.').

or remove directors without cause.[274] Alternative governance mechanisms may also serve as substitutes.[275]

Internal and external governance mechanisms further interact.[276] For example, scholars have devoted the greatest effort to attempting to assess the impact of antitakeover mechanisms on corporate performance based on the premise that, by reducing the disciplinary effect of the market for corporate control, antitakeover mechanisms reduce board and management accountability. Studies of any specific antitakeover mechanism are difficult to evaluate, however, in that an issuer's susceptibility to a takeover is a function of a multiplicity of governance mechanisms that may include a poison pill and staggered board, a state antitakeover statute, and judicially adopted legal standards for review of a board's conduct in the takeover context.[277]

The second challenge in evaluating governance mechanisms is that their effectiveness depends on firm-specific characteristics, including the firm's existing management team, its shareholder base, and its life-cycle stage. A firm with a long-term, imperial CEO, for example, may require greater director independence. A mature company may be run by managers who are unduly inclined to engage in empire-building mergers or to retain excessive cash flows. Firms owned by a high percentage of retail investors may face excessive free-riding and apathy, while those with many activist owners may be influenced by short-termism or conflicting shareholder objectives. The very governance mechanisms that are valuable for some firms impose excessive costs upon others. In particular, increasing board accountability by enhancing shareholder power is likely to be valuable for poorly managed firms and wasteful, at best, for well-run issuers.[278]

Finally, the governance needs of issuers are dynamic. In addition to the firm-specific factors described above, which can change over the life cycle of an issuer, a variety of market, economic, and even political developments can disrupt the equilibrium between management and shareholder power.[279] The dramatic increase in the institutionalization of the US securities markets, for example, has increased the potential disciplinary effect of shareholder voting power.[280] The adoption by many firms of majority voting is likely to have a similar effect.[281] In contrast, the Delaware Supreme Court's adoption of the *Unitrin*

[274] See Coates (2001: 1352 tbl.3) (finding that these provisions made the staggered boards ineffective for 18% of issuers in the study).

[275] See Hallman, Hartzell, and Parsons (2004: 3–5) (describing the substitution effect of two governance mechanisms in management compensation—the threat of termination and pay for performance).

[276] See Gillan, Hartzell, and Starks (2003) (explaining that such mechanisms 'interact to determine a firm's governance environment').

[277] See, e.g., Fisch (1995: 471) (reviewing Roberta Romano's *The Genius of American Corporate Law* (1993)) (questioning event studies that analyse the wealth effect of antitakeover mechanisms without controlling for other factors that affect the firm's vulnerability to execute a takeover).

[278] See Fisch (1995: 469) (explaining how provisions that increase management discretion may increase the value of well-managed firms but decrease the value of poorly managed firms).

[279] Similarly, such developments can change the effect of specific governance mechanisms. Robert Daines conducted a highly publicized study concluding that Delaware incorporation was associated with increased firm value (2001: 555).

[280] See Fisch (2010b: 879–80) (citing statistics on the growth in institutional ownership of publicly traded equity).

[281] See Verret (2007: 1009) (explaining how majority voting 'could serve to alter significantly the balance of power between shareholders and board members').

standard[282] enhanced management power by reducing the susceptibility of issuers to the discipline of the takeover market.[283]

Several distinctive features render state corporate law robust to firm-specific differences and market and regulatory developments, as discussed in more detail below. First, state law is largely enabling, rather than mandatory. Second, state law is subject to regulatory competition.[284] Third, the development of state law is incremental. These features, which are absent in federal securities regulation, enable state law to maintain an equilibrium in the allocation of power between managers and shareholders.

Although state corporation statutes constrain some issuer choices, in most cases, state statutes provide default rules that enable issuers to customize their governance structures. With respect to shareholder power to elect directors, for example, statutes offer a variety of choices, allowing shareholders to elect directors through majority or plurality voting, permitting supermajority voting requirements, and authorizing special voting structures, such as staggered boards, cumulative voting, tenured voting, and non-voting stock (Easterbrook and Fischel 1983: 408–10). Statutes enable firms to allocate voting rights among multiple share classes and, in some cases, permit corporations to grant non-shareholders the right to elect directors.[285] State law also permits issuers to adopt charter and by-law provisions that limit or condition shareholder nominating power, such as qualification requirements for directors and advance notice by-laws.[286]

This enabling character allows firms to fine-tune their governance structures to reflect differences in their shareholder bases, the extent to which they have a high percentage of institutional investors, the need to protect distinctive shareholder groups such as founding families, the extent to which managers are substantial shareholders, and so forth. Fundamentally, the range of available choices reflects the fact that the optimal structure and distribution of voting power will not be identical for all firms and that customization will increase the efficiency of the shareholder franchise. The enabling approach also furthers experimentation. Issuers can introduce a variety of mechanisms for increasing shareholder participation in the selection of directors, and their workability and legality can be assessed on a case-by-case basis.[287]

[282] *Unitrin, Inc. v. Am. Gen. Corp.*, 651 A.2d 1361, 1373–4 (Del. 1995).

[283] In *Unitrin*, the Delaware Supreme Court clarified that proportionality review under *Unocal* required an assessment of whether the defensive measure was 'preclusive' or 'coercive' and, if not, whether it fell within a 'range of reasonableness' (*Unitrin*: 1387–9); see also Regan (2001: 967–8) (explaining how the *Unitrin* decision disrupted the director–shareholder balance of power).

[284] Although issuers can elect to incorporate in any state, the majority of public corporations incorporate in Delaware (Fisch 2000). I have argued that the flexibility and responsiveness of Delaware corporate law are distinctive features that explain, in part, Delaware's attractiveness as a state of incorporation (see Fisch 2000: 1064). Consequently, the following discussion focuses heavily on Delaware law.

[285] See, e.g., N.Y. Bus. Corp. Law § 703(a) (McKinney 2003) (authorizing the certificate of incorporation to provide bondholders with the right to elect one or more directors).

[286] See, e.g., *JANA Master Fund, Ltd. v. CNET Networks, Inc.*, 954 A.2d 335 (Del. Ch. 2008) (upholding board power to adopt advance notice by-laws).

[287] See Strine (2008: 1098) (explaining how the enabling approach enables 'livable practices . . . to emerge and awkward ones to be discarded', judicial review to test the validity of new practices, and 'state statute writers' to address dissatisfaction with the judiciary's treatment).

The flexibility provided by enabling statutes is further enhanced by regulatory competition. Corporate law allows corporations to choose the state in which they are incorporated and, as a result, the law that will govern the corporation's internal affairs. Regulatory competition enables issuers to choose from a menu of corporate structures and features and creates a natural experiment in the effectiveness of specific governance provisions. Regulatory competition provides two independent values. First, state differences allow product differentiation. Nevada offers a legal regime that is particularly management friendly,[288] for example, and North Dakota recently adopted a distinctively shareholder-friendly regime.[289] Second, individual states provide laboratories for experimentation with innovations that can be subjected to a market test and, if successful, adopted more broadly. State antitakeover statutes[290] and statutes authorizing director exculpation provisions in corporate charters[291] are two examples in which such innovations spread and, over time, were adopted by the majority of states.[292]

Third, the development of state law is incremental.[293] State judicial decisions employ a common law methodology that maintains consistency and stability while providing the flexibility for courts to adapt legal rules to new developments.[294] The Delaware cases concerning the scope of director fiduciary duties in the takeover context,[295] for example, involved a series of adjustments to the relative power of shareholders and boards, adjustments that were able to reflect changes in the structure of hostile tender offers, the development of financing structures, such as junk bonds, and the interaction of state fiduciary principles with other regulatory developments, such as state antitakeover statutes and the Williams Act.[296]

[288] See Subramanian (2002: 1856) (describing Nevada's distinctive provisions and observing that 'Nevada has 15% of the non-Delaware out-of-state incorporations market').

[289] See N.D. Cent. Code § 10-35-01 to -33 (2007).

[290] See Carney (1998: 735–6) (describing the spread of state antitakeover statutes).

[291] See Romano (1990: 1160) (describing how Delaware's innovative provision authorizing director exculpation 'diffused rapidly among the states').

[292] See Carney (1998: 737–41) (citing other examples of provisions that spread among states).

[293] See Strine (2005: 683) (describing incremental evolution of Delaware corporate law through Chancery Court decisions).

[294] See, e.g., Calabresi (1982: 4):

> The incremental nature of common law adjudication meant that no single judge could ultimately change the law, and a series of judges could only do so over time and in response to changed events or to changed attitudes in the people.

[295] A similar evolution can be seen in the Delaware decisions over the duty of good faith. Initially, a series of decisions seemed to articulate good faith as a distinctive fiduciary duty, supplementing the pre-existing duties of care and loyalty. E.g., *Emerald Partners v. Berlin*, 787 A.2d 85, 90 (Del. 2001) ('The directors of Delaware corporations have a triad of primary fiduciary duties: due care, loyalty, and good faith.'). Perhaps in response to subsequent lawsuits that suggested that the duty had the potential to create excessive litigation, thereby chilling the board's discretionary decision-making, the courts cut back, retreating from the characterization of good faith as a separate duty and limiting the scope of its reach. E.g., *Stone v. Ritter*, 911A.2d 362, 370 (Del. 2006) ('[T]he obligation to act in good faith does not establish an independent fiduciary duty that stands on the same footing as the duties of care and loyalty.').

[296] See Regan (2001: 951–70) (recounting the evolution of Delaware case law concerning director fiduciary duties in the takeover context).

Legislative intervention, which frequently occurs as a response to issues that have been developed through the factual context of specific disputes, offers a corrective measure for reconsideration of judicially created rules. Unlike federal regulation, which is typically an initial regulatory response, corporate legislation is frequently a second step, taken after courts have attempted to apply existing legal rules to a variety of fact patterns and the legislature has been able to observe the consequences.[297] As Ed Rock (1997: 1102) explains, '[T]he Delaware legislature and courts cannot promulgate *ex ante* the standards to govern new situations until they see a variety of cases and figure out how well or badly people behaved'. Thus, after the Delaware Supreme Court's decision in *Smith v. Van Gorkom*[298] appeared to subject outside directors to excessive liability risk, the legislature authorized director exculpation charter provisions (Romano 1990: 1160). When the Supreme Court rejected a proxy reimbursement by-law as invalid under Delaware law,[299] the legislature amended the statute to authorize proxy reimbursement by-laws.[300]

19.5.2 Federalizing Proxy Access

Federal proxy access offers none of the advantages of state corporate governance described in the preceding subsection 19.5.1. As a general matter, federal regulation does not provide the opportunities for experimentation and variation offered by state law. Federal regulation imposes mandatory and uniform rules on issuers and limits the options for opting out of these rules.[301] Mandatory rules increase the stakes involved for regulators such as the SEC in ascertaining the optimal regulatory structure. They also reduce the potential for competition and the market to discipline politically motivated choices that may be inefficient (Romano 1993: 82–3). In contrast, rules that allow issuer-specific choice produce valuable evidence on the efficiency of regulatory choices, both directly by producing the variation needed to assess the effects of the rules and indirectly by prompting issuers to opt out of inefficient regulation.[302]

That is not to say that mandatory rules are always inappropriate. As the preceding subsection 19.5.1 has explained, however, uniform national rules are likely to be suboptimal tools for regulating corporate governance. In particular, shareholder nominating power is embedded in the state regulatory framework of shareholder voting. State law is the source of shareholder voting power. State law provides the tools by which issuers can customize shareholder voting power through charter and by-law provisions. State law supplies the

[297] See Strine (2008: 1098) ('[I]f either the stockholders or managers are dissatisfied by the judiciary's treatment of those proposals, pressure will be put on state statute writers to address their concerns.').

[298] 488 A.2d 858 (Del. 1985).

[299] *CA, Inc. v. AFSCME Emps. Pension Plan*, 953 A.2d 227, 239–40 (Del. 2008).

[300] Del. Code Ann. tit. 8, § 113 (Supp. 2011).

[301] See Romano (1993: 86–96) (summarizing arguments in the debate over mandatory versus enabling corporate law).

[302] An example is the takeover context. Empirical studies reported a substantial negative price effect on issuers that were subject to the restrictive Pennsylvania antitakeover statute. See, e.g., Chandy et al. (2008: 403). Because the statute provided an opt-out provision, however, issuers could and did avoid the price effect by exercising their ability to opt out.

fiduciary principles that limit management power to interfere with shareholder voting rights.[303] Shareholder nominating rights interact with both the scope of their substantive voting rights and the structural mechanisms that govern the voting process.

Both this interaction and the difficulty of evaluating the effect of corporate governance regulation create challenges for the regulation of shareholder nominating power. Federal regulation is poorly suited for the kind of experimentation that is particularly valuable in an area in which it is difficult, *ex ante*, to identify the optimal regulatory approach.[304] The process is complicated by the heavily politicized nature of the SEC rulemaking process. The massive letter-writing campaigns and lobbying efforts associated with the SEC's consideration of proxy access contributed to regulatory gridlock and vastly complicated the task of structuring the regulation. The nature of proxy access, which involves a shift of power from concentrated and well-funded corporate managers to dispersed investors with comparatively small stakes, increased the potential that the rulemaking record would be distorted.[305] Under private ordering, issuers could vary their nominating procedures, and one issuer's approach could differ from that of its competitor. This variation eliminates the pressure to ensure that a single mandated rule is optimal.

Nor can federal regulation be defended, in the context of proxy access, as a necessary response to the inability of shareholders to obtain minimally acceptable levels of proxy access through state law and private ordering.[306] First, as indicated above, the level of proxy access that Rule 14a-11 provided to investors was truly minimal. To the extent that few, if any, shareholders would have qualified to use Rule 14a-11 and that those few qualifying shareholders already had sufficient access to the proxy by mounting an election contest, Rule 14a-11 did not remedy any existing obstacles.[307] Second, federal regulation, not state law, has historically been the dominant obstacle to private ordering. The SEC rules, not

[303] See, e.g., *Blasius Indus. v. Atlas Corp.*, 564 A.2d 651, 661 (Del. Ch. 1988) (articulating the heightened standard of 'compelling justification' for review for board decisions that interfere with the shareholder franchise).

[304] As Vice Chancellor Strine (2010: 7) explains, private ordering through issuer-specific by-laws enables 'the market [to] assess what works best without the high costs that come with the imposition of an unproven, invariable mandate'.

[305] See Komesar (1994: 62–3) (explaining how concentrated groups with large stakes can present distorted pictures of the public interest to political officials); cf. Letter from Joseph A. Grundfest, Co-Dir., Rock Ctr. on Corporate Governance, to Elizabeth M. Murphy, Sec'y, SEC (18 Jan. 2010), available at <www.sec.gov/comments/s7-10-09/s71009-599.pdf> (attaching a working paper for the purpose of 'drawing the Commission's attention' to two highly flawed empirical studies that demonstrated, according to the commentator, that 'proxy access . . . is inimical to the best interests of the shareholder community as a whole').

[306] Some commentators argued that a mandatory federal proxy access rule was necessary because of the limitations on shareholder ability to establish proxy access procedures through private ordering. See, e.g., Letter from Julie Gresham, Corporate Sec'y, Shareowner Educ. Network, and Ann Yerger, Exec. Dir., Council of Inst. Investors, to Mary Schapiro, Chairman, SEC (18 Nov. 2009), available at <http://www.sec.gov/comments/s7-10-09/s71009-568.pdf>.

[307] The extent of those obstacles may also be overstated. For example, the SEC identified various limitations on shareholder power to amend the by-laws to establish proxy access procedures. Adopting Release, *supra* note 12, at 56,673. However, only about 4% of Russell 3000 companies do not permit shareholders to amend the by-laws (Young 2009). In addition, market developments suggest that institutional investors are making substantial progress in increasing shareholder voting power, despite the SEC's resistance to their efforts (see Choi, Fisch, and Kahan 2010: 872–6).

state law, prevent the use of a universal ballot that would afford shareholders the freedom to choose from a complete list of issuer and shareholder candidates.[308] The SEC rules, not state law, burden shareholder attempts to engage in collective action in connection with the election process by regulating such attempts as proxy solicitations. And the SEC rules impose compliance costs, including filing requirements, on shareholders seeking to exercise their state law nominating power.

Third, and most importantly, while state law cannot provide shareholders with the ability to overcome existing federal regulatory obstacles, it can nonetheless undercut the minimum level of nominating power afforded by a federal rule. Thus, to the extent that Rule 14a-11 was an effort to respond to limitations in state law or private ordering, it was inadequate.

Rule 14a-11 explicitly provided that it was subject to the availability of shareholder nominating rights under state law.[309] Accordingly, state legislatures could have completely nullified the effect of the rule by eliminating shareholder nominating power—such as by vesting such power in the board or a board nominating committee. Similarly, after the rule's adoption, commentators immediately suggested that issuers consider implementing director qualification by-laws.[310] Although Rule 14a-11 did not permit an issuer to exclude a shareholder nominee from the ballot on the basis that the nominee did not meet the company's qualification requirements (Emmerich 2010), nothing in the SEC rules required a company to seat a director that did not meet its qualification requirements.[311] Similarly, issuers could have thwarted shareholder efforts at group formation by adopting low-threshold poison pills.[312] One academic outlined fifteen possible ways of limiting shareholder nominating power (Verret 2011: 404–15), and it seems difficult to imagine the SEC precluding these responses without taking on a much more substantive role in regulating corporate governance—a role extending well beyond the authorization in Dodd-Frank.

Finally, state regulation of corporate governance offers extensive safeguards against excessive or inefficient shareholder activism. Individual issuers can limit proxy access, in the same manner that Rule 14a-11 did, by imposing minimum ownership and holding period requirements.[313] To the extent that such by-laws unduly restrict shareholder nominating power, state courts and legislatures have a variety of responses available, ranging from the use of judicially

[308] See 17 C.F.R. § 240.14a-4(d)(4) (2011) (prohibiting the inclusion of director candidates on proxy cards without their consent); accord Kouwe (2009) ('Currently, shareholders in most contested corporate elections, including Target's, receive two proxy cards and can vote only for one slate of candidates.').

[309] Adopting Release, *supra* note 12, at 56,674:

> The rule defers entirely to State law as to whether shareholders have the right to nominate directors and what voting rights shareholders have in the election of directors.

[310] See, e.g., Emmerich (2010) (suggesting that companies review their director qualification by-laws and stating that 'companies may, subject to state law, preclude nominees from serving as directors for failure to satisfy reasonable qualification requirements').

[311] Indeed, there is case authority suggesting that the election of a director who did not, at the time of his election, meet the company's qualification requirements would be invalid. See Bishop (2010) (citing and discussing *Waterbury v. Temescal Water Co.*, 105 P. 940 (Cal. Ct. App. 1909)).

[312] See, e.g., *Versata Enters. v. Selectica, Inc.*, 5 A.3d 586 (Del. 2010) (upholding the validity of a pill with a 4.99% trigger).

[313] Cf. *JANA Master Fund, Ltd. v. CNET Networks, Inc.*, 954 A.2d 335, 340–6 (Del. Ch. 2008) (upholding the validity of an advance notice by-law but reading it narrowly); Carlson and Hartlin (2008: 1) (advising clients on how to revise advance notice by-laws to reflect concerns raised by recent Delaware decisions).

imposed limits on the extent to which these by-laws can limit shareholder voting rights[314] to legislative requirements that such limitations be included in the corporate charter (and thus approved by shareholders) rather than being implemented through a director-adopted by-law.[315]

19.6 An Alternative Regulatory Approach

This chapter has questioned the SEC's motives in adopting a federal proxy access rule and challenged the SEC's competence to establish appropriate criteria for modifying the balance of power between shareholders and management in determining the composition of the board of directors. Although existing political forces are likely to preclude the SEC from responding to the DC Circuit decision in the short term, the invalidation of Rule 14a-11 should cause the SEC to reconsider its overall approach to shareholder participation in the nomination of directors.

The solution to the deficiencies described in this chapter, along with the concerns identified by the DC Circuit, is not to return to the pre-Rule 14a-11 status quo. As the SEC itself recognized, both the promulgation and interpretation of the federal proxy rules directly interfere with the exercise of shareholder power and shareholder attempts to reallocate the balance of authority at individual issuers with respect to both the composition of the board of directors and other governance issues. Rather than attempting to determine an appropriate balance of power, the SEC should simply stop trying to regulate corporate governance. Instead, the SEC should revise the federal proxy rules to remove the impediments that currently limit the ability of states, issuers, and shareholders to experiment with, vary, and improve governance structures.

Removing these impediments is easy. Instead of trying to structure proxy access, the SEC should allow state law to determine both the circumstances under which shareholders have the power to nominate director candidates and the appropriate qualifications for nominating shareholders and their nominees. State law can make these determinations in a variety of ways. State statutes can set forth the scope of shareholder nominating power. Similarly, state statutes can, as Delaware already does, explicitly authorize issuers to adopt individually tailored nominating procedures and to describe the manner for doing so. Under the traditional enabling approach of state law, issuers can establish individually tailored nominating procedures directly, through charter and by-law provisions, and indirectly, by specifying director qualification requirements, advance notice rules, annual meeting procedures, and so forth. Overreaching by either shareholders or corporate management can be constrained through judicial review—state courts can evaluate the permissible scope of issuer-specific provisions and restrictions consistent with shareholders' statutory voting authority and management's fiduciary obligations. Federal proxy rules should, instead, focus on the SEC's core competency—disclosure.

[314] See *JANA Master Fund, Ltd.*, 954 A.2d at 338 (determining whether CNET's advance notice by-law, if construed broadly, should be held invalid as 'an unreasonable restriction on [the] shareholder franchise').

[315] E.g., Del. Code Ann. tit. 8, § 141(d) (Supp. 2008) (permitting issuers to establish classified boards through charter provision but not through director-adopted by-law).

Accordingly, this chapter advocates the following regulatory changes. First, the SEC should amend Regulation 14A to require issuers to disclose in their proxy statements all properly nominated director candidates, whether the nominations are made by a nominating committee, a shareholder, or some other mechanism.[316] State law, including case law, state corporation statutes, and the issuer's governing documents (to the extent those documents are consistent with state law), would determine whether a nomination is proper. This amendment would enable individual issuers to experiment with varying criteria, such as the ownership threshold or holding period, to determine the extent to which their choices affected the quality and quantity of shareholder nominations. It would also allow issuers to experiment with other mechanisms for increasing shareholder input, such as expense reimbursement or shareholder representation on nominating committees. Issuers would also have the power to adopt mechanisms to limit the extent of shareholder input, including imposing qualification requirements and establishing methods for determining priority among director candidates.

In terms of disclosure, federal law would require that the issuer provide comparable disclosure in the proxy statement for all director candidates, including the directors' employment, compensation, other directorships, and qualifications. Nominating shareholders and their nominees would be required to supply this information to the issuer as a condition of inclusion in the proxy statement. Issuers would also be required to disclose, in the proxy statement and for each director candidate, the source of that director's nomination (e.g., issuer nominating committee or shareholder). If the issuer's proxy statement includes a statement in support of any of the board-nominated director candidates, Regulation 14A would require the board to give nominating shareholders the opportunity to include a supporting statement of equal length for their nominees.

Second, consistent with the disclosure in the proxy statement, the SEC should amend Rule 14a-4 to require the issuer's proxy card to give shareholders the opportunity to vote for any of the candidates included in the proxy statement. The proxy card would thus constitute a universal ballot for all properly nominated candidates.

Third, the SEC should adopt exemptions from sections 13(d) and 16(b) for collective shareholder action in connection with the election of directors so long as the shareholders do not, individually or collectively, seek to obtain economic control of the issuer. Specifically, the exemption should provide that collective shareholder action does not, itself, create a group for purposes of 13(d) or result in the aggregation of shareholder holdings for purposes of 13(d) or 16(b). Such exemptions should extend to both the nomination and the election of directors and the collective action associated with proposed by-law amendments concerning director qualifications, nominating procedures, and similar issues.

Finally, the federal proxy rules should directly facilitate issuer efforts to experiment with different mechanisms for private ordering. In particular, the SEC should extend the

[316] In 2002, Les Greenberg and James McRitchie filed a rulemaking petition with the SEC proposing an amendment to Rule 14a-8 that, although structured somewhat differently from the proposal in this chapter, would have had the similar effect of providing 'that the solicitation of proxies for all nominees for Director positions, who meet the other legal requirements, be required to be included in the Company's proxy materials'. Request for Rulemaking to Amend Rule 14a-8(i) to Allow Shareholder Proposals to Elect Directors, U.S. Sec. & Exch. Comm'n (1 Aug. 2002), available at <http://www.sec.gov/rules/petitions/petn4-461.htm>.

disinterested shareholder exemption under Rule 14A2(b)(1) to exempt shareholders engaging in collective action for the purpose of nominating director candidates pursuant to their issuer's nominating procedures from the notice and filing requirements of the federal proxy rules. This change would remove the important existing impediment to nominating procedures that require a minimum number of shareholders to support or second a nomination.

A major advantage of this proposal is that it enables shareholders and issuers to experiment with a broader range of options for increasing shareholder input into board composition. Rule 14a-11 was, after all, roughly modelled on a proxy access procedure developed by shareholders.[317] Absent regulatory interference, issuers could develop a variety of alternative procedures. Issuers could use the existing nominating committee to nominate two candidates for each board position. This approach meets some of the current objections to proxy access by enabling the nominating committee to maintain control over director selection, control that addresses concerns over director qualifications, conflicts of interest, and overall board composition, while increasing the degree of shareholder choice. Another approach could authorize corporations to increase board size to accommodate shareholder-nominated candidates without displacing existing issuer nominees. This approach would increase shareholder input without creating an active contest that might displace sitting directors.

In experimenting with proxy access procedures, investors and issuers might also look to the experiences of other common law countries.[318] Australia and Canada, for example, allow nominations by 5% shareholders without the requirement of a minimum holding period.[319] Australia also authorizes nominations by groups of 100 shareholders.[320] Although caution is necessary in importing the governance approaches of countries with different corporate structures and ownership models, the experiences of these countries cast doubt on the objections posed by critics of proxy access. Shareholder candidates are rarely nominated and still less frequently elected. Rather than inciting frequent contested elections, the Australian system, for example, is said to promote the peaceful transition of directors in whom investors have lost confidence.[321]

An alternative approach would provide minority shareholder groups of sufficient size with the right not merely to nominate director candidates but to secure board representation. Under the voting list approach taken by Italy and Spain, for example, minority shareholders can propose a list of shareholder nominees that competes with the official list of candidates and ensure that at least one of their representatives obtains a director seat.[322]

317 See *supra* notes 45–52 and accompanying text (discussing the *AFSCME* decision and the SEC's response).

318 Examining proxy access from a global perspective suggests the availability of alternative governance rights that might substitute for increased nominating power as well. Shareholders in some common law countries have the right to amend the corporation's charter and the right to call an extraordinary shareholders meeting at which they can take actions such as removing directors with whom they are dissatisfied (see Hill 2008).

319 Letter from Michael O'Sullivan, President, Austl. Council of Super Investors, to Elizabeth M. Murphy, Sec'y, SEC 1 (14 Aug. 2009) (hereinafter O'Sullivan Letter), available at <http://www.sec.gov/comments/s710-09/s71009-195.pdf>; McDermott and Farrell (2012).

320 O'Sullivan Letter, *supra* note 319, at 1.

321 O'Sullivan Letter, *supra* note 319, at 1.

322 Ventoruzzo (2010: 35–6). See generally Wilcox, Segni, and Erede (2009) (describing list voting in Italy); Erede (2009: 20–4) (describing Italian law provisions protecting rights of minority shareholders).

One commentator reports that the system, which has been in effect in Italy since 2006, has worked 'smoothly' and has affected the board composition of listed companies (Ventoruzzo 2010: 36).

Another option is shareholder participation on the issuer's nominating committee. In Sweden, the nominating committee consists of shareholders rather than directors.[323] The Swedish shareholder nominating committee approach has recently been publicized by the Centre for Tomorrow's Company, a think tank that had urged United Kingdom corporations to adopt a similar structure for selecting directors.[324] A variation on this approach might be a nominating committee jointly comprised of shareholders and independent directors.

It is, of course, beyond the scope of this chapter to evaluate the relative costs and benefits of these and other alternatives. The point is that the corporate structure contains a variety of methods and mechanisms for increasing shareholder input into the selection of directors. In the absence of empirical or normative justification for the SEC's chosen approach, it is imprudent to prevent states and issuers from considering these alternatives.

The amendments proposed by this chapter might not result in effective shareholder nominating rights. Issuers might respond by adopting by-law provisions that impose procedural requirements, director qualifications, filing deadlines, or conditions for nominating shareholders that are impossible to meet. Indeed, private ordering may lead to more limited nominating rights than those the SEC attempted to provide through Rule 14a-11. Critically, however, regulating shareholder nominating rights as a component of corporate governance offers a variety of fail-safes and counterbalances that limit potential managerial overreaching in the way that a restrictive federal rule does not. As we have seen in recent years, private ordering and state regulation have enabled corporate governance mechanisms to adapt to firm and market developments. Innovations, such as majority voting and firm-specific modifications like the elimination of staggered boards, shift the balance of power between shareholders and management. In the current environment, the pump is primed for reform of nominating procedures. The SEC just has to get out of the way.

19.7 Conclusion

There was no need for the SEC to try to determine the optimal level of shareholder nominating power. The area would have been free for state law and issuer-specific experimentation if the SEC had simply held seventy years ago that issuers were required to disclose the existence of all properly nominated director candidates on the issuer's proxy statement and to provide shareholders with a chance to vote on the election of such candidates. Instead, the SEC viewed its responsibility with respect to proxy access too broadly. The SEC's expertise with respect to market regulation, disclosure, and investor protection does not translate into expertise over corporate governance. Nothing in the SEC's structure, composition, or

[323] See Tomorrow's Co., Tomorrow's Corporate Governance: Bridging the UK Engagement Gap through Swedish-Style Nomination Committees 3 (2010) (describing the Swedish system), available at <http://www.forceforgood.com/Uploaded_Content/tool/243201011485875.pdf>.

[324] Tomorrow's Co., Tomorrow's Corporate Governance, at 9, 42–3, 45, 47.

experience indicates that it is better positioned than state legislatures, state courts, and corporations themselves to determine who should sit on corporate boards or to allocate power between shareholders and managers to decide this question.[325]

The SEC's adoption of a proxy access rule in 2010 was misguided. Market and legal developments had reduced the need for a mandated form of proxy access, and the SEC's rule was so narrow and restrictive that it was unlikely to enhance shareholder nominating power. At the same time, the SEC's attempt to funnel shareholder nominating efforts through the federal procedure would likely have frustrated experimentation with more effective alternatives. In adopting Rule 14a-11, the SEC acted as corporate governance czar—displacing existing state law governance mechanisms in order to decide how much governance power shareholders should enjoy.

In responding to the DC Circuit's decision, the SEC should reconsider a regulatory approach that continues to impede shareholder efforts to impose accountability on corporate boards. Specifically, the SEC should modify its proxy rules to facilitate shareholder choice about nomination procedures. This chapter has identified minor amendments to the federal proxy rules that would reduce federal interference with private ordering. Although issuer-specific experimentation may not produce the perfect proxy access procedure, it—unlike the SEC's regulatory process—is likely to produce experiential data that, at a minimum, can facilitate more informed governance choices. In the absence of federal interference, issuers, state legislatures and courts, and investors themselves can respond to that experience.

References

Aguilar, M. K. (2009). Proxy Access Debate Rages On, *Compliance Week* (18 Aug.), available at <http://www.complianceweek.com/article/5545/proxy-access-debate-rages-on>.

Akyol, A. C., Lim, W. F., and Verwijmeren, P. (2012). Shareholders in the Boardroom: Wealth Effects of the SEC's Proposal to Facilitate Director Nominations, *Journal of Financial and Quantitative Analysis* 47(5), 1029.

[325] See Troy A. Paredes, Comm'r, SEC, Statement at Open Meeting to Propose Amendments Regarding Facilitating Shareholder Director Nominations (20 May 2009), available at <http://www.sec.gov/news/speech/2009/spch052009tap.htm> ('The Commission is not well-positioned to decide "who is in" and "who is out" '.). Whether Congress can or should make those determinations is a separate matter. Since the adoption of Sarbanes-Oxley, Congress has made increasing, albeit cautious, inroads into the type of policy determinations over corporate law and governance that previously had been left exclusively to state law and, to an extent, private ordering. See Bainbridge (2003: 26, 28) (describing the increasing federal control of corporate law). Dodd-Frank provides fragments of the most aggressive federalization of corporate law to date with its inclusion of provisions concerning shareholder approval of executive compensation, the composition of compensation committees, the separation of the positions of CEO and chairman of the board, and the promulgation of self-regulatory organization standards specifying director duties. *See* Pub. L. No. 111-203, §§ 763(a), 951, 972, 124 Stat. 1778, 1899, 1915 (2010) (codified as amended at 15 U.S.C. §§ 78j, 78n (Supp. IV 2010)). To date, however, the federalization remains largely a piecemeal effort. With the limited exception of Say on Pay, see *supra* note 252, which is, in any case, a non-binding advisory vote, Dodd-Frank does not modify the substantive issues upon which shareholders can vote or the procedures by which they exercise that voting power.

Allen, T. (2010). Showdown over Special Meetings, *ISS* (20 Jan.), available at <http://blog.issgovernance.com/gov/2010/01/showdown-over-special-meetingssubmitted-by-ted-allen-publications.html> .

Anabtawi, I. (2006). Some Skepticism about Increasing Shareholder Power, *UCLA Law Review* 53, 561.

Atkins, P. (2010). The SEC's Sop to Unions, *Wall Street Journal* (27 Aug.), at A15, available at <http://online.wsj.com/article/SB10001424052748703632304575451343422958522.html>.

Bainbridge, S. M. (2003). The Creeping Federalization of Corporate Law, *Regulation* 26(1), 32.

Bainbridge, S. M. (2006). Response, Director Primacy and Shareholder Disempowerment, *Harvard Law Review* 119, 1735.

Ballard, J. G. (2009). Regulatory Watch: SEC Extends Comment Period for Proposed Director Nomination Rule, *Business Law Currents* (15 Dec.), available at <http://currents.westlaw-business.com/Articles/2009/12/20091215_0022.aspx?cid=&src=E100629001&sp=>.

Bebchuk, L. A. (2005). The Case for Increasing Shareholder Power, *Harvard Law Review* 118, 833.

Bebchuk, L. A. (2010). Another View: Don't Gut Proxy Access, *New York Times Dealbook* (21 June), available at <http://dealbook.nytimes.com/2010/06/21/another-view-dont-gut-proxy access/>.

Bebchuk, L. A., Coates, IV, J. C., and Subramanian, G. (2002). The Powerful Antitakeover Force of Staggered Boards: Theory, Evidence, and Policy, *Stanford Law Review* 54, 887.

Becker, B., Bergstresser, D., and Subramanian, G. (2011). Does Shareholder Proxy Access Improve Firm Value? Evidence from the Business Roundtable Challenge, Harvard Business School, Working Paper No. 11-052, available at <http://www.hbs.edu/research/pdf/11-052.pdf>.

Bishop, K. P. (2010). Director Qualification Requirements, Nominations & Proxy Access, *California Corporate and Securities Law* (7 Sept.), available at <http://calcorporatelaw.com/2010/09/director-qualification-requirements-nominations-proxy-access/>.

Black, B., Cheffins, B., and Klausner, M. (2006). Outside Director Liability, *Stanford Law Review* 58, 1055.

Boston Globe (2011). Overhaul Forces Loan Wording Change, *Boston Globe* (6 Jan.), at 8.

Bratton, W. W. (2007). Hedge Funds and Governance Targets, *Georgetown Law Journal* 95, 1375.

Calabresi, G. (1982). *A Common Law for the Age of Statutes* (Cambridge, MA, Harvard University Press).

Carlson, R. R. and Hartlin, J. T. (2008). Revisiting Advance Notice Bylaws In Light of Recent Delaware Decisions, available at <http://www.paulhastings.com/assets/publications/981.pdf>.

Carney, W. J. (1998). The Production of Corporate Law, *Southern California Law Review* 71, 715.

Cernich, C., Fenn, S., Anderson, M., and Westcott, S. (2009). *Effectiveness of Hybrid Boards*, available at <http://irrcinstitute.org/pdf/IRRC_05_09_EffectiveHybridBoards.pdf>.

Chandy, P. R., Foster, Jr, C. M., Braswell, M. K., and Poe, S. L. (2008). The Shareholder Wealth Effects of the Pennsylvania Fourth Generation Anti-Takeover Law, *American Business Law Journal* 32, 399.

Check, C. and Miller, M. (2009). Determining Shareholder Access: Examining Shareholder–Management Relationships through the Differing Lenses Used by the SEC and the 'Common Law' of Corporate Bylaws, *Wake Forest Law Review* 44, 297.

Cheffins, B. R. (2009). Did Corporate Governance 'Fail' During the 2008 Stock Market Meltdown? The Case of the S&P 500, *Business Lawyer* 65, 1.

Choi, S. J. and Fisch, J. E. (2008). On Beyond CalPERS: Survey Evidence on the Developing Role of Public Pension Funds in Corporate Governance, *Vanderbilt Law Review* 61, 315.

Choi, S. J., Fisch, J. E., and Kahan, M. (2010). The Power of Proxy Advisors: Myth or Reality?, *Emory Law Journal* 59, 869.

Choi, S. J., Pritchard, A. C., and Fisch, J. E. (2005). Do Institutions Matter? The Impact of the Lead Plaintiff Provision of the Private Securities Litigation Reform Act, *Washington University Law Quarterly* 83, 869.

CNNMoney (2011). Fortune 500 2011: Top 500 American Companies – Mattel (23 May), available at <http://money.cnn.com/magazines/fortune/fortune500/2011/snapshots/272.html>.

Coates, IV, J. C. (2001). Explaining Variation in Takeover Defenses: Blame the Lawyers, *California Law Review* 89, 1301.

Colvin, G. (2007). The Gadfly in the Ivory Tower, *Fortune* (16 Apr.), at 40.

Compliance Intelligence (2010). White House Intervenes to Weaken Corporate Governance Bill, *Compliance Intelligence* (18 June), available at <http://complianceintel.com/articleprint.aspx?articleid=2603470&single=true>.

Connelly, J. (2010). Proxy Access: Worth Little More Than a Hill of Beans, *Corporate Board Member* (Third Quarter), at 50.

Cooper, H. (2010). Obama Signs a Contentious Overhaul of the US Financial System, *New York Times* (22 July), at B3.

Cox, J. D. and Thomas, R. S. (2002). Leaving Money on the Table: Do Institutional Investors Fail to File Claims in Securities Class Actions?, *Washington University Law Quarterly* 80, 855.

Daines, R. (2001). Does Delaware Law Improve Firm Value?, *Journal of Financial Economics* 62, 525.

Davis, G. F. (2008). A New Finance Capitalism? Mutual Funds and Ownership Re-Concentration in the United States, *European Management Review* 5, 11.

Dennis, B. (2010). Senate Passes Landmark Bill in Triumph for Obama, *Washington Post* (16 July), at A1.

Dent, Jr, G. W. (2010). The Essential Unity of Shareholders and the Myth of Investor Short-Termism, *Delaware Journal of Corporate Law* 35, 97.

Easterbrook, F. H. and Fischel, D. R. (1983). Voting in Corporate Law, *Journal of Law and Economics* 26, 395.

Emmerich, A. O. (2010). Shareholder Proxy Access: Time to Get Ready, *Harvard Law School Forum on Corporate Governance and Financial Regulation* (16 Sept.), available at <http://blogs.law.harvard.edu/corpgov/2010/09/16/shareholder-proxy-access-time-to-get-ready/>.

Erede, M. (2009). Governing Corporations with Concentrated Ownership Structure: Can Hedge Funds Activism Play Any Role in Italy? (unpublished manuscript), available at <http://ssrn.com/abstract=1397562>.

Fisch, J. E. (1993). From Legitimacy to Logic: Reconstructing Proxy Regulation, *Vanderbilt Law Review* 46, 1129.

Fisch, J. E. (1995). Picking a Winner, *Journal of Corporation Law* 20, 451.

Fisch, J. E. (2000). The Peculiar Role of the Delaware Courts in the Competition for Corporate Charters, *University of Cincinnati Law Review* 68, 1061.

Fisch, J. E. (2001). Aggregation, Auctions, and Other Developments in the Selection of Lead Counsel under the PSLRA, *Law and Contemporary Problems* 64, 53.

Fisch, J. E. (2002). Lawyers on the Auction Block: Evaluating the Selection of Class Counsel by Auction, *Columbia Law Review* 102, 650.

Fisch, J. E. (2008). The Transamerica Case, in J. R. Macey (ed.), *The Iconic Cases in Corporate Law* (St Paul, MN, Thomson West).

Fisch, J. E. (2010a). The Overstated Promise of Corporate Governance, *University of Chicago Law Review* 77, 923.

Fisch, J. E. (2010b). Securities Intermediaries and the Separation of Ownership from Control, *Seattle University Law Review* 33, 877.

Frankel, A. (2002). Class Warfare, *American Lawyer* (Mar.), at 76.

Georgeson (2009). 2009 Annual Corporate Governance Review.

Gibson Dunn (2009). SEC Grants No-Action Relief to Activist Shareholders Seeking to 'RoundOut' Short Slates with Each Other's Nominees (2 Apr.), available at <http://www.gibsondunn.com/publications/pages/SECGrantsNo-ActionReliefToActivistShareholdersSeekingtoRoundOutShortSlates.aspx>.

Gillan, S., Hartzell, J. C., and Starks, L. T. (2003). Explaining Corporate Governance: Boards, Bylaws, and Charter Provisions, John L. Weinberg Ctr. for Corporate Governance, Working Paper No. 2003-03, available at <http://ssrn.com/abstract=442740>.

Goldfarb, Z. A. (2009). SEC Pick Pledges to Ratchet Up Oversight, *Washington Post* (16 Jan.), at D1.

Goodman, A. L., Olson, J. F., and Fontenot, L. (2010). *Practical Guide to Sec Proxy and Compensation Rules* (5th edn) (New York, Aspen Publishers).

Graybow, M. (2009). Schapiro Braces for Fight over Proxy Access, *Reuters* (29 Apr.), available at <http://www.reuters.com/article/idUSTRE53S6I520090429>.

Grossman, R. J. and Denton, J. R. (2009). Never Mind Equal Access: Just Let Shareholders 'Split Their Ticket', *M&A Lawyer* (Jan.), at 28.

Grundfest, J. A. (2010). Measurement Issues in the Proxy Access Debate, Rock Center for Corporate Governance at Stanford University Working Paper No. 71; Stanford Law and Economics Olin Working Paper No. 392, available at <http://ssrn.com/abstract=1538630>.

Hall, C. (2010). Dodd–Corker Fed Bill May Contain Left-Wing 'Shareholder' Power Grab (3 Mar.) *Competitive Enterprise Institute*, available at, <http://cei.org/news-releases/dodd-corker-fed-bill-may-containleft-wing-shareholder-power-grab>.

Hallman, G., Hartzell, J. C., and Parsons, C. (2004). Carrots and Sticks: The Threat of Dismissal and Incentive Compensation (21 Oct.) (unpublished manuscript), available at <http://www.areuea.org/conferences/pdf/52/723.pdf>.

Harris, L. (2010). Missing in Activism: Retail Investor Absence in Corporate Elections, *Columbia Business Law Review* 2010, 104.

Hill, J. (2008). Evolving 'Rules of the Game' in Corporate Governance Reform, *International Journal of Corporate Governance* 1, 28.

Hollis, M. (2002). Enron Losses Trigger Scrutiny of State Panel, *Sun-Sentinel* (Fort Lauderdale, FL) (24 Mar.), at 6B.

Holz, J. and Berman, D. (2010). Investors Gain New Clout, *Wall Street Journal* (26 Aug.), at A1.

Jensen, M. C. and Meckling, W. H. (1976). Theory of the Firm: Managerial Behavior, Agency Costs and Ownership Structure, *Journal of Financial Economics* 3, 305.

Kahan, M. and Rock, E. (2011). The Insignificance of Proxy Access, *Virginia Law Review* 97, 1347.

Kirdahy, M. (2008). Say-on-Pay Edges Closer to Law, *Forbes* (11 Nov.), available at <http://www.forbes.com/2008/11/11/say-on-pay-lead-compensation-cx_mk_1110corpgovernance.html>.

Kirkpatrick, G. (2009). Corporate Governance Lessons from the Financial Crisis, *OECD-Financial Market Trends*, available at <http://www.oecd.org/finance/financial-markets/42229620.pdf>.

Komesar, N. K. (1994). *Imperfect Alternatives: Choosing Institutions in Law* (Chicago, University of Chicago Press).

Kouwe, Z. (2009). Ackman and Target Tangle in Ballot Brawl, *New York Times Dealbook* (21 Apr.), available at <http://dealbook.nytimes.com/2009/04/21/ackman-and-target-tangle-in-ballot-brawl/>.

Larcker, D. F., Ormazabal, G., and Taylor, D. J. (2010). The Regulation of Corporate Governance (unpublished manuscript), available at <http://rockcenter.stanford.edu/wp-content/uploads/2010/05/The-Regulation-of-Corporate-Governance_Larcker.pdf>.

Lipton, M. and Rosenblum, S. A. (1991). A New System of Corporate Governance: The Quinquennial Election of Directors, *University of Chicago Law Review* 58, 187.

Loewenstein, M. J. (1994). The SEC and the Future of Corporate Governance, *Alabama Law Review* 45, 783.

Lynch, S. N. (2009). Activists, Take Note: SEC Delays a Proxy Vote, *Wall Street Journal* (3 Oct.), at B3.

McDermott, R. and Farrell, S. (2004). Canada, in *Global Corporate Governance Guide 2004*, available at <http://www.globalcorporategovernance.com/n_namericas/134_140.htm>.

Macey, J. R. (2007). Too Many Notes and Not Enough Votes: Lucian Bebchuk and Emperor Joseph II Kvetch about Contested Director Elections and Mozart's Seraglio, *Virginia Law Review* 93, 759.

Macey, J. R. (2008). *Corporate Governance: Promises Kept, Promises Broken* (Princeton, NJ, Princeton University Press).

McKinney, M. (2009). Shareholders OK 'Say on Pay', *Star Tribune* (Minneapolis, MN) (26 June), at D1.

McRitchie, J. (2009). Proxy Access (20 Aug.), available at <http://corpgov.net/2009/08/proxy-access/>.

Morgenson, G. (2006). All's Not Lost, Disgruntled Investors, *New York Times* (1 Oct.), at B1.

Newman, P. M. (2008). Legal Considerations in Forming a Mutual Fund, in P. M. Newman (ed.), *ALI–ABA Course of Study: Investment Company Regulation and Compliance* (New York, American Law Institute), available at <http://files.ali-cle.org/thumbs/datastorage/skoobesruoc/pdf/CW009_chapter_02_thumb.pdf>.

Nicholson, H. A. (2004). Note, Securities Law: Proxies Pull Mutual Funds into the Sunlight: Mandatory Disclosure of Proxy Voting Records, *Oklahoma Law Review* 57, 687.

Ovide, S. (2010). Marty Lipton: Why I Invented the Poison Pill, *Wall Street Journal Deal Journal Blog* (29 Dec.), available at <http://blogs.wsj.com/deals/2010/12/29/marty-lipton-why-i-invented-the-poison-pill/>.

Palmiter, A. R. (1994). The Shareholder Proposal Rule: A Failed Experiment in Merit Regulation, *Alabama Law Review* 45, 879.

Pender, K. (2001). CalPERS Had Enron Because Many Did, *San Francisco Chronicle* (9 Dec.), at G1.

Regan, P. L. (2001). What's Left of Unocal?, *Delaware Journal of Corporate Law* 26, 947.

Reichart, K. R. (2009). Is Your Manager Trading Too Much?, *Morningstar* (18 Aug.), available at <http://news.morningstar.com/articlenet/article.aspx?id=304376>.

Rock, E. B. (1997). Saints and Sinners: How Does Delaware Corporate Law Work?, *UCLA Law Review* 44, 1009.

Romanek, B. (2010). Doing the Math: How Many Proxy Access Comment Letters This Decade?, *The Corporate Counsel Blog*, available at <http://www.thecorporatecounsel.net/Blog/2010/02/math-of-comment-letters.html>.

Romano, R. (1990). Corporate Governance in the Aftermath of the Insurance Crisis, *Emory Law Journal* 39, 1155.

Romano, R. (1993). *The Genius of American Corporate Law* (Washington, DC, American Enterprise Institute Press).
Romano, R. (2001). Less Is More: Making Institutional Investor Activism a Valuable Mechanism of Corporate Governance, *Yale Journal on Regulation* 18, 174.
Scannell, K. (2009). Corporate News: Policy Makers Work to Give Shareholders More Boardroom Clout, *Wall Street Journal* (26 Mar.), at B4.
Smith, D. G., Wright, M. G., and Hintze, M. K. (2011). Private Ordering with Shareholder Bylaws, *Fordham Law Review* 80, 125.
Stevens, W. H. (1926). Stockholders' Voting Rights and the Centralization of Voting Control, *Quarterly Journal of Economics* 40, 353.
Strine, Jr, L. E. (2005). The Delaware Way: How We Do Corporate Law and Some of the New Challenges We (and Europe) Face, *Delaware Journal of Corporate Law* 30, 673.
Strine, Jr, L. E. (2008). Breaking the Corporate Governance Logjam in Washington: Some Constructive Thoughts on a Responsible Path Forward, *Business Lawyer* 63, 1079.
Strine, Jr, L. E. (2010). One Fundamental Corporate Governance Question We Face: Can Corporations Be Managed for the Long Term Unless their Powerful Electorates Also Act and Think Long Term?, *Business Lawyer* 66, 1.
Subramanian, G. (2002). The Influence of Antitakeover Statutes on Incorporation Choice: Evidence on the 'Race' Debate and Antitakeover Overreaching, *University of Pennsylvania Law Review* 150, 1795.
USA Today (2002). The Enron Scandal, *USA Today* (21 Jan.), at 3B.
Ventoruzzo, M. (2010). Empowering Shareholders in Directors' Elections: A Revolution in the Making, European Corporate Governance Institute, Working Paper No. 147/2010, available at <http://ssrn.com/abstract=1558467>.
Verret, J. W. (2007). Pandora's Ballot Box, or a Proxy with Moxie? Majority Voting, Corporate Ballot Access, and the Legend of Martin Lipton Re-Examined, *Business Lawyer* 62, 1007.
Verret, J. W. (2011). Defending Against Shareholder Proxy Access: Delaware's Future Reviewing Company Defenses in the Era of Dodd-Frank, *Journal of Corporation Law* 36, 391.
Walton, N. (2011). On the Optimal Allocation of Power between Shareholders and Managers, University of Southern California Law School, Law & Economics Working Paper Series, Paper No. 118, available at <http://law.bepress.com/cgi/viewcontent.cgi?article=1172&context=usclwps>.
Wilcox, J., Segni, A. D., and Erede, M. (2009). Italy's 'Vote by Slate' – An Innovative Method to Elect Minority Directors, in K. Eddy (ed.) *International Corporate Governance Network 2009 Yearbook* (London, International Corporate Governance Network).
Yan, X. S. and Zhang, Z. (2009). Institutional Investors and Equity Returns: Are Short-Term Institutions Better Informed?, *Review of Financial Studies* 22, 893.
Young, B. (2009). The Limits of Private Ordering: Restrictions on Shareholders' Ability to Initiate Governance Change and Distortions of the Shareholder Voting Process, Harvard Law School Forum on Corporate Governance and Financial Regulation (24 Nov.), available at <http://blogs.law.harvard.edu/corpgov/2009/11/24/the-limits-of-private-ordering/>.

C.

Law Reform: The Burden of Persuasion

CHAPTER 20

HEDGE FUND ACTIVISM: WHAT DO WE KNOW AND NOT KNOW?

JOHN C. COFFEE, JR

Beginning sometime around 2005, shareholder activism changed. Specifically, a number of hedge funds changed their basic business strategy. Instead of picking stocks expected to perform well, they began to focus on underperforming stocks—in effect, 'dogs'. As tactics developed, they would deliberately acquire an equity position that required disclosure of their beneficial ownership (i.e., 5% of a class or more under the US's Williams Act[1]), and then announce, as necessitated by SEC disclosure rules, their proposed program of reforms. Their 'reforms' might range from major changes (such as selling the company, spinning off non-core divisions, or firing the CEO) to lesser changes (such as stock buy-backs, increased dividends, or simply governance reforms). These announcements of a corporate governance campaign (typically on the SEC's Schedule 13D) usually triggered an immediate stock price improvement, which might later erode (but on average not disappear). Often (but not always), a proxy fight would follow, as the insurgents would seek to elect a minority (or 'short') slate of two or three directors to the target's board. Within two years, the hedge fund typically exits, selling its block (sometimes back to the issuer) at a profit. This strategy has been highly successful for the hedge funds employing it, and predictably success has bred imitation. According to FactSet SharkWatch, there have been 1,115 such campaigns between 2010 and June 2014 (Hoffman and Benoit 2004).

The scale of these efforts has also grown, with the targets becoming significantly larger. Consider just three examples from 2014. First, Elliott Capital Management settled a bitter proxy fight on terms that compelled Hess Corporation, a major oil refiner, to sell its retail arm for $2.6 billion and invest the proceeds in stock repurchases (De La Merced 2014). Next, Third Point LLC, a particularly aggressive hedge fund, won three seats on Sotheby's board,

[1] At the outset, it is useful to note that Section 13(d)(1) of the Securities Exchange Act, 15 U.S.C. § 78m(d)(1), requires any person or 'group' acquiring beneficial ownership of more than 5% of a class of equity securities of a 'reporting' company to disclose such ownership, along with additional information, including the purpose behind the stock acquisition, within ten days thereafter. As later noted, this ten-day window is more than twice the applicable period in Europe.

running on a platform that called for Sotheby's CEO to be fired. Although it lost its battle in the Delaware Chancery Court,[2] Third Point easily won the proxy war. Finally, Pershing Square Capital joined with Valeant Pharmaceuticals International Inc. to make an over $50 billion tender for Allergan Inc. Although they were ultimately outbid, they demonstrated that hedge funds could team with strategic bidders to seek control (Gelles, De La Merced, and Stevenson 2014).[3]

In the wake of these high-profile cases, many pundits have announced that this is the heyday of hedge fund activism. Fund managers now hold the whip hand, they argue, and managements must appease these new activists and accommodate their agendas. This could well prove to be true (although in fact Sotheby's was uniquely exposed because its board and management held less than 1% of their company's stock, while, as discussed below, the activist hedge funds had accumulated over 30% of Sotheby's stock by the time of the vote). Nonetheless, much of the commentary on hedge fund activism has missed the forest for the trees. Much ignored has been the obvious fact that hedge funds have their own self-interests, which are not perfectly aligned with those of the other shareholders. Conflicts of interest therefore arise, and special attention needs to be given to both the entry and exit strategy of hedge funds in these campaigns. Even more repressed has been the macro-economic impact of hedge fund activism: Does it imply increased leverage, less corporate investment in research and development, and a shorter investment horizon across the corporate landscape?

Why have these issues been slighted? Particularly among academics (for whom all glory lies in being the first to announce a paradigm shift), the commentary to date has tended to be one-sided, often approaching cheerleading. Many legal academics view hedge fund activism as an uncomplicated morality play with 'good' hedge funds fighting an 'entrenched' management that was seeking to use a 'discriminatory' poison pill to block the shareholders' 'true' will. These academics have bought into the view that hedge funds and other activist investors are the catalysts who will at long last arouse institutional investors from their rational apathy and induce them to assert themselves as owners.[4] This view will likely persist, both because academics tend to herd and because they have not examined the underlying evidence with sufficient care. Viewing this topic through a more skeptical lens, this short chapter will review the empirical evidence on hedge fund activism and find it to be inconclusive at best on a number of issues; then, it will turn to the issues surrounding the activist's new tactics, as illustrated by the Sotheby's litigation. This author cannot claim complete objectivity because he did serve as an expert witness for Sotheby's in the foregoing litigation. Precisely for that reason, however, the focus of this chapter will not be on the 'inside

[2] Third Point sued to invalidate Sotheby's poison pill, which had a two-tier structure, permitting 'passive' shareholders to acquire up to 20% of its stock, but limiting 'active' shareholders to 10%. The Chancery Court found this disparity justifiable. See *Third Point LLC v. Ruprecht*, 2014 Del. Ch. LEXIS 64 (2 May 2014). In the settlement, announced just days after this decision, the Sotheby's board was expanded from twelve to fifteen and the three Third Point nominees were seated (along with the Sotheby's nominees); Third Point accepted a 15% standstill restriction (and was reimbursed for $10 million of its expenses) (see Foley 2014). In short, the judiciary sided with Sotheby's, but the shareholders went with Third Point.

[3] Noting 9.7% stake in target acquired by Pershing Square.

[4] For the leading (and impressive) articles in this new genre, see Bebchuk (2013); Gilson and Gordon (2013). Hordes of other articles are following.

baseball' of the Sotheby's case, but rather on the empirical evidence and the broader policy issues. That focus is relevant because the Sotheby's battle will likely foreshadow many proxy fights to come, as imitation is the sincerest form of flattery.

In terms of how these governance campaigns play out, there are four practical lessons to be learned from the Sotheby's battle, the first two of which are uncontroversial and the last two both controversial and counter-intuitive. These tactical conclusions then set the stage for examining the empirical and policy issues.

Lesson One. Defendants Can Continue To Use the Same Tactics Against Hedge Funds That They Long Have Used Against Hostile Bidders![5] In the Sotheby's litigation, Third Point, the insurgent, argued that Sotheby's two-tier poison pill offended the Delaware standard (which traditionally requires a compelling justification for any curtailment of voting rights[6]) because Sotheby's was seeking in its view to thwart a proxy contest and thus impede voting rights. Unsurprisingly, this view was squarely rejected by the Delaware Chancery Court. If a proxy context exception had been grafted onto *Unocal, Unocal* would have become meaningless. That Sotheby's two-tier pill discriminated in favour of 'passive' shareholders and against 'active' shareholders did concern Vice Chancellor Parsons, but ultimately did not move him, perhaps because all flip-in pills are 'discriminatory' (in that they dilute only the acquirer who crosses the defined threshold). Ultimately, the pill's focus on 'active' shareholders struck him as a proportionate response to the threat of a 'creeping control' acquisition and the impact of the gathering of a 'wolf pack' (in his phrase) of hedge funds. For the future, we can expect that activist hedge funds will have to stay within the ownership limits imposed by the target's poison pill (usually around 15%). But, as next discussed, the impact of that constraint is waning.

Lesson Two: The Traditional Tactics No Longer Work! Winning the War in the Courtroom Does Not Win the War on the Proxy Battlefield! Sotheby's won a complete legal victory but settled on terms that implied its defeat in the marketplace. Sotheby's pill was upheld, but so what? Sotheby's still had to sue for peace and accept all three insurgent directors (even though the key proxy advisor, Institutional Shareholder Services ('ISS'), had only recommended votes for two of them). That Sotheby's paid Third Point's legal and proxy expenses (some $10 million) will only convince other activists that they too can achieve costless victories. Also, Third Point's counsel made great use in court of emails showing some Sotheby's directors to share Third Point's doubts about internal governance and compensation levels at Sotheby's. Legally, this evidence may demonstrate the independence of the Sotheby's directors and illustrate a robust and candid internal debate. But at the practical level, it tended to convince those still undecided voters that new voices were needed on the Sotheby's board. For the practitioner, the lesson here is that directors need to realize that, when litigation is

[5] See *Blasius Industries, Inc. v Atlas Corp.*, 564 A.2d 651 (Del. Ch. 1988); *Unocal Corp. v. Mesa Petroleum Co.*, 493 A.2d 946 (Del. 1985). The most important recent decision is probably *Yucaipa American Alliance Fund II, L.P. v Riggio*, 1 A.3d 310 (Del. Ch. 2010) (involving a similar fact pattern).

[6] That standard has, however, been diluted. In a later case, the Delaware Supreme Court held that the *Blasius* standard applies:

> only when the primary purpose of the board's action is to interfere with or impede the exercise of the shareholder franchise and the shareholders are not given a full and fair opportunity to vote effectively.
>
> *MM Cos. v Liquid Audio, Inc.*, 813 A.2d 1118, 1130 (Del 2003).

foreseeable, every email among directors and/or senior executives effectively begins with the implicit caption: 'Dear Ladies and Gentlemen of the Jury'.[7]

Lesson Three: Hedge Fund Activism Causes Losses as Well As Gains. Although Sotheby's stock price rose on Third Point's announcement of its campaign, it has fallen thereafter, and it fell further on the announcement that Third Point had been awarded three seats on Sotheby's board in a settlement. Who then won this battle? On the evidence to date, the clearest winner to date has been Christie's, Sotheby's major rival. Together, the two firms share a virtual duopoly in a unique market for personal and financial services that is dependent on 'relationships'. Instability at Sotheby's can and will be exploited by its rival, Christie's. More generally, factionalized boards (which the new activist tactics virtually ensure) may accelerate employee departures, customer turnover, and business instability.

On this score, Sotheby's may have been uniquely vulnerable. The most important clients for both Sotheby's and Christie's are the limited number of executors of major estates who need to auction art portfolios that may have aggregate values in the multibillion range. Often, this business requires special services, extended negotiations, sizable financial guarantees, and handshake deals. In such a 'relationship' environment, the fact that Third Point probably sought to fire the CEO and senior management of Sotheby's implies that any eventual successor management at Sotheby's may not be aware of, or feel bound by, understandings reached by the current management. Even if this problem can be addressed, Christie's can still assert that the current Sotheby's management is too preoccupied with governance matters to give their full attention to clients. Unless the new board can play nicely together in the corporate sandbox, the most valuable clients—current and prospective—may be seduced away by rivals.

Even if Sotheby's is more vulnerable than most targets, its position is not unique. If one examines carefully the empirical data and looks beyond simply the mean return to consider also the distribution of returns, one finds enormous variance in the stock price impact of activist campaigns. Put simply, an activist campaign often faces the target with the prospect of 'boom or bust'. Well-known examples —J. C. Penney and Yahoo—illustrate this danger and show that proxy battles can both increase and decrease value for shareholders. Sometimes, this is because such battles produce internal disruption and instability. Other times, it is because hedge fund managers have no operational skills and do not understand the industry.

Lesson Four: The Poison Pill May Be Losing its Toxicity in Many Cases! In part, this development reflects the power of the proxy advisors (most notably, ISS), who are forcing target companies to adopt only a weaker, shorter-term poison pill (at least in the absence of a shareholder vote). Indeed, in the Sotheby's contest, Sotheby's adopted a two-tier poison pill that was by design a kinder, gentler pill because it did not bar a 100% tender offer, but only a 'creeping' acquisition. Largely unnoticed by the press, Sotheby's two-tier shareholder rights plan permitted anyone to make a 100% tender offer (including even Third Point). All it barred was a 'creeping control' campaign (that is, crossing a specified threshold of the target firm's shares without offering to buy all the shares). This is a 'shareholder-friendly' approach to takeovers that both redefines the role of the poison pill and actually may bring

[7] I recognize, of course, that jury trials do not occur in the Delaware Chancery Court, but they do occur in the Court of Public Opinion, when proxy fights are tried.

US practice into closer conformity with Europe and England (where partial bids and creeping acquisitions are largely blocked by statute). Desirable as this goal is, however, it may not be obtainable without legal change.

This may be the key issue for the future. Do shareholders need protection from 'creeping control' acquisitions? In the past, the poison pill gave them such protection, but it may not be capable of performing that role for the future.

20.1 The Evidence on Activism

The case for hedge fund activism rests heavily on the claim that interventions in corporate governance by activist investors enhance value for shareholders. The most frequently cited study supporting this conclusion appeared in the *Journal of Finance* in 2008 and found an average abnormal return of 7% to 8% around the filing of a Schedule 13D announcing the activist's acquisition of a 5% or greater stake in the target (see Brav et al. 2008). But this evidence goes only to the short-term return over the twenty-day window on both sides of that announcement. If we look instead to the long-term abnormal returns in this same study, we find that over the period beginning one month prior to the announcement of the activist's position and concluding with the activist's exit from that position, the returns are widely variant and can be negative. Indeed, one-quarter of the firms in this sample had a size-adjusted, long-term abnormal return of -25% or worse, and 50% experienced a size-adjusted, long-term abnormal return of only 0.3% or less (Brav et al. 2008: 1761). Thus, the shareholders of half of all the firms in this sample received a return that was either negligible or worse (and 25% incurred very negative returns). To be sure, the mean return was 14.3% on this same basis, but that was largely because the return was very high to the top 25% of the firms in this sample.[8] Put more simply, the target firm stalked by the activist fund in this study seemingly faces a very bipolar, long-term future—either a feast or a famine. That should concern a reasonable board of directors, who manage not a portfolio of bets (as financial managers do), but a single company facing a risky future.

What is going on here? A careful study in the *Journal of Financial Economics* found that the long-term returns from shareholder activism are concentrated in those firms that ultimately get acquired, while targets that remain independent do not experience any long-term share price improvement (see Greenwood and Schor 2009). Several other studies find little evidence of long-term positive abnormal returns in the years following the initial price jump on the filing of the Schedule 13D.[9] A more recent study in 2013 does find that targeted

[8] According to Table VI in this study, the top 1% earned a 439% annualized size-adjusted return and the top 5% earned a 146% similar return on the same basis (Brav et al. 2008: 1761). The top 25% earned on this same basis a roughly 25% return.

[9] See, e.g., Bebchuk, Brav, and Jiang (2014: 22) (finding no statistically significant evidence of abnormal stock performance for the three- and five-year periods after the filing of the Schedule 13D). They interpret this evidence as showing no long-term underperformance by stocks targeted by activists, but the evidence also does not strongly support superior performance. For a more sceptical view, see Clifford (2008: 324–6, 332). Others find a positive impact on long-term returns, but only in cases where the Schedule 13D was filed by a hedge fund or investor engaged in a hostile campaign (see Klein and Zur, (2009: 220)).

firms experience positive abnormal returns on average over the two years following the commencement of an activist hedge fund's campaign, but also that the distribution of these returns is again heavily skewed (see Khorena et al. 2013). In fact, 52% of the targets in this study showed negative excess returns over both the one- and two-year periods. Thus, while the mean long-term abnormal return was positive in this study, the majority of firms actually experienced a negative long-term abnormal return. Again, this shows that the extraordinary returns in those cases where activism produces a takeover drive the aggregate results (and hide the reality that roughly half the companies in these samples experience negative returns). For the holder of a diversified portfolio, this is of little concern, but for a board of directors of a single company, it is central because their fiduciary duty is to protect their own company, not maximize the investor's portfolio.

The evidence of activism's impact on operational performance and reported profits is more mixed, but several studies find no improvement between the year before the filing of the Schedule 13D and the year after.[10] At least two studies also find a significant decrease in investment levels at the target firm and a concomitant increase in leverage (see Greenwood and Schor 2009; Klein and Zur, Chapter 9, this volume). This evidence is read by these scholars to be 'consistent with [the] hypothesis that activists have few levers in creating shareholder value over the long-term rather than a takeover' (Greenwood and Schor 2009: 371). From this perspective, the long-term gains from hedge fund activism may reflect simply an increase in the prospect of a takeover. One can model the price of any stock as composed of two elements: (1) its value under current management; and (2) the takeover premium that another firm will offer, discounted by the probability of such an offer being made. Even when no takeover materializes, the increased prospect of one may linger, affecting the firm's stock price for some time thereafter.

In general, although hedge fund managers may be good stock pickers, there is little reason to believe that they have much managerial experience or competence. And their hunches often prove disastrously wrong. That was the case in Pershing Square's intervention at J. C. Penney. There, Pershing Square acquired a 16.5% stake in the firm. William Ackman then attempted a new strategy and imposed a new CEO at the firm; the result was disaster. While J. C. Penney's shares went up initially, its share price declined by 59.5% over the period between the initial schedule 13D filing and Pershing Square's eventual exit. All this occurred while the market as a whole soared over the same period.[11] Other examples are easily found.[12]

The empirical studies also demonstrate another counter-intuitive finding: while a Schedule 13D filing or the announcement of a proxy contest may spur a stock price increase, it does not usually matter who wins. One well-known study by Mulherin and Poulsen (1998) finds no difference in abnormal returns between contests in which the dissident wins a board seat and contests in which the dissident loses. They generalize that the gains come not

[10] See Greenwood and Schor (2009: 329–31) (finding no significant change in return on assets, operating return on assets, payout ratio, asset growth, or share growth in year before and after filing of Schedule 13D); Bebchuk, Brav, and Jiang (2014: 9–10) (no increase in industry-adjusted return on assets for firms targeted by activists). Brav et al. (Chapter 8, this volume) did find improvements in operating performance under some tests, but not others (Brav et al. 2008: 1769–72).

[11] For a critical review of Ackman's hubris in undertaking this campaign, see Surowiecki (2013).

[12] For a series of case studies involving thirteen companies targeted by two prominent hedge fund activists, see Lee and Schloetzer (2014).

from the identity of the victor, but from the predictable tendency of the incumbent management to implement the 'specific changes' sought by the insurgents (Mulherin and Poulsen 1998: 300–2). The Sotheby's contest was consistent with this pattern, as in 2014 (well after the hedge funds had begun to circle around Sotheby's) Sotheby's announced a combined dividend and stock repurchase totalling $450 million (or roughly 15% of its $3 billion market capitalization).

Some studies actually find that the average abnormal returns in proxy contests are higher when the incumbent management wins (see Alexander et al. 2010: 4435), and at least one has found negative abnormal returns (and also declining operational performance) following proxy contests in which the insurgent wins seats (see Ikenberry and Lakonishok 1993). All this evidence is consistent with a basic story: if the incumbent management will modify its policies in response to the challenge, shareholders are better off than in the case of an insurgent victory (probably because shareholders are spared the risk of inexperienced, headstrong, or even egomaniacal insurgents taking control of the company). The wealth gains from proxy contests appear to largely stem from (1) expected takeovers premiums; (2) bondholder wealth transfers (as the result of increased leverage); and (3) large dividends and dispositions of assets. In fairness, there is some evidence that hedge funds do curtail excessive executive compensation and cash hoarding. But little suggests that the market expects significantly improved operational performance in the wake of an insurgent proxy victory (nor do we observe such improvements in fact).

One last cautious observation must be made about the empirical evidence. Many of these studies go back for decades. Yet, the contemporary activism of a Pershing Square, a Third Point, or a Carl Icahn is really only about five years old. Moreover, as the odds of victory increase, more campaigns, based on weaker justifications, become likely. Future studies need to focus on the long-term success of this new breed of activist.

20.2 New Tactics and the Role of the Poison Pill

The new hedge fund activism is the result of a confluence of several legal and institutional factors: (1) the decline in popularity of the staggered board (which decline makes a control challenge much more feasible); (2) the enhanced power of the proxy advisors (and their willingness to support 'short slates' in proxy contests, without the insurgent needing to offer any control premium); (3) the success of proxy advisors in forcing target companies to place a short time limit on their 'poison pills' (usually one year) under the threat that the proxy advisors would otherwise recommend a vote against management's nominees in any proxy contest; and (4) the uniquely long ten-day window under Section 13(d) of the Williams Act before a 5% beneficial holder must disclose its position. This last legal factor enables the insurgent to buy 5% quietly and cheaply and then tip its allies in the institutional investor community, who can then buy heavily during this window period before the public announcement is made.

In response, target firms have also experimented with new tactics. The Sotheby's proxy contest featured an atypical form of shareholder rights plan that was the focus of much attention because of three distinctive features: (1) it imposed a 10% ceiling on shareholders who filed a Schedule 13D, but only a 20% ceiling on shareholders filing a Schedule 13G; (2) it did not apply to any tender offer for 100% of the shares (provided that the offer was kept open for at least 100 days in order to permit a value-maximizing auction); and (3) it had a duration of only one year (unless extended by a shareholder vote).

Of these three features, most of the public attention focused on the least important one: namely, the distinction it drew between the ceilings on 'active' and 'passive' shareholders. Conventional wisdom views Schedule 13D filers as more active and likely to challenge management than Section 13G filers (who must represent that they will not seek to influence control to use this simpler form). Third Point saw this disparity as 'discrimination' against 'active' shareholders, arguing that shareholders who filed a Schedule 13D were more likely to vote against management than Schedule 13G filers.

In fact, this 'discriminatory' feature has considerable precedent supporting it. In my expert report in Sotheby's litigation, I tabulated that some seventy-three corporations have adopted shareholder rights plans that distinguished 'active' from 'passive' investors and permitted higher ownership levels for the latter.[13] These date back to 1986 when United Continental Holdings did it first; the most recent such adoption was by Avid Technology in January 2014. Some 40.3% of these shareholder rights plans place the ceiling for activist shareholders at 10%, while another 54.2% use a 15% ceiling for 'active' shareholders (the overall average ceiling was 13.2%). The ceiling for passive investing was typically placed at 20%.

Why is this disparity justifiable? In my judgment, it has a thoroughly defensible and even commendable purpose: it protects against a 'creeping control' acquisition. In the Sotheby's litigation, the chief executive officer of MacKenzie Partners, a major proxy solicitation firm, submitted an expert report estimating that 32.86% of Sotheby's stock was then held by hedge funds. He further estimated that the level of hedge fund ownership had risen from 13% of all Sotheby's shares (as of a year earlier) to 23.22% as of the record date for the Sotheby's annual 2014 meeting. Thus, if Third Point had won the right that it sought to increase its ownership level to 20%, then on that basis over 43% of the Sotheby's stock would be held by hedge funds. As a practical matter, that would mean that the ballgame was over.

Nonetheless, some academic colleagues respond to this evidence by telling me: 'You do not know that the hedge funds will vote as a group'. True only in theory, such an assertion mainly illustrates the academic tendency to wear self-imposed blindfolds. This rapid build-up in hedge fund ownership is evidence of the recurrent pattern that Vice Chancellor Parsons described in his Sotheby's decision as the formation of the 'wolf pack' that justified the use of the poison pill.[14] The reality is that there is no plausible explanation for the sudden

[13] Although I have reviewed the documents, the identification of these seventy-three cases was made by The Analysis Group, which also computed the averages.

[14] See *Third Point LLC v. Ruprecht*, at *58 to *59. Vice Chancellor Parsons actually stated:

> The Board also was informed by its advisors that it was not uncommon for activist hedge funds to form a group or 'wolfpack' for the purposes of jointly acquiring large blocks of a target company's stock. Based on these facts, ... I cannot conclude that there is a reasonable probability that the Board did not make an objectively reasonable determination that Third Point posed a threat of forming a control block for Sotheby's with other hedge funds without paying a control premium.

In short, the danger that control could pass in a 'creeping' acquisition without payment of a control premium justified the use of the poison pill.

interest of hedge funds in a relatively small company in a low-growth market—other than the opportunity to make a short-term profit from the proxy contest (and, more specifically, from the announcement of the Schedule 13D filing).

The simple truth then is that 'birds of a feather will flock together'. Why? If hedge funds can learn of an activist campaign in advance of the Schedule 13D filing, they are assured of an almost certain profit (unless they hold for the long-term and the stock declines). One hedge fund tipping another does not amount to insider trading under the law to date because there is no breach of a fiduciary duty. Only if one hedge fund tipped another of an approaching tender offer would the securities laws be violated (and only then if the prospective bidder had already taken a 'substantial step' towards commencing the tender offer[15]). This ability to engage in 'conscious parallelism' (in Vice Chancellor Parson's apt phrase) without becoming a member of a Section 13(d) 'group' probably fuels much hedge fund activism because it combines high return with low risk.

20.3 The Significance of the 'Wolf Pack'

To their supporters, 'activist' hedge funds are the needed catalysts that arouse and unite slumbering indexed institutional investors for their common good (because the indexed investor is typically rationally apathetic, disabled by collective-action problems). Indeed, this may happen. But an alternative view is that activist hedge funds simply see a low-risk, high-profit opportunity in the following tactic: buy before the Schedule 13D is disclosed and sell sometime later (possibly to the target) before the possibility of a takeover has faded. Neither view is inconsistent with the other, but the 'wolf pack' need not appraise carefully (or even agree with) the lead hedge fund's strategy if a short-term stock gain is likely. Whether or not its strategy is sound, the assembly of this 'wolf pack' gives the lead hedge fund its leverage and forces the target firm to negotiate with it from a position of weakness. Once the target knows that 20% or more of its stock is held by activists, it knows it must appease them, typically by structuring a large liquidity 'event' (typically, a stock buy-back or special dividend).

This phenomenon of wolf pack formation is implicit in Figure 20.1, which shows both the stock price appreciation and the extraordinary stock accumulations in the ten-day window before the filing of a Schedule 13D (see Brav et al. 2008: 1756). In this figure, the spike in both the stock price and the trading volume begins between eight and ten days before the Schedule 13D's filing and then declines sharply at four days after its filing.

As Figure 20.1 shows, most of the stock price appreciation occurs before the Schedule 13D's filing, and most of the abnormal trading volume also occurs before that filing. After the filing, things cool down relatively quickly.

The lead hedge fund will rationally seek to buy its stake slowly and quietly so as not to affect the stock's price (although it may also buy more stock in the ten-day window). Most of the abnormal buying volume before the Schedule 13D is filed thus seems to be the result of informed trading by the lead hedge fund's allies. These allies may learn of the impending

[15] See SEC Rule 14e-3(a), 17 C.F.R. See SEC Rule 14e-3(a), 17 C.F.R. § 240. 14e-3(a).

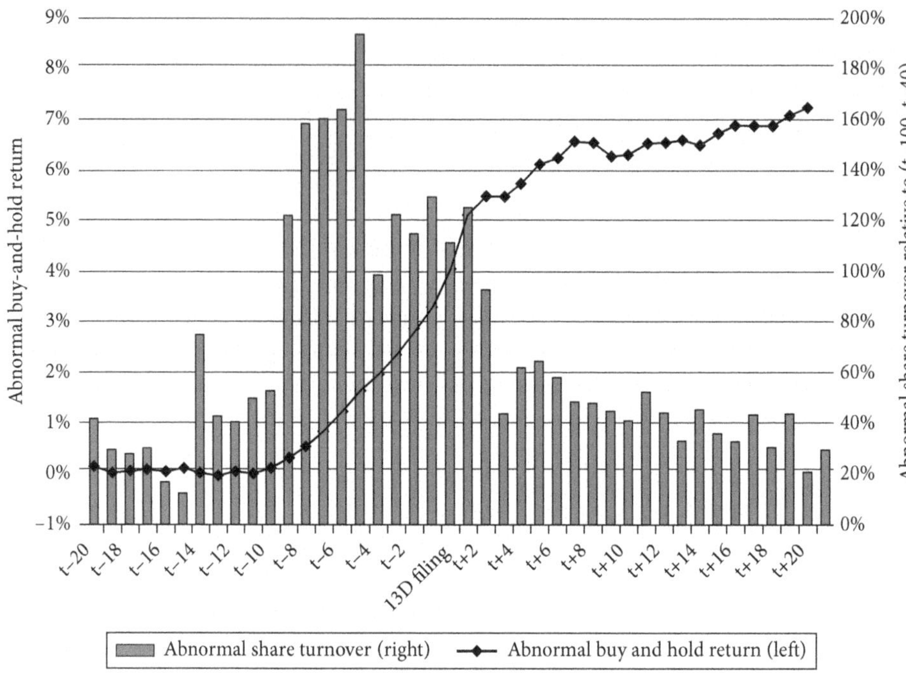

FIGURE 20.1 Day-to-day abnormal returns over the window period

announcement at different points, but they know they have to buy quickly before the information becomes public.

From a policy perspective, the 'wolf pack' is a very loosely knit organization, and many of the members are probably focused on their exit strategy from the day that they buy. Hedge funds, operating in this fashion, should not be assumed to be the champion of all the shareholders, for at least four reasons:

First, when the activist hedge fund 'wolf pack' acquires something like 30% of the issuer's stock (as they did in Sotheby's), they are displacing institutional investors, who are selling to 'informed' traders who are utilizing material, non-public information. This may not legally constitute insider trading, but it may be considered ethically troubling by many. Indeed, under European rules, this might well constitute unlawful insider trading.

Second, precisely because assembling the 'wolf pack' is an activity that combines high profit with low risk, it is likely to be overused. The wolf pack's members are much like IPO buyers pursuing an allocation in a 'hot' IPO because they know there is generally a first-day price jump. Such buyers care less about the company because they know (and only know) that a scare allocation in a 'hot' IPO has value. Over time, the stock market will probably learn that not every Schedule 13D announcement implies beneficial changes or a lucrative takeover. In the interim, however, excessive volatility and a 'bubble-like' price movement is likely to be associated with this activity.

Third, the hedge fund member of a wolf pack will be predictably focused on a profitable 'exit' strategy. Already, there is evidence of a new resurgence of 'greenmail' transactions led by activist hedge funds. According to the *Wall Street Journal*, over the last year, at least ten public companies have repurchased blocks of stock held by activist hedge funds in transactions that closely resemble traditional 'greenmail' (see Hoffman and Benoit 2004: 22).[16]

Finally and most importantly, the 'wolf pack' phenomenon can lead to 'creeping control' acquisitions, which deny public shareholders their opportunity for a control premium. Traditionally, the key responsibility of the target's board of directors in the takeover context is to protect this opportunity. This danger of a lost opportunity for a control premium can result under either of two alternative scenarios. First, the participating hedge funds may assemble a de facto control block of, say, 30% or more. Such a block carries what Delaware Chief Justice Leo Strine has recently termed 'negative control'.[17] Based on this block, the hedge funds (or their leader) might negotiate a merger between the target and a chosen acquirer on terms that assure the acquirer that it will not become subject to a value-inflating auction.[18] If a 30% block stands behind the acquirer, a rival acquirer will be less likely to challenge the transaction for a variety of reasons.[19] A variation on this first scenario is that the hedge fund could partner up, itself, with a strategic acquirer and make a joint tender offer at a price below what otherwise would have to be paid in a more open market. Such an arrangement resembles Pershing Square's position in its joint bid with Valeant for Allergan, and it refutes the claim that hedge funds never seek control.

Alternatively, the hedge fund might itself seek to exercise control over the target as its largest shareholder with one or more seats on its board. It might do this either in the belief that it knows more about the business (as Pershing Square seemed to believe it did in its disastrous intervention at J. C. Penney) or in order to obtain the 'private benefits of control'. The 'private benefits of control' are diverse and include prestige and public importance. In this light, it is relevant that Daniel Loeb, the CEO of Third Point, is an avid art collector. The opportunity to be the chairman or CEO of Sotheby's could interest him simply for the ego gratification inherent in such visibility. Economists tend to overlook this factor, but it explains much human behaviour. By analogy, if this author had a multibillion-dollar hedge fund behind him, he might seek to buy a 40% (and controlling) interest in the New York Yankees—in order to play its general manager. Ultimately, the private benefits of control include the 'right to play with the trains'. But in both my hypothetical case and that of Loeb, the result of such megalomania is likely to be disastrous for the other shareholders. Confident as I may be of my baseball acumen, cooler heads may believe that I know less about the business of baseball than the typical general manager. In the case of Sotheby's, a

[16] These repurchases differ slightly from classic 'greenmail' because they are not at a premium to the market (although it is also doubtful that a large blockholder could sell its stake at the market).

[17] As Chief Justice Strine (2014: 497) has recently explained, 'The pill works to prevent a creeping takeover whereby effective negative control over a corporation is acquired without the payment of a control premium'. He goes on to explain that such a block would be a 'huge deterrent to any potential acquirer' (Strine 2014: 497).

[18] Bidders in fact often seek 'support agreements' from institutional blockholders under which the latter agree to vote for a proposed acquisition. If the first bidder obtains such an agreement from major hedge funds holding a 20% block or more, rival bidders will be unlikely to challenge its offer.

[19] Even in the absence of a support agreement favouring the first bidder, a second bidder will know that to effect a 'squeeze out' merger and consolidate the target, it will need to establish the 'intrinsic fairness' of its merger proposal, unless it can obtain a 'majority of the minority' vote. Unless it has the support of the large blockholders, such a vote will be difficult.

passionate art collector might make its worst possible CEO (because the avid collector and the auctioneer have very different perspectives and valuations).

The irony in all the criticism focused on Sotheby's poison pill is that it was less toxic and blocks much less than the traditional pill. Basically, it only prevented (and for only a limited period) a creeping control acquisition. Thus, it neither stops a hostile tender offer nor forces the bidder to conduct a contemporaneous proxy fight to redeem the poison pill. This both gives the bidder greater flexibility as to timing (i.e., it need not wait for the annual meeting) and reduces the bidder's overall costs. Finally, the Sotheby's pill only lasted for one year (unless extended by a shareholder vote). All in all, the Sotheby's pill was far more shareholder-friendly than most of its predecessors. Probably, it was so structured to comply with ISS's guidelines,[20] but nonetheless, the bottom line is this: the significance of the poison pill may be diminishing. It is becoming more a road bump than a barrier.

For the future, other potential targets seem unlikely to copy the two-tier 'discriminatory' feature in Sotheby's shareholder rights plan. Because the Chancery Court's decision upheld a 10% limit, there may be little reason to give 'passive' shareholders a higher, 20% ceiling. Few institutional investors want to go to the 20% level because such ownership will take them over the 10% line that triggers Section 16(b)'s 'short swing' profits provision. Crossing that line seriously restricts the liquidity that they much desire. No shareholder crossed this 10% line in the Sotheby's battle.

Thus, the future may see many poison pills, probably adopted shortly after the filing of a Schedule 13D by an activist investor, that will have a short, one-year duration and do not block a 100% bid. If so, hedge fund activism should only increase, as its goal would be to put the target in play, with the 'wolf pack' acquiring in the aggregate as much as a 20% to 35% block. Such a block could usually elect at least a short slate of directors. ISS appears to favour short slates, and its support could swing most proxy contests to the insurgent, at least in the initial round.

Ultimately, this strategy appears significantly dependent on the current ten-day 'window' under Section 13(d) of the 1934 Act, which gives both the activist hedge fund and its allies a longer period than they enjoy in Europe to increase their holdings before public disclosure of their ownership is required.[21] Undeniably, this state of affairs motivates hedge funds to activism, but by the same token it diminishes any control premium or enhanced share price to those shareholders who sell while the 'wolf pack' is increasing its aggregate holding to 30% or more. In short, there are winners and losers in this process.

Despite this appearance of 'insider-like' trading, the standard (and knee-jerk) response from the activist side is that large profits to those who buy before the Schedule 13D's filing are justifiable because they motivate a desirable activism. Yet, Mr Ackman and Pershing Square are reported to have quickly generated over a $1 billion paper profit when they

[20] ISS objects to any poison pill adopted by the board that has a duration of greater than one year. A longer duration in its view should require shareholder approval. If a proxy contest is under way, ISS's support can be crucial and may swing between 10% and 30% of the vote (see Ertimur, Ferri, and Oesch 2013).

[21] See Section 13(d)(1) of the Securities Exchange Act, 15 U.S.C. § 78m(d)(1). Under the Transparency Directive, Europe has limited this period to four trading days. See Transparency Directive, Council Directive 2013/50/EU, 2013 O.J. (L294) at art. 9(i). The UK uses an even shorter two-trading-day window.

announced their campaign for Allergan.[22] That may be more incentive than anyone needs. Finally, those studies that show as many companies losing value as gaining value from hedge fund activism call into question whether more incentive is even desirable. The more that one doubts (or considers unproven) the long-term beneficial effects of hedge fund activism, the more the case grows for shortening the Section 13(d) 'window'. The more that the poison pill seems to be losing its blocking power (as the Sotheby's case seemingly shows), the more that 'closing the §13D window' becomes the best and most feasible option that will work without precluding hedge fund activism.

What do we not yet know? The impact of hedge fund activism on target companies remains uncertain, particularly with respect to the impact on operating performance and investment in research and development. The existing evidence falls well short of the level sufficient to justify relaxing transparency or reducing shareholder protections against 'creeping control' acquisitions. Indeed, we do not yet know whether the apparent gains from hedge fund activism reflect anything more than a marginally increased prospect of a takeover or merger.

What will happen next? It remains unclear whether hedge fund activists can strike an alliance with longer-term institutional investors (who tend to be indexed and thus more concerned about the macro-economic impact of activism on their entire portfolio). The test case and next battleground will likely prove to be the coming struggle over proxy access. Major public corporations may be on the verge of granting shareholders the right to nominate a director on the corporation's own proxy statement, provided that the nominating shareholder group have held at least a three percent block for three years.[23] If so, few hedge funds will be able to satisfy this three year holding period requirement and will need to find allies within the longer-term institutional investor community. This will require very case-specific negotiations, and longer-term investors may gain a greater voice and leverage in this process.

Given those uncertainties, what should regulators do? The least restrictive alternative is the preferable option. Here, this implies that increased transparency (which would be the consequence of shortening the current ten-day window under the Section 13(d)) is the simplest, safest reform.[24]

References

Alexander, C. R., Chen, M. A., Seppi, D. J., and Spatt, C. S. (2010). Interim News and the Role of Proxy Voting Advice, *Review of Financial Studies* 23, 4419–54.

Bebchuk, L. A. (2013). The Myth That Insulating Boards Serves Long-Term Value, *Columbia Law Review* 113, 1637–94.

[22] Pershing Square acquired a 9.7% stake in Allergan for approximately $4 billion, and Allergan's shares quickly rose over 36%. Later a rival bidder won the auction at an even higher price, adding to Pershing Square's profits.

[23] This is the formula that General Electric has accepted (see Morgenson 2015). As she discusses, some institutional investors (including Vanguard) would prefer an even longer five year holding period.

[24] Another possible reform would be to deem tippees of the hedge fund to belong to a 'group' with it, thus tripping the Section 13(d) tripwire when the 'group' assembled 5%. Although the SEC is unlikely to adopt any such rule, it would chill the formation of the 'wolf pack'.

Brav, A, Jiang, W., Partnoy, F. and Thomas, R., Hedge Fund Activism (2008). Corporate Governance, and Firm Performance, Journal of Finance, 63, 1729–75.

Bebchuk, L., Brav, A., and Jiang, W. (2014). The Long-Term Effects of Hedge Fund Activism, Working Paper, available at <http://ssrn.com/abstract=2291677>.

Clifford, C. P. (2008). Value Creation or Destruction? Hedge Funds As Shareholder Activists, *Journal of Corporate Finance* 14, 323–36.

De La Merced, M. J. (2014). Slimming Down, *New York Times Dealbook* (23 May), at B-7.

Ertimur, Y., Ferri, F., and Oesch, D. (2013). Shareholder Votes and Proxy Advisors: Evidence from Say on Pay, Working Paper, available at <http://ssrn.com/abstract=2019239>.

Foley, S. (2014). Sotheby's Bows to Loeb over Board Seats in Fresh Victory for Activists, *Financial Times* (6 May), at 1.

Gelles, D., De La Merced, M. J., and Stevenson, A. (2014). An Unusual Hostile Bid for the Maker of Botox; Hedge Fund Manager Allies With Drug Maker to Acquire Allergan, *International New York Times* (23 Apr.), at 15.

Gilson, R. J. and Gordon, J. N. (2013).The Agency Costs of Agency Capitalism: Activist Investors and the Revaluation of Governance Rights, *Columbia Law Review* 113, 863–928.

Greenwood, R. and Schor, M. (2009). Investor Activism and Takeovers, *Journal of Financial Economics* 92, 362–75.

Hoffman, L. and Benoit, D. (2004). Activist Funds Dust off 'Greenmail' Playbook, *Wall Street Journal (Europe)* (13 June), at 22.

Ikenberry, D. and Lakonishok, J. (1993). Corporate Governance Through the Proxy Contest: Evidence and Implications, *Journal of Business* 66, 465–504.

Khorena, A., Hooper, E., Shivdasani, A., Sigurdsson, G., and Zhang, M. (2013). Rising Tide of Global Shareholder Activism, *Citi Corporate and Investment Banking* 2013, 13.

Klein, A. and Zur, E., (2009) Entrepreneurial Shareholder Activism: Hedge Funds and Other Private Investors, Journal of Finance, 64, 187–229.

Lee, R. and Schloetzer, J. D. (2014). The Activism of Carl Icahn and Bill Ackman, Directors Notes, The Conference Board (May), available at <http://www.conference-board.org/directornotes>.

Morgenson, G., (2015), Airing Out Stagnant Boardrooms, New York Times, (23 February) at BU-1.

Mulherin, J. H. and Poulsen, A. B. (1998). Proxy Contests and Corporate Change: Change Implications for Shareholder Wealth, *Journal of Financial Economics* 47, 279–313.

Strine, Jr, L. E. (2014). Can We Do Better By Ordinary Investors? A Pragmatic Reaction to the Dueling Ideological Mythologists of Corporate Law, *Columbia Law Review* 114, 449–502.

Surowiecki, J. (2013). When Shareholder Activism Goes Too Far, *The New Yorker* (15 Aug.).

CHAPTER 21

THE CASE AGAINST SHAREHOLDER EMPOWERMENT

WILLIAM W. BRATTON AND MICHAEL L. WACHTER

21.1 Introduction

In 2006, shareholder empowerment figured prominently in a well-publicized law-reform agenda presented by the Committee on Capital Markets Regulation, a private group concerned about the competitiveness of US capital markets. The Committee's report connected shareholder power to market control, reasoning that enhanced shareholder rights provide accountability and that accountability means lower agency costs, higher market prices, and, accordingly, a more competitive equity marketplace.[1] In addition, the Committee argued that strong shareholder rights invite more dependence on market discipline of managers and 'go hand in hand with reduced regulation or litigation' (Committee on Capital Market Regulation 2006: 16). Restating, 'accountability' means market control, which means lower agency costs. The Committee thereby weighed in on corporate law's leading structural question: who should decide how best to maximize long-term value for the shareholders' benefit—the managers or the shareholders themselves?[2] The question holds out a choice

[1] See Committee on Capital Markets Regulation (2006: 93) (arguing that enhanced shareholder rights in the areas of takeover defences and remedy selection will reduce expected agency costs and incentivize entry into US public markets). The Committee's report focused on shareholder ratification of poison pills adopted by a staggered board, majority voting for boards of directors, shareholder access to the director nomination process, executive pay, and contractual alternatives to litigation (Committee on Capital Markets Regulation 2006: 16–18).

[2] This is often referred to as the debate over 'shareholder primacy'. But shareholder primacy has two aspects, the first going to the objective of the corporation and the shareholders' place as legal beneficiary, and the second going to the allocation of power within the corporation. This chapter takes the first aspect as settled in favour of the shareholders and focuses on the second aspect. To avoid confusion, we avoid the term entirely, instead using the phrase 'shareholder empowerment'.

between a shareholder-driven, agency model of the corporation, guided by informational signals from the financial markets, and the prevailing legal model, which vests business decision-making in managers who possess an informational advantage regarding business conditions. The shareholder side contends that the prevailing model fails to provide a platform conducive to aggressive entrepreneurship and instead invites management self-dealing and conservative decision-making biased toward institutional stability. It looks to a shareholder community populated with actors in financial markets for corrective inputs. Unlike the managers, who are conflicted and risk averse, the shareholders come to the table with a pure financial incentive to maximize value. It is a high-stakes debate. For the Committee on Capital Markets Regulation, along with many other proponents of shareholder empowerment, the nation's global competitive fitness hangs in the balance.

Even so, shareholder proponents have shifted their emphasis in the wake of the financial crisis of 2008.[3] Although 'accountability' remains the ultimate goal, we hear fewer references to market control as the means to that end, presumably because it resonates equivocally in light of recent market failures. Proponents instead hold out the need to restore 'trust'.[4] We illustrate this approach with the comments of former Securities and Exchange Commission (SEC) Chairman Arthur Levitt on the meltdown in the financial sector,[5] which was still in its early phase when he wrote in the summer of 2008. For Levitt, the subprime collapse, the Bear Stearns implosion, and revelations of poor risk management at large financial firms had 'injected a dangerously large degree of mistrust into the markets' (Levitt: 2008). He believes that managers and boards should have raised the alarm, and that enhanced shareholder voice, '[w]hile not a panacea, . . . would go a long way in helping to restore trust' (Levitt: 2008).

The trust characterization resonates because it focuses on management culpability, and the managers who now have (or recently have had) to rely on government largesse do bear primary responsibility for the decisions that precipitated the financial crisis. Executive pay has become a flashpoint political issue as a result of the culpability designation, and the resulting popular picture is not pretty.[6] Managers of financial companies appear as quick-buck artists who used their compensation schemes to siphon millions of dollars from

[3] But see, e.g., CII (2009) (quoting CII Chair and CALPers CIO Joseph A. Dear, who stated that the proposed act was needed 'to promote market discipline and accountability').

[4] See The Causes and Effects of the Lehman Brothers Bankruptcy: Hearing Before the H. Comm. on Oversight and Gov't Reform, 110th Cong. 4 (2008) (statement of Nell Minow, Editor, *The Corporate Library*) (connecting shareholder power with the restoration of credibility); Zingales (2009: 24–7) (connecting trust and accountability, and contending that shareholder nominations will channel shareholder inputs to long-term value and deter managing to the market); Schumer (2009) (emphasizing the need to restore confidence through greater accountability and shareholder empowerment); cf. Lowenstein (2009) (arguing that shareholder-nominated board members will cause shareholders to shift from a short-term view, in which exit is the primary means of expressing discontent, to a long-term view, in which 'the less forceful, but more supple "voice" ' is used effectively). For a bank chairman's thoughts on the need to restore trust, see Green (2009: 3).

[5] See Levitt (2008) (advocating for the repeal of prior SEC decisions in order to increase shareholder control and accountability).

[6] See, e.g., Solomon and Fitzpatrick (2009) (reporting that the Treasury Department's 'special master' for compensation objected to Bank of America CEO Kenneth D. Lewis's 2009 compensation, pushing Lewis to agree to forego salary for the year).

companies on the brink of collapse.[7] Their shareholders, as the primary bearers of losses incurred, emerge as victims along with the taxpayers.[8]

Blame for managers means sudden political traction for a long-standing law-reform agenda put forward by proponents of shareholder empowerment. We have already seen 'Say on Pay' mandates imposed on Troubled Asset Relief Program (TARP) recipients, along with substantive constraints on modes and amounts of compensation.[9] Broad 'Say on Pay' mandates appear in prominent proposed legislation[10] and in the administration's reform agenda.[11] There is also a high-profile SEC proposal to amend the proxy rules to require inclusion of shareholder board nominees in management proxy statements.[12]

[7] Shareholder rights advocates often use this imagery. See, e.g., Lowenstein (2009: 11) ('[M]anagers cannot be trusted not to (grossly) overpay themselves . . .'); Schumer (2009) ('[T]he leadership at some of the nation's most renowned companies took too many risks and too much in salary . . .' (internal quotation marks omitted) (quoting Senator Schumer)); cf. Zingales (2009: 23–4) (noting the image, but arguing against direct regulation of pay).

[8] See Shareholder Bill of Rights Act of 2009, S. 1074, 111th Cong. § 2 (describing legislative findings and noting that a lack of accountability 'led to the loss of trillions of dollars in shareholder value, losses that have been borne by millions of Americans who are shareholders through their pension plans, 401(k) plans, and direct investments').

[9] See Emergency Economic Stabilization Act of 2008 (EESA), Pub. L. No. 110-343, § 111(b)(2)(A), 122 Stat. 3765, 3777, amended by American Recovery and Reinvestment Act of 2009, Pub. L. No. 111-5, sec. 7001, § 111, 123 Stat. 115, 516–20 (to be codified at 12 U.S.C. § 5221) (requiring sellers of troubled assets to have:

> limits on compensation that exclude incentives for senior executive officers of a financial institution to take unnecessary and excessive risks that threaten the value of the financial institution during the period that the Secretary holds an equity or debt position in the financial institution).

Subsequent Treasury guidelines require that for all TARP recipients, executive base pay be limited to $500,000 and that any incentive pay must be granted in the form of restricted stock, although these rules can be waived by shareholders except for those companies receiving 'exceptional financial recovery assistance'. Press Release, US Department of the Treasury, Treasury Announces New Restrictions on Executive Compensation (4 Feb. 2009), available at <http://www.treasury.gov/press-center/press-releases/Pages/tg15.aspx>; see also American Recovery and Reinvestment Act of 2009 §§ 7000–7002, §§ 111, 109(a), 123 Stat. at 516–21 (amending EESA and limiting incentive payments to the CEO and the twenty next-highest-paid executives of large TARP recipients to one-half of the executive's salary (other than payments required under earlier contracts and restricted stock), prohibiting golden parachutes and defined 'luxury' expenditures, and mandating 'Say on Pay' votes). The SEC has proposed a rule implementing the 'Say on Pay' mandate. See Shareholder Approval of Executive Compensation of TARP Recipients, 74 Fed. Reg. 32,474 (proposed 8 July 2009) (to be codified at 17 C.F.R. pt. 240) (amending proxy rules to help implement EESA requirements).

[10] See Shareholder Bill of Rights Act of 2009, S. 1074 § 3 (amending prior acts to require that proxies 'include a separate resolution subject to shareholder vote to approve the compensation of executives').

[11] See US Department of the Treasury, Financial Regulatory Reform: A New Foundation (2009: 29–30), available at <http://www.treasury.gov/initiatives/Documents/FinalReport_web.pdf> (expressing the Department's intent to support increased transparency in compensation practices and supporting 'Say on Pay' legislation).

[12] Facilitating Shareholder Director Nominations, 74 Fed. Reg. 29,024 (proposed 18 June 2009) (to be codified in scattered parts of 17 C.F.R.) (proposing to 'require companies to include shareholder nominees for director in the companies' proxy materials' in certain circumstances). In addition, the New York Stock Exchange has amended its rules to eliminate broker discretionary voting for election of directors (for companies not registered under the Investment Company Act of 1940) (NYSE 2009: § 402.08(B)(19)).

While this reaction is perfectly understandable, it remains highly questionable as a policy matter. This chapter states the contrary case, showing that the financial crisis, far from concluding the matter in the shareholders' favour, bolsters the case for the prevailing legal model. A shareholder-based agency model of the corporation sends management a simple instruction: in all circumstances, manage to maximize the market price of the stock. And that is exactly what managers of some critical financial firms did in recent years. They managed to a market that focused on their ability to increase observable earnings and, as it turned out, failed to factor in concomitant increases in risk that went largely unobserved.

Risk-taking is at the heart of the capitalist system, but so is the incentive-compatible rule that the risk-takers internalize not only the expected higher returns but also the expected higher systematic risk. For the financial institutions judged too big to fail, and apparently for others as well, risk internalization has not proven to be the case. The economic rescue's net costs amount to an externalization of the risks taken and an uninvited external shock to the political economy.

A negative implication follows for shareholder empowerment. If managers misunderstood the quantum of risks they were taking, then shareholders with more limited access to the relevant information certainly were no better informed and accordingly had no role to play in preventing externalization. Even as managers must shoulder the blame for the crisis, current complaints about management irresponsibility can legitimately be restated as complaints about management to the market. At the same time, management's risk aversion—its long-derided willingness to accept reduced risk in exchange for institutional stability—all of a sudden holds out advantages. Managers are risk averse because they fear losing their jobs in bankruptcy. Whereas bankruptcy is a natural element in the 'winds of creative destruction',[13] those winds blow no good when the losses are externalized to the US Treasury.

The prevailing legal structure of the corporation holds out a robust framework. Corporate law has always performed a balancing act with management discretion and shareholder power. The balance, however, has always privileged the directors and their appointed managers in business policymaking because they are better informed than the shareholders and thus better positioned to take responsibility for both monitoring and managing the firm and its externalities. As between directors and shareholders, it is the directors who have the best access to information and are best able to serve as the monitors of the managers, increasing the likelihood of compliance with continuing and emerging regulations. As between managers and shareholders, the managers are the ones who have the day-to-day knowledge of the company, its history, policies, opportunities, vulnerabilities, and challenges. The managers are likely to have the information and institutional perspective suited to anticipate points of conflict with the outside political economy and to formulate a responsive strategy. As long as they remain faithful, they are best suited to maximize the value of the corporation and thus the shareholders' residual claim.

The case outlined above must confront two responses from proponents of shareholder empowerment: first, shareholder incentives are correctly aligned and their business-policy preferences accordingly superior to those of conflicted managers; therefore, shareholder authority would reduce agency costs and increase the value of the corporation. Second, the

[13] Cf. Abernathy and Clark (1984) (describing Joseph Schumpeter's theory that innovation acts as a force of 'creative destruction', reducing the value of existing competence and inspiring new growth).

efficiency of stock prices ameliorates the problem of information asymmetry and reliably communicates both the value implications of corporate policy to the shareholders and the business preferences of the shareholders to the managers. This chapter rebuts this depiction of a win–win combination of shareholder power and market-sensitive management.

Section 21.2 frames the terms of debate. We ground our conceptual case for the prevailing legal model in Eugene Fama and Michael Jensen's description of the governance of publicly traded corporations. For Fama and Jensen, the prevailing legal model follows from an agency-cost trade-off. The model divides the economic rights attached to the residual claim both from the power to set corporate policy, which goes to the managers, and from the responsibility to monitor the agents who execute the policy, which goes to the board. This separation follows from a natural allocation of interest, information, and expertise. It does so for the purpose of reducing the agency costs that would result if shareholders that are both dispersed and diversified had the power to impose policy inputs. Agency costs do result, but as an embedded and inevitable result of dispersed ownership.

Section 21.3 looks into the debate's economic stakes, pushing back against the shareholder claim that systemic slack results in enormous agency costs that can be reduced only through fundamental law reform. We ground our response in Michael Jensen and William Meckling's seminal theory of agency costs and its projection of a dynamic, market-based process of agency-cost reduction. The shareholder proponents depict agency costs as a static, ahistorical constant. We question this picture from a historical perspective, asserting that even though agency costs tied to shareholder disempowerment had a moment of high salience during the 1980s, their importance diminished in subsequent years. The diminution followed from a dynamic pattern of response to underlying market forces, both inside boardrooms and outside in the markets. Inside, management reoriented itself and adopted key points from the shareholder agenda into corporate business plans, facilitating mergers and restructurings and stepping up cash payouts to shareholders. Outside, shareholders got stronger. The rationally apathetic investor waned as the institutional shareholder voice rose in volume and increasingly independent boards of directors got into the habit of listening. In our view, the shareholder case emerges denuded of urgency.

Section 21.4 steps into the brave new world projected by the shareholder proponents, to see how things will work. We draw on financial economic theory to identify serious problems under the new regime. The claim of market price robustness rests on the assertion that recent advances in the stock market's informational efficiency render fluid, unaffiliated groups of shareholders well enough informed to make wise choices on many corporate matters. Unfortunately, the stock price has two material shortcomings when viewed as a source of day-to-day instructions for business policy: first, stock prices are not fully informed because of informational asymmetries enjoyed by managers. Second, stock prices can be influenced by speculative factors unrelated to fundamental value, factors highlighted in the recent finance literature on heterogeneous expectations. Serious risks of unintended negative consequences follow when management decisions are directed to stock price reactions. It has long been known that financial markets display more volatility than the volatility in the underlying economy could ever justify. Asking managers to manage to the market could inject that higher degree of financial market volatility into the real economy.

Section 21.5 turns to the financial crisis. The fact that management bears primary responsibility for the crisis does not by itself effect a policy connection between increased shareholder power and regulatory reform. A connection obtains only if increased shareholder power would have imported more effective risk management in advance of the crisis. No plausible grounds exist for making such a case. If anything, the managers responsible had incentives too closely aligned with those of their shareholders due to equity incentive compensation. Compensation, accordingly, is the topic on which the crisis holds out a lesson for corporate governance. If trust is to be restored, equity incentive plans must be restructured to discourage management to the market. Shareholder empowerment, far from getting us to that result, would get in the way. Section 21.6 concludes.

21.2 Framing the Issues: The Prevailing Legal Model, Shareholder Empowerment, and Agency Costs

The prevailing legal model of the corporation privileges the decision-making authority of the board of directors. The board, in the classic expression, wields 'original and undelegated'[14] powers that follow directly from the organizational form provided by the law rather than from a delegation of authority from the shareholders. Even though the shareholders elect the board, they have no right to tell it what to do. They can only proceed indirectly, by removing it or replacing it at the next annual meeting.[15] As a legal matter, directors are not agents of the shareholders.

Proponents of shareholder empowerment propose an alternative regime of shareholder choice regarding matters of business policy. Under their contrasting model of the corporation, the shareholders emerge as principals in an agency relationship.[16] From this point of view, the board's decision-making power stems from the shareholders' delegation of that power. It follows that what the shareholders delegate they should also be able to withdraw.

This chapter makes a policy case to support the present legal allocation of power. This section lays out the basic terms of the debate in which we intervene. We begin, in Section 21.2.1, by contrasting the economic framework in which we ground our case with the economic framework that undergirds the case for shareholder empowerment. Section 21.2.2 lays out shareholder proponents' law-reform agenda.

21.2.1 The Economic Stakes: Trade-off Versus Win–Win

The shareholder case has historical roots in *The Modern Corporation and Private Property*, by Adolf Berle and Gardiner Means (1932). Berle and Means famously showed that

14 *People ex rel. Manice v. Powell*, 94 N.E. 634, 637 (N.Y. 1911) (internal quotation marks omitted) (quoting *Hoyt v. Thompson's Ex'rs*, 19 N.Y. 207, 216 (1859)).

15 See Del. Code Ann. tit. 8, § 141(k) (2001) (providing for removal of the boards of directors of Delaware corporations).

16 See, e.g., Hansmann and Kraakman (2001: 439–40) (asserting that legal regimes worldwide have converged on corporate law systems characterized by 'shared ownership by investors' and 'delegated management' to a board).

ownership and control of public corporations had separated, charging that resultant management power needed significant substantive constraint, constraint that earlier in history had been exercised by shareholder-owners.[17]

We base our case for the prevailing legal model on Eugene Fama and Michael Jensen's rebuttal of the Berle and Means diagnosis.[18] Fama and Jensen reframed the separation of ownership and control as a rational allocation of risk-bearing and decision-making functions. Expertise, access to information, and complexity emerge as neutral, economic explanations for what Berle and Means described in economic terms as intrinsically problematic and in political terms as illegitimate management empowerment.

21.2.1.1 *The Trade-off*

Fama and Jensen substitute contract for property as the mode of analysis and ask why public corporations have survived in history. They suggest that organizational contracts must perform two functions: (1) the allocation of the residual claim, and (2) the allocation of decision rights (Fama and Jensen 1983a: 302).[19]

In Fama and Jensen's depiction, shareholders contract for the right to the net cash flows, thus taking the residual claim. Decision management and decision control, in contrast, go inside the organization, subject to shareholder retention of the right to vote for the board and matters reserved for their ratification.[20] This holds out an economic advantage: the residual risk holders 'are not required to have any other role in the organization' (Fama and Jensen 1983b: 328). This frees them to specialize in risk-bearing, leaving others to specialize in initiating and implementing business decisions and in monitoring their effectiveness (Fama and Jensen 1983b: 330). The alternative of cutting the shareholders into business decision-making could be costly: '[M]ost of the diffuse residual claimants are not qualified for roles in the decision process' (Fama and Jensen 1983a: 309). After all, wealth and willingness to bear risk do not by themselves assure needed skills.[21] It follows that the delegation

[17] See Hansmann and Kraakman (2001: 124):

> The concentration of economic power separate from ownership has, in fact, created economic empires, and has delivered these empires into the hands of a new form of absolutism, relegating 'owners' to the position of those who supply the means whereby the new princes may exercise their power.

[18] See Fama and Jensen (1983a: 301–2) (rebutting Berle and Means's analysis by arguing that organizations where ownership and control are separated survive because they benefit from specialization of these roles and are able to control agency problems by separating 'the ratification and monitoring of decisions from initiation and implementation of the decisions'); see also Fama and Jensen (1983b: 331–2) (recapping the thesis of Fama and Jensen (1983a) and noting that devices for separating these roles include 'decision hierarchies', boards of directors, and 'incentive structures that encourage mutual monitoring among decision agents').

[19] Note that this two-part division of functions precisely identifies the two contested zones in corporate law's political economy.

[20] See Fama and Jensen (1983a: 313) (explaining that shareholders vote on 'auditor choice, mergers, and new stock issues' in addition to board membership).

[21] See Fama and Jensen (1983a: 312) (commenting that, because managerial skills are not necessarily tied to wealth or willingness to bear risk, specialization enhances a complex organization's ability to adapt to changes in the economic environment and lowers the cost of risk-bearing services).

of decision management and control to actors inside the corporation is efficient (Fama and Jensen 1983a: 309).

Decision rights, thus sent inside the organization, are split between two groups. The powers of initiation and implementation go to management.[22] Thus management is separated from residual risk-bearing. The reason is agency-cost reduction. Given a complex business organization with knowledge diffusion, business decision-making should go to agents with relevant knowledge.[23] At the same time, controls need to be imposed to protect the residual claimants from expropriation by the managers. This second aspect of agency-cost reduction calls for having a separate decision controller to monitor and ratify management decisions (Fama and Jensen 1983a: 308–9). The two decision functions, management and monitoring, must be separate 'almost by definition' (Fama and Jensen 1983a: 304). As a result, a board of directors that includes outsiders performs the monitoring function.[24] The board retains 'ultimate control over internal agents' and their decisions (Fama and Jensen 1983a: 313) and stands in for the classical owner-entrepreneur[25] of Berle and Means. Backstopping the board as agency-cost controllers are a host of public and private external monitors—the courts and regulatory agencies on the public side, and the stock market and the takeover market on the private side (Fama and Jensen 1983a: 312–13).

What becomes of ownership in Fama and Jensen's contractual model? The model, rather than separating it from control, divides it up along with control. The classical owner-entrepreneur performs all three of the functions they identify—he/she sets business policy, monitors corporate agents, and bears the residual risk. Fama and Jensen in effect take these ownership incidents and distribute them across the organization. The shareholders emerge as owners-in-part, bearing the residual risk and, as voters, sharing in control at a step removed from business decision-making and direct monitoring. It follows that management and the board share in ownership. This sharing of ownership functions implies nothing radical; it is just a contractual adjustment of the classical model that accounts for the evolution of corporate law and practice during the twentieth century.

Thus Fama and Jensen rebut the notion that corporate governance is dysfunctional because a traditional shareholder-owner is absent. But the rebuttal, effective though it may be, does not by itself determine the outcome of today's contest between the shareholder-directed agency model and the prevailing legal model. It does, however, clear noise from the screen, facilitating a meaningful statement of the policy issue. The noise comes from the conceptual legacy of unitary ownership and the teaching that shareholders are owners who are natural principals in an agency relationship with corporate management. Once the noise is filtered out and the division of ownership is recognized, the question becomes whether the allocation of authority in public corporations makes economic sense. Fama and Jensen answer in the affirmative for the reasons just given.

[22] See Fama and Jensen (1983a: 303–4) (defining the activities involved in decision initiation and implementation).

[23] See Fama and Jensen (1983a: 307–8) (noting that this model reduces agency costs).

[24] See Fama and Jensen (1983a: 313, 315) (discussing the incentives of outside directors).

[25] See Fama and Jensen (1983a: 309):

> Separation and diffusion of decision management and decision control—in effect, the absence of a classical entrepreneurial decision maker—limit the power of individual decision agents to expropriate the interests of residual claimants.

21.2.1.2 *The Win-Win*

The shareholders' basic claims can be accessed through Henry Hansmann and Reinier Kraakman's identification of two touchstone points that ground a general consensus in their favour: first, 'ultimate control over the corporation should rest with the shareholder[s]', and second, the market price of the corporation's stock should provide 'the principal measure of its shareholders' interests' (2001: 440–1).

'Ultimate control' takes us to an agency framework[26] favouring shareholder inputs. The supporting economic case focuses on agency costs and incentives. All other things equal, agency-cost reduction enhances value, and enhanced principal control can conceivably lower agency costs.[27] So the question is whether shareholders, as principals, are well suited to provide value-enhancing inputs, or, as Fama and Jensen asserted, are not well suited.

The suitability case begins with shareholder incentives: their capital investment[28] in the residual interest lends them an undiluted, pure financial incentive to maximize the value of the firm.[29] From an incentive point of view, shareholders contrast favourably with managers and independent directors, whose incentives are comprised by interests in compensation and job retention.

The question then becomes whether these pure shareholder incentives can be harnessed by the governance system despite the fact that dispersed, diversified shareholders labour under information asymmetries and lack business expertise. Hansmann and Kraakman's second proposition—that the market price of the stock provides the 'principal measure' of the shareholder interest—holds out the means to this end. If the stock price provides an objective and accurate measure of the purely motivated shareholder directive to maximize value, it provides the best source of instructions for governance and business policy. After all, it is in the financial market where shareholders, using the Holmström and Kaplan metaphor, 'put their money where their mouth is' (2001: 138).[30] From this it follows that a manager-agent with correct incentives should manage to the market price.[31]

[26] The phrase 'ultimate control' is imprecise. The assertion in the text reflects our interpretation. The legal model already vests the franchise in the shareholders and directs the board to manage in their interests. Arguably, this amounts to an allocation of 'ultimate control'. Hansmann and Kraakman accordingly imply more in the way of shareholder authority. To see why, compare Hansmann and Kraakman's conception with that of Fama and Jensen, who assign 'ultimate control' to the board of directors, subject to the shareholder vote (see Fama and Jensen 1983a: 313). This would not suffice for Hansmann and Kraakman, for whom 'ultimate control' at a minimum means shareholder choice on tender offers, as they consider trust-based outcomes favouring management discretion to be inefficient (see Hansmann and Kraakman 2001: 467). Even as today's shareholder agenda goes much farther, the term 'ultimate control' easily accommodates it.

[27] See Committee on Capital Markets Regulation (2006: 16) (asserting that '[s]hareholder rights serve the critical function of reducing . . . agency costs' and that inadequate shareholder rights cause shares to trade at a discount to fundamental value).

[28] See Holmström and Kaplan (2001: 138) ('[I]f resources are to shift . . . the market may have a role to play in funneling capital toward the new companies').

[29] See Hansmann and Kraakman (2001: 449) ('[I]f the control rights granted to the firm's equity-holders are exclusive and strong, they will have powerful incentives to maximize the value of the firm').

[30] See also Dent (2008: 1213, 1225) ('Although share prices do not exactly match fundamental value, no measure is better').

[31] This chapter continues a line of analysis that begins in Wachter (2003).

Thus do the shareholder proponents contemplate a species of market control.[32] They want the market price—which is, after all, set by shareholders investing at the margin—to be the ongoing and determining source of shareholder input. It bids those managers who are effective agents to manage to the stock market in formulating business policy, thereby accessing the high-quality instructions embedded in stock market prices. With the market price as the management yardstick, value-enhancing opportunities to merge, sell, or dissolve will no longer be frustrated by the managers' desire to hold on to control; resources will no longer be misdirected to suboptimal executive compensation plans; and governance arrangements will import appropriate constraints and incentives.[33] Managing to the market price also is thought to import administrative coherence, because the yardstick provides a means with which to evaluate management performance.[34]

Value maximization pursued with a long-term time horizon is said to follow.[35] Here the proponents refer to basic principles of valuation, which teach that long-term value is impounded in the present market price.[36] It follows that managing to the market price is incentive compatible with regard to the time horizon because both short-term and long-term investors have incentives to maximize long-term value.[37]

Shareholder proponents do not deny that the market price is set under conditions of information asymmetry and thus is not fully informed.[38] The implied assertion is that any resulting divergence between market price and fundamental value will not hold out perverse effects, given management to the market price. An ameliorating factor has also been noted: some studies show that market prices have become better informed over the past half-century.[39] The information gap between those inside and outside of the corporation has narrowed, due in part

[32] See Committee on Capital Markets Regulation (2006: 16) (asserting that strengthened 'shareholder rights go hand in hand with reduced regulation [and] litigation').

[33] See Bebchuk (2005: 840, 850) (noting that, in the absence of shareholder intervention, management tends not to adopt 'game-ending decisions' because such decisions also end the managers' control).

[34] See Holmström and Kaplan (2001: 138–9) (explaining that long-term management effects, especially in times of change, are difficult to measure absent share prices).

[35] See Hansmann and Kraakman (2001: 451):

> The ability of standard-model firms to expand rapidly in growth industries is magnified . . . by access to institutional investors and the international equity markets . . . . Over time, then, the standard model is likely to win the competitive struggle on the margins. . . . As the pace of technological change continues to quicken, this competitive advantage should continue to increase.

[36] See Black and Kraakman (2002: 522) (explaining that intrinsic or 'hidden' value can be assessed by a board but is invisible to shareholders).

[37] In the view of shareholder proponents, accountability suffers under the prevailing regime, leading to inefficient regulatory responses, including shareholder litigation. See Committee on Capital Markets Regulation (2006: 16, 93–6). Therefore, systemic reform designed to facilitate shareholder intervention is appropriate because the inherited model affords management discretionary space to disregard the price directive.

[38] See Gordon (2007: 1548–63) (discussing the factors that have narrowed the scope of information asymmetry and thereby increased stock price information, but not suggesting perfect symmetry).

[39] For a description of the empirical literature, which focuses on an increase in idiosyncratic volatility, see *infra* notes 132–5 and accompanying text.

to stricter mandatory disclosure requirements and in part to more liquid markets and a larger sector of information intermediaries.[40]

Summing up, shareholder proponents seek to reform the prevailing legal model of the corporation (or what might be called the 'Fama–Jensen corporation') to ensure that shareholder inputs directly impact both business decision-making and monitoring. The supporting theoretical case rests upon three assumptions: first, that information asymmetries can be ignored (or alternatively, that managers cannot be trusted to use their superior knowledge in the best interest of the corporation); second, that business instructions following from pure financial incentives have agency-cost reductive effects; and, third, that the market price accurately communicates these instructions.

21.2.2 The Law-reform Agenda

The shareholders' law-reform agenda took shape in response to the takeover wars of the 1980s. State lawmakers and state courts, in particular the Delaware courts, responded to the outbreak of hostile activity by restating and reinforcing the legal model's allocation of authority to management.[41] The shareholder case coalesced as a protest against that outcome, and the context was ideally suited to the shareholder position. Recall that Fama and Jensen defended the legal model on the assumption that a vigorous market for corporate control operated as a check on subpar managers.[42] If courts and legislatures had impaired that market's operation, the impairments needed to be removed. Moreover, the takeover context minimized the importance of the shareholders' debilities respecting information and expertise. In the information-enriched environment created by the disclosure requirements of a contested battle for control, shareholders were deemed informed enough to choose rationally between the value of two or more competing corporate strategies.[43]

[40] See Gordon (2007: 1548–63) (attributing stock prices' increased information value to SEC and Financial Accounting Standards Board (FASB) disclosure regulations, as well as to the rise in investment analysts and information-dissemination mechanisms).

[41] This response raised questions about the terms of fiduciary duty. It took a decade and four famous cases before the Delaware courts delivered a definitive answer respecting the scope of the fiduciary duty. See *Unitrin, Inc. v. Am. Gen. Corp.*, 651 A.2d 1361, 1388 (Del. 1995) (ruling that refusal to redeem a poison pill survives review if it is neither 'preclusive' nor 'coercive' and falls within a 'range of reasonableness'); *Paramount Commc'ns, Inc. v. Time Inc.*, 571 A.2d 1140, 1154 (Del. 1989) (sustaining the 'just say no' defence based on a business plan implemented by the board of directors); *Moran v. Household Int'l, Inc.*, 500 A.2d 1346, 1351–7 (Del. 1985) (sustaining the poison pill as a structural matter and applying *Unocal* scrutiny); *Unocal Corp. v. Mesa Petroleum Co.*, 493 A.2d 946, 955–6 (Del. 1985) (applying proportionality scrutiny to management defence tactics). When the answer finally came, trust trumped agency, forcing hostile offerors to resort to the shareholder franchise in the form of a proxy fight for board control in order to put to the shareholders the choice between the offer price and management's claim that its business plan held out greater value on a long-term basis. That is, the board was left with the power to block offers to protect the business plan, thereby remitting the exercise of shareholder choice not to the market for shares but to the exercise of the franchise. See Gilson and Schwartz (2001: 788) (emphasizing that, because of the ubiquity of the poison pill, corporate control changes occur principally by election rather than through the market).

[42] See *supra* text accompanying notes 22–5.

[43] The Delaware courts disagreed even so, channelling the contested control transaction into the even richer information environment of the proxy contest. See *Paramount Commc'ns*, 571 A.2d at 1154–5

Furthermore, shareholders were seen as having been on the right side of the era's valuation questions. The capital markets emerged from the 1980s with an enhanced reputation as drivers of productivity. The era's corporate restructurings were deemed to have been a productive success. It followed that capital markets had a comparative advantage over appointed managers in effecting structural reforms necessitated by deregulation and technological change.[44] Firms tend to be experts in existing technologies, products, and processes. Markets came to be thought to have the advantage when it comes to recognizing the implications of new technologies, products, and processes—the markets move the capital to higher-valuing users who then put the capital into more productive projects.[45]

Shareholder empowerment emerged from the takeover era as the leading issue in corporate law, with a consistent consensus in its favour. The list of agenda items continued to grow during the period of institutional adjustment that followed. The shareholders, dissatisfied with the legal outcome and led by now-dominant institutions, lost their passivity.[46] 'Governance' became a zone of ongoing engagement between managers, institutional shareholders, and a new class of professional intermediaries. Independent boards of directors assumed greater institutional salience.[47]

Even so, shareholder empowerment remained elusive[48] and so emerged as the focus of a law-reform agenda. If the shareholders could not surmount collective action problems

(permitting a corporation's board of directors to forego unsolicited tender offers it perceives as threats to corporate policy despite shareholder support, thereby forcing a bidder to use alternative means of acquiring control).

44 See Holmström and Kaplan (2001: 122) ('The real drivers behind the increased dominance of capital markets . . . can be traced to deregulation . . . and to new information and communication technologies. . . .'). We note that while Holmström and Kaplan expect the 1980s experience of market advantage to persist over time, they also acknowledge the possibility of changed conditions under which market price guidance could lose its productive quality (Holmström and Kaplan 2001: 140–1) (suggesting that if stock markets slow, reliance on them may also decrease).

45 See Holmström and Kaplan (2001: 137–8) ('Markets are more effective than managers when it comes to moving capital from declining industries to emerging industries.'); cf. Hansmann and Kraakman (2001: 450–1) (noting that shareholder input will favour aggressive development of new product markets and abandonment of inefficient investments).

46 Shareholders can be counted on to vote against antitakeover amendments and in favour of redeeming poison pills. See Kahan and Rock (2002: 898) (noting that, when possible, shareholders prevented the adoption of 'takeover inhibiting charter amendments' while voting in favour of proposals to redeem poison pills).

47 See Gordon (2007: 1511) (noting the 'increasingly tight link between the independent board and the priority of shareholder value').

48 The post-takeover era began with a vision of direct institutional investor control through aggressive use of the shareholder franchise. See Black (1990: 525, 585–9) (discussing shareholder monitoring as a concept that had not yet come to fruition and analysing factors that influence whether shareholders remain apathetic or not). It was hoped that institutional holdings had reached a level of concentration that would render collective action barriers surmountable, with US institutions stepping into the role played by blockholders in other governance systems. See, e.g., Gilson and Kraakman (1991: 884–8) (suggesting that institutional investors could organize on a subscription basis and fund correctly incentivized candidates for board seats). But no such movement to self-help by spontaneous order occurred. Far from yielding, collective action barriers instead emerged much reinforced in the new environment. The free-rider problem continued to discourage investment managers from incurring the costs of governance challenges—gains that must be shared with competitors who do not share the costs do not advance investment managers' careers. See Fisch (1994: 1019–25) (discussing the free-rider problem as disincentivizing investors from monitoring because the benefits spread to competitive

themselves, then law reform directed at lowering the costs and expanding the payoffs of shareholder intervention made sense. Today's shareholder law-reform agenda serves these dual purposes.

Proposals on the agenda fall into two categories. The first, a narrower category, accepts the existing legal model in its broad outline and focuses on process reforms designed to expand the range of shareholder choices in the election process and to facilitate shareholder contests. The second type would give the shareholders the option to legislate their way out of the prevailing model, to an agency model holding out direct control of business policy. Cost concerns are present in both categories. Some reforms are designed to enhance the impact of existing low-cost activist strategies like 'just vote no' campaigns. All of the rest include transfers from the corporate treasury to intervening shareholders.

The list of improvements proposed for the present election system is lengthy. The first items are designed to facilitate rejection of selected candidates and protest voting. These include majority (as opposed to plurality) voting and confidential voting, both of which have already been adopted voluntarily by many corporations.[49] Reformers want shareholders to have the option of a 'no' vote (as opposed to the present 'withhold' vote expression of negativity) and a right to replace all incumbents every two or three years.[50] Other provisions hold out more in the way of power shifting. They would clear a way for shareholder nomination of board candidates, not only by opening access to the proxy statement but by providing for reimbursement of solicitation expenses.[51]

The second legislative category is more radical. The shareholders already have the power to amend the by-laws under state codes.[52] But, even cabined in a tight zone of process-based subject matter,[53] the power has been unexercised because shareholders, while they do have the power to put a by-law amendment to a shareholders' meeting, have neither access to management's proxy statement nor state law power to trump contrary board-adopted by-laws. The reformers would grant both.[54]

investors but the cost is only borne by the monitor); Rock (1991: 473–4) (acknowledging that money managers have no selective incentives to actively improve diversified funds because doing so would simultaneously benefit the managers to whom they are compared).

At the same time, many fund advisors sell services to managers, importing an independent business reason to stay cooperative. See, e.g., Bainbridge (2006: 1751–4) (describing the incentive problems of financial institutions). Finally, mutual fund investors can redeem at any time, inhibiting investment in large, illiquid blockholder positions that would carry boardroom influence.

49 See Allen (2007) (demonstrating that majority voting has become standard practice among large public companies).

50 See Bebchuk (Chapter 3, this volume) (suggesting these election reforms as part of a broader reform scheme to make directors accountable to shareholders).

51 See Bebchuk (Chapter 3, this volume) (noting that threshold requirements would be needed). For the SEC's recent proposal, see Facilitating Shareholder Director Nominations, 74 Fed. Reg. 29,024 (proposed 18 June 2009) (to be codified in scattered parts of 17 C.F.R.), and *supra* note 12 and accompanying text.

52 See, e.g., Del. Code Ann. tit. 8, § 109 (2001) (granting shareholders the power to adopt, amend, or repeal by-laws even when directors share this power).

53 See *CA, Inc. v. AFSCME Employees Pension Plan*, 953 A.2d 227, 231–40 (Del. 2008) (answering questions certified from the SEC regarding a proposed by-law that improperly sought to 'remove the subject of election expense reimbursement' from the board's discretion).

54 See Bebchuk (Chapter 3, this volume) (arguing that shareholder-adopted by-laws should be facilitated while boards' power to adopt by-laws should be constrained). The SEC's current proposed

At the same time, there are definite limits on what can be accomplished through by-law amendment. By-laws are limited to process matters and cannot surmount the reservation to the board of the power to manage the business, a reservation read broadly by the Delaware courts.[55] Only a charter amendment can delimit the board's powers,[56] and state corporate codes accord the board agenda control over charter amendments.[57] The agency reformers accordingly would open the door to shareholder-initiated charter amendments and accord power to initiate a change of jurisdiction of incorporation, with expense reimbursement.[58] They contemplate that once the door is opened, shareholders can allocate to themselves the power to force a sale or liquidation of the firm,[59] or to force a large dividend (and the leveraged financing thereof) or a subsidiary spin-off.[60] Present proposals respecting business policy stop at this point. But we note an implicit open end: once any door to the reversal of board business judgment is opened, there will be no principled basis for containing shareholder mandates respecting business policy.

Finally, 'Say on Pay' initiatives would similarly allow the shareholders to cross the line to control of business policy, but in ratification mode and on a mandated annual basis. Here the idea is to put the top executives' total compensation package to the shareholders for an up/down advisory vote.[61]

21.2.3 Summary

The shareholders' reform agenda reflects their view that the prevailing model is out of date. By hypothesis, it remained defensible only so long as collective action problems rendered shareholder exercise of discretionary powers infeasible. But, as we have seen, concentrated institutional shareholdings have not by themselves removed this barrier. Accordingly, if the firm is to be reconstituted along agency lines,[62] the shareholder collective action problem

rules include a limited by-law access provision, keyed to 'shareholder proposals that would amend, or that request an amendment to, a company's governing documents regarding nomination procedures or disclosures related to shareholder nominations . . .' (Facilitating Shareholder Director Nominations, 74 Fed. Reg. at 29,024).

55 See *CA, Inc.*, 953 A.2d at 232 (noting that shareholders lack the broad management power statutorily allocated to the board of directors).

56 See Del. Code Ann. tit. 8, § 242(a)(2) ('[A] corporation may amend its certificate of incorporation . . . [t]o change, substitute, enlarge or diminish the nature of its business or corporate powers and purposes . . .').

57 See Del. Code Ann. tit. 8, § 242(b)(1) ('Every amendment authorized by subsection (a) . . . shall be made . . . in the following manner: . . . [the] board of directors shall adopt a resolution setting forth the amendment proposed . . .').

58 See Bebchuk (2005: 865–70) (suggesting that shareholders should be empowered to change things like the corporate charter and the state of incorporation).

59 See Bebchuk (2005: 895–901) (addressing the effects on agency costs of shareholder power to participate in 'game-ending' decisions).

60 See Bebchuk (2005: 901–8) (analysing the impact of shareholder power to make 'scaling-down' decisions).

61 Initiatives presently on Washington reform agendas fall into the first, narrower category addressed to the shareholder franchise. See *supra* note 9 and accompanying text.

62 See Black (1990: 608) (noting that shareholder voice is an idea that has never been tried, rather than an idea that has failed).

must first be solved by changing the terms of shareholding itself through a system of subsidies for activists. With that accomplished, the shareholders would get the power to opt out of the prevailing model on a firm-by-firm basis.

Significantly, the shareholder proponents do not anticipate that these reforms would open the door to hundreds of issue-based proxy contests. They instead point to an *in terrorem* effect. They project that the threat of shareholder intervention by itself will influence management conduct, forcing managers to focus on the stock price in order to avoid triggering destabilizing and disempowering shareholder action.[63]

The projection is fair.[64] But therein lies the problem. The shareholder proponents dismiss the prevailing legal model too quickly, eliding two critical points. The first of these is taken up in Section 21.3. There we show that in the years since the takeover era, the legal model has proven highly responsive to shareholder interests and demands, meliorating agency costs. The second point is addressed in Section 21.4. The shareholders, even as they plausibly expect that an agency model would further reduce agency costs, fail to confront new costs that would result from the change, in particular suboptimal results stemming from managing to the market. In our view, once these countervailing points are on the table, the

[63] See Bebchuk (2005: 878) ('Introducing the [shareholder] power to intervene would induce management to act differently in order to avoid shareholder intervention.').

[64] In making this projection, shareholder proponents effectively respond to a point made by their critics, who warn that pure financial incentives posited by shareholder proponents will not obtain efficiency in all cases and that empowered activists may have private agendas. See Anabtawi (2006: 586–93) (explaining how the interests of certain types of shareholders may differ from the interests of others). Since the bite lies in the threat, any problems of self-dealing can be dealt with by fiduciary law, and any incentive misalignments in actual contests will come out and impact the vote. Note also that if the bite lies in the threat, any shareholder incentive problems will be minimal because the shareholders who actually wield the power will be the market price setters, actors who do indeed act with undiluted incentives to maximize value.

The critics make two additional points. First, they project governance incoherence in the move from oligarchic to democratic governance, citing information asymmetries and conflicting interests within the group of newly empowered constituents. See, e.g., Bainbridge (2006: 1745) (citing Arrow 1974: 68–70) (arguing that authority-based decision-making structures, grounded in central agencies empowered to make binding decisions, are necessary when the organization's constituencies suffer from information asymmetries and have differing interests). Second, they predict that shareholder empowerment will impose a short-term time horizon with consequent perverse effects. See, e.g., Anabtawi (2006: 579–80) (noting how pressure from short-term shareholders can cause companies to neglect long-term focus).

Shareholder proponents similarly rely on the market price to rebut the first criticism. They pose the market price as the focal point for decision-making, thereby obviating any coherence problem. If the market price is indeed suited to guide business policymaking, the shareholder proponents win this point. Emphasis accordingly needs to be directed away from theories of government to financial economics, where the inquiry should focus on the interplay between information asymmetry, investor expectations, and market pricing. We conduct this inquiry in Section 21.4. This analysis also applies to the short-term time horizon objection. Under basic principles of valuation, short-term and long-term investors both have incentives to maximize long-term value, and the market price subsumes all time horizons—short, intermediate, and long. See Black and Kraakman (2002: 532–3) (asserting that 'even short-term investors have an incentive to maximize the firm's long-term value, because only by doing so can they maximize the price at which long-term investors will buy the shares that the short-term investors will soon want to sell'). If the market price does so accurately, then there should be no perverse effects.

Thus, the shareholder proponents rely entirely on the robustness of the market price of the stock as a predictor of fundamental value.

shareholder empowerment case falls well short of surmounting the burden of proof that ordinarily confronts proposals for fundamental structural change.

21.3 Systemic Responsiveness

We have seen that the shareholder proponents' win–win scenario predicts that shareholder empowerment will cause agency costs to decline and capital to flow to the best use, and that agency costs will persist absent shareholder empowerment. Agency-cost reduction and shareholder empowerment move in lockstep in this picture—you do not get one without the other. This *sine qua non* posits constant, highly salient agency costs and claims that fundamental law reform is the only way to reduce them. This in turn implies that the corporate governance system leaves big money on the table in the ordinary course, a proposition that to us is counter-intuitive.

This section challenges the shareholder *sine qua non*. Our challenge follows from the lesson Jensen and Meckling taught in their classic work on agency costs: institutions change in response to market incentives. In Jensen and Meckling's framework, managers and shareholders address agency costs as they arise over time, in the managers' case by bonding their fidelity and in the shareholders' case by monitoring their investments (Jensen and Meckling 1976: 308). To the extent agency costs remain unaddressed, it is because they are too costly for the parties to remove themselves.[65] Agency-cost reduction, then, is as much an endogenous incident of the system's operation as are agency costs themselves. A prediction results for corporate governance: as new agency costs appear, we can expect the system to find ways to reduce them, even as a residual component of agency costs will persist in the wake of the system's adjustments.

The shareholder *sine qua non*, in contrast, follows from a static picture of agency costs and corporate governance institutions. This holds that managers will systematically fail to maximize value in predictable ways. They will favour conservative, low-leverage capital structures, misinvest excess cash in suboptimal projects, fail to reduce excess operating costs, and resist premium sales of control. All of these missed opportunities amount to agency costs that could be reduced if the law provided for greater shareholder input.

This fixed picture of systemic shortcomings derives less from economic theory than from a particular time and governance context. The time was the 1980s, and the context was the debate over hostile takeovers. At the time, the management predilection for institutional stability had significant negative implications for productivity, with an open playing field for hostile bids as the agency-cost corrective of choice.[66] This section uses Jensen and Meckling's framework as a lens for reviewing subsequent history, contending that the corporate governance system has been dynamic rather than static in addressing agency costs. Indeed, developments on the front lines of business practice have led to a series of

[65] See Jensen and Meckling (1976: 308) (explaining how many agency costs can be avoided through principal monitoring and agent bonding expenditures, and referring to the remaining agency costs as the 'residual loss').

[66] See, e.g., Kraakman (1988: 897–901) (offering two hypotheses on the sources of discounted share prices).

agency-cost-reductive changes. We use four critical examples to indicate that recent history bears out the Jensen–Meckling prediction of responsive agency-cost reduction both by actors inside corporations and actors in the financial markets. First, managers emerged from the 1980s sensitized to the benefits of shareholder-value maximization even as the board of directors emerged as a more robust monitoring institution. Hostile takeovers lost their place at the cutting edge of corporate governance as a result. Second, the revival of private equity buyouts showed that disciplinary merger activity can proliferate even in the absence of either actual or threatened hostile bids. Third, the appearance of hedge fund activists showed, much to the surprise of many, that the prevailing legal model of the shareholder franchise can be well suited to shareholder intervention. Finally, a shareholder-directed break in a long-standing pattern of corporate cash payouts accompanied the hedge funds' appearance.

Cumulated, these developments show that the governance system works dynamically within the prevailing legal model to remove money on the table stemming from excess agency costs. Shareholder empowerment proponents have played an important role in this process by exerting continuing pressure on directors and managers. They are deservedly applauded for their efforts (as are directors and managers who weigh in against them in the public debate). Even so, a question arises as to the need for greater shareholder empowerment.

21.3.1 Corporate Governance and the Market for Corporate Control

We start with an evolutionary account of the corporate governance system put forward by Bengt Holmström and Steven Kaplan in 2001. They surveyed the evolution of shareholder–manager relations, noting that a regime of market-oriented corporate governance emerged in the wake of the 1980s. They depicted the takeover wars as a reaction to an external shock caused by economic factors such as deregulation, globalization, and new information and communications technologies. The financial markets, they observed, showed a comparative advantage over management in undertaking the structural adjustments made necessary by the changes (Holmström and Kaplan 2001: 122–3). Viewed from this perspective, the shift to market control followed neither from its intrinsic superiority respecting capital allocation nor from a structurally embedded level of excess agency costs but from transitory economic factors.[67] A different economic environment, said Holmström and Kaplan, could trigger a shift away from the markets.[68]

[67] See Kraakman (1988: 137) (suggesting that 'markets have come to play a bigger role not because they have become better at allocating capital and not because managers misbehaved, but rather because the market's comparative advantage has been favoured by economy-wide trends in deregulation, globalization, and information technologies').

[68] In discussing potential future developments, Holmström and Kaplan stated:

> We have argued that at least some of the efficiency gains associated with these changes can be traced to the comparative advantage of markets in undertaking large-scale change. Since these effects are temporary, it is possible that the current level of market influence on the governance and organization of firms is going to abate. It is not hard to build a scenario in which the pursuit of shareholder value becomes a less important guideline to managers in the next few years.... If the stock markets are flat or down for the next few

For Holmström and Kaplan, the takeover shock in turn caused a governance response: shareholder-oriented economic assumptions took hold within corporate boardrooms. Incentive realignment was essential in bringing this about, and the move to equity-based management compensation duly encouraged managers to see things the shareholders' way. Thus, restructuring found its way into strategic business planning in the ordinary course. Corporate governance practices changed, too, with the emergence of the independent monitoring board. By all available indicators, the move to board independence and more vigorous monitoring continues unabated.[69]

Significantly, none of this required any changes in the prevailing legal model. The emergence of the independent board did occasion some pushing and shoving in the private sector, manifested in the gestation of the American Law Institute Corporate Governance Project.[70] But it can still be fairly described as a joint effort by directors and investors seeking best corporate practices. Regulatory mandates came after the fact.[71] The system, in sum, became more cognizant of the need to reduce agency costs, with private ordering as the means to the end.[72]

Hostile takeovers decreased in policy salience as the market context changed. Merger volume reached new records, and the transactions were overwhelmingly friendly.[73] Managers proved willing to sell. Stock options and exit compensation provided a carrot, and majority-independent boards held out a stick in the form of a rising rate of CEO dismissals.[74] Hostility became less a fundamental transactional distinction and more a secondary strategy choice determined by cost–benefit calculations at the acquiring firm.[75] The hostile offer's diminishing importance is further confirmed by the diminishing incidence of defensive devices in corporate contracts. Staggered boards (which together with poison pills afford the maximum available protection) among Standard & Poor's (S&P) 100 companies

years, then the extensive reliance on stock options may again dissipate, leading managers to have less focus on stock prices (Holmström and Kaplan 2001 at 140).

[69] See Kahan and Rock (2008) (surveying the range of pertinent empirical measures of changes in boards of directors). We make the same assertion respecting § 162(m) of the Internal Revenue Code, enacted in 1994, which limits the corporate tax deductability of salaries to $1 million (I.R.C. § 162(m) 2006). Had the governance system not changed its views first, we doubt it would have occurred to Congress to add the section.

[70] See Macey (1993: 1218) (describing conflicting views between the American Law Institute and corporate management).

[71] The stock exchange rules mandating committees arrived only after Enron. These, for the first time, hardwire the majority-independent board of directors (NYSE 2009: § 303A.01). Not only is an independent director majority now mandated, but independence is formally defined (NYSE 2009: § 303A.02). Accompanying mandates include separate meetings for outside directors and for all independent nominating, compensation, and audit committees (NYSE 2009: §§ 303A.03–.06).

[72] Thus did Hansmann and Kraakman declare an end to corporate law history at the new century's start (2001: 439) ('There is no longer any serious competitor to the view that corporate law should principally strive to increase long-term shareholder value.').

[73] See Kahan and Rock (2002: 878–80, 879 tbl.2) (detailing trends in M&A activity from 1988 to 2000).

[74] See Kahan and Rock (2002: 881–4) (describing the effects of having independent board members).

[75] See Schwert (2000: 2,600) (suggesting that 'the distinction between hostile and friendly offers is largely a reflection of negotiation strategy').

declined from 44% to 16% between 2003 and 2008; the decline among S&P 500 companies was from 57% in 2003 to 36% in 2007.[76]

Meanwhile, the private equity buyout is the segment of the mergers and acquisitions (M&A) market most likely to entail the post-closing governance discipline sought by the shareholder camp, a segment that experienced a remarkable revival beginning in the mid-1990s. Buyout firms act as aggressive blockholders, closely monitoring management performance and imposing performance targets.[77] The private equity business model includes and depends on an active threat of manager removal even as it includes and depends on the participation of management incumbents and incentivizes them with a share of the equity. Leverage enhances the threat by interpolating the possibility of downside disaster and magnifying the financial payoff for success.[78] Discipline, accordingly, is wrought into these companies' governance structures. Pre-closing hostility, however, is avoided. When the recent buyout boom peaked in 2006, buyouts comprised 42% of total merger activity as measured by number of transactions (Bratton 2008: 513 fig.1).

All of this shows the corporate governance system acting out the Jensen and Meckling model. Managers bonded themselves by playing ball with the independent board, aligning their personal wealth with that of the shareholders, and, in a growing number of cases, giving up their takeover defences. Investors simultaneously stepped up their monitoring. Agency-cost reduction was the end in view on both sides. The market power that first registered in the conflicts of the 1980s continued to register,[79] but in a more cooperative framework. Shareholder value creation became embedded in corporate practice under the prevailing legal model. No fundamental, facilitative legal change was needed.[80]

A shareholder proponent might counter these observations by noting that legally sanctioned antitakeover measures increase the costs of takeovers and thereby diminish the intensity of market discipline and lead to increased agency costs. That point certainly carries for some firms at some times.[81] But the Jensen and Meckling model anticipates these costs,

[76] Kahan and Rock (2008: 21–2). The trend of decline is also evident in smaller firms, but the magnitude is less—in 2007, 58% of S&P 400 mid-cap firms and 55% of S&P 600 small cap firms had staggered boards (Kahan and Rock 2008: 22).

[77] See Cheffins and Armour (2007) (noting that 'management will be forced to adhere to strict, results-oriented financial projections').

[78] See Cheffins and Armour (2007) (observing that '[t]he overall result is a more dynamic and challenging boardroom style than prevails in public companies').

[79] See Holmström and Kaplan (2003: 7–8) ('[T]he accomplishments of the 1980s were by no means forgotten. By the 1990s U.S. managers, boards, and institutional shareholders had seen what LBOs and other market-driven restructurings could do.').

[80] See Kahan and Rock (2002: 897–9) (observing that 'the use of adaptive devices seems to work reasonably well').

[81] We note, however, that empirical results on the economic effects of takeover defences across the board are mixed. The literature on takeover defences provides a good example of the empirical back and forth. Many assert that takeover vulnerability influences stock prices even today. Gompers, Ishii, and Metrick (2003: 144) compared portfolios made up of firms with 'strong' and 'weak' shareholder protections (with 'weak' including antitakeover protection) and showed that, between 1990 and 1998, a long position in strong-protection firms and a short position in weak-protection firms would have earned an annual abnormal return of 8.5%. Bebchuk and Cohen (2005: 421) conducted a subsequent test focused on the staggered board, which, together with the ubiquitous poison pill, makes for a state-of-the-art defensive barrier. They show a statistically significant reduction in firm value at the 99% confidence level. They also test for economic significance, finding that a staggered board lowers Tobin's

too, with its residuum of irreducible agency costs. Given all of the adjustments described above, it is hard to project a revival for the hostile takeover, quite apart from the costs incident to anti-takeover regulation.

21.3.2 New Blockholders

Shareholders who own large blocks of stock suffer no lack of empowerment, whether they own controlling blocks or non-controlling blocks of sufficient size to assure board representation and inside influence. Shareholder proponents have long bemoaned the relative absence of these blockholders in US equity capital structures, speculating that they might, if we had them, make up the disciplinary deficit under the prevailing legal model. They once looked to blockholding arrangements in corporate governance systems in other countries to see if conditions favourable to blockholding could be replicated here, but without success.[82] Yet, in recent years, after all hope seemed lost, home-grown blockholders did appear, but not in the form predicted.

Q by 17 points (Bebchuk and Cohen 2005: 424). A number of complementary studies show connections between antitakeover provisions and specific undesirable results—bad mergers, higher wages, and low management turnover. See Borokhovich, Brunarski, and Parrino (1997: 1496) (correlating antitakeover adoption and higher levels of compensation); Masulis, Wang, and Xie, (2007: 1883) (studying 3,333 acquisitions from 1990 to 2003 and showing lower abnormal bidder returns for firms with antitakeover provisions, controlling for product market competition, equity-based pay, institutional ownership, and board characteristics); Mikkelson and Partch (1997: 206) (comparing management turnover in two periods, 1984–88 and 1989–93).

None of this is conclusive. Endogeneity problems prevent the studies from proving conclusively that antitakeover provisions cause lower stock prices. Gompers, Ishii, and Metrick's abnormal positive returns could represent unanticipated benefits of good governance or may reflect environmental changes unrelated to governance. See Becht, Bolton, and Röell (2005: 43) (warning of the limitations of Gompers, Ishii, and Metrick's findings). In addition, the market may take antitakeover provisions as a signal of poor management quality or a lack of shareholder orientation. See Coates (2000: 301–2) (acknowledging that market reaction to antitakeover measures will depend on investors' prior beliefs about management and shareholder orientation). Other unobservable variables may be in play. Market actors may simply overestimate the salience of the takeover threat. Chief executives may do the same thing. Finally, a study of the performance of the Gompers, Ishii, and Metrick portfolio after 2003 reverses the performance result, suggesting that the original result was sensitive to the distinct performance patterns of technology firms during the study period. Core, Guay, and Rusticus (2006: 681–4) (showing that the poor-governance-performance portfolio outperformed the good-governance-performance portfolio during 2000–03, and finding no evidence of a causal relationship between governance and operating performance).

It should also be noted that other studies of takeover defences reach the opposite conclusion. One study of the subsequent performance of firms adopting takeover defences finds no performance decline. See Johnson and Rao (1997: 660, 669) (surveying a range of financial measures with respect to more than 600 antitakeover amendments adopted between 1979 and 1985 and finding no adverse effect). Later performance improvement has even been detected. See Field and Karpoff (2002: 1883) (comparing initial public offering (IPO) firms with and without takeover defences and finding that defenceless firms underperform for the first two years but that there are no significant performance differences thereafter).

[82] See Roe (1994: 223–4) (discussing how US concentration trends slowed in the early 1980s and how, in the 1990s, they were only moving slightly toward the large blocks present in Japan and Germany); Gilson and Kraakman (1993: 1006–9) (mentioning several empirical studies that show a 'mildly positive relationship between active large-block shareholders and corporate performance'). It turned out that the incentives that supported blockholding abroad could not be replicated domestically. Path dependencies

Activist hedge funds broke the mould. They take significant equity stakes in target companies—generally 5% to 15% of the target's stock is the range. They mount hostile challenges to managers and business plans at publicly traded firms worldwide. They are impatient shareholders, who look for value and want it realized in the near or intermediate term. They tell managers how to realize the value and challenge publicly those who resist the advice, using the proxy contest as a threat. The strategy proved successful during the bull market run up to 2008.[83] The leading empirical study looks at the period 2001 to 2006 and pairs 236 activist hedge funds with 1059 publicly traded targets (Brav et al., Chapter 8, this volume). These activist engagements persist, albeit in diminished numbers since the financial collapse.[84] Whether the number of targets rises or falls in the future is unclear, because an upward stock market and ready credit together played an important role in facilitating the phenomenon.

The activist funds have drawn heavily on the financial agenda in the shareholders' agency-cost playbook.[85] There are four main means to the end of agency-cost reduction and value creation: increasing leverage, returning excess cash to shareholders, realizing premiums through the sale of going-concern assets, and cutting operating costs. The activists for the most part drew on the first three plays, using their newly discovered power to prompt borrowing, force the disgorgement of large cash accounts and the sale of operating divisions, and, in some cases, force the sale of the target company itself.[86] In contrast, the record on cost-cutting initiatives, which tend to require expertise and knowledge respecting internal operations, is sketchier (Bratton 2007: 1413–15).

Meanwhile, the activists' record of success further testifies to the capital markets' ability to adapt within the prevailing legal framework. The strategy, while hostile, only rarely looks to the market for corporate control (Bratton 2007: 1426–7). Instead, the players act out a game of threat and resistance, in which victory lies in either the target's diffusion of the threat with a governance concession or, in the larger number of cases, with the insurgent's entry to the boardroom as a minority blockholder. Payoff through board membership means taking the benefit of the richer informational base available inside the company and, in many cases, movement toward a cooperative outcome (Bratton 2007: 1428).[87]

within the system retarded its adaptability. At the same time, blockholding in other countries followed from their different political environments, particularly their stronger social democratic systems. See Bebchuk and Roe (1999: 169) (positing that path dependence causes advanced economies to differ in their ownership structure, despite pressures to converge); Roe (1996: 644–6) (describing how both path dependence and chaos theory account for variations in institutions, within a range of acceptable economic efficiency).

[83] See, e.g., Brav et al. (Chapter 8, this volume) (listing and discussing five motives for hedge fund activism and describing two examples of activist events).

[84] See, e.g., Hyatt (2009) (discussing how, despite decreasing hedge fund assets, the hedge fund industry still appeals to risk-taking activist investors looking for undervalued companies); Squire (2009) (describing the perfect situation for activist shareholders: enthusiasm for shareholder rights and distressed equity markets); Zuckerman (2009) (noting that while the flow of new activist engagements continues, funds have lost value in lockstep with market averages, leading to investor withdrawals).

[85] See *supra* text accompanying note 66.

[86] See Bratton (2007: 1390–401) (listing and describing four ways in which an activist investor with influence can get an immediate return on investment: get the target to sell itself, get the target to sell a major asset, get the target to pay out spare cash, or have the target change its long-term business plans).

[87] At the same time, activist hedge funds rely on trading-market liquidity to facilitate exit at a time of their own choosing (Bratton 2007: 1412–13).

Significantly, the appearance of these new blockholders can be explained by reference to the alignment of incentives bound up in their shareholding. Hedge funds are independent actors, where other institutional investors are not. They do not sell services to the class of companies they target and so, unlike conventional mutual fund advisors, are unconflicted (Bratton 2007: 1384). They lock up investor money for longer periods than do mutual funds and thus have time horizons better suited to governance activism (Bratton 2007: 1384). Finally, the funds in question concentrate on fundamental analysis (Bratton 2007: 1383) and so pick their targets on a fuller informational basis than customarily is the case with institutional equity investors.

It follows that the barriers to shareholder intervention embedded in the prevailing legal model are less salient than previously assumed. The problem lies less with the legal model and more with incentive constraints bound up in institutional shareholding. The landscape, however, is dynamic. The hedge funds have inspired interventions by large, mainstream investment advisors; they also have depended on and received the support of other, more passive institutional investors.[88] The emerging picture bespeaks the robustness of a system that channels shareholder inputs through the board-election franchise.

The point is not that hedge fund activism by itself reduces agency costs to zero.[89] Indeed, activist shareholder intervention, whether from a hedge fund blockholder or in the course of a private equity buyout, confirms the continued presence of the agency costs that shareholder proponents seek to control.[90] The point instead is that, given agency costs and the right incentive alignment, the system will address them aggressively, just as Jensen and Meckling predicted. With managers, the critical incentive change involved incentive compensation. With shareholders, the incentive barrier stemmed from the shareholders' own institutional frameworks. Once a framework conducive to governance intervention finally appeared, the capital markets provided ready support and the prevailing legal model proved facilitative.

21.3.3 Cash Payouts

Cash disgorgement is a leading shareholder agenda item. According to an account that Michael Jensen articulated in the 1980s, managers habitually hold on to their spare cash,

[88] See Kahan and Rock (2008: 14–17) (discussing changes in mutual funds, such as more activist behaviour, which is usually expected from hedge funds, and cooperation with hedge funds designed to pressure a target's management).

[89] Private equity, which carries blockholding to its logical conclusion, presents a telling comparison case. It has had a mesmerizing effect on some agency theorists, who have proposed ownership by private equity funds as a strong-form solution to the problem of separated ownership and control. See Gilson and Whitehead (2008: 231–2) (theorizing that private owners can transfer risk in discrete slices to parties who can manage or diversify away those risks, which serves as a lower-cost substitute for traditional risk capital); Jensen (1989) (encouraging private equity ownership as a solution to 'the conflict between owners and managers over the control and use of corporate resources').

[90] It also should be noted that agency costs at target companies do not by themselves necessarily trigger the requisite financial incentives for outside intervention. Buyouts thrive on cheap, available credit and occur cyclically with its availability (Bratton 2008: 521–3). Unsurprisingly, '[p]rivate equity volume plummeted 69 percent in 2008 because of the lack of credit' (Fortado 2009). Since then, many deals have been restructured, with equity swapped for debt. See Kelly and Keehner (2009) (discussing firms' employment of tools such as debt exchanges and equity infusions to restructure and save deals).

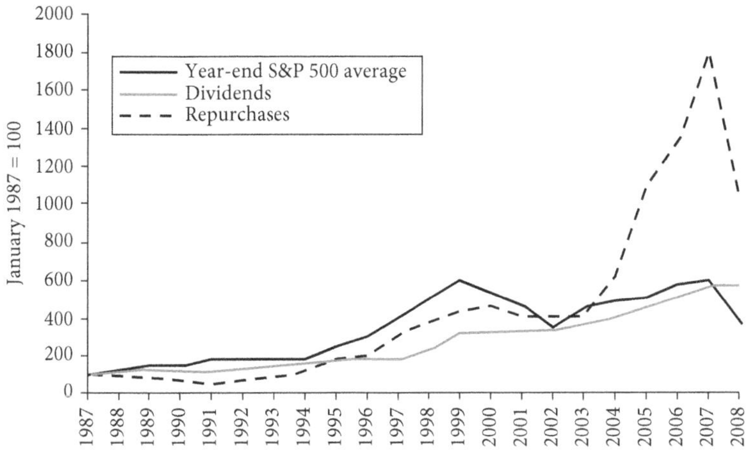

FIGURE 21.1 Payouts, 1987–2008

tending to reinvest it in suboptimal projects (1986: 323). Suboptimal reinvestment, together with conglomerate bust-up, was widely held to be the motivation for 1980s takeovers. It remains at the top of the shareholder financial agenda, even as empirical studies of the problem of suboptimal reinvestment of cash flow have produced mixed results.[91]

Whether or not cash retention remains a serious governance problem, the cash-disgorgement agenda registered in boardrooms with unprecedented success during the later stages of the most recent bull market. Figure 21.1 below tracks shareholder payouts in the form of dividends and stock repurchases by the companies in the S&P 500 from 1987 to 2007. The year 1987 is taken as the start date because it marks the beginning of a three-decade trend of increased resort to open-market repurchases by public companies.[92] The 1987 year-end S&P 500 average (247), the companies' total annual dividend payments in 1987 ($44.3 billion), and their 1987 total repurchases ($32.5 billion) are pegged at 100 on the vertical axis. Figure 21.1 shows relative increases and decreases to 2008, when the S&P 500 closed at 366, total dividends were $247 billion, and total repurchases were $340 billion. A break in two long-standing trends occurred in 2004. Prior thereto, increases in levels of dividends and levels of repurchases roughly tracked increases in stock prices (with both tending to lag behind the market). There was also a trend of rough parity between total dividends and total repurchases. Both trends ended in 2003 in favour of an increase in net amounts paid out, with the lion's share of the increase in the form of repurchases. In 1987, repurchases amounted to 1.6% of average market capitalization, and total payout amounted to 3.8%; in 2007, repurchases amounted to 4.6%, and total payout amounted to

[91] Compare Servaes (1994: 254) (looking at over 700 takeover targets during the period of 1972 to 1987 and finding overinvestment only in the larger firms in the sample and in the oil and gas industry), with Titman, Wei, and Xie (2003).

[92] The crash of 1987 amounted to an external shock that moved payout policy in the direction of repurchases. See Bratton (2005a: 871) ('[The] OMR [(open market repurchase)] advantage was first discovered in the wake of the stock market crash of 1987. The crash brought an unprecedented increase in OMR programs. . . .').

6.3%. The dollar amount of annual repurchases increased eighteenfold from 1987 to the peak year of 2007.[93]

Clearly, managers had become more attuned to the shareholder agenda.[94] Whether hedge fund activism played a role is a matter of speculation, but the suggestion arises.[95] The suggestion in the end leads us back to the Jensen and Meckling model. Given excess cash available for distribution, market-based demands for distribution will follow in the ordinary course.[96] The notable increase in overall levels paid out suggests an additional point: once the market input registers, many managers can be expected to respond voluntarily.

21.3.4 Summary

This section's title, 'Systemic Responsiveness', summarizes our reading of institutional changes within corporate governance. It is an agency-cost story that starts out at the same place and time as the shareholder story—namely, with the external shocks of the 1980s. The shocks—deregulation, globalization, and new technology—were exogenous to the corporate governance system but stemmed from endogenous adjustments elsewhere in the economy. The shareholder story freezes the frame at the end of the 1980s conflicts, making its case for law reform by depicting the governance system as static and unresponsive. We move the frame forward in time to show that the corporate governance system made a series of endogenous adjustments addressed to agency-cost control both in the boardroom and in the financial markets. Significantly, none of the changes described required resort to new regulation.

The prevailing legal model emerges as a constant factor in this picture of dynamic change. The constancy follows from the legal model's capaciousness. It sets out a minimal list of mandates—management by the board, annual election by the shareholders, and the managers' duty of loyalty. Within this framework, parties may conduct governance as they deem appropriate. Thus the model can accommodate management domination and shareholder passivity on the one hand and shareholder activism and management disempowerment on the other. Particular results follow from incentives, which in turn originate in contracts between the corporation and its managers and contracts between investing entities and their investors.

Our argument puts agency costs, as discussed in policy contexts, back in touch with their theoretical roots. Jensen and Meckling predicted not only dynamic adaptation toward the end of removing money from the table but an agency-cost residuum too costly for removal

[93] The pattern changed in other respects as well. Prior to 2004, numbers of outstanding shares tended to remain constant even as repurchase activity increased, with new issues of shares incident to merger activity and employee stock option exercises matching or exceeding numbers repurchased. From 2004 to 2007, in contrast, 65.1% of S&P 500 repurchasers reduced numbers of shares outstanding (Standard & Poor's 2007).

[94] The financial crisis materially chilled buyback activity in 2008, when 'S&P 500 buybacks reached $339.6 billion—a 42.3% drop from the record setting $589.1 billion spent during 2007' (Standard & Poor's 2008).

[95] A second factor also should be noted. As between dividends and repurchases, managers holding unexercised stock options have a financial incentive to make repurchases (Bratton 2005a: 872–6).

[96] Even as the pattern began to change in 2004 and 2005, Wall Street analysts were complaining that corporations were husbanding cash at historically high levels. See, e.g., Bratton (2007: 1394) (noting that in 2006 'the S&P 500's cash accounts stood at the highest point since the early 1980s' and that shareholders maintained the position that free cash flow should be paid out).

through private ordering. An important point follows: persistent residual agency costs do not by themselves justify regulatory intervention. The cost–benefit case for reducing residual agency costs by regulation must be made independently, and it may lead to the conclusion that the participants are better off bearing the residual costs. The shareholders emphasize benefits only, ignoring the costs implied by their suggested reforms. Section 21.4 confronts these costs.

We close this section with three caveats respecting normative implications. First, this is a positive account, put forward to import balance to the factual background in which shareholder reform proposals are evaluated and to denude it of any suggestion of economic urgency. Second, the endogenous changes we describe have contractual origins and so benefit from a normative presumption in their favour. But normative questions are by no means foreclosed. We will ask a few of our own, respecting equity incentive pay, in Sections 21.4 and 21.5. Third, our picture of systemic responsiveness would, if extended to the extreme, imply that law is irrelevant. We would not make this extension. To the contrary, we think that law matters here because it accords the board of directors a zone of discretion in which to make informed business decisions disfavoured by the market, a view presented more fully in Section 21.4.

21.4 Shareholder Empowerment and Economic Theory

Everybody agrees that managers know more than shareholders. Everybody also agrees that agency costs arise when managers use this informational advantage for their own gain. The result is one of the paradigmatic problems that corporate law tries to solve. Shareholder advocates would address the problem by giving the shareholders sufficient power to impress their preferences, as expressed in market price signals, upon the managers. This gives rise to two key questions: what do the shareholders whose trades shape market prices actually know, and what does the market price teach the wider group of shareholders? Shareholder empowerment assumes that the price setters know quite a bit and that the wider group learns a lot from the price the former set, including not only the true value of the corporation but answers to specific questions such as whether or not managers are doing a good enough job to deserve the compensation proposed by the board of directors. In this section, we appraise these assumptions, addressing the question of what shareholders actually know and taking into account not only the traditional literature on information asymmetries but also the emerging literature on heterogeneous expectations.

We begin on the positive side of the street, stating the best case for shareholder empowerment. This conjoins the semi-strong form of the Efficient Capital Market Hypothesis (ECMH) and the Capital Asset Pricing Model (CAPM) to depict a world in which market prices, although reflecting only information from past market prices and current publicly available information, accurately reflect expectations respecting future fundamental value. We show that the market price, thus modelled, can indeed signal a need to reduce agency costs. But we also highlight a problem of diminishing returns. The market price sends reliable governance signals only in a subset of cases characterized by clear-cut issues and minimal information asymmetries. As governance issues become more complex and information asymmetries more pervasive, market signals become difficult to read.

We then cross to the negative side of the street to confront a critical question: if management's informational superiority presents a paradigmatic problem, how does the stock price surmount the information asymmetry barrier? The answer is that it does not. Strong-form efficiency, under which the stock price impounds all private as well as public information, does not hold; hence, managers know more than they disclose and the stock price does not impound the undisclosed information. Traditional ECMH makes a relatively modest claim respecting the informativeness of the market price. Its implications for corporate governance are therefore modest.

Finally, we tread deeper into negative territory to ask what happens when managers shape business policy to cater to uninformed market prices. This inquiry upsets the neatness of even the limited claims that market efficiency holds for corporate governance. New corporate finance models based on heterogeneous expectations make particularly stark projections of suboptimal results. The heterogeneity models show that the information conveyed by the price sometimes can be misleading for purposes of business policymaking. These periods, although limited, are important.

We go on to explore these models' implications for corporate governance, reaching two critical conclusions: First, shareholder empowerment will make it much more difficult for a good board of directors to resist pressures to manage to the market. This can lead to bad business decisions, either due to information asymmetry or a run of speculative mispricing. Second, incentive-compatible executive compensation and shareholder empowerment are inconsistent goals. If executive compensation can be fixed by requiring longer holding periods, it is then turned around and unfixed if managers are encouraged to manage the market as a response to shareholder empowerment.

We note a methodological constraint. We confine our economic evaluation to the rational-expectations framework held out by traditional financial economics. We think this 'high church' literature more than suffices to undercut the case for shareholder empowerment. At the same time, we acknowledge a significant body of behavioural work on market pricing, both theoretical and empirical.[97] We omit reference to it for simplicity, toward the end of avoiding an unnecessary excursion onto disputed methodological territory.

[97] These studies focus on sentiment, investment styles, and asset tastes. For a review of the behavioural finance literature, including studies in trading activity, research in corporate finance, and analyses of stock returns, see Subrahmanyam (2007). Traditional pricing theory holds that the prices of two assets move together as a result of co-movement in fundamental value. But, given market frictions, limits to arbitrage, and irrational (or 'sentimental') investors, co-movement might have other causes. Coordinated demand, then, influences prices. See Baker and Wurgler (2006: 1648–50) (examining sentiment's impact on the cross section of stock returns from 1963 to 2001 and showing that high-sentiment investors gravitate to young, small, unprofitable growth stocks or distressed issues, while low-sentiment investors like large, profitable dividend payers, and that abrupt changes in sentiment result in demand shocks for sensitive stocks); Barberis, Shleifer, and Wurgler (2005: 284) (showing that investors group assets into categories); Barberis and Shleifer (2003: 162–4) (examining the impact of style investing on institutional and individual investors); Gompers and Metrick (2001: 244) (showing that institutions like large, liquid stocks with relatively low returns in the year prior to purchase, and that institutional demand for large issues accounted for nearly 50% of the issues' relative price appreciation of large over small stocks across the period 1980 to 1996); Kumar and Lee (2006: 2453–4) (showing that retail investors tend to nest in small firms, lower-price firms, firms with relatively low levels of institutional ownership, and value firms).

Section 21.4.1 shows what market pricing efficiency can and cannot do for the shareholder case. Section 21.4.2, describing the pricing salience of information asymmetries, shows that the best case is incomplete. Section 21.4.3 details the impact of heterogeneous investor expectations and the value-destructive effects of managing to a speculative market.

21.4.1 Pricing Efficiency and the Case for Shareholder Empowerment

If financial markets were strong-form efficient, stock prices would fully and correctly reflect all relevant information, both public and private. In such a state of the world, the shareholder proponents' case would be compelling, and the paradigmatic problem of corporate law would vanish. Shareholders could know as much as the managers if they carefully scrutinized the stock price and attended to public disclosures and leaks of material non-public information. Powerful implications for corporate governance would obtain.

If shareholders were thus informed, directors might understandably view themselves more as agents of the shareholders and less as their trustees. As faithful agents, the directors would seek to learn their principals' wishes. The financial market would hold out the best source of this information, since the movement of stock prices would reveal the shareholders' well-informed preferences respecting corporate developments. Managers might even vet investment decisions with the market and observe the pricing effect, adopting strategies leading to stock price increases and abandoning those leading to stock price declines.

But this is not the state of the world according to the modern corporate finance literature, a literature with complex and easily misunderstood implications for corporate governance. We explore these below and contend that one thing is clear: shareholder proponents wrongly assume that agency costs can be reduced without countervailing negative effects when directors act more like agents and manage to shareholder preferences signalled in market prices.

21.4.1.1 *ECMH, CAPM, and the Value of a Share*

Markets would be strong-form efficient if they priced in all information—material non-public information as well as all public information. It is, however, generally accepted that financial markets are not strong-form efficient.[98] In contrast, ECMH's semi-strong form is generally accepted. This, sometimes called 'informational efficiency', posits that the capital markets embed all publicly available information into security prices.[99] It has

[98] See, e.g., Ross, Westerfield, and Jaffe (2002: 359) ('Even the strongest adherents to the efficient-market hypothesis would not be surprised to find that markets are inefficient in the strong form.').

[99] See Malkiel (1992: 739). ECMH asserts that the stock market possesses efficiency attributes in terms of three alternative, progressively more inclusive information sets (see, e.g., Malkiel 1992: 739–41). The first, or weak form, defines market efficiency in terms of past market prices. The market is efficient according to the weak form if investors cannot predict future stock price movements based on an information set containing all past price movements. As noted in the text, the second, or semi-strong form, defines market efficiency in terms of all publicly available information. The third, or strong form, includes non-public information as part of the information set. Markets are efficient according to the strong form if stock prices include all non-public information as well as public information.

two implications: first, that no trading strategy based on public information can regularly outperform the market,[100] and, second, that insiders who possess non-public information can outperform the market when trading in their own stock.[101] The latter point is hardly surprising since it means that insiders, even after making all required disclosures, remain better informed than outsiders. Add this up and an important point emerges for our argument: informational asymmetries exist in tandem with 'informational efficiency', with the managers and directors having the informational advantage.

Now for a second key point: the informational efficiency posited by ECMH does not imply that the share price equals the pro rata value of the discounted free cash flows of the corporation.[102] This is a point that is often misunderstood. To say that no investment strategy can outperform the market does not in itself say anything about the stock price's accuracy in measuring the corporation's fundamental value—that is, the discounted value of expected future free cash flows. ECMH only requires that stock price movements mirror a random walk (Brealey, Myers, and Allen 2006: 333–41), and, as long as stock price movements are random, outguessing the market is not possible. Whether the random walk moves around, away from, or ultimately always stumbles into the correct price is another matter. To evaluate this possibility, we must look to CAPM.

The corporation is a collection of assets and its value is the free cash flow that those assets are expected to generate into the indefinite future. CAPM provides the discount rate needed to state those expected future free cash flows as a present value.[103] The discount rate reflects the riskiness of the expected flows—the more risky the flows, the higher the discount rate and the lower the present value. CAPM is a theory of risk that boils down to the assertion that a given corporation's discount rate will be proportional to its expected future free cash flows' covariance with the economy's free cash flows.

With these building blocks, we can further investigate the question whether efficient stock prices provide an accurate measure of the fundamental value of the corporation—that is, the discounted value of the firm's expected future free cash flows. All turns on the word 'expected' in the concept of 'expected free cash flows'. Since future results are unknowable, fundamental value turns on expected rather than actual cash flows. Nothing in the theory even remotely suggests that these future expectations will be borne out by the passage of time. Expectations can turn out to be wildly incorrect.

Consequently, if the strong form were to hold, an investor who was privy to both private and non-private information could not consistently earn abnormally large investment returns.

[100] See Malkiel (1992: 739) (asserting that under the 'semi-strong form of EMH ... an analysis of balance sheets, income statements, announcements of dividend changes or stock splits or any other public information about a company ... will not yield abnormal economic profits').

[101] See Meulbroek (1992: 1696) ('The analysis suggests that insider trading increases stock price accuracy by moving stock prices significantly.'); see also Jenter (2005: 1906) (showing that managers trade as contrarians and earn excess returns on their trades, but that the excess returns disappear after controlling for size and book-to-market effects).

[102] See Campbell, Lo, and MacKinlay (1997: 24–5) (discussing reasons why 'perfect [stock] efficiency is an unrealistic benchmark that is unlikely to hold in practice').

[103] See Lintner (1965: 27) ('The analysis thus justifies viewing market values as riskless-rate present values of certainty-equivalents of random future receipts ....' (italics omitted)); Sharpe (1964: 436–42) (describing the 'consistent relationship between ... expected returns and what might best be called *systematic risk*').

Despite this, the statement that 'stock market prices are always correct' remains near to being definitionally true. The syllogism is the following: first, financial markets do capture future expectations more reliably than any other mechanism; second, fundamental value turns on expectations of the future free cash flows. Since the market provides the most reliable estimate of future expectations, it is reasonable to define value in terms of market price.

The market-based definition of value is particularly appealing for corporate law because it follows from the valuations of willing buyers and sellers. A key assumption in this line of reasoning, homogeneity of expectations, further enhances its appeal.[104] CAPM assumes that all individuals have access to all of the publicly available information and reach the same expectations about the future. As a result, CAPM assumes that all investors employ the same valuation metrics and share prevailing market expectations. Shareholders, market price setters, and passive proxy voters alike become one. Under this model of value, the shareholders expeditiously can deliver governance instructions through the market price. To see how, imagine that a shareholders' meeting was convened to set a value on the company. Under this unitary model of the shareholder, the resulting value would be the market price; it follows that the meeting need not be called in the first place. More generally, under an agency model of the corporation, the manager-agents should look to the market price for the principal's instructions.

Of course, expectations do differ among investors in the real world. One still might believe that the market price reflects the average shareholder's expectations and so provides a reliable proxy for fundamental value. As we shall see below, however, switching to an assumption of heterogeneous expectations generates results that lead to profoundly different implications for corporate law.

21.4.1.2 *Implications for the Case for Shareholder Empowerment*

Shareholder proponents take the market price, as modelled in traditional financial economics, as the best available projection of a corporation's expected future cash flows. They then hold it out as an essential point of reference in the detection and reduction of management agency costs. They do not deny the existence of information asymmetries but, at least implicitly, assume them to have been minimized by increases in market efficiency and a thick layer of disclosure requirements.[105]

A hostile tender offer for a publicly traded company presents the best case for this approach. Hypothesize an offer at a substantial premium over the market price and incumbent managers who contend that their business plan holds out superior prospects for long-term value enhancement. How should the target's directors respond? With minimal information asymmetries, the answer is clear: the directors should accept the voice of the shareholders as expressed through the market price, which elevates the bid price over the incumbents' business plan.

The case is easy because information asymmetries do not complicate it. In the shareholder proponents' view, when management holds out its business plan as superior in the

[104] See Sharpe (1964: 433–4) (assuming 'homogeneity of investor expectations' as a condition for equilibrium in capital markets).

[105] See Gordon (2007: 1548–63) (describing the increase in the content and scope of mandated disclosures over the last fifty years and suggesting a causal role in the rise of the independent board).

teeth of the market's rejection, it inappropriately uses its position of informational superiority as an excuse for what amounts to self-interested entrenchment. In the informationally rich environment of the takeover market, it can be argued that informational asymmetries are at their lowest level. Given this, the shareholders know the value of the corporation substantially as well as the managers do. It follows that the market price is the only metric needed to decide the appropriate outcome and that the legal rule should allow shareholders to decide the contest for control at the tendering stage.

Now consider a more difficult case, which concerns the selection of the terms of an executive compensation scheme. In theory, a given scheme should be geared to the recent performance of the individual executives. This recent data, however, will not be fully available to the public. Even given the full set of data, choices remain respecting the terms of the performance-based compensation scheme. The actor designing the package must exercise judgment, for, in practice, there is no generally accepted template that sets out the terms of an optimal package.[106] Now imagine a package assembled and submitted to the shareholders pursuant to a 'Say on Pay' mandate. How will the shareholders evaluate the plan? Given all of the above, the vote likely will reflect levels of satisfaction with recent price performance rather than considered views about optimal incentive pay or the full set of performance data, much of which will remain unobservable.

More generally, as information asymmetries become greater in scope, which occurs as business-policy choices become more complex, the stock price becomes less an objective report on a particular value outcome and more an input for interpretation. Policymaking becomes an exercise calling for inside information, experience, and sound business judgment. The tie between inputs garnered from shareholder votes, which in turn reflect overall levels of satisfaction with price performance, and the reduction of particular agency costs becomes much attenuated.

Shareholder proponents do not deny this even as they seek to open doors to shareholder intervention. They avoid the trap of recommending that uninformed shareholders routinely make business decisions by focusing on deterrent effects.[107] Shareholder intervention emerges as a potential threat that managers will avoid by managing to the market. The proponents' case accordingly turns on an implicit assertion: information asymmetries are small relative to the agency costs at stake, so that managing to the market either brings positive results or does no harm.

We disagree with the assertion. The importance of information asymmetries relative to agency costs is an empirical question to which no one has an answer. The best that can be said for the shareholders is that their agenda's credibility improves to the extent that information asymmetries are minimal. But minimal information deficits cannot safely be assumed. Section 21.4.2, which follows, shows that information asymmetries are real. Section 21.4.2 goes on to address the claim that managing to the market can do no harm, showing that managing to an uninformed market price can result in suboptimal business policy. That problem reemerges in more acute form in Section 21.4.3, which discusses speculative overpricing under heterogeneous expectations.

[106] For a presentation of the range of positions taken in the literature, see Bratton (2005b: 1562–75) (reviewing Bebchuk and Fried 2004).

[107] See *supra* text accompanying note 63.

21.4.2 The Information Asymmetry Problem

We have seen that strong-form efficiency would support a nearly unassailable case for shareholder empowerment. But financial markets are not strong-form efficient. Information asymmetries are real. Empirical studies confirm this point beyond doubt, showing that managers who trade in their corporation's shares earn abnormally high returns.[108]

Information asymmetries make it difficult for the market to project accurately the free cash flows that the corporation will produce. The difficulties extend to ascertainment of a capitalization rate,[109] as well as to the projection of future free cash flows. This subsection explores the implications of these difficulties for corporate governance. It makes two points. First, information asymmetries are not going to go away. Second, the evidence confirms their status as a salient factor in business policymaking. Systemic change that forced management to the market price would enhance their salience, increasing agency costs. An uninformed market is structurally incapable of sending business policymakers a determinative signal. It follows that, given asymmetric information, market signals need to be interpreted on a continuous basis rather than followed blindly. The job of interpretation is an intrinsic management function.

21.4.2.1 *Persistence*

If information asymmetries would just go away, the case for shareholder empowerment would be straightforward. Yet shareholder proponents do not seek a level informational playing field. There is no call for full disclosure in the form of a requirement that corporations disclose all relevant information,[110] a requirement presently absent from both the federal securities laws and state corporate law.

Nor should there be. Corporate finance theory holds that full disclosure by the firm is prohibitively costly.[111] Full (or fuller) disclosure carries costs of reduced incentives, increased regulation, and the proprietary cost that follows from sharing private information with competing firms. It also holds out benefits. Better quality disclosure can reduce the firm's equity cost of capital and enhance the liquidity of its publicly traded securities. In equilibrium, the

[108] See Baker, Ruback, and Wurgler (2007: 149) (asserting that 'corporate managers have superior information about their own firm', which 'is underscored by the evidence that managers earn abnormally high returns on their own trades').

[109] It bears noting that the informational imbalance impacts both sides of the valuation exercise—the ascertainment of the discount rate as well as the projection of future free cash flows. See Wachter (2003: 792–3) (discussing the inability of existing models to accurately estimate the discount or market capitalization rates). CAPM provides the most common approach for accessing the risk premium in the discount rate. More specifically, it employs an empirically derived single risk factor, beta(β), that measures a given stock's contribution to the systematic risk in the market portfolio. Although betas customarily are estimated from market data, the true underlying beta depends on the covariance of the firm's free cash flows with the overall market's free cash flows, factors that may be better known by the managers than the market.

[110] We have seen that this is Fama and Jensen's basic point. See *supra* text accompanying note 23.

[111] See Grossman and Hart (1980: 323–4) (illustrating formally that full disclosure presupposes three conditions: (1) that investors know that firms possess the information; (2) that affirmative misrepresentation does not occur; and (3) that disclosure is costless).

level of disclosure follows from a trade-off of these costs and benefits, with different firms gravitating to different disclosure levels.[112] Several mechanisms reduce the asymmetry without eliminating it—the mandatory disclosure system, the work of financial analysts, and the investigations of large, activist shareholders.[113] The magnitude of the resulting imbalance varies from firm to firm, becoming more severe as the duration of the firm's investments increases, the firm's business plan focuses on growth, and the firm's size is smaller.[114]

21.4.2.2 *Evidence and Effects*

Information asymmetries figure prominently in leading economic accounts of corporate financial practices.[115] Simply, managers take advantage of market overvaluation to tap the equity markets. The pattern shows up both with initial public offerings (IPOs) and equity offerings by seasoned issuers. For example, studies show that IPOs are positively correlated with *ex ante* indicators of overpricing, such as the industry's market-to-book ratios and stock indices.[116]

[112] See Core (2001: 442–4):

> This choice involves trading off the reduction in the information asymmetry component of the cost of capital that results from increased disclosure quality against the costs of reduced incentives, litigation costs, and proprietary costs. (citations omitted).

[113] See Stein (2003: 115) (noting that even as governance processes, capital structure, incentive contracts, intermediation, and the mandatory disclosure regime reduce informational distortions, some remain unresolved and relevant in equilibrium).

[114] For example, a long-established business with no growth opportunities confronts a relatively small information asymmetry problem. It, accordingly, will have little incentive to go beyond mandated disclosure items. In contrast, a firm with abundant growth opportunities and a more complicated information set has a more serious information asymmetry problem. Depending on the interplay of costs and benefits, its managers may find it advantageous to make additional voluntary disclosures. See Core (2001: 443) (examining which firms will find it optimal to make voluntary disclosures); see also Healy and Palepu (2001: 420–5) (examining the motives behind voluntary disclosure). Investor relations also influence these choices—firms with large analyst followings and large populations of institutional investors tend to disclose more. See Healy and Palepu (2001: 416–18) (suggesting that management might voluntarily disclose where analysts give favourable ratings); Healy, Hutton, and Palepu (1999: 488–90) (noting that a multivariate analysis demonstrated that 'increased disclosure is related to . . . growth in institutional ownership and analyst coverage'). Finally, as the shareholder proponents assert, agency costs also play into the mix. Managers have incentives to make self-serving disclosures. See Healy and Palepu (2001: 421, 425) (explaining that managers have incentives to make capital-cost-lowering disclosures). Ultimately, the credibility of any firm's disclosures (and hence the firm's proximity to the optimal level and quality of disclosure) depends on the effectiveness of its governance. See Core (2001: 444) ('[I]t is the governance structure that constrains the manager to follow optimal policy.'). Empirical literature supports all of the foregoing points. See Leuz and Wysocki (2008: 23–38).

[115] See, e.g., Leland and Pyle (1977: 372) (noting that while an entrepreneur may not be able to directly convey inside information, he/she may be able to signal that information to potential shareholders based on the fraction of equity that he/she retains); Miller and Rock (1985: 1031) (arguing that 'managers know more than outside investors about the true state of the firm's current earnings'); Ross (1977: 27–31) (developing a model that establishes a signalling equilibrium based on the assumption that managers have inside information).

[116] See Baker, Ruback, and Wurgler (2007: 159–60) (surveying literature that suggests equity issuance is correlated with overvaluation); Lerner (1994: 293–4, 299) (finding, in a comparison of the number of IPOs and a biotechnology equity index, that venture capitalists time IPOs and that 'IPOs coincide with the peaks in equity valuations'); Loughran, Ritter, and Rydqvist (1994: 166) (finding that, in fourteen of

Seasoned issuers keep an eye out for market windows: a survey of corporate CFOs shows that two-thirds look for market overvaluation before issuing equity.[117] Studies also show that IPO issuers underperform relative to comparables for years after the offering,[118] with the underperformance serving as *ex post* confirmation of overpricing at the time of the offering. The same result occurs in the years after seasoned issuers sell more stock—the range of underperformance relative to the market is 20% to 40% during the subsequent five years.[119] Unsurprisingly, the asymmetrically informed markets react negatively to the very announcement of a new stock offering. This limits the availability of equity as a financing alternative, particularly when the managers deem their stock to be underpriced or correctly priced.[120]

Perceived undervaluation also drives financing choices, but in the opposite direction. These companies finance with debt rather than equity.[121] And, instead of selling more stock, they repurchase stock previously issued. Subsequent returns on repurchased stock are positive, running 12% above those on comparables over four years.[122] Significantly, although the announcement of

the fifteen countries examined, 'IPO volume is positively correlated with the inflation-adjusted level of the stock market'); Pagano, Panetta, and Zingales (1998: 28) (finding that 'the main factor affecting the probability of an IPO is the market-to-book ratio at which firms in the same industry trade').

[117] See Baker, Ruback, and Wurgler (2007: 159):

> Several lines of evidence suggest that overvaluation is a motive for equity issuance.... [Two-thirds] of CFOs of public corporations... state that 'the amount by which our stock is undervalued or overvalued was an important or very important consideration' in issuing equity. (citations omitted).

[118] See Ritter (1991: 3) (contending that 'in the long-run, initial public offerings appear to be overpriced', and finding that 'in the 3 years after going public these firms significantly underperformed a set of comparable firms matched by size and industry'). Several empirical studies have also found that for IPOs declining profitability and investment after the IPOs suggest that the issuances were incidences of market timing. See Pagano, Panetta, and Zingales (1998: 28–9) ('Our finding that investment and profitability decrease after the IPO points to the [attempt-to-time-the-market] explanation.').

[119] See Baker, Ruback, and Wurgler (2007: 160) ('[O]n average, US equity issues under-perform the market somewhere in the ballpark of 20–40% over five years'); see also Baker and Wurgler (2000: 2219):

> When equity prices are too high, existing shareholders benefit by issuing overvalued equity. When equity prices are too low, issuing debt is preferable. Consistent with this timing hypothesis, firms issuing equity have poor subsequent performance.

[120] Managers who believe their stock to be correctly priced or underpriced will avoid selling new equity, financing with debt or internal cash flow. See Stein (2003: 118–19) (examining models of debt financing or cash-flow financing). Managers of firms with good potential investments but constraints on these sources of financing must sell new equity or forego the investments. They are forced to time their financing, and hence their investment, to the under-informed market price, with a sacrifice of flexibility. See Baker, Stein, and Wurgler (2003: 986–90) (showing that investment by firms with financing constraints is sensitive to the market price).

[121] See Hovakimian, Opler, and Titman (2001: 3–4) (determining that 'firms with higher current stock prices (relative to their past stock prices, book values, or earnings) are more likely to issue equity rather than debt and repurchase debt rather than equity' and that this finding is 'consistent with agency and information asymmetry models where managers are either reluctant to issue equity at low prices or have an incentive to boost their leverage when the stock prices are low'); Marsh (1982: 133) (finding that the total amount of UK companies' equity and debt issues is related to the performance of the stock and bond markets).

[122] See Ikenberry, Lakonishok, and Vermaelen (1995: 184) ('Beginning in the month following the repurchase announcement, the average buy-and-hold return over the next four years is more than 12% above that of a control portfolio.').

a repurchase program means a small bump for the stock price, the pattern of positive subsequent returns shows that the market does not fully assimilate the signal's informational content.[123]

Information asymmetries also lead to complications for corporate investment policy. The complications arise when managers manage to the market, factoring expected stock price reactions into their decisions. To see the complications, hypothesize a company with a new, long-term investment project. The new project is complicated and so presents the market with a costly and lengthy exercise in valuation. As a result, the new project is likely to be mispriced by the market.[124] Given managers who cater to the stock price, the risk of underpricing may lead management to pass up the opportunity.[125] The greater the stress on keeping up the stock price, the more likely this suboptimal result.

Given an uninformed market and managers inclined to cater to the price, investment decisions may be keyed to what the market expects—its schematized picture of the company and its strategy and prospects. When a manager sees an opportunity not yet in the market's picture of the company and predicts that the market will react negatively to a shift in emphasis, he/she must undertake a process of informational mediation. The result is costly delay.[126] Contrariwise, if the market expects a company to invest in a line of business that the market believes will be highly

[123] See Ikenberry, Lakonishok, and Vermaelen (1995: 184) ('The most striking finding . . . is that the information conveyed by open market share repurchases is largely ignored.').

[124] See Shleifer and Vishny (1990: 148) ('The time to disappearance of mispricing depends on how fast . . . investor misperceptions are corrected. . . .'). There are numerous articles providing empirical confirmation of this mispricing. See, e.g., Holden and Lundstrum (2005: 3–4) (showing that firms selected for long-term traded options (and hence a lower cost of trading on long-term information) increased their research and development (R&D) to sales ratios 23% to 28% compared with matching firms not selected for long-term traded options in the two years following selection); see also Stein (1988: 63–7) (showing formally that, even absent agency costs, managers of a firm threatened by a takeover will sell an underpriced asset).

We note that direct empirical testing of these assertions is difficult. This follows from the nature of the phenomenon predicted—underinvestment tends to be unobservable by the market. See Stein (1988: 131) (noting that models of investment can be difficult to test because underinvestment occurs in 'activities that are not directly observable by the market' (emphasis omitted)). Market-timing studies showing that firms issuing equity have strong operating numbers two years prior to the issuance and weak numbers thereafter provide indirect evidence, with underinvestment prior to the offering as a possible cause of the earnings pattern. See Stein (1988: 132) (examining studies where circumstantial evidence of underinvestment results from such an earnings pattern).

[125] See Kihlstrom and Wachter (2003: 551–6) (showing formally that managers vulnerable to a hostile offer and having better information about prospective investments will forego unpopular investment opportunities and fail to maximize the value of the corporation); Stein (1989: 667) (modelling suboptimal investment where managers maximize a weighted average of near-term stock prices and long-run value); see also Miller and Rock (1985: 1031–3) (presenting a model of shareholder investment and management decision-making where asymmetric information leads to suboptimal levels of investment); Narayanan (1985: 1469–70) (showing that reputational incentives can lead to underinvestment).

[126] See Aghion and Stein (2008: 1025) (creating a model in which managers can devote resources to either increasing sales growth or improving per-unit profit margins and arguing that devoting resources to one end necessarily means sacrificing the other). As modelled, the market puts more weight on growth metrics when it sees a growth firm and more weight on cost-cutting metrics when it sees a business plan focused on profit margins (Aghion and Stein 2008: 1032–5). Problems arise for a manager who decides, as events unfold in the product market, to move from a growth posture to present-profit maximization. The manager devises strategies in a two-way feedback process with the market and so delays shifting resources from growth to cost cutting until such time as the market can appreciate the business wisdom

profitable in the future, the managers will feel pressured to make the market-favoured investment even if they understand that it is suboptimal based on their superior, contrarian information.[127]

Excessive concern about stock price effects also leads to earnings management, which can in turn lead to underinvestment. In a world where institutional fund managers benchmark portfolios by reference to quarterly earnings per share (EPS),[128] sensitivity to stock market reactions implies a focus on quarterly earnings numbers.[129] Once management prioritizes meeting the market's EPS expectations, investments that enhance long-term value but impair near-term earnings may be delayed or foregone.[130] Unsurprisingly, the more sensitive a given CEO's pay is to the stock price, the higher the level of earnings management at the firm.[131]

of the shift (Aghion and Stein 2008: 1027, 1042–3). The delay is suboptimal, and the later change of direction is abrupt. The more the manager cares about the stock price, the more dramatic the oscillation (Aghion and Stein 2008: 1035).

[127] See Bebchuk and Stole (1993: 720) (demonstrating that, where information about long-term investment is available to investors, overinvestment may result because long-term investment may be seen as a signal of a positive long-term outlook). Carrying this out a step, similarly situated managers with reputational concerns may 'herd' into a subset of favoured but suboptimal investments (see Stein 2003: 132–3); see also Fisch (2006: 672) (describing the connection between overvalued stock and value-destroying decision-making).

[128] See Rappaport (2005: 65) (discussing investors' and managers' 'mutually reinforcing obsession with short-term performance'). In addition, those who actively manage their portfolios tend to hold stocks for short periods (Rappaport 2005: 66–8).

[129] Managers have been shown to be more sensitive to accounting earnings than to cash flows. See Graham, Harvey, and Rajgopal (2005: 6) ('[A]ccounting earnings matter more to managers than cash flows for financial reporting purposes. . . .').

[130] Investment activity can negatively impact near-term earnings because the amount funded must be expensed, as is the case with R&D costs. Prioritizing earnings can also mean delaying other expenses, such as maintenance or advertising, even though management believes that present action enhances long-term firm value. Alternatively, managers making a capital investment decision can face a choice between one project with higher later cash flows and higher present value (but lower near-term earnings) and a project with higher earlier cash flows and lower present value (but higher near-term earnings). For one study which examines such choices, see Bhojraj and Libby (2005: 2). Maximizing long-term value signals the first investment, while maximizing near-term EPS signals the second.

Numerous scholars have tested this empirically. See Bushee (1998: 306–7, 319–30) (showing that a responsive reduction of R&D spending is likely in firms with low institutional holdings, but that in firms whose predominant owners are institutions with high portfolio turnover and momentum trading strategies ('transient' institutions), earnings management through R&D cuts is very likely); Bushee (1999: 2–3) (showing a weak institutional preference for near-term earnings amongst institutions as a whole, but a strong preference for near-term earnings within the transient subset, along with a concomitant tendency to hold companies whose stock is mispriced); see also Cheng, Subramanyam, and Zhang (2005: 1–4) (using voluntary earnings guidance as a proxy for managing to the market). There is also survey evidence of this phenomenon. See Graham, Harvey, and Rajgopal (2005: 32–5, 35 fig.5) (surveying 401 chief financial officers and reporting that nearly 80% said that they would decrease discretionary spending on R&D or advertising to meet earnings targets, and just over 55% said that they would delay a new project despite a small sacrifice in value); see also Graham, Harvey, and Rajgopal (2006: 9–10) (reporting that only 59% of the same group of executives would approve a high net present value project if it entailed missing earnings by .10).

[131] See Bergstresser and Philippon (2006: 512–13) (finding evidence that CEOs whose compensation is more closely tied to share price 'more aggressively use discretionary components of earnings to affect their firms' reported performance'). Otherwise, the underinvestment problem can be expected to be

In summary, maximizing the corporation's fundamental value and maximizing its stock price can amount to distinct objectives in the presence of information asymmetries. Directors can attach a value to the corporation that is not only different from that reflected in the market price but better informed. When directors opt to maximize the stock's present appeal they may in the end sacrifice long-term shareholder value. Consequently, managing to an under-informed market price holds out intrinsic risks for business policy, particularly investment policy.

21.4.2.3 *Idiosyncratic Volatility*

We note that a recent line of empirical studies is thought to cut against the foregoing results. These studies assert that the shareholders' information asymmetry problem diminished substantially as the securities markets developed and deepened over the last half-century. They track the quantum of stock price variation explained by movements across the market as a whole, showing a substantial diminution over time, along with a concomitant increase in firm-specific, or 'idiosyncratic', volatility.[132] The more particular implication, according to proponents of one reading of the data, is that market traders have somehow obtained enhanced access to private information.[133] How that might have happened, however, is not explained. The evidence, moreover, is indirect, inferential, and in dispute.[134] The literature holds out at least four competing explanations of the data,[135] resulting in a state of explanatory gridlock.

at its most acute when management has particularly strong incentives to please the market, as happens when new equity finance is needed or with takeover pressure.

[132] According to one study, it was thirty times higher in 1997 than in 1962. See Campbell et al. (2001: 24 fig.5) (showing that variance for a typical firm was thirty times higher in 1997 than in 1962, while the equally weighted average R^2 statistic of a market model declined from 0.26 to 0.08 across the same period). The studies follow from Richard Roll (1988), which showed that market models could explain a lesser quantum of daily volatility than previously had been assumed (Roll 1988: 542–3).

[133] If that is the case, then the information asymmetry problem has been ameliorated to some extent. Carrying this point a step further, some proponents posit that good managers look to the stock price to get good instructions for business policy, claiming not only well-informed but accurate stock prices. See Durney et al. (2003: 798–9) (evidencing an empirical connection between low R^2 and the informativeness of the stock price, and, by implication, its accuracy); Durney, Morck, and Yeung (2004: 89) (finding better-quality investment decision-making at low R^2 firms, thus suggesting that informative stock prices facilitate efficient investment); see also Chen, Goldstein, and Jiang (2007: 620–3) (showing a further correlation between stock price variation and the sensitivity of the firm's level of investment to its stock price).

[134] Even the studies' authors point to their weaknesses: the evidence as to price informativeness is only indirect, the implications are a matter of 'theoretical conjecture', and other factors could be involved (Durney, Morck, and Yeung 2004: 69); see also Chen, Goldstein, and Jiang (2007: 625):

> Admittedly, it is . . . possible that our measures are correlated with other factors. . . . We believe that our extensive robustness tests mitigate this concern to a large extent. But, it remains possible that something else is behind our results.

Idiosyncratic volatility, then, does not prove that the price has become better informed and more accurate—it only suggests such.

[135] The stepped-up volatility could also reflect (1) trading 'frenzy unrelated to concrete information' (Roll 1988: 566); (2) increased cash flow volatility within the companies (Campbell et al. 2001: 37–40); (3) speedier information dissemination over time (Campbell et al. 2001: 39); or (4) increased volatility in investor discount rates (Campbell et al. 2001: 39–40). Empirical evidence has been marshalled to

Gridlock or not, evidence that the market has become better informed does not by itself imply that information asymmetries have actually decreased. Both public and non-public information may have improved, leaving the gap between the two unchanged. Consequently, there is simply no evidence to prove the assertion that the gap between private and public information available to the market has narrowed materially.

21.4.3 Heterogeneous Expectations

We now turn to the emerging literature of heterogeneous expectations.[136] This line of financial economics has developed in an attempt to explain pricing bubbles, but it has broader implications for the debate over shareholder empowerment. Not long ago, many thought of bubbles as historical anomalies that happened before financial markets became as efficient as they are today. The historical parade of bubbles, and the busts that followed, include the Dutch tulip bubble of 1630–37, the South Sea bubble of 1710–20, the British railway boom from 1845–46, the subsequent US railway boom and bust in 1873, and the dramatic rise and crash of the US stock market of the 1920s. But the bubble-to-bust experience of Japan between the 1980s and 1990s[137] and our own recent Internet bubble caused researchers to ask how such events can occur in a world where financial markets are thought to be generally efficient. As a consequence, explanations for bubbles are being integrated into broader financial models.

Heterogeneous expectations models integrate pricing bubbles into the conceptual framework of 'high church' financial economics by assuming rational behaviour by all investors. Investors are not only rational but assumed to have access to the same information, to employ standard valuation techniques, and to trade on fundamentals rather than on noise. The models depart from the asymmetric information literature in two critical respects.

support each of the four alternatives. See Wei and Zhang (2006: 261–2) (showing that a decline in return on equity and, hence, greater uncertainty explains the increase in volatility, and attributing two-thirds of the increased volatility to newly listed firms); Xu and Malkiel (2003: 614) (finding from cross-sectional regressions that idiosyncratic volatility is related to trading volume, institutional ownership, and a growth posture); Brandt et al. (2008: 13–14) (conjecturing that idiosyncratic volatility is related to speculative euphoria); Fink et al. (2005: 12–17) (showing a significant rise in idiosyncratic risk stemming from a drastic increase in the number of younger, riskier IPO firms in the market and demonstrating that after controlling for the proportion of young firms there is no time trend respecting idiosyncratic risk). Other studies have begun to undermine some of the literature's basic assumptions. The conclusion that prices have become better informed is refuted by a study that ties the stepped-up volatility to increased opacity due to deteriorating accounting practices and increased dispersion of analysts' forecasts (see Rajgopal and Venkatachalam 2008). The consistent upward trend of volatility has also been challenged. See Brandt et al. (2008: 6–8, 37 fig.2) (showing that the idiosyncratic volatility trend spiked during the period 2002–04 and declined sharply thereafter through 2007, and identifying an earlier but shorter-lived trend toward increased volatility during the period 1926–33); Brockman and Yan (2006: 12–14) (documenting a downward trend in idiosyncratic volatility from 1926–62).

[136] For the original model, see Miller (1977: 1151). We do not claim to be the first to introduce this work in the legal literature. For two papers that have previously discussed its implications, see Stout (1997: 482–92, 2003: 639–50). For heterogeneous expectations approaches to merger pricing, see Booth (1991) and Stout (1990).

[137] For a heterogeneous expectations analysis of the Japanese bubble, see Barsky (2009).

First, the models assume symmetric information not only among investors but between those inside and outside of the corporation. Second, the models drop the classical assumption of homogeneous investor expectations. Here, each investor is informed by the same set of information but develops his/her own estimate of fundamental value,[138] an estimate that at any given moment may differ from the market price. Some investors form more optimistic expectations, while others are more pessimistic.

Models with heterogeneity of expectations have three primary implications for corporate governance: (1) the market price may no longer represent the views of the shareholders as a whole or even of a majority of the shareholders; (2) the market price may not represent the pro rata value of the corporation; and (3) mispricing is likely to affect investment behaviour within the corporation, and this investment behaviour may be detrimental to the corporation.

21.4.3.1 *The Models*

In the leading heterogeneous expectations models, investors overweigh their own estimates of firm value and undervalue the estimates of other investors. This generates optimists and pessimists and trading where the optimists buy stock from the pessimists. As information flows, any particular investor may change from being optimistic to pessimistic or vice versa. Such changes in position explain the high volume of trading that is typically observed during bubbles.[139]

Critically, the models depict stock prices as having two components: first, the fundamental value of the stock; and second, the present owner's option to sell her stock to an even more optimistic investor.[140] The result is that, even in equilibrium, the stock price may exceed the valuation of the most optimistic investor. Even as this investor values the firm based on optimistic expectations as to future value, the speculative component makes this investor willing to pay an even higher price for the stock because of the option value of selling the stock to an even more optimistic investor.[141] As a result, prices can differ systematically from fundamental value.

This prediction will sound radical to an observer steeped in ECMH and CAPM.[142] But this literature in fact resonates quite well with 'high church' financial economics. We note three important points of connection.

First, there is no claim that financial markets always operate in a state where heterogeneity of expectations causes prices to diverge from fundamental value expectations.

[138] This is frequently framed in terms of Tobin's marginal Q.

[139] See Scheinkman and Xiong (2003: 1185) (noting that optimists and pessimists oscillate, changing their forecasts as information flows).

[140] For the original model of speculative behaviour in a marketplace, see Harrison and Kreps (1978: 325–8).

[141] The more pronounced the differences of opinion among investors, the more salient the speculative element. See Patrick Bolton, Scheinkman, and Xiong (2006: 578–80) (explaining the effects of differences of opinion on speculative behaviour and thus fluctuating stock valuation).

[142] If CAPM's assumption of homogeneous expectation is relaxed, and some investors are well informed while others are misinformed, the theory's prediction no longer holds. See Fama and French (2007: 669) (concluding that disagreement between dissimilarly informed investors moves pricing away from CAPM).

Heterogeneity is likely to occur when there is a change in technology, when glamour companies emerge, or when companies running newer businesses with less established track records become an important part of the market.[143]

Second, the literature yields a picture of bubbles that can be read together with semi-strong ECMH. Bubbles have two defining empirical markers: (1) a period of rapidly rising prices followed by a subsequent collapse; and (2) an unusually high volume of trading that cannot be explained by changes in fundamentals. Under the first marker, a bubble can only be identified after it has burst; rapidly rising stock prices do not constitute a bubble unless or until followed by a sharp decline or collapse.[144] *Ex post* identification is not problematic for semi-strong efficiency, however, since there is no claim that a bubble can be identified *ex ante*. It follows that there is no implicit claim that a contrarian trading strategy can be developed that yields reliable profits from a bubble.

Third, the models do assume constraints on short selling that prevent arbitrageurs from eliminating upward bias in the stock price stemming from optimistic purchases. This assumption might have put them outside the 'high church' tent twenty years ago.[145] Today, however, the economic literature recognizes real-world limitations on the arbitrage correction function.[146]

21.4.3.2 *Implications for Business Policy and Corporate Governance*

The heterogeneous expectations models change a single classical assumption, homogeneous investor expectations, to drive a wedge between stock prices and fundamental value without resort to information asymmetries. Information asymmetry and heterogeneous expectations thus emerge as separate tracks for projecting the potential adverse effects of managing to the market.

21.4.3.2.1 Implications for Shareholder Voting

When shareholder proponents ask for shareholder voting on business-policy matters, they assume that the stock price offers a reliable proxy for fundamental value and so provides the shareholders with informational guidance. The information picture changes with heterogeneous expectations. Increases in the speculative component of the stock price provide little or no information on fundamental value enhancement, and a shareholder basing a vote

[143] See Panageas (2005).

[144] For example, then Federal Reserve Chairman Alan Greenspan (1996) made his famous speech on 'irrational exuberance' in December 1996. The stock market would come near to doubling over the next several years, with the bubble only bursting in late 2000.

[145] Traditional ECMH proponents never denied that many investors are uninformed and that their trading activities push the market price away from fundamental value. They instead posited that mispricing presents a risk-free arbitrage opportunity and that the arbitrage corrective will be complete, assuring that stocks have flat demand curves and insulating market prices from shocks stemming from shifts in supply and demand having no relation to fundamental value. See Scholes (1972: 179–82) (discussing various hypotheses regarding arbitrage opportunities resulting from market imperfections).

[146] Arbitrage in corporate stocks is risky. Individual stocks do not have perfect substitutes. Arbitrage hedges accordingly carry the risk that the two streams of returns do not cancel out. See Wurgler and Zhuravskaya (2002: 585–6) (reporting the results of an empirical test of stocks that join the S&P 500 and finding that no substitutes that would hedge away more than 25% of the daily return variance could be located). That risk must be compensated for by additional returns, which in turn cause a

on market price information could be greatly misled in supporting the company's management. Shareholder voting would reward those companies whose prices had an increased speculative component. As a consequence, managers interested in securing shareholder support for a business decision, such as executive compensation, would have an incentive to skew business policy in directions that excited speculative reactions in the market.

21.4.3.2.2 *Implications for Business and Investment Strategy*

We now inquire into the distortionary potential of speculative prices for decision-making in corporate boardrooms, irrespective of shareholder voting. The models have two noteworthy features: first, their time frames cover only the period during which the bubble is still growing, thus excluding the effects of the bubble's bursting; second, they assume that the managers' duty is to maximize the stock price for the benefit of the current shareholders. Given these parameters, what is a fiduciary to do in a speculative market?

The directions are clear. In order to maximize the wealth of the corporation's current shareholders, management should first sell additional overpriced stock, thereby effectively lowering the company's cost of capital.[147] Having sold the stock, managers should then approve increased capital expenditures. In a model from Stavros Panageas, this investment serves two 'efficiency' purposes. 'One is to increase the "long run fundamentals" of the company *according to the beliefs of the current owners*', since the high stock price presumably indicates a high present value of growth opportunities.[148] The other is to increase the speculative element, permitting the current owners to capture a larger resale value when they sell their stock.[149]

José Scheinkman and Wei Xiong reach a similar conclusion.[150] Like Panageas, they see stock ownership as including an option to profit from other investors' overvaluations (2003: 1184). Patrick Bolton joins Scheinkman and Xiong by pointing this out in an article

reduction in the number of attractive plays and reduce the volume of corrective trading. The smaller the number of corrective traders, the more risky their plays become. Moreover, even if an arbitrageur's fundamental-value analysis is flawless, a given play succeeds only when the rest of the market comes to share the analysis and moves the stock in the predicted direction. As the time to correction lengthens, so does the play's duration and risk. All of this calls for a substantial base of capital, which further depresses the number of potential players.

Regulatory and institutional constraints also dampen demand for shorting activity. See Gilson and Kraakman (2003: 725–31) (analysing the difficulties of successful arbitrage in financial markets); see also Shleifer and Vishny (1997: 38–43) (positing a model for agency constraints on arbitrage activity). But cf. Asquith, Pathak, and Ritter (2005: 245) (showing empirically that only a handful of stocks on the US markets are short-sale constrained due to an unavailability of loanable shares). The average ratio of short interest to shares outstanding in February 2000 was only 2%. See Ofek and Richardson (2003: 1118) (calculating average short interest to be approximately 2% of shares outstanding as compared with almost 3% for Internet stocks). This is an increase from a less than 1% average during the period 1973–79. See Figlewski (1981: 471–2, 472 tbl.1) (listing the average short interest for stocks on the S&P 500 from 1973–79 as a percentage of total stock outstanding).

[147] See Panageas (2005: 17) (noting that new investment does not increase long-run fundamental value but rather short-term resale price).

[148] Panageas (2005: 17) (emphasis added).

[149] See Panageas (2005: 17) (noting that the speculative element arises because of disagreement over the fundamental valuation of the corporation and captures the current owners' resale premium).

[150] Their focus is on management self-interest, and they find that managers may themselves profit by adopting strategies that boost the option or speculative component. See Scheinkman and Xiong (2003: 1208) ('Firm managers may be able to profit by adopting strategies that boost the speculative component.').

on executive compensation.[151] In this model, executives divide their time between increasing the fundamental value of the corporation and increasing the value of the speculative component in the stock price.[152] In order to maximize the wealth of the current shareholders, the optimal compensation contract actually 'overemphasize[s] short-term stock performance to induce managers to take actions that may increase the speculative component in stock prices' (Bolton, Scheinkman, and Xiong 2006: 578). Indeed,

> [w]hen it is possible for future investors to overvalue the firm due to their optimism, it is in the interest of current shareholders to cater to such potential sentiment even at the expense of firm long-term fundamental value. (Bolton, Scheinkman, and Xiong 2006: 597)

In other words, it is in the interests of current shareholders for managers to have a short-termist view so as to maintain the speculative element in the stock price and give the current shareholders the possibility of selling to even more optimistic investors.

To get a better sense of the models' implications, hypothesize a stodgy technology company (hereafter 'Stodgy') in the year 1998, at the heart of the high-tech bubble. Its managers want more momentum in the company's profile. They get an opportunity to buy an Internet operation that recently has gone public (hereafter 'Cybershares'). Cybershares has never made a profit and is investing heavily in a number of innovative, web-related projects. Prospects for revenues, however, are shadowy. Cybershares' stock, initially sold to the public for $20, now trades at $60. Stodgy's managers negotiate the acquisition of Cybershares at a still higher premium price and submit the transaction to a special committee of its independent directors for approval. The independent directors take a dim view of the Internet's revenue-generating prospects and believe Cybershares to be overpriced. They do, however, expect the Internet price bubble to persist for at least the intermediate term, even as they perceive little fundamental value and predict an eventual bust. The shareholders are expected to favour the merger overwhelmingly. How should the independent directors of Stodgy vote?

Within the parameters of the heterogeneous expectations models, Stodgy's directors should vote in favour of the acquisition because the models define their fiduciary duties in terms of present stockholders, and the deal holds out the benefit of a speculative price enhancement for the company's stock that would generate present stock price maximization. The result holds for investment policy in general: even if the purchase of Cybershares reduces the fundamental value of Stodgy, the purchase improves the wealth of its current shareholders as long as the increase in the speculative component of the stock price outweighs the diminution of value in the fundamental component of the stock price.[153]

As already noted, the models focus only on pricing effects inside the bubble and do not factor in the likelihood of the bubble bursting. Let us relax this parameter in the merger case, allowing market participants to factor in the possibility of an eventual pricing correction. We now find Stodgy's directors facing a difficult choice. An investment made to increase the speculative element in the price but lacking in supporting fundamental value will benefit

[151] See Bolton, Scheinkman, and Xiong (2006: 578) ('The holder of a share then has not only a claim to future dividends but also an option to sell the stock to a more optimistic investor in the future.').

[152] See Bolton, Scheinkman, and Xiong (2006: 579) (explaining managers' short-term behaviour in terms of the speculative component).

[153] See Polk and Sapienza (2009: 187–90) (arguing that managers may rationally make investments that decrease long-term value in order to secure short-term gains).

only those who sell before the bubble bursts, with longer-term holders and new investors left holding the deflated remains.[154] The directors have no inside information but believe that the probability of the bubble bursting is higher than the probability assessment built into the market price. Unfortunately, the directors cannot convince the optimistic market that their own pessimistic expectations are correct. As long as the bubble persists, it will appear that they turned down a good deal in the eyes of their shareholders.

In the constrained context of the models, including their interpretation of corporate law, the directors should ignore their own business judgment. The result follows from the models' assumption of symmetric information. Given this, the directors' conclusion differs from the market's only with respect to subjective expectations about future outcomes; it does not follow from a position of informational superiority. There is no reason for the directors to assume that they have a better answer than the market; accordingly, they should give the current shareholders what they want.

21.4.3.2.3 *Implications for the Legal Model of the Corporation*

The prevailing legal model works differently because it instructs the directors to maximize the value of the 'corporation' and not the stock price. Remember that in the bubble models, the stock price has both a fundamental value component and a speculative component. In our hypothetical, the speculative component is positive, which is why the merger can reduce the fundamental value yet still result in a higher stock price. The move to the legal model permits the Stodgy directors to take the fundamental value information into account in making their decision. This gives them a basis to vote against the merger in accord with their own business judgment.

Thus, the legal model, in holding out 'corporate' value maximization, opens up a zone of discretion. Within it, Stodgy's directors may ignore the most optimistic shareholders who set the market price. Because the legal model imposes no duty to manage to the market when the directors' views about value differ from the market's view, the directors have no duty to approve the merger simply for the purpose of allowing those shareholders to sell their stock to more optimistic shareholders. More generally, the legal model permits the directors to consider a longer time horizon. In the hypothetical, long-term value is maximized accordingly.

Compare this with the Cybershares merger case under a hypothetical legal regime that models the directors as agents of the shareholders. This makes the merger much more difficult to resist, reducing the zone of directorial freedom of action to maximize long-term value. The market, which serves as a proxy for shareholder preferences, favours the deal. Under an agency model, the principal's preferences should control. The directors can still vote against the deal, citing fundamental value as a defence. But this defence no longer provides a complete answer under the law because it privileges the interests of one subset of principals (the pessimistic, long-term holders) over another (the optimistic, short-term holders). Here, where the assumption of a unitary shareholder has failed, the board must choose winners and losers within the group of principals. Arguably the market price, as objective money on the table, holds out the more principled decision rule.[155]

[154] See Polk and Sapienza (2009: 187–90) (arguing that shorter-term investors will benefit from 'catering' on the part of management).

[155] What of the impact of the shareholder franchise in the hypothetical? More facts would be needed. If the directors approve the merger, the subsequent shareholder vote will be in favour of the merger, but

21.4.3.2.4 *Controlling Shareholders Compared*

In the above cases, directors face a dilemma in exercising their business judgment when it conflicts with the views of their shareholders as expressed in market prices. The heterogeneous expectations models contrast the case where there is a controlling shareholder, positing that controlling shareholders are likely to have a longer-term rather than a shorter-term outlook.[156]

The incentive shift toward long-term value maximization arises because the controller cannot or does not want to sell his/her shares, despite what he/she believes to be an inflated price. Constraints on the ability of controlling insiders to sell their stock have a number of sources, including IPO-related resale restrictions and negative tax consequences from capital gains realization. Perhaps more importantly, the sale of a large enough block causes the seller to lose his/her power as a controller.[157]

The locked-in controller will adopt a conservative investment policy consistent with the view that he/she will still be in control when the bubble bursts and the speculative component of the stock price goes to zero. In particular, he/she has no incentive to consider speculative mispricing when determining investment policy and no reason to accept negative-net-present-value investments that increase the value of the speculative component. On the other hand, the controlling shareholder can profitably adopt one prong of the non-controllers' short-termist strategy by causing the firm to sell additional shares into the overpriced market, thereby lowering the firm's cost of capital. Since the funds so raised need not be used for investment purposes, they can be put aside to repurchase the shares after the bubble has burst.[158]

21.4.3.2.5 *Implications for Management Compensation*

The perverse effects predicted by the models follow only to the extent that the managers have the option of selling into the market and do not hesitate to exercise it. As we have seen, when frictions prevent sales, the managers have no stake in managing to the speculative element in the stock price, and fundamental value information determines investment

only so long as the bubble has not yet burst. Indeed, if the pessimistic shareholders are not locked into their shareholdings, they will vote yes on the ground that the best course in the wake of board approval is to vote yes and sell. Only shareholders that, for whatever reason, cannot sell will vote no. If the board turns down the merger, no shareholder vote occurs. The shareholder franchise comes into play at the next annual meeting. If the bubble has not burst, the directors presumably will be punished. Indeed, even if the bubble has burst, shareholders may still be inclined toward punishment due to the missed opportunity to sell.

[156] See Panageas (2005: 21) ('Long-termism is just the extent of 'entrenchment' of current 'major' shareholders in the firm.').

[157] The controller might also face insider trading restrictions under Rule 10b-5 (17 C.F.R. § 240.10b-5 2009).

[158] See Bolton, Scheinkman, and Xiong (2006: 595) (explaining that during speculative episodes, 'the cost of capital is below the firm's long-run value'). The reduction in the cost of capital is consistent with the controller's belief that the expected return on the shares will be lower in the future.

Note that the controlling shareholder's time horizon lengthens to the extent that access to the trading markets is restricted. Given a partial constraint on liquidation of its position, the firm's investment policy would be partially open to short-term incentives—the controlling shareholder would determine investment using 'some weighted average between share price and long term value' (Panageas 2005: 22).

policy.[159] It follows that equity-based compensation schemes that lack constraints on market sales exacerbate the suboptimal-investment problem.[160] It also follows that compensation plans should seek to mimic as closely as possible the incentives of a controlling shareholder, the shareholder who will be deterred from selling into an overpriced market by the need to maintain the control position and its accompanying value.[161]

Now consider the impact of shareholder empowerment respecting the terms of compensation plans, given these choices. Presumably, shareholders who are asked the hypothetical question of whether they prefer directors to have long- or short-term incentives will most of the time express a preference for the long-term. This is because the long-term strategy maximizes the current stock price, at least in normal times when stocks trade without a speculative element. Given these conditions, shareholders can be expected to support compensation plans that constrain executive resales.

Contrast this with a company that has an upward-trending stock price subject to speculative influence. Here, shareholder voting preferences should shift to follow the stock price. After all, if the stock price is inflated, it is because the shareholders have bid it up in the hope that the trend will continue. Resale constraints are undesirable because they would discourage the managers from stoking the trend. From a policy perspective, then, shareholder empowerment can work at cross purposes with the goal of reducing value-destroying short-termist behaviour.

21.4.3.2.6 Summary

We have shown that information asymmetries can open a gulf between managing to maximize long-term fundamental value and managing to maximize the market price of the stock. We have also shown that speculative pricing under heterogeneous expectations can have the same result. In both cases, managing to the market leads to suboptimal results, with negative implications for shareholder empowerment.

When market prices are taken as governance inputs they accordingly need to be interpreted as a matter of business judgment. In our view, the prevailing legal model gets it right when it remits the judgment to the directors and their appointed managers. A recent empirical study confirms that directors do indeed use their discretion to the advantage of fundamental value. The study finds that managers look to the stock price when investing only in limited circumstances, and when so doing they successfully separate the fundamental value signal from the speculative signal.[162] This positive report card underscores the case favouring the prevailing legal model's zone of directorial discretion.

[159] See Panageas (2003) (noting that if managers do not have frictionless access to markets, investment decisions are based on fundamental value).

[160] See Bolton, Scheinkman, and Xiong (2006: 578–9) (explaining that an incentive compensation scheme keyed to short-term stock price enhancement at the sacrifice of long-term value can be optimal for a group of speculative shareholders).

[161] Short-termist incentives will not, however, be entirely absent. A controlling shareholder retains the incentive to sell additional shares into the overpriced market in order to reduce the cost of capital, an incentive shared with all managers of all companies.

[162] See Bakke and Whited (2006) (finding 'that investment does respond to legitimate information in price movements, but only for firms that rely on outside equity financing and whose shares are *not* mispriced' (emphasis added)).

21.5 Shareholders, Managers, Markets, and the Financial Crisis of 2008

In this section we turn to the recent financial crisis and the claim that shareholder empowerment is the regulatory response that will restore trust in the system.[163] Leading executives of financial firms—particularly those whose firms had to be saved by the federal government—have emerged as the poster children for the evildoers who caused the crisis. But did the problem arise because the managers were fiduciaries who violated the shareholders' trust, or because the managers were acting more like agents by managing to the market? Does manager culpability translate, as Arthur Levitt would have us believe,[164] into a case for shareholder empowerment? Or did the shareholders take the lead on the road to crisis, rewarding the financial companies that took on the most leverage with higher stock prices, and penalizing those that did not?

In Section 21.5.1 we examine the financial crisis through the lens of the shareholders of the financial firms at its epicentre. In so doing, we highlight the place of managing to the market in the chain of causation. As we show, the evidence suggests that shareholders first fell in love, and then fell out of love, with the financial companies that were taking on the most risk and the most leverage. In Section 21.5.2 we turn to the question of the proper role of corporate governance in post-crisis law reform, focusing on executive compensation and its central role both in fomenting the crisis and in fixing the system. Doing so removes shareholder empowerment from the reform picture.

21.5.1 Financial Risk and Shareholder Inputs

Figure 21.2 tracks the performance of the subset of bank stocks included in the S&P 500 index against that of the entire S&P 500 from January 2000 to March 2009. It shows that prior to the autumn of 2007, the banks handsomely outperformed the market as a whole, in rough correlation with its ups and downs.[165] They then underwent a precipitous fall that presaged and outstripped that of the market as a whole, which began a year later. We note that Figure 21.2 understates the performance gaps. The relative weight of the financial sector within the S&P 500 grew from 13.0% in 1999 to 22.3% in 2006,[166] only to retreat back to 13.6% in mid-2009.[167] It follows that the S&P 500, excluding finance, neither rose nor fell as much as the line indicates.

The stock market favoured the banks between 2000 and 2007 because of rising earnings that resulted from wide spreads between expected returns on lending and the costs of increasing leverage in a stable economic environment. The problem, which became more

[163] See *supra* notes 1–12 and accompanying text. [164] See *supra* text accompanying note 5–6.

[165] The correlation of the two number series is 0.48.

[166] Bespoke Investment Group, Current and Historical Sector Weightings of the S&P 500 (24 Apr. 2008), available at <http://bespokeinvest.typepad.com/bespoke/2008/04/current-and-his.html>.

[167] Select Sector SPDR Trust, Sector Returns by Year 2003–2012, available at <http://www.sectorspdr.com/shared/pdf/SPDR-Periodic-Table-web.pdf>.

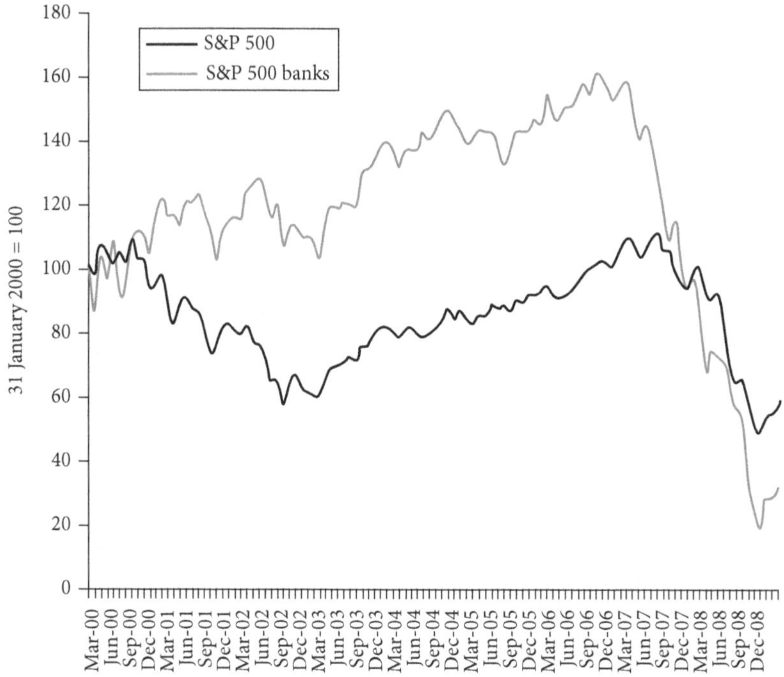

FIGURE 21.2 S&P 500/S&P 500 banks, 2000–09

and more apparent in 2007, was that the banks had been making high-yield loans into the residential-mortgage sector (including, but not limited to, subprime loans) that were much riskier than had been appreciated. Securitization[168] had turned these risky loans into AAA paper on the assumption that the price of the real estate securing the loans would continue to rise.[169] At the same time, the rise in real estate prices was built in part on increasing demand for housing fuelled by ever-riskier real estate financing.[170]

Was the crash of financial stocks the result of a system that gave managers too much power, or did it follow from managers catering to stockholders as they expressed their views through stock prices? Some evidence to answer the question can be found by breaking out individual financial stocks that were the poster children of the crisis, with each playing a different role. Figure 21.3 depicts the individual share prices of Countrywide Financial, JPMorgan Chase, and Bank of America against the S&P 500 Bank index. Countrywide is now one of the clear villains in the story. But it also was the clear market favourite, at least until mid-2007. Countrywide expanded at a torrid pace after 2000 by making riskier loans, both in the subprime and prime sectors, and financing the

[168] See generally Schwarcz (1994) (explaining how securitization works and how companies benefit from it).

[169] See, e.g., Norris (2007) (explaining the riskiness of AAA securities backed by subprime mortgages).

[170] See, e.g., Pavlov and Wachter (2009: 3) (linking recent use of aggressive mortgage lending instruments and the underlying house price volatility).

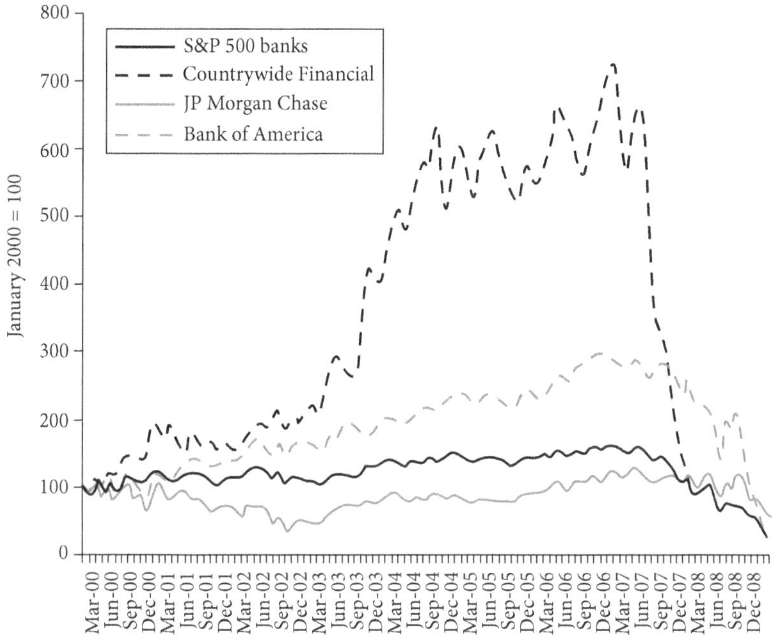

FIGURE 21.3 Sectoral variations

expansion on a short-term basis in the repurchase and commercial paper markets.[171] Countrywide's line in Figure 21.3 stops in mid-2008 because portfolio losses forced it into a defensive merger with Bank of America.

It appears the stock market failed to appreciate the risks held out by the sector's higher fliers. In our view, this lack of appreciation can be traced partly to the information asymmetry

[171] In 2003, Countrywide was the star of its sector, having returned 23,000% on its equity between 1982 and 2003. See Tully (2003) ('Most amazing of all is that Countrywide boasts the best stock market performance of any financial services company in the FORTUNE 500. . . .'). Countrywide built itself into an industry leader with a strictly prime-lending operation, entering the subprime market only in 1999. Between 1999 and 2003, Countrywide got its growth in earnings and market share from an aggressive mortgage refinancing operation. That strategy depended on historically low interest rates. When rates climbed in 2003, it had to look elsewhere to continue its stellar performance. See Richard and Feldheim (2004) (concluding that investors were moving money into asset-backed securities, creating a possible 'bonanza' for consumer borrowing). Subprime lending was a part of the solution but only undertaken with a view to securitizing all mortgages originated. Prime lending remained a much greater part of the business. But here the company took a notably aggressive approach, originating adjustable rate mortgages highly exposed to declines in real estate prices. See Haggerty (2006) (raising the possibility that Countrywide was less cautious than rivals in granting adjustable rate mortgages). The right side of Countrywide's balance sheet also changed. Shareholders' equity, 16% of total assets in 1999, declined to 7% of total assets in 2006. Compare Countrywide Credit Indus., Inc., Annual Report (Form 10-K), at F-4 (29 Feb. 2000), with Countrywide Fin. Corp., Annual Report (Form 10-K), at F-3 (28 Feb. 2008). In 1999, the overwhelming portion of Countrywide's outside borrowing was medium term. By 2006, it was relying on short-term credit in the form of repurchase obligations and commercial paper. See Countrywide Fin. Corp., Annual Report (Form 10-K), at F-3 (28 Feb. 2008) (reporting that repurchase obligations, while constituting 0% of liabilities in 1999, were 23% in 2006, while longer-term 'notes payable' declined from 79% of liabilities in 1999 to 39% in 2006).

problem described in Section 21.4.2. As we noted there, markets can easily fail to measure the risk factors incorporated into discount rates.[172] What was unusual here was the magnitude of the underestimation.

A full account of these events is beyond the scope of this chapter, but a few useful points should be noted. Banks historically have been low-beta stocks. The banks, operating with less leverage than recently has been the case, made their profits on the spread between borrowing and lending rates. Since this spread does not generate enormous returns, the banks were steady earners with high dividends. Furthermore, by doing their best to match the duration of their assets with their liabilities and maintaining large reserves of safe, liquid assets, they contained their risk, and hence their returns.[173]

This all changed as some banks made riskier loans, became more involved in buying and selling securitized assets, and operated with more leverage. Such a change in business strategy meant a move to greater expected returns and greater risk. In the stable economic environment of 2003–07, these banks generated much higher profits with little volatility. The stock market fell in love with this combination of unexpectedly high returns and apparently constant low risk. Higher stock prices resulted.

For a management dedicated to maximizing shareholder value, the instruction manual was clear: get with the program by generating more risky loans and doing so with more leverage. Any bank whose managers failed to implement the new math of high returns and low beta got stuck with a low stock price.[174] For an example, look at JPMorgan Chase in Figure 21.3. It suffered from loan and other investment losses from 2001 to 2004, and then, as the housing bubble expanded, recovered while adhering to strict risk management policies.[175] Consequently, its stock lagged behind the bank index until the crisis began to unfold and then overtook the index. Unsurprisingly, its managers laboured under considerable pressure to follow the strategies of competing banks (Tett 2009: 124–42). JPMorgan Chase had merged with a view to dominating the securitization business (Tett 2009: 120). In 2005, the new bank cranked up a production line for collateralized debt obligations based on subprime mortgages but never flicked the start switch because its managers could not find a way to make the risk/return numbers add up (Tett 2009: 121–8).

As long as the economy was expanding, the riskier business strategies worked well. But when the economy slowed, the higher risk became observable. High returns went along with higher risk after all, and the realization caused stock prices to fall.

Now let us turn back the clock to 2005 and hypothesize a newly appointed CEO at a bank that has been pursuing the high-growth/high-leverage strategy. The bank has been originating mortgages, both prime and subprime, whose soundness depends on continued rising real estate prices. Although it funnels most of its subprime originations into securitizations, some of these mortgages will be retained on its increasingly levered balance sheet. How would this CEO evaluate the policy? The stock market has been sending a strong signal

[172] See *supra* note 109 and accompanying text.

[173] For a description of the process by which banks went from regulatory constraint to high-risk investing, see Posner (2009: 41–74).

[174] For a smaller bank, that meant becoming an attractive merger target as the industry concentrated.

[175] See Kelly (2009: 194–6) (describing JPMorgan Chase CEO Jamie Dimon's approach as 'steer[ing] the bank away from risky holdings'); Tett (2009: 110–42) ('Dimon believed strongly that risks must be properly managed... .').

that the shareholders love the new approach. If the CEO is shareholder sensitive, he/she will be inclined to view the new strategy as terrific. If that is the case, then the bank's fortunes are set. However, suppose the new CEO, who has had a long banking career, believes that the market is underestimating the risk of the high-growth/high-return strategy built around originating risky mortgages on a more levered balance sheet. The new CEO accordingly decides against taking on more leverage and orders the managers to stop originating both subprime mortgages and 'teaser rate' mortgages, prime mortgages requiring no down payment, and instead orders them to sell off as many as possible, even if that means realizing a loss and incurring other transaction costs.

Does the CEO's insightful move improve the stock price? The bank, which is forced to lower its earnings forecast substantially, can fully explain the development as a return to a lower-risk corporate strategy that it believes will pay off when the economy cools and the returns on the subprime mortgages turn negative. But the result of not giving the market what it wants can be painful. The new corporate policy is unlikely to be rewarded precisely because the stock market believes the existing high-leverage corporate strategy, duly ratified by a rising stock price, is the correct one. The hypothetical thus ends with the bank's stock price dropping substantially and the managers' stock options going underwater. The story, in short, tracks Section 21.4's analysis of the problems confronting managers making investment decisions given speculative stock pricing under heterogeneous expectations.

Now return to the question asked in this chapter's Introduction: would increased shareholder power have moderated the bank's risky business practices? We think the answer is no. While many of the CEOs of adversely affected financial institutions certainly must have agreed with the strategy, some might not have. It is not as if contrarian warnings were not on the table for all to see. *The Economist* began a series of warnings about real estate price bubbles in 2002.[176] Managers at JPMorgan Chase saw warning signs in the subprime market in 2005 and so decided to stay out (Tett 2009: 122–4). Insiders at other banks must have posited similar conclusions.[177] The question is whether increased shareholder empowerment would have emboldened these informed insiders into abandoning the strategy so popular on Wall Street or would have deterred them. The inference from the evidence lies clearly with the latter result. Citigroup's then CEO, Charles Prince, spoke publicly of his own second thoughts in 2007, late in the game. He chose to stick with the program despite his second thoughts: 'When the music stops, in terms of liquidity, things will be complicated.... But as long as the music is playing, you've got to get up and dance. We're still dancing.'[178] His upwardly bouncing stock price surely set the motivating rhythms.[179]

[176] See *Economist* (2002) (warning then Federal Reserve Chairman Alan Greenspan to look out for a boom in share prices or house prices combined with a big increase in debt and overinvestment by firms). The warning became more focused by 2004 (*Economist* 2004) (predicting a crash of the UK housing market).

[177] Cf. Scannell and Emshwiller (2009) (reporting SEC allegations that Countrywide executives saw warning signs and decided not to disclose that information to investors).

[178] Kotkin (2009) (reviewing and quoting from Grant 2008).

[179] A recent empirical study of executive compensation at financial companies compares those that did badly in the financial crisis (such as AIG, Bear Stearns, Citigroup, Countrywide, and Lehman) with those that did better (such as Berkshire Hathaway, Goldman Sachs, JPMorgan Chase, and Wells Fargo) (Cheng, Hong, and Scheinkman 2009: 5–10, 22–6). The study finds (a) a statistically and economically significant connection between executive compensation and price-based measures of risk such as beta and stock return volatility; (b) that higher-paying firms were more likely to be in the tails of

The financial sector undertook high-risk/high-return strategies to enhance return on equity and raise stock prices.[180] The executives who danced to the rhythm were compensated with stock options and restricted stock in addition to cash bonuses, and so had incentives roughly in alignment with those of their shareholders.[181]

At least in retrospect we know that the market underestimated the risk being taken and thus failed to provide an objective, critical reference point for monitoring purposes. To the contrary, stock prices confirmed the strategies until well past the point of no return. We think that Arthur Levitt got it exactly wrong. Shareholder power was a part of the problem and is not a part of the solution.

21.5.2 The Changing Policy Context

Financial collapse reorients policy agendas. Is the shareholder agenda helped or hurt by these developments? As noted above, a large clientele believes that market exuberance can be fixed by giving shareholders more say. We think the policy implications go in the opposite direction. What is needed is incentive compatibility for managers. Incentive compatibility and shareholder accountability, however, do not yield the same results.

We noted in Section 21.4 that the heterogeneous expectations models have an important implication for executive compensation plans.[182] Equity-based incentive-alignment schemes need to filter out speculative market inputs. Long-term holding constraints, whether attached to restricted stock or stock options, are the means to the end. Professors Sanjai Bhagat and Roberta Romano recommend prohibiting resales of 80% to 85% of the equity granted until two to four years after the manager leaves the company, with such restrictions extending down the hierarchy to cover bonus plans for traders.[183] The idea is to drive a wedge between the incentives of shareholders who are active in the market and those of managers. As we also noted in Section 21.4, managers taking equity compensation under resale restrictions resemble blockholders more than the dispersed shareholders on whom reform proponents continue to focus.

performance; and (c) a positive relation between residual compensation and subprime exposure (Cheng, Hong, and Scheinkman 2009: 5–10, 22–6.); see also Fahlenbrach and Stulz (2009: 12) (reporting on an empirical study and showing:

> that there is no evidence that banks with a better alignment of CEOs' interests with those of their shareholders had higher stock returns during the crisis and some evidence that banks led by CEOs whose interests were better aligned with those of their shareholders had worse stock returns and a worse return on equity).

180 See, e.g., Cohan (2009) (criticizing the testimony of financial executives to Congress who alleged that the financial crisis was unavoidable).

181 The mix among stock options, restricted stock, and cash bonuses varied from company to company and from executive to executive within each company. For example, in 2006, Citibank disclosed a heavier weighting to cash bonuses, whereas Bank of America relied more on stock options. Compare Citigroup Inc., Definitive Proxy Statement (Schedule 14A), at 39–52 (14 Mar. 2006), with Bank of Am. Corp., Definitive Proxy Statement (Schedule 14A), at 22–7 (20 Mar. 2006).

182 See *supra* text accompanying notes 159–61.

183 The authors reason that a two-year minimum suffices to diffuse the incentive to manage earnings; by the end of four years the intermediate-term effects of the manager's contribution will have worked their way into the stock price (ibid: 7).

The manager/shareholder wedge has a second significant effect. Market shareholders tend to diversify their holdings in order to minimize risk.[184] Resale-constrained managers are under-diversified and presumptively carry more risk than portfolio investors. As they bear more risk, they tend toward risk-averse investment strategies. Thus does the emerging consensus favouring strict resale constraints reverse long-held views respecting equity-based compensation, views shaped during the 1980s.[185] Stock options, which build in sensitivity to upside gain and insensitivity to downside loss, long have been deemed the compensation mode of choice because they counterbalance the risk aversion that accompanies the undiversified investments of human capital that executives make in their companies. Up until now, management stock resales have been viewed as a matter for contractual trade-off—because they make it possible for the executives to diversify their investment portfolios, they increase the value of the compensation plan to the recipient and so reduce costs of compensation to the corporate employer and its shareholders.[186]

The times have changed. Even bank CEOs now acknowledge a need for boards to be scrupulous about compensation structures and incentives, toward the goal of 'trust restoration'.[187] Bhagat and Romano, even as their proposal addresses the TARP compensation constraints for financial companies, nonetheless commend its resale restrictions for the boards of all publicly traded companies (2009: 3–4). Bebchuk and Spamann go further still, at least with regard to TARP recipients, contending that any equity-based compensation scheme holds out a possibility of incentivizing excessive risk-taking, due to the combination of high leverage and the equity's limited liability (2009: 3–4). They recommend basing incentive compensation on enterprise value rather than shareholder value—that is, rewards should be based on the value of a package of common stock, preferred stock, and bonds.[188]

These new views on executive compensation bespeak a seismic shift in thinking about shareholder–manager relations. Compensation is the margin on which business policymakers align the incentives. Formerly, the shareholders were seen as a unitary population for whose interest the stock price provided a robust proxy. Now we see that at certain critical times the shareholder interest can disaggregate, with some shareholders' interests diverging from near-term stock price maximization. In such times, maximizing the market price provides faulty instructions to managers, undermining the claims of shareholder proponents and supporting the need for managers to exercise their business judgment independently. Recent changes in notions about appropriate management incentives accordingly come as no surprise. The new model, which seeks to cast management in the mould of a

[184] See Easterbrook and Fischel (1991: 30) ('[T]he vast majority of investments are held by people with diversified portfolios.'); Murphy (2002: 858–9) (factoring free transferability and hedging into the opportunity cost of a stock option).

[185] See generally Jensen and Murphy (1990: 261–2) (finding the relation between executive wealth and shareholder wealth to be small, partly because executive compensation structures were not highly sensitive to performance at the time).

[186] Critics of compensation plans have questioned this analysis in part, recommending resale restraints that balance the long-term time horizon with the executive's interest in liquidity and diversification. See Bebchuk and Fried (2004: 174–6) (concluding that the efficient balance between restrictions on cashing out vested options and executives' interest in liquidity and diversification will vary from firm to firm). But cf. Bratton (2006: 75) (recommending across-the-board resale constraints).

[187] See Green (2009: 3) ('Public trust depends on a responsible, measured attitude to compensation.').

[188] Green (2009: 5–6); see also Acharya et al. (2009: 193–4).

long-term holder, may be more hypothetical than descriptive of actual shareholders at many companies.

21.6 Conclusion

This chapter bases its case against shareholder empowerment on the modern financial economics of market pricing. It cites information asymmetry and new financial economic theories of speculative overpricing. We underscore the importance of the new economics by reference to bank stocks during the period 2000 to 2008—a reference that leads ineluctably to consideration of the implications of the financial crisis for corporate law's political economy. There, on the critical topic of executive compensation, we already see the shareholder interest, as manifested in the market price, retreating in the corporate governance system's rearview mirror.

Shareholder proponents will object, pointing out that banks are different. Their businesses are built on assets and liabilities with mismatched durations, necessitating a protective deposit-insurance regime. That in turn holds out moral hazard in the form of speculative investment, with prudential regulation following to square the circle. Producers of goods and services in other sectors do not hold out these special risks. As to them, the shareholder case remains intact, or so goes the argument.

We see it differently. Our case, albeit brought home at the extreme, is not thereby limited. We have shown that excessive reliance on market pricing poses problems for corporate governance. We certainly do not claim that shareholder inputs shaped by market prices are intrinsically unreliable. We do claim that mispricing is a salient possibility, more so in times of economic volatility. It follows that price signals need to be interpreted by an agent exercising sound business judgment, with the independent board of directors bearing that burden.

The shareholder case, in contrast, follows from a theory that merges agency-cost reduction, value maximization, and price signals into a unitary whole to yield a one-size-fits-all governance instruction. This chapter breaks open this holistic theoretical construct. Once that is accomplished, the shareholder proponents have no riposte because they have never thought it necessary to confront the difficulties of balancing the benefits and detriments of market inputs and to restate their case in a realistic cost–benefit framework. We have no idea what such a robust shareholder empowerment case might look like. Pending its articulation, we think any reform following from the shareholder agenda to be inopportune in the present context. The prevailing governance system has proven itself quite responsive to market inputs. Shareholder power has waxed over the past several decades as an endogenous market response to changes in the economic environment. The high residual agency costs of thirty years ago have been cured by cost-effective increases in market monitoring and director bonding. Money on the table has that effect.

Now, in the aftermath of the financial crisis of 2008, the question is whether the self-adjusting market mechanism proved overly responsive to shareholder pressure by staking executive fortunes on short-term price effects. If the financial crisis teaches us anything, it is that managing to the market is the problem that needs to be addressed. That calls for recalibration of compensation mechanisms, not legislative change to increase shareholder power.

More generally, today's regulatory questions concern the constraint of business discretion in the wake of market failure, in particular, risk-taking in pursuit of shareholder gain. Despite the shareholder proponents' recent reframing of their case in terms of trust, shareholder empowerment remains what it always has been—a strategy that looks to regulatory reform that enhances market control over the zone of discretion in which directors make business judgments.

Regulatory reform strategies henceforth could proceed in the opposite direction. The pure financial incentives that advantage shareholder inputs in expansive, deregulatory times register equivocally in the face of public demands for control of market risk-taking. Debates on executive pay are beginning to bear out this point. Regulations that seriously address risk-taking will bypass the shareholders to impose constraints on financial corporations directly, narrowing their zone of freedom of action. As between managers and shareholders, such initiatives cause power to flow the managers' way. With regulation comes the responsibility to comply, a burden that falls on directors and officers. The more extensive the forthcoming regulatory intervention, the more irrelevant the shareholder empowerment strategy will become. This strategy has, in our view, reached the outer limits of its effectiveness for the time being.

References

Abernathy, W. J. and Clark, K. B. (1984). Innovation: Mapping the Winds of Creative Destruction, *Research Policy* 14, 3–22.

Acharya, V. A., Carpenter, J. N., Gabaix, X., John, K., Richardson, M., Subrahmanyam, M. G., Sundaram, R. K., and Zemel, E. (2009). Corporate Governance in the Modern Financial System in V. A. Acharya and M. Richardson (eds.), *The Modern Financial Sector in Restoring Financial Stability: How to Repair a Failed System* (Hoboken, NJ, John Wiley & Sons Inc.), 185–96.

Aghion, P. and Stein, J. C. (2008). Growth versus Margins: Destabilizing Consequences of Giving the Stock Market What It Wants, *Journal of Finance* 63, 1025–58.

Allen, C. H. (2007). Study of Majority Voting in Director Elections, available at <http://blogs.law.harvard.edu/corpgov/2007/11/23/study-of-majority-voting-in-director-elections/#more-312>.

Anabtawi, I. (2006). Some Skepticism about Increasing Shareholder Power, *UCLA Law Review* 53, 561–99.

Arrow, K. J. (1974). *The Limits of Organization* (New York, W. W. Norton & Company).

Asquith, P., Pathak, P. A., and Ritter, J. R. (2005). Short Interest, Institutional Ownership, and Stock Returns, *Journal of Financial Economics* 78, 243–76.

Bainbridge, S. M. (2006). Director Primacy and Shareholder Disempowerment, *Harvard Law Review* 119, 1735–58.

Baker, M., Ruback, R. S., and Wurgler, J. (2007). Behavioral Corporate Finance in E. Eckbo (ed.), *Handbook of Corporate Finance: Empirical Corporate Finance* (vol. 1) (Amsterdam, Elsevier North-Holland), 145–88.

Baker, M., Stein, J., and Wurgler, J. (2003). When Does the Market Matter? Stock Prices and the Investment of Equity-Dependent Firms, *Quarterly Journal of Economics* 118, 969–1005.

Baker, M. and Wurgler, J. (2000). The Equity Share in New Issues and Aggregate Stock Returns, *Journal of Finance* 55, 2219–57.

Baker, M. and Wurgler, J. (2006). Investor Sentiment and the Cross-Section of Stock Returns, *Journal of Finance* 61, 1645–80.

Bakke, T.-E. and Whited, T. M. (2006). Which Firms Follow the Market? An Analysis of Corporate Investment Decisions (18 Nov.) (unpublished manuscript), available at <http://ssrn.com/abstract=891570>.

Barberis, N. and Shleifer, A. (2003). Style Investing, *Journal of Financial Economics* 68, 161–99.

Barberis, N., Shleifer, A., and Wurgler, J. (2005). Comovement, *Journal of Financial Economics* 75, 283–317.

Barsky, R. B. (2009). The Japanese Bubble: A 'Heterogeneous' Approach, National Bureau of Economic Research, Working Paper No. 15052, available at <http://www.nber.org/papers/w15052>.

Bebchuk, L. A. (2005). The Case for Increasing Shareholder Power, *Harvard Law Review* 118, 833–914.

Bebchuk, L. A. and Cohen, A. (2005). The Costs of Entrenched Boards, *Journal of Financial Economics* 78, 409–33.

Bebchuk, L. A. and Fried, J. (2004). *Pay Without Performance: The Unfulfilled Promise of Executive Compensation* (Cambridge, MA, Harvard University Press).

Bebchuk, L. A. and Roe, M. J. (1999). A Theory of Path Dependence in Corporate Ownership and Governance, *Stanford Law Review* 52, 127–70.

Bebchuk, L. A. and Spamann, H. (2009). Regulating Bankers' Pay, John M. Olin Center for Law, Economics, and Business, Discussion Paper No. 641, available at <http://ssrn.com/abstract=1410072>.

Bebchuk, L. A. and Stole, L. A. (1993). Do Short-Term Objectives Lead to Under-or Overinvestment in Long-Term Projects?, *Journal of Finance* 48, 719–29.

Becht, M., Bolton, P. and Röell, A. (2005). Corporate Governance and Control, European Corporate Governance Institute, Finance Working Paper No. 02/2002, available at <http://ssrn.com/abstract=343461>.

Bergstresser, D. and Philippon, T. (2006). CEO Incentives and Earnings Management, *Journal of Financial Economics* 80, 511–29.

Berle, Jr, A. A. and Means, G. C. (1932). *The Modern Corporation and Private Property* (Buffalo, NY, William S. Hein & Co., Inc.).

Bhagat, S. and Romano, R. (2009). Reforming Executive Compensation: Focusing and Committing to the Long-Term, Yale Law & Economics Research Paper No. 374, available at <http://ssrn.com/abstract=1336978>.

Bhojraj, S. and Libby, R. (2005). Capital Market Pressure, Disclosure Frequency-Induced Earnings/Cash Flow Conflict, and Managerial Myopia, *Accounting Review* 80, 1–20.

Black, B. S. (1990). Shareholder Passivity Reexamined, *Michigan Law Review* 89, 520–608.

Black, B. and Kraakman, R. (2002). Delaware's Takeover Law: The Uncertain Search for Hidden Value, *Northwestern University Law Review* 96, 521–66.

Bolton, P., Scheinkman, J., and Xiong, W. (2006). Executive Compensation and Short-Termist Behaviour in Speculative Markets, *Review of Economic Studies* 73, 577–610.

Booth, R. (1991). Discounts and Other Mysteries of Corporate Finance, *California Law Review* 79, 1053–117.

Borokhovich, K. A., Brunarski, K. R., and Parrino, R. (1997). CEO Contracting and Antitakeover Amendments, *Journal of Finance* 52, 1495–517.

Brandt, M. W., Brav, A. P., Graham, J. R., and Kumar, A. (2008). The Idiosyncratic Volatility Puzzle: Time Trend or Speculative Episodes?, University of Texas McCombs School of Business, Research Paper No. FIN-02-09, available at <http://ssrn.com/abstract=1141219>.

Bratton W. W. (2005a). The New Dividend Puzzle, *Georgetown Law Journal* 93, 845.

Bratton, W. W. (2005b). The Academic Tournament over Executive Compensation, *California Law Review* 93, 1557–84.

Bratton, W. W. (2006). Supersize Pay, Incentive Compatibility, and the Volatile Shareholder Interest, *Virginia Law and Business Review* 1, 55–100.

Bratton, W. W. (2007). Hedge Funds and Governance Targets, *Georgetown Law Journal* 95, 1375–434.

Bratton, W. W. (2008). Private Equity's Three Lessons for Agency Theory, *European Business Organization Law Review* 9, 509–33.

Brealey, R. A., Myers, S. C., and Allen, F. (2006). *Principles of Corporate Finance* (8th edn) (New York, McGraw Hill).

Brockman, P. and Yan, X. S. (2006). The Time-Series Behavior and Pricing of Idiosyncratic Volatility: Evidence From 1926 to 1962 (Sept.) (unpublished manuscript), available at <http://ssrn.com/abstract=1117284>.

Bushee, B. J. (1998). The Influence of Institutional Investors on Myopic R&D Investment Behavior, *Accounting Review* 73, 305–33.

Bushee, B. J. (1999). Do Institutional Investors Prefer Near-Term Earnings over Long-Run Value? (Apr.) (unpublished manuscript), available at <http://ssrn.com/abstract=161739>.

Campbell, J. Y., Lettau, M., Malkiel, B. G., and Xu, Y. (2001). Have Individual Stocks Become More Volatile? An Empirical Exploration of Idiosyncratic Risk, *Journal of Finance* 56, 1–43.

Campbell, J. Y., Lo, A. W., and MacKinlay, A. C. (1997). *The Econometrics of Financial Markets* (Princeton, NJ, Princeton University Press).

Cheffins, B. and Armour, J. (2007). The Eclipse of Private Equity, European Corporate Governance Institute, Law Working Paper No. 082/2007, available at <http://ssrn.com/abstract=982114>.

Chen, Q., Goldstein, I., and Jiang, W. (2007). Informativeness and Investment Sensitivity to Stock Price, *Review of Financial Studies* 20, 619–50.

Cheng, I.-H., Hong, H. G., and Scheinkman, J. A. (2009). Yesterday's Heroes: Compensation and Creative Risk-Taking (Oct.) (unpublished manuscript), available at <http://ssrn.com/abstract=1502762>.

Cheng, M., Subramanyam, K. R., and Zhang, Y. (2005). Earnings Guidance and Managerial Myopia (Nov.) (unpublished manuscript), available at <http://ssrn.com/abstract=851545>.

CII (Council of Institutional Investors) (2009). Press Release, CII Applauds Introduction of Shareholder Bill of Rights Act (19 May), available at <http://pressrelated.com/press-release-cii-applauds-introduction-of-shareholder-bill-of-rights-act.html>.

Coates, IV, J. C. (2000). Takeover Defenses in the Shadow of the Pill: A Critique of the Scientific Evidence, *Texas Law Review* 79, 271–382.

Cohan, W. D. (2009). Op-Ed., A Tsunami of Excuses, *New York Times* (12 Mar.), at A23.

Committee on Capital Markets Regulation (2006). Interim Report, available at <http://www.capmktsreg.org/pdfs/11.30Committee_Interim_ReportREV2.pdf>.

Core, J. E. (2001). A Review of the Empirical Disclosure Literature: Discussion, *Journal of Accounting and Finance* 31, 441–56.

Core, J. E., Guay, W. R., and Rusticus, T. O. (2006). Does Weak Governance Cause Weak Stock Returns? An Examination of Firm Operating Performance and Investors' Expectations, *Journal of Finance* 61, 655–87.

Dent, Jr, G. W. (2008). Academics in Wonderland: The Team Production and Director Primacy Models of Corporate Governance, *Houston Law Review* 44, 1213–74.

Durney, A., Morck, R., Yeung, B. Y. (2004). Value-Enhancing Capital Budgeting and Firm-Specific Stock Return Variation, *Journal of Finance* 59, 65–105.

Durney, A., Morck, R., Yeung, B. Y., and Zarowin, P. (2003). Does Greater Firm-Specific Return Variation Mean More or Less Informed Stock Pricing?, *Journal of Accounting Research* 41, 797–836.

Easterbrook, F. H. and Fischel, D. R. (1991). *The Economic Structure of Corporate Law* (Cambridge, MA, Harvard University Press).

Economist (2002). See To Burst or Not to Burst?, *Economist* (7 Sept.), at 68.

Economist (2004). Will It Be Different This Time?, *Economist* (9 Oct.), at 22.

Fahlenbrach, R. and Stulz, R. M. (2009). Bank CEO Incentives and the Credit Crisis, European Corporate Governance Institute, Finance Working Paper No. 256/2009, available at <http://ssrn.com/abstract=1439859>.

Fama, E. F. and French, K. R. (2007). Disagreement, Tastes, and Asset Prices, *Journal of Financial Economics* 83, 667–89.

Fama, E. F. and Jensen, M. C. (1983a). Separation of Ownership and Control, *Journal of Law and Economics* 26, 301–26.

Fama, E. F. and Jensen, M. C. (1983b). Agency Problems and Residual Claims, *Journal of Law and Economics* 26, 327–49.

Field, L. C. and Karpoff, J. M. (2002). Takeover Defenses of IPO Firms, *Journal of Finance* 57, 1857–89.

Figlewski, S. (1981). The Informational Effects of Restrictions on Short Sales: Some Empirical Evidence, *Journal of Financial & Quantitative Analysis* 16, 463–76.

Fink, J., Grullon, G., Fink, K., and Weston, J. (2005). IPO Vintage and the Rise of Idiosyncratic Risk (4 Feb.) (unpublished manuscript), available at <http://ssrn.com/abstract=661321>.

Fisch, J. E. (1994). Relationship Investing: Will It Happen? Will It Work?, *Ohio State Law Journal* 55, 1009–48.

Fisch, J. E. (2006). Measuring Efficiency in Corporate Law: The Role of Shareholder Primacy, *Journal of Corporation Law* 31, 637–74.

Fortado, L. (2009). Linklaters Tops Deal Advisers as M&A Volume Plummets 38 Percent, *Bloomberg* (2 Jan.), available at <http://www.bloomberg.com/apps/news?pid=newsarchive&sid=aNZBdBiog9_o>.

Gilson, R. J. and Kraakman, R. (1991). Reinventing the Outside Director: An Agenda for Institutional Investors, *Stanford Law Review* 43, 863–906.

Gilson, R. J. and Kraakman, R. (1993). Investment Companies as Guardian Shareholders: The Place of the MSIC in the Corporate Governance Debate, *Stanford Law Review* 45, 985–1010.

Gilson, R. J. and Kraakman, R. (2003). The Mechanisms of Market Efficiency Twenty Years Later: The Hindsight Bias, *Journal of Corporation Law* 28, 715–42.

Gilson, R. J. and Schwartz, A. (2001). Sales and Elections as Methods for Transferring Corporate Control, *Theoretical Inquiries in Law* 2, 783–814.

Gilson, R. J. and Whitehead, C. K. (2008). Deconstructing Equity: Public Ownership, Agency Costs, and Complete Capital Markets, *Columbia Law Review* 108, 231–64.

Gompers, P., Ishii, J., and Metrick, A. (2003). Corporate Governance and Equity Prices, *Quarterly Journal of Economics* 118, 107–56.

Gompers, P. A. and Metrick, A. (2001). Institutional Investors and Equity Prices, *Quarterly Journal of Economics* 116, 229–59.

Gordon, J. N. (2007). The Rise of Independent Directors in the United States, 1950–2005: Of Shareholder Value and Stock Market Prices, *Stanford Law Review* 59, 1465–568.

Graham, J., Harvey, C., and Rajgopal, S. (2005). The Economic Implications of Corporate Financial Reporting, *Journal of Accounting and Economics* 40, 3–73.

Graham, J., Harvey, C. R., and Rajgopal, S. (2006). Value Destruction and Financial Reporting Decisions (6 Sept.) (unpublished manuscript), available at <http://ssrn.com/abstract=871215>.

Grant, J. (2008). *Mr. Market Miscalculates: The Bubble Years and Beyond* (Mt Jackson, VA, Axios Press).

Green, S. (2009). Group Chairman, HSBC Holdings plc, Speech at the British Bankers' Association Annual International Banking Conference: Restoring Governance and Trust (30 June).

Greenspan, A. (1996). Chairman, Federal Reserve Board, Remarks at the Annual Dinner and Francis Boyer Lecture of The American Enterprise Institute for Public Policy Research: The Challenge of Central Banking in a Democratic Society (5 Dec.), available at <http://www.federalreserve.gov/boarddocs/speeches/1996/19961205.htm>.

Grossman, S. J. and Hart, O. D. (1980). Disclosure Laws and Takeover Bids, *Journal of Finance* 35, 323–34.

Haggerty, J. R. (2006). Do Countrywide's Loans Stack Up?, *Wall Street Journal* (25 July), at C3.

Hansmann, H. and Kraakman, R. (2001). The End of History for Corporate Law, *Georgetown Law Journal* 89, 439–68.

Harrison, J. M. and Kreps, D. M. (1978). Speculative Investor Behavior in a Stock Market with Heterogeneous Expectations, *Quarterly Journal of Economics* 92, 323–36.

Healy, P. M., Hutton, A. P., and Palepu, K. G. (1999). Stock Performance and Intermediation Changes Surrounding Sustained Increases in Disclosure, *Contemporary Accounting Research* 16, 485–520.

Healy, P. M. and Palepu, K. G. (2001). Information Asymmetry, Corporate Disclosure, and the Capital Markets: A Review of the Empirical Disclosure Literature, *Journal of Accounting and Economics* 31, 405–40.

Holden, C. W. and Lundstrum, L. L. (2005). Costly Trading, Managerial Myopia and Long-Term Investment (Sept.) (unpublished manuscript), available at <http://ssrn.com/abstract=809507>.

Holmström, B. and Kaplan, S. N. (2001). Corporate Governance and Merger Activity in the United States: Making Sense of the 1980s and 1990s, *Journal of Economic Perspectives* 15, 121–44.

Holmström, B. and Kaplan, S. N. (2003). The State of US Corporate Governance: What's Right and What's Wrong?, Euro*Stanford Law Review Stanford Law Review* pean Corporate Governance Institute, Finance Working Paper No. 23/2003, available at <http://ssrn.com/abstract=441100>.

Hovakimian, A., Opler, T., and Titman, S. (2001). The Debt-Equity Choice, *Journal of Financial and Quantitative Analysis* 36, 1–24.

Hyatt, J. (2009). Getting Smaller, But Not Quieter, *CFO* (Feb.), at 17.

Ikenberry, D., Lakonishok, J., and Vermaelen, T. (1995). Market Underreaction to Open Market Share Repurchases, *Journal of Financial Economics* 39, 181–208.

Jensen, M. C. (1986). Agency Costs of Free Cash Flow, Corporate Finance, and Takeovers, *American Economic Review* 76, 323–9.

Jensen, M. C. (1989). Eclipse of the Public Corporation, *Harvard Business Review* (Sept.–Oct.), 61–74.

Jensen, M. C. and Meckling, W. H. (1976). Theory of the Firm: Managerial Behavior, Agency Costs and Ownership Structure, *Journal of Financial Economics* 3, 305–60.

Jensen, M. C. and Murphy, K. J. (1990). Performance Pay and Top-Management Incentives, *Journal of Political Economy* 98, 225–64.
Jenter, D. (2005). Market Timing and Management Portfolio Decisions, *Journal of Finance* 60, 1903–49.
Johnson, M. S. and Rao, R. P. (1997). The Impact of Antitakeover Amendments on Corporate Financial Performance, *Financial Review* 32, 659–702.
Kahan, M. and Rock, E. B. (2002). How I Learned to Stop Worrying and Love the Pill: Adaptive Responses to Takeover Law, *University of Chicago Law Review* 69, 871–915.
Kahan, M. and Rock, E. B. (2008). Embattled CEOs, European Corporate Governance Institute, Law Working Paper No. 116/2008, available at <http://ssrn.com/abstract=1281516>.
Kelly, J. and Keehner, J. (2009). Private Equity Indigestion Comes with Bain Bloomin' Onion Debts, *Bloomberg* (11 Mar.), available at <http://www.bloomberg.com/apps/news?pid=news archive&sid=apUN4GkGPA.I&refer=home>.
Kelly, K. (2009). *Street Fighters: The Last 72 Hours of Bear Stearns, The Toughest Firm on Wall Street* (New York, Portfolio/Penguin Group).
Kihlstrom, R. E. and Wachter, M. L. (2003). Corporate Policy and the Coherence of Delaware Takeover Law, *University of Pennsylvania Law Review* 152, 523–75.
Kotkin, S. (2009). A Bear Saw Around the Corner, *New York Times* (4 Jan.), at BU2.
Kraakman, R. (1988). Taking Discounts Seriously: The Implications of 'Discounted' Share Prices as an Acquisition Motive, *Columbia Law Review* 88, 891–941.
Kumar, A. and Lee, C. M. C. (2006). Retail Investor Sentiment and Return Comovements, *Journal of Finance* 61, 2451–86.
Leland, H. E. and Pyle, D. H. (1977). Informational Asymmetries, Financial Structure, and Financial Intermediation, *Journal of Finance* 32, 371–87.
Lerner, J. (1994). Venture Capitalists and the Decision to Go Public, *Journal of Financial Economics* 35, 293–316.
Leuz, C. and Wysocki, P. (2008). Economic Consequences of Financial Reporting and Disclosure Regulation: A Review and Suggestions for Future Research (Mar.), (unpublished manuscript), available at <http://ssrn.com/abstract=1105398>.
Levitt, Jr, A. (2008). Op-Ed., How to Boost Shareholder Democracy, *Wall Street Journal* (1 July), at A17.
Lintner, J. (1965). The Valuation of Risk Assets and the Selection of Risky Investments in Stock Portfolios and Capital Budgets, *Review of Economics and Statistics* 47, 13-37.
Loughran, T., Ritter, J., and Rydqvist, K. (1994). Initial Public Offerings: International Insights, *Pacific-Basin Finance Journal* 2, 165–99.
Lowenstein, R. (2009). A Seat at the Table, *New York Times* (7 June) (Magazine), at 11.
Macey, J. R. (1993). The Transformation of the American Law Institute, *George Washington Law Review* 61, 1212–32.
Malkiel, B. G. (1992). Efficient Market Hypothesis, in P. Newman, M. Milgate, and J. Eatwell (eds.), *The New Palgrave Dictionary of Money and Finance* (London, Palgrave Macmillan), 739.
Marsh, P. (1982). The Choice between Equity and Debt: An Empirical Study, *Journal of Finance* 37, 121–44.
Masulis, R. W., Wang, C., and Xie, F. (2007). Corporate Governance and Acquirer Returns, *Journal of Finance* 62, 1851–89.
Meulbroek, L. K. (1992). An Empirical Analysis of Illegal Insider Trading, *Journal of Finance* 47, 1661–9.

Mikkelson, W. H. and Partch, M. M. (1997). The Decline of Takeovers and Disciplinary Managerial Turnover, *Journal of Financial Economics* 44, 205–28.

Miller, E. M. (1977). Risk, Uncertainty, and Divergence of Opinion, *Journal of Finance* 32, 1151–68.

Miller, M. M. and Rock, K. (1985). Dividend Policy under Asymmetric Information, *Journal of Finance* 40, 1031–51.

Murphy, K. J. (2002). Explaining Executive Compensation: Managerial Power versus the Perceived Cost of Stock Options, *University of Chicago Law Review* 69, 847–69.

Narayanan, M. P. (1985). Managerial Incentives for Short-Term Results, *Journal of Finance* 40, 1469–84.

Norris, F. (2007). Market Shock: AAA Rating May Be Junk, *New York Times* (20 July), at C1.

NYSE (New York Stock Exchange) (2009). Listed Company Manual, available at <http://nysemanual.nyse.com/LCM/sections/>.

Ofek, E. and Richardson, M. (2003). Dot-Com Mania: The Rise and Fall of Internet Stock Prices, *Journal of Finance* 58, 1113–38.

Pagano, M., Panetta, F., and Zingales, L. (1998). Why Do Companies Go Public? An Empirical Analysis, *Journal of Finance* 53, 27–64.

Panageas, S. (2003). Speculation, Overpricing, and Investment—Theory and Empirical Evidence (15 Nov.) (unpublished manuscript), available at <http://www.cepr.org/meets/wkcn/1/1609/papers/panageas.pdf>.

Panageas, S. (2005). The Neoclassical Theory of Investment in Speculative Markets (16 Apr.) (unpublished manuscript), available at <http://ssrn.com/abstract=720464>.

Pavlov, A. and Wachter, S. (2009). Subprime Lending and House Price Volatility, University of Pennsylvania Institute for Law & Economics, Research Paper No. 08-33, available at <http://papers.ssrn.com/abstract=1316891>.

Polk, C. and Sapienza, P. (2009). The Stock Market and Corporate Investment: A Test of Catering Theory, *Review of Financial Studies* 22, 187–217.

Posner, R. A. (2009). *A Failure of Capitalism: The Crisis of '08 and the Descent into Depression* (Cambridge, MA, Harvard University Press).

Rajgopal, S. and Venkatachalam, M. (2008). Financial Reporting Quality and Idiosyncratic Return Volatility over the Last Four Decades (Sept.) (unpublished manuscript), available at <http://ssrn.com/abstract=650081>.

Rappaport, A. (2005). The Economics of Short-Term Price Obsession, *Financial Analysts Journal* (May–June), at 65.

Richard, C. and Feldheim, D. (2004). Asset-Backed Securities Gain Favor, *Wall Street Journal* (25 May), at C5.

Ritter, J. R. (1991). The Long-Run Performance of Initial Public Offerings, *Journal of Finance* 46, 3–27.

Rock, E. B. (1991). The Logic and (Uncertain) Significance of Institutional Shareholder Activism, *Georgetown Law Journal* 79, 445–506.

Roe, M. J. (1994). *Strong Managers, Weak Owners: The Political Roots of American Corporate Finance* (Princeton, NJ, Princeton University Press).

Roe, M. J. (1996). Chaos and Evolution in Law and Economics, *Harvard Law Review* 109, 641–68.

Roll, R. (1988). R^2, *Journal of Finance* 43, 541–66.

Ross, S. A. (1977). The Determination of Financial Structure: The Incentive-Signalling Approach, *Bell Journal of Economics* 8, 23–40.

Ross, S. A., Westerfield, R. W., and Jaffe, J. (2002). *Corporate Finance* (6th edn) (New York, Irwin/McGraw Hill).

Scannell, K. and Emshwiller, J. R. (2009). Countrywide Chiefs Charged with Fraud, *Wall Street Journal* (5 June), at C1.

Scheinkman, J. A. and Xiong, W. (2003). Overconfidence and Speculative Bubbles, *Journal of Political Economy* 111, 1183–219.

Scholes, M. S. (1972). The Market for Securities: Substitution versus Price Pressure and the Effects of Information on Share Prices, *Journal of Business* 45, 179–89.

Schumer, C. (2009). Press Release, The Office of Senator Charles Schumer, Schumer, Cantwell Announce 'Shareholder Bill of Rights' to Impose Greater Accountability on Corporate America (19 May), available at <http://www.schumer.senate.gov/new_website/record.cfm?id=313468>.

Schwarcz, S. L. (1994). The Alchemy of Asset Securitization, *Stanford Journal of Law, Business and Finance* 1, 133–54.

Schwert, G. W. (2000). Hostility in Takeovers: In the Eyes of the Beholder?, *Journal of Finance* 55, 2599–640.

Servaes, H. (1994). Do Takeover Targets Overinvest?, *Review of Financial Studies* 7, 253–77.

Sharpe, W. F. (1964). Capital Asset Prices: A Theory of Market Equilibrium under Conditions of Risk, *Journal of Finance* 19, 425–42.

Shleifer, A. and Vishny, R. W. (1990). Equilibrium Short Horizons of Investors and Firms, *American Economic Review* (Papers and Proceedings) 80, 148–53.

Shleifer, A. and Vishny, R. W. (1997). The Limits of Arbitrage, *Journal of Finance* 52, 35–55.

Solomon, D. and Fitzpatrick, D. (2009). Czar Blocks BofA Chief's Pay, *Wall Street Journal* (16 Oct.), at A1.

Squire, K. (2009). A Golden Age for Activist Investing, *Barron's* (16 Feb.), at 30.

Standard & Poor's (2007). S&P 500 Buybacks: Three Years and $1.3 Trillion Later.

Standard & Poor's (2009). Press Release, S&P 500 Stock Buybacks Retreat 66% in Fourth Quarter; Off 42% in 2008 (26 Mar.).

Stein, J. C. (1988). Takeover Threats and Managerial Myopia, *Journal of Political Economy* 96, 61–80.

Stein, J. C. (1989). Efficient Capital Markets, Inefficient Firms: A Model of Myopic Corporate Behavior, *Quarterly Journal of Economics* 104, 655–69.

Stein, J. C. (2003). Agency, Information and Corporate Investment, in G. M. Constantindes, M. Harris, and R. M. Stulz (eds.), *Handbook of the Economics of Finance* (vol. 1A) (Amsterdam, Elsevier North-Holland), 111–65.

Stout, L. A. (1990). Are Takeover Premiums Really Premiums? Market Price, Fair Value, and Corporate Law, *Yale Law Journal* 99, 1235–96.

Stout, L. A. (1997). How Efficient Markets Undervalue Stocks: CAPM and ECMH Under Conditions of Uncertainty and Disagreement, *Cardozo Law Review* 19, 475–92.

Subrahmanyam, A. (2007). Behavioural Finance: A Review and Synthesis, *European Financial Management* 14, 12–29.

Tett, G. (2009). *Fool's Gold: How the Bold Dream of a Small Tribe at J.P. Morgan was Corrupted by Wall Street Greed and Unleashed a Catastrophe* (New York, Free Press).

Titman, S., Wei, K. C. J., and Xie, F. (2003). Capital Investments and Stock Returns, National Bureau of Economic Research, Working Paper No. 9951, available at <http://www.nber.org/papers/w9951>.

Tully, S. (2003). Meet the 23,000% Stock, *Fortune* (15 Sept.), at 204.

Wachter, M. L. (2003). Takeover Defense When Financial Markets Are (Only) Relatively Efficient, *University of Pennsylvania Law Review* 151, 787–824.

Wei, S. X. and Zhang, C. (2006). Why Did Individual Stocks Become More Volatile?, *Journal of Business* 79, 259–92.

Wurgler, J. and Zhuravskaya, E. (2002). Does Arbitrage Flatten Demand Curves for Stocks?, *Journal of Business* 75, 583–608.

Xu, Y. and Malkiel, B. G. (2003). Investigating the Behavior of Idiosyncratic Volatility, *Journal of Business* 76, 613–44.

Zingales, L. (2009). The Future of Securities Regulation, Chicago Booth School of Business, Working Paper No. 08-27; FEEM Working Paper No. 7-2009, available at <http://ssrn.com/abstract=1319648>.

Zuckerman, G. (2009). Activists Must Adjust Their Aim, *Wall Street Journal* (27 Apr.), at C10.

Index

The manufacturer's authorised representative in the EU for product safety is Oxford University Press España S.A. of El Parque Empresarial San Fernando de Henares, Avenida de Castilla, 2 - 28830 Madrid (www.oup.es/en or product.safety@oup.com). OUP España S.A. also acts as importer into Spain of products made by the manufacturer.
Printed and bound by CPI Group (UK) Ltd, Croydon, CR0 4YY
18/09/2026
02218912-0001